THE DORAMA ENCYCLOPEDIA

THE DORAMA ENCYCLOPEDIA
A Guide to Japanese TV Drama since 1953

Jonathan Clements & Motoko Tamamuro

Stone Bridge Press • Berkeley, California

Published by
STONE BRIDGE PRESS
P. O. Box 8208, Berkeley, CA 94707
TEL 510-524-8732 • sbp@stonebridge.com • www.stonebridge.com

We want to hear from you! Updates? Corrections? Comments? Please send all
correspondence regarding this book to **doramainfo@stonebridge.com**.

Printed in the United States of America.

10 9 8 7 6 5 4 3 2 1   2008 2007 2006 2005 2004 2003

LIBRARY OF CONGRESS CATALOGING-IN-PUBLICATION DATA
Clements, Jonathan, 1971-
   The dorama encyclopedia : a guide to Japanese TV drama since 1953 /
Jonathan Clements & Motoko Tamamuro.
        p. cm.
   Includes bibliographical references and index.
   ISBN 1-880656-81-7
1. Television plays, Japanese–History and criticism–Encyclopedias.
2. Television programs–Japan–History–Encyclopedias. I. Tamamuro,
Motoko. II. Title.
PN1992.3.J3 C58 2003
791.45'6–dc22
                                              2003018182

To Lee Brimmicombe-Wood

CONTENTS

THE DORAMA ENCYCLOPEDIA

ILLUSTRATIONS

INTRODUCTION

The idea of television was first discussed at the end of the 19th century, when futurists imagined not only hearing words and music, but also seeing pictures transmitted from a distant source. The French artist and writer George du Maurier depicted the idea in 1879 in *Punch* magazine, showing a couple sitting in front of their fireplace, with a screen above the mantelpiece showing a tennis match. His concept is still prescient today, since it not only evokes the 21st century's plasma widescreen giants, but also interactivity, as du Maurier envisaged the viewers communicating with the people onscreen.

By 1882, another Frenchman, Albert Robida, predicted that this as-yet uninvented device would be able to bring images of distant wars into a family's home, make it possible to learn from teachers far away, shop without leaving an armchair, and even, once the ladies of the house were safely tucked away, peruse gentlemen's entertainment of a more salacious nature.

In 1884, the German Paul Nipkow invented the "Nipkow disk," a rotating disc whose spiral perforations permitted light to scan back and forth across its target. Though the Nipkow disc and other

mechanical patents were later supplanted by electronic devices, their appearance allowed others to experiment further with the moving image.

As radio technology spread throughout the world, it dragged speculation about television in its wake. Inspired by the same *Punch* cartoons that fired European and American inventors, Kenjirō Takayanagi wrote of his hopes for the coming medium in 1924. He experimented with primitive broadcasting technology, and in 1926, Takayanagi was able to recreate a fuzzy image of the character "I" from the Japanese *katakana* syllabary. It was the first thing to appear on a TV screen in Japan.

A FALSE START

The *Nippon Hōsō Kyōkai*, Japan Broadcasting Corporation, or NHK, was formed in 1926 by the merging of three independent radio stations in Tokyo, Nagoya, and Osaka. Charged with being the voice of the Japanese government, NHK also began early experiments in television on 13 May 1939.

The first television drama to be broadcast in Japan was *Before Dinner* (*Yūgemae*, 1940), written by Uhei Ima, and directed by Tomokazu Sakamoto and Ryūji Kawaguchi. A 12-minute short about a family evening, it features two children waiting for their mother to return home. While the daughter, Kimiko (Shihoko Seki) prepares dinner, the son, Atsushi (Kiyoshi Nonomura) reads about a bus crash in the newspaper and begins to fret about his mother's safety. Mother (Izumiko Hara) eventually returns safely, clutching a photograph, which both children assume is a potential marriage partner for the other. Instead, it turns out to be a memorial picture of their father, presumed dead in the war in China, adding a poignant dose of pathos to an otherwise everyday scene.

Few people, however, got to see *Before Dinner*, as television sets were not on sale to the Japanese public. Soon afterward, in June 1941, NHK suspended all television experiments in preparation for the coming war.

Defeat, occupation, and reconstruction meant that television did not reappear in Japan until the 1950s. World War II also halted most TV activity abroad, but the Allied victors were soon continuing their experiments. Regular network broadcasting began in earnest in both America and Britain in 1946, giving the TV industry of the English-speaking world a further five-year head start on its Japanese counterpart. This gap in development would prove to be crucially important in later years.

FIRST STEPS

Just as the demilitarized Japanese manufacturing industry was steered into toys and consumer durables, the nascent new TV medium was urged to avoid controversy. Toward the end of the Occupation, the Japanese were encouraged to emulate American soap operas. NHK continued its experiments, making another test broadcast with the light comedy *Newly Wed Album* (*Shinkon Album*, 1952). NHK's TV arm was established in a licensing model after the fashion of the British Broadcasting Corporation, funded through subscriptions paid by TV set owners. However, there was already competition among other companies for the right to begin commercial broadcasting—in other words, a TV station that gained its financing from sponsorship and advertising. The first to acquire a license was Nihon TV (NTV), an affiliate of the *Yomiuri Shinbun* newspaper, but NHK was still ahead in development. Consequently, the first official TV broadcast to the people of Japan was an NHK production on 1 February 1953. At the time, Japan had only 866 television sets that could receive it.

This first true broadcast was a nod to dramatic tradition—Act IV Scene I of the famous kabuki play *Yoshitsune and the Thousand Cherry Trees*. It features Shizuka, the mistress of **YOSHITSUNE**, as she walks with a shape-shifting fox, who protects both her and the drum she carries, which was made from his parents' hides.

Just three days later, NHK showed a drama that had been specially commissioned for the screen, not lifted from another medium—*Flute on the Mountain Path* (*Yamaji no Fue*), written by Kayoko Sugi and directed by Tsuneo Hatanaka. Based on a northern Japanese folktale, it depicted a sad love story between musician Tōjirō (Tsutomu Shitamoto) and his wife/ guardian angel (Michiko Ōtsuka). With limited resources, the drama had to be broadcast live, leading to Japanese TV's first blooper, when a cameraman mistakenly left

© 2003 Steve Kyte

Japanese TV's first blooper

the camera pointing at Ōtsuka during one of her costume changes.

Other programming in the early days attempted to find subjects that could be exploited by the limited broadcasting resources of the day. Deals were struck with radio stations to have cameras present at news bulletins and musical performances, essentially adding little but a visual gimmick to programming already available on the radio. Sports, however, proved to be a far better use of the new medium, particularly if it was something like wrestling, boxing, or *sumo,* where the competitors could be expected to spend most of their time in a small area that could be covered by a single locked-off camera. With their Yomiuri Group affiliations, NTV soon began covering baseball in great detail, particularly the exploits of the Yomiuri Giants team.

Television soon came to be known as the "brown screen," in contrast to the silver screen of the movie theater—a pejorative comparison that the movie world did everything in its power to encourage. An average 17-inch set retailed at 245,000 yen, or just under $700, at a time when the starting salary for a college graduate was only $42 a month. A private TV set was far beyond the means of the average citizen, and the early broadcasts were aimed at the wealthy and a popular audience of sports fans who could be expected to cluster to watch important matches. In order to encourage greater consumption, NHK placed sets in public halls as a form of pauper's cinema, while NTV followed suit with TVs in prominent positions on main thoroughfares, causing traffic jams but also generating much-needed publicity.

EARLY CONVENTIONS AND TV FIRSTS

As late as 1955, Japanese television was still only broadcasting an average of five hours a night. News programs and sporting events helped fill much of the schedules, along with vaudeville performances by comics and musicians. As the initial gimmick faded, television was shunned by a cinema acting community that saw it as a threat, while its drama serials lacked the financial resources to truly compete with radio—where, as the saying goes, the pictures were still better.

Returning from a study trip in America, director Hiroshi Nagayama initiated Japan's first period drama, commissioning writer Kiyoyuki Nishikawa to adapt an old samurai detective story by former kabuki playwright Kidō Okamoto. Remade many times since, most recently in 1997, HANSHICHI began as a 40-minute drama, and the production of several sequels over the following years made it not only the first true period drama on Japanese TV, but also the first series and the first franchise.

The early 1950s also saw the first appearance of the "Home Drama" genre, emphasizing family ties. Director Tsutomu Ogata's *Sunday Diary of My Home* (*Waga Ya no Nichiyō Nikki*, 1953) showed everyday life for a family of parents, children, and aging mother-in-law. Written for NTV by Yoshikazu Yamashita and featuring Kazuo Mayumida and Setsuko Horikoshi, its 25 half-hour episodes focused on generational differences and the contradictions of being a loving family in a confined space, outlining a style of drama that lives on to this day in shows such as MAKING IT THROUGH and LADY OF THE MANOR. To early TV directors, one of the appeals of kitchen-sink drama was that the camera rarely had to move far from the kitchen sink.

Not to be outdone by its commercial rival, NHK tried its own variation on the home drama format in the 13-episode *Ups and Downs Toward Happiness* (*Kōfuku e no Kifuku*, 1953). Written by Izumi Kyō, its protagonists, the wealthy Kanō family, are rendered penniless after World War II and forced to struggle for existence in a miserable tale that would be imitated in later generations by OSHIN and INOCHI: LIFE.

The search for a style and identity remained one of trial and error. Since TV was a completely new technology, there was no older generation with a resumé of relevant experience. Instead, it attracted talent from other, established media, creating tensions between two chief factions. Those who transferred from radio knew about live performances and tightly timed broadcasts, but had little appreciation of the limitations and pitfalls of a visual medium. Others had a background in the film world, whose antipathy to TV was such that anyone leaving to work in the new medium was unlikely to be welcomed back. These refugees were used to filming out of sequence on multiple sets and locations, but had little or no experience of sequential shooting or the terrifying prospect that every project had to be executed in a single half-hour take. A third faction was formed of the very young, those with no experience of either earlier medium, who had accepted low-paying jobs as underlings and learned the new technology on the job. Within a few years, these early continuity girls, floor managers, and cameramen would form the next generation of directors and producers.

These early productions saw a flurry of firsts as crews tried new ways of using their equipment. NHK's *Poems From Heaven*

(*Tenraku no Shishū*) attempted the brave feat of filming a story live on 12 separate sets, while NTV's *I Kept My Promise* (*Watashi wa Yakusoku o Mamotta*) experimented with rear projection to put a more impressive vista behind the foreground action. The first true special effect on Japanese TV is believed to be a flying dog in NHK's fantasy *The Dog Is Alive* (*Inu wa Ikiteiru*).

By 1955, the talent was confident enough to experiment with the new medium. *Hanshichi* director Hiroshi Nagayama made the detective drama *Pursuit* (*Tsuiseki*) for NHK, from a script by Naoya Uchimura. Featuring two detectives on the trail of a smuggler, the one-hour show was shot live on location in Tokyo's Tsukishima area and Osaka's Dōtonbori district, as well as studio sets in both cities. Though technical achievement took precedence over the simplistic story line, the groundbreaking show won an award for its innovation.

Producers also went in search of new sources of material to adapt. August 1955 saw the first televisual adaptation of a *manga*, when Hajime Akiyoshi's *Todoroki Sensei* leapt from the pages of the *Yomiuri Shinbun* onto the screen. The bold, unflappable Mr. Todoroki was played by comedian Roppo Furukawa, in a drama which ran at the same time every weekday. Called "strip scheduling" in the West, this daily broadcasting came to be known in Japan as *obi dorama,* or "belt drama."

The two original networks gained another competitor the same year, with the first broadcasts from KRT (now known as Tokyo Broadcasting Systems, or TBS). The new network immediately specialized in "television novels," based on the successful book adaptations and radio plays that ran on its radio affiliate. The network's first hit was *Mr. Himana Jumps Out* (*Himanashi Tobidasu*), a mystery series concocted by film critics Jūzaburō Futaba and Toshiko Minami. Inspired in equal parts by *Sherlock Holmes* and American hard-boiled fiction, it featured the crime-solving adventures of photographer Shinsuke Himana (Yasuo Kubo) and his assistant Daisuke (Toshio Takahara). Running for a total of seven years, the program was also the first to have a regular sponsor, Sankyō Pharmaceuticals, whose patronage ensured a scene in which Mr. Himana would visit his local pharmacy to buy one of the corporation's vitamin drinks. *Mr. Himana Jumps Out* was a great success for KRT, eventually gaining a peak rating of 61.5%. However, despite such high viewing figures, Japanese TV drama was still beaten in the ratings by big sporting events and its greatest foe, foreign imports.

THE ALIEN INVASION

By 1956, television was expanding in all directions. As the price of individual sets came down, private ownership was rising exponentially. The channels were extending their programming beyond a mere few hours in the evening, and there were now three channels to choose from. This incredible growth created a new problem—Japan simply did not have enough technicians, talent, equipment, or facilities to meet this new demand. Television was now a gaping maw that needed to be filled with programming, and the industry that made the programming was incapable of doubling in size every year. An obvious source of new programming lay in the archives of Japan's movie studios, but the cinema industry refused to cooperate with its upstart rival. The Japanese TV industry, like its counterparts in most other countries, looked abroad for new programming, and its chief source was the ten-year-old broadcast industry of the United States of America.

As Japanese television was still struggling to develop an identity of its own, it was inundated with better made, higher budget shows from the glamorous, rich nation that had recently defeated it in WWII. Initially, such imports were confined to the children's market, partly because children's programming is often the place where cheap "filler" is stuffed, while primetime keeps the higher profile. The first American series to be shown on Japanese television was the Fleischer brothers' animated *Superman* in 1955, soon followed by *Popeye, Huckleberry Hound,* and *The Flintstones.* When two cultures are very different, cartoons are often easier to transform into local products—dubbed dialogue is harder to spot, and children are less likely to notice anyway.

Before long, live-action shows followed for the adult audience. An entire generation grew up watching Caucasian faces speaking overdubbed Japanese in their living rooms and often preferred these early imports over the offerings from their own local TV industry. Tough American law enforcers, such as the car chases of *Highway Patrol* and the fact-focused *Dragnet,* competed in the schedules against *Buffalo Bill, Annie Oakley,* and *Hopalong Cassidy.* By 1958, the highest rated show of *any* kind on Japanese television was the live-action *Adventures of Superman* starring George Reeves on KRT, watched by 74.2% of all TV sets in Japan.

Writers Hirokazu Fuse and Kuniko Mukōda responded with *Dial 110* for NTV,

a police drama made with the cooperation of real-life law enforcers, and utilizing a deliberately documentary touch to add a note of realism. Meanwhile, with KRT's imported *Superman* dominating the schedules, the channel decided to steal from its own success with a local product, commissioning Japan's first superhero, the **MOONLIGHT MASK**. The prospect of a Japanese version of *Superman* struck a chord, and the series was one of the few homegrown products to share the top ten ratings with American imports.

Mixing the documentary thrills of *Dial 110* with the amateur sleuthing of *Mr. Himana Jumps Out,* producer Kazuo Shimada created *Crime Journalist (Jiken Kisha).* Focusing not only on mysteries, but also on competition between rival journalists to get a scoop, the show was the first "workplace drama," creating a subgenre of Japanese TV that survives in shows such as **HOTEL** and **FEMALE ANNOUNCERS**.

The late 1950s saw the arrival of industrial video tape, which revolutionized a television studio's ability to record and edit programming. Multiple sets, multiple takes, non-sequential shooting, and location work were now all within the grasp of Japanese TV crews, significantly improving the quality of shows in the new medium, and producers' chances of making extra money through reruns.

KRT's one-off drama *I Want to Be a Shellfish (Watashi wa Kai ni Naritai,* 1958) was the first to be shot on video, with the first 50 minutes taped at several locations, and its closing half broadcast live from a single set. It also courted controversy with its tale of a kindly barber, Toyomatsu (Frankie Sakai), unexpectedly arrested as a C-class war criminal. In the ensuing courtroom drama, it is revealed that Toyomatsu executed a downed American pilot during the war. Though he argues that he would have been killed by his own superior officers if he had disobeyed them, he is sentenced to death. As he awaits the gallows, he writes to his wife: "*I have lost hope in humanity. If I am ever reborn, I want to be a shellfish. Then I won't be drafted.*" Directed by Itsuhiko Okamoto, the award-winning drama carried a powerful message of the Japanese people's anger and frustration with the wartime system, and the postwar culture of blame and guilt.

THE EFFECT OF FOREIGN TV

Foreign imports went through two periods of boom and decline. In the early years, TV's original audience comprised the wealthy upper middle-class, often learning English and keenly interested in America. As television sets spread throughout the country and filtered down to the lower classes, TV channels began to receive complaints about the amount of foreign programming. Viewers in rural areas protested that the cowboy adventures of *The Lone Ranger* and the inscrutable occidental humor of *I Love Lucy* meant little to them and that it was often difficult for them to tell the foreign actors apart. Channels soon obliged by making more acceptable local products, and foreign imports tailed off, only to repeat the cycle with the arrival of color television in 1960. The flood of foreign products only truly slowed in the late 1960s after a decade of influence, by which time many "traditions" of modern Japanese TV drama had already been established, both in imitation of it and reaction to it.

The influx of foreign shows is at least partly responsible for the strange trend for "three-dimensional" nomenclature in modern Japanese shows. Japanese titles often seem to have a foreground name and a background qualifier (e.g. *Superdimensional Fortress* + *MACROSS*), which is likely to have grown out of foreign shows with a descriptive onscreen Japanese title subordinate to the original English name. Such additions were commonplace in early television, leading to a tradition of show titles containing the original foreign name, with a qualifying prefix, such as *Detective Columbo, Detective Kojak, Lawyer Preston* (*The Defenders*), or *Lawyer Judd* (*Judd for the Defense*).

Translation of foreign shows also led to changes in emphasis, particularly with regard to the all-important hook that caught the viewer's eye and encouraged tuning in. *Sergeant Preston of the Yukon* was renamed *Police Dog King* to imply closer affinity with the popular *Famous Dog Lassie* and *Famous Dog Rin Tin Tin*. *Tallahassee 7000* was renamed *Dial 7000*, implying a relationship with *Dial 110*. Theme songs would often be reprised by Japanese performers. Some, such as *Batman*, had lyrics *added* in order to help explain the show: "*With a black mask and a cloak like a cloud, a golden belt that shines and boots of dynamic blue, bright red fire shoots from his jet-car, as the engine burns and away he goes, at full speed . . . Batman! Batman! Batman!*" Not all alterations were accurate—the New York crime story *The D.A.'s Man* was incorrectly transliterated as *Dazman*, while a well-known humanist science fiction series was first broadcast in Japan as *Great Battle in Space Star Trek*.

Japan also saw a succession of American comedies centered on a female lead. Since housewives traditionally held the purse strings and were the target for most early advertising, producers were inspired by the thought of programming in which women had the upper hand, however temporarily. Consequently, after the release of titles known in Japan as *My Wife Is on the Case* (*Glynis*), *My Wife Is a Big Star* (*Mona McCluskey*), and *My Wife Is a Company Employee* (*The Cara Williams Show*), local networks responded with shows such as MY WIFE IS 18 and MAMA IS MY RIVAL.

Two of the most influential shows fetishized women as fantasy creatures with magical properties, known in Japan as *My Wife Is a Witch (Bewitched)* and *Cute Witch Jeannie (I Dream of Jeannie)*. Their influence led to the creation of Mitsuteru Yokoyama's COMET-SAN, and subsequent *anime* serials such as *Little Witch Sally* (*AE) and *Marvelous Melmo* (*AE). Treated as a wholly juvenile genre in Japan, the idea soon split into two distinct subsets of animation—girls' stories about sorcerous minxes who could transform, *Cinderella*-style, into an older, more sophisticated version of themselves and boys' stories about guys with magical girlfriends. The transformation idea of the first is difficult to achieve with live-action (but see MY WIFE IS 18), although the magical girlfriend subgenre lives on in shows such as MINAMI'S SWEET-HEART and STEEL ANGEL KURUMI—PURE.

IN LIVING COLOR

Japanese TV reached a state of maturity at the end of the 1950s. Fuji TV and Nihon Educational Television (*Nihon Kyōiku Terebi* or NET, later known as TV Asahi) both commenced broadcasting in 1959, while TV ownership jumped rapidly in the weeks before the Royal Wedding of Crown Prince Akihito to Michiko Shōda. A love match between the future Heisei Emperor and a commoner he had met on a tennis court, the marriage was the culmination of a real-life *Cinderella* story for Japan's middle-classes, and an effective bait to encourage latecomers to buy televisions after a decade of resistance. By this point, there were 43 broadcasting stations in Japan, mostly affiliated to the four commercial networks.

Mere months after the happy TV owners of Japan had watched the Royal Wedding on their new monochrome sets, the networks introduced the new gimmick of color transmission. One in three people now had their own black-and-white TV, meaning that the new conspicuous consumer accessory was a color set. Such sets cost more than two and half years of a graduate's salary, and were as unaffordable to the general population as monochrome sets had been a decade earlier. There was a renewed interest in foreign shows thanks to the greater amount of color in the U.S. industry, and Japanese programmers responded with content of their own.

The year 1958 saw NHK's *Off the Bus Route* (*Bus Dōri Ura*) directed by Masao Tateno from a script by Izuho Sudō and Keisuke Tsutsui. Explicitly aimed at an audience of housewives, it featured the relationship between two families, the schoolteacher Akazawas and the beauty-salon Kawadas. Lifting much of its style and dialogue from earlier radio dramas, *Off the Bus Route*'s style was not particularly innovative, although its method of delivery was. Screened in 15-minute sections broadcast after the morning and evening news every weekday, it seized the attention of the nation's women, demonstrating that specific markets could be targeted at different times of the day. Such information was of little practical use to NHK, which remained publicly funded, but was of great interest to advertisers on other networks. Though NHK's later morning serials (or *asa-dorama*) such as NON-CHAN'S DREAM are largely outside the scope of this book, they remain an important ratings-magnet outside the hours of primetime.

NHK's first true Serial TV Novel (*Renzoku Terebi Shōsetsu*) was *My Daughter and I* (*Musume to Watashi*) by Yoshikazu Yamashita, based on the autobiographical radio drama by Bunroku Shishi. Expecting its "viewers" to be half occupied with household chores, the drama utilized radio conventions such as expository narrations and kept one foot in the real world with an onscreen clock—no housebound viewer would ever be caught with her feet up watching TV when the kids came home.

With children at school and menfolk at work during the daytime, Fuji TV decided to target NHK's newfound audience of housewives. Fuji's lunchtime slot, formerly occupied by educational programs on cooking and housekeeping, was replaced in 1960 with *Days of Infidelity* (*Hibi no Haishin*), the tale of a torrid affair between a company chairman and his married lover. Soap opera antics, star-crossed lovers, and doomed affairs began to form their own subgenre within Japanese TV drama, creating a sector of infidelity dramas that survives to this day in shows such as PARFUM DE LA JALOUSIE.

In evening slots, Japanese television was flooded with American courtroom dramas, a challenge which NET met with the legal series *The Verdict* (*Hanketsu*, 1962). Written by Hideo Honda and directed by Taku Yatsuhashi, the series drew its inspiration from real life in the style of *Dial 110*. However, real-life Japanese courtrooms lack the adversarial excitement of those in the Western world, and the program makers were obliged to find other topics to fill their episodes. Consequently, *The Verdict* reinforced the traditions of the growing workplace drama, focusing not on the jobs that needed to be done, but on human relationships within the office and the theoretical problems presented by each case. Such a structure also led to *The Verdict* dealing with a number of social problems in post-war Japan, such as the gap between the law and reality in matters of divorce, discrimination, and education. The show lasted for four years, but suffered in later seasons from censorship during the Olympics and the Vietnam War. Eventually dropped through the withdrawal of sponsorship, it became the subject of a petition for reinstatement. The show never went back into production, although its fans were grudgingly rewarded with a long period of reruns.

THE *TAIGA* DRAMA

Brooks and Marsh, the chroniclers of American television history, cite the late 1950s and early 1960s as the era of "Adult Westerns." As a natural result of Japan's hunger for new programming, serials such as *Rawhide, Wanted: Dead or Alive,* and *The Virginian* soon made their way to the Far East, where their alien obsessions with wandering lawmen, cattle rustlers, and gunfights were beamed at the Japanese audience for several years. Notably, these Westerns were assembled on film by American movie studios forced into an uneasy truce with the TV world.

Such a cooperative venture was impossible in Japan, where movie theater audiences were falling fast—in fact, a 60% drop in box-office receipts since 1958, the year in which Japanese TV got its hands on video tape. The movie studios resented the fast growth and easy access of television and not only lambasted television as an inferior medium devoid of interesting content or true spectacle, but also forbade all stars under studio contract from appearing in television shows.

This deadlock in Japanese entertainment was eventually broken in 1963 by Taiji Nagasawa, the director of NHK's Department of Entertainment. Like many others in Japan (such as the creators of **THE SAMURAI**), when he watched American Westerns, he did not see cowboys and Indians so much as stories from a nation's recent past. The time, he thought, was right for Japan to have its own period drama, and he drew up plans for an epic. As befitted NHK's educational remit, the show was designed to teach the public about an important historical figure, but Nagasawa also intended it to be a rambling history like a French *roman-fleuve*. The idea of a novel "like a great river" inspired him to use a similar term in Japanese: *taiga*. His greatest coup, however, lay in the casting of Shōchiku star Keiji Sada in the lead role, effectively breaking the studio ban on movie stars appearing on TV. The result, **LIFE OF A FLOWER,** elevated TV's status and laid the groundwork for the modern Japanese medium. It also created the tradition of an annual *taiga* from NHK, which continues every Sunday, every year. Other networks soon jumped on the period-drama bandwagon, particularly Fuji with its long-running **THREE SWORDSMEN** and TBS with **MITO KŌMON**.

NHK TAIGA DRAMA CHRONOLOGY

1963 Life of a Flower	1983 Tokugawa Ieyasu
1964 *Akō Rōshi* (see Chūshingura)	1984 Burning Mountains and Rivers
1965 *Taikōki* (see Hideyoshi)	1985 Spring Swell
1966 Yoshitsune	1986 Inochi: Life
1967 Three Sisters	1987 Masamune the One-Eyed Dragon
1968 Ryōma Departs	1988 Shingen Takeda
1969 Heaven and Earth	1989 Kasuga the Court Lady
1970 The Fir Tree Left Behind	1990 As If in Flight
1971 Slope in Spring	1991 Taiheiki
1972 New Tale of the Heike	1992 Nobunaga
1973 Land Thief	1993a Wind of the Ryūkyū Islands
1974 *Kaishū Katsu* (see Ryōma Departs)	1993b The Fire Still Burns
1975 *Genroku Taiheiki* (see Chūshingura)	1994 War of Flowers
1976 Wind, Cloud, and Rainbow	1995 Yoshimune
1977 Kajin	1996 Hideyoshi
1978 Days of Gold	1997 Mōri Motonari
1979 The Grass Aflame	1998 Tokugawa Yoshinobu
1980 Time of the Lion	1999 Chūshingura
1981 *Hideyoshi's Women* (see Hideyoshi)	2000 Aoi
1982 *Group at the Ridge* (see Chūshingura)	2001 Hōjō Tokimune
	2002 Toshiie and Matsu
	2003 Musashi
	2004 Shinsengumi

THE OLYMPIAN IDEAL

The 1960s saw Japan unexpectedly commence exporting TV programming to other countries. Though some live-action shows did make it abroad, by far the most lucrative export was, and still is, animation. As with the early American cartoons that came into Japan in the 1950s, it was much easier to transform a cartoon into something resembling a product of the foreign viewers' native culture, and so it was that *Astro Boy* (*AE) and *Kimba the White Lion* (*AE) reached America, with their Japanese origins carefully concealed.

Japan's involvement in the world

Japanese TV ownership jumped in 1964.

© 2003 Steve Kyte

increasing the number available in Japanese homes. With the support of American President John F. Kennedy, NHK also began tests of satellite relay broadcasting, ready to beam the opening ceremony to the watching world. On the day of the high-profile first experiment, Kennedy agreed to utilize the new technology by sending a message to the Japanese viewers on 22 November 1963, intending to broadcast from Texas, where he was on a tour in preparation for the following year's election. However, instead of a goodwill speech from Kennedy, the first satellite relay brought news of his assassination just after midday in downtown Dallas.

The Tokyo Olympics opened on 10 October 1964, deliberately shifted to later in the year in order to avoid the hot Japanese summer. The ceremony was not merely a symbol of Japan's rapid growth and renewal, but also of the country's acceptance back into the international community—Japan was originally supposed to hold the Olympics in 1940, only to lose the chance over the war in China. The ceremony's ratings peaked at 89.9%—a record that is unlikely to be broken, and the sports hysteria of the Japanese reached fever pitch when the women's volleyball team won a gold medal. The high ratings for the Olympics would lead to a number of TV dramas based on sports, such as *Straight Line for Jūdō* (*Jūdō Itchokusen*), **THE SIGN IS V**, and **BEAUTIFUL CHALLENGER**, as well as anime sports dramas such as *Attack Number One* (*AE), *Star of the Giants* (*AE), and *Tomorrow's Joe* (*AE).

Japanese broadcasters had finally won the battle for the attention of their audience—1964 was the first year that not a single foreign show occupied the top twenty

community reached new heights as the preparations began for the Tokyo Olympics in 1964. Sports fans took the plunge at last and purchased color television sets, greatly

ratings slots. Foreign imports remained part of the scheduling, but returned to their first foothold in the children's viewing hours or migrated to the late-night and midnight slots. Prime time was now exclusively Japanese, and would stay that way.

BEYOND THE NUCLEAR FAMILY

The year 1964 also saw a new type of Home Drama, *Seven Grandchildren* (*Shichinin no Mago*). Instead of the nuclear family dramas in imitation of American serials in earlier shows, *Seven Grandchildren* introduced an extended family—the grandfather, grandmother, parents, and seven sons and daughters, all living in the same house. Writer Kuniko Mukōda would go on to write **LIKE ASHURA**, and several other dramas that stretched the boundaries of an otherwise unappealing genre. The same period saw *Eleven of Us for Now* (*Tadaima Jūichinin*), written in part by *Oshin*'s Sugako Hashida, in which a businessman struggled to support a family that included his wife and nine offspring. Though a family of such dimensions was highly unusual in post-war Japan, the spread of the children's ages from nine to 30 allowed for a far greater number of plots—a vital aid to hard-pressed writers, particularly at a time when the average drama episode increased in length from a simple 30 minutes to a whole hour. So it was that, when *The Waltons* was eventually broadcast on Japanese TV under the title *My Family Has Eleven People* (TBS, 1973), it was regarded by many as an American knockoff of a Japanese original. The popularity of multi-generational family dramas, both with writers who like expanded plotting possibilities and also with audiences of different ages who all identify with at least someone

onscreen, continues to this day with the ongoing success of such shows as *Making It Through*.

The following year saw another important milestone—*What Is Youth?* (*Seishun to wa Nan da*), in which a passionate new schoolteacher tried against all odds to turn a sports club full of no-hopers into a team of national renown. The idea of a *Seishun Dorama* (Youth Drama) that celebrated the students even as it offered redemption to their mentors, was to become ingrained in Japanese television, creating a subgenre of unlikely educators in **FLY! YOUTHS**, **ZEALOUS TIMES**, **KINPACHI SENSEI**, and **GTO**. Dramas about unlikely sports and unlikely successes also flourished, and today have grown beyond television to form a staple part of the Japanese movie world, in films such as *Water Boys* and *Ping Pong*.

The disparate elements of the "Youth" and the "Home" dramas were soon combined by Fuji in 1966 with *The Young Ones* (*Wakamonotachi*), in which a sister and four brothers, almost all of school-leaving age or older, tried to stick together after the death of their parents, despite occasional clashes of motivation and personality. Director Tokihisa Morikawa claimed that he planned the series in direct opposition to the Confucian values of earlier dramas, setting up the kind of problem that in other series would call for the benign and wise father figure, and then forcing the young cast to solve the situation themselves. The group dynamics of young people forced together by circumstances would become an important feature of the later "Trendy" dramas of the 1990s, and popular shows of later years such as **ALL ABOUT YOUNG PEOPLE** and **UNDER ONE ROOF**.

Such a discrete rebellion against

tradition was making itself felt elsewhere in Japanese culture, particularly as the 1960s came to an end, and Japanese university students began fighting the Japanese system in a series of protests, riots, and incidents of civil obedience. In 1968, the year's *taiga* drama was RYŌMA DEPARTS, in which a hero of modernizing Japan fought against the stuffy, oppressive regime that he would eventually overthrow. Possibly in a more conservative reaction to the unrest that was fomenting among the young, conservative TV fought back with a series that glorified mothers, not only as the center of the family, but as a tough, unflappable center of daily life—be it as businesswomen, preparers of food, or nurturers of the family. In Yumie Hiraiwa's *Mother Intrepid* (*Kimottama Kaasan*), lead character Isako (Masako Kyōzuka) is a widow who must deal with the tensions between herself and her daughter-in-law, keep her family on an even keel, but most importantly run a business. *Mother Intrepid* was the first of many dramas in which women struggled in the commercial sector, leading to later occupational dramas such as IT'S TIME and Hiraiwa's own THANK YOU.

NEW TYPES OF HERO

Television is only slightly older than the Baby Boom generation. There were more children around to *watch* TV in the late 20th century—a situation that has led to its great power with the young. Children's willingness to suspend disbelief has often been exploited by broadcasters as an excuse for low budgets, particularly obvious in the early puppet shows on Japanese TV. *Chirorin Village* and *The Hakkenden* were regarded as disposable by their broadcasters that few ʾdes are extant today, while *Madcap*

Island was criticized for its thinly veiled attacks on adult figures and institutions. As the Space Race and the Cold War began to dominate the news, sci-fi puppetry was the order of the day, and Japanese children were entertained by the voyages of the spaceship *Silica* and the futuristic wonders of *Aerial City 008*.

The puppet shows of the late 1960s were heavily influenced by the works of Gerry Anderson, particularly *Thunderbirds* (NHK, 1966). Although puppetry was already losing out to animation in the battle for ratings, the miniature special effects work in *Thunderbirds* was to inspire a radically different type of children's entertainment. With a tug-of-war between TBS and NTV over the rights to *The Twilight Zone*, movie special effects director Eiji Tsuburaya capitalized on the interest by offering several channels a similar show. The ideas that eventually manifested as OPERATION MYSTERY, UNBALANCE, and most importantly, ULTRA Q, all began as attempts to integrate a mystery show with special effects work. Tsuburaya's studio found a way of integrating *Thunderbirds*-style miniature effects with full-size human actors, by creating a plot which allowed for giant superheroes to clash in tiny cities—ULTRAMAN.

While TBS capitalized on the success of *Ultraman*, TV Asahi commissioned a rival from the Tōei studios, which streamlined the superhero formula for its maximum merchandising potential. Using a story idea from manga author Shōtarō Ishinomori, Tōei plumped for not one but *five* color-coded heroes like the Tracy brothers of *Thunderbirds*, each with a doll and a vehicle toy waiting to be sold. They called it a *sentai,* or "battle team." The result was GORANGER, a franchise of such power that its producers would not let the copyright rest with a single individual. Instead, they registered the idea to one "Saburō Yade" (a name that could be translated as Third Son of Eight Hands), a mysterious figure who continues to claim the credit for successive hero shows in Japan. The authors were intensely impressed with his achievements over the years, until we began to suspect that he, like his anime colleague "Hajime Yadate" at Bandai, was actually a pseudonym designed to assign copyright in new shows to a studio-owned entity. Mr. Yade first appeared in company documents when Tōei entered negotiations with Marvel comics over several projects designed to bring Marvel Comics properties to Japan. Though a couple of anime spin-offs did finally appear, the only live-action result was the Japanese **SPIDER-MAN** series. Plans to follow it with *Captain America* eventually transformed into **BATTLEFEVER J** (for which Mr. Yade took the credit), and the series that would eventually be known as the "Super Sentai" series remained a resolutely Japanese production ever since.

THE RISE OF THE MINI-SERIES

The 1970s were a time of reassessment by the masters of Japanese media. The year 1971 saw the success in the pop charts of the song "Children Who Never Knew the War" (Sensō o Shiranai Kodomotachi) by the Zeroes—an attempt to remind the older generation that those now coming of age had no part in the folly of WWII, and wanted nothing to do with its memory or its shame. Similarly, as American TV continued its exports of hard-bitten cop shows and action movies, the United States endured a humiliating retreat from

SUPER SENTAI SERIES CHRONOLOGY

1975 Goranger	1994 Kakuranger ☞
1977 Jaqk	*Power Rangers sea-*
1978 (no official show,	*son three*
but see Spider-	1995 Ohranger ☞ *Power*
Man)	*Rangers Zeo*
1979 Battlefever J	1996 Carranger ☞ *Power*
1980 Denziman	*Rangers Turbo*
1981 SunVulcan	1997 Megaranger ☞
1982 Goggle V	*Power Rangers in*
1983 Dynaman	*Space*
1984 Bioman	1998 Gingaman ☞ *Power*
1985 Changeman	*Rangers Lost*
1986 Flashman	*Galaxy*
1987 Maskman	1999 Gogo Five ☞ *Power*
1988 Liveman	*Rangers Lightspeed*
1989 Turboranger	*Rescue*
1990 Fiveman	2000 Timeranger ☞
1991 Jetman	*Power Rangers*
1992 Zyuranger (see	*Time Force*
Mighty Morphin'	2001 Gaoranger ☞ *Power*
Power Rangers)	*Rangers Wild Force*
1993 Dairanger ☞ *Power*	2002 Hurricanger ☞
Rangers season	*Power Rangers*
two	*Ninja Storm*
	2003 Abaranger

Vietnam. Japan's answer to these times came in the form of **MEN'S JOURNEY**, an adventure series in which the central cast were not soldiers or gun-wielding cops, but humble security guards. Led by an old soldier who constantly reminds them that they are powerless, they must deal with the threats of the modern world without resorting to the temptations of force—a true internalization of the values forced on Japan by the Allied powers, but apparently forgotten already by the victors.

Behind the scenes, the tensions between cinema and television were still high. Because television was still primarily an advertising delivery system aimed at women, the movie industry had concentrated its efforts on attracting a male audien

Japanese movies of the period had become increasingly violent or erotic, reaching a point by the 1970s when many of them were regarded as unsuitable for broadcast without cuts. Rather than attack popular films with censorious scissors, the TV companies decided to make their own tele-features, and the 1970s saw a rise in the number of 90- and 120-minute movies made for television.

Foreign television of the period was similarly characterized by big productions and mini-series, several of which also exerted their influence on the Japanese market. The Italian docudrama *Life of Leonardo da Vinci* inspired the Japanese to answer with their own *Biography Without Borders: The Members of the Coudenhové Family* (*Kokkyō no nai Denki: Coudenhové-ke no Hitobito*, 1973). Directed by Naoya Yoshida to mark the 20th anniversary of NHK as a TV broadcaster, the series starred Sayuri Yoshinaga not only as the real-life Mitsuko Aoyama, a woman of the Meiji period who married Heinrich Coudenhové, Earl of Calergi in Austria, but also as the reporter who investigates her story in the present day.

The biggest and most infamous of the mini-series was, in effect, a Japanese-American hybrid. Broadcast across eight consecutive nights on TV Asahi in 1981, *James Clavell's Shōgun* featured notable local stars such as Yōko Shimada, Frankie Sakai, and Toshirō Mifune, but was not well-received by Japanese viewers. The audience resistance stemmed from the script's fictionalization of numerous historical figures, which, to a Japanese audience reared on *taiga* dramas, seemed pointless. After all, why have a "John Blackthorne" Richard Chamberlain, still famous in n as *Doctor Kildare*) when the historical

Will Adams was just as interesting and would have made for a more interesting subject on the rival NHK network? Indeed, it is no coincidence that the *taiga* drama two years later did just that and chronicled the life of the chief inspiration for "Lord Toranaga"—**TOKUGAWA IEYASU**.

YUPPIES AND TRENDIES

As Japan entered the 1980s, a generation had grown up watching TV and was now working in it. NTV was able to celebrate its 25th anniversary with **MONKEY**, a landmark series that celebrated the growth of TV in Japan by employing two whole generations of stars and guest stars—alongside former pop idols, the cast included a model whose first public success had only come a year earlier. *Monkey* united Japan and gave two years of *taiga* dramas serious competition during its broadcasts.

As the 1980s saw Japan recover from the Oil Shocks, the economic boom-time gave rise to two influential serials. In 1983, Sugako Hashida's *Oshin* lionized a suffering heroine who endures hardships throughout the 20th century. It firmly codified the already well-established formulae of the NHK "television novel" for a new generation, but it also found an international audience, albeit escaping the notice of most English-language territories. *Oshin* encouraged primetime shows to imitate the misery and struggle of daytime women's TV, most notably in **CHILD WITHOUT A HOME** and the later *taiga* drama **INOCHI: LIFE**, in a genre that extends to the present day with such blockbusters as **100 YEARS**.

While *Oshin* warned Japanese women to cherish their traditional virtues and not be tempted by the deceptive allure of modern values, Toshio Kamata's **FRIDAY'S WIVES** featured three disenchanted homemakers seeking extramarital thrills while their husbands were at work. Though little different in basic form from 1960's *Days of Infidelity*, *Friday's Wives* clung resolutely to images of conspicuous consumption and the yuppie lifestyle, inadvertently establishing a desire in its upwardly mobile audience to see more of the same.

As America itself observed with *The Big Chill* (1983) and *Thirtysomething* (1987), the Baby Boomers of the late 1940s and early 1950s were now leaving their youth behind. The largest young audience in TV history, which had in its time swelled the ratings for children's cartoons and teen movies, was now witnessing friends pairing off, marrying, and having children of their own. The time was right to make dramas for this new demographic, and TV producers elected to mix the lost hopes (or steely optimism) of the thirtysomethings with a mid-youth crisis among twentysomethings, perhaps inspired by the seven directionless graduates of *St. Elmo's Fire* (1983). The most conspicuous results were **ODD APPLES** and **SEVEN PEOPLE IN SUMMER**, with large casts allowing for several interlocking love triangles and plots, and a concentration on urban life in the materialistic 1980s.

Rating as high as some of the lesser *taiga* serials, *Seven People in Summer* was soon refined into the first of the "Trendy Dramas" that defined the late 1980s. Featuring beautiful people in creative professions so achingly cool that they required foreign words to describe them such as *journalism, design,* and *broadcasting,* the Trendy Dramas that began with **I WANT TO HUG YOU!** found a new audience among singletons.

The Trendy Dramas that flourished in the late 20th century did so in a newly created market. Previously, early morning and early evening shows were confined to kids' stuff. During the day, housewives were the only audience expected to be watching TV. In the later evening, maybe something hard-boiled or crime-ridden for Dad, back from a hard day at the office. The economic boom-time of the 1980s bubble economy changed all that. Suddenly, Japanese households were more likely to have two or even three televisions. Women under 25, generally living at home until marriage, and therefore blessed with a massive disposable income, became an important advertising demographic. Certain producers realized that these young girls would no longer be pouting in the living room while Dad watched the latest samurai drama. In theory, they could be watching their own portable set in their bedroom and obey the commercials' purchase suggestions for foreign holidays, exotic face creams, and hair products.

RECESSION AND RECOVERY

The Japanese economic boom, however, soon gave way to bust, and with the flop of **PARADISE OF LOVE**, the Trendy Drama was pronounced dead. However, rumors of its demise were greatly exaggerated—before long, **TOKYO LOVE STORY** achieved monster ratings by recreating many of the earlier traditions of Trendy Drama, and itself inspired numerous imitators. Some, such as **IN THE NAME OF LOVE** and **101ST PROPOSAL**, sought to replay the clichés of Trendy Drama with a more bittersweet touch. Others, seeing the success as having something to do with *Tokyo Love Story*'s origins in a manga, sought to adapt other popular comics for a TV audience. Cr

Fumi Saimon in particular, saw most of her manga works snatched up for TV adaptation, including later hits such as **ASUNARO CONFESSIONS** and **AGE 35**, but other manga adaptations included titles for a younger audience that still watched anime, such as **YOUNG KINDAICHI FILES** and **MASK OF GLASS**.

The introduction of a character in a wheelchair in **UNDER ONE ROOF** reawakened a disability subgenre that had been dormant in primetime drama since the 1970s show **KANTARŌ TERAUCHI AND FAMILY**. The quintessential disability drama was the autistic ingenue played by Emi Wakui in **PURE**—to this day, when Japanese producers announce a "Pure Drama," they mean a show whose plot turns on some form of disability or infirmity. Such topics have included HIV in **PLEASE GOD! JUST A LITTLE MORE TIME**, blindness in **EDGE OF THE WORLD**, deafness in **HEAVEN'S COINS**, and multiple personality disorder in **MPD PSYCHO**. Initially a brave attempt at inclusion and education, the 1990s vogue for disabled characters soon collapsed into a clichéd carnival of afflictions, thrown into many new dramas like just another character quirk.

With *trendy* now little more than a signifier of a young cast and little leeway for escape from budgetary constraints, it was left to scriptwriters to find a new direction. Other genres also underwent changes— not so much overhauls as recombinations of earlier traditions. Successes in the 1990s included **BAYSIDE SHAKEDOWN**, a lighthearted police drama with additional romantic undertones, the gangster turned schoolteacher comedy of *GTO*, and the disability romance of **BEAUTIFUL LIFE**. The 1990s also ᵥ a resurgence in horror and thrillers, ᵏs chiefly to a succession of waves of

interest ushered in by **NIGHT HEAD**, *The X-Files*, the *Ring* movie, and its later offspring such as the **RING** TV series and other thrillers like **TRICK** and **UNSOLVED CASES**. Amidst these hybrid plots, the old favorites jostled for airtime—tough detectives, cheating couples, ghost stories, and samurai dramas.

The 1990s also saw the reversal of the movie world's antipathy toward television. After initial frosty relations, the film world admitted defeat by the 1980s, when cinemas often became little more than venues where films would be previewed as loss-leaders for eventual video sales. The career path of actors on TV also ensured that the medium provided the movies with most of their new talents. Where once the movie and TV industries literally refused to communicate or share resources, they now enjoy symbiotic links so permeable that many Japanese movies are spin-offs of television series and often incomprehensible without prior knowledge of the original. In an age of cinema spin-offs and of rental and retail video, recent TV series such as *Bayside Shakedown*, **YIN-YANG MASTER**, *Ring*, **HYPNOSIS**, and **HEAVEN'S COINS** have capitalized on the increased exposure of a cinema release. Instead of fading from public view after the usual 12 weeks, shows are kept in the public eye by occasional TV specials until such time as a movie is ready, which itself generates advertising for the retail video release of the original series. Long regarded as an almost completely disposable and transient form of entertainment, earlier seasons of TV dramas are now often available for perusal long after their original broadcast. Not only should this hopefully force some of the lazier producers to stop recycling the same plots with only minor alterations, but it has already created a new market for Japanese TV drama outside Japan.

THE RISE OF THE HARIZU

The end of the 20th century saw several attempts to make a landmark TV drama. Prime contenders were TBS, which made the epic *100 Years*, and NHK, whose 2000 *taiga* was the multigenerational historical drama **AOI**. However, it was Fuji that truly won the race to come up with a glimpse of the future, in their internationally-themed drama **LOVE 2000**.

Drama in the 21st century has been characterized by a new influence—the genre's popularity in other parts of Asia. TV drama found a new and unexpected audience in Korea, Taiwan, Hong Kong, Malaysia, and Singapore, spreading through piracy, cable channels, and home-taping. For those who had to defer to their parent's viewing choices on the home television, the availability of Japanese dramas on VCD afforded a new opportunity, since the video format was readily playable on any computer's CD-ROM drive. This latter option was particularly influential on the spread of Japanese TV into the People's Republic of China, where impoverished students without TV sets could still watch new shows using college computers.

In a pattern that has been repeated before with the influx of manga in the 1970–80s and anime in the 1980–90s, initial pirate editions of Japanese products in the rest of Asia created a demand that was eventually met with legitimate exports. In 1997, the Japanese drama *Tokyo Love Story* (as *Dongjing Aiqing Gushi*) in mainland China and **LONG VACATION** (as *Youchang Jiaqi*) in Hong Kong enjoyed such impres-

METAL SERIES CHRONOLOGY	
1982 Gavan	1989 Jivan
1983 Shaliban	1990 Winspector
1984 Shider	1991 Solbrain
1985 Juspion	1992 Exidraft
1986 *Spielban* (see VR Troopers)	1993 Jan Person
	1994 Blue Swat
1987 Metaldar ☞ *VR Troopers #2*	1995 *Bee Fighter* (see Beetleborgs)
1988 Jiraiya	1996 *Bee Fighter Kabuto* ☞ *Beetleborgs #2*

sive word-of-mouth that Japanese dramas became the trendy topic of conversation in fashion magazines the following year. This was particularly noticeable in Hong Kong, where *Long Vacation* was the first pop culture artifact to arrive after the former colony's handover to China and regarded by many as an uncensored alternative to state-approved television. By 2000, the shows had received legitimate broadcasts on Asian TV networks, and by 2001, *riju*, as Japanese drama is known in Mandarin (*yatkehk* in Cantonese) was a fundamental feature of local youth-oriented programming. In Taiwan, local slang even coined a new term for its aficionados—the *harizu*.*

Japanese TV producers were not slow to exploit the genre's newfound popularity. A number of internationally themed dramas began production around the turn of the century, featuring guest stars from other Asian territories. Faye Wong appeared in **FALSE LOVE**, Vivian Hsu in *Lady of the*

---

* *Harizu*. The name includes the characters for "[Rising] Sun" and "Tribe," preceded by an onomatopoeic character designed to recall the Pekinese lap-dog *habagou*, a slang term for those who kowtow to foreigners. It is also a pun on *hanizu*—a minority.

© 2001 Comic Ritz Productions Co. Ltd.

Meteor Garden, the Taiwanese remake of *Hana Yori Dango*

Manor, Yoon Son-ha in **FIGHTING GIRL,** and Takeshi Kaneshiro in *Love 2000*—guaranteeing instant audience expansion in the actors' homelands. The year 2002 also saw the first genuine Japan-Korea TV coproduction in the form of the short hands across the water romance **FRIENDS,** starring Won Bin and Kyōko Fukada.

Meanwhile, the popularity of Japanese drama led to a rush by producers to copy the formula—though they disagreed on what exactly "the formula" was. The manga-based *GTO* and *Asunaro Confessions* were cloned for Taiwanese TV, while other producers opted to buy the adaptation rights to unfilmed manga, hoping to recreate a ʲanese feel but with local casts. Hence,

the beginning of the 21st century has seen a live-action Mandarin adaptation of *Hana Yori Dango* (*AE) under the title *Meteor Garden,* followed by *Marmalade Boy* and *The Story of Tarō Yamada,* all starring Taiwanese actors.

America was not excluded from this wave of interest. Not only did many Chinese-Americans adopt the same *harizu* attitude as their Asian cousins, but the local immigrant population had access to original Japanese drama, often with English subtitles. Over a hundred shows have been subtitled and broadcast on TV in Hawaii, leading to the beginnings of an American fan community, particularly on the West Coast of the United States with access to channels such as KTSF and KSCI. Other series have been shown untranslated on networks such as NGN in America, and JSTV in Europe. Some members of Japanese animation fandom, long equipped to prepare and distribute amateur subtitles of foreign-language shows, retooled their interests to encompass live-action drama—fansubs began to appear of famous shows like *Ring.* DVD, VCD, and internet distribution sped up the availability of TV drama outside Japan and created a market for it.

The success of Japanese TV drama in English remains most powerful in the children's demographic, where it has maintained a constant profile since the late 1970s. **MONKEY, STAR FLEET,** and **THE WATER MARGIN** dominated children's television in the U.K. during the early 1980s, but the medium's greatest live-action success came with the long-awaited U.S. breakthrough of a *sentai* show. Heavily bowdlerized and featuring an all-American cast out of costume, *Dinosaur Battle Team Zyuranger* was retooled as **MIGHTY MORPHIN' POWER RANGERS**, creating a franchise that is still running to this day. As we prepare this book for the press, *Power Rangers* is approaching its 500th episode in the United States—not bad for a foreign show. Other *sentai* series, including **MASKED RIDER** and several fragments of the Metal Series, have followed the Power Rangers onto American networks, though their early time slots and juvenile content have kept them safe from most kinds of academic scrutiny—this book is the first to place the *sentai* shows in their televisual context.

ABOUT THIS BOOK

Everyone can think of at least one Japanese drama, even if they only know it through its movie adaptation or its manga inspiration. The lucky ones, particularly in Hawaii and the West Coast of the United States, may have even had the chance to watch some TV dramas on local TV stations. Whatever your current knowledge of Japanese TV drama, this book is designed to expand it exponentially. Each entry comes with cross-references to point out similar shows and is fully indexed. An actor's career can be traced through the index at the back of the book, and much of the fun we have had in writing the book has come from those moments when we have not only discovered a new favorite writer or director, but the opportunity to explore their other work.

Though this book is a stand-alone work, it contains cross-references to Stone Bridge Press's *Anime Encyclopedia* (2001), in order to provide extra information on the strong ties between television and the worlds of Japanese comics and animation. The presence of "(*AE)" in an entry indicates that further information can be found in the *Anime Encyclopedia*, as many serials such as **JOURNEY TO THE WEST**, **SAZAE-SAN**, and **MASK OF GLASS** also exist in animated incarnations.

Following government crackdowns on "rockabilly" sounds and a concerted effort to keep the Swinging Sixties from having too much effect on Japan, the music industry came to be dominated by talent agencies, a situation which led in turn to a situation in which *talento* became the main pool of recruitment for drama stars. Sadly, this media mix does not always work to the advantage of the shows on offer. Quite often, it merely gives people who can't sing an excuse to prove that they can't act either. Frustratingly for Japan's many decent actors, some shows have been ruined by the presence of inadequate costars, and many display the clear signs of having been flung together as little more than a high concept vehicle for a "big-name" performer with limited range. It should be remembered, however, that the rise of the *talento* is not a recent phenomenon, but has been part of Japanese media since the earliest days of TV. Without the ossified traditions of apprenticeship and loyalty of art forms such as kabuki or classical theater, TV offered a fast track for many new stars, and success in one sector of it often led to work elsewhere. Many of today's older character actors were once *talento* themselves, such as *Bayside Shake-down*'s Chōsuke Ikariya (formerly the bass player with the Drifters) and *Lady of the Manor*'s Ittoku Kishibe (formerly with the Tigers).

However, in lasting this long, the stars of yesteryear have proved their abilities are not mere flashes in the pan. Viewers of the contemporary dramatic scene have no way of knowing who will still be onscreen in 30 years, but it's fair to imagine that a few of today's celebrities will be thankfully absent. Lip-synching to bubblegum pop music in a shopping mall might be a career choice for some, but can be irritating when parleyed into an excuse to torture us over an evening's viewing. Every so often, the "talent" system produces a performer with genuine star power, such as Takuya Kimura, but such finds are rare indeed. The early evening slots, sometimes termed the "kidult" genres in English-language broadcasting, are often an offense to acting, and several of the worst criminals have even managed a successful escape to primetime.

You have been warned—not all of the shows we discuss in this book are programs we can honestly, objectively rate as "entertainment." However, our experience in the anime world has taught us that it is crucial to give readers the opportunity to separate the good from the bad. An appraisal with no frame of reference would be like trying to convince someone of the landmark status of *Hill Street Blues,* devoid of its historical context and without the opportunity to compare it with *Saved by the Bell.*

While we generally regard the best of American TV (*ER, Murder One, The West Wing*) as the best in the world, not all of its

virtues are immediately apparent to the Japanese. Though many shows reach Japan in translation, there is no guarantee that they come across with the same level of impact or quality. The Japanese translator of one well-known American series was so poorly paid that he could only make ends meet if he translated three entire episodes every day. Though most translators insist on a script and a video, he was forced to work blind, with nothing but the show's audio soundtrack as material. Lines naturally drifted in meaning, and references to onscreen events became garbled—if the U.S. producers ever wondered why their show was less of a success than it could have been in Japan, they should have asked themselves whether it was the same show by the time it reached its new audience.

Nevertheless, America often provides Japanese producers with new ideas. When in search of producer's possible inspiration, it is fruitless counting back a year or so to see what was on at the Japanese cinema. TV people don't seem to go to the movies, although they do rent videos and watch foreign films on television—this book includes mentions of inspirations where we believe them to be obvious, and the time lag implies that many productions are inspired by the release of big movies on rental video, not their theatrical first-run.

Where we see an obvious or potential link with a foreign show, we often give information on it. However, such parallels should not be taken as statements that the Japanese or American producers are ripping each other off—merely that they may have been inspired by some of the other material onscreen at the time. It is certainly cause for speculation on cross-pollination between two cultures—we'll probably never know if the broadcast of **GOOD MOURNING** in California had any influence on the germination of *Six Feet Under,* but it is an interesting thought.

When discussing a possible foreign inspiration for these dramas, we restrict ourselves to the most likely impetus—*Ally McBeal* never did anything that the plays of Dennis Potter didn't do two decades before, but the works of Dennis Potter were not on Japanese TV every week while producers were planning **HERO** and **UNMARRIED FAMILY**. Similarly, we only suggest evidence of inspiration where it appears plausible—there are coincidental similarities between **HEAVEN CANNOT WAIT** and the shelved *God Squad* project by *Moonlighting*'s Glenn Gordon Caron, but it is highly unlikely that the producers of one had any knowledge of the other.

There are several Osamu Tezukas in the Japanese entertainment business, including a composer (*AE) and the famous creator of *Astro Boy.* A third Osamu Tezuka, the producer of *Purple Eyes in the Dark,* is listed as "Osamu Tezuka (b)" to avoid confusion.

TV SPECIALS

We only include TV movies where they relate directly to a given series, or where, such as Takashi Miike's **TENNEN SHŌJO MANN**, a series generally comprises movie-length episodes. Thus, we mention TV movies such as the spin-offs of the series *Bayside Shakedown,* but not failed pilots. We were originally heartbroken that we could not include **THE SNIPER** and elated when the last-minute arrival of a sequel turned it from a one-shot TV movie into a two-part series, and hence qualified for inclusion. Limitations of space, however, have forced

us to severely curtail our coverage of TV movies.

Many serials often exist in feature-length "TV movie" editions, comprising the highlights of the first third or two-thirds, and broadcast partway through the original run in an attempt to snare extra viewers for the remainder of the story. Where we know these "specials" to exist, we have mentioned them, but there are likely to be far more that have faded into the schedules and gone unnoticed.

Our estimations of running times are approximate and are based on the scheduled times in Japanese TV guides, minus time allowed for commercial breaks. Many TV series also have a first or last episode that is noticeably longer than the 45-minute norm. Where we know this to be the case, we have noted it, but it is highly likely that many other series also have an opener of perhaps 70 minutes, deliberately designed to make a splash on the schedules and attract attention. Accordingly, our running times should be cited with care, and episode counts preceded by a "ca." are pure supposition.

ENGLISH RELEASE

Over 15% of the titles in this book, more than 150 titles, have already been broadcast in English. Where all or part of a TV series is available in a *legal* English version, we have put an asterisk next to the title. This generally means that the series has had a subtitled broadcast on an American TV channel, though occasionally it can mean a dubbed broadcast in the U.K. (*Monkey*) or Australia (**PHANTOM AGENTS**), or perhaps even the use of some of the footage within another show, for which the plot and characters have been greatly changed

(**Beetleborgs**). Considering the great influence that TV exerts on the Japanese film industry, although many TV series have not been translated, their movie spin-offs have (*Yin-Yang Master, Bayside Shakedown*). In such cases, we still list the series as untranslated. The only exception is those English-language "movies" which have been assembled wholly from footage from the TV series (**Mighty Jack**). In such cases, we count the show's English availability as "partial" and add an asterisk.

RATINGS

Where available, we also include peak ratings for the landmark shows. These figures are based on the estimated percentage of Japanese households with a set tuned to the show in question—thus, the 35.7% rating for the last episode of *GTO* means that just over a third of all households in Japan were tuning in to Fuji TV. The highest drama rating in recent years was *Oshin* (62.9%), a stunningly high figure, unlikely to be beaten as the proliferation of channels gives viewers more choices.

The Japanese ratings system relies not on who is watching a TV set, but merely whether it is on. Accordingly, the percentiles listed in this book are for *households,* not the individual viewers chronicled by the American system. Thus, we can say *Oshin* was seen in 62.9% of Japanese homes with a TV set, but this statement does not necessarily mean that 62.9% of the Japanese population were watching, nor is it any guarantee that the houses in question did not have a second or third set, each turned to a different channel.

Despite this slight difference in statistical methods, Japanese figures were commensurate with those of American

GAIJIN THEME TUNES
Just a few of the Westerners who have provided the themes for Japanese TV drama:

Debbie Gibson—*About Men*
Whitney Houston—*August Love Song*
Maxi Priest—*Bayside Shakedown*
Richie Sambora—*Beach Boys*
Jane Birkin—*Beauty*
Diana Ross—*Boyfriend*
The Beatles—*Come Out and Play*
Celine Dion—*Eve, My Lover*
Rolling Stones—*Face*
Paul McCartney—*Family Weathermap*
Brian Ferry—*Gift*
Paul Anka—*Golden Bowl*
Carly Simon—*Hotel*
Elton John—*Iguana's Daughter; The Sun is Not Silent*
John Lennon—*Last Song, Precious Friend*
Swing Out Sister—*Midday Moon*
Frank Sinatra—*Mid-Life Crisis; Sometime Somewhere*

Simon and Garfunkel—*No Longer Human*
Robbie Williams—*OL Way of Saving*
Nana Mouskouri—*100 Years*
Chicago—*Singles*
The Eagles—*Second Time Around*
Elvis Costello—*The Smile Has Left Your Eyes*
Abba—*Strawberry on the Shortcake; Love is a Battlefield!*
Garth Brooks—*Sunflowers on the Hill*
Wham—*Tomoko and Tomoko*
The Carpenters—*Underage; Where is Love?*
Amber—*Unmarried Family*
Diana Ross—*Until This Becomes a Memory*
Sting—*Yasha*
Bee Gees—*Young Generation*
Mariah Carey—*You're under Arrest*

networks until the 1980s—in fact, the most-watched drama in American TV history was *Roots* (1977), which gained a share of 71%. However, as the American networks fragmented into increasingly disparate "narrowcasts" of affiliates, syndicates, and niche-interest programming, the chances of a single broadcast attaining such a wide audience declined at great speed. In the early years of the 21st century, where viewers can be corralled into niche channels that pander to particular subgenres, U.S.

networks often fight over single percentile points. While such narrowcasting also exists in Japan, modern TV drama continues to hold the interest of a huge sector of the population.

SINGERS AND COMPOSERS

We mention theme music where known, and also list composers where they are known to have a crossover appeal with the anime-watching audience. Music over the opening and closing credits (the OP and ED, in Japanese media slang) is often part of a cross-promotional deal, and our experience in the anime world has taught us that entire new fanbases can be created through a well-placed tie-in. This is certainly the rationale behind the prevalence of media tie-ins in Japan, where even TV commercials tend to have an onscreen credit detailing the identity and availability of their theme music. Consequently, we have added the details of the theme music to all shows where such information was available to us, discovering in the process a surprising number of non-Japanese performers moonlighting in the TV drama world (see sidebar on previous page).

FOREIGN SHOWS

Since hundreds of shows seen by Japanese viewers are not Japanese at all, we have also included a list of over a thousand series from around the world in the first appendix, listed along with their Japanese broadcast channels and, where known, their Japanese broadcast dates and names.

Sometimes this renaming can create a bizarre taxonomy of title changes, as in the case of the TV show known to the Japanese as *Burn! 0011*. To translate the title correctly, we would first need to know that the spy show *The Man From U.N.C.L.E.* was broadcast in Japan in 1965 as *0011 Napoleon Solo,* which both implied a relationship with 007 and shifted the show's emphasis further onto the dark, handsome (and presumably, honorably Asian) Robert Vaughan. Meanwhile, Bruce Lee's movie *Enter the Dragon* was released in Japan as *Burn! Dragon.* It's only armed with these two precedents that a researcher without reference material stands any chance of working out that *Burn! 0011* is actually the cartoon series *Hong Kong Phooey,* retitled to convey the secret agent and Kung-fu elements to a Japanese audience.

A second appendix lists the most common Mandarin titles for the 150 serials that have spearheaded Japanese drama's popularity in the rest of Asia, designed to aid viewers and scholars in China, Taiwan, and Singapore.

EXTRAS

In addition, the book is sprinkled with sidebars of bonus information. Some of the best moments are plot twists, which we have given out of context in our "spoiler" sidebars. If you don't want to know which show involves a pastiche of *Spartacus* in the final sequence, simply stay away from the answer given on the following page.

Following the publication of Stone Bridge Press's *Anime Encyclopedia,* several readers expressed an interest in knowing the authors' own favorite shows, all the better to gauge how likely our opinion was to match their own. Accordingly, both Jonathan Clements (JC) and Motoko Tamamuro (MT) have provided subjective lists of their favorite shows, actors and actresses, alongside more statistically compelling evidence from Japanese surveys.

IMAGES

We have tried diligently to obtain permissions for all copyright images used in this book. If we have inadvertently omitted or incorrectly listed the name of a rights-holder, we will gladly correct the error in the next edition. We honor the rights of creators and acknowledge their work.

We had hoped, after the success of the *Anime Encyclopedia,* that Japanese rights-holders would realize the value of publicity for their works. Sadly, only a few have been prepared to cooperate with us at all, while others were forced to demand reproduction fees beyond the means of a small publisher, or simply did not return our calls. In many cases, we have been literally stunned by the lack of interest displayed by some promotions offices in promoting their material to foreign audiences. We would like to point out, to those foreign authors who have experienced similarly dispiriting difficulties in dealing with the Japanese, that having a native Japanese speaker on the team seems to make no difference at all! Luckily, representatives of several companies were prepared to help, while others did what they could within the restrictions of their own bureaucracies. Japanese publishing practice has a very different view of what constitutes "fair use," and some companies are used to charging high fees for images, even when they are giving them to a magazine for an advertorial puff-piece. Such a stranglehold has been crippling to criticism in Japan, and, we believe, seriously hindered the development of Japanese television in markets abroad.

This book contains many illustrations and images, but we had hoped it would contain many more. Like many books about television in Japan itself, we have plugged a number of gaps with specially-commissioned artwork—in this case from renowned illustrator Steve Kyte. We hope that his illustrations add to your enjoyment of this book, and we shall persist in trying to talk him into authorizing a *Geisha Detective* T-shirt.

ACKNOWLEDGMENTS

The following people have all contributed in some way to the task of writing this book, through the supply of information, materials, images, gossip, and sometimes just a shoulder to cry on:

John Ainsworth, Chikahiro Andō, Amelia Bedford, Laura Block, Lee Brimmicombe-Wood, Beth Cary, Stephen Cremin, Merlin David, Lisa DeBell, Carole Eichner, Chelsey Fox, Kimberly Guerre, Kimiyo Hayakawa, Charlotte Howard, Petra Howard-Wuertz, Osamu Ichihara, Setsuko Ichihara, Tomoyuki Imai, Simon Jowett, Tony Kehoe, Steve Kyte, Masaki Koide, Richard Larcombe, Gilbert Mackay, Gerry Malir, Victor Marino, Akiko Matsuda, Naomi Matsuda, Helen McCarthy, James McLeod, Tom Mes, Chrys Mordin, Katsuyuki Motohiro, Yoshiko Nakano, Adam Newell, Yukari Ogura, Lisa Richards, Lynn Robson, Anna Sargent, Mark Schilling, Fumiko Shiromoto, Toren Smith, Jim Swallow, Sachiko Tamamuro, Elizabeth Tinsley, Brad Warner, Leigh Williams, and Shōko Yamamoto.

Special thanks go to Andrew Deacon for his Mandarin romanizations in Appendix Two, Barry Harris, who found whole new uses for Microsoft Word's index functions, and Steve Kyte for his many black and white illustrations. And, as ever, Peter Goodman of Stone Bridge Press, who always looks upon the positive side of being handed a manuscript three times the size he was expecting.

Eleven entries contained in this book were published previously in *Newtype USA* magazine and are reprinted here with the kind cooperation of Newtype USA, Inc. and its editorial team.

THE DORAMA ENCYCLOPEDIA

ABBREVIATIONS AND KEY
The following abbreviations are used throughout the listings:

*	available in English
JPN	official Japanese title
AKA	"also known as" (alternative title)
PRD	produced by
DIR	directed by
SCR	script by
CAST	main cast members
CHN	broadcasting company
DUR	running time, episode number, broadcast dates
N/C	not credited
N/D	no data available
??	uncertain data (usually broadcast date)
ca.	circa, approximately
ep., eps.	episode(s)
mins.	minutes
BOLDFACE TYPE	cross-reference to main entry

ABARANGER

2003. JPN: *Bakuryū Sentai Abaranger*.
AKA: Explosive Dragon Battle Team
Abaranger. PRD: Gō Nakajima, Jun
Higasa, Hideaki Tsukada. DIR: Hajime
Konaka. SCR: Minehisa Arakawa. CAST:
Kōchirō Nishi, Shō Tomita, Aiko Itō,
Kaoru Abe, Kōen Okumura, Michi
Nishijima. CHN: Asahi. dur: 25 mins. x
ca. 50 eps.; Sun 16 February 2003–.
Peace and quiet in Tokyo is suddenly
interrupted by a dinosaur attack—the
gentle ancient beasts have been pro-
voked into such violent behavior by the
evil Evallion. Black Ranger Asuka
(Abe), an inhabitant of the parallel
Dino Earth, comes to our world to stop
Evallion's acts but needs the help of
locals to form a battle team. With
token high school girl Emiri
(Nishijima), he gathers coffee shop
owner Ryūnosuke (Okumura), Ranru
(Itō) from Fukuoka to be the Yellow
Ranger, Yukito (Tomita) from Sapporo
to be the Blue Ranger, and Ryōga
(Nishi) to be the Red Ranger. The
newly formed team then fights to save
the city from the dinosaur invasion in
the most recent incarnation of the
MIGHTY MORPHIN' POWER RANGERS
franchise to appear on Japanese
screens before this book went to press.
Presumably, these adventures will
appear on U.S. screens as the 12th
Power Rangers series sometime in 2004.

ABARE HATCHAKU

1979. AKA: *Wild Boy*. PRD: N/C. DIR:
Shūji Matsuo. SCR: Yasushi Ichikawa,
Narimitsu Taguchi. CAST: Tomonori
Yoshida, Eishin Higashino, Chiharu
Kuri, Yukako Hayase, Miwako Fujitani.
CHN: Asahi. DUR: 45 mins. x 327 eps.;
Sat 3 February 1979–8 March 1980
(#1); 22 March 1980–27 March 1982
(#2); 10 April 1982–26 March 1983
(#3); 2 April 1983–23 February 1985
(#4); 2 March 1985–21 September
1985 (#5).
Eleven-year-old Chōtarō (Yoshida) specializes in fighting and mischief-mak-
ing in the classroom. Though he has a
reputation as a bully, he'll happily do
anything for a girl, as long as she asks.
Based on the manga by Hisashi
Yamanaka, *AH* managed the tricky
accomplishment of appealing both to
children and adults—the former mar-
veling at the pranks he got away with,
the latter cooing at what a cute kid he
was underneath it all. Four sequels followed, but Chōtarō's youthful cuteness
was a difficult quality to maintain.
Consequently, though his father was
always played by Higashino, successive
seasons of *AH* have featured new actors
playing Chōtarō. The second season
Otoko! AH (*AH, the Man!*, 1980) featured additional directors Eizō
Yamagiwa and Keishi Kawashima, with
Atsushi Kurimata replacing the lead.
He in turn was replaced by Naoya
Araki for the 1982 season, while
Chōtarō was played by Takayuki
Sakatsume in 1983 and by Kazuyoshi
Sakai in the 1985 season.

ABARENBŌ SHOGUN *

1978. AKA: *Unruly Shogun*. PRD: Eisuke
Ozawa. DIR: Eisuke Ozawa, Tsutomu
Tomari, Haruo Ichikura, Hirofumi
Morimoto. SCR: Eisuke Ozawa, Bunjin
Imamura. CAST: Ken Matsudaira,
Saburō Kitajima, Jōji Yamamoto,
Tamao Nakamura, Yuki Matsumura,
Hiroharu Shimizu. CHN: Asahi. DUR: 45
mins. x ?? eps.; Sat 7 January
1978–2 May 1978 (#1); 5 March
1983–7 March 1987 (#2); 9 January
1988–29 September 1990 (#3); 6
April 1991–26 April 1992 (#4); 3 April
1993–26 March 1994 (#5); 8 October
1994–20 January 1996 (#6); 13 July
1996–25 January 1997 (#7); 12 July
1997–7 March 1998 (#8); 7
November 1998–30 September 1999
(#9); 30 March 2000–14 September
2000 (#10); 5 July 2001–10
December 2001 (#11); 8 July 2002–9
September 2002 (#12).
AS dramatizes the life of **YOSHIMUNE**
(1684–1751), the eighth Tokugawa
shogun. Inheriting the fief of Kishū
(now known as Wakayama and Mie
prefectures) at the age of 22, he
became shogun at age 33, following
the death of his 8-year-old predecessor.
According to this TV drama version, he
also found the time to fight crime, disguising himself as Shinnosuke
(Matsudaira), a lordless samurai.
Without the knowledge of the other
nobles, "Shin-san" wanders the back-
streets of Edo, helping local salt-of-the-
earth firefighter Tatsugorō (Kitajima)

deal with criminals and other wrong-doers.

The historical Yoshimune was reputedly a good martial artist (as if anyone would tell him he wasn't!) and also a friend of commoners. Part of his down-to-earth nature was attributed to his mother, a peasant girl who became a bath attendant on his father's estate. This story is alluded to in the drama version, when Yoshimune becomes the ruler of Japan and invites his mother (Nakamura) to join him in Edo Castle—ashamed of her humble birth, she refuses. The series also makes much of Yoshimune's love life—the original was married to an aristocrat at 23, but widowed just four years later. For the drama version, he is repeatedly encouraged to take another wife but instead occupies himself with his three pretty concubines.

Actor Matsudaira was originally selected to play Yoshimune/Shin-san because of his sword-fighting abilities—he formerly trained under Shintarō Katsu, one of the best actors in samurai movies. However, his maturation during the series has paralleled that of the historical character he plays, making his portrayal of the role much more than a series of sword fights. Further seasons of *AS* followed in 1983, 1988, and 1991. From 1992 to 2001, there was a new season of *AS* every year except 1995.

The most recent series focuses on Jūbei Shiranui (Shimizu), a gang leader with a lust for jewelry, who has terrorized the area for three months. Shinnosuke (i.e., the disguised Yoshimune) visits Jūbei at a gambling den but gets into a fight with Eikichi (aka Eigorō, played by Matsumura), the new chief of firefighters. The struggle ruins the cockfight Jūbei is trying to organize, and the two combatants are held at gunpoint by angry gangsters. Jūbei decides to kill them, but the pair are rescued at the last minute by the firefighters (who also functioned as a form of city watch during the Edo period). Soon, Shin-san forms a new friendship with Eikichi, and the dis-

guised shogun is pitching in to help a firefighter beat a murder charge, as well as saving a small child from a burning building. Such heroism leads the misty-eyed Eikichi to comment: *"Master, you are the best shogun. But when you are here as Shinnosuke Tokuda, you are also my friend."* The series was broadcast with English subtitles in the U.S. on KIKU TV. For another nobleman disguised as a commoner, see **MITO KŌMON**.

ABOUT MEN

1990. JPN: *Otoko ni Tsuite*. PRD: Ken Matsumoto. DIR: Ken Matsumoto. SCR: Toshiharu Matsubara. CAST: Yūko Asano, Ayumi Ishida, Masanori Sera, Eiji Bandō, Yū Hayami, Toshiaki Karasawa. CHN: TBS. DUR: 45 mins. x 11 eps.; Fri 12 October 1990–21 December 1990.

Thirty-year-old nurse Tsukiko (Asano) is still hurt that her father Kanichi (Bandō) had an affair eight years ago while her mother was dying. Now, she is approached by an unknown woman called Akari (Ishida), who tells her that Kanichi is dying of cancer, in a drama that centers on the strange relationship between Tsukiko and her father's lover. Though the female relationships are nicely done, depictions of men in the workplace seem somewhat false. Bandō, in particular, looks far too healthy to be a cancer patient. Compare to **PLEASE GOD! JUST A LITTLE MORE TIME**. Theme: Debbie Gibson—"Without You."

ACCOMMODATING WOMAN

1993. JPN: *Tsugō no Ii Onna*. PRD: Shunsaku Kawake. DIR: Shunsaku Kawake, Tōru Hayashi. SCR: Makiko Uchidate. CAST: Yūko Asano, Shin Takuma, Morio Kazama, Narimi Arimori, Tamaki Hosokawa. CHN: Fuji. DUR: 45 mins. x 11 eps.; Thu 14 October 1993–23 December 1993. Dressmaker Nao (Asano) has been going out with Junichirō (Takuma) for three years, but he has been growing steadily distant for the last few months—he has stopped bringing her

gifts and won't even kiss her anymore. Nao suspects he is seeing someone else but still holds out hope that he will marry her. In fact, Junichirō already has a fiancée and regards Nao as an idle diversion. One night, Nao sees Junichirō with Yōko (Hosokawa), the sister of her best friend Sachiko (Arimori). In a fit of pique, she drunkenly seduces the taxi driver who is taking her home. She begins a relationship with the driver (Kazama), a former student revolutionary who is now stuck in a rut with a wife and two kids. However, Junichirō eventually sees the error of his ways, ditches Yōko, and asks Nao to marry him. But Nao decides that she will never be an accommodating woman again. Controversial in its day for its first episode, in which the lead character had sex with a stranger in a public lavatory, *AW* was an early success for writer Makiko Uchidate, who would revisit similar territory with **LUCKILY I WASN'T SO IN LOVE**. Uchidate, a former office worker, presented a dissenting voice popular among women in their twenties, who were justifiably concerned that Japan's bubble economy wasn't all it was cracked up to be. Uchidate's cynical view of fairy-tale endings was a welcome change from the happily-ever-afters of many other dramas. Theme: Eri Hiramatsu—"Modorenai Michi" (The Unweeping Road).

AD BOOGIE

1991. PRD: Yasuo Yagi. DIR: Makoto Kiyohiro. SCR: Kazuhiko Yūkawa. CAST: Taishū Kase, Masatoshi Hamada, Kōji Matoba, Yui Asaka, Haruko Sagara, Yōko Moriguchi, Hikari Ishida. CHN: TBS. DUR: 45 mins. x 10 eps.; Fri 18 October 1991–20 December 1991. Kazushige (Kase) starts a career as an assistant director at a TV production company, only to discover that it is nothing like the glamorous profession he imagined. The "AD" position is also known as a "3Ds" job (difficult, demanding, and dangerous), and Kazushige is under constant pressure from his superiors. Kumi (Asaka) recruits him to pose as her boyfriend in an elaborate attempt to convince her father that she is unable to move back into the family home. Predictably, the couple soon begin dating for real, although Kazushige does not really understand Kumi's carefree lifestyle.

Meanwhile, Takumi (Hamada) has been an AD for seven years and believes that he will lose his girlfriend Naoko (Sagara) unless he gets to direct his own drama series soon. Fellow production assistant Takayuki (Matoba) secretly adores nurse Riyoko (Moriguchi), though he callously has a one-night stand with the broken-hearted makeup artist Akane (Ishida). Akane cries on Kazushige's shoulder and soon begins to develop feelings for him as well.

As Takumi's drama gets underway, Kumi leaves Kazushige to work for a fashion company but soon discovers that it is not as glamorous as it looks. Riyoko leaves for Kagoshima, leaving Takayuki behind in Tokyo. Takumi's drama is finally completed, but as he is showing it to Naoko, he receives news of his father's collapse. Although his drama is warmly received, he decides to leave television and return to his native Osaka to run his family's rice store. Naoko, realizing how much Takumi loves his job, volunteers to run the rice shop for him so he can stay in Tokyo.

On Christmas Eve, Takayuki is waiting for Riyoko at the airport, hoping that she has used the airplane ticket he gave her and that she will agree to marry him. Instead, he only finds a stewardess, who hands him a Dear John letter and returns his ring. Meanwhile, Kazushige asks Akane out, only to have her refuse to be anyone's second choice. Wondering what she meant, Kazushige walks home alone, where he encounters Kumi, who apologizes and embraces him.

Turning aside from TV drama's usual obsession with glamorous newscasters, journalists, or actors in the fashion of **GOOD NEWS** or **STAR STRUCK**, *AD Boogie* is a convincing look behind the

scenes of drama itself, blessed with strong supporting characters amid the traditional clichés. The story was reprised once more on 9 October 1992 in the feature-length TV special *AD Returns*. Theme: Seishirō Kusunoki—"Hottokenaiyo" (I Can't Leave It Alone).

ADULT'S CHOICE, AN

1992. JPN: *Otona no Sentaku*. PRD: Hiroshi Ōtani. DIR: Takamichi Yamada. SCR: Shizuka Ōishi. CAST: Seiko Matsuda, Shin Takuma, Tetsuya Bessho, Hitomi Takahashi. CHN: TBS. DUR: 45 mins. x 11 eps.; Fri 10 January 1992–20 March 1992.

Six years after her parents were presumed lost at sea, Miki (Matsuda) leaves her boyfriend Kōji (Bessho) to marry Yōichirō (Takuma). It could be argued that she is attracted to Yōichirō because he lost his own parents in a similar tragedy, but he is also conveniently handsome, rich, and endowed with better prospects than Kōji, the impoverished assistant to a manga artist. Kōji tries to win back Miki's heart, eventually becoming a rich manga artist in his own right, with an impressive red sports car. But Shizuka Ōishi's script includes many unexpected twists—though it may be a silly romance at heart, it also explores a more pragmatic theme, that love alone is not enough to sail through married life. Matsuda is known as the "queen of the *burikko*," or the embodiment of cutesified Japanese girlhood—her performance in this drama would not disappoint her fans but does seem somehow stuck in a 1980s time warp. For another tale of manga creation, see **KING OF EDITORS**. Theme: Seiko Matsuda—"Kitto Mata Aeru" (We'll Certainly Meet Again).

AERIAL CITY 008

1969. JPN: *Kūchū Toshi 008*. PRD: N/C. DIR: N/C. SCR: Takagaki Aoi. CAST: (voices) Toshiko Ōta, Genzō Wakayama, Kyōko Satomi, Michiko Hirai, Kazuo Kumakura, Arihiro Fujimura, Tomoko Matsuhima. CHN: NHK. DUR: 15 mins.

Aerial City 008

x ca. 200 eps.; Mon 7 April 1969–3 April 1970.

Aerial City 008 is the pinnacle of 21st-century science, an ideal dwelling place for mankind, in a future where all the major cities of the world are connected by supersonic jets that reduce traveling time to a maximum of three hours. Eleven-year-old Hoshio (Ōta) is the son of prominent scientist Yūsuke (Wakayama), and lives in this high-tech utopia with his mother Saeko (Satomi) and sister Tsukiko (Hirai).

Later in the series, Hoshio's family become involved in the fight against the Black Cat criminal organization. A group of master thieves determined to steal priceless antiques like the Sword of Genghis Khan and the fabled Ring of the Queen's Eye, the Black Cat gang also dabbles in espionage and ongoing attempts to ruin efforts to put up a permanent moonbase.

Heavily influenced by Gerry Anderson's *Thunderbirds* (NHK, 1966) and *Captain Scarlet* (TBS, 1968), this puppet show used modern "super-marionettes" rather than the more traditional puppets found in shows such as **CHIRORIN VILLAGE** and **THE HAKKENDEN**. The puppets were created by Tokyo University aeronautical engineering graduate Kinosuke Takeda,

After School

who also put his experience to good use designing the futuristic look of the aerial city. The story itself was based on *Aozora Monogatari* (Blue Sky Story), a tale by **JAPAN SINKS** creator Sakyō Komatsu.

Despite high production values and an accomplished voice cast including Toshiko Ōta from *Secret Akko-chan* (*AE) and Michiko Hirai from *Little Witch Sally* (*AE), *Aerial City 008* was a failure. Producers at the time claimed that science fiction was too difficult for children to handle (a strange excuse in the wake of both **SILICA** and **SPACE PATROL**) or that Japanese children were frightened by the more realistic marionettes used in the show. A generation later, **STAR FLEET** would also use marionettes, also use science fiction, and also flop spectacularly in Japan. Theme: Chinatsu Nakayama—"Kūchū Toshi 008" (Aerial City 008).

AFRICA NIGHTS
1999. JPN: *Africa no Yoru*. PRD: Masatoshi Yamaguchi. DIR: Rieko Ishizaka, Narihide Mizuta, Shunsaku Kawake, Shizuka Ōishi. CAST: Kyōka

Suzuki, Kōichi Satō, Rie Tomosaka, Yasuko Matsuyuki, Shigeru Muroi. CHN: Fuji. DUR: 45 mins. x 11 eps.; Thu 15 April 1999–24 June 1999.
Twenty-nine-year-old Yaeko (Suzuki) has only been married for a short while when her husband is arrested for embezzlement. She tries to start a new life, quitting her job to become a lecturer at a cram school and renting a room at the Maison Africa apartment block. This brings her into contact with her eccentric neighbors, including Reitarō (Satō), whom she briefly dated eight years before. Reitarō is a former film director whose sole production was the movie *Africa Night*. He has since become a business consultant who insists on using charts scrawled with arcane symbols. Reitarō is now dating another Maison Africa resident, the actress/model Yuka (Matsuyuki), who is so obsessed with hygiene that she takes three baths a day. While the women compete for Reitarō's affections, they are both held at bay by Midori (Tomosaka), his overly possessive teenage sister. Meanwhile, the lovelorn women seek advice from

local delicatessen owner Mizuho (Muroi). She offers them consultations on affairs of the heart but secretly has problems of her own—having undergone cosmetic surgery to disguise her identity, she is hiding from the police, who want her for her husband's murder. Compare to **LEAVE IT TO ME**, although *AN* owes its greatest debt to Rumiko Takahashi's *Maison Ikkoku* (*AE), which similarly throws together mismatched residents at an apartment block. *AN* was shown unsubtitled in the U.S. on the International Channel. Theme: Speed—"Breakin' Out to the Morning." Peak rating: 13.4%.

AFTER SCHOOL
1992. JPN: *Hōkago*. PRD: Kōji Shiozawa. DIR: Mamoru Hoshi. SCR: Masashi Todayama. CAST: Arisa Mizuki, Issei Ishida. CHN: Fuji. DUR: 45 mins. x 5 eps.; Thu 15 October 1992–12 November 1992.
Azusa (Mizuki), vice president of her high school class, returns to the school grounds to retrieve something one balmy summer's evening. There she

and fellow student Kōji (Ishida) are struck by lightning, causing them to swap bodies. Based on a manga by **ABARE HATCHAKU** creator Hisashi Yamanaka, with a clear debt to Rumiko Takahashi's *Ranma 1/2* (*AE). The original comic featured lead characters at an elementary school, whereas the drama adaptation brings them up to high school age—making it easier to circumvent the filming restrictions imposed on child actors. The story was previously filmed as the Nobuhiko Ōbayashi movie *Transfer Students* (*Tenkōsei*, 1982), starring Satomi Kobayashi and Toshinori Omi as teenagers at a *junior* high school— whatever the ages, the high concept still works. It is also worth remembering that Hollywood, often seen as a rich source of material by Tokyo, was swamped with body-swap stories in the late 1980s, including the TV remake of *Freaky Friday* (1995) and movies such as *Like Father Like Son* (1987), *Vice Versa* (1988), and *18 Again!* (1988). *After School* was remade yet again in 2002, this time by NHK, as **WHICH IS WHICH?** Compare to **MINAMI'S SWEETHEART** and **CHANGE!**. Theme: Arisa Mizuki— "Shake Your Body for Me."

AFTER SCHOOL DANGER

1999. JPN: *Abunai Hōkago*. PRD: Hitoshi Fuse, Kagenobu Kuwata. DIR: Noboru Sugiyama. SCR: Miyuki Noe. CAST: Kazuya Ninomiya, Subaru Shibuya, Ai Katō, Kōichi Iwaki, Saya Takagi. CHN: Asahi. DUR: 45 mins. x ca. 11 eps.; Mon 12 April 1999–14 June 1999.
Intellectual teenager Katsuyuki (Ninomiya, from Johnny's Juniors) suddenly gains a sporty stepbrother Haru (Shibuya, also from Johnny's Juniors) when their single parents marry. Though they despise each other, the mismatched pair soon form a crack investigative team in their neighborhood, solving school murders and other mysteries. With leads ill-prepared to occupy starring roles and "mysteries" that are often lacking verve or clarity, *ASD* rarely looks like anything more than a pallid copy of **YOUNG KINDAICHI**

FILES. Theme: V6—"Believe Your Smile."

AFTER THE CHILDREN HAVE GONE TO BED

1992. JPN: *Kodomo ga Neta Ato de*. PRD: Yoshiki Tanaka. DIR: Nozomu Amemiya. SCR: Kazuhiko Ban. CAST: Kyōhei Shibata, Yōichi Miura, Tōru Kazama, Tomoko Yamaguchi. CHN: NTV. DUR: 45 mins. x 11 eps.; Sat 18 April 1992–27 June 1992.
Tarō (Shibata) is a children's story writer who despises kids; Ryōsuke (Miura) is a slacker who has just returned to Tokyo after two years in Okinawa; Hideki (Kazama) is the Romeo bartender at their local drinking establishment. All three suddenly discover that they are fathers and are forced to cope with new responsibilities under the disapproving eye of nursery school teacher Yamaguchi. Compare to **DON'T CALL ME PAPA** and **BASICALLY NICE**. Theme: Noriko Makihara—"Mō Koi wa Shinai" (Won't Love Again).

AGE 35

1996. JPN: *Age 35 Koishikute*. AKA: *Age 35, I Miss*. PRD: Hiroyoshi Koiwai. DIR: Michio Mitsuno. SCR: Miho Nakazono, Taeko Asano. CAST: Kiichi Nakai, Misako Tanaka, Asaka Seto, Kippei Shiina, Miyuki Kōsaka. CHN: Fuji. DUR: 45 mins. x 11 eps.; Thu 18 April 1996–27 August 1996.
Married father-of-two Hideyuki (Nakai) has been cheating on his wife Akemi (Tanaka). He has been conducting an affair with Misa (Seto), a secretary at his company but decides he must return to his family and break up with her. Misa tells him that she is pregnant. Meanwhile, Akemi meets Shin (Shiina), an old friend from art college, now working as a ceramics artist. Shin confesses that he has always had feelings for Akemi, and, discovering that her husband has been having an affair, she finds herself attracted to him. **TOKYO LOVE STORY** creator Fumi Saimon, who wrote the original *Age 35* manga for *Big Comics* magazine, artfully

questions the nature of marriage and couples, in a similar way to her later **UNMARRIED FAMILY**. Theme: Sharan Q —"Iiwake" (Excuse).

AIRPORT 92

1992. JPN: *Daikūkō 92—Ai no Tabidachi*. AKA: *Airport 92—Love's Voyagers*. PRD: N/C. DIR: Kazuhiko Yamaguchi. SCR: Gorō Hanawa. CAST: Hitoshi Ueki, Hiroshi Fuse, Keiko Saitō, Maki Mizuno, Kōkai Nakajima. CHN: Asahi. DUR: 25 mins. x 10 eps.; Thu 15 October 1992–17 December 1992.
Shinozaki (Ueki) is assigned to a new role as the chief of airport security after the airport suffers a spate of embarrassing incidents. He sets about bringing things into line but faces opposition from his second-in-command Munakata (Fuse), an embittered transfer from the quarantine section who would much rather be back in his old job. Compare to the similarly ground-hugging **BIG WING**. Theme: Nobumitsu Maeda—"Christmas for You."

AKEMI'S DEPARTURE

1976. JPN: *Akemi no Kadode*. PRD: Seiji Akiyama. DIR: Noriaki Ikemura, Ryōzō Yoshida. SCR: Hiroko Kishi. CAST: Yumiko Asai, Aiko Uchida, Manabu Tanaka, Chiyoko Komine. CHN: NHK. DUR: 25 mins. x 6 eps.; Mon 16 February–25 February 1976.
In an effort to prevent her remote mountain village from being drowned by a new dam development scheme, country girl (Akemi) begs the local villagers to band together and buy back the land. Based on the story of the same name by Chiyo Hayafune.

ALL ABOUT YOUNG PEOPLE

1994. JPN: *Wakamono no Subete*. PRD: Chihiro Kameyama, Atsuhiro Sugio. DIR: Isamu Nakae, Tatsuteru Kimura, Yūji Usui. SCR: Yoshikazu Okada. CAST: Masato Hagiwara, Takuya Kimura, Anju Suzuki, Shinji Takeda, Keiko Tōyama, Sayaka Yamaguchi, Ebi, Masato Irie, Takao Ōsawa, Eri Fukatsu. CHN: Fuji.

DUR: 45 mins. x 10 eps.; last ep: 90 min; Wed 19 October 1994–21 December 1994.

A disparate group of friends lend help to each other in times of trouble. Tetsuo (Hagiwara) lost his parents in an accident three years ago. Now he runs his father's garage and looks after his sister Taeko (Yamaguchi), who has been suffering from autism since her parents' death. Tetsuo's friend Mamoru (pop idol Ebi) helped him steal some money from yakuza to help pay his debts and has been a vegetable ever since because of the beating he suffered. Tetsuo's friend Keisuke has spent the last two years trying, without success, to be accepted into a medical university. Office worker Kaoru (Suzuki) returns to her friends after quitting her job, itself the result of a breakup with her fiancé Yūichi (Irie). Ryōko (Fukatsu) wants to be an actress and whiles away the time by working in a bank. When her big break comes, she discovers she is pregnant and is forced to reject the part, quit her job, and marry Shinsuke (Ōsawa). From this seemingly random selection of independent lives, scriptwriter Yoshikazu Okada weaves an engrossing portrait of the troubles of twentysomethings in Japan, as each of his characters struggles to escape from the aimless years that precede the start of the drama. Be it drifting without a proper career, burial in false hopes, mental anguish, or exam failure, the *AaYP* cast are all stuck in some sort of rut, with little to help them but their friends. Okada's depiction of male friendship in particular was regarded as fresh and genuine, devoid of macho posturing. This was Okada's first original script—he had previously adapted others' stories, such as **MINAMI'S SWEETHEART** and would go on to write 1990s classics such as **BEACH BOYS** and **BAYSIDE SHAKEDOWN**. Theme: Mr. Children—"Tomorrow Never Knows."

ALTHOUGH SHE'S MY MOTHER . . .

1995. JPN: *Uchi no Haha Desu ga . . ..* PRD: Toshiaki Iwashiro. DIR: Ken Matsu-

moto. SCR: Masao Yajima. CAST: Masami Hisamoto, Nae Yūki, Tsurutarō Kataoka, Masao Kusakari, Yoshiko Kuga. CHN: Asahi. DUR: 45 mins. x 10 eps.; Thu 20 April 1995–22 June 1995.

When 16-year-old Kiyomi (Hisamoto) gets pregnant by musician Makoto (Kusakari), she realizes that the news would destroy his career. She has the child in secret, and her daughter Sayumi (Yūki) grows up unaware of her true father. However, when she reaches 18, Makoto comes back into their lives, now a successful composer. From the writer of **BIG WING**. Theme: B-Wish—"Ai ga Nakucha ne" (Gotta Have Love).

ALWAYS IN LOVE WITH SOMEONE

1990. JPN: *Itsumo Dareka ni Koishiteru.* PRD: Kazuhiko Takahashi. DIR: Kazuhiro Onohara. SCR: Yūko Kanaya. CAST: Rie Miyazawa, Kurōdo Maki, Hikaru Nishida, Kazuko Katō, Mie Hama. CHN: Fuji. DUR: 45 mins. x 11 eps.; Thu 11 January 1990–22 March 1990.

While vacationing in Okinawa, teenager Satoko (Miyazawa) is rescued from drowning by the handsome Kizuku (Maki). He becomes a fantasy figure for her, like a modern-day knight in shining armor, though that all changes when he transfers to her school. The idealized holiday romance soon sours when Satoko discovers more about Kizuku's true nature, and that while he may have saved her life, he is a juvenile delinquent. Theme: Rie Miyazawa—"No Titlist."

ALWAYS THE TWO OF US

2003. JPN: *Itsumo Futari.* PRD: Yoshihiro Suzuki. DIR: Takeshi Nakazawa, Kazuhiro Kobayashi. SCR: Yūko Aizawa. CAST: Takako Matsu, Kenji Sakaguchi, Takashi Kawashibara, Ryōko Hasegawa, Aya Hirayama, Eita, Hiromi Satō, Masahiko Nishimura. CHN: Fuji. DUR: 45 mins. x 11 eps.; Mon 6 January 2003–24 March 2003.

Realizing that she's 26 years old and that it's now or never, country girl Mizuho (Matsu) packs her things and

heads for Tokyo. She has always wanted to be a wealthy writer with a prestigious Daikanyama address apartment and is prepared to give it one last shot before she gives up on her dreams. But as she struggles to sell her work, she encounters Keita (Sakaguchi), her old childhood friend, now a scriptwriter for a popular TV show. Keita has no ambition, but always seems to luck into the right jobs, whereas Mizuho's life is a constant struggle against poverty and rejection.

ANESTHESIA

1994. JPN: *Masui.* PRD: Yūichi Fujita. DIR: Yukio Fukamachi. SCR: Katsumi Okamoto. CAST: Tetsuya Watari, Tsurutarō Kataoka, Keiko Takahashi, Maki Mizuno. CHN: Yomiuri. DUR: 45 mins. x 10 eps.; Sat 15 January 1994–26 March 1994.

Kuniko (Takahashi), the wife of Takanobu (Watari), has been hospitalized for uterine cancer. The anesthesiologist Nonaka (Kataoka) explains that he will use only local anesthesia, as it is a routine operation. However, due to surgical mistakes, she falls into coma. Based on a novel by **LOST PARADISE** creator Junichi Watanabe, but not as successful. Theme: Tokiko Katō—"Ai ga Todokanai" (Love Does Not Reach).

ANIMAL DOCTOR

2003. JPN: *Dōbutsu no Oishasan.* PRD: Kōtarō Takahashi, Kazuhisa Shimoda. DIR: Shimako Satō, Masahiro Kuno, Takashi Yamazaki. SCR: Rie Yokota, Masaki Fukasawa, Ryōta Furusawa, Michiru Etō. CAST: Yū Yoshizawa, Emi Wakui, Tōru Emori, Kyōko Kishida, Masao Kusakari. CHN: Asahi. DUR: 45 mins. x ca. 11 eps.; Thu 17 April 2003–?? June 2003.

Teenager Kimiteru (Yoshizawa) is merely passing by the Veterinary Science Department of H University when a mysterious professor tells him that he will become a vet. He does somehow decide to study veterinary science at university, where he soon discovers that his human associates are even weirder than the animals. A human comedy in the style of **ROCINANTE**, based on the 1987 manga published by Noriko Sasaki in *Hana to Yume* magazine. Theme: Mio Isayama—"Asahi no Naka de Hohoende" (Smile in the Morning Sun).

ANJU AND ZUSHIŌ

1976. JPN: *Anju to Zushiō*. PRD: Kanae Mayuzumi. DIR: Minoru Hanabusa. SCR: Sumie Tanaka. CAST: Kimiko Ikegami, Satoru Hasegawa, Keiko Tsushima, Kyūzō Kawabe, Hideyo Amamoto, Satoshi Morizuka, Ryō Matsui, Kiyoshi Kinoshita, Junkichi Orimoto, Mariko Nakano, Kyōko Kishida. CHN: NHK. DUR: 20 mins. x 4 eps.; Mon 20 December 1976–23 December 1976.

Masauji Hangan (Kawabe) is the lord of Ōshū, the area covered by modern-day Fukushima, Miyagi, Iwate, and Aomori prefectures. His wife Yashio (Tsushima), his children Anju (Ikegami) and Zushiō (Hasegawa), and their nurse Taki travel to visit him at the capital Kyoto. When they reach Naoi no Ura in Niigata one month later, they cannot find an inn to stay overnight. Because slave traders are working in that area, the local officials have banned inns from offering beds to strangers. They decide to sleep out in the open, but Tayū (Morizuka) offers them shelter. Yashio and Taki in one boat, Anju and Zushiō in another, they drift out to sea and are separated. They come to realize that Tayū is a slave trader and they have been tricked. Taki throws herself into the sea. Yashio is taken to Sado Island, Anju and Zushiō are brought to Yura in Tango (now in Hyōgo Prefecture), where they are sold as slaves to Sanshō the Bailiff (Amamoto). Some time later, Anju helps Zushiō escape, and he flees to Kyoto. There, Motochika Fujiwara (Orimoto), the governor of Umezu, grants him an audience but reveals that his father Masauji is dead. The Emperor offers Zushiō his late father's lands, but Zushiō instead chooses to be governor of Tango. Returning as a powerful official, he discovers that Anju has been tortured and

Another Heaven

© 2000 Asahi

killed. He is tempted to execute Sanshō the Bailiff and his family but instead orders them to free their slaves and give them money. He then journeys to Sado Island, where he is reunited with his aged, blind mother. Based on Ōgai Mori's novel *Sanshō the Bailiff*, which was also made into a live-action film by Kenji Mizoguchi in 1954, as well as the 1961 anime adaptation *The Littlest Warrior* (*AE). Compare to **SON OF THE GOOD EARTH**.

ANOTHER HEAVEN

2000. JPN: *Another Heaven: Eclipse*. PRD: Hiroko Yako, Hajime Sasaki. DIR: Jōji Iida, Kenzō Maihara, Osamu Takigawa. SCR: Jōji Iida. CAST: Takao Ōsawa, Yōsuke Eguchi, Haruhiko Katō, Manami Motoue, Shigeru Muroi, Yoshio Harada, Chiharu Niiyama, Takashi Kashiwabara. CHN: Asahi; 45 mins. x 11 eps.; Thu 20 April 2000–29 June 2000.

Akimi (Muroi) is a former detective with the Tokyo Metropolitan Police, now running a small private investigation office. He is hired by Keiichi Inahata (Yutaka Matsushige), whose beautiful fiancée Sachiko (Hinako Saeki) disappeared on a moonlit night and has not been seen since. Taking the case, Akimi enlists the aid of his former deputy Gorō (Ōsawa), an officer who has been suspended for indirectly allowing a female drug addict to die. Meanwhile, Tokyo is plagued by a strange serial murder case, in which the corpses of young men are found with their heads severed and their brains cooked. Discovering that several other women have gone missing in the same fashion as Sachiko, Akimi begins to suspect that the disappearances of the men and women are somehow related. It is a spooky series in the *The X-Files* mode, capitalizing on the success of **RING** and **UNSOLVED CASES**, and

© 2001 Fuji

Antique

tied symbiotically to the simultaneous release of the movie version, directed by Jōji Iida. Weaving subplots of child abuse and paranormal activities, the story is interesting and the cast is stellar, but the extremely complicated plot turned a number of viewers off. Theme: Luna Sea—"Gravity."

ANTIQUE

2001. JPN: *Antique—Seiyō Kottō Yōgashi Ten.* AKA: *Antique—Western Style Confectionery; Cake Shop.* PRD: Ichirō Takai. DIR: Katsuyuki Motohiro. SCR: Yoshikazu Okada. CAST: Hideaki Takizawa, Kippei Shiina, Naoto Fujiki, Koyuki, Kazuki Enari, Taeko Nishino, Kazunobu Tsuji, Kaori Manabe, Hiroshi Abe, Manami Konishi, Susumu Kobayashi, Kaoru Yachigusa. CHN: Fuji. DUR: 25 mins. x 11 eps.; Mon 8 October 2001–17 December 2001.
Successful boxer Eiji (Takizawa) mysteriously quits at the height of his powers and disappears from the public eye. Newspaper reporter Momoko (Koyuki) suspects something is going on and discovers that he has taken a job as an assistant in the titular café, a former antique store converted into a cake shop by bored rich kid Keiichirō (Shiina). In a parody of the didactic

asides of sports serials and martial-arts stories, Eiji is studying under the Master of Cake, genius chef Yūsuke (Fujiki). He learns about the Meaning of Cake in the world at large—how it can bring lovers together and form indelible memories even as it is consumed. Meanwhile, Momoko digs deeper into Eiji's big secret, while other cast members reveal the skeletons in their own closets that have conspired to bring them together. A menagerie of guest stars appear in cameo roles—any occasion that requires cake, of course, is bound to have a story attached to it, from one couple's discovery that they are going to have a baby to the sham wedding of a lonely girl.

Based on Fumi Yoshinaga's manga *Western Style Confectionery,* serialized in the girls' magazine *Wings, Antique* was a return to television by **BAYSIDE SHAKEDOWN** director Motohiro after the high-profile movie *Space Travelers* (*AE). With a workplace serving as the focus for the lives and loves of customers and staff, the premise is nothing new, particularly in the crowded gourmet subgenre that also brought us **THE CHEF, DELICIOUS LIAISONS,** and **SOMMELIER.** However, as Fuji's big drama of the season, directed by a box-office winner and starring an idol at his peak, elements of *Antique's* execution appear noticeably sumptuous—from Keiichirō's Ferrari to Momoko's clothes, this show cost more than average. The store itself is an Art Nouveau masterpiece, and the camerawork often lingers for expensive, unfakeable close-ups on the Master of Cake at work. The conspicuous consumption even applies to the soundtrack—no obscure pop tie-in here; instead the *Antique* producers snapped up the rights to several entire *albums* by the best-selling group Mr. Children, allowing for a constantly altering theme song and background music that is a veritable hit parade of Japanese chart-toppers from recent years.

However, *Antique* sometimes takes too long admiring the view. It takes its

sweet time resolving mysteries and building up to climaxes, with a languid pace that might put some viewers off. Ironically, it's also possible that the kind of female audience who might have truly enjoyed this romantic sitcom in the style of *Chocolat* could have been scared away by opening scenes in the boxing ring, which served to make the drama look much more testosterone-heavy than it really was. As a former athlete who assesses calorie consumption by the miles that need to be jogged in penance, Eiji is the perfect hero for the diet-conscious, and heartthrob Takizawa plays him with consummate charm, making this a real treat for his fans, as long as they can take the wait.

One would think that dramas about sportsmen with improbable second careers would be few and far between, but see **KING OF EDITORS** and **DEAR WOMAN.**

ANYTHING I CAN DO FOR YOU

1992. JPN: *Kimi no Tame ni Dekiru Koto.* PRD: Kazuhiko Takahashi. DIR: Hideaki Matsuda. SCR: Akiyo Takigawa, Miho Nakazono. CAST: Eisaku Yoshida, Yuriko Ishida, Yōko Minamino, Chikara Takeuchi, Sae Isshiki. CHN: Fuji. DUR: 25 mins. x 13 eps.; Mon 6 July 1992–28 September 1992.
Successful advertising executive Tatsuya (Yoshida) quarrels with his girlfriend Akiko (Ishida). Before the pair can kiss and make up, he is killed in a car accident. Refusing to admit he is dead, Tatsuya's soul occupies the body of brain-dead patient Masaki (also played by Yoshida). Though he tries to get on with his life, including winning back Akiko, his quest is somewhat hampered by his new body—Masaki is the driver who caused Tatsuya's death. An interesting premise that combines the benign haunting of *Ghost* (1990) with the body-swap conceit of *Quantum Leap* (1989)—compare to **HEAVEN'S KISS.** Theme: Masatoshi Ono—"You're the Only."

AOI *

2000. JPN: *Aoi—Tokugawa Sandai*. AKA: *Hollyhock—Three Generations of the Tokugawa*. PRD: N/C. DIR: Mitsunobu Ozaki. SCR: James Miki. CAST: Masahiko Tsugawa, Toshiyuki Nishida, Shima Iwashita, Tōru Emori, Ryō Tamura, Toshio Kurosawa, Mitsuko Kusabue, Toshiyuki Nishida, Kisuke Yamashita. CHN: NHK. DUR: 45 mins. x 49 eps. (eps. 1 and 49: 70 mins.); Sun 9 January–17 December 2000.

Stealing the thunder of TBS's modern romance **100 YEARS**, NHK welcomed in the new millennium with a similarly ambitious multi-generational tale, featuring the first three rulers of Japan's Tokugawa shogunate—Ieyasu, Hidetada, and Iemitsu.

HIDEYOSHI, leader of the Toyotomi family, has left a panel of five regents to rule Japan until his son Hideyori reaches maturity. However, the regents are split by factionalism between Hideyori's loyal representative Mitsunari Ishida and the ambitious Ieyasu Tokugawa (see **TOKUGAWA IEYASU**). They eventually go to war, and the two opponents meet on the battlefield at Sekigahara in 1600. After the epic opening episode, the story jumps back to the death of Hideyoshi in 1598, tracing the escalation of the enmity between Ieyasu and Mitsunari. The narrative only catches up in episode 13, as Ieyasu bestows rewards upon his generals in the aftermath of the battle, though he snubs his son Hidetada for arriving late. Mitsunari is hunted down and captured and berates his captors for their disloyalty, even as he is hauled off for execution.

Sekigahara effectively marked the end of the long wars that dominated Japanese history in the middle ages, and many of *Aoi*'s later episodes are concerned with political intrigues and discussions of the sweeping reforms introduced by Ieyasu. A generation of schoolchildren must have welcomed the dramatization of such dry topics as Ieyasu's seizure of the silver mines of Fushimi or his iron grip on the trading ships that soon become Japan's only official contact with the outside world. By 1607 (episode 22), Ieyasu has "retired" on the advice of **MASAMUNE**, and handed over the reins of power to Hidetada. However, like the "retired emperors" of old, he still exercises considerable authority of his own. *Aoi* presents a believable picture of the decline of Japan's military aristocracy as the massive samurai class, trained for war since birth, have trouble adjusting to a time of peace. Embittered at their marginalization, many thousands of samurai attempt to overthrow the Tokugawa family, resulting in the 1614 summer and winter campaigns in the Osaka region. With the death of Hideyori (immolated in his besieged castle in episode 30), Ieyasu's hold on power is finally secure, though he soon dies (episode 31), leaving his family to squabble over the succession.

Like his father before him, Hidetada relinquishes his shogunal title in favor of "retirement," leaving his own son Iemitsu as the next shogun in 1622 (episode 39). In addition to intrigues among the nobles, the Tokugawa remain at odds with the imperial family despite familial connections—Iemitsu's sister is the wife of Emperor Gomizunō and mother of the heir to the throne. The Emperor causes the greatest trouble by announcing his abdication in favor of his four-month-old child in 1627 (episode 44). In order to avoid such a public-relations disaster, Hidetada comes out of retirement to offer help, much to Iemitsu's embarrassment. For a more spectacular and fanciful dramatization of these intrigues, see **THE YAGYŪ CONSPIRACY**. Hidetada calls in representatives from the Mito clan (see **MITO KŌMON**), and an angry Iemitsu banishes him from polite society. Hidetada dies in 1632, but his influence lives on after his death. Iemitsu discovers that his own brother Tadanaga has built a shrine to their father without first seeking his permission. He angrily confiscates Tadanaga's fief and sends him into exile at Takasaki Castle, where the grief-stricken samurai takes his own life. In control but deprived of his beloved family members, Iemitsu faces the future alone. Shown subtitled in the U.S. on KIKU TV.

ARE YOU IN THE GOODBYE CLUB?

1977. JPN: *Kimi wa Sayonara Zoku ka*. PRD: N/C. DIR: N/C. SCR: Izuho Sudō. CAST: Nobuo Gosō, Ippei Kimura, Keiko Tomita, Rie Sugiyama, Aritsune Amano, Kichizaburo Tomita, Masao Okabe, Jun Funaki, Kentarō Fujiki. CHN: NHK. DUR: 20 mins. x 12 eps.; Mon 14 February 1977–3 March 1977.

Twelve-year-old Yukio (Gosō) likes painting but hates school. After a minor head injury, his doctor advises him to stay at home for two or three days but his jubilation soon turns to boredom. He goes to visit his grandfather (Amano) but what begins as a happy tale of "dropping out" (for just a while . . . this being Japan, after all!) gradually changes in tone. In fact, Yukio's illness is life-threatening, he is soon hospitalized, and his observations of the lives and deaths of those around him leave him a changed person. Based on a novel by Tadaaki Mori.

ARE YOU ON THE MOVE?

1993. JPN: *Hikkosemasu ka*. PRD: N/C. DIR: Shintarō Sofue. SCR: Hideyoshi Nagasaka, Chikane Yamada. CAST: Yasuo Daichi, Keiko Takahashi, Kyōka Suzuki, Tomoko Nakajima, Pinko Izumi, Rie Yamaguchi, Ken Ishiguro. CHN: NTV. DUR: 45 mins. x 12 eps.; Wed 7 July 1993–22 September 1993.

After four years at his company's South East Asia office, Gosuke (Daichi) returns to Japan. He decides to move out of rented accommodation and buy a detached house but is conned by Riichirō (Ishiguro), a bank manager he foolishly thinks he can trust. Now he is in serious financial difficulty, causing his wife Suzue (Takahashi) and three daughters (Suzuki, Nakajima, and Yamaguchi) to rally round. Compare to similar homemaking difficulties in **EXCUSE ME AGAIN** and Kōki Mitani's movie *All About Our House*

Army of the Apes

(2001). Theme: GAO—"Tsuki ni Hoeru Asa" (A Morning Barking at the Moon).

ARMY OF THE APES *

1974. JPN: *Saru no Gundan*. AKA: *The Ape Corps; Time of the Apes*. PRD: Matakazu Takahashi, Masashi Tadakuma. DIR: Kiyosumi Fukazawa, Shunichirō Kazuki. SCR: Keiichi Abe, Narimitsu Taguchi, Bunzō Wakatsuki. CAST: Reiko Tokunaga, Hiroko Saitō, Masaaki Kaji, Wataru Ōmae, Tetsuya Ushio, Baku Hatakeyama, Kazue Takita, Noboru Nakataya, Hitoshi Ōmae, Hiroyuki Kawase. CHN: TBS. DUR: 25 mins. x 26 eps.; Mon 6 October 1974–30 March 1975.
Cryogenic researcher Kazuko (Tokunaga) is fooling around in the laboratory with her friends Jirō (Kaji) and Yurika (Saitō) when the facility is struck by a major earthquake. Hiding inside the Cold Sleep chambers for protection, they are inadvertently frozen. They emerge years later to find the world ruled by highly evolved apemen, who have all but exterminated the human race. Teaming up with human survivor Gōdo (Ushio), they become involved in a growing strife between gorillas and chimpanzees, all the while searching for a way to somehow reverse their trip in time. This they eventually do with the aid of a convenient flying saucer, though when they finally awake in the wrecked lab, it is suggested that their adventures *might* have been a dream all along. . . .

Army of the Apes was broadcast a mere month after the U.S. debut of the *Planet of the Apes* TV series (which itself reached Japan on Fuji TV in 1975) and was similarly inspired by the 1968 movie and the spin-offs that followed. Despite this obvious pedigree, the idea for the Japanese series was credited to SF writers Sakyō Komatsu, Kōji Tanaka, and Aritsune Toyota. Since the ape actors were not able to speak lines through their masks, their dialogue was added in postproduction by a number of voice actors who were better known for their work in anime, including Ichirō Nagai, Hiroko Kikuchi, and Kōji Yada. Part of the series was dubbed for the U.S. market by Sandy Frank in a 90-minute movie edit under the title *Time of the Apes* (1975), in which form it graced the TV show *Mystery Science Theater 3000*. For this version, the leads were renamed Kathryn, Johnny, and Caroline.

ARRANGED MARRIAGE

2000. JPN: *Omiai Kekkon*. AKA: *The Matchmaker*. PRD: Atsuhiro Sugio. DIR: Takao Kinoshita. SCR: Noriko Yoshida. CAST: Takako Matsu, Yūsuke Santamaria, Yōsuke Kubozuka, Judy Ong, Tamao Satō, Ayako Kawahara, Ayumi Ishida. CHN: Fuji. DUR: 45 mins. x 11 eps.; Tue 11 January 2000–?? March 2000.
Former stewardess Setsuko (Matsu) goes to the wedding of a old work colleague who found her husband through the "arranged marriage" tradition of *omiai*, in which prospective partners are set up by their families or by professional matchmakers. She returns home to celebrate the birthday of her own fiancé Hiroshi, only to be surprised by his lover, who has arrived to tell Hiroshi she is pregnant. Meanwhile, company man Kōtaro (Santamaria) is told that a transfer to Milan is in the offing for him, so long as he can find himself a wife at short notice—the company does not permit single representatives abroad. His boss's wife Mrs. Sakuraba (Ong) volunteers to find a wife for him and discovers that her friend Kinue (Ishida) has a daughter who has recently come on the market—naturally, it turns out to be Setsuko. Setsuko, however, is uneasy at the idea of arranged marriages and, though she attends the formal *omiai* meeting, declines to take things further. Later, however, she meets Kōtaro at a party where the couple seem to hit

it off. Learning that they have met socially by chance and without official interference, Mrs. Sakuraba sets up another meeting between them.

Entertainingly focusing on some of the more farcical aspects of love and dating, *AM* examines the various ways of finding a spouse. With typical Japanese pragmatism, it questions the sanity of the romantic ideal, pointing out the folly of waiting eternally for Cupid's random arrows, when Japanese tradition offers professional help. However, it is also evenhanded, noting the equally bizarre idea of marrying first and hoping love will follow and that not every *omiai* results in fairy-tale success. Compare to NARITA DIVORCE, which similarly approaches human relationships with a touch that is both humorous and incisive.

ARREST YOUR EYES

1988. JPN: *Kimi no Hitomi o Taiho Suru*. PRD: Yoshiaki Yamada, Tōru Ōta. DIR: Shunsaku Kawake. SCR: Izō Hashimoto. CAST: Takanori Jinnai, Hiroshi Mikami, Yūko Asano, Toshirō Yanagiba, Shizuka Kudō. CHN: Fuji. DUR: 45 mins. x 12 eps.; Mon 4 January 1988–21 March 1988.
Three mismatched detectives fight crime at Dōgenzaka police station in Shibuya, Tokyo. The hot-tempered Sawada (Jinnai), polite Domon (Yanagiba), and elite fast-tracker Tajima (Mikami) not only walked the beat but also became involved in romantic and comedy situations in the course of the series, making *AYE* an arguable forerunner of the trendy drama phenomenon that was to dominate the 1990s. Yanagiba in particular would maintain a high profile in cop shows with his role in BAYSIDE SHAKEDOWN nearly ten years later. Theme: Toshinobu Kubota—"You Were Mine."

ARTISTIC SOCIETY

1990. JPN: *Geinō Shakai*. PRD: Yasuhide Ikenaga. DIR: Yūchi Aizuki. SCR: Takako Shigemori. CAST: Saburō Tokitō, Yōko Minamino, Ayako Sawada, Mariko Kaga, Daijirō Harada. CHN: TBS. DUR: 45 mins. x 12 eps.; Sat 5 July 1990–27 September 1990.
Yoshikazu (Tokitō) is the manager of pop idol Mutsuko (Sawada) and is used to arranging every detail of her life. After he arranges her wedding celebrations with her fiancé Sakaki (Harada), he waves them off on their honeymoon but the couple then disappear without a trace. He sets off to find them, teaming up with third-generation Japanese American Aiko (Minamino). Theme: Akiko Kobayashi—"Kokoro no Honoo" (Flame in My Heart). Based on a story by Yumie Hiraiwa.

AS IF IN FLIGHT

1990. JPN: *Tobu ga Gotoku*. PRD: Takayuki Hirayama. DIR: N/C. SCR: Mieko Osanai. CAST: Toshiyuki Nishida, Takeshi Kaga, Yūzō Kayama, Hideki Takahashi, Kaho Minami, Eri Ishida, Yūko Tanaka, Noriko Sakai, Naoto Ogata, Chikako Kaku. CHN: NHK. DUR: 45 mins. x ca. 48 eps.; Sun 7 January 1990–9 December 1990.
For its *taiga* historical drama for 1990, NHK created this lavish tale about the end of an era. Considering its shooting schedule, it must have gained extra poignancy when overtaken by historical events. It would have been in production at the time of the death of the Shōwa Emperor Hirohito, grandson of the Meiji Emperor whose restoration forms a central part of the narrative. The source material was a novel by the Japanese historian Ryōtaro Shiba, also known for the movie *Taboo*, as well as TOKUGAWA YOSHINOBU, RYŌMA DEPARTS, KAJIN, and LAND THIEF. Like many of his books, *As If in Flight* concentrates on a period of history barely known outside Japan itself—the infighting and struggles that characterized Japan's modernization, from the arrival of foreign interference to the beginning of Japan's martial expansion. Japanese were forced to deal with the fact that the shogun, appointed originally to quell foreign barbarians, was powerless to resist the superior technology of the Western powers, who were determined to open Japan to trade and shipping. Progressive factions in the government understood that Japan's self-imposed seclusion was over, and that the time had come to learn from the West before Japan was divided among foreign powers in the same fashion as neighboring China. Conservative factions preferred to see the shogun's impotency as a temporary setback, best solved by the appointment of a new shogun—preferably one of their own choosing.

At the end of Edo period, civil servants Yoshinosuke Saigō (Nishida) and Toshimichi Ōkubo (Kaga) become involved in political infighting in the feudal domain of Satsuma (now Kagoshima Prefecture). Saigō (later to take the name Takamori Saigō) supports the reformist faction of Nariakira Shimazu (Kayama) while Ōkubo supports the traditionalist Hisamitsu Shimazu (Takahashi). At 28 years of age, Saigō accompanies Nariakira to the shogun's base in Edo, where Nariakira arranges a marriage between his daughter Atsuhime and the 13th shogun Iesada Tokugawa. However, after a while, Nariakira falls ill, and it is Hisamitsu's son who takes over the top post in Satsuma. As Hisamitsu's right-hand man, Ōkubo persuades Hisamitsu to recall Saigō but the new chief has little time for Saigō and banishes him to an island.

In 1867, Saigō returns from exile to participate in the overthrow of the 15th and final shogun Yoshinobu. Imperial rule is officially restored (i.e., government is now conducted in the name of the Meiji Emperor) and Ōkubo sets off on a fact-finding mission to the West, accompanied by Takayoshi Kido and Tomomi Iwakura. Saigō stays to help in negotiations with Korea, which is in the midst of an anti-Japanese campaign and refuses to sign any treaties with the Meiji government.

After his wishes are ignored regarding negotiations with the Koreans, Saigō heads for Kagoshima, a virtually independent feudal domain within Japan, where he establishes a school.

© 1976 Tsuburaya Productions

Astekaiser

However, when the Chōshū region (see **MŌRI MOTONARI**) is pressured to sign on with the new Meiji system, the area revolts and Saigō becomes the leader of the resistance.

In the style of many modern TV dramas, *As If in Flight* contrasts its lead characters with opposing traits—Saigō is depicted as an emotional man, while Ōkubo is coolly rational. Such a division of characteristics makes the leads in *AIiF* immediately accessible to a modern audience able to compress their characters into a shorthand suitable for discussing, say, Shunsaku and Shinji of **BAYSIDE SHAKEDOWN**. It also helps to conceal the vast downloads of historical data buried in the sprawling story, covering the period which saw the last gasp of the samurai era and the first stirrings of Japan as a modern world power. Shiba's original novel covered the period from the Meiji Restoration in 1867 to the assassination of Toshimichi Ōkubo in 1878—all previous events covered in this synopsis were added to ease the audience gently into the central events.

ASTEKAISER

1976. JPN: *Pro-wres no Hoshi Astekaiser.* AKA: *Pro-wrestling Star Astekaiser.* PRD: Masaru Yoshitsu, Kimihiko Etō, Matakazu Takahashi. DIR: Kiyosumi Fukazawa, Akira Okazaki, Kanji Ōtsuka, Shōhei Tōjō. SCR: Bunzō Wakatsuki, Keiichi Abe, Susumu Takahisa. CAST: Yoshiteru Shimamura, Asao Matsumoto, Futoshi Kikuchi, Tadayoshi Kura, Nagata Tamagawa, Rika Yazaki, Hitoshi Ōmae, Eiichi Miura, Shunsuke Ikeda, Shōhei Yamamoto, Kōichi Nara. CHN: NET (Asahi). DUR: 25 mins. x 26 eps.; Thu 7 October 1976–31 March 1977. The savage Lure begin their inexorable assault on our reality, extending the influence of the Black Mist. Each week, Satan Demon (Yamamoto) sends a champion fighter to test the best that Earth has to offer, including such super-powered enemies as Dark Gladiator, Iron Buster, Blue Bison, and Garrison Snake. Earth's only hope is professional wrestler Shun (Shimamura), who secretly transforms into the superhuman champion of justice Astekaiser (Nara). Based on an idea by

Gō Nagai and Ken Ishikawa, the creators of *Getter Robo* (*AE) but released as a coproduction with **ULTRAMAN** studio Tsuburaya, *Astekaiser* featured a mixture of live-action material and animation in the style of the same year's **BORN FREE**. Animation was by Studio Dart under the control of Atsushi Takagi. In the final episode, Astekaiser got to fight with Satan Demon himself.

ASTRO BOY

1959. JPN: *Tetsuwan Atomu.* PRD: Matsuzaki Pro, Mikasa Eiga. DIR: Hiroshi Yoshikawa, Akira Shiwa, Hideo Ōhashi, Toshio Nanba. SCR: Isohachi Shibuya, Shigetoshi Iwata, Haruo Kōrogi. CAST: Masahito Segawa, Akio Tanaka, Gorō Morino. CHN: Fuji. DUR: 25 mins. x 65 eps.; Sat 7 March 1959–28 May 1960. Deserted by his callous creator, super-powered robot Atom (Segawa) is adopted by the kindly Professor Ochanomizu (Tanaka, later replaced by Morino). With Ochanomizu's advice, he fights for justice in this black-and-white live-action adventure series that preceded the more famous anime *Astro Boy* (*AE) by several years. The live-action incarnation of Osamu Tezuka's famous superhero comic enjoyed five story-arcs in the course of its broadcast history—one for each season. These were, in order, *The ZZZ (Three-Zee) Gang, Mexico, Franken vs. Atom, Flight to Mars,* and finally *Vapor Human.* However, despite its apparent success, the live-action *AB* has been quietly buried in the history of Japan's most famous manga creator—Tezuka was reputedly aghast at what was done to his creation by the independent producers that made the TV series and resolved to do it *his* way in the later anime incarnation. Another Tezuka manga was filmed as **SPACE GIANTS**.

ASUNARO CONFESSIONS

1993. JPN: *Asunaro Hakusho.* AKA: *Ordinary People.* PRD: Chihiro Kameyama. DIR: Tatsuaki Kimura, Takehiko Shinjō. SCR: Eriko Kitagawa. CAST: Hikari Ishida, Michitaka Tsutsui,

Anju Suzuki, Takuya Kimura, Hidetoshi Nishijima, Asuka Kurosawa. CHN: Fuji. DUR: 45 mins. x 11 eps.; Mon 11 October 1993–20 December 1993. University students Narumi (Ishida), Kakei (Tsutsui), Toride (Kimura from SMAP), Seika (Suzuki), and Matsuoka (Nishijima) form the Asunaro book club. But other tensions lie beneath the discussions of the novels—Narumi likes Kakei, but Kakei is already dating a non-member called Tokie (Kurosawa). On a club beach trip, Narumi and Kakei become closer and eventually sleep together. Meanwhile, Toride secretly admires Narumi, while both Seika and Matsuoka lust after Kakei.

Tiring of life at his current college, Kakei decides to try Kyoto University instead, upsetting his new relationship with Narumi. On Christmas Eve, which has of late become the accepted time in Japan for people to pop the question, Matsuoka tells Kakei of his own feelings for him, only to flee when he sees Kakei's horrified reaction. While Matsuoka seeks solace with Seika, Narumi tires of waiting for Kakei in front of the campus Christmas tree. Eventually, she finds comfort in the arms of another; when Kakei visits her the next day to apologize, he finds her in bed with Toride.

Matsuoka dies in an accident, Kakei gets into Kyoto University, and Toride goes abroad, while Seika discovers that she is pregnant with Matsuoka's child and moves to Kobe. With the Asunaro club dispersed, it all seems over but the members reunite after four years to evaluate their lives and look back at the good old days. As with SEVEN PEOPLE IN SUMMER, IN THE NAME OF LOVE, and numerous other dramas that draw their inspiration from *The Big Chill* (1983) and *St. Elmo's Fire* (1985), AC

also gives two unrequited lovers one last chance to get together. The series was reprised on 30 December 1993 in a feature length edit, *Asunaro Confessions: One More Time.* Based on the manga serialized in *Big Comics* by TOKYO LOVE STORY creator Fumi Saimon, this series not only consolidated the stardom of Kimura but would encourage producer Kameyama and scenarist Kitagawa to reunite later for the even more successful LONG VACATION. The manga was also a success in Taiwan, where it was published as *Aiqing Baipishu* (Love Confessions) and later remade as the Mandarin drama series *Aiqing Baipishu: Tomorrow* (2002). Theme: Fumiya Fujii—"True Love."

AT SEVENTEEN

1994. JPN: *17-sai.* PRD: Hisao Ogura. DIR: Mashiro Suzuki. SCR: Masashi Todayama, Yoshikazu Okada. CAST: Yuki Uchida, Sae Isshiki, Shinji Takeda, Tarō Yamamoto, Miyoko Asada. CHN: Fuji. DUR: 45 mins. x 14 eps.; Thu 28 April 1994–1 September 1994. Takumi (Uchida) returns to her home-town, where she tries to help her old school friends Midori (Isshiki) and Kyōichi (Takeda) escape from a run of bad luck. However, everything she tries only seems to drag them deeper into trouble—although her heart remains in the right place.

ATTENTION PLEASE

1970. PRD: N/C. DIR: N/C. SCR: N/C. CAST: Hiroko Kii, Asako Minagawa, Kenji Sahara. CHN: TBS. DUR: 45 mins. x ca. 40 eps.; Sun 23 August 1970–28 March 1971. After the success of the live-action manga adaptation THE SIGN IS V, TBS followed straight on in the same Sunday slot with this version of Chieko Hosokawa's manga from *Shōjo Friend.*

Though originally written for a female audience, a series about seven glamorous flight attendants in uniform had obvious crossover appeal to a male viewership. The appeal of foreign travel and handsome pilot suitors aside, the show also helped establish the workplace-related subgenre in Japanese TV drama—in a way, the "stewardess" occupation we see here is the first of the exotic *katakana* jobs that would return as a fundamental feature of the trendy dramas a generation later—see I WANT TO HUG YOU! Inspiring imitators such as STEWARDESS SWEETHEART, as well as flight attendant characters in other dramas such as YAMATO NADESHIKO, *AP* took place in and around Tokyo's Haneda Airport, a location that would appear faintly quaint after the opening of the larger Narita Airport in 1978. Thereafter, Haneda lost much of its exotic appeal to the TV audience, eventually becoming the setting for the satirical BIG WING. Theme: The Bars—"Attention Please."

AUGUST LOVE SONG

1996. JPN: *Hachigatsu no Love Song.* PRD: Norihiko Imamura. DIR: Ryōko Hoshida. SCR: Mitsuo Kuroto. CAST: Riona Hazuki, Masaya Katō, Sae Isshiki, Ken Ogata, Uchihiro Ōkawa. CHN: NTV. DUR: 45 mins. x 11 eps.; Mon 1 July 1996–9 September 1996. The downtrodden and broken-hearted finally find love, as lonely widower chef Eizō (Ogata) takes on a handsome new assistant Kitarō (Katō) in his restaurant, much to the interest of his daughter Chika (Hazuki), who is a talented songwriter forced to allow others to take the credit for much of her work. Theme: Whitney Houston—"All at Once."

B

BABEL

2002. JPN: *Babel—The Tower of Babel*. PRD: Yū Hirose, Yū Moriya. DIR: Nobuyuki Takahashi. SCR: Shunpei Okada. CAST: Takashi Kashiwabara, Ryō, Junichi Inoue, Manami Konishi, Ryōko Hirosue, Meikyō Yamada. CHN: BS Fuji. DUR: 30 mins. x 12 eps.; Fri 4 January 2002–22 March 2002.
Babel is an underground secret medical organization, run by brilliant doctors, including two, Kyōichi Hamura (Kashiwabara) and Kaoru Kizaki (Ryō), who use the latest technology to cure the supposedly incurable. The series goes on to reveal their mysterious pasts, in the style of NIGHT HEAD, mixed with medical suspense in the spirit of *Black Jack* (*AE). Shown in a late-night slot on Fuji's satellite channel, this near future sci-fi thriller soon attracted a cult following. Episodes 2, 3, 4, and 9 were rerun in May 2002 at three in the morning—presumably, only doctors on shiftwork would be awake to see it.

BAD GIRLS HIGH SCHOOL

1990. JPN: *Ikenai Joshi Kō Monogatari*. PRD: Yūji Tōjō. DIR: Ken Inoue. SCR: Masao Yajima. CAST: Yūko Kotegawa, Katsuhide Uegusa, Yōichi Miura, Hirohide Yakumaru, Kin Sugai. CHN: NTV. DUR: 45 mins. x 11 eps.; Sat 13 January 1990–24 March 1990.
Misuzu (Kotegawa) is a teacher at an elite mission high school for girls but lives a life far removed from the educa-tional ideal. She lives in an apartment with university student Takashi (Uegusa) who is several years her junior and the couple cherish ambi-tions of making it big in rock music—she as a singer and he as a guitarist. The staff and pupils at the school, how-ever, heartily disapprove of her chosen lifestyle. Theme: Chisato Moritaka—"Seishun" (Youth).

BAKUMATSU EXCHANGE STUDENTS

1994. JPN: *Bakumatsu Kōkōsei*. PRD: Osamu Tezuka (B). DIR: Mamoru Hoshi. SCR: Kōichi Nakamura. CAST: Fumie Hosokawa, Shinji Takeda, Tarō Yamamoto, Megumi Kobayashi, Renji Ishibashi. CHN: Fuji. DUR: 45 mins. x 5 eps.; Sat 15 January 1994–12 February 1994.
Popular school teacher Meg (Hosokawa) treats her pupils to an educational trip to a film set where period dramas are made. While they look around, the area is struck by an earthquake, transporting them back in time to the real-life 19th century. Compare to TIME TRAVELER. Based on an idea credited to Taku Mayumura (see BAKUMATSU TIME TRAVELERS).

BAKUMATSU TIME TRAVELERS

1977. JPN: *Bakumatsu Miraijin*. AKA: *Future Persons at the Close of the Bakufu Period*. PRD: Kaoru Kanō. DIR: Kazuya Satō, Osamu Koyama. SCR: N/C. CAST: Toshiharu Hoshino, Masakazu Sawamura, Keizō Kanie, Hiroshi Inuzuka, Masayo Banri, Noboru Ichiyama, Yūko Kotegawa, Akio Tanaka, Tetsuo Morishita, Nancy Meadows. CHN: NHK. DUR: 40 mins. x 16 eps.; Mon 5 September 1977–29 September 1977.
While visiting the battleship *Mikasa* on the coast at Yokosuka, schoolboys Fumihiko Wada (Hoshino) and Mitsugu Itō (Sawamura) are transport-ed back in time to the year 1862. Arriving at the foreigners' settlement in Yokohama, they are suspected of being criminals and forced to evade officers of the law. Finding themselves living in a crucial period of Japanese history (see also AS IF IN FLIGHT) dur-ing which the shogun's rule faded and conspirators plotted to restore the emperor, the children meet several famous historical figures and inadver-tently change the course of history. In particular, they accidentally cause the death of Sōshi Okita, who was/would have been a major figure in the Meiji Restoration. Based on the story *A Memorable Summer* (*Omoi Agari no Natsu*) by Taku Mayumura, who was also credited with the original ideas for the later BAKUMATSU EXCHANGE STUDENTS, CHALLENGE FROM THE FUTURE, MYSTERIOUS NEW STUDENT, MYSTERIOUS PENFRIEND, and SCHOOL IN PERIL. Another of Mayumura's time travel stories was animated as *Time Stranger* (*AE). Mayumura was not the only Japanese SF novelist to tackle time

travel—his stories competed with Yasutaka Tsutsui's TIME TRAVELER and Sakyō Komatsu's MY TIME TRAVEL JOURNEY WITH MARI.

BAROM ONE

1972. PRD: Tōru Hirayama, Hisashi Sano. DIR: Katsuhiko Taguchi, Itaru Orita, Minoru Yamada, Akio Koyama. SCR: Masaru Igami, Hisashi Yamazaki, Mari Takizawa, Masayuki Shimada, Yōsuke Maekawa. CAST: Hiroyuki Takano, Hideo Murota, Yoshiki Iizuka, Keisuke Asakawa, Kiyoshi Kobayashi, Akio Terajima, Shōzō Iizuka. CHN: Yomiuri. DUR: 35 mins. x 35 eps.; Sun 16 April 1972–26 November 1972.

Kobū (Terajima), the personification of light, has been locked in an age-long battle with Doruge (Murota, voice: S. Iizuka), the personification of darkness. Believing itself to be dying, Kobū happens across two Japanese boys with a remarkably strong bond of friendship. If combined in the right way, their skills and energies will mesh together to create Barom One, an agent of justice that can defend the Earth from the evil Doruge. So it is that the smart junior high schooler Kentarō (Takano) gets to join forces with his sports-jock classmate Takeru (Y. Iizuka), forming the brains and brawn, respectively, of a new superhero. Meanwhile the evil Doruge comes to Earth, where he walks among men as flamboyant billionaire "Mr. Doruge"— not the world's most impenetrable disguise. However, in the style of many evil masterminds from GORANGER onward, Doruge rarely enters combat himself but instead sends mutants to fight his battles for him. Based on the manga by Takao Saitō, who also drew a comic version of JAPAN SINKS but is best known as the creator of *Golgo 13* (*AE). For its 30th anniversary in 2002, *Barom One* returned to Japanese television screens as an animated series. Theme: Ichirō Mizugi—"Bokura no Barom One" (Our Barom One).

BASEBALL DETECTIVES

1980. JPN: *Bokura Yakyū Tanteidan.*

Baseball Detectives

AKA: *We Are Baseball Detectives.* PRD: Takao Kondō, San Tsuburaya, Atsushi Ōki. DIR: Tōru Sotoyama, Hiroshi Okamoto, Kiyosumi Fukazawa. SCR: Hideyoshi Nagasaka, Hirohisa Soda, Keiichi Abe, Akiyoshi Sakai. CAST: Daijirō Tsutsumi, Guts Ishimatsu, Setsuko Numazaki, Yōsuke Takemura, Jō Shishido. CHN: TV Tokyo. DUR: 35 mins. x 18 eps.; Tue 22 April 1980–22 September 1980.

Tenma (Tsutsumi) and his fellow young members of the One Packs baseball team prove to be successful amateur sleuths. While the evil villain Akamanto (The Scarlet Cape) continues to outwit camp detective Kanari (Ishimatsu) and his steely assistant Doro (Shishido), the children manage to outfox every one of his schemes. *BD* was loosely based on the *Boy Detectives Club* children's books by crime novelist Ranpo Edogawa, an ever-popular series of teen mysteries that was filmed

for TV during the 1960s under its original title *Shōnen Tanteidan* and as the anime series *Naughty Detectives* (*AE). Moving the action to a baseball club seems to have been little more than a gimmick—clutching at straws in order to compete with the simultaneous broadcast of a new ULTRAMAN series on the rival Asahi network. Despite, or perhaps because of this, *BD* never quite enjoyed the popularity of its 1960s forerunners. Teen sleuthing, however, remains a popular area in Japanese TV, most notably in recent years with the success of YOUNG KINDAICHI FILES.

BASICALLY NICE

2002. JPN: *Hito ni Yasashiku.* PRD: Kensaku Sawada. DIR: Kensaku Sawada, Daisuke Tajima. SCR: Osamu Suzuki, Yoshihiro Izumi. CAST: Shingo Katori, Mitsuru Matsuoka, Kōji Katō, Kenta Suga. CHN: Fuji. DUR: 45 mins.

x 11 eps.; Mon 7 January 2002–
?? March 2002.

Tough guys Zen (Katori from SMAP), Tarō (Matsuoka), and Ken (Katō) are Harajuku punks who accidentally find themselves baby-sitting timid first-grader Akira (Suga). One of them may be Akira's father, forcing all three to try to act responsibly. Comedic high jinks ensue as Zen becomes a regular and unwelcome visitor to Akira's school and the unwitting love interest of Akira's teacher Nozomi. One of many Japanese TV dramas in which unlikely candidates become surrogate parents (compare to **DON'T CALL ME PAPA** and **AFTER THE CHILDREN HAVE GONE TO BED**), though this particular serial's greatest debts are to *Three Men and a Little Lady* and the TV series *My Two Dads*.

BATTLEFEVER J

1979. PRD: Kazutake Ochiai, Susumu Yoshikawa, Itaru Orita. DIR: Hirokazu Takemoto, Shigeho Hiroda, Minoru Yamada, Kimio Hirayama. SCR: Susumu Takahisa, Masamitsu Uehara, Takashi Ezure, Hirohisa Soda. CAST: Hironori Tanioka, Yūhei Kurachi, Takeshi Itō, Naoya Ban, Kenji Ōba, Diane Martin, Naomi Hagina. CHN: Asahi. DUR: 25 mins. x 52 eps.; Sat 3 February 1979–26 January 1980.

General Kurama of the National Defense Ministry forms a secret task force to deal with super-powered complications and "monster incidents," equipped with the newest technology and special vehicles, including the first giant robot to grace a Super Sentai show. The team comprises secret agents who fight with a martial arts skill based on dances from around the world. The leader is the red-helmeted Masao (Tanioka), codenamed Battle Japan, who fights with the power of "kung fu dance." His second in command is Kyōsuke (Kurachi), codenamed Battle France (Kurachi), who fights with the power of Spanish Dance—your eyes do not deceive you. When that turns out not to work too well, he also has a rapier as backup. Despite a headdress that makes him look like an Egyptian

Pharaoh, the orange-clad Kosaku (Itō) is the Battle Cossack, who fights with the power of Russian dancing and uses Chinese martial arts weapons. He was killed off during the series and replaced later on by Makoto (Ban), Battle Cossack II. Shiro (Ōba) is Battle Kenya, who fights with the power of Tropical Dance and also has the ability to communicate with animals. The token female member of the team is Diane (who plays herself), who has mastered the art of Disco Dancing and hence becomes Miss America. Diane has joined the team in order to avenge the death of her FBI agent father but after being heavily wounded in a battle, she returns to America and is replaced by fellow agent Maria (Hagina).

The team's chief enemy is the international Egos Corporation, led by the purple-robed criminal mastermind Satan Egos. Along with his son, his pretty assistant Salome (the world's strongest woman), and an army of gray-clad Cutmen minions, Satan is determined to seize control of the world, and only the Battlefever J team stand in his way. To help in their struggle, they have the submarine Battle Shark, which splits in two to release their giant robot, the Battlefever Robo.

Battlefever J began development as a follow-up to the **SPIDER-MAN** series—producers originally planned an adaptation of Marvel's *Captain America* but instead opted for this international team show, reviving in the process the "Sentai" battle team franchise that began with **GORANGER** to make this "Super Sentai" show. Based on an idea by former *Combattler V* and *Starbirds* (*AE) creator Saburō Yade, *Battlefever J* was completely mad, even by the standards of Japanese television. In the Super Sentai chronology, *Battlefever J* comes after **JAQK** and before **DENZIMAN**. Writer Ezure would reappear nearly two decades later scripting **THE CURSE**. Music by Michiaki Watanabe.

BAYSIDE SHAKEDOWN

1997. JPN: *Odoru Daisōsasen*. AKA: *Dancing on the Line of Enquiry;*

Wangan Police Station; Dancing Detective; Bayside Dragnet. PRD: Chihiro Kameyama, Shōji Hidefumi. DIR: Katsuyuki Motohiro, Kensaku Sawada. SCR: Ryōichi Kimizuka. CAST: Yūji Oda, Eri Fukatsu, Chōsuke Ikariya, Toshirō Yanagiba, Miki Mizuno, Yūsuke Santamaria, Sōichirō Kitamura, Akira Saitō, Takehiko Ōno. CHN: Fuji. DUR: 45 mins. x 11 eps.; Tue 7 January 1997–18 March 1997; + specials 100 mins. x 3 eps., 40 mins. x 1 ep.

Disaffected computer salesman Shunsaku Aoshima (Oda) changes careers at the ripe age of 29, becoming a detective at the Wangan police station. Though he is initially ignored by most of the officers, he demonstrates an early skill for empathizing with victims and is able to draw important evidence out of uncooperative interview subjects. His chief nemesis is Shinji Muroi (Yanagiba), a self-made man from Akita, who has fought his way up through the Police Board Criminal Council despite snobbish opposition from the Tokyo University graduates who make up most of its numbers. Though the two men are permanently at odds, the emotional Shunsaku and the logical Shinji eventually form an uneasy partnership.

Their friendship flourishes in the course of several episodes that introduce other members of the team. Old hand Heihachirō (Ikariya) is due for retirement but trying to settle some of his outstanding cases. One comes back to haunt him, when an old adversary sends him a booby-trapped office chair, forcing him and Shunsaku to stay completely still while the rest of the office try to defuse the bomb—a steal from a similar setup in *Lethal Weapon 3*. Sumire (Fukatsu) is Shunsaku's would-be love interest in the Department of Theft, whose cold exterior hides an abused past. She attracts a stalker who is convinced that she is the earthly incarnation of the anime character Pink Sapphire (a thinly veiled homage to *Sailor Moon*, *AE), whom Shunsaku and Shinji must stop before he turns into a killer.

Bayside Shakedown

Bayside Shakedown is one of the landmark shows of the 1990s, remaining high on viewer polls half a decade after its release. Though the high concept is nothing new, it struck a chord with the *Friends* and *Ally McBeal* generation, offering last-chance wish fulfillment for twentysomething viewers that there was still a possibility to change careers and start afresh. The glossy production values and pop video sensibilities glamorized the world of police work—instead of the rumpled look of NINZABURŌ FURUHATA, the *BS* officers try very hard to play it young and cool. They achieve this through an unobtrusive anti-intellectualism that derides academic achievement in favor of simple attitude and instinct. When a team of criminal profilers arrive at Wangan, they are depicted as incompetent college boys

whose charts and graphs are no substitute for door-to-door enquiries and knowledge of the streets. There is similar comedic bungling from the Three Amigos (Kitamura, Saitō, and Ōno), a group of unashamedly brownnosing senior officers who preside over the younger officers with an air of benevolent incompetence. The series aims several pop culture references squarely at animation fans, including an arrest at an Image Club where visitors can hire prostitutes dressed as famous anime characters, and the regular recurrence of music from Shirō Sagisu's soundtrack to *Evangelion* (*AE). Viewers are also advised to keep an eye out for each episode's token foreigner, including theme song collaborator Maxi Priest, though our personal favorite remains the suspect who can

be heard loudly protesting, *"But I am from* Finland*!"*

Later episodes adopt a more serious tone, as the team go on the trail of a cop killer who has also seriously wounded police chief's son Masayoshi Mashita (Santamaria). It ends with Shunsaku temporarily demoted but with the promise of future collaboration with Shinji as he rises through the ranks. It also achieves neat narrative closure with the arrival of Yukino (Mizuno) in the Traffic department—a crime victim in the first episode, she has been inspired by her contact with Shunsaku to seek a career in law enforcement.

The series stayed in the public eye through a novelization and several seasonal TV movies. *The End of the Year Special* (1997) features Shunsaku's return to Wangan Police Station after serving punitive time as a beat cop. However, there is no room for him at any department and he eventually lands in Traffic. A routine investigation at an elementary school escalates into a drugs enquiry and eventually into a volatile hostage situation, with a murderer kidnapping the Three Amigos. *Wangan Side Story: The Female Cop* (1998) features the arrival of new officer Natsumi (pop idol Yuki Uchida), forced to partner-up with a shrewish older officer for a pointless tale of traffic cops—apart from the Wangan location, it seems to have little to do with the original. Yūji Oda returned to the series with *The Autumn Crime Eradication Special* (1998), in which his character is shown coming back to Wangan after "a period under cover." He and Sumire are put onto a case in which an arsonist is found to be working for a woman who was abused by the victim, creating a complicated circle of blame and responsibility. He also discovers that Shinji has been bugging the phones at Wangan, creating a tense standoff once more between the factions at the office. The cast returned in the movie *Bayside Shakedown* (1999), which capitalized on two years of specials and video releases to gain high box office in Japan. The movie sets up a suitable coda to the series with the kidnapping of the chief of police. As Shunsaku and Shinji collaborate in the search to find him, Heihachirō reminisces about his youth, when he too partnered with a hotshot. Like the young officers, Heihachirō and his old friend split police work between them—one to stay on the streets, the other to fight his way through office politics. The movie was promoted with the broadcast of a spoof 40-minute mini-drama starring the Three Amigos, *The Three Baddest Guys in Wangan* (1999), for which crew members were interviewed as murder suspects—some sources mistakenly file this as another full-length TV special. The cast were reunited in a second movie, *Bayside Shakedown: Blockade the Rainbow Bridge* (2003).

When illness forced Oda to miss filming on his new series **ROCKET BOY** in 2001, episodes 2, 5, 9, 10, and 11 of *BS* were rebroadcast to fill up the missing month of airtime under the title *That's Odoru Daisōsasen* with new framing footage starring Santamaria. Theme: Yūji Oda and Maxi Priest—"Love Somebody." In parts of Asia, the *BS* series is sometimes referred to by the erroneous title *Rhythm and Police,* though this is actually the name of its unforgettable disco/samba instrumental opening music, by FFSS. Peak rating 23.1%.

BEACH BOYS

1997. PRD: Chihiro Kameyama. DIR: Eriko Ishizaka. SCR: Yoshikazu Okada. CAST: Takashi Sorimachi, Yutaka Takenouchi, Ryōko Hirose, Yuki Akimoto, Mike Maki, Ryōko Shinohara, Kano Kimura, Izumi Inamori. CHN: Fuji. DUR: 45 mins. x 12 eps. (eps. 1 and 12: 65 mins.); Mon 7 July 1997–22 September 1997.

Kicked out by his girlfriend, Hiromi (Sorimachi) heads to a seaside with his car *"because it's summer!"* and because he has no place else to go. At the Diamond Head seaside hotel, he meets Kaito (Takenouchi), a former elite trading company rep recently ousted from his project after making a critical business error. Both think that it is too early for a summer holiday but there are worse places to sit and think about future plans. While they try to pick up the pieces of their lives, they take part-time jobs at the inn, which is run by Masaru (Maki), an old man who claims to have been the first surfer in Japan. Their arrival is a dream come true for two would-be love interests: Masaru's granddaughter Makoto (Hirose) and Haruko (Inamori), the owner of the local Bar Nagisa.

BB was an immediate hit with the female audience, chiefly for featuring beautiful Saipan beach scenes and beautiful boys—former model Takenouchi and future **GTO** heartthrob Sorimachi. However, unlike other beach-bum dramas like **BEACH WARS**

MIX and **NEVER LAND**, the lazy life by the seaside does not equate with shallow storytelling. Instead of heavy dramatic twists or sappy romance, *BB* concentrates on the subtle development of the leads' male friendship, telling the story with notable attention to character development for the supporting roles. *BB* is therefore successful on two levels, not only in its stated aim of feel-good summer holiday nostalgia but also as an entertaining drama that can hold its own with the best. A feature-length special was screened on 3 January 1998 and was set three months after the boys left Diamond Head. See also **ALL ABOUT YOUNG PEOPLE**, another Okada piece, as well as the suspiciously similar **BOY HUNT**. Theme: Takashi Sorimachi with Richie Sambora—"Forever."

BEACH WARS MIX

2001. JPN: *Saotome Typhoon.* PRD: Akemi Tōyama, Yasuhide Yamashita, Susumu Nakazawa. DIR: Hitoshi Ōne, Hiroaki Hobo, Naoki Tamura. SCR: Shinji Ohara. CAST: Haruhiko Katō, Yū Yoshizawa, Ryōko Shinohara, Masanori Ishii, Sae Isshiki. CHN: Asahi. DUR: 45 mins. x 11 eps.; Sat 7 July 2001–22 September 2001.

Wild card Taifū Saotome (Katō) returns to his seaside birthplace of Ōtake after three years of traveling. Claiming to have experience at all the world's beaches, he signs up for the local lifeguards and immediately causes trouble with his carefree attitude. Taifū's old friend Akiko (Shinohara) is pleased to have him back but beach boss Jun (Ishii) is a frustrated bodybuilder with little interest in lifesaving, while his earnest assistant Kazuhisa (Yoshizawa) is so obsessed with beach rules and sign writing that it's easy to believe he would prefer the beach to be completely deserted. This is exactly what local Head of Tourism Mr. Mizuno is hoping for—one more drowning in the local waters and he will be able to shut down the pleasure beach and sell it to property developers for a new marina and hotel

© 2000 TBS

Beautiful Life

complex. His assistant Ikumi (Isshiki) has other ideas, however. Without a beach to manage, she will be forced to take a new job promoting the local delicacy (repulsive *nattō* bean products) and she promises herself that the resort will have its best summer yet.

Based on the manga by Ikuko Kujirai (creator of *Madonna*, *AE) in *Big Comics Superior,* the standard tropes of Japanese drama are all here for the taking, from the prodigal maverick with a "natural" understanding of the spirit of [insertjobtitlehere], to the displaced local hero, and the uptight beauty who needs to let her hair down. Unfortunately, it's the actors who are the letdown with a uniformly hammy cast mugging at each other as if they were in a children's pantomime. Nobody in the production seems to have any faith in the material they are performing, and even the local weather seems to have given up and gone home. *BWM* was presumably filmed off-season or in the early mornings to avoid gawping crowds and it shows, with many outdoor scenes overcast and the sun-kissed beach life looking distinctly chilly—compare to the genuine

summer warmth that seems to suffuse NEVER LAND. Later attempts to introduce a revenge plot only make things seem even more laughable, as Mizuno reveals Taifū originally left town because "*He killed my brother.*" An unsuccessful attempt to introduce the formula of **GTO** into the genre of *Baywatch*.

BEAUTIFUL CHALLENGER
1971. JPN: *Utsushiki Challenger*. PRD: N/C. DIR: Mikio Koyama. SCR: N/C. CAST: Kayoko Suda, Ritsuko Nakayama, Emiko Namiki, Toshie Ishii, Mieko Nomura, Emi Shindō, Kōji Moritsugu. CHN: NTV. DUR: 45 mins. x ca. 26 eps.; Sun 4 April 1971–17 October 1971. Midori (Shindō) and her group of female tenpin bowlers challenge the male establishment in a variation of the earlier sports-related dramas such as THE SIGN IS V. The drama was credited with initiating a massive wave of interest in bowling among women, much to the annoyance of the male old guard in the bowling establishment and ironically reprising the onscreen tension in the real world. Compare to GOLDEN BOWL. Theme: Toshiko

Fujita—"Utsukushii Challenger" (Beautiful Challenger).

BEAUTIFUL LIFE *
2000. JPN: *Beautiful Life: Futari de Ita Hibi*. AKA: *Days We Spent Together; Meili Rensheng*. PRD: Hiroki Ueda. DIR: Jirō Ikuno, Nobuhiro Doi. SCR: Eriko Kitagawa. CAST: Takuya Kimura, Takako Tokiwa, Miki Mizuno, Hiroyuki Ikeuchi, Kōji Matoba, Atsurō Watabe, Takanori Nishikawa, Koyuki. CHN: TBS. DUR: 45 mins. x 11 eps. (ep 1: 70 mins.); Sun 16 January 2000–26 March 2000. Beautician Shūji (Kimura from SMAP) is nearly knocked off his motorbike by Kyōko (Tokiwa), a wild-haired girl in a sports car, who is too busy on her cell phone to notice him. After exchanging harsh words (for Japan, anyway!) in the street, the couple meet again at the library, where they fight over a parking space. Shūji is surprised when Kyōko produces a wheelchair from her car and even more taken aback when he goes looking for a chemistry textbook and discovers that Kyōko is the librarian who must help him. She accuses him of building a bomb and he archly notes that her hair has "already

exploded." When he needs a model for a magazine makeover competition, he offers to bury the hatchet by featuring her, though his winning photo-story leads to accusations from some quarters that he has exploited her wheelchair-bound status.

Mixing the basic formula of love-comedy with a sensitive portrayal of the plight of the disabled, *BL*'s ratings eclipsed those of every other trendy drama in the previous decade, much to the surprise of its commissioning channel TBS. Its success did not translate into critical acclaim, however—Kimura's HERO came out in the same year and scooped most of the awards.

Embittered at the condescending attitude of the able-bodied, Kyōko develops a grudging respect for Shūji—in arguing with her and refusing to cut her any slack, he is one of the few people who treat her as a normal person. In a touching moment, she and her fellow librarian keep a long vigil as they wait for him to return a book on the due date. The scene conveys what any viewer will have been expecting but life throws more obstacles in the path of true love. Shūji's newfound media profile turns him into a celebrity stylist at the Hot Lip salon, leaving him with less time for Kyōko. Shūji must deal with political infighting at the salon, such as the theft of his designs by fellow employee Satoru (Nishikawa) or the rapid rise and subsequent fall from grace of Takumi (Ikeuchi), a younger stylist tempted by offers from a rival boutique. Shūji breaks his arm trying to protect Kyōko at a concert and discovers firsthand just how little provision there is for the disabled in Japan. Meanwhile, the couple's friends Sachie (Mizuno) and Masao (Watabe) begin their own relationship in the obligatory romantic subplot. Later episodes introduce Shūji's prodigal ex-girlfriend Satsuki (Koyuki) whom Kyōko confronts, only to collapse under the strain. Shūji, preoccupied with a fashion show, discovers secondhand that Kyōko's condition is worsening and tragedy looms on the

horizon. One of the slew of disability dramas that began in the late 1990s—compare to the similar PURE, SUMMER SNOW, UNDER ONE ROOF, and WHEN THE SAINTS GO MARCHING IN. Shown subtitled in the U.S. on KIKU TV. Theme: B'z—"Konya Tsuki no Mieru Oka ni" (Tonight on the Moonlit Hill).

BEAUTY *

1999. JPN: *Utsukushii Hito*. AKA: *Le Bel Homme*. PRD: Kazuhiro Itō. DIR: Nobuhiro Doi, Ken Yoshida, Tamaki Endō. SCR: Shinji Nojima. CAST: Masakazu Tamura, Takako Tokiwa, Takao Ōsawa, Chizuru Ikewaki, Rina Uchiyama, Hiroyuki Miyasako, Aiko Morishita. CHN: TBS. DUR: 45 mins. x 10 eps. (eps. 1 and 10: 70 mins.); Fri 15 October 1999–17 December 1999. Kyōsuke (Tamura) is a well-to-do plastic surgeon who cherishes his teenage daughter but is unable to escape the memory of his beloved violinist wife, who died in an accident four years earlier. He is approached by Miyuki (Tokiwa), a beautiful woman desperate for cosmetic surgery. She has fled from an abusive husband, and the only way to be truly free of him is for her to completely change her identity. Against his better judgement, he gives her the best face he can think of—that of his dead wife.

Rivaling the same writer's LIPSTICK in its sheer originality, *Beauty*'s love beyond the grave is not its only unexpected thrill. Miyuki's husband Jirō (Ōsawa) is no ordinary wife beater but a respected officer in the police force—if anyone can track a woman down, it's him. Meanwhile, Kyōsuke is tormented by his own hubris—he has brought his wife back from the dead but with the mind of an independent woman who does not necessarily return his adoration. As he later confesses, the original didn't either and he feels history repeating itself.

Before long, the resourceful Jirō has obtained closed-circuit camera footage of someone using Miyuki's card at an ATM and the trail leads him closer to Kyōsuke. Miyuki is torn between her

vows to Jirō (she is still married, after all) and her growing feelings for Kyōsuke. The eventual showdown leads to a shooting and Kyōsuke's impromptu return to life-or-death surgery.

An attempt to broaden Tamura's repertoire from his famous recurring role as detective NINZABURŌ FURUHATA, *Beauty* was less popular with his fans, who were used to the sight of him taking control of a situation and solving crimes instead of waiting helplessly for them to happen to him. Despite this lukewarm reaction, *Beauty* is loaded with the plot twists and innovations that have made Nojima such a popular writer—who else would combine *Unlawful Entry* with *Face/Off*? Aside from the artful way Tokiwa's face is never shown until after Miyuki has had the fateful operation, the most impressive element is the slow-burning way in which Jirō's nature is revealed. When he first appears he is undercover as a gangster, making Miyuki's plight all the more sympathetic. It is only later that the "gangster" is revealed as a cop amid adoring members of the public, hammering home the fact that nobody is going to believe Miyuki if she claims he has assaulted her. Compare to AFRICA NIGHTS, which also features a spouse on the run with the aid of cosmetic surgery. Shown subtitled in the U.S. on KIKU TV. Theme: Jane Birkin—"L'Aquoiboniste." Peak ratings: 22.7%.

BEAUTY AND POWER *

1997. JPN: *Onnatachi no Teikoku*. AKA: *Women's Empire*. PRD: N/D. DIR: N/D. SCR: N/D. CAST: Sumiko (aka Junko) Fuji, Yukiyo Toake, Ryūzō Hayashi, Mayumi Wakamura, Akira Nakao. CHN: NHK. DUR: 90 mins. x 2 eps.; [broadcast dates unknown]. Kyōko (Toake) is Head of Sales at Imperial Cosmetics and has literally worked her way up from the shop floor. She puts the company's future on the line by throwing all its resources behind the latest product, a makeup line of her own design called "Speak." However, Kyōko's life is thrown into turmoil when unsubstantiated reports in the press claim that the new cosmetic causes an allergic reaction in some consumers and that the spokesmodel Mizue (Wakamura) has been forced into hiding with an embarrassing rash. Matters are not helped by the appearance of a virtually identical cosmetics line at a rival company, and Kyōko becomes the subject of an internal investigation, spearheaded by the privileged Nobuko (Fuji), who, it is said, is only Head of Purchasing because she is the illegitimate daughter of the company founder.

As sales take a drastic dive, the two women realize that they are being set up. Someone is making a play for a takeover bid of Imperial Cosmetics, and they must unite to track down the culprit. Suspicion ultimately falls on Nobuko's husband Takashi (Hayashi), particularly when photos appear of him at a clandestine meeting with Mizue. Shown subtitled in the U.S. on KIKU TV—the American broadcast was divided into four episodes.

BEAUTY OR THE BEAST

2003. JPN: *Bijo ka Yajū*. PRD: Satoshi Nagabe. DIR: Hiroshi Nishitani, Hidetomo Matsuda. SCR: Tomoko Yoshida. CAST: Nanako Matsushima, Masaharu Fukuyama, Ikkei Watanabe, Norito Yajima, Kuranosuke Sasaki, Miho Shiraishi, Masaru Nagai, Papaiya Suzuki, Kanako Fukaura, Kiyoshi Kodama. CHN: Fuji. DUR: 45 mins. x ca. 11 eps.; Thu 9 January 2003–?? March 2003.

Makoto (Matsushima) has a law degree from Tokyo, an MBA from Harvard, and years of experience at several high-profile news networks. While working on an important scoop in Paris, she is approached by representatives from Japan's JBC network, who make her an offer she can hardly refuse—an extremely high salary and the chance to handpick her team, so long as she agrees to return to Japan and turn around JBC's ailing news program.

Makoto arrives back in Japan with plenty of ideas, only to discover that she is not the only VIP at the JBC news desk. Hiromi (Fukuyama) is a troublesome variety presenter, subject of endless scandals and reprimands, who has been demoted to the news department as his last chance to make good. The stern lady journalist and the unpredictable star are soon fighting on and off screen—compare to **STRAIGHT NEWS** and **NEWS WOMAN**.

BEAUTY SEVEN

2001. PRD: Kenji Ikeda. DIR: Michihito Ozawa, Tarō Ōtani. SCR: Tomoko Yoshida. CAST: Takako Uehara, Yūko Nakazawa, London Boots, Anna Umemiya, Uno Kanda, Takashi Fujii, Kaori Momoi, Kōshirō Matsumoto, Misaki Itō, Mami Uematsu, Takako Katō, Shōko Takada. CHN: NTV. DUR: 45 mins. x 11 eps.; Wed 4 July 2001–30 September 2001.

Plain-Jane country girl Akari (Uehara from Speed) comes to Tokyo in search of her boyfriend but gets stood up. She applies for a job at Lespoire, a beauty salon hard-hit by the recession whose staff doubts that it can continue to ride out the bad times. Matters are not helped by the demarcation in the salon that sends the top-notch customers to Sakura (Kanda), Hazuki (Itō), and Reiko (Uematsu), while Miyako (Nakazawa), Kimie (Katō), and Ryōko (Takada) are forced to fight over less well-off clients. Soon after Akari starts, Mr. Okano (Matsumoto), an executive at the salon chain's head office, sends the go-getting Shōko (Momoi) down to Lespoire, giving her three months to turn the boutique's fortunes around. She begins making sweeping changes, not all of which the staff regard as wise. Smartly exploiting its setting for all it is worth, *Beauty Seven* not only introduces the requisite number of starlets to attract passing male channel surfers but also throws in many beauty tips to add to the show's "educational" value. Every now and then they also mention that it's what's on the inside that counts, as you might expect. Compare to **BEAUTY AND POWER** and **PLASTIC BEAUTY**.

Beetleborgs (U.S. version)

BEETLEBORGS *

1995. JPN: *Jūkō Beetle Fighter*. AKA: *B-Fighter, B-Fighter Kabuto, Big Bad Beetleborgs*. PRD: Jun Kaji, Nagafumi Hori, Jun Higasa. DIR: Osamu Kaneda, Shinichirō Sawai, Tetsuharu Mitsumura, Tarō Sakamoto, Hidenori Ishida, Katsuya Watanabe. SCR: Shūichi Miyashita, Nobuo Ōgisawa, Kyōko Sagiyama, Akira Asaka, Yasuko Kobayashi. CAST: Daisuke Tsuchiya, Shigeru Kanai, Reina Hazuki, Chigusa Tomoe, Takashi Sasano, Keiko Konno, Hideaki Hikuda, Toshimichi Takahashi, Jirō Okamoto, Takeshi Watabe. CHN: Asahi. DUR: 25 mins. x 53 eps.; Mon 5 February 1995–25 February 1996.

A group of teenagers team up to save the world from invaders from the alternate Jamal Dimension by transforming into the metallic Beetle Fighters. Takuya (Tsuchiya) is the Blue Beetle, Daisaku (Kanai) is the Green Beetle, while the female Red Beetle is played Rei (Hazuki) for the first 21 episodes and Mai (Tomoe) thereafter. Their enemies include Emperor Gaum of Jamal (Watabe), his general Gigaro (Takahashi), and Shadow the Black Beetle Warrior (played by Okamoto until episode 43, thereafter replaced by Keisuke Tsuchiya). In other words, a perfectly unremarkable team show in the style of Metal Series stories such as **SHIDER**, based on an original concept from Super Sentai ideas man Saburō Yade. Music by Kōji Kawamura. Theme: Shinichi Ishihara—"Jūkō Beetle Fighter" (Armored Beetle Fighter).

After a further 52 episodes the next year, retitled *B-Fighter Kabuto*, the series might well have faded without a trace but for the fact that it began production during the 1990s Sentai golden age initiated by the foreign success of the **MIGHTY MORPHIN' POWER RANGERS**. So it was that *B-Fighter* gained a new lease of life with Saban Entertainment's English-language adaptation, retitled *Big Bad Beetleborgs* and first broadcast in the U.S. on 9 July 1996.

Ditching most of the original plot in the *Power Rangers* style, the U.S. version replaced the nonfighting footage with a backstory of its own. For the *Beetleborgs* incarnation, the stars are Drew (Wesley Barker), Roland (Herbie Baez), and Jo (Shannon Chandler, then Brittany Konarsewski), three all-American children forced to hide out in a haunted house by local bullies. There they encounter the "funtastic phantom" Flabber (Billy Forrester) who grants them each a wish. They choose to ask for the ability to transform into the Big Bad Beetleborgs, who, in a triumph of cross-promotion, already exist as comic characters—young viewers can thus emulate their heroes by running straight out to buy the tie-in comics. However, the same magical powers also accidentally release the comic's evil Vexor (Rick Tane) and his Magnavor servants, who are determined to seize control of the world. It's fortunate the children didn't wish for something innocuous like a puppy, otherwise evil would reign supreme—luckily, they can now become superheroes to resist the very evil that they have unleashed! *Beetleborgs* has much less of the sci-fi tone of *Power Rangers*, preferring instead to play for laughs and concentrating on the haunted house theme with cameos from vampires, mummies,

and werewolves. It was succeeded by the *B-Fighter Kabuto* season, renamed *Beetleborgs Metallix*, in which inventor Arthur Fortunes creates new suits for the kids. Now wearing their Chromium Gold, Titanium Silver, and Platinum Purple suits, the kids are enlisted to help save the world from Arthur's brother Lester. Regarded by the *Power Rangers* generation as rather childish, if you can imagine that.

BELOVED COP

1992. JPN: *Itoshi no Deka*. PRD: N/C. DIR: Keiichi Ozawa. SCR: Motozō Mineo. CAST: Tetsuya Watari, Hiroshi Tachi, Shin Takuma, Mio Takagi, Fumie Hosokawa. CHN: Asahi. DUR: 45 mins. x 20 eps.; Sun 18 October 1992– 21 March 1993.

Detective Hayama (Tachi) and Detective Kawamura (Takuma) are buddies at Jōsei Police Station, working hard to solve crimes under chief detective Takakura (Watari). *BC* was a show cast in the same mold as **HOWL AT THE SUN** (which also featured Watari) but its standard cop show clichés left it with little success. It would take **BAYSIDE SHAKEDOWN** to revitalize the tired genre some years later. Theme: Hiroshi Tachi—"Nureta Kuchibiru ni Kuchizuke" (Kiss Your Wet Lips).

BENKEI

1986. JPN: *Musashibō Benkei*. PRD: N/C. DIR: N/C. SCR: N/C. CAST: Kichiemon Nakamura, Keiko Oginome, Kaori Takahashi, Teruko Nagaoka, Tarō Kawano, Yumi Asō. CHN: NHK. DUR: 45 mins. x ca. 40 eps.; Wed 9 April 1986–3 December 1986.

After being carried in his mother's womb for three years, Benkei is born with long hair and teeth and the body of a small child. It is said that he immediately laughed and commented on the brightness of the outside world, leading local people in his native Kii (modern Wakayama) to proclaim that he is a devil. Abandoned on a mountainside, he is adopted by Dainagon, a Kyoto resident who rears him until age seven when he leaves to become a

monk. Thrown out of the monastery for his violent behavior, Benkei wanders Japan in search of enlightenment, though only trouble seems to find him. After accidentally causing a temple to burn down, he decides to begin a quest to defeat 1,000 of the hated Heike samurai in battle and donate their swords to a temple. Obtaining the first 999 swords proves relatively easy but the final weapon belongs to **YOSHITSUNE** (Kawano), a young boy whose appearance belies his great skill as a warrior. After a prolonged battle, Benkei admits defeat and swears allegiance to Yoshitsune, becoming his loyal companion throughout the events also covered in the **TALE OF THE HEIKE** and **THE FIRE STILL BURNS**. Though only occasionally mentioned in the historical records of the 12th century, Benkei has become a popular figure since his appearances onstage in plays such as *Ataka* (nō), its kabuki version *Kanjinchō*, and Kurosawa's movie remake of the same story *Those Who Tread on the Tiger's Tail* (1945). A colorful supporting character in other adaptations, here he takes center stage in a drama that has every appearance of the year's *taiga* but is not. Possibly it was being held in reserve by NHK in case the actual 1986 *taiga* **INOCHI: LIFE** ran into difficulties.

BEST DAD IN THE WORLD

1998. JPN: *Sekai de Ichiban Papa ga Suki*. PRD: Ichirō Takai. DIR: Masayuki Suzuki. SCR: Ryōichi Kimizuka. CAST: Sanma Akashiya, Ryōko Hirosue, Masato Hagiwara, Masahiko Tsugawa, Yoshinori Okada. CHN: Fuji. DUR: 45 mins. x 12 eps.; Fri 7 August 1998– 23 September 1998.

Eighteen-year-old Tami (Hirosue) is forced to move in with her father Zenzō (Akashiya) when her mother dies. But Tami has barely seen him for 13 years, partly because neither she nor her mother had any desire to associate with the man who deserted them. For his part Zenzō continues to live a bachelor lifestyle and has kept his daughter's existence secret from everyone he knows. Her arrival causes him considerable difficulties, particularly when she decides to study to be a doctor and approaches her estranged father for financial help. Compare to **GENTA IKENAKA 80 KILOS**. Note that the American sitcom *The Donna Reed Show* was an early success on Fuji TV in 1959, with a Japanese title that translates as *Best Mama in the World*. Theme: Tube— "Kitto Dokokade" (Surely Somewhere). Peak rating: 21.1%.

BEST FRIEND
1995. PRD: Toshiji Matsumura, Yūya Fujii. DIR: Hisao Ogura, Yūichi Satō. SCR: Miho Nakazono. CAST: Yasuko Matsuyuki, Eri Fukatsu, Katsunori Takahashi, Mikihisa Azuma, Maki Mizuno, Masahiro Matsuoka, Keiko Tōyama, Masaaki Sakai, Kanako Enomoto. CHN: NTV. DUR: 45 mins. x 9 eps.; Mon 16 October 1995– 11 December 1995.
Kōhei (Takahashi) asks his girlfriend Kaede (Matsuyuki) to marry him. He also reveals that his company is going to transfer him to the London office and that he would like his bride-to-be to come along. As Kaede walks home she bumps into Yūko (Fukatsu), a girl from far-off Yaizu who has come to town for a meeting with her ex-boyfriend's business partner. The girls inadvertently swap address books in the confusion, leading Kaede to discover that Yūko has a meeting planned with Kōhei. She immediately expects the worse, in a farce modeled on the yuppie identity-swap comedy *Taking Care of Business* (aka *Filofax,* 1990). Theme: Tatsurō Yamashita—"Sekai no Hate Made" (To the Ends of the Earth).

BEST FRIENDS
1999. JPN: *Best Friend.* PRD: Noriko Nishiguchi, Mitsunori Morita. DIR: Mitsunori Morita, Katsunori Tomita. SCR: Masao Yajima. CAST: Ai Katō, Ai Maeda, Ryūichi Ōura, Miyoko Asada, Yūichi Haba. CHN: Asahi. DUR: 45 mins. x 9 eps.; Mon 18 October 1999–13 December 1999.

Country girl Makoto (Maeda) comes to Tokyo, hoping to become a famous singer like Hikaru Utada. She stays at the home of prissy city girl Kiyoka (Katō) where her innocent and friendly nature wins her many friends despite Kiyoka's snooty objections. Kiyoka tries to talk Makoto out of her outgoing attitude, warning her that talking to people and taking an interest in their problems is simply not the done thing in Tokyo. Kiyoka is not merely jealous of Makoto's attitude but of her ambition—Kiyoka once wanted to be a rock star but was prevented from doing so by her domineering father Yuzuru (Haba). In order to hit Makoto with some harsh realities, Kiyoka introduces Maeda to her former manager Fukahori (Ōura) but much to her annoyance he decides that Makoto shows unbridled talent. Far from getting Makoto banished back to the countryside, Fukahori encourages her to pursue her career, a situation which means that Makoto is around to witness the spectacular breakup of Kiyoka's family. Kiyoka's mother Shizuka (Asada) discovers that Yuzuru is having an affair, leading to intense family turmoil. Meanwhile, Kiyoka is diagnosed with myocarditis, the same disease that killed Bobby Simone (Jimmy Smits) in *NYPD Blue* the previous year, and given six months to live. Makoto is wracked with guilt and unable to sing, but Kiyoka encourages her to live her dreams for the benefit of them both—compare to the Bette Midler vehicle *Beaches* (1988, released in Japan as *Forever Friends*). NB: we have pluralized the Japanese title in order to distinguish this show from **BEST FRIEND**, although both series had the same title in Japanese. An unexpectedly weepy series from the writer of **BIG WING**—compare to **JUST THE WAY WE ARE**.

BEST PARTNER *
1997. PRD: Mitsunori Morita. DIR: Mitsunori Morita, Katsunori Tomita, Kenjirō Kuranuki. SCR: Kenji Nakazono, Kōnosuke Takahashi. CAST: Teruyoshi

Uchimura, Atsurō Watabe, Maki Sakai, Saya Takagi, Yōko Nogiwa, Nana Kinomi, Misato Tanaka, Tsuyoshi Ihara, Chieko Matsubara, Megumi Kobayashi. CHN: TBS. DUR: 45 mins. x 11 eps.; Sun 12 October 1997–21 December 1997.
Ichirō Suzuki (Uchimura) marries Asuka (Sakai), a girl from another part of the printing company where he works and meets her boss for the first time at the wedding. His name is *also* Ichirō Suzuki (Watabe), although he seems to be far more popular and successful, and Underling Ichirō is somewhat dismayed to discover they have been assigned to work together. The two Ichirōs start off on the wrong footing when Underling Ichirō successfully gains a contract that Boss Ichirō has been chasing for a whole year. The understandable confusion of their names ensures that praise and blame for various acts are misdirected, including the news that *"Ichirō's wife is pregnant,"* which spreads around the company before either Ichirō or their spouses has confirmed it.
A slice-of-life thirtysomething comedy, *BP* throws a series of difficulties at its tortoise and hare protagonists. These include Underling Ichirō's conviction that he only has a few months to live, Boss Ichirō's discovery that he's not as strong as he used to be (he throws his back out), and Asuka's torn allegiances between supporting the career path of her husband or her boss. Later episodes introduce more serious tensions, as Boss Ichirō suspects that his wife Kaoru is having an affair with her boxercise coach Tōru, while the death of Underling Ichirō's father-in-law tempts him away from the print business and into a rice cracker company. Shown subtitled in the U.S. on KIKU TV.

BEST TABLE, THE
1997. JPN: *Saikō no Shokutaku.* PRD: Fumio Igarashi. DIR: Mitsunori Morita. SCR: Masao Yajima, Miaki Onozawa. CAST: Hidekazu Akai, Anju Suzuki, Akiko Hinagata, Harumi Inoue, Katsuhide Uegusa, Takeo Chii. CHN: Asahi. DUR:

Big Wing

45 mins. x 11 eps.; Thu 17 April 1997–26 June 1997.
Tatsuo (Chii) is the chef-owner of an Italian restaurant, but is losing his clientele as the quality of his cuisine declines. His daughter Nao (Suzuki) wants to hire a new chef to turn the restaurant's fortunes around but the only person her father trusts is Yūtarō, a maverick cook whose whereabouts are currently unknown. When Nao eventually tracks Yūtarō down, she discovers that he has lost his sense of taste. Compare to **KING'S RESTAURANT** or **THE CHEF**.

BETTER FAMILY PLAN
1995. JPN: *Akarui Kazoku Keikaku*. PRD: Nariaki Odagiri. DIR: Nariaki Odagiri. SCR: Yuki Kiyomoto. CAST: Yasuo Daichi, Momoko Kikuchi, Junji Takada, Naomi Hosokawa, Kae Okuyama. CHN: Fuji. DUR: 45 mins. x 11 eps.; Thu 12 January 1995–23 March 1995.
Widower Hikotarō (Daichi) has struggled for eight years to bring up his four children alone while continuing to

hold down a job at a rubber company producing everything from tires to condoms. He announces his intention to marry Riko (Kikuchi), a girl who is 24 years his junior and wholly unprepared for life as a stepmother.

BETTER WATCH OUT FOR US
1996. JPN: *Oretachi ni Ki o Tsukero*. PRD: Yūya Fujii. DIR: Kaneta Nakamura. SCR: Akiyo Takigawa, Tokio Tsuchiya. CAST: Naoki Hosaka, Yoshihiko Hakamada, Miki Nakatani, Toshiyuki Nagashima, Keiko Oginome. CHN: NTV. DUR: 45 mins. x 11 eps.; Mon 15 April 1996–24 June 1996.
Elite lawyer Takumi (Hosaka), unemployed Yūsuke (Hakamada), and locksmith Tōru decide to go into business as criminals. They plot a safecracking heist to steal from criminals, promising that they will put their ill-gotten gains to good use.

BIG MONEY
2002. PRD: Akira Wada, Ken Tsuchiya. DIR: Masaki Nishiura. SCR: Keiko Hata.

CAST: Tomoya Nagase, Taizō Harada, Hitoshi Ueki, Aya Okamoto. CHN: Fuji. DUR: 45 mins. x 12 eps.; Thu 11 April 2002–6 June 2002.
Unemployed twentysomething Norimichi (Nagase) leeches off his parents and scrapes a living playing *pachinko*. He is recruited by Taihei (Ueki), a disgruntled former stock trader with Matsuba Bank who has sworn to destroy the company for its evil deeds. The unlikely pair then begin their campaign against the elite brokers of Matsuba and its lead trader Fumihiko (Harada).

Perhaps realizing that the previous year's **GOODBYE MR. OZU** would have been much more fun without the unnecessary distractions of a high school basketball team, Fuji replayed the story of a vengeful outcast from the banking world but this time keeping the story firmly in the financial arena.

BIG WING *
2001. PRD: Mitsunori Morita. DIR: Mitsunori Morita, Katsunori Toyota, Kenichirō Kuranuki. SCR: Masao Yajima. CAST: Yuki Uchida, Takashi Kashiwabara, Yōko Nogiwa, Maki Sakai, Hiromasa Taguchi. CHN: TBS. DUR: 45 mins. x 10 eps.; Mon 1 January 2001–31 March 2001.
Kumiko Yoshikawa (Uchida) wants to be the best ground attendant at Haneda Airport. Though others may scoff (the authors certainly do), it's a heartfelt wish since it's what her mother, who died in childbirth at the airport, would have wanted. Kumiko is perkiness personified—she might run as if her elbows have been stapled to her sides but she has a heart of gold, loves children, and always respects her elders. Ground Manager Shōko (Nogiwa), a no-nonsense middle-aged woman who times each takeoff with pinpoint accuracy, realizes that only Kumiko understands the spirit of ground attendancy, while the other girls have forgotten what it means to truly serve the customer.

Played deadly straight yet still as camp as Christmas, *BW* is almost a parody of all the other work-oriented dramas. Whereas other airline staff might elect for the glamour and travel of **YAMATO NADESHIKO**, Kumiko keeps her feet firmly on the ground, giving out tourist information and paging lost travelers in Haneda, once the exotic location of **ATTENTION PLEASE** but now an also-ran airport that chiefly serves domestic flights.

Cartoony characterization is perhaps only to be expected, since *BW* was adapted from the three-volume manga in *Big Comics* by Masao Yajima (see also **MAGNIFICENT ADVENTURES OF KOHARU THE GEISHA**) and Shinji Hikino but the cast earnestly strive to impart their jobs with the same *gravitas* as brain surgery or police work. So it is that the harsh pretty boy taskmaster Kuriyama (Kawashibara) drills Kumiko in the importance of her job and that She Must Never Leave Her Post, only to find the softhearted girl deserting leaflet distribution in order to carry an old woman to her plane and again to help an old man find his wallet. Like the similarly mundane **BUS STOP**, transitory guest stars bring plots to the rest of the cast—a hard up actor in trouble with the yakuza, a rock star whom Kumiko has adored since her school days, and the predictable little boy lost are just some of the sappy, yet immensely enjoyable subplots. Shown subtitled on KIKU TV in the U.S. We thought *Big Wing* was very silly but then we found **EVIL WOMAN**.

BINTA
1990. PRD: N/C. DIR: Hiroshi Akabane. SCR: Kenichi Ōnishi. CAST: Chikako Kaku, Kōjirō Shimizu, Saki Takaoka, Hideo Takamatsu, Tatsuo Umemiya. CHN: TBS. DUR: 45 mins. x 12 eps.; Tue 9 January 1990–27 March 1990.
Hibari (Kaku)'s father Shirō (Takamatsu) owns an exclusive traditional Japanese inn. After Shirō's sudden death, several boys (the Bakumatsujuku group) arrive to collect their inheritance, claiming to be Shirō's long-lost sons.

BIOMAN
1984. JPN: *Chōdenshi Bioman*. AKA: *Super Electric Bioman*. PRD: Moritaka Kato, Yasuhiro Tomita, Takeyuki Suzuki, Seiji Abe. DIR: Nagafumi Mori, Kazushi Hattori, Minoru Yamada. SCR: Hirohisa Soda, Kunio Fujii, Kyōko Sagiyama, Masaru Yamamoto, Jō Narumi. CAST: Ryōsuke Sakamoto, Naoto Ōta, Akihito Ōsuga, Yuki Yajima, Sumiko Tanaka, Michiko Makino, Munemaru Kōda, Ichirō Murakoshi. CHN: Asahi. DUR: 25 mins. x 51 eps.; Sat 4 February 1984–26 January 1985.
After arriving 500 years ago in the Bio Robo spaceship, robot guardian Peebo finds the time has come to reveal that Earth is in danger. Evil genius Doctor Man (Kōda) was once the human Doctor Kageyama but now wants to conquer the world with his army of Machine Men. Only the five members of the Bioman team—descended from humans irradiated with Bioenergy by the arrival of Peebo all those centuries earlier—can stop him. Their leader is Shirō (Sakamoto), a former shuttle pilot who is now Bioman Red One and responsible for the Bio Radar. Shingo (Ōta) is Green Two, the team's driver and Bio Scope specialist. Ryuta (Ōsuga) is Blue Three, a submersible pilot and Bio Ear (sonar) operator. Mika (Yajima) is Yellow Four, who specializes in Electro Holography. After the untimely death of Mika in an early battle with the Machine Men, she is replaced by Jun (Tanaka) as Yellow Four II, who is also an archer. A second girl, Hikaru (Makino), is Pink Five, who is able to track enemies with her Bio Beam Light and also uses the special Pink Barrier attack. As if that wasn't enough to keep her busy, she is also a flutist.

Bioman was something of a departure from the traditional Super Sentai layout, since it not only had two female team members but also jettisoned the word "sentai" from its title. In other respects, however, it was still born from the same cookie-cutter formula first perfected in **GORANGER**, with a five-member team battling garish monsters of the week, with the aid of their toy tie-in super-vehicles—in this case, Bio Jets One and Two, which combine to form the giant Bio Robo. The presence of two female members also led to a broadening of the usual action figure merchandizing into a new girl-friendly area—*Bioman* fans could also buy dressable dolls of Yellow Four and Pink Five. In addition to Doctor Man's Machine Men, the team had to fight the Big Three, a trio of minions named Mason, Farrah, and Monster, as well as Silva, a shiny robot hunter specially designed to hunt down anything containing bio-particles. "Based on an idea by Saburō Yade," *Bioman* was preceded in the Super Sentai series by **DYNAMAN** and followed by **CHANGEMAN**. Music by Tatsumi Yano.

BLACK HOOD THE MASTER THIEF
1976. JPN: *Kaiketsu Kurozukin*. PRD: Kanae Mayuzumi. DIR: Susumu Yasue. SCR: Ikuko Ōyabu. CAST: Yasosuke Bandō, Kaoru Sugita, Satoru Mizuno, Akifumi Inoue, Kōichi Hayashi, Seiichirō Kameishi. CHN: NHK. DUR: 20 mins. x 8 eps.; Mon 22 November 1976–2 December 1976.
At the close of the Edo period, Mitsuwa (Sugita) and her brother Tamasaburō (Mizuno) are living in abject poverty in a tenement block so shabby that they can see the stars through their ceiling when they go to bed at night. They are searching for their missing father Tsuchiyuki and brother Genichirō—Tsuchiyuki was a military historian, whose legacy to his children was a map demonstrating the weak points in the defenses of Edo Castle. Several prominent officials, particularly Yatagorō Akaoni (Inoue), are determined to get the map from the children. Meanwhile, the children go undercover in search of more information about their father—Mitsuwa taking a job as a lady-in-waiting at the estate of Akaoni's superior, while Tamasaburō sneaks into the jail where local Christians are held prisoner. Trouble often breaks out for the children but whenever they think

Blue Bird

all hope is lost they are rescued by the mysterious heroic figure known only as the Black Hood. Based on a story by Hitomi Takagaki, serialized in *Shōnen Club* magazine in 1935.

BLOCKS COME TUMBLING DOWN
1983. JPN: *Tsumiki Kuzushi: Oya to Ko no 200-nichi Sensō*. AKA: *200 Day Parent-Child War*. PRD: Seiji Kuroda. DIR: Takeharu Hidaka. SCR: Itsuo Kamijō. CAST: Tomoko Takabe, Akira Maeda, Mayumi Ogawa, Ikkō Furuya. CHN: TBS. DUR: 45 mins. x 7 eps.; Tue 15 February 1983–29 March 1983.
Actor Nobuhiko (Maeda) and his wife Mieko (Ogawa) have been overprotective with their daughter Kaori (Takabe) ever since she was diagnosed at age four with an abdominal tumor. Having grown up to be a shy and selfish girl, she has fallen out with her father and is eternally suspicious of her parents. Now a high school student, she is tormented by bullies because of her brown hair—a side effect of the medication she had to take. She becomes a bully herself, starting fights with pupils from other schools and stealing money. Her parents initially blame the school for her bad behavior and take her elsewhere but her attitude does not improve in her new school. Now a

crazy-haired Goth girl, Kaori develops a habit for sniffing paint-thinner, wrecking her home both physically and metaphorically. The distraught parents turn to psychologist Takeuchi (Furuya) for help, and he advises them that the root of Kaori's problem lies with her parents' lack of love.

With a peak of 45.3%, the last episode of this docudrama (based on a true account by actor Takanobu Hozumi of his rebellious daughter) was one of the highest rated shows in its year of broadcast, beaten only by the annual New Year's Eve singing contest and by the unassailable **OSHIN**. One is tempted to suggest that the way to a wayward daughter's heart is *not* to write a book about her misdeeds but the public lapped up the confessional nature of the story—soon after the original book was released Hozumi's daughter was arrested again, which only added to the publicity. The story was also later adapted into Kosei Saitō's live-action movie *Domino* (*Tsumiki Kuzushi*, 1983), starring Noriko Watanabe and Ayumi Ishida. Beyond the voyeuristic opportunity to spy on a star's problems, the drama also garnered praise for its frank depiction of the domestic problems that could affect any family with a run of bad luck—compare to **CALL ME A BAD GIRL** and **RED**. Theme: Takao Kisugi—"Mukuchi na Yoru" (Taciturn Night).

BLUE BIRD *
1997. JPN: *Aoi Tori*. AKA: *L'Oiseau Bleu* [*sic*]. PRD: Seitarō Kijima. DIR: Nobuhiro Doi, Kanji Takenoshita. SCR: Hisashi Nozawa. CAST: Etsuji Toyokawa, Yui Natsukawa, Anne Suzuki, Hiromi Nagasaku, Shirō Sano, Maiko Yamada. CHN: TBS. DUR: 45 mins. x 11 eps.; Fri 10 October 1997–19 December 1997.
Strong, silent type Yoshimori (Toyokawa) is a train station attendant in a remote village who falls for new arrival Kahori (Natsukawa). Appearing drunk one night at Yoshimori's station, Kahori confesses that she is unhappy with her new husband Hiromu (Sano), who is the son of the richest man in

town but uncaring toward her and her daughter Shiori (Suzuki). The couple begin a clandestine relationship, risking the lethal gossip and rumor of a small town.

Like writer Nozawa's later **WEDNESDAY LOVE AFFAIR**, *BB* can be clearly divided into two distinct halves, with the opening story only distantly related to the closing chapters. Just as the tension mounts in the Yoshimori-Kahori-Hiromu love triangle, Yoshimori leaves town and goes on the run with his lover and her daughter. The trio are forced progressively further north—unable to register Shiori at a new school and constantly on the lookout for Hiromu, the idea of a lovers' paradise soon sours. Eventually, at the end of the line in Hokkaidō, Kahori dies under mysterious circumstances and Yoshimori is imprisoned for her murder.

Six years later, an older Shiori (Yamada) confronts Yoshimori and hears the truth about her mother's death. The two decide to go on the vacation that the trio planned but never took. Hiromu, now running for mayor, forces Yoshimori to leave town and Shiori insists on accompanying him. Though Yoshimori asks Hiromu to collect her, Hiromu refuses, not only because he is busy with his political campaign but also because he has realized the publicity might be beneficial to him if he claims that Shiori has been kidnapped. The couple run off to an island that was a favorite destination for Kahori, and as they wait for the end Yoshimori tries to cheer Shiori up by relating the story of the *Blue Bird of Happiness*. As in Maurice Maeterlinck's original 1908 play (see also *AE*), the characters have searched all over for this nebulous avian MacGuffin, only to discover that it was at home all along. For this TV homage, the searching serves a dual purpose as a travelogue, with Yoshimori's romantic quest taking him and his surrogate family to plenty of Japanese tourist spots. Shown subtitled in the U.S. on KIKU and KTSF TV. A 1997 Boxing Day TV special with the cumbersome title of *Painful Love Once More—Tears and Emotions Memorial: Blue Bird Yoshimori's Terminus Beneath the Sea and Sky of Saipan,* comprised a digest of favorite moments from the series, spliced with new footage of Yoshimori ten years on.

BLUE SCATTERS

1983. JPN: *Ao ga Chiru.* PRD: Mitsuru Yanai. DIR: Yutaka Takahata, Mamoru Yamada, Yasuo Yagi, Akio Yoshida. SCR: Seita Yamamoto. CAST: Ken Ishiguro, Yurie Nitani, Kōichi Satō, Maiko Kawakami, Yoshikazu Shimizu. CHN: TBS. DUR: 45 mins. x 13 eps.; Fri 21 October 1983–27 January 1984.

Undecided about whether he should register for his university or not, Ryōhei (Ishiguro) suddenly has his mind made up for him when he sees beautiful lady in red Natsuko (Nitani). At the freshman fair, Kaneko (Satō) convinces Ryōhei and his newfound friend Yūko (Kawakami) to join the tennis club. Ryōhei tries to convince Natsuko to join, but she is not interested in him. They then discover that the university has no tennis court but hope that if they build it, more members will come. Sure enough, after three months, the court is ready and the tennis club is booming. The team members manage to convince Anzai (Shimizu) to join them—a former tennis star, he gave it up due to illness and makes the ideal ringer for the university's collegiate matches. Eventually, even the prissy Natsuko joins up.

Though the plot seems unbearably derivative in the wake of similar quirky sports movies such as *Water Boys* and *Sumo Do Sumo Don't, Blue Scatters* is a whole decade ahead of these latecomers. COMING HOME author Teru Miyamoto's original book was set in the Kansai region (i.e. Osaka) in the 1960s and moved to contemporary Tokyo for this remake. Much of the cast and crew, particularly leads Ishiguro and Nitani, were noticeably inexperienced, adding a naive quality that only highlighted the serial's charm, making *Blue Scatters* an extremely influential series

in the college romance genre—compare to later imitators such as ODD APPLES. Theme: Seiko Matsuda—"Aoi Photograph" (Blue Photograph).

BLUE SWAT

1994. PRD: Jun Kaji, Nagafumi Hori. DIR: Satoru Tsuji, Michio Konishi, Masao Minowa, Tetsuji Mitsumura, Hidenori Ishida. SCR: Junichi Miyashita, Nobuo Ōgisawa, Kyōko Sagiyama, Hirohisa Masuda, Yasuko Kobayashi, Akira Asaka. CAST: Sōji Masaki, Yūka Shiratori, Hiroshi Domon, Yūki Tanaka, Tomoko Higata, Shigeru Sano, Toshikazu Yokota, Shigeru Araki, Mitsue Mori. CHN: Asahi. DUR: 30 mins. x 51 eps.; Sun 30 January 1994–29 January 1995.

After the Blue Swat alien counteroffensive base is destroyed by invaders, only three team members survive. Shō (Masaki), Sara (Shiratori), and Shigu (Domon) are blamed for the disaster but resolve to confront their alien enemies with whatever equipment they can salvage—chiefly their high-tech battle suits, which despite their name are demonstrably purple in hue. Later episodes saw the addition of extra teammates Seiji (Tanaka) and Sumire (Higata), presumably to make the Blue Swat group of equivalent size and dynamic to the average battle team in the style of MIGHTY MORPHIN' POWER RANGERS and its ilk. *Blue Swat* replaced JAN PERSON in the Sunday morning fight slot on TV Asahi.

BODYGUARD, THE

1997. PRD: Tetsuya Kuroda, Tadahisa Sakamoto. DIR: Takamichi Yamada, Shingo Matsubara, Hiroshi Ikezoe. SCR: Saburō Kurodo. CAST: Tsuyoshi Nagabuchi, Naomi Zaizen, Atsushi Ōnita, Kaoru Hatsuse, Isao Natsuyagi. CHN: Asahi. DUR: 45 mins. x 11 eps.; Thu 10 July 1997–18 September 1997.

Shin (pop star Nagabuchi) is a supercompetent bodyguard who saves the life of a foreign dignitary. Along with his comic relief partner (Ōnita), he is recruited by retired police officer

Yamada (Natsuyagi) to guard endangered widow Megumi (Zaizen). Unnecessary slapstick and unconvincing stage blood mars a show that unashamedly rips off the Kevin Costner vehicle *The Bodyguard* (1992), though singer Nagabuchi impressively holds his own in martial arts scenes with former wrestler Ōnita—see also RUN. Theme: Tsuyoshi Nagabuchi—"Himawari" (Sunflowers).

An earlier series, also called *The Bodyguard,* was shown on the channel when it was still known as NET in 1974. Written by Toshio Abe and directed by Yasushi Nagano, it featured a group of four men and six females, each with a martial arts specialty, led by Shinichi "Sonny" Chiba.

BORDER

1999. JPN: *Border—Hanzai Shinri Sōsa File.* AKA: *Border—Criminal Psychology Investigation File.* PRD: Ryūta Inoue, Mamoru Koizumi. DIR: Nobuhiro Kamikawa, Kōichi Okamoto. SCR: Toshiyuki Morioka. CAST: Akina Nakamori, Michitaka Tsutsui, Hitomi Satō. CHN: NTV. DUR: 45 mins. x 8 eps.; Mon 11 January 1999–8 March 1999.

A criminal drama featuring Nakamori as a psychological profiler, though her investigations were cut short by the star's ill health, leaving the series with a messy ending and an absent lead. *Border* ran during the same TV season that saw thrillers swamping Japanese TV schedules but its lack of staying power and confused denouement allowed UNSOLVED CASES and RING to seize all the audience attention. Compare to similar filming problems on ROCKET BOY. Theme: Akina Nakamori—"Ophelia."

BORN FREE

1976. JPN: *Kyōryū Tankentai Born Free.* AKA: *Dinosaur Investigators Born Free; Return of the Dinos; Dinosaur Park.* PRD: Akira Tsuburaya, Kiyoshi Iwagami. DIR: Kōichi Takano, Haruyuki Kawajima, Jun Ōki, Toshitsugu Suzuki. SCR: Keiichi Abe, Atsuhiro Andō, Tadaaki Yamazaki, Narimitsu Taguchi. CAST: Atsunori Mori,

Born Free

Shingo Kanemoto, Kyōnosuke Ue, Yōko Kuri, Kazue Takahashi. CHN: NET (Asahi). DUR: 25 mins. x 25 eps.; Sun 1 October 1976–25 March 1977.
In 1996, Comet Arby's approach to Earth causes major upheavals. Dinosaurs, long thought extinct, begin to wander the planet. In the Japanese outpost of an international alliance devoted to controlling the problem, Professor Tadaki forms the Born Free group, a team of dinosaur catchers that aims to protect the creatures from the evil hunter King Battler. The title was inspired by the unrelated U.S. TV series *Born Free* (1974).

The otherwise unremarkable *BF* took its place in the history books by combining animated footage with live-action modelwork, superimposing cel-animated characters drawn by the Sunrise Studio onto the high quality modelwork for which the Tsuburaya studio was famed. Tsuburaya would follow the success of *Born Free* with the similar dinosaur show **EISENBORG**.

BORN OF LIES
1998. JPN: *Ai Tokidoki Uso*. AKA: *Love Sometimes Lies*. PRD: Mikiko Umehara. DIR: Hiroshi Yoshino, Ryōichi Itsukida. SCR: Yukari Tatsui. CAST: Yasuko Matsuyuki, Masato Hagiwara, Hiroshi Abe, Hikaru Nishida, Harumi Inoue, Hideaki Itō. CHN: NTV. DUR: 45 mins. x 12 eps.; Wed 8 April 1998–25 June 1998.
After five years of marriage, surgeon Ayuko (Matsuyuki) and her pediatrician husband Ryōsuke (Hagiwara) discover that there is no chance whatsoever that she will ever conceive a child. They resign themselves to life without offspring, though their existence is upset by the arrival of a man who claims to be Ryōsuke's younger brother (Itō). Compare to the same writer's later drama about another controversial medical issue—**SEMI DOUBLE**. Theme: Yasuko Matsuyuki—"Ai no Sekai" (World of Love).

BOSS'S BAD YEAR, THE
1993. JPN: *Kachō-san no Yakudoshi*. PRD: N/C. DIR: Hironobu Kuwata. SCR: Hirokazu Fuse. CAST: Kenichi Hagiwara, Eri Ishida, Teppei Yamada, Megumi Matsushita, Kyōzō Nagatsuka. CHN: TBS. DUR: 45 mins. x 13 eps.; Sun 4 July 1993–3 October 1993.
Mr. Terada (Hagiwara) is a 43-year-old employee at a large textile company, who becomes convinced that the next twelve months are going to be bad luck for him. He is promoted to sales manager but the apparent good fortune soon turns bad, as his new job title requires him to relocate out of Tokyo to the hellish Osaka office. There, his arrival comes at the same time as a massive downturn in sales and his family starts to resent him for their misfortunes. Based on the story by Musashi Kanbe.

BOY CHASER
1998. JPN: *Osorubeshi Otonashi Karen-san*. AKA: *Awesome Karen Otonashi*. PRD: Yūji Tōjō. DIR: Kazuhisa Imai. SCR: Yoshikazu Okada. CAST: Kanako Enomoto, Yoshinori Okada, Rena Komine, Miho Kanno, Kirari. CHN: Asahi. DUR: 45 mins. x 10 eps.; Mon 5 January 1998–16 March 1998.
Teenager Karen (Enomoto) falls in love with Gunshi (Okada), an older boy at the same high school. But when she realizes that she could not be farther away from "his type," she transforms into a schoolgirl stalker. Presumably a younger version of the previous year's **STALKER'S INESCAPABLE LOVE**, played more for laughs and based on the 1993 manga by **REIKO SHIRATORI I PRESUME** creator Yumiko Suzuki. Theme: Deeps—"Happiness."

BOY HUNT
1998. PRD: Takuya Kaneko, Chihiro Kameyama. DIR: Tatsuaki Kimura, Takehiko Shinjō. SCR: Fumie Mizuhashi, Junya Yamazaki. CAST: Arisa Mizuki,

Asaka Seto, Issei Ishida, Miki Sakai, Tomomi Kahara. CHN: Fuji. DUR: 45 mins. x 12 eps.; Mon 6 July 1998–21 September 1998.

Chalk-and-cheese college girls Riri (Mizuki) and Chisato (Seto) are good friends but almost fall out over Kei (Ishida), a handsome DJ whose plans to date them both go horribly awry. Deciding that they are both better off without him, they head for a southern beach, where their friend Erika (Kahara) owns a hotel. They resolve to spend the entire summer "hunting boys," though the hot-tempered Chisato mellows when her first victim, surfer Takenosuke (Daijirō Kawaoka) pretends to have been injured to win her affection. Riri, for her part, is unable to put Kei out of her mind. Learning that he has left a message on her answering machine, she returns to Tokyo, while Chisato hides her own feelings for him and encourages her friend to get back together with him. The two couples seem to have navigated their way out of their romantic difficulties until, toward the end of the summer, Kei surprises Chisato by confessing that he still has feelings for her. Chisato is forced to choose between the man she adores and her best friend in a female-oriented reworking of the previous year's **BEACH BOYS**, from the same producer Chihiro Kameyama. Like its predecessor, *Boy Hunt* ticks off all the boxes of a summertime drama, beginning with a carefree travelogue, cruising with a burgeoning romance, and then hitting the viewers with the bittersweet realization that all summers eventually must end. Theme: Convertible (a group featuring Arisa Mizuki)—"Oh Darling."

BOYFRIEND
1997. JPN: *Kare*. PRD: Kazuo Yamada, Isao Araki. DIR: Yasuyuki Kusuda. SCR: Hiroshi Takeyama, Masaya Ozaki. CAST: Hiroko Shino, Gorō Inagaki, Hiromi, Masato Ibu, Yasuko Sawaguchi. CHN: Kansai. DUR: 45 mins. x 11 eps.; Tue 7 January 1997–18 March 1997.

Sayoko (Shino) is the manager of the Madonna beauty salon. With her husband Seiji (Ibu) addicted to gambling, she is more open that she might have expected to the prospect of hiring broken-hearted hunk Toshiya (Inagaki), a hair and makeup artist introduced to her by her geisha client Ryōko (Sawaguchi). The two older women develop a great interest in Toshiya's love life in this adaptation of a novel by Hiroshi Takeyama. Compare to **BEAUTY SEVEN**. Theme: Diana Ross—"Promise Me You'll Try." Peak rating: 20.2%.

BRAND
2000. PRD: Akira Wada, Masatoshi Katō. DIR: Masaru Hirano. SCR: Kumiko Tabuchi. CAST: Miki Imai, Kyōko Enami, Somegorō Ichikawa, Eisaku Yoshida, Aiko Satō, Akira Hiraizumi. CHN: Fuji. DUR: 45 mins. x 11 eps.; 13 January 2000–23 March 2000.

Thirty-five-year-old PR lady Midori (Imai) is a workaholic, devoted to selling the fashion brand Dion. Forced to take a week off by her manager Haruko (Enami), she realizes that she has no idea what to do with her life when she is not working. Meanwhile, twentysomething Sōichirō (Ichikawa) is the master-designate of a tea school. Given three years' freedom before he must take his post, he returns to Japan in search of a job. He feels stifled by his traditional track, and hopes to change careers—as chance would have it, he has found a post at Midori's company by the time she returns to work. She is initially skeptical at such a traditionalist in her PR company but soon comes to respect Sōichirō when the firm has to attend a corporate tea ceremony. Although he is annoyed that his talents are being exploited and embarrassed that his own father Jōtaro (Hiraizumi) is in attendance with a number of tea masters, Sōichirō is the perfect host.

A predictable love polygon unfolds, as Sōichirō realizes he has feelings for Midori, despite already having a fiancée chosen by his parents and also basking in the unrequited adoration of his co-worker Yuri (Satō). Meanwhile, Midori's colleague and former boyfriend Horiguchi (Yoshida) falsely claims to Sōichirō that the couple are still an item. While Midori battles with her feelings for the two men, the Dion brand comes under attack from rival company Angela.

As well as the interlocking male-female romantic intrigues (with what the authors believe to be six separate sides but we could have missed one), *Brand*'s complex drama also features a classically Japanese juxtaposition of duty and emotion. Sōichirō must choose between his preordained life as tea master and husband or face ostracism for taking up with a business-woman ten years his senior. The cultural clash of old and new morals was accentuated with the casting of Ichikawa in the role of Sōichirō—like fellow drama star Takako Matsu, he is the descendant of a long line of kabuki actors and brings a certain gravity to his role. In an ironic turnabout, this satire on public relations proved to be a lucrative opportunity for product placement for Christian Dior, who supplied all the clothes sold as the "Dion" brand. Theme: Miki Imai—"Goodbye Yesterday."

BRIDE BEHIND THE CURTAIN
1994. JPN: *Daikazoku Dorama: Yome no Deru Maku*. AKA: *Great Family Drama: The Curtain Whence Comes the Bride*. PRD: Yūji Tōjō. DIR: Masahiro Kunimoto. SCR: Hirokazu Fuse. CAST: Yasuko Sawaguchi, Hiroshi Fuse, Akiho Sendō, Isamu Hashizume, Kin Sugai. CHN: Asahi. DUR: 45 mins. x 11 eps.; Thu 14 July 1994–22 September 1994.

Uptown girl Etsuko (Sawaguchi) gets engaged to downtown boy Yūichi (Fuse), the eldest of ten siblings. Claiming that the couple are from opposite sides of the tracks and unlikely to ever enjoy a successful marriage, Etsuko's father refuses to allow them to wed unless Yūichi comes to live with Etsuko's family. *BBtC* is another in-law appeasement drama in the style of **LADY OF THE MANOR** and **SHOTGUN**

MARRIAGE but one which forces both marriage partners to confront the unsuitability of their spouse's relatives. Theme: Akiho Sendō—"Setsunai Yūki" (Heart-rending Courage).

BRIDE IS SIXTEEN, THE

1995. JPN: *Hanayome wa Jūroku-sai.* PRD: Masayuki Morikawa. DIR: Noboru Sugiyama. SCR: Toshiya Itō. CAST: Hidemasa Nakayama, Rie Tomosaka, Hideki Takahashi, Masaki Kyōmoto, Akiko Hinagata. CHN: Asahi. DUR: 45 mins. x 10 eps.; Mon 14 October 1995–18 December 1995.

When rich girl Koyuri (Tomosaka) runs away from home, her family hires teenage orphan look-alike Natsumi (Tomosaka again) to take her place. Natsumi must act her role perfectly, even to the extent of marrying the wealthy boss of Tachibana Construction, who turns out to be not quite the ogre she has been led to expect. A modern fairy tale, stealing from *The Prince and the Pauper* and *Pretty Woman* (1990) in equal amounts. Compare to **THE STAND-IN** and **FORBIDDEN FRUITS**. Theme: Katsunori Takahashi—"Unbalance."

BRIDE-TO-BE *

1995. JPN: *Tatakau O-yome-sama.* AKA: *Fighting Bride.* PRD: Yoshiki Tanaka. DIR: Nozomu Amemiya. SCR: Toshio Terada. CAST: Akiko Matsumoto, Naoki Hosaka, Isao Hashizume, Miho Takagi. CHN: NTV. DUR: 45 mins. x 9 eps.; Wed 18 October 1995–13 December 1995.

Atsuko (Matsumoto), a young girl who works in a china company, tells her boyfriend Shunpei (Hosaka) that she is pregnant. They decide to get married but never seem to find the right time to tell Atsuko's father Masaichi (Hashizume). Based on the manga by Eiko Kera—compare to **SHOTGUN MARRIAGE**.

A feature-length TV sequel *Bride-to-Be: Honeymoon Special* (1996) has the newlyweds forced to move in with Shunpei's mother after their apartment burns down. In-law tensions build but Masaichi falls for a friend of Shunpei's mother, reuniting the cast for one more romantic dilemma. Shown subtitled in the U.S. on KIKU TV.

BROKEN DOWN ROBOT TAIHEI

1978. JPN: *Ponkotsu Robot Taiheiki.* AKA: *Chronicle of the Broken Down Robot.* PRD: Kanae Mayuzumi. DIR: Kazuya Satō. SCR: Mamoru Sasaki. CAST: Michikazu Yamada, Sanae Nakahara, Masaaki Waguri, Takao Yamada, Gijirō Satō, Rabbit Sekine, Miyuki Kojima, Toshie Negishi, Noboru Mitsutani, Eri Tsuruma, Hirō Oikawa. CHN: NHK. DUR: 15 mins. x 4 eps.; Mon 25 December 1978–28 December 1978.

At his lab, the doctor (Mitsutani) fixes secondhand electrical appliances. He has also invented Taihei (voiced by Oikawa), a robot who works part time at a nearby noodle restaurant. Matsuda (Satō) and Tsukiko (Kojima), Takemoto (Yamada) and Yukiji (Negishi), Umemura (Sekine) and Hanae (Tsuruma) are three couples who meet and fall in love at the noodle restaurant and decide to marry there with Taihei as a witness. However, their plans meet with opposition from the local Christian and Shinto priests, who regard the novelty of a "robot wedding" as unfair competition with their more spiritual services. The couples reluctantly agree to more traditional services but still attempt to schedule their own ceremonies at the noodle bar with Taihei. Eventually, all is resolved and the triple wedding takes place with robot, Shinto, and Christian all as witnesses. Recalling the British sitcom *Metal Mickey* (1979), this bizarre Christmas SF comedy was based on a story by Eisuke Ishikawa, adapted for the screen by prolific anime writer Mamoru Sasaki (*AE) and mystifyingly changes tack in its final episode to become a religious farce. The Japanese title is a pun alluding to the medieval *Taiheiki* chronicle also filmed as **TALE OF THE HEIKE**.

BROTHERS

1998. PRD: Miwako Kurihara. DIR: Kōzō Nagayama. SCR: Atsuko Hashibe. CAST: Masahiro Nakai, Yoshino Kimura, Gorō Kishitani, Yoshio Harada, Tsubasa Imai, Ryōtarō Akashi. CHN: Fuji. DUR: 45 mins. x 12 eps.; Mon 13 April 1998–29 June 1998.

Widower Manabu (Harada) runs a large Buddhist temple in Tokyo, and hopes that one of his four sons will take over the "family business." However, eldest son Shinbu (Kishitani) is more interested in becoming a sportswriter, arriving to conduct services in Buddhist robes but with a crash helmet on his head ready for a speedy getaway. He also runs a nightclub, where Nana (Kimura) used to be a dancer. She wakes up in bed next to second brother Shinjin (Nakai from SMAP) and claims that they have slept together. He attempts to shoo her off the temple precinct, but she sees Manabu's ad for a housekeeper and applies for the job. Comedy then ensues, as the harassed girl becomes a surrogate mother for the slobbish family. In a variation of the in-law appeasement series such as **LADY OF THE MANOR**, nothing Nana does goes according to plan—she never gets Shinbu's eggs just right, she throws out the old washing machine that is a memento of the boys' mother, and she becomes an unwitting accomplice in the secret tobacco habit of third son Shin (Imai). To prove that truly nothing is sacred any more, the black-robed family line up in front of the temple incense burner with guitars to perform the theme song for the credit sequence. Compare to similar religious high jinks in **SISTER STORIES**. Theme: SMAP—"Taisetsu" (Importance). Peak rating: 24.3%.

BROTHER'S CHOICE, A

1994. JPN: *Oniichan no Sentaku.* PRD: Mitsuru Yanai. DIR: Mitsuru Yanai. SCR: Michio Shimizu. CAST: Takanori Jinnai, Miyuki Imori, Tōgo Shimura, Misako Konno, Yoshiki Kobayashi. CHN: TBS. DUR: 45 mins. x 12 eps.; Sun 9 October 1994–25 December 1994. Engaged couple Shūji (Jinnai) and

Chikako (Konno) have bought an apartment prior to their wedding. Soon after Shūji moves in, his sister Yōko (Imori) and brother Izumi (Shimura) become sudden, unexpected, and not entirely welcome, boarders with the couple. As the fateful wedding day approaches, Shūji realizes that his aged father is now living on his own, while Chikako feels obliged to look after her mother. An in-law appeasement comedy in the style of LADY OF THE MANOR, in which a modern couple learn that marriage is seldom about just two people. Theme: Misa Jōnouchi—"Kimi no Koe ga Kikitai" (I Want to Hear Your Voice).

BUNNY KNIGHTS

1999. JPN: *Sennen Ōkoku Sanjūshi Bunny Knights*. AKA: *Millennium Kingdom Three Musketeers Bunny Knights; Vanny Knights*. PRD: Takeshi Nakajima. DIR: Kenzō Maihara, Atsushi Shimizu, Mikio Hirota, Toshikazu Nagae. SCR: Atsushi Maekawa, Reiko Yoshida, Daisuke Habara, Kazuya Hatazawa, Tetsuki Kondō. CAST: Mie Kuribayashi, Rie Masuko, Luna Nagai, Kei Watanabe, Erika Yamakawa, Yūki Ōkawa. CHN: Asahi. DUR: 25 mins. x 20 eps.; Sat 3 April 1999–19 September 1999.
Anime fan Kazuyoshi (Watanabe) injures himself in the company canteen and is assigned the lovely Alice (Kuribayashi) as a home helper. Little does he know that Alice and her friends, would-be model Akira (Masuko) and tough girl Airi (Nagai), are secret identities for the Knights of Arest, sworn defenders of justice and truth. Within Kazuyoshi himself sleeps the spirit of Arest Horn, the only warrior who can defeat the coming attack of the vampire Amor Gore. For this he will need to acquire the Millennium Saber, and the girls will transform into the miniskirted Bunny Knight supersoldiers.

A mind-boggling show from the makers of MASKED ANGEL ROSETTA, combining the monster-of-the-week angle popularized by the MIGHTY

MORPHIN' POWER RANGERS, with the late-night titillation of 1990s girlie anime—*BK* was screened at two o'clock in the morning, which is why some sources list it as a very late Friday show rather than a very early Saturday show. The show incorporated animated transformations in homage to *Sailor Moon* (*AE), for which the knights assumed a cartoon form designed by Haruhiko Mikimoto and animated by the popular studio KSS. For a much more adult drama from scenarist Yoshida, see PARFUM DE LA JALOUSIE.

BURNING MOUNTAINS AND RIVERS

1984. JPN: *Sanga Moyu*. PRD: N/C. DIR: Yūji Murakami. SCR: Shinichi Ichikawa. CAST: Kōshirō Matsumoto, Toshiyuki Nishida, Daijirō Tsutsumi, Reiko Ōhara, Yōko Shimada, Kenji Sawada, Toshirō Mifune. CHN: NHK. DUR: 45 mins. x ca. 45 eps.; Sun 8 January 1984–23 December 1984.
The three Amaba brothers are second-generation Japanese Americans, whose allegiances are torn by the bombing of Pearl Harbor. Determined to show his loyalty to his adopted country, Isamu (Tsutsumi) volunteers for the U.S. Army and is shipped off to fight in Europe. A second brother, studying in Japan at the outbreak of hostilities, is conscripted to fight against the Americans as a Japanese soldier. The third brother Kenji (Matsumoto) avoids conflict by enlisting as a military interpreter, in which capacity he witnesses the war crimes trials that followed Japan's defeat. He is led to question the nature of homeland and patriotism and was inspired to do something to help Japan regain its lost honor. In a departure for NHK's *taiga* period drama series, *BM&R* turned away from Japan's distant past to tackle controversially recent events. Adapting Toyoko Yamazaki's novel *Futatsu no Sokoku* (*Two Homelands*), the show led to significant embarrassment for its commissioning channel, as Americans of Japanese descent resented the implication that their loyalties were divided

between the U.S. and a country many of them had never seen, while the older generation of Japanese viewers reacted unfavorably to a chronicle of Japan's wartime activities. Though the TV adaptation was something of a ratings disaster, Yamazaki's novel was inspired by the true story of Akira Itami, the chief language monitor at the war crimes trial, himself a second-generation Japanese American, who eventually committed suicide in 1950. Compare to 100 YEARS, which also examined the loyalties of Japanese emigrants, and the vastly more successful 20th-century *taiga* drama INOCHI: LIFE.

BUS STOP

2000. PRD: Miwako Kurihara. DIR: Michio Mitsuno, Hideki Takeuchi. SCR: Yoshihiro Izumi. CAST: Naoko Iijima, Teruyoshi Uchimura, Taichi Kokubu, Rina Uchiyama, Toshirō Yanagiba, Yū Yoshizawa, Mari Hoshino, Ryūta Kawabata. CHN: Fuji. DUR: 45 mins. x 12 eps.; Mon 1 July 2000–30 September 2000.
Marketing girl Natsuo (Iijima) is left out on a limb when her boss/lover Kojirō (Yanagiba) leaves for New York. Before long, she is demoted to data manager and instructed to turn around the fading fortunes of a rundown Tōkyō bus company. The result is an absurdly hilarious drama, as if an

Buska

airport soap opera was forced to manage with buses when someone set fire to the budget. Natsuo is the *"maverick who doesn't play by the book,"* which in bus driver terms means she prefers private transport and is not averse to passing in bus-only lanes. Driver Musashi (Uchimura), meanwhile, is the friendly Japanese everyman, who treats his vehicle as if it were a jumbo jet and merrily addresses his passengers as if passing on details of their altitude and cruising speed. As Natsuo, Iijima does her usual poor little rich girl routine (her role here is very similar to that in her 2001 movie vehicle *Messengers*) but she soon develops a romantic interest in Musashi, adding extra dramatic tension when Kojirō predictably returns from America to form the requisite love triangle. Compare to the equally silly **BIG WING**. Theme: Mr. Children—"Not Found."

BUSKA

1966. JPN: *Kaijū Būsuka*. AKA: *Booska*. PRD: Kōji Morita, Yōzō Nagai. DIR: Jūkichi Takemae, Minoru Manda, Toshitsugu Suzuki, Tetsuhiro Kawasaki, Kazuo Kimata. SCR: Masahiro Yamada, Keisuke Fujikawa, Shinichi Sekisawa, Tetsuo Kinjō, Shinichi Ichikawa, Kōichi Yamano,

Shōzō Uehara. CAST: Seikichi Nakamura, Kunio Suzuki, Tetsuo Yamamura, Tomohiro Miyamoto, Nekohachi Edoya, Kazuko Hata, Junko Nakahara, Yoshiyuki Fujie, Hiroshi Nakajima. CHN: TVT. DUR: 25 mins. x 47 eps.; Wed 9 November 1966–27 September 1967. The sequel *Buska! Buska!!*; DUR: 25 mins. x 38 eps.; Sat 2 October 1999–24 June 1999.

Boy inventor Daisaku (Miyamoto) has created an all-purpose machine that gets him out of bed in the morning, brushes his teeth, and ejects him from the house with his backpack attached. He also tries to create a Godzilla-style monster by feeding a chemical cocktail to his pet iguana Buska. Owing to an amount of old baking powder past its sell-by date, the resulting "monster" is a gentle, charming creature with large round eyes and a buck-toothed expression not unlike a squirrel. However, it also has amazing physical strength and (in the style of **MONKEY**) a magical crown made of the element Buskanium, which allows it to shrink in size to just 50cm tall. It likes noodles and hates turtles.

As one might expect from a Tsuburaya show, human life is soon threatened by a number of bizarre opponents, forcing Daisaku's creation

to save the world from monsters and aliens, including a Glacier Witch and a giant sponge. From episode 26, the series also introduces Buska's mischievous "brother" Chamegon, formed from Daisaku's experimental combination of an alien and a squirrel. Chamegon has the power of superspeed, shoots a Monster Beam from his tail, and can also transform into anything, so long as it has a supply of walnuts.

In the heart-rending final episode, a space mission to Planet R requires an alien pilot to endure the 20-day round-trip. Buska and Chamegon are delighted to volunteer, and only Daisuke realizes that time dilation effects will mean that each day in space will mean a whole year will have elapsed on Earth—compare to similar relativistic tragedy in Hideaki Anno's *Gunbuster* (*AE). Daisuke waves them off with tears in his eyes, never expecting to see his friends again.

However, 33 years later, the series *was* resurrected as *Buska! Buska!!*, this time featuring Daisuke's son Yūsaku (Masaaki Tachizawa) as the main character. Missing the obvious chance to bring back the original creatures from their space voyage, the new series simply featured the creation of an all new Buska, as Yūsaku attempts to create a superhero "Miracle Mirror King" but accidentally adds *ramen* noodle sauce to the mix. Despite, or perhaps because of its generation-old pedigree, the new *Buska* series was regarded as slightly old-fashioned by the modern audience. Although it remained a heartwarming children's comedy like the old series, the production team tried to appeal to new audiences by injecting extra gags and some female eye candy, before eventually admitting defeat and canceling the series 13 episodes early. See also **CHIBIRA** and for reptilian pals of a different kind **DAUGHTER OF IGUANA**.

BY THE SEA *

1998. JPN: *Umi Made Go Fun*. AKA: *Five Minutes From the Sea*. PRD: Tetsuo Ichihara. DIR: Yasuo Inoshita. SCR:

Satoshi Suzuki. CAST: Hirohide Yakumaru, Yasuko Sawaguchi, Yumi Shirakawa, Shirō Itō. CHN: TBS. DUR: 45 mins. x 12 eps.; Mon 28 June–20 September 1998.

Newlyweds Kōhei (Yakumaru) and Shōko (Sawaguchi) are still waiting for their new apartment to be ready in October. They reluctantly move in with her parents, Daisuke and Asako Umino, for the summer and Kōhei consoles himself with the fact that his in-laws' home is *"only five minutes from the sea."* Before long, however, Shōko's other two siblings are also forced to move back, along with their significant others. Little sister Kuriko is made to stop subsidizing her education by working nights in a hostess bar, while third sister Junko idles away her time at home hoping to become a professional photographer. After Kuriko's boyfriend Takuzō sees Junko naked in the shower, she convinces *him* to become an underwear model, much to her sister's distress. Meanwhile, Junko's boyfriend Ittetsu becomes increasingly distant. . . . Is he the right man for her?

A textbook case of the in-law appeasement subgenre, also found in shows such as **SHOTGUN MARRIAGE** and **LADY OF THE MANOR**. A newlywed couple is forced to experience the bride's parents at closer range than recommended, the husband fights and befriends her siblings, and the oldies resign themselves to appreciating that times may change but Family is the greatest thing in the world. The cast is also faced with the traditional obstacles to harmony—Kōhei is offered a posting abroad (in conservative TV drama terms, about as welcome as an alien abduction), while several old flames and new prospects offer a whole rack of temptations. Daisuke confronts his wife over her college-era boyfriend and sulkily arranges a rendezvous with a fancy woman of his own. Meanwhile, Shōko has kicked Kōhei out after a quarrel and both arrange a secret meeting with new suitors. Needless to say, all three couples have chosen the same venue. All is resolved by the end of the summer, when it is time for the various couples to go their separate ways. Junko and Ittetsu finally prepare for marriage but a drunken Daisuke is arrested and must race to get to the church on time. Shown subtitled in the U.S. on KIKU TV.

C

CALIFORNIA DREAMING

2002. JPN: *Yume no California*. PRD: Yoshitaka Setoguchi. DIR: Nobuhiro Doi, Shinichi Mishiro, Shunichi Hirano. SCR: Yoshikazu Okada. CAST: Tsuyoshi Dōmoto, Ryōko Kuninaka, Kō Shibasaki, Kenichirō Yasui, Seiichi Tanabe, Kankurō Kudō. CHN: TBS. DUR: 45 mins. x 11 eps.; 12 April 2002–28 June 2002.

College boy Owaru (Dōmoto) goes to his junior high school reunion, where he discovers that Keiko (Kuninaka), the girl he worshipped from afar, still has no idea who he is. In fact, the only people who remember him are the reunion organizers Kōhei (Yasui) and Kotomi (Shibasaki), who presumably have written reminders to help them. As the festivities wind down, the four characters sneak into the school and discuss their lives. Keiko is depressed after failing a university entrance exam. Kotomi is beautiful but pathologically shy. Owaru is tired of being constantly compared to his smarter, funnier brother. Kōhei, however, merely listens in silence before asking the others if they think things are ever likely to improve. When they are unable to provide an answer, he climbs up onto the school roof and throws himself off.

Combining writer Okada's earlier friendship in adversity of **ALL ABOUT YOUNG PEOPLE** with his coastal retreat of **BEACH BOYS**, the three surviving classmates decide it is time to drop out of the rat race by moving to the seaside to work in a surfing shop called California. The story's central conceit traces a line back through writer Okada's earlier **IN THE NAME OF LOVE**, through **SEVEN PEOPLE IN SUMMER**, to the ultimate inspirations for many Japanese dramas, *The Big Chill* (1983) and *St. Elmo's Fire* (1985).

CALL ME A BAD GIRL

1984. JPN: *Furyō Shōjo to Yobarete*. PRD: Chiharu Kasuga, Hiroshi Arakawa, Yūzō Higuchi. DIR: Tōgorō Tsuchiya. SCR: Takashi Ezure. CAST: Maiko Itō, Yūki Matsumura, Shingo Tsurumi, Nana Okada, Tomiyuki Kunihiro, Akira Nagoya, Kazue Itō, Masaya Takahashi, Tayo Iwamoto. CHN: TBS. DUR: 45 mins. x 24 eps.; Tue 17 April 1984–25 September 1984.

Verbally abused by her mother at every opportunity, Shōko (M. Itō) has become a nervous, self-destructive wreck. She falls in love with Tetsuya (Kunihiro), whom she sees as her rescuer and takes a new job at a canteen. However, Tetsuya's mother confronts her at work and orders her never to see her son again, as he is already engaged to Kyōko (Okada). While she is still trying to extricate herself from this delicate situation, she is arrested while trying to help some friends on the wrong side of the law and sent to a juvenile correctional facility—compare to **LIPSTICK**.

Although Shōko has given up on Tetsuya, he cannot forget her and dumps his fiancée, who duly attempts to commit suicide. Obligated to care for his recuperating ex, Tetsuya fails to visit Shōko, who breaks out in search of him. Seeing Tetsuya and Kyōko together, Shōko runs away and falls in with an all-girl biker gang, though she is eventually persuaded to return to the center.

Meanwhile, the correctional facility is in search of a new music teacher—a job for which the foolhardy Tetsuya volunteers. He soon realizes that Makoto (K. Itō), one of the girls in his class, is really his long-lost sister Yōko. Tetsuya's father eventually explains that Yōko is really the daughter of his mistress, whom he was unable to see because he was already married to Tetsuya's mother and was unable to leave her as it would have cost him his professorship. The mistress (whose name really *was* Makoto) committed suicide after her daughter was adopted by Tetsuya's family, leaving Yōko to turn into a runaway who would eventually be sent to the correctional facility on a murder charge. In order to avenge her mother's death, Yōko decides to arrange a series of terrible trials for Tetsuya and his true love Shōko . . . because presumably, somewhere in Crazyland, it must all be *his* fault!

Despite an intensely illogical set of character motivations, this drama in the style of **BLOCKS COME TUMBLING DOWN** is supposedly based on a true story—the early life of musician Shōko Hara. But the *Cinderella* formula is well used here, with the added bonus of cat-fighting Japanese girls in Goth make-up. Theme: MIE—"Never."

CAMPUS NOTES

1996. JPN: *Campus Note*. PRD: Akira Isoyama. DIR: Akio Yoshida. SCR: Yumie Nishiogi. CAST: Yuki Uchida, Masato Hagiwara, Keiko Tōyama, Mari Nishio. CHN: TBS. DUR: 45 mins. x 11 eps.; Fri 12 January 1996–22 March 1996. Former badminton protégé Haruka (Uchida) is now a freshman physics student at Shōnan University and something of a late bloomer. She is warned away from Kuwata (Hagiwara), a senior with a reputation for selling off everything that isn't nailed down, though as with many TV drama rogues, he has a heart of gold—it turns out that he's not a drug addict but the struggling single parent of a three-year-old son. Typical drama love triangles soon ensue in a disappointing series from the writer of SWEET HOME. Theme: Yuki Uchida—"Shiawase ni Naritai" (I Want to be Happy).

CAN I CALL YOU PAPA?

1992. JPN: *Papa to Yobasete*. PRD: N/C. DIR: Tatsuzō Inohara. SCR: Yukie Senhara. CAST: Cha Katō, Hikaru Nishida, Yoshie Ichige, Akira Enomoto. CHN: TVT. DUR: 45 mins. x 6 eps.; Sun 12 January 1992–16 February 1992. Ichirō (Katō) works for a marine product company. He is now living in the warehouse in Tokyo while his wife and children are living back home in Tateyama. One day his company decides to rent out part of the warehouse, and Ichirō finds himself forced to share space with Fukino (Nishida), a high school girl in need of a paternal figure in her life.

CAN YOU TELL A WHITE LIE?

1990. JPN: *Utsukushii Uso o Tsukemasu ka*. PRD: N/C. DIR: Nariaki Odagiri. SCR: Kyōhei Nagaoka. CAST: Akira Onodera, Maiko Okamoto, Satomi Tezuka, Yumi Takigawa. CHN:

Asahi. DUR: 45 mins. x 5 eps.; Thu 14 June 1990–12 July 1990. When Sōsuke (Onodera) discovers that he only has three months to live, he sets off in search of Yūko (Takigawa), the mother of his daughter and the woman he divorced eight years previously.

CAN'T HURRY HAPPINESS

1992. JPN: *Shiawase o Isoganaide, Haken OL Koi Monogatari*. AKA: *Temp Office Lady Love Story*. PRD: N/C. DIR: Akira Nagamine. SCR: Noriko Nakayama. CAST: Isako Washio, Hiroshi Fuse, Hisahiro Ogura. CHN: TVT. DUR: 45 mins. x 6 eps.; Sun 23 February 1992–29 March 1992. Asako (Washio) quits her job using marriage as an excuse. However, instead of quitting the workplace to be a wife and mother, she becomes a wandering temp, posted to various companies-of-the-week. A strangely uncharacteristic Japanese drama, combining the workplace-oriented character with the wandering lifestyle of a rōnin—though LONE WOLF AND CUB never worked in a toy factory, a record company, or a construction yard.

CAN'T HURRY LOVE

1998. JPN: *Koi wa Aserazu*. PRD: Yū Moriya, Takashi Ishihara, Kō Wada. DIR: Setsurō Wakamatsu, Hiroshi Nishitani, Masataka Takamatsu. SCR: Mitsuru Tanabe, Naoya Takayama. CAST: Yūji Oda, Shingo Katori, Anju Suzuki, Tamao Satō, Koyuki. CHN: Fuji. DUR: 45 mins. x 12 eps.; Wed 15 April 1998–1 July 1998. Akira (Oda) leaves the resort island of Okinawa and takes the long trip to Tokyo where he becomes a bartender, thinking that it is a good way to pick up girls. His friend Ryō (Katori from SMAP) is a gifted noodle chef but prefers to concentrate his efforts on con tricks, particularly at Akira's expense. Throw in Akira's would-be girlfriend from back home (Suzuki) and the scene is set for a typical comedy love polygon. As befitting his status as Japan's biggest TV star post-BAYSIDE

SHAKEDOWN, Oda's series purloined from a Hollywood name of similar standing, with blatant steals from the Tom Cruise vehicle *Cocktail* (1988). Cruise must be something of a lucky charm for Oda—he also took the Maverick role in the *Top Gun* rip-off *Best Guy* and appeared as another Cruise-alike in JUSTICE FOR ALL. Theme: Yūji Oda—"Shake it Up." Peak rating: 22.4%.

CAN'T LIVE WITHOUT LOVE

1991. JPN: *Aisazu ni Irarenai*. PRD: N/C. DIR: Motoya Satō. SCR: Hiromi Kawase, Makoto Hayashi. CAST: Eisaku Yoshida, Mikihisa Azuma, Naomi Zaizen, Akiho Sendō. CHN: NTV. DUR: 45 mins. x 11 eps.; Wed 16 October 1991–25 December 1991. Years after they last saw each other, childhood friends Yūko (Zaizen) and Isamu (Azuma) meet at a party. A lot has changed since then—Isamu has now taken a job as a division chief at his father's construction company. However, Yūko avoids mentioning the central event in her own life—her recent breakup with Tsutomu (Yoshida), another old schoolfriend.

CAN'T TELL ANYONE

1993. JPN: *Dare ni mo Ienai*. PRD: Seiichirō Kijima. DIR: Jirō Shōno. SCR: Ryōichi Kimizuka. CAST: Chikako Kaku, Shirō Sano, Chisato Yamazaki, Yōko Nogiwa, Yūichi Haba. CHN: TBS. DUR: 45 mins. x 12 eps.; Fri 9 July 1993–24 September 1993. Newlyweds Shingo (Haba) and Kanako (Kaku) move into a new apartment and prepare for married life. However, their honeymoon bliss is interrupted by Mario (Sano), Kanako's embittered ex-boyfriend, who moves in next door. He begins making advances to her once more, though it is initially unclear whether he is trying to win her back or avenge his wounded pride by scaring her to death.

With Sano's obsessive character, it could almost be a sequel to I TRULY LOVED YOU. Compare to the later drama THE STALKER. Theme: Yumi

Carranger

Matsutoya—"Manatsu no Yoru no Yume" (Midsummer Night's Dream).

CAPRICIOUS INDEX

1973. JPN: *Kimagure Shisū*. PRD: N/C. DIR: Ryō Kusakabe, Isamu Koyama. SCR: Seita Yamamoto. CAST: Masataka Tanba, Arihiro Fujimura, Yuriko Kaku, Michiko Miyoshi. CHN: NHK. DUR: 25 mins. x 6 eps.; Mon 16 April 1973–25 April 1973.

Mystery writer Kuroda (Tanba) believes that he can commit the perfect crime. With the aid of his girlfriend Sumiko (Kaku), he steals a statue of Buddha from the famous Matsudaira collection. However, he does not count on the particular abilities of the Buddha's owner Saeko (Miyoshi), who enlists the help of local Shinto priest and amateur sleuth Makino (Fujimura). A rare children's drama from NHK in that it uses all adult actors, *CI* was based on a story by prolific SF author Shinichi Hoshi.

CAPTAIN ULTRA

1967. PRD: Tōru Hirayama, Yasuji Ueda, Kunio Kumagai. DIR: Hajime Satō, Akira Kajima, Hirokazu Takemoto, Minoru Yamada, Katsuhiko Taguchi, Yoshiharu Tomita. SCR: Susumu Takahisa, Norio Osada, Arashi Ishizu, Minoru Yamada, Masaki Tsuji,

Takeo Kaneko. CAST: Hirohisa Nakata, Nenji Kobayashi, Jirō Sagawa, Ichirō Izawa, Yuki Shirono, Shigeru Yasunaka. CHN: TBS. DUR: 30 mins. x 24 eps.; 16 April 1967–24 September 1967.

Captain Ultra (Nakata) fights to protect the Earth from monsters in a series that might look on the surface like a Tsuburaya production but was in fact made by their rivals Tōei. With Tsuburaya's **ULTRAMAN** series forced to finish early due to the time lag between filming and broadcast, Tōei stepped into the breach with this new look-alike show, featuring **BIOMAN** and **MASKED RIDER AMAZON** star Nakata.

CARRANGER *

1996. JPN: *Gessai Sentai Carranger*. AKA: *Racing Battle Team Carranger; Power Rangers Turbo*. PRD: Atsushi Kaji, Tarō Iwamoto, Kenji Ōta, Kōichi Yada, Shigeki Takadera. DIR: Yoshiaki Kobayashi, Tarō Sakamoto, Katsuya Watanabe, Ryūta Tazaki, Noboru Matsui, Noboru Takemoto. SCR: Yoshio Urasawa, Hirohisa Soda, Toshihisa Arakawa. CAST: Yūji Kishi, Akihiro Masujima, Yoshihiro Fukuda, Yuka Motohashi, Atsuko Kurisu, Mari Maruta, Yoshitada Ōtsuka, Hiroshi Ōtake, Rika Nanase. CHN: Asahi. DUR: 25 mins. x 48 eps.; 1 March 1996–7 February 1997.

The Earth is threatened by the alien Borzoku. Five young Earthlings are imbued with stellar energy, giving them Kurumagic powers that allow them to transform into the Carranger team, who also moonlight as the Pegasus racing team. Leader Kyōsuke (Kishi) is the Red Racer, best driver and test pilot of the Pegasus vehicle. Naoki (Masujima) is the Blue Racer, master of speed and designer of the Pegasus. Minoru (Fukuda) is the Green Racer, business manager for the Pegasus team and occasional figure of fun. Nazumi (Motohashi) is the team's female mechanic and also the Yellow Racer. Yōko (Kurisu) is the team's accountant and also, when numbers fail her, the Pink Racer. They are occa-

sionally aided by the mysterious Signalman (Ōtsuka), a Ranger-like loner who functions as a kind of super-policeman. Their enemies are the minions of the Borzoku, served by their monsters-of-the-week and their multicolored Wampa cannon-fodder minions. Alien princess Sonnet (Nanase) might be working for the bad guys but she is also secretly in love with the Red Racer.

The Carranger team each have a color-coded racing car, which can transform into a humanoid robot. The cars can also combine to form the Carranger Robo and its Victory Twin Star super mode, while the double trailer combination that carries the Carranger vehicles around can itself transform into the giant Victrailer robot. Signalman had his own Polispeeder motorcycle and patrol car, which could transform into a police robot.

Carranger was soon adapted into the fifth incarnation of the **MIGHTY MORPHIN' POWER RANGERS** franchise in the U.S. as *Power Rangers Turbo*, which characteristically dumped most of the non-SFX footage and bolted newly filmed sections around the remains. The team's new enemy was named Space Pirate Divatox (Carol Hoyt/Hilary Shepard), whose powers were regarded as too strong to be challenged by the Power Rangers' Zeo abilities (see the previous series **OHRANGER**). Instead, they become the new Turbo Rangers with their Turbo Zords, though Blue Ranger Rocky (Steve Cardenas) injures his back and is replaced by Justin (Blake Foster). Later in the season, the cast was completely changed, with the departure not only of the rest of the remaining Rangers but also of the long serving mentor figures of Zordon and Alpha-5. Justin was joined by new Rangers TJ (Selwyn Ward), Carlos (Roger Velasco), Ashley (Tracy Lynn Cruz), and Cassie (Patricia Ja Lee). They also gained a new ally in the form of the Blue Senturion (Davis Walsh), who occasionally fought on their side and eventually departed for space. However, in this series, the bad guys were victorious—Divatox successfully destroyed the Power Rangers' base. Justin stayed behind on Earth while the rest of the cast, now equipped with Rescue Zords, launched into space in an attempt to save the departed Zordon, thereby setting the scene for the *Power Rangers in Space* series, itself based on the following year's Super Sentai show **MEGARANGER**. Music for the original was by Toshihiko Sahashi. Note that in the U.S. version, Carol Hoyt played both the first incarnation of Divatox *and* the Power Rangers' new mentor Dimitria.

CARRIED ON THE SEA BREEZE
1991. JPN: *Umikaze o Tsukamaete.* PRD: N/C. DIR: Michihiko Obimori. SCR: Izumi Konno. CAST: Hiroaki Murakami, Azusa Watanabe, Yōko Moriguchi, Etsuji Takahashi. CHN: TVT. DUR: 45 mins. x 6 eps.; Sun 13 October 1991–17 November 1991.
Police academy graduate Chiaki (Watanabe) is posted to a special criminal investigation unit covering the Tokyo Bay area. She is detailed to cover a firearms smuggling case but the clumsy rookie keeps on making mistakes. Her captain Katagiri (Murakami) encourages her to persevere and she eventually becomes a prized member of the team. For a much more successful use of the same police district, see **BAYSIDE SHAKEDOWN**.

CASABLANCA STORY
1990. JPN: *Casablanca Monogatari; Kaitō ni Kuchizuke o.* AKA: *Kiss the Phantom Thief.* PRD: N/C. DIR: Toshikazu Kobayashi. SCR: Hirokazu Fuse. CAST: Tōru Kazama, Azusa Nakamura, Harue Akagi. CHN: TVT. DUR: 45 mins. x 6 eps.; Sun 15 July 1990–19 August 1990.
Shinya (Kazama) lives in room 101 of the Casablanca apartment block. When he is posted to Greece by his company, his room is rented by Nobuko (Nakamura), a struggling animator. However, when Shinya returns to his apartment, he sees a man behaving suspiciously, in a drama that mixes the mismatched neighbors of **AFRICA NIGHTS** with a criminal heist.

CEREMONIAL OFFICIATOR
1996. JPN: *Kankonsōsai Buchō.* PRD: Noriaki Asao. DIR: Tōru Moriyama. SCR: Michio Shimizu. CAST: Kenichi Hagiwara, Miyoko Asada, Yasunori Danta, Masahiko Tsugawa, Azusa Nakamura. CHN: TBS. DUR: 45 mins. x 12 eps.; Sun 7 January 1996–24 March 1996.
Unassuming salaryman Ryūhei (Hagiwara) is a successful salesman for a large property development company. He is promoted to deputy division chief but his rise up the ranks also leads to his unexpected removal from the department where he has spent his entire working life. Now, he finds himself in charge of the Ceremonial Occasions Division—his first job is to organize the funeral of a fellow employee. Compare to **GOOD MOURNING** and **WEDDING PLANNER**. Theme: Kenichi Hagiwara—"Nakeruwake ga Naidaro" (I Couldn't Cry, Could I?).

CHAIRMAN WAKA DAISHŌ
1992. JPN: *Shachō ni Natta Waka Daishō.* AKA: *Young Captain Becomes the Boss.* PRD: N/C. DIR: Ryōichi Itsukida. SCR: Akiko Hamura. CAST: Yūzō Kayama, Tōru Hayakawa, Kaori Koshiba, Hisaya Morishige. CHN: TBS. DUR: 25 mins. x 16 eps.; Thu 16 April 1992–30 July 1992.
Former valedictorian Yūichi Tanō (Kayama) is now the president of Tanō Trading Company. Since the death of his wife, Chikako (Wakako Sakai), he has worked hard to rear his son, Yūsuke (Hayakawa) and daughter, Yuri (Koshiba), and they have grown into fine young people. Without telling his father, Yūsuke successfully applies for a job at Tanō Trading, only to get into trouble on his first day when he arrives late.
Leading man Yūzo Kayama is the son of 1930s idols Ken Uehara and Yōko Kozakura. He became a star in his own right during the 1960s after the release of the movie *The University's Young Captain* (1961, *Daigaku no Waka Daishō*). In a series of sequels the idol was packed off to many exotic destinations, living the kind of luxurious life that would later be offered to the Japanese middle classes for real during the time of the bubble economy. The innocent movie series ended in 1971, when its preppy "twentysomething" hero was pushing middle age, though there was a brief and unsuccessful revival with *Waka Daishō Returns* (1981, *Kaette Kita Waka Daishō*). Realizing that the original teen audience would now be viewers in their fifties, the TBS network planned a six-month TV revival in the form of this look at life for the "Young Captain" twenty years after his heyday. However, the show was canceled early due to low ratings.

CHAKO-CHAN SERIES
1962. PRD: N/C. DIR: Eizō Yamagiwa. SCR: N/C. CAST: Harumi Yomo, Yasuyuki Miyawaki, Toshie Takada, Hideo Satō. CHN: TBS. DUR: 30 mins. x ca. 260 eps.; 15 October 1962–24 May 1963 (#1); 17 July 1964–2 October 1964 (#2); 4 February 1965–7 January 1966 (#3); 3 February 1966–30 March 1967 (#4); 6 April 1967–28 March 1968 (#5); 4 April 1968–27 March 1969 (#6).
This series was one of the most important children's home dramas of the 1960s, depicting the everyday life of Chako (Yomo). Chako first appeared in *Papa's Childcare Diary*, in which her parents were played by her real-life father and mother, Shōji Yasui and Miki Odagiri. However, stunt parents Jun Tatara and Yukari Itō replaced the real ones for the second series, *Chairman Chako-chan*, themselves replaced by Hideo Satō and Toshie Takada for the third installment *Chako-chan Hi,* which also added Natsuko Shigehara as a kindly grandmother. Her real parents returned to play themselves in *Chako-chan,* only to disappear again for *Chako Nee-chan,* which restored Satō and Takada—such switching of casts is not uncommon in TV shows with the child

actors, but not with the adults! *Chako Nee-chan* (*Big Sister Chako*) introduced a brother for the heroine in the form of Ken'ichi (Miyawaki). The pair starred together in the fifth season *Chako and Ken-chan* and in a spin-off movie in 1969. Thenceforth, with "little Chako" now a hulking teenager, the series was rebranded as **KEN-CHAN**, in which form it enjoyed another decade of success. In the early 21st century, the series found a new lease on life on DVD as a nostalgia product, as two generations of parents tried to interest their own children in what they viewed when they were younger.

CHALLENGE FROM THE FUTURE
1977. JPN: *Mirai kara no Chōsen*. PRD: Kanae Mayuzumi. DIR: Yoshiyuki Itō, Minoru Hanabusa, Isamu Koyama. SCR: Yasuo Tanami. CAST: Toshiya Kumagai, Masumi Sakamoto, Teresa Noda, Hiroyuki Satō. CHN: NHK. DUR: 20 mins. x 20 eps.; Mon 10 January 1977–11 February 1977.
Kōji (Satō) transfers to Tsukioka Junior High School, where he has trouble keeping up with his diligent and super-efficient classmates. He discovers that many of them also attend the elite "Eikō" prep school but meets with considerable opposition when he tries to find out more about it. After student rep Michiru (Sakamoto) tries to set up a student hall patrol with the power to punish all wrongdoers and *suspected* wrongdoers, Kōji tries to organize a student resistance. When he is apprehended as a ringleader, the principal of the Eikō School offers to welcome him into their ranks if he stops causing trouble. When Kōji refuses, he discovers that the Eikō facility is run by a group of psychic fascists from the future who are using the school system to brainwash children of the year 1975 to do their bidding. Kōji is imprisoned in another time, while the future agents send an android version of him back to 1975 to talk his fellow students out of further resistance. However, the other children fight against their enemies with guerrilla tactics.

Challenge from the Future is an intriguing mixture of opposing elements—the clever conceit that one's teachers genuinely are fascist mutants who need to be stopped from taking over the world juxtaposed with the need to sanitize and somehow deal with the images of student unrest that had dominated Japanese TV screens in the late 1960s and early 1970s. The series was based on *two* books by SF author Taku Mayumura—*Talent from Hell* (*Jigoku no Sainō*) and *Nerawareta Gakuen* (remade as **SCHOOL IN PERIL**). Mayumura also wrote the original novels on which **BAKUMATSU TIME TRAVELERS** and **BAKUMATSU EXCHANGE STUDENTS** were based.

CHANCE!
1993. PRD: Shōji Shiosawa. DIR: Hisao Kogure. SCR: Eriko Kitagawa, Kazuyuki Morosawa. CAST: Hiroshi Mikami, Hikaru Nishida, Satomi Tezuka, Leo Morimoto, Mikihisa Azuma. CHN: Fuji. DUR: 45 mins. x 12 eps.; Thu 14 April 1993–30 June 1993.
Rock musician Jōji Honjō (Mikami) leaves Japan for New York at the height of his popularity. He returns two years later to discover that the fickle media world has already forgotten him. Instead, the new pop star is Hyūga (Azuma), who used to be Jōji's backing singer. Jōji's decides to start a pop career again from square one with the help of his new manager (Nishida). *Chance!* was an early script from **LONG VACATION** creator Eriko Kitagawa and attracted a bonus audience who wanted to see real-life pop idol Nishida behaving like a hard-nosed business-woman. Theme: Toshinobu Kubota—"Yume with You" (Dream with You).

CHANGE!
1995. PRD: Masato Kimura (#1); Noboru Sugiyama (#2). DIR: Kazuhiro Mori (#1); Setsuo Wakamatsu (#2). SCR: Masaya Ozaki (#1); Toshio Terada (#2). CAST: Ken Ishiguro, Minako Ta-naka, Haruhiko Katō, Misato Hayase, Shingo Yanagisawa (#1); Atsuko Asano, Yuka Nomura, Ryūya Fujiwara,

Tsuyoshi Ujiki, Hiroshi Abe (#2). CHN: Asahi. DUR: 45 mins. x 8 eps., Tue 25 July 1995–12 September 1995 (#1); 45 mins. x 10 eps., 12 October 1998–14 December 1998 (#2).
Authoritarian high school teacher Tatsuma (Ishiguro) magically swaps minds with slacker student Yōichi when the two bump into each other. Both are forced to live their lives in each other's bodies while searching for a way to undo the curse in one of a glut of Japanese imitations of the late 1980s Hollywood craze for body-swap movies (see **AFTER SCHOOL**). Theme: To Be Continued—"Truth."
Three years later, TV Asahi showed another series with a similar high concept, also called *Change!*, though the 1998 version had a title written in the katakana syllabary, instead of the 1995 version's roman letters. The 1998 version centers on middle-aged actress Mizuho (Asano), who constantly quarrels with her teenage daughter Saori (Nomura). However, the two suddenly swap bodies when they are struck by lightning, forcing Saori to confront Mizuho's work-related pressures. The second series was released simultaneously with a manga version of the same story. Compare to **MINAMI'S SWEETHEART** and **WHICH IS WHICH?**. Theme: Penicillin—"Butterfly."

CHANGEMAN
1985. JPN: *Dengeki Sentai Changeman*. AKA: *Electro Assault Battle Team Changeman*. PRD: Sanetaka Katō, Yasuhiro Tomita, Takeyuki Suzuki. DIR: Nagafumi Hori, Minoru Yamada, Takeo Nagaishi. SCR: Hirohisa Soda, Kunio Fujii, Kyōko Sagiyama. CAST: Haruki Hamada, Hiroshi Kawai, Shirō Izumi, Hiroko Nishimoto, Mai Ōishi, Seizō Katō, Shōhei Yamamoto. CHN: Asahi. DUR: 25 mins. x 55 eps.; Sat 2 February 1985–22 February 1986.
When news arrives of imminent attack by the invading Gozma race, Earth Force recruits a five-member team of specialists to save the world. Each is a former member of a branch of Earth

Force, now styled after a mythical beast from Earth's past and able to channel that energy into fighting their enemies. The leader is former pilot Hiryū (Hamada) the Change Dragon, who fights with Dragon Power and his Change Sword. Shō (Kawai) is Change Gryphon, once a ranger with Earth Force, now a martial arts master with the Changeman team. Yūma (Izumi) is a former officer with the Earth Force Land Division, now the blue-clad Change Pegasus and an aerial battle specialist. As in the previous year's Super Sentai show BIOMAN, there are two female team members. Former operations officer Sayaka (Nishimoto) is Change Mermaid, endowed with super-speedy Mermaid Power. Mai (Ōishi) is Change Phoenix, former Earth Force intelligence officer now wielder of Phoenix Power. Their equipment includes the flying Shuttle Base, which launches the three supervehicles Landchanger, Helichanger, and Jetchanger, which in turn can combine to form the giant Change Robo. Their archenemy is armless, legless cyborg Star Emperor Bazoo (voiced by Katō), who sends a different monster to fight the Changeman team every week, aided by his army of egg-hatched cannon fodder, who are known as the Hitlers. The following year's Super Sentai series was FLASHMAN. Music by Tatsumi Yano.

CHANGERION

1996. PRD: N/C. DIR: Takao Nagaishi, Hajime Konaka, Masao Minowa. SCR: Toshiki Inoue. CAST: Takeshi Hagino, Atsushi Ogawa, Jirō Okamoto, Kazunari Aizawa, Noboru Ichikawa, Mariko Akama, Yuka Matsui. CHN: TVT. DUR: 25 mins. x 39 eps.; Wed 3 April 1996–25 December 1996.
Fun-loving private detective Akira (Hagino) is investigating a routine case of a missing person, though he suspects that several child kidnappings in the neighborhood may be linked. However, he is enveloped in "crystal power" when he bumps into a vehicle owned by the secret SAIDOC task

Cheap Love

force. The experience gives him the chance to become Changerion, the warrior of light, charged with fighting off the predations of the Gingar, a creature of darkness. Gingar is only one of many ancient monsters waking from centuries of sleep in a nearby Dark Dimension. Despite an obvious debt to the monster-of-the-week formula of ULTRAMAN, *Changerion* has its moments of unconventionality, particularly in its leading man, who rejects the unwritten superhero code of justice in favor of having a good time and only reluctantly drags himself away from spending sprees and eating binges to save the world. It also contains moments of arch comedy, such as the time that Akira and his sidekick Hayami (Aizawa) are forced to dress as women to stake out a shoe store where creatures from the Dark Dimension are kidnapping female shoppers.

CHEAP LOVE *

1999. PRD: Tamon Tanba. DIR: Jun Yasuda, Hiroshi Matsubara. SCR: Makoto Hayashi. CAST: Takashi Sorimachi, Mayu Tsuruta, Yū Yoshizawa, Mami Kurosaka, Takashi Naitō, Hisashi Igawa, Naoko Nagamine, Ikki Sawamura. CHN: TBS. DUR: 45 mins. x 10 eps.; Fri 15 October 1999–17 December 1999.
Junichi (Sorimachi) has been a talent scout for a hostess bar for the last seven years but he lacks the steely resolve that the job really requires. His scouting partner Ryō (Yoshizawa) tries to recruit Nanami (Tsuruta), a 29-year-old music teacher, who is justifiably angered by both the approach and by Junichi's protestations that she is "too old." Juri, one of Junichi's earlier acquisitions, causes trouble for the bar, and Junichi finds himself owing one million yen in compensation. The boys launch into a succession of question-

able moneymaking schemes, including adult video production and even trying to win the money at the horse races. Nanami accidentally becomes involved in their schemes, first unwittingly then with some degree of interest as she finds herself inexorably attracted to the rough diamond Junichi. Her friend Ayumi reminds her that she is engaged and that the wedding is fast approaching. Ayumi is torn between Junichi and her fiancé but Junichi is on the run from the police and his former boss, and time is running out.

Capitalizing on Sorimachi's lovable rogue image from the previous year's **GTO**, *CL* throws in further underworld thrills influenced by **THE STAND-IN**. The drama plays up the romantic formula of two people from "different worlds" (compare to **STAR STRUCK**) but the depiction of Junichi's gangland life tries to have its cake and eat it too— tutting dolefully at the excesses of the underworld, while simultaneously hoping to titillate its audience. Shown subtitled in the U.S. on KIKU TV. Theme: Northern Bright—"Wildflower." Peak rating: 15.9%.

CHEF, THE *

1995. PRD: Akira Koyama. DIR: Ryūichi Inomata. SCR: Masahiro Yoshimoto. CAST: Noriyuki Higashiyama, Akiho Sendō, Naomi Kawashima, Tōru Emori, Taichi Kokobu, Harue Akagi. CHN: NTV. DUR: 45 mins. x 9 eps.; Sat 21 October 1995–16 December 1995.
Businesswoman Reiko (Kawashima) is charged with organizing a swish hotel party for her company. However, the kitchen staff go on strike and she is forced to call in a one-man culinary A-Team, Takumi Ajisawa (Higashiyama), a world-class chef who charges a fortune but delivers the impossible. The result is a drama that mixes the journeyman troubleshooter of *Black Jack* (*AE) with the gourmet pretensions of **SOMMELIER**. Based on the 1985 manga, written by Mai Kenmei and drawn by Tadashi Katō. Shown subtitled in the U.S. on KIKU TV. Theme: Namie Amuro—"Chase the Change."

CHIBIRA

1970. JPN: *Chibira-kun*. AKA: *Little Chibira*. PRD: Akira Tsuburaya, Yoshikazu Morita. DIR: Kazuo Kimata, Toshitsugu Suzuki, Tatsumi Andō, Tomoya Kittomi, Kiyotsugu Tani, Shōhei Tōjō, Jun Ōki. SCR: Keisuke Fujikawa, Namie Shima, Kan Tamura, Yumi Ichikawa, Masako Kae, Tadashi Konō, Toyohiro Andō, Bunzō Wakatsuki, Chizuko Kamichi. CAST: Kenbō Kaminarimon, Junpei Takiguchi, Ichirō Murakoshi, Kyōko Fujinami, Kazuo Kumakura, Ado Mizumori, Kazue Takahashi, Shingo Kanemoto, Rika Yamagishi. CHN: NTV. DUR: 15 mins. x 78 eps.; Mon 30 March 1970–25 September 1970.
Chibira Hattaru (child star Kaminarimon) is a baby monster, who tries to live a normal family life with his monster family Papagon, Mamagon, and pet Pochipochi. Chibira represented an attempt by the Tsuburaya studio to duplicate the success of its earlier cute-monster comedy **BUSKA**, and featured singer and illustrator Ado Mizumori as the voice of Chibira's bullying rival Gakinko.

CHILD IN THE WIND

1974. JPN: *Kaze no Naka no Kodomo*. PRD: Masaharu Morita. DIR: Yoshiyuki Itō. SCR: Izuho Sudō. CAST: Hiroyuki Satō, Shigeyuki Hatamoto, Mihoko Inagaki, Shōji Miyai. CHN: NHK. DUR: 24 mins. x 6 eps.; Tue 27 August 1974–4 September 1974.
Eleven-year-old Zenta (Satō) and his eight-year-old brother Sanpei (Hatamoto) amuse themselves by climbing a tree in their garden and admiring the breeze and the view from the branches. However, their life is thrown into turmoil when their father Ichirō (Miyai) is framed for embezzlement at his company. With Ichirō under arrest and mother Setsuko (Inagaki) forced to work in a hospital, Sanpei is cared for by their uncle, much to his wife's displeasure. Meanwhile, Akazawa, one of the colleagues who framed Ichirō, harasses their new landlord to have them

thrown out of their rented accommodation. Ichirō begins to plead his case in court, while Akazawa is himself arrested for arson. The authorities discover that Akazawa had embezzled the money himself in order to cover some bad debts on the stock market and was planning to let Ichirō take the blame and destroy the evidence by burning down the factory. Ichirō returns to his family and normality is restored in this adaptation of the novel of the same name by Jōji Tsubota.

CHILD WITHOUT A HOME

1994. JPN: *Ie Naki Ko*. PRD: Atsushi Satō. DIR: Hidenobu Hosono. SCR: Masaya Takatsuki, Toshiya Itō. CAST: Yumi Adachi, Rumiko Koyanagi, Naoki Hosaka, Maki Mizuno, Yoshiko Tanaka. CHN: NTV. DUR: 25 mins. x 25 eps.; Sat 16 April 1994–2 July 1994 (#1); 15 April 1995–8 July 1995 (#2).
With her mother in hospital and her drunken stepfather (Takashi Naitō) permanently impoverished, little Suzu (Adachi, in the role that made her a star) also has to deal with bullies at school. Her only friend is her dog, Ryū. She steals a friend's money in order to pay for her mother's surgery and is unrepentant when caught by a teacher, boldly proclaiming *"I need money!"* The teacher tries to reason with her but she merely laughs at him, proclaiming *"If you love me, give me money!"* The line was to become a catchphrase for the series, whose tough girl heroine was regarded as an antidote to the stoic sufferer of **OSHIN**.

With an original story credited to the ever-inventive Shinji Nojima (creator of **LIPSTICK** and **BEAUTY**), the controversially pugnacious Suzu led to a jammed switchboard at NTV, as rightwingers and concerned parents complained about its amoral attitude. However, the general audience soon warmed to a new type of heroine who was tough, shrewd, and scathing. The last episode of the first season gained a rating of 37.2%, making it NTV's highest scoring drama series of the 1990s. Compared against other networks and excluding the greatly higher figures for NHK morning and period dramas, *Child without a Home*'s record was only beaten at the very end of the decade by **BEAUTIFUL LIFE**.

Such success led to the inevitable movie adaptation in December 1994 and a disappointingly cartoonish second season. With her mother dead at the end of series one, Suzu learns that the wealthy Ichijō family is looking for a long-lost granddaughter and swindles them into believing that she fits the bill. The Ichijō family is then torn asunder by a violent feud over the inheritance.

Director Hosono has since claimed that the show's original inspiration was a combination of *Dog of Flanders* (*AE) and the aforementioned *Oshin*, although there are other, possibly inadvertent parallels with *Sans Famille,* the children's story by Hector Malot that was made into an anime on NTV in 1970 with a very similar Japanese title (see *Nobody's Boy*, *AE). The second season of *Child without a Home* resembles another Malot adaptation, *Nobody's Girl* (*AE), which was broadcast in 1978. Themes: Miyuki Nakajima—"Sora to Kimi no Aida ni" (Between the Sky and You); "Tabibito no Uta" (Song of Travelers).

CHILDHOOD
1976. JPN: *Yōnen Jidai*. PRD: Tomoyoshi Hagiwara. DIR: Minoru Hanabusa, Masaki Uehara. SCR: Toshirō Ishidō. CAST: Natsuho Miyakai, Terumi Niki, Akemi Negishi, Noboru Nakatani. CHN: NHK. DUR: 25 mins. x 6 eps.; Mon 19 January 1976–29 January 1976.
Ten-year-old Terumichi (Miyakai) is often prevented from seeing his real parents by his cold-hearted stepmother Hatsu (Negishi). Her reason is that Terumichi's father is a samurai, whereas his mother is only a humble maid and their marriage across class boundaries is an embarrassment to the family. The pretty Tee (Niki) is also in the same circumstances and is looked after by Hatsu. When Terumichi's father dies, his mother is thrown out of the family home, and Terumichi goes looking for her with the family dog Shiro. He starts praying for her safety in front of a *jizō* statue, where he is found and taken in by a kindly Shinto priest. He realizes that he has feelings for Tee but she is already betrothed in an arranged marriage. Lonely once more, Terumichi heads off in search of Tee, in a story based on an autobiographical work by Saisei Muroo, written in 1918.

CHILDHOOD'S END
1994. JPN: *Yumemiru Koro o Sugitemo*. PRD: Toshihiro Iijima. DIR: Mitsunori Morita. SCR: Toshio Terada. CAST: Naoki Hosaka, Riona Hazuki, Ryūji Harada, Fumie Hosokawa, Naoki Miyashita. CHN: TBS. DUR: 45 mins. x 11 eps.; Fri 14 October 1994–23 December 1994.
Asuka (Hazuki) is in her last year at University but is having trouble finding a job. She takes a short vacation in the Yatsugatake Mountains with her boyfriend Junichi (Harada) and friends. Though the original plan was to use the country setting to think about her career options, she is instead entranced and charmed by the simplicity of country life. In particular, she is taken with the easygoing farm worker Tamon (Hosaka)—an interest which soon causes tension with her jealous boyfriend.

CHINESE CUISINE SERVED STAR LEO STYLE
2003. JPN: *Netsuretsu Chūka Hanten*. AKA: *Ardent Chinese Restaurant*. PRD: Tadashi Makino. DIR: Masayuki Suzuki, Toshiaki Kimura, Takashi Narita. SCR: Tsukasa Morihiro. CAST: Kyōka Suzuki, Kazunari Ninomiya, Asaka Seto, Shirō Itō. CHN: Fuji. DUR: 45 mins. x 11 eps.; Wed 8 January 2003–26 March 2003.
The *Star Leo* ocean liner plies a route from Japan to Hong Kong and on its next trip is also scheduled to be the site for a high-class cooking competition between the four major schools of Chinese cuisine. Passengers will be able to sample the dry and crunchy wonders of Beijing food, the hot chili dishes of Sichuan, the soft squishy delicacies of Canton, and the sweet and sour seafood of Shanghai, prepared for them by four world-class chefs. Miss Tachibana (Suzuki) is the Hong Kong business school graduate responsible for the whole venture who finds herself in serious trouble when the four chefs refuse to come aboard in protest of some of her working practices. As the *Star Leo* sets sail, Tachibana is forced to throw herself at the mercy of the only three cooks left onboard—the unskilled lazybones Sakota, the overeager trainee Nanami, and Mr. Noguchi, the restaurant food buyer.

Chinese Cuisine mixes several of Japanese drama's most common clichés—the team of no-hopers, the snooty career woman, and a gourmet specialty, combining them in an exotic seafaring location.

CHINTARO'S DIARY
1975. JPN: *Chintarō Nikki*. PRD: Seiji Akiyama. DIR: Sasahara, Maeda, Sano, Watanabe. SCR: Yukio Doi. CAST: Takahito Igarashi, Hitoshi Takagi, Momoko Sawai, Masa Yamada, Michiyo Kuki, Tadakazu Kitami, Kayoko Horiya, Seiji Niima, Haruo Itō, Shōhei Nishimura. CHN: NHK. DUR: 25 mins. x 12 eps.; 29 May 1975–11 June 1975.
Chintarō (Igarashi) is a twelve-year-old mischievous boy, whose father (Takagi) is a long-suffering translator and whose mother (Yamada) is a tireless nag. When his millionaire uncle comes to visit from Osaka, he takes him to a local temple, though the uncle is incensed at the temple's special line in

---

WEDDINGS FROM HELL

"I object!" "No! I object"

In a pastiche of Spartacus, the priest asks "if anyone has a reason why these two should not be wed?" Most of the bride's guests stand up and object in turn. The groom's family then charge across the aisle for a punch-up. ☞

Chirorin Village

religious favors—pray there and it guarantees a death without suffering. Chintarō also has two sisters, Toshiko (Sawai) and Ritsuko (Kuki). Architect Kitazawa (Itō) and vet Kōno (Nishimura) are competing for Toshiko's affections. In the midst of all this familial chaos, the millionaire uncle announces that he wants to adopt Chintarō and rear him as his own son.

CHIRORIN VILLAGE
1956. JPN: *Chirorin Mura to Kurumi no Ki.* AKA: *Chirorin Village and Kurumi/Walnut's Tree.* PRD: N/C. DIR: N/C. SCR: N/C. CAST: (voices) Tetsuko Kuroyanagi, Kyōko Satomi, Michiyo Yokoyama, Taeko Shimada. CHN: NHK. DUR: 15 mins. x ca. 1000 eps.; 16 April 1956–3 April 1964.
Kurumi (Satomi) the walnut, Tonpei (Yokoyama) the onion, and Piko (Kuroyanagi) the peanut solve a variety of conflicts and arguments between fruits and vegetables in one of Japan's first ever children's shows. This magical puppet series gained a new lease of life in 1966, when it was transferred to Fuji TV. The voice actors remained the same, and Fuji secured an agreement from the sponsors that children's viewing pleasure would not be marred by any commercial breaks. The series was

resurrected in 1992 as a 170-episode animated series (*AE). Compare to *Tomato-Man* (*AE) and MADCAP ISLAND.

CHIYO NO FUJI STORY, THE
1991. JPN: *Chiyo no Fuji Monogatari.* PRD: N/C. DIR: Mitsuru Shimizu. SCR: Makiko Uchidate. CAST: Naoki Miyashita, Raita Ryū, Kō Hashimoto, Yōko Asagaya. CHN: Kansai. DUR: 45 mins. x 4 eps.; Sun 2 June 1991–23 June 1991.
Mitsugu (Miyashita) has been good at sports since childhood and breaks athletic records when he is still at junior high. His talent as an athlete gets him accepted to a prestigious high school ahead of all of his classmates, who jealously sign him up for a sumo competition without telling him. This drama is a fictionalized biography of the real-life sumo wrestler Chiyo no Fuji, detailing his discovery by Master Kue and his eventual victory in the Japanese championships after much hardship.

CHRISTMAS EVE
1990. PRD: Tamaki Endō. DIR: Tōru Moriyama. SCR: Makiko Uchidate. CAST: Nobuko Sendō, Eisaku Yoshida, Shin Takuma, Misa Shimizu, Yuki Matsushima. CHN: TBS. DUR: 45 mins. x 11 eps.; Fri 12 October 1990–21 December 1990.
Yukiko (Sendō) and Misaki (Shimizu) are bank employees vacationing in Australia who discover that their work colleague Kurumi (Matsushima) has just split up with office hunk Tsuyoshi (Yoshida). Yukiko begins a relationship with Tsuyoshi back in Tokyo, while Misaki continues her secret affair with the manager Murakami (Takuma). Tsuyoshi asks Yukiko to marry him, but she has doubts after hearing more about his ex-girlfriend and does not respond positively. The crushed Tsuyoshi has a one-night stand with Misaki, causing Yukiko to decide to leave the bank and find a job elsewhere. Murakami persuades Yukiko to stay and also persuades her into his bed. The couple eventually forgive each other and Tsuyoshi promises to

be home from a Hokkaidō business trip on Christmas Eve. However, he is stuck there by bad weather, and the lovers are finally reunited on Boxing Day. *Christmas Eve* is another wry look at modern manners from the writer of AN ACCOMMODATING WOMAN and LUCKILY I WASN'T SO IN LOVE. Theme: Midori Shinjima—"Silent Eve."

CHURASAN *
2001. PRD: Yasuhiro Suga. DIR: Takayasu Enoto, Kazuki Watanabe, Takashi Ōtomo, Ren Takahashi, Satoshi Endō. SCR: Yoshikazu Okada. CAST: Ryōko Kuninaka, Kenji Kobashi, Kyōko Mano, Gori, Takayuki Yamada, Miho Kanno, Aiko Satō, Yoshiko Tanaka, Masaaki Sakai. CHN: NHK. DUR: 15 mins. x ca. 300 eps.; Wed 4 April 2001–29 September 2001 (#1); 31 March 2003–?? June 2003 (#2).
Eri (Mirai Umino) is an eleven-year-old girl from Okinawa, who, with her brother Yoshinobu (Yūta Murakami), befriends the two Uemura brothers whose family have just moved to the island from Tokyo. However, Kazuya Uemura (Yūya Endō) has a terminal disease and, as his life slips away, he asks Eri to promise to marry his brother Fumiya (Shūichi Yamauchi) when she grows up. The friends dutifully grant his dying wish but then the bereaved Uemura family moves back to Tokyo. Time passes and the couple lose touch.

A grown-up Eri (Kuninaka) heads to university in Tokyo and works part time at a themed Ryūkyū Islands restaurant. Grown-up Yoshinobu (Yamada) flees Okinawa to stay with her, hoping to become a pop star in the big city, though Eri has other worries and is struggling to train as a nurse, unaware that the grown-up Fumiya (Kobashi) is now studying to become a doctor nearby.

With similarities to the amnesiac romance of the anime *Love Hina* (*AE), *Churasan* also shows the hallmarks of a Yoshikazu Okada drama, concentrating not just on the love story but on the bonds between friends in the style of his earlier **ALL ABOUT YOUNG PEOPLE**. *Chura*, incidentally, is "beautiful" in the Okinawan dialect. Shown with English subtitles in the U.S. on KTSF TV.

CHŪSHINGURA *

1999. JPN: *Genroku Ryōran*. AKA: *Treasury of Loyal Retainers, 47 Rōnin*. PRD: N/C. DIR: Makoto Ōhara, Keiji Kataoka, Kazuhiro Motoki. SCR: Takehiro Nakajima. CAST: Kankurō Nakamura, Ken Matsudaira, Kōji Ishizaka, Rie Miyazawa, Shinobu Ōtake, Machiko Kyō, Eisaku Yoshida. CHN: NHK. DUR: 45 mins. x 49 eps.; Sun 10 January 1999–12 December 1999.

In 1678, Kuranosuke Ōishi (played by kabuki actor Nakamura) is the trainee chief counselor for the Akō samurai clan. Visiting the Yoshiwara pleasure quarter for the first time, he befriends Matashirō Irobe, a vassal of the Uesugi clan.

In 1680, the era of **MITO KŌMON**, Tsunayoshi becomes the fifth Tokugawa shōgun, taking a woman called Sonoko as his concubine. However, his mother Keishōin takes an immediate dislike to the new arrival— somewhat justifiably, since Sonoko secretly loves the lower-ranking samurai Tadatsugu Okajima of the Numata clan. Eventually, Keishōin wins out and Sonoko is packed off to be the mistress of counselor Yoshiaki Yanagisawa.

Tsunayoshi abolishes the Numata clan, and Tadatsugu heads for Edo following the suicides of his disgraced father and brother. There, he witnesses the misfortunes of Tsunayoshi, who loses his young heir and grows increasingly paranoid about his plotting courtiers. Paramount among them is Kōzukenosuke Kira, a nobleman determined to make his own son the head of the Uesugi clan. As the years pass, Kira's influence becomes increasingly powerful, while Tsunayoshi's reforms and decrees lead to civil unrest and an attempt on his life. Meanwhile, tensions grow between Kira and Kuranosuke's capricious master Takumi no Mikoto, leading to a fateful day in 1701 when Takumi draws his sword and attacks Kira.

Takumi is forced to atone for his misdeed by committing suicide and Kuranosuke is faced with a difficult decision. Asked to surrender the Akō castle, he agrees but resolves to avenge the death of Takumi. Vendettas are legal if they are registered, but official notification will only make Kira impossible to reach. Instead, Kuranosuke gathers 46 of his most loyal retainers and organizes a secret mission. His plan is to kill Kira and then commit mass suicide, the only way the honor of the Akō clan can be restored.

The vendetta of the 47 rōnin is one of the most famous stories in Japan, best known through its numerous fictionalizations in the kabuki theater. *Chūshingura* chooses the best of both worlds, telling the true story of the tragedy but as a backdrop to a tale of star-crossed lovers that mixes historical and fictional characters. It takes 20 episodes to set up the complex series of attachments and intrigues that lead to the stabbing of Kira, bounding across 23 years of drama before slowing to a crawl for a blow-by-blow account of the events of 1701 and beyond. There is thus plenty of time to set up the shadowy evil of Kira (who spends much of the series behind the scenes like the Prince of Darkness), as well as the dangerously capricious nature of Takumi. As befits an NHK drama, there is also plenty to entertain the female audience, with much talk of noble sacrifice and bedroom intrigues. Ironically, it is some of the drama's more unbelievable incidents that are actually true, most notably an ongoing farce about protecting dogs. The historical Shogun Tsunayoshi genuinely *did* order the execution of anyone who killed a dog and insisted that citizens address canines with high-level terms of honor and respect.

The following year's NHK *taiga* drama was **AOI**, which covered the events of the preceding half-century, and could almost be described as a prequel. See also the anime *Woof Woof 47 Rōnin* (*AE), which took the canine theme to extremes by portraying the central cast *as* dogs. This 1999 *Chūshingura* was not the first; the story was previously made into the *taiga* drama *Rōnin of Akō* (1964), starring Kazuo Hasegawa. It was also adapted as the 1975 *taiga* drama *Genroku Taiheki*, which focused on the figure of Yoshiyasu Yanagisawa (Kōji Ishizaka), a secretary to the fifth shogun Tsunayoshi. During May of the production year, the set was visited by Britain's Queen Elizabeth II, in a publicity event that must have been exactly the kind of international legitimization the *taiga* producers had been hoping for.

It was adapted once again as a *taiga* drama in 1982: *The Group at the Ridge* (*Tōge no Gunzō*), starring Ken Ogata and Daisuke Ryū, this time using a novel by Taichi Sakaiya, which compared the fall of the 47 rōnin to the upheaval caused by the bankruptcy of a 20th-century company. See also **WHITE RIDGE**.

The 1999 version was shown subtitled in the U.S. on KIKU TV.

CITIZEN'S DECISION

1996. JPN: *Jiken*. AKA: *Shimin no Hanketsu*. PRD: Hideo Amino. DIR: Haruhiko Mimura. SCR: Akihiro Ishimatsu, Masa Furuta. CAST: Tsunehiko Watase, Ayako Sawada, Tōru Watanabe, Haruko Satsuki. CHN: TVT. DUR: 45 mins. x 11 eps.; Mon 7 October 1996–16 December 1996.

High school teacher Sada (Watase) is appointed to be a juror at the Criminal Investigation Examination. The CIE is a system for victims of dropped cases. The jurors are chosen at random and the chosen person cannot refuse. Sada is not keen to do it but he attends the examination. Theme: Rumiko Kyuhō—"Memai" (Vertigo).

CLASSMATES

1989. JPN: *Dōkyūsei*. PRD: Yoshiaki Yamada, Tōru Ōta. DIR: Michio Kōno. SCR: Yūji Sakamoto. CAST: Narumi Yasuda, Naoto Ogata, Momoko Kikuchi, Shin Takuma, Tomoko

© 2003 Steve Kyte

Cold Moon

Yamaguchi, Junichi Ishida, Miho Nakai. CHN: Fuji. DUR: 45 mins. x 13 eps.; Mon 3 July 1989–25 September 1989. College sweethearts Chinami (Yasuda) and Kamoi (Ogata) separate shortly before graduation. Though both begin relationships with others, they meet again after 15 months to realize that that they still have feelings for each other. Based on the manga by **TOKYO LOVE STORY** creator Fumi Saimon. Theme: Ziggy—"Gloria."

COACH *

1996. PRD: Shizuo Sekiguchi. DIR: Hisao Ogura. SCR: Ryōichi Kimizuka. CAST: Atsuko Asano, Kōji Tamaki, Junichi Ishida, Anju Suzuki, Masahiko Nishimura. CHN: Fuji. DUR: 45 mins. x 12 eps.; Thu 4 July 1996–19 September 1996.
Nagisa (Asano) is a section leader at a high-class trading company, transferred to a remote sardine factory outpost after blowing an important deal at the head office. She finds herself in a run-down facility where Seitarō

(Tamaki) and his fellow workers care more about baseball than their jobs. The head office then decides to shut the factory down and move operations abroad but Nagisa resolves to instill a unified spirit in her workforce, if not through work then through sport. The result is a story that reverses the cast genders of the U.S. movie *A League of their Own* (1992, released in Japan as *Pretty League*). One of many TV dramas in which sport champions over everyday adversity—compare to **GOODBYE MR. OZU**. Reputedly shown subtitled on U.S. TV. Theme: Kōji Tamaki—"Den-en" (Fields and Gardens).

COLD MOON

1998. JPN: *Tsumetai Tsuki*. PRD: Yoshinori Horiguchi. DIR: Akihiro Karaki. SCR: Akiyo Takigawa, Masaya Ozaki. CAST: Akina Nakamori, Hiromi Nagasaku, Kōji Matoba, Tōru Karawatari, Yasuyo Shiroshima, Takurō Tatsumi. CHN: Yomiuri. DUR: 45 mins. x 10 eps.; Mon 12 January 1998–16 March 1998.

Newscaster Kōhei (Tatsumi) is involved in a hit-and-run accident but his actions are reported to the police by pregnant passerby Misaki (Nagasaku). With his public image ruined by the scandal, Kōhei commits suicide. The shock causes his pregnant wife Kiyoka (Nakamori) to miscarry her child. She is taken to the hospital, where she is enraged to see Misaki has happily given birth—Kiyoka swears to avenge herself on the woman who has destroyed her happy life. After winning Misaki's trust, Kiyoka tries to murder Misaki's baby and seduce her husband. Realizing she is in danger, Misaki threatens to stab Kiyoka but is unable to commit the crime. Instead, Kiyoka stabs herself with a knife and accuses Misaki of doing it. Misaki is incarcerated for attempted murder and Kiyoka marries Misaki's husband, bringing up her child Yū as if he was her own—and feeding him Kōhei's powdered ashes in his milk.

Despite overt similarities to *The Hand That Rocks the Cradle* (1992), *Cold*

Moon is one in a long tradition of Japanese bunny boiler dramas, to be filed alongside THE CURSE, WEDNESDAY LOVE AFFAIR, and PARFUM DE LA JALOUSIE. This one goes particularly far, since Kiyoka's revenge does not end with Misaki in prison, her child in her arms, and her husband in her bed. A former surgeon, Kiyoka plots to trick Misaki into a hospital, drugging her so that she can give her a hysterectomy. Marvelously evil. Theme: Akina Nakamori—"Kisei: Never Forget" (Homecoming: Never Forget).

COLD MORNING

1978. JPN: *Tsumetai Asa*. PRD: Motozō Tsubaki. DIR: Takamasa Suzuki, Mitsuo Maeda, Ryūnosuke Sano. SCR: Shirō Ishimori. CAST: Takaharu Yoshimoto, Yasuharu Umeno, Yumiko Yoshida, Toshie Takada, Aritsune Amano, Kiyoshi Shimizu. CHN: NHK. DUR: 20 mins. x 12 eps.; Mon 27 February 1978–16 March 1978.

High school friends Shigeo (Yoshimoto) and Tomiko (Yoshida) are suddenly turned into step-siblings by their formerly single parents—father Sadaichi (Umeno) and mother Sachiko (Takada) think their children need a complete family and are determined to see they get one at all costs. Despite the initial comedic potential of two single-sex households suddenly forced to become one harmonious whole, *Cold Morning* veers off in a more dramatic direction, preferring to concentrate on troubles at school and issues such as teen suicide. Based on a story by Yōjirō Ishizaka, though possibly with something of a debt to the U.S. TV series *The Brady Bunch* (1969). Relations by marriage are a common device in Japanese drama, allowing for chaste friendship as here, a variation on the reluctant buddies genre as in AFTER SCHOOL DANGER, and even the not quite incest of STRAWBERRY ON THE SHORTCAKE.

COME LIVE WITH ME

1995. JPN: *Heya (Uchi) ni Oide yo*. AKA: *Come on Over to My Place*. PRD:

Susumu Ōoka. DIR: Akio Yoshida. SCR: Yumiko Kamiyama. CAST: Misa Shimizu, Tatsuya Yamaguchi, Toshio Kakei, Naomi Hosokawa, Naoko Iijima. CHN: TBS. DUR: 45 mins. x 11 eps.; Fri 13 January 1995–24 March 1995.

Aya (Shimizu) is a music teacher by day but works at night as a pianist in a hotel bar. She falls in love with Mikio, a student cameraman and the two of them move in together, though events often seem to conspire to keep them apart. Based on the 1990 *Young Sunday* manga by Hidenori Hara. Theme: Kenji Ozawa—"Sore wa Chotto" (Hang on a Minute).

COME OUT AND PLAY

1988. JPN: *Asobi ni Oideyo*. PRD: Akihiro Daikoku. DIR: Yoshihito Fukumoto, Setsuo Wakamatsu. SCR: Toshio Okumura, Chigusa Shiota. CAST: Yuki Saitō, Tadahiko Takamoku, Hiro Furumura, Shigeru Muroi, Shinji Yamashita. CHN: Fuji. DUR: 45 mins. x 12 eps.; Mon 4 July 1988–19 September 1988.

Nijiko (Saitō) works at the food section at a department store but is suddenly promoted to division chief of planning as part of an affirmative action program. The result finds the 21-year-old stripling forced to butt heads with middle-aged managers old enough to be her father. Comedy soon ensues. Theme: The Beatles—"Help!"

COME TO MAMA'S BED

1994. JPN: *Mama no Bed ni Irasshai*. AKA: *Hey Boy! Come in Mama's Bed*. PRD: N/C. DIR: Takeshi Matsumoto. SCR: Kazuhiko Ban. CAST: Miwako Fujitani, Tōru Kazama, Ikkō Furuya, Hitomi Kuroki, Hiroko Tanaka. CHN: Asahi. DUR: 45 mins. x 11 eps.; Thu 13 October 1994–29 December 1994.

Kōsuke (Kazama) doesn't just lose his girlfriend Kyōko (Fujitani), he loses her to his Dad, Kōzō (Furuya)! Before long, he's gained a young stepmother, who acts as if they were never lovers and presides over the uneasy situation in the household. Eventually, Kōsuke gets his revenge by finding a new girl-

friend of his own—his Dad's ex-lover Masuko (Kuroki). Theme: Mikako Fujitani—"Spare Key—Ai Saretemo Shō ga Nai" (Spare Key—Gotta Be Loved).

COMET-SAN

1967. PRD: N/C. DIR: Eizō Yamagiwa, Toshirō Kagetsu. SCR: Mamoru Sasaki, Kōei Yoshihara, Shinichi Ichikawa, Takahito Ishikawa, Kimitaka Ōhashi. CAST: Yumiko Konoe, Haruko Mabuchi, Hiroshi Ashino, Shirō Ōtsuji, Takayoshi Kura, Gen Funabashi, Midori Nishizaki. CHN: TBS. DUR: 30 mins. x 77 eps.; Mon 3 July 1967–30 December 1968 (#1); 30 mins. x 68 eps.; 12 June 1978–24 September 1979 (#2).

Comet, a mischievous alien girl, is such a handful on her homeworld of Beta that her school principal sends her off to work for the Peace Corps in the middle of nowhere—Earth. The trip does nothing to mellow Comet and she even defaces a star with graffiti on her way. Taking a job as a housemaid, she inspires the suspicions of boys Takeshi and Kōji, though few believe them when they claim that their housekeeper can make wishes come true with a magic wand or that she is in a constant struggle to protect the Earth from invaders. Although parallels with *Bewitched* (1964) and *I Dream of Jeannie* (1965) seem obvious, *Comet-san* was officially adapted from a girls' manga serialized in *Margaret* magazine by Mitsuteru Yokoyama, who also created GIGANTOR and JOHNNY SOKKO AND HIS GIANT ROBOT. In a Japan that was still getting used to animation on TV, *Comet-san* added special effects by integrating live-action with animation provided by future anime director Tadao Nagahama. After the 20th episode, the monochrome series burst into full color, adding to its innovative look. Theme: Yumiko Konoe—"Comet-san."

The series has been remade twice. The 1978 version featured idol Kumiko Ōba as Comet-san, who flies from Virgo to Earth in a flying saucer that can shrink and be camouflaged as a false tooth. She comes to stay with a music teacher played by Kōhei Sawano, intending to find *"a really beautiful thing"* to complete her final assignment at star school. She becomes popular through her use of magic but is not allowed to use it without permission from her mother. Characters from the **ULTRAMAN** series also appeared in cameo roles.

The most recent version of the series was a fully animated 2001 version (*AE), aimed at a considerably younger audience.

COMING HOME

1994. PRD: Chiharu Kasuga. DIR: Hiroshi Okamoto. SCR: Takashi Ezure. CAST: Takako Tokiwa, Junko Sakurai, Kōyō Maeda, Yumiko Fujita, Tatsuo Umemiya, Nana Okada, Tetsurō Tanba. CHN: TBS. DUR: 45 mins. x 12 eps.; Fri 8 July 1994–23 September 1994. Shintarō Shirota (Umemiya) lives with his wife Atsuko (Fujita), his four children, Shitarō's father Fukuzō (Tanba), and a dog. However, in the manner of in-law appeasers throughout the history of Japanese TV, he is forced to make room for his sister Megumi (Okada) and her children, as well as an unexpected lodger from Hungary. Based on a story by Teru Miyamoto, who also wrote **BLUE SCATTERS**.

COMPLETE LOVE

1993. JPN: *Tetteiteki ni Ai wa.* PRD: Tamaki Endō. DIR: Tamaki Endō, Osamu Katayama, Yoshikazu Kaneko. SCR: Shizuka Ōishi. CAST: Nobuko Sendō, Eisaku Yoshida, Takeshi Naitō, Michiko Yamamura, Kiwako Harada. CHN: TBS. DUR: 45 mins. x 11 eps.; Fri 15 October 1993–24 December 1993. Passport officer Junko (Sendō) takes a vacation away from the Ministry of Foreign Affairs where she works and heads off to L.A., where she promptly loses her passport. She calls her colleagues in Tokyo and begins a flirtatious phone relationship with Kōichirō (Naitō), who works in the section next to hers. Meanwhile, Junko finds herself falling for her married colleague Ronpei (Yoshida), who also happens to

be in L.A. and offers to help her out. Although Sendō's character was supposed to be honest with her feelings, she was not popular with the female audience or indeed with writer Ōishi, who announced that she preferred the supporting cast member career-girl Teruno (Kiwako Harada). Ōishi's other dramas include **AFRICA NIGHTS** and **DAUGHTER-IN-LAW**. Sendō and Yoshida sang the theme tune "Ima o Dakishimete" (Embrace This Moment) under the group name NOA.

CONCERTO *

1996. JPN: *Kyōsōkyoku.* PRD: Yasuo Yagi. DIR: Makoto Kiyohiro, Kanji Takenoshita. SCR: Toshikazu Ikehata. CAST: Masakazu Tamura, Takuya Kimura, Rie Miyazawa, Saburō Ishikura, Kei Satō, Masami Hisamoto. CHN: TBS. DUR: 45 mins. x 10 eps.; Fri 11 October 1996–13 December 1996. Kakeru (Kimura from SMAP) is a young architect struggling to make ends meet but supported 100% by his loving girlfriend Hana (Miyazawa). The couple find a confused man in a tuxedo wandering out of the sea and take him home to recover. Some time later, Kakeru goes looking for work at the Tokyo office of famous architect Kōsuke (Tamura), only to discover that he is the same man. Though the two men settle their differences and begin working together, they are less cooperative when it comes to Hana—Kōsuke eventually steals her away from Kakeru and the two are married while Kakeru is busy on a new building project.

As the years pass, Kakeru develops a set of lucrative contracts for industrialist Tatsumi (Satō) and is making plans to marry Tatsumi's daughter Kyōko (Yoshino Kimura). However, he discovers that Hana and Kōsuke are no longer together and cannot resist getting back together with her. The wrath of his jilted fiancée loses him much of his work and as he swings back from riches to rags, Hana walks out on him. The two architects meet once more, only to discover that Hana is not living with either of them. . . .

A popular drama of the mid-1990s, *Concerto* capitalizes on its generation-gap love triangle—Kōsuke is presented as an aging boy who never grew up but who gets everything he wants, while Kakeru is a bright young thing who must make grave compromises to get ahead. It gained extra attention through the profiles of its stars—Miyazawa had been absent from TV for four years since **TOKYO ELEVATOR GIRL**, while Kimura's meteoric career path included a 1996 guest role in Tamura's more famous vehicle, **NINZABURŌ FURUHATA**. Also published as a novel, credited to screenwriter Ikehata. Shown subtitled in the U.S. on KIKU TV and KTSF TV. Theme: Vanessa Williams—"Alfie." Note also the liberal amounts of Burt Bacharach music on the soundtrack. Peak rating: 28.2%.

CONDITION WHITE

1994. JPN: *Shiro no Jōken.* PRD: Takahiro Kasaki. DIR: Hiroki Yamada. SCR: Yoshihisa Aiba. CAST: Ari Nakae, Hisako Manda, Azusa Nakamura, Masanori Sera, Tōru Masuoka. CHN: Kansai. DUR: 45 mins. x 9 eps.; Mon 4 April 1994–30 May 1994. After the death of the chairman of Nomura Hospital under suspicious circumstances, his three daughters Ryōko (Manda), Risako (Nakamura), and Yōko (Nakae) discover that they have inherited his 15-million-yen debt. In order to solve the mystery surrounding her father's death and debt, Yōko becomes a trainee doctor under Hirose (Sera), the surgeon who operated on her father. Based on the 1991 manga by Naka Marimura—compare to **THREE SISTER DETECTIVES**. Theme: Class—"Holiday."

CONFUSED LIFE

2001. JPN: *Fure-Fure Jinsei.* PRD: Ryūta Inoue. DIR: Kazuhiro Mori. SCR: Rie Yokota. CAST: Yuki Matsushita, Junichi Ishida, Hidekazu Akai. CHN: NTV. DUR: 45 mins. x 11 eps.; Mon 2 July 2001–10 September 2001. When she discovers that her friend Shiori has left her husband and children for a job in the sex industry, an Akita woman (Matsushita) goes in search of her. She leaves behind her unappealing boyfriend and meets a supermarket manager (Akai) who also knows Shiori.

CONVENIENCE STORE STORY

1990. JPN: *Convenience Monogatari*. PRD: N/C. DIR: Akira Nagamine. SCR: Hiroyuki Uchimura. CAST: Mitsuyoshi Uchimura, Kiyotaka Nanbara, Akira Maeda, Aki Takejō. CHN: TVT. DUR: 45 mins. x 6 eps.; Sun 8 April 1990–13 May 1990.

Hiatari (Uchimura) starts a part-time job at a convenience store, where senior Kitajima (Nanbara) agrees to show him the ropes. One day, Hiatari takes an interest in a young child who comes in everyday to buy a packed lunch—shouldn't his mother be making it for him . . . ? A funny and heart-warming story from the comedy duo Uchimura and Nanbara, which would have the ultimate compliment paid to it eight years later by **FOR LONELY LITTLE YOU**, which seems suspiciously similar. Theme: The Minx—"Pash."

COP, THE

1990. JPN: *The Keiji*. PRD: N/C. DIR: Tōgorō Tsuchiya. SCR: Hanabusa Ogawa, Sanshirō Kuramoto. CAST: Yutaka Mizutani, Tsurutarō Kataoka, Ikue Sakakibara, Yōsuke Eguchi. CHN: Asahi. DUR: 45 mins. x 26 eps.; 15 April 1990–30 September 1990. Detectives from Roppongi Police Station solve urban crimes. Yutaka Mizutani played a cool detective (shortly before his stint on **COP CLAN**), while Kataoka's role is more emotional—compare to the similar chalk-and-cheese partnering of **ARREST YOUR EYES** and **BAYSIDE SHAKEDOWN**. Their colleague, played by Eguchi, is a loner who refuses to see criminals as human beings but slowly changes his ways through exposure to the human feelings of Kataoka. Theme: Ayumi Nakamura—"It's All Right."

Concerto

COP CLAN

1990. JPN: *Deka Kizoku*. PRD: Norio Hatsukawa, Yoshio Nakamura, Kazu Takeda, Hiroki Asatsu. DIR: Yasuharu Hasebe, Tōru Kinoshita, Shinobu Murata. SCR: Yutaka Kaneko, Hiroshi Kashiwabara, Kazunari Huruuchi, Toshimichi Ōkawa, Junichi Miyashita, Motokazu Mineo, Yoshirō Oka. CAST: Hiroki Matsutaka, Hiroshi Tachi, Hiromi Gō, Hitomi Kuroki, Hiroshi Fuse, Yutaka Mizutani. CHN: NTV. DUR: 45 mins. x 37 eps., Fri 13 April 1990–22 March 1991 (#1); 45 mins. x 40 eps.

(1st ep. 90 mins.), 12 April 1991–20 March 1992 (#2); 45 mins. x 25 eps., 17 April 1992–25 December 1992.

Cops at the Jōnan Police Precinct are presented as a family away from home, as detectives Shunsuke (Tachi) and Sudō try to break up a long-running feud between two criminal gangs. Other officers from Daikan Police Station include Yumiko Shimura (Kuroki), Hiroshi Izumi (Fuse), and Nobuo Iwata (Toshikazu Fukawa) but the initial focus of the show remained on Shunsuke, who appeared to combine *Columbo* and DETECTIVE STORY by driving around in a battered Mustang. However, one season into the first broadcast run, Tachi left the series—his character died in episode 16—to be replaced by former FBI agent Akira Kazama (Gō), who accidentally stumbles onto a drug ring when he investigates what he believes to be a run-of-the-mill art robbery.

An obvious attempt to remake HOWL AT THE SUN for the 1990s, to the extent of lifting entire episodes of the 1970s classic. A second season of *CC* was unafraid to jettison as much of the cast as it liked and introduced new leading men Shintarō Honjō (Mizutani) and Minoru Harada (Minoru Tanaka), whose first job is to crack a ring of passport forgers, only to discover that their prime counterfeit suspect is already dead. *CC2* moved the focus away from the crimes themselves and onto the relationships between the officers (compare to HAGURE KEIJI) and also reached the stage where the restless cast and casting director seem to have settled down—the lineup and style remained relatively unchanged for the third and final season. The show was replaced by NAKED COP in the same slot.

COUNTING THE SLEEPLESS NIGHTS

1992. JPN: *Nemurenai Yoru o Kazoete.* PRD: Keiko Take. DIR: Noriaki Asao. SCR: Toshio Kamata. CAST: Misako Tanaka, Kunihiko Mitamura, Tsurubei Shōfuku-tei, Nenji Kobayashi, Miyoko Asada.

CHN: Asahi. DUR: 45 mins. x 11 eps.; Thu 16 April 1992–25 June 1992.

Tomoko (Tanaka) is posted to Shinjuku Sakae Central Police Station as a deputy section chief. She graduated from Tokyo University and has passed the advanced civil servant exam, which leads to her being regarded as something of an *objet d'art* by the rough and tough detectives. Coming so soon after *Silence of the Lambs* (1990), it was only to be expected that this series veered away from mundane police work and into realms of suspense and psychological drama. Theme: Mariko Takahashi—"Hagayui Kuchibiru" (Impatient Lips).

COUNTRY LIVING

1999. JPN: *Inaka de Kurasō yo.* AKA: *Let's Move to the Country.* PRD: Hiroshi Tōsai. DIR: Takemitsu Satō. SCR: Yūko Kinya. CAST: Masanobu Takashima, Natsumi Nanase, Sōichirō Kitamura, Yuriko Hoshi, Shingo Yanagisawa, Kōichi Miura, Tsuyoshi Kimura, Reiko Kusamura, Takashi Itō. CHN: TVT. DUR: 45 mins. x ca. 11 eps.; Wed 14 July 1999–?? September 1999.

Although they have always made their home in Tokyo, it has been a lifelong dream for Mr. and Mrs. Okamura to move out to the country and live a simple life. Mr. Okamura suddenly decides that it's now or never and forcibly relocates his yuppie family to a remote mountain village. The Okamuras immediately begin experiencing difficulties with the close-knit locals and soon discover that life in the country without urban conveniences is not quite the picnic they thought it would be. Compare to FROM THE NORTH and LADY OF THE MANOR.

COUSINS

1992. JPN: *Itoko Dōshi.* PRD: Kei Koyama. DIR: Nozomu Amemiya. SCR: Masahiro Yoshimoto. CAST: Masanobu Takashima, Tomoko Yamaguchi, Shigeru Muroi, Etsuji Toyokawa, Tokuma Nishioka. CHN: NTV. DUR: 45 mins. x 11 eps.; 14 October 1992–23 December 1992.

Artist Emiko (Yamaguchi) realizes that she is working in the same company as her long-lost cousin Atsushi (Takashima), a former advertising salesman who disappeared after a family quarrel five years earlier. Theme: Seishirō Kusunose—"Hoshi ga Mieta Yoru" (The Night We Watched the Stars).

CRAM SCHOOL BOOGIE

1990. JPN: *Yobikō Boogie.* PRD: Yasuo Yagi. DIR: Tamaki Endō. SCR: Kazuhiko Yūkawa. CAST: Naoto Ogata, Kōji Matoba, Yūji Oda, Misako Tanaka. CHN: TBS. DUR: 45 mins. x 12 eps.; Fri 20 April 1990–6 July 1990.

Shigeki (Ogata) is on his way to take an important university exam when a woman on his train falsely accuses him of feeling her up. He is dragged off to a police station and is unable to perform in the exam, necessitating a year of studying for re-takes at a cram school alongside fellow students Kaoru (Oda) and Ichirō (Matoba).

At their first English class, he realizes the lecturer is the woman who claimed that he was a pervert. Both he and Kaoru soon find themselves drawn to Yuki (Tanaka), but she rebuffs their advances. Meanwhile, Shigeki begins dating college student Megumi (Marina Watanabe), though she soon realizes that his mind is on someone else. To complete the traditional love polygon, Ichirō secretly loves Megumi.

Kaoru and Yuki quit school after the summer vacation, and by January, Shigeki is getting good grades in the mock exams. Ichirō, however, looks set to fail. On the day of the actual entrance exam for Nippon University, it is Ichirō who passes, while Shigeki fails. A depressed Shigeki encounters Kaoru the dropout, who has decided to be a film director and is inspired to try harder. However, he also fails to make the grade for Waseda University and is forced to re-enroll at the cram school for another year, hoping to be more lucky in life and in love. Compare to SWEET HOME.

CROSS OF ROSES

2002. JPN: *Bara no Jūjika.* PRD: Reiko Kita, Tadashi Makino. DIR: Michio Kōno, Narihide Mizuta, Tatsuaki Kimura. SCR: Taeko Asano. CAST: Hiroshi Mikami, Yuriko Ishida, Masanobu Katsumura, Aiko Satō, Tetsuji Tamayama, Mayuko Nishiyama, Masashi Aida, Tsubaki Nekoze, Yūki Amami. CHN: Fuji. DUR: 45 mins. x 11 eps.; Thu 10 October 2002–?? December 2002.

Commercial director Tōgo (Mikami) is continually getting into trouble for trying to make advertisements with a little more creative spark than his workaday colleagues' results. Although his mother constantly pressures him to have a child with his wife Sumiko (Ishida), it appears that one or both of them is unable to have children. Tōgo resigns himself to a childless marriage, until he meets the pretty career woman Akira (Amami). Akira claims to have no interest in men ever since a traumatic childhood incident. However, she still wants a baby and asks Tōgo if he will be the father—she offers him no strings, no relationship, no publicity. Tōgo eventually agrees and the couple draw up a careful set of rules, agreeing not to see each other again once the baby is born. However, they later have a change of heart and Tōgo is tempted to leave Sumiko for Akira and his child. When Sumiko finds out, she plots an elaborate scheme of revenge suitable for a bunny boiler drama—compare to PARFUM DE LA JALOUSIE and BORN OF LIES.

CURSE, THE *

1998. JPN: *Sōzetsu! Yome Shūtome Sensō: Rasetsu no Ie.* AKA: *Gruesome! Bride vs. Mother-in-Law War: House of Devil; Bridal Wars.* PRD: Kenji Matsumura, Fumio Igarashi. DIR: Kyū Kojima, Mio Ezaki. SCR: Takashi Ezure. CAST: Noriko Katō, Yōko Yamamoto, Naoki Hosaka, Ryō Tamura, Kazue Itō. CHN: Asahi. DUR: 45 mins. x 12 eps. (1st ep 90 mins.); Thu 9 April–25 June 1998.

Yōko (Katō) is a typical Japanese office lady who looks forward to marriage and starting a family. When her boyfriend Takashi (Hosaka) finally pops the question, she readily agrees and he proudly takes her to meet his parents. She is warmly welcomed by her new mother-in-law Ayano (Yamamoto) but discovers Sumiyo, Ayano's half-mad mother-in-law, has been kept prisoner in an annex of the house ever since Ayano caused the death of her husband. Despite warnings from her sister-in-law Saeko and threats from Takashi's vindictive cousin Suzuka, Yōko resolves to go through with it.

Takashi is posted abroad, forcing Yōko to move in with her in-laws and experience their company firsthand. She must deal with rancid miso soup and the presence of a cat in her bed, but such pranks are only the beginning. Takashi neglects to mention his mother in a letter home, causing Ayano to fly into a rage. Yōko discovers that she is pregnant but loses the baby due to Ayano's interference. Takashi grows increasingly distant, particularly after Ayano suggests that Yōko may have been having an affair with her own father-in-law, Takao!

It transpires that Takao does indeed have a mistress (can you blame him!), who is introduced as Fumiko. She is pregnant. Prepared to try anything to escape from the family, Yōko puts a curse on Ayano and prepares to head for her own family home but her mad mother-in-law slashes her own wrists in an attempt to keep her close.

Based on the manga by Chikae Ide, *The Curse* combines in-law appeasement à la LADY OF THE MANOR with a grand guignol of tortures, creating an endlessly inventive series of torments and vendettas that makes CHŪSHINGURA look like a picnic. Ayano is TV drama's most remorseless enemy, prepared to use bribery, violence, and threats to get her own way, but she is by no means the only "soul-eater" in the show who makes others' lives a misery. The titular affliction is not merely a magical spell but growing old in an uncaring society with no one to rely

Cyber Girls Thelomea

upon but resentful relatives. It takes Sartre's maxim that "hell is other people," and asks if even that is preferable to loneliness—playing on the primal fears of the 20th-century yuppie generation by presenting marriage as a Faustian pact, destroying young freedoms with a series of invasive obligations, infidelities, and betrayals. Though the script acknowledges that Yōko's desired fairy-tale marriage is a theoretical possibility, it loads each scene with dire portents that Takashi is not The One. With the arrival of Itsurō, a doctor who carries a torch for her, the traditional drama love triangle is altered into a life-or-death decision, with no second chance.

Sadly, the execution of *The Curse* is not quite as entertaining as its high concept—in the age of trendy dramas and location-shooting, the cardboard sets and (frankly) cardboard acting in *The Curse* make it appear considerably older than it is. Shown in the U.S. on KIKU TV, where the local audience warmed to its peculiar mixture of language-class Japanese and psychological horror writer Ezure was also responsible for the insane Sentai show BATTLEFEVER J.

CYBER GIRLS THELOMEA

1998. JPN: *Cyber Bishōjo Teromea.* PRD:

Takeshi Nakajima, Iwao Yutani, Tomohiko Hamada. DIR: Takeshi Nakajima, Toshikazu Nagae. SCR: Masahiro Yokotani, Takeo Kasai. CAST: Tsugumi, Yōko Kamon, Hitomi Miwa, Tatsuya Fujiwara, Shintarō Tanabe, Yoshimasa Nakamaru, Akitoshi Ōtaki, Sōichirō Kitamura, Akira Tanabe, Hiroko Mori. CHN: Asahi. DUR: 25 mins. x 11 eps.; Sun 5 April 1998–28 June 1998.

Asagi (Tsugumi), Lena (Kamon), and Itsumi (Miwa) are super-powered school girls at Invisibility High. They spend a lot of time in the Atomic Research Institute, where children with super-power potential are tested with the aid of Cyber Suits, until the day when an experiment goes disastrously wrong and test subject Shū (Tanabe) runs amok and kills staff members. The girls discover that they are the end results of a secret genetic-engineering program begun some 17 years earlier and that they are really commodities made to order for the shadowy Alpha Syndicate. But have their various abilities already been stolen from them in the form of the mysterious girl Psi (Mori), who could be a hybrid of each girl's best genetic material? A live-action answer to the 1990s success of *Evangelion* (*AE), with a late-night broadcast time that allowed for the fights with monsters of the week to swiftly devolve into ripped clothing and a distinctly sadomasochistic streak. The Cyber Suits, in particular, look like something from a bondage catalogue. Though it was shown after midnight and hence technically on Sunday morning, some sources still list it as a Saturday night program. Compare to **BUNNY KNIGHTS** and **GAZER**.

DAIRANGER *

1993. JPN: *Gosei Sentai Dairanger.* AKA: *Five Star Battle Team Dairanger; Mighty Morphin' Power Rangers (Series Two).* PRD: Kyōzō Utsunomiya, Atsushi Kaji, Takeyuki Suzuki, Shinichirō Shirokura. DIR: Yoshiaki Kobayashi, Shōhei Tōjō, Tarō Sakamoto, Takeru Ogasawara, Katsuya Watanabe. SCR: Noboru Sugimura, Tsunehisa Arakawa, Susumu Takahisa, Kunio Fujii. CAST: Keiichi Wada, Tatsuya Nōmi, Akira Hanemura, Keisuke Tsuchiya, Natsuki Takahashi, Hisashi Sakai, Rintarō Nishi, Yōko Amematsuri, Madoka Tamura. CHN: Asahi. DUR: 25 mins. x 50 eps.; 19 February 1993–11 February 1994.

The Goma Clan is once more on the rise 6,050 years after it was defeated by magical power. Only the descendants of their mortal enemies, the Dai Clan, stand any chance of saving the world, forming the Dairanger team of heroes, each with a theme based on a creature from Chinese mythology. Leader Ryō (Wada) is a cook in a Chinese restaurant who dreams of bringing proper *jiaozi* dumplings to the people of Japan. He is also the red Dragon Ranger, who fights with twin Dragon Swords. Daigo (Nōmi) works in a pet shop and hopes one day to become the world's greatest swordsman. He is also the green Lion Ranger and fights with a Lion Staff. Shōji (Hanemura) dreams of becoming the world boxing champion. He is also the blue Pegasus Ranger

and fights with the Pegasus Nunchaku. Tomo (Tsuchiya) is a fashion-conscious beautician and is also the yellow Kirin Ranger. He fights with the Kirin Kusarigama (a kind of blade-and-chain ninja weapon). Token female Ling (Takahashi) is a foreign exchange student from China. She is also the pink Phoenix Ranger and fights with the Phoenix Wand. They are joined later by Kō (Sakai), the only non-Dai member of the team, whose allegiances are torn between the warring tribes. However, once on the Dairanger team, Kō becomes the white Fang Ranger. He not only fights with the White Tiger Sword but regularly asks the sentient weapon for advice.

Though the standard mode of transport for the team was a set a personal motorcycles, their obligatory super-vehicles were modeled after their totem animals—a Dragon, Lion, Pegasus, Kirin, Phoenix, and Tiger. Kō's One Tiger could transform into a humanoid robot mode, while all the vehicles could combine to form the Fang King giant robot. The team also had access to Twisting Dragon and Great Turtle giant robots.

Inspired in equal parts by *Superman II* (1980) and the early-1990's Gulf War, the Dairanger enemies are a trio of leather-clad Goma super-warriors, named Saddam (Nishi), Kara (Amematsuri), and Zaidos (Tamura). In fact, Saddam is the true enemy—all other adversaries have been created by

him from mud, including his monsters-of-the-week and the cannon fodder Kotpotro minions. The show also included flashback sequences to pre-historic China, featuring the ancestors of the modern-day rangers.

By the time *Dairanger* was released in Japan, its predecessor *Zyuranger* had already made the leap to the U.S. market in the heavily rewritten form of the **MIGHTY MORPHIN' POWER RANGERS.** Plans were already afoot to continue *Power Rangers* using footage from this newer show but instead of wiping the slate clean and beginning anew, the U.S. producers elected to continue their storyline and simply find excuses for the changes in lineup and vehicles. The new footage, coupled with standard TV series attrition, caused some changes in the cast for the American *Power Rangers* show. Tommy (Jason Frank), who had left the series as the Green Ranger, returned as the White Ranger and team leader. The cast also gained a new Red Ranger Rocky (Steve Cardenas), Black Ranger Adam (Johnny Yong Bosch), and Yellow Ranger Aisha (Karan Ashley)—the previous Rangers having decided to go to a peace conference in Switzerland. Original Blue and Pink Rangers David Yost and Amy Jo Johnson stayed with the series. The *Power Rangers* series also avoided the Saddam subplot, preferring to shoot new footage using stand-in Carla Perez for the original Japanese Bandora/Rita Repulsa enemy and introduced a new adversary of their own—Lord Zedd (Robert Axelrod). For the flashback sequences set in ancient China, the American version moved the location to the old Wild West in the style of *Back to the Future III* (1989), claiming to be depicting the life of the *American* cast's ancestors.

NB—Kirin is translated here as the Japanese variant of *qilin*, while Pegasus is used as a European approximation of *tenma*. Inspired as usual "by an idea from Saburō Yade" and featuring music from Kōji Kawamura. *Dairanger* was followed in the Japanese Super Sentai chronology by **KAKURANGER**.

DAISUKE HANAMURA

2000. JPN: *Hanamura Daisuke*. AKA: *Great Lawyer, The*. PRD: Yūji Tōjō, Kazuhisa Andō. DIR: Renpei Tsukamoto. SCR: Masaya Ozaki. CAST: Yūsuke Santamaria, Issei Ishida, Miki Mizuno, Naomi Kawashima, Hitoshi Nakayama. CHN: Kansai. DUR: 45 mins. x ca. 11 eps.; Tue 4 July 2001–?? September 2001.

When senior partners of a giant legal firm realize that their best lawyers are snowed under by small claims and minor cases, they decide to hire a dogsbody. Daisuke (Santamaria) is a poorly paid lawyer who never stands much of a chance of becoming a high-powered international litigator like his boss. Placed in charge of cases that would only waste the valuable time of his superiors, he continues to approach each assignment with enthusiasm and originality, until his activities do more for the corporation's reputation than its biggest paying cases. A comedy about the Japanese legal system, drawing on the early seasons of *Ally McBeal* (when interesting cases still diverted the cast from their love lives), *DH* was a whole season ahead of the more famous legal drama **HERO**, which would win high ratings the following year. Theme: Yuki Kimura—"Love and Joy."

DANGEROUS ANGEL X DEATH HUNTER

1997. JPN: *D X D*. AKA: *Dangerous Angels*. PRD: Kiyosuzu Inoue, Satoshi Suzuki. DIR: Tōya Satō. SCR: Tetsuya Ōishi, Daisuke Uhara. CAST: Tomoya Nagase, Junichi Okada, Yasufumi Terawaki, Sawa Suzuki, Ai Maeda. CHN: NTV. DUR: 45 mins. x 11 eps.; Sat 5 July 1997–20 September 1997.

Satoru Aizawa (Nagase from TOKIO) is critically injured and recovers from his near death experience to discover that he has gained psychic powers. He teams up with Toranosuke Kihara (Okada from V6), a private detective who also has a psychic power, and they begin investigating a series of disappearances at a children's daycare center that is scheduled for demolition. Their research reveals the wandering spirit of a boy, who died there long in the past and is still waiting to be picked up by his mother, who was killed in an accident herself on her way to the school. Much like the earlier psychic investigators of **NIGHT HEAD**, the team uses its powers to dispel the ghost's influence and he departs, allowing them to reveal a more earthly concern—the corruption behind the mayor's deal with the land developers over the daycare center's grounds. Later cases involve the boys opposing the plans of a mysterious man called Father, who is determined to turn Shinjuku into a Babylon of black magic. Theme: Tomoya Nagase with 3T—"Eternal Flame."

DANGEROUS DETECTIVE

1986. JPN: *Abunai Deka*. AKA: *Yokohama Cop Story*. PRD: N/C. DIR: Yasuharu Hasebe, Hiroki Tezeni, Tōru Murakawa, Kiyoshi Nishimura, Haruo Ichikura. SCR: Shōichi Maruyama, Machiko Nasu, Hiroshi Kashiwabara, Toshimichi Ōkawa, Toshiyuki Tanabe, Motokazu Mineo, Mitsuru Arai. CAST: Hiroshi Tachi, Kyōhei Shibata, Tōru Nakamura, Atsuko Asano, Shizuo Nakajō, Nana Kinomi, Michihiro Yamanishi. CHN: NTV. DUR: 45 mins. x 51 eps., Sun 5 October 1986–27

September 1987; *More Dangerous Detective*: 45 mins. x 25 eps., 7 October 1988–31 March 1989.

Toshiki "Dandy" Takayama (Tachi) and partner Yūji "Sexy" Ōshita (Shibata) make life hell for their subordinate Tōru Nakamura, who would like to have the nickname "Pretty" but is stuck with "Sloth," courtesy of his unforgiving colleagues. All three are mothered by the big-sisterly Kaoru Mayama (Asano), a detective in the juvenile crime section.

Yūji's maverick policing methods go horribly wrong when he attempts a raid on suspected political extremists without backup, leading to a chase through the streets with stolen firearms and the complete leveling of a nightclub in the path of Yūji and his prey. While the other detectives pick through the mess, witnesses describe the lead criminal as an underage boy who will reach his majority on his birthday the next day. Ōshita decides to arrest him as a juvenile criminal and hopes for adult punishment to follow on a technicality.

Despite apparent similarities to *Lethal Weapon* (1987), *Dangerous Detective* must have already been in production when Richard Donner began making his explosive mismatched buddy series in Hollywood. Set in Yokohama, *DD* was a precursor of the trendy drama phenomenon of the 1990s, leaning on the charms of future "trendy" star Atsuko Asano and foreshadowing the style of later cop shows such as **ARREST YOUR EYES** and **BAYSIDE SHAKEDOWN**. After an equally successful second season, the series jumped to the movie theaters, where it flourished as *Dangerous Detective* (1987), *Dangerous Detective Again* (1988), *The Most Dangerous Detective* (1989), *Dangerous Detective Returns* (1996), and *Dangerous Detective Forever* (1998). Hideaki Anno, the director of *Evangelion* (*AE), had a cameo role as a gun maniac in the final film.

DANGEROUS JOB FOR A SCHOOL GIRL

1991. JPN: *Joshi Kōsei! Kiken na Arbeit.* AKA: *School Girl! Dangerous Job.* PRD: N/C. DIR: N/C. SCR: Masahiro Yoshimoto. CAST: Yumiko Takahashi, Miki Fujitani, Toshikazu Fukawa, Shingo Yamashiro, Miho Takagi. CHN: TBS. DUR: 45 mins. x 3 eps.; Wed 10 September 1991–12 September 1991.

Manga editor Seyama (Yamashiro) and manga artist Yuki (Takagi) consider themselves experts on speaking to the female high school audience but Seyama's daughter Hazuki (Fujitani) is a rebellious teen who doesn't listen to her father's sage advice. Compare to **KING OF EDITORS**.

DANGEROUS LIAISONS

1999. JPN: *Kiken na Kankei.* AKA: *Dangerous Relationship.* PRD: Masatoshi Yamaguchi. DIR: Isamu Nakae, Tatsuaki Kimura, Narihide Mizuta. SCR: Yumiko Inoue. CAST: Etsuji Toyokawa, Norika Fujiwara, Gorō Inagaki, Ryōko Shinohara, Yoshiko Tokoshima, Kimiko Yo, Ken Ishiguro. CHN: Fuji. DUR: 45 mins. x 11 eps.; Thu 14 October 1999–23 December 1999.

Yukiko (Fujiwara) is having trouble at work, where the other detectives look down on her for being a woman. She also risks suspension on trumped-up charges of sexual harassment, brought by the owner of the Miyakoya super-market chain, a high-class shopping business that she suspects, **SOMMELIER**-style, of packaging low-grade wine in high-class bottles. She is just about to climb into a taxi when she is stopped by her impoverished boyfriend Takao (Inagaki), a freelance writer permanently low on cash, who needs to borrow some money. The taxi drives on without her. . . .

After the death of his daughter and his divorce from his wife Hitomi (Tokoshima), taxi driver Shinji (Toyokawa) has led a miserable single life. Having just lost his latest fare, he ends up at Narita airport, where by bizarre coincidence the next passenger

to get into his cab is his former class-mate Yūichirō Tsuzuki (Ishiguro). Yūichirō has been living in Hong Kong for 17 years and has only returned to Japan as the beneficiary of his rich father's will. Barely recognizable after having been away for so long, Yūichirō taunts Shinji with tales of his success and lectures him about the importance of having the right label. In a moment of rage, Shinji murders Yūichirō. While he is clearing evidence from the hotel room, he is approached by Chihiro (Shinohara), a secretary newly assigned to Yūichirō by his father's company. Shinji realizes that not even Yūichirō's family knows what their son looks like and decides to play along. His deception even fools Yūichirō's mother Ayako (Yo), and the imposter becomes the new president of the Tsuzuki family supermarket chain Miyakoya.

Trying to forget his moment of mad-ness, Yūichirō leads a successful, law-abiding life. However, Miyakoya is still under investigation by Yukiko, who is sure that "Yūichirō" looks familiar but can't quite work out where she has seen him before. Her arrival on the scene, voicing her suspicions that *"low-class is posing as high-class"* among the supermarket shelves, causes Shinji to lose his cool. He is prepared to do any-thing to hang on to his newfound life, and is petrified that his former life and heinous crime will catch up with him.

Though some claimed that *DL* was a homage to the Alain Delon vehicle *Plein Soleil* (1959), nobody was really fooled—the more obvious modern inspiration was *The Talented Mr. Ripley* (1999), which was similarly adapted from the novels of Patricia Highsmith. *DL* shares much in common with the superb **OUT**, which also ran on the Fuji network during the same season. Similarities include a female detective fighting office discrimination who becomes romantically involved with a criminal, as well as the discovery of a corpse whose identification threatens the murderer like a ticking time bomb. Compare to **I DON'T NEED LOVE**.

Theme: Mariko Ide—"There Must Be an Angel (Playing With My Heart)." Peak rating: 17.7%.

DAUGHTER-IN-LAW *

1994. JPN: *Chōnan no Yome.* AKA: *Bride of the Eldest Son.* PRD: Seiichirō Kijima. DIR: Jirō Shōno, Hideki Isano, Katsuo Fukuzawa. SCR: Shizuka Ōishi. CAST: Yūko Asano, Junichi Ishida, Yōko Nogiwa, Yasunori Danta, Miki Sakai, Tetsuya Yamaguchi, Masanori Kujo, Akio Kaneda, Kōichi Yamamoto, Rumi Matsumoto, Shirō Sano. CHN: TBS. DUR: 45 mins. x 24 eps., Thu 14 April 1994–7 July 1994 (#1); 45 mins. x 11 eps., 12 October 1995–21 December 1995 (#2).

Happily married life for Misato (Asano) is suddenly disrupted by the death of her father-in-law Shōchirō (Yamamoto). She is forced to live with the surviving members of the Nakamura family, sharing the house with her husband Kenichirō (Ishida), his fearsome mother Setsuko (Nogiwa), and her other two sons. Before long, youngest son Kōsaburō (Yamaguchi) invites someone else to stay: his girlfriend and fellow theater troupe performer Tamako (Sakai). Afraid that Setsuko will kick her out, Tamako pretends that she is pregnant with Kōsaburō's child. When Setsuko discovers the deception, she is so angry that she moves out to stay with second son Yūjirō (Danta). However, she is soon back at home when her spiky temper causes her to fall out with Yūjirō's wife Erika (Anju Suzuki).

Misato is overjoyed to discover that she is pregnant herself, though the family's joyous celebration is curtailed by a miscarriage. While recovering she must mediate between Yūjiro and his wife as they teeter on the brink of divorce. Misato becomes pregnant again but soon before the arrival of the baby, Kenichirō confesses his wish to be transferred to Singapore—but falls prey to a duodenal ulcer. Misato goes back home after Kenichirō's operation only to find Tamako is in labor, this time for real. She sends Kōsaburō and

Daughter of Iguana

© 1996 Asahi

Tamako off to the hospital but soon after that her own labor starts. She drags herself to a hospital and gives birth to a boy.

One of the in-law appeasement dramas that regularly recur on Japanese TV (compare to **BY THE SEA** and **LADY OF THE MANOR**) and likely to enjoy increasing popularity as rising house prices and aging baby boomers make living with one's relatives an increasingly likely occurrence. Deliberately planned as an opening salvo in the ratings war with Fuji, *DiL* eventually trounced its Thursday night rival **LIVE FOR THIS LOVE** with a rating of 25.8%—though writer Ōishi would eventually defect to Fuji with the script for **VINGT-CINQ ANS WEDDING**. A novelization was published by Shūeisha, credited to screenwriter Ōishi. Like the same screenwriter's **MY FATE**, the story was planned for two seasons instead of the traditional stand-alone. An eleven-episode second season, *Daughter-in-Law 2* (1995) replaced the familial tensions with work-related issues—Kenichirō gets a new job as a bank employee, while Misato struggles with freelance life as a *tonkatsu* cook. Both series were broadcast in the U.S. with English subtitles on KIKU TV. Themes: Dreams

Come True—"Wherever You Are," Mari Ōguro—"Aishitemasu" (Love).

DAUGHTER OF IGUANA

1996. JPN: *Iguana no Musume.* AKA: *Iguana's Daughter.* PRD: Yūji Tōjo. DIR: Kazuhisa Imai. SCR: Yoshikazu Okada. CAST: Miho Kanno, Yoshinori Okada, Naomi Kawashima, Masao Kusakari, Reina Komine, Kanako Enomoto, Hitomi Satō. CHN: Asahi. DUR: 45 mins. x 11 eps.; Mon 15 April 1996–24 June 1996.

Rika (Kanno) is a Japanese high school student with a crush on Noboru (Okada). Though she wishes she could talk to him, she is painfully shy because she has never received any approval from her mother Yuriko (Kawashima). Her father Masanori (Kusakari) has always loved her but Yuriko is convinced that Rika is not a human being at all but an iguana. Consequently, she has rebuffed Rika for her entire life, lavishing her attentions on her perky younger daughter Mami (Enomoto).

A highly original twist on the high school romance genre, *Daughter of Iguana* discards Japanese drama's regular *Cinderella* formula in favor of a template derived from *The Little Mermaid.* Amid the usual teenage angst, take

your pick as to which is the more horrific: a girl convinced that she is a reptile or a mother who is prepared to tell her that it's true! After early scenes seemingly inspired by the U.S. sci-fi series *V* (1984), in which a mother screams at her first sight of her scaly offspring, Rika's early life is swiftly glossed in a series of scenes of outstanding maternal neglect. After she spends her savings on a scarf she knows her mother wants, only to be rebuffed yet again, the young Rika tries to commit suicide, only to be saved by a passing boy who predictably turns out to be Noboru. Before long, she has matured into Kanno, who plays her role with the same endearing wallflower clumsiness that characterizes her later **WHERE IS LOVE?** and gamely performs many sequences in a convincing iguana mask whenever she is called upon to appear as her mother sees her.

Opposed by her rival Kaori (Komine) and on occasion by her own sister, Rika hopes to win the heart of her handsome prince, ever fearful that he will find out "her secret" and reject her on reptilian grounds. Meanwhile, Rika hopes to go to the same university as Noboru, where she hopes to become a researcher in abnormal psychology—with her family background, who can blame her?

Based on the manga by Moto Hagio, who also created **THEY WERE ELEVEN**, *Daughter of Iguana* shares its theme with the previous year's *Key the Metal Idol* (*AE), which featured a similar protagonist with severe self-esteem issues. Some small solace is offered by a framing device in which an older Rika tells the iguana's tale as a bedtime story for her own child, thereby reassuring viewers that a happy ending will eventually be forthcoming. The titular "Iguana's Daughter," it transpires, is not the traumatized heroine at all, but the happy girl we see her playing with in each episode's closing credits. Theme: Elton John—"Your Song."

DAWN IN SILVER

1973. JPN: *Akatsuki wa Tada Gin-iro.*

PRD: Kazuo Shibata. DIR: Minoru Hanabusa. SCR: Yoshiki Iwama. CAST: Taizō Sayama, Kyōji Kobayashi, Miyuki Hayata, Satoshi Morizuka, Takao Yamada, Harumi Yomo, Nobuko Suzuki, Hitoshi Ishii. CHN: NHK. DUR: 45 mins. x 6 eps.; Mon 2 April 1973–11 April 1973.

When transfer student Rika (Hayata) arrives at their middle school, all the boys fall in love with her and Ken (Sayama) is no exception. He is ecstatic when the ethereal beauty decides to join his photography club, though initial elation turns to disappointment when she agrees to be their new model, only to have all their photographs somehow fail to come out. But Ken has already realized that there's something out of the ordinary about Rika. Convinced he has seen Rika dematerialize in a shower of silver particles, he visits her hometown where he discovers a letter written in mysterious characters. Rika is actually an alien on a mission to protect the people of Earth from an invasion by her enemies, the people of planet NN83 Minus. The evil inhabitants of NN83 Minus plan to convince the people of Earth that pollution is completely harmless, thereby hastening the destruction of the planet. Such a disaster would also ruin Rika's homeworld, which is bathed in the light reflected from the surface of the Earth—we're not sure how this is supposed to stop happening just because everyone is dead. Ken goes out to rescue Rika from the fourth dimension, while scholars decode the letter and submit the matter to the government, which refuses to take them seriously.

Based on a children's story by Ryū Mitsuse, the author of WIPE OUT THE TOWN, *Gemini Prophecies* (*AE), and several episodes of *Soran the Space Boy* (*AE). Compare to TIME TRAVELER and SCHOOL IN PERIL. Music by Seiichirō Uno.

DAYS

1998. PRD: Yoshikazu Kobayashi. DIR: Isamu Nakae, Hideki Takeuchi,

Narihide Mizuta. SCR: Shizuka Ōishi. CAST: Tomoya Nagase, Miho Kanno, Miki Nakatani, Ken Kaneko. CHN: Fuji. DUR: 45 mins. x 10 eps.; Mon 12 January 1998–23 March 1998.

Factory workers Tetsuya (Nagase from TOKIO) and Shōta (Kaneko) head out for a night on the town, determined to find some women who'll put out. Instead, they end up meeting nail salon beauticians Mayumi (Nakatani) and Sasaki (Kanno) and Tetsuya tears the long sleeve of Mayumi's expensive kimono. A retread of Nagase's earlier nice-but-shy-guy dramas such as THOSE WERE THE DAYS but with added edge in its treatment of the older generation. In the wake of the youth oriented success of BAYSIDE SHAKEDOWN, *Days* was prepared to present the over-thirties as feckless, incompetent, and conniving idiots, such as one scene in which Tetsuya rescues a man from muggers, only to find himself accused of the crime by the drunken and ungrateful victim. Theme: Tamio Okuda—"Sasurai" (Wandering). Peak rating: 23.7%.

DAYS OF GOLD

1978. JPN: *Ōgon no Hibi*. PRD: Susumu Kondō. DIR: Kiyū Okamoto. SCR: Shinichi Ichikawa. CAST: Somegorō Ichikawa (aka Kōshirō Matsumoto), Jinpachi Nezu, Komaki Kurihara, Tetsurō Tanba, Masahiko Tsugawa, Kōji Tsuruta, Ken Ogata, Masako Natsume. CHN: NHK. DUR: 45 mins. x ca. 52 eps.; Sun 8 January 1978–24 December 1978.

Sukezaemon Ruson (Ichikawa) is a merchant who imports vases from the Philippines. The vases are highly valued as tea utensils and he makes a huge profit. Made after the previous year's KAJIN left the entire audience dazed and confused, this was the first *taiga* drama to concentrate on the lives of commoners and the reviled merchant class of the Tokugawa period. *DoG* documents the rise and fall of the merchant city of Sakai, as seen by its most famous resident, the semilegendary Ruson. The story was plotted

by Saburō Shiroyama, who specialized in books with a heavy economic content and was the first *taiga* to be filmed outside Japan. Peak rating: 34.4%.

DEAR BELOVED

1992. JPN: *Shinai naru mono e*. PRD: Tōru Ōta. DIR: Tatsuaki Kimura, Tōru Hayashi, Takeshi Nakazawa. SCR: Hisashi Nozawa. CAST: Yūko Asano, Toshirō Yanagiba, Megumi Yokoyama, Reona Hirota, Aki Mukai, Shigemitsu Ogi, Kaori Koshiba, Miyuki Nakajima, Chōichirō Kawarazaki, Keiko Saitō, Kōichi Satō. CHN: Fuji. DUR: 45 mins. x 12 eps.; Thu 2 July 1992–17 September 1992.

Nagiko (Asano) and Nozomu (Yanagiba) are a happily married couple without children. Nagiko works for a bed company and Nozomu is a sales person at a real estate agency. Nagiko

---

THINGS I LEARNED FROM WATCHING JAPANESE DRAMA

Rain makes you sneeze.
Any injury can be healed with a white sticking-plaster on the cheek.
Sex always leads to pregnancy.
Nothing good will come of foreign travel.
Women in white are psychos (unless they are getting married).
Old women are either mad or Kaoru Yachigusa.
Every Japanese home has a spare green-ink divorce application form.
It's impossible to find a deserted rooftop from which to throw oneself.
If you have a college reunion, someone is going to have an affair.
If you have a college reunion, someone is going to die.
Episode one marriage ☞ episode one widow.
End with a wedding, but not the one everyone expects.

bumps into ex-boyfriend Seiichirō (Satō), who is now separated from his wife and child. Meanwhile, Nozomu begins having clandestine Thursday meetings with Ruiko (Yokoyama), the girl to whom he proposed before he met Nagiko. Seiichirō tells Nagiko that he wants her to have his baby and she confesses that she remains childless with Nozomu because it is Seiichirō's child that she wants. Upon seeing Nozomu and Ruiko together, Nagiko swiftly accepts it as confirmation of his infidelity and sleeps with Seiichirō, which leads to Nozomu demanding a divorce. However, neither can forget the happy days they shared and they meet again with the help of counselor Hondō (Ogi), who brings them back to the seaside resort where they share happy memories and where Nagiko later aborted Nozomu's child. With its terrible misunderstandings, flirtatious expectation, and histrionic drama, *DB* set the tone for an entire subgenre of infidelity dramas, of which two of the most entertaining recent examples are **WEDNESDAY LOVE AFFAIR** and **PARFUM DE LA JALOUSIE**. A novelization was also published, credited to scenarist Nozawa. Miyuki Nakajima, who wrote and sang the theme tune "Asai Nemuri" (Shallow Sleep), appears in a cameo role in the second and last episodes.

DEAR MOTHER

1975. JPN: *Zenryaku Ofukuro-sama*. PRD: Hidehiro Kudō. DIR: Tomoki Tanaka. SCR: Sō Kuramoto. CAST: Kenichi Hagiwara, Tatsuo Umemiya, Mitsuko Oka, Kaoru Yachigusa, Kaoru Momoi, Ryōko Sakaguchi, Hideo Murota, Takuzō Kawatani, Kinuyo Tanaka. CHN: NTV. DUR: 45 mins. x ca. 50 eps.; 17 October 1975–9 April 1976; ?? October 1976–?? April 1977.
Sabu (Hagiwara) leaves his mother (Tanaka) in Yamagata to train as a chef at an exclusive Japanese restaurant at Fukagawa in downtown Tokyo. Sabu falls in love with the technique of his boss Hidetsugu (Umemiya) and they build up a master-apprentice relation-

ship—compare to the later **ANTIQUE**. As befits a script from Sō Kuramoto, writer of **FROM THE NORTH**, much of the action is glossed in epistolary monologues as Sabu writes home to his beloved mother. Kuramoto's own mother died the year before *DM* went into production, leading to a sharp observation of human beings and parent-child relationships, and its subsequent regular appearance on best-ever drama lists, nearly three decades after its original broadcast. A sequel followed in 1976. Actress Kinuyo Tanaka herself passed away four days before the broadcast of the episode in which Sabu attended his mother's funeral.

DEAR WOMAN

1996. PRD: Kazunori Shiokawa. DIR: Akio Yoshida. SCR: Miho Nakazono, Misato Hayashi. CAST: Noriyuki Higashiyama, Shinobu Ōtake, Tomoya Nagase, Marina Watanabe, Yōko Nogiwa. CHN: TBS. DUR: 45 mins. x 10 eps.; Sun 13 October 1996–22 December 1996.
Former sportsman Tamon (Nagase from TOKIO) retires and seeks a job in the real world. Much to his annoyance, he winds up in the personnel division of a big Tokyo company, where his tough superior Kyōko (Ōtake) forces him to work on a project that raises awareness of women's issues and sexual harassment in the workplace. As he grudgingly eases himself out of the all-male world of sports and into the corporate world where women have an equal say, he finds that he is falling in love with Kyōko, though she has a dark secret that she has shared with him alone—compare to **KING OF EDITORS**, another fish-out-of-water story with a sportsman in the main role. There was also a TV special, though we have been unable to determine if it was a sequel or a clip-show using footage from earlier episodes. Theme: Seiko Matsuda— "Sayōnara no Shunkan" (The Moment We Said Goodbye).

DECADE OF TWO

1992. JPN: *Jūnen Ai*. PRD: Yasuo Yagi.

DIR: Akio Yoshida. SCR: Kazuhiko Yūkawa. CAST: Misako Tanaka, Masanori Hamada, Senri Ōe, Keiko Saitō, Anju Suzuki, Kazuya Kimura. CHN: TBS. DUR: 45 mins. x 11 eps.; Fri 16 October 1992–25 December 1992.
In 1982, Aozora Tani (Tanaka) is hastily sneaking out of her married boss's room, where the couple have been conducting a secret affair. She meets Arashi (Hamada), who just escaped from his lover's jealous husband. It transpires that Arashi is also a friend of Masakazu (Ōe), who is dating Aozora's best friend Fumi (Saitō). Aozora decides to confess to Masakazu that she has feelings for him, only to inadvertently do so on Masakazu and Fumi's wedding day. Masakazu jilts Fumi at the altar and runs away with Aozora—the couple eventually marry and have a daughter, Masami. Aozora returns to work, where she begins to have an affair with her subordinate Kōichi (Kimura). At the same time, Masakazu sleeps with Fumi.

Masakazu decides to leave Fumi to start again with Aozora but the vengeful Fumi kidnaps Masami, and Masakazu goes trying to save her. Aozora's mother Aiko (Yumi Shirakawa) suggests to the distressed Aozora that they should run a small hotel. However, Aiko dies in an accident.

In 1992, Arashi returns, having divorced Aozora's younger sister Miyuki (Suzuki), whom he married on the rebound after their disastrous courtship. Aozora opens the hotel to realize her mother's dream and lives there happily with Arashi and Masami—even Fumi comes along to help out! Aozora toys with the idea of marrying Arashi but he is reluctant, considering what happened last time.

One day, the Tokyo police call on Aozora because the pregnant Miyuki has quarreled with her new boyfriend, Kōsuke, over her refusal to marry him. Miyuki wants to live independently like her mother before her. On the way back to her own hotel, Aozora listens a tape that Arashi recorded, in which he says that he has made his mind up to marry her. On Christmas Day, while Arashi delivers gifts to Masami dressed as Santa Claus, Aozora falls down a cliff after slipping on a snowy road. Arashi sets off to look for her in the evening but an accident with a candle causes the hotel to catch fire.

Pure distilled TV drama—where the U.S. series *24* (2001) would cram an hour into 45 minutes, *DoT* crowbars an entire *year* into the same period, shoving 365 days into every episode. A special feature-length TV movie version was broadcast on 8 October 1993, which depicted the events of the entire series as a dream and instead showed the *real* events of Aozora and Arashi's decade—in which they get married, only for him to realize that her heart lies elsewhere. Compare to **INOCHI: LIFE**. Theme: Senri Ōe—"Arigatō" (Thank You).

DELICIOUS LIAISONS

1996. JPN: *Oishii Kankei*. PRD: Yoshikazu Kobayashi. DIR: Shunsaku Kawake. SCR: Hisashi Nozawa, Atsuko Hashibe. CAST: Miho Nakayama, Toshiaki Karasawa, Naoko Iijima, Shin Takuma, Tsuyoshi Kusanagi. CHN: Fuji. DUR: 45 mins. x 10 eps.; Mon 14 October 1996–16 December 1996. When she is 20 years old, rich girl Momoe (Nakayama) is treated to a meal by her gourmet father in celebration of her finding her first job. However, as Momoe savors the most fantastic consommé soup she has tasted in her life, her father collapses and is rushed to hospital. Five years later, Momoe's life is a wreck—her father's death led to the seizure of the family home and Momoe's desertion by her fiancé. She enters a restaurant called Le Petit Lapin and is stunned to discover that she has finally found the chef who made the consommé she can never forget. Meeting chef Oda (Karasawa), she begs him to teach her, in a food oriented variation on the traditional love story—compare to **THE CHEF, SOMMELIER,** or **ANTIQUE**. Based on a 1993 manga by Satoru Makimura,

who also created **IMAGINE**. Theme: Miho Nakayama with MAYO—"Mirai e no Present" (A Present for the Future). Peak rating: 25.5%.

DENZIMAN

1980. JPN: *Denji Sentai Denjiman*. AKA: *Electric Battle Team Denjiman*. PRD: Kazutake Ochiai, Yūyake Usui, Susumu Yoshikawa. DIR: Hirokazu Takemoto, Shigeo Hiroda, Kimio Hirayama, Yoshiaki Kobayashi, Yoshikazu Yoshikawa, Kazushi Hattori. SCR: Masakazu Uehara, Takashi Ezure, Hirohisa Soda, Susumu Takahisa. CAST: Shinichi Yūki, Kenji Ōba, Eiichi Tsuyama, Naoya Uchida, Akira Koizumi, Machiko Soga, Tōru Ōhira. CHN: Asahi. DUR: 25 mins. x 51 eps.; Sat 2 February 1980–31 January 1981.

Three thousand years after they fled from the victorious Vader Clan, the Denzi alien crew of the starship Denziland arrive in the Sol system. With the Vaders close behind them, the Denzi select five "Denziman" protectors to help save the Earth. Unsurprisingly, the Denziman team are a color-coded squad not dissimilar to every other Super Sentai show. They are led by Ippei (Yūki) the Denzi Red, who is a master of karate. Daigorō (Ōba) is Denzi Blue, a former circus acrobat and master of the deadly Blue Screw Kick. Jun (Tsuyama) is Denzi Yellow, a genius scientist and, when brains inevitably fail, master of the Denzi Suplex special attack. Tatsuya (Uchida) is Denzi Green, a former police officer who has sworn to avenge the death of his father at the hands of a Vader-created monster. He is an accomplished marksman and uses the Green Spin Kick as his special attack. The token female is Akira (Koizumi) as Denzi Pink, a former tennis star who has now mastered aikido (more useful for fighting alien invaders) and uses the Denzi Thunder special attack. As well as a jeep and motocycle sidecar combo, the forces of good also have a Denzi Tiger and Denzi Fighter assault vehicles, which can transform and combine into the Dai Tenji giant robot.

Their alien enemies are led by the evil Queen Hedorian (Soga), an interdimensional invader-bitch who experiences extreme pleasure at the sound of human suffering. Hedorian's cohorts include Hedora Shogun, lady spies Mila and Kela, and of course the Vader monster-of-the-week, which she hatches from an egg and sends in to thwart the Denziman team.

Coming after **BATTLEFEVER J** and before **SUNVULCAN** in the Super Sentai chronology, *Denziman*'s greatest claim to fame was the introduction of the goggle/visor helmet design that was to become mandatory on all later installments of the series—one more step closer to the look and feel of the **MIGHTY MORPHIN' POWER RANGERS**. Note that *Battlefever J*'s Battle Kenya, actor Kenji Ōba, graduates from team mascot to second in command in this show. Based on an idea by Saburō Yade—though one is tempted to wonder how long it took "him" to retool the same old Sentai template for another year. With *The Empire Strikes Back* released in 1980, the name "Vader" was particularly popular—it also turned up in the following year's anime *Thunderbirds 2086* (*AE), though it was romanized as "Beyda" for the U.S. audience. Music by Michiaki Watanabe.

DEPARTMENT STORE

1991. JPN: *Depāto! Natsu Monogatari, Depāto! Aki Monogatari*. AKA: *Department Store! Summer Story, Department Store! Autumn Story*. PRD: Kazuko Nozoe. DIR: Masaharu Segawa. SCR:

Takeru Ishihara. CAST: Masahiro Takashima, Hikaru Nishida, Nenji Kobayashi, Yumi Morio, Hidemasa Nakayama, Natsumi Nanase. CHN: TBS. DUR: 45 mins. x 10 eps.; Wed 2 July 1991–3 September 1991 (#1); 45 mins. x 11 eps.; Wed 13th October 1992–22nd December 1992 (#2).

Daisuke (Takashima) is a new recruit at a department store, whose strong sense of fair play puts him at odds with Customer Complaints Manager Suzuki (Kobayashi). But will it win the heart of Daisuke's fellow new arrival Reiko (Nishida)? A sequel series tracked the store's progress through another season. Theme: Hikaru Nishida—"Tokimeite" (Heart Aflutter), Masahiro Yakajima—"Nakiyamanaide" (Don't Stop Crying).

DESSIN *

1997. AKA: *Making It Up to You*. PRD: Motoki Umehara. DIR: Ryōichi Itsukida, Tomoaki Koga, Kazuki Kaneda. SCR: Junya Yamazaki. CAST: Takao Ōsawa, Tomoyo Harada, Shizuka Kudō, Tetsuya Bessho. CHN: NTV. DUR: 45 mins. x 12 eps.; Wed 2 July 1997–17 September 1997.

Art teacher Satoshi (Ōsawa) used to be a painter but gave up two years previously after the suicide of his bitter rival Masato. He meets Masato's former fiancée Sae (Harada) in an art shop and discovers that she has yet to recover from the traumatic events. Feeling partly responsible for her condition, he tries to help out but does not reveal his former association with Masato. Satoshi is drawn to Sae but she has other problems on her mind—her father Toshio is critically ill and the only way she can afford the medical payments is if she agrees to marry Keiichi, the son of one of her father's clients. Meanwhile, Satoshi begins to paint again with Sae as his model and muse. Keiichi suspects (rightly) that there is more to Satoshi's relationship with Sae and checks up on his background. Meanwhile, Keiichi's ex-girlfriend Shōko claims that she is pregnant with his child.

When Satoshi is wounded defending Sae from an attacker, Toshio discovers both the evil nature of Keiichi and Satoshi's guilty secret. However, he agrees to keep Satoshi's rivalry with Masato secret and gives Satoshi his blessing. Satoshi and Sae eventually move in together but a vengeful Keiichi organizes a hostile takeover of Toshio's construction company. The shock proves fatal for Toshio.

Determined to have Sae at all costs, Keiichi sends her a wedding dress but she rebuffs his advances. Faced with a choice between a miserable rich life with Keiichi or happy poverty with Satoshi, she chooses the latter, only to discover that Satoshi is critically ill. Realizing that this is his chance, Keiichi offers another deal. This time, he will pay for Satoshi's medical treatment but the price is Sae's hand in marriage.

True enough, the "kingdom" is Asō Construction, and Keiichi lacks a top hat and twirling moustache but with a loyal princess, ailing father, and evil suitor, *Dessin* is a modern fairy tale. Sae is left with a classic choice between her duty and her emotions. The Japanese drama aspect makes itself felt in the presence of the suicidal fiancée and a consumptive hero—compare to its more successful imitators **LIPSTICK** and **PLEASE GOD! JUST A LITTLE MORE TIME**. Shown subtitled in the U.S. on KIKU TV.

DETECTIVE IN PURSUIT

1996. JPN: *Keiji Ou!*. PRD: Nagafumi Hori. DIR: Kon Ichikawa, Tadayoshi Kurahara, Eiichi Kudō, Yasuo Furuhata, Junya Satō, Toshio Masuda, Seiji Izumi, Shingo Matsubara, Shinichirō Sawai, Tōru Murakawa, Yasuharu Hasebe. SCR: Tatsuo Nogami, Takako Shigemori. CAST: Kōji Yakusho, Hiroshi Fuse, Mieko Harada, Eisuke Tsunoda, Noriko Watanabe. CHN: TVT. DUR: 45 mins. x 25 eps. (1st ep 90 min); 8 April 1996–23 September 1996. Kentarō Sawaki (Yakusho) and Naoharu Majima (Fuse) from the Metropolitan Police are involved in

various cases, in a detective series made as a co-production with Tōei, which drafted in many movie directors to make their own episodes—e.g. journeyman director Hasebe, *Tasmanian Story*'s Furuhata, and Kudō, who made some of the movies in the **SURE DEATH** series. Note the presence of Kon Ichikawa, as well. *DiP* was the first Japanese series to address the issue of internet crime.

DETECTIVE STORY

1979. JPN: *Tantei Monogatari*. PRD: N/C. DIR: Tōru Murakawa, Kiyoshi Nishimura, Yukihiro Sawada, Yasuharu Hasebe, Akira Katō, Keiichi Ozawa, Mitsuyoshi Tobikawa, Yōnosuke Koike. SCR: Shōichi Maruyama, Machiko Nasu, Susumu Saji, Hirokazu Nakajima, Yuki Miyata, Yoshio Shirosaka, Hiroshi Kashiwabara, Eiichi Uchida, Akio Ido, Chiho Katsura, Yōzō Tanaka. CAST: Yūsaku Matsuda, Mikio Narita, Mitsuko Baishō, Michihiro Yamanishi, Nancy Cheney, Kahori Takeda. CHN: NTV. DUR: 45 mins. x 27 eps.; Tue 18 September 1979–1 April 1980. Former cop Shunsaku Kudō (Matsuda) returns from a five-year stint on the streets of San Francisco and sets up office as a private investigator in a shabby building. His time in America has turned him into something of a rebel, riding a white Vespa P150X scooter, smoking foreign Camel cigarettes, and constantly obsessing about the ideal blend of coffee. He also dresses outlandishly, in a black or white suit with colorful shirt, fedora, and sunglasses—undercover surveillance is clearly not his forté, though his experience abroad has made him an excellent marksman. Two penniless girls, wannabe model Nancy (Cheney) and wannabe actress Kahori (Takeda), live in the same building, and eternally fret over whether he is eating properly and wrapping up warm.

Many of Shunsaku's cases involve missing persons (or even a Persian cat), though occasionally he finds himself reluctantly dragged into underworld business such as hunting down lost yakuza money (episode 4) or a missing diamond (episode 24). In the surreal ninth episode, he is hired to find a girl who, according to her brother, has been abducted by aliens. Because Shunsaku has eaten "alien money" (chocolate), he discovers that he is obliged to do the boy's bidding. The high point of the series comes close to the end of its run, in episode 25, when Shunsaku's friend and rival Detective Hattori (Narita) is accused of corruption by a new chief of police. Hattori's subordinate Detective Matsumoto (Yamanishi) asks Shunsaku to help clear Hattori's name—a story which involves Shunsaku fighting opposition from both the criminals and the police.

Supposedly, action-star Matsuda was expected to play his character as an archetypal, hard-boiled cop, although one look at him as Jiipan in HOWL AT THE SUN is enough to establish his rebel credentials. Famously reared in a brothel and a onetime resident of San Francisco himself, his laid-back, talkative private eye was a breath of fresh air for the genre, creating a wave of popularity in Japan equivalent to that of *Magnum P.I.* (1980) in the U.S., and placing *Detective Story* high on top ten lists to this day. However, part of the show's longevity may derive from the tragic fate of Matsuda, who died of cancer at 40, shortly after completing his first big international movie role as the bad guy in Ridley Scott's *Black Rain* (1989). *Detective Story* director Murakawa would go on to make DETECTIVE IN PURSUIT and other crime dramas, while the lead character's name, Shunsaku, would be handed on to the star of the next generation's big detective series, BAYSIDE SHAKEDOWN. Theme: Shōgun—"Bad City."

Detective Story

DEVIL SUMMONER

1997. JPN: *Shin Megami Tensei Devil Summoner.* AKA: *True Goddess Reborn Devil Summoner.* PRD: Yasuharu Okada, Tomoyuki Imai, Akinori Okagawa, Yasushi Fujii. DIR: Atsushi Shimizu, Iwao Takahashi, Mitsunori Hattori, Mikio Hirota, Masaki Daikuwara. SCR: Daisuke Habara, Katsuhiro Takada, Yūki Okano, Mitsuru Hosokawa. CAST: Sōji Masaki, Chiharu Kawai, Hiroko Sakurai, Ayaka Nanami, Akira Ōtani. CHN: TV Tokyo. DUR: 25 mins. x 25 eps.; Sun 5 October 1997–29 March 1998. Private investigator Kyōji (Masaki) ekes out a precarious existence in downtown Yokohama. However, he is no ordinary detective but the inheritor of his father's magical devil-summoning powers. With his shamaness partner Li (Kawai) and her sorceress mother Mari (Sakurai), he fights demonic crime. The first half of the series introduces school girl Kumiko (Nanami), who awakens Kyōji's dormant powers, as well as the evil plot of the demonic Princess Inaruna, who wants to destroy the Earth. Later episodes throw in some more young assistants and add some miniskirted female Dark Summoners to aid Kyōji in his struggles against alternate dimensions. They also introduce handsome male Dark Summoner Tōichirō, played by heart-throb Anza Ōyama, formerly better known as the male lead in the *Sailor Moon* musical. *DS* was the third Tsuburaya show to appear on TV Tokyo in its late-night slot, after WIZARD OF DARKNESS and SCHOOL IN PERIL. It was originally based on the same *Megami Tensei* computer game that was the inspiration for the anime *Digital Devil Story* and *Tokyo Revelation* (*AE). *DS* kept the franchise in the public eye until the release of a further incarnation, the *Pokémon*-inspired *Devichil* in 2000. Though it was broadcast after midnight and hence technically on Sunday morning, some sources still list it as a Saturday night show.

© 2003 Steve Kyte

DEVIL'S KISS

1993. JPN: *Akuma no Kiss*. PRD: Keisuke Miyakegawa. DIR: Tōru Hayashi, Nobuhiro Kamikawa. SCR: Noriko Yoshida. CAST: Yoshie Okuyama, Takako Tokiwa, Eri Fukatsu, Hidetoshi Nishijima, Fukumi Kuroda, Tōru Masuoka. CHN: Fuji. DUR: 45 mins. x 12 eps.; Wed 7 July 1993–22 September 1993.

Misao (Okuyama) has come to Tokyo from Shizuoka to study to become an illustrator for children's books. She takes a part-time job in a kiosk at a train station and unexpectedly meets two old schoolfriends. Mariko (Tokiwa) is also at university but paying the rent through much more dangerous moneymaking schemes, while Sachiko has got a full-time job but signs over large parts of her wages to a religious cult after being raped by her mother's lover. Misao also finds herself in a delicate situation when her new boss, popular artist Rei Kitahara (Kuroda), tries to entice her into a lesbian affair.

Devil's Kiss is a dark study of the different ways temptation can lead people from the path of righteousness, which soon devolves into troubling scenes of rape and violence. It is still notorious a decade later for featuring Tokiwa in an infamous nude scene. Trapped by mounting debt, Mariko is forced to work in the sex industry by loan shark Kaneda (Masuoka). Her pimp Kyōhei finds her a highly stressful but well-paying client and offers her cocaine to numb the experience. This, of course, is all part of the plan and instead of getting out of debt, Mariko has to work even harder to fund her addiction. Kaneda then sends a videotape to her family showing her having sex with a client and threatens to release it as a porn film unless she pays him off. Mariko takes an overdose and is hospitalized, causing her family to hand over the money, though the evil Kaneda releases the video anyway. An irate Kyōhei stabs Kaneda and is killed by Kaneda's vengeful subordinate. Meanwhile, Sachiko must deal with a suicide attempt by her lover's wife, and Rei

attempts to bribe Misao into keeping silent about her lesbianism. Also published as a novel, credited to scriptwriter Yoshida. Theme: Southern All Stars—"Erotic Seven."

DEVIL'S SEASON

1995. JPN: *Ma no Kisetsu*. PRD: Fukuko Ishii. DIR: Yasuo Inoshita. SCR: Akemi Shimizu. CAST: Keiko Matsuzaka, Ayumi Ishida, Kunihiko Mitamura, Ken Tanaka, Jun Inoue. CHN: TBS. DUR: 45 mins. x 12 eps.; Thu 13 April 1995–29 June 1995.

Kyōko (Matsuzaka) lives with her husband Kōsuke (Mitamura) and two children. She attends a class reunion, where she remains incredibly popular with all her old classmates—and speculates as to whether she is happy with the choices she has made in life. The menfolk are particularly taken with her, most notably Yutaka (Tanaka), now a supermarket owner and determined to win her heart no matter what the consequences.

DIAMOND GIRL

2003. PRD: Hideki Inada, Azuma Yabuki. DIR: Hisao Ogura, Masanori Murakami. SCR: Sumino Kawashima, Yūdai Yamaura. CAST: Arisa Mizuki, Shōsuke Tanihara, Gorō Kishitani, Sachie Hara, Masanobu Katsumura, Yumi Shirakawa. CHN: Fuji. DUR: 45 mins. x ca. 11 eps.; 9 April 2003–.

Reika (Mizuki) is 26 years old and a firm believer that it is a woman's sacred duty to be as beautiful as possible. She goes to Australia, supposedly to study English, although she does little except frequent beauty salons and tanning parlors. It is thus not too surprising that the only people she meets are other Japanese nationals, including handsome rookie lawyer Shinichirō Natsume (Tanihara). The couple fall in love but Shinichirō is transferred back to the Morris Makimura Law Firm in Japan. As he prepares to leave, he asks Reika to marry him and the lovestruck girl begins to make preparations for a ceremony to take place after her graduation. She has already ordered a

wedding dress when Shinichirō calls to break it off.

The irate woman dashes back to Japan for an explanation, only to discover that Shinichirō has tired of her superficial ways and her obsession with superficial beauty. Determined to prove that there is more to her than that, she takes a job at his law firm, in a series that combines the American comedy of *Ally McBeal* with the class comedy of REIKO SHIRATORI I PRESUME. Some might also detect an element of the Reese Witherspoon vehicle *Legally Blonde*, here retooled for Arisa Mizuki, the star of LEAVE IT TO THE NURSES.

DIVORCE PARTY

1993. JPN: *Rikon Party*. PRD: N/C. DIR: Shinji Fukuda, Tadakazu Koike. SCR: Takako Suzuki. CAST: Mako Ishino, Naomi Akimoto, Hozumi Gōda, David Itō, Kazuyuki Asano, Hiromi Nakamura. CHN: TBS. DUR: 25 mins. x 40 eps.; Mon 24 May 1993–16 July 1993.

Sawako (Ishino) is a twice-divorced woman, who has turned her experience to her advantage. She now works as a television pundit, advising callers to her program on affairs of the heart and refusing to be ashamed that her marriages have not worked out with fairy-tale endings. Since 20% of all real-life TBS broadcasts comprise news-related, panel-based "wide shows" such as those featured in this series, the set budget must have been easy to maintain.

DO WE HAVE A TOMORROW?

1991. JPN: *Oretachi ni Asu wa Kuru no ka*. PRD: N/C. DIR: Makoto Kiyohiro. SCR: Michio Shimizu. CAST: Nenji Kobayashi, Manabu Fukuhara, Kumiko Akiyoshi, Itaru Takashina. CHN: TBS. DUR: 45 mins. x 5 eps.; Sun 27 January 1991–26 May 1991.

Ichirō (Kobayashi) pocketed five million yen from work. He runs away from Tokyo with his lover Taeko (Akiyoshi) and his eleven-year-old son Tomoo (Fukuhara). The trio start living and working at the remote Tsukamoto Farm, although Ichirō is an idle laborer, preferring to steal from others instead of doing an honest day's work. Compare to COUNTRY LIVING and BLUE BIRD.

DO WE LOVE EACH OTHER!

1989. JPN: *Aishiatteru kai!*. PRD: Yoshiaki Yamada, Tōru Ōta. DIR: Yasuyuki Kusuda, Kōzō Nagayama. SCR: Shinji Nojima. CAST: Takanori Jinnai, Kyōko Koizumi, Toshirō Yanagiba, Emi Wakui, Ritsuko Tanaka, Atsushi Kondō. CHN: Fuji. DUR: 45 mins. x 10 eps.; Mon 16 October 1989–18 December 1989.

Ippei (Jinnai) is a teacher at South Aoyama High School. Fubuki (Koizumi) is a teacher at the neighboring Omotesandō Girls High. Though the pair are supposed to set an example for their students, they cannot help arguing every time they meet, an upbeat variant on *Much Ado About Nothing* for the 20th century.

The series was capped on 4 April 1990 by a feature-length edit and coda, replaying the final episode with additional footage. At the student graduation, Ippei addresses his students using the words of the drama's title: *"Do we love each other, or what?"* Meanwhile, Fubuki confesses to Ippei's student Jun (Tanaka) that she genuinely does have feelings for Ippei, even though she is unable to resist fighting with him. She prepares to leave quietly for England where she can be away from his influence. The would-be lovers are finally united at Narita airport, where Ippei confesses his feelings for Fubuki. After they have kissed, she stares deeply into his eyes and says, *"I still don't like you."* An early series for the master dramatist Shinji Nojima, *DWLEO* was followed by another comedy, LOVE IS A WONDERFUL THING. Compare to I WANT TO HUG YOU!, another of the series that set the pace for 1990s trendy drama, complete with the telltale exclamation mark in the title. Theme: Kyōko Koizumi— "Gakuen Tengoku" (School Heaven).

DOCTOR HIIRAGI

1995. JPN: *Gekai Hiiragi Matasaburō*.

AKA: *Surgeon Hiiragi*. PRD: Masaru Takahashi. DIR: Masahiro Nakano. SCR: Mitsuo Kuroto. CAST: Kenichi Hagiwara, Naoki Hosaka, Saya Takagi, Izumi Igarashi, B-saku Satō. CHN: Asahi. DUR: 45 mins. x 23 eps.; Thu 6 July 1995–28 September 1995; 17 October 1996–19 December 1996.

Surgeon Matasaburō Hiiragi (Hagiwara) is placed at a notorious hospital. He prays before every operation to the Big Dipper and his colleagues regard him as an eccentric nuisance at first but soon come to respect him. At the end of the first 13-episode season, Matasaburō leaves to become a volunteer doctor in Africa (a decision pastiched in 24-HOUR ER), only to be called back for the second season when Chairwoman Kyōko (Kaoru Yachigusa) asks him to help reorganize the hospital. Broadcast without English subtitles in the U.S. on KTSF TV. Theme: B'z—"I Love You."

DOCTOR, THE

1999. JPN: *Za Doctor*. PRD: Mitsunori Morita. DIR: Mitsunori Morita, Takamichi Yamada, Miki Nemoto, Kenjirō Kurata. SCR: Kenji Nakazono. CAST: Shinichi Tsutsumi, Kazushige Nagashima, Yōko Nogiwa, Takaoki Saki, Riona Hazuki. CHN: TBS. DUR: 45 mins. x ca. 11 eps.; Sun 4 July 1999–?? September 1999.

Rivalry between a surgeon and a specialist in internal medicine, but the surgeon is played by Nagashima, the real-life son of the manager of the Yomiuri Giants baseball team. This, apparently, is enough to get some dramas commissioned.

DOCTOR ON CALL

1992. JPN: *Ōshin Doctor no Jiken Carte*. PRD: N/C. DIR: Makito Takai. SCR: Shinichi Ishikawa. CAST: Kyōhei Shibata, Chiaki Matsubara, Masayuki Watanabe, Harumi Inoue, Leo Morimoto. CHN: Asahi. DUR: 45 mins. x 11 eps.; Thu 13 October 1992–22 December 1992.

Former prison doctor Yūki (Shibata) is

invited to help his old friend Onodera (Morimoto) at a Shinjuku clinic. But Onodera is killed in an accident, which his wife Atsuko (Matsubara) claims to have been the result of drunk driving. Yūki inherits Onodera's practice and also a deepening mystery as to the exact events that led to the death of his friend. Theme: Masaki Ueda— "Wagamama" (Selfishness).

DOKU

1996. PRD: Mikako Kurihara. DIR: Tatsuaki Kimura. SCR: Yoshikazu Okada. CAST: Narumi Yasuda, Shingo Katori, Kippei Shiina, Miho Kanno, Rikako Murakami. CHN: Fuji. DUR: 45 mins. x 10 eps.; Thu 17 October 1996–19 December 1996.

Frustrated office lady Yuki (Yasuda) realizes her true vocation while on holiday in Vietnam. Back in Tokyo, she quits her former job and passes the exams to teach English as a foreign language. Her horrified family fret that now she will never find a husband, while her friend Amamiya (Shiina) also disapproves but only because it will reduce his opportunities to confess his true feelings for her. Missing the kind of food she ate on vacation, Yuki enters a Vietnamese restaurant, only to find that Doku (Katori from SMAP), the boy who first inspired her to become a teacher, is working there. Intending to study at Japan's prestigious Waseda University, he has come to Tokyo to learn Japanese and coincidentally happens to be in the first Japanese class that Yuki is assigned to teach.

Doku is an entertaining mix of romance and internationalism and a prophetic vision of things to come. Five years after it was voted best drama of its season, Japanese television was awash with similar fish-out-of-water dramas, partly shot abroad for additional exoticism and produced with an injection of foreign money. For a non-Japanese audience (which accounts for most readers of this book), part of the appeal lies in the recreation of familiar stereotypes and situations from

Doku

Japanese language classes and, indeed, from *gaijin* life in Japan—you never forget the first time a Japanese cop stops you in the street just for being a foreigner. Similar comedy classrooms also appear in **FALSE LOVE** and **THE SNIPER**. Theme: Miki Imai—"Pride." Peak rating: 19.8%.

DON'T CALL ME PAPA

1972. JPN: *Papa to Yobanaide*. PRD: Tōru Ueno. DIR: Hiroshi Senno. SCR: Hiroshi Matsuki. CAST: Tetsuo Ishidate, Kaoru Sugita, Miyako Nagauchi, Shirō Ōsaka, Chieko Misaki, Manami Fuji. CHN: NTV. DUR: 45 mins. x ?? eps.; [broadcast times unknown].
After the death of his sister, harassed salaryman Sakyō (Ishidate) is forced to care for his niece Chiharu (Sugita). An immensely successful show in its time, *DCMP* still appears on viewers' popularity polls to this day, with influences that can still be felt in contemporary reluctant surrogate parent dramas from **NEWS WOMAN** to **BASICALLY NICE**. Ishidate's exasperated *"Chi-bō!"* (pet name for Chiharu) catchphrase entered into 1970s slang, while the series even drew a crowd of non-comedy fans, keen to gawk at Sugita, whose offscreen love tribulations kept the series in the public eye.

DON'T CALL ME PRIME MINISTER

1997. JPN: *Sōri to Yobanaide*. AKA: *Farewell Mr. Premier*. PRD: Shizuo Sekiguchi. DIR: Masayuki Suzuki. SCR: Kōki Mitani. CAST: Masakazu Tamura, Honami Suzuki, Michitaka Tsutsui, Masahiko Nishimura. CHN: Fuji. DUR: 45 mins. x 11 eps.; Wed 8 April 1997–17 June 1997.
With his party at their lowest ever ebb in the opinion polls, a new prime minister (Tamura) has political office unexpectedly thrust upon him. Knowing there is little chance of hanging on to power for long, he determines to do the best he can and tries to avoid setting a record for the shortest ever term. A political satire set in an imaginary country, starring **NINZABURŌ FURUHATA**'s Tamura as a politician who seeks homespun advice from his maid and his plucky daughter. Shown unsubtitled in the U.S. on the cable channel WMBC. Compare to **MAYOR IN LOVE**. Peak rating: 22.6%.

DON'T CRY KIYOKO

1975. JPN: *Kiyoko wa Nakumon ka*. PRD: Seiji Akiyama. DIR: Kimio Hatada, Hiroshi Watanabe. SCR: Yoshiki Iwama. CAST: Hiroyo Funabashi, Takato Igarashi, Jun Funaki, Toshie Kobayashi, Manami Furui, Baku Numata. CHN: NHK. DUR: 25 mins. x 6 eps.; Mon 17 March 1975–26 March 1975.
Kiyoko (Funabashi) is an eleven-year-old girl who lives in a shabby apartment near a factory. Her classmate Masao (Igarashi), aka Beramatcha, lives in the same block. Kiyoko writes a love letter to her classmate Ishino, for which she is teased by her classmates Tomoko and Hisae. Beramatcha also makes fun of her, though secretly he has a crush on her himself. The two are brought together through the efforts of Kiyoko's neighbor Uchida (Numata), a salesman who dreams of living on a remote island. When the children both do poorly in a math exam, it is Uchida who tells Kiyoko how bad Beramatcha is feeling and encourages her to study with him—Beramatcha's sister (Furui) has run off with her boyfriend, making life even lonelier for the boy.
A poor man's **OSHIN**, as an impoverished schoolgirl dreams about a richer, happier life and befriends a boy who is similarly downtrodden. Meanwhile, Kiyoko's drunken father (Funaki) gets into trouble with the yakuza, though Beramatcha saves the day by scaring them off. Based on the story *Machikado no Kaze* (*Breeze on a Street Corner*) by Ryōji Kawakami.

DON'T LEAVE ME ALONE

1995. JPN: *Hitori ni Shinaide.* PRD: Kazuhiko Takahashi. DIR: Shōji Fujita. SCR: Noriko Yoshida. CAST: Chikako Kaku, Takanori Jinnai, Mikihisa Azuma, Miki Mizuno, Masaya Katō. CHN: Fuji. DUR: 45 mins. x 12 eps.; Fri 7 July 1995–22 September 1995.

Import/export company communications director Chiharu (Kaku) fully expects to settle down one day with fellow employee Mikami (Katō), just as soon as they both overcome their shyness. She is therefore somewhat taken aback when Mikami proudly announces that he will shortly be marrying someone else—leading Chiharu to storm off in anger to a baseball batting range, where she meets another romantic possibility and one she's less prepared to allow to slip away. Theme: Globe—"Feel Like Dance."

DON'T NEED A MAN

1994. JPN: *Otoko wa Iranai.* PRD: Shunichi Kobayashi. DIR: Shunichi Kobayashi. SCR: Hirokazu Fuse, Yūko Kanaya. CAST: Pinko Izumi, Yasuko Matsuyuki, Harue Akagi, Teruhiko Saigō, Hanako Miyagawa. CHN: Yomiuri. DUR: 45 mins. x 10 eps.; Thu 20 October 1994–22 December 1994.

Fourteen years after divorcing her womanizing husband, the plucky Tokiko (Izumi) is an employee at a business cleaning company and a part-time private investigator. Her daughter Yuki (Matsuyuki) thoroughly disapproves of her mother's lifestyle and decides to go in search of her long-lost father. A minor diversion for Izumi, the regular star on several long-running serials including **MAKING IT THROUGH.**

DON'T WORRY

1998. PRD: Toyohiko Wada, Yūji Ōhira. DIR: Yasuyuki Kusuda, Satoru Nakajima. SCR: Satoko Okudera, Akira Tomozawa, Masahiro Yoshimoto. CAST: Masahiko Kondō, Maiko Kikuchi, Kumiko Endō, Shunsuke Nakamura. CHN: Kansai. DUR: 45 mins. x 12 eps.; Wed 14 April 1998–30 June 1998.

Deep in debt, Shintarō (former pop idol Kondō) takes a job as a driver for the debt collector to whom he still owes money. He rents a room on the second floor of a run-down building but the previous owner's "Private Investigations" business sign keeps attracting unwelcome visitors. Eventually, Shintarō realizes that there could be money in it and instead of turning clients away, he begins to pose as a detective. Theme: Masahiko Kondō—"King and Queen."

DON'T YOU LIKE IT?

1992. JPN: *Kirai ja Nai ze.* PRD: N/C. DIR: Ikuhiro Saitō. SCR: Izō Hashimoto. CAST: Hironobu Nomura, Naomi Zaizen, Shōko Aida, Toshinori Kanda, Ari Nakae, Ryūji Harada. CHN: TBS. DUR: 45 mins. x 12 eps.; Thu 2 July 1992–24 September 1992.

Keigo (Nomura) is posted to the Aiga System School at the foot of Mount Fuji as a teacher. When he gets there, he is surprised to see bars on every window of the classrooms. His fellow traveler, student Misato (Harada), is taken away when he shows a rebellious attitude. Keigo realizes that this institution is not like other schools in the area. . . . Compare to **CHALLENGE FROM THE FUTURE.**

DOUBLE KITCHEN

1993. PRD: Chihiro Kameyama, Seiichirō Kijima. DIR: Tatsuaki Kimura, Akio Yoshida. SCR: Yumie Nishiogi, Toshiharu Matsubara. CAST: Tomoko Yamaguchi, Masanobu Takashima, Yōko Nogiwa, Shirō Itō, Shirō Sano, Megumi Yokoyama. CHN: TBS. DUR: 45 mins. x 11 eps.; Fri 16 April 1993–25 June 1993.

When they return from their honeymoon, newlyweds Miyako (Yamaguchi) and Shinobu (Takashima) discover that they are now forced to share a house, not merely with Miyako's parents Machiko (Nogiwa) and Keizo (Itō) but also with her two troublesome younger sisters. *DK* features in-law appeasement in the style of **LADY OF THE MANOR** and **DAUGHTER-IN-LAW,**

Double Score

but is a disappointing offering from the writer of the superior **CAMPUS NOTES** and **SWEET HOME.** Shown unsubtitled in the U.S. on the International Channel. Theme: Princess Princess—"Dakara Honey" (So, Honey . . .).

DOUBLE SCORE

2002. PRD: Hisao Kogure. DIR: Makoto Hirano, Masanori Murakami, Yoshinori Kobayashi. SCR: Toshio Terada, Higashi Yabuki. CAST: Takashi Sorimachi, Manabu Oshio, Risa Sudō, Yoshinori Okada, Kazuyuki Aijima, Rikako Murakami. CHN: Fuji. DUR: 45 mins. x 11 eps.; Tue 8 October 2002–?? December 2002.

Maverick cop Shinnosuke (Sorimachi) has an arrest record of 95% but wastes a large amount of time filling in paperwork to answer all the complaints brought about by his unorthodox methods. Much to his annoyance, he is assigned the straight-laced Etsurō (Oshio) as a partner. The idea of mismatched buddies must appear old even to those whose memories only extend as far back as **BAYSIDE SHAKEDOWN.** And yet, presumably such ideas become clichés because they work—Fuji TV's press release had the gumption to call this a "new kind of police story," despite drawing comparisons with

© 2002 Fuji

Miami Vice and *Beverly Hills Cop!*
Theme: Chemistry—"It Takes Two."

DOWN AND OUT *

1998. JPN: *Pu Pu Pu*. PRD: Tamon
Tanba. DIR: Ken Yoshida, Nobuhiro Doi,
Fuminori Kaneko. SCR: Machiko Nasu,
Yuriko Takeda. CAST: Gō Morita, Ken
Miyake, Junichi Okada, Akiko Kinouchi,
Momoko Kurasawa, Jōji Tokoro. CHN:
TBS. DUR: 45 mins. x 11 eps.; Fri 9
October 1998–18 December 1998.
Hayato (Morita), Rikuo (Miyake), and
Kazuya (Okada) are three rebellious
teens who meet up at Narita Airport.
All three are heading for Los Angeles
despite their parents' opposition but
arrive to discover that their trendy
school has gone bankrupt—compare
to a similar setup in *Tenamonya Voyagers*
(*AE). Conned by a fellow Japanese
citizen, they are deported by U.S.
immigration and arrive back in Japan
penniless and downhearted. They
begin a series of moneymaking ventures, including working in an illegal
casino and selling tickets to an "air
stewardess party" which lacks any air
stewardesses. Their parents are soon
back on the scene with a series of disapproving glances but the boys struggle on. Girlfriend troubles and house
hunting add to their problems, though
the series eventually takes a turn for
the maudlin, as some of the characters
are forced to face up to their responsibilities to their families and ultimately
to each other.

The three stars are the three
youngest members of the boy band V6,
collectively known as Coming Century.
A promising American beginning is
shown up to be little more than a
sneak vacation for the cast, as the series
swiftly returns to everyday Japan and a
typical drama of semi-rebellion.
Broadcast in the U.S. with English subtitles on KIKU TV. Theme: V6—"Over."
Peak rating: 15.9%.

DOWNTOWN DETECTIVES

1991. JPN: *Downtown Tanteigumi '91*.
PRD: N/C. DIR: Hideo Sakurai. SCR:
Katsuyuki Nakamura. CAST: Morio

Kazama, Kirin Kiki, Azusa Nakamura,
Miyako Yamaguchi, Ai Yasunaga. CHN:
Asahi. DUR: 45 mins. x 10 eps.; Mon 7
October 1991–16 December 1991.
After thirteen generations as a power-
ful yakuza syndicate, the Minatogumi is
dissolved by its last leader Shintarō
(Kazama) who sets up a private investi-
gation service with his sister Yuki
(Yasunaga) and his henchmen Taku
(Yūsuke Mikado) and Satoru (Shinichi
Sawato).

DREAMS OF ROMANCE *

2001. JPN: *Koi wa Nannen Sundemasu
ka*. AKA: *How Many Years to Wait for
Love; No Lover; Are You In Love?*. PRD:
Michihiko Umezawa, Ikuhide Yokochi,
Kōichi Nagata. DIR: Shimako Satō,
Renpei Tezuka. SCR: Reiko Yoshida,
Noriko Gotō. CAST: Kyōko Koizumi,
Naoko Iijima, Hitomi Kuroki, Tōru
Nakamura, Hideaki Itō, Akiko Yada,
Yūichirō Yamaguchi, Kazufumi
Miyazawa. CHN: TBS. DUR: 45 mins. x
10 eps.; Fri 19 October 2001–21
December 2001.
Yūko (Koizumi) is a thirtysomething
wife and mother trying not to admit
that she is unhappy. Her husband
Ryōhei (Nakamura) won her over by
comforting her when she was suffering
from a broken heart, and although she
does not believe he is the one perfect
Mr. Right, she tells her acquaintances
at the local beauty parlor that she is as
happy as can be expected. She reasons
that it would have been counterpro-
ductive to wait for "true love"—hence
the show's interrogative Japanese title
and the characters' glib answer: a million years. Deep down, Yūko is faintly
envious that her old friends still get to
have careers and parties, while she is
seeing the children off to school. She
also yearns for her old high school
flame Kenichi (Miyazawa), never
expecting to meet him again. Unsurprisingly (for us), when her family goes
to a furniture store to buy a new dining
table, carpenter Kenichi turns out to
be the owner, though he and Yūko initially pretend they have never met
before.

Meanwhile, fellow beauty parlor customer Mayumi (Iijima) is also faintly
disappointed with life. She fell in love
with husband Ichirō when he was
appearing onstage in *Hamlet* but now
finds herself supporting a depressed,
unemployed actor. In an entertaining
reversal of the traditional "honey I'm
home" scenario, Ichirō gamely tries to
reinvent himself as a househusband,
only to become sullen and resentful
when his breadwinner wife does not
come straight home from the office.

Sakiko (Kuroki), the owner of the
beauty parlor, has difficulties of a different nature. While her husband is
away on business, she is trying to set up
her daughter Risa (Yada) with a suitable boy. She attends an *omiai* meeting
with Hiroshi (Itō), one of her husband's juniors but when Risa fails to
turn up, the two dine together and
Sakiko finds herself flirting with the
man she is supposed to be introducing
to her daughter. Meanwhile, Risa, who
later claims to have been detained by a
crisis at the house of one of her female
friends, is keeping a secret from her
mother. In fact, she is having an affair
with a married man—Yūko's husband
Ichirō!

Writer Yoshida, who so successfully
strafed modern morals in **ARRANGED
MARRIAGE** and **NARITA DIVORCE**, returns
for another run here, presumably also
recycling a little of her research for
WIPE YOUR TEARS to supply the carpenter character of Kenichi. Unlike the
sensationalist **PARFUM DE LA JALOUSIE**,
which played on TV Asahi during the
same season and on the same day, *DoR*
builds tension with a confidently slow
pace—we are well into the second
episode before the shadow of infidelity
starts to fall. Such a leisurely attitude
allows the audience to enjoy Iijima cast
against type as a housewife, as well as
numerous amusing Freudian hints of
what is to come, such as Hiroshi's habit
of inadvertently dipping his tie in his
dinner whenever he talks to his blush-
ing would-be mother-in-law. Also published in novel form, credited to writer
Yoshida. Broadcast in the U.S. with

English subtitles on KIKU TV and KTSF TV and Asahi Homecast. Theme: Yuki Koyanagi—"Remain—Kokoro no Kagi" (Remain—Key to Your Heart).

DRUM CANNA

2002. JPN: *Drum Canna no Bōken*. AKA: *Adventures of Drum Canna*. PRD: N/C. DIR: N/C. SCR: Yasunari Suda. CAST: (voices) Juri Ihata, Tomoharu Sugaya, Keiko Han, Ryūzō Ishino. CHN: NHK2. DUR: 15 mins. x 36 eps.; 9 September 2002–19 December 2002.
Canna Mochizuki (Ihata) is a young girl who is transported by a magical trash can to the alternate world of Gomilly Hills (Jpn. *gomi* = trash), where she meets residents, all of whom are made of trash. This modern NHK puppet show in the spirit of the classic **Madcap Island** was augmented with animation and computer graphics from anime studio 4°C. NB—a *drumcan* in Japanese is an oil drum.

DYNAMAN *

1983. JPN: *Kagaku Sentai Dynaman*. AKA: *Science Battle Team Dynaman*. PRD: Moritaka Katō, Yasuhiro Tomita, Seiji Abe, Takeyuki Suzuki. DIR: Shōhei Tōjō, Kazushi Hattori, Minoru Yamada, Nagafumi Hori. SCR: Hirohisa Soda, Takayoshi Miki, Kyōko Sagiyama, Takeshi Terada, Isamu Matsumoto, Ichirō Yamanaka, Shunsuke Yoshida. CAST: Satoshi Okita, Junichi Kasuga, Shōji Unoki, Yū Tokita, Sayoko Hagiwara, Takeshi Watabe. CHN: Asahi. DUR: 25 mins. x 51 eps.; Sat 5 February 1983–28 January 1984.
The long-forgotten Jassinca ("*Evil*ution") race, who have hidden in the depths of the Earth for centuries, return to seize control of the surface world. Professor Hiroshi Yumeno, a researcher into dream therapy, realizes that the Jassinca are coming and recruits the five-member Dynaman team to hold off the invasion and make their dreams a reality. The team leader is Hokuto (Okita) or Dyna Red, whose dream is to make a power source that does not pollute the environment. When not thinking inventive thoughts, he fights with a Dyna Sword. Ryū (Kasuga) is Dyna Black, whose dream is to make contact with extraterrestrials. He is also the descendant of the Iga ninja clan and a specialist in covert operations. Yōsuke (Unoki) is Dyna Blue, whose dream is to be able to live and breathe permanently underwater with the aid of artificial gills. Kōsaku (Tokita) is Dyna Yellow, a part-time gardener whose dream is to create ideal yields from crops. Rei (Hagiwara) is the token female Dyna Pink, whose dream is to acquire a machine that will enable her to communicate with animals. Nine-tailed Emperor Aton (Watabe) is the dastardly leader of the Jassinca, while seven-tailed General Kar is his subordinate and leader of the army of single-tailed Tailmen who form the cannon fodder of his invasion. Greater dangers provided by the obligatory monster of the week are thwarted by the Dynaman team's special vehicles. Dyjupiter is a giant caterpillar track vehicle, from which the team can launch in their big rig, tank, and jet mini-vehicles. These in turn can combine to make a sword-wielding giant robot, called Dyna Garry. No, really—"based on an idea by Saburō Yade," who obviously thought Garry would be a great name for a robot. *Dynaman* was preceded in the Super Sentai series by **Goggle-V**, and followed by **Bioman**. Music by Kensuke Kyō.

Six episodes of *Dynaman* were later dubbed in parody form for the USA Network, and broadcast in 1988 as part of the show *Night Flight*—this is the only appearance of the series in the English language.

E

E.S.
2001. JPN: *Kiken na Tobira: Ai o Tejo de Tsunagu Toki*. AKA: *Dangerous Door: When Handcuffs Love*. PRD: Katsuhiro Masui. DIR: Shinori Yoshida, Keita Motohashi. SCR: Junya Yamazaki. CAST: Jun Toba, Chiaki Hara, Yūko Itō, Shigeki Hosokawa, Masakazu Mimura, Wakana Sakai, Rie Tomosaka, Kōichi Iwaki. CHN: Asahi. DUR: 45 mins. x 11 eps.; Sat 14 April 2001–30 June 2001.

Detective Izumi (Hara) is solving a murder case at a hospital, in a drama that manages to disappoint, despite featuring piles of dead bodies and a love affair between Izumi and the prime suspect Yū (Toba).

EDGE OF THE WORLD *
1994. JPN: *Kono Yo no Hate*. AKA: *End of This World*. PRD: Tōru Ōta. DIR: Isamu Nakae. SCR: Shinji Nojima. CAST: Honami Suzuki, Hiroshi Mikami, Sachiko Sakurai, Etsuji Toyokawa, Ryūichi Ōura, Megumi Yokoyama, Kazuko Yoshiyuki, Masaru Matsuda. CHN: Fuji. DUR: 45 mins. x 12 eps.; Mon 10 January 1994–28 March 1994.

After she caused her sister's blindness in a fire, Maria (Suzuki) is holding down two jobs as a postal worker by day and a nightclub hostess at night in order to pay for a restorative operation. She saves former pianist Shirō (Mikami) from an accident and, discovering that he has amnesia, takes him home. The two become lovers but Shirō's wife Yuriko eventually ruins their fun by asking for him back. After Maria tries to injure his hand, Shirō realizes that she wants him free of his career and smashes his own hand so that he can never play the piano again.

Meanwhile, Maria's sister Nana (Sakurai) is working at a flower shop and meets Jun (Ōura) who has a scar on his left cheek. Although she opens her heart to him, she soon refuses him when she learns that he is a convenience store robber.

Jealous of Shirō's relationship with Maria, Rumi (Yokoyama) turns him into a cocaine addict. Maria announces that she is pregnant but miscarries after she is assaulted by Shirō. The distraught woman throws herself in front of a car to commit suicide but survives. As she recuperates, Maria decides to marry the wealthy Kamiya (Toyokawa) who has been trying to win Maria's heart.

Nana starts living with her mother Yūko (Yoshiyuki) who soon dies, leaving her corneas to her blind daughter. With her sight restored, Nana realizes that the man who has been sending her love letters in braille is Jun, the rebuffed robber writing to her from jail.

Shirō tries to extort money from Kamiya, claiming that he needs to be paid off if he is to stay away from Maria. But Kamiya reminds him that Maria has made her own decision and that Kamiya is no longer part of her life. Meanwhile Rumi's ex-boyfriend Sasaki throws acid in her face in revenge for being dumped. The disfigured Rumi kills Sasaki and lures Maria to a deserted warehouse but she is stopped by her new boyfriend Ino (Matsuda), who plucks out his own eyes to assure her that her looks don't matter to him.

One doesn't need to look at the credits to realize this a Shinji Nojima drama, in the spirit of his later **LIPSTICK**. Piling on melodramatic favorites, from a blind flower seller to a man *"who'll never play the piano again,"* *EotW* has to be one of Nojima's darkest dramas, even to the bittersweet finale, in which Shirō puts in an appearance at Kamiya's wedding to Maria. Broadcast with English subtitles in the U.S. on the multicultural channel KTSF TV, though the reaction of San Francisco Bay Area citizens to its Greek tragedy roster of maimings, blindings, stalkings, and suicides is not recorded. Theme: Yutaka Ozaki—"Oh My Little Girl." Note that pop idol Ozaki himself died aged 27 in 1992, making the choice of this song from his first album particularly poignant for the Japanese audience.

EISENBORG
1977. JPN: *Kyoryū Daisensō Aizenborg*. AKA: *Dinosaur War Eisenborg*. PRD: Takashige Niimi. DIR: Kanji Ōtsuka, Kazuho Manda, Jun Ōki, Toshihiko Nakajima. SCR: Keiichi Abe, Hiroyasu

Yamaura, Kazuo Takagiwa, Bunzō
Wakatsuki, Narimitsu Taguchi, Yasushi
Hirano. CAST: Kyōnosuke Kami, Yōko
Asagami, Shingo Kanemoto, Junpei
Takiguchi, Tetsuo Mizushima, Jun
Hazumi. CHN: TV Tokyo. DUR: 25 mins. x
39 eps.; Fri 7 October 1977–30 June
1978.
The dinosaurs have survived in secret
to the present day, hidden in underground caverns. Their leader Ulul
(Takiguchi), a dinosaur with an IQ of
over 300, decides it is time to reclaim
the surface world. Professor Tachibana
is killed trying to stop them and his
children Ai (Asagami) and Zen (Kami)
are gravely injured. Tachibana's fellow
scientists give them cybernetic augmentation to save their lives, and they
become the newest members of the
anti-dinosaur taskforce Team D. They
can also fuse together to form the
Super Aizen cyborg when the day calls
for a giant robot, which is rather often.
The follow-up to **BORN FREE**, splicing
stop motion and cel animation into the
live-action sections. After episode 20,
the dinosaur threat was replaced by
Goddess the Evil Witch-Queen
(Hazumi), who invaded with aliens
from planet Gazaria.

ELIGIBLE
1994. JPN: *Tekireiki*. PRD: Takamichi
Yamada. DIR: Toshiyuki Iijima. SCR:
Kenichi Iwasa. CAST: Hiroshi Mikami,
Momoko Kikuchi, Tomoko Nakajima,
Yasufumi Terawaki, Hitomi Takahashi.
CHN: TBS. DUR: 45 mins. x 12 eps.; Fri
15 April 1994–1 July 1994.
Highly-paid yuppie researcher Shōhei
(Mikami) is looking forward to his
imminent marriage to Makoto
(Kikuchi), when he receives a shocking
message from his home village. His
elder brother has been adopted as heir
by the childless neighboring manor,
obligating Shōhei, as the next in line,
to return to the remote countryside
and manage the family farm. Compare
to **COUNTRY LIVING** and **LADY OF THE
MANOR**. Theme: Hiroshi Mikami—"A
Place in the Heart."

ELOPEMENT APPROACHES
1995. JPN: *Kakeochi no Susume*. PRD:
Keiji Tatara. DIR: Keiji Tatara. SCR:
Satsuo Endō. CAST: Tomoya Nagase,
Hiromi Nagasaku, Takashi Naitō, Mai
Takarao, Pierre Taki. CHN: Asahi. DUR:
45 mins. x 9 eps.; 3 July 1995–11
September 1995.
Tamotsu (Nagase) and his private tutor
Yui (Nagasaku) go on vacation to a hot
springs resort, where they begin an
illicit affair. Just as they are getting into
bed together, they are disturbed by
Gorō (Naitō) and his mistress Hinako
(Takarao), who rush in from the next
room in a panic after a botched double
suicide.

EMERGENCY HEART SURGERY
1999. JPN: *Kyūkyū Heart Chiryōshitsu*.
PRD: Tadashi Shibata, Kazushisa Andō.
DIR: Yasuyuki Kusuda, Yoshishige
Miyake. SCR: Noriko Nakayama. CAST:
Naomi Zaizen, Kotomi Kyōno. CHN: Fuji.
DUR: 45 mins. x ca. 11 eps.; Tue 6 July
1999–?? September 1999.
A young lady doctor (Kyōno) only
knows how to play by the book and
soon angers the maverick nurse
(Zaizen) who is assigned as her assistant. The reluctant partners must learn
to respect each other, in a medical variation on the mismatched buddies so
often found in police dramas.

ENOUGH OF YOUR LIES
1988. JPN: *Kimi ga Uso o Tsuita*. PRD:
Yoshio Yamada, Tōru Ōta. DIR: Yasuyuki
Kusuda. SCR: Shinji Nojima. CAST:
Hiroshi Mikami, Senri Ōe, Hiroshi
Fuse, Honami Suzuki, Yumi Asō. CHN:
Fuji. DUR: 45 mins. x 9 eps.; Sat 24
October 1988–19 December 1988.
Ryō (Mikami) and Akiko (Asō) meet at
a party and start a relationship.
However, they did not tell truth about
themselves—Ryō claims to be a lawyer,
while Akiko pretends to be from a
wealthy family. After each discovers the
other's deception, they try to struggle
on but the relationship finishes on
Christmas Eve (traditionally the time
for couples to commence longer-last-
ing commitments). *EoYL* was the debut

Eisenborg

drama from scriptwriter Nojima—com-
pare to **BORN OF LIES** and **FRIENDS**.
Theme: Princess Princess—"Get
Crazy!"

ENVOY OF ALLAH
1960. JPN: *Allah no Shisha*. PRD: N/C.
DIR: N/C. SCR: N/C. CAST: Shinichi
"Sonny" Chiba, Hitoshi Ōmae, Kyōko
Mizushima. CHN: NET (Asahi). DUR: 25
mins. x 26 eps.; Thu 7 July 1960–27
December 1960.
The prince of the Middle Eastern kingdom of Kabayan goes in search of four
pieces of an ancient map, which he
believes will lead him to a great lost
treasure. Oriental adventure in the
style of the *Arabian Nights* (*AE), based
on an idea by **MOONLIGHT MASK** creator Yasunori Kawauchi. Leading man
Chiba would still be working over 40
years later, playing a fearsome father-
in-law in **SHOTGUN MARRIAGE**. The
mythical kingdom and many of the
characters who inhabited it were
named after the show's sponsor,
Kabaya Confectionery.

ETCHAN
1974. PRD: N/C. DIR: Hiroshi Takei,
Tōru Kusakabe, Ryūnosuke Sano. SCR:
Mutsuaki Saegusa. CAST: Mayumi
Hattori, Baku Numata, Kanako
Nakamura, Yōko Takagi, Shōhei
Nishimura, Misato Nakura. CHN: NHK.

DUR: 25 mins. x 12 eps.; Mon 27 May 1974–19 June 1974.

Three years after the death of her mother, Etchan (Hattori) has to deal with a new woman in her father's life. Papa (Numata) has decided to marry Kaoru (Takagi), an irritating woman who has made a lot of money translating a well-known textbook on child psychology. As the unspoken battle of wills begins between Etchan and Kaoru, the little girl also comes to realize that there is someone more suitable already in her father's life. She immediately tries to set him up with pretty department store clerk Kyōko (Nakura), whom she would much prefer as a stepmother. Based on the story by Bunroku Shishi—compare to COLD MORNING.

ETERNAL CHILD

2000. JPN: *Eien no Ko.* AKA: *Forever Child.* PRD: Susumu Kondō, Norimasa Ikeda, Norihiko Imamura, Takao Tsujii. DIR: Yasuo Tsuruhashi, Junji Kadō. SCR: Takehiro Nakajima. CAST: Miki Nakatani, Kippei Shiina, Atsurō Watabe, Yuriko Ishida, Mira Murano, Yōsuke Asari, Ryō Katsuji, Ken Izawa, Tomoka Kurotani, Masato Furuoya, Eiko Nagashima, Mariko Fuji. CHN: Yomiuri TV. DUR: 45 mins. x ca. 11 eps.; Mon 10 April 2000–30 June 2000.

After suffering terrible abuse 18 years earlier, Yūki (Nakatani) works as a nurse in a mental hospital. Her brother Satoshi (Izawa) has been accused of rape but manages to arrange an out-of-court settlement through his tough lawyer Nagase (Watabe). In order to work off the debt incurred, Satoshi agrees to take a job at Nagase's law firm. Nagase needs the extra help because he has to spend more time with his aged mother, who has developed Alzheimer's disease. However, Nagase has a past he has tried to forget, a history of child abuse at the hands of his mother, which he only recalls now that the old woman relies on him to bathe and clothe her. He also remembers his time at a children's hospital when he was a boy, when he

and his childhood friend Arisawa mistook the young Yūki for an angel when they met her on a beach—at the time, she claimed to have no name.

Arisawa (Shiina) grew up to become a cop but has trouble keeping his cool on child abuse cases. After almost killing a man who has imprisoned his family, Arisawa goes to visit one of the surviving children in the hospital, where he meets Yūki and Nagase and rekindles their childhood friendship. However, the trio and their acquaintances soon find themselves at the center of a series of bizarre murders, in a thriller in the style of the earlier SLEEPING FOREST, based on a novel by Arata Tendō. Reputedly shown unsubtitled in the U.S. Compare to FROM THE HEART, which was broadcast on TBS during the same season.

EVE—SANTA CLAUS DREAMING

1997. AKA: *Santa Claus Dreaming.* PRD: Miwako Kurihara. DIR: Michio Mitsuno, Kensaku Sawada. SCR: Arisa Kaneko. CAST: Toshiaki Karasawa, Riona Hazuki, Katsunori Takahashi, Chōsuke Ikariya, Mari Hoshino, Ami Onuki, Yumi Yoshimura, Takashi Sorimachi. CHN: Fuji. DUR: 45 mins. x 10 eps.; Thu 16 October 1997–18 December 1997.

Santa (Karasawa) is a psychologist fallen on hard times. His wife died in a car accident while dosed up on tranquilizers, his daughter refuses to get a grown-up life, and he has trouble making his rent payments. He is approached by Koshiba (Ikariya), an assistant to a rich industrialist, who has a special task for him. He is assigned to counsel the industrialist's daughter Saori (Hazuki) without her knowledge, in order to prevent her causing harm to herself. Santa knows that she is in danger, since it was he who saved her from taking a drunken plunge off the hospital roof a scant nine months earlier. He agrees to take the case, despite the questionable medical ethics of "stealth counseling," partly because he needs the money but also because her condition reminds him of the death of his late wife. But while Santa feigns

friendship with Saori, he realizes that she has already formed an attachment with his surgeon colleague Shunsuke (Takahashi). She believes that Shunsuke is the man who saved her from death because she mistakenly believes it was him she saw wearing a distinctive Santa Claus hat.

Eve is a clever study of the psychology of transference, showing how even the sane invest their feelings in the approval of another—Saori's shattered esteem through the neglect of her father, Santa's desire to assuage his own guilt over his wife by helping Saori, and, of course, the inevitable love triangle that develops. Flashbacks to the rooftop incident, coupled with the inexorable advance of Christmas at the end of the fall season, ensure that *Eve* maintains a seasonal feel throughout, accentuated by the extensive use of rearrangements of well-known carols applied to the soundtrack for dramatic effect. Note pop idols Puffy (Onuki and Yoshimura) in the cast, as well as GTO's Sorimachi in a minor role. Theme: Puffy—"Mother," Celine Dion—"Be the Man."

EVEN IF YOU LIE

1993. JPN: *Uso Demo Ii Kara.* PRD: Yūji Tōjō. DIR: Masahiro Kunimoto. SCR: Miyuki Noe. CAST: Kanako Higuchi, Gorō Inagaki, Mitsuko Baishō, Masaki Kanda, Kazuhiko Nishimura. CHN: Yomiuri. DUR: 45 mins. x 9 eps.; Sat 23 October 1993–18 December 1993.

Thirty-five-year-old Ayako (Higuchi) is the single manager of a juice shop in Tokyo. She answers the phone one day to hear a handsome-sounding man on the other end of the line. It is a wrong number but she promises to go on a date with him. When she arrives to meet him, she finds Fumiya (Inagaki), a young stripling of 22. Compare to WHERE IS LOVE?, which similarly features a relationship with a large age difference, conducted through telephonic happenstance. Theme: Seizo Ise—"Never."

Evil Woman

EVIL WOMAN

1992. JPN: *Waru*. PRD: N/C. DIR: Kazuo Yamamoto. SCR: Yumiko Kamiyama. CAST: Hikari Ishida, Hiroshi Fuse, Marina Watanabe, Masatoshi Nagase, Mitsuko Baishō, Shinobu Yūki. CHN: NTV (Yomiuri). DUR: 45 mins. x 11 eps.; Sat 18 April 1992–27 June 1992.
Marilyn Tanaka (Ishida) starts her career with hopes and enthusiasm, only to find herself assigned to the Office Supplies Room, also known as Solitary Confinement. She remains resolutely perky and her senior Negishi (Baishō) sees the potential in her for a meteoric office lady career. She begins to educate her in company history, the Way of Management, and the little tips that are vital for success—keeping an eye on the hallway in front of the chairman's office, and always remembering the name of the cleaning lady. At the next office reshuffle, Marilyn is reposted to the secretarial pool but discovers that her "dream job" is not all she hoped for. She is now required to be submissive and obedient—not qualities she learned as the Mistress of Paper Clips back in the Office Supplies Room. The only person who treats her with any kindness now is chief secretary Natsume (Yūki) but Natsume and Negishi once fought over the same man and both have sworn vengeance. Based on the 1988 manga by Jun Fukami in *Be Love* magazine, *Evil Woman* is a classic to rival the sublimely inconsequential **BIG WING**. It also invites comparison with the Hollywood movie *Working Girl* (1988), whose heroine climbs from the typing pool to the boardroom, whereas Marilyn's sights are set significantly lower. See also **POWER OFFICE GIRLS** and **OL POLICE**.

EXCUSE ME AGAIN

1994. JPN: *Maido Gomen Nasai*. PRD: Toyohiko Wada. DIR: Yasuyuki Kusuda. SCR: Masahiro Yoshimoto. CAST: Yasuko Matsuyuki, Naoki Hosaka, Yukari Morikawa, Takashi Sorimachi, Jun Murakami, Akiko Hinagata. CHN: TBS. DUR: 45 mins. x 12 eps.; Tue 5 July 1994–20 September 1994.

When their father is transferred elsewhere on business, sisters Sakura (Matsuyuki), Yuri (Ai Sasamine), and Ayame (Hinagata) have the run of a the family's newly built house in Tokyo. However, the house is riddled with faults and problems and the girls are constantly forced to complain to the developers. Compare to **ARE YOU ON THE MOVE?** Theme: Be-B—"Dōmu—Kaze ni Mukatte" (Longing Dream—Toward the Wind).

EXIDRAFT

1992. JPN: *Tokusō Exidraft*. AKA: *Special Investigation Exidraft*. PRD: Kyōzō Utsunomiya, Nagafumi Hori. DIR: Michio Konishi, Tetsu Mitsumura. SCR: Shūichi Miyashita, Naoyuki Sakai. CAST: Shigeki Kagemaru, Mamoru Kawai. CHN: Asahi. DUR: 25 mins. x 49 eps.; Sun 2 February 1992–24 January 1993.

A detective in a super-fast flying car (that can make it from Tokyo to Osaka in ten minutes flat) fights evil criminals. **EXIDRAFT** comes between **SOLBRAIN** and **JAN PERSON** in the Metal Series chronology and is credited as usual to the pseudonymous "Saburō Yade." Theme: Takayuki Miyauchi—

"Goal wa Mirai" (The Future is Our Goal).

EYE OF THE JAGUAR

1959. JPN: *Jaguar no Me*. PRD: Shunichi Nishimura. DIR: Sadao Funatoko. SCR: N/C. CAST: Kōichi Ōse, Keiko Kondō, Yoshio Kitahara, Takashi Mita, Satoshi Tenshin, Shingo Ōsawa, Masayasu Takatō. CHN: KRT (TBS). DUR: 25 mins. x 38 eps.; Sun 12 July 1959–27 March 1960.

The Blue Dragon secret society plans to steal the treasure of Genghis Khan, which is guarded by the fabled Panther of Justice. They intend to use their own "Evil Panther" to do so but are foiled by a Japanese orphan who is searching for his long-lost elder brother. Only he can stop their conspiracy to restore ancient tyranny, in a series of adventures that leapt from the Gobi Desert to Shanghai, Singapore, and Hong Kong. Based on a prewar novel serialized in *Shōnen Club*, *EotJ* was broadcast as the follow-up to **MOONLIGHT MASK**. It was an immense success with the Japanese baby-boom generation, who were yet to really experience foreign travel for themselves—compare to **HARIMAO**.

EYE OF THE STORM

2002. JPN: *Shin Ai no Arashi*. AKA: *New Storm of Love*. PRD: N/D. DIR: Yoshikazu Kaneko. SCR: Shōichirō Ōkubo. CAST: Miki Fujitani, Jun Kaname, Yoshizumi Ishihara, Hiroyuki Watanabe, Kazuko Katō, Kinya Aikawa. CHN: Fuji. DUR: 15 mins. x 65 eps.; Tue 7 July 2002–?? September 2002.

In 1927, two years after the crowning of the Shōwa Emperor, wealthy heiress Hikaru Saegusa (Fujitani) has fallen in love with orphan Takeshi (Kaname), who has been brought into the family to help her father with his business. However, the pair are forced to keep their love a secret, especially since the fortunes of the Saegusa family take a downward turn as war approaches. Faced with financial ruin, Hikaru's father orders her to save the family by marrying the wealthy self-made man Yūsaku (Ishihara), in a plot often repeated in women's drama—compare to **100 YEARS** and **PEARL BEAUTY**. A remake of a 1986 series, which itself was followed by two sequels, *Flower of the Storm* (1988) and *Summer Storm* (1989).

FACE (1)

1997. PRD: Hiroharu Morita. DIR:
Yasuyuki Kusuda. SCR: Masahiro
Yoshimoto, Masaya Ozaki. CAST: Shinji
Takeda, Ryō, Akiko Hinagata,
Masahisa Ikuse, Kii Negishi. CHN:
Kansai. DUR: 45 mins. x 12 eps.; Tue
1 July 1997–16 September 1997.
Natsuki (Takeda) regards women as a
source of income. He is dating hospital
owner's daughter Misato (Hinagata)
purely in order to get money out of
her. However, his life changes when he
meets bar girl Aya (Ryō) at a hostess
club and falls in love with her. But the
course of love does not run true when
one of the lovers is revealed to have a
multiple personality disorder—compare to **MPD PSYCHO**. Theme: The
Rolling Stones—"Angie."

FACE (2)

2003. JPN: *Kao*. PRD: Kazuhiko
Takahashi, Hiroyuki Gotō. DIR: Masato
Hijikata, Hideaki Matsuda, Junichi
Tsuzuki. SCR: N/C. CAST: Yukie Nakama,
Jō Odagiri, Kotomi Kyōno, Ken Kaitō,
Tōru Masuoka. CHN: Fuji. DUR: 45 mins.
x ca. 11 eps.; 15 April 2003–.
Mizuho Hirano (Nakama) is an artist
who works for the police sketching
criminal portraits. Despite being marginalized in a society of male law
enforcement officers, she insists on
investigating cases herself, in the style
of **INVESTIGATOR MARIKO**. Though
based on a story by Hideo Yokoyama,
this adaptation adds a love story

between Mizuho and her cop colleague Kōsuke (Odagiri), as well as an
amnesiac past in an orphanage that
recalls **SLEEPING FOREST**. Not to be confused with the 1997 **FACE (1)** listed
above.

FACE: UNKNOWN LOVER

2001. JPN: *Face: Mishiranu Koibito*.
PRD: N/C. DIR: Ryūichi Inomata. SCR:
Emiko Wakao. CAST: Yūichirō
Yamaguchi, Yukie Nakama, Katsunori
Takahashi, Minako Tanaka, Hiroko
Hatano, Marina Watanabe, Karin
Yamaguchi. CHN: NTV. DUR: 45 mins.
x 9 eps.; Wed 10 January 2001–7
March 2001.
Saki (Nakama) is having an affair with
her married boss Okada (Yamaguchi).
One day a man named Tōru
(Takahashi) forces Okada to open the
safe to steal the money inside. After the
criminal flees, the boss's son Takumi
(Takahashi again) also disappears. Saki
goes looking for Takumi and discovers
that he and Tōru are two personalities
warring for control of the same body.
Takumi is appointed chairman of
Yokohama Trading by his father, who
does not realize that Takumi's sec-
ondary personality is conducting an
affair with his own stepmother
(Yamaguchi)! Saki, too, is a victim of
the twin personalities—she begins an
affair with Takumi, only to discover
that she has inadvertently slept with
the carefree Tōru, who has got her
pregnant.

As if the above synopsis was not confusing enough, *F:UL* was cut short due
to falling ratings, resulting in an
intense compression of events and revelations. Later episodes are a true
rollercoaster ride, as writer Wakao desperately tries to cram in the rest of the
plot. One of several mind-bending
schizo dramas of the late 1990s, tracing
a triple ancestry back to **ONLY YOU
CAN'T SEE IT** and the amnesiac courier
of **GIFT**, as well as to *Fight Club* (1999),
whose release probably excused this
rehash of an idea already covered
rather well in **FACE**.

FALSE LOVE

2001. JPN: *Uso Koi*. PRD: Kazuhisa
Andō, Naoki Satō, Yōichi Arishige.
DIR: Toshiyuki Mizutani, K. Kataoka,
Shinichi Yokozuka, Hiroshi Ikezono.
SCR: Natsuko Takahashi. CAST: Kiichi
Nakai, Yukie Nakama, Faye Wong,
Shunsuke Nakamura, Akira Fuse,
Patrick Haran, Clifford Ripple, Teah,
Yurai. CHN: Fuji. DUR: 45 mins. x 12
eps.; Tue 3 July 2001–17 September
2001.
While shopping for a wedding ring for
his rich fiancée Emi (Nakama), struggling photographer Akira (Nakai) has
his wallet stolen. It falls into the hand
of Chinese immigrant Faye (Wong),
who uses Akira's stolen credentials to
acquire a marriage certificate in their
names. This allows her to extend her
residency in Japan for another month,
in which she hopes to secure legal

False Love

© 2001 Fuji

employment as a fashion designer. However, the news that he already has a wife (albeit one he has never met) could not come at a worse time for Akira, who hears it as he is marching down the aisle with Emi. Refusing to believe such a ludicrous story, he goes through with the wedding anyway and hires a private detective to track Faye down and arrange a divorce before Emi's wealthy parents discover their new son-in-law is an inadvertent bigamist.

FL is one of several early 21st-century serials designed to exploit Japanese drama's popularity in the rest of Asia. Like LADY OF THE MANOR, which presents a different angle on the theme of an unwelcome spouse, it peppers its dialogue with snatches of English and Mandarin for added exoticism. Like LOVE 2000, it literally steals a cast member from the films of Hong Kong director Wong Kar-Wai—in this case, the impeccably gamine Wong. Its other antecedent is the comedy NARITA DIVORCE, in which a similarly reluctant couple struggle with their feelings for each other *after* they have officially decided to end their relationship. While Akira regards Faye as nothing more than a nuisance, she claims to have genuinely fallen for him after see-

ing one his photographs. This is enough for some viewers, though others will see nothing more than a spoiled, arrogant minx who pleads poverty but wears designer clothes, lies to get what she wants, and has no thought for the chaos she causes.

Some suspension of disbelief is called for, particularly regarding the desperate measures to which Faye resorts—there are far easier ways to get a one-month visa extension in Japan, starting with simply asking for one! However, *FL* never claims to be anything more than a comedy, as suggested in the opening scene, when civil servant Tsunoda (Katsuhisa Namase) reveals that he is a part-time feng shui master and predicts that dire misfortunes will befall Akira unless he moves a potted plant from an inauspicious sector.

Some of the more priceless scenes feature Faye's foreign housemates, who practice ruses for cheating the Japanese system. In a parody of the saccharine internationalism of most language classes, Faye's friends learn outrageously ill-mannered phrases such as "*It's all that guy's fault!*" With all the synchronicity to be found in situation comedies, they usually get the chance to try their newfound insults out, to Akira's eternal disadvantage.

FAMILY A

1994. JPN: *Kazoku A*. PRD: Tamaki Endō. DIR: Atsushi Moriyama. SCR: Akira Tomozawa, Akio Endō. CAST: Hironobu Nomura, Yui Natsukawa, Takuzō Kawatani, Yoshio Harada, Akiko Urae. CHN: TBS. DUR: 45 mins. x 9 eps.; Thu 13 October 1994–8 December 1994. Forced to move in with his in-laws while he saves for a house, Shunpei (Nomura) finds that his relationship with his wife Akiko (Natsukawa) is stretched to the breaking point. Father-in-law Daigorō (Harada) is a particular problem in another in-law appeasement drama—compare to SHOTGUN MARRIAGE. Theme: Ryōji Kurihara—"Aoi Yoru" (Blue Nights).

FAMILY VALUES *

1999. JPN: *Tōi Shinseki Chikaku no Tanin*. AKA: *Combat in the Kitchen*. PRD: N/C. DIR: N/C. SCR: Yumie Nishiogi. CAST: Noriko Sakai, Shima Iwashita, Ryūji Harada, Jō Shishido, Minako Tanaka. CHN: NHK. DUR: 45 mins. x ca. 11 eps.; [broadcast dates unknown]. A daughter (Sakai) of an exclusive restaurateur in Akasaka is working as an office lady. One day, however, she is destined to become the restaurant owner, a fate that causes her eccentric aunt (Iwashita, of course) to come back to Japan to "educate" her. Auntie has been married to an English aristocrat but still epitomizes traditional Japanese womanhood. As in the later LADY OF THE MANOR, Iwashita's feminine ideal includes lessons in the correct use of a *naginata* pole sword, a bit of comedy business that alludes to Iwashita's many roles in *taiga* dramas. Meanwhile, the pregnant Sakai does her best to keep her head down. Shown with English subtitles in the U.S. on KTSF TV.

FAMILY WEATHERMAP

1980. JPN: *Kazoku Tenkizu*. PRD: Kanae Mayuzumi. DIR: Kazuya Satō, Takamasa Suzuki, Tatsuya Saegusa. SCR: Isamu Seki. CAST: Yoshio Tsuchiya, Chitose Kobayashi, Chiaki Matsubara, Masayuki Kikuchi, Natsuho Miyakai, Yukari Saitō. CHN: NHK. DUR: 30 mins. x 12 eps.; Mon 22 December 1980–27 December 1980; 23 March 1981–26 March 1981. Average mom Hiroko Morioka (Kobayashi) is surprised to find hundreds of letters in her mailbox. Her youngest daughter Minako (Saitō) has advertised for a pen pal in a girls' magazine and has got more replies than she bargained for. Hiroko and her husband are less pleased when they discover that each of Minako's pen pals has been treated to a diatribe about the Morioka parents and how much Minako hates them. Minako also receives an unexpected visitor— teenage runaway Tomoko, who has fled from Sendai to see her pen pal.

However, Minako's father Kunio (Tsuchiya) talks Tomoko out of her depression, revealing that he too ran away from home when he was a child but then discovered how much his parents loved him.

Meanwhile, the Moriokas' second son Mitsuhiko (Miyakai) tries to help a school friend who is on the run from police. Eldest son Yōichi (Kikuchi) studies so hard that he becomes the top of the class—but his success causes the former top pupil to commit suicide in embarrassment. This in turn causes a media circus to descend on the Morioka family. Their problems continue when Hiroko must deal with the death of her former boyfriend and when Kunio is threatened with blackmail after he gives evidence against a group of rapists.

Family Weathermap was a deliberate attempt by NHK to create a documentary-style "home drama" for a juvenile audience, in reaction to the SF and fantasy that characterized most children's entertainment at the time. As Japan's bubble economy brought apparent prosperity everywhere, scenarist Seki was encouraged to put a typical Japanese family through unexpected adversity in the style of *The Little House on the Prairie* (1973, see also *AE). Theme: Paul McCartney—"Junk."

FANTASY AND REALITY IN MARRIAGE

1991. JPN: *Kekkon no Risō to Genjitsu*. PRD: Chihiro Kameyama. DIR: Yūtarō Kawamura. SCR: Kazuhiko Ban. CAST: Masatoshi Nakamura, Misako Tanaka, Junichi Ishida, Kazuko Katō, Megumi Yokoyama, Ayaka Ōno. CHN: Fuji. DUR: 45 mins. x 11 eps.; Thu 10 January 1991–21 March 1991.

Yasuhiko (Nakamura) works for a stationery company and lives at the company apartment with his wife Asako (Tanaka) and a daughter Kaede (Ōno). His colleague Kōhei and wife Saki (Katō) live in the same block but Kōhei is conducting a secret affair with Yasuhiko's subordinate Shinobu

(Yokoyama). Theme: ZARD—"Goodbye My Loneliness."

FATE IN 2001

2001. JPN: *2001-nen no Otoko Un*. AKA: *Luck with Men in 2001; New Year's Resolution*. PRD: Kazuhisa Andō, Yōko Matsui. DIR: Satoru Nakajima, Shinichi Iijima. SCR: Miyuki Noe. CAST: Miho Kanno, Seiichi Tanabe, Manabu Oshio, Nana Katase, Mirai Yamamoto, Kurume Arisaka, Mitsuru Fukikoshi, Aya Enjōji. CHN: Fuji. DUR: 45 mins. x 11 eps.; Tue 9 January 2001–20 March 2001.

Ataru (Kanno) rushes home from work to surprise her live-in lover Ken on Christmas Eve, only to discover that he has moved out. She goes looking for him at the house of his friend Kaoru (Oshio), only to find that Kaoru, too, will be lonely this Christmas. Discovering that Ataru was ready to settle down with Ken, Kaoru offers her a shoulder to cry on and Ataru faces the 21st century with a new resolve to find herself a good man—like many other drama heroines, she may have already done so. . . . Theme: Judy and Mary—"Lucky Pool."

FATHER

1990. JPN: *Otōsan*. PRD: Tōya Satō. DIR: Nozomu Amemiya. SCR: Masato Kaneko. CAST: Ikkō Furuya, Yoshie Ichige, Yuki Hoshino, Yōko Kuga. CHN: NTV. DUR: 45 mins. x 9 eps.; Sat 13 October 1990–8 December 1990.

Former ship builder Kōsaku (Furuya) has spent the last five years as a part-time organizer at a wedding hall. At one wedding reception, he goes up onto the stage with the back of his trousers torn. The shameful event is featured in a photo magazine and proves that no publicity is bad publicity, since the number of bookings for the hall go up. Compare to CEREMONIAL OFFICIATOR and WEDDING PLANNER. Theme: Mariko—"Gūzen" (Coincidence).

FEMALE ANNOUNCERS

2001. JPN: *Joshi Ana [i.e., Announcer]*.

AKA: *News Planet*. PRD: Shizuo Sekiguchi, Kenichirō Yasuhara. DIR: Hiroshi Nishitani, Masato Hijikata. SCR: Yōichi Maekawa, Arisa Kaneko. CAST: Miki Mizuno, Rie Tomosaka, Hideaki Itō, Yū Yoshizawa, Shunsuke Nakamura, Frank O'Connor, Aiko Satō, Nagisa Katagiri. CHN: Fuji. DUR: 45 mins. x 11 eps.; Tue 9 January 2001–20 March 2001.

Ever since a film crew came to her remote fishing village when she was a child, Makoto (Mizuno) has wanted to be a TV reporter. Now she's a twentysomething rookie at the Tōkyō Pacific News Network, gamely donning animal costumes for freezing early-morning outside broadcasts, hoping all the while to make it as an anchorwoman. Her chief rival is Mariko (Tomosaka), the coldhearted, ambitious daughter of a famous journalist, bitterly resentful that she has nothing more interesting to do than report on the weather—perhaps a snide reference to the actress's role in FROM THE HEART. The two women find themselves fighting over handsome breakfast show presenter Kōji (Itō), and dueling for the approval of retiring anchorwoman Ryōko (Katagiri), who is likely to have some say in who replaces her in the top anchorwoman job.

A lighter-hearted comedy from the writer of the superb OUT, *FA* demonstrates an in-depth knowledge of TV behind the scenes, as Makoto battles with surly film crews, talentless presenters, and hawk-eyed paparazzi. Her difficult hours and stressful lifestyle destroy her relationship with her high school sweetheart Ryūji, and the newshound is herself hounded when a series of misunderstandings lead to press speculations about her private life. Meanwhile, her fellow broadcasters are the traditional Japanese menagerie of quirky no-hopers, including a Pets Corner presenter who is afraid of animals.

Part of *FA*'s appeal lies in the series of slapstick disasters that befall Makoto on air. These include her accidentally catapulting her cameraman into mid-air on an amusement park ride, beating up a child when he tries to cheat at video games, and inadvertently hitting a senior presenter in the face with a bowl of super-hot chili. Whereas the star of **News Woman** was a reporter at the top of her game, Makoto is still learning on the job and *FA* shows the perils of broadcasting, from the importance of clear diction to checking that one's animal costume isn't on backward. The humorless Mariko, meanwhile, has problems of her own, including the unwelcome attentions of sex-mad British film director Johnson (O'Connor), who tries to feel her up while promoting his movie *Say Goodbye Vietnam. FA* is particularly good on the sheer triviality of most TV and is not afraid to show its cast battling to get a scoop, only to discover they have been knocked off air by a more "newsworthy" event on another channel—sometimes, much to Makoto's embarrassment, a news item about *her.*

Note that *FA* is often referred to as *News Planet,* probably because the opening credits of the show within a show are actually more eye-catching than those of *FA* itself! The series was broadcast unsubtitled on the U.S. network NGN. Compare to **Tabloid** and **Straight News**.

FEMALE NEWSCASTERS

1990. JPN: *Onna Caster Monogatari.* prd: N/C. DIR: Masayuki Yamane. SCR: Keiji Nagao. CAST: Misako Konno, Mari Torikoshi, Itsumi Ōsawa, Hirohide Yakumaru. CHN: TVT. DUR: 45 mins. x 6 eps.; Sun 26 August 1990–30 September 1990.

Natsumi (Konno)'s dream is to become a newscaster. Although she gets a job at Yamato TV, she finds that reality does not live up to her expectations and begins to believe that her superiors are doing everything they can to keep her off the air. Her colleague Yōko (Ōsawa) is chosen to present a cooking program, which only leads Natsumi into a deeper depression. However, like the Japanese hero-

ines of so many other news show shows, she perseveres.

FEMALE TEACHER

1998. JPN: *Onna Kyōshi.* PRD: Yūji Tōjō. DIR: Kazuhisa Imai. SCR: Kazuyuki Morosawa. CAST: Reiko Takashima, Yasufumi Terawaki, Akiko Hinagata, Yōko Nogiwa. CHN: Asahi. DUR: 45 mins. x 12 eps.; Thu 2 July 1998–17 September 1998.

Misako (Takashima) quit her teaching job after she was attacked by a pupil. She reluctantly returns to teaching when she sees an advertisement for a temporary teacher and is accepted by the stern senior teacher (Nogiwa). However, when she reaches the staff room, she discovers that her ex-husband Sugimoto (Terawaki) is teaching the first grade. Theme: Chez Vous—"Kitto Itsuka . . ." (Maybe One Day).

FIGHT ELEGY

1973. JPN: *Kenka Elegy.* PRD: Kazuo Shibata. DIR: Kanae Mayuzumi. SCR: Izuho Sudō. CAST: Masanao Yamada, Junkichi Orimoto, Keiko Takeshita, Masashi Koike, Naoya Makoto, Paiton Balmore, Harumi Matsukaze. CHN: NHK. DUR: 30 mins. x 6 eps.; Mon 28 May 1973–6 June 1973.

In 1933, 13-year-old Kiroku (Yamada) loses his mother. His sailor father Junkichi (Orimoto) arranges for him to stay with Tomiko (Matsukaze), whose daughter Michiko (Takeshita) is a year older than the new arrival. Kiroku becomes a chorister at a local church and soon agrees to perform an important task for Michiko at the next Sunday Mass—it's also her birthday and he hopes to impress her. His church attendance causes him to miss out on athletics practice, causing his high school seniors to beat him up in punishment. Ringleader Nagaoka (Makoto) continues to bully Kiroku on a regular basis, until Kiroku's church friend "Snapping Turtle" offers to teach him how to protect himself. Kiroku's fighting skills improve so swiftly that he soon wins a fight with a gang from a rival school, causing his

teachers to ban him from athletics meets anyway!

Demonstrating considerable lack of smarts, Nagaoka taunts Kiroku about his relationship with Michiko, causing Kiroku to proclaim that she is "his Virgin Mary" and to hammer the point home by beating Nagaoka to a pulp. Reprimanded once more, not only by the school but by the military police, Kiroku decides to leave town with Snapping Turtle, and goes in search of his uncle Moriyama. However, Moriyama is arrested as a Communist sympathizer, leading Kiroku to be boarded with yet another relative. That summer, Turtle reports that he has joined the army and that Michiko has decided to become a nun.

A year later, Kiroku is a sensitive young poet who hears that Michiko is dying. He visits her at her sanatorium to say goodbye. Turtle chooses this moment to announce that he is being posted to Manchuria, causing Kiroku to put aside any thought of fighting again. However, his stand makes little difference, as Michiko wastes away, and Turtle eventually dies in Burma. Japanese children's television is not *always* this depressing. Based on the novel by Takashi Suzuki.

FIGHTING GIRL

2001. PRD: Kazuki Nakayama. DIR: Takao Kinoshita, Hideaki Matsuda. SCR: Yumiko Kamiyama. CAST: Kyōko Fukada, Aya Hirayama, Yoon Son-Ha, Kenji Sakaguchi, Masanobu Katsumura, Takashi Sasano, Hironobu Nomura, Shigeru Izumiya. CHN: Fuji. DUR: 45 mins. x ca. 11 eps.; Wed 4 July 2001–26 September 2001.

Pushy, overbearing bad girl Sayoko (Fukada) dyes her hair blonde, gets her belly button pierced, and insults the customers at the clothes shop where she works. None of this impresses her widowed metal worker father, who frets constantly about his blind younger daughter Fuyumi (Hirayama) and just wishes Sayoko would get her life in order and go to college. Sayoko loses her job and her boyfriend, followed shortly by her self-esteem when Korean exchange student Ami (Yoon) berates her on the train for having no consideration for others. Later, Fuyumi trips at the train station and the relentlessly helpful Ami escorts her home.

After an argument with her father, Sayoko sulks at the beach, where she witlessly agrees to go home with a bored rich kid, who immediately attempts to rape her in his grandfather's waterfront mansion. Saved by the timely arrival of the boy's new tutor, she returns home, only to find that her train nemesis Ami has been invited for dinner by her grateful father.

FG plays like three completely different scripts smashed together in a freak car accident, each attempting to repeat some of the glories of recent hits. It even deals the disability card from the bottom of the deck by introducing Sayoko's blind sister at regular intervals. All of these clichés could be forgiven in a Japanese drama but not the way that we are introduced to our supposed romantic lead when he tries to sexually assault the heroine. If any good came of *Fighting Girl*, it was that it set the stage for further cooperation between Japanese and Korean TV, most notably in the later Fukada vehicle FRIENDS.

FIR TREE LEFT BEHIND, THE
1970. JPN: *Momi no Ki wa Nokotta.* PRD: Taiji Nagasawa. DIR: Naoya Yoshida, Makoto Ōhara. SCR: Sōsuke Shigeki. CAST: Mikijirō Hira, Komaki Kurihara, Sayuri Yoshinaga, Masayuki Mori, Kinya Kitaōji, Kei Satō, Eiji Okada, Kyōko Kagawa, Kazuyo Mita. CHN: NHK. DUR: 45 mins. x 52 eps.; Sun 4 January 1970–27 December 1970.

After the death of MASAMUNE THE ONE-EYED DRAGON, the rulership of northern Japan remains in the hands of his descendants in the Date clan through the 17th century. Masamune's grandson Tsunamune, third chief of the Date, is forced to retire due to his inappropriate behavior, passing the reins of

power on to his two-year-old son Tsunamura. Since a regency is called for until Tsunamura is old enough to run the fiefdom himself, his great uncle Hyōbu Date (Satō), the youngest son of Masamune, volunteers to act as Tsunamura's guardian. Soon, he becomes the unchallenged master of the area, ruling in Tsunamura's name with the assistance of his subordinate Kai Harada (Hira).

After a decade of misrule, the conservative Aki Date (Mori) makes an official complaint to the government about Hyōbu's activities. All relevant parties are summoned to an official hearing in Edō in 1671, where the regents find their alibis and excuses have little weight with the officers present. As the situation becomes tense, Aki taunts Kai in an antechamber and the two warriors fight a brief but savage duel. Kai cuts Aki down, only to fall himself to the sword of Geki Shibata, one of the samurai summoned by the sounds of the commotion.

As a result of this incident, known to Japanese historians as the Date Strife, all the men in the Harada family are executed and Hyōbu is sent into exile. The Date lands are restored to Tsunamura, and the Harada family fades from history.

The events of the Date Strife are a subject of some debate among modern Japanese scholars. The trial of Harada was originally limited to a question of who drew his sword first, though, as with CHŪSHINGURA, the matters at stake clearly extended much further than the two individuals involved in the duel. Harada has been painted as the villain of the piece in many earlier dramatic works, such as the kabuki play *Meiboku Sendai Hagi* (1777) but this 300th-anniversary *taiga* drama follows the plot of a novelization by Shūgorō Yamamoto that paints him as a faithful servant of his clan. Instead of power-crazy manipulator, the *taiga* Harada is a loyal retainer who realizes that Hyōbu Date plans to split the Date domain with the shogunate, betrayed by Hyōbu and dying in valiant defense of his

clan—compare to similar historical conjecture in THE FIRE STILL BURNS. Yamamoto was reputedly inspired by his discovery that Harada is still regarded as a hero in his birthplace, lending a provincial perspective to a well-known historical story in the approved spirit of the *taiga* drama tradition. The fir was Kai Harada's favorite tree and employed as a symbol of the stigma he suffers. As befits its kabuki origins, an earlier dramatization of the novel was broadcast on TV Tokyo in 1964, featuring Nobuwaka Jitsukawa in the lead role alongside many kabuki actors such as Tamasaburō Bandō.

FIRE STILL BURNS, THE
1993. JPN: *Honoo Tatsu.* PRD: Keiji Shima. DIR: Masami Kadowaki. SCR: Takehiro Nakajima. CAST: Ken Watanabe, Yūko Kotegawa, Hiroaki Murakami, Tsunehiko Watase, Kōtarō Satomi, Kyōka Suzuki, Naomi Zaizen, Etsuji Toyokawa, Tatsurō Nadaka, Tengai Shibuya, Kazuhiro Murata, Kei Satō, Kenji Niinuma, Hiroharu Nanbara, Keizō Kanie, Kōichi Satō, Hironobu Nomura, Kyōzō Nagatsuka, Tomoko Nakajima, Eisuke Tsunoda. CHN: NHK. DUR: 45 mins. x ca. 50 eps.; 4 July 1993–13 March 1994.

Following the success of WIND OF THE RYŪKYŪ ISLANDS, NHK producer Keiji Shima authorized a second *taiga* drama to observe Japanese history from the margins. On this occasion, he chose to focus on the events of Japan's Genpei War from the perspective of the northern tip of Honshū. Whereas most dramas (see **GRASS AFLAME**) prefer to approach the conflict in the traditional manner, through the eyes of the warring siblings Yoritomo and **YOSHITSUNE**, *TFSB* instead weaves a story around the Fujiwara family, who famously harbored Yoshitsune during the civil war, only to betray him at his time of greatest need.

As with the later **AOI**, *TFSB* also compresses a number of decades by looking at several successive generations—the first part features family founder Tsunekiyo, the second part a feud between his sons Kiyohira and Iehira. For the third part, the focus shifts to Kiyohira's son Hidehira, and *his* notorious son Yasuhira.

At the beginning of the 11th century, the northern area of Ōshū (the modern Tōhoku district, occupying the north of Japan's main island) is ruled by the Abe family. Nobleman Tsunekiyo Fujiwara (Watanabe) attends the wedding of Abe heir Sadatō (Murata) and the beautiful princess Ryūrei (Zaizen). There he meets Yū (Kotegawa), the daughter of Yoriyoshi.

In 1051, the Abe family rebels against the central government—the First Nine-Year War. The central government sends Yoriyoshi Minamoto (Kei Satō) to watch over Mutsu (now Iwate and Aomori prefectures). Yoriyoshi's son Yoshiie (Kōichi Satō) meets Ryūrei and falls in love with her—later in the series, when Yoshiie grows up, he becomes Ryūrei's lover. Ambitious Yoriyoshi decides to damage the fortunes of the Abe family by putting Tsunekiyo and Nagahira Taira (Niinuma) on the front line. However, when Tsunekiyo discovers that Nagahira has been killed through Yoriyoshi's negligence, he switches sides and helps the Abe family win the battle. Although Tsunekiyo learns that Yoriyoshi and Yoshiie escape disguised as Abe's soldiers, he lets them go.

Yoriyoshi seeks refuge in the Kiyohara domain in Dewa (now Yamagata and Akita prefectures). There, he also falls in love with Ryūrei. Yoshiie visits Tsunekiyo to thank him for saving his life and the two enemies exchange swords as a mark of friendship.

The Abe family is attacked once more by an alliance of the Minamoto under Yoriyoshi, assisted by the Kiyohara family. On the retreat, Sadatō Abe begins to suspect that a spy in the Abe camp is informing his enemies about his plans and kills his wife when he realizes her treachery. Sadatō dies in battle and Tsunekiyo is killed by Yoriyoshi, thus ending the First Nine-Year War.

A generation later, Kiyohira (Murakami), the son of Tsunekiyo and Yū, is now a man. His father's friend Yoshiie becomes the ruler of Mutsu, and orders Kiyohira to divide Ōshū between himself and his half-brother Iehira (Toyokawa). Iehira resents Kiyohira for being a higher-ranking official and conspires to overthrow him. When the time comes to pay the land tax, Iehira seizes Kiyohira's family as hostages but does not expect his half-brother to join forces with Yoshiie and crush his army. Iehira begs for forgiveness but is beheaded. However, Yoshiie is not rewarded for putting down the uprising—instead, the central government dismisses him from his post and treats the brothers' feud as a private matter not deserving government assistance. So ends the Later Three-Year War, with Yoshiie feeling as if he has been used by Kiyohira.

A generation passes, and Kiyohira tries to make northern Japan a cultured area to rival the Imperial Capital. In 1125, he completes Chūsonji, the Golden Temple Mortuary in his new northern capital of Hiraizumi. Now it is Kiyohira's son Hidehira (Watase), the head of the Fujiwara clan, who is visited in 1184 by Yoshiie's great-great-grandson Yoshitsune. Yoshitsune becomes close to Hidehira's daughter Kaoruko (Nakajima) but is forced to leave Ōshū to help his brother Yoritomo fight a war against the rival

Taira clan. Yoshitsune's martial prowess brings victory for the Minamoto clan, much to his brother's displeasure. Persecuted in southern Japan, Yoshitsune seeks refuge in the north and is welcomed by Hidehira in Hiraizumi. However, Hidehira dies in 1187, and although he makes his children swear to remain allies with Yoshitsune, his heir Yasuhira (Watanabe) is unwilling to disobey Yoritomo. Now calling himself Shogun, Yoritomo insists that Yasuhira hands the nobleman over. As Yoshitsune's presence in Hiraizumi becomes increasingly troublesome, Yasuhira argues with his own family about the way to deal with the problem. His brother Tadahira (Tsunoda) tries to kill him but Yasuhira slays him. He then sends Tadahira's remains to Yoritomo, claiming that they are those of Yoshitsune and then helps Yoshitsune to flee. Yoritomo learns the truth and attacks Hiraizumi, killing the last of the northern Fujiwara and ending almost exactly a century of their rule.

Based on a story by Katsuhiko Takahashi, *TFSB* draws on later northern folktales which suggest that Yoshitsune survived his famous last stand and lived to fight another day—some even suggested that he later conquered China using the pseudonym Genghis Khan! However, it remains scrupulously accurate in its depiction of the lives of the northern Fujiwara and only hints at alternate readings of historical events.

FIREMAN

1973. PRD: San Tsuburaya, Kimihiko Etō, Hiroshi Saitō, Yoshikazu Morita. DIR: Jun Ōki, Hiromi Higuchi, Toshitsugu Suzuki, Hiroshi Okamoto, Tatsumi Andō. SCR: Kazuo Sagawa, Jun Ōki, Iwatarō Ishii, Masao Kobayashi. CAST: Naoya Makoto, Gorō Mutsu, Keiko Kurihara, Mitsuru Saijō, Shin Kishida, Tadashi Hiraizumi. CHN: Fuji. DUR: 30 mins. x 30 eps.; Sun 7 January 1973–31 July 1973.
A mysterious meteorite lands in the sea near Japan, causing rising water

temperatures and mysterious glowing phenomena. Dr. Gunpachi Unno and members of the Marine Development Center find dinosaurs at the crash site and are saved from peril by the arrival of the superhero Fireman. The incident leads to the establishment of a Scientific Attack Force (SAF), whose members include geologist "Daisuke Misaki," who is secretly Fireman, a warrior from the subterranean Avan Empire.

Fireman was created to mark the tenth anniversary of Tsuburaya Productions, and was a deliberate effort to recreate the studio's famous **ULTRAMAN** in a more science-fictional setting, with more realistic enemies. However, this attempt to appeal to older viewers was not well received (compare to **MIGHTY JACK**) and the tone of the series shifted in its latter half to comedy.

Fireman

FIREMEN AFLAME

1996. JPN: *Honnō no Shōbōtai*. PRD: Tetsuya Kuroda. DIR: Setsuo Wakamatsu. SCR: Shōichirō Ōkubo. CAST: Tōru Nakamura, Mikihisa Azuma, Saya Takagi, Natsuho Toda, Izumi Igarashi. CHN: Asahi. DUR: 45 mins. x 11 eps.; Thu 11 April 1996–26 June 1996.

Late in his twenties, Takeshi (Nakamura) changes careers to become a firefighter, though the emotional new recruit enjoys an uneasy relationship with the cold, logical lead fireman Yōhei (Azuma)—compare to similar rivalry in the later **BAYSIDE SHAKEDOWN**. Tensions in the station house become even more strained when it is revealed that 18 years earlier, a fire started by Yōhei left Takeshi's sister Yuka (Toda) wheelchair-bound—a mix of the 1990s vogue for disability drama and the recent popularity of the Naoto Takenaka fireman movie *119* (1994). Theme: Tsuyoshi Nagabuchi—"Tomo yo" (Friend).

FIRST LOVE

2002. PRD: Hiroki Ueda. DIR: Jirō Shōno, Natsuki Imai, Hiroshi Matsubara. SCR: Shizuka Ōishi. CAST: Atsurō Watabe, Kyōko Fukada, Hiroyuki Ikeuchi, Yōko Kuga, Nami Kazuto, Yōko Naitō, Emi Wakui. CHN: TBS. DUR: 45 mins. x 11 eps.; Wed 17 April 2002–26 June 2002.

Nao Tōdō (Watabe) is a popular classical literature teacher at a high school. Nasumi Ezawa (Fukada), one of many female students who adore him, sends him daily commentaries on classical love poems from classical literature. Though Nao is attracted to her, he is unable to act on his feelings because of his status as a teacher—though after a year of denial, the two eventually kiss. Soon afterward, Nao leaves the school, and Nasumi tries to locate him without success.

Five years later, Nasumi graduates from university and starts working at a wedding hall. Her sister Tomoko (Wakui), a popular essayist, calls the family together to present her fiancé—much to Nasumi's surprise, it is Nao but both pretend never to have met before. Nasumi reluctantly realizes that she still has feelings for Nao, though he does not seem to reciprocate.

Meanwhile, Nao is approached by his former student Seiichi (Ikeuchi), now a teacher at the school. Seiichi confesses that he secretly adores Nasumi and asks Nao for advice on winning her heart. Though Seiichi and Nasumi appear to begin a relationship, Nao comes home one day to find Nasumi waiting for him. She cannot forget her feelings. Sibling love rivalry soon ensues in the style of **MERRY CHRISTMAS IN SUMMER**, with the added bonus of bucketloads of references to classical literature, especially love poems. Added mystery comes in the unfolding tale of why Nao left the school in such a hurry five years earlier and a dark secret that Tomoko is trying to hide from the rest of her family. Theme: Hikaru Utada—"Sakura Drops."

FIRST TIME

2002. JPN: *Hatsutaiken*. AKA: *First Experience*. PRD: Toshihiro Inada, Takeshi Tsuchiya. DIR: Takao Kinoshita, Masahito Shikata. SCR: Yumiko Kamiyama. CAST: Miki Mizuno, Naoto Fujiki, Ryōko Shinohara, Jō Odagiri,

Hiroko Hatano, Kōtaro Koizumi, Maki Sakai, Haruko Katō. CHN: Fuji. DUR: 45 mins. x 11 eps.; Tue 8 January 2002–19 March 2002.

Machi Takanashi (Mizuno) is a disaffected vet, annoyed that life didn't turn out to be as interesting as she had hoped. Having studied hard to follow in the animal doctor footsteps of her grandmother Masae (Katō), she has neglected other areas of her life and is still a virgin. She resolves that, Mr. Right or not, she will lose her virginity at 28. She goes to a love hotel with a man she just met but is not able to go through with it. She attends a class reunion secretly hoping to give herself to her former grade school crush Takumi (Fujiki). However, the years have changed Takumi into a self-centered, arrogant man (compare to the same season's POWER OF LOVE). Theme: Do as Infinity—"Hi ni Ataru Sakamichi" (Hillside in the Sun).

FIVE

1997. AKA: Five Spies. PRD: Atsushi Satō. DIR: Ryūichi Inomata, Tarō Ōya, Makoto Naganuma. SCR: Yasuyuki Nojiri, Izō Hashimoto. CAST: Rie Tomosaka, Rina Chinen, Kumiko Endō, Tomoe Shinohara, Sarina Suzuki, Kanako Enomoto. CHN: NTV. DUR: 45 mins. x 11 eps.; Sat 19 April 1997–28 July 1997.

Nanaka (Suzuki), Madoka (Chinen), Izumi (Endō), Kayo (Shinohara), and Eri (Enomoto) are five former teenage convicts, who now work as agents for the man who helped them break out of jail. Their missions are aimed at defeating an evil consortium, though the police are still on their trail, forcing them to work above the law—if they're caught, they will be sent back inside. A modern-day variation on the delinquents-turned-cops of SUKEBAN DEKA but also with a certain debt to *Charlie's Angels*, which was first shown in Japan on NTV in 1977 as *Chijō Saikyō no Bijotachi Charlie's Angel* (*World's Strongest Pretty Women Charlie's Angels*). Broadcast unsubtitled in the U.S. on NGN. Theme: Moon Child—"Escape."

FIVEMAN

1990. JPN: *Chikyū Sentai Fiveman*. AKA: *Earth Battle Team Fiveman*. PRD: Kyōzō Utsunomiya, Takeyuki Suzuki. DIR: Takao Nagaishi, Shōhei Tōjō, Kiyoshi Arai, Masao Minowa. SCR: Hirohisa Soda, Asami Watanabe, Kunio Fujii, Toshiki Inoue. CAST: Toshiya Fuji, Kei Shindachiya, Ryōhei Kobayashi, Kazuko Miyata, Keiko Hayase, Chika Matsui, Takeshi Ishikawa. CHN: Asahi. DUR: 25 mins. x 48 eps.; Fri 2 March 1990–8 January 1991.

Unluckily, Earth is one of a thousand worlds selected for destruction by the spacefaring empire of Zorn. As Zorn destroys the planet Shidon, two loving parents send their five children into space, hoping that they will reach Earth, grow up among the local inhabitants, and find a way to stop the Zorn attack before it's too late. They also find the time to create a set of supervehicles to aid their offspring in their quest and Arthur G6, a robot who watches over them. Eldest son Manabu (Fuji) is a psychology lecturer but also Five Red, the wielder of the V Sword. Younger brother Ken (Shindachiya) is a judo teacher but also Five Blue, who fights with yo-yos and Frisbees. Third son Bunya (Kobayashi) is a language teacher but also Five Black, a karate expert and wielder of the Power Cutter. Big sister Sumi (Miyata) is a mathematics teacher but also Five Pink, the team computer expert and wielder of the Cutie Circle. Baby sister Remi (Hayase) is a music teacher but also Five Yellow, a kung fu expert who uses her flute as a weapon in the devastating Melody Cut. The Fiveman team travels on motorcycles but, courtesy of their parents, also have a big rig combination—the Sky Alpha truck, which transforms into a plane, pulling the Carrier Beta trailer. Carrier Beta contains the Land Gamma car but also combines with the other sections to form the obligatory Five Robo. The brothers and sisters can also separately combine their vehicles to make the Star Carrier and Super Five Robo.

Their enemy is Medo (Matsui) the Galactic Emperor, who is incensed that only Earth holds out among the thousand worlds he has decided to conquer. Each week, from his battleship Valgaia, he instructs his loyal but incompetent Captain Garoa (Ishikawa) to send more cannon fodder minions to attack the world, and when they inevitably fail, a monster-of-the-week in true Super Sentai style. *Fiveman* was preceded in the Super Sentai chronology by TURBORANGER and followed by JETMAN. Music by Akihiko Yoshida.

FLASHMAN

1986. JPN: *Chōshinsei Flashman*. AKA: *Supernova Flashman*. PRD: Sanetaka Katō, Takeyuki Suzuki. DIR: Nagafumi Hori, Minoru Yamada, Shōhei Tōjō, Takao Nagaishi. SCR: Hirohisa Soda, Kunio Fujii, Toshiki Inoue, Mitsuru Shimada. CAST: Fujita Tarumi, Kihachirō Uemura, Yasuhiro Ishiwatari, Yōko Nakamura, Mayumi Yoshida, Kazunori Ishizuka, Hiroharu Shimizu, Eiichi Onoda. CHN: Asahi. DUR: 25 mins. x 50 eps.; Sat 1 March 1986–21 February 1987.

Five human children are saved from alien hunters by the Flash race. Returned to Earth as teenagers, they are charged with protecting their homeworld from the invading alien Mes Empire. Evil ruler La Deus (Ishizuka) and right-hand man Professor Le Kefren (Shimizu) send a weekly monster to challenge the strength of the Flashman team, aided by a cannon fodder army of Beast Warriors. The good guys are led by trainee scientist Jin (Tarumi) who transforms into Red Flash and wields a Prism Sword. Dai (Uemura) is Green Flash, whose chief attack is a super-strength punch. Bun (Ishiwatari) is Blue Flash who fights with a Prism Ball and Star Dust. Sara (Nakamura) is Yellow Flash who fights with her Prism Baton. Rū (Yoshida) is Pink Flash, whose special item is her gravity-defying Prism Boots. The Flashman team boasts a personal motorcycle each, as well as an array of extra vehicles including Jet Delta, Tank Command, and the shuttle Star Condor.

Unlike previous Super Sentai shows, *Flashman* really pushed the giant robot connection, starting with the combination robot Flash King. However, perhaps inspired by Optimus Prime from the previous year's *Transformers* (*AE), the writers introduced a new robot after episode 17. This comprised a 12-wheeler truck-trailer combination—the trailer transforming into the Flash Titan robot, while the rig transformed separately into Titan Boy.

For some reason, though the original idea is still the responsibility of the Super Sentai regular "Saburō Yade," the *Flashman* staff boasts an uncommonly large number of scenarists from the anime world, as well as music from composer Kōhei Tanaka (*Gunbuster* *AE). *Flashman* was preceded in the Super Sentai chronology by CHANGEMAN and followed by MASKMAN.

FLIGHT BY NIGHT *
1999. JPN: *Yonigeya Honpo*. AKA: *Angels on Loan*. PRD: Hikaru Suzuki, Norihiko Nishi. DIR: Takahito Hara. SCR: Sumio Ōmori, Yukio Nagasaki. CAST: Masatoshi Nakamura, Tomoe Shinohara, Taichi Kokubu, Mikihisa Azuma, Akiko Hinagata, Nobuko Tachikawa. CHN: NTV. DUR: 45 mins. x 20 eps. (final ep 90 mins.); Wed 13 January 1999–17 March 1999 (#1); 16 April 2003–?? June 2003 (#2).
Masahiko (Nakamura) runs Rising Sun, a reputable financial consultancy in Tokyo. However, he has another line of business after hours: helping people in impossible situations to leave their old lives behind and start anew. When bankruptcy claims and lawsuits fail, Masahiko's people can help you disappear, in a mind-boggling finance-oriented variant on *Mission: Impossible* (1996). In the style of THE STAND-IN, Masahiko's business operates above the law but rarely seems to find a client who doesn't deserve his help. They help a businessman who has kept his company's bankruptcy secret from his pregnant wife and a singer who wants to perform one last number for a special someone before he runs out on his

debts. Based on the 1992 *Young Jump* manga by Yasutaka Nagai and broadcast in the U.S. with English subtitles on KTSF TV and KIKU TV. The series returned for a second season in April 2003. Compare to LOVE SEPARATION SERVICE. Theme: Namie Amuro—"I Have Never Seen."

FLIPSIDE OF NAOJIRŌ THE TOFU SELLER, THE
1992. JPN: *Tōfuya Naojirō no Ura no Kao*. AKA: *True Face of Naojiro*. PRD: Yoshio Fukunaga, Yasutaka Kitahata, Gō Yamaguchi. DIR: Hiroyuki Ohara. SCR: Hiroshi Kashiwabara. CAST: Kenichi Hagiwara, Eriko Watanabe, B-saku Satō, Akiko Inagaki, Ryūji Kataoka. CHN: Asahi. DUR: 45 mins. x 10 eps.; Tue 7 July 1992–15 September 1992.
Tofu seller Naojirō was once a notorious robber but has kept the fact secret from everyone around him, including his wife Machiko (Watanabe). Suzuki (Kataoka), who works at the bank where Naojirō deposited most of the money he earned in his criminal career, discovers his secret and uses it to blackmail him. Unless Naojirō agrees to rob a nearby *pachinko* parlor, Suzuki will let his secret out.

FLOW ME TO THE SEA
1990. JPN: *Watashi o Umi made Nagashite*. PRD: Kimio Shindō. DIR: Eizō Sugawa. SCR: Takehiro Nakajima. CAST: Keiko Takahashi, Tatsurō Nadaka, B-saku Satō, Saya Takagi, Chisako Hara, Masaharu Hayami. CHN: Asahi. DUR: 45 mins. x 4 eps.; Thu 19 July 1990–9 August 1990.
Ayako (Takahashi) comes back to her parents' home with her teenage son Tomokazu (Hayami). She insists that she has to do it to cure her son's truancy but the real reason is to live separately from her husband Yasuhiko (Satō).

FLOWERS FOR ALGERNON
2002. JPN: *Algernon ni Hanataba o*. PRD: Yūji Tōjō, Tatsuya Itō, Kazuhisa Andō. DIR: Takehiko Shinjō, Renpei Tsukamoto. SCR: Yoshikazu Okada.

CAST: Yūsuke Santamaria, Miho Kanno, Yū Yoshizawa, Tomoko Nakajima, Tōru Masuoka, Kei Ishibashi, Hiromasa Taguchi, Kanako Enomoto, Ayumi Ishida. CHN: Kansai. DUR: 45 mins. x 11 eps.; Tue 8 October 2002–?? December 2002.
Haru (Santamaria) is a fully-grown adult, but only has the mind of a child. He has always been an object of ridicule in his neighborhood but has a sunny disposition and never lets the tormenting get to him, if indeed he notices that he is the butt of many jokes at all. He adores Erina (Kanno), a teacher at a local center for the disabled, who cares for him as if he were her younger brother. When Erina's associates at an experimental laboratory ask for a test subject for a new program, Erina persuades Haru to volunteer. He is pitted against a superintelligent mouse, Algernon, in a series of tests and later undergoes surgery to increase his own mental capabilities. Within days, Haru's IQ has leapt from 68 to 150. He becomes a fully-functioning adult for the first time and charms Erina, who is tempted to leave her boyfriend and begin a relationship with her former pupil. Haru remains attached to his old "rival" Algernon but notices one day that the mouse's intelligence seems to be reverting to its old level. He realizes that he, too, may shortly find his newfound awareness slipping away and desperately struggles to retain his new life. In adding science fiction to the mix, this adaptation of Daniel Keyes' tragedy could well be the last word in the disability genre that dominated the 1990s—compare to its contemporary TRANSPARENT. Keyes' original won the 1960 Hugo award as a short story, the 1966 Nebula for its novelization, and an Oscar when filmed as the movie *Charly* (1968).

FLUTIST, THE
1977. JPN: *Fuefuki Dōji*. AKA: *Flute-Playing Boy*. PRD: N/C. DIR: N/C. SCR: Yasuo Tanami. CAST: (voices) Shinsuke Chikaishi, Rihoko Yoshida, Kenbō Kaminarimon. CHN: NHK. DUR: 15 mins.

x 220 eps.; Mon 4 April 1977–17 March 1978.

During the Muromachi Period, Full Moon Castle in Tanba is raided by pirates. Hagimaru, heir to the castle, and his flute-playing brother Kikumaru throw out the usurpers and then embark on a quest to avenge their dead father, in a puppet show based on a story by Toshio Kitamura. Compare to the earlier NHK Puppet Shows TEN BRAVE WARRIORS OF SANADA and THE HAKKEN-DEN. With the desultory archival treatment that seems endemic to so many Japanese puppet shows, little of the series remains extant—only the first and last episodes have survived.

FLY! YOUTHS

1972. JPN: *Tobidase! Seishun*. PRD: N/C. DIR: Masahiro Takase, Tōgorō Tsuchiya, Hidekazu Nagahara. SCR: Toshio Kamata, Hidekazu Nagahara, Itsuo Kamijō, Katsuya Suzaki. CAST: Takenori Murano, Wakako Sakai, Ichirō Arishima, Kei Satō, Takanobu Hozumi, Yoshitaka Atamashi, Pepe Hozumi, Tatsuhito Gō, Yutaka Mizutani, Hiroshi Yagyū. CHN: NTV. DUR: 45 mins. x 43 eps.; Sun 20 February 1972–18 February 1973.

Sugimoto (Arishima) is principal of Taiyō Academy, with a policy of accepting any students, even dropouts from other schools. Chairman Motokura (Satō) is unhappy with the resultant anarchy and orders the senior teacher Egawa (Hozumi) to clean up the troublesome students and invite well-behaved children from all over the country to come to their school. Meanwhile, new teacher Kōno (Murano) arrives at the school and is placed in charge of the hopeless soccer club. He tries to organize a match against the elite Higashi High but the snooty coach of the Higashi team refuses to pit his sportsmen against such a weak and dishonorable team. The Taiyō team members are furious at the snub and are preparing to start a fight with the Higashi boys at the beach when Kōno suggests there is a better way: steal their pants!

Though Kōno often clashes with his students, he always appreciates their viewpoint and eventually his charges come to respect him. Meanwhile, untrustworthy authority figures like Egawa and fellow teacher Tsukamoto (Yagyū) are waiting anxiously for students to cause trouble so that they can be permanently removed from the school.

As well as marking the debut of Takenori Murano, *FY* is a landmark in school dramas, establishing a formula that has been repeated for the ensuing three decades. The most obvious inheritor was ZEALOUS TIMES, in which Yutaka Mizutani, a student in *FY*, played one of the teacher's roles. Later retreads of the same idea include KINPACHI SENSEI, GTO, and GOODBYE MR. OZU. Scriptwriter Kamata also wrote FRIDAY'S WIVES.

FOOD FIGHT

2000. AKA: *Food Frenzy*. PRD: Norihiko Nishi, Shinji Nojima. DIR: Tōya Satō. SCR: Junya Yamazaki. CAST: Tsuyoshi Kusanagi, Kyōko Fukada, Shirō Sano, Rie Miyazawa, Toshio Kakei, Somegorō Ichikawa, Sachiko Sakurai, Issei Ishida. CHN: NTV. DUR: 45 mins. x ca. 11 eps. (last ep is 90 mins.); Sat 1 July 2000–30 September 2000.

Former orphanage resident Mitsuru (Kusanagi from SMAP) now tries to repay the institution that raised him by entering "all you can eat" contests and turning over the prize money. Produced but not written by LIPSTICK's Shinji Nojima, *FF* is a tongue-in-cheek pastiche of martial arts dramas, as Mitsuru enters a criminal underworld where a shadowy kingpin (the boss at his day job, of course) sets him up with a series of all-devouring opponents. Meanwhile, he fights off the attentions of the boss's wife (Miyazawa) and tries to help Yūta, an eight-year-old boy whose single surviving parent has been sentenced to prison. Beyond the slapstick eating contests, there is also a subtler subtext, as Mitsuru fights to prove in family-oriented Japan that there should be no stigma attached to being

an orphan. He wins through in the end and hopes to win the heart of the young orphanage manager played by Fukada. Fellow SMAP group member Takuya Kimura guests in each episode by providing the voice of Mitsuru's companion (a talking crow) while the final episode features a pointless cameo from girl group Morning Musume. A later TV special pastiches *Speed* (1994), with Mitsuru trapped on a train and forced to take on an opponent per carriage until he works his way up to the front, where a bomb has been concealed. Compare to LOVE ME. Broadcast in the U.S. without subtitles on KTSF TV. Theme: SMAP—"Lion Heart."

FOR LONELY LITTLE YOU

1998. JPN: *Hitoribotchi no Kimi ni*. PRD: Makoto Kiyohiro. DIR: Makoto Kiyohiro, Naoyuki Yokoi. SCR: Toshio Sekine. CAST: Masanori Hamada, Gaku Hamada, Hiromi Nagasaku, Mariko Kaga, Risa Sumina. CHN: TBS. DUR: 45 mins. x 12 eps.; Thu 2 July 1998–17 September 1998.

Shintarō (Hamada) comes to Tokyo to run his aunt's convenience store but is plagued by Yūta (Hamada), a young child who persistently steals from him. He tracks the child to a lonely apartment, where he finds him living apparently alone without any food and running a high fever. Yūta learns that his mother is dead and attempts to commit suicide. Shintarō takes the boy to a hospital and looks after him all night, eventually volunteering to take him in until the end of summer. His motives are not that pure but are a thinly disguised attempt to impress Yūta's teacher Shiraishi (Sumina). However, before long, immature adult Shintarō and wise child Yūta become true friends. Compare to CONVENIENCE STORE STORY. Theme: Fayray—"Taiyō no Gravity" (The Sun's Gravity).

FOR YOU

1995. PRD: Miwako Kurihara. DIR: Rieko Ishizaka. SCR: Miho Nakazono. CAST: Miho Nakayama, Masanobu

Takashima, Hiroko Moriguchi, Katsunori Takahashi, Shingo Katori, Megumi Yokoyama, Ryōtarō Akashi. CHN: Fuji. DUR: 45 mins. x 11 eps. (last ep 90 mins.); Mon 9 January 1995–20 March 1995.

At age 19, Yayoi (Nakayama) had a tempestuous affair, only to lose her lover in an aircraft accident. She decides to bring up her son alone, without any help from others. Five years later, she gets a new job and finds herself falling for work colleague Tōru (Takashima). However, she has kept the fact she is a single mother hidden from him and cannot think of the right time to break the news. Compare to BEST DAD IN THE WORLD. Shown unsubtitled in the U.S. on KTSF TV. Theme: Miho Nakayama—"Hero." Peak rating: 22.7%.

FORBIDDEN FRUIT

1997. JPN: Fukigen na Kajitsu. AKA: Sulky Fruit, Inappropriate Fruit. PRD: Akira Isoyama. DIR: Jirō Shōno, Osamu Katayama, Makoto Kondō. SCR: Miho Nakazono. CAST: Yuriko Ishida, Kenichi Okamoto, Takeshi Naitō, Ikkei Watanabe, Kyōko Kishida. CHN: TBS. DUR: 45 mins. x 11 eps.; Thu 9 October 1997–18 December 1997.
Bored housewife Mayako (Ishida) falls for younger man Kōichi (Watanabe). While she is still trying to put her feelings in order, she meets her ex-lover Nomura (Naitō) and rekindles their old relationship. Still reeling from her new situation, she meets music critic Michihiko (Okamoto) and faces yet another moral dilemma. Like the earlier ACCOMMODATING WOMAN, much of FF's impact on the Japanese audience lay in its ability to shock, as it contrived to set its heroine up with another opportunity for sex each episode. At heart, however, it belongs to the genre of dramas that question modern morals—such as what makes Mayako's actions forbidden and whether her behavior would be so shocking if she were a man. Compare to ARRANGED MARRIAGE, which similarly challenges society's assumptions about relation-

ships and FORBIDDEN LOVE, which similarly invites the audience to enjoy watching the results. Theme: UA—"Kanashimi Johnny" (Sad Johnny).

FORBIDDEN FRUITS

1994. JPN: Kindan no Kajitsu. PRD: Ken Inoue. DIR: Nozomu Amemiya. SCR: Kazuhiko Yūkawa, Michiru Etō. CAST: Misako Tanaka, Kenichi Okamoto, Reiko Katō, Tomoko Ōshima, Keiji Matsuda, Yoshie Ichige. CHN: NTV. DUR: 45 mins. x 13 eps.; Wed 6 July 1994–28 September 1994.
Popular actress Yōko (Tanaka) succumbs to an unknown illness in the middle of an important shoot. While visiting her in the hospital, her agent Asako (Ichige) discovers that local nurse Tsukiko (Tanaka again) looks exactly like the famous star and convinces her to impersonate her for the remainder of the filming. Neither of the women stops to wonder if Tsukiko will want to return to her everyday life afterward or if Yōko will want to return to the public eye. Compare to THE BRIDE IS SIXTEEN, another role-swapping drama from the following year and STAR STRUCK, which also questions the glamour of life in the spotlight. Note that we have pluralized the "fruits" of the title in order to distinguish this drama from the similarly named Fukigen na Kajitsu, which is filed above as FORBIDDEN FRUIT. Theme: Miki Imai—"Miss You."

FORBIDDEN GAMES

1995. JPN: Kinjirareta Asobi. PRD: Kazuo Yamamoto. DIR: Masahiro Kunimoto. SCR: Keiko Uyama, Masaya Ozaki. CAST: Rina Katase, Takako Tokiwa, Kōichi Iwaki, Megumi Okina, Tetsuta Sugimoto. CHN: Yomiuri TV. DUR: 45 mins. x 12 eps.; Thu 13 April 1995–29 June 1995.
Ayumi (Tokiwa) comes to Tokyo for a wedding, staying with her elder sister Eiko (Katase). Psychologist Eiko has been married to salaryman section chief Yōhei (Iwaki) for 15 years but Ayumi's arrival causes the couple's happy façade to slip. Though they put

on a brave face to keep up appearances, they have been living in a sexless marriage for some time and both decide that perhaps the time is right for a change. Compare to ACCOMMODATING WOMAN. Theme: C + C + T.K.—"Silent Lover."

FORBIDDEN LOVE *

1999. JPN: Majo no Jōken. AKA: A Witch's Condition, Innocent Witch, Farewell from the Witches. PRD: Yasuo Yagi. DIR: Nobuhiro Doi, Kazuhiro Nanba, Osamu Katayama. SCR: Kazuhiko Yūkawa. CAST: Nanako Matsushima, Hideaki Takizawa, Hitomi Kuroki, Kazunaga Tsuji, Yumi Shirakawa, Naomi Nishida, Maiko Yamada, Yūichirō Yamaguchi, Rin Ozawa, Ryōsei Tayama, Yōichi Nukumizu. CHN: TBS. DUR: 45 mins. x 11 eps.; Thu 8 April 1999–17 June 1999.
Twentysomething school teacher Michi (Matsushima) falls for Hikaru (Takizawa from Johnny's Juniors), a teenager transferred to her class. She breaks

up with her fiancé Masaru (Tetsuya Bessho) and conducts an affair with Hikaru that begins with road trips and continues with romantic encounters in the school library. As a whispering campaign spreads, she is pressured to resign and confesses her feelings before the entire school. Michi and Hikaru run away together but are pursued by Hikaru's overbearing mother Kyōko (Kuroki) and the rejected Masaru, who inform the authorities that Michi has seduced a minor. Michi is arrested for statutory kidnapping but Hikaru secures her release by pretending that he has "come to his senses" and no longer has any feelings for her. Hikaru is packed off to Los Angeles to finish his studies, while the desolate Michi discovers that she is pregnant with his child. . . .

One of the highest-rated dramas of the year, *FL* presents a winning combination—for the boys, the thought of Nanako Matsushima falling in love with them; for the girls, the chance to speculate on how they could mother Hideaki Takizawa; and for the adults, a decent quantity of *Schadenfreude* as the youngsters ruin their lives. Replaying the earlier TBS show **HIGH SCHOOL TEACHER** from a slightly different viewpoint, *FL* is a typical Japanese tale of doomed love. A tragic ending is only to be expected—the audience merely watches to observe the *nature* of the unhappiness, though writer Yūkawa follows the lead of **LIPSTICK** in leaving the finale open to several interpretations. Whereas Hollywood storytelling champions "freedom" as the right to love and happiness, *FL* is in love with the idea of persecution. Though it pays lip service to the idea that *"we make our own freedom,"* everyone who tries in *FL* seems to end up worse off! From references to Galileo to the "Witch's Condition" of the Japanese title, *FL* depicts any attempt to fight conservative values as a futile sacrifice, likely to end in tears. Like a religious apostate or a Mafia inductee, Hikaru is forced to prove his lack of faith in Michi by burning a photograph of her—just one

of many scenes that play up the suffering true love has to endure. *FL* pulls all the usual tricks of a doomed romance, including the *Romeo and Juliet* cliché of misdirected letters and its modern narrative equivalent—poor mobile phone connections. It also piles on the pathos as the lovers sacrifice middle-class security and luxury to be together—their room is a textbook recreation of the dingy love nest of Yutaka Ozaki's infamous pop dirge "I Love You," in which a couple have nothing but misery and each other.

A couple of common subplots add little to the drama, including a clandestine affair between Michi's confidante Kiriko (Nishida) and the jilted Masaru, as well the collapse of Michi's parents' marriage—now that she is old enough to make her own mistakes, her mother wants to dump her husband and return to her former career as a musician. The most effective is the slow decline of Hikaru's widowed mother Kyōko, whose desire to control her son causes her to sacrifice not only her job but also her sanity. Her attempt to drag her son into an unwitting double suicide is just one of several Oedipally suspect scenes—Michi's love for Hikaru might be irresponsible and inappropriate but his yearning for a mother substitute runs much deeper, a factor of blame which Kyōko eventually realizes, to her great distress. Compare to **LOST PARADISE** and **PLEASE GOD! JUST A LITTLE MORE TIME**, though it's fair to say that most seasons of Japanese TV offer something that looks a lot like *FL*. Shown subtitled in the U.S. on KIKU TV and KTSF TV. Theme: Hikaru Utada—"First Love." Peak rating: 29.5%.

FRESHLY BREWED BEGINNINGS

1997. JPN: *Bancha mo Debana*. PRD: Asahi Wada. DIR: Yasuo Inoshita. SCR: Sugako Hashida. CAST: Pinko Izumi, Maki Ichiji, Tatsuya Yamaguchi, Hiroshi Abe. CHN: TBS. DUR: 45 mins. x 25 eps.; Mon 20 October 1997–26 March 1998.
Maruta Removal Company is facing a

crisis. Director Shintarō faces bankruptcy and has to sell his house and land to pay the creditors. Shintarō's daughter Kayo (Izumi) gives up her marriage to rebuild the company. *"Bancha mo debana"* is a Japanese saying meaning that even poor quality tea tastes good when freshly brewed. In other words, everyone has the chance to shine at least once in their life and even an unhappy marriage was once fresh and exciting. Theme: Maki Ichiji—"Ameagari no Hoshizora" (A Starry Sky after Rain).

FRIDAY'S LOVERS *

2000. JPN: *Kinyōbi no Koibitotachi e.* AKA: *Dear Friday's Lovers.* PRD: Mitsunori Morita. DIR: Mitsunori Morita, Kenjirō Kuranuki. SCR: Noriko Nakayama. CAST: Norika Fujiwara, Katsunori Takahashi, Maki Mizuno, Ikko Furuya, Yōko Nogiwa. CHN: TBS. DUR: 45 mins. x 10 eps.; Fri 14 January 2000–?? March 2000.
Madoka (Fujiwara) is a saleswoman on the fast track to management, who speaks Indonesian and hopes to be posted abroad. After a disastrous day in which she loses her appointment book and is dumped by her boyfriend, she discovers that she has been demoted to the secretarial pool. Though she finds herself falling for security guard and frustrated musician Haruki (Takahashi), she has trouble adjusting to her new lowly role and decides to fight for the chance to get back into sales when the company announces a new restaurant chain in Italy. Broadcast with English subtitles in the U.S. on KIKU TV. Theme: Glay—"Happiness."

FRIDAY'S WIVES

1983. JPN: *Kinyōbi no Tsumatachi e.* AKA: *Dear Friday's Wives.* PRD: Toshihiro Iijima. DIR: Toshihiro Iijima, Ken Matsumoto. SCR: Toshio Kamata. CAST: Ikkō Furuya, Tomoko Ogawa, Shigeru Izumiya, Eri Ishida, Aki Takeshiro, Hikaru Nishikawa, Kenichi Katō, Ayumi Ishida. CHN: TBS. DUR: 45 mins. x ca. 30 eps.; Fri 11 February 1983–13 May 1983 (#1); 6 July 1984–5

October 1984 (#2); 30 August 1985–6 December 1985 (#3).

A departure from conventional large family dramas, *FW* focuses on several nuclear families with style and disposable income. Three couples in a newly developed suburb of Tokyo form a social circle but their outward happiness hides extramarital affairs and housewives' dissatisfaction with full-time homemaking. As a sign of the popularity of the show, *Kintsuma* (Friday wife) entered Japanese slang as a term for infidelity—compare with **WEDNESDAY LOVE AFFAIR**. The third and final season was the most popular, in which a couple who separated at the altar meet each other again by chance and rekindle their relationship, even though they are both now married to other people—compare to **MY LOVER**.

To an audience tired of the ceaseless misery of in-law appeasement dramas, *FW*'s stylish and sophisticated yuppie couples had fresh appeal. The concentration on fashion, home accessories, and classy restaurants also made *FW* a forerunner of the later trendy drama style typified by **I WANT TO HUG YOU**. Writer Kamata continued the love polygon approach in his **SEVEN PEOPLE IN SUMMER**.

FRIENDS (1)

2000. PRD: Makoto Kiyohiro. DIR: Makoto Kiyohiro, Osamu Katayama. SCR: Toshio Sekine. CAST: Masanori Hamada, Emi Wakui, Kōji Miyamoto, Sawa Suzuki, Kazuhiro Murata, Tatsuya Yamaguchi, Yuiko Takeuchi. CHN: TBS. DUR: 45 mins. x 11 eps.; Fri 7 July 2000–15 September 2000.

Thirty-five-year-old freelance photographer Junpei Kōda (Hamada) takes photographs of a celebrity couple at a baseball stadium. The pictures are published in the weekly magazine *Zoom* and inadvertently include Risa (Wakui), an office worker who has called in sick to attend the game. Sacked by her irate boss when he sees the photo, Risa takes a job at a photographic lab, where she is less than pleased to see Junpei.

Risa's boyfriend Naoya (Miyamoto) tries to commit suicide by jumping into a river and is later chastised by Junpei for placing Risa in such a stressful position. Meanwhile, fellow freelance photographer Osamu (Yamaguchi) has fallen in love with Miyuki, and Risa begins to nurse Junpei when he develops a headache, which turns out to be a brain tumor. Risa's friend Fumio (Suzuki) tries to drag her failing antique shop away from the brink by considering the offer of a two million yen dowry if she agrees to marry shy cab driver Ryūichi (Murata).

Despite a title deliberately designed to recall the 1994 U.S. TV comedy, this Japanese incarnation owes a greater debt to such series as **ALL ABOUT YOUNG PEOPLE**, in which a group of mismatched acquaintances offer support to each other. Theme: Fayray—"Tears." Note: we have added the numeral (1) to distinguish this series from the unrelated later *Friends* listed below.

FRIENDS (2)

2002. PRD: Hideki Isano, Kan Byong-Mon. DIR: Nobuhiro Doi, Han Chul-Soo. SCR: Yoshikazu Okada, Hwan Soon-Young. CAST: Kyōko Fukada, Won Bin, Akiko Yada, Yukiyoshi Ozawa, Lee Dong-Gun, Han Hae-Jin, Dok Young-Jae, Kim Su-Kyoung, Sonwu Eun-Sook, Naho Toda, Keiko Takeshita, Kelly Chen. CHN: TBS. DUR: 90 mins. x 2 eps.; Mon 4 February 2002–5 February 2002.

Tokyo shopgirl Tomoko (Fukada) takes a Hong Kong vacation with her work colleague Yūko (Yada) but Yūko deserts her to see her local boyfriend. Stuck in a foreign country where she doesn't speak the language, Tomoko mistakes Korean visitor Jihoon (Won) for a bag snatcher and almost causes his arrest. Jihoon is supposed to be making an amateur movie in Hong Kong but has lost his leading lady. With nothing better to do, Tomoko agrees to take the role, which seems to involve a lot of running.

Though they can only communicate

Friends (2)

in broken English, the two stay in contact when they return to their homes. They confess to their previous deceptions (he claimed to be a professional film director, she a fashion designer) and take stumbling steps to learn each other's language. When the chance comes to visit Seoul, Tomoko tries to set up a meeting but local love rival Hye-Jin (Han) deletes her message. She spends a lonely couple of days waiting by the phone in her hotel room, only to accidentally meet Jihoon outside his favorite cinema. Similar problems ruin Jihoon's later visit to Japan. Attending a film festival nearby, he travels to meet Tomoko but is scared off by her jealous co-worker Shōta (Ozawa), who tells him in notably fluent English to disappear if he cannot guarantee he will make her happy. The heartbroken Jihoon returns to Korea and enlists for two years' military service, until Shōta confesses to Tomoko what he has done.

Billed as the first-ever Japanese-Korean drama coproduction and broadcast in the run-up to the soccer World Cup, *Friends* is a 21st-century story in the style of **LADY OF THE MANOR** and **FALSE LOVE**, perhaps capitalizing from contacts made during the making of the earlier Fukada vehicle FIGHTING GIRL. The original script reputedly called for the lovers' first meeting to take place in New York (home of the U.S. *Friends* and starting point for VIRGIN ROAD) but the 9/11 terrorist attacks made filming there impossible. Ironically, this may have been to the show's benefit, since the use of Hong Kong as a backdrop for the first 20 minutes secured the attention of the larger overseas Chinese market. The rest of the series is split evenly between Seoul and Tokyo as the would-be lovers conduct an epistolary relationship, while complementary confidantes and rivals look on. As a romance it is pedestrian but still endearing, though some may rightfully distrust the sincerity of a love based on little more than sign language and the chance coincidence of their names (the *Ji* of Jihoon and the *Tomo* of Tomoko are written with the same character). However, as the couple become closer through e-mail and language learning, it becomes a love story that's difficult to dislike. The second part loses its way, since much of it simply marks time until Jihoon finishes military service. Tomoko takes a job as a tour guide in Seoul but though the lovers' linguistic and geographical differences are reconciled, she must still deal with the opposition of Jihoon's traditionalist parents, who react to her cheery "*Konnichi wa*" with comedic revulsion. Released on DVD in Japan with additional features such as Korean and Japanese pronunciation guidelines—a sensible recognition of its value as a learning aid for romantics on both sides of the Straits of Tsushima. See also the previous year's ONE MORE KISS.

FRIENDS AND LOVERS

1997. JPN: *Tomodachi no Koibito.* AKA: *Friend's Lover.* PRD: Kazuhiro Itō. DIR: Ken Yoshida, Hiroshi Matsubara, Jun Nasuda. SCR: Erika Komatsu. CAST: Sachiko Sakurai, Asaka Seto, Masanobu Andō, Haruhiko Katō, Jovijova. CHN: TBS. DUR: 45 mins. x 12 eps.; Thu 10 April 1997–26 June 1997.

Arts college classmates Mako (Sakurai) and Aki (Seto) are the best of friends, though Mako has never admitted that she secretly loves Aki's boyfriend Kashiwagi (Andō). Compromising on her ambitions after graduation, Mako becomes an office lady at a Tokyo company, only to discover that Kashiwagi is working at the company next door. The neighboring company is owned by Kashiwagi's domineering father, whose worsening illness has caused Kashiwagi to split up with Aki and enter everyday society as a company man. Meanwhile, Aki is also being worshiped from afar, this time by the head (Katō) of the college drama society, which has fallen on hard times ever since they lost Kashiwagi, their star actor. This run-of-the-mill romantic drama also features an improbable kidnapping subplot. Theme: Four Trips—"Wonder."

FRIENDS IN NEED *

1995. JPN: *Jinsei wa Jōjō da.* AKA: *Life is Good.* PRD: Yasuo Yagi. DIR: Akio Yoshida. SCR: Kazuhiko Yūkawa. CAST: Masatoshi Hamada, Takuya Kimura, Naoko Iijima, Yuriko Ishida. CHN: TBS. DUR: 45 mins. x 11 eps.; Fri 13 October 1995–22 December 1995.

Hachirō (Hamada from the comedy duo Downtown) is a former boxer, now working as a debt collector for a finance company. He is sent to collect money from Kazuma (Kimura from SMAP), a former trainee doctor who has fallen on hard times ever since the suicide of his girlfriend. Hachirō pursues Kazuma into a bank, where Kazuma convinces the staff that the debt collector is in fact an armed robber. Although he is falsely arrested, Hachirō develops a liking for the roguish renegade and even offers to help him evade other debt collectors. The two mismatched buddies begin working together on a series of swindles and ventures in the style of CHEAP LOVE but romance catches up with them. Hachirō is sent to collect debts from the beautiful violinist he worships from afar, while a hospital manager's daughter confesses to a crush on Kazuma.

Broadcast with English subtitles in the U.S. on KIKU TV. Theme: SMAP—"Oretachi ni Asu wa Aru" (There Is a Tomorrow For Us). Peak rating: 23.2%.

FROM THE DINING ROOM WITH LOVE

1998. JPN: *Shokutaku kara Ai o Komete.* PRD: Kazuhiko Takahashi. DIR: Akiji Fujita. SCR: Yūko Kaneya. CAST: Chikako Kaku, Takeshi Naitō, Aki Hano, Ryōko Sakuma, Kei Tani. CHN: TVT. DUR: 45 mins. x 10 eps.; Wed 14 October 1998–16 December 1998.

After company bankruptcy forces them out of their corporate apartment, Haruka (Kaku) and Shūichi (Naitō) have no choice but to move in with Shūichi's parents (Tani and Sakuma). Shūichi finds another job but the salary is far less than before. Haruka decides to take a part-time job to help the household income.

FROM THE HEART *

2000. JPN: *Kimi ga Oshietekureta Koto.* AKA: *Things I Learned From You.* PRD: Tsuneaki Yamazaki. DIR: Ken Yoshida, Susumu Ōoka, Makoto Uchida. SCR: Yuriko Takeda. CAST: Rie Tomosaka, Takaya Kamikawa, Tatsuya Fujiwara, Miwa Mukunoki, Eriko Hatsune, Cha Katō, Kengo Mizushima. CHN: TBS. DUR: 45 mins. x 12 eps.; Thu 13 April 2000–30 June 2000.

Mayuko (Tomosaka) is an autistic woman who has a fascination with all kinds of weather. Not only is she hypnotized by any kind of rain or snow, she pays such close attention to the environment around her that she has developed an uncanny ability to predict the weather. She meets Shinichi (Kamikawa) in the middle of a storm, when she rebukes him for not bringing his umbrella after the "obvious" signs of approaching rain. He is unnerved by her intense interest in his keychain and inadvertently leaves it behind. Coincidentally, Mayuko's brother Jun (Fujiwara) is a medical student in the psychology class Shinichi teaches—he has developed an understandable interest in "high-functioning" autistics.

He rightly suspects that Mayuko wants to spend more time in everyday society and fears that she will suffer without her family's protection.

As Mayuko is tracked down and recruited by WeatherWorld, a meteorological company unaware of her condition, she begins seeing Shinichi for counseling. He, however, has a secret of his own—he is suffering from post-traumatic stress disorder ever since the death of his girlfriend. As their sessions continue, Mayuko learns from Shinichi about ways of coping and dealing with others, while he finds himself benefiting, too—he is learning how to love again, even though loving a patient is against the ethics of psychotherapy. Meanwhile, Mayuko is lured into the campaign of a politician who wishes to exploit her talents for his own ends.

Yet another disability drama from the infestation that dominated the late 1990s, *FtH* nonetheless presents a sensitive portrayal of its lead—there is often a fine line between autism and the clumsiness/emotional immaturity of many point-of-view characters in Japanese drama, and *FtH* is at least honest about Mayuko's condition. Like fairy-tale characters from *Pinocchio* to *Star Trek*'s Spock, Mayuko is an innocent keen to learn about human emotions—Shinichi teaches her that there is more to a hug than simple entwining of arms and she earnestly enquires if the pain she feels at the death of her cat has any relation to sadness.

Later episodes reveal that Mayuko's condition was itself brought about by psychological trauma and that like the heroine of **SLEEPING FOREST** she is the survivor of a past crime, the perpetrator of which is still at large. The sudden change in tone brought about by this revelation suffices to drag *FtH* from merely good to simply excellent and Tomosaka's performance is equally superb. Compare to **TRANSPARENT**, which added a science fictional spin to the idea of a "disabled" character unaware of his affliction and also **ETERNAL CHILD**, which similarly fea-

tured a relationship between a psychotherapist and an autistic patient and was broadcast during the same season on Japanese TV. Tomosaka plays another woman obsessed with weather (albeit in a very different way) in **FEMALE ANNOUNCERS**. Broadcast subtitled in the U.S. on KIKU TV. Theme: Shela—"Love Again . . . Eien no Sekai" (Love Again . . . Eternal World).

FROM THE NORTH
1981. JPN: *Kita no Kuni Kara.* PRD: Toshio Nakamura, Narimichi Sugita, Takaharu Yokoyama. DIR: Narimichi Sugita. SCR: Sō Kuramoto. CAST: Kunie Tanaka, Hidetaka Yoshioka, Tomoko Nakajima, Keiko Takeshita, Kōichi Iwaki, Ayumi Ishida. CHN: Fuji. DUR: 45 mins. x 24 eps.; Fri 9 October 1981–26 March 1982.
When his wife Reiko (Ishida) leaves him for another man, Gorō (Tanaka) decides that Tokyo is no longer the place for him. With his children, nine-year-old Jun (Yoshioka) and eight-year-old Hotaru (Nakajima), he returns to his remote home village of Furano in Hokkaidō. The children have particular trouble adjusting to a new home without electricity or plumbing and Jun even tries to escape back to his mother in the capital. Eventually, the household gains an additional member in the form of Reiko's sister Yukiko (Takeshita). Fleeing a disastrous relationship with a married man, she joins the northern commune as well, until all four members return to Tokyo in the penultimate episode for Reiko's funeral.

A back-to-nature series that reduces the concerns of family soap operas to basic human needs, *FtN* mixes beautiful unspoiled scenery with the simple concerns of rural living. **DEAR MOTHER** writer Kuramoto moved up to Furano himself for four years while writing the first series, and the story was shot on location in genuinely remote spots. The filming of the series forced a similar country lifestyle on the cast and crew, a condition that adds a palpable note of realism to incidental details

like chopping wood and walking on snow. Like its characters, the series is not afraid of solitude or silence—dialogue is often laconic and entire scenes pass with nothing said at all. The result is a drama of great emotional depth and one that has been regularly resurrected in feature-length specials that follow the characters' lives over the next 21 years.

In *FtN Fuyu* (Winter), shown on 24 March 1983, Gorō returns from seasonal work to find that Jun's friend Masakichi (Yoshihito Nakazawa) has run away from home. While the children fret about their missing friend, Gorō must contend with the return of one of Furano's conquering heroes. After 30 years in Tokyo, original Furano pioneer Matsukichi comes back to the village where he is a living legend. Meanwhile, Gorō finds himself obliged to help Midori (Michiko Hayashi), the mother of the missing child, who is in debt to the tune of seven million yen.

FtN Natsu (Summer), shown on 27 September 1984, features another clash of the opposing city and country lifestyles, when Jun's friend Tsutomu (Makoto Mutsuura) visits him from Tokyo. The children are impressed by Tsutomu's computer, but hurt when he insults their father. After a long gap, in which the "children" became hulking teenagers, *FtN Hatsukoi* (First Love) was broadcast on 27 March 1987. With its tale of Jun's obsession with local girl Rei (Megumi Yokoyama) and with his plan to build a wind-powered electric generator for his father's birthday, it is cited by many viewers as their favorite installment in the series. *FtN Kikyō* (Coming Home), shown on 31 March 1989, picks up the story two years later, after Jun's earlier happy ending has been reversed. Last seen heading off to boarding school in Tokyo with Rei, Jun now returns after failing his exams, just in time to witness Hotaru's first love and broken heart. Gorō welcomes his son but insists that he return to Tokyo to give himself another chance.

In the two-part *FtN Sudachi* (Leaving the Nest) shown on 22 and 23 May 1992, Hotaru graduates from high school. The focus, however, shifts to Jun working in Tokyo and struggling to cope with the news that his girlfriend Tamako is pregnant with his child. By the middle of the trendy drama boom of the 1990s, *FtN* seems to adopt similar characteristics with *FtN Himitsu* (Secret), shown on 9 June 1995, in which Jun is now conducting a long-distance love affair with Rei, who remains in Hokkaidō's major city of Sapporo. Meanwhile, Hotaru has been conducting an affair with a 43-year-old married man, Dr. Kuroki, and eventually runs away with him.

FtN Jidai (Epoch), was shown on 10 and 11 July 1998 to commemorate the 40th anniversary of Fuji TV—compare to similar anniversary showpieces such as **OSHIN** and **MONKEY**. Hotaru returns to Furano with her ex-lover's child and Masakichi offers to make an honest woman of her. Local patriarch Sōta (Iwaki) plans a big ceremony for them but dies in a fatal accident.

The final installment of the series came on 6 and 7 September 2002 with *FtN Yuigon* (Testament). Jun and Masakichi inherit Sōta's cattle farm, only to find their initial exuberance ruined by unpaid bills. In order to pay off Sōta's debts, the two friends separate to find employment elsewhere. Meanwhile, Hotaru works as a nurse, while the aged Gorō enjoys semi-retirement and baby-sits his grandson. The ever-unlucky Jun begins to date Yui

(Yuki Uchida) but discovers that her missing husband Hiroshi (Gorō Kishitani) has returned to reclaim her. Gorō agrees to build a house for a friend's newly wed daughter but is struck by sudden pains in his abdomen.

The ratings for the final episodes of *FtN* peaked at 38.4%—only to be expected for a series that is regularly ranked in the top three drama events of all time by viewer's polls. It is difficult to quantify the reasons for its success—Kuramoto himself regards it as a form of production retreat that happened to produce occasional TV shows, while many in the audience simply like the idea of watching the characters grow and change *in real time,* not compressed into a single season like most dramas. Part of its appeal may also rest in the simple return to homespun, farm town values, an atavistic urge also welcomed in **COUNTRY LIVING** and **LADY OF THE MANOR**. Music by Masashi Sada.

FROZEN SUMMER
1998. JPN: *Kōritsuku Natsu.* PRD: Motoko Kimura. DIR: Masahiro Kunimoto. SCR: Michiru Etō, Rie Yokota. CAST: Shigeru Muroi, Shirō Sano, Yōko Nogiwa, Saya Takagi, Sayaka Yamaguchi. CHN: NTV. DUR: 45 mins. x 11 eps.; Mon 6 July 1998–14 September 1998.
Successful lady lawyer Natsuki (Muroi) marries successful businessman Kenichi (Sano) and gains an instant family when she becomes the stepmother of his three children from a previous marriage. Another reluctant parenting drama in the style of **BASICALLY NICE** and **DON'T CALL ME PAPA**. Theme: Sachiko Suzuki—"Tashikamete Ite yo" (Please Make Sure).

FUGITIVE, THE
1992. JPN: *Tōbōsha.* PRD: N/C. DIR: Hiroshi Akabane. SCR: Misao Yajima. CAST: Toshihiko Tahara, Emi Wakui, Hidekazu Akai, Yukiharu Takahashi. CHN: Fuji. DUR: 45 mins. x 12 eps.; Wed 1 July 1992–16 September 1992.

Eiji (Tahara) works at the loan division of Tōzai Bank. He is ordered to sign a suspicious document that is later used to frame him for embezzlement. He goes on the run from the police and attempts to avenge himself against his persecutor Shimazu (Takahashi), who raised Eiji as his own son. The American series *The Fugitive* (1963) was formerly broadcast on TBS in 1964 under the same title. Theme: Toshihiko Tahara—"Ame ga Sakendeiru" (Rain Calls Out).

FULL HOUSE
2000. JPN: *Tadaima Manshitsu.* PRD: Ikuhide Yokochi, Kazuo Yamamoto. DIR: Shunji Muguruma. SCR: Mika Ōmori. CAST: Kanako Enomoto, Ikki Sawamura, Hiroyuki Miyasako, Jun Miho, Raita Ryū, Manami Fuji. CHN: Asahi. DUR: 45 mins. x ca. 11 eps.; Sun 14 October 2000–30 December 2000.
School teacher Momo (Enomoto) is forced to change jobs when her mother dies, taking over the family business the Hotel Eileen. Episodic adventures then ensue in the style of **HOTEL**, as a series of idiosyncratic guests arrive with stories to be told, while Momo simultaneously tries to fight off business enemies who want Hotel Eileen shut down or demolished. Compare to **TAKE ME TO A RYOKAN** and **SEESAW GAME**.

FULL OF THE SUN
1998. JPN: *Taiyō ga Ippai.* PRD: Takuharu Morita. DIR: Takao Kinoshita. SCR: Tokio Tsuchida. CAST: Masatoshi Nakamura, Riho Makise, Shigeki Hosokawa, Mayuko Takada. CHN: Kansai. DUR: 45 mins. x 10 eps.; Tue 13 January 1998–17 March 1998.
Yūichi (Nakamura), widowed for ten years, suddenly wins 150 million yen in a lottery. At work, he is ordered to see the chairman of the company, who asks him to marry his daughter Mariko (Makise). Theme: Nanase Aikawa—"Kanojo to Watashi no Jijō" (Her Secret, My Secret).

FURTHER ADVENTURES OF MUSASHI

1964. JPN: *Sorekara no Musashi.* AKA: *And Then, Musashi . . . .* PRD: N/C. DIR: N/C. SCR: N/C. CAST: Ryūnosuke Tsukigata, Chiyonosuke Azuma. CHN: NET. DUR: 45 mins. x 52 eps.; Mon 23 March 1964–12 April 1965.

The aging warrior MUSASHI prepares to fight a duel with his sworn enemy Kojirō Sasaki but disappears. The locals presume that he has fled but he is found by the local lord's daughter carving an oar into a wooden sword. The forthcoming duel is more than just a fight between two men—rival lords are backing the opponents and their combat is a ritualized war between the clans. Sasaki's people, however, lack Musashi's honor—they fully intend to murder Musashi, even if he wins.

Though Musashi bests Sasaki, he feels empty, and his thoughts turn to Okō, the love of his life, who is seriously ill—Okō is only one of several doomed women who fall in love with Musashi in the course of the series. He wanders Japan acquiring a few new pupils and fighting more duels, losing another beloved in the process and gaining Iori, an adopted son he rescues as a child from a burning village. Eventually, as death nears, the frail Musashi writes his famous tactical manual *The Book of Five Rings.*

Although Musashi's modern-day fame rests on the series of novels by Eiji Yoshikawa, some stories of his life remain public domain legends, and it is these which have now been adapted on three separate occasions. Presumably for legal reasons, the three drama series detailing events of the later life of Japan's "Sword Saint" rename many of the characters already familiar from Eiji Yoshikawa's famous novels, thereby making them fair game for a TV series without having to pay Yoshikawa for any remake rights. The story was adapted again as five TV movies, all shown on the same day in January 1981 and starring Kinnosuke Yorozuya (aka Kinnosuke Nakamura) in the title role. The most recent version, starring Kinya Kitaōji as Musashi, also added extra subplots revolving around THE YAGYŪ CONSPIRACY. Musashi is offered the post of fencing instructor, but turns it down, leading to the recruitment of his sworn enemy Munenori Yagyū. Yagyū's agents fan out across Japan, claiming to be teachers of swordsmanship but actually charged with a mission to subvert the authority of all lords who resist the authority of the Shogun.

Musashi also becomes involved in another war-by-proxy, the intrigues between the Spanish and the Dutch for the chance to keep Japanese trade to themselves. The Dutch win in the propaganda war and convince the Shogun that the Catholic religion preached in the Nagasaki region by the Spanish will lead to trouble and rebellion. As the shogunate clamps down savagely on Christianity in the region, Musashi helps Princess Yuri (another woman hopelessly in love with him) to save Christian children who would otherwise be put to the sword by Yagyū agents.

Musashi is approached by Lord Hosokawa, an old friend whose rule is threatened by the attempts of his frail father, the former lord, to regain the authority he once had before he resigned. Yagyū intrigues encourage Hosokawa retainers to make life difficult for the new lord, and Musashi's sworn enemy Mondo starts another vendetta in a fit of pique when Lord Hosokawa promises Musashi the hand of Princess Yuri in marriage. Musashi's final duel, against Jūbei Yagyū himself, ends with the samurai's final victory and his retreat into retirement to write. The Kinya Kitaōji *Musashi* also dominated the schedules on New Year's Day 1996. The Yagyū also appeared as the ultimate enemy in LONE WOLF AND CUB.

G

GAORANGER *

2001. JPN: *Hyakujū Sentai Gaoranger*.
AKA: *One Hundred Beasts Battle Team
Gaoranger; Power Rangers Wild Force*.
PRD: Kenji Ōta, Kōichi Yada, Jun
Higasa, Takahiro Yokozuka. DIR: Toshi
Morota, Katsuya Watanabe, Tarō
Sakamoto, Noboru Matsui, Kenzō
Maihara, Noboru Takemoto, Shōjirō
Nakazawa. SCR: Yoshiki Takeue,
Masataka Akaboshi, Naoyuki Sakai,
Chiejirō Nakasu. CAST: Noboru Kaneko,
Kei Horie, Takeru Shibaki, Kazuyoshi
Sakai, Mio Takeuchi, Tetsuji
Tamayama, Rei Saitō. CHN: Asahi. DUR:
25 mins. x 51 eps.; Sun 18 February
2001–10 February 2002.

At the beginning of the 21st century,
the Earth is threatened by the Org devil clan. Power Animals, who live in an
ethereal aerial island, choose five
young human warriors to defend the
planet. Former veterinarian Sō (Kaneko) is now Gao Red, King of Beasts, the
incarnation of the lion, who fights with
Lion Fang punches. Former pilot cadet
Gaku (Horie) is Gao Yellow, King of
Birds, an eagle incarnate who can control the winds. Tenacious hunter Kai
(Shibaki) is Gao Blue, King of Water, a
shark incarnate who specializes in
underwater combat. Former sumo
wrestler Sōtarō (Sakai) is Gao
Black, King of the Prairie, a bison
incarnate and subject to fits of berserk
rage. Sae (Takeuchi) is Gao White,
Queen of the Forests, a tiger incarnate
and a martial arts specialist. The team

is later joined by Osamu (Tamayama)
as Gao Silver, a warrior who fought
against the Org a thousand years ago,
who is now a wolf incarnate and 1062
years old.

Gaoranger was soon adapted by
Saban Entertainment for the U.S. market as the tenth season in the **MIGHTY
MORPHIN' POWER RANGERS** series,
under the title *Power Rangers Wild Force*.
The U.S. version is set 3000 years after
the magical kingdom of Animaria was
last threatened by Master Org (Ilya
Volokh) and his Org warriors. For all
that time, Princess Shayla (Ann Marie
Crouch) has lain dormant in Animaria,
which is now a floating island, with five
Wild Zords that can be used to defend
it if it is ever attacked again. The Org
have been locked in an earthbound
prison for many centuries but their
bonds have been weakened by contemporary pollution. Shayla begins recruiting modern teenagers to help her and
eventually assembles Yellow Ranger
Taylor (Alyson Kiperman), Blue
Ranger Max (Philip Jeanmarie), White
Ranger Alyssa (Jessica Ray), and Black
Ranger Danny (Jack Guzman). The
series begins with the recruitment of
the final team member, Red Ranger
Cole (Ricardo Medina, Jr.), a kid from
the wilderness who leaves his tribe in
search of civilization. The Rangers also
fight against and then recruit Merrick
(Philip Andrew), the mythical sixth of
the original legendary warriors, who
temporarily turned to the dark side

after donning a cursed wolf mask in an
attempt to defeat Org's last attack. In
the Super Sentai chronology, *Gaoranger*
came after **TIMERANGER** and before
HURRICANGER and was, as usual, credited to the imagination of one "Saburō
Yade."

GARRET IN THE SKY

1974. JPN: *Kūchū Atelier*. PRD: Seiji
Akiyama. DIR: Noriaki Sasahara. SCR:
Yukio Doi. CAST: Hiroyo Funabashi, Tayo
Iwamoto, Yūsuke Tozawa, Aki Yamada,
Kenji Tanaka, Kazumi Yokota. CHN:
NHK. DUR: 25 mins. x 9 eps.; Mon 23
September 1974–9 October 1974.

Yuri (Funabashi) is a meek and bright
12 year old. Her mother (Iwamoto) is
an eccentric painter who behaves as if
the rest of the world is invisible while
she is working at her canvas. Her easel
always dominates the room and consequently this symbol of the workplace
interferes in Yuri's own life. Mother
concentrates so hard on her painting
and a forthcoming exhibition that she
forgets to go to the Parents' Day at
Yuri's school. Based on a novel by
Mizue Takekawa.

GAVAN

1982. JPN: *Uchū Keiji Gaban*. AKA:
Space Cop Gaban. PRD: Susumu
Yoshikawa, Itaru Orita. DIR: Yoshiaki
Kobayashi, Atsuo Okunaka, Hideo
Tanaka, Kazushi Hattori, Takeru
Ogasawara. SCR: Shōzō Uehara,
Susumu Takahisa, Mikio Matsushita,

Kazue Abe, Tatsurō Nagai, Tomomi Tsutsui. CAST: Kenji Ōba, Takako Towa, Toshiaki Nishizawa, Kyōko Myōdai, Masayuki Suzuki, Jun Tatara, Michio Iijima, Ken Nishida, Noboru Mitani. CHN: Asahi. DUR: 30 mins. x 44 eps.; Fri 5 March 1982–25 February 1983.

The evil Makū Space Crime Organization destroys a space colony and establishes a base on Earth but is pursued by Gavan (Ōba), a half-alien cosmic law enforcer determined to save the planet as it is the birthplace of his mother. Gavan's high-powered armor puts him on equal terms with the monsters he must battle, who include mutated Earth animals, a sea monster that preys on Japanese shipping, and a Makū agent using an antique alien helmet which turns the wearer invisible. The Makū forces are prepared to try anything, including the kidnapping of pacifists to ensure that belligerent factions seize control of the government (compare to PHANTOM AGENTS), starting up schools designed to turn innocent children into future footsoldiers (compare to CHALLENGE FROM THE FUTURE), and manipulating the media to imply that Gavan is kidnapping children instead of saving them.

Star Ōba formerly appeared as a comedy sidekick in Super Sentai shows such as BATTLEFEVER J and DENZIMAN but got to be the dashing lead in *Gavan*, which was to become the first of the loosely linked "Metal Series." Where GORANGER and its successors in the rival Super Sentai series featured teams of superheroes in super-cool vehicles, the Metal Series preferred to encase its actors in armored battle suits. The series continued with SHALIBAN (who was introduced toward the end of the series as Gavan's earthbound replacement when the Space Sheriff was promoted to captain), SHIDER, JUSPION, *Spielban* and METALDAR (combined and adapted for the U.S. as VR TROOPERS), JIRAIYA, JIVAN, WINSPECTOR, SOLBRAIN, EXIDRAFT, JAN PERSON, BLUE SWAT, and the two *Bee-Fighter* serials (which were combined and adapted for the U.S. as BEETLEBORGS).

Gavan was also adapted into manga form by Minoru Nonaka. Supposedly based, as usual, on "an idea by Saburō Yade," the series contained some innovative and paranoid plot twists. Makū's cunning knows no bounds—the empire is prepared to offer sportsmen miracle drugs if they do their bidding (an idea used again in the later *Black Jack,* *AE) and kidnap the family of a scrupulous scientist in order to force him to work on an illegal virus. Meanwhile, Gavan searches incessantly for his long-lost father, who eventually appears in the 43rd episode, played by golden age superhero Shinichi "Sonny" Chiba. Theme: Akira Kushida—"Uchū Keiji Gaban" (Space Detective Gavan).

GAZER

1998. JPN: *Bishōjo Shinseiki Gazer*. AKA: *Beautiful Girl New Century Gazer*. PRD: Gō Nakajima, Tomoyuki Imai, Hiroki Ōta. DIR: Atsushi Shimizu, Katsuhito Ueno. SCR: Baku Kamio, Daisuke Habara. CAST: Kazue Fukiishi, Atsuko Sudō, Tomofumi Uno, Ryūgo Hashi, Daisuke Honda, Sayaka Kimura, Miyuki Kojima, Akira Ōtaka, Kirina Mano, Yōko Nagasogabe, Erika Kuroishi, Masami Horiguchi, Kazuhiko Nishimura. CHN: Asahi. DUR: 30 mins. x 6 eps.; Sun 22 August 1998–26 September 1998.

Schoolgirl Moe Mikasa (Fukiishi) is troubled by mysterious dreams. She heads off for a day out with her friends Hitomi (Sudō), Ayako (Kimura), and Yūji (Hashi), ostensibly for a picnic but really to see whether a recent "meteorite" in Shinrin Park was really a UFO. However, the park has been sealed off, and after they see a luminous object in the sky, the group is pursued by armed individuals. Moe escapes with the help of Yūji and her journalist uncle Akira (Nishimura), only to discover that her parents have been murdered by serial killed Kō (Uno).

Pursued by a mysterious woman called Rio (Mano), Moe goes on the run. She discovers that she was really adopted and that as a child she was abducted by aliens and injected with the Ekidona virus. Developed by Kirigami (Horiguchi), the chief of the Vector Life Science Lab, and his lover Asō (Nagasogabe), Ekidona hybridizes human and alien DNA. Those on whom the virus only exerts a partial effect are transformed into android mutants like Kō and Rio. However, as the original vector for the virus, Moe has the chance to become a living goddess and Kirigami wants to control her. Kō tries to save Moe from the hand of Kirigami. Meanwhile, Asō approaches Rio to create more powerful mutants and to steal a march on Kirigami.

Heavily influenced by *The X-Files* (1993), first screened on TV Asahi in 1995, *Gazer* adds monster combat in the long tradition of Tsuburaya shows—compare to similar late-night serials such as BUNNY KNIGHTS and MASKED ANGEL ROSETTA. Though it was broadcast after midnight and hence technically on Sunday morning, some sources still list it as a Saturday night show. Music by Takashi Nakagawa and Takuya Nishimura.

GEISHA DETECTIVE

1999. JPN: *Maiko-san wa Meitantei*. AKA: *The Geisha Is a Famous Detective, Investi-Geisha, Modern Geisha*. PRD: Takashi Inoue. DIR: Takashi Inoue. SCR: Izō Hashimoto, Kazu Sunamoto, Hiromi Tanaka. CAST: Miki Sakai, Ryūji Harada, Eiichirō Funakoshi, Kyōko Kishida. CHN: Asahi. DUR: 45 mins. x ca. 11 eps.; Thu 15 April 1999–?? June 1999.

Kogiku (Sakai) is a trainee geisha living in Japan's former capital Kyoto, where she has a reputation for putting her foot in it—in the first episode alone, we see her archly comment that a tourist's sketches *"are almost there,"* only to discover later that she is talking to famous artist Sawaki (Harada). Amid the kabuki performances, geisha dances, and samisen serenades, Kyoto's geisha quarter is plagued by a series of crimes, mystifying the local detective (Funakoshi). Only Kogiku's in-depth

Geisha Detective

unmasked through their inability to match seasonal patterns on their kimono or their inadequate knowledge of the tea ceremony. In a genre that has become dominated by the American cop show, there is something refreshingly ludicrous about a chase sequence in which kimono-clad samisen players pursue a fleeing criminal while teetering on their traditional *geta* clogs and something touchingly sweet about a script that *doesn't* attempt to play all this for laughs. Despite the crew's deadly serious intent, the result is one of the funniest Japanese dramas ever made, with plenty of Kyoto scenery as an added bonus. Based on a mystery by Misa Yamamura, and a somewhat unexpected screen adaptation credit for Izō Hashimoto, the cowriter of *Akira* (*AE). Compare to THE MAGNIFICENT ADVENTURES OF KOHARU THE GEISHA and another crime fighter from Kyoto, INVESTIGATOR MARIKO. Theme: ZARD—"Sekai wa Kitto Mirai no Naka" (The World Lies in the Future).

GENTA IKENAKA 80 KILOS

1980. JPN: *Ikenaka Genta 80 Kilo*. PRD: Tadashi Nakajima. DIR: Kan Ishibashi. SCR: Toshiharu Matsubara. CAST: Toshiyuki Nishida, Ryōko Sakaguchi, Yōichi Miura, Junichi Inoue, Miwako Fujitani, Toshie Takada, Kaoru Sugita, Kanako Arima, Tomokazu Miura, Satoka Abiko. CHN: NTV. DUR: 45 mins. x 48 eps.; Sat 5 April 1980–28 June 1980 (#1); 4 April 1981–29 August 1981 (#2); 8 April 1989–6 May 1989 (#3). Photojournalist Genta Ikenaka (Nishida) marries widow Tsuruko (Mitsuko Oka) who has three daughters—15-year-old Eri (Sugita), 11-year-old Miku (Arima), and 6-year-old Yako (Abiko). However, Tsuruko dies unexpectedly, and although her relatives intend to split the girls up and rear them themselves, Genta insists on keeping them together and carrying out his duties as a responsible surrogate parent. Though they welcome the news that they won't be separated, the sisters still find the process of acclimat-

knowledge of geisha tradition, coupled with her impressive ability in judo, can help the police solve the crimes. Meanwhile, despite Kogiku's initial insults, the artist decides to stay around a while—he likes this geisha more than he lets on.

Geisha Detective is simply one of the most mind-boggling series we have seen, with an unbeatable mixture of ancient tradition, daft plotting, and cardboard sets. For those viewers who

are not defeated by the impenetrable Kyoto accent and geisha dialect, it is an entertaining treasure trove, mixing amateur sleuthing in the style of Agatha Christie's Miss Marple with cultural footnotes à la LADY OF THE MANOR. In one typical example, Kogiku reasons that a geisha suicide is no such thing, noting that the victim's *obi* sash appears to have been tied by someone else after her death. Murderers and imposters are

ing to their new parent difficult at times. Yako refuses to answer her teacher when she calls roll using her new surname and Eri constantly compares Genta to her biological father.

Over time, Genta wins the girls over but his fatherly advice is not always appreciated. He advises Yako to stand up to bullies, only to receive a complaint from Miku's school that she has copied her sister and reduced a boy to tears. Genta must also juggle his job and private life with his newfound stepchildren.

In his first major role, Nishida (who formerly played the lecherous Pigsy in **MONKEY**) set the tone for two further decades of dramas in which a career-minded adult with a heart of gold is suddenly forced to become a surrogate parent—compare to **GOOD MOURNING, NEWS WOMAN**, and **BEST DAD IN THE WORLD**.

After the success of the initial 13-episode run, the series returned for a 21-episode second season the following year. Genta returns from a nine-month stint in Cambodia, where he has been photographing refugee camps. During his absence, the house has burned down (compare to **MASTERS OF TASTE**), leading to the girls being scattered among distant relatives. Genta's colleague Akiko (Sakaguchi), whom he had left in charge of the girls, is stuck in the hospital after breaking her leg in the fire and Genta is shocked to discover that nobody thought to tell him any of this while he was away.

After Genta regrouped his step-family in the second season, the story was updated on 3 April 1986 in a feature-length TV movie, depicting the approach of Genta and Akiko's long-awaited wedding. A second special on 6 October the same year focused on Eri's courtship with dentist Okumura (Miura), a single father whose child Eri teaches in her new job at a kindergarten.

A short four-episode third season (with a little editing, it could probably have been released as another one-shot special) picked up the family's story 13

years after the death of Tsuruko. Akiko and Eri are both pregnant, Miku is a fully grown college student, and Yako is preparing for her high school entrance exam. It ends with Genta becoming a father and a grandfather on the same day.

The series finally bowed out with one final "Goodbye" TV special on 6 October 1992. Miku is planning a wedding of her own and Yako wants to be a photographer *"just like Dad."* Genta realizes that, just as his little girls have grown up, other youngsters are muscling in on his career but it doesn't stop him being a proud parent and step-parent one last time.

GIFT

1997. PRD: Yoshiki Tanaka, Masatoshi Yamaguchi. DIR: Shunsaku Kawake, Isamu Nakae, Kensaku Sawada. SCR: Jōji Iida, Yumiko Inoue. CAST: Takuya Kimura, Shigeru Muroi, Satomi Kobayashi, Ryōko Shinohara, Masayuki Imai. CHN: NTV. DUR: 45 mins. x 11 eps.; Wed 16 April 1997–25 June 1997.

Naomi (Muroi) plans on fleeing the country with her boyfriend and 50 million yen in cash but when she arrives at the allotted meeting place, her boyfriend and her money are nowhere to be seen. Instead, she follows a trail of blood to the safe, where she finds Yukio (Kimura), a naked man with no knowledge of who he really is or how he got there. Reasoning that Yukio's lost memories are the only way of tracking down her missing cash, Naomi employs Yukio as a courier—the things he delivers and the people he meets often jogging his memory with snippets of his past life. Naomi also tries to use other methods to cure Yukio's amnesia and is not beneath hiring another girl (Shinohara) to pose as his "forgotten" girlfriend. Meanwhile, Yukio is also pursued by a female detective, who has been tracing the missing money for three years and has also realized that the key lies somewhere in Yukio's mind.

On the surface, *Gift* is yet another

work-oriented drama, depicting episodic adventures in the life of a courier as Yukio delivers everything from a love letter to a corpse. He becomes involved in blackmail attempts and kidnappings and stands up for right in true Japanese leading man style. However, as might be expected from the writer of **NIGHT HEAD**, the series also features a gripping subplot that prefigures **SLEEPING FOREST**, as the traumatized Yukio slowly pieces together images from his past. Arriving out of order and devoid of context, the images slowly form into a flashback that details the events that caused him to lose his memory. As with Christopher Nolan's movie *Memento* (2000), which *Gift* resembles in certain ways, such revelations force Yukio to question who his real friends are—the restoration of his old life ruining the new one he has enjoyed for three years. The series was also the cause of a minor media scandal in Japan when it was blamed for encouraging children to carry knives. Theme: Brian Ferry—"Tokyo Joe."

GIGANTOR *

1960. JPN: *Tetsujin 28-gō.* AKA: *Ironman #28.* PRD: N/C. DIR: Santarō Marune, Hiroyuki Shiwa. SCR: Santarō Marune, Haruo Kōrogi. CAST: Shōichi Naitō, Santa Arikiyama, Yōichirō Mikawa, Setsuko Ogata, Kumiko Nōtomi, Kōtarō Bandō, Osamu Kanai. CHN: NTV. DUR: 25 mins. x 13 eps.; Mon 1 February 1960–25 April 1960.

Large robots are being used to commit crimes by the secret QX criminal organization. Orphan Shōtaro (Naitō) realizes that they are military machines created by his scientist father during World War II, long presumed destroyed by Allied bombing. In fact, the robots survived the war and have fallen into the wrong hands. Former researcher Professor Shikashima (Mikawa) helps Shōtaro find Ironman #28, the last and strongest of the prototypes. They decide to use #28 to fight crime and restore the good name of Shōtaro's father.

Based on the 1956 manga in *Shōnen*

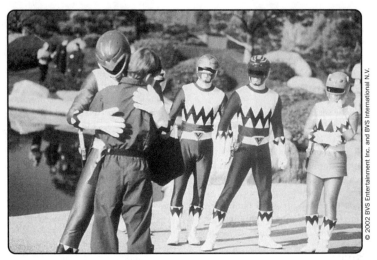

Gingaman

Magazine, written by **WATER MARGIN**'s Mitsuteru Yokoyama, *Gigantor* was later transformed into a more successful animated series (see *AE) that ran for considerably longer than this single black-and-white season. As might be expected, the limits of live-action filming took their toll, most obviously in the titular robot, whose height was a mere two meters, hardly the "bigger than big" of the later anime version. Episodes of the series were released in the U.S. in a feature-length edit under the title *Brain 17.*

GINGAMAN *
1998. JPN: *Seijū Sentai Gingaman.* AKA: *Star-Beast Battle-Team Galaxy-Man; Power Rangers Lost Galaxy.* PRD: Kenji Ōta, Kōichi Yada, Shigeki Takadera. DIR: Ryūta Tazaki, Masato Tsujino, Takeo Nagaishi, Hajime Konaka, Toshi Moroda. SCR: Yasuko Kobayashi, Yoshiki Takeue, Minehisa Arakawa, Tsuyoshi Kida, Kei Murakami, Tetsuo Okita. CAST: Kazuki Maebara, Hiroshi Sueyoshi, Hide Teru, Nobuteru Takahashi, Juri Miyazawa, Teruaki Ogawa, Rokurō Nōya, Hidekazu Shibata, Kei Mizutani, Norio Wakamoto. CHN: Asahi. DUR: 25 mins. x 50 eps.; Sun 22 February 1998–14 February 1999. Three thousand years after the first

Gingaman team locked the Baruban Space Pirates beneath the sea, the evil creatures escape from their watery prison during an underwater earthquake. The creatures of the Ginga forest recruit five modern warriors to fight the old battle again, led by Ginga Red Ryōma (Maebara), wielder of the Star Beast Sword and imbued with the spirit of fire. Hayate (Sueyoshi) is Ginga Green, sometime flute player and warrior imbued with the spirit of wind. Gōki (Teru) is Ginga Blue who draws his powers from the spirit of water. Hikaru (Takahashi) is Ginga Yellow who fights with the spirit of thunder. Token female Saya (Miyazawa) is Ginga Pink who fights with the power of flowers. The team is also occasionally joined by Hyūga (Ogawa), the Dark Knight and former lone warrior of justice. Their allies in this include their five color-coded Star-Beasts, each of which has a robot version that can combine to form the Gingaio (Ginga King) robot, as well as other robots such as the Gigantis Buster and Brutaus. The team also have all-black versions of their steeds, which can combine to make the Gingaio Black superrobot. Their enemies include four Baruban generals led by the sexy space bitch Cerinda (Mizutani). Actress Kei

Mizutani also appeared in numerous anime/manga tie-ins, including *Weather Woman* (*AE), *Kekko Kamen* (*AE), and *The Ladies' Phone Sex Club,* and Juri Miyazawa appeared in **DANGEROUS ANGEL X DEATH HUNTER.** Note also popular anime voice actor Wakamoto (*Gunbuster,* *AE) as the series narrator. "Based on an idea by Saburō Yade," and featuring music by Toshihiko Sahashi.

Gingaman was adapted into the seventh incarnation of the U.S. TV show **MIGHTY MORPHIN' POWER RANGERS,** under the title *Power Rangers Lost Galaxy.* After the apocalyptic events of *Power Rangers in Space* (see the **MEGARANGER** synopsis), there were only a few tenuous links between this show and the former continuities. The U.S. plot features stowaway Leo (Danny Slavin) onboard the colony vessel Terra Venture, who becomes embroiled in an attempt by space villain Scorpius (Kim Strauss) to invade a distant world. Alien warrior Maya (Cerina Vincent) asks for the humans' help and the group eventually draw magical Quasar Sabers from a stone, transforming them into the new Power Rangers—Red Leo, Yellow Maya, Blue Kai (Archie Kao), Green Damon (Reggie Rolle), and Pink Kendrix (Valerie Vernon). Leo's long-lost brother Mike (Russell Lawrence) also appears occasionally in symbiosis with the long-lived space warrior Magna Defender. After acquiring their new Zord beasts/robots, the Power Rangers fight off Scorpius but lose Kendrix. Believing her to be dead, the earlier series' former evil-invader-princess-restored-to-good Karone (Melody Perkins) becomes the new Pink Ranger. After a prolonged battle with new enemies Captain Mutiny (Mike Reynolds), Deviot (Bob Pappenbrook), and Trakeena (Amy Miller), the Rangers restore normality. The Gingaman Rangers would also have cameo roles in the following series in the Super Sentai chronology, **GOGO FIVE,** released in the U.S. as *Power Rangers Lightspeed Rescue.*

GIRL ACROSS TIME

1994. JPN: *Toki o Kakeru Shōjo*. PRD: Yūji Iwata. DIR: Masayuki Ochiai. SCR: Ryōichi Kimizuka. CAST: Yuki Uchida, Yoshihiko Hakamada, Gamon Kaai, Leo Morimoto, Yasutaka Tsutsui, Namie Amuro. CHN: Fuji. DUR: 45 mins. x 5 eps.; Sat 19 February 1994–19 March 1994.

Seventeen-year-old Kazuko Yoshiyama (Uchida) sniffs a lavender-scented potion at the high school laboratory and unknowingly gains a supernatural power. She kisses her classmate Kazuo (Hakamada) but he rejects her advances, claiming to have come from the 27th century to experiment on 20th-century humans with homemade chemicals. He only arrived three weeks earlier but has planted false memories in all his acquaintances, so that they believe he has known them all their lives. Kazuko is scandalized that her experience of first love and first kiss has been led astray by mind-altering drugs, but forgives him when she realizes it was Kazuo's love for her that made him "augment" her feelings.

Kazuo reveals that he is developing a new chemical which should allow him to return to his own time. Before he leaves the 20th century, he takes Kazuko back to an incident seven years in her own past, when she watched paralyzed as her younger sister Miyoko almost drowned. Though Kazuko hopes that reliving the incident will help her overcome her trauma, her ethereal time-travel body makes it impossible for her to intervene and she must endure the anguish a second time. Returning to the present day, Kazuo erases Kazuko's memories of him and his abilities. However, later Miyoko talks to Kazuko about the incident and assures her that she would not have survived without her—it was Kazuko calling her name that snapped her out of her unconsciousness after she was pulled from the water. Theme: Nokko—"Ningyo" (Mermaid).

A remake of Yasutaka Tsutsui's TIME TRAVELER by screenwriter Kimizuka, who, if he could see his *own* future, would see BAYSIDE SHAKEDOWN looming in it not long afterward.

GIRL COMMANDO IZUMI

1987. JPN: *Shōjo Commando Izumi*. PRD: N/C. DIR: Toshio Ōi, Morio Maejima. SCR: Masayoshi Azuma, Junki Takegami, Kazuhiko Kōbe, Akihiko Kakizaki. CAST: Izumi Igarashi, Yumi Tsuchida, Masami Katsuragawa, Takeo Chii, Hiroyuki Watanabe, Takeyuki Yue, Yuki Sukegawa. CHN: Fuji. DUR: 25 mins. x 15 eps.; Thu 5 November 1987–18 February 1988.

Tokyo schoolgirl Izumi (Igarashi) hides her elite fighting skills and has trouble explaining where she got them from—in fact she is the "ultimate warrior" and target of numerous monsters of the week. Teaming up with local detective Eiji (Chii), she tries to defend her school and friends from attacking terminators. In order to know her lost past, she fights against the organization that turned her into a weapon. In the final episode, she finally gets to blow the chairman of the organization away with a bazooka. A camp bad-girl-high-school series in the tradition of SUKEBAN DEKA but with classroom differences settled with the aid of recoilless rifles and heavy artillery. Compare to the anime *Project A-ko* (*AE). James Cameron's *Terminator* (1984) was a great influence on Japanese sci-fi, not the least for its ability to integrate a futuristic plot with low-cost contemporary locations. Theme singer A-jari appeared in a cameo role in the episode "Aim for the Concert." Theme: A-jari—"Just for Love."

GIRLFRIEND SHE HATES, THE

1993. JPN: *Kanojo no Kirai na Kanojo*. PRD: N/C. DIR: Kazuo Yamamoto. SCR: Atsuko Sagara. CAST: Yuriko Ishida, Mieko Harada, Ryūji Harada, Hiroshi Fuse. CHN: Yomiuri. DUR: 45 mins. x 11 eps.; Sat 17 April 1993–26 June 1993.

Satsuki (Ishida) works at the administration department in an import-export company. She decides to leave her freelance photographer boyfriend Kanō (Ryūji Harada) and change her life. She is successfully transferred to the sales department but the new boss Reiko (Mieko Harada) is so efficient that she makes her feel inadequate. Theme: ZARD—"Kimi ga Inai" (You're Not There).

GIRLS IN HOT WATER

1994. JPN: *Yukemuri Joshidaisei Sōdō*. AKA: *College Girls in Hot Water*. PRD: Yoshio Gōda. DIR: Masaharu Ōta. SCR: Yuki Kiyomoto. CAST: Saki Takaoka, Takako Tokiwa, Shingo Kusuyama, Makoto Nonomura, Robert Hoffman. CHN: Asahi. DUR: 45 mins. x 5 eps.; Tue 15 February 1994–15 March 1994.

Serika (Takaoka), Reiko (Tokiwa), and two other girls are members of a hot spring club who win a night at an exclusive hot springs hotel in a quiz. Arriving to discover that their destination has been accidentally double-booked, they are forced to head to Ichinotaki Inn, a run-down hotel that is so quiet it faces closure. Like the heroines of TAKE ME TO A RYOKAN and WOMEN OF THE ONSEN, the girls decide to stay and help, in a series whose glimpses of naked female flesh guaranteed a boost to the ratings from furtive male voyeurs.

GIVE ME GOOD LOVE

1990. JPN: *Kimochi Ii Koi Shitai*. PRD: Yūzō Abe. DIR: Yasuyuki Kusuda. SCR: Noriko Nakayama, Keiko Nobumoto. CAST: Narumi Yasuda, Minako Tanaka, Yumi Morio, Eisaku Yoshida, Masao Kusakari. CHN: Fuji. DUR: 45 mins. x 13 eps.; Mon 2 July 1990–24 September 1990.

Kana (Yasuda), Eri (Tanaka), and Yuki (Morio) are three carefree office ladies who work as travel agents. They live for foreign travel and fun with their friends, although Kana causes tension in the group when she discovers a new interest: a boyfriend called Takashi (Yoshida). *GMGL* is a historical document, preserving a 1990s trend in aspic—the heroines are all "*oyaji gals*," or young women whose interests bizarrely mirror those of old men.

Living with their parents while waiting to be snapped up by a financially solvent Mr. Right, these women have a supremely high disposable income, fattened still further by regular bonuses. Consequently, these bright young things behave like salarymen with a windfall, betting on horses, drinking sake by the gallon, and playing golf as if their lives depend on it. The term was originally coined by manga artist Yukko Chūsonji in her 1989 work *Sweet Spot* and fast fell from visibility and use as the 1980s boom turned to bust in the 1990s. Theme: Pink Sapphire—"P.S. I Love You."

GIVE US LOVE

1995. JPN: *Bokura ni Ai o*. PRD: Tōru Ōta. DIR: Isamu Nakae. SCR: Yumie Nishiogi. CAST: Yōsuke Eguchi, Anju Suzuki, Shinji Takeda, Kōsuke Toyohara. CHN: Fuji. DUR: 45 mins. x 11 eps.; Mon 17 April 1995–26 June 1995.

Fired from his company job, Shinkai (Eguchi) goes to stay with his sick aunt. Soon he finds himself taking over her run-down boarding house. As Shinkai tries to come to terms with the change in his lifestyle (compare to **AFRICA NIGHTS**), he finds a new interest in the neighboring high-class apartments, namely in the form of Sayuri (Suzuki), one of the attractive air stewardesses who live there. Theme: L-R—"Knockin' on Your Door."

GLASS SLIPPERS *

1997. JPN: *Garasu no Kutsu*. PRD: Yoshiki Tanaka. DIR: Nozomu Amemiya, Takaya Kurata, Hiroshi Yoshino. SCR: Toshio Terada. CAST: Noriko Katō, Shirō Sano, Naoki Hosaka, Kōsuke Toyohara, Ritsuko Tanaka, Fukumi Kuroda. CHN: NTV. DUR: 45 mins. x 12 eps. (first and last eps. 90 mins.); Wed 9 April 1997–25 June 1997.

Rich draper's heir Tōru (Hosaka) falls in love with orphan girl Natsu Andō (Katō), a timid librarian who is convinced everyone calls her "*An* Donuts," as in red beanpaste *an*, behind her back. Natsu's brother Ryūtarō (Sano) is a humble shoemaker, who depends almost exclusively on Tōru's family firm for his livelihood. Natsu encourages Ryūtarō to test his shoemaking ability with ladies' shoes and foreign contracts. When Tōru asks Natsu for her hand in marriage, his stepmother Masako (Kuroda) does everything she can to force them apart. Meanwhile, Masako's daughter Yuriko is jealous of Natsu's happiness and arranges for Ryūtarō to be blackmailed by his former best friend.

As might be expected of any television series whose plot synopsis contains the words "one day, Ryūtarō is attacked by some angry shoemakers," *Glass Slippers* is a faintly ridiculous modern fairy tale in the style of **TOKYO CINDERELLA LOVE STORY** or **MRS. CINDERELLA**. Though it bravely tries to include a succession of fairy tale setups, the unlikeliness of some of the coincidences and plot twists stretch even the suspension of disbelief of the forgiving drama audience. The final *deus ex machina* involving the whereabouts of Natsu's long-lost father is stolen straight from the script of a Christmas pantomime but since this drama series openly wears its inspiration on its sleeve, it seems pointless to deride it for its lack of realism. Fairytale motifs are often buried just beneath the surface of TV drama plots, but most, such as the red shoes that feature in **WHERE IS LOVE?**, are included with considerably more subtlety. However, *Glass Slippers* brazenly tugs at its viewers' heartstrings with the introduction of an ugly stepsister, an evil stepmother, a failed artist and his blind daughter, and of course, a load of cobblers. Broadcast with English subtitles in the U.S. on KIKU TV. Theme: Aska—"One."

G-MEN 75 *

1975. PRD: Teruo Kondō, Hiroo Hara, Yūzō Higuchi. DIR: Tatsukazu Takamori, Kazuhiko Yamaguchi, Michio Konishi, Shinji Murayama, Hajime Satō, Kashiwa Yamauchi, Yukio Noda, Yoshiji Fukasawa, Junya Satō, Norihito Komatsu, Masaharu Segawa, Hirokazu Takemoto, Junnosuke Takasu, Makoto Naitō, Nagafumi Hori. SCR: Susumu Takahisa, Mieko Osanai, Yūichi Ikeda, Hajime Satō, Mitsuru Arai, Kuniaki Oshikawa, Hiroshi Nishijima, Akiyoshi Sakai, Tatsurō Nagai, Akihiro Kakefuda, Eiji Yamamura. CAST: Tetsurō Tanba, Daijirō Harada, Yasuaki Kurata, Fujita Okamoto, Mihoko Fujita, Yū Fujiki, Yōsuke Natsuki, Gō Wakabayashi, Tsuyoshi Ibuki, Maria Mori, Mari Natsuki, Takeshi Kaga. CHN: TBS. DUR: 45 mins. x 354 eps., 24 May 1975–27 March 1982; 45 mins. x 17 eps., 3 October 1982–13 March 1983.

When stewardess Rumi Takano is shot dead, assistant inspector Ichirō Sekiya (Harada) and his subordinate Tsusaka (Okamoto) are put on the case. They suspect foul play and track Rumi's suspicious-looking colleague Keiko to an airport locker. There, she leaves a stuffed animal she bought in San Francisco, where it is picked up by the real criminal. Realizing he is being followed, he tries to give the cops the slip and hijacks a bus in the process.

By episode two, the unlucky cops have been co-opted into the G-men, an organzation that takes its cue from the hard-boiled espionage atmosphere of the earlier **KEY HUNTER**. Sekiya proves his worth by agreeing to enter a prison undercover to bust an international crime organization and is rewarded with the formation of a counter-crime squad of his own. The original members are the superintendent Kuroki (Tanba), superintendent Odagiri (Natsuki), detective Yamada (Fujiki), detective Hibiki (Fujita), detective Kusano (Kurata), assistant inspector Sekiya (Harada), and detective Tsusaka (Okamoto). Their mission, should they choose to accept it, is to prevent international crime from impacting on Japan locally.

Although it often recycled old plots and even episodes from *Key Hunter*, *G-Men* jettisoned its predecessor's humorous interludes. In place of the comedy, *G-Men* made much of its international credentials—most detectives on the squad were bilingual and showed off their talents in English, French, Cantonese, Vietnamese, and Spanish. A number of foreign embassies and actors took part in the filming, and in episode 21, the squad even temporarily gained a visiting member from New York—compare to the arrival of Kanuka Clancy in *Patlabor* (*AE). The show's international angle paid off in foreign attention—as *Fierce Dragon Special Police Squad*, it was screened in Hong Kong six months after airing in Japan and some episodes were reputedly shown in the U.S. as part of a "Japan Night" strip around 1979.

With beautifully choreographed action sequences from Yasuaki Kurata and an overall sense of style, *G-Men* enjoyed a long run of success. After a grand finale TV special on 3 April 1982 set in France and Denmark, the series enjoyed a two-season hiatus. It returned for a final 17 episodes later in the year, rebranded as *G-Men 82* and rescheduled against TV Asahi's **SEIBU POLICE**. However, its rival won the ratings war and the 17 episodes in the new time slot were to be the *G-Men*'s last.

GOD OF LOVE

2000. JPN: *Koi no Kamisama*. AKA: *Cupid's Arrow*. PRD: Tamon Tanba. DIR: Akio Yoshida, Hiroshi Matsubara. SCR: Yumiko Aoyagi. CAST: Yoshino Kimura, Issei Ishida, Takashi Kashiwabara, Ken Kaneko. CHN: TBS. DUR: 45 mins. x ca. 11 eps.; Fri 14 January 2000–17 March 2000.
English teacher Ibuki (Kimura) and struggling model Kōshin (Ishida) have been together for six years but the security of their relationship is threatened when Kōshin is suddenly thrust into the media limelight. As Kōshin's work takes him further away from Ibuki and for longer, she is pursued by Reiji (Kashiwabara), a man from the Ministry of Finance who thinks he can offer her what her boyfriend cannot. Compare to **STAR STRUCK** and

FORBIDDEN FRUITS. Theme: Makoto Kawamoto—"Binetsu" (Slight Fever).

GODDESS OF VICTORY

1996. JPN: *Shōri no Megami*. PRD: Kazuhiko Takahashi. DIR: Masanori Murakami. SCR: Kumiko Tabuchi. CAST: Masahiro Nakai, Yasuko Matsuyuki, Tōru Kazama, Takanori Jinnai, Toshiyuki Kitami. CHN: Fuji. DUR: 45 mins. x 11 eps.; Tue 16 April 1996–25 June 1996.
Easygoing college senior Kōhei (Nakai) takes a job at a *juku* (cram school) where Japanese children are intensively coached in ways of passing competitive university entrance exams. With his attitude that there should be more to life than passing exams, he is well-liked by his five pupils but thrown into conflict with Katagiri (Jinnai), a straight-laced, snooty graduate of an elite Tokyo college. Math teacher Katagiri has arrived with his five star pupils, who have inherited their teacher's attitude and cause conflict with Kōhei's more laid-back charges. Compare to **LEGENDARY TEACHER**. Theme: Ulfuls—"Banzai—Suki de Yokatta" (Banzai—So Glad You Like It).

GOGGLE-V

1982. JPN: *Daisentai Goggle Five*. AKA: *Great Battle Team Goggle Five*. PRD: Yūki Usui, Seiji Abe, Takeyuki Suzuki. DIR: Shōhei Tōjō, Kazushi Hattori, Minoru Yamada, Satohi Tsuji, Michio Konishi. SCR: Hirohisa Soda, Tomomi Tsutsui, Isamu Matsumoto, Akiyoshi Sakai, Kyōko Sagiyama, Kei Yuki. CAST: Ryōji Akagi, Junichi Kasuga, Shigeru Ishii, Sanpei Godai, Megumi Ōkawa, Yōsuke Naka. CHN: Asahi. DUR: 25 mins. x 50 eps.; Sat 6 February 1982–29 January 1983.
In order to fight off an invasion from the evil scientists of the Desdark Empire, a computer in the Institute of Future Science selects a five-person team to defend planet Earth. Each is imbued with the spirit of an ancient Earth culture, starting with Kenichi (Akagi) whose Goggle Red uniform is

set with a ruby from Atlantis. Supersmart Kanpei (Kasuga) is the head of the university chess club but also Goggle Black, bearer of an Asian emerald and representative of all that is noble in Asian cultures. Saburō (Ishii) is Goggle Blue whose sapphire represents the glory that was Egypt. Tai (Godai) is Goggle Yellow whose opal represents the lost Asian continent of Mu. And token female Miki (Ōkawa) is Goggle Pink whose diamond contains the spirit of the ancient American cultures of the Maya and the Aztecs. Attentive readers may like to note that none of the Goggle Five seems to think that Europe ever had any culture worth saving—so much for Greece, Rome, and all those other also-rans of world history.

A trio of super vehicles, the Goggle Dump, Goggle Tank, and Goggle Jet can launch from the massive Goggle Ceasar vehicle, which resembles a brightly colored version of the Jawas' Sandcrawler from *A New Hope*. Once outside the Goggle Caesar, the three vehicles can combine to make a giant robot, the Goggle Five. Their enemies include Desdark President Taboo, "Retired" Leader Desmark (who still insisted on interfering, compare to his historical inspiration in **AOI**) and an army of camouflage-wearing Madaramen. Based on "an idea by Saburō Yade," *Goggle-V* came after **SUNVULCAN** and before **DYNAMAN** in the

Gogo Five

Super Sentai series. Music by Michiaki Watanabe.

GOGO FIVE

1999. JPN: *Kyūkyū Sentai Gogo Five*. AKA: *Power Rangers Lightspeed Rescue*. PRD: Kenji Ōta, Ken Fukuyoshi, Kōichi Yada, Jun Higasa. DIR: Hajime Konaka, Katsuya Watanabe, Takao Nagaishi, Toshi Morota, Hiroshi Futsuda. SCR: Yoshiki Takegami, Shunichi Miyashita, Yasuko Kobayashi, Ryōta Yamaguchi. CAST: Ryūichirō Nishioka, Masashi Taniguchi, Atsushi Harada, Kenji Shibata, Monika Sakaguchi, Mike Maki, Miho Yamada. CHN: Asahi. DUR: 25 mins. x 50 eps.; Sun 21 February 1999–6 February 2000.

The Saima clan gathers negative energy to revive their great witch-queen Grandienne, inadvertently causing chaos on Earth. Dr. Mondo of the Tatsumi clan, who have been noble firefighters since the Edo period, sets up the Tatsumi Laboratory for Disaster Prevention. Nepotism being what it is in the world of sentai shows, he appoints his own children as the members of the Gogo Five team. Ten (Nishioka) formerly worked as a member of the Capital Fire Fighters Bureau (CFFB) but is now Go Red. His old CFFB colleague Rumi (Taniguchi) is a calm and level-headed man and rebranded as Go Blue. Gentle-natured Shō (Harada) was once a pilot with the CFFB Aerial Division and is now Go Green. Sharpshooter Daimon (Shibata) was once a police officer but is now Go Yellow with a strong sense of justice. The token female team member is Sai (Sakaguchi), a former emergency nurse at National Rinkai Hospital and now Go Pink. In a departure from previous shows in the Super Sentai continuity, the emphasis with *Gogo Five* was not merely on fighting evil but on conducting rescue missions—compare to Gerry Anderson's *Thunderbirds* (1964). Note that *Gogo Five* takes place in the "present-day," whereas its predecessors JETMAN and OHRANGER were both set in the "future year" of 1999.

With predictable speed, the series was co-opted by Saban as the eighth in their MIGHTY MORPHIN' POWER RANGERS series and exported to the U.S. as *Power Rangers Lightspeed Rescue*. The U.S. version finds the futuristic city of Mariner Bay built on a forgotten demonic burial ground. Passing nomads unwittingly release the four demons, forcing the defense organization Lightspeed to immediately recruit five teenagers to defend the city from its new enemies. The rangers are Carter/Red (Sean Johnson), Chad/Blue (Michael Chatarantabut), Joel/Green (Keith Robinson), Kelsey/Yellow (Sasha Williams), and Dana/Pink (Allison MacInnes). They are later joined by Ryan (Rhett Fisher), a troubled youth who occasionally appears as the Titanium Morpher, using technology he has stolen from his estranged father, Bill Mitchell (Ron Roggé). Bill (surely not a reference to the 1920s aviator who predicted the Pacific War!?) is the mentor of the five-strong team, along with Angela Fairweather (Monica Louwerens), the scientist who designed Mariner City. Their efforts are concentrated on defeating the minions of the Saima Clan before the long-awaited Grand Cross celestial conjunction (a vestige of the original Japanese plot), at which point their evil nemesis Queen Bansheera (Diane Salinger) will return from exile to wreak havoc. On occasion, the team also rescues people with a giant robot whose arms contain extending ladders. *Gogo Five* comes after GINGAMAN in the Super Sentai chronology and was followed by TIME RANGER. Music by Toshiyuki Watanabe.

GOING HOME WITH SOMEONE SOMEDAY

1990. JPN: *Itsuka Dareka to Asakaeri*. PRD: Kazuhiko Takahashi. DIR: Kazuhiro Onohara. SCR: Yūko Kanaya. CAST: Rie Miyazawa, Tōru Kazama, Hikaru Nishida, Taishū Kase. CHN: Fuji. DUR: 45 mins. x 10 eps.; Thu 18 October 1990–20 December 1990.

When her parents travel abroad, teenager Ritsuko (Miyazawa) is forced to stay alone at her aunt's apartment, until her quiet is disrupted by the arrival of her cousin Hideka (Nishida) who returns unexpectedly from studying in America, bringing her handsome boyfriend Keisuke (Kase) with her. A clash of two titans of yesteryear, as pop idols Miyazawa and Nishida duke it out for control of the screen. Theme: Rie Miyazawa—"Game."

GOKENIN ZANKURŌ

1995. prd: N/D. dir: N/D. scr: Narito Kaneko. cast: Ken Watanabe, Tōru Masuoka, Jun Karasawa, Yukiko Kishi, Mayumi Wakamura, Sansei Shiomi, Kyōko Kishida. chn: Fuji. dur: 45 mins. x ca. 50 eps.; 11 January 1995–1 March 1995; 8 January 1997–19 March 1997; 15 October 1997–21 January 1998; 13 January 1999–17 March 1999; 13 November 2001–26 March 2002.

Zankurō Matsudaira (Watanabe) is a low-grade vassal of the Tokugawa Shogun, forced to moonlight as a bodyguard and executioner to make ends meet. He also has a drinking problem, an overeating mother, and a propensity to protect the oppressed, all of which eat into his finances. His confident mother Masajo (Kishida) is the descendant of a famous family of shogunal retainers and a mistress of the pen and sword, who regards her son as a failure.

Based on the novel by Renzaburō Shibata, GZ has entertained Japanese audiences at intermittent intervals for almost a decade. Zankurō remains permanently penniless, and is jilted by his fiancée, who has now married another man and become a mother. He enjoys a turbulent relationship with geisha Tsutakichi (Wakamura) and continues to search for new ways of making money. In his recent 2002 series, he is trying to work off his massive drinks tab by serving drinks in a Tōhachi tavern. There, he meets Riku (Tamao Nakamura), a mother whose son Senmatsu has failed to return a year after his kimono shop apprenticeship should have ended. When Zankurō's police friend Saji (Shiomi) discusses a murderous robbery that seems to have involved a family's servants, Zankurō suspects that one of the missing servants could be the missing Senmatsu and hunts him down. Although Senmatsu tries to flee his murderous fellows, he still dies in his mother's arms. This incident leaves Zankurō alone once more, unlikely to get much thanks from Riku and forced to head off in search of more employment—compare to LONE WOLF AND CUB.

GOKUSEN

2002. PRD: Kazuho Masuda, Masatoshi Katō. DIR: Tōya Satō. SCR: Michiru Etō, Eri Yokota, Yūko Matsuda. CAST: Yukie Nakama, Misaki Itō, Yūko Nakazawa, Jun Matsumoto, Katsuhisa Namase, Ken Kaneko, Jun Oguri, Takuma Ishigaki, Hiroki Narimiya, Tomohiro Waki. CHN: NTV. DUR: 45 mins. x 12 eps.; Wed 17 April 2002–3 July 2002.

All-male high school Shirogane Academy is welcoming two female teachers for the first time in its history. Shizuka (Itō) is advised by school nurse Kikuno (Nakazawa, formerly of Morning Musume) to wear clothes suitable for running in, a warning whose meaning becomes clear when fellow teacher Kumiko (Nakama) is pelted with objects thrown by her troublesome students. However, Kumiko has a secret—she is the heiress to a *yakuza* fortune, trying to live a life on the right side of the law in honor of her late father's wishes. She meets a handsome man on the bus and finds herself falling in love with him, only to discover that he is emphatically not marriage material—he is a detective. Based on the 2002 *You Comics* manga by Kozueko Morimoto, *Gokusen* begins in the style of **GTO**, but soon veers off course into a criminal variant of *Romeo and Juliet*. Though probably rushed into production in the wake of *The Sopranos,* the series has a local pedigree as well, with resemblances to earlier shows such as **DOWNTOWN DETECTIVES** and **THE QUIET DON**. The story came back for the December TV movie *Gokusen Returns* (2002) and a 2003 special. Theme: V6—"Feel Your Breeze."

GOLDEN BOWL

2002. PRD: Kazuho Masuda, Hibiki Itō, Kazuhisa Kitajima. DIR: Ryūichi Inomata. SCR: Shinji Nojima. CAST: Takeshi Kaneshiro, Hitomi Kuroki, Hideaki Ōtaki, Muga Takewaki, Kanako Enomoto, Eiko Segawa. CHN: NTV. DUR: 45 mins. x 11 eps.; Sat 20 April 2002–7 June 2002.

Tokyo stockbroker and bowling hobbyist Shū Akutagawa (Kaneshiro) visits the Golden Bowl[ing] Alley almost every day after work. The manager Michio (Ōtaki) presents him with the titular golden ball, downheartedly explaining that, as his best customer, he should keep it as a souvenir when the troubled alley is demolished to make way for a love hotel.

The employees rally round to oppose the closure of the alley, convincing Michio to tear up the contract but exciting the wrath of local gangster Tsutomu (Shigemitsu Ogi). In the midst of wranglings over the future of the business (compare to **GOOD LUCK** and **SISTER STORIES**), Shū must fight off the not entirely unwelcome advances of a whole group of lady bowlers. He tells them all that he has a girlfriend who lives a long way away and does not admit the truth—that he was left heartbroken after the death of his true love in an accident. Eventually, the fate of the alley is to be decided by a match between male-female pairs. The gangsters bring in professional ringers, leaving Shū stuck with Chiaki (Segawa) when he would much rather be teamed with Hitomi (Kuroki), a married woman who always bowls with a pink ball. Compare to its original inspiration, the classic series **BEAUTIFUL CHALLENGER**. Theme: Paul Anka—"You Are My Destiny."

GOLDEN KIDS *

1997. JPN: *Kin no Tamago.* AKA: *Golden Egg.* PRD: Noriko Nishiguchi. DIR: Takamichi Yamada, Shinbo Matsubara, Hiroshi Ikezoe. SCR: Toshio Sekine. CAST: Yūko Asano, Tsurutarō Kataoka, Taichi Kokubu, Hisano Yamaoka, Chisa Nomura. CHN: TBS. DUR: 45 mins. x 12 eps.; Thu 3 July 1997–18 September 1997.

Pushy mother Izumi (Asano) is convinced that she married below her station and is determined that her daughter Marimo (Nomura) should be a star. Despite the objections of her husband Kōtarō (Kataoka) and mother-in-law (Yamaoka), she enrolls her in a performing arts troupe, run by a child-hating musician (Kokubu). Marimo soon wins a minor role on TV but Izumi is never satisfied with her daughter's successes.

Like STAR STRUCK and BEST FRIENDS, *GK* peeks behind the scenes of an actor's life, stripping away the glitz and glamour to reveal an unending treadmill of casting calls and disappointments. Marimo would far rather play with her friends and go on school trips but is constantly dragged away from her regular childhood to fulfill her mother's ambitions. Izumi, for her part, grows insanely boastful about her daughter's talents, and must face inevitable embarrassment when Marimo loses a prime part to her friend Reina. For a conservative TV genre that glorifies family ties, *GK*'s revelation that Kōtarō will have to leave his wife and child behind in Tokyo when he is transferred to another city has an impact of scandalous proportions. The struggle to balance real life with the media provides much of the farcical energy of *Golden Kids,* as Izumi tries to simultaneously attend a press call and a school sports event, while the pressures of a movie part eventually prove to be too much for Marimo, at least at this point in her life. Ironically, the child actors in this show are rather better than average, even when they are pretending to act badly. Shown subtitled in the U.S. on KIKU TV. Theme: Komi Hirose—"Natsu Damon" (Because It's Summer).

GOOD CHILDREN'S ALLY

2003. JPN: *Yoiko no Mikata.* PRD: Ken Inoue, Masatoshi Katō. DIR: Tarō Ōtani, Makoto Naganuma. SCR: Mika Umeda. CAST: Shō Sakurai, Yuki Matsushita, Kazue Fukiishi, Hideko Yoshida, Mari Hamada, Shōzō Endō. CHN: NTV. DUR: 45 mins. x ca. 11 eps.; Sat 18 January 2003–?? March 2003.
In order to cover someone's maternity leave Taiyō (Sakurai) becomes the only man in the otherwise all-girl Himawari

Kindergarten. Led by the fearsome Kiyoko Yoshikawa (Yoshida), the other teachers are deeply distrustful of this new arrival and the nursery school is beset with problem parents, including an irate couple who demand to know how their child could have broken his shoulder while in the teachers' care. Compare to LOVE ME and WATCH OUT NURSERY CHIEF. Theme: Arashi— "Tomadoi Nagara" (Being Confused).

GOOD COMBINATION

2001. AKA: *Good Buddies.* PRD: Hisao Wakaizumi. DIR: Mitsuru Hirose, Yoshio Yashikawa. SCR: Nao Morishita, Shigeo Motoo. CAST: Jun Toba, Yumi Adachi, Daijirō Kawaoka, Akiko Kinouchi, Yoshihiko Hakamada, Kanpei Hazama. CHN: NHK. DUR: 45 mins. x 5 eps.; Tue 12 June 2001–10 July 2001.
Lonely teenage slacker Ryūhei (Toba) joins the Osaka Owarai Talent School, an academy of the performing arts that specializes in stand-up comedy. Through improvisation and performances with his fellow misfits, he comes to terms with his teen angst— the titular combination of the title is *"the miracle of friendship and the gift of laughter."* Compare to WHO DID THIS TO ME?.

GOOD LUCK *

1996. PRD: Yoshinobu Kosugi. DIR: Nozomu Amemiya. SCR: Toshio Terada. CAST: Akiko Matsumoto, Shirō Sano, Isamu Hashizume. CHN: NTV. DUR: 45 mins. x 11 eps.; Wed 3 July 1996–11 September 1996.
Rinko (Matsumoto) is a directionless bank employee, whose life is thrown into turmoil when she inherits her father's *pachinko* parlor. Suddenly she is forced to make tough business decisions, fend off local gangsters, and turn the troubled gambling arcade into a profit-making venture. Enlisting the help of her friends Yūji and Toshio, she competes against local property developers Kurobe Kōsan for control of the site. Toshio volunteers two million yen of his own money but neglects to mention that he has already

promised the sum to his fiancée Kaori, who is understandably angry. The building is scheduled for demolition, and as the final moments approach, Rinko and her friends struggle to prove that the property developers have no right to tear it down. Broadcast with English subtitles in the U.S. on KIKU TV. Theme: Kyōsuke Himuro—"Squall." Not to be confused with GOOD LUCK!!, whose two exclamation points make all the difference.

GOOD LUCK!!

2003. PRD: Hiroki Ueda. DIR: Nobuhiro Doi, Katsuo Fukuzawa, Shunichi Hirano. SCR: Yumiko Inoue. CAST: Takuya Kimura, Shinichi Tsutsumi, Kō Shibazaki, Rina Uchiyama. CHN: TBS. DUR: 45 mins. x 10 eps.; 19 January 2003–23 March 2003.
Hajime (Kimura from SMAP) is a newly qualified jet liner co-pilot, who hopes one day to become a captain. En route to Narita airport from Honolulu, his chief pilot Kōsaku (Kōichi Iwaki) suddenly falls ill, compelling the inexperienced Hajime to land the plane himself. Though he succeeds, he is mocked by pretty ground crew chief Ayumi (Shibazaki), who regards his landing prowess as highly suspect. Disciplined by his supervisor Kazuki (Tsutsumi) for daring to land the plane unsupervised (what was he supposed to do?!), Hajime soon gets into more trouble and is suspended from flying. His bosses hope he will take the hint and resign but he refuses to quit.

Meanwhile, he must fight off the advances of Urara (Uchiyama), a gold-digging stewardess in the YAMATO NADESHIKO mode, who wants a pilot for a husband. Though Hajime denies it, his real attraction seems to be for the mechanically minded Ayumi but the level-headed ground crew girl claims to have no interest in pilots—compare to similar high jinks in BIG WING. Theme: Tatsurō Yamashita—"Ride on Time." Not to be confused with GOOD LUCK, a series *sans* exclamation points shown seven years earlier on NTV.

Good Mourning

GOOD MORNING TEACHER

1980. JPN: *Ohayō Sensei Konnichi wa.*
AKA: *Hello, Teacher Good Morning;
Hello Mister Ohio?* PRD: Kanae
Mayuzumi. DIR: Minoru Hanabusa,
Kazuya Satō, Haruo Yoshida,
Takamasa Suzuki. SCR: Yasuo Tanami.
CAST: Dwight Waldron, Ichirō Arishima,
Yumi Shirakawa, Kazuya Ōsaka, Miyuki
Yoshida, Rie Katsuragi, Hiroko
Isayama, Yoshitaka Kashirashi, Haruka
Morita, Yoshio Ōmori, Hiroshi
Yanagitani, Norihiko Yamamoto,
Hiroyuki Takano. CHN: NHK. DUR: 30
mins. x 8 eps.; Fri 4 August 1980–11
August 1980.
Peter McQueen (Waldron) comes to
Japan to teach English at a local school
and stays at the home of doctor
Tadamasa (Arishima), whose wife
Nobuko (Shirakawa) is wary of foreign-
ers. While hitchhiking to the town (an
incredibly *foreign* thing to do, in
Japanese eyes), Peter befriends Toshio
(Takano), a student from the high
school where he is going to teach. He
lends him a tape, only to discover that
his kindness led to Toshio's persecution and the boy's injury in a fight.

Struggling with unfamiliar Japanese
rules and customs, Peter tries to understand his students, who soon adore
him because he treats them like small
adults. They give him the nickname
Ohayō, in one of the first dramas to
grapple with Japan's *gaijin* complex—
the nation's constant alternation
between blind adoration of foreigners
and bigoted hatred of them. By the
end of the series, Peter is given the
chance to become *much* closer to the
Japanese, when Tadamasa sets him up
with a local girl. However, her ardor
cools when Peter reveals that he
intends to *stay* in Japan and he is jilted
by his prospective bride.

GOOD MOURNING

1994. PRD: Tōru Ōta. DIR: Tatsuaki
Kimura. SCR: Yumie Nishiogi. CAST:
Atsuko Asano, Kiichi Nakai, Morio
Kazama, Shigeru Muroi, Masao
Kusakari. CHN: Fuji. DUR: 45 mins. x 11
eps.; Thu 14 July 1994–22 September
1994.
College lecturer Minori (Asano) falls
in love with handsome funeral director
Kenichi (Kusakari). Eventually the pair
are married but Kenichi unexpectedly
drops dead three days into the honey-
moon. Returning to Japan as a widow,
Minori finds she has inherited a surly
stepson and a funeral business that is
80 million yen in debt. A black comedy
from the writer of CAMPUS NOTES and
SWEET HOME, inviting comparison with
the later TV serials CEREMONIAL
OFFICIATOR and, in the U.S., *Six Feet
Under.* Shown without English subtitles
in the U.S. on KTSF TV. Theme: The
Waves—"Baila! Baila! Baila! Good
Mourning!"

GOOD NEWS *

1999. PRD: Seiichirō Kijima, Hideki
Isano. DIR: Makoto Kiyohiro, Fuminori
Kaneko, Hideki Isano. SCR: Ryōichi
Kimizuka. CAST: Masahiro Nakai, Mayu
Tsuruta, Shirō Sano, Yasunori Danta,
Ran Itō, Akiko Yada, Ryūnosuke
Kamiki, Chitose Kobayashi, Kōichi
Yamamoto. CHN: TBS. DUR: 45 mins. x
12 eps.; Sun 11 April 1999–?? June
1999.

Jōichi (Nakai from SMAP) is a young staffer at struggling movie company Human Pictures, who receives the good news that he is to be given an assistant directorship on a forthcoming production. Mixing the karmic satire of **HEAVEN CANNOT WAIT** with media comedy in the style of **AD BOOGIE**, each piece of good news Jōichi receives is accompanied by an equivalent scrap of bad, such as when he goes scouting for a child actor at a local kindergarten and is mistaken for a kidnapper. Akiko (Tsuruta), the mother of the child he is accused of snatching, turns out to be a yuppie publisher and the couple discover that they have feelings for each other. With an 80 million yen debt hanging over the film company (coincidentally, the same debt that appears in **GOOD MOURNING**), Jōichi convinces Akiko to license one of her firm's books for a movie adaptation. However, as production gets underway, Jōichi's succession of bad luck payoffs ensue, including the news that the boss's daughter now has control of production and that one of the major investors in the production is Akiko's vengeful ex-husband. Broadcast with English subtitles in the U.S. on KIKU TV. Theme: Tomoyasu Hotei—"Nobody's Perfect." Peak rating: 15.9%.

GOOD OLD DAYS: FOUR GRADUATIONS

1996. JPN: *Ii Hi Tabitachi: Yottsu no Sotsugyō*. AKA: *Four Graduations and a Wedding*. PRD: N/C. DIR: Setsuo Wakamatsu. SCR: Chiho Shioda. CAST: Yumiko Takahashi, Hiroshi Abe, Masayuki Sakamoto, Kuniyoshi Matsumura, Emiri Henmi. CHN: Kansai. DUR: 45 mins. x 4 eps.; 4 March 1996–25 March 1996.
Madoka (Takahashi) married her childhood sweetheart Noboru (Abe), now an assistant professor at a university. However, the couple's happy new life is disrupted by having to share a house with Noboru's father, a senior lecturer. Though obviously an in-law appeasement drama in the style of **BRIDE-TO-BE**, the plotting of *Good Old*

Days reflects that of the British movie *Four Weddings and a Funeral* (1993) but using the passing of the academic year to mark time. Theme: Yumiko Takahashi—"Makete mo Ii yo" (Even If I Lose).

GOOD PERSON

1997. JPN: *Ii Hito*. AKA: *Good Man*. PRD: Hideki Inada, Yūji Ōhira. DIR: Mamoru Hoshi, Masanori Murakami. SCR: Mitsuru Tanabe, Kōshiro Mikami, Mayumi Nakatani. CAST: Tsuyoshi Kusanagi, Miho Kanno, Naomi Zaizen, Yuka Nomura, Miho Yabe, Shirō Itō. CHN: Fuji. DUR: 45 mins. x 11 eps.; Wed 15 April 1997–24 June 1997.
Hokkaidō graduate Yūji (Kusanagi from SMAP) takes a job in a sportswear manufacturing firm, much to the concern of his girlfriend Asako (Kanno), who frets that his mild-mannered "good-guy" nature will be exploited by the canny tricksters of Tokyo. However, Yūji's insistence on "helping" others often causes more trouble for them than it does for him, in a comedy that pits homespun country wisdom against the customs of Japan's bustling capital city. Although the original *Big Comics* manga by Shin Takahashi was published in 1993, this TV adaptation seemed to have been commissioned in the wake of *Forrest Gump* (1994), to which it is often compared. Theme: SMAP—"Celery."

GOODBYE ANTS

1994. JPN: *Ari yo Saraba*. PRD: Tamaki Endō. DIR: Tamaki Endō. SCR: Hiromi Saitō, Takako Suzuki. CAST: Eikichi Yazawa, Kyōzō Nagatsuka, Ryōsuke Miki, Tatsuo Matsumura, Midori Kiuchi. CHN: TBS. DUR: 45 mins. x 12 eps.; Fri 15 April 1994–1 July 1994.
Ryōta (Yazawa), a postgraduate entomologist with a particular interest in ants, is approached by his old principal Hanaoka (Matsumura) and asked to fill in as a teacher at a high school. However, Ryōta is not a "people person," and finds himself stuck with the seniors who are just about to enter Japan's notorious Exam Hell—a never-

ending treadmill of cramming for university entrance tests. Theme: Eikichi Yazawa—"Ari yo Saraba" (Goodbye Ants).

GOODBYE MR. OZU *

2001. JPN: *Sayonara Ozu Sensei*. PRD: Shizuo Sekiguchi. DIR: Makoto Hirano, Keita Kawano. SCR: Ryōichi Kimizuka. CAST: Masakazu Tamura, Yūsuke Santamaria, Naomi Nishida, Kotomi Kyōno, Asami Mizukawa, Kei Tani, Asaka Seto, Fumiyo Kohinata. CHN: Fuji. DUR: 45 mins. x 11 eps.; Tue 9 October 2001–18 December 2001.
After he is arrested by the FBI for insider trading, prominent banker Nanpei Ozu (Tamura) serves twelve months in an American prison. Ostracized by his Wall Street firm, he returns to Japan to discover that his bosses at Kōyō Bank have not only made him the scapegoat for their unethical schemes but have also dragged his name through the Japanese gutter press. Divorced by his scandalized wife and unemployable in the financial world, he is forced to take the only job available—teaching economics at a run-down Tokyo high school.

With TV drama still reeling from the success of **GTO**, it was only a matter of time before someone turned the concept on its head, pitching a maverick businessman against a class full of would-be gangsters. The pitch for *Ozu* sounds suspiciously like a hundred American classroom dramas—will the lovable teacher see the inner goodness in his bad-seed pupils? But this time it is Ozu himself who is in search of redemption. He is a dead man walking, likened to a "ghost" by family, friends, and colleagues alike, fallen from the pinnacle of success (much of the first episode is shot in New York, no less) to the very bottom of the scrap heap, with little hope of regaining his shattered self-esteem. Thus, he finds himself identifying with similar write-offs, particularly the five troubled transfer students who comprise the woefully inept boys' basketball team. Even though his banker bosses soon beg him to return to high finance, he becomes the school's basketball coach, coaxing his teen truants up from zeroes to heroes.

Soon revealing its true colors as a sports tale in the tradition of *Slam Dunk* (*AE), *Ozu* half-heartedly throws in a supporting class of listless, lovelorn teachers. However, its mumbling, shuffling center remains Tamura, an actor supremely confident that he can try anything because he will always be welcome back at NINZABURŌ FURUHATA. His acting style is thus fearlessly naturalistic, with realistically poor posture, slurred diction, and inexpressive movements that accentuate his state of benign failure. The viewer waits in vain for him to snap at his pupils' outrageously rude behavior, since there is nothing wrong with his charges that a few sharp blows to the head wouldn't cure. But he is everyman taken to extremes and silently endures the embarrassment like the rest of us probably would. Reputedly shown subtitled on NGN TV in the U.S. Compare to SCHOOL TEACHER, which played against it during the same season on TBS.

GOODBYE ONCE MORE

1992. JPN: *Sayonara o Mō Ichidō*. AKA: *Goodbye Again*. PRD: Yutaka Kiyono. DIR: Shūsaku Kawake. SCR: Fumie Mizuhashi. CAST: Junichi Ishida, Kumiko Akiyoshi, Shin Takuma, Ken Ishiguro, Masumi Miyazaki, Yuriko Ishida. CHN: Fuji. DUR: 45 mins. x 11 eps.; Wed 15 April 1992–24 June 1992.
Kyōko (Akiyoshi) is a newscaster with TV Japan, whose show is losing the ratings war. Going to the hospital for a check-up, she encounters Shūhei (Ishida), her former boyfriend, whom she threw aside in favor of her career. The couple resume their relationship, although Kyōko's illness proves to be terminal. Compare to PLEASE GOD! JUST A LITTLE MORE TIME and BEAUTIFUL LIFE, which also feature a fiery relationship challenged by a medical condition. Theme: Laura Fiji— "Hitomi no Sasayaki" (Whispering of Your Eyes).

GOODBYE TO THE OLD ME

1992. JPN: *Kinō no Watashi ni Sayonara*. PRD: N/C. DIR: Kyū Kojima. SCR: Shōji Imai. CAST: Marina Watanabe, Iyo Matsumoto, Yukari Morikawa, Yūki Matsumura, Russell Ishii, Yōko Ōkawa. CHN: TV Tōkyō. DUR: 45 mins. x 8 eps.; Sun 8 September 1992–27 October 1992.
Rinko (Watanabe) is a gym instructor asked by the manager Sawai (Ishii) to make plans for an affiliate gym on another site. Though she initially welcomes the challenge, she discovers that she has a rival in the form of Kana (Ōkawa), Sawai's jealous lover.

GORANGER

1975. JPN: *Himitsu Sentai Goranger*. AKA: *Secret Battle-Team Goranger*. PRD: Takashi Ogino, Tōru Hirayama, Susumu Yoshikawa, Michi Fukazawa. DIR: Hirokazu Takemoto, Minoru Yamada, Itaru Orita, Katsuhiko Taguchi, Hidetoshi Kitamura, Michio Konishi. SCR: Shōzō Uehara, Susumu Takahisa, Mitsuru Arai, Hirohisa Soda, Kimio Hirayama, Keisuke Fujikawa. CAST: Naoya Makoto, Hiroshi Miyauchi, Baku Hatakeyama, Jirō Daruma, Mitsuo Andō, Risa Komaki, Yukio Itō (aka Takeshi Masamichi). CHN: NET (Asahi). DUR: 25 mins. x 84 eps.; Mon 5 May 1975–26 March 1977.
Earth is attacked by the Black Crucifix army of the alien Great Shogun (Andō) and only the secret Earth Guard League and their Goranger team can save the planet. Utilizing the latest scientific technology, the team is led by Takeshi the Red Ranger (Makoto), who fights with a whip and a gun. His second in command is the rakish Blue Ranger Akira (Miyauchi), who fights with a bow. Ōta the Yellow Ranger (Hatakeyama) is a curry-loving brawler who fights with "demon power" (a hand on the end of a stick!), though not for long, since he quit the series, ostensibly to run the Eagle Kyūshū base. He was replaced by a new Yellow Ranger Daigorō (Daruma), though the original actor returned before the series ended. Love interest

Peach Ranger Peggy (Komaki) is the team's explosives specialist (her bombs are shaped like hearts, of course), while the team's youngest member is boomerang-wielding 17-year-old Green Ranger Kenji (Itō).

In the style of the MASKED RIDER (another show created by manga artist Shōtarō Ishinomori), the team have a set of souped up motorcycles, though the Peach and Yellow Rangers are forced to ride in sidecars rather than having their own vehicles. The motorcycles are carried in a red and white helicopter gunship called the Baribrun, launching from it down a long ramp that extends from the front like a tongue.

The first of the Super Sentai series, *Goranger* incorporated elements of the popular ULTRAMAN superhero show and the PHANTOM AGENTS spy series to create an all-new franchise. With an original concept by a manga author, the staff also poached several writers from the anime world, as well as composer Michiaki Watanabe, who created music for several early sentai shows. The idea of a five-person team, colorcoded for ease of identification, with action figure and merchandising tie-ins, would be repeated with only the most superficial of alterations in many other series; like some of the long-running anime franchises it resembled (e.g. *Time Bokan*, *Brave Saga* *AE), the Super Sentai series had a target audience that often genuinely was too young to remember the previous incarnations and would not question the incessant repetition. The next to be released was JAQK, but the Super Sentai series is still running to this day—now credited to "Saburō Yade" as creator, rather than Ishinomori. Though *Goranger* was never released in English, its popularity set the tone and paradigm for its many successors, including the **MIGHTY MORPHIN' POWER RANGERS** that were to dominate children's television in the mid-1990s.

GRADUATION

1990. JPN: *Sotsugyō*. PRD: Yasuo Yagi. DIR: Kunimasa Kondō. SCR: Eriko Komatsu. CAST: Miho Nakayama, Atsuko Sendō, Yūji Oda, Masatoshi Nagase, Michiko Kawai. CHN: TBS. DUR: 45 mins. x 12 eps.; Fri 12 January 1990–30 March 1990.
Kaori (Nakayama) is in the second grade at a junior college. She has only four months until graduation but has not found a job and she has no connections or skills. And to make things worse, she is not from, in, or around Tokyo. Finally she visits a small company that she finds in a job hunting magazine.

GRASS AFLAME, THE

1979. JPN: *Kusa Moyuru*. AKA: *The Grass Burns*. PRD: Taiji Nagasawa. DIR: Makoto Ōhara. SCR: Takehiro Nakajima. CAST: Kōji Ishizaka, Shima Iwashita, Hiromi Gō, Saburō Shinoda, Ken Matsudaira, Sakae Takita. CHN: NHK. DUR: 45 mins. x ca. 45 eps.; Sun 7 January 1979–23 December 1979.
In the 12th century, noble lady Masako Hōjō (Iwashita) falls in love with Yoritomo Minamoto (Ishizaka) who has been exiled to Izu by Kiyomori Taira (see **TALE OF THE HEIKE**). Despite her family's opposition, she marries him. After Yoritomo becomes the *de facto* ruler of Japan, setting up the shogunal government in Kamakura, his interest in Masako fades and he conducts several affairs. Upon his death, their son Yoriie (Gō) is the rightful heir but looks set to be usurped by more powerful factions. Taking matters into her own hands, Masako becomes regent in a coalition with her father Tokimasa Hōjō and

brother Yoshitoki (Matsudaira). Yoriie is locked away in the Shuzenji temple at Izu and his younger brother Sanetomo becomes the next shogun. However, Sanetomo is merely a nominal ruler, while the real power lies with Yoshitoki, who eventually has him assassinated. The trio then invite the former Shogun's distant relative Yoritsune to come from Kyoto and take the Shogunate—Yoritsune is only two years old, allowing Masako to become regent once more.

Based on the novel *Hōjō Masako* by Michiko Nagai, this *taiga* drama takes the innovative route of making its lead sympathetic to modern audiences. More noticeable for viewers was the foregrounding of a female character from history but one with thoroughly understandable problems. Unlike the hysterical empresses and witches of old, Masako (1157–1225) is presented as a charming woman who loves her husband too much to go on vendettas and loves her children too much to resort to murdering them, often treating the regency as if it were an unwelcome stint of baby-sitting, which in many ways, it probably was. The drama added to its approachable attitude by using noticeably modern dialogue, instead of the *thou's* and *thee's* of previous period pieces—compare to its chief rival in the year's ratings, NTV's **MONKEY**, which similarly modernized its dialogue. **YOSHITSUNE** and **THE FIRE STILL BURNS** are set in roughly the same historical period. Peak rating: 34.7%.

GRAVE OF THE WILD CHRYSANTHEMUMS

1975. JPN: *Nogiku no Haka*. PRD: Masaharu Morita. DIR: Minoru Hanabusa. SCR: Toshirō Ide. CAST: Satoshi Hasegawa, Akiko Koyama, Makoto Arashi, Mayumi Miura, Midori Takei, Ryūnosuke Kaneda, Sumiko Abe, Setsuko Horikoshi. CHN: NHK. DUR: 25 mins. x 9 eps.; Mon 1 September 1975–17 September 1975.
The 15-year-old Tamiko (Takei) is sent to learn manners by staying with the

upper-class Saitō family. The lady of the house Chiyo (Koyama) and her daughter Yoshiko (Miura) teach her how to do housework properly, and Tamiko befriends the son Masao (Hasegawa), who is two years younger. Chiyo tells Tamiko and Masao not to be too friendly in public but her admonition only brings them closer together. One day when they are weeding in the grounds, they find a wild chrysanthemum, prompting Tamiko to tell Masao a story she heard from her grandmother, who once told her that she was a reincarnation of the flower. Masao confesses that he likes—even loves—chrysanthemums, and Tamiko jokingly compares him to a gentian flower. The two happy children return home to find the family in a somber mood—Masao is to be sent away to boarding school. Before he leaves, he gives a love letter to Tamiko, who pines for him but is kept from meeting him again by a series of unhappy coincidences. Eventually, she returns to her family and is married off to a doctor but becomes critically ill after a miscarriage. After a prolonged and painful illness, she eventually dies, clutching Masao's love letter and photograph in her hand. When Masao hears the news, he visits her grave to find wild chrysanthemums growing all around it. An utterly miserable tale of doomed love, based on the book of the same name by Sachio Itō, which was also adapted as one of the *Animated Classics of Japanese Literature* (*AE).

GREATEST FEELING, THE

1995. JPN: *Saikō no Kataomoi*. AKA: *White Love Story*. PRD: Reiko Kita. DIR: Shunsaku Kawake. SCR: Miyuki Noe. CAST: Masahiro Motoki, Eri Fukatsu, Tetta Sugimoto, Narimi Arimori, Tomoya Nagase, Harumi Inoue. CHN: Fuji. DUR: 45 mins. x 11 eps.; Wed 11 January 1995–22 March 1995.
Kōhei (Motoki) is a salaryman who goes skiing every winter. It's a good chance for him to catch up with his old college ski club buddies and to pursue Noriko, the former classmate he still

worships from afar. Noriko, however, has no interest in Kōhei, since she is hopelessly devoted to a married man who thinks little of her. Meanwhile, Kōhei meets Kurumi (Fukatsu), a travel agent who works in the building next to his. Finding that she has developed feelings for Kōhei, Kurumi follows him and his friends on their next skiing trip to Hokkaidō, in a classic love polygon tale in the style of **TOKYO LOVE STORY** and **WHERE IS LOVE?**, and actionably similar to the earlier **IN THE NAME OF LOVE**. Broadcast without subtitles in the U.S. on the WNYC channel. Theme: Masaharu Fukuyama—"Hello."

GREATEST LOVER, THE

1995. JPN: *Saikō no Koibito*. PRD: Kōtarō Takahashi. DIR: Kazuhisa Imai. SCR: Yoshikazu Okada. CAST: Gorō Inagaki, Yumiko Takahashi, Ryūichi Ōura, Izumi Yamaguchi, Kei Tani. CHN: Asahi. DUR: 45 mins. x 11 eps.; Mon 17 April 1995–25 June 1995.
As a child Michio (Inagaki) fell in love with Yūko (Takahashi), who came into his life when his mother remarried. He has always adored his stepsister but she regards him as a true brother and seems to have no interest in him. He is forced to admit his feelings when old friend Takao (Ōura) returns from America, hoping to marry Yūko himself. Compare to **COLD MORNING** and **STRAWBERRY ON THE SHORTCAKE**. Theme: Yumiko Takahashi—"Suki Suki Suki" (Like It Like It Like It).

GROWN-UP KISS

1993. JPN: *Otona no Kiss*. PRD: Yoshiki Tanaka. DIR: Hiroshi Yoshino. SCR: Toshio Kamata. CAST: Kyōhei Shibata, Junichi Ishida, Jun Fubuki, Fukumi Kuroda, Eri Fukatsu. CHN: NTV. DUR: 45 mins. x 9 eps.; Sat 23 October 1993–18 December 1993.
Sachiko (Fubuki) files for divorce after discovering that her husband Shūichi (Shibata) has kissed Reiko (Fukatsu). At the same time, used car salesman Naoto (Ishida), an inveterate womanizer, also gets one of the distinctive

green ink forms from his own wife Chiharu (Kuroda). Presumably, the women end up swapping husbands, in a rehash of Kamata's earlier *Otokotachi ni Yoroshiku* (*Give My Regards to the Men,* 1987), commissioned by NTV in a bid to compete with the higher ratings of rivals TBS and Fuji.

GTO

1998. AKA: *Great Teacher Onizuka*. PRD: Tadashi Shibata, Kazuhisa Andō. DIR: Hiroshi Akabane, Satoru Nakajima. SCR: Kazuhiko Yūkawa, Yoshiyuki Suga. CAST: Takashi Sorimachi, Nanako Matsushima, Yōsuke Kubozuka, Miki Kuroda, Kirari, Hiroyuki Ikeuchi, Yoshimasa Kondō, Naohito Fujiki, Yumi Shirakawa, Aimi Nakamura, Erika Mabuchi, Nana Katase. CHN: Kansai. DUR: 45 mins. x 12 eps.; Tue 7 July 1998–22 September 1998.
After seven years at a low-grade college, former biker Eikichi Onizuka (Sorimachi) finally graduates. Despite reservations about his attitude, the short-handed staff of Musashino Seirin High School hire him and put him in charge of the notorious Year Two, Class Four. Bad boy Yoshito (Kubozuka) immediately tries to entrap him, photographing his new teacher in a clinch with scantily clad schoolgirl Nanako (Kirari). However, Onizuka proves to be an earnest educator and wins his class around through his interest in their problems. When that fails, he can always call on his cop roommate or former biker associates to rough up the bullies—in a parody of **MITO KŌMON**, a motorcycle gang saves the day, their leader pointing at Onizuka and saying: *"Don't you know who this is . . . ?"* Despite repeated altercations, leading to Onizuka walking around the school with a resignation letter permanently stored in his top pocket, he gains the love and respect of the students and teachers.
Critics described *GTO* as a harder-hitting remake of **KINPACHI SENSEI**, a fact acknowledged by the program makers in the first episode, when Onizuka turns away from his habitual

GTO

schoolgirl porn in the video store and asks to rent copies of the famous classroom drama instead. It struck a chord with teenage viewers for its willingness to deal humorously with contemporary classroom issues and for the subtext of an educator who genuinely cares for the children in his charge—it may be a hoary cliché, but there is a first time for every viewer when it appears fresh, and it seems that *GTO* was a first time for many. The virginal Onizuka lives between the worlds of students and teachers: he is young enough to understand the children's problems, yet still a member of the adult establishment. The teachers, particularly would-be love interest Azusa (Matsushima), regard him suspiciously, though they are forced to admit that his unorthodox methods can effectively cut through some educational Gordian knots.
 GTO achieved a peak rating of 35.7% in its native Japan and was also a hit across the rest of East Asia. It inspired a new wave of imitators, particularly a business version in **SALARYMAN KINTARŌ**, a female alter ego in **NAOMI**, a role reversal in **GOODBYE MR. OZU**, and even the Mandarin series *An Outstanding Teacher of a Delectable Subject* (*Mala Miaoxian Shi,*

aka *Taiwan GTO,* aka *Happy Campus*). However, its hero existed in manga form long before many of his modern fans were out of kindergarten. Onizuka first appeared in the 1990 biker manga *Shōnan Pure Love Gang* by Tōru Fujisawa, before getting *GTO* as his own spin-off series in *Shōnen Magazine* in 1997. The manga version is slightly more risqué, including more violent scenes and a younger hero (22 versus TV's 25) who unashamedly takes a teaching post in order to chase school-girls. The character of Azusa is also different—the manga version is supportive of Onizuka and regards teaching as her dream job, whereas the live-action incarnation is repulsed by his tough guy image and wants to leave teaching to become an air hostess. Such a reversal of characterization allows for the traditional drama formula of mismatched romantic leads who must talk each other into admitting their true feelings and adds an extra in-joke. Azusa has a poster in her bedroom of Yutaka Takenouchi, who starred alongside Sorimachi in **BEACH BOYS**, while actress Matsushima is married to Sorimachi in real life.

Although Sorimachi went on to other projects such as **CHEAP LOVE**, *GTO* remained in the public eye for a further two years—compare to **BAYSIDE**

SHAKEDOWN, which similarly retained a fan base long after its initial broadcast. After the publication of a novelization by scenarist Yūkawa, a *GTO* TV special followed in December 1998, comprising a movie-length edit of the highlights of the series with additional blooper footage. After a brief 1998 radio serial, *GTO* returned to Japanese TV screens in 1999 as a 42-part anime series (*AE), which featured writer Yoshiyuki Suga on staff—presumably some of his live-action scripts were recycled. For the anime version, the voice of Onizuka was provided by Wataru Takagi.

Sorimachi returned for an all-new TV special in August 1999, in which Onizuka finally loses his virginity to Azusa and heads off to a new posting, which turns out to be an all-girls convent school. However, he almost ruins his chances with Azusa when he attempts to beat up a man holding her hand, only to discover it is her father. He eventually impresses the old man in time to set up the *GTO* theatrical movie, in which he is moved again, this time to Azusa's home prefecture of Hokkaidō. In *GTO: The Movie* (1999), Onizuka reaches his posting to discover a desolate town, whose local economy has been ruined by the bankruptcy of a local Canadian theme park (*sic*).

With Norika Fujiwara co-starring as a local reporter, Onizuka successfully turns the town's fortunes around. Theme: Takashi Sorimachi—"Poison."

GUARD MAN, THE

1965. PRD: N/C. DIR: N/C. SCR: N/C. CAST: Ken Utsui, Jun Fujimaki, Yūsuke Kawazu, Isamu Kuraishi, Shizuo Nakajō, Masao Shimizu, Yoshio Inaba. CHN: TBS. DUR: 45 mins. x ca. 400 eps.; Fri 9 April 1965–24 December 1971.

Security guards in the Tokyo Patrol (an organization based on the real-life security company SECOM) become secret crimefighters. Though they have no jurisdiction, they know what is "right," and pursue criminals who regard themselves as above the law. Some critics regarded security guards as unlikely law enforcers (clearly these people have never heard of **GEISHA DETECTIVE**), but actor Utsui plays his role so convincingly that the series enjoyed a long run of success on Japanese TV. Mixing serious incidents with more tongue-in-cheek supernatural cases on occasion, *The Guard Man* was greatly influential on later action series, particularly **KEY HUNTER**. Peak rating: 39.9%.

HR

2002. AKA: *Home Room.* PRD: Shizuo Sekiguchi, Takeshi Tsuchiya. DIR: Kōki Mitani, Keita Kawano. SCR: Kōki Mitani. CAST: Shingo Katori, Tomohiko Imai, Takehiko Ono, Jun Kunimura, Miki Sakai, Ryōko Shinohara, Akira Shirai, Keiko Toda, Shidō Nakamura. CHN: Fuji. DUR: 45 mins. x 24 eps.; Wed 9 October 2002–?? March 2003.

Mild mannered Shingo (Katori from SMAP) is determined to do the best job he can and finds himself working as an English teacher at a night school (compare to GODDESS OF VICTORY). His fellow staff member is Tomohiko (Imai), a sociology lecturer who is not quite as cool as he thinks he is. Their students are the archetypal drama collection of misfits and dropouts, including middle-aged electrician Takehiko (Ono), old carpenter Shunichi (Kunimura), high school dropout Akira (Shirai), bad boy Mikihiro (Nakamura), former nightclub hostess Ryōko (Shinohara), clumsy housewife Keiko (Toda), and super-shy schoolgirl Miki (Sakai). Claimed by Fuji TV as "Japan's first sitcom," as in a situation comedy in the heretofore unseen American style, *HR* is a welcome return for writer Mitani, who also brought us THE PASSWORD IS BRAVERY and DON'T CALL ME PRIME MINISTER. In accordance with its roots in a particularly un-Japanese style of television, the show was recorded each week in front of a live studio audience, using only

three sets—the classroom, staff room, and cafeteria.

HAGURE KEIJI *

1988. JPN: *Hagure Keiji Junjōha.* AKA: *Stray Pure Cop.* PRD: N/D. DIR: Kazuki Yoshikawa, Yasutada Nagano, Mikio Koyama, Tōru Murakawa, Kiyoshi Miyakoshi. SCR: Kikuma Shimoiizaka, Kazuo Miyakawa, Akihiro Ishimatsu, Susumu Takahisa, Isamu Matsumoto. CAST: Makoto Fujita, Tatsuo Umemiya, Rei Okamoto, Junji Shimada, Osamu Bonchi, Kane Kosugi. CHN: Asahi. DUR: 45 mins. x ca. 360 eps.; Wed 6 April 1988–21 September 1988 (#1); 5 April 1989–4 October 1989 (#2); Wed 4 April 1990–3 October 1990 (#3); 19 April 1991–9 October 1991 (#4); 8 April 1992–23 September 1992 (#5); 7 April 1993–6 October 1993 (#6); 6 April 1994–21 September 1994 (#7); 12 April 1995–11 October 1995 (#8); 10 April 1996–25 September 1996 (#9); 2 April 1997–1 October 1997 (#10); 1 April 1998–30 September 1998 (#11); 31 March 1999–?? September 1999 (#12); 5 April 2000–27 September 2000 (#13); 4 April 2001–26 September 2001 (#14); 3 April 2002–2 October 2002 (#15).

Detective Yasuura (Fujita) is a shambling, unkempt investigator who shuns violence but always gets his man through deduction and reason. Some storylines straddle a couple of episodes but most of Yasuura's cases are dealt with in the span of a single evening,

although the relentless march of the program has caused the writers to go in search of ever more inventive cases for him to pursue. These include a manslaughter case that transforms into murder, when a hit-and-run driver is found to be stone-cold sober, a man found dead in a movie theater with no obvious murderer, a disabled girl accused of attacking her bullies, and an ex-convict accused of murdering his loud karaoke-loving neighbor.

Sensibly for a long-running drama, *Hagure Keiji* also prefers to involve the audience in the lives of Yasuura's subordinates, a motley crew of officers and detectives whose relationships and past lives can add extra depth to the case-of-the-week formula. Thus, more often than not, the occupants of the station house are not faced with the cliché of a murder to which they are called, so much as they are dragged into events in the lives of people around them— Yasuura has investigated the murder of his favorite barber, helped a fellow detective's ex-husband beat a murder rap, and even delved into the past of his brother, who died long ago in World War II. This personal, emotional involvement is nothing new in crime shows but may have been something of an influence on later shows such as BAYSIDE SHAKEDOWN, which simply marginalizes the veteran Yasuura-type character to make his hapless but more photogenic assistants the focus of all the action.

Hagure Keiji's most obvious debt lies in the portrayal of its main character, who closely resembles Peter Falk in *Columbo* (1971), broadcast on NHK in 1974. Reflecting the concerns of its middle-aged audience, *Hagure Keiji* has also devoted many episodes to Japan's aging society. Yasuura's case work often brings him into contact with issues of euthanasia, pension fraud, and the stress of caring for aging relatives. In this regard, it bears a certain similarity to the work of best-selling manga star Kenshi Hirokane, particularly the old-timer love stories of *Shooting Stars in the Twilight*.

Compare to Yasuura's chief rival in the detection stakes, Masakazu Tamura's **NINZABURŌ FURUHATA**. The four most recent seasons have been broadcast with English subtitles in the U.S. on KIKU TV. In a sure sign of the show's popularity with programmers and audiences, season #14 of *Hagure Keiji* began its KIKU broadcast on 1 July 2002—in other words, before the Japanese run was more than halfway done. Theme songs include: Takao Horiuchi—"Ai ga Miemasu ka" (Does it Seem Like Love?), "Jidaiya no Koi" (Modern Love).

HAKKENDEN

1973. PRD: Takashi Nakayama. DIR: Takamasa Suzuki, Yukiharu Itō, Mari Sasaki, Tōru Minegishi, Hiroshi Kubota, Kōichirō Hatano. SCR: Tōru Ishiyama. CAST: (voices) Kyū Sakamoto, Shinsuke Konseki, Kiyoshi Kawakubo, Takashi Saitō, Nobuaki Sekine, Hideo Kinoshita, Keiko Hanagata, Hiroko Suzuki, Sumiko Abe, Takanobu Hozumi, Mamoru Hirata, Makio Inoue. CHN: NHK. DUR: 15 mins. x 464 eps.; Wed 2 April 1973–28 March 1975. Five hundred years ago, the castle of feudal lord Yoshisane Satomi (Konseki) is surrounded by the army of his local rival Kagetsura Anzai. Jesting in the face of imminent defeat, Yoshisane tells his dog Yatsufusa that he will give him his daughter Princess Fushi in marriage if the dog returns with Anzai's head. By the end of the night, Yatsufusa does so and though the fortunes of the Satomi family improve, the dog refuses to leave Fushi's side. Yoshisane become furious and tries to kill the dog but Fushi throw herself in front of her father's spear. Insisting that her father keep his word, the princess leaves the castle with the dog.

In fact, the dog has been possessed by the evil spirit of Tamaazuma, a warrior slain long ago by Yoshisane and his retainer Daisuke Kanamari (Hozumi). Eventually, Fushi and the dog are found living together in a cave, where they are killed (he on purpose, she by accident) by Yoshisane and Daisuke. At the time, Fushi was staring at her own reflection in a pool, thinking that she could see herself developing canine features. As the princess dies, the eight beads of her necklace scatter into the sky and become eight puppies. Daisuke becomes a monk and travels around the country searching for eight young warriors that Princess Fushi left. His only clues are their ownership of a beautiful jewel or a peony shaped birthmark.

The eight young warriors encounter each other without any knowledge of their background or shared origin. Meanwhile Tamaazuma's evil spirit plays with the young men's destiny. But Sadamasa Ōgigayatsu, the governor general of the Eastern provinces, is plotting to invade Yoshisane's territory and only the eight dog-warriors have the power to stop him.

Based on the multi-volume 19th-century novel by Kyokutei Bakin, this fifth NHK puppet show was the very first period drama in the series, borrowing techniques from kabuki and bunraku theater and utilizing archaic words and phrases in its script. Despite these apparent obstacles, it was more successful than its predecessors, attracting an audience of children and adults. Though some parts of the series have since been re-released on DVD, many of the original episodes were deleted long ago, and only fragments remain. A film version of the early chapters, using all-new footage, was shot in 1975 by Tōei and a live-action movie adaptation followed from Kinji Fukasaku in 1983. The most recent incarnation of the series was an anime version in 1990 (*AE), whose crew publicly acknowledged their inspiration from this famous puppet series.

HALF DOC

2001. JPN: *Han Doku*. AKA: *Half Doctor*. PRD: Hiroki Ueda. DIR: Yukihiko Tsutsumi, Fuminori Kaneko. SCR: Shizuka Ōishi. CAST: Tomoya Nagase, Rina Uchiyama, Kazuya Ninomiya, Hitomi Manaka, Rei Okamoto, Kazuki Sawamura, Yōko Nogiwa. CHN: TBS. DUR: 45 mins. x 10 eps.; Wed 3 October 2001–12 December 2001. Former Ikebukuro gang member Ichiban Hazama (Nagase from TOKIO) unexpectedly passes the national medical examinations and is sent to the elite Genpaku Sugita Memorial Hospital in Tokyo. Alongside snooty fellow medical interns Michiko Kojima (Uchiyama) and Megumi Kisaragi (Manaka), he is introduced to stern super-surgeon Kazushi Shindo (Sawamura), who is said to have *"the hands of God,"* and refuses to entertain the notion of failure among his staff. He curtly informs the new arrivals that they will succeed in all things or be summarily fired.

Half Doc's finest moment is its opening dream sequence, a pastiche of *Black Jack* (*AE) in which Ichiban imagines himself as a scar-faced surgeon working miracles while a dewy-eyed schoolgirl looks on adoringly. From then on, it's a slow spiral into the everyday, as the **IKEBUKURO WEST GATE PARK** team try to engineer a medical version of **GTO**. Needless to say, Ichiban is a maverick whose passion for his patient's feelings is supposed to excuse his tomfoolery and insubordination. The script dutifully engineers some amusing collisions of initially unrelated events, setting up absurdist moments of comedy in the style of *Seinfeld,* such as Ichiban being set upon by hospital security on his first day and his attacking a closed-circuit

TV camera with a lobster. Later episodes pile on additional melodrama but this often sits uneasily with the initial comedy style.

HANDS OFF THE THIEF

1990. JPN: *Dorobō ni Te o Dasuna*. PRD: N/C. DIR: Isamu Nakatsugawa. SCR: Shōichirō Ōkubo. CAST: Yoshiko Tanaka, Kōichi Satō, Kanta Ogata, Rei Okamoto. CHN: TVT. DUR: 45 mins. x 11 eps.; Wed 17 October 1990–26 December 1990.

Konno (Satō) and Mayumi (Tanaka) are a newlywed couple with a difference. She is a respected detective but he has a secret identity as the master thief Dark Cat. Returning from their honeymoon, Konno hears of the discovery of a famous Old Master painting and decides to steal it. A comedy mystery based on a story by Jirō Akagawa, *HotT* resembles a role reversal of the famous *Cat's Eye* (*AE) in which the male lead was the detective and the female lead was the thief.

HANDSOME MAN

1996. PRD: Akihiro Hisano. DIR: Akiyoshi Imazeki. SCR: Hiroki Shimoto, Machiko Iida. CAST: Hiroshi Nagano, Kunihiro Matsumura, Shinju Ozawa, Fumie Hosokawa. CHN: Asahi. DUR: 45 mins. x 10 eps.; Mon 8 January 1996–11 March 1996.

Tobio (Nagano) is a smart young surgeon who has his pick of the ladies. A malicious deity decides that he needs to rethink his private life and punishes him. Now, whenever he thinks about sex, he transforms into the unattractive Tobio Mark Two (Matsumura). Theme: Coming Century (V6)—"Theme of Coming Century."

HANGMAN, THE

1981. PRD: Hiroshi Sakuma, Kuniya Ōkuma, Tetsuo Okuda. DIR: Umetsugu Inoue, Akinori Matsuo, Kuniya Ōkuma, Tadashi Mafune, Keiichi Ozawa, Michio Konishi, Kōichi Gotō, Kiyotada Mizuno, Yōichi Maeda, Michihiko Obimori, Kiyoshi Nishimura, Yasuharu Hasebe. SCR: Takayuki Yamada, Katsuyuki Naka-

mura, Hiroshi Nagano, Yū Tagami, Masaru Takesue, Tatsuhiko Kamoi, Tomomi Tsutsui, Toshiaki Matsushima, Hiroyasu Yamaura, Katsuaki Chaki, Noboru Sugimura. CAST: Ryūzō Hayashi, Toshio Kurosawa, Hitoshi Ueki, Shizue Abe, Yōko Natsuki, Shinichi Kase, Dion Ram, Jaguar Gorson, Tatsuo Nadaka, Sō Yamamura. CHN: Asahi. DUR: 45 mins. x 51 eps.; 14 November 1980–6 November 1981 (#1); 4 June 1982–24 December 1982 (#2); 29 July 1983–10 February 1984 (#3); 21 August 1984–5 April 1985 (#4); 7 February 1986–22 August 1986 (#5).

The Hangman (*sic*) is a private group that punishes evildoers who operate above the law. They take their orders from a leader with the codename "God" (Yamamura), and specialize not in killing their prey but in driving them to confess their crimes to the world at large. The members are Toshiya Tsuzuki, aka Black (Hayashi); Kōsuke Kusakabe, aka Mite (Kurosawa); Yūtarō Tsuji, aka Ban (Ueki); Reiko Asami, aka Penny (Abe); Gorō Dōmon, aka Bike (Kase); and Kiyoyasu Ryū aka Dragon (Ram).

This modern-day revamp of the SURE DEATH premise was more popular than expected and recommissioned for a further 26 episodes. However, by the time of the second series, some of the original cast had other commitments and were replaced. In the second season which aired six months later, the hard-boiled elements were downplayed in favor of a newfound concentration on the agent's daily lives—God assigns them jobs in the real world to aid in covering their tracks.

The third series featured all new members, including a replacement God (Shigeru Amachi) and initiated a slow decline into camp that would reach its nadir with the cartoonish fourth season, in which another new God (Frankie Sakai) got the members to form a taxi company as part of their cover. When the members head out for a "hanging," a robot transforms a cab into a Hangmanmobile.

The last series dropped God entirely in favor of a housewife as the leader (Yōko Yamamoto). Instead, a man called Maeo (Yoshio Tsuchiya) became the manager and commissioned the hangmen.

HANSHICHI *

1997. JPN: *Shin Hanshichi Torimonochō*. AKA: *New Detective Stories of Hanshichi*. PRD: N/D. DIR: Masami Kadowaki, Yoshio Fukumoto, Takahisa Gotō, Keiki Nakadera. SCR: Hisashi Yamanaka, Kimi Saitō, Toshimichi Saeki, Kimiko Saitō, Rin Takagi. CAST: Hiroyuki Sanada, Riho Makise. CHN: NHK. DUR: 45 mins. x 18 eps.; Fri 4 April 1997–1 August 1997.

Two years after the untimely death of his beloved wife, Hanshichi (Sanada) lives alone in a run-down building in old Edo. His sister-in-law Okume (Makise), who nurses a crush on him, often comes round to "*see that he is all right,*" but Hanshichi stalwartly resists her advances in honor of his wife's memory. He works as an assistant to the local law enforcers but his true vocation is detective work, and Tokugawa-era Edo provides him with plenty of cases to test his sleuthing mettle. His first involves a girl found dead in the river—a local woman becomes suspicious about the circumstances of the death, only to discover more misfortune wrapped in the tragedy. Yes, the girl was murdered but she was also the mistress of the woman's husband, upon whom the suspicion now falls.

This series is only the latest in a long line of TV adventures for Hanshichi. The story was first dramatized in 1953 by NHK as the very first period drama on TV. It was repeatedly made into TV dramas, such as in 1955 by NHK, 1956 by KRT (now TBS), 1960 by NTV, 1966 by TBS, 1971 by NET (now Asahi), 1979 by Asahi, and 1991 by NTV. However, its pedigree stretches even further back, as Hanshichi was originally created in 1917 and is a pillar of Japanese crime fiction to rival **HEIJI ZENIGATA**. First appearing in *The Soul of Obun*, serialized in *Bungei Club* magazine, Hanshichi featured in 68 novels by author Kidō Okamoto, who conceived his hero as a Japanese answer to Sherlock Holmes. His character and outlook are certainly very similar, although Okamoto never included a recurring Watson character for Hanshichi to bounce ideas off and the series also included several forays into the supernatural.

Hanshichi's clients are often beleaguered women who claim (sometimes truly) to have been framed. They include a spinster who fears she is cursed because all of her fiancés meet with tragic ends, an heiress whose feckless brother is striking a secret deal with a rival clan, and a troubled wife supposedly caught red-handed holding a knife over the dead body of her father-in-law. This last crime, we might surmise, was rather common in Edo-era Japan, since Hanshichi must deal with a very similar case soon after, this time with a wife accused of murdering her husband! Other cases include a couple who claim to be haunted by the ghost of their stepdaughter, who ran away from home after the childless pair finally conceived children of their own, and a corrupt police officer stalked by a convict newly released from jail. Broadcast with English subtitles in the U.S. on KIKU TV. Theme: Tamio Okuda—"Yō."

HAPPINESS IN BLOOM
2003. JPN: *Shiawase Saita*. PRD: N/C. DIR: N/C. SCR: N/C. CAST: Kaori Taka-hashi, Shōko Nakajima, Kōji Higuchi, Yorie Yamashita, Narumi Kayashima. CHN: Fuji. DUR: 25 mins. x ca. 26 eps.; 6 January 2003–?? June 2003.

Saki (Takahashi) discovers that her husband of three years has cheated on her and summarily divorces him. She vows never to get married again but finds herself volunteering for a job at a marriage broker (see **ARRANGED MARRIAGE**), where it becomes her responsibility to coach and support others as they go in search of someone with whom they can spend the rest of their lives. Based on the three volume manga of the same name published in 1997 by Kuni Arisaka.

HAPPY
1999. JPN: *Happy—Ai to Kandō no Monogatari*. AKA: *Happy—A Tale of Love and Emotion; Go Happy Go*. PRD: Kaori Hashimoto. DIR: N/C. SCR: Miaki Onosawa, Yuki Kiyomoto. CAST: Saki Takaoka, Hideki Takahashi, Kōsuke Toyohara, Seiko Takada. CHN: TV Tokyo. DUR: 45 mins. x 22 eps.; Wed 14 April 1999–?? June 1999 (#1); 19 July 2000–20 September 2000 (#2).

After being blinded in a skiing accident, 22-year-old Kaori (Takaoka) is deserted by her boyfriend and forced to start a new life. Her situation improves when she acquires the friendly seeing-eye dog Happy. Not only does the dog bring her immediate mobility and companionship but his presence leads to her meeting a new love, Noboru, who eventually asks her to marry him.

Based on the 1995 manga by Nobuko Hama serialized in *Be Love* magazine, *Happy* returned to Japanese screens in a feature-length edit, which was then followed by a second season, *Happy 2*. The second season introduces a second dog owner, Madoka (Kumiko Endō) who keeps a whole kennel-full of canines at a run-down warehouse. Compare to **ROCINANTE**, another animal tale. Both TV movie and series were shown without subtitles on the U.S. channel KTSF TV. Themes: Alma—"Mahoroba no Oka de" (At the Enchanting Hill), Tomato Cube—"Utakata" (Ephemeral).

HAPPY MANIA
1998. PRD: Masatoshi Katō. DIR: Takao Kinoshita, Makoto Hirano. SCR: Hiromi Kusumoto, Mika Umeda. CAST: Izumi Inamori, Norika Fujiwara, Kazumi Moroboshi, Ken Kaneko, Sakura Uehara. CHN: Fuji. DUR: 45 mins. x 11 eps.; Wed 8 July 1998–23 September 1998.

Kayoko (Inamori) is the titular happy maniac, a girl whose obsession is male attitudes toward relationships, making it something of a victimless crime—though her quarries often regard her as an irritating stalker who keeps developing crushes on them. She is alternately helped and hindered in her pursuits by Hiromi (Fujiwara), the friend whose apartment she is forced to share after being thrown out of her own. Based on the manga by Moyoko Anno, whose other publications include *Chameleon Army, Flowers and Bees,* and *Angelic House*. Theme: Southern All Stars—"Paradise." Peak rating: 20.8%.

HARD-WORKING MAN, A
2002. JPN: *Yoisho no Otoko*. PRD: Yūji Tōjō, Tatsuya Itō. DIR: Kazuyuki Morozawa, Fuminori Kaneko, Katsuo Fukuzawa, Renpei Tsukamoto, Arata Katō. SCR: Kazuyuki Morozawa, Yōko Iino. CAST: Gorō Inagaki, Somegorō Ichikawa, Akiko Yada, Hiroko Hatano, Nenji Kobayashi, Yūko Asano, Hatsunori Hasegawa,. CHN: TBS. DUR: 45 mins. x 11 eps.; Sun 14 April 2002–?? June 2002.

Kōtarō Sakurai (Inagaki from SMAP) is a salesman for Akebono Insurance. He is good at currying favor and is promoted more rapidly than colleagues such as Eiji (Ichikawa), who regard him with some envy. However, when his company is merged with Global Life, all his bosses lose their authority, to be replaced by an emissary from the new owners. Makiko (Asano) is also known as The Iron Lady, a ball-breaking manager with (a sure sign of trouble on the horizon . . .) an MBA from America. Makiko immediately starts shaking up the company, leading many staff members to threaten strike action, all except Kōtarō, who sees his chance to suck up to the new boss.

On the day of the boycott, only three people turn up for work—Makiko, Kōtarō, and Kōtarō's girlfriend Naomi (Yada). Makiko receives a phone call from a major client threatening to cancel a contract and Makiko and Kōtarō must take the chairman Iwamori (Sei Hiraizumi) out for dinner to assuage his fears. After Iwamori becomes lewd and unreasonable, Makiko gets furious with him, but Kōtarō is happy to apologize to Iwamori for Makiko's behavior. He explains to Makiko that it often costs nothing to express gratitude or contrition and that he would rather speak up and be hated than hold his peace and repent at leisure. An intriguing contrast of Japanese and Western social/managerial attitudes ensues, in a drama that also has many similarities to **GOOD PERSON**, which featured Inagaki's fellow SMAP member Tsuyoshi Kusanagi.

HARIMAO

1960. JPN: *Kaiketsu Harimao*. AKA: *Harimao the Marvel*. PRD: Shunichi Nishimura. DIR: Sadao Funatoko. SCR: Masaru Igami, Junichi Ōmura. CAST: Toshiyuki Katsuki, Keiko Kondō, Fuyukichi Maki, Izumi Machida, Masayuki Naitō, Kōji Matsuyama, Tamaki Matsunaga, Toshi Yagisawa, Jōji Sakisaka, Tamotsu Ōtake, Masako Izumi. CHN: NTV. DUR: 25 mins. x 65 eps.; Tue 5 April 1960–27 June 1961. The Malaysian government is looking for Harimao, a local rebel who is interfering with their activities. However, their only information about the thorn in their side is that he appears to be of Japanese extraction. Tarō is caught in possession of a gun but released soon after without being charged. When he reaches his uncle's house, he is met by an ethnic Chinese, Chan Xiuming, who promises to take him to his uncle

the following day, although that night Tarō discovers that there is more to his family than meets the eye.

Harimao was also known as the "Malaysian Coxinga" or the "Tiger of Malay." Under the latter title, he was the subject of a World War II propaganda movie, a mythical figure who fought to rescue the people of Southeast Asia from the oppressive white colonial powers. In reality, Harimao was a concoction of Japanese wartime intelligence but his reappearance in an exotic TV series loaded with supposedly foreign locations and actors (chiefly Japanese staffers painted brown!) was a real treat for young Japanese viewers at the time. Harimao's disguise, as far as we can make out from the photographs, appears to comprise a pair of sunglasses, a turban, and half a woman's *sari,* but then again, that is still more likely to hide his true identity than, for example, Zorro's mask or Clark Kent's spectacles.

The TV series was complemented by a manga in *Weekly Shōnen Magazine,* written by Katsuo Yamada and drawn by Shōtarō Ishinomori. As a roguish master thief, Harimao has clear similarities with Monkey Punch's later creation *Lupin III* (*AE), a fact acknowledged in the TV movie *Lupin III and the Treasure of Harimao* (1995). Theme: Michiya Mitsuhashi—"Kaiketsu Harimao" (Harimao the Master Thief).

HARMONIA

1998. JPN: *Harmonia, Kono Ai no Hate.* AKA: *Edge of This Love.* PRD: Hiroko Haseyama. DIR: Yukihiko Tsutsumi, Takaya Kurata. SCR: Shinji Ohara, Shinichi Hisamatsu. CAST: Kōichi Dōmoto, Miki Nakatani, Akiko Yada, Satomi Tezuka. CHN: NTV. DUR: 45 mins. x 9 eps.; Sat 11 July 1998–12 September 1998. Professional cellist Hideyuki (Dōmoto) supplements his income by teaching part time. He needs money for the treatment of his brother Kenshi, who is suffering from heart disease. He is

A Hard-Working Man

drafted into an experimental scheme to help Yuki (Nakatani), a girl with an incurable brain disease that has robbed her of the power of human speech. Communicating through music, Hideyuki begins Yuki's therapy, only to discover that the mute girl also has paranormal powers and can channel her unspoken rage at others. Hideyuki organizes a piano recital but, one after another, all the people invited are mentally attacked. Hideyuki loses his confidence and stops teaching Yuki but she starts playing cello for the first time of her own free will. Her therapist Fukatani realizes that she plays for Hideyuki alone and asks him to come back. Pleased with what he regards as progress on the Yuki case, Hideyuki asks his girlfriend Yasuko to perform with her in another piano recital but Yuki uses her powers to crush Yasuko's fingers.

The guilt ridden Hideyuki prepares to leave Japan but Yuki refuses to accept that he will never come back to her and refuses to play the cello any more. After failing the exam he must pass to gain a foreign placement, Hideyuki visits Yuki once more and she stuns him by perfectly mimicking the playing of a world-class cellist she has only seen on video. However, Yuki remains mute and apparently autistic, unable to do anything but copy others. Fukatani confesses that he may know why Yuki does not speak and begs Hideyuki to help her achieve her "potential."

Based on SF love story by Setsuko Shinoda, in a similar vein as the obsessive love of **EDGE OF THE WORLD** and the repressed memories of **SLEEPING FOREST**. Theme: Shōnentai—"Ai to Chinmoku" (Love and Silence).

HATCHŌBORI SEVEN *

2002. JPN: *Hatchōbori no Shichinin.* PRD: Katatoshi Kawada, Hisakazu Uesaka, Yoshitsugu Kojima. DIR: Heiji Izumi, Mitsumasa Saitō. SCR: Gorō Shima, Katsukage Chaki, Kunio Fujii. CAST: Tsurutarō Kataoka, Saburō Ishikura, Hiroaki Murakami, Jindai Yamashita, Masao Orimo, Kazumi Tanimoto, Yōko Saitō, Nobuto Okamoto, Rin Ozawa, Katsumasa Uchida. CHN: Asahi. DUR: 45 mins. x ca. 27 eps.; 13 January 2000–16 March 2000 (#1); 18 January 2001–?? March 2001 (#2); 7 January 2002–11 March 2002 (#3).

Edo period policeman Hachibei Futsuda (Kataoka) is called in on an incident by his colleague Heisuke Matsui (Yamashita). A man has taken a woman hostage at a bank. When they get there, a samurai has just released the hostage and killed the criminal, telling witnesses that the criminal did not deserve to live. The samurai's name is Hisazō Aoyama (Murakami) and he is their new boss at the police station.

We have deliberately used these anachronistic terms to convey some of the feel of *Hatchobori Seven*—often it literally seems as if a busload of cast and crew from **HAGURE KEIJI** have crashed into the TV Asahi period props department and been forced to perform a modern-day drama wearing historical costumes. Featuring "seven warriors" (an obvious gag) fighting crime in 19th-century Tokyo, *H7* has returned for two further seasons, in which their misadventures continue to appeal to

fans of their NHK rival **HANSHICHI**. Many cases, as expected, are staples of thrillers the world over—a suicide that turns out to be murder, a pregnant woman in search of her baby's father, and an arsonist who holds the paper-walled city ransom. Others are more peculiar to 19th-century Japan, such as a hooker arrested for prostitution *"without a license."* Some of the seven cops' more intriguing cases include a girl who must solve a mystery in days or be forced to make good on a promise to sell herself into slavery, a group of ruffians who attack Aoyama on the street because he has accidentally taken a lantern belonging to their true target, and an artist who has nursed a grudge for decades against a famous kabuki actor. Meanwhile, chief Aoyama remains an intensely stoic center for the action, like an old Dirty Harry finally put in charge of his precinct and often ready with a word of sympathy for the circumstances that created criminals as well as their victims. All three seasons have been broadcast in the U.S. with English subtitles on KIKU TV. Themes: Keizō Nakanishi—"Bug," Tako Kisugi—"Chijō no Speed" (Speed of the Worlds), Masayuki Suzuki—"Dakishimetai" (I Wanna Hold You).

HEART BEAT

2000. PRD: Shōichi Kanayama, Kōichirō Fuchiyama, Jun Tsubaki, Kim Tegwan, Hiroteru Ōta, Takashi Fujita. DIR: Atsushi Shimizu, Kim Tegwan. SCR: Yūki Okano, Kim Tegwan. CAST: Mika Kaneda, Saori Nara, Yuka Hirata. CHN: TVT. DUR: 25 mins. x 13 eps.; Wed 4 October 2001–27 December 2001. Schoolgirl Itsumi Takeuchi (Kaneda) has five boyfriends but still craves true love. Kaori Misaki (Nara) is a lonely girl who is somewhat eccentric and obsessed with fairy tales. Nagisa Tachibana (Hirata) dreams of becoming an idol singer. After an accidental meeting, the three runaways discover a music system called Heart Beat that makes its listener ecstatically happy. They decide to delve into Heart Beat's origins, in a late-night drama that mix-

es the media mystery of **RING** with pretty late-night schoolgirl eye candy. Note—most broadcast listings refer to this as a Wednesday night show, though technically it went on at one o'clock on a Thursday morning.

HEAVEN AND EARTH

1969. JPN: *Ten to Chi to.* PRD: N/D. DIR: N/D. SCR: Katsuo Nakai, Yoshinori Sugiyama. CAST: Kōji Ishizaka, Yukiji Takahashi, Kōtarō Nakamura, Mitsuteru Nakamura, Fumie Kashiyama, Tamao Nakamura. CHN: NHK. DUR: 45 mins. x 45 eps.; Sun 5 January 1969–28 December 1969. Torachiyo (K. Nakamura) is a son of Tamekage Nagao, the deputy guardian (*shugo*) of Echigo (now Niigata Prefecture). Unloved by his parents and persecuted by his elder brother, he grows up to take over his father's post, along with a new name Kenshin Uesugi (now played by actor Ishizaka). Five times in single decade, Kenshin fights with his rival **SHINGEN TAKEDA** (Takahashi) from Kai (now Yamanashi Prefecture) in a civil war that eventually engulfs all of Japan.

Heaven and Earth was the first *taiga* drama to be filmed in color, a decision that reputedly also led the producers to commission a script set in the time of Kenshin, since that period was famed for its brightly colored suits of armor. The gamble paid off, particularly in the stunning depiction of the battle of Kawanakajima. The series was based on a story by Chōgorō Kaionji published in *Weekly Asahi* from 1960 to 1962. It was also adapted into a movie of the same name in 1990 and apocryphal events from the same time also feature in the Kurosawa movie *Kagemusha.* Peak rating: 32.4%.

HEAVEN CANNOT WAIT *

1999. JPN: *Tengoku ni Ichiban Chikai Otoko.* AKA: *The Man Closest to Heaven; I Don't Wanna Die.* PRD: Sanae Suzuki, Akira Isoyama. DIR: Akio Yoshida, Osamu Katayama, Fuminori Kaneko. SCR: Masato Ochi. CAST: Masahiro Matsuoka, Takanori Jinnai,

Megumi Okina, Yoshihiko Hakamada, Yōsuke Kubozuka, Takami Matsumoto, Sōichirō Kitamura, Hiroshi Ikeuchi, Ikkei Watanabe. CHN: TBS. DUR: 45 mins. x 11 eps.; Fri 6 January 1999–24 March 1999.

Hapless 21-year-old youth Shirō Amakusa (Matsuoka from TOKIO) lives permanently in the shadow of his three successful elder brothers. He has failed the university entrance exams on three occasions and lives a wasted life in Tokyo. He is confronted by Yoshimi Tendō (Jinnai), his leather-clad guardian angel, who informs him that he is scheduled to die soon, unless he can catch up with the life he should have led—compare to I'LL BE BACK and HEAVEN'S KISS. In a cross between *Highway to Heaven* and *Quantum Leap*, he is assigned a different project each week, successful completion of which will gain him another few days' respite and the chance to chase his would-be girlfriend, Koharu (Okina).

His missions revolve around a Tokyo company, where Koharu works as secretary to the boss Junichi (Kitamura) and gains a rival for Koharu's affections in the form of the boss's son Satoru (Kubozuka). Shirō comes to realize that every one of his actions affects others, starting when he steals someone else's taxi and causes a chain of events that almost leads to the suicide of a disenchanted salaryman. With the emphasis on farce and physical comedy, the missions are often more like party game forfeits than life-threatening crises—Shirō must kiss an older woman or cry real tears, but such apparently mundane acts can save his life. Shirō soon finds himself working at Koharu's company, where a series of tasks in the real world add to the fun. By episode two, Koharu has accidentally mailed the boss's vacationing wife a parcel destined for his mistress, forcing the staff members to race across Japan and stop the delivery. The result is the surreal sight of Shirō, dressed in a life-sized teddy bear costume, hanging onto the back of a runaway delivery truck as it careens through the lanes of

an Alpine ski resort followed by a fist-fight with a resolute postman in the forest, as a near-sighted hunter slowly takes aim at what he believes to be a wild animal.

Later episodes find Shirō resolving his issues with his brothers and fending off the attempts of Koharu's father to find her a more suitable fiancé. He must also evade a vengeful criminal who mistakes him for a double-crossing drug dealer. Shirō and Koharu become closer when both are bitten by a poisonous viper and Shirō must decide who gets the single available shot of serum. Meanwhile, there are elements of *Wings of Desire* (or rather, its 1998 remake *City of Angels*) as Tendō begins to fall for pretty widow Ruri (Matsumoto) and reveals that his own life is anything but perfect.

Note that Shirō Amakusa's historical namesake was the leader of the Christian rebels who held out against the samurai in 17th-century Shimabara. Who would have guessed that a famous Christian martyr would lend his name to a TV show 300 years later, featuring a credit sequence in which the entire cast does the can-can dressed as Tarantino's Reservoir Dogs, while someone throws buckets of water at them?

A two-hour TV special followed, in which Tendō returns to Earth to aid another mortal—this time, schoolgirl Hikaru who has drifted into teenage prostitution and petty theft. This was followed by a full second season in April 2001, *HCW—The Teacher*, featuring Matsuoka as the titular educator Kazuya Okinoshima, Jinnai again as the tormenting angel, and new cast members Ai Katō and Shō Sakurai. To date, *The Teacher* is the only part of the franchise not to have been screened subtitled on KIKU TV in the U.S. See also I'LL SAVE THE WORLD and SKY HIGH. Theme: TOKIO—"Oh! Heaven." Peak rating: 14.5%.

HEAVEN'S COINS *
1995. JPN: *Hoshi no Kinka*. AKA: *Die Sterntaler*. PRD: Miki Umehara. DIR:

Heaven's Coins

Hiroshi Yoshino. SCR: Yukari Tatsui, Junya Yamazaki. CAST: Noriko Sakai, Takao Ōsawa, Yutaka Takenouchi, Minako Tanaka, Naomi Hosokawa, Ikki Sawamura, Tomomi Nishimura. CHN: NTV. DUR: 45 mins. x 24 eps. (ep 12: 90 mins.); Wed 12 April 1995–12 July 1995 (#1); 9 October 1996–25 December 1996 (#2/*Zoku*). Remake: 45 mins. x ca. 11 eps.; 25 April 2001–24 June 2001.

Deaf Aya (Sakai) comes to Tokyo in search of Shūichi (Ōsawa), the boy she fell in love with, who has mysteriously failed to return to Hokkaidō. With the help of his half brother Takumi (Takenouchi), Aya tracks Shūichi down to a hospital ward—but he has lost all memory of her after an accident. In order to be close to him, she takes a job as a nurse at the hospital, only to be flung into takeover intrigues and the deadly relationship between Shūichi and Shōko (Hosokawa), the girl who caused him to lose his memory. Meanwhile, Takumi finds Aya strangely attractive and she must fend off the advances of one brother whilst trying to remind the other of the promise he made to marry her.

Heaven's Coins was one of the highest-rated dramas of its time, mixing the hospital intrigue of **24-HOUR ER** and the ever popular disability subplot seen in **PURE**, **UNDER ONE ROOF**, or **SUMMER SNOW**. In fact, *Heaven's Coins* required considerably more effort on the part of its cast, since many of them were obliged to learn sign language in order to have believable onscreen communication with the Sakai character—compare to the later Japanese hearing-impaired movie *I Love You* (2001) and the following season's **SAY YOU LOVE ME**. Nor does the series scrimp on its melodramatic obligations, throwing aside Japanese drama's traditional *Cinderella* template in favor of *Die Sterntaler* by the brothers Grimm (hence the show's alternate title)—a folktale in which an orphan girl gives away all her possessions to help others, to be rewarded by golden coins raining from the sky. However, even the traditionally misery-loving Japanese viewers were heard to complain that Aya does not seem to get much of a reward for all her troubles—after suffering much physical and mental abuse, she seems to end up back where she started.

Like all Japanese good girls, Aya has a lot of suffering to endure—her enemy Shōko is a prize manipulator and is not above resorting to physical assaults, suicide attempts, and pregnancy blackmail to get what she wants. Though Aya eventually bends to the pressure and retreats to Hokkaidō in the feature-length 12th episode, the series soon returned as *Zoku Hoshi no Kinka* (*More Heaven's Coins*) the following year. Aya finally accepts Takumi's proposal of marriage, only to discover that Shūichi is suddenly back on the market—she realizes, a little too late, that it is still Shūichi that she really loves. Meanwhile, the second season piles on the histrionics, killing off major characters from the previous series, introducing an incarcerated mother, and involving Shūichi in a custody battle over his new son—even if Aya gets her man, she'll still be volunteering for a reluctant parent sequel with added in-law appeasement! The serial's progressively darker tone reaches its peak with the resolution of the hospital takeover bid, in which the dastardly criminals almost get their just desserts. Peak rating: 23.9%.

The series was rounded off with a long TV movie, which recapped the previous story with extra bridging footage of Aya—now back in Hokkaidō and pregnant with a child of her own. Both series and the concluding TV movie were broadcast in the U.S. with English subtitles on KIKU TV and KTSF TV. Themes: Noriko Sakai—"Aoi Usagi" (Blue Rabbit) and "Kagami no Doresu" (The Dress in the Mirror).

The story returned in 2001 as *Shin Hoshi no Kinka* (*New Heaven's Coins*), a complete remake starring Mari Hoshino in the Sakai role. This time, the put-upon deaf heroine comes to Tokyo in search of her long-lost mother.

HEAVEN'S KISS

1999. JPN: *Tengoku no Kiss*. AKA: *Tokyo Ghost Story*. PRD: Masaaki Itō, Satoko Uchiyama. DIR: Akihiro Karaki, Masahiro Hisano, Jun Akiyama. SCR: Hiromi Kusumoto. CAST: Megumi Okina, Taka, Tatsuya Fujiwara, Mai Hōshō, Junji Takada, Nana Katase, Aya Hirayama, Jun Matsuda, Kurume Arisaka, Keiko Toda, Hiroko Shimabukuro, Takashi Fujii, Satoko Ōshima, Tomoko Nakajima, Kyōko Fukada. CHN: Asahi. DUR: 45 mins. x ca. 11 eps.; Mon 12 July 1999–13 September 1999.

Rock star Shū (Taka from Lacrima Christi) swears never to sing again after the death of his girlfriend (Shimabukuro from Speed). Okina plays a ghost with solid, human form, who will not be permitted to become an angel until she engineers Shū's return to society as a singer. However, while she tries to manipulate things on Earth so that they can both get on with their lives, she finds herself falling for a normal human being at her high school. Like the same year's **HEAVEN CANNOT WAIT**, *HK* seems to have taken its theme from *City of Angels* (1998), appealing to a wider audience through the use of many prominent guest stars. Themes: Hiroko Shimabukuro—"As Time Goes By," Lacrima Christi—"Eien" (Forever).

HEIJI ZENIGATA

1966. JPN: *Zenigata Heiji*. PRD: N/C. DIR: Yasushi Sasaki, Yoshiyuki Kuroda, Masahiko Izawa, Shizuo Okamoto. SCR: Tatsuo Nogami, Kikuma Shimoiizaka, Katsuyuki Nakamura, Hide Ogawa, Akira Yokobori, Hitoshi Endō, Minoru Takahashi, Ken Hakuma, Heihachi Komaki, Yoshiki Yasutoshi. CAST: Hashizō Ōkawa, Yoshiko Kayama, Chinpei Hayashiya, Kaoru Yachigusa, Hachirō Azuma, Akiko Hyūga, Masaki Kyōmoto, Tatsurō Endō, Yoshie Ichige, Kensaku Morita. CHN: Fuji. DUR: 45 mins. x 888 eps.; Wed 4 May 1966–4 April 1984 (#1); 29 May 1991–2 October 1991 (#2); 15 July 1992–25 November 1992 (#3); 29 May 1993–10 November 1993 (#4); 27 July 1994–14 December 1994 (#5); 8 March 1995–12 July 1995 (#6); 23 July 1997–3 September 1997 (#7); 28 January 1998–25 February 1998 (#8).

Heiji Zenigata (Ōkawa) is an impoverished assistant law enforcement officer in Edo-era Japan, sometimes nicknamed "the Failure" because of his recurring habit of freeing criminals for whose plight he feels sympathy. His subordinate Hachigorō (Jūrō Sasa) is his eyes and ears on the city streets, regularly arriving to report the latest gossip or scandal, and the two form an uneasy crime-fighting team. The hard drinking, heavy smoking Heiji has only a few things in his favor—the love of his wife Shizu (Yachigusa), the thanks of the lower-class individuals he protects from corrupt samurai, and a neat talent for hurling coins, using them to stun fugitives with unfailing accuracy.

First appearing in Kodō Nomura's story *A Virgin in Gold* (1931), detective Zenigata went on to feature in another 338 print adventures, rivaling **HANSHICHI** in the attention of the Japanese crime reading audience. This long-running TV adaptation of the franchise started out as a deliberate attempt to put modern crimes and concerns in an attractive samurai-era setting, and starred former samurai movie actor Ōkawa as the lovable, compassionate hero.

This famous series was not the first TV adaptation of the *Zenigata* stories. KRT ran its own *Zenigata* drama in 1958 and another in 1962 after the channel had changed its name to the more familiar TBS. After Ōkawa died in 1984, the NTV network tried to steal the Zenigata myth with its own version but the attempt backfired, as loyal Ōkawa fans begrudged the channel its attempt to replace their idol. Fuji eventually renewed the series with Kinya Kitaōji as Zenigata and initially tried to keep all other elements as similar as possible to the much loved Ōkawa "original." Once the audience had learned to accept a new actor as Zenigata, the channel began to introduce changes on a gradual basis, shifting the focus of some episodes onto the supporting cast in the style of HAGURE KEIJI. The popularity of the series also led to the creation of two apocryphal modern-day descendants, the Inspector Zenigata who doggedly chases Monkey Punch's manga master thief *Lupin III* (*AE) and the teenage detective *Ai Zenigata* (*Keitai Keiji Ai Zenigata*, 2002), whose late-night exploits on Asahi's BS-i satellite channel involved her fighting crime with her mobile phone. Theme: Kazuo Funaki—"Zenigata Heiji." Peak rating: 31.5% (in 1970).

HELP!
1995. PRD: Kōji Shiozawa. DIR: Mamoru Hoshi. SCR: Ryōichi Kimizuka. CAST: Arisa Mizuki, Junichi Ishida, Masahiko Nishimura, Ayako Ōmura. CHN: Fuji. DUR: 45 mins. x 10 eps.; Fri 13 January 1995–17 March 1995.
Nana (Mizuki) is asked to baby-sit two children of Shūichi (Ishida) for a single night. However, Shūichi disappears, leaving Nana to discover that the contract she has signed obliges her to look after the kids until *"such time as Shūichi returns."* Reluctant parenting from the writer of BAYSIDE SHAKEDOWN, with

something of a debt to the U.S. movie *Adventures in Babysitting* (1987).

HERE'S LOOKING AT YOU
2002. JPN: *Kimi o Mi Agete*. AKA: *Here's Looking Up at You*. PRD: Shinsuke Naitō, Hideo Tsuchiya. DIR: Tomoaki Iso, Mitsuru Kubota. SCR: Sumio Ōmori. CAST: Tsuyoshi Morita, MIKI, Masanori Ishii, Kōtarō Takada, Mireiyu, Kazuki Kitamura, Takuzō Kadono, Naoko Ōtani, Masaya Katō. CHN: NHK. DUR: 45 mins. x 4 eps.; Tue 12 February 2002–12 March 2002 .
Shōji Takano (Morita), a safecracker who prefers to keep his own company, is hired by a Thai criminal for a heist in Bangkok. On the plane to Thailand, he meets Eiko (MIKI), a tall Japanese woman who towers above him and forces him to look up whenever he talks to her. In Bangkok, he is taken blindfolded to a suburban house where he must open a safe that has lain undisturbed since World War II. When he succeeds, the contents of the safe cause the surrounding observers to burst into tears.

Back in central Bangkok, he meets Eiko once again and the pair enjoy a brief holiday romance, truncated by her return to Tokyo, and Shōji's realization that he will always be too short for her. The two still see each other back in Tokyo, but Eiko's brother Shinya (Takada) does not approve of Shōji and sets her up with the tall, handsome club owner Kitaoka (Kitamura). Eiko and Shōji break off their relationship but two months later Eiko is kidnapped by criminals who need Shōji to open a safe for them and retrieve incriminating evidence about trafficking in illegal immigrants.

Something of a departure for NHK, this modern drama mixes the glamorous gangster lifestyle of CHEAP LOVE with the international travelogue of FRIENDS, based on the novel of the same name by Taichi Yamada, who also created SUNFLOWERS ON THE HILL. Theme: Eiko Matsumoto—"Kimi ni Aitai" (I Want to See You).

HERO
2001. PRD: Takashi Ishihara, Kō Wada. DIR: Masayuki Suzuki, Makoto Hirano, Kensaku Sawada. SCR: Ken Ōtake, Yasushi Fukuda. CAST: Takuya Kimura, Takako Matsu, Nene Ōtsuka, Hiroshi Abe, Masanobu Katsumura, Tomohito Hachijima, Takuzō Kadono. CHN: Fuji. DUR: 45 mins. x 11 eps.; Mon 8 January 2001–19 March 2001.
Kōhei (Kimura from SMAP) is a former delinquent from the far northern city of Aomori who never graduated high school but somehow passed the difficult exams to become a public prosecutor. Arriving in Tokyo, he demonstrates all the outward appearances of a hick—dressing in inappropriately casual clothes, believing every word he hears on trashy talk shows, and spending much of his salary on ridiculous devices from the home shopping channel. But his simple behavior is just an act, for Kōhei has a bright legal mind and a winning allure with *almost* everyone he meets. His bespectacled colleague Maiko (Matsu) thinks herself immune to his charms and snootily ignores many of his ideas and hunches, until she is forced to admit that he is very smart and rather handsome.

With madcap lawyers running riot in an office fraught with dangerous romance and bizarre cases, *Hero* is Japan's answer to *Ally McBeal* (NHK, 1998, as *Ally My Love*), uniting two of the country's top stars in an ideal vehicle. Kimura in particular is ideally suited to his role—few actors have the natural charisma to carry off such a part but he bravely underplays it like a young NINZABURŌ FURUHATA, calmly reasoning his way through each case, while the rest of the cast bump into each other like the Keystone Cops.

Cases include an underwear thief whose alibi rests on a tape of the (fictional) *Miracle Girl* anime he religiously records, a murder suspect who pleads self-defense after causing the death of his assailant, and a man accused of threatening to kill his mistress when she threatens to dump him.

© 2001 Fuji

Hero

Meanwhile, plucky lady lawyer Mizuki (Ōtsuka) is conducting a clandestine office affair with Susumu (Abe), who is supposedly a happily married man. Tatsuo (Katsumura) is a young prosecutor who shamelessly bosses around his older counterpart Takayuki (Fumiyo Kohinata) and also believes that *he* is dating Maiko—this is news to her. In just one of many innovative twists, the titular "hero" is revealed not to be Kōhei at all but a brave security guard forgotten by everyone except his family.

Later episodes deal with the possibility that, successful or not, Kōhei's straight talking makes him a lot of enemies in Tokyo, where his rural origins and lack of a university education will always keep him an outsider—compare to the attitude toward Shinji in **BAYSIDE SHAKEDOWN**. As Kōhei fights a losing battle to stay in Tokyo, the suspense in the closing episodes lies in whether he

will be able to secure justice in his last case and if he will be leaving alone or with someone special. At the time of the original broadcast, a sizable fraction of the 36.8% peak audience never found out, since they neglected to stay tuned through the end of the closing credits of the final episode and missed a scene in which we, along with one of his ex-colleagues, visit Kōhei at his idyllic new posting.

HE'S LIKE A DEVIL
1975. JPN: *Akuma no Yō na Aitsu*. PRD: Teruhiko Hisayo. DIR: N/C. SCR: Kazuhiko Hasegawa. CAST: Kenji Sawada, Tatsuya Fuji, Tomisaburō Wakayama, Ichirō Araki, Seiko Miki, Hiroko Shino, Michiyo Yasuda. CHN: TBS. DUR: 25 mins. x 17 eps.; ?? June 1975–?? September 1975.
Early in the morning of 10 December 1968, a police officer stopped a security van in the middle of a rainstorm. He

told the security guards in the van that the destination bank had been bombed and that there was a chance that the vehicle was carrying a similar device. Smoke started to billow from the van while he was searching it, and he yelled at the security guards to take cover. However, as they ran from the vehicle, the "police officer" calmly climbed into the front seat and drove away with ¥300 million.

The perpetrator of this real-life crime was never caught, leading writer Hasegawa to speculate what might have happened—depicting the thief as a naive man caught up in events. In the drama, the criminal is Ryō Kamon (Sawada), who has blown all the money over six years and is now anxiously awaiting the day when the statute of limitations runs out on the crime. However, he is unlikely to enjoy his imminent freedom from prosecution, as he is suffering from a brain tumor that could kill him within six months. He is also working as a gigolo, pimped by his bisexual lover Shūji (Fuji), a childhood friend who was once a high-ranking detective but who resigned when he realized who was responsible for the 1968 robbery. Shūji's old colleague Isoroku (Wakayama) is still working on the case and suspects Ryō as he struggles to find a way of pinning the crime on him. As if this did not present enough problems in Ryō's life, he must fight off the advances of an army of adoring women, including his own sister Izumi (Miki).

The former frontman for the Tigers band, Sawada had pursued a glam-rock solo career as "Julie" since the band split up in 1971. With his androgynous good looks and little boy lost attitude (you can also see him getting abused in Paul Schrader's *Mishima*), he gained a substantial female following but this drama series represented an attempt to move into the acting world, like his former rival, Tempters lead singer Kenichi Hagiwara. However, for reasons unknown, this original-sounding story was only screened once and disappeared for over two decades until it was revived for a limited edition DVD release in 2001.

HIDDEN SECRET

2002. JPN: *Haha no Kokuhaku.* AKA: *Mother's Confession.* PRD: Masahiko Okumura, Kazuo Hirano, Toshiki Shimazaki, Takao Komatsu. DIR: Masahiko Okumura. SCR: Yoshinori Watanabe. CAST: Hitomi Takahashi, Tomiyuki Kunihiro, Yasuyo Mimura, Takeo Nakahara, Naomi Akimoto. CHN: Fuji. DUR: 15 mins. x 60 eps.; Mon 7 January 2002–29 March 2002.

Sixteen-year-old Haruna (Mimura) is a popular girl in the neighborhood, often described as having the good looks of her mother Ai (Takahashi) and the brains of her father Shiro (Kunihiro). They have kept a secret from her—she was conceived by artificial insemination by donor after her parents spent five years trying without success for a baby of their own. However, Haruna starts to suspect that something is amiss after she receives an anonymous birthday card and several crank calls. Eventually, her parents are forced to reveal that she is the offspring of sperm donated from Doctor Kadokura, a bitter man who has recently lost his wife and daughter—a girl who looked just like Haruna. Based on the novel *Kyōen* by Masao Takahashi, serialized in the *Nihon Keizai Shinbun* from 1998. Compare to BORN OF LIES.

HIDEYOSHI

1996. PRD: N/C. DIR: Mikio Satō. SCR: Hiroshi Takeyama. CAST: Naoto Takenaka, Yasuko Sawaguchi, Tetsuya Watari, Masanobu Takashima, Tōru Watanabe, Hiroyuki Sanada, Takako Matsu, Masahiko Nishimura, Hiroaki Murata, Hideaki Akai, Shin Takuma. CHN: NHK. DUR: 45 mins. x ca. 50 eps.; Sun 7 January 1996–22 December 1996.

In an age of civil strife, Mitsuhide Akechi kills warlord NOBUNAGA in battle in 1582, leaving Nobunaga's former associate Hideyoshi Toyotomi (1536–1598) to seize the reins of power. Hideyoshi marches against Akechi and by 1590 has united all of Japan under his rule.

After the previous year's *taiga* drama YOSHIMUNE, NHK took a different tack for their follow-up: the life of the man who joined Nobunaga's army as a common soldier, only to work his way through the ranks, become Nobunaga's trusted confidante, and take his niece as his favorite concubine. After uniting Japan, Hideyoshi founded the city known today as Tokyo, attempted a disastrous invasion of Korea, and died in 1598, leaving no legitimate heir but a five-year-old son born of his concubine. Consequently, Japan eventually falls under the rule of Ieyasu Tokugawa (see TOKUGAWA IEYASU)—events also depicted in the later AOI.

Scenarist Takeyama discards historical realism in favor of a medieval Japanese take on *The Godfather,* presenting HIDEYOSHI as a sympathetic character caught in unpleasant times, a working-class hero trying to make good in a world full of evil. As Hideyoshi, comic actor Naoto Takenaka was acclaimed for bringing a "breath of fresh air" to the *taiga* series—restoring some of the humanity and approachability last seen in Shima Iwashita's GRASS AFLAME, though part of the show's appeal must also rest with the director Satō, who ensured that it cracked along at a far brisker pace than some of its more sedate predecessors.

Hideyoshi's life has previously been adapted into a *taiga* form in 1965, as *Taikōki,* which controversially opened with a shot of a bullet train. Eschewing samurai combat in favor of historical minutiae and realistic historical information, *Taikōki* won over a large salaryman audience by presenting the lot of a samurai as notably similar to that of a modern-day businessman—trapped in a large organization, weighed down with debts of obligation.

The story was adapted from yet another perspective for the *taiga* drama of 1981. A year before she would make her name with OSHIN, writer Sugako Hashida scripted *Hideyoshi's Women* (*Onna Taikōki*), which presented the whole tale from the viewpoint of his wife. *Hideyoshi's Women* featured Yoshiko Sakuma in the lead role and also reunited Toshiyuki Nishida from MONKEY with Masako Natsume in what would be one of the actress's last roles before her untimely death. Peak rating: 37.4%.

HIGH SCHOOL GREAT ESCAPE

1991. JPN: *High School Dai Dassō.* PRD: N/C. DIR: Hidekazu Nakayama. SCR: Masahiro Kobayashi. CAST: Eri Fukatsu, Masami Nakagami, Emi Kodaka, Minori Yoshinaga. CHN: TVT. DUR: 45 mins. x 12 eps.; Wed 9 January 1991–27 March 1991.

New student Tsugumi (Fukatsu) comes to Bel Air Academy, a school that treats its pupils as society's elite and aims to educate the future rulers of Japan, in the style of CHALLENGE FROM THE FUTURE.

HIGH SCHOOL NOTEBOOKS

1989. JPN: *High School Rakugaki.* PRD: N/C. DIR: Akio Yoshida. SCR: Kiyota Yamamoto. CAST: Yuki Saitō, Nenji Kobayashi, Shirō Itō, Jōji Tokoro. CHN: TBS. DUR: 45 mins. x 24 eps.; Fri 6 January 1989–24 March 1989 (#1); 13 July 1990–28 September 1990 (#2).

Pretty teacher Izumi (Saitō) is posted to a technical high school and placed in charge of the first-year mechanics class, where the students are initially uninterested in learning from a woman. Theme: The Blue Hearts—"Jōnetsu no Bara" (Rose of Passion).

HIGH SCHOOL TEACHER

1993. JPN: *Kōkō Kyōshi.* PRD: Kazuhiro Itō. DIR: Shinichi Kamoshita, Ken Yoshida, Tōru Moriyama. SCR: Shinji Nojima. CAST: Hiroyuki Sanada, Sachiko Sakurai, Tōru Negishi, Noriko Watanabe, Hidekazu Akai, Emiko Nakamura. CHN: TBS. DUR: 45 mins. x 11 eps.; Fri 8 January 1993–19 March 1993.

Academic Takao Hamura (Sanada)

High School Teacher

becomes a temporary teacher at a girls high school while on sabbatical leave—compare to **GOODBYE ANTS**. He helps his student Mayu (Sakurai) evade punishment for fare dodging and the girl follows him back to his apartment, where the couple are surprised by Takao's fiancée Chiaki. The daughter of his college professor, Chiaki is immediately suspicious about their relationship. Each day as Takao arrives at school and stores his shoes, he finds a message which reads simply *"Help me."*

Meanwhile, life at the school is taking on a certain amount of notoriety. Student Naoko flirts with her teacher Fujimura (Masaki Kyōmoto) and is raped by him in an incident caught on videotape. Perhaps inspired by this incident, lesbian schoolgirl Asami (Nakamura) becomes jealous of the attention Takao lavishes on Mayu in his role as basketball captain and files a complaint claiming that Takao has raped *her.* Takao's class is boycotted by his students but Mayu stands by him. Later, Takao discovers that his fiancée Chiaki has been having an affair. He breaks off the engagement but the end of his relationship with Chiaki also causes him to fall out with her father and essentially brings an end to his potential academic career.

Takao cries on Mayu's shoulder and the two are witnessed leaving a hotel together. This incident leads to Mayu's suspension from school and Takao resolves to stay away from her for her sake. Meanwhile, Fujimura blackmails Naoko into having a sexual relationship with him and the pregnant school girl asks Mayu to lean on Takao for help. Takao visits Mayu at her home, where he witnesses her hellish home life firsthand and ends up stabbing her father. The couple go on the run together, in a hard-hitting drama from Shinji Nojima, which set the tone for a whole subgenre of romantic thrillers in the 1990s, of which **BLUE BIRD** and **FORBIDDEN LOVE** are perhaps the most representative. With a rating of 33.0%, *HST* dominated the schedules in its season and also led to a novelization, credited to Nojima. The story was reprised, presumably with extra footage, in the TV movie *HST: Another Story of Mayu,* which was broadcast in November 1993. For Nojima's part, *HST* represents the beginning of his darker period, leading to his scripts for **EDGE OF THE WORLD, NO LONGER HUMAN, LAST SONG,** and the similar **LIPSTICK.** Theme: Dōshi Morita—"Bokutachi no Shippai" (Our Failure).

The series returned in a sequel/remake in January 2003, starring Naohito Fujiki and Aya Ueto. Both set and broadcast exactly a decade after the original, the new story featured another doomed romance but this time it is the *teacher* who hides a dark secret from the rest of the world.

HIS AND HER CIRCUMSTANCES

1994. JPN: *Kare to Kanojo no Jijō.* PRD: Akira Koseki. DIR: Ken Matsumoto. SCR: Masahiro Yoshimoto, Yukiko Okazaki. CAST: Saburō Tokitō, Kaho Minami, Toshirō Yanagiba, Hiroshi Abe, Maho Toyota. CHN: Asahi. DUR: 45 mins. x 12 eps.; 14 April 1994–7 July 1994. Two former university buddies become roommates when they meet after two years apart. Noboru (Yanagiba) offers his old friend Hiroshi (Tokitō) a place to live, after the unemployed Hiroshi splits up with his faithless wife Shiori (Minami). Despite the similar title, this has no relation to the *His and Her Circumstances* anime series (*AE). Theme: T-BOLAN—"Love."

HIS AND HER TEA CUPS

2000. JPN: *Heisei Meoto Jawan—Dokechi no Hanamichi; Getting By.* AKA: *Modern Era His-and-Her Tea Cups: A Flower Way of Stinginess.* PRD: Kazuhiko Yūkawa, Kazuho Masuda, Futoshi Ōhira. DIR: Takaomi Saegusa, Makoto Naganuma, Masahiko Kiki. SCR: Yoshiko Morishita. CAST: Noriyuki Higashiyama, Atsuko Asano, Gaku Hamada, Honami Tajima, Hoka Asada, Keita Saitō, Shōta Saitō, Yūka, Anju Suzuki, Sarina Suzuki. CHN: NTV. DUR: 45 mins. x ca. 20 eps.; 12 January 2000–?? March 2000 (#1); 9 January 2002–?? March 2002 (#2). Mantarō (Higashiyama) is an optimistic man who dreams of being rich one day. His wife Setsu (Asano) is a stingy woman who runs the noodle restaurant that Mantarō inherited from his mother. They have five children: Un (Hamada), Kō (Tajima), Kan (Shunji Matsuzaki), Fuku (K. Saitō), and Raku (S. Saitō), and all are kept under Setsu's strict money saving regime. However, her husband always blows the cash. In the second episode, Mantarō gets the idea for a mock kidnapping to get rich quickly. He looks for children he might be able to abduct. Meanwhile, he learns that his own daughter Kō and her friend have truly been abducted and that the penny-pinching Setsu has suddenly come up with two million yen from nowhere.

For a Japanese audience still reeling from the collapse of the bubble economy, there was something endearing in the idea of a wife who could always balance her checkbook, no matter what the pressure. However, the series took an unexpected turn with its second season, set a year after Setsu's sudden death. Mantarō is deeply in debt, while Un has taken a job as a newspaper delivery boy to help support the family. Daughter Yuki inherits Setsu's penny-pinching role and controls her three younger brothers with an iron hand.

However, Mantarō introduces them to their would-be stepmother, 20-year-old beauty Akari (Yūka), a girl from a rich family who will solve all of Mantarō's problems. The children try to talk her out of it but she smiles resolutely and insists that her love for Mantarō cares nothing for his poverty. Yuki in particular cannot accept someone else is taking the maternal role but she tries to explain her late mother's system to Akari.

The truth soon comes out—Akari and Mantarō are rushing into marriage because Akari is pregnant. The children run away from home but Un realizes that all is not as it seems. He believes he has seen Akari's face on a pornographic video cover and in several magazines, too. Eventually, the ghost of Setsu appears to him and warns him that his suspicions are correct and that Akari, a woman of loose morals, is trying to con her father. Meanwhile, Mantarō is working to open another noodle bar, counting on Akari's wealthy parents' money.

Compare to GENTA IKENAKA 80 KILOS and ETCHAN, in which children are similarly reluctant to accept a parent's new spouse.

HŌJŌ TOKIMUNE *

2001. AKA: *Tokimune*. PRD: N/C. DIR: Yoshiyuki Yoshimura, Kunio Yoshikawa. SCR: Yumiko Inoue. CAST: Motoya Izumi, Atsurō Watabe, Atsuko Asano, Shinnosuke Ikehata, Shirō Itō, Ken Watanabe, Masakazu Tsukayama. CHN: NHK. DUR: 45 mins. x 49 eps.; Sun 7 January 2001–9 December 2001.

In the year 1247, Japan is still ruled by the Hōjō regency. Tokiyori (Watanabe) is the fifth Hōjō regent (great-grand-nephew of Masako from THE GRASS AFLAME) but his power is threatened by Yasumura Miura (Tsukayama), the leader of a clan who feel their position has been usurped by the Hōjō. To strengthen their position, the Hōjō family prepares to marry into the allied Mōri clan, brokering a wedding between Tokiyori and Akirako, the daughter of the head of the Mōri clan. However, the Mōri clan ally with the hated Miura and the Hōjō go to war. The Hōjō are victorious and Akirako is given as a bride to Tokiyori. Tokiyori's concubine Lady Sanuki has a child first but three years later, Akirako gives birth to Tokiyori's son Shōjumaru. Much to the annoyance of Sanuki, Tokiyori recognizes the new son as his true heir, causing her to fear for the future of her own son Hōjumaru.

Akirako's mother Fujiko tries unsuccessfully to stir up a revolt among the remnants of the Miura clan. When she is unsuccessful, she commits suicide, entreating her daughter to do likewise and to murder both of Tokiyori's children before she does so. However, Akirako refuses.

In 1255, the half brothers go out into the streets of Kamakura for the first time and are shocked by the poverty they encounter. They also meet with Nichiren, a Buddhist priest who has gained a strong following among the common people. The boys are scolded for their misdeeds but little of a traditional childhood remains for them. At his ceremony of manhood, the elder brother Hōjumaru receives the name Tokitoshi, a surname denoting the influence behind the scenes of the Ashikaga family, who are hoping to use him as a puppet. Two years later, Tokiyori prepares to abdicate at age 30 and in Shōjumaru's naming ceremony officially designates him as his heir by giving him the name Tokimune.

After several youthful adventures, including a romantic interlude and an attack by pirates, the full grown Tokimune (Izumi) is present in 1260 when the priest Nichiren warns the government of the impending danger of an invasion from overseas. However, he is ignored in favor of more pressing local matters, such as the growing feud between the children of Tokiyori's two wives. After Tokimune embarrasses one of his stepsiblings at an archery match, the angry Sanuki starts a fire that burns down the mansion and causes the death of another concubine.

Sometime later, after the suspicious death of Tokiyori by poisoning, Tokimune is slowly promoted through the ranks of the Hōjō. During his tenure, Japan is rocked by the arrival of emissaries from the Mongol ruler Khublai Khan, demanding that Japan open its doors to foreign trade. The Emperor decides to offer no reply at all, an act which angers the shogun's council and leads to the abdication of the former regent and the appointment of Tokimune. As Japan enters its time of greatest crisis, Tokimune is now the man in charge of defending it—at age 17.

As the years pass, the threat of Mongol invasion grows increasingly great. An attempted coup leads Tokimune to mistakenly sentence one of his own brothers to death for treason. Tokimune has barely recovered from the scandal when news comes that Khublai Khan has successfully suppressed an uprising in Korea and that now the way is open for him to invade Japan with a fleet of 1000 ships.

After an unsuccessful first attempt, the Mongols arrive in south Japan's vast Hakata Bay with an army of 140,000. The fighting is long and hard but the Japanese hold them off, until a divine wind, the *kamikaze*, destroys the Mongol fleet.

Based on a story by Katsuhiko Takahashi, this *taiga* dramatization of the meteoric career of Tokimune (1251–1284) was distinguished by a strong supporting cast—as in history itself, Tokimune often seems swamped by the more colorful characters that surrounded him. Broadcast in the U.S. with English subtitles on KIKU TV.

HOME AND AWAY

2002. PRD: Ichirō Takai. DIR: Kensaku Sawada. SCR: Ryōichi Kimizuka. CAST: Miho Nakayama, Naomi Nishida, Kōtarō Koizumi, Wakana Sakai. CHN: Fuji. DUR: 45 mins. x 11 eps.; Mon 7 October 2002–16 December 2002.

In the ten years since her mother's funeral, Kaede (Nakayama) has refused to speak to her distant father. Though there was little he could have done, Kaede resents him for not being at his wife's side when she died. Now, as Kaede's fairy-tale wedding to an elite businessman approaches, her brother recommends that she invite her father to the ceremony. She heads off to see her father but is forced to take a long route, thanks to a series of mishaps, as well as her own terrible sense of direction. The result is a mini-travelogue of Japan, as the angelic Kaede meets new guest stars of the week, each with a problem that needs to be dealt with or an argument that needs solving. Meanwhile, the embittered Kaede slowly comes to realize that she has the power to help others in need, including her own estranged father. **BAYSIDE SHAKEDOWN** creator Ryōichi Kimizuka retells *The Littlest Hobo*, with Miho Nakayama taking the role of the wandering German Shepherd! Broadcast without subtitles in the U.S. on the International Channel.

HOMEWORK

1992. AKA: *Housework*. PRD: Tamaki Endō. DIR: Tamaki Endō. SCR: Satsuo Endō. CAST: Toshiaki Karasawa, Misa Shimizu, Akiko Urae, Masaharu Fukuyama. CHN: TBS. DUR: 45 mins. x 11 eps.; Tue 6 October 1992–25 December 1992.

Keisuke (Karasawa) has just transferred from the sales department to the accounting department at a stationery company. At home with his parents, he finally has had enough of his politician father's strongly held opinions and of his mother's constant willingness to defer to whatever he says. He moves out of the family home and in with his girlfriend Uran (Urae)—an office lady who runs a small import business in the evenings. Life for the couple starts off well but the cracks soon start to show when Uran demonstrates a complete inability to do any housework. Keisuke starts to find himself attracted to Sachiko (Shimizu), a girl who works at a law firm and reminds him of his own mother. However, Sachiko is living with Shūji (Fukuyama), an unsuccessful musician. Another home drama from Tamaki Endō, the writer also responsible for **UNTIL THE MEMORY FADES** and **RINTARŌ**. Compare to **DREAMS OF ROMANCE**. Theme: Kanichi Inagaki—"Christmas Carol no Koro ni wa" (While Christmas Caroling).

HOT DOG

1990. PRD: Susumu Ōoka. DIR: Tōru Moriyama. SCR: Yūki Shimizu. CAST: Toshirō Yanagiba, Atsuko Sendō, Hideo Murota, Mie Nakao. CHN: TBS. DUR: 45 mins. x 11 eps.; Thu 19 April 1990–28 June 1990.

Shin (Yanagiba) is a short-tempered gangster, assigned by his boss to look after the children of fellow mob henchman Nakanishi while he serves a prison sentence. An intriguing combination of the reluctant parenting of **DON'T CALL ME PAPA** with the gangland-meets-normality satire of *Married to the Mob* (1988). Compare to **OUT**. Theme: Eikichi Yazawa—"Pure Gold."

HOT BLOODED NEWBIE

1991. JPN: *Nekketsu! Shinnyū Shain Sengen*. AKA: *Hotblood! Proclamation of New Employee*. PRD: Mitsunori Morita. DIR: Ken Matsumoto. SCR: Akira Momoi. CAST: Yōichi Miura, Hiroshi Abe, Katsuhide Uegusa, Hitomi Kuroki, Yasuko Matsuyuki, J. Bucks. CHN: TBS.

DUR: 45 mins. x 11 eps.; Tue 9 April 1991–18 June 1991.

New banking employee Hanyū (Uegusa) is bullied by the manager Tsutsumi (Miura), who is in charge of the bank's orientation program. After surviving the grueling induction process, Hanyū and fellow newbies Mike (Bucks) and Jinbō (Abe) are posted to the branch where Tsutsumi works. The first job he gives them is to rob the bank.

HOTEL *

1990. PRD: Teruo Kondō. DIR: Masaharu Segawa. SCR: Yoshi Yokota. CAST: Hiroki Matsukata, Misako Konno, Masanobu Takashima, Tetsurō Tanba, Nenji Kobayashi, Michael Tomioka, Hiroki Matsukata, Mariko Fuji, Azusa Nakamura, Akira Akasaka. CHN: TBS. DUR: 45 mins. x 83 eps.; Thu 11 January 1990–22 March 1990 (#1); 9 January 1992–26 March 1992 (#2); 7 April 1994–22 September 1994 (#3); 13 April 1995–28 September 1995 (#4); 9 April 1998–18 June 1998 (#5).

Ippei (Takashima) is a new employee at Hotel Platon. He is late from the very first day and has some trouble with the customers. However, he resolves to become the perfect hotel manager, in this long-running adaptation of the 1984 manga by **MASKED RIDER** creator Shōtarō Ishinomori, presumably itself inspired by the American series *Hotel* (1993).

Few Japanese dramas last for more than a couple of seasons at best, so few can take advantage of the kind of natural workplace attrition that has allowed *ER*, for example, to replace almost all of its central cast in the course of its run. *Hotel*, however, runs through the 1990s, and with a title that emphasizes the building rather than the contents, it has remained flexible enough to move with the times and public tastes.

For the fourth season, the workplace was shaken up by the arrival of Keisuke (Fujioka), a no-nonsense businessman from Los Angeles with no time for the "Japanese way" of doing things—compare to HARD-WORKING MAN. He is forced to run a hotel whose surly new staff include former air stewardess Noriko (Nakamura), while old hands such as Ippei and hotel doctor Izumi (Fuji) try to keep the peace. However, it would appear that the fourth season marked the high point of *Hotel*'s ratings—there was no *Hotel* the following year, although Takashima all but reprised his role in another TBS show, SHINKANSEN. Both seasons three and four had enjoyed runs twice as long as the average TV drama but the final fifth season was reduced to the standard 11 episodes. In a flash of exoticism, Ippei and fellow manager Akira (Akasaka) are dispatched to a new affiliate hotel in Hawaii and ordered to turn its fortunes around.

The fourth season was broadcast in the U.S. with English subtitles on KIKU TV. A 2001 special, in which an employee's strange behavior is traced back to his debts to organized crime, was also broadcast in Hawaii. Themes: Emiko Shiratori—"Let the River Run," Kaho Shimada—"Kimi ni Dekiru Koto" (Anything You Can Do), Carly Simon—"Let the River Run," Miju—"Couples."

HOTEL DOCTOR

1993. PRD: N/C. DIR: Makito Takai. SCR: Yoshi Shinozaki. CAST: Kōichi Satō, Kumiko Akiyoshi, Kazukiyo Nishikiori, Shigeyuki Nakamura, Tetsurō Tanba. CHN: Asahi. DUR: 45 mins. x 11 eps.; Tue 12 January 1993–23 March 1993.

Ryōsuke (Satō) starts working at a clinic in the Sheraton Hotel where his junior Namihiko (Nishikiori) is the director. For a self-proclaimed bachelor like Ryōsuke, it's the perfect life, with full room service and, so he hopes, only occasional medical emergencies. Doubtless annoyed by the ongoing success of the TBS HOTEL franchise, Asahi tried to match it with this interesting clone, adding a medical spin into the bargain.

HOTEL WOMAN

1991. PRD: Yōko Yamazaki. DIR: Seiji Izumi. SCR: Takuya Nishioka. CAST: Yasuko Sawaguchi, Yōko Akino, Hitomi Takahashi, Takeshi Naitō, Yōko Nozawa. CHN: Kansai. DUR: 45 mins. x 11 eps.; Mon 7 October 1991–23 December 1991.

While Shūko (Sawaguchi) is studying in New York, she falls in love with Ryōichi (Ken Tanaka), an executive for an exclusive hotel group in Japan. When Ryōichi commits suicide after a failed business merger, the pregnant Shūko returns to Tokyo and takes a job in one of his company's hotels. Theme: B'z—"Alone."

HOTMAN

2003. PRD: Yōko Matsui, Toyohiko Wada. DIR: Satoru Nakajima. SCR: Masataka Kashida. CAST: Takashi Sorimachi, Akiko Yada. CHN: TBS. DUR: 45 mins. x ca. 11 eps.; Thu 10 April 2003–?? June 2003.

Enzō (Sorimachi) is a former gangster, now become a respectable fine arts teacher and the reluctant guardian of his four younger siblings. He gains an extra member of the family when he finds five-year-old Nanami on his doorstep attached to a note from an anonymous woman, claiming that Nanami is the daughter Enzō never knew he had. Nanami also suffers from a severe dermatological condition that swiftly turns her presumed father into a health food nut. As actor Sorimachi nears his thirties, producers have obviously decided that it is almost time for him to settle down, in a series that marries his earlier tough guy role from GTO to a reluctant parenting drama in the spirit of PAPA SURVIVAL. The story was based on a manga serialized in *Young Jump* by Shō Kitagawa, whose other works include *Blue Butterfly Fish* (*AE) and *Nineteen* (*AE). Theme: Exile—"Together."

HOUSE OF THE DEVILS

1999. JPN: *Oni no Sumika.* AKA: *Don't Be a Cry-Baby.* PRD: Hiroyoshi Koiwai. DIR: Utahiko Honma, Tatsuaki Kimura.

Continued on p. 123

SCR: Yuki Fujimoto, Junya Yamazaki. CAST: Kyōko Fukada, Kelly Chen, Kumiko Okae, Aimi Nakamura, Katsuhisa Namase, Naohito Fujiki, Akira Nishikino, Mari Hoshino. CHN: Fuji. DUR: 45 mins. x 11 eps.; Tue 12 January 1999–23 March 1999.

After her parents are killed in a car crash, Ayumi (Fukada) and her brother are separated and sent to live with relatives. Ayumi must leave her friends behind, quit school, and work at the Water Inn, a hot spring hotel owned by her evil uncle. Bullied and persecuted by family members and guests, Ayumi's only allies are her kindly aunt and Li (Chen), an illegal Chinese worker. Later, she attracts the attention of handsome local politician Yuzuri

(Fujiki). However, the more interest Yuzuri shows in Ayumi, the angrier her uncle becomes, since he is hoping to set Yuzuri up with his own daughter, Ayumi's unkind cousin Yuriko (Nakamura). As implied by the orphan servant girl, domineering father figure, ugly sister, and handsome prince, *HotD* is another modern *Cinderella* drama in the style of THE CURSE or GLASS SLIPPERS. Theme: Siam Shade— "Kumori Nochi Hare" (Cloudy Later Sunny).

HOUSEKEEPER, THE *

1998. JPN: *Service*. AKA: *At Your Service*. PRD: Yoshiki Tanaka. DIR: Nozomu Amemiya, Kazuki Kaneda. SCR: Miyuki Noe. CAST: Akiko Matsumoto, Ryūji Harada, Yasufumi Terawaki, Masako Miyaji, Rei Takagi. CHN: NTV. DUR: 45 mins. x 11 eps. (first ep 90 mins.); Wed 7 January 1998–3 March 1998.

Housekeeper Chiharu (Matsumoto) arrives at a high-class apartment for her new posting, only to discover that the client, Akira (Harada), is the spitting image of her fiancé Yuichi, who died three years earlier. The coldhearted Akira has thrown himself into his restaurant business in a failed attempt to forget the suicide of his own wife, while his six-year-old daughter Mari fantasizes that her mother is still alive. Though Chiharu and Akira initially quarrel about the best way to deal with his late wife's belongings and the best way to help Mari deal with her grief, Chiharu soon admits to herself that she has feelings for him. However, Akira has to overcome his bitterness and realize that it's time to move on—a process made all the more difficult by an impending threat to the restaurant. Another fairy tale in the tradition of TOKYO CINDERELLA LOVE STORY, this time aimed at a significantly older audience—*The Housekeeper* was unpopular with the general trendy drama crowd because it lacked cover girl beauties. It also bears a certain resemblance to the following year's BEAUTY, which similarly featured a stranger in the image of a long-lost spouse. Theme: Akiko Matsumoto—"Soon."

HOUSEWIFE AND DETECTIVE

1999. JPN: *Mamachari Deka*. PRD: Kazuhiro Itō. DIR: Hiroshi Matsubara, Jun Nasuda, Tamaki Endō. SCR: Eriko Komatsu. CAST: Yūko Asano, Misako Tanaka, Tōru Masaoka, Shingo Murakami, Katsumi Takahashi, Shirō Sano. CHN: TBS. DUR: 45 mins. x 11 eps.; Thu 7 January 1999–18 March 1999.

Housewife Hinako cannot resist talking to her detective husband about the cases he is working on. When he is reluctant to discuss work, the keen amateur sleuth hooks up with Kaoru, a lady detective who is also a divorcée. Two level female heads inevitably prove better than the confused male officers with whom Kaoru must work, and the unlikely team solves crimes all around Tokyo. Deliberately designed to appeal to a family audience (with no bloodshed), *Housewife and Detective* is an unapologetically comedic take on Japan's unending penchant for mysteries. Theme: Mayo Okamoto— "Takaramono" (Treasure).

HOW TO MARRY A BILLIONAIRE

2001. JPN: *Okumanchōja to Kekkon Suru Hōhō*. AKA: *How to Marry a Billionaire; Wealth Marriage*. PRD: Hiroki Wakamatsu, Mamoru Koizumi. DIR: Tarō Ōtani, Takaomi Saegusa, Futoshi Ōhira. SCR: Yumiko Aoyagi. CAST: Norika Fujiwara, Mai Takarao, Maho Toyota, Jō Shishido, Naoyuki Fujii, Naoko Ken, Kōichi Iwaki, Ryō Fukawa, Michitaka Tsutsui; NTV. DUR: 45 mins. x 11 eps.; Mon 15 July 2002–13 September 2002.

Kazuka (Fujiwara), Fujiko (Toyota), and Kaori (Takarao) are working in the sex trade. One night, Kazuka is entertaining Yūzō Kanamaru (Shishido), a chief executive of a prominent construction company. Her service is so "extensive" that the exhausted Kanamaru dies on the bed during the act. Kazuka asks Fujiko and Kaori for help (compare to OUT) and the girls are locked up for the night by the police. Some time later, they realize that each of them has an identical key, which turns out to be for a house in Hayama that Kanamaru was saving for his three absent daughters. Moving in to the deserted dwelling, they decide to pose as Kanamaru's wealthy heiresses, in the hope of landing rich husbands. Each successive week then sees the girls chasing a different victim, from ballroom dancers to gangsters, in an entertaining black comedy, regarded by some critics as a sign of declining 21st-century morals, although its true inspiration lies in the movie *How to Marry a Millionaire* (1953), a vehicle for Marilyn Monroe, Betty Grable, and Lauren Bacall. The U.S. movie also had a 52-episode TV spin-off which was broadcast in Japan on Fuji in 1959. A mere *million* yen, of course, is not even enough to buy a car, hence the inflation in numbers.

HOWL AT THE SUN

1972. JPN: *Taiyō ni Hoero*. PRD: Akiyoshi Okada. DIR: Susumu Takebayashi. SCR: Hide Ogawa, Toshio Kamata, Shinichi Ichikawa, Mineaki Hata. CAST: Yūjirō Ishihara, Shigeru Tsuyuguchi, Raita Ryū, Tappei Shimokawa, Akira Onodera, Keiko Sekine, Kenichi Hagiwara, Hidemi Aoki, Yūsaku Matsuda. CHN: NTV. DUR: 45 mins. x 718 eps.; Fri 21 July 1972–14 November 1986.

At the Criminal Investigation Section in Shinjuku's Nanamagari precinct, section chief "Boss" Tōdō (Ishihara) leads a group of detectives: Yama-san (Tsuyuguchi), Gori-san (Ryū), Chō-san (Shimokawa), and "His Highness" Denka (Onodera). Hayami (Hagiwara) is a young detective posted to the section, immediately ridiculed for his pantaloon suit and long hair. Denka suggests that they should call him Macaroni because he resembles a cowboy from a "macaroni" Western film. While the cops are arguing, the phone rings with news of a new murder case. Macaroni immediately dashes out, while Yama prepares to fight crime at a more languorous pace.

No discussion of Japanese cop shows would be complete without mention of *Howl at the Sun*, still voted high in viewers' polls two decades after its conclusion. Producer Okada's aim was to create a youth drama in which the cast happened to be detectives, placing emphasis on developing personalities and personal lives of the youthful officers—without *Howl at the Sun*, there would never have been a DANGEROUS DETECTIVE or BAYSIDE SHAKEDOWN. Conversely, scenarist Ogawa preferred to concentrate on the motives of the criminals themselves, creating a truly human drama, while older viewers were drawn in by the sight of former movie tough guy Ishihara, the star of the original film of SEASON OF THE SUN, who had sworn never to work in television.

The cast of young detectives gained extra appeal through regular culls—just as in real life, no one was safe from the Grim Reaper. The first to die was Detective Macaroni, killed off after actor Hagiwara decided there was nothing left for him to do in the role. He died ignominiously, stabbed at a construction site while taking a toilet break but his death scene attracted such high ratings that it set a new formula for the production team.

Macaroni was replaced by an even more popular character, Jiipan (Matsuda), who got his nickname from the denim outfit or "jean pants" he favored. With long, permed hair and a preference for karate over gunplay, the rebel Jiipan cut a dashing swath through the series, both on and off screen. Despite his popularity as a character, arguments between actor Matsuda and the production team led to his being written out—Jiipan was killed by a man he was trying to rescue, while actor Matsuda was soon reborn as the loner hero of DETECTIVE STORY.

As well as becoming a fertile breeding ground for the writers of future successes like SEVEN PEOPLE IN SUMMER and DAYS OF GOLD, the show outlasted most of its cast members—many new cops arrived, stood their ground, and

eventually met with tragic deaths. However, Ishihara remained the core of the series as Boss, despite the same ill health that plagued him on SEIBU POLICE. Knowing that the end was in sight, both Ishihara and the production team called it a day. In his final episode, Ishihara's Boss talked a criminal into giving himself up in a five minute improvisation, which was to be his farewell to his fans. Eight months later, he was claimed by liver cancer, dying at the relatively young age of 52. Theme: Katsuo Ōno—"Taiyō ni Hoero." Peak rating: 40.0% (in 1979).

The series returned in 2001 for a one-off TV movie, made to commemorate the 13th anniversary of the death of Matsuda. Boss was played by Hiroshi Tachi, while Ken Kaneko filled the role of a newcomer cop, albeit without one of the nicknames that characterized the original series. The show also featured Keiko Takahashi reprising her old role as Jiipan's girlfriend Nobuko, now a criminal profiler and a cameo from manga artist Hiroshi Kurogane, who helps the team assemble a portrait of their suspect.

HURRICANGER

2002. JPN: *Ninpū Sentai Hurricanger*. AKA: *Ninja Battle Team Hurricanger, Power Rangers Ninja Storm*. PRD: Kōichi Yada, Jun Higasa, Sayoko Matsuda. DIR: Katsuya Watanabe, Satoshi Morota, Hajime Hashimoto. SCR: Shūichi Miyashita, Atsushi Maekawa, Naoyuki Sakai. CAST: Shunya Shioya, Nao Nagasawa, Kōhei Yamamoto, Ken Nishida, Shōko Takada, Yūjirō Shirakawa, Nobuo Kyō. CHN: Asahi. DUR: 25 mins. x 35+ eps.; 17 February 2002–.

There are two rival schools of *ninjutsu*—the Hayate branch, who police "*the highways of history*" and the Ikazuchi branch, who police "*the byways.*" Presumably, one needs to be an initiate to work out what that's supposed to mean. The two schools meet for their annual contest, only to be surprised by a third school of ninja, the space faring Jakanja, who wipe out all

but three survivors—Takasuke (Shioya), Nanami (Nagasawa), and Kōta (Yamamoto), who skipped school that morning. They are contacted by their school principal Hyūga (Nishida), who has evaded death by transforming himself into a hamster. His daughter Doctor Oboro (Takada) recruits the three survivors to be the Hurricane Ninja Team, with the impetuous but good-natured laborer Takasuke as Hurricane Red. The smart and highly competitive Nanami is Hurricane Blue and also a part-time country singer. The coolheaded Kōta is Hurricane Yellow and also a part-time homecare assistant.

Hurricanger comes after GAORANGER in the Super Sentai continuity and became the eleventh incarnation of the MIGHTY MORPHIN' POWER RANGERS series from Saban Entertainment in 2003, under the title *Power Rangers Ninja Storm*. In the American version, teen skateboarder Shane (Pua

Continued from p. 121
TV Tokyo: Established as Tokyo Channel 12 in 1964 by the Foundation for Science and Technology.
WOWOW: Subscription satellite broadcaster formed in the 1990s by a consortium of companies who wished to provide a commercial alternative to NHK's satellite services.
During the 1990s, the Ministry of Post and Telecommunications permitted the establishment of many smaller channels, particularly on cable, where Rupert Murdoch's J Sky B eventually managed to buy out the digital channel PerfecTV, now known as SKY PerfecTV. In the 21st century, satellite and cable have become the niche market homes of foreign programming, while terrestrial channels remain resolutely Japanese in their output.

Magasiva), motocross rider Dustin (Glenn McMillan), and surfer girl Tori (Sally Martin) are all initiates into a secret ninja school in their hometown of Blue Bay Harbor. There, they are trained by the kindly Sensei (Grant McFarland) until the day that evil space ninja master Lothor transforms Sensei into a guinea pig *(sic)*. The three original Wind Ninja, colored Red, Yellow, and Blue respectively, join forces with members of the rival Thunder Ninja clan—Hunter the Crimson Power Ranger (Adam Tuominen) and Blake the Navy Power Ranger (Jorge "Jorgito" Vargas)—in order to fight off Lothor's evil schemes. They are later joined by yet another, the Green Samurai Ranger (Jason Chan). *Hurricanger* was followed by **ABARANGER** in 2003.

HYPNOSIS

2000. JPN: *Saimin*. PRD: Hideki Inada. DIR: Hiroshi Nishitani, Masanori Murakami. SCR: Akihiro Tago. CAST: Gorō Inagaki, Asaka Seto, Akiko Yada, Michiko Hata, Tatsuya Fuji, Miyoshi Shiomi, Daisu. CHN: TBS. DUR: 45 mins. x 11 eps.; Fri 9 July 1999–?? September 1999.

One year after a murder case in which the criminal used hypnosis as a weapon, psychiatrist and hypnotherapist Saga (Inagaki from SMAP) has lost confidence in his ability and left the hospital. Instead, he earns a precarious living as a fortune-teller, until the day that Yuka (Seto) comes to see him as a client. She has amnesia and soon she has his attention as the pair begin to fall in love.

Meanwhile, a number of men are meeting their deaths under mysterious circumstances in public places. The only common factor is that each corpse is found with a purple bruise at its throat. Detective Sotoyama (Shiomi) and Muta (Daisu) visit Saga asking him to help them but Saga is reluctant. Ever since he was unable to help a girl with multiple personality disorder a year earlier, he has foresworn all police activity. However, the police convince him to change his mind after they reveal that the men are all former boyfriends of Yuka and that his new girlfriend is a prime suspect. In order to help her, Saga decides to go back to the hospital.

Based on a story by Keisuke Matsuoka, *Hypnosis* is a direct sequel to the movie of the same name, released in June of the same year. Theme: Tina—"Meiro" (Labyrinth).

I

I AM A MAN

1971. JPN: *Ore wa Otoko Da.* PRD: Kichinosuke Shiraishi. DIR: Kazuo Nakaarai. SCR: Akihiko Sugano. CAST: Kensaku Morita, Kumi Hayase, Tatsuo Matsumura, Keiko Tsushima, Chōichirō Kawarazaki. CHN: NTV. DUR: 30 mins. x ca. 50 eps.; Sun 21 February 1971–13 February 1972.

Eighty percent of the students at Aoba High School are girls. Hirokazu (Morita, in his first drama appearance) stands up for the male minority and also acts as captain of the *kendō* club. Unlike previous dramas, which tended to focus equally on students and teachers, *I Am A Man* focused almost exclusively on the students. Though it was held up as a macho treatise for oppressed men to stand up to shrill feminists, it was based on a manga written by a woman, Natsumi Tsugumo.

I AM YOUR ALLY

1995. JPN: *Watashi, Mikata desu.* PRD: Toshihiro Iijima. DIR: Takamichi Yamada. SCR: Kenichi Iwasa, Yoshihisa Aiba. CAST: Hiroshi Tachi, Azusa Nakamura, Ken Ishiguro, Junko Sakurai, Kotono Shibuya. CHN: TBS. DUR: 45 mins. x 11 eps.; Thu 12 January 1995–23 March 1995.

Rinpei (Tachi) is a passionate detective who often meddles in other people's business, whether he is welcome or not. His half brother Satoshi (Ishiguro) is studying to pass the judicial exams but starts working with Rinpei, causing all sorts of conflicts as one sibling tries to get results while the other is scrupulously insistent on playing by the book. Theme: Masayuki Suzuki—"Adam na Yoru" (Night Like Adam).

I BORROWED MONEY FROM HER

1994. JPN: *Boku ga Kanojo ni Shakkin o Shita Ryū.* PRD: Yasuo Yagi. DIR: Jirō Shōno. SCR: Toshikazu Ikehata. CAST: Hiroyuki Sanada, Kyōko Koizumi, Michitaka Tsutsui, Keiko Saitō, Tsurube Shōfukutei. CHN: TBS. DUR: 45 mins. x 11 eps.; Fri 14 October 1994–23 December 1994.

Kunihiko (Sanada) has a satisfactory life, with a good job at a construction company and a nice house in the suburbs. However, his wife Michiko (Saitō) is unable to control her spending habits, resulting in threats from Nao (Tsutsui), a representative of the credit card company. Kunihiko borrows money from Yuki (Koizumi), a woman who lives in the neighboring apartment, leading to a comedy in which the fluctuating amount owed is displayed onscreen each episode. Theme: Kyōko Koizumi—"Tsuki Hitoshizuku" (A Drop of the Moon).

I CAN'T GO ON

1995. JPN: *Gaman Dekinai!* PRD: Yoshiki Miruta. DIR: Hidekazu Matsuda. SCR: Izō Hashimoto. CAST: Kyōka Suzuki, Kazuhiko Nishimura, Masato Ibu, Ayako Sawada, Minako Tanaka. CHN: Kansai. DUR: 45 mins. x 8 eps.; Mon 9 January 1995–27 February 1995.

Kiwami (Suzuki) and Kenji (Nishimura) have been married for two years. However, after they are forced to move back in with Kenji's parents, their happiness is short-lived, in yet another in-law appeasement drama. Based on a manga by Tamiko Akaboshi, creator of LOVE AFTER DIVORCE and I CAN'T GO ON ANY LONGER. Theme: trf—"Crazy Gonna Crazy."

I CAN'T GO ON ANY LONGER

1996. JPN: *Mō Gaman Dekinai!* PRD: Toshimasa Noda. DIR: Hidekazu Matsuda. SCR: Izō Hashimoto. CAST: Mayumi Wakamura, Kōji Matoba, Morio Kazama, Wakako Sakai. CHN: Kansai. DUR: 45 mins. x 12 eps.; Tue 2 July 1996–17 September 1996.

Sayaka (Wakamura) is living with her in-laws. After she has a baby, her mother-in-law Sonoko (Sakai) insists that she should quit her job and become a housewife. Sayaka ignores Sonoko's instruction and goes back to work soon after. But when she comes home from work, there is always a list of things she must do. Another adaptation of a manga by Tamiko Akaboshi, commissioned after the success of the previous year's I CAN'T GO ON. Theme: Lindberg—"Green Eyed Monster."

I CAN'T SEE YOU

1994. JPN: *Kimi ga Mienai.* PRD: Hiroshi

Doi. DIR: Ryōko Hoshida. SCR: Toshio Terada, Akio Sekita. CAST: Chikako Kaku, Satomi Tezuka, Kazue Itō, Katsuyuki Mori, Yōsuke Natsuki. CHN: Kansai. DUR: 45 mins. x 8 eps.; Mon 6 June 1994–25 July 1994.

For the last nine years Sawako (Kaku) has nursed her feelings of terrible guilt after being the sole survivor of a double suicide pact with a man who had a wife and child. With her friend's help, she gets a new job assisting a late-night radio DJ and finds herself rearing the dead man's daughter. Compare to the same writer's later **KIDNAP**.

I DON'T NEED LOVE

2002. JPN: *Ai Nante Iraneeyo Natsu.* PRD: N/C. DIR: Yukihiko Tsutsumi. SCR: Yukari Tatsui. CAST: Atsurō Watabe, Ryōko Hirosue, Tatsuya Fujiwara, Gorgo Matsumoto, Kazuma Suzuki, Mayuko Nishiyama, Leo Morimoto, Ryōko Sakaguchi. CHN: TBS. DUR: 45 mins. x 10 eps.; Fri 12 July 2002– 13 September 2002.

Recently released after a six-month stint in prison, Reiji (Watabe) hears that recently deceased computer magnate Shunsuke Takazono has left much of his fortune to his blind daughter Ako (Hirosue). Another part of the inheritance is earmarked for Sakiko (Sakaguchi), the stepmother with whom Ako has been feuding for 15 years. In theory, a third portion has been set aside for Shunsuke's son, also called Reiji, although nobody has seen him for years. With debts of three-quarters of a billion yen, Reiji decides he has nothing to lose if he impersonates his missing namesake and tries to swindle Ako out of her fortune. However, Reiji knows exactly where Ako's real brother is—he has been looking after his apartment while he was in prison. Compare to **DANGEROUS LIAISONS** and the same writer's earlier **PURE**.

I LOVE TEACHER

1990. JPN: *Aishiteruyo! Sensei.* PRD: Masayuki Morikawa. DIR: Shirō Nakayama. SCR: Izō Hashimoto. CAST: Mami Yamase, Hiroshi Abe, Chizuru

Azuma, Kazuhiko Kanayama. CHN: TBS. DUR: 45 mins. x 8 eps.; Tue 10 July 1990–28 August 1990.

Mayu (Yamase) passes her teaching exam and is assigned to teach a sixth grade class. Although she is supposed to set an example for her young charges, she is unable to admit that she is allergic to vegetables and cannot eat them in the school canteen. Theme: Crayon Sha—"Broken Heart: Namida wa Niji ni Nare" (Broken Heart: Make Your Tears A Rainbow).

I LOVE YA!

1995. JPN: *Sukiyanen.* PRD: Michihiko Umetani. DIR: Ikuhiro Saitō. SCR: Man Izawa. CAST: Yoshiko Mita, Masami Hisamoto, Ryūji Harada, Akiko Hinagata. CHN: Yomiuri. DUR: 45 mins. x 12 eps.; Thu 6 July 1995–21 September 1995.

Shy Kokage (Hisamoto) looks completely different from her beautiful mother Chiharu (Mita). As a result she is slightly afraid of men and is still a virgin at 26 years old. Her search continues for Mr. Right and she begins to suspect she may have found him in the shape of a salaryman from Osaka. Compare to **FIRST TIME**. Theme: Voice—"Sukiyanen: But Game Is Over" (I Love You: But Game Is Over).

I LOVE YOU

1993. JPN: *Aishiteruyo!.* PRD: N/C. DIR: Toshiaki Iwaki. SCR: Masao Yajima. CAST: Toshihiko Tahara, Yōko Minamino, Yumi Adachi, Ikkei Watanabe. CHN: Asahi. DUR: 45 mins. x 11 eps.; Mon 11 October 1993–27 December 1993.

Stuntman Shinsuke (Tahara) loses his partner Shin in an accident. Shin's daughter Megumi (Adachi) tells him that her father was the son of the principal of an exclusive girls' school. Hoping to snatch a share of the inheritance for himself, Shinsuke visits the school, claiming to be Megumi's guardian. Theme: T-BOLAN— "Wagamama ni Daki Aetanara" (If We Hug Each Other Selfishly).

I TRULY LOVED YOU

1992. JPN: *Zutto Anata ga Sukidatta.* PRD: Seiichirō Kijima. DIR: Jirō Shōno. SCR: Ryōichi Kimizuka. CAST: Chikako Kaku, Hiroshi Fuse, Masumi Miyazaki, Shirō Sano, Yōko Nogiwa. CHN: TBS. DUR: 45 mins. x 13 eps.; Fri 3 July 1992–25 September 1992.

Miwa (Kaku) works at a wedding hall in Tokyo, where her father is trying to arrange her own marriage. She reluctantly returns to her hometown of Sendai for an *omiai* marriage meeting with Tokyo University graduate Fuyuhiko (Sano), with whom she is distinctly unimpressed. However, while visiting her old high school, she bumps into her former boyfriend Yōsuke (Fuse).

Finally agreeing to marry Fuyuhiko, she discovers that her husband has a severe mother complex and refuses to even touch her. Meanwhile, she begins seeing Yōsuke in secret, angering her father and mother-in-law Etsuko (Nogiwa). Deciding to get a divorce, Miwa is tricked into staying with her husband and becomes pregnant after a single night spent with him. However, Fuyuhiko refuses to believe the child is his, causing Miwa to run to Yōsuke for comfort, only to be imprisoned in her house by Etsuko and her father. Fuyuhiko finally accepts her wish for a divorce but blames his mother for interfering—he stabs Etsuko with a piece of glass. Turning himself in to the police, he tells Miwa that now they are both free. As Miwa leaves to spend the rest of her life in Kyūshū with Yōsuke, Fuyuhiko tells her that he has loved her ever since he saw her in elementary school.

Though starting off as a traditional TV drama, *I Truly Loved You* was heavily influenced by *Twin Peaks* (1990)—former supporting character Fuyuhiko came to dominate the series and actor Sano gained critical acclaim for his sinister portrayal, along with Nogiwa, who became one of Japanese drama's most fearsome in-laws as Etsuko. Later dramas in the same vein included **JEALOUSY**, **DEVIL'S KISS**, **EDGE OF THE WORLD**, and **CAN'T TELL ANYONE**, in which Sano played a similarly obsessed character. Theme: Southern All Stars— "Namida no Kiss" (Kiss in Tears). Peak rating: 34.1%.

I WANT TO BE BEAUTIFUL

1992. JPN: *Kirei ni Naritai*. PRD: Yūji Tōjo. DIR: Kazuo Yamamoto. SCR: Miyuki Noe. CAST: Yuri Nakazawa, Kae Okuyama, Takeshi Kaga, Miho Takagi, Jun Fubuki. CHN: Yomiuri. DUR: 45 mins. x 11 eps.; Sat 17 October 1992– 26 December 1992.

Trainee teacher Fūko (Nakazawa) has lived with her mother Kyōko (Fubuki) ever since her parents' divorce several years earlier. Her father Shinya (Kaga) now runs a beauty salon. When a man she adores makes fun of her apple cheeks, Fūko decides to take a part-time job at her father's salon to learn how to change her looks. Compare to BEAUTY SEVEN. Theme: Fumina Hisamatsu—"Tenshi no Kyūsoku" (Sleep of Angels).

I WANT TO BE HAPPY

1992. JPN: *Shiawase ni Naritai! Heisei Arashiyama Ikka*. AKA: *I Want To Be Happy: Heisei [-era] Arashiyama Family*. PRD: N/C. DIR: Satoshi Tsuji. SCR: Yoshihisa Aiba. CAST: Reiko Katō, Takeo Chii, Yōko Asagaya. CHN: TVT. DUR: 45 mins. x 8 eps.; Sun 31 May 1992–2 August 1992.

Aki Arashiyama (Katō) is an office lady working for a well-known company, who hails from an argumentative family from downtown Tokyo. One day, their former lodger Seiji (Kōjiro Shimizu), a carpenter, comes back to live with them—but Aki has never noticed before how handsome he is.

I WANT TO HUG YOU!

1988. JPN: *Dakishimetai*. PRD: Yoshiaki Yamada, Tōru Ōta. DIR: Shunsaku Kawake, Michio Kōno. SCR: Toshiharu Matsubara. CAST: Atsuko Asano, Yūko Asano, Masahiro Motoki, Junichi Ishida, Tomoko Ikuta, Kōichi Iwaki, Yōko Nogiwa. CHN: Fuji. DUR: 45 mins. x 12 eps.; Thu 7 July 1988– 22 September 1988.

Asako Ikeuchi (A. Asano) is a single stylist, while her friend of 25 years Natsuko Hayakawa (Y. Asano) is a housewife married to Asako's ex-boyfriend, interior designer Keisuke (Iwaki). Natsuko discovers that Keisuke is having an affair with Chika (Ikuta), a younger woman who falsely claims to be pregnant. The heartbroken Natsuko moves in with Asako and the two women try to scare Chika away, though she refuses to back off. Meanwhile, magazine editor Shūji (Ishida) and makeup artist Jun (Motoki) duel over Asako's affections. Though she accepts a marriage proposal from Shūji, she still has secret feelings for Keisuke, which Keisuke reciprocates.

I Want to Hug You! was a watershed production in Japanese drama and the first of the "trendy dramas" that have characterized Japanese TV until the present day. Instead of mouthing didactic platitudes or moral messages, its two leads gossiped about men and work, vocalizing the feelings of a young audience of twentysomethings. Spoiled rich girl Natsuko eternally drags the gullible Asako into her schemes and moans endlessly about her job, although for many viewers the cast all had dream lives. Instead of mundane salaryman occupations, the cast of *IWTHY!* all have fashionable *katakana* jobs (i.e., occupations written with trendy foreign words), parade around in the latest designer clothes, drive expensive cars, and live in superstylish yuppie apartments. Amid a succession of imitators, such as ALWAYS IN LOVE WITH SOMEONE and YOU ARE MY FAVORITE IN THE WORLD, the producers copied their own success with shows such as I'M IN LOVE WITH YOUR EYES! and DO WE LOVE EACH OTHER! Although the trendy drama fad was officially over with the collapse of the 1980s boom economy (and the flop of PARADISE OF LOVE), they never really went away. Producer Ōta soon returned with TOKYO LOVE STORY, and while contemporary trendy dramas are less openly materialistic, they can still

trace a line back to this pioneer show. Note that the serial's Japanese title is also that of the Japanese version of the Beatles song "I Wanna Hold Your Hand." Theme: Carlos Toshiki & Omegatolive—"Aquamarine no Mama de Ite" (Stay Aquamarine).

The show returned for a feature-length TV special in October 1999, picking up the characters' lives ten years on. Discovering that Keisuke is having another affair and even had a child with his latest woman, Natsuko moves back in with Asako and announces that this time she *really will* divorce him. Natsuko immediately starts interfering in Asako's life again, earnestly informing her that she will be a romantic failure if she isn't married by the millennium and pushing her into a relationship with photographer Inagaki (Ryūya Kamikawa). However, just when things seem to be settling down, Jun returns from a ten-year sojourn in America.

I WANT YOU MORE THAN I SHOULD

1995. JPN: *Kimi o Omou Yori Kimi ni Aitai*. AKA: *I Want You More Than I Desire*. PRD: Makoto Ogawa. DIR: Akihiro Karaki. SCR: Tokio Tsuchiya. CAST: Masatoshi Nakamura, Yuki Saitō, Mieko Harada, Gamon Kaai, Hayaru Hagiwara. CHN: Kansai. DUR: 45 mins. x 11 eps.; Mon 17 April 1995–26 June 1995.

In the three years since the accidental death of their son, bank manager Kōichirō (Nakamura) and his wife Yukiko (Harada) have been unable to continue with their lives. Kōichirō has become increasingly distant and has thrown himself into his work. His life is turned around when he is sent to foreclose on a restaurant that is loaded with heavy debts. Theme: Masatoshi Nakamura—"Aritakke no Ai o Atsumete" (Gather All the Love Possible).

IDEAL BOSS, AN *

1997. JPN: *Risō no Jōshi*. AKA: *Perfect Boss*. PRD: Tamon Tanba. DIR: Shinichi

An Ideal Boss

Kamoshita, Ryō Moriyama, Sanae Suzuki. scr: Hiromi Kusumoto, Makoto Hayashi. cast: Kyōzō Nagatsuka, Yasuko Matsuyuki, Yuriko Ishida, Yoshino Kimura, Ikki Sawamura, Jun Fubuki, Akira Maeda, Karin Yamaguchi. chn: TBS. dur: 45 mins. x 12 eps.; Sun 13 April 1997–29 June 1997.

After five years working overseas, Tokio (the ever reliable, ever paternal Nagatsuka) is posted back home to Japan, where he is made assistant branch manager of a travel agency. Before he has even made it out of Narita airport, he sees two of his new staff members demonstrating hopeless inability to cope with herding demanding tourists, and he realizes that he will have a difficult job ahead of him. Branch manager Tsuge (Maeda) sternly warns him that the two useless travel agents Marika (Matsuyuki) and Emiko (Ishida), as well as the equally hopeless new recruit Nanako (Kimura), must all improve noticeably or they will be fired. Tokio tries to maintain staff morale by hiding the manager's dissatisfaction but the girls continue to do an extremely poor job in the slapstick style of BIG WING. He comes to realize

that the girls are doing their very best in difficult circumstances—Marika is nursing a broken heart after being dumped by her boyfriend (who adds insult to injury by getting married and booking his honeymoon with the firm!), while Emiko is struggling to prove to her wealthy Niigata family that she can make it on her own in the big city. As hard times strike the travel agency (compare to the similar recession-struck holiday company in SPRING IN BLOOM), the girls risk dismissal by taking second jobs. Meanwhile, a menagerie of human interest stories masquerading as holiday makers traipse through each episode, such as a man who wants to buy one last vacation for his terminally ill wife and a coach party of fearsome grannies. The girls are threatened by the evil actions of a scheming staff member and temptation arrives in the form of Michiko (Yamaguchi), a beautiful former schoolmate of Tokio's, who is now a rich divorcée with her own travel firm. Matters come to a head in the finale, when a tour bus crash leaves cast members critically injured and Tokio makes the career suicide decision to put an

injured staff member ahead of a local VIP for medical treatment. He puts his staff before his own well-being because he has now become "the ideal boss," while his kind attentions have finally transformed his employees into the ideal staff. Unrelated to the previous season's IDEAL MARRIAGE, despite being screened on the same channel. Shown with English subtitles in the U.S. on KIKU TV. Theme: Jeho—"Sayonara Seishun" (Goodbye Youth).

IDEAL MARRIAGE, AN

1997. jpn: *Risō no Kekkon*. aka: *Wedding Story*. prd: Seiichirō Kijima. dir: Nobuhiro Doi, Katsuo Fukuzawa. scr: Takao Kinoshita, Toshinori Nishimae, Yumiko Aoyagi. cast: Takako Tokiwa, Akiko Matsumoto, Takashi Naitō, Izumi Inamori, Ikki Sawamura, Shigeki Hosokawa, Shirō Itō, Kanako Enomoto, Yōko Nogiwa. chn: TBS. dur: 45 mins. x 10 eps.; Fri 17 January 1997–21 March 1997.

Osaka girl Mari (Tokiwa) is sexually harassed while working at a Tokyo company and is fired after she berates her boss with her distinctive local dialect. Unwilling to admit to her family that she has fallen off the career ladder, she takes a job as a waitress in a restaurant. Jilted by her boyfriend of six months, the heartbroken Mari meets Ben (Yutaka Takenouchi), an elite salaryman and Tokyo University graduate, who has also recently been dumped. The two begin a courtship of their own, but Mari's no-nonsense Osaka attitude often conflicts with Ben's straight-laced, upper-class Tokyo reserve. She also has to contend with his feisty 16-year-old sister Megumi (Enomoto), who has long prided herself on being the only woman in his life. Theme: ZARD—"Kimi ni Aitakunattara" (When I Want to See You). Peak rating: 21.7%.

IF A CHILD COULD FLY

1972. jpn: *Tobetara Honko*. prd: Kazuo Shibata. dir: Michiyasu Kaji. scr: Masahiro Yamada. cast: Yoshio Arima, Nobu Yano, Manami Fuji, Shin

Sotonomura, Shinji Osada, Mochihisa Maruyama, Kumeko Urabe. CHN: NHK. DUR: 30 mins. x 4 eps.; Sat 6 May 1972–27 May 1972.

Believing his parents do not understand him, runaway Kazuo (Arima) leaves home and follows a monster through the streets of Tokyo. The creature is actually Gatler, a promotional mascot for a new Tsuburaya movie, and when "it" returns to the cinema, Kazuo meets the theater's owner, a mysterious old woman called Some (Urabe). Claiming that she fears her son and daughter-in-law are plotting to rob her of her fortune, Some asks Kazuo to pose as her long-lost relative but he returns home. There, he discovers that his father has stabbed his mother and fled. After being berated by his injured mother, he runs away from home again, steals pills from a department store pharmacy, and takes an overdose. Waking up in the hospital, he is asked where he lives and makes up a false address, only to discover that his real uncle and aunt live there, and that their own son, also coincidentally called Kazuo, was killed in the wartime Tokyo air raids. They welcome Kazuo as their own son, in a story based on a comic by Hisashi Yamanaka, who also created **ABARE HATCHAKU, AFTER SCHOOL,** and **TO BE AS I AM.**

IF I LOVE AGAIN
1995. JPN: *Koi mo Nidome Nara*. PRD: Masaru Kamikura. DIR: Nobuo Mizuta. SCR: Yasuhiro Koshimizu. CAST: Sanma Akashiya, Kōichi Satō, Miyoko Asada, Riona Hazuki. CHN: NTV. DUR: 45 mins. x 10 eps.; Wed 11 January 1995–15 March 1995.

Kōsuke (Akashiya) is a married man who keeps a secret mistress when he is transferred to Osaka. He plans on ditching her when he returns to Tokyo but arrives home to discover that his wife has filed for divorce. To make the matter worse, his mistress follows him from Osaka. Theme: Chisato Moritaka—"Futari wa Koibito" (We Are Lovers).

IF MY WISH COMES TRUE
1994. JPN: *Moshimo Negai ga Kanau Nara*. PRD: Yasuo Yagi. DIR: Akio Yoshida. SCR: Kazuhiko Yūkawa. CAST: Miho Nakayama, Masatoshi Hamada, Takashi Hamazaki, Hiroshi Okada, Marina Watanabe, Tsuyoshi Ujiki. CHN: TBS. DUR: 45 mins. x 12 eps.; Fri 7 January 1994–25 March 1994.

Mirai (Nakayama) has shunned all contact with her family since childhood but must admit her past when she becomes engaged to wealthy businessman's son Ken (Ujiki). Soon afterward, her long-lost brothers Torao (Hamada), Ryūji (Hamazaki), and Takashi (Okada) arrive to cause trouble. Though the tension is between siblings rather than two generations, the result is much the same as any other in-law appeasement drama—and the lead woman is still the one who has to deal with it all. Theme: Miho Nakayama—"Tada Nakitaku Naru no" (Makes Me Want To Cry).

IKEBUKURO WEST GATE PARK
2000. PRD: Akira Isoyama. DIR: Yukihiko Tsutsumi, Hideki Isano, Fuminori Kaneko. SCR: Kankurō Kudō. CAST: Tomoya Nagase, Ai Katō, Yōsuke Kubozuka, Aiko Morishita, Ryūta Satō, Tomohisa Yamashita, Ken Watanabe, Satoshi Tsumabuki, Issei Takahashi, Shin Yazawa. CHN: TBS. DUR: 45 mins. x ca. 11 eps. (ep 1: 70 mins.); Fri 14 April 2000–?? June 2000.

Makoto (Nagase) is a 17-year-old tough guy in the Tokyo district of Ikebukuro. He occasionally tends to his mother's fruit shop but can earn much better money challenging suckers to bowling contests. Makoto remains friends with some of his high school buddies—one of whom is Takashi, the ultra-violent leader of the Tokyo G-Boys gang. Catching would-be artist Shun shoplifting, Makoto puts him to work drawing portraits in the street—Shun prefers to draw headless corpses but needs to work off his debt to the thuggish Makoto. It is while harassing passersby to sit for a portrait that Makoto meets Rika, a part-time prostitute whose

death in a hotel room is just about to change his life.

Somewhere beneath its glamorized violence and its loutish behavior, *IWGP* was once a comedy about crazy kids putting one over on the adults—tracing a line back through *Top Cat* to *Sergeant Bilko*. But the episodic incidents in which Makoto cons, outwits, and outsmarts the local police are soon replaced by a more sinister plot that grows from the show's more violent moments. He enlists his fellow thugs to help track down Rika's murderer themselves—though it is tempting to point out that the police would have had better resources to investigate, if only Ikebukuro hooligans would stop deflating their tires, harassing passersby, and starting fights.

IWGP plays like the results from a focus group of little boys, asked what they see in the recent **GTO** and **CHEAP LOVE** and unable to articulate an interest in anything apart from the fights. Described by many critics as the low point of Japan's post-modern gangster chic, at heart this is merely a *yakuza* story for sullen teenagers—one waits in vain for some *real* tough guys to turn up and kick some sense into them. The success of *IWGP* started a new cycle of imitators—see also **GOODBYE MR. OZU, HALF DOC,** and **KISARAZU CAT'S EYE.** The gang returned in a 2003 TV special.

I'LL BE BACK
1999. JPN: *Kimi to Ita Mirai no Tame ni: I'll be Back*. AKA: *I'll Be Back for the Future I Had with You; Back to Our Future*. PRD: Ken Inoue, Satoshi Suzuki. DIR: Tōya Satō, Akihiro Karaki. SCR: Tetsuya Ōishi. CAST: Tsuyoshi Dōmoto, Kimiko Endō, Yukie Nakama, Shirō Sano, Takeshi Naitō. CHN: NTV. DUR: 45 mins. x 10 eps.; Sat 6 January 1999–20 March 1999.

Atsushi (Dōmoto) is a directionless teen who works in a supermarket, much to the despair of his widowed father Hiroshi (Naitō). At midnight on New Year's Eve 1999, he has a heart attack in an almost deserted cinema, and *something* gives him a second chance. He wakes up to discover that it is 1995 again, and he must relive the 1990s once more but with his memories of the previous cycle intact.

IBB begins as a Japanese riff on the idea of *Groundhog Day* (1993), with just a dash of *Run Lola Run* (1998) and *It's a Wonderful Life* (1946). However, with a running time far greater than a mere movie, it has ample opportunity to experiment with its themes. Atsushi's early attempts to improve his life end in tragedy, only to find him awakening back in 1995 again.

Over several cycles, he begins to piece together the circumstances of his mother's death and suspects that he is not the only person who jumps back in time every five years. Later episodes reveal the shadowy figure of Yūsuke Mayuzumi (Sano), a Machiavellian sorcerer seen on New Year's Eve standing on a rooftop inside a glowing pentacle, waving a pocket watch at the sky. Seemingly retaining memories of previous cycles, he begins stalking Atsushi's group with manipulative letters signed with a simple "M" and has a sinister agenda of his own.

IBB is one of Japanese TV's most cleverly plotted dramas, literally allowing its leading man to alter critical decisions as if replaying a video game. The other characters are well realized enough that their own lives are changed by his decisions but can also continue independently of him. After one cycle ends in a painful breakup between him and his lover Sayaka, he decides to avoid even meeting her the next time around, only to encounter her anyway when she begins dating a friend. He learns that general trends seem unchanged from cycle to cycle but that events sometimes happen in the wrong order—not for him the touchstone future sports almanac that allows Biff Tannen to amass a fortune in the *Back to the Future* movies. True to Japanese dramatic tradition, he must also work out which of several girls is Miss Right.

Compare to similar second chances in **HEAVEN CANNOT WAIT**, while New Year's Eve 1999 also formed the opening moments of **LOVE 2000**. Theme: Kinki Kids—"Yamanaide, Pure" (Don't Stop, Pure). Peak rating: 19.0%.

I'LL NEVER LOVE AGAIN

1991. JPN: *Mō Daremo Aisanai*. PRD: Yūzō Abe. DIR: Yoshiyuki Kusuda. SCR: Masahiro Yoshimoto, Noriko Nakayama. CAST: Eisaku Yoshida, Minako Tanaka, Tomoko Yamaguchi, Takurō Takumi, Hiroyuki Yakumaru, Arisa Mizuki. CHN: Fuji. DUR: 45 mins. x 12 eps.; Thu 11 April 1991–27 June 1991.

When a male corpse is found in a lake under suspicious circumstances, the resultant police investigation is watched with some interest by Tōtō bank driver Takuya (Yoshida) and bank worker Sayuri (Tanaka). This is because the body belongs to someone *they* hired, a criminal instructed to rape Sayuri's colleague Miyuki (Yamaguchi) in front of Miyuki's fiancé Osamu (Yakumaru) and her sister Yayoi (Mizuki). When the criminal attempted to turn the tables and threatened to go to the police with details of his mission, Sayuri killed him and enlisted Takuya's help in dumping his body in the lake.

The two conspirators believe that the ends justify the means—Takuya needs money to hire a lawyer to defend his father, who is currently in prison for a crime he did not commit. For her part, Sayuri needs Miyuki's money in order to liberate herself from her lover Toshiki (Takumi), an arrogant billionaire who treats her as if she is his property.

After the rape, Miyuki cancels the wedding with Osamu, who swears revenge on the traumatized girl because she has made his family lose face! Meanwhile, Takuya offers Miyuki a shoulder to cry on. Miyuki decides that the best way to help Takuya is to "borrow" some money from Toshiki's overstuffed account. Toshiki discovers that the money is missing and has Miyuki arrested. Toshiki takes over the

company formerly run by Miyuki's father but is ousted by Sayuri and Takuya, who engineer a corporate takeover.

Learning that Sayuri and Takuya are responsible for her misery, Miyuki begins a program of revenge, becoming a company director and causing Takuya to lose his job and his mobility in an accident. Takuya then discovers that the man for whom he has committed so many crimes is not really his father at all!

Made as the yuppie bubble economy turned sour on the Japanese, *I'll Never Love Again* was the first of the so-called subgenre of "roller-coaster" dramas, with histrionic plots whose complexity made it almost impossible to unravel if viewers allowed their attention to waver. Writer Yoshimoto continued the same formula in **ONLY YOU CAN'T SEE IT** and **FACE**. Compare also to such Sidney Sheldon sagas as **THE OTHER SIDE OF MIDNIGHT**. **LONG VACATION** star Tomoko Yamaguchi established herself with this drama. Theme: Billy Hughes—"Todokanu Omoi."

I'LL SAVE THE WORLD

2002. JPN: *Boku ga Chikyū o Sukuu*. PRD: Akira Isoyama. DIR: Osamu Katayama, Akio Yoshida, Shinichi Hirano. SCR: Miho Nakazono. CAST: Teruyoshi Uchimura, Hitomi Manaka, Arata Furuta, Yoshihiko Hakamada, Noboru Kaneko, Ken Horiuchi, Shō Aikawa. CHN: TBS. DUR: 45 mins. x 11 eps.; Thu 4 July 2002–?? September 2002.

After falling down a staircase, everyday salaryman Yūsaku (Uchimura) discovers that he can hear everything his workmates are thinking for a limited time. His former classmate Jūzō (Aikawa) convinces him not to cast aside his gift and he begins to use it to help those whose troubled thoughts he hears. Combining **TRANSPARENT** with *What Women Want* (2000), this telepathic comedy also bears a certain resemblance to the same channel's earlier **HEAVEN CANNOT WAIT**, whose protagonist similarly found himself forced to solve other's problems within a time limit.

I'M IN LOVE WITH YOUR EYES!

1989. JPN: *Kimi no Hitomi ni Koishiteru!* PRD: Yoshiaki Yamada, Tōru Ōta. DIR: Shunsaku Kawake, Michio Kōno, Masahiro Nakano. SCR: Kazuhiko Ban. CAST: Miho Nakayama, Momoko Kikuchi, Tomoko Fujita, Kōyō Maeda, Eisaku Yoshida, Minako Tanaka, Junichi Ishida, Kazuko Katō, Gitan Ōtsuru. CHN: Fuji. DUR: 45 mins. x 10 eps.; Mon 16 January 1989–20 March 1989.

Hitomi (Nakayama), Machiko (Kikuchi), and Teruyo (Fujita) start living together in Tokyo's fashionable Daikanyama quarter. College students Gen (Maeda) and Kōhei (Ōtsuru) move into the next room to theirs, and the young people become attracted to each other despite constant quarrels. As suggested by the telltale final exclamation point, this is another in the early trendy dramas as typified by I WANT TO HUG YOU! and DO WE LOVE EACH OTHER!. Theme: Mariko Murai—"Dōshiyōmonaku Love Affair" (Helpless Love Affair).

IMAGINE

2000. PRD: Yoshishige Miyake. DIR: Takehiko Shinjō, Toshinori Nishimae. SCR: Michiru Egashira. CAST: Kyōko Fukada, Hitomi Kuroki, Shunsuke Nakamura, Hiroshi Abe. CHN: Kansai. DUR: 45 mins. x ca. 11 eps.; Tue 11 January 2000–?? March 2000.

Teenage Tokyo singleton Yū (Fukada) has an office job and often seems mature beyond her years. However, her mother Mitsuko (Kuroki) behaves like a rebellious teenager, causing much trouble for her long-suffering daughter. Though Yū begins courting new workmate Yōhei (Nakamura), she is also dragged into her mother's relationship with her new boyfriend Toshihiko (Abe). Considering the Japanese drama penchant for portraying young women as irritatingly infantile ditzes, *Imagine* is a refreshing change and is redolent of the British

comedy series *Absolutely Fabulous*, in which a similarly straight-laced daughter must fret over an immature mother. It was also a good opportunity for Fukada to be cast against type, although she was soon back to playing the ingénue in STRAWBERRY ON THE SHORTCAKE. Based on the 1994 manga by Satoru Makimura, who also wrote DELICIOUS LIAISONS. Theme: Kyōko Fukada—"Kirameki no Shunkan" (The Moment You Shine).

IN A BRIGHT SEASON

1995. JPN: *Kagayaku Kisetsu no Naka de.* AKA: *Into a Bright Moment.* PRD: Chihiro Kameyama. DIR: Tatsuaki Kimura, Takehiko Shinjō. SCR: Yoshikazu Okada. CAST: Hikari Ishida, Naoki Hosaka, Masahiro Nakai, Ryōko Shinohara, Miyuki Imori, Kyōko Toyama, Kyōzō Nagatsuka. CHN: Fuji. DUR: 45 mins. x 11 eps. (final ep 70 mins.); Thu 20 April 1995–29 June 1995.

Six years into their studies, trainee doctors Kanako (Ishida), Shunsuke (Hosaka), and Shinichi (Nakai from SMAP) begin their medical internships. Under the tutelage of strict Doctor Takasugi (Nagatsuka), they prepare for their final exam. A medical retread of ASUNARO CONFESSIONS, contrasting the class backgrounds of several students and allowing the mix of rich and poor to create extra tensions in addition to the usual love polygons. Theme: Field of View—"Kimi ga Ita kara" (Because You Were There).

IN CASE OF FIRE

1990. JPN: *Hino Yōjin.* PRD: Nobuo Komatsu. DIR: Hiroshi Yoshino. SCR: Sō Kuramoto. CAST: Takaaki Ishibashi, Noritake Kinashi, Kumiko Gotō, Kaori Momoi. CHN: NTV. DUR: 45 mins. x 11 eps.; Sat 7 July 1990–29 September 1990.

Sonoji is a Japanese noodle restaurant that has almost 200 years of history. Toki (Atsuko Ichinomiya), the wife of the previous owner, has all the decision-making power in the restaurant, or so she thinks. She is approached

one day by the manager Kaki (Momoi), who introduces her to Heikichi (Kinashi), a man who claims to be the illegitimate son of the previous owner. If he is telling the truth, then Mrs. Toki has no stake in the restaurant, although she is ready with the offer of a compromise. Theme: Tunnels—"Dōnika Narusa" (We'll Make It Somehow).

IN THE NAME OF LOVE

1992. JPN: *Ai to Iu Na no Moto ni.* PRD: Tōru Ōta. DIR: Kōzō Nagayama. SCR: Shinji Nojima. CAST: Honami Suzuki, Toshiaki Karasawa, Yōsuke Eguchi, Yoriko Dōguchi, Tamotsu Ishibashi, Hiromi Nakajima, Hideo Nakano, Raita Ryū, Leo Morimoto. CHN: Fuji. DUR: 45 mins. x 12 eps.; Thu 9 January 1992–26 March 1992.

Three years after graduating from university, former boat club members Takako (Suzuki), Kengo (Karasawa), Tokio (Eguchi), Noriko (Dōguchi), Jun (Ishibashi), Naomi (Nakajima), and Atsushi (Nakano) hold a reunion. Tokio and Kengo had fought over Takako by holding a diving competition, though Takako reveals that she and Kengo have now split up—

EVERYTHING I KNOW ABOUT JAPANESE HISTORY I LEARNED FROM NHK TAIGA DRAMAS . . .

WIND, CLOUD, AND RAINBOW— (935–941)
FIRE STILL BURNS, THE— (1051–1189)
HŌJŌ TOKIMUNE—(1247–1281)
TAIHEIKI—(1305–1358)
WAR OF FLOWERS—(1449–1490)
MŌRI MOTONARI—(1499–1571)
HIDEYOSHI—(1582–1598)
AOI—(1598–1632)
CHŪSHINGURA—(1678–1703)
TOKUGAWA YOSHINOBU— (1839–1867)
AS IF IN FLIGHT—(1867–1878)
SPRING SWELL—(1871–1911)
INOCHI: LIFE—(1945–1986)

although they were once engaged, she found herself unable to keep up with his ambitions to become a politician and instead left him to become a teacher. Meanwhile, Tokio has returned from an extended stay in America and found himself a job in a *pachinko* arcade, while Noriko reveals that she is pregnant with Jun's child but unwilling to marry him. Naomi is working as a model and unhappily functioning as the mistress of a married man. Finally, Atsushi steals money from his workplace for a Philippina club hostess and hangs himself when his crime is discovered.

All the friends are deeply affected by Atsushi's death—Kengo stands up to his corrupt father, Naomi contemplates finding a husband of her own, and Jun starts working at a center for the disabled. Noriko has her baby and encourages Jun to take a more active interest in her life, leaving Takako single and lonely, but never truly alone as long as she has her friends.

Despite being one of writer Nojima's lesser dramas, complete with self-consciously naturalistic dialogue, *ItNoL* achieved massive ratings of 32.6% and led to the Fuji network extending the final episode by 15 minutes—now a regular occurrence with many popular shows. The *Big Chill* idea of friends reunited by the death of an old classmate would be recycled many times, including GREATEST FEELING, STAR GAZING, and CALIFORNIA DREAMING. Reputedly broadcast without subtitles on a Japanese language station in the New York area. Theme: Shōgo Hamada—"Kanashimi wa Yuki no Yō ni" (Sadness Is Like Snow).

INCLEMENT LOVER

2000. JPN: *Tenki Yohō no Koibito*. AKA: *Unpredictable Lover; Fairweather Lover*. PRD: Ichirō Takai, Shunji Matsumura. DIR: Yoshiko Hoshida, Kensaku Sawada. SCR: Yoshikazu Okada. CAST: Kōichi Satō, Izumi Inamori, Eri Fukatsu, Hiroyuki Yabe, Ryōko Yonekura, Mieko Harada, Ikkei Watanabe. CHN: Fuji. DUR: 45 mins. x

12 eps.; Mon 10 April 2000–30 June 2000.
FM Sofia radio personality Shōko (Fukatsu) has a beautiful voice but is convinced that nobody would find her attractive in the flesh—consequently, she uses a pseudonym on-air and advises callers about romance, even though she herself has never been in love. In fact, much of the wisdom she dispenses is not hers at all but comes from pretty single mother Sachi (Inamori), a waitress in the FM Sofia canteen, who often supplies Shoko with the pithy advice that the listeners adore. When a persistent fan Shōichi (Yabe) from the weather department insists on meeting her for real, she enlists the help of Sachi to impersonate her. Unavoidably detained, Shōichi instead sends his divorced, single parent meteorologist manager Katsuhiko (Satō), whom both the ladies agree is something of a catch. Both girls start competing for the affections of the handsome weatherman but neither can work out whether he is interested in the voice and personality of Shōko or the looks and wisdom of Sachi. A modern update of *Cyrano de Bergerac*, though likely to have been more directly inspired by *The Truth About Cats and Dogs* (1996), *Inclement Lover* was broadcast in the U.S. without subtitles on the NGN network. Theme: Ayumi Hamasaki—"Seasons."

INFRARED MUSIC

1975. JPN: *Sekigai Ongaku*. PRD: Masaharu Morita. DIR: Kazuya Satō. SCR: Toshio Kamata. CAST: Kazuo Monma, Hideo Satō, Kaoru Endō, Ranko Mizushiro, Junichi Takeoka, Junko Arai, Kō Hirano, Toyoaki Yoshida, Hideyo Amamoto. CHN: NHK. DUR: 25 mins. x 6 eps.; Mon 7 April 1975–16 April 1975.
Schoolboy Norio (Monma) realizes that nobody else in his family can hear Strauss's *Blue Danube* waltz being played on the radio. He is contacted by his classmate Asako (Endō), who reveals that the music originates from the Mutant Scientific Research

Institute (MSRI)—a secret organization dedicated to nurturing and protecting children with special powers. Such children can *hear* in infrared, allowing them to pick up sounds at a different frequency from normal people. A voice on the radio instructs those who can hear it to assemble at Tokyo Tower, from where they are brought to the MSRI. Doctor Hijiri (Amamoto) gives each of them an "R6" box that enables them to communicate with each other before asking them to return in a week. Back home, Norio and his newfound friends try to explain what has happened but lose consciousness every time they are about to mention the MSRI. Eventually, they learn that the Earth is scheduled for demolition and that they have been selected by aliens as creatures worth saving. Norio must choose between life off-world as an alien or dying on Earth in the coming disaster.

With stylish scarlet backgrounds to amaze the growing number of viewers with color television sets, *Infrared Music* was supposedly based on a novel by Hiroshi Sano, although its central premise seems suspiciously similar to the British series *The Tomorrow People* (1973), which was itself broadcast on NHK the following year with the Japanese title *Chikyū Bōeitai* (*Earth Defense Force*).

INHERITANCE OF THE FUKUI FAMILY

1994. JPN: *Fukui-sanchi no Isan Sōzoku*. PRD: Junichi Kōzuki. DIR: Naosuke Kurosawa. SCR: Chigusa Shiota. CAST: Yuki Saitō, Hiroshi Fuse, Tetsuya Bessho, Haruko Katō, Hōsei Komatsu. CHN: Kansai. DUR: 45 mins. x 9 eps.; Mon 1 August 1994–26 September 1994.
After the death of Mr. Fukui, the chairman of a confectionery company, plans are made to divide his estate of 600 million yen between his wife and sons. However, a week after the funeral, the family are approached by the widow (Saitō) of Mr. Fukui's third son, who demands that she also has a right to a

share. Theme: Takako Okamura—"Yama Ari Tani Ari" (There Are Mountains and There Are Valleys).

INOCHI: LIFE *

1986. JPN: *Inochi*. AKA: *Life*. PRD: Taiji Nagasawa. DIR: Shizuhiro Iyoda. SCR: Sugako Hashida. CAST: Yoshiko Mita, Pinko Izumi, Kōji Yakusho, Mako Ishino, Masato Ibu, Kin Sugai, Harue Akagi, Shirō Ōsaka. CHN: NHK. DUR: 45 mins. x ca. 50 eps.; Sun 5 January 1986–14 December 1986.

Miki (Mita) is a 20-year-old college student at the end of the war, whose father is still missing and whose mother's illness led to her early death due to lack of treatment and facilities. Returning to her home in northern Japan's Aomori, Miki opens a medical practice in a village that has no other doctor. After a while, she goes to the U.S. to study medicine, returning to marry Gōzō (Ibu), a widower with two children.

After the embarrassing reaction to World War II *taiga* drama BURNING MOUNTAINS AND RIVERS, NHK would be forgiven for staying away from modern times. However, the recent success of the channel's non-*taiga* drama OSHIN led producers to commission this 20th-century follow-up, that, by beginning in 1945 and sharing the same writer, was a retread of *Oshin* in all but name. Broadcast during the middle of Japan's bubble economic boom, *Inochi* was a stern warning for Japanese women not to forget their traditional virtues of sincerity and compassion in an increasingly materialistic age, and the series was rewarded with peak ratings of 36.7%, making it the tenth most successful *taiga* drama ever. *Taiga* drama entered a new renaissance, with the following year's MASAMUNE THE ONE-EYED DRAGON continuing the success and 1988's SHINGEN TAKEDA achieving *taiga*'s highest ratings of 25 years. Meanwhile *Inochi* went on to become the first *taiga* drama to be broadcast in English, in an extremely truncated form, when the 37-hour running time was hacked into four 25-minute episodes and screened with subtitles during a 1987 Japan Season on the U.K.'s Channel Four. For the U.K. broadcast, fierce editing forced the plot to advance at a rate of literally a year every two minutes, making Miki's life through the 20th century often appear more like time-lapse photography than natural aging.

INVESTIGATOR MARIKO *

1999. JPN: *Kasōken no Onna*. AKA: *Investigator Woman*. PRD: Osamu Tezuka (b), Takashi Inoue. DIR: Masahito Tsujino, Hajime Hashimoto, Kazuo Ōi. SCR: Yūichi Higure, Hakaru Sunamoto, Junji Takegami, Hideaki Tsukada. CAST: Yasuko Sawaguchi, Takeshi Naitō, Akinori Hano, Yūko Itō, Makoto Matsui, Nenji Kobayashi, Ikkei Watanabe, Yuriko Hoshi. CHN: Asahi. DUR: 45 mins. x 27 eps. (final ep 90 mins.); Thu 21 October 1999–?? December 1999 (#1); 19 October 2000–?? December 2000 (#2); 1 November 2001–?? December 2001 (#3).

FBI-trained Mariko (Sawaguchi) is a police forensic scientist in Kyoto, who faces heavy opposition in a world dominated by male officers, particularly her doubting ex-husband (Watanabe), now the Chief Detective with whom she must remain civil despite their differences. Where the men often believe only evidence seen with their eyes, Mariko uses her scientific abilities to crack seemingly impossible cases.

Investigator Mariko draws on a broad international tradition of canny ladies who outwit the local menfolk on a regular basis but never seem to win their respect—compare to *Prime Suspect*, *Silent Witness*, and HOUSEWIFE AND DETECTIVE. Its appeal to the female audience is obvious, while the use of technology to solve crimes also made it a winner with viewers of *The X-Files* inspired shows, such as RING and UNSOLVED CASES. Many of Mariko's adventures turn out to have a twist in the tale, and often her battles with authority revolve around defenses of the wrongly accused or her suspicions of foul play in a seemingly clear case of innocence. These include a professor suspected of murdering his research assistant, a jealous lover masquerading as a terrorist, and a suspected case of snuff movie-making.

The show also seems to take particular joy in the dramatic possibilities of the mobile phone—one episode features a corpse whose life is reconstructed through its mobile's memory, while another has a bank robber whose activities are secretly broadcast to the outside world by an undercover policewoman who inadvertently becomes one of his hostages. Episodes showcase widgets of the week, including internet surveillance, crime reenactment, ultraviolet scans, X-rays, dialect analysis, and facial reconstruction. However, personal drama also remains a high priority in the style of BAYSIDE SHAKEDOWN, not just for the weekly guest stars but also for the regular cast members, most notably in the cat-and-dog rivalry between the divorced leads. For another Kyoto crime fighter, see GEISHA DETECTIVE. Compare to TAEKO SASHŌ'S LAST CASE.

All three seasons have been broadcast with English subtitles in the U.S. on KIKU TV. Themes: ZARD—"Kono Namida Hoshi ni Nare" (Turn These Tears into Stars), Kyōsuke Himuro—"Outside Beauty," Kobukuro—"Miss You."

INVISIBLE DORI-CHAN

1978. JPN: *Tōmei Dori-chan*. PRD: Tanetake Ochiai, Susumu Yoshikawa. DIR: Hirokazu Takemoto, Minoru Yamada, Kōichi Takemoto, Kimio

---

WEDDINGS FROM HELL

Finger Food

This wedding is disrupted by an insane grandmother, who sees her stolen ring on the bride's finger and tries to bite it off her hand, wrecking the dining hall in the ensuing struggle. ☞

Hirayama. SCR: Shōzō Uehara, Hideyoshi Nagasaka, Michihiko Saijō, Tomomi Tsutsui. CAST: Sumiko Kakizaki, Seiichi Andō, Mitsuru Satō, Yoshiko Yoshino, Machiko Soga, Kazuo Andō, Yūji Takeda, Kazuaki Yoshiyama, Toshiaki Noda, Hiroyuki Yahata, Takeshi Fujiki, Risa Komaki, Arihiro Fujimura. CHN: Asahi. DUR: 30 mins. x 25 eps.; Sat 7 January 1978–1 July 1978.

Midori (Kakizaki) and her brother Torao (S. Andō) are kidnapped by fairies. The fairy President-King Ganvas (Fujimura) tells them that he is their real father but the children cannot forget the human world and ask to be sent back. Ganvas permits this, on the condition that the children help to *"make people's dreams,"* and bestows upon them the power of invisibility to help this happen.

Based on a manga by Shōtarō Ishinomori, *Invisible Dori-chan* was the first live-action magical girl series to be made after **COMET-SAN** and helped establish the traditions of the genre that continue to this day. Ishinomori also wrote the lyrics of the theme tune "Tōmei Dori-chan" that was sung by Kumiko Ōsugi.

INVISIBLE MAN

1996. JPN: *Tōmei Ningen.* PRD: Yoshinobu Kosugi. DIR: Ryūichi Inomata. SCR: Kazuhiko Ban. CAST: Shingo Katori, Eri Fukatsu, Junichi Ishida, Hitomi Kuroki, Leo Morimoto, Satsuki Ariga. CHN: NTV. DUR: 45 mins. x 13 eps.; Sat 13 April 1996–6 July 1996.

Hanzō (Katori from SMAP) is a photo-journalist from Ogasawara, who comes to find work in the big city. Teaming up with reporter Hijima (Fukatsu) to work on a crime investigation, he accidentally acquires a potion that allows him to become completely invisible. He uses his newfound talent to solve crimes, in a comedy that takes a more serious turn toward the end of the series. Thanks to the nature of Hanzō's invisibility, the actor playing him could usually expect to end up naked at least

once each episode, reputedly leading Katori to have each of his buttocks insured for 100 million yen. We are not exactly sure how this would have helped but it added to the show's pre-broadcast hype. Theme: Southern All Stars—"Ai no Kotodama: Spiritual Message" (Spirit of Love: Spiritual Message).

IN-LAWS, THE

2003. JPN: *Gibo to Issho ni.* AKA: *With My Mother-in-Law.* PRD: Atsuhiro Sugio, Mamoru Koimizu. DIR: Daisuke Tajima, Masataka Takamaru. SCR: Arisa Kaneko, Erina Tanaka. CAST: Miki Mizuno, Tortoise Matsumoto, Ken Kaitō, Shun Oguri, Maki Miyamoto, Yōko Kuga, Hitomi Takahashi, Ken Utsui, Kyōko Suizenji. CHN: Fuji. DUR: 45 mins. x 11 eps.; Tue 7 January 2003–?? March 2003.

Losing her mother when she was five years old and her father at twenty, Tamayo (Mizuno) has little family of her own. Married for three years, she finds herself living with her mother-in-law Mayu (Miyamoto), a no-nonsense divorcée in her fifties, who has struggled to raise three sons after she threw out their drunken father. But when Tamayo's husband dies suddenly, the twentysomething woman finds herself trapped at Mayu's family lunch box operation, arguing about everything from balancing the family budget to who uses the bath first. In-law appeasement in the style of **LADY OF THE MANOR**, featuring Ulfuls lead singer Tortoise Matsumoto.

IS MAMA BEAUTIFUL!?

1991. JPN: *Mamatte Kirei!?* PRD: Yasuo Yagi. DIR: Akio Yoshida. SCR: Akiko Yamanaga, Shizuka Ōishi. CAST: Atsuko Asano, Masahiro Motoki, Kōji Matoba, Shinji Yamashita, Shigeru Muroi. CHN: TBS. DUR: 45 mins. x 11 eps.; Fri 11 January 1991–22 March 1991.

Newly divorced illustrator Yōko moves house with her daughter but foolishly places her trust in a TV weatherman. As a result, she is drenched in an unexpected downpour and curses the

anonymous voice forever, only to discover that her sworn enemy is Susumu (Motoki), who has also just moved into her neighborhood. Theme: Psy-S—"Friends or Lovers."

ISN'T BEING CUTE ENOUGH?

1999. JPN: *Kawaii Dake ja Dame Kashira?.* PRD: Yūji Tōjō, Tetsuya Kuroda. DIR: Kazuhisa Imai, Renpei Tsukamoto. SCR: Kazuyoshi Okada. CAST: Kanako Enomoto, Sayaka Yamaguchi, Toshinori Okada, Naomi Kawashima, Masao Kusakari. CHN: Asahi. DUR: 45 mins. x 10 eps.; Mon 11 January 1999–?? March 1999.

Yūko (Enomoto) is a fashion-conscious student at a short-term college, who begins a series of bitter contests with her self-proclaimed rival Setsuko (Yamaguchi). Based on the manga by Yumiko Suzuki, who also created **REIKO SHIRATORI I PRESUME** and played by the actors in a fittingly cartoony style—compare to Enomoto's similar campery in **THE STAND-IN**. Theme: Deeps—"Brand New Heaven."

IT STARTED WITH A KISS

1996. JPN: *Itazura na Kiss.* AKA: *Teasing Kiss, Mischievous Kiss.* PRD: Mitsunori Morita. DIR: Mitsunori Morita. SCR: Hiromi Kusumoto, Harumi Mori. CAST: Takashi Kashiwabara, Aiko Satō, Takeshi Naitō, Miyoko Asada, Mayu Ozawa. CHN: Asahi. DUR: 45 mins. x 9 eps.; Mon 14 October 1996–16 December 1996.

Ever since they accidentally kissed at a school ceremony, flaky teenager Kotoko (Satō) has had a crush on Naoki (Kawashima), the class president and captain of the basketball team. She tries to confess her feelings for him on her 18th birthday, but he rebuffs her for being strange. The heartbroken girl returns home only to find her house is on fire. With nowhere to live, her chef father Shigeo (Naitō) decides they have to move in with some childhood friends of his, though to Kotoko's cringing embarrassment, they turn out to be Naoki's parents. Naoki is equally mortified, and tells Kotoko that she is not to mention their arrangement at school and she is to keep two meters away from him at all times. Naoki's mother (Asada) is eternally trying to push the couple together and confesses that she has always wanted a daughter. She shows Kotoko photographs of a young Naoki dressed as a girl, which Kotoko successfully uses to blackmail Naoki into tutoring her for a forthcoming exam. The effort of teaching her forces Naoki to study hard for the first time in his life and both students make it into the top hundred (after a bizarre scene in which the teachers try to keep Kotoko's grade secret because she comes from a "lower class"—welcome to Japan!). However, a photo of them in a misleadingly compromising position is posted on the school notice board, leading other classmates to believe the couple are already an item. Based on the 1990 manga in *Margaret* magazine by Kaoru Tada, who also created *Night For Loving* (*AE), the reluctant step-siblings of *It Started with a Kiss* resemble those in other dramas such as **COLD MORNING** and **STRAWBERRY ON THE SHORTCAKE**. There are also numerous anime parallels, particularly in the accidental kiss scene that resembles a similar incident in *Kimagure Orange Road* (*AE) and high school one-upmanship in the spirit of *His and Her Circumstances* (*AE). Theme: Speed—"Steady."

ITABASHI MADAMES
1998. PRD: Shizuo Sekiguchi. DIR: Keita Kōno, Masato Hijikata, Makoto Hirano. SCR: Hiroshi Hashimoto. CAST: Junko Sakurai, Saya Takagi, Masako Miyaji, Emily Henmi, Katsunori Takahashi. CHN: Fuji. DUR: 45 mins. x 10 eps.; Wed 14 October 1998–16 December 1998.
Falling on hard times, the Kiyonuma family are forced to move to the run-down public housing projects of Itabashi. The shock is soon too much for Kōhei (Takahashi), the golf-loving middle-class aspirant father, and he deserts his wife and children. Wife Takako (Sakurai) is forced to struggle to make ends meet with the help of several other tough neighborhood wives. Based on a presumably true story by the real Takako Aonuma, this comedy series was used as a vehicle for actress Sakurai—part of the appeal to audiences lay in the young office lady character of the same year's **POWER OFFICE GIRLS** portraying a harassed housewife. Theme: Toshihiko Sahashi—"Peach."

IT'S TIME
1970. JPN: *Jikan Desu yo*. PRD: Teruhiko Kuze. DIR: Teruhiko Kuze. SCR: Sugako Hashida, Kuniko Mukōda. CAST: Mitsuko Mori, Eiji Funakoshi, Eitarō Matsuyama, Mayumi Ōzora, Kirin Kiki, Masaaki Sakai, Akira Kawaguchi, Nekohachi Edoya. CHN: TBS. DUR: 45 mins. x ca. 120 eps.; 4 February 1970–26 August 1970.
Matsu (Mori) runs a public bath, aided and abetted by her husband (Funakoshi) and employees (Sakai and Kiki). An important human drama that spawned sequels in 1971, 1973, and 1974, *It's Time* is often held up by critics for its use of future scriptwriting giants Kuniko Mukōda (**LIKE ASHURA**) and Sugako Hashida (**OSHIN**), though much of its ratings popularity also rested on the regular doses of female nudity it provided. The show was also a good career move for comedians Sakai (who went on to star in **MONKEY**) and Kiki, who were left to provide comic relief while the leads got on with the serious story lines. The 1971 series introduced Mari Amachi, then an unknown, while the 1973 episodes offered an early role for Miyoko Asada.

After a long absence from the airwaves, the story was revived as *It's Time Again* (1987) with the comedy duo The Tunnels in the lead roles. The new incarnation was followed by a further sequel in 1988 and two specials.

The series was rebranded again for *It's Time Heisei Gannen* (1989), a title which capitalized on the beginning of the new Imperial Heisei era. The 1989 version adopted a different drama cliché, replaying *Romeo and Juliet* with Fumiya Fujii and Miho Tsumiki as the heirs to rival bath houses who fall in love. This most recent series also featured Masahiro Nakai, Tsuyoshi Kusanagi, and Shingo Katori from SMAP as supporting characters, in their first significant drama roles.

J

JAN PERSON

1993. JPN: *Tokusō Robo Jan Person*. AKA: *Special Detective Robot Jan Person*. PRD: Jun Kaji, Nagafumi Hori. DIR: Michio Konishi, Masao Minowa. Tetsuji Mitsumura, Hidenori Ishida, Osamu Kaneda. SCR: Jūichi Miyashita, Nobuo Ōgisawa, Kyōko Sagiyama, Hirohisa Soda, Naoyuki Sakai. CAST: Yūichi Komine, Shōya Torii, Tomoko Kawashima, Mikio Tomita, Hideki Ishikawa, Noboru Ichikawa, Kazuki Takahashi. CHN: Asahi. DUR: 25 mins. x 50 eps.; Sun 31 January 1993–23 January 1994.

Jan Person (Komine) and his partner Gan Gibson (Torii) are robot cops, fighting to keep three separate crime syndicates in line. JP's arsenal of weaponry includes the Break Knuckle (a fist that flies off his arm) and a small cannon concealed in his kneecap, while GG's weapon of choice is a giant bazooka called the Spindle Cannon. In times of trouble they can hit their power-up buttons for extra energy, in an early morning kids kung fu show that nevertheless gained a small adult following, drawn to the strangely camp idea of a superhero in purple battle armor assisted by a motorcycling deputy dressed in a cowboy outfit. *JP* began life as an attempt to buck contemporary trends in Japanese superhero shows, starting with the substitution of the "-man" suffix of ULTRAMAN with the clumsy but well-meaning "-person." The hero also seems to have been designed as a loner, only to have various sidekicks forced upon him by merchandising concerns. Compare to similar *Robocop* clones such as JIBAN and SHIDER and the following year's equally purple BLUE SWAT. "Based on an idea by Saburō Yade," and with music from Kei Wakakusa. Theme—"Hitori de Doko e Yuku" (Where Are You Going All Alone?).

JANBORG A

1973. PRD: Toyoaki Tan. DIR: Yoshiyuki Kuroda, Shōhei Tōjō, Sei Okada, Hiroshi Shimura, Toshitsugu Suzuki. SCR: Hiroyasu Yamaura, Narimitsu Taguchi, Toyohiro Andō, Fumikazu Wakatsuki. CAST: Naoki Tachibana, Toshiaki Amada, Chieko Sakurada, Toshiya Wazaki, Shōichirō Maruyama, Toshio Nakamura, Shigehiro Takahashi, Michiharu Sakamoto, Mitsuru Saijō. CHN: Mainichi Broadcasting (MBS). DUR: 30 mins. x 50 eps.; Wed 17 January 1973–29 December 1973.

In order to protect Earth from the alien invaders of Planet Glose, Naoki (Tachibana) is given the robot Janborg A. Unlike ULTRAMAN, with whom this monster-of-the-week show might otherwise be confused, Naoki remains a normal human being who merely pilots the giant Earth-defending machine, which is otherwise disguised as an innocuous Cessna aircraft at the aviation company where Naoki has a day job. This leads to occasional work-based conflicts, as when Naoki needs the aircraft to transform into Janborg A and save the world, whereas other employees are busy using it for something else, such as giving aerial tours to old ladies.

JAPAN SINKS *

1974. JPN: *Nihon Chinbotsu*. PRD: Tomoyuki Tanaka, Susumu Saitō, Tadashi Ogura, Yōji Hashimoto, Takao Yasuda. DIR: Jun Fukuda, Kiyoshi Nishimura, Taku Nagano, Eizō Yamagiwa, Minoru Kanaya, Tadashi Mafune. SCR: Yūichirō Yamane, Hideyoshi Nagasaka, Toshio Ishidō. CAST: Keiju Kobayashi, Takenori Murano, Kaoru Yumi, Toshio Kurosawa, Toshiyuki Hosokawa, Noboru Nakatani, Kunie Tanaka, Asao Uchida, Kenji Sahara, Isamu Hashimoto, Nobuto Okamoto, Ayako Sawada. CHN: TBS. DUR: 45 mins. x 26 eps.; Mon 6 October 1974–30 March 1975.

Mini-sub pilot Toshio Onodera (Murano) leaves late for an observation dive near the foot of Mount Fuji, thanks to the arrogant behavior of his client Dr. Tadokoro (Kobayashi). While the crew observe strange undersea fissures in the seabed off Izu, the area is struck by an earthquake. Toshio's land-based fiancée Etsuko (Mariko Mochizuki) is closer to the epicenter and dies under a pile of rubble.

While the depressed Toshio blames himself for her death (why!?), a second earthquake in the Himeji region causes consternation among scientists.

Though earthquakes are nothing unusual in Japan, Himeji has always been earthquake free, while recent tremors have even caused an entire island to disappear beneath the waves. After further investigations in Toshio's submarine, Tadokoro predicts that the new seismic disturbances threaten to plunge all of Japan beneath the sea. Few people believe him but Tadokoro convinces Toshio by taking his vessel below crush depth to observe more strange phenomena.

Back in Tokyo, Toshio is introduced to a wealthy beauty Reiko (Yumi) and appears to begin a new life and a new romance. But the professor's predictions are found to be quantifiably accurate—Japan is going to sink and the only issue now is how long the island has left. The Japanese, a race long accustomed to earthquakes, tidal waves, and volcanoes, must come to terms with the fact that their sacred nation, supposedly created by the gods themselves, will shortly disappear. Though some refuse to leave, others become involved in a desperate effort to convince foreign nations to take in literally millions of refugees. Meanwhile, the quakes and eruptions occur with increasing frequency, bringing a fresh new disaster each week.

Sakyō Komatsu, creator of **MY TIME TRAVEL JOURNEY WITH MARI** and sometime scenarist on **ARMY OF THE APES**, established his reputation as a preeminent science fiction author with the publication of the *Japan Sinks* novel in 1973. A series of coincidences ensured it received massive media attention, commencing with an unexpected volcanic eruption in Japan on its day of publication and continuing with the economic catastrophe of the early 1970s "oil shocks" that threatened to bankrupt the nation. The population of Japan was also jumpy about the "next big disaster," as 1973 was the 50th anniversary of the Great Tokyo Earthquake (see **100 YEARS**). As history was to testify, however, the next big earthquake to hit Japan was still twenty years away.

Janborg A

© 1973 Tsuburaya Productions

A movie soon followed from Tōhō in 1973, released in bowdlerized form in the U.S. as *Tidal Wave* in 1975, and this increased exposure helped gain the novel several foreign language deals. A terrifying study of a nation's lost psyche to the Japanese and an entertaining dose of *schadenfreude* for most other nations, *Japan Sinks* became a high-profile export in the age of disaster movies, once leading Brian Aldiss to describe Komatsu as the most widely read SF author in the world. Exploiting know-how from the earlier film version, this television remake nevertheless had an enormous budget for its time—half a billion yen, of which 40% went to special effects and, we might cruelly suggest, about two bucks to haircuts. The story was also released in a 1973 manga adaptation from Takao Saitō, creator of *Golgo 13* (*AE) and **BAROM ONE**.

JAQK

1977. JPN: *Jacker Dengeki Tai*. AKA: *Jacker Attack Force*. PRD: Takashi Ogino, Yoshiaki Koizumi, Susumu Yoshikawa. DIR: Hirokazu Takemoto, Atsuo Okunaka, Kimio Hirayama, Katsuhiko Taguchi, Minoru Yamada. SCR: Shōzō Uehara, Kuniaki Oshikawa, Susumu Takahisa, Hikaru Arai, Kimio Hirayama, Keisuke Fujikawa. CAST: Hiroshi Miyauchi, Yoshitaka Tanba, Hirayama Itō (aka Shichirō Gowa), Michi Love, Yūsuke Kazato, Masashi Ishibashi. CHN: Asahi. DUR: 25 mins. x 35 eps.; Sat 2 April 1977–24 December 1977.

A series of cyborgs is designed, each with the ability to control a particular form of energy. For reasons known only to themselves, their masters decide to have a unifying theme for the team, naming them all after playing cards. Gorō the Spade Ace (Tanba) is able to wield atomic energy as a weapon, using his bow to shoot it at his opponents in arrow form. Former boxer Ryū the Dia[mond] Jack (Itō) controls electricity, focusing it in his Elecky Sword. Bunta the Clover King (Kazato) has mastered the power of gravity, which he wields through his Crab Megaton—a weight on the end of a chain which he twirls around his head. Karen the Heart Queen (Love) controls magnetic energy through her Heart Q, which is a big pink Q. The team is led by Sōkichi the Big One (Miyauchi, already familiar to fans from the previous show GORANGER), who is able to use his Special Stick to combine the other four energy types, transforming the Jaqk team into a truly formidable force. Their obligatory vehicles are chiefly cars, though Clover King has a motorcycle, each of which can fly into their aircraft mothership, the Sky Ace.

The Jaqk Team's enemy is the Iron Claw (Ishibashi), an international arms dealer and drug smuggler, leader of the CRIME international syndicate, who favors a sequined cape and an unfeasibly large Afro hairdo. As in other Super Sentai shows, the Iron Claw has two sets of minions—anonymous cannon fodder (Jokers in this show) and ludicrously costumed monsters of the week, each of which singularly fails to defeat the trusty heroes. Based once again on an idea by Shōtarō Ishinomori, this second Super Sentai series gained an older audience, supposedly through its more serious themes—though it is more likely that it simply retained the viewers of its predecessor, GORANGER. After *Jaqk*, the producers attempted to exploit American ideas in SPIDER-MAN but the next true Super Sentai show in the series was BATTLEFEVER J. Music by Michiaki Watanabe.

JEALOUSY
1993. PRD: Yoshiki Tanaka. DIR: Ryōichi Itsukida. SCR: Toshio Terada, Michiru Etō. CAST: Junichi Ishida, Hitomi Kuroki, Hitomi Takahashi, Narimi Arimori, Mayu Tsuruta. CHN: NTV. DUR: 45 mins.

x 11 eps.; Wed 6 January 1993–24 March 1993.
In 1985, neuropathologist Masato (Ishida) begins an affair with his patient Yūko (Kuroki), only to have a change of heart and dump her on Christmas Eve—a traditional night in Japan for *reaffirming* romance, not ending it. Seven years later, the vengeful Yūko comes back into Masato's life, this time as an employee at his clinic. Compare to PARFUM DE LA JALOUSIE. Theme: Yuiko Tsubokura—"Je T'aime."

JETBOY
1959. JPN: *Shōnen Jet*. PRD: Tsunayoshi Takeuchi. DIR: N/C. SCR: N/C. CAST: Hirofumi Nakajima, Ken Tsuchiya, Munehiko Takada, Tamaki Matsunaga, Toshi Yagisawa, Masako Izumi, Setsuko Midorikawa. CHN: Fuji. DUR: 30 mins. x 83 eps.; Wed 4 March 1959–28 September 1960.
Ken Kitamura (Nakajima) is an assistant boy detective who solves cases with his dog Shane. He rides a scooter called Rabit. His ultimate weapon is his loud voice (!). His chief rival Black Devil has many dastardly schemes for ruling the world but never kills people. The result is the perfect show for young boys—a cool career, a cool vehicle, man's best friend, and a gun when things get boring. From June 1960, the Jetboy was played by Ken Tsuchiya. Music by Hideo Miyagi.

JETMAN
1991. JPN: *Torihito Sentai Jetman*. AKA: *Birdman Battle Team Jetman*. PRD: Kyōzō Utsunomiya, Jun Kaji, Takeyuki Suzuki. DIR: Keita Amemiya, Shōhei Tōjō, Kiyoshi Arai, Masao Minowa, Tarō Sakamoto. SCR: Toshiki Inoue, Kenichi Araki, Hiroyuki Kawasaki, Toshihisa Arakawa, Asami Watanabe, Kunio Fujii, Naoki Yawatari, Takahiko Masuda. CAST: Kōtarō Tanaka, Toshihide Wakamatsu, Tomihisa Naruse, Rika Kishida, Sayuri Uchida, Maho Maruyama, Takumi Hirose, Daisuke Tachi, Hideaki Kusaka. CHN: Asahi. DUR: 25 mins. x 51 eps.; Fri 15 February 1991–14 February 1992.

In 1999, as the Viram creatures try to invade the Earth from another dimension, the avian Jetman race arrives riding on a Bartnick Wave. They have sent a five-member team to defend the world, led by Ryū (Tanaka), who is not only a Sky Force officer but also Red Hawk. Kai (Wakamatsu) is Black Condor, a maverick team member who doesn't play by the book and often quarrels with the leader. Kindhearted Raita (Naruse) likes handicrafts and experimenting with cooking but is also the fearsome Yellow Owl. Kaoru (Kishida) is a clumsy team member as the White Swan but what she lacks in ability she makes up for in an obsession with always winning. Ako (Uchida) is still in high school, where she excels at sports and also rehearses for a career as a pop idol, none of which is much help to her role on the team as Blue Swallow. As well as motorcycles and cars, the Jetman team have a set of super-vehicles—the Jet Hawk, Jet Condor, Jet Owl, Jet Swan, and Jet Swallow. These can combine to form the Jetman super-plane, and also transform to make three giant robots—Tetra Boy, Bird Garuda, and Great Icarus. Their enemies in the next dimension reside in the demonic fortress of Virock, with a strangely minimalist and monochrome interior ruled over by the evil Empress Juza.

The most famous anime team show *Battle of the Planets* (*AE) also had an avian unifying theme, but *Jetman* added extra influences through the presence of many anime writers and *Zeiram* director Amemiya. The result was a Super Sentai show that gained a much more adult audience than many of its predecessors and which set the stage for a new boom in sentai popularity. *Jetman* was preceded in the Super Sentai chronology by FIVEMAN and followed by *Zyuranger*, better known today as MIGHTY MORPHIN' POWER RANGERS.

JINBE
1998. PRD: Atsuhiro Sugio. DIR: Kōzō Nagayama, Tatsuaki Kimura. SCR: Noriko Yoshida. CAST: Masakazu

Tamura, Takako Matsu, Tsuyoshi Kusanagi, Reiko Takashima. CHN: Fuji. DUR: 45 mins. x 11 eps.; Mon 12 October 1998–22 December 1998. Marine biologist Jinbe (Tamura) has reared his daughter Miku (Matsu) single-handedly since the death of her mother when she was only three. As Miku reaches her 20th birthday, he confesses that he is not actually her real father. Based on the manga in *Big Comics Superior* by Mitsuru Adachi, creator of KŌSHIEN AND OUR YOUTH. Theme: Reika Mirai—"Umi to Anata no Monogatari" (Story of the Sea and You). Peak rating: 22.6%.

JIRAIYA
1988. JPN: *Sekai Ninja Sen Jiraiya.* AKA: *The World Ninja War Jiraiya, Earth Ninja War Jiraiya.* PRD: Kyōzō Utsunomiya, Susumu Yoshikawa, Itaru Orita. DIR: Satoshi Tsuji, Tetsuji Mitsumura, Akihisa Okamura, Itaru Orita, Kiyohiko Arai. SCR: Akira Nakahara, Susumu Takahisa, Kunio Fujii, Norifumi Terada, Takashi Kyūki, Nobuo Ōgisawa, Tsuyoshi Koike. CAST: Takumi Tsutsui, Yoshiaki Hatsumi, Megumi Sekiguchi, Takumi Hashimoto, Kazunari Hirota, Tomoko Taya, Hitoshi Ōmae, Junichi Haruta, Hiromi Nohara, Aya Nagamine, Machiko Soga, Hizuru Uratani, Hiroshi Nagasawa, Shōzō Iizuka, Shingo Nagamori. CHN: Asahi. DUR: 30 mins. x 50 eps.; Sun 24 January 1988–22 January 1989.

Ninja from all over the world fight against evil monsters who are trying to get hold of Pako, an element that can allow them to rule the world. However, the monsters turn out not to be all bad—they have their own system of ethics and philosophy, and some even switch sides to aid ninja warrior Tsutsui save the planet. Another entry in the Metal Series, coming between METALDAR and JIVAN. Theme: Akira Kushida—"Jiraiya."

JIVAN
1989. JPN: *Kidō Keiji Jivan.* AKA: *Robot Detective Jivan.* PRD: Kyōzō Utsunomiya, Susumu Yoshikawa, Itaru Orita,

Nagafumi Hori. DIR: Michio Konishi, Akihisa Okamoto, Kiyohiko Miyasaka, Takeru Ogasawara, Tetsu Mitsumura. SCR: Shō Sugimura, Kunio Fujii, Nobuo Ōgisawa, Kenichi Araki. CAST: Shōhei Kusaka, Konomi Mashita, Michiko Enokida, Kunio Konishi, Hajime Izu, Akira Ishihama, Ami Kawai, Leo Melendy, Akemi Furukawa, Yōko Asakura, Shōzō Iizuka, Kazuko Yanaga. CHN: Asahi. DUR: 25 mins. x 52 eps.; Sun 29 January 1989–28 January 1990.

Naoto Tamura (Kusaka) is mortally wounded in an accident, only to be revived by Dr. Igarashi (Izu). He is now Jivan the robot detective, designed to work as a lone crusader of justice. Coming in between JIRAIYA and WINSPECTOR in the Metal Series, *Jivan* was something of a departure in its concentration on a robot hero, not a transforming team. Its Japanese inspiration can be traced back to ROBOT DETECTIVE and through it, to the anime series *8th Man* (*AE). Theme: Akira Kushida—"Kidō Keiji Jivan" (Mobile/Robot Cop Jivan).

JOHNNY SOKKO AND HIS GIANT ROBOT *
1967. JPN: *Giant Robo.* PRD: Shinichi Miyazaki, Tōru Hirayama, Yasuharu Ueda. DIR: Minoru Yamada, Hirokazu Takemoto, Katsuhiko Taguchi, Itaru Orita, Kōichi Takemoto, Michio Konishi. SCR: Masaru Igami, Tomio Matsuda, Hisashi Abe, Kana Hichijō. CAST: Mitsunobu Kaneko, Akio Itō, Masasaburō Date, Yumiko Katayama, Hideo Murota, Kōji Miemachi, Tomomi Kuwabara, Mitsuo Andō, Hirohiko Satō. CHN: NET (Asahi). DUR: 25 mins. x 26 eps.; Wed 11 October 1967–1 April 1968.

Evil Emperor Guillotine (Satō), ruler of the Planet Gargoyle, crashes his flying saucer in the Pacific Ocean. The Earth authorities believe he is dead. Meanwhile, in another part of the Pacific, Japanese boy Daisaku/Johnny (Kaneko) is on a cruise liner. The ship is attacked by Dagora (U.S.: Dracolon), one of many monsters who have come

to Earth along with Guillotine. As the ship sinks, Daisaku escapes with his newfound writer friend Jūrō/Gerry (Itō) and the pair are washed up on a seemingly deserted island. There they meet Doctor Over/Professor Guardian (Andō), a scientist who has been forced by Guillotine to build a super-powered robot. However, as his project nears completion, the scientist has realized he cannot go through with the evil deed and he booby-traps his lair with an atomic bomb. The professor's lair is attacked by the Gargoyle Gang/Big Fire (agents of Guillotine), and the Doctor urges Daisaku and Jūrō to escape while he stays behind to fight them off. However, instead of being destroyed in the explosion, Giant Robo is activated by it. The robot is designed to recognize the first voice it hears as its master—Daisaku speaks into the fob watch containing a radio transmitter and Giant Robo becomes his to command.

Spider (Date), leader of Guillotine's Gargoyle Gang, orders Dagora to attack Tokyo but Daisaku and Jūrō climb into Giant Robo's hand and command him to fly them there. When they arrive, Daisaku orders Giant Robo to fight Dagora, and the first of many monster battles is won. In later episodes, Guillotine sends other monsters to threaten the safety of the world, including Globar the Devil-Ball

(U.S.: Nucleon), Satan Rose (U.S.: Gargoyle Vine the Space Plant), Gangar (U.S.: The Giant Claw), Dorogon (U.S.: Dragon the Ninja Monster), Ikageras (U.S.: Scanlon the Starfish Monster), and Draculan the Space Vampire (same in the U.S., for once!).

Though one Tōru Hirayama shared part of the credit for the series, its origins were chiefly the responsibility of "co-creator" Mitsuteru Yokoyama, the manga author whose other works included COMET-SAN, GIGANTOR, and WATER MARGIN, as well as numerous works later adapted into anime, such as *Babel II* (*AE). Though equally as influential as Osamu Tezuka, Yokoyama seems to have lost out in the battle for the limelight—Tezuka was undoubtedly the better self-publicist and had his own studio to push his products. Published in *Shōnen Magazine* in 1956, Yokoyama's original *Giant Robo* manga had a similar monster-of-the-week storyline, although the manga robot was originally created as part of a secret World War II project—possibly we can see Hirayama's influence here, carefully sanitizing the original with an eye to foreign sales. If that was the case, he got his wish—the series was broadcast in the U.S. in 1969 as *Johnny Sokko and His Giant Robot* and then in Australia during the 1970s. The U.S. production was overseen by producer Salvatore Billiteri, who also produced the American version of *Prince Planet* (*AE), with a rewritten script credited to Reuben Guberman. The voice of Johnny was provided in the American version by Prince Planet actor Billie Byers. Several episodes of the series were re-cut into a feature-length edition, released in the U.S. as *Voyage into Space* (1970). Compare to other early dramas imported into the English-speaking world, such as SPACE GIANTS and PHANTOM AGENTS. The story was also radically remade as a straight-to-video anime series in 1992—see *Giant Robo* (*AE). Music by Takeo Yamashita.

JOURNEY TO THE WEST

1993. JPN: *Saiyūki*. PRD: Nobuo Komatsu. DIR: Haruo Ichikura, Katsuo Kadona, Rokurō Sugimura, Shinobu Murata, Keiichirō Yoshida. SCR: Eizaburō Shiba, Takeshi Tagami, Masaki Fukasawa, Motozō Mineo, Masaaki Wakui, Kenichi Onishi, Masaya Ozaki. CAST: Toshiaki Karasawa, Riho Makise, Akira Enomoto, Hisahiro Ogura, Shingo Yanagisawa, Kimiko Amari, Noboru Takachi. CHN: NTV. DUR: 45 mins. x 17 eps.; Fri 8 April 1993–23 September 1993.

Five hundred years after he is cast out of Heaven, the Monkey King Sun Wukong (Karasawa) is offered a chance to redeem himself, if only he will escort the Buddhist monk Tripitaka (Makise) from China to India to collect some sacred scrolls. Over a decade after the landmark series MONKEY and with the channel's 40th anniversary imminent, NTV tried to revisit past glories with this remake of its previous remake of the Wu Cheng-En novel, even to the extent of casting another actress to play the boy priest Tripitaka. Sadly, Makise suffered in comparison to the late Masako Natsume. Theme: Inflix—"Kizudarake no Tenshi ni Nante Naritai to wa Omowanai" (Don't Think I Want to Become a Wounded Angel).

JUNE BRIDE

1995. PRD: Hiroki Ueda. DIR: Jirō Shōno, Osamu Katayama, Takashi Hashimoto. SCR: Haruo Masutani, Hana Takahashi. CAST: Naomi Zaizen, Hiroshi Fuse, Saya Takagi, Yoshihiko Hakamada, Hiroshi Abe. CHN: TBS. DUR: 45 mins. x 12 eps.; Fri 14 April 1995–30 June 1995.

Haughty receptionist Naomi (Zaizen) is forcibly transferred to the sewing machine division of the electrical appliance company where she works. Her bitter rival Saeko (Takagi) has been posted to the same section from the secretarial pool, and the girls are forced to cooperate with each other in order to turn around the fortunes of the troubled division. In other words,

two modern girls ironically defending one of the last bastions of "women's work"—compare to the mismatched buddies of TABLOID who fight to *stay* in a man's world, not to leave it. Theme: Junko Yamamoto—"Itsudemo Yume ni Hanataba o" (Always Give Flowers to the Dream).

JUNGLE PRINCE

1970. PRD: N/C. DIR: N/C. SCR: N/C. CAST: Keiji Yano, Takako Fuji, Hiroshi Katō. CHN: NTV. DUR: 25 mins. x 26 eps.; Mon 6 July 1970–10 August 1970 (b/w).

An orphan boy grows up in the jungle and helps defend it from the predations of the evil Robora, in a show that transplants the monster-of-the-week adventure of ULTRAMAN into the jungle setting popularized by the 1966 Japanese broadcast of *Tarzan*. However, any chances *JP* might have had were ruined by the circumstances of its production—filmed years before it was actually broadcast, the monochrome show was fatally left on the shelf until all its newer rivals were being shown in color. In episode 19, our jungle hero discovered that his father came from Tokyo—a trifle obvious since he'd been speaking Japanese all his life. Compare to JUSPION.

JUNIOR: LOVE CONNECTION

1992. JPN: *Junior: Ai no Kankei*. PRD: N/C. DIR: Akiji Fujita. SCR: Hideyoshi Nagasaka. CAST: Masanobu Takashima, Masaya Katō, Kimiko Ikegami, Minako Tanaka, Yasuko Matsuyuki, Isao Hashizume. CHN: Fuji. DUR: 45 mins. x 11 eps.; Thu 16 April 1992–25 June 1992.

Hirama (Takashima) is a son of Tokuzen (Hashizume), the Minister of the Environment. While working for the Japanese Environmental Protection Agency, Hirama befriends Ryūichi (Katō), a politician's secretary and the son of the important mover and shaker Sakigake (Shigezō Hayasaka). Additional realism is added by the presence on the production staff of Shigezō Hayasaka, a former secretary to the real-life Japanese Prime Minister Kakuei Tanaka, now a political commentator and adviser on the production. Compare to **HOMEWORK** and **MAYOR IN LOVE**. Theme: Yang Sukyong—"Itsuka Kitto Hohoemi E" (It Will Turn to Smile One Day).

JURISDICTION

2000. JPN: *Shokatsu: Real Police Story*. PRD: Takahiro Kasaoki. DIR: Keita Kōno, Junichi Tsuzuki. SCR: Masashi Todayama, Naoya Takayama. CAST: Masahiro Matsuoka, Misako Tanaka, Isao Hashizume, Saya Takagi, Hironobu Nomura, Yoshihiko Hakamada. CHN: Fuji. DUR: 45 mins. x 12 eps.; Tue 11 April 2000–27 June 2000.

Toma Hamura (Matsuoka) graduates *summa cum laude* from the Tokyo University Law Department and finds a job with the Metropolitan Police. The elite rookie is sent to the Jōnan area for his training, where he is unsurprisingly teamed with an inappropriate partner—ambitious tomboy Ayano Kujō (Tanaka), who has clawed her way up from rock bottom. With little faith in Toma's abilities, Ayano carries the caseload herself, leading to a series of blowouts between the mismatched couple as they try to find a way to work together. The result is a predictable cop show, based on the manga of the same title by Kazuhiko Satake with a script from **NINZABURŌ FURUHATA** writer Keita Kōno. Theme: TOKIO—"Ai wa Nude" (Love Is Nude).

JUSPION

1985. JPN: *Kyojū Tokusō Juspion*. PRD: Susumu Yoshikawa, Itaru Orita, Yūki Usui. DIR: Yoshiaki Kobayashi, Takeru Ogasawara, Michio Konishi, Satoshi Tsuji, Haruya Yamazaki, Shōhei Tōjō. SCR: Shōzo Uehara. CAST: Akira Kurosaki, Kiyomi Tsukada, Noboru Nakatani, Junichi Haruta, Atsuko Koganezawa, Hiroshi Watari, Toshimichi Takahashi, Hirotaka Sekine, Misa Nirei, Kyō Anan, Junko Takahashi, Yukie Kagawa, Shōzo Iizuka. CHN: Asahi. DUR: 25 mins. x 46 eps.; Fri 15 March 1985–24 March 1986.

Raised in the wild in the company of giant beasts, the orphan Juspion (Kurosaki) must travel to Earth to save it from the evil Satangorse, who intends to use alien beasts to rule the galaxy. Arriving on Earth in the transforming mother ship Dileon, Juspion discovers that the planet is already threatened by Satangorse's son Mad Galan. With his faithful assistant Android Anri, Juspion dons his Metaltex suit and prepares to save the world, in yet another entry in the Metal Series, coming after **SHIDER** in the series chronology. Less successful than the earlier robot detective shows that began with **GAVAN**, *Juspion* was criticized for poor special effects. Nevertheless, the producers had high hopes for it and even included an English theme song in an attempt to win foreign attention. *Juspion* was not sold abroad but the next show in the Metal Series, *Spielban*, did make it to America—see **VR TROOPERS**. Music is by Hiroaki Watanabe.

JUST ANOTHER J-LEAGUE

1993. JPN: *Mō Hitotsu no J-League*. PRD: N/C. DIR: Takahito Hara. SCR: Masaki Fukasawa. CAST: Toshihiko Sakakibara, Yumiko Takahashi, Maki Mochida, Masami Nakagami, Kazue Itō. CHN: NTV. DUR: 45 mins. x 7 eps.; Fri 22 October 1993–3 December 1993.

Hitoshi (Sakakibara) has passed the trials to join the J-League team Tokyo Saints. But the path of the professional soccer player is fraught with peril, and Hitoshi is humiliated by the fine performance of Yūji (Nakagami), a player who has honed his soccer skills abroad. However, he gets extra support from Yōko (Takahashi), a high school junior who shyly waits for the moment to tell him she loves him. Compare with another soccer story, **OUR OLÉ!** Theme: Keizō Nakanishi—"Tatta Hitotsu no Ai o" (One and Only Love To You).

JUST THE WAY WE ARE

1992. JPN: *Sugao no Mamade*. AKA:

With a Naked Face. PRD: Kōji Shiozawa. DIR: Michio Mitsuno. SCR: Eriko Kitagawa. CAST: Narumi Yasuda, Akina Nakamori, Kōji Matoba, Mikihisa Azuma, Shingo Tsurumi, Kiyoshi Kodama. CHN: Fuji. DUR: 45 mins. x 12 eps.; Mon 13 April 1992–29 June 1992.

Still traumatized by the abortion she had when she was a teenager, librarian Yumiko (Yasuda) has given up on the dating game and relies on her father Shūzō (Kodama) to set her up with *omiai* marriage meetings. She misses the latest, with doctor Yoshihiko (Tsurumi), because she is caught in the rain. Instead, she meets Kanna (Nakamori), a girl from out of town who has come to Tokyo to become a stage star, and the unlikely couple become firm friends . . . until they fall in love with the same man. Compare to **BEST FRIENDS** and the ultimate inspiration for both, the Bette Midler vehicle *Beaches* (1988). Theme: Kome Kome Club—"Kimi ga Iru Dake de" (Just to Have You Here). Peak rating: 31.9%.

JUSTICE FOR ALL

1995. JPN: *Seigi wa Katsu*. AKA: *Justice Will Win*. PRD: Kōji Shiozawa. DIR: Setsuo Wakamatsu. SCR: Masashi Todayama, Yasushi Asai. CAST: Yūji Oda, Mayu Tsuruta, Shigeru Muroi, Yasunori Danta, Harumi Inoue. CHN: Fuji. DUR: 45 mins. x 10 eps.; Wed 18 October 1995–20 December 1995.

Junpei Takaoka (Oda) is an extremely capable lawyer who has not lost any of his last 25 cases and recently voted into the fifth partnership of the Central Law firm. He is assigned with admiring rookie lawyer Kyōko (Tsuruta) to defend the Big Stone International corporation, which is being sued by Mrs. Mizunuma, the widow of an employee who died abroad—she insists he was there on business, the company insists that he was there on vacation and that consequently it has no legal obligation to pay damages.

While researching the case, Junpei discovers that the dead Mizunuma had been sending large amounts of money from Big Stone to Central Law—with the large bills legal firms are notorious for charging, Central Law is being used as the perfect money laundering service. Even more troubling for Junpei is the discovery that Big Stone is the new name for Kurobishi Trading, a company whose unscrupulous business practices led to the dismissal and eventual suicide of his own father. However, when the vengeful Junpei announces to his boss Ōuchi that he has cracked the case, he is framed for embezzlement. Junpei manages to get the evidence somewhere safe and, although he loses his lawyer's license, is able to enlist the help of Tsukada, his late father's lawyer. With Tsukada's help, Junpei is able to arrange for the arrest of Ōuchi. In court, Ōuchi is defended by the elite of Central Law's defense counsels but buckles on the stand when Junpei calls himself as a witness.

Oda had formally taken the Tom Cruise role in the *Top Gun* rip-off *Best Guy* (1990)—here he reprises his Hollywood alter ego's success in *A Few Good Men* (1992) and *The Firm* (1993). See also **CAN'T HURRY LOVE**, another Cruise-alike for Oda. Theme: Yūji Oda—"Ai Made Mō Sugu Dakara" (Not Far To Love).

K

KAJIN

1977. AKA: *Flower God, Vassal*. PRD: Tsuneo Narushima. DIR: Akira Saitō, Yūji Murakami, Hiroyuki Eguchi, Masami Kadowaki, Akira Mitsui. SCR: Yasuko Ōno. CAST: Umenosuke Nakamura, Masatoshi Nakamura, Mariko Kaga, Ruriko Asaoka, Toshiyuki Nishida, Saburō Shinoda, Jūkichi Uno, Kumiko Akiyoshi, Tarō Shigaki, Shinobu Ōtake, Isao Bitō. CHN: NHK. DUR: 45 mins. x ca. 50 eps.; Sun 2 January 1977–25 December 1977.

When the Japanese army attacks the rebellious domain of Chōshū in the 1860s, local village doctor Kuraroku Murata (later called Masujirō Ōmura, played by U. Nakamura) is appointed to lead an army that can overthrow the shogun—compare to RYŌMA DEPARTS. An unexpectedly level-headed tactician, the doctor is also blessed with an army of passionate royalists such as Shinsaku Takasugi and Hajime Inoue. He also applies European-style methods of training, drill, and discipline, previously unheard of in Japan's samurai society—an era later covered by Hollywood in *The Last Samurai* (2003). Such policies allow him to defeat the government army, end the reign of the discredited shogun, and restore Imperial rule in the form of the Emperor Meiji. The doctor's new model army becomes the basis for the entire Japanese military after the Meiji Restoration—a force that includes men from all backgrounds, not merely the descendants of samurai, though many disgruntled nobles choose instead to join the navy. He also institutes a national conscription system, obligating all men over 20 years to perform military service, although in practice the upper classes and eldest sons of most families manage to find ways to exempt themselves.

The story was based on *Kajin, Yo ni Sumu Hibi* (Days Nested in the World), *Jūichibanme no Shishi* (The 11th Royalist), and *Tōge* (Mountain Pass)—all novels by Ryōtarō Shiba, who also created AS IF IN FLIGHT, LAND THIEF, and TOKUGAWA YOSHINOBU. Unfortunately, the attempt to adapt four entire books seems to have defeated the production team on this *taiga* drama, with an already complex historical period rendered almost impossible to understand at some points. In search of a new gimmick to keep the *taiga* franchise afloat, NHK responded the following year with DAYS OF GOLD, the first to be filmed outside Japan. Music by Mitsuru Hayashi.

KAKURANGER *

1994. JPN: *Ninja Sentai Kakuranger*. AKA: *Ninja Battle Team Hidden-Ranger*. PRD: Jun Kaji, Susumu Yoshikawa, Takeyuki Suzuki, Naruki Takadera. DIR: Yoshiaki Kobayashi, Shōhei Tōjō, Tarō Sakamoto, Takeru Ogasawara, Katsuya Watanabe, Hiroshi Futsuda. SCR: Noboru Sugimura, Tsunehisa Arakawa, Kunio Fujii, Susumu Takahisa, Hirohisa Soda. CAST: Teruaki Ogawa, Hitomi Hirose, Dai Tsuchida, Hide Kawai, Kane Kosugi, Kazuki Yao, Hidemasa Shibata, Enjō Sanyūtei. CHN: Asahi. DUR: 25 mins. x 53 eps.; Fri 18 February 1994–24 February 1995.

Four hundred years after valiant ninja sealed the passageway that allowed demons access to Earth, the forces of evil break through once more into our own dimension. Earth's last hope is a band of modern ninja, led by Sasuke (Ogawa), a descendant of legendary ninja Sasuke Sarutobi (see *Magic Boy*, *AE). Sasuke is Ninja Red, a master of ninja techniques, who fights with the spirit of a monkey. His second in command is, surprisingly for sentai shows, a woman, Tsuruhime (Hirose) the Ninja White, the 24th generation leader of the Crane Clan and mistress of the Crane fighting art. Seikai (Kawai) is Ninja Yellow, a descendant of famous warrior Miyoshi Seikai Nyūdō, who fights with the power of a bear. Saizō (Tsuchida) is Ninja Blue, a descendant of famous ninja Saizō Kirigakure who fights with the super-swiftness of a wolf. American Jiraiya (Kosugi) is the descendant of famous ninja JIRAIYA, who fights with the power of a toad and is the master of the mid-air death blow.

Their enemy in Gaikotsu Castle is the Demon King and their chief adversaries his five pretty *kunoichi* assistants—deadly female ninja who lead the obligatory cannon fodder minions and a series of monsters of the week. The team's Bear, Crane, Monkey, Wolf, and Toad vehicles can combine to form the Super Stealth King, though there is little stealthy about a giant robot. In fact, the *Kakuranger* cast had one of the biggest arsenals of giant robot shows in sentai history, including later additions such as the Jūgun (Beast-General) and Super Jūgun, as well as individual pilotable robots.

Kakuranger was keen to establish links with many earlier ninja stories, including the manga of Sanpei Shirato and Fujihiko Hosono, as well as earlier updates such as **PHANTOM AGENTS**. The producers even cast the son of *Nine Deaths of the Ninja* star Shō Kosugi as Ninja Black in yet another attempt to tie *Kakuranger* indelibly to the assassins of popular myth. Ironically, *Kakuranger* lost most of its cultural references in the transition abroad to become the next installment of the **MIGHTY MORPHIN' POWER RANGERS** series, where it formed the third distinct saga in Saban Entertainment's radically revised version after **DAIRANGER** and *Zyuranger*.

In America, the crossover from the former series was achieved by the introduction of Rita Repulsa's brother Rito (Kerrigan Mahan), who stole the team's powers. After a trip to the Temple of Power, the Rangers received new powers and new Ninja Zords, later augmented by Shogun Zords. The line-up changed once more, with Kimberley leaving to train for the Pan Global Games, replaced by new Pink Ranger Catherine (Katherine Hilliard). A new Yellow Ranger arrived in the form of Tanya (Nakia Burrise). Footage from *Kakuranger* also appeared in *Power Rangers Alien Force*, a mini-story arc that supposedly took place while the original cast were searching for their new powers. For these episodes, the Earth was defended by stand-in extraterrestrial heroes, who also used special effects footage lifted from *Kakuranger*. Once the cast returned, the stage was set for yet another lineup change in *Power Rangers Zeo*, which

used footage from the next show in the Super Sentai chronology, **OHRANGER**.

KASUGA THE COURT LADY

1989. JPN: *Kasuga no Tsubone*. PRD: Yasuo Shibuya. DIR: Masayuki Tomizawa, Masahide Kenzai, Hisashi Ichii, Yoshiori Komiyama. SCR: Sugako Hashida. CAST: Reiko Ōhara, Yoshiko Sakuma, Tōru Emori, Yōsuke Eguchi, Shinji Yamashita, Shirō Ōsaka, Aiko Nagayama, Hiroshi Itsuki, Kiyoshi Nakajō, Ikuzō Yoshi, Guts Ishimatsu, Hiroshi Fujioka, Takuya Fujioka, Masatoshi Nakamura, Tetsurō Tanba. CHN: NHK. DUR: 45 mins. x 50 eps.; Sun 1 January 1989–17 December 1989.

Ever since her father Mitsuhide Akechi caused the death of **NOBUNAGA**, Lady Kasuga (Ōhara) has been shunned by polite society and treated as the daughter of a traitor. The Shogun Ieyasu Tokugawa (see **TOKUGAWA IEYASU**) appoints her as a nanny for Hidetada's son Takechiyo, who will later be known as the third Shogun Iemitsu. Given a new role in the new order, Kasuga thrives and becomes involved in many intrigues at Edo Castle, although she remains eternally at odds with Hidetada's first wife Eyo, who is a niece of Nobunaga. During a turmoil of civil war, she longs for peace.

As with Sugako Hashida's two earlier *taiga* adaptations, *Hideyoshi's Women* (see **HIDEYOSHI**) and **INOCHI: LIFE**, history is examined from the point of view of a female lead. Though traditionally portrayed as a tough, uncompromising soul, this Kasuga was played as an honest, devoted woman in a script that, although criticized for excess amounts of exposition, was strongly supported by female viewers. Peak rating: 39.2%.

KEEP IT UP, DETECTIVE

1973. JPN: *Soreyuke Meitantei*. PRD: N/C. DIR: Hiroshi Takei. SCR: Toshiharu Matsubara. CAST: Makiko Sawa, Jun Sawaki, Eizaburō Takahashi, Shunji Fujimura, Tetsuji Taniguchi, Shirō Shimizu, Tarō Towada. CHN: NHK. DUR:

25 mins. x 6 eps.; Mon 3 September 1973–12 September 1973.

Sanshirō (Sawaki), Sanae (Sawa), and Tonpei (Takahashi) are undependable detectives, tracking the Black Gang of master thieves who have stolen 300 million yen. With a pedigree that stretched back to Ranpo Edogawa's *Boy Detectives' Club*, this short-lived series was based on *Tantei Reijo* (Detective Lady) by Rei Kido.

KEN-CHAN SERIES

1969. PRD: N/C. DIR: N/C. SCR: N/C. CAST: Yasuyuki Miyawaki, Masaki Maeda, Kumiko Kishi, Mayumi Sakuma, Nobuo Tsukamoto, Keiko Yanagawa, Tomokazu Muta, Kazuko Yoshiyuki, Keizō Yamada, Tomoko Nagaharu, Yukari Saitō. CHN: TBS. DUR: 30 mins. x ?? eps.; 3 April 1969–26 February 1970 (#1); 5 March 1970–4 March 1971 (#2); 11 March 1971–2 March 1972 (#3); 9 March 1972–1 March 1973 (#4); 8 March 1973–28 February 1974 (#5); 7 March 1974–27 February 1975 (#6); 6 March 1975–26 February 1976 (#7); 4 March 1976–24 February 1977 (#8); 3 March 1977–23 February 1978 (#9); 2 March 1978–22 February 1979 (#10); 1 March 1979–28 February 1980 (#11); 6 March 1980–26 February 1981 (#12); 5 March 1981–25 February 1982 (#13); 4 March 1982–30 September 1982 (#14).

After being introduced in the long-running **CHAKO-CHAN** series, Kenichi (Miyawaki) became the star of his own show, although little of the original continuity was preserved. First introduced in *Chako Nee-chan* (1966), Kenichi was presented to the Japanese public as a little brother for the popular Chako character, though his original big sister was nowhere to be seen. His first series as headliner was *Jan Ken-chan* (a reference to the scissors-paper-stone game *jan-ken-pon*), in which his parents were played by Masaki Maeda and Kumiko Kishi. Toko-chan (Sakuma), a younger sister for Ken, was introduced the following year in

Ken-chan Toko-chan, with the ever shifting parents now played by Nobuo Tsukamoto and Keiko Yanagawa.

The third season, *Ken-chan at the Sushi Restaurant,* established a new format wherein Ken's parents would find an occupation that would be interesting for the children—with parents Tomokazu Muta and Kazuko Yoshiyuki and Megane (Yamada), a bespectacled playmate named for his glasses. The formula and cast were repeated for the fourth season *Ken-chan at the Cake Shop,* and while the pattern stayed the same for the fifth season *Ken-chan at the Toy Shop,* Ken's parents were now Maeda and Kishi once more. The toy shop arc also introduced Ken's new sister Mako-chan (Nagaharu) for the first time.

As with the previous *Chako-chan* series that launched Miyawaki, a perennial problem with cute child actors is that they grow up all too fast. The sixth season *Ken the Big Brother* began preparing for disaster by introducing Ken's younger sibling Kenji (Hiroya Oka). The parents were played by Muta and Kishi, who stayed as parents of the week for a while. The boys also appeared in the seventh season *Ken-chan at the Noodle Restaurant,* which introduced yet another sister Chako played by Yukari Saitō—if ever anyone needed proof that aliens were kidnapping people in the 20th century, the *Chako-chan* and *Ken-chan* series provides all the evidence you need, with more lineup changes than any other TV show. With little Kenji now safely installed as the new "Ken-chan," the time was right for Miyawaki to bow out, which he did gracefully in *Ken-chan at the Fruit Shop* after ten years of loyal service to TV drama.

The series soldiered on without him with *Sports Ken-chan* and *Ken-chan at the Bakery,* with Oka in the lead as Kenji and Muta's final performance as Ken's father. For the eleventh season *Ken-chan at the Curry Restaurant,* Ken's ever-mutating father was now played by Sumio Takatsu. Ratings were beginning to decline as the show entered its second decade, leading the producers to

aim for the nostalgia market, and reintroduce a sister called Chako (Keiko Kume) for the twelfth season *Ken-chan Chako-chan.* Oka's last season was the thirteenth, *Ken-chan and Chums,* and although Kume tried to carry on the torch in the following year's *Chako-chan Ken-chan,* the series finally ground to a halt in 1982.

KEY HUNTER

1968. PRD: Teruo Kondō. DIR: Kinji Fukasaku. SCR: Susumu Takahisa. CAST: Tetsurō Tanba, Yōko Nogiwa, Shinichi "Sonny" Chiba, Hayato Tani, Eiko Ōkawa, Hiroshi Kawaguchi, Hiroshi Miyauchi, Tadao Nakamaru, Masaya Oki. CHN: TBS. DUR: 45 mins. x 262 eps.; Sat 6 April 1968–7 April 1973. As increasing numbers of criminals manage to avoid the law, a secret group is formed within the police force—captain Tetsuya Kuroki (Tanba), former journalist Yōsuke Kazama (Chiba), linguist and magician Keiko Tsugawa (Nogiwa), stunt driver Tatsuhiko Shima (Tani), and Yumi Taniguchi (Ōkawa), who is blessed with an exceptional memory. Ignoring for a moment the character-plus-trait construction so prevalent in modern sentai shows such as MIGHTY MORPHIN' POWER RANGERS, this hard-boiled cop thriller was played completely straight and became well-known for its superb action sequences. This is hardly surprising, considering the presence of movie martial artists like Tanba and Chiba, in a show which added to its crime fighting appeal with the faux-exoticism that comes from fighting showy international criminal syndicates, not mundane local ones. *Key Hunter* was an important landmark in the history of Japanese cop shows, also imitated in Edo-era form as SURE DEATH, and when its long run came to an end, its star and even some of its scripts were recycled in G-MEN 75. Director Fukasaku went into the cinema, where he would eventually gain international notoriety for *Battle Royale* (2000). Note the presence of a very young and gorgeous Yōko Nogiwa in miniskirt and calf-length boots. Like

Chiba, she is still acting in TV dramas 35 years later. Theme: Yōko Nogiwa—"Hijō no License" (License to Chill).

KEYS TO THE CITY

1997. JPN: *Bokura no Yūki Miman City.* AKA: *Our Heroism; The Kids are in Charge, Miman City.* PRD: Yūko Hasegawa. DIR: Yukihiko Tsutsumi, Kenji Ikeda. SCR: Satsuo Endō, Shinji Ohara. CAST: Tsuyoshi Dōmoto, Kōichi Dōmoto, Mai Hōshō, Hidemori Tokuyama, Jun Matsumoto, Akiko Yada, Yūki Ohara. CHN: NTV. DUR: 45 mins. x 10 eps.; Sat 18 October 1997–20 December 1997. News reports announce that the city of Mokuhara has been struck by a terrible earthquake and that all the roads are closed. Concerned for the safety of his friends, Yamato (K. Dōmoto from Kinki Kids) decides to head for the city anyway. En route he meets Takeru (T. Dōmoto also from Kinki Kids), who is also heading for Mokuhara in search of his sister. However, once they reach the city, they discover that the situation is worse than they had imagined. There has been no earthquake after all—instead, Mokuhara and the surrounding regions have been contaminated with micro-organisms from a meteorite strike. All the adults in the city have been killed, and the government has sealed off the area to prevent the spread of a plague that kills everyone older than their teens. The two newcomers try to restore order in the city, until they discover that even this secret version of events has been concocted to cover up *something else.* When they realize who is really responsible, they decide to take on the government, in a strange mix of *Lord of the Flies* and NEVER LAND. Theme: Kinki Kids—"Ai Sareru Yori Ai Shitai" (Want To Love You More Than Being Loved).

KIDNAP

2000. JPN: *Tsugumi e.* AKA: *For Tsugumi . . . ; Kidnap of the Heart.* PRD: Satoko Uchiyama. DIR: Masaaki Odagiri, Masahiro Hisano. SCR: Toshio Terada. CAST: Mayu Tsuruta, Tōru Nakamura, Tsutomu Yamazaki, Tamao Satō, Ken

© 1972 Asahi

Kikaida

Kaneko. CHN: Asahi. DUR: 45 mins. x ca. 11 eps.; Thu 6 July 2000–14 September 2000.

Yūmi (Tsuruta) and Takashi (Nakamura) are a middle-class couple who have just moved into a new neighborhood. When their young daughter Tsugumi develops a toothache, Yūmi takes her to the dentist, Masaki (Kaneko). However, Masaki begins stalking Yūmi, until Takashi is sulkily forced to take the morning off work and warn off the obsessed man. Before long, their daughter disappears, and Masaki becomes the prime suspect.

Kidnap was one of the critical hits of its season, shocking Japanese audiences with its portrayal of how easily a secure lifestyle could be upset by a madman, even in safe, "crime-free" Japan. Amassing believable events to create unbelievable situations in the style of OUT, *Kidnap* drags the audience away from their safe TV world into a horrific place, putting its superb cast through a gamut of emotions from

terror to loss to revenge—unlike most Japanese dramas, there is no guarantee here of a happy ending. Shot with the uncompromising naturalism of a docudrama, it is noticeably different from its peers, with a languorous pace and none of the comedy business so common to Japanese TV. It also ensures that the identity of the kidnapper (by episode three, killer) is known from the beginning, even to his mother, who steadfastly refuses to cooperate with the police. As in *Silence of the Lambs* and *The Vanishing*, such prior knowledge changes the nature of the drama, discarding the detective formula of murder mystery in favor of an analysis of the process by which the criminal is brought to justice—in fact, he is himself hounded by a determined detective (Yamazaki), who suspects him from the start. The emotional tension is raised through several peripheral torments, all of which combine to force the couple into a living hell comparable to THE CURSE. These include

the attitude of the police (who cut corners by writing Tsugumi's death off as an accident, only to be embarrassed by the parents' own investigation) and the intrusive behavior of the media and paparazzi. Even everyday life takes on a new, menacing aspect—in one scene, Yūmi returns from a frenzied search for her daughter to discover that Takashi, with little else to occupy him, is calmly catching up on some work from the office.

See also **LIMIT**, another kidnapping drama that ran during the same season on Yomiuri TV. Themes: Suzuki—"The Rose," Jeanne D'arc—"Chizu no Nai Bashō" (Unmapped Place).

KIKAIDA *
1972. JPN: *Jinzō Ningen Kikaidā*. PRD: Tōru Hirayama, Susumu Yoshikawa. DIR: Hidetoshi Kitamura, Toyohiko Seyama, Yasutada Nagano. SCR: Masaru Igami, Hideyoshi Nagasaka, Kuniaki Oshikawa, Shōji Shimazu. CAST: Daisaku Ban, Mitsuo Andō, Jun Mizunoe, Masahiro Kamiya, Hajime Izu. CHN: NET (Asahi). DUR: 25 mins. x 89 eps.; Sat 8 July 1972–5 May 1973 (#1); 12 May 1973–30 March 1974 (#2).

Doctor Kōmyōji (Izu) is forced to create cyborg warriors for the evil Dark Destruction Corps. However, he loses his memory after an accident in his laboratory, allowing his latest creation, Kikaidā (Ban), to escape. Taking the name Jirō and hiding out with the doctor's children Mitsuko (Mizunoe) and Masaru (Kamiya), Kikaida fights evil monsters of the week, although he can be temporarily turned to the Dark side if he hears the music of a flute played by his evil nemesis Doctor Gill (Andō).

Unsurprisingly, as it was created by **MASKED RIDER**'s Shōtarō Ishinomori in collaboration with Tōru Hirayama, *Kikaida* has many similarities to other anti-heroes of its day, such as *Cyborg 009* (*AE). Few of its contemporaries have enjoyed such longevity in their original state—reruns of *Kikaida* continue to charm new fans a whole generation after it originally ended.

Only a week after the close of the

first series, but supposedly three years after the final defeat of the Dark Destruction Corps, Kikaida returned in a new incarnation, confusingly titled *Kikaida 01*. Remnants of the Dark band together to form Hakaida, a new evil organization that is battled chiefly by the original Kikaida's "older brother," a cyborg that preceded him on the production line. Since "Jirō" is a common name for a second son, this earlier Kikaida took the human name of "Ichirō," or "first son." As well as fighting off Hakaida's minions, and Gill's new incarnation as "Boss Hakaida," the brothers must fight off a trio of similar Blue, Red, and Silver cyborgs, known collectively as the Hakaida Squad. However, with the eventual defeat of the Haikaida Squad, Gill was resurrected once more, this time by the Shadow Murder Force, yet another criminal organization. Shadow Murder hopes to kill off a billion human beings as part of its plan for world domination, giving Ichirō (Jirō's actor having left to star in the new series *Inazuman*) a new cause to fight for. Meanwhile, Shadow Murder troops constantly try to kidnap two young Japanese boys, Akira and Hiroshi, each of whom has the plans for a super-weapon hidden in his back—compare to a tongue-in-cheek pastiche of this situation in *Those Who Hunt Elves* (*AE).

The original series was broadcast subtitled on KIKU TV in Hawaii in 1974 and the channel has since become known as the "home of Kikaida," keeping both original series in reruns and even arranging for the *Generation Kikaida* (2001) retrospective broadcast. *Kikaida* was released in a subtitled DVD format in the U.S. in 2002. The series was also resurrected in animated form in 2001 (*AE), while Kikaida's sworn enemy got his own spin-off movie, *Mechanical Violator Hakaida* (1995).

Note, the exact spelling of the name Kikaida has been a subject of constant and wearying debate among fans of the show–technically speaking the final "a" should have a macron in English and

be "ā," though this has been dropped in the U.S. Although some still adhere to the "Kikaider" spelling used on Japanese documents of the time, even the series' translators have given in to the inertia of fandom and rendered it as "Kikaida" for the recent American DVD release. "Kikaida" is phonetically more accurate in the U.S., where final "R's" are emphasized. Other countries find it quite mystifying, since both variants are pronounced exactly the same in Britain and Australia.

KINDNESS ALONE MAKES NOT THE MAN

1990. JPN: *Yasashii Dake ga Otoko ja nai*. PRD: N/C. DIR: Tadashi Mafune. SCR: Izō Hashimoto. CAST: Masayuki Watanabe, Akio Ishii, Takayasu Komiya, Satomi Tezuka, Aya Sugimoto. CHN: TV Tokyo. DUR: 45 mins. x 6 eps.; Sun 7 January 1990–11 February 1990.
Makoto (Watanabe) is a salaryman in an electrical goods firm with a reputation as an inveterate womanizer. He eventually marries his girlfriend Hiromi (Sugimoto) but seems unable to give up chasing other women. After only a year, Hiromi tells him that she wants them to break up—compare to **NARITA DIVORCE**. This drama was based on a story by the suspiciously named *Hiromi* Arikawa—possibly someone was settling an old score.

KING OF EDITORS

2000. JPN: *Henshū Ō*. PRD: Yū Moriya, Kenichirō Hobara. DIR: Yūichi Satō. SCR: Takehiko Hata. CAST: Taizō Harada, Kotomi Kyōno, Hitomi Manaka, Katsumi Takahashi, Rei Kikukawa, Yoshinori Okada, Shinobu Ōtake. CHN: Fuji. DUR: 45 mins. x ca. 11 eps.; Tue 10 October 2000–27 December 2000.
Kanpachi (Harada) has been obsessed with the boxing manga *Tomorrow's Joe* (*AE) since he was a child—compare to **HALF DOC**'s love of *Black Jack* (*AE). It inspires him to become a boxer himself but his promising career is cut tragically short by a detached retina. With no idea of what direction he should

take in life, the unemployed former sportsman takes a job at the manga publishers Daigakukan (a thinly disguised combination of the real-life manga publishers Kōdansha and Shōgakukan). He arrives to discover that the company's main cash cow, the schoolgirl superheroine series *Blue Sailor Moon*, is experiencing difficulties. Its creator Kodomari (Okada) has become disenchanted with the direction he has been forced to take his manga—periodic audience feedback calls for more violence and more T&A, and Kodomari cannot bring himself to do it. Meanwhile, the publishers call for an armed response team when they receive a bomb threat at a *Blue Sailor Moon* idol singer audition. Caught in the girls' locker room trying to perform a conjuring trick, Kanpachi is mistaken for a pervert by one of the female editors and chased around the building by an overeager SWAT team.

Despite his run of bad luck, he soon becomes an indispensable part of the editorial team on *Young Shout* magazine, a comic anthology whose artists are plagued by a series of problems. As well as Kodomari's crisis of confidence, Kanpachi must deal with Aki Yashiro (Ōtake), a drunken spinster with an eccentric way of assembling her pages. He must also nurture Sayuri, a pretty newcomer whose moving manga wins a company prize but who is then unceremoniously forced to draw the ludicrous *Sumo First Love* story by *Young Shout*'s uncompromising editor. Sayuri perkily does her best, and Kanpachi's associates help her out by posing as reference. When *Sumo First Love* does not appear to be catching the public eye, Kanpachi begins a guerrilla marketing campaign in local bookshops (compare to the same actor's similar activities in **WEDNESDAY LOVE AFFAIR**), loudly laughing at the strip and then eagerly buying a copy at dozens of local stores.

King of Editors began life in 1993 as a manga itself, drawn by Seiki Tsuchida for the pages of Shōgakukan's *Big Comics Spirits* anthology. The television adaptation dutifully lifts large parts of

Kinpachi Sensei

Tsuchida's original, including footnotes on the manga production process which scroll across the screen at relevant points and on-screen titles keeping the viewer up to date with who's who, at least in the fictional universe. Sadly but understandably, neither manga nor TV version makes it too easy for viewers to guess exactly which if any real-life manga creators are being lampooned. Kanpachi regularly daydreams himself into re-enactments of famous scenes from *Tomorrow's Joe,* and *Blue Sailor Moon*'s inspiration in *Sailor Moon* (*AE) is obvious, but otherwise the viewer is left to indulge in scandalous speculation about which well-known manga artist might have a drinking problem, which readers' darling has been known to abandon cute puppies by the roadside, and which young talent might have used feminine wiles to secure her first contract. Meanwhile, Kanpachi is a veritable manga character come to life—he develops a nosebleed when he sees a girl's panties, he insists on stripping off before going to the bathroom, and his boxing background allows for regular slapstick moments. Its over the top, comedic approach aside, *King of Editors* remains an informative lesson in how

the manga business really works, and amid the farce and slapstick are some detailed analyses of marketing, editorial, and publishing practices in the Japanese industry. However, the TV version took several years to make it off the drawing board—perhaps certain publishers were not 100% happy about the way they were portrayed. Theme: Triceratops—"Fall Again."

KING'S RESTAURANT *
1995. JPN: *Ōsama no Restaurant.* AKA: *Belle Equipe.* PRD: Shizuo Sekiguchi. DIR: Masayuki Suzuki. SCR: Kōki Mitani. CAST: Kōshirō Matsumoto, Michitaka Tsutsui, Tomoko Yamaguchi, Kyōka Suzuki, Masahiko Nishimura. CHN: Fuji. DUR: 45 mins. x 11 eps.; Wed 19 April 1995–5 July 1995.

The famous French restaurant Belle Equipe goes into a slump after the owner Noritomo (Nishimura) loses interest. Noritomo's father dies but his will exhorts Noritomo's half brother Rokurō (Tsutsui) to help turn around the fortunes of the restaurant. Rokuro dutifully tracks down the restaurant's former star chef Sengoku (Matsumoto), a difficult personality but with an undeniable talent with food. Though the other members of the staff rebel, they eventually come to appreciate that Sengoku's maverick methods will win back the customers. He also inspires the listless waitress Shizuka (Yamaguchi) to study to be a cook herself. However, these methods also cause tension, as when the perfectionist Sengoku calls for the dismissal of the patisserie chef Inage (Zen Kajihara), claiming that the Belle Equipe desserts are not up to gourmet standard.

When Rokurō and Sengoku arrive as customers, Shizuka is forced to put her newfound talents through their paces to cook a meal, while Inage risks his job by creating a new dessert for Sengoku—compare to ANTIQUE. Though Sengoku still has reservations, he applauds Inage's style.

NINZABURŌ FURUHATA creator Kōki Mitani claimed that his original inspiration for this gourmet drama was the

U.S. baseball movie *Bad News Bears* (1976), in which a similar group of no-hopers succeed against overwhelming odds. After two sequels, the second of which featured the titular Bears playing in Japan, the subsequent 1979 TV series gained a 24.1% rating with the Japanese audience.

In combining food with the clichés of other dramas, Mitani helped create a healthy subgenre of TV drama, imitated a mere two seasons later in THE CHEF and subsequently in SOMMELIER and DELICIOUS LIAISONS. However, Mitani's plotting was nothing too original on its own, with roots that stretch back to *Oishinbo* (*AE) and Jūzō Itami's ultimate food movie *Tampopo* (1986). However, Mitani did manage to cut costs by shooting almost all his series in the restaurant itself and assembled an interesting cast from radically different disciplines, including kabuki actor Kōshirō Matsumoto as the stoic chef and LONG VACATION's Yamaguchi as the female lead. The cooking was supervised by Yukio Hattori, director of the East Japan Culinary School Association and the chief executive of the French Culinary Academy Association in Japan, known to American viewers from his appearances in *Iron Chef.* Broadcast in the U.S. with English subtitles on KTSF TV. Theme: Tsuyoshi Hirai—"Precious Junk." Peak rating: 20.4%.

KINPACHI SENSEI *
1979. JPN: *San-nen B-gumi Kinpachi Sensei.* PRD: Mitsuru Yanai. DIR: Jirō Shōno, Kanji Takenoshita, Keiichi Satō, Yutaka Takahata. SCR: Mieko Osanai, Takako Shigemori. CAST: Tetsuya Takeda, Mitsuko Baishō, Harue Akagi, Yūko Natori, Ichirō Zaitsu, Kaoru Sugita, Toshihiko Tahara, Yoshio Nomura, Masahiko Kondō, Shingo Tsurumi, Satomi Kobayashi, Junko Mihara. CHN: TBS. DUR: 45 mins. x ca. 120 eps.; Fri 26 October 1979–28 March 1980 (#1); 3 October 1980–27 March 1981 (#2); 10 October 1988–26 December 1988 (#3); 12 October 1995–28 March

1996 (#4); 14 October 1999–30 March 2000 (#5); 11 October 2001–28 March 2002 (#6).

New teacher Kinpachi Sakamoto (long-haired former folk singer Takeda) is posted to Sakura Junior High, where he is placed in charge of ninth grade students facing a high school entrance exam. Unlike many other teachers (but exactly like the protagonists of **FLY! YOUTHS** and **ZEALOUS TIMES**, to name but two predecessors), Kinpachi is filled with a passion for education and idealism for his students' potential. However, his rather old-fashioned, innocent optimism about teaching must face up to some hard knocks from life in the modern world, including a 15-year-old girl, Yukino (Sugita), who becomes pregnant by her classmate Tamotsu (Tsurumi). Tamotsu's parents arrange for him to move to another school but he elects to stay when Yukino reveals that she is keeping the baby. Ever one for a moral message, Kinpachi uses the incident as a chance to give his class a lecture about the meaning of love—compare to actor Takeda's role in the later **101ST PROPOSAL**. He also confronts those teachers whose attitudes toward such teen problems are simply to sweep them under the carpet.

Released at the height of media hand-wringing about the pointless high pressure "exam hell" of the Japanese school system, *KS* was unafraid to deal with serious themes alongside perennial school drama favorites—bullying, conformity, corrupt teachers, and growing pains. After the success of the initial two seasons, the series went into partial hiatus—three of the boys from the first season of *KS*, Toshihiko Tahara, Masahiko Kondō, and Yoshio Nomura, went on to become an idol group, the Tanokin Trio. *KS* returned in numerous TV-movie specials throughout the 1980s, in October 1982, 1983, 1984, and 1985; December 1985, 1986, and 1987; March 1989; and December 1990.

During that period, the series settled into the public consciousness as the archetypal school drama. Takeda, who took his role so seriously that he reputedly used to control the child actors *offscreen* as well as on, became known as the nation's favorite teacher since *Botchan* (*AE). After an abortive third season in 1988, the series returned in earnest in 1995, a whole generation after its premier. With its original child/parent audience now a generation older and ready to watch the show in the company of their grandchildren/children, *KS* enjoyed a powerful renaissance and remains a Japanese cultural icon. Successive seasons have repeated the *KS* formula, of the earnest teacher inspiring his young charges, throwing in issues of the day such as environmental pollution and gay rights. Meanwhile, Kinpachi loses his wife to cancer and discovers that his son Kosaku has developed a type of leukemia—true to the spirit of the teacher's vocation, Kosaku encourages his father to concentrate on his pupils, even as he himself undergoes chemotherapy. Other modern-themed episodes include a girl who is kidnapped by a man she meets on the Internet and a student whose father is wrongly accused of murder and happened to be a litigation lawyer, much to the distress of the journalists who printed the original accusation. Old episodes remain a good back catalogue cash cow on video, as they often depict the TV debuts of the drama stars of the future.

The specter of *KS* hovers over any other attempt to make a drama about an educator, leading to blatant copies such as **SCHOOL TEACHER** or shows made in deliberate reaction to it, such as **GTO**. More recent seasons have been broadcast in the U.S. with English subtitles on KIKU TV.

Theme: Kaientai—"Okuru Kotoba" (A Word I Give to You). This song was recorded by Takeda's old band in 1980 and not only soared to the top of the Japanese pop charts but also remains a regular feature of many middle and high school graduations.

KINSHIRŌ TŌYAMA'S BEAUTY SALON

1994. JPN: *Tōyama Kinshirō Biyōshitsu.* PRD: Yoshinobu Kosugi. DIR: Nobuo Mizuta. SCR: Masaki Fukasawa, Hiroshi Matsuki. CAST: Toshiyuki Nishida, Rina Katase, Mari Natsuki, Minako Honda, Shunsuke Matsuoka, Ryūhei Uwashima. CHN: NTV. DUR: 45 mins. x 11 eps.; Sat 9 July 1994–24 September 1994.

After the death of his father, Kinshirō (Nishida) continues to run the small family barbershop business. His debt-ridden brother Ginpei (Uwashima) sells off his 50% share of the business to a developer, who insists on converting the shop into a fashionable beauty salon. With little choice but to do as he is told, Kinshirō finds himself forced to take a job there as a lowly shampoo boy. A tongue-in-cheek retelling of the legendary stories of **TŌYAMA NO KINSAN**. Theme: Kazumasa Oda—"Manatsu no Koi" (Midsummer Love).

KISARAZU CAT'S EYE

2002. PRD: Akira Isoyama. DIR: Fuminori Kaneko. SCR: Kankurō Kudō. CAST: Junichi Okada, Shō Sakurai, Wakana Sakai, Sadao Abe, Aiko Morishita, Hiroko Yakushimaru. CHN: TBS. DUR: 45 mins. x ca. 11 eps.; Fri 18 January 2002–?? March 2002.

Twenty-one-year-old Kōhei (Okada from V6) is a former high school baseball player, who works in his Dad's barber shop. One day, he is told that he has cancer and that he only has six months to live. In order to realize some of his life's ambitions, he forms a gang of thieves with his old school buddies, who still play on weekends for the baseball team Kisarazu Cats. They name the gang Cat's Eye and target their former high school baseball team manager Nekota (Abe), who blamed Kōhei for losing a very important match before graduation. When the gang succeed in stealing Nekota's car, Kōhei tells his friends about his illness. **IKEBUKURO WEST GATE PARK** writer Kudō takes another angle on the kids playing as criminals idea here,

Koseidon

pastiching Tsukasa Hōjō's manga/anime *Cat's Eye* (*AE). Theme: Arashi—"A Day in Our Life."

KANTARŌ TERAUCHI AND FAMILY

1974. JPN: *Terauchi Kantarō Ikka*. PRD: Mitsuhiko Hisayo. DIR: Mitsuhiko Hisayo. SCR: Kuniko Mukōda. CAST: Asei Kobayashi, Hideki Saijō, Chiho Yūki, Meiko Kaji, Miyoko Asada, Tatsuya Fuji, Haruko Katō. CHN: TBS. DUR: 45 mins. x ca. 26 eps.; Wed 16 January 1974–9 October 1974 (#1); ?? April 1975–5 November 1975 (#2). Kantarō (Kobayashi) is a stone mason like his father and his father before him. The straight-talking, gruff artisan also places great stock in human relationships and resolutely corrects any error he makes without a word or a second thought. In short, he is the archetypal Japanese father, an idealized image often regarded as a fossil from the good old days, whenever they were.

He lives with his family—wife Satoko (Katō), his mother Kin (Yūki), his son Shūhei (Saijō), and his daughter Shizue (Kaji), who was crippled owing to an accident for which Kantarō blames himself. The final family member is Miyoko (Asada), their maid.

Created by the same Kuniko Mukōda who gave Japan **IT'S TIME** and who reputedly used her own father as inspiration, *KT&F* is packed full of sharp observations on the minutiae of family life—unafraid to make its viewers laugh (Kin has a teenager's obsession with male idol singers), cry, or even shift uncomfortably (Kantarō must face up to the fact that his own son has been charged with sexual assault). The inclusion of a disabled character shattered many taboos of the time and set the scene for the vast number of disability dramas that would be created by the next generation of writers in the 1990s. The show was also

unafraid of experimenting with the TV format, with such gimmicks as onscreen recipes for the meals the Terauchi family were seen eating. Artist Tadanori Yokō, who worked on designs for the series, also appeared in a cameo role. Actress Chiho Yūki later changed her name to Kirin Kiki, by which she is known in 1990s drama cast lists.

KŌENJI SHOPPING MALL

1990. JPN: *Kōenji Junjō Shōtengai*. PRD: N/C. DIR: Nobuo Yamashō. SCR: Motofumi Tomikawa. CAST: Tatsuya Fuji, Yoshie Ichige, Natsuko Kahara, Shōhei Yamamoto, Yasuko Sawaguchi. CHN: Asahi. DUR: 45 mins. x 4 eps.; Thu 12 April 1990–3 May 1990. In 1962, there are about 80 shops in front of Kōenji station. Shōichi (Yamamoto) works in the family shop selling dried foods and witnesses the changes brought about by time and economic shifts in Japan. Based on a novel of the same name by Shōichi Nejime, *KSM* cunningly approaches life in a shopping arcade as if it were the last refuge of traditional village life in the modern world. Where else would the world comprise just a handful of families, forced into everyday proximity and also to band together against outside threats? Compare to *Abeno Bridge Magical Mall* (*AE). Theme: Kyū Sakamoto—"Ue o Muite Arukō" (I'll Walk with My Head Up). NB: The song was previously released in the U.S. in 1963 under the title "Sukiyaki," and became the only Japanese song to ever reach number one on the *Billboard* charts.

KOSEIDON

1978. JPN: *Kyōryū Sentai Koseidon*. AKA: *Dinosaur Task Force Koseidon*. PRD: Hiroshi Ishikawa, Atsushi Ōki, San Tsuburaya. DIR: Tōru Sotoyama, Shōhei Tōjō, Kimio Hirayama. SCR: Masaki Tsuji, Narimitsu Taguchi, Hiroyasu Yamaura, Yasushi Hirano, Bunzō Wakatsuki, Nanase Nishizawa. CAST: Tetsuya Ōnishi, Keiji Mikei, Takako Kawasaki, Miyuki Ichijō, Hiroyuki

Kumagai, Machiko Nagahama, Nanami Murano, Tetsuo Yamamura, Tōru Kawai. CHN: TVT. DUR: 45 mins. x 52 eps.; Thu 7 July 1978–29 June 1979. The members of the Time Patrol Koseidon team are obliged to save the Earth from attack by aliens in the distant past. The Godmes race have chosen to invade Earth during the age of the dinosaurs and are using creatures of the time, such as the triceratops and tyrannodon, to carry out their evil mission. The heroically named Gō Toki (Ōnishi, his character's name means "Go Time!") leads the team, whose secret weapon is the Human Cannon Koseider. The series was immensely successful—Tsuburaya's studio history proudly recalls how the famous "Beat" Takeshi Kitano even discussed it on his radio show. Accordingly, as the initial 26 episodes came to a close with the defeat of the Godmes Emperor, the series was allowed to continue and became the first Tsuburaya program to have an unbroken year-long run. For the latter half of the run, the Koseidon team became time detectives, searching for criminals who had evaded justice by leaping back to the time of the dinosaurs. Compare to BORN FREE and EISENBORG, previous Tsuburaya shows that replaced the traditional alien monsters of ULTRAMAN with creatures that owed at least some relationship to real creatures from the Earth's past. The next Japanese kids' show to use dinosaurs was over a decade away but it would be MIGHTY MORPHIN' POWER RANGERS.

KŌSHIEN AND OUR YOUTH
1983. JPN: Dakara Seishun Nakimushi Kōshien. PRD: Atsumi Yajima. DIR: Noriaki Sasahara, Tetsushi Nakamura. SCR: Man Izawa. CAST: Kinya Aikawa, Yōko Kikuchi, Rika Abiko, Junichi Nitta, Jirō Esawa, Seiichi Matsumoto, Takeshi Ōta. CHN: NHK. DUR: 25 mins. x 13 eps.; Wed 14 June 1983–11 October 1983.
Ryūnosuke (Aikawa) is the coach of Aoba High School baseball club. His daughter Natsuko (Kikuchi) loathes

baseball because her father was too busy looking after his baseball team to care for her dying mother. She discovers that her father plans to invite his old teammate's son Asahi (Ōta) onto the team and bitterly plots against them. Meanwhile, she is courted by Shingo (Esawa), an ace pitcher from Yōmei High School but rebuffs his advances. Asahi helps Ryūnosuke to build up a decent baseball team and Natsuko starts to develop an interest in him. When she learns that his parents met each other through baseball, she decides to join the club to look after the boys and help fulfill her father's dream of winning at Kōshien, the semi-annual national high school baseball championship. Based on the manga Ah! Seishun no Kōshien (Ah! Kōshien of Our Youth) by JINBE creator Mitsuru Adachi, whose baseball-themed works were also animated—e.g., Touch (*AE), Slow Step (*AE), Miyuki (*AE), and Nine (*AE). Compare to the previous year's KŌSHIEN AND OUR SUMMER HOPE.

KŌSHIEN AND OUR SUMMER HOPE
1982. JPN: Oretachi Natsuki to Kōshien. PRD: Kanae Mayuzumi. DIR: Noriaki Sasahara, Tetsushi Nakamura. SCR: Yumiko Takahoshi. CAST: Natsuki Aida, Yoshinori Ninohe, Masakazu Sawamura, Hitoshi Hirao, Akira Yamaguchi, Tōru Minegishi. CHN: NHK. DUR: 30 mins. x 5 eps.; Mon 2 August 1982–6 August 1982.
Natsuki (as herself) is an all-girls school student who deliberately transfers to a coed establishment with the best baseball team in the area. Announcing to the coach (Minegishi) that she wants to join the baseball team, she is laughed out of his office but she persists in asking him every day. When he jokingly tells her to shave her head she does so and he eventually relents. Natsuki faces opposition from many other members of the establishment and gamely endures the same tests and hazings as the boys on the team. However, she is defeated by district rules, which do not permit girls to

play on a boys' baseball team and is forced to sit out the season's first game. When a team member is injured, the other team members debate whether to allow Natsuki to replace him. They eventually decide to let her play, even though they know this violation of the rules will disqualify them from playing in the finals at Kōshien Stadium if they make it that far.
The story began as Yakyūkyō no Uta o Utau Musume (The Girl Who Sang the Baseball-Crazy Song), submitted by Takahoshi to a script-writing contest and snapped up for adaptation in the days when Mitsuru Adachi's Touch (*AE) was one of Japan's most popular new manga—see KŌSHIEN AND OUR YOUTH. Note that "summer hope" in Japanese is written natsu-ki. Theme: Yoshimi Iwasaki—"Moshimo" (If Only).

KŌSUKE MIZUMORE
1974. JPN: Mizumore Kōsuke. PRD: Tōru Ueno, Takamasa Yamamoto. DIR: Shigeo Tanaka. SCR: Hiroshi Matsuki. CAST: Tetsuo Ishidate, Hiromi Murata, Daijirō Harada, Harue Akagi, Hiromi Murachi, Hisaya Morishige. CHN: NTV. DUR: 45 mins. x 25 eps.; Sun 13 October 1974–30 March 1975.
Kōsuke (Ishidate) leaves home to become an itinerant rock drummer. His father Yasutarō (Morishige), realizes that he has little choice but to pass on the family plumbing business to Kōsuke's younger brother Teruo (Harada). Six years after Kōsuke's departure, Yasutarō falls seriously ill and confesses to the boys that he is not their real father. In fact, their father was a military chief, who died saving Yasutarō's life in battle. When their mother died soon afterward, the boys were left orphaned, leading Yasutarō to adopt them. In time, his neighbor Takiyo (Akagi) moved in with her daughter Asami (Murachi), whom the boys have always assumed was their half sister.
Obliged to return and care for his family, Kōsuke tries to become a

plumber but fails spectacularly. He prepares to run from his new career but his siblings accuse him of never standing up to his responsibilities. Somehow, he gets his family through the hard times, in a drama that would later influence **UNDER ONE ROOF**. Theme: Singers Three—"Mizumore Kōsuke."

KOWLOON RENDEZVOUS

2002. JPN: *Kowloon de Aimashō*. AKA: *See You in Kowloon*. PRD: Shunji Muguruma. DIR: Moto Sasaki, Takayuki Sashida, Akiko Kamiyama. SCR: Miyuki Noe. CAST: Yuriko Ishida, Ryūichi Kawamura, Kyōko Hasegawa, Tsuyoshi Ihara, Mikihisa Azuma. CHN: Asahi. DUR: 45 mins. x ca. 11 eps.; Fri 12 April 2002–28 June 2002.
Kaoru Saegusa (Ishida) is a 30-year-old office lady working for Ōedo Travel and secretly conducting an affair with her married boss Kōsuke Akazawa (Ihara). Her colleague Shūtaro in the Hong Kong office worships her from afar but is too shy to make his feelings known. Meanwhile, the half-Chinese Jasmine (Hasegawa) doggedly pursues Shūtarō's womanizing colleague Dai (Azuma).

Based on a manga by Fumi Saimon, *KR* replays the love polygon of her earlier **TOKYO LOVE STORY** but with a foreign focus typical of a high-profile drama in the 21st century—further proof, if ever there was any doubt, of the author's ability to keep moving with the times. Note Ryūichi Kawamura, former member of rock band Luna Sea, cast against type here as a guy who never seems to get the girls. Theme: Ryūichi Kawamura—"Sugar Lady."

KYOTO UNSOLVED CASES

1999. JPN: *Kyōto Meikyū Annai*. PRD: Takashi Ido. DIR: Naosuke Kurosawa, Mitsumasa Saitō. SCR: Masato Hayashi, Yoshinori Watanabe, Yūichi Higure, Katsuaki Chaki. CAST: Isamu Hashimoto, Yōko Nogiwa, Nanako Ōkōchi, Kazuhiko Nishimura, Bengal. CHN: Asahi. DUR: 45 mins. x 46 eps.; Thu 14 January 1999–11 March 1999 (#1); 20 January 2000–16 March 2000 (#2); 18 January 2001–21 June 2001 (#3); 10 January 2002–21 March 2002 (#4).
Journalist Sugiura (Hashimoto) moves to Kyoto to work at the press club at the Kyoto Metropolitan Police, leaving

his wife behind in Tokyo. Though he often talks to his wife on the phone (*Columbo*-style, she never appears), he becomes so engrossed in the Kyoto crime scene that he never goes home. Instead, he helps solve Kyoto crimes by using his knowledge of incidents from the past—much more sensible than his local counterpart, the **GEISHA DETECTIVE**.

The second season lost Bengal and added Emi Ōji and Kōji Matoba to replace Nanako Ōkōchi and Kazuhiko Nishimura. By the third season, the series' success was assured and the number of episodes was doubled. However, the third season also saw noticeable changes. Narrative coherence was maintained through the rare step of having a single writer (Takuya Nishioka) producing all the scripts but since he was not one of the original team, he allowed the formula to alter. After the arrival of Nishioka as his rival, Sugiura became less proactive in sniffing out cases, whereas his old self would be champing at the bit to start investigating. The offscreen Mrs. Sugiura was only mentioned once thereafter. Theme: Rumiko Kubo—"Perfect Circle."

LABYRINTH

1999. PRD: Osamu Shigematsu, Yoshiki Tanaka. DIR: Nozomu Amemiya. SCR: Toshio Terada. CAST: Atsurō Watabe, Sachiko Sakurai, Takeshi Naitō, Naoki Hosaka, Yōko Moriguchi. CHN: NTV. DUR: 45 mins. x 11 eps.; Wed 21 April 1999–30 June 1999.

After a patient dies as the result of a surgical error, nurse Natsuko (Moriguchi) cannot live with the guilt and throws herself from the roof. Although her life is saved, she becomes a vegetable and dies a year later, uttering a single word: *"papillon."* Her brother Yūichirō (Watabe), who saw her fall, finds a letter when sorting through her belongings which brings the nature of her "suicide" into question. Suspecting that head doctor Katsuhiko Sonobe (Naitō) is somehow responsible for his sister's death, Yūichirō takes a job at the hospital and starts planning his revenge. Compare to HEAVEN'S COINS. Theme: Toshiyuki Makihara—"Hungry Spider."

LADY DOCTOR'S CASE FILE

1991. JPN: *Geka Byōtō Joi no Jiken File.* PRD: N/C. DIR: Haruo Kazukura. SCR: Hideyoshi Nagasaka, Yū Kaneko. CAST: Yūko Kotegawa, Saburō Tokitō, Mami Yamase, Kōichirō Shimizu, Ayaka Ōno. CHN: Asahi. DUR: 45 mins. x 11 eps.; Thu 11 July 1991–19 September 1991.

Tomoko (Kotegawa) is a surgeon and a police medical officer. In collaboration with medical examiner Mutō (Tokitō), she helps solve cases, such as saving a mother and daughter from an unsuccessful suicide bid.

LADY PROSECUTOR'S CASE FILE

1993. JPN: *Onna Kenji no Jiken File.* PRD: N/C. DIR: Minoru Matsushima. SCR: Katsuyuki Nakamura. CAST: Yasuko Sawaguchi, Masanobu Takashima, Yōko Nogiwa, Saya Takagi, Yōsuke Natsuki. CHN: Asahi. DUR: 45 mins. x 10 eps.; Thu 21 October 1993–16 December 1993.

Yoshika (Sawaguchi) just started working as a prosecutor. She solves cases with the aid of her wise seniors Shizue (Nogiwa) and Sonoko (Takagi), supported by her journalist husband Kazuki (Takashima). Theme: Class—"Mō Kimi o Hanasanai" (I Won't Let You Go).

LADY OF THE MANOR

2001. JPN: *Honke no Yome.* AKA: *My Married [sic], Bride of the Estate.* PRD: Masahiro Kunimoto, Hitoshi Tsugiya, Hiroya Fujii, Michihiko Suwa. DIR: Hiroya Fujii, Masahiro Kunimoto, Kōichi Okamoto. SCR: Mayumi Nakatani. CAST: Shima Iwashita, Vivian Hsu, Shunsuke Nakamura, Mie Nakao, Toshie Negishi, Tarō Ishida, Saki Takaoka, Kei Tani, Yoshiko Tanaka, Ittoku Kishibe, Judy Ong, Noriko Sakai. CHN: Yomiuri (NTV). DUR: 45 mins. x 10 eps.; Mon 8 October 2001–12 December 2001.

Seven months after their marriage in Taiwan, businessman Shinji Yamada (Nakamura) and his half-Chinese wife Nozomi (Hsu) visit his wealthy landowner family in Okunosato, a tiny country hamlet outside Tokyo. They arrive to find Shinji's elder brother Yutaka has been disinherited after running out on the family. Shinji is now expected to become the lord of the manor on his father's death, and fearsome matriarch Kin (Iwashita) sternly disapproves of her grandson's yuppie wife.

Nozomi doesn't make the best of impressions—she inadvertently addresses her in-laws as *"the honorable old bats,"* scatters the ancestral memorial tablets, prepares a banquet of repulsive Chinese delicacies, and even (the horror!) spits out her sashimi. Kin icily informs her that Shinji should find a more acceptable *Japanese* spouse—as if on cue, his former high school sweetheart Yuriko (pop star Sakai in a cameo role) soon comes round for tea. But Nozomi refuses to leave her husband's side until the family accepts her. Though she enjoys limited support from Shinji's father Takashi (Kishibe), mother Haruko (Tanaka), and sister Reiko (Nakao), she incurs the undying enmity of the aforementioned trio of "old bat" aunties and *all* quake in fear of Kin's wrath. Nozomi comes to realize that Kin herself was once an outsider in the family and that much of the hazing is merely a test to ensure that she has the strength of character to survive life as a future lady of the manor and mother of the son and heir. The obligatory romantic subplot comes in the form of Shinji's sister Reiko, who is conducting a secret affair with Noboru, the firstborn son of the rival Okuyama clan, who have been feuding with the Yamadas for over a century over an unmentionable insult. Meanwhile, a succession of troublesome guests tramp through the Yamada mansion, including Nozomi's feisty mother Anhua (Ong) and Americanized brother Takuya, whose trip to Japan inspires him to become a florist.

Based on the *Office You* manga serial by Rika Okada, *Lady of the Manor* seems tailor-made for the 21st-century drama audience. As with its near contemporaries **FIGHTING GIRL** and **LOVE 2000**, it plays to the wider viewership in neighboring Asian countries. Nozomi and Anhua are painted as ultra-modern, liberated women, pluckily blowing the cobwebs away from dusty Japanese tradition. Or at least, that's how the show might look to a foreign audience—Japanese viewers get to laugh at hapless foreign *nouveaux riches* who have never arranged a flower in their lives, stumble awkwardly in kimono, and stick out a mile amid the sophisticated country elite. There are thus two sides to every joke, guaranteeing that *LotM* is a show that pleases most of its audience most of the time. However, Nozomi can only ruin dinner or trash a tea ceremony so often—as with the similar in-law appeasement of **SHOTGUN MARRIAGE**, the episodes occasionally fall into a formulaic rut of misunderstanding, argument, sulking, and reconciliation, albeit padded with a survey of Japanese country customs that is interesting in itself. The cast's behavior becomes increasingly juvenile as the series progresses, but the story is held together by Shima Iwashita, still radiant in her sixties, whose sternly deadpan performance as Kin is scheming and scary, sporadically sympathetic, but always funny. She effortlessly dominates her

every scene, although when she argues with Nozomi's mother, the battle is the scariest on Japanese screens since Godzilla versus Mothra. Compare to other in-laws from hell in **THE CURSE** and **HOUSE OF THE DEVILS**. Theme: Dreams Come True—"Marry Me."

LADY REPORTER: KEIKO TACHIBANA

1992. JPN: *Jikenkisha Tachibana Keiko*. PRD: Atsushi Satō. DIR: Mitsunori Morita. SCR: Mitsuo Kuroto. CAST: Yuki Saitō, Narimi Arimori, Nenji Kobayashi, Karin Yamaguchi, Michiko Haneda, Yasushi Mukōsawa. CHN: Asahi. DUR: 45 mins. x 11 eps.; Thu 9 April 1992–18 June 1992.

Keiko (Saitō) is a reporter with ATB TV station who receives coded messages from Sugiyama (Mukōsawa), a man who expresses extreme hatred for her father. The next day, a special unit from the public prosecutor's office places Matsuno Products, her father's firm, under investigation. Theme: Maki Ōguro—"Stop-motion: Eien ni" (Stop-motion: Forever).

LAKE OF MIST

1974. JPN: *Kiri no Mizuumi*. PRD: Masaharu Morita. DIR: Minoru Hanabusa. SCR: Kazuya Sunada. CAST: Yukari Uehara, Isao Kimura, Hitomi Nakahara, Taizō Sayama, Hiroo Oikawa. CHN: NHK. DUR: 25 mins. x 6 eps.; Mon 9 September 1974–18 September 1974.

Teenage runaway Kumiko Uno (Uehara) accepts a lift from middle-aged man Tadahira Ōike (Kimura). He offers her a place to stay at the lakeside bungalow next to his, whose landlord is apparently absent. She awakes the next day to find that Tadahira has gone, leaving only a boat floating in the lake and all the appearance of a watery suicide.

As the returning landlord and the police begin an investigation, Kumiko conceals her true identity, afraid of the repercussions if she admits to having run away from home. The police already want Tadahira on an embezzle-

ment charge and believe Kumiko is the mysterious "Kaori" with whom he was on the run. The police find a bottle of sleeping pills in Tadahira's room and are prepared to believe the suicide story, but his wife, brother Kōhei (Kimura again), and son Takashi (Sayama) suspect that Kumiko has murdered him.

However, Kumiko suspects that the true murderer is Kōhei, who posed as his own brother to take her to the lake in the hopes that she will confirm the story as the closest thing to a witness. Kōhei gives himself away by addressing her by her real name, which he can't possibly have known unless he was the man who drove her to the lake. He confesses to the murder of Tadahira and to faking the suicide in order to atone for his brother's embezzlement shame.

Released and relieved, Kumiko returns home and apologizes to her family, only to see Tadahira and the real Kaori in a café a few days later. Based on the story *Hada-Iro no Tsuki* (*Skin-Colored Moon*) by Jūran Hisao, and far too good for the children's audience at which it was supposedly aimed.

LAND THIEF

1973. JPN: *Kunitori Monogatari*. PRD: Taiji Nagasawa. DIR: Akira Saitō. SCR: Yasuko Ōno. CAST: Mikijirō Hira, Hideki Takahashi, Masaomi Kondō, Junko Ikeuchi, Keiko Matsuzaka, Shōhei Hino. CHN: NHK. DUR: 45 mins. x ca. 50 eps.; Sun 7 January 1973–30 December 1973.

Dōsan (Hira), aka The Viper, is an oil trader in the 16th century who claws his way up the social ladder until he is a lord. A servant of the Nagai family, themselves attached to the Sanuki clan who protect Mino, he destroys his boss, seizes power from the deputy protector Saitō, and changes his name to Dōsan *Saitō* to imply he deserves the post. Destroying the Mino clan, Dōsan becomes the protector of the Mino region, before being beheaded by his own son in 1556.

The death of Dōsan allows his old

rival **Nobunaga** (Takahashi), who has lain in wait since marrying Dōsan's daughter Koihime (Matsuzaka), to extend his own power into the Mino region. Now in a position to dominate an important strategic area of Japan, Nobunaga jumps at the chance to "help" his ally Yoshiaki, using the request for aid as an excuse to invade Kyoto and install Yoshiaki as the new Ashikaga Shogun. Thereby, Nobunaga is able to become the real ruler of Japan, through the puppet Shogun, setting up the events of the later **Hideyoshi**. Based on a novel by **As If in Flight** creator Ryōtarō Shiba, which impressively dramatized a period of "*gekokujō*," in which the "low dominated the high."

LAST LOVE *

1997. JPN: *Saigo no Koi*. PRD: Seiichirō Kijima. DIR: Jirō Shōno, Naoyuki Yokoi. SCR: Eriko Kitagawa. CAST: Masahiro Nakai, Takako Tokiwa, Naomi Hosokawa. CHN: TBS. DUR: 45 mins. x 11 eps.; Fri 11 July 1997–19 September 1997.

Sixth-year medical student Tōru (Nakai from SMAP) callously rebuffs an approach from prostitute Aki (Tokiwa). Some time later, the couple meet again at Keiyū Hospital, when Aki is revealed to be the sister of Tōru's first patient, a boy called Jun. Of course, Aki is a "good girl" after all, forced to sell herself to pay for her brother's operation. Tōru tries to dissuade Aki from her career but she points out that he can offer no alternative. Aki takes a job in the Royal Staff brothel and eventually Jun's operation is paid for. Once Aki's sisterly duties are discharged, Jun is adopted by a couple from Shizuoka, leaving his sister alone with her debts and her inadvertent new career. Poorly concealing the fact that he is falling for Aki, Tōru begins to ask her out on dates and even arranges for her to travel to Shizuoka to see her beloved brother. However, his colleague Misako (Hosokawa) wants him for herself and tries several ruses to separate him from

Aki. Tōru tries to reintroduce Aki into "civilized" society, but her old life soon catches up with her—compare to **Please God! Just a Little More Time**, which has a different way of disapproving.

The world's oldest profession is also the source of one of drama's oldest clichés—the hooker with a heart of gold. *Pretty Woman* (1990) glamorized prostitution for a materialist decade but also offered viewers a fairy-tale ending. We are led to believe that its leads were meant for each other and that their roles as tart and trick were merely an obstacle to be overcome, like a guardian dragon or a fast flowing river. *Last Love* takes a similar attitude, presenting the viewer with two lovable middle-class leads, one of whom has fallen on hard times and merely seeks a temporary career in the sex trade out of a Confucian sense of filial piety. It asks if it is possible to save her now that she has tasted forbidden fruit—like the protagonist of **Lipstick**, Tōru wonders whether the girl he loves is a wife-in-waiting or irredeemably damaged goods.

Such debates should be contrasted with the *enjo kōsai* (subsidized dating) epidemic that was supposedly rocking Japan at the time—overenthusiastic tabloids alleged that schoolgirls were selling themselves so they could afford designer accessories. Such scaremongering aside (it doesn't *only* happen in Japan, and it's as if the media preferred their hookers to be starving drug addicts), *Last Love* was one of several dramas that seemed to have been indirectly inspired by the scandal—see also **The Stand-In**, **Single Life**, and **Tennen Shōjo Mann**. Broadcast in the U.S. with English subtitles on KIKU TV. Theme: Kazumasa Oda—"Tsutaetai Koto ga Arunda" (I Have Something To Tell You). Peak rating: 20.4%.

LAST SONG, THE

1998. JPN: *Seikimatsu no Uta*. AKA: *End of the Century Song, The*. PRD: Takashi Umehara. DIR: Hidenobu Hosono, Tomoaki Koga, Tarō Ōtani. SCR: Shinji

Last Love

Nojima. CAST: Yutaka Takenouchi, Yoshino Kimura, Megumi Matsumoto, Tsutomu Yamazaki, Hinano Yoshikawa, Ryōko Hirosue, Keiko Tōyama, Yōsuke Saitō, Erika Oda, Eiko Nagashima. CHN: NTV. DUR: 45 mins. x 11 eps.; Wed 14 October 1998–23 December 1998.

Noa (Takenouchi) has been jilted at the altar. Natsuo Momose (Yamazaki) is deeply in debt to loan sharks after failing to win a hard-fought election for university chancellor. Both men decide to throw themselves off a building but are deterred by a passerby and decide to do something else. They move in together and begin work on a submarine—a Noah and Moses for the modern age! Their relationship also allows writer Nojima, creator of **Beauty** and **Lipstick**, to explore philosophical questions about love, such as when Noa meets Sumire (Hirosue), a female ghost who is invisible to her former lover because he does not believe love is eternal. By meeting Sumire, Noa realizes that his relationship with his former fiancée was not real love and he begins a quest to find it through observing a succession of self-contained romantic tales with big name guest stars. Blind Kyōko (Tōyama) is blissfully happy in her relationship with the middle-aged Kōrogi (Saitō) but deserts him after an operation restores her sight and with it her greed. Itsumi (Oda) has a medical condition that means she cannot be exposed to sunlight, although she commits suicide by doing just that in order to prove her love for Noa.

Later episodes include similar meditations, introducing artful twists and dilemmas to straightforward romances. A father must decide between keeping his daughter by his side or losing her to allow her to pursue her own dreams. A relationship is destroyed after a niggling doubt assumes giant proportions; a genius demands to be loved to a higher degree than "normal" people (compare to **TRANSPARENT**); and a widow debates how best to show her love—suicide or living with the memories. The script is not afraid to stray into areas of science fiction—the episode on narcissism concentrates on a scientist who has lost his family due to his obsession with his research, who has now recreated them in the form of undiscerning clones who make no unwelcome demands. Such frictions are also the subject of the ninth episode, which questions whether the course of true love should always run smooth—can a couple have a row and still be in love?

The final episodes turn the lens of inquiry onto the leads themselves, as the dying Natsuo asks Noa to find his one true love, Fuyuko (Nagashima)—note that the winter *fuyu* complements the summer *natsu*, but do opposites really attract? However, Fuyuko is revealed to be a pragmatic woman who has already put the past behind her, whereas Natsuo clings to the memory of what they once had.

LS is a fascinating exercise in TV drama and a good illustration of Shinji Nojima's writing style at work—he wrote that it was his own odyssey to discover the nature of true love. Each episode destroys another romantic notion but this is not Nojima's trademark pessimism. Instead, he deliberately strips away all the conventions and traditions of modern romance,

hoping to find *true* true love as whatever remains at the end. The theme song seems deliberately chosen as an ironic counterpoint, its optimism and assurance constantly opposed by on-screen events until the final moments of the series.

Reputedly shown unsubtitled on U.S. TV. Theme: John Lennon—"Love," also John Lennon—"Stand by Me."

LEAVE IT TO ME *

1998. JPN: *Makasete Darling*. PRD: Kagenobu Kuwata. DIR: Sanae Suzuki, Naoyuki Yokoi. SCR: Makoto Hayashi. CAST: Takanori Jinnai, Chikako Kaku, Chizuru Azuma, Baijaku Nakamura. CHN: TBS. DUR: 45 mins. x 12 eps.; Sun 11 January 1998–22 March 1998. Kagetora (Jinnai) has been away from Tokyo for seven years, running a remote branch office for his company in the countryside. He is elated when he is asked to relocate to the big city, regarding it as an opportunity to get back onto the promotional ladder. However, although Tokyo has not changed at all, Kagetora's family seem indelibly altered by their time in the countryside. Assigned to a cramped corporate dormitory beset by nosy neighbors and bitchy company wives, Kagetora's wife Minako (Kaku) and children begin to wish that they had never left the relative freedom of the sticks. Kagetora is forced to deal with the hang-ups and conflicts of his fellow employees at "home" as well as at the office. Meanwhile the traditional temptations arrive to lure him away from the true path—envy ensues when he is spotted lunching with an ex-girlfriend, his father offers him the chance to run the family steel mill, and a conspiracy grows behind the scenes to sell off the land on which the dormitory is built. Compare to the following year's **AFRICA NIGHTS**, which similarly exploited the chance proximity of larger-than-life characters to create a successful comedy. Broadcast with English subtitles in the U.S. on KIKU TV. Theme: Tatsuya Ishii featuring Nora—"Rhythm."

LEAVE IT TO RYŌMA

1996. JPN: *Ryōma ni Omakase*. PRD: Takashi Umehara. DIR: Hidenobu Hosono. SCR: Kōki Mitani. CAST: Masatoshi Hamada, Shirō Itō, Tamaki Ogawa, Takashi Sorimachi, Masahiko Nishimura. CHN: NTV. DUR: 45 mins. x 12 eps.; Fri 12 April 1996–26 June 1996.

At the end of Edo period, the famous samurai Ryōma Sakamoto (Hamada from Downtown) is living at Chiba Dōjō. So far, historically accurate, though this bizarre retelling of the story of **RYŌMA DEPARTS** soon takes a turn for the comedic. Deliberately played for laughs and cluttered with anachronisms such as headphones and televisions, it features samurai dueling not with swords but with Twister in the style of *Bill and Ted's Excellent Adventure* (1988). Theme: H jungle with T—"Friendship."

LEAVE IT TO THE NURSES

1996. JPN: *Nurse no O-shigoto*. AKA: *A Nurse's Job*. PRD: Ayako Ōga, Kazuyuki Morosawa. DIR: Hitoshi Iwamoto, Hideki Takeuchi, Tōru Hayashi. SCR: Michiru Egashira. CAST: Arisa Mizuki, Yuki Matsushita, Masahiro Matsuoka, Kyōzō Nagatsuka, Kazumi Moroboshi, Harumi Inoue, Kōki Okada, Naohito Fujiki, Yumi Adachi. CHN: Fuji. DUR: 45 mins. x 63 eps.; Tue 2 July 1996–24 September 1996 (#1); 14 October 1997–23 December 1997 (#2); 11 April 2000–19 September 2000 (#3); 2 July 2002–24 September 2002 (#4). Izumi (Mizuki) disgraces herself by getting drunk at her graduation ceremony—she is rushed to the very hospital where she is due to start work as a nurse. This is only the beginning of a series of disasters for the clumsy new arrival. When she phones her boyfriend Mikami (Moroboshi from Hikaru Genji) while she is supposed to be alert and on-call, senior nurse Shōko (Matsushita) advises her to quit before her negligence leads to the death of a patient. However, the plucky nurse perseveres, in a comedy that has hung on for almost a decade.

Later seasons of *LittN* have shifted focus slightly—initially simply for variety's sake, although it should also be noted that the concerns of the series seem to be aging along with its audience. In the second season, Izumi has to balance her struggling career with a new love in her life, while by the third, she and her fellow nurses are fretting over marriage, childcare, and the problems of holding down a career and a family.

In 1998, many of the cast and crew reunited for **SISTER STORIES** which, although based on a completely different source, essentially allowed them to reprise their roles and characters. A movie spin-off, *Leave It to the Nurses* (2002) officially formed the "50th" episode of the series, in which an armed gunman takes over the hospital and holds the nurses as hostages. However, this was not the last gasp of the franchise, but an extended trailer for the fourth season, which began a few weeks later.

Beginning with Izumi returning from her long-delayed honeymoon with husband Kentarō (Fujiki), the fourth season throws in a super-efficient new recruit Hiromi (Adachi), who puts the other nurses to shame and promotes Shōko to a managerial level, where she is rebuffed by her snooty colleagues. Meanwhile, married life for Izumi becomes an in-law appeasement drama, as she is forced to live with Kentarō's mother. Her ability to manage her home life is as chaotic as her workplace ineptitude, as when she shouts at her mother-in-law not to call her at work, only to discover the old lady was merely trying to take her out for her birthday. Compare to **NURSE STATION** and **WHITE SHADOW**. Broadcast in the U.S. without subtitles on NGN. Themes: Arisa Mizuki— "Promise to Promise," "Days."

LEFT BEHIND ON LIBERTY HILL

1990. JPN: *Jiyū no Oka ni Watashi ga Nokotta*. PRD: N/C. DIR: Teruhiko Kuze. SCR: Hitoshi Nozawa. CAST: Yumi Asō, Eisaku Yoshida, Haruko Katō, Chōsuke Ikariya. CHN: Asahi. DUR: 45 mins. x 4 eps.; Thu 10 May 1990–31 May 1990. Ordinary office lady Yasuko (Asō) becomes bored with everyday life and runs away with her photographer boyfriend Shunichi (Yoshida). When her family makes no attempt to contact her, she eventually becomes worried and returns home, only to find it creepily empty.

LEGENDARY TEACHER

2000. JPN: *Densetsu no Kyōshi*. PRD: Kenji Ikeda. DIR: Takaya Kurata, Tarō Ōya, Ryūichi Inomata. SCR: Takeryū Ishihara, Tomoko Yoshida. CAST: Masahiro Nakai, Hitoshi Matsumoto, Hiromi Nagasaku. CHN: NTV. DUR: 45 mins. x ca. 11 eps.; Sat 15 April 2000–30 June 2000.
Easygoing teacher Nanami (Matsumoto) is happy to simply serve time at his high school and hopes his pupils learn more about life than passing exams. Such an attitude puts him head-to-head with Kazami (Nakai from SMAP), a fiercely competitive teacher who is determined to make the world a better place, starting with curing his students from their apathy. The two chalk-and-cheese educators become reluctant buddies in an attempt to turn their school's fortunes around, in a retread of **GODDESS OF VICTORY**. Broadcast in the U.S. without English subtitles on the NGN and KTSF channels. Theme: Hi-Lo's—"Seishun" (Youth).

LEND ME YOUR WINGS

1996. JPN: *Tsubasa o Kudasai*. AKA: *Give Me Your Wings*. PRD: Kōji Shiozawa. DIR: Isamu Nakae. SCR: Yūji Sakamoto. CAST: Yuki Uchida, Takashi Sorimachi, Kōichi Satō, Akiko Yada, Naomi Hosokawa, Maki Kurodo, Miki Mizuno. CHN: Fuji. DUR: 45 mins. x 12 eps.; Mon 1 July 1996–23 September 1996.
Tōko (Uchida) is an orphan girl, reared by her aunt on the remote island of Amami Ōshima and reluctant to form attachments with anyone. The boy she adores from afar is Atsuya (Sorimachi), the star of the school rugby team, who gives her his runner-up medal when his team fails to win the inter-schools final. Told by talent scout Hiroshi (Satō) that she could make it in the entertainment business, she heads for Tokyo, only to find that Hiroshi's business has been in a two-year slump and that he is thinking of quitting show business altogether. The disappointed Tōko initially returns to Amami Ōshima but soon volunteers to come back to Tokyo and help Hiroshi turn his luck around. The fact that her unrequited sweetheart Atsuya is studying at a Tokyo college may also have something to do with her desire to return to the capital. Sorimachi plays a talent scout himself in **CHEAP LOVE**. Theme: Yuki Uchida with M.C.A.T.— "Ever and Ever." Peak rating: 15.5%.

LET'S GO NAGATACHŌ

2001. PRD: Kazuho Masuda, Nobuo Mizuta, Tetsuhiro Ogino, Yūichi Koike. DIR: Hitoshi Iwamoto, Makoto Naganuma. SCR: Kazuhiko Ban. CAST: Takaaki Ishibashi, Kōichi Iwaki, Tōru Emori, Rei Kikukawa, Yoshimasa Kondō, Sachiko Sakurai, B-saku Satō, Kō Shibazaki, Anju Suzuki, Takeshi Naitō, Masahiko Nishimura, Issa Hentona. CHN: Nihon TV. DUR: 45 mins. x 10 eps.; Wed 10 October 2001– 12 December 2001.
Gorin Tsutsui (Ishibashi) works for Diet politician Ichirō Inayama (Nishimura), supposedly as a secretary, though he finds himself working on many other tasks, including entertaining unhappy lobbyists and briefing surly journalists. Other staff include the senior secretary Ryōzō Ezaki (Satō), policy adviser Nobuko Takayanagi (Hideko Yoshida), and his private assistant Reiko Hirose (Shibazaki). Assistant secretary Kenta Okumura (Hentona), a suspicious character with dyed hair, has also just joined the group. Times are tough for Inayama, as he is out of favor with the government—he belongs to the largest faction of his party, led by former Prime Minister Kōtarō Nomoto

(Emori), although the incumbent Prime Minister is reformist Shunichirō Izumi (Iwaki), who gained his position chiefly thanks to the popularity of the Foreign Minister Maiko Tazaka (Shigeru Muroi).

Fellow Diet member Masaki Aosawa (Naitō) announces that he and several younger members are planning on forming their own political group, to which Inayama is invited. Knowing that Aosawa belongs to the rival faction, Inayama should refuse but he accepts on the understanding that the new group will lobby to keep him in his district. However, the prime minister's office also wants to keep the support of the corporations and threatens to reveal Inayama's affair with a nightclub hostess unless he keeps the lobbyists supporting the party.

Reuniting much of the crew of **STRAIGHT NEWS**, including writer Kazuhiko Ban, *LGN* may seem like a rip-off of *The West Wing* (1999), but is actually based on a manga that finished in 1991. The original, *Hyōden no Tractor* (Electoral Tractor) written by political journalist Kenny Nabeshima and drawn by Tsukasa Maekawa, compared secretaries to heavy machinery laboring in the fields of political capital. It lent itself perfectly to an adaptation satirizing Japan's contemporary Koizumi government and was updated with a few more timely references and the addition of comedian Ishibashi in the lead role. The result is a drama that cleverly makes the opaque and confusing world of politics much more approachable and entertaining. Compare to **ONE HOT SUMMER**. Theme: Da Pump (featuring Issa Hentona, who also appeared in the show)—"All My Love to You."

LET'S GO TO SCHOOL

1991. JPN: *Gakkō e Ikō*. PRD: Chihiro Kameyama. DIR: Shunsaku Kawake. SCR: Kazuhiko Yūkawa. CAST: Yūko Asano, Miho Takagi, Hiroshi Fuse, Taishū Kase, Sae Isshiki. CHN: Fuji. DUR: 45 mins. x 12 eps.; Mon 8 April 1991–24 June 1991.

Thirtysomething English teacher Yuki (Asano) is a spirited, resolutely single woman, quick to act and hard to stop. Her colleague Eri (Takagi) is an easy-going music teacher, who prefers to take the path of least resistance in every aspect of her life. Both women are shaken up by the arrival at their school of handsome sports teacher Mr. Inamura (Kase), who becomes the unwitting subject of a duel for his attention. Compare **GODDESS OF VICTORY** and **LEGENDARY TEACHER**. Theme: The Checkers—"How're You Doing Guys?"

LET'S MEET ON CHRISTMAS EVE

1995. JPN: *Christmas Eve ni Aimashō*. AKA: *Christmas Eve Rendezvous*. PRD: Nobuto Nagasaka. DIR: Yukihiko Tsutsumi. SCR: Yasunori Ikeda, Shinji Ohara. CAST: Tomoko Nakajima, Nobutaka Satō, Leo Morimoto. CHN: TVT. DUR: 45 mins. x 10 eps.; Mon 16 October 1995–18 December 1995.

Shiori (Nakajima) is experiencing dizzy spells and creepy bouts of déjà vu. She goes to the hospital, where she is treated by assistant therapist Yūji (Satō). Later, it appears that each of her dizzy spells seems to coincide with a series of serial killings in the neighborhood, making Shiori a prime suspect even though she has no memory of the incidents. Compare to **GIFT** and **FACE**. Theme: trf—"Brand New Tomorrow."

LIFE FROM THE EYES OF A PROFESSOR

2002. JPN: *Tensai Yanagisawa Kyōju no Seikatsu*. AKA: *Life of Genius Professor Yanagisawa*. PRD: Akira Wada, Kumiko Nakajima. DIR: Masayuki Suzuki, Masanori Nishiura. SCR: Hideo Tsuchida, Arinori Fujimoto. CAST: Kōshirō Matsumoto, Chieko Matsubara, Keiko Toda, Fumiyo Kohinata, Tōko Miura, Akiko Kawahara, Tomomitsu Yamaguchi, Ryōko Kuninaka, Ryūta Satō. CHN: Fuji. DUR: 45 mins. x 9 eps.; Wed 16 October 2002–11 December 2002.

Yoshinori Yanagisawa (Matsumoto)

teaches economics at International Cultural University. He has a blinkered outlook on life and refuses to entertain the idea of ever doing anything that is not in complete adherence to "The Rules," whatever they may be. Consequently, he insists on always walking on the right side of the sidewalk and refuses to cross the street anywhere except at crosswalks. His long-suffering wife Masako (Matsubara) endures his eccentricities but their daughter Setsuko (Kuninaka) cannot bear her father's attitude. Determined to prove Setsuko wrong, Yoshinori carefully studies the traffic laws and discovers not only that he is in the right but that everyone else in Tokyo is a law-breaker. He begins berating those who leave their bicycles on the sidewalk and attempts to remove a shopfront sign that *"obstructs the passage of pedestrians."* Although the police are soon called to the scene, he uses his academic rhetoric to bully them into believing that his insane outlook on life has some merit—just one incident from a series based on the 1988 manga by Kazumi Yamashita which ran for 14 years in *Comic Morning* magazine. Its closest relative on Japanese TV is the similarly manga-based *Genius Idiot Bakabon* (*AE).

LIFE OF A FLOWER

1963. JPN: *Hana no Shōgai*. PRD: Taiji Nagasawa. DIR: Hiroshi Inoue. SCR: Makoto Hōjō. CAST: Keiji Sada, Shōroku Onoe, Chikage Awashima, Shikaku Nakamura, Kaneko Iwasaki. CHN: NHK. DUR: 45 mins. x 39 eps.; Sun 7 April 1963–28 December 1963.

The very first *taiga* drama was based on a book by historical novelist Seiichi Funabashi, its title a metaphor for the brief flourishing of its lead character who was cut down all too soon. Naosuke Ii (Onoe) is a feudal lord who is appointed as the Shogun's chief minister. In 1858, when he is pressured by U.S. Consul-General Townsend Harris to sign a commercial treaty, he does so without first seeking the approval of the Emperor. Such approval is little more than a rubber stamp in an era when all real power rested with the Shogun, but this is perhaps the first time in centuries when the emperor's divine authority was truly under threat. It is also a tacit admission by the Shogun, appointed originally to protect Japan from barbarians, that he is unable to perform his job. Ii's act prompts loyalists to the Emperor to call for the restoration of his authority (see As If In Flight), while others fight over the Shogun's right to stay in power (see Shinsengumi).

Meanwhile, the search continues for a suitable heir for Shogun Iesada, who has recently passed away. Reformists recommend Yoshinobu Hitotsubashi as an ideal candidate, but Ii instead chooses Yoshitomi Tokugawa (known to posterity as Iemochi). His decision angers both factions—those loyal to the emperor and the reformists—forcing him to instigate draconian measures to prevent the criticisms and public demonstrations from getting out of hand. In 1860, Ii is assassinated by a royalist.

Life of a Flower was a gamble by Taiji Nagasawa, the director of NHK's Department of Entertainment. Nagasawa planned to combat the hostility of the movie studios (who forbade TV work) with a deliberately high-class drama: a sprawling epic retelling a great story from Japanese history, mixing the big picture of Japan's opening to the West with human drama in the form of Ii's dilemma and scandalous improvisation in a subplot that suggested Ii conducted an affair with the beautiful Takajo Murayama, who later worked as a spy for him. *Life of a Flower* not only began the annual *taiga* tradition that continues to this day but also effectively elevated TV's status and laid the groundwork for the modern Japanese media. The following year's *taiga* drama, *Rōnin of Akō* (see Chūshingura) was the first to begin in January and run for the whole year and was followed in turn by *Taikōki* (see Hideyoshi).

The story was remade by TV Tokyo in 1988, with a script by Kazuya Kasahara, and Kinya Kitaōji in the lead role.

LIFE OF BANGAKU

2002. JPN: *Bangaku no Isshō*. PRD: Ryūnosuke Endō, Kenichirō Yasuhara. DIR: Kon Ichikawa. SCR: Sadao Yamanaka, Megumi Tamura. CAST: Kōji Yakusho, Kyōka Suzuki, Saburō Ishikura, Tsuyoshi Ujiki. CHN: Fuji. DUR: 45 mins. x 9 eps.; Tue 9 March 2002–?? June 2002.

Bangaku (Yakusho) is a masterless samurai who is unable to put aside his personal belief in justice. Like Lone Wolf and Cub, he wanders Edo-era Japan, meeting a completely new supporting cast each week and then saving them from evil. The original *Bangaku Ajikawa* (1932) was a series of stories by Kyōji Shirai that ran in Japanese magazines for a whole decade. In 1933, it was adapted into a film of the same name by director Sadao Yamanaka, whose shooting script was supposedly the basis for this remake.

LIFE SCORNED, A

1977. JPN: *Shikarare Jinsei*. PRD: Kanae Mayuzumi. DIR: Tōru Minegishi, Yoshiyuki Itō. SCR: Mamoru Sasaki. CAST: Junichi Hasegawa, Tomoe Hiiro, Takeshi Katō, Mari Satō, Taka Itō, Satoka Yazaki. CHN: NHK. DUR: 20 mins. x 16 eps.; Mon 30 May 1977–23 June 1977.

When his parents separate, Hachirō (Hasegawa) is sent to live with his father (Katō) but still goes to meet his mother (Hiiro) in secret. His father is extremely angry when he discovers the deception and Hachirō begins to develop a psychosomatic itch. The pain becomes so unbearable that he goes to school one day wearing nothing but his underwear, which leads to his expulsion. On the advice of an old man (Itō), Hachirō heads to Hachijō Island to recuperate, where he teaches a budding poet (Yazaki) how to write and realizes that he has found his true vocation. A dramatization of the early life of poet Hachirō Satō, poems from whose first collection were recited at

the close of each episode. Compare to a similar authorial biography in Shirobanba.

LIFE WITH DAD *

2003. JPN: *Otōsan*. AKA: *Father*. PRD: N/C. DIR: N/C. SCR: N/C. CAST: Masakazu Tamura, Naoko Iijima, Miki Nakatani, Ryōko Hirosue, Kyōko Fukada, Ryōko Moriyama, Taichi Kokubu. CHN: TBS. DUR: 45 mins. x ca. 11 eps.; Sun 5 January 2003–?? March 2003.

Shirō (Tamura) is a lonely widower who owns his own noodle bar and has raised his four daughters single-handedly. He is very proud of his girls but at least part of his satisfaction comes from his daughters' unwillingness to confess when things go wrong. Eldest daughter Yū (Iijima) is on the brink of divorce and plans on moving back into the family home as soon as she can think of a way to break the news of her misfortune to Shirō. Akira (Nakatani) has always been the reliable one but now plans on moving *out* of the family home and finally trying to live her own life, instead of clearing up after everyone else. Nurse Makoto (Hirosue) is so afraid of introducing her father to her boyfriend that she has kept him completely secret, even to the extent of renting an apartment where she can see him without having to resort to family territory. And youngest daughter Kei (Fukada) is a piano prodigy who is waiting for the right moment to tell Dad that she has had enough of music and wants to quit. But before any of these issues can be raised, Dad drops a bombshell of his own. He intends to remarry, much to his daughters' horror. Broadcast in the U.S. with English subtitles on KIKU TV and KTSF.

LIKE ASHURA

1979. JPN: *Ashura no Gotoku*. PRD: N/C. DIR: Ben Wada. SCR: Kuniko Mukōda. CAST: Kaoru Yachigusa, Ayumi Ishida, Haruko Katō, Jun Fubuki, Toshinobu Sawake. CHN: NHK: 45 mins. x ca. 50 eps.; Sat 13 January 1979–27 January 1980.

Four sisters discover that their aged father Kōtarō (Sawake) has a son by a previously unknown mistress. Tsunako (Katō), Makiko (Yachigusa), Takiko (Ishida), and Sakiko (Fubuki) meet to discuss the situation civilly, but it soon becomes clear that they have little in common and that their polite chats hide problems and enmities of their own. Mukōda's kitchen-sink drama was written specifically to play to the director's strength—but since Wada was

known primarily for hard-boiled stories of cops and bankers, the observations and human conflicts became noticeably sharp. Perhaps for this reason, this drama still scores high on viewer polls a whole generation after it was originally screened. Now in her seventies, Yachigusa remains a popular face on Japanese TV to this day, when she seems to be the default setting for any drama series that requires a kindly grandmother—see ANTIQUE.

LIKE LOVE IN A STORM

1993. JPN: *Arashi no Naka no Ai no Yōni*. PRD: Shunji Okamoto. DIR: Kan Ishibashi. SCR: Masahiro Yoshimoto, Mie Nakazono. CAST: Yasuko Sawaguchi, Ruriko Asaoka, Mikihisa Azuma. CHN: Yomiuri. DUR: 45 mins. x 12 eps.; Sat 3 July 1993–25 September 1993.

Mio (Sawaguchi) has a job interview at a fashion brand KYOKO, where her designs impress the owner Kyōko (Asaoka) and her son Takayuki (Azuma). Based on a story by Hitomi Fujimoto, ideally suited to the exotic foreign jobs favored by the trendy drama generation. Theme: Yōko Takahashi—"Blue no Tsubasa" (Blue Wings).

LIMIT

2000. JPN: *Limit—Moshimo, Waga Ko ga . . . .* AKA: *Limit—If Only, My Child Were . . . .* PRD: Yoshinori Horiguchi. DIR: Yasuo Tsuruhashi. SCR: Hisashi Nozawa. CAST: Narumi Yasuda, Misako Tanaka, Kōichi Satō, Takanori Jinnai, Miki Yamamoto, Ikki Kitamura, Satoshi Tsumabuki, Chiharu Niiyama. CHN: Yomiuri. DUR: 45 mins. x ca. 11 eps.; Mon 3 July 2000–30 September 2000.

A female police officer sees civilian life in a new light after her own child is kidnapped. Compare to KIDNAP, which ran during the same season on TV Asahi, and writer Nozawa's earlier wife meets underworld drama OUT.

LIONMARU

1972. JPN: *Kaiketsu Lionmaru*. AKA: *Swift Hero Lionmaru*. PRD: Tomio

Washizu, Shigeru Shinohara, Takanobu Bessho. DIR: Kōichi Ishiguro, Tatsumi Andō, Keinosuke Tsuchiya. SCR: Susumu Takahisa, Bunzō Wakatsuki, Tatsuo Tamura, Tomio Shinoda, Toshiaki Matsushima, Haruya Yamazaki. CAST: Tetsuya Ushio, Akiko Kujō, Norihiko Umechi, Kōji Tonohiro, Yoshitaka Fukushima, Shin Tokudaichi, Jūzaburō Akechi, Kazu Kamoshida, Kyōko Miyano, Tsunehiro Arai, Kiyoshi Kobayashi. CHN: Fuji. DUR: 25 mins. x 80 eps.; Sat 1 April 1972–4 April 1973 (#1); 14 April 1973–29 September 1973 (#2).

Ninja warrior Shishimaru (Ushio), his pretty female assistant Kazumi (Kujō), and token child Kōsuke (Umechi) wander samurai-era Japan, defending the inhabitants from monsters sent by Devil Gōsun (Kobayashi), an evil mastermind determined to seize control of the world. Shishimaru has numerous items of ninja gear to help him, including a magic sword that allows him to transform into Lionmaru (Kamoshida), a frankly ridiculous stuffed animal costume involving a red suit, dark cloak, and a huge lion's head. Meanwhile, Kōsuke brings up the rear with a bag of explosives and a flute that transforms into a blowpipe, which he can also use to summon Hikarimaru, the team's Pegasus (or if you prefer, a mystified and slightly bored horse, to which someone in the props department has glued some wings). The result is an intensely enjoyable festival of camp martial arts action, which reaches new heights at the serial's midpoint with the arrival of Tora Jōnosuke (Tonohiro), aka Tiger Joe, Lionmaru's eyepatch-wearing, transforming tiger nemesis—compare to another one-eyed warrior in THE YAGYŪ CONSPIRACY. Based on an idea by SPECTREMAN creator Sōji Ushio with Takanobu Bessho. Insane, but in a good way. Jōnosuke actor Kōji Tonohiro died in an accident at a location hotel, and was replaced from episode 42 by Yoshitaka Fukushima.

The original 54-episode run was renewed for a shorter second season, retitled *Fū-Un Lionmaru* (Wind-Cloud Lionmaru), easily distinguished by the color of Lionmaru's fur—it's white in season one and brown-gold in season two. Theme: Yūki Hide—"Let's Go, Lionmaru."

LIPSTICK

1999. AKA: *Fallen Angel*. PRD: Atsuhiro Sugio. DIR: Kensaku Sawada, Kōzō Nagayama, Isamu Nakae. SCR: Shinji Nojima. CAST: Ryōko Hirosue, Hiroshi Mikami, Issei Ishida, Ayumi Itō, Minako Tanaka, Yumi Asō, Chizuru Ikewaki, Yōsuke Kubozuka, Aimi Nakamura. CHN: Fuji. DUR: 45 mins. x 12 eps.; Mon 12 April 1999–23 June 1999.

Frustrated artist Yū (Mikami) secretly longs for his dead brother's flutist fiancée Chihiro (Asō). In his day job as a guard at a unisex young offenders' institution, he develops a strange relationship with laconic remand inmate Ai (Hirosue) after he agrees to look after her cat. In successive interviews, it is he who bears his soul to *her* and his life outside takes new and unexpected turns.

A superb series, right from the wordless opening sequence, in which Ai assaults a couple in Tower Records while Yū sketches passersby in a swish café. The love polygons of Japanese drama are stretched to absurd lengths on both sides of the prison bars—innocent-seeming pretty boy inmate Kōki (Kubozuka) is revealed as a criminal kingpin, who pimped his own girlfriend Anna (Nakamura) and even forced her to attempt suicide. New arrival prison guard Takao (Ishida) saves Anna, only to find that she now wants to repay him with sexual favors—although her ardor soon cools and he is forced to impress her with ever more foolhardy acts of self-mutilation, using thumb tacks and ballpoint pens. For his part, Kōki begins a brooding relationship after hours in the library with ball-breaking female prison guard Yukino (Tanaka)—as the series goes on, she proves to be the *least* pathological of the prison staff, most of whom

turn out to be in greater need of locking up than the inmates. Meanwhile, Ai's cellmates are the world's least convincing criminals: supposedly in the slammer for alleged drug offenses, assaults, and attempted murders, none of them look as if they could hurt a fly. This, however, only adds to the entertainment, particularly when jockeying for position as cellblock queen leads to nude beatings in the showers, spoon fights, assault with curry, and fiery games of table tennis and badminton.

Hirosue is a remarkably still and brooding presence, avoiding all eye contact and initially most opportunities for speech, crouching in the corner and daring the cast to find out her terrible secret. She manages to keep her character believable and mysterious, while around her the storyline careens from hard-hitting subplots of incest, prostitution, and suicide to less credible comedy business such as the acquisition of a pet ant and Yū's ongoing attempts to replace his dead brother, both in the art gallery (compare to **DESSIN**) and in the affections of Chihiro. Some suspension of disbelief is required regarding the competence of the Japanese prison system, but once past this hurdle, *Lipstick*'s twists and turns never fail to surprise. Excellent fun and a good opportunity for language students to learn phrases like: *"Please do not set fire to your defense counsel's hair again."* Theme: Rebecca—"Friends." Peak rating: 19.4%.

LIVE FOR THIS LOVE

1994. JPN: *Kono Ai ni Ikite*. PRD: Reiko Kita. DIR: Shunsaku Kawake. SCR: Hisashi Nozawa. CAST: Narumi Yasuda, Gorō Kishitani, Etsuji Toyokawa, Eri Fukatsu, Jun Miho, Fumio Watanabe, Kyūsaku Shimada. CHN: Fuji. DUR: 45 mins. x 12 eps.; Thu 14 April 1994–30 June 1994.

Seiichi (Toyokawa) leaves his wife Tatsuko (Miho) to live with the pregnant Akemi (Yasuda), a girl with whom he has been having an affair. Six years later, Akemi believes they are a happy couple with a young child but discovers

Continued from p. 159

Romeo's friend Mercutio finds Tybalt doctoring company documents and is injured in a fall when he tries to stop him. Reunited at Mercutio's bedside at Apothecary Hospital, the cast realize that Romeo is innocent. Romeo is exonerated of all accusations, but Juliet slips away, to prepare to fly abroad for her posting in Taiwan. Romeo rushes to the airport, where he stops her just before she gets on her plane. In a surprise twist, Rosalind meets Mercutio as he is discharged from hospital, and confesses that she has fallen in love with him. At the double wedding that follows, Juliet and Rosalind both throw their bouquets, which are caught by Nurse and Doctor Apothecary, who smile shyly at each other.

that Seiichi has been secretly seeing Tatsuko. Akemi drowns her sorrows at a local bar, where she is mistaken for a call girl by depressed detective Yūsaku (Kishitani). Despite this ominous first encounter, the two began to conduct an affair of their own but in the course of one of their clandestine meetings Akemi leaves her young son Kazu unattended. The boy is kidnapped and murdered, and a distraught Akemi leaves Seiichi after their wedding to pursue a career as a prostitute.

Tatsuko's father Shigeki (Watanabe) tells Akemi that it was Yūsaku's discredited colleague Shūhei (Shimada) who murdered her son. Akemi asks Yūsaku to reinvestigate the case but when he is unable to turn up any new evidence, Akemi murders Shūhei herself. She is arrested but keeps silent, and the Public Prosecutor's Office is unable to pin the crime on her.

Released without charge and desiring to put her actions behind her, Akemi fights off a jealous Tatsuko (who stabs Yūsaku) and then prepares to begin life again with Seiichi, planning a vacation in the remote romantic spot where they first met. However, the jilted Yūsaku suspects her motives—he has discovered that Kazu was really murdered by Thai business associates of Seiichi's in revenge for a botched blackmail attempt. Yūsaku suspects that Akemi's reunion with Seiichi is nothing of the sort and that she intends to murder him in revenge for the death of their child.

An excellent bunny boiler drama from OUT's Hisashi Nozawa, *LFTL* opens in the style of I'LL NEVER LOVE AGAIN, hitting the audience with a succession of stunning twists and then leaving the viewer to savor the unraveling of the stored tension. Buried within its modern trappings, it also contains an element of 19th-century melodrama. Nowhere is this clearer than in the character of Yūsaku, who is given a succession of duty versus emotion dilemmas to rival those of HANSHICHI, including a directive to arrest the prostitute he loves before she can kill the ex-husband *he* hates in revenge for the death of the child *she* bore, which ruined the marriage of the woman who stands before him begging for *his* help, who doesn't realize that by doing so *he* will be forced to destroy Akemi's previous alibi and thereby implicate *her* in the murder of Shūhei. We love it. See also BLUE BIRD for another drama by Nozawa starring Etsuji Toyokawa. Theme: Izumi Tachibana—"Eien no Puzzle" (Eternal Puzzle).

LIVEMAN

1988. JPN: *Chōjū Sentai Liveman*. AKA: *Super-Beast Battle Team Liveman*. PRD: Kyōzō Utsunomiya, Takeyuki Suzuki. DIR: Takeo Nagaishi, Shōhei Tōjō, Minoru Yamada. SCR: Hirohisa Soda, Kunio Fujii, Toshiki Inoue. CAST: Daisuke Shima, Kazuhiko Nishimura, Megumi Mori, Masao Yamaguchi, Shinobu Kawamoto, Jōji Nakada. CHN: Asahi. DUR: 25 mins. x 49 eps.; Sat 27 February 1988–18 February 1989. The evil Bolt Cyber Army attacks and destroys the Scientific Academy, leaving only three survivors. Joining with

some new recruits, they form the Liveman team to save the Earth. Their leader is Yūsuke (Shima) the Red Falcon who fights with Falcon Power and his Falcon Sword. Jō (Nishimura) is the Yellow Lion who fights with Lion Power and his powerful Lion Punch. Megumi (Mori) is the Blue Dolphin who fights with (you guessed it) Dolphin Power and shoots Dolphin Arrows. These three original survivors of the attack are joined by Tetsuya (Yamaguchi) the Black Bison, who fights with the Bison Rod and whose older brother died in the enemy assault, Junichi (Kawamoto) who is the Green Jackal and fights with his Jackal Cutter to avenge the death of his baby sister at the hands of Bolt. Launching from the Machine Buffalo mobile base, their Lion, Dolphin, and Falcon vehicles combine to form Live Robo, while the Bison and Jackal vehicles combine separately to make the smaller Live Boxer robot. Both robots can themselves combine to make Live Combination Five.

Their archenemy is Pierce (Nakada), the chief scientist and master of Dark Arts, who leads an army of cannon fodder Jinma minions, as well as a selection of monsters of the week. He has also recruited three of the Liveman team's fellow humans to fight on his side, though their plans are always foiled. "Based on an idea by Saburō Yade" and featuring music from Tatsumi Yano. *Liveman* was preceded in the Super Sentai chronology by MASKMAN and followed by TURBORANGER.

LIVING BY THE SWORD

1998. JPN: *Kenkaku Shōbai*. PRD: Yōichi Nōmura, Tetsuo Sao. DIR: Akira Inoue, Yoshiki Onoda, Nobuyuki Sakai, Shinji Harada, Masahiro Takase. SCR: Naruhiko Kaneko, Tsutomu Nakamura, Tatsuo Nogami, Megumi Tamura, Akira Tasaki. CAST: Makoto Fujita, Makiya Yamaguchi, Shinobu Terajima, Ayako Kobayashi, Kōichi Miura, Gen Kimura, Toshio Yamauchi, Eri Satō, Meiko Kaji, Mikijirō Hira. DUR: 45 mins. x 37 eps.;

Tue 13 October 1998–16 December 1998 (#1); 8 December 1999–15 March 2000 (#2); 5 June 2001–24 July 2001 (#3); 21 January 2003–?? March 2003 (#4). During the Edo period, the capital is ruled by the consul Okitsugu Tanuma (Hira). Kōhei Akiyama (Fujita) is a former swordsman, now enjoying retirement in the company of Oharu (Kobayashi), a wife 40 years his junior. His son by a previous marriage, Daijirō (Yamaguchi) runs a school of swordsmanship and has little time for anything except martial arts. Kōhei, however, devotes himself to upholding the spirit of the law, defending innocent members of the public from predations of corrupt officials and legal loopholes—compare to MITO KŌMON. The fourth season introduces Mifuyu (Terajima), the illegitimate daughter of the consul, who is both a femme fatale in the fight scenes and a fitting love interest for Daijirō. Based on the stories by Shōtarō Ikenami, creator of ONIHEI THE INVESTIGATOR, which have reportedly sold over 10 million copies in Japan.

LIVING LIKE AN ANGEL

1992. JPN: *Tenshi no Yō ni Ikitemitai*. PRD: Naoyuki Yokoi. DIR: Masaharu Segawa. SCR: Toshimichi Saeki. CAST: Minako Tanaka, Ken Ishiguro, Miho Takagi, Takeshi Naitō, Tomoko Nakajima. CHN: TBS. DUR: 45 mins. x 13 eps.; 3 July 1992–Fri 25 September 1992. When Sakurako (Tanaka) goes to donate blood, she meets Koume (Nakajima), who is studying to be a social worker. Sakurako becomes interested in the job and starts studying with Koume but is thrown into a social worker's job before she is truly qualified when a boy who lives next door suddenly collapses. Theme: JAM Cream—"19-ban Tango" (Tango #19).

LIVING ROOM

1993. JPN: *Ocha no Ma*. PRD: Yūji Saitō. DIR: Yūya Fujii. SCR: Satoko Okudera. CAST: Marina Watanabe, Akitsugu

Narita, Etsushi Toyokawa, Wakako Sakai. CHN: Yomiuri. DUR: 25 mins. x 11 eps.; Sat 9 January 1993–20 March 1993.

Sonoko (Watanabe) leaves college and starts work at a construction company. She decides to move to Tokyo and try living alone but her boyfriend Kaoru (Narita) insists that they should live together and settles in her new apartment. Theme: Anzen Chitai—"Hitoribotchi no Yell" (Lonely Yell).

LIVING SINGLE

1996. JPN: Hitori Gurashi. PRD: Seiichirō Kimijima. DIR: Jirō Shōno. SCR: Yumiko Aoyagi. CAST: Takako Tokiwa, Katsunori Takahashi, Hiromi Nagasaku, Saya Takagi, Kei Shimizu. CHN: TBS. DUR: 45 mins. x 13 eps.; Fri 10 October 1996–13 December 1996.

Miho (Tokiwa) sells ladies' shoes at a Tokyo department store and decides that now that she has a job, it's time to live independently of her family. She goes looking for a place of her own, much to the annoyance of her best friend Kyōko (Nagasaku), who was hoping to move in with her. After a disastrous love affair, Miho feels lonely and isolated but Kyōko pointedly shuns her. Theme: Yūmi Matsutoya—"Saigo no Uso" (Final Lie).

LOCAL NEWS: DEPARTMENT THREE *

2001. JPN: Kochira Daisan Shakaibu. PRD: Kazushi Morishita. DIR: Kinta Nakamura, Makoto Kiyohiro, Atsushi Kurosawa. SCR: Shōji Imai, Masakazu Ōkubo, Yayoi Yoshida, Rei Izumi. CAST: Ken Watanabe, Yumi Asō, Masato Hagiwara, Miki Sakai, Hidehiko Ishizuka, Kenji Sakaguchi, Keiko Toda, Kaori Iida, Ai Kago, Hisaya Morishige, Masaki Kyōmoto, Masahiko Tsugawa. CHN: TBS. DUR: 45 mins. x 11 eps.; Mon 10 October 2001–17 December 2001.

Jirō (Watanabe) is a newly appointed editor at the Daishin newspaper, appalled to discover he has been placed in charge of Local News Department Three, the notorious

dead-end posting where the corporation sends its no-hopers, flakes, and incompetents, as another company does with its POWER OFFICE GIRLS. When the leader of a local volunteer group is murdered, Jirō galvanizes his staff into hunting down the murderer and the motive, discovering in the process that just as Department Three has been left to rot, society itself is in the habit of writing off entire groups of people. Compare to TABLOID. Broadcast with English subtitles in the U.S. on KTSF TV.

LONE WOLF AND CUB

1973. JPN: Kozure Ōkami. PRD: Kiyoharu Nakaoka, Norio Katō. DIR: Makito Takai, Minoru Matsushima, Norizō Tanaka, Akinori Matsuo, Mitsumasa Saitō, Kazuo Ikehiro. SCR: Ichirō Ikeda, Masato Ide, Katsumi Okamoto, Saburō Shibahide, Kengo Inomata. CAST: Kinnosuke Yorozuya, Kazutaka Nishikawa, Eiji Okada, Akira Nishimura, Kiwako Taichi, Kei Satō. CHN: NTV. DUR: 45 mins. x 78 eps.; Sun 1 April 1973–30 September 1973 (#1); 7 April 1974–29 September 1974 (#2); 4 April 1976–26 September 1976 (#3); 14 October 2002–9 December 2002 (remake #1), 7 July 2003– (remake #2).

Ittō Ogami (Yorozuya), a former public executor in the Edo period, becomes a lordless samurai after his family is killed by the Yagyū clan (see YAGYŪ CONSPIRACY). In order to retaliate, the sword master and Daigorō (Nishikawa), his three-year-old son, wander around the country assassinating for money. They go through many crises together until Ittō finally faces Retsudō (Satō), the head of the Yagyū clan, in a final showdown redolent of MUSASHI.

Based on Kazuo Koike and Gōseki Kojima's manga masterpiece, published in Manga Action magazine from 1971 to 1976, LW&C also exists as a series of movies. In the lead role, actor Yorozuya brings an unnerving gravity to his character, particularly when surrounded by more everyday TV actors

and the cloyingly cute Nishikawa as Daigorō. After Yorozuya's death, a remake of the series, starring HEIJI ZENIGATA actor Kinya Kitaōji alongside Akira Kobayashi, was broadcast in the winter of 2002 on TV Asahi. Theme: Yukio Hashi—"Kozure Ōkami" (Lone Wolf and Cub).

LONG FOR LOVE

1997. JPN: Konna Koi no Hanashi. AKA: Story of Love. PRD: Shizuo Sekiguchi. DIR: Hisao Kogure. SCR: Masaki Fukasawa, Rumi Takahashi. CAST: Hiroyuki Sanada, Kōji Tamaki, Nanako Matsushima, Naho Toda. CHN: Fuji. DUR: 45 mins. x 12 eps.; Thu 3 July 1997–18 September 1997.

Coldhearted billionaire Shūichirō (Sanada) discovers that he only has three months to live and is talked into living out his last days as a good man by fellow patient Kōnosuke (Tamaki), a pauper who feels he is rich in spirit because of all the help he gives other people. Compare to Akira Kurosawa's Ikiru (1952). Theme: Kōji Tamaki—"Mr. Lonely."

LONG LOVE LETTER

2002. JPN: Long Love Letter Hyōryū Kyōshitsu. AKA: Long Love Letter Drifting Classroom. PRD: Masatoshi Yamaguchi. DIR: Narihide Mizuta, Hideki Takeuchi, Tatsuaki Kimura. SCR: Mika Ōmori. CAST: Takako Tokiwa, Yōsuke Kubozuka, Tomohisa Yamashita, Takayuki Yamada, Satoshi Tsumabuki, Ren Ōsugi, Hiromi Nakajima. CHN: Fuji. DUR: 45 mins. x 11 eps.; Wed 9 January 2002–20 March 2002.

Flower seller's daughter Yūka (Tokiwa) loses contact with her would-be boyfriend Akio (Kubozuka) through a series of unlucky coincidences. Some time later, she bumps into Akio when she is making a delivery at her local high school and finds him lying on the library floor under a semi-naked schoolgirl. He is now a (very) popular teacher at the school, and Yūka returns to see him a second time, only to get involved in a row about their relationship. Their shouting is interrupted by

Long Love Letter

an earthquake, during which the school and everyone in it is suddenly transported to an unknown desert. Some students adjust faster than others—Sekiya (Nakajima) manages to establish control of the school's dwindling food supply and uses it to exert a new and unwelcome authority. The school is attacked by unknown assailants, leaving Akio critically injured and the students' supplies running dangerously low. Over time, the students come to realize that they have somehow been transported a generation into the future after an indeterminate apocalypse.

Based on a 1972 manga by Kazuo Umezu, mixing *Lord of the Flies* with *Fist of the North Star* (*AE), *LLL* toys with its audience's expectations, running the first episode like a standard romance, only to hit its cast with the earthquake at the end. The cast only discovers their whereabouts through tantalizing tidbits—a wrecked bullet train here, a garbled Global Positioning System response there—leading them to believe that, somehow, they are in the year 2020. Mika Ōmori's script skillfully updates Umezu's original, concentrating on the modern terror of mobile phones unable to get a signal and populating the school with a menagerie of

misfit students—hardly any of the cast seem to have standard-issue black hair. With a group of unfortunates who are only in the building in the first place because they are remedial cases, early scenes recall the teen detention movie *Breakfast Club* (1984). The shift to a presumably post-apocalyptic future causes a radical change in priorities—bad girls breaking into the staff room to read the answers to a forthcoming exam are suddenly transformed into competent survivalists, while the school grind demands to know if the time-slip will affect his test results. Running through the plot are numerous debates about life decisions and paths not taken. Before the disaster, viewers are treated to portents of time gone awry—a pencil falls from a desk in a quantum manner and Yūka witnesses a balloon that both floats away *and* stays attached to the little girl who has just bought it. Such science fictional moments prepare the audience for more traditional dramatic crises. Yūka was once a teacher who sacrificed her former career to prevent a promising student from expulsion. He, however, let her down by dropping out to become a sushi chef and now waits expectantly back in the real world, gazing into the crater where the school once was.

Umezu's original manga was also adapted into a 1991 movie, directed by Nobuhiko Ōbayashi and featuring Troy Donahue. Broadcast without English subtitles in the U.S. on KSCI TV. Theme: Tatsurō Yamashita—"Love Land Ai Land."

LONG VACATION

1996. PRD: Chihiro Kameyama. DIR: Kōzō Nagayama. SCR: Eriko Kitagawa. CAST: Takuya Kimura, Tomoko Yamaguchi, Takako Matsu, Yutaka Takenouchi, Izumi Inamori, Kōsuke Toyohara, Leo Morimoto. CHN: Fuji. DUR: 45 mins. x 11 eps.; Mon 15 April 1996–24 June 1996.

When her fiancé fails to turn up at the altar, 30-year-old Minami (Yamaguchi) storms round to his apartment, still

wearing her wedding dress. However, the groom has disappeared, leaving only his bewildered roommate Hidetoshi (Kimura from SMAP). A poor little rich girl, now bankrupted by the disappearance of her fortune along with her fiancé (compare to GIFT), Minami is forced to move in with Hidetoshi and jump-start her flagging modeling career. She decides to treat the desertion as a "long vacation," a respite from the rat race granted to her by God as she stood alone at the altar. Hidetoshi wants to be a concert pianist but lacks confidence, preferring instead to develop a hopeless crush on fellow musician Ryōko (Matsu), who, just to make matters worse, begins a relationship with Minami's brother Shinji (Takenouchi).

Giving up on modeling, Minami takes a new job as an assistant to photographer Tetsuya (Toyohara), who soon sleeps with her, asks her to move in with him, and only then reveals that he is a divorcé with a child. Minami moves out of Hidetoshi's apartment anyway after the two quarrel about Tetsuya's motives—the 25-year-old Hidetoshi is jealous of Tetsuya and resentful that Minami hasn't fallen for *him*. Minami moves out, the two sulk for a while, and Hidetoshi loses interest in music, only to be forced to confront his attitude when Minami decides to start learning the piano herself. Inspired by her passion, he enters a music contest—Minami, of course, is listening in secret, with tears streaming down her face. She leaves early but Hidetoshi tracks her down outside the apartment. He has won a trip to Boston and asks her to come with him . . . for a finale that may bring poetic and narrative closure to the "long vacation" of the title, but which was regarded by many viewers as an unnecessary coda.

Taking its cue from *When Harry Met Sally* (1989), with two ideal partners sublimating their true feelings for each other in fights and spats, *LV* is one of the landmark dramas of the 1990s along with TOKYO LOVE STORY, gaining a peak rating of 36.7%. Writer Kitagawa's dialogue is so snappy that some of her "best quotes" were published in their own separate cash-in book, while director Nagayama was unafraid of running entire scenes without any words at all. *LV* hypnotizes its viewers with the *will-they-won't-they* tension of Hidetoshi and Minami as they grow closer together, only to have old flames, family troubles, and new suitors regularly drag them apart. Meanwhile, there is added *frisson* in the rare sight of a relationship between a younger man and an older woman, particularly when the woman is 1990s star Yamaguchi and the man is 21st-century heartthrob Kimura, in his first major role.

The series also exists in novelized form, credited to Kitagawa. A feature-length October 1997 TV special replayed the last few episodes from the perspective of supporting cast members Momoko (Inamori) and Professor Sasaki (Morimoto) and helped keep the series in the public eye ready for its video release. *LV* was much imitated in later Japanese dramas, particularly LOVE GENERATION, LOVE ON HOLD, and OVER TIME, although its greatest influence was felt abroad. Even as its cast and crew went on to the next show and the next drama season, consigning the 11 weeks of *LV*-mania to history, pirated copies of the series turned it into an underground hit in Hong Kong—to such an extent that there were reports of people ostracized from social circles if they had no opinion on the show. Illegal editions of *LV* pioneered the spread of Japanese drama in the former colony and led to its legal broadcast on local television in 2000. Such exposure has given the series a far greater longevity than many others and initiated a whole new market for Japanese drama outside its territory of origin. It was also broadcast with English subtitles in the U.S. on KTSF TV. Theme: Toshinobu Kubota and Naomi Campbell—"La La La Love Song."

LOST PARADISE
1997. JPN: *Shitsurakuen*. AKA: *Paradise Lost*. PRD: Shunji Okamoto, Shin Kondō. DIR: Akira Katō, Junji Hanadō. SCR: Takehiro Nakajima. CAST: Ikkō Furuya, Naomi Kawashima, Miho Kanno, Ryūichi Ōura. CHN: NTV. DUR: 45 mins. x 12 eps.; Mon 7 July 1997–22 September 1997.

Hisaki (Furuya) is a middle-aged publisher who is marginalized at work and unhappy in his marriage. When his daughter Chika (Kanno)'s engagement is canceled by her fiancé Sōgo (Ōura), Hisaki confronts him for an explanation. Sōgo confesses that he has found a better love in the form of Rinko (Kawashima), a young calligrapher with whom Hisaki soon begins a highly inappropriate affair that is guaranteed to end in tears. The couple's relationship becomes increasingly obsessive (and steamy) until tragedy beckons.

LP was based on a 1995 story by Junichi Watanabe and serialized in the *Nihon Keizai Shinbun*, whose readership of middle-aged businessmen turned the story into a hit, both in its original form and in its later republication as a novel. It was also adapted into a 1997 live-action film, starring Kōji Yakusho and Hitomi Kuroki. Controversial sex scenes were part of the appeal of the story in all its incarnations, but were all the more eye-opening on conservative Japanese network television. The producers made sure the public was aware how shocking it would all be by releasing equally provocative stills to the press. After the success of *LP*, harassed editors also featured in LOVE STORY and WEDNESDAY LOVE AFFAIR. Note: although the title seems intended as a reference to John Milton's *Paradise Lost*, popular discussion of the movie has already established it as *LP*, leading us to reluctantly file it here. For another Watanabe dramatization, see ANESTHESIA. Theme: ZARD—"Eien" (Eternity).

LOVE AFTER DIVORCE
1999. JPN: *Wakaretara Suki na Hito*.

PRD: N/C. DIR: Hiroshi Akabane. SCR: Mika Umeda. CAST: Yuki Saitō, Hidemasa Nakayama, Keizō Kanie, Yōko Yamamoto, Yasutaka Tsutsui. CHN: TVT. DUR: 45 mins. x 10 eps.; Wed 6 January 1999–?? March 1999.

Momoe (Saitō) is a daughter of an acupuncturist. Divorcing her unfaithful and timid husband (Nakayama) after he has an affair, she starts studying to be a beautician. However, soon after the divorce, her husband's company is bankrupted and he comes to her to live with her. Based on the manga by I CAN'T GO ON creator Tamiko Akaboshi—compare to FALSE LOVE and NARITA DIVORCE. Broadcast unsubtitled in the U.S. on KTSF TV.

LOVE AGAIN
1998. PRD: Noriko Nishiguchi. DIR: Takamichi Yamada, Takehiko Shinjō. SCR: Toshiya Itō. CAST: Atsurō Watabe, Hikari Ishida, Miho Kanno, Shinji Takeda. CHN: TBS. DUR: 45 mins. x 9 eps.; Thu 16 April 1998–11 June 1998.

Yūta (Watabe) finally gets lucky with Kaori (Kanno), who attends the horseback riding club where he works. The couple sleep together, but the following morning Yūta meets his old flame Mizuki (Ishida). Though the two have not seen each other for seven years, Mizuki still has feelings for Yūta and confesses that she wants him back. However, Mizuki has commitments of her own, such as her wedding to the unsuspecting Kōichi (Takeda), which is only days away. *LA* begins with what might be the happy ending of another series, only to go horribly wrong when ghosts from the past threaten to interfere with our romantic leads (who would play a less troubled couple in the later WHERE IS LOVE?)—a rare drama to tackle the eternal truth that sometimes people just want what they can't have. Theme: The Brilliant Green—"There Will be Love There: Ai no Aru Basho."

LOVE AND EROS
1998. JPN: *Love to Eros*. PRD: Akira

Isoyama. DIR: Jirō Shōno, Osamu Katayama. SCR: Miho Nakazono. CAST: Atsuko Asano, Tomoya Nagase, Fumiya Fujii. CHN: TBS. DUR: 45 mins. x 12 eps.; Thu 2 July 1998–17 September 1998.

Ten years after the sudden death of her husband, Kasumi (Asano) struggles to rear her son alone, working in a bentō shop to make ends meet. Her husband's best friend Ryūichi (Fujii) proposes to her at the funeral of his own father, but his half brother Jirō (Nagase from TOKIO) desires her for himself. When Ryūichi tells her his intention to give up his share of his inheritance in favor of Jirō, Kasumi is moved and decides to marry him. However, when she meets Jirō and he tells her of his sad and lonely childhood in an orphanage, her feelings swing toward him. Broadcast in the U.S. without English subtitles on NGN. Theme: Fumiya Fujii—"Wara no Inu" (Straw Dog). Peak rating: 12.8%.

LOVE AND JUSTICE

2001. JPN: *Ai wa Seigi*. AKA: *Love Is Justice*. PRD: N/C. DIR: Toshihiro Itō, Kenkō Satō. SCR: Izō Hashimoto. CAST: Tamao Nakamura, Akira Kimura, Harumi Inoue, Aki Kawamura, Masayuki Imai. CHN: Asahi. DUR: 45 mins. x ca. 11 eps.; Fri 12 January 2001–?? March 2001.

Kimura plays a lawyer in a law firm whose senior partner (Nakamura) is an eccentric old woman, leading to courtroom comedy and romantic subplots in the style of *Ally McBeal*. Eclipsed in the ratings by the quantifiably more successful legal drama **HERO**.

LOVE AND LIES

1996. JPN: *Gimu to Engi*. AKA: *Duty and Performance*. PRD: Kagenobu Kuwata. DIR: Kagenobu Kuwata. SCR: Taeko Azuma. CAST: Yūko Asano, Hitomi Kuroki, Shirō Sano, Ryūichi Ōura, Fumie Hosokawa, Ken Kaneko, Chiharu Niiyama, Zen Kajihara, Hiromitsu Suzuki. CHN: TBS. DUR: 45 mins. x 11 eps.; Thu 10 October 1996–19 December 1996.

After six years of marriage, Shōko (Asano) devotes more time to her struggling lighting design company than she does to her husband Yoshihiko (Sano), a kindly veterinarian. Sex for the couple has become the perfunctory effort of the Japanese title—he does so out of a sense of *duty*, while she creates the *performance* of having enjoyed it. However, Shōko finds no need to fake it when she meets Kenji (Ōura), a married man who feigns tiredness at home with his wife but is ready and willing to give Shōko what she craves. Compare to **WEDNESDAY LOVE AFFAIR**, another drama of marital infidelity. Based on a story by Makiko Uchidate, who also created **LUCKILY I WASN'T SO IN LOVE** and **THE WAY YOU WERE WHEN WE FIRST MET**. Theme: Mariya Takeuchi—"Lonely Woman."

LOVE AND PEACE *

1998. PRD: Ken Inoue, Takuya Nakagomi. DIR: Tōya Satō, Tarō Ōya, Tetsuhiro Ogino. SCR: Tetsuya Ōishi, Akihiro Tago. CAST: Masahiro Matsuoka, Aiko Satō, Sakura Uehara, Shinsuke Itsutsu. CHN: NTV. DUR: 45 mins. x 12 eps.; Sat 18 April 1998–4 July 1998.

Kenta (Matsuoka from TOKIO) is engaged to his childhood sweetheart Asuka (Satō) and starting a new job as a detective, but is forced to juggle childcare when his brother dies and he must care for his nephew Yōhei and nieces Hazuki and Futaba. Asuka defies her father and moves in with Kenta but he is preoccupied with difficult times at the police station and his stepchildren's own oddities—young Yōhei starts bullying other children at school while little Hazuki tries to borrow money from the yakuza. Kenta also discovers that his brother was heavily in debt when he died and that he has "inherited" the repayments on a loan of 3.5 million yen.

As in actor Matsuoka's later **HEAVEN CANNOT WAIT**, he is beset with every imaginable problem, inheriting all the stages of parenthood at once, from rebellious teen Hazuki to terrible toddler Futaba. But in mixing reluctant parenthood (see **NEWS WOMAN**) with the trendy detective of the previous year's **BAYSIDE SHAKEDOWN**, *L&P* puts a police procedural spin on family life. It is not enough that Yōhei and his girlfriend go missing in the woods, they go missing on the day that a murderer is on the loose. Similarly, when Hazuki brings home a friend whose father has been absent for years, Stepdad Detective discovers that his fingerprints match those at an unsolved crime scene. The series ends with Kenta and Asuka preparing for their wedding, while he pushes away the unwelcome advances of another woman and the children go missing from protective custody after someone tries to blow up Futaba's kindergarten. Compare to **FIGHTING GIRL**, another attempt to throw in everything but the kitchen sink. Broadcast with English subtitles in the U.S. on KIKU TV and KTSF TV. Theme: TOKIO—"Love and Peace."

LOVE COMPLEX

2000. PRD: Kō Wada. DIR: Kensaku Sawada, Narihide Mizuta. SCR: Ryōichi Kimizuka. CAST: Takashi Sorimachi, Toshiaki Karasawa, Yoshino Kimura, Naomi Nishida, Koyuki, Ryō, Nami Ichinohe, Misaki Ito, Yasunori Danta, Hitomi Takahashi, Kyōko Enami. CHN: Fuji. DUR: 45 mins. x ca. 11 eps.; Thu 12 October 2000–21 December 2000.

After an unknown criminal embezzles a fortune from Wonder Electronics, rakish investigators Gō (Karasawa) and Ayumu (Sorimachi) are transferred to the executive floor to hunt down the suspect. It soon becomes apparent that none of the executives can actually use their computers, absolving them of any involvement in the electronically perpetrated crime but causing suspicion to fall on their seven beautiful secretaries. Each of the girls has an intense loyalty to the others and each has a different reason for thinking that men are the scum of the earth, making it very unlikely that they will cooperate with the investigators. Screened in the

Thursday night thriller slot, this mystery-comedy hybrid failed to achieve the success of previous Sorimachi vehicles such as **CHEAP LOVE**, though some readers may be intrigued by the plotline's resemblance to any of a dozen well-known dating simulations—e.g., *Tokimeki Memorial* (*AE). The original script was reputedly called *Top Secret*, though the final version reflects a change in emphasis along the lines of **POWER OFFICE GIRLS**. As with such computer games, the hero must sift out the bad girls and ensure that he gets a good one for himself by the end. Perhaps through an overdose of *Ally McBeal* on the part of scriptwriter Kimizuka, the script does appear to go overboard with post-modern references, piling on sudden moments of slow-mo, freeze-frames, an episode introduced by the director, and even a parody of *The Blair Witch Project* (1998). Broadcast in the U.S. on the International Channel and NGN, but without English subtitles. Theme: Takashi Sorimachi—"Free."

LOVE FROM OREGON
1984. JPN: *Oregon Kara Ai*. PRD: Toshio Nakamura. DIR: Takuji Tominaga. SCR: Mitsuo Kuroto. CAST: Ikkō Furuya, Nana Kinomi, Ran Itō. CHN: Fuji. DUR: 45 mins. x ca. 11 eps.; Wed 10 October 1984–?? December 1984.
Akira loses his parents in an accident and is invited to stay with his uncle (Furuya) and aunt (Kinomi) who are farmers in Oregon. Depicting a child's life in the beautiful, inscrutable Occident, exotic American scenery led to the serial's success, and it was recycled into five feature-length specials during the following summer.

LOVE GENERATION
1997. PRD: Hiroyoshi Koiwai. DIR: Kōzō Nagayama, Tatsuaki Kimura. SCR: Taeko Asano, Masaya Ozaki. CAST: Takuya Kimura, Takako Matsu, Takeshi Kurosaki, Masaaki Uchino, Risa Junna, Norika Fujiwara, Shinsuke Itsutsu, Ryūta Kawabata, Yōko Moriguchi, Ippei Shiina. CHN: Fuji. DUR: 45 mins. x 11

Love Generation

eps.; Mon 13 October 1997–22 December 1997.
Teppei (Kimura from SMAP) misses the last train home and witnesses a spectacular breakup between Riko (Matsu) and her fiancé Mitsuru (Kurosaki). He suggests that Riko accompanies him to a hotel, where his attempt at seduction is singularly unsuccessful. The following day, a company reshuffle pushes him out of his flamboyant job as creative director for advertising and into the Stepfordesque Operations Department, where all individuality must be checked at the door. He is shocked to discover that Riko works there as an office lady, and the steely girl cuts him no slack when he has trouble fitting in. Though they

fight all the time, they are both broken-hearted—she over the end of her relationship with Mitsuru, he over the loss of his childhood sweetheart Sanae (Junna), who has impressively dumped Teppei in order to marry his elder brother Sōichirō (Uchino).

Riko's wise friend Erika (Fujiwara) warns her that opposites attract, and sure enough Teppei and Riko soon become an item. Meanwhile, Sōichirō and Teppei try to pretend that the Sanae situation is fine (compare to similar incestuous intrigue in **COME TO MAMA'S BED**), while Sōichirō begins a clandestine association with Nami (Moriguchi), his former girlfriend, cast aside because her mother's criminal record could jeopardize Sōichirō's career. Worried that the arrival of Nami will put a strain on Sōichirō's relationship with his fiancé, Teppei arranges a meeting with her but his encounter is misinterpreted by Riko, who now thinks *he* is having the affair!

Retreating to her parents' house in far Nagano, Riko is pursued by Teppei to a local hilltop, where he proposes to her under the stars. He promises to come back for her answer in a week, but the eager Riko cannot wait. She returns to Tokyo early, only to see Teppei in the company of another woman. Though it is another perfectly innocent misunderstanding, she storms off. Meanwhile, Teppei heads for Nagano after a work presentation, but is unable to get there when his car breaks down. Eventually, Riko finds him in Tokyo and tells him her answer.

Heavily influenced by **TOKYO LOVE STORY**, and with a title designed to recall **LONG VACATION**, *LG* was by no means the highest-rated drama of the 1990s, but famously achieved record Fuji viewing figures of 31.3% on its first episode—a likely sign of the growing star power of Kimura, who would find even greater success with **HERO** and **BEAUTIFUL LIFE**. The show's peak ratings were a satisfactory 32.5%.

As a maverick in a staid salaryman world, the outspoken nature of Kimura's character does not merely extend to his argumentative flirting with Matsu—Teppei scandalously suggests, for example, that air stewardesses, the glamorous ideal of so many TV dramas, are nothing more than aerial office ladies, whose job is to serve tea and look pretty. The script also includes several sly references to popular anime of the time—Teppei's old classmate Tamio is obsessed with *Evangelion* (*AE), while Teppei's induction into his new workplace is signified by the cutting off of his ponytail in a homage to *Princess Mononoke* (*AE). He also teases Riko by withholding her precious *Hello Kitty* (*AE) toy.

A feature-length TV edit, *Love Generation 98—Start With the Happy End* was broadcast on 6 April 1998, confus-

ing matters by stopping short of the finale and cutting to new footage of Matsu and Kimura, who comment on the story so far, both as themselves and as their characters. The story was also published as a novelization, credited to scenarists Asano and Ozaki. Theme: Eiichi Ōtaki—"Shiawase na Ketsumatsu" (Happy End).

LOVE HAS YET TO COME

1995. JPN: *Mada Koi wa Hajimaranai*. PRD: Chihiro Kameyama. DIR: Masayuki Suzuki. SCR: Yoshikazu Okada. CAST: Kyōko Koizumi, Kiichi Nakai, Maki Sakai, Takako Tokiwa, Yutaka Takenouchi. CHN: Fuji. DUR: 45 mins. x 9 eps.; Mon 16 October 1995–18 December 1995.

A couple who committed love suicide in the Edo period are reincarnated in the modern age. Kōichirō (Nakai) is divorced by his wife, while Akane (Koizumi) is proposed to by Satoshi (Takenouchi), a man four years younger than her age. The couple are faced with the opportunity to do things right this time. Theme: Kyōko Koizumi—"Beautiful Girls."

LOVE IS A BATTLEFIELD!

2003. JPN: *Koi wa Tatakai!* AKA: *Love is a Fight!; Love and Fight!*. PRD: Takehiko Senno. DIR: Satoshi Katayama. SCR: Masaya Ozaki. CAST: Manami Honjō, Miki Sakai, Takeshi Ihara, Shigeru Muroi. CHN: Asahi. DUR: 45 mins. x ca. 11 eps.; Thu 9 January 2003– 13 March 2003.

Lady journalist Hanako (Honjō) gives help and advice to her friends as they try to find love in Tokyo, offering her thoughts on every subject from Christmas Eve dating etiquette to the way to tell Mr. Right from afar. All the while, she hopes that some of her own advice will land her a Mr. Right of her own. Based on the "Hanako" magazine column and doubtless intended as a sanitized version of Sex and the City. Theme: Abba—"Dancing Queen."

LOVE IS A WONDERFUL THING

1990. JPN: *Suteki na Kataomoi*. PRD:

Tōru Ōta. DIR: Shunsaku Kawake. SCR: Shinji Nojima. CAST: Miho Nakayama, Toshirō Yanagiba, Yū Aihara, Ken Ishiguro, Emi Wakui, Mikihisa Azuma, Kiwako Harada. CHN: Fuji. DUR: 45 mins. x 10 eps.; Mon 15 October 1990–17 December 1990.

Keiko (Nakayama) is a Tokyo banker with troubles in life and love whose new associate Tomomi (Wakui) tries to set her up with Shunpei (Yanagiba). Keiko gets on with Shunpei on the phone, but backs out when she realizes that he is the same man who saw her falling down at the train station—compare to a similar farce in **ARRANGED MARRIAGE**. Later, Keiko and her friend Taeko (Aihara) meet Shunpei at the video store, where Taeko engineers a double date by volunteering to bring him a tape he wants to see. Out on the town with Shunpei and his friend Yutaka (Ishiguro), Taeko urges Keiko to leave with Yutaka, so that she can have Shunpei to herself. Shunpei however, recognizes Keiko's voice when she calls Taeko later. To throw him off the scent, Keiko claims that her name is Nana, forcing her to maintain a false identity as she finds herself falling for Shunpei herself. Meanwhile, she begins seeing Yutaka, who with dramatic predictability is passionately in love with her but finds his feelings unrequited.

Naturally, "Nana" is unable to agree to meet Shunpei, since he will discover that she is really Keiko. "Nana" refuses to see Shunpei, and the jilted man begins to develop an interest in Keiko. In an attempt to forget "Nana" and out of respect for Yutaka's love of Keiko, Shunpei begins a new relationship with his colleague Ikumi (Harada). However, Shunpei becomes angry with Keiko when she dumps Yutaka and the two have a falling out, only to be reunited on Christmas Eve, when Ikumi brings Shunpei evidence that "Nana" and Keiko are one and the same.

An innocent romance with tense comedy business, setting the pace for **TOKYO LOVE STORY** and **101ST PROPOSAL**, *LiaWT* was an early drama from **BEAUTY**'s Shinji Nojima. Inadvertent false identities would also feature in **WHERE IS LOVE?**. Theme: Miho Nakayama—"Aishiterutte Iwanai!" (I Won't Say I Love You!).

LOVE ME

2000. JPN: *Ai o Kudasai*. AKA: *Give Me Your Love*. PRD: Kazuki Nakayama, Miyuki Nashimoto. DIR: Akiji Fujita, Hidekazu Matsuda. SCR: Jinsei Tsuji. CAST: Miho Kanno, Yōsuke Eguchi, Hideaki Itō, Sachie Hara, Yuka Kurotani, Toshio Kakei, Tetta Sugimoto, Takanori Jinnai. CHN: Fuji. DUR: 45 mins. x ca. 11 eps.; Wed 5 July 2000–?? September 2000. Kirika (Kanno) intends to throw herself from one of the Hakodate mountain cable cars, but is talked down by Motojirō (Eguchi). In order to keep her alive, he becomes her pen pal and confidante—he draws up ground rules forbidding face to face meetings and ruling out any romantic involvement between the two. Kirika returns to her day job in a nursery school, where the parents resent her for lecturing them on good parenting when her own family background is far from ideal—compare to similar tensions in **FOOD FIGHT**. She also lives a double life as a busker, singing songs on street corners (one of which is both the theme to the series and a successful single released during the broadcast run) and avenging her childhood self by seducing the fathers of some of the children in her care. All the while, Motojirō tries to keep her on the straight and narrow in a constant stream of letters; somehow quaint in the digital age, when people in the real world were already communicating by mobile and e-mail. Shown unsubtitled in the U.S. on the NGN network. Theme: Miho Kanno—"Zoo: Ai o Kudasai" (Zoo: Give Me Your Love).

LOVE MEANS NO REGRETS

1996. JPN: *Ai to wa Kesshite Kōkai Shinai Koto*. PRD: Takamichi Yamada. DIR: Miki Nemoto. SCR: Masao Yajima. CAST: Naoto Ogata, Nene Ōtsuka, Megumi Yokoyama, Masaki Kanda.

CHN: TBS. DUR: 45 mins. x 11 eps.; Fri 12 January 1996–22 March 1996. Yasuhiro (Ogata) works at a publishing company, where he is engaged to the editor Tomoko (Yokoyama). Yasuhiro's sister Kayo (Ōtsuka) is always with her brother and tries to monopolize his attention. Compare to **IDEAL MARRIAGE**. Theme: Tunnels—"Omae ga Hoshii" (I Want You).

LOVE ON HOLD *

1997. JPN: *Koi no Vacance*. AKA: *In Love and Loving It*. PRD: Toshio Akabane, Katsumi Kamikura. DIR: Nobuo Mizuta, Futoshi Ōhira. SCR: Yasuhiro Koshimizu. CAST: Sanma Akashiya, Anju Suzuki, Ryō, Reiko Takashima, Katsuhisa Namase, Mari Hamada, Takeshi Masu, Ittoku Kishibe. CHN: NTV. DUR: 45 mins. x 10 eps. (1st ep 90 mins.); Wed 8 January 1997–12 March 1997. Kankurō (Akashiya, in a role that was made for him) is a businessman seen leaving a Tokyo bar drunk with his boss's pretty secretary Aki (Suzuki). Though the couple never make it to the bedroom, the circumstantial evidence is enough for some office gossips, and Kankurō and Aki are presumed to be an item. Though the pair try to end the rumors, nobody believes their denials—even when they try to avoid each other, their workmates simply assume there has been a lovers' quarrel and try to get them "back together." However, Kankurō is supposed to find a wife anyway (as in **ARRANGED MARRIAGE**, the company frowns on unwed middle managers) and is soon pressured into dating Aki's sister-in-law Chiharu. Meanwhile, Aki's sister Tamao suspects that her husband Kensaku (Chiharu's brother) is sleeping around, while Kankurō's junior assistant Taichi (Namase) harbors secret feelings for Aki.

Love on Hold is an unadulterated farce, as each of Kankurō's ideas saves him from one difficult situation, only to make things ten times worse. It reaches its insane peak when Kankurō is forced to climb out of the window of

his own apartment and phones the *four* women waiting for him there to try and extricate himself from yet another marital misunderstanding. As in **FALSE LOVE**, Kankurō is presented with a forged marriage certificate by one desperate wife and eventually considers permanent bachelorhood as a welcome alternative.

The Japanese/French title translates literally as *Love Vacation*, a blatant attempt to imply non-existent links with Fuji's popular **LONG VACATION**. A TV special followed on 10 October the same year. Broadcast with English subtitles in the U.S. on KIKU TV. Theme: Mr. Children—"Everything (It's You)."

LOVE ON WINGS

1992. JPN: *Koi wa Tsubasa ni Notte*. PRD: N/C. DIR: Chichū Tachi. SCR: Kaoru Sugiya. CAST: Mai Kitajima, Tetsuya Bessho, Mariko Kaga, Tōru Minegishi. CHN: TVT. DUR: 45 mins. x 6 eps.; Mon 19 April 1992–24 May 1992. Momo (Kitajima) works in a Yotsuya printing company, until one fateful day when a new employee joins the firm. It is her mother Sakura (Kaga), who abandoned her and disappeared when she was only a child.

LOVE QUOTIENT

2002. JPN: *Ren'ai Hensachi*. PRD: Miwako Kurihara, Kiichi Iguchi. DIR: Yūichi Satō, Tetsuji Kubota, Takao Kinoshita. SCR: Hiroshi Tsuzuki, Yoshihiro Izumi, Yūji Sakamoto. CAST: Miki Nakatani, Tomohiro Sekiguchi, Junichi Okada, Rei Kikukawa, Tomoko Nakajima, Tae Kimura, Takako Tokiwa, Gorō Inagaki, Tomomitsu Yamaguchi, Sayaka Kaneko, Naomi Zaizen, Kō Shibazaki, Takashi Yashibara, Toshirō Yanagiba, Tsunku, Ken Kaito. CHN: Fuji. DUR: 45 mins. x 12 eps.; Thu 4 July 2002–19 September 2002. A cunning way of keeping several plates spinning at once, as producer Kurihara sells the Fuji network on a "series" that effectively comprises three completely separate romances—compare to the same season's **100 GHOST STORIES**. They are supposedly linked by a common thread, but the alleged unifying theme of "love for the modern woman" is found in almost *all* Japanese serials! In many ways, the result is little different from a multi-character drama like WHERE IS LOVE?, just with less overlap and with the subplots presented sequentially instead of simultaneously. Though there are some common characters, such as Ayumu (Tsunku), it is far more likely that the linking factor resides in several behind the scenes concerns—the setup makes it possible to work with several casts and crews simultaneously, reducing the chances of holdups like that experienced by ROCKET BOY. The presence of so many famous names is a marketer's dream, allowing the commercials to show them all together, even if their characters never meet. And while feature-length re-edits are common in Japanese TV drama, the size of each mini-story makes it possible to make several, with less wasted footage—this is TV with an eye on video sales.

[*Part One: Until the Fire Has Almost Burned Out*] Twenty-eight-year old Reiko (Nakatani) is dumped by Kōichirō (Sekiguchi), her boyfriend of five years. Her performance at work takes a nosedive and her depression drives her toward borderline anorexia. She comes to realize that every aspect of her former "happy" life was founded on the belief that she was in a secure relationship, and without one, she is a nervous wreck. Somewhat misguidedly, she decides that the answer to her problems will be to fall head-over-heels in love with the next man she meets.

[*Part Two: Party*] Kotoko (Tokiwa) is a woman with expensive tastes, working in the high-class Marunouchi district, living in salubrious Daikanyama, and spending nights on the town in luxurious Aoyama. Her life is thrown into turmoil when her cushy job with one of the foreign affiliates collapses. Desperate to hang onto the lifestyle to which she has become accustomed, she realizes her chances might lie in marriage to Natsume (Inagaki), a rich trader she meets at a party. However, she

finds more fulfillment with the geeky Junpei (Yamaguchi), the owner of a glass factory. Taking a job alongside TV drama's usual catalogue of societal misfits, she starts to find a new place for herself.

[*Part Three: Fighting Among Themselves*] Tamako is a successful Marunouchi businesswoman in her mid-thirties, regarded by other employees as past her prime. She despises the company's yearly intake of office ladies, regarding them as empty-headed bimbos with no appreciation for the finer things in life. She is also conducting a secret affair with Shirō (Yanagiba), though she secretly admits it is going nowhere. Chie (Shibazaki) is a 22-year-old office lady, forever dreaming of finding her Mr. Right and pretty sure that he isn't her current boyfriend, unemployed actor Tsukasa (Kaito). When the handsome Yukihiko (Yashibara) is head-hunted from a New York office and brought to Tokyo, both women decide that he is The One and begin competing for his affections.

LOVE REVOLUTION

2001. PRD: Utahiko Honma, Kimiyasu Hiraga. DIR: Kōzō Nagayama, Kazuhiro Kobayashi. SCR: Yuki Fujimoto. CAST: Makiko Esumi, Ryōko Yonekura, Naoto Fujiki, Manabu Oshio, Miki Sakai, Maiko Toda. CHN: Fuji. DUR: 45 mins. x 12 eps.; Mon 9 April 2001–25 June 2001.

Kyōko (Esumi) is a doctor whose brisk manner has led many of her associates to believe she has no need for a man in her life. Nothing, however, could be further from the truth, and she earnestly prays for a boyfriend at the Church of Saint Valentine in Rome, where she has gone on vacation with her air stewardess buddy Mariko (Yonekura). Though a gypsy predicts that Kyōko will soon return to the church in a bridal carriage, the women laugh it off and head back to Japan. On the return flight, Kyōko's medical skills save the life of a portly Italian restaurateur, who now believes it is his mission to find her a man. His initial

matchmaking attempts include the secretary of a prominent politician and an out of work actor who moonlights as a bartender. But it's the bad boy that gets Kyōko's attention, when a man (Fujiki) suddenly kisses her in the hospital hallway—little does she know he is a scheming journalist, intending to use her as cover while he digs for dirt on the politician. Broadcast without English subtitles in the U.S. on KSCI TV. Theme: Ken Hirai—"Kiss of Life."

LOVE SEPARATION SERVICE

2001. JPN: *Wakaresaseya*. PRD: Kimihiko Imamura. DIR: Junji Kadō, Yūya Fujii. SCR: Tadashi Morishita. CAST: Rikako Murakami, Megumi Okina, Shunsuke Nakamura, Yōko Nogiwa, Tsunehiko Watase, Takeshi Naitō, Takuzō Kadono. CHN: Yomiuri. DUR: 45 mins. x ca. 11 eps.; Mon 8 January 2001–?? March 2001.

Dumped by her husband, the depressed Miyo (Murakami) finds herself working for the private espionage organization PPI, whose specialty is arranging temptations, reconciliations, and embarrassments designed to break up relationships. Their clandestine activities allow their clients to walk away from relationships without any guilt or blame, combining the thrills of *Mission: Impossible* (reborn in movie form since 1996) with the satire of THE STAND-IN. Compare to FLIGHT BY NIGHT.

LOVE STORY

2001. PRD: Hiroki Ueda. DIR: Jirō Shōno, Nobuhiro Doi, Natsuki Imai. SCR: Eriko Kitagawa. CAST: Etsushi Toyokawa, Miho Nakayama, Yūka, Shingo Katori, Haruhiko Katō. CHN: TBS. DUR: 45 mins. x 11 eps.; Sun 15 April 2001–24 June 2001.

Misaki (Nakayama) is an outspoken, go-getting publisher's employee whose willingness to pick at apparently minor inconsistencies has made her excellent editor material, but extremely unlucky in the relationship stakes. She is assigned to deal with Kō (Toyokawa), an eccentric author whose romances once commanded immense sales, but now appears to be in a slump—he has not written a story in two years and faces being dropped by his publisher. While the other editors fawn around him, she makes incisive criticisms, which lead to a reprimand from her boss but the grudging respect of the author, even if he doesn't like what he hears.

In the wake of LOST PARADISE, the editor's life became a popular theme for dramatists, with troubled authors · also appearing in WHERE IS LOVE? and WEDNESDAY LOVE AFFAIR. In its romance between straight-talking lady and obsessive-compulsive writer, *LS* also owes a debt to the Jack Nicholson vehicle *As Good As It Gets* (1997), even to the extent of a chalk-and-cheese conflict between the author and his neighbor—in this case bleached blonde charmer Kyōji (Katori from SMAP), who leaves a trail of broken-hearted women behind him. Taking an idea from the *Friends* "Central Perk" set-up, *LS*'s leads live upstairs from the friendly Sunset Café coffee shop, whose well-meaning owner initially mistakes the nervous Misaki for one of Kyōji's ex-girlfriends. Meanwhile, Kō's doting grandmother owns a nearby rice cracker shop and diligently sets up her single grandson on a blind date with her favorite customer. Naturally, the "nice young girl" turns out to be the argumentative Misaki whom Kō is trying so hard to avoid—compare to similarly disastrous matchmakings in ARRANGED MARRIAGE and WITH LOVE. Notable also for the classic line: *"If you were Nobita, I'd be your Doraemon,"* a reference to the mismatched pals of the long-running *Doraemon* series (*AE). Theme: Spitz—"Haruka ni" (To the Distance).

LOVE SUICIDES AT YOKOHAMA

1994. JPN: *Yokohama Shinjū*. PRD: Katsumi Kamikura. DIR: Masahiro Tsurugi. SCR: Nobuyuki Matsui, Michiru Etō. CAST: Kōichi Satō, Isako Washio, Chiharu Komatsu, Junichi Kasuga. CHN: NTV. DUR: 45 mins. x 11 eps.; 12 January 1994–23 March 1994.

Love 2000

Aoi (Washio) believes that Shūhei (Satō) murdered her fiancé, but when the killer is put on trial, he convinces the court that he was only acting in self-defense. Eager for justice to be done, Aoi begins to stalk Shūhei, only to fall in love with him. Compare to TABLOID. Theme: Kōji Yamada—"Himawari" (Sunflower).

LOVE 2000

2000. JPN: *Nisennen no Koi*. AKA: *Love in the Year 2000; AD 2000–Don't Shoot Her!* PRD: Hiroyoshi Koiwai. DIR: Renpei Tsukamoto. SCR: Yuki Fujimoto. CAST: Miho Nakayama, Takeshi Kaneshiro, Johnny Yoshinaga, Kazufumi Miyazawa, Mikihisa Azuma, Mitsuru Murata, Fayray. CHN: Fuji. DUR: 45 mins. x ca. 11 eps.; Mon 10 January 2000–?? March 2000. Software engineer Rieru (Nakayama) meets fellow employee "Nogami" (Kaneshiro) while monitoring Y2K problems at the Ministry of Foreign Affairs on New Year's Eve. Little does she know that "Nogami" is really Yuri, an assassin from the Ural Republic, sent to Japan to execute his defecting

scientist father Malueff (Yoshinaga). Yuri is a desperate man—his mother and sister are being held hostage to ensure the successful completion of his mission and he has already had to kill his own brother to save him from capture. Rieru is unwittingly used as Yuri's cover during a failed assassination attempt at the opera and helps him evade the police at a hotel stakeout.

Yuri's handler Naomi (Fayray) plans to kill Rieru, ostensibly because *"she knows too much,"* but really because Naomi is jealous of Yuri's feelings for her. Yuri's mission is successful, but he is shot by Malueff's minder Saeki (Miyazawa) and hides out at a church near Rieru's house, where Rieru finds him and nurses him in secret.

Meanwhile, Rieru's sister Maria has a raft of troubles that would be enough for any other drama in themselves. Forced into debt by her abusive, drug-dealing, slacker boyfriend Seiji, she raises money through appearing in pornographic films but eventually finds out that she is pregnant. Seiji, for his part, discovers that he has been used to smuggle evidence against Yuri past the police and tries to blackmail Rieru.

Saeki confronts Rieru (whom he too is falling for) with the evidence that Yuri's mother and sister are already dead—he has no reason to do his government's bidding anymore. However, Naomi is determined to kill Yuri before he switches sides and begins a vengeful campaign against the lovers that includes poisonings, bombings, and an assault on Maria. Matters come to a head when Ulanov, a prominent Ural politician, visits Japan, and Yuri prepares a new mission of his own. . . .

Love 2000 was fortunate to be released in the period between the end of the Cold War and the shock of the 9/11 attacks in America—stories about misunderstood terrorists were not so popular 18 months later, in a climate which saw the swift burial of TV Asahi's lighthearted comedy **THE SNIPER** and the recession that features in **FRIENDSHIP**. *Love 2000* was also the harbinger of a new era of TV drama, featuring stars with pan-Asian appeal—the trilingual Kaneshiro's regular appearances in Wong Kar-Wai films making him one of the region's truly international heartthrobs. Adding the traditions of Japanese TV to the conventions of the techno-thriller, it jumps from family melodrama and star-crossed romance to counterespionage in the style of the Korean blockbuster *Swiri*. Its originality was all the more impressive on its initial release, since it premiered simultaneously across East Asia, with few plot details revealed in advance. The international angle was repeated often in the early years of the 21st century with stars from Hong Kong (**FALSE LOVE**), Korea (**FRIENDS**), and Taiwan (**LADY OF THE MANOR**).

In a more traditional thriller, Saeki would have been the hero. He is the supercompetent investigator, traumatized by the death of his parents at the hands of terrorists, who desires the female lead and doggedly hunts the foreign assassin. But it is Yuri who gets all the limelight, as hinted in the early

opera sequence, where Rieru explains the plot of Wagner's *Tristan and Isolde.* Like Isolde, Rieru is unable to give up her man even when she finds out who he really is, though Yuki Fujimoto's screenplay also seems unable to quit while it is ahead, losing momentum in the later chapters before collapsing in a disappointing B-movie ending.

New Year's Eve 1999 also provided the opening moments of another drama, **I'LL BE BACK**. Theme: Do As Infinity—"Yesterday and Today."

LOVE YOU FOREVER

1991. JPN: *Kimi Dake ni Ai o Love Forever.* AKA: *Love Only You Love Forever.* PRD: Kunisuke Hirabayashi. DIR: Hidenobu Hosono. SCR: Yūko Miyamura. CAST: Hironobu Nomura, Yuki Matsushita, Michiko Kawai, Hitomi Shimizu, Miki Fujitani, Etsushi Takahashi, Reiko Matsunaga. CHN: NTV. DUR: 45 mins. x 11 eps.; Sat 12 January 1991–23 March 1991.

Tōru (Nomura) and Namiko (Matsushita) are "waiting for the right time" to tell her domineering father Gōzō (Takahashi) that they are dating. On the way to see Namiko, Tōru kills a man in a car accident, whose sister (Matsunaga) loses her eyesight. The result is an outstandingly melodramatic in-law appeasement series—like **SHOTGUN MARRIAGE** with added death, and a ticking time bomb in the form of one cast member who will reveal the nature of Tōru's crime the moment her sight returns. Look on the bright side, how could things ever get worse . . . ? Theme: Shinpei Watanabe—"Yorikakatte Only You" (Lean On Me, Only You).

LOVERS ON THE SAND

1999. JPN: *Suna no Ue no Koibitotachi.* AKA: *Seaside Lovers.* PRD: Yūji Ōhira, Shintarō Suzuki. DIR: Akiji Fujita, Kazuhiro Onohara. SCR: Kazuhiko Ban. CAST: Tomoya Nagase, Manami Honjō, Megumi Okina, Miho Kanno, Masato Hagiwara. CHN: Kansai. DUR: 45 mins. x 11 eps.; Tue 12 October 1999–21 December 1999.

Akira (Nagase)'s girlfriend (Kanno) is killed in a vacation accident in Australia and the grieving Akira soon finds himself falling for Reiko (Honjō), the guilt-ridden girl responsible for the death. Theme: ACO—"Yorokobi ni Saku Hana" (The Joyful Flower Blooms). Peak rating: 15.2%.

LOVE'S HESITATIONS

1997. JPN: *Koi no Tamerai.* AKA: *Hesitation of Love.* PRD: Hideki Isano, Kazunori Shiokawa. DIR: Ken Yoshida, Akio Yoshida, Tōru Moriyama, Hideki Isano. SCR: Ryō Iwamatsu. CAST: Naoto Takenaka, Anju Suzuki, Miki Nakatani, Tōru Masuoka, Sawa Suzuki, Shinya Tsukamoto, Shinobu Ōtake. CHN: TBS. DUR: 45 mins. x 11 eps.; Fri 10 October 1997–19 December 1997.

Middle-aged salaryman Akio (Takenaka) finds himself out of a job and having to start all over again. He is tempted to throw in his lot with Hiroko (Suzuki), an antique seller's daughter with whom he formerly had an *omiai* marriage meeting, since at least he will get a wife and a job out of the deal. However, he is soon tempted by two other choices: an energetic minx who is far too young for him and an old flame who just might have been the love of his life. Theme: Naoto Takenaka—"Kimi ni Hoshi ga Furu" (Stars Falling Down on You).

LUCKILY I WASN'T SO IN LOVE

1998. JPN: *Ai Shisuginakute Yokatta.* AKA: *Feeling Relief Is Easy.* PRD: Satoko Uchiyama. DIR: Ken Matsumoto, Masahiro Nakano. SCR: Makiko Uchidate. CAST: Noriyuki Higashiyama, Ryō, Miki Sakai, Tatsuya Fujiwara. CHN: Asahi. DUR: 45 mins. x 11 eps.; Thu 8 January 1998–19 March 1998.

Bored with life in Tokyo, Natsumi (Ryō) quits her job and prepares to return to her hometown in the sticks. However, on her last night in the big city, she meets and falls in love with playboy Yōtaro (Higashiyama). Though she arrives back in her little hometown, her heart remains in Tokyo. . . . She eventually returns, determined to win Yōtaro for herself, though he is recovering from a messy divorce and busily sowing wild oats while Natsumi meekly waits for him to come to his senses. THE WAY YOU WERE WHEN WE FIRST MET creator Makiko Uchidate adapted the screenplay from her own original story, which had also been turned into a manga in 1996 by artist Noriko Irie.

LULLABY DETECTIVE
1991. JPN: *Lullaby Keiji 91/92/93.* PRD: N/C. DIR: Tōgorō Tsuchiya. SCR: Hiroshi Nagano. CAST: Narumi Arimori, Tatsuo Umemiya, Tsurutarō Kataoka, Yūki Matsumura. CHN: Asahi. DUR: 45 mins. x ca. 34 eps.; Sun 20 October 1991–5 April 1992; ?? April 1993–?? June 1993.

Miyuki (Arimori) is the new deputy section chief at the West Shinjuku police station, much to the annoyance of the male detectives who are expected to obey her orders. Theme: X-Japan—"Say Anything."

LXIXVXE
1999. AKA: *Live.* PRD: Hiroki Ueda. DIR: Jirō Shōno, Kanji Takenoshita, Natsuki Imai. SCR: Keiko Nobumoto, Miki Aiuchi. CAST: Eriko Imai, Tatsuya Fujiwara, Akiko Kinouchi, Hitoe Arakaki, Rina Uchiyama, Mari Hoshino, Kenji Harada. CHN: TBS. DUR: 45 mins. x ca. 11 eps.; Fri 9 April 1999–?? June 1999.

Keen saxophonist Misaki (Imai from Speed) transfers to a new high school in Yokosuka, where she joins the brass band to make new friends. The band, however, is in extreme disarray and on the verge of disbandment. The band leader Seiichi (Harada) assigns Misaki to play the flute but when she hears fellow saxophonist Yūki (Arakaki from Speed) practicing on the waterfront, she decides to turn the band's fortunes around. Possibly inspired by the British movie *Brassed Off* (1996), *LxIxVxE* jettisons its forerunner's political bite in favor of a simple tale of musicians in search of success. Quirky people building self-esteem with offbeat hobbies are commonplace in Japanese drama—compare to TIME OF YOUR LIFE, BLUE SCATTERS, and the movies *Water Boys, Shall We Dance?,* or *Sumo Do Sumo Don't.* Theme: Amika Hattan—"Shooting Star."

M

MADCAP ISLAND

1964. JPN: *Hyokkori Hyōtanjima*. AKA: *Pop-Up Gourd Island*. PRD: N/C. DIR: Shōichi Yuki, Hiroshi Chii, Yūichi Yamaguchi. SCR: Hisashi Inoue. CAST: (voices) Arihiro Fujimura, Kazuo Kumakura, Kyōji Kobayashi, Toshie Kusunoki, Chinatsu Nakayama, Toshiko Fujita. CHN: NHK. DUR: 15 mins. x 1224 eps.; Mon 6 April 1964–4 April 1969.

After the unexpected eruption of Mount Gourd, the nearby island drifts free and floats across the ocean, bringing its inhabitants into contact with numerous strange kingdoms, such as Tamure, ruled by a lion, and the state of Buldokia, where dogs rule over people. Meanwhile, the peripatetic islanders have an election to determine their leader and eventually vote for the optimistic and broadminded Don Gavacho (Fujimura). His sometime associates include pirate-turned-businessman Torahige (Kumakura), who claims to have plundered the seven seas and 108 rivers, and Dandy (Kobayashi), a gangster who escaped from captivity by using his umbrella to parachute from a transport plane. Now a sheriff on Madcap Island, Dandy harbors secret desires for the pretty local schoolteacher Miss Sandy (Kusunoki). A gentle soul who is adored by all the local children, Miss Sandy is also a martial artist.

One of the most successful serials ever shown on Japanese children's television, the puppet show *Madcap Island* appealed to its young audience by destroying almost all the logic of the adult world. It also attracted an appreciative audience of knowing parents, who ignored the silly floating island and instead enjoyed the subtle satirical notes—compare to similar jibes in CHIRORIN VILLAGE. At the time of its initial broadcast, NHK received several complaints about "violence and bad language" in the show. Creator Hisashi Inoue would later become one of the writers on *The Moomins* (*AE), while the puppet show and its happy theme song would also appear in the anime *Only Yesterday* (*AE).

Partway through its original TV run, the series was also made into a 61-minute animated movie, *Madcap Island* (1967), directed by Taiji Yabushita. In this form it has been shown at several film festivals but the original puppet incarnation has not fared so well. Only eight of the 1224 original episodes survive to this day, but the series was remade for a new generation in 1991 for NHK's BS-2 satellite channel. In this latest incarnation, Akira Nagoya took over the role of Don Gavacho, as the original actor Arihiro Fujimura had since died. For more popular puppetry, see THE HAKKENDEN and SUN WUKONG.

MAGNIFICENT ADVENTURES OF KOHARU THE GEISHA, THE

1991. JPN: *Geisha Koharu no Karei na Bōken*. PRD: N/C. DIR: Shūichi Nakayama. SCR: Masao Yajima. CAST: Nobuko Miyamoto, Yū Hayami, Mitsuru Hirata, Shizuo Nakajō. CHN: Asahi. DUR: 45 mins. x 11 eps.; Thu 11 April 1991–20 June 1991.

After the death of her mother, Koharu (Miyamoto) has no choice but to help out in the geisha house where she was born and raised. She befriends Miki (Hayami), a part-time serving girl, who reveals that she used to be a journalist and that she is busy writing an exposé of life in the red-light district.

A timely look at life in the geisha world, doubtless inspired by the infamous Sōsuke Uno case two years before, in which a geisha broke traditional confidentiality to admit she was having an affair with the prime minister. Scenarist Yajima also wrote the manga *Human Scramble* (drawn by Kenshi Hirokane) and BIG WING. For more kimono-clad adventures, see GEISHA DETECTIVE.

MAKING IT THROUGH *

1990. JPN: *Wataru Seken wa Oni Bakari*. AKA: *Surrounded by Devils in Life*. PRD: Fukuko Ishii. DIR: Yasuo Inoshita. SCR: Sugako Hashida. CAST: Pinko Izumi, Hisano Yamaoka, Takuya Fujioka, Harue Akagi, Aiko Nagayama, Yoshiko Nakada, Mami Nomura, Tomoko Fujita, Shōko Nakajima, Toshiji Kishida, Kaoru Okunuki, Katsuhide Uegusa, Utako Kyō. CHN: TBS. DUR: 45 mins. x ca. 350 eps.; Thu 11 October 1990–26 September 1991 (#1); 15

April 1993–31 March 1994 (#2); 4 April 1996–27 March 1997 (#3); 1 October 1998–24 December 1998 (#4); 7 January 1999–25 March 1999 (#5); 5 October 2000–?? March 2001 (#6); 4 April 2002–?? October 2002 (#7).

Family problems such as life after retirement, problems with in-laws, and children's independence are all examined through the life of Daikichi (Fujioka) and Setsuko Okakura (Yamaoka) and their five daughters: Satsuki (Izumi), Ayako (Nakada), Yayoi (Nagayama), Yōko (Nomura), and Nagako (Fujita). Created at the height of the trendy drama boom by OSHIN writer Sugako Hashida and resolutely flying in the face of the glossy, superficial concerns of the 1980s generation, MIT has proved to be a blue-chip success. It has steadily gained audiences in a run that has lasted over a decade and allows its viewers to pick a point of identification, which then ages with them.

With five daughters, each of whom has a relationship and a circle of friends to fret over, the Okakura family are guaranteed to have enough drama to keep them busy, and the multi-generational structure allows them to flit between in-law appeasement and child rearing on a weekly basis. In fact, the entire family assembles only rarely, allowing for actors to drop in and out of the central cast when their careers require it. It also regularly allows new viewers points to jump on—there are new arrivals and subplots that need to be explained on a weekly basis, allowing for a structure that invites new viewers and then tricks them into staying. Their restaurant business also permits a third theater of action, where the family members are forced to deal with rotating staff and work-related disputes. Meanwhile, in-laws dabble in everything imaginable, from crane driving to hydroponics.

With the opening of the "Kōraku" family restaurant business at the end of season three, matriarch Setsuko sets off for New York for a long-deserved vacation, only to die abroad. Season four is taken up with the arrangements for her funeral and the troubles caused by the arrival of interfering aunt Taki (Nomura). With the restaurant short-staffed, family members fight over who should put their "real" career on hold to keep the business afloat, while Fumiko's child reveals that he is in trouble with the police—a bout of delinquency that eventually brings his divorced parents back together. Yayoi's son marries a woman who is pregnant by another man, whereas the widowed mother-in-law of one of the daughters announces that she intends to marry a doctor and hand over the inheritance to her hospital to her new steps.on. Meanwhile, the daughters fight over the best plan of action to take with the widowed Daikichi—should they let him mourn in peace or attempt to set him up with new marriage material.

MIT is also unafraid of references to the modern world. One grandson becomes the subject of family gossip when he is discovered to be seeing a girl he met on the internet, while a granddaughter decides to put her family ahead of a part she has been offered in a TV drama—the ultimate way for the cast and crew to pay homage to the values of their humble fans.

As the 21st century dawns, the family is troubled by the disappearance of trusted staff member Seiko (Nakajima) with millions of yen. The seventh series sees Kimi (Akagi), the manageress of the Kōraku business, bringing her son-in-law Kenji (Kishida) in to run the restaurant's packed-lunch concession. He in turn drafts in his fiancée Mitsuko (Okunuki), leading to resentment among the family and the initiation of a series of hazings. Meanwhile, Nagako's husband Eisaku (Uegusa) is transferred to a new office and lives alone, forcing Nagako to leave her daughter in the hands of her mother-in-law Tsuneko (Kyō) and seek a new job. The perils of leaving one's man to look after himself, however, are soon realized when Eisaku collapses at work.

Seasons 1–5 have been broadcast in the U.S. with English subtitles on KIKU TV.

MAKING MEMORIES

1981. JPN: Omoidezukuri. PRD: N/C. DIR: Shinichi Kamoshita, Yasuo Inoshita, Ryūtarō Toyohara. SCR: Taichi Yamada. CAST: Masako Mori, Yūko Kotegawa, Yūko Tanaka, Kyōhei Shibata, Takehiko Maeda, Sumiko Sakamoto, Kiyoshi Kodama, Sumie Sasaki, Kenichi Katō, Jinpachi Nezu. CHN: TBS. DUR: 45 mins. x ca. 11 eps.; Fri 18 September 1981–25 December 1981. Office ladies played by Masako Mori, Yūko Kotegawa, and Yūko Tanaka face the big 25, the age that was once regarded as the time limit for a good marriage—1980s popular slang referred to such women as "Christmas Cakes," unsellable after the 25th. The women are torn between their desires for a romantic wedding and their wish to enjoy their twenties and have some happy memories to cherish as the misery of married life sets in. Broadcast at the same time as the first run of FROM THE NORTH, the ratings battle between this series by ODD APPLES creator Yamada and his great writing rival Sō Kuramoto became the subject of some media debate.

MAMA IS AN IDOL

1987. JPN: Mama wa Idol. PRD: N/C. DIR: N/C. SCR: Masahiro Yoshimoto. CAST: Miho Nakayama, Kunihiko Mitamura, Kumiko Gotō. CHN: TBS. DUR: 45 mins. x 10 eps.; Tue 14 April 1987–16 June 1987. Widowed junior high school teacher (Mitamura) marries a young starlet (Nakayama) without his daughter's approval. Now daughter (Gotō) is stuck with a stepmother who is adored by all the boys in her class and whose fame seems to outshine her at every turn—compare to YAGAMI'S FAMILY TROUBLES and MY WIFE IS 18. An early performance from Nakayama, who rather conveniently was a teen idol and ideally suited to the role. Feature-length specials followed in 1987 and 1988, and the show was later ripped off for the anime *Paradise Without Stars* (*AE).

MAMA IS MY RIVAL

1972. JPN: *Mama wa Rival*. PRD: Chiharu Kasuga. DIR: Ryūichi Okaya. SCR: Mamoru Sasaki. CAST: Yūki Okazaki, Etsushi Takahashi, Alice Atsushi. CHN: TBS. DUR: 45 mins. x ca. 40 eps.; Wed 4 October 1972–26 September 1973.

A teenage girl (Okazaki) has mixed feelings when her widowed father (Takahashi) announces that he intends to remarry. His chosen bride is one of his daughter's classmates (Atsushi), a decision which brings classroom rivalry to the evening dinner table and domestic disputes into the school. A retread of Okazaki's earlier MY WIFE IS 18, compare to COME TO MAMA'S BED and MAMA IS AN IDOL. Theme: Machiko Sasaki—"Mama wa Rival."

MAMA'S GENES *

2003. JPN: *Mama no Idenshi*. PRD: N/C. DIR: N/C. SCR: N/C. CAST: Hiroko Yakushimaru, Takaya Kamikawa, Jōtarō Koike, Eran Mochizuki, Ayako Sawada, Raita Ryū, Yū Yoshizawa. CHN: TBS. DUR: 45 mins. x 10 eps.; [broadcast times unknown].

Wataru (Kamikawa)'s parents have scrupulously remodeled their house to provide living space for Wataru's elder brother and his family. But when the elder brother unexpectedly relocates to Osaka, Wataru finds that his parents now want him to move in. His wife Nanami (Yakushimaru) can think of nothing worse, as she does not get on with her mother-in-law and dreads the chaos her children are likely to wreak on Wataru's family home. In-law appeasement in a city setting—compare to BY THE SEA and LADY OF THE MANOR. N.B. We obtained information on this show from TBS's own website but although the channel gives information on this show, it cannot possibly have been broadcast at the time they claim, as it would have had to share a signal with the remake of HIGH SCHOOL TEACHER. Broadcast in the U.S.

with English subtitles on KIKU TV. Theme: Rag Fair—"Asatte wa Sunday" (The Day after Tomorrow is Sunday).

MAMA'S GRADUATION CEREMONY

1976. JPN: *Mama no Sotsugyōshiki*. PRD: Seiji Akiyama. DIR: Mikio Hatada. SCR: Yoshio Iwama. CAST: Rieko Hiramatsu, Masao Okabe, Michiko Hirai, Yōichi Sase, Hiroyo Funabashi. CHN: NHK. DUR: 25 mins. x 9 eps.; Tue 2 March 1976–27 March 1976.

Tomoko Kobayashi's mother Chieko (Hiramatsu) is a PTA member busy attending meetings to organize Tomoko and her classmates' graduation ceremony. One day, Tomoko sees a postcard advising her mother that her own graduation is imminent—Chieko's elementary school never officially presented its students with their certificates, owing to wartime distractions. The event gives Chieko the opportunity to tell her daughter about World War II, when she herself was Tomoko's age 28 years earlier.

MAN HATER

1994. JPN: *Otoko Girai*. PRD: Yasuo Yagi. DIR: Makoto Kiyohiro. SCR: Noriko Yoshida. CAST: Momoko Kikuchi, Senri Yamazaki, Akiko Matsumoto, Masami Hisamoto, Kōji Matoba, Shirō Itō. CHN: TBS. DUR: 45 mins. x 11 eps.; Thu 14 July 1994–22 September 1994.

When his eldest daughter Fuyuko (Hisamoto) marries an unsuitable candidate, priest Ryōtaku (Itō) begs his other daughters Akio (Kikuchi), Natsumi (Matsumoto), and Chiharu (Yamazaki) to find husbands who might be interested in taking over the running of the temple when he retires. They, however, have no interest in getting married—compare to BROTHERS.

MAN OF THE DOMESTIC RELATIONS COURT

1993. JPN: *Kasai no Hito*. PRD: N/C. DIR: Kazufumi Ōki. SCR: Yūki Shimizu. CAST: Tsurutarō Kataoka, Nobuko Sendō, Tōru Kazama. CHN: TBS. DUR: 45 mins. x 12 eps.; Thu 7 January 1993–25 March 1993.

Kyōko (Sendō) becomes an investigator at the domestic relations court, where civil disputes between family members are heard and hopefully settled before they become matters for higher courts to rule upon. She discovers that the weird man she catches listening to a tree in the yard is actually Judge Yoshio (Kataoka), appointed to this low-level venue after rejecting an offer to work at the Supreme Court—compare to HERO. Judge Yoshio solves problems that are familiar to the viewers and brings them reconciliation. Based on a manga written by Jinpachi Mōri and drawn by Osamu Uoto. Theme: Taeko Ōnuki—"Haru no Tegami" (Letter in Spring).

MANTEN

2002. AKA: *The Whole Sky*. PRD: Yoshinori Komiyama. DIR: Tomochika Kasaura. SCR: Nozomi Makino. CAST: Mao Miyaji, Atsuko Asano, Hidekazu Akai, Tatsuya Mihashi, Nobuko Miyamoto. CHN: NHK. DUR: 15 mins. x ca. 150 eps.; 30 September 2002–29 March 2003.

Eighteen-year-old Manten (Miyaji) visits the Tanegashima Space Center, where she meets Mamoru Mōri, the Japanese astronaut who went into orbit on the Space Shuttle *Endeavor* in 1992. She has cherished a childhood ambition of becoming an astronaut and studies to become one while paying the bills by working at a meteorological office.

What might have been a modern drama in the style of ROCKET BOY took on new meaning on 1 February 2003—just as the fictional Manten was about to board a shuttle, the real-life *Columbia* exploded on reentry, thrusting this morning drama into the media spotlight. NHK added title cards conveying its condolences to the *Columbia* victims but did not take the series off the air, pressing on with a story that emphasized that space travel was no picnic and fraught with danger, but ultimately for the benefit of the entire human race.

MARIA

2001. PRD: Kōichi Funatsu. DIR: Ryōko Hoshida, Nobuyuki Takahashi. SCR: Yūji Hashimoto, Katsuhide Suzuki. CAST: Atsuko Asano, Kumiko Okae, Maki Gotō, Nagisa Katahira, Seiko Takada, Kyōko Kishida. CHN: TBS. DUR: 45 mins. x ca. 11 eps.; Wed 4 July 2001–?? September 2001.

Four kindhearted sisters run a Shinjuku medical practice, although their policy of putting their patients first has brought them close to financial ruin. Meanwhile, a nearby rival firm without their scruples gains customers and power in the local market, dazzling patients with new technology and fancy treatments. Theme: S.E.N.S.—"Maria."

MARIKO

1974. PRD: Masaharu Morita, Minoru Hanabusa. DIR: Yoshiyuki Itō. SCR: Yōko Matsuda. CAST: Mayumi Asano, Atsushi Negami, Reiko Chikamatsu, Toshie Takada, Kiyoshi Kinoshita. CHN: NHK. DUR: 25 mins. x 6 eps.; Mon 28 January 1974–6 February 1974.

Since she was four years old, Mariko (Asano) has been living with her widowed father Daisuke (Negami) and grandmother Kiyo (Chikamatsu). She is therefore shocked to discover that her father has been dating Shizuko (Takada) for seven years and keeping the relationship secret from her. When Daisuke is injured in a car accident, Shizuko cares for him at the hospital but Mariko is still reluctant to befriend her until Kiyo tells her that her father would leave, and in fact *has left* Shizuko, for his daughter's sake. Mariko guiltily visits Shizuko, and asks her to marry her father. Mariko's would-be boyfriend Masaya (Kinoshita) convinces her that life is not so terrible as all that and she wishes her new stepmother well on her wedding day.

Based on the novel *Shizuka ni Jishū Seyo* (Study Quietly By Yourself) by Reiko Takaya—compare to ETCHAN and COLD MORNING.

MARRIAGE AVERSION SYNDROME

1991. JPN: *Kekkon Shinaikamoshirenai Shōkōgun.* PRD: N/C. DIR: Hidenobu Hosono. SCR: Yūko Kanaya. CAST: Yumi Asō, Misako Konno, Chizuru Azuma, Shin Takuma, Shingo Tsurumi, Takurō Tatsumi, Shigeru Yazaki. CHN: NTV. DUR: 45 mins. x 10 eps.; Sat 19 October 1991–21 December 1991.

Freelance writer Fumika (Asō) has broken up with her boyfriend Toshio (Tsurumi), magazine editor Naoko (Konno) is dumped by her boyfriend Tōru (Tatsumi), and bank clerk Shoko (Azuma) conducts a clandestine affair with Etō (Yazaki). *MAS* is distinguished by its origins—it is based on a work of nonfiction by Shiho Tanimura, which investigated the behavior of women who cannot decide between marriage and independence. When published in 1990, it was immensely popular with a female audience but roundly condemned by the male establishment. Some commentators even facetiously noted that if readers took its message to heart, nobody would breed and the population would be wiped out! However, despite this controversial genesis, Tanimura's book fast acquires the appearance of any other trendy drama, soon devolving into just another tale of friends helping each other through adversity, in the style of WHERE IS LOVE?, ALL ABOUT YOUNG PEOPLE, and countless others.

MARRIAGE: DO YOU LIKE ME?

1993. JPN: *Kekkon: Watashi ga Sukidesuka.* PRD: N/C. DIR: Akiji Fujita. SCR: Akiyo Segawa. CAST: Chiharu Komatsu, Rie Hatada, Naoko Kawai, Kimiko Ikegami, Takeshi Naitō. CHN: Asahi. DUR: 45 mins. x 19 eps.; Tue 13 April 1993–21 September 1993.

Newly hired journalist Momoko (Komatsu) is commissioned to write a feature in collaboration with photographer Hayasaki (Naitō). Although she is attracted to him, he is her sister's ex-boyfriend.

MARRIAGE STARTS WITH A LIE

1993. JPN: *Usotsuki wa Fūfu no Hajimari.* PRD: N/C. DIR: Shirō Nakayama. SCR: Yuki Kiyomoto, Toshiya Itō. CAST: Eisaku Yoshida, Kaho Minami, Anju Suzuki, Ikkei Watanabe, Ichirō Zaitsu. CHN: NTV. DUR: 45 mins. x 12 eps.; Wed 14 April 1993–30 June 1993.

Kitchen unit salesman Ryōta (Yoshida) and hand model Masumi (Minami) are swindled into buying the same apartment, but decide to pose as husband and wife in order to hang onto it. Compare with MARRY ME! Theme: Toi et Moi—"Aru Hi, Totsuzen" (One Day, Suddenly).

MARRY ME! *

1996. JPN: *Kekkon Shiyō yo.* AKA: *Let's Get Married.* PRD: Yukio Matsuda. DIR: Kagenobu Kuwata. SCR: Masashi Todayama. CAST: Yōsuke Eguchi, Hikari Ishida, Yumi Asō, Hiroki Matsukata, Erika Mabuchi, Tsuyoshi Kusanagi. CHN: TBS. DUR: 45 mins. x 12 eps.; Thu 11 April 1996–27 June 1996.

Interior designer Keitarō (Eguchi) was deserted three years ago by his scheming wife Nagisa (Asō), who has fled to Canada to pursue a career in jewelry. Through her lawyers, Nagisa informs him that she will apply for permanent custody of their six-year-old son Ren, unless Keitarō finds himself a wife within two months. The desperate Keitarō places an advertisement in the newspaper, which is swiftly answered by Miwa (Ishida), a failure of a door-to-door saleswoman, who has been forced to spend a fortune buying her own products to hit her sales targets. The two have already met and do not get on, but agree to a marriage of convenience (see VIRGIN ROAD). Though they believe they have foiled Nagisa's lawyer, they are forced to live together for real after a flood at Miwa's apartment. This proves doubly difficult when Miwa's mother drops in for a surprise visit—naturally she knows nothing about her daughter's sudden wedding.

Despite its leaden predictability (you just *know* that Nagisa is going to return when she is least wanted and that Miwa is going to get jealous when she sees her "husband" in the arms of another woman), *MM* entertainingly recycles many clichés of the 1990s drama, including reluctant roommates, surrogate parenting, and in-law appeasement. Compare to SPRING IN BLOOM and FALSE LOVE, and the movies *Green Card* (1990) and *A Walk in the Clouds* (1995). Broadcast with English subtitles in the U.S. on KIKU TV. Theme: Yōsuke Eguchi—"Traveling Boy."

MASAMUNE THE ONE-EYED DRAGON

1987. JPN: *Dokuganryū Masamune*. PRD: Katsufumi Nakamura. DIR: Masahiro Higuchi, Yoshiyuki Yoshimura, Yoshiki Nishimura, Yukinori Kida, Akio Suwabe. SCR: James Miki. CAST: Ken Watanabe, Kinya Kitaōji, Shima Iwashita, Junko Sakurada, Kumiko Akiyoshi, Keiko Takeshita, Teruhiko Saigō, Tomokazu Miura, Yoshio Harada, Chōsuke Ikariya, Eiji Okuda, Masahiko Tsugawa, Shintarō Katsu. CHN: NHK. DUR: 45 mins. x 50 eps.; Sun 4 January 1987–13 December 1987.
Developing smallpox at age five, young lord Masamune Date survives but loses the sight in his right eye. His domineering mother (Iwashita) causes him to channel his frustrations in a new direction, and in adulthood (played by Watanabe), he becomes feared throughout Japan as the "one-eyed dragon." Becoming the feudal lord of Mutsu in Japan's far north (modern Aomori Prefecture), Masamune is the ruler of all of northern Japan, until he is forced to surrender to the army of HIDEYOSHI in 1590. Still a major power in the region, Masamune is witness to the struggles that follow during the civil war era (see LAND THIEF) and sees the rulership of Japan pass from Nobunaga to Ieyasu and the Tokugawa heirs. In 1613, Masamune sends a messenger out of Japan, who travels through Mexico to Spain and then Rome itself, where he hopes to strike a deal with the Pope. However, Christianity is outlawed in Japan and Masamune is forced to give up his scheme.

Based on *Date Masamune* by Sōhachi Yamaoka, *Masamune* was one of the most successful *taiga* dramas and marked a triumphant return to the genre's feudal origins after the previous year's INOCHI: LIFE. It defeated all its *taiga* predecessors with a peak rating of 47.8%, only to be trounced itself by SHINGEN TAKEDA the following year. Also notable for *Masamune* were the show's *average* ratings, which maintained a steady 39.7% throughout its year-long broadcast. It was the first major role for Ken Watanabe and it made his name as one of the most acclaimed TV actors. For a sequel of sorts, see THE FIR TREE LEFT BEHIND.

MASK OF GLASS

1997. JPN: *Garasu no Kamen*. PRD: Yoshiki Miruta, Satoko Uchiyama. DIR: Toshinori Nishimae, Noboru Sugiyama, Kazuhisa Imai. SCR: Fumie Mizuhashi, Miyuki Noe. CAST: Yumi Adachi, Seiichi Tanabe, Megumi Matsumoto, Yōko Nogiwa, Mariko Fuji. CHN: Asahi. DUR: 45 mins. x 23 eps.; Mon 7 July 1997–15 September 1997 (#1); 13 April 1998–29 June 1998 (#2).
Famous actress Chigusa Tsukikage (Nogiwa) is left hideously disfigured after an accident and is forced to quit the stage to teach. However, her career inspires two girls to audition for her academy. One is Maya (Adachi), an innocent girl who is thrilled to be joining her idol's theater troupe. The other is Ayumi (Matsumoto), a privileged rich girl and already a veteran of the stage while still a teenager. Chigusa sees potential in them both but hopes to train Maya to the height of dramatic perfection, so that she may perform the supposedly "unperformable" lead in *Red Angel*, to which Chigusa owns the rights. Leaving her family to move in with the drama group, Maya discovers that Chigusa is a supremely tough teacher with fiercely high standards. Furthermore, other students are jealous that this newcomer has snagged their teacher's interest and subject Maya to a succession of pranks and practical jokes. Maya thus becomes the put-upon *Cinderella* heroine of so many manga and drama series with the obligatory secret admirer—a man who sends her purple roses on the nights of her performance, who turns out to be the despised Masami (Tanabe), a theatrical entrepreneur who hopes to buy the rights to *Red Angel* from the frail Chigusa.

When adapting any well-known story for a different medium, there is always a danger that it will not live up to reader's expectations. The problem is compounded in *MoG* since the script calls upon the girls to perform "as genius actresses," which is difficult to fake—compare to GOLDEN KIDS. Reputedly, creator Suzue Miuchi resisted previous attempts to make a live-action TV adaptation of her work but relented in this case because of the star names attached: veteran thespian Nogiwa and Adachi, the former child star of CHILD WITHOUT A HOME. But while the young stars do their best to appear inspired and brilliant, they still end up looking like a group of typical Japanese TV starlets, although Nogiwa is spectacularly smoldering (compare to NEVER LAND) as the embittered, superstrict Chigusa, encapsulating the very essence of her character from the manga, and with a luxuriant wig of manga-style hair to match. Mariko Fuji, who plays Maya's ailing mother in season one, previously played the protégé Ayumi in a 1980s stage version of the story. The tale also exists in anime form (*AE). Theme: B'z—"Calling."

MASKED ANGEL ROSETTA

1998. JPN: *Kamen Tenshi Rosetta*. PRD: Hiromi Ōta, Kyō Fujii. DIR: Mitsunori Hattori, Iwao Takahashi, Mikio Hirota, Kenzō Maihara, Atsushi Shimizu. SCR: Takahiko Masuda, Tsuyoshi Koike, Jun Maekawa, Hiroshi Kanno, Akimasa Niima. CAST: Rei Yoshii, Tetsuya Ushio, Tsuyoshi Sasaki, Yuriko Hishimi. CHN: TVT. DUR: 30 mins. x 13 eps.; Sun 5 July 1998–26 September 1998.
Ordinary teenager Asuka Kami (Yoshii) is attacked by a vampire but is able to defend herself with the help of her father Kenichirō (Ushio), transforming herself into Masked Angel

Rosetta. When she recovers, she is informed by Kenichirō that her family's duty has always been to resist the predations of the evil creatures of Duatos. It is now Asuka's turn, in the style of *Devil Hunter Yohko* (*AE), to become a vampire hunter, mixing the fighting style of the **MASKED RIDER** series with a certain debt to TV's *Buffy the Vampire Slayer* (1997). A video spin-off, *MAR: Black Flare* concentrated on more mundane issues such as Asuka's school life. Though we have listed it as a Sunday show, many sources list this post-midnight broadcast as belonging to the Saturday that preceded it. Compare to **WIZARD OF DARKNESS**.

MASKED RIDER *

1971. JPN: *Kamen Rider*. PRD: Tōru Hirayama, Itaru Orita, Seiji Abe, Susumu Yoshikawa. DIR: Hideyuki Kimura, Kōichi Takemoto, Minoru Yamada, Hiroo Kitamoto, Toshiaki Kobayashi, Michio Konishi, Ryūta Tazaki. SCR: Masaru Igami, Takashi Ezure. CAST: Hiroshi Fujioka, Akiji Kobayashi, Jirō Chiba, Gorō Naya, Takeshi Sasaki, Linda Yamamoto, Eisei Amamoto, Kenji Ushio, Matasaburō Tanba, Hiroshi Miyauchi, Akira Yamaguchi, Chizuru Ono, Hideki Kawaguchi, Ken Sakuma, Shinji Nakae, Fumiya Nakamura, Ryō Hayami, Naoki Miyama, Jun Tazaki, Tōru Okazaki, Satoshi Matsuda, Shigeru Araki, Machiko Soga, Kyōko Okada, Hiroaki Murakami, Nobuo Tsukamoto, Shunsuke Takasugi, Shun Sugata, Tetsuo Kurata, Ayumi Taguchi, Akemi Inoue, Susumu Kurobe, Masanori Jisen, Masaki Kyōmoto, Takahito Horiuchi, Kohisa Ishikawa, Jō Odagiri, Toshiki Kashū, Jun Kaname, Yūsuke Tomoi, Takamasa Suga, Yukari Kaga, Takehito Handa. CHN: Asahi. DUR: 25 mins. x 501 eps. (+ Ryuki ca. 50 eps., + Phi's ca. 50 eps.); Sat 3 April 1971–10 February 1973 (#1); 17 February 1973–9 February 1974 (#2); 16 February 1974–12 October 1974 (#3); 19 October 1974–29 March 1975 (#4); 5 April 1975–27 December 1975 (#5); 5 October 1979–10

Masked Rider

October 1980 (#6); 17 October 1980–3 October 1981 (#7); 4 October 1987–9 October 1988 (#8); 23 October 1988–24 September 1989 (#9); 30 January 2000–21 January 2001 (#10); 28 January 2001–29 January 2002 (#11); 3 February 2002–19 January 2003 (#12); 26 January 2003– (#13).

Though only one of its many TV incarnations has been translated into English, the *Masked Rider* remains an important ambassador for Japanese TV abroad, particularly outside the English-speaking world, where many more of its heroes flourish from Italy to Brazil. Most of its seasons have also been broadcast on U.S. TV, albeit without English subtitles, on local channels for the Japanese community in Hawaii and California. Unlike the "Super Sentai" series and its **MIGHTY MORPHIN' POWER RANGER** spin-offs, *MR* has an ongoing continuity resembling that of **ULTRAMAN** and is consequently listed

here in one large entry, instead of a dozen separate ones. We simply do not have the space to note all the *MR* reunions, TV specials, and alliances here, and have instead limited ourselves to a basic roundup of the series continuity.

Mortally injured in a motorcycle accident, science student and keen racer Takeshi Hongo (Fujioka) is rescued by the sinister Shocker Organization, who plan to turn him into a cyborg warrior to carry out their evil deeds—compare to creator Shōtarō Ishinomori's earlier *Cyborg 009* (*AE). Rescued by his former teacher before Shocker can reprogram his mind for evil, Takeshi becomes a thorn in the side of his would-be masters, fighting their evil schemes with his robotic abilities and also with the motorcycling prowess he has retained from his previous life. Reaching a certain speed on his motorcycle allows him to transform into the Masked Rider, and his bike into the Cyclone superbike. Takeshi is aided in his fight against evil by his former motorcycling instructor Tobei (Kobayashi), and FBI agent Kazuya (Chiba). After episode 74, he also acquires the assistance of the Masked Rider Boys' Squad—a group of children who maintain a vigil for signs of evil activities by Shocker. Like all the other MRs that would follow him, Takeshi must not only deal with monsters of the week, but is occasionally forced to fight off evil versions of himself, which supposedly look exactly the same, but can *always* be identified by a telltale yellow scarf.

One of the few actors to perform his own stunts, Hiroshi Fujioka broke his leg when he hit a telephone pole in episode ten, forcing the program makers to shoot around his recuperation. When it became clear that three weeks of stunt doubles and stock footage would not suffice to get Fujioka back on his feet (compare to similar difficulties on ROCKET BOY), the original MR was temporarily written out.

Off to Europe to fight a particularly evil Shocker scheme, Takeshi leaves Japan under the protection of MR 2, former photographer Hayato (Sasaki). Hayato's induction is similar to that of his predecessor—he is *another* intended Shocker soldier, but is rescued by Takeshi, once more conveniently after he has been cybernetically enhanced, but before he has been brainwashed.

Actors Sasaki and Fujioka then double-teamed the series for the remainder of its 98-episode run, allaying the producers' fears of production delays but also creating the sense of an international MR cooperative that would run through later episodes. Episodes could dwell on Takeshi's European adventures, some of which crossed over into Hayato's sphere, leading the two actors to share episodes in which they fought evil together. Meanwhile, the producers happily doubled the amount of merchandise, first with the arrival of the unexpected new character, then a second time when the heroes gained new powers. Officially,

Takeshi returned from Europe after allowing himself to be recaptured and retooled by his former Shocker masters, gaining augmented powers, a new suit, and the ability to transform at will. Similarly, Hayato disappeared to South America for several episodes to fight the Geldam organization, returning with new vigor thanks to a masochistic program of crocodile wrestling and voluntary exposure to snake poisons!

The second series of *MR*, confusingly named *MR V3* since it referred to the Rider not the season, introduced a new hero, Shirō (Miyauchi) who unwittingly invites danger when he comes to the aid of distressed damsel Junko (Ono). The Destron terrorist organization, an offshoot of the previous serial's Gel-Shocker axis (in fact, later MR enemies almost always turn out to be puppets of the original MR's nemesis, the "Great Leader"), targets Shirō and his family, murdering his parents and sister. However, Shirō is saved by the timely arrival of his chemistry teacher Takeshi, who transforms into MR. The former season's two riders refuse to allow Shirō to have cyborg augmentation, as, like the same creator's KIKAIDA, they mourn the loss of their humanity and have no desire to inflict it on someone else. However, Shirō is injured saving them from an attacker and they are forced to give him a cyborg body to save his life . . . not a moment too soon, since they are themselves soon missing in action after saving Tokyo from an atomic monster, and the third MR becomes the sole hero, aided by Takeshi's old mentor Tobei. Maintaining the pattern established by the first season, the new MR is not alone for long and eventually befriends Jōji (Yamaguchi), a former Destron scientist, who switches sides after Destron mastermind Marshall Armor (Nakamura) almost kills him. However, "Riderman," as he becomes known, is only initially interested in avenging himself on his former boss and often clashes with Shirō. He is finally redeemed when he is presumed killed in a nuclear blast after saving

Japan, leading Shirō to deliver a eulogy proclaiming Jōji as the "fourth MR."

A fifth MR soon arrived in the third season *MR X*, which ran for a much shorter period—35 episodes against the original's 98 and the sequel's 52. Daisuke Jin (Hayami) is the son of a scientist who undergoes cybernetic modification to save his life after he is mortally wounded by agents of the sinister Government of Darkness. He receives help, like his predecessors, from Tobei and also teams up with all former MRs for the movie *Masked Rider X: Five Riders vs. King Dark* (1974). Questions of how three of the earlier Riders were able to survive a nuclear blast were left unanswered.

Series #4 introduced the sixth Rider, *MR Amazon*, and a *Tarzan*-influenced story in the style of JUNGLE PRINCE. Orphaned in a plane crash in the South American jungle, the superstrong Daisuke Yamamoto (Okazaki) is raised in the wild and eventually returns to his homeland, where he saves the young Masahiko (Matsuda) from a spider monster by transforming into a magical warrior. The monster is revealed to be the handiwork of the Geddon organization, who have already killed off the inhabitants of Daisuke's village in search of his magical armband. The only MR whose suit did not resemble an insect, and the first who was not a cyborg, MR Amazon instead transformed into a green, sharp-toothed creature resembling a chameleon. His story chronicles not only the usual MR conventions of defending Japan from invaders but also his slow acclimatization to his native culture, as he learns to speak Japanese and reintegrate into civilization.

Amazon was soon replaced for a fifth season with *MR Stronger*—vengeful youth Shigeru Jō (Araki), who volunteers for cybernetic augmentation with the Black Satan group and then turns against his masters in time-honored MR tradition. With the letter "S" proudly emblazoned on his chest in presumed homage to *Superman*,

Shigeru also had the assistance of a female cyborg, Yuriko (Okada), who was able to transform into his fighting assistant Tackle. The fifth series of *MR* was clearly expected to be the last, reintroducing all previous MRs for the last five episodes, and ending with an elegiac montage and a farewell from series narrator Shinji Nakae. *MR Stronger* is regarded as the end of the first era of *MR*, not only for the four-year production gap that followed, but also since it was the last time that all former MRs were able to assemble on-screen in the presence of their unifying mentor Tobei.

After a gap of several years, the sixth season *New MR*, also known as *Skyrider*, features hang gliding enthusiast Hiroshi (Murakami), who witnesses agents of terrorist organization Neo Shocker as they attempt to kidnap scientists. Though he fights them off, he is later mortally wounded, and, like many MRs before him, augmented into a cyborg minion, only to rebel (you would think that terrorist organizations would have learned their lesson after so many failed attempts). Joining forces with MR Stronger and new mentor Jirō Tanihara (Tsukamoto), the new cyborg continues to fight evil—his unique ability to fly like a Marvel superhero leading both friends and foes to address him as "Skyrider."

A seventh season ran straight on, featuring a slightly different origin story. MR Super One begins life in America as Japanese astronaut Kazuya (Takasugi), who volunteers for cybernetic augmentation in preparation for a deep-space mission. When the U.S. base is attacked by the Dogma Kingdom, Kazuya is the sole survivor and makes his way to Japan to resist the Dogma invasion. *MR Super One* was the first *MR* series not to rely heavily on former continuity—though Jirō appeared as a mentor figure, the other MRs only arrived for the movie spin-off and were not seen in the TV series.

MR Super One was followed by another gap of several years, broken only by the one-shot TV special *Birth of the*

Tenth MR: Riders Come Together (1984). Teenage pilot Ryō Murasawa (Sugata) and his sister are kidnapped by the evil terrorists of the Badan Empire. The sister dies but the brother is transformed into the cyborg warrior Silver Cross, who eventually rebels against his masters to become MR ZX. However, despite all the appearance of the origin-story for a new series, MR ZX disappeared from sight and was only seen in a cameo role for a few episodes of *MR Rider Black RX* (see below).

The *MR* series proper did not return until the eighth season in 1987, *MR Black*. After his parents are murdered by the savage Golgom cult, Kōtaro (Kurata) is raised by the Akizuki family, whose son Nobuhiko (Horiuchi) shares the same birthday as his. In fact, the Golgom cult is deliberately trying to engineer a race of super-warriors and believe the 19-year-old boys, born on the day of a solar eclipse, to be perfect material. The kidnap attempt is successful but Kōtaro escapes the brainwashing process to become the 11th MR, unaware that his friend also survived and has been transformed into his enemy Shadowmoon (Jisen).

Kurata stayed in the lead role for the ninth series, *MR Black RX*, which begins with him captured by the Crisis Empire and launched into space, where solar energy causes him to change into a more advanced hero and one with multiple forms, such as his RX suit, as well as the Roborider and Biorider variants. He was also the only MR to have a car in addition to the usual motorcycle and benefited from the help of all ten previous MRs, including the short-lived ZX, for the final confrontation with the Crisis Empire.

The *MR* series continued, but it was the *Black RX* incarnation that made it to the U.S. mass-market, when it was released by Saban Entertainment as *Masked Rider* (1995). In the tradition of other Americanized versions such as **BEETLEBORGS** and **VR TROOPERS**, much of the fighting and special effects

footage remained, though the cast members out of costume were replaced with local actors. Dex (Ted Jan Roberts) is the alien prince who arrives from space and defends the Earth from the predations of his own uncle. However, the English-language *MR* did not achieve the longevity of its Saban stablemates and soon disappeared.

Meanwhile, the Japanese *MR* series entered another lull after *Black RX*, broken by occasional movie and video outings that singularly failed to develop into another series. Discounted by many fans as non-canonical, the straight-to-video production *New MR* (1990) features Shin (Ishikawa), a youth whose DNA is combined with that of a grasshopper to give him the ability to transform into a superhero—in other words, this masked rider doesn't actually wear a mask at all, like *MR Amazon*, nor is he a cyborg.

Similar issues surrounded the short theatrical movies *MR ZO* (1993), directed by **JETMAN**'s Keita Amemiya with costumes by Yasushi Nirasawa and featuring Hiroshi Tsuchikado as a hero created from mixing locust DNA with a human being and cybernetics, and *MR J* (1994), starring Yūta Mochizuki as a reporter who transforms into a grasshopper cyborg in order to defend the world from the alien Fog Mother. As a further sign of producers messing with the old formula, MR J also had the ability to transform into a giant version of himself in the style of **ULTRAMAN**. These characters appeared in two other spin-off movies, but pointedly in association with each other, not with earlier incarnations.

The tenth season of *MR* did not arrive until 2000, with *MR Cougar,* which similarly eschewed some of the old conventions. Yūsuke (Odagiri) tries on a mummy's belt taken from an archeological site and finds that it gives him the power to transform into an insectoid hero that can itself transform a second time into several elemental-themed speciality forms to combat the ancient Grongi tribes who have reawakened in Japan. *Cougar* ushered in a new wave of interest in *MR* from an unexpected source, as ratings revealed that the show's largest audience (after its target of 4–12s) comprised women in their 30s. In other words, the handsome, athletic Odagiri drew an audience not just of young children but of their lonely mothers! Consequently, at the show's close, its star walked into several high-profile roles in night-time drama, such as **PARFUM DE LA JALOUSIE** and the *MR* formula began to skew toward a different perception of its audience.

The eleventh season, *MR Agito,* reacted to the "Odagiri Effect" by having not one, but *three* handsome young men as fighting heroes. Its lead, amnesiac Shōichi (Kashū), develops special powers after being rescued by a professor but his companions include the searingly handsome police agent Makoto (Kaname), who can don the G3 fighting armor to help Shōichi. A second assistant, Ryō, can transform into the superpowerful MR Gilos, but the process causes him great pain and threatens to eventually kill him. This trio of troubled heroes was another hit with the Mom audience, although long-term (i.e., male) fans did not approve, and the tie-in movie *MR Agito Project G4* (2001) still took over a billion yen at the box office.

The twelfth season, *MR Ryūki,* was the cause of further controversy, with

accusations that it deviated a step too far from the original formula devised by Shōtarō Ishinomori. It begins with the standard template, with journalist Shinji (Suga) and his senior Reiko, investigating missing persons cases but finding themselves sucked into a mirror world where they must fight to save the Earth. Though he has the ability to transform into MR Ryūki, Shinji takes several severe beatings at the hands of the evil Dragledder, until help arrives in the form of fellow Masked Rider, MR Knight (Matsuda). Meanwhile, the cast becomes involved in a series of romantic intrigues and office flirtations more suited to an evening drama than a children's sci-fi show. The show eventually acquired a veritable army of *13* masked riders, including the franchise's first Lady Rider, Natsuki Katō, regarded by the fan community as the last straw, but sufficient to propel *MR Ryūki* to successful ratings.

In the most recent incarnation of the series, *MR Phi's* (2003), the company director of the mysterious Smartbrain organization enlists the help of his daughter and her two handsome male friends in the ongoing battle against the Orphenc group (presumably inspired by "Orthanc" from *Lord of the Rings*), an evil syndicate hell bent on destroying the human race. To transform, the latest Masked Rider must take out his special mobile phone and type the sequence "555"— see **HEIJI ZENIGATA** for details of *Ai Zenigata,* an investigator the previous year who also made good use of her mobile.

MASKED WOMAN

1998. JPN: *Kamen no Onna.* PRD: Kazuko Noe, Kyōko Fukutomi. DIR: Satoshi Isaka, Yoshimasa Fujie. SCR: Taketatsu Ishihara. CAST: Akiko Hinagata, Junichi Ishida. CHN: TBS. DUR: 45 mins. x 10 eps.; Thu 15 October 1998–17 December 1998.
Former marathon runner Kuroku (Ishida) changes his name and disappears from public view to seek a career in medicine, only to find himself rail-

roaded into coaching a new athlete. Based on a book by Daikichi Terauchi. Theme: trf—"EMB race."

MASKMAN

1987. JPN: *Kōsentai Maskman.* AKA: *Shining Battle Team Maskman.* PRD: Kyōzō Utsunomiya, Takeyuki Suzuki. DIR: Takao Nagaishi, Shōhei Tōjō, Minoru Yamada. SCR: Hirohisa Soda, Kunio Fujii, Toshiki Inoue. CAST: Ryōsuke Umezu, Kōichi Kusakari, Kazunari Hirota, Yuki Nagata, Kanako Maeda, Seizō Katō, Mina Asami, Hiroshi Takeda. CHN: Asahi. DUR: 25 mins. x 51 eps.; Sat 28 February 1987–20 February 1988.
When the subterranean Tube Empire attempts to seize control of the surface world, the five-member Maskman team is assigned to defend the human race. They are led by former racing driver Takeru (Umezu) as Red Mask, a master of karate and the wielder of the Masky Blade. Ken (Kusakari) is Black Mask, a kung fu master from the distant mountain provinces and wielder of the Masky Rod. Akira (Hirota) is Blue Mask, master of Chinese *kempō* (we're not sure how this is supposed to differ from kung fu in the eyes of a child audience!) who fights with the Masky Tonfa. Haruka (Nagata) is Yellow Mask who fights with the Masky Rotor, but also helps the team with the ninja skills that have been passed down through her family. Momoko (Maeda) is Pink Mask who fights with Taiqi or with her Masky Ribbon. Red Mask drives a racing car, while the other team members have their own motorcycle. They also have special vehicles such as the Masky Jet and Masky Tank, which combine to form the Great Five robot. In later episodes, a bigrig combination was introduced (compare to the previous year's **FLASHMAN**) that transformed into the Land Galaxy robot.

Their enemy underground is King Saber (voiced by Katō), whose faction was responsible for transforming the peaceful subterranean world into the belligerent Tube Empire. He fights them with his army of cannon fodder

Angura Warriors, and also wakes monsters of the week from various caves in his domain. However, Saber also has enemies within—since supporters of the peace-loving Igamu faction still reside in his kingdom and would prefer it if he stopped fighting the surface people. Katō previously voiced the evil emperor Bazoo in CHANGEMAN, while composer Gōrō Ōmi was yet another anime alumnus (see *Grey: Digital Target*, *AE). "Based on an idea by Saburō Yade"; the following year's Super Sentai show was LIVEMAN.

MASTERS OF TASTE *

1995. JPN: *Aji Ichi Monme*. AKA: *Pinch of Flavor*. PRD: Osamu Tezuka (b), Fumio Igarashi. DIR: Ikuhiro Saitō, Hiroshi Ikezoe. SCR: Kazuyuki Morozawa. CAST: Masahiro Nakai, Ritsuko Tanaka, Kumiko Okae, Nenji Kobayashi, Yōko Nogiwa, Shingo Katori, Kirin Kiki, Hiroshi Fuse. CHN: Asahi. DUR: 45 mins. x 21 eps.; Thu 12 January 1995–16 March 1995 (#1); 11 January 1996–21 March 1996 (#2).

Satoru (Nakai from SMAP) has wanted to be a master chef ever since he was a child. He is given an internship at the traditional Restaurant Fujimura, where the customers and fellow staff are initially disdainful of his maverick culinary skills.

In the eleven-episode second season, Satoru returns from intensive training in Kanazawa, only to be reposted to a struggling bistro in Kyoto when the Restaurant Fujimura burns down. Despite all his earlier successes, he is back among strangers and must impress a completely new crowd with his knowledge of culinary arts. Based on the 1986 *Big Comics Superior* manga by Yoshimi Kurata and Zenta Abe which ran for 33 volumes and over a decade, guaranteeing an audience of all ages. Both seasons were broadcast in the U.S. with English subtitles on KIKU TV. Themes: Maki Ōguro—"La La La," "Aaah."

MATASABURŌ THE WIND IMP

1976. JPN: *Kaze no Matasaburō*. PRD: Kanae Mayuzumi. DIR: Masami Uehara. SCR: Minoru Bessho. CAST: Natsuho Miyakai, Noboru Mitsuya, Shigeyuki Sunouchi, Kazuto Andō, Kenichirō Hase, Naoki Wakayama, Masayuki Kumagaya. CHN: NHK. DUR: 20 mins. x 4 eps.; Mon 6 December 1976–9 December 1976.

Transfer student Saburō Takada (Miyakai), aka Matasaburō, comes to a small school in a village where his father is a mining engineer. The local kids are surprised by Matasaburō, who wears Western-style clothes while all the others wear kimono, but chiefly because every time he moves, a breeze seems to swirl around him. Ichirō (Sunouchi), Kasuke (Andō), Etsuji (Wakayama), Satarō (Kumagaya), and Kōsuke (Hase) take Matasaburō out in the field to play but by the time they have bonded and become true friends, Matasaburō has gone, leading the other children to speculate that they have been playing with a spirit. Based on a classic children's story by Kenji Miyazawa and also adapted into an anime in 1988 (*AE).

MATRON INVESTIGATES

1997. JPN: *Meitantei Hokenshitsu no Obasan*. AKA: *Famous Detective School Matron*. PRD: Ryōichi Satō, Noboru Sugiyama, Hitoshi Fuse. DIR: Kazuhisa Imai, Shirō Nakayama, Noboru Sugiyama. SCR: Michiru Egashira. CAST: Ken Miyake, Yasuko Matsuyuki, Kotomi Kyōno, Riona Hazuki. CHN: Asahi. DUR: 45 mins. x 10 eps.; Mon 6 January 1997–10 March 1997.

Sakurako (Matsuyuki) is a bespectacled high school nurse with a penchant for solving mysteries who joins forces with eager teenager Kamimiya (Miyake from V6) to fight crime in her neighborhood—whipping off her glasses and letting down her hair to become a beautiful lady detective before scurrying back to her humdrum school life once the mystery is solved. Not quite as eye-popping as GEISHA DETECTIVE but heading there. Based on a manga in

Margaret magazine by Akiko Miyawaki, whose other works include *Predestined Lover* and *The Mirror of Janus*. Theme: Yasuko Matsuyuki—"Sorappo no Ai no Arashi" (Storm of Love in the Sky).

MATTIE AND DAI

1973. JPN: *Mattie to Dai-chan*. PRD: Seiji Akiyama. DIR: Noriaki Sasahara, Ryūnosuke Sano, Hiroshi Watanabe. SCR: Akito Mizuhara, Tomoaki Saegusa. CAST: Reiko Kōzaki, Shinzō Segawa, Hiroko Fujioka, Akihisa Shimazaki, Masanari Hanetō, Mikio Terashima, Yayoi Tsuda, Yasuko Hayashi, Satomi Ōhashi, Mami Matsunaga, Yuriko Kita, Takehisa Naitō, Masatoshi Ikuki, Shigeko Ōmori, Naomi Yamada, Shinichi Kozuka. CHN: NHK. DUR: 25 mins. x 12 eps.; Mon 26 November 1973–12 December 1973 (#1); 3 February 1975–26 February 1975 (#2).

Machiko "Mattie" Hara (Kōzaki) has been lifelong friends with the boy next door, Daigo (Hanetō), but the two argue more often now that they are teenagers. Their classmate Mitsuyo (Ōhashi) has been absent from school for some time while caring for her mother who was injured in a car accident, and Daigo volunteers to call on her to deliver the classwork she has missed. Mattie, however, flies into a jealous rage. Meanwhile, Daigo resents Mattie's blind adoration of idol singer Akihiko Shiratori, in a sweet evocation of first crushes and first love.

Two years after the original nine episode series, Mattie would return for a new story, *Mattie and Her Happy Friends* (*Mattie to Yukai na Nakamatachi*). With "lifelong friend" Daigo nowhere to be seen but with actress Kōzaki reprising her role, the second season focused on another teenage couple's refusal to admit their true feelings for each other—the audience for *Mattie* would grow up to adore TOKYO LOVE STORY. Mattie is taken aback when her "lifelong friend" Shinichi (Kozuka) dedicates a song on the school's lunchtime broadcast to another girl. When she confronts him, he tells her that it was a mistake on the part of the presenter and that he intended for the song to be dedicated to her. However, Hamako (Yamada), the girl who mistakenly received the dedication, now believes that Shinichi likes her, and the kind-hearted Mattie convinces Shinichi to ask her out on a date to save her feelings. Mattie is jealous but keeps her feelings to herself, though Hamako is heartbroken when she discovers the truth and soon leaves for the countryside.

MAYOR IN LOVE

2002. JPN: *Koi Suru Top Lady*. PRD: Takahiro Kasaoki, Hisao Ogura. DIR: Hiroshi Nishitani, Keita Kōno. SCR: Michiru Tanabe. CAST: Miki Nakatani, Toshirō Yanagiba, Megumi Okina, Yū Yoshizawa, Sayaka Yamaguchi. CHN: Fuji. DUR: 45 mins. x 11 eps.; Tue 8 January 2002–19 March 2002.

Chiharu (Nakatani) is a girl in her mid-twenties with a perfectly average life, one she has cultivated in reaction to her father's profession—he is the high-profile mayor of Tatehama City. However, upon his sudden death, Chiharu finds herself "inheriting" his post as part of a public relations exercise by her late father's spin doctors. Shunsaku (Yanagiba) is her father's gruff chief of security, who objects in principle to the former mayor's daughter being railroaded into carrying on her father's work. But when he is assigned to protect Chiharu, he finds his feelings slowly turning to romance.

Shunsaku is not the only member of the public who begins by doubting Chiharu's potential. Local cable network anchorwoman Yūko (Okina) is intensely distrustful of the new mayor, and not only because Chiharu seems unqualified. Yūko harbors secret feelings for her cameraman Yūsuke (Yoshizawa), whereas *he* once attended the same school as Chiharu and worships her from afar, much to the displeasure of Shunsaku. Meanwhile, Shunsaku has new security headaches in the form of Mari (Yamaguchi), Chiharu's best friend and sole confidante, who often sleeps over at the

mayoral residence after a hard night on the town. Little does he suspect that Mari spends so much time with the mayor because *she* has fallen for Shunsaku! *MiL* features political comedy in the style of DON'T CALL ME PRIME MINISTER—someone was going to crash *Ally McBeal* into *The West Wing* eventually, and it would appear that writer Tanabe got there first.

MEANWHILE YOU GOT MARRIED

1994. JPN: *Sono Uchi Kekkon Suru Kimi e*. AKA: *To You Who Are About to Marry*. PRD: Nobuo Komatsu. DIR: Nozomu Amemiya. SCR: Satsuo Endō. CAST: Miwako Fujitani, Tōru Nakamura, Maki Sakai, Satoshi Ikeda, Shōko Ikeda, Masanori Sera. CHN: NTV. DUR: 45 mins. x 11 eps.; Sat 15 January 1994–26 March 1994.

Keiko (Fujitani) and Nobuto (Nakamura) are forced to delay their wedding for three months after an accidental double booking at the hotel where they planned to hold the ceremony. The hotel manager apologizes for his error, only to reveal himself as Kenji (Sera), Keiko's long-lost ex-boyfriend, for whom she still has secret feelings. Theme: Satoshi Ikeda—"Omoidasanai Yoru wa Nai Darō" (Wasn't It an Unforgettable Night?).

MEDICAL JURISPRUDENCE CASE FILES

1992. JPN: *Hōigaku Kyōshitsu no Jiken File*. PRD: N/C. DIR: Kunihiko Yamamoto. SCR: Shōji Imai. CAST: Yūko Natori, Shin Takuma, Kaho Minami, Nagisa Katahira. CHN: Asahi. DUR: 45 mins. x 25 eps.; Thu 2 July 1992–24 September 1992 (#1); 1 July 1993–23 September 1993 (#2).

Saki (Natori) is an assistant professor at the Medical Jurisprudence Room at a University hospital. Her husband Kazuma (Takuma) is a detective. Her sister Miyuki (Minami) becomes an assistant to Saki and together they solve crimes. Compare to RED TURNIP, whose lead also returned in numerous TV movies after the end of the original series. Later installments of *MJCF* were

screened as TV movies on 9 July 1994, followed by 22 April 1995, 22 July 1995, 11 May 1996, 26 October 1996, 5 April 1997, 3 January 1998, 9 May 1998, 31 October 1998, 2 January 1999, 26 June 1999, 1 July 2000, 3 February 2001, 26 May 2001, 8 December 2001, and 13 July 2002.

MEGARANGER *

1997. JPN: *Denji Sentai Megaranger*. AKA: *Electromagnetic Battle Team Megaranger; Power Rangers in Space*. PRD: Kenji Ōta, Kōichi Yada, Shigeki Takadera, Naomi Takebe. DIR: Takao Nagaishi, Noboru Takemoto, Ryūta Tazaki, Masato Tsujino, Tarō Sakamoto. SCR: Yoshiki Takeue, Minehisa Arakawa, Shigeru Yanagawa, Yasuko Kobayashi. CAST: Kunihiko Ōshiba, Junji Ehara, Masaya Matsukaze, Eri Tanaka, Asami Higashiyama, Shigeru Kanai, Ryūsaburo Ōtomo, Tetsuo Morishita, Asami Jō. CHN: Asahi. DUR: 25 mins. x 51 eps.; Fri 14 February 1997–15 February 1998.

Faced with imminent invasion by the war-like cyber-realm of Negiregia, the peace loving International Science Alliance embarks on the Megaproject. Using computer games to test the qualifications of applicants, they recruit a group of high school students, and use them to form the Megaranger team. Their leader Kenta (Ōshiba) is the hot-headed Mega Red who fights with a giant drill. Kōichirō (Ehara) is computer boffin and marksman Mega Black, constantly quarreling with Kenta over who should be leading the team. Shun (Matsukaze) is the level-headed Mega Blue who specializes in mind games and also works at a computer graphics company. Chie (Tanaka) is a cameraman's assistant and lists her hobbies as sports and singing but also moonlights as Mega Yellow. Miku (Higashiyama) is the youngest and clumsiest member of the team as Mega Pink. These team members are later joined by their own boss Yusaku (Kanai), who becomes the all-powerful Mega Silver.

Their chief enemy is Cyberking Javius I (Ōtomo) of Negiregia who is determined to invade the three-dimensional world with an army of monsters of the week, his henchman Ugande and Dr. Hinera (Morishita), and an army of cannon fodder androids. Additionally, Hinera is aided by Shiborena (Jō), an android replacement for the daughter he lost during a scientific experiment—compare to many anime equivalents from *Astro Boy* onward (*AE).

A virtual reality spin on the traditional sentai show, ironically one also attempted with the U.S. version of the much earlier **METALDAR** in **VR TROOPERS**, *Megaranger* was more basic than the previous year's **CARRANGER**, perhaps a sign that the previous year's show overreached its budgetary limits. The special vehicles were limited to a series of numbered star fighters, which would of course combine to make robots such as the Super Galaxy Mega and the Voyager Machine. "Based on an idea by Saburō Yade," and featuring music in the original version from Toshihiko Sahashi.

Megaranger was adapted into the sixth incarnation of the U.S. TV show **MIGHTY MORPHIN' POWER RANGERS**, under the title *Power Rangers in Space*. Deprived of their Red member and eager to find their kidnapped mentor Zordon (see **CARRANGER** synopsis), the Rangers head into space. Meanwhile, a conference of all the series' previous bad guys (played by their American stand-ins) acknowledges the new supremacy of Dark Specter (Christopher Cho). Dark Specter assigns the evil Princess Astronema (Melody Perkins) to destroy the Power Rangers. They, however, have gained new allies in the form of alien Red Ranger Andros (Christopher Khayman Lee) and his Silver Ranger colleague Zhane (Justin Nimmo). In the ensuing series of battles, Andros discovers that Astronema is really his long-lost sister Karone and converts her back to the forces of good under her original name. The final episodes wiped much of the slate clean, with the loss in battle of most of the Power Rangers' robots

Megaranger (U.S. cast)

© 2002 BVS Entertainment Inc. and BVS International N.V.

and the destruction of Zordon's tube, which conveniently sends out a shockwave destroying all the Power Rangers' old enemies. The next show in the Super Sentai chronology was the following year's **GINGAMAN**, adapted for the U.S. market under the title *Power Rangers Lost Galaxy*.

MELODY

1997. PRD: Teruhiko Kuze. DIR: Noriaki Asō, Tatsuzō Inohara, Teruhiko Kuze. SCR: Hiroshi Takeyama. CAST: Kyōko Koizumi, Kaoru Kobayashi, Kōji Tamaki, Ken Kaneko, Tomoko Tabata, Haruko Katō, Rieko Miura, Kazumi Moroboshi. CHN: TBS. DUR: 45 mins. x 13 eps.; Sun 5 January 1997–30 March 1997.

After a messy divorce from her husband who is working overseas, Sachiko (Koizumi) moves away with her son Masakazu. She is forced to take a room at her mother-in-law's house and searches for a new job. She finds one at a struggling local cable TV station (compare to **NEWS WOMAN**), whose producer Ōyama (Kobayashi) is desperately trying to increase ratings. He decides to hire the controversially scandalous newscaster Sakurai (Tamaki), in a show crammed to the brim with pop idols old and new. Theme: Spitz—"Scarlet."

MEN WHO PRETEND TO BE ASLEEP

1995. JPN: *Netafuri Shiteru Otokotachi*. PRD: Tomoko Kobashi. DIR: Yasuo Tsuruhashi. SCR: Makiko Uchidate. CAST: Akira Kobayashi, Ayumi Ishida, Shinsuke Ashida, Shin Takuma, Yuki Kudō. CHN: Yomiuri. DUR: 45 mins. x 9 eps.; Thu 12 January 1995–9 March 1995.

Madoka (Ishida) lives alone after splitting up with her husband Kōhei (Kobayashi). One day, young office lady Yuriko (Kudō) moves into her neighborhood, and, after the women become friends, announces that she has fallen in love with her boss, who predictably turns out to be Kōhei. Theme: Akira Kobayashi—"Ude no Niji Dake" (Only Rainbow on My Arm).

MEN WHO WANT TO MARRY

1991. JPN: *Kekkonshitai Otokotachi*. PRD: Seiichirō Kijima. DIR: Jirō Shōno. SCR: Toshiharu Matsubara. CAST: Tsurutarō Kataoka, Hiroshi Fuse, Tōru Kazama, Kaho Minami, Tomoko Yamaguchi. CHN: TBS. DUR: 45 mins. x 12 eps.; 5 July 1991–20 September 1991.

Morihiko (Kataoka) is a sales person at a real estate agency keen to marry before his company transfers him to

Borneo. He meets Mai (Minami) at a singles' party. She is a divorcée who works at an accounting office. Compare to **ARRANGED MARRIAGE**. Theme: Senri Ōe—"Kakkowarui Furarekata" (Blind Rejection).

MEN'S JOURNEY

1976. JPN: *Otokotachi no Tabiji*. PRD: Susumu Kondō. DIR: Katsufumi Nakamura, Kiyoshi Takano, Masayuki Tomizawa. SCR: Taichi Yamada. CAST: Kōji Tsuruta, Yutaka Mizutani, Kensaku Morita, Toshio Shiba, Kaori Momoi, Junko Igarashi, Gin Maeda, Kentarō Shimizu, Kayoko Kishimoto. CHN: NHK. DUR: 60 mins. x ca. 12 eps.; Sat 28 February 1976–13 March 1976 (#1); 5 February 1977–19 February 1977 (#2); 12 November 1977–3 December 1977 (#3); 10 November 1979–24 November 1979 (#4).

Shintarō Yoshioka (Tsuruta) walks into an office occupied by six new employees and asks them to attack him. This is a security company and the recruits must demonstrate their fighting skills, but Shintarō defeats them all without effort. He warns them that they face a life of restrictions—security guards do not have the power of arrest nor can they carry weapons, giving them all the risks of police work with none of the defenses.

After their boot camp training experience the rookie guards are sent out into the world. Shintarō takes Yōhei (Mizutani) and Tatsuo (Morita) to guard a skyscraper and prevent anyone from committing suicide by jumping off its roof for a two-month period. Tatsuo tries to treat it like a war game, though Yōhei refuses to take the "mission" seriously. The depressed Etsuko (Momoi) sneaks into the building, evades the guards, and prepares to jump to her death but Shintarō talks her down with stories about World War II. He tells her that death was around every corner in the 1940s and that people do not have the right to decide when they will die until they have made the best of living.

A subtler, more pacifist answer to America's cop show and wartime adventure exports, *MJ* offers an allegory of Japan's own military might in the postwar period—compare to the identity crisis of the previous year's **JAPAN SINKS**. While **G-MEN 75** happily imitated *The Untouchables* and *Kojak, MJ* features a group of heroes unable to employ the traditional tools of American heroism. Devoid of guns or the moral high ground, the cast is neatly contrasted both on and off screen. Actor Tsuruta genuinely had experienced World War II and made unsubstantiated claims to having been a member of a kamikaze squad. Meanwhile, his weary but noble failure is offset against bright young things born after the end of the war—the cast includes former child actors such as **I AM A MAN**'s Kensaku Morita, and Yutaka Mizutani from **ZEALOUS TIMES**. The genuine tension between the two generations led to great popularity with the Japanese public, and future **ODD APPLES** writer Yamada was able to piggyback some potentially controversial ideas into his scripts, such as the treatment of the elderly and disabled.

In later episodes, thwarted suicide Etsuko joins the team and immediately causes trouble with her new-age attitude. Although she successfully apprehends a shoplifter, she refuses to take the woman (an impoverished housewife) to the police but instead offers to buy her coffee, causing Shintarō to fly into a rage. Etsuko, who has *returned* the stolen goods on the thief's behalf, refuses to see that there is still a criminal to be punished—a brilliant evocation of the difference in generational attitudes at the time. Meanwhile, the true connections between today's Japanese and yesterday's are made clearer when Tatsuo discovers that Shintarō not only knows his mother but was an old wartime flame of hers who left for a reason that mere kids *"couldn't possibly understand."*

After the series officially ended, the cast was reunited one last time in a 1982 TV movie.

MERRY CHRISTMAS IN SUMMER *

2000. JPN: *Manatsu no Merry Christmas*. PRD: Hiroki Ueda. DIR: Jirō Shōno, Natsuki Imai. SCR: Tō Shimizu. CAST: Yutaka Takenouchi, Miki Nakatani, Ai Katō, Ren Ōsugi, Tetta Sugimoto, Maiko Yamada. CHN: TBS. DUR: 45 mins. x 10 eps.; Fri 13 October 2000–15 December 2000.

Okinawan orphan Haru (Nakatani) comes to Tokyo after the death of her foster mother, ostensibly to see her old friend, aspiring actress Natsumi (Katō). However, her secret target is Natsumi's brother Ryō (Takenouchi), another former orphanage kid who left town to become a boxer. In fact, Ryō has fallen on hard times and now works as a sparring partner and part-time hoodlum. He is at Haneda airport on the trail of a con man who specializes in tricking provincial girls into a life of prostitution—naturally, it is Haru who he saves, though he does not recognize her at first. The two begin a tentative relationship, although Haru insists that Ryō can only take her out with money that he earns honestly. However, his old underworld connections surround him, and he risks arrest and the loss of any chance of gaining a boxing license. Just as the couple's problems seem to resolve themselves, Haru discovers evidence that they are actually brother and sister—causing them to radically rethink their relationship. But though they move in together as siblings, neither is able to stomach the idea of the other forming a loving relationship with someone else.

After beginning like an inverted version of **HEAVEN'S COINS** (a girl comes from the Deep South, instead of the Far North, in search of a long-lost lover), *MCiS* suddenly veers off course to become another not quite incest drama in the style of **STRAWBERRY ON THE SHORTCAKE** or **COME TO MAMA'S BED**. Broadcast in the U.S. with English subtitles on KIKU TV. Theme: The Brilliant Green—"Angel Song: Eve no Kane" (Angel Song: Chime on the Eve).

MERRY CHRISTMAS JUST FOR YOU

1991. JPN: *Kimidake ni Merry Christmas*. PRD: N/C. DIR: Akimitsu Sasaki. SCR: Shōji Sasaki. CAST: Tomoko Fujita, Toshikazu Fukawa, Rina Takahashi, Masumi Okada, Hiroko Arisawa. CHN: TVT. DUR: 45 mins. x 6 eps.; Sun 24 November 1991– 29 December 1991.

Female doctor Akane (Fujita) bumps into Shunichi (Fukawa), her former boyfriend who disappeared on Christmas Eve two years ago. She finds out that he was with Masako (Takahashi), her best friend and a pharmacist, at her clinic on the day he disappeared. Sometime later, Shunichi's current girlfriend Hiromi (Arisawa) visits Akane. She has cardiovalvulitis and she warns Akane not to see him again.

MESSAGE

2003. JPN: *Message: Kotoba ga Uragitteiku*. AKA: *Words of Betrayal*. PRD: Yūya Fujii. DIR: Masahiro Kunimoto. SCR: Nao Morishita. CAST: Hitomi Manaka, Ryō, Masato Ibu, Ryūdō Uzaki, Ken Tanaka, Mitsuko Baishō. CHN: Yomiuri. DUR: 45 mins. x 11 eps.; Mon 13 January 2003– ?? March 2003.

Kyōko (Manaka) is transferred from a newspaper section to a glossy scandal magazine. Arriving at a hospital to report on a suspected case of medical malpractice, she meets Yonekura, the father of the baby victim. Though he is initially distrustful, she wins his trust by recounting the death of her sister's child nine years earlier, in what the family suspected was another case of malpractice. Interviewing the supervising Dr. Hayashi, Kyōko discovers that he administered drugs to induce labor, without seeking consultation from the patient or her next of kin. Hayashi denies any accusations, but Kyōko's photographer Adachi (Ibu) makes another discovery—on the day of the fateful incident, Hayashi appears to have been in attendance at his mentor's birthday party. For anyone whose

memory does not stretch back to TABLOID and THE SUN IS NOT SILENT. Theme: Fayray—"Sukida nante Ienai" (I Can't Say I Love You).

METALDAR *

1987. JPN: *Chōjinki Metaldar*. AKA: *Super Robot Metaldar*. PRD: Susumi Yoshikawa, Itaru Orita, Jun Mikasa, Yūki Usui, Akira Koseki. DIR: Takeru Ogasawara, Yoshiharu Toyota, Itaru Orita. SCR: Susumu Takahisa, Haruya Yamazaki, Kunio Fujii, Shōzō Uehara. CAST: Hikaru Senoo, Hiroko Aota, Hiroshi Kawai, Shinji Tōdō, Yūko Mitsui, Emiko Yamamoto. CHN: Asahi. DUR: 25 mins. x 39 eps.; Mon 16 March 1987–17 January 1988.

During World War II, Professor Kōga is a scientist working for the Japanese Empire on a secret project to defend his country with an army of robot warriors. Hearing that his son has been killed fighting in the Pacific, the grieving Professor turns away from his work, refuses to involve himself in the war effort, and disappears from sight, reputedly taking his best prototype with him. Forty years later, his former assistant Makoto (Tōdō) now calls himself Emperor Neross, and is the leader of an international crime syndicate. Neross orders the assassination of the Professor but Kōga survives to reach his secret hideout, where he activates his "robot son" Ryūsei (Senoo). Ryūsei witnesses his father's death at the hands of Neross agents and swears revenge, discovering in the process that one of his talents is the ability to transform from a life-like human being into a new improved variant of the original military design—Metaldar. His sole true companions are Springer, a robotic dog he also finds in his father's laboratory, and plucky lady photographer Mai (Aota).

With obvious similarities not only to KIKAIDA but also to ASTRO BOY and the anime series *Big X* (*AE), there is a certain irony in the producer's claim that the "original" idea was created by their house pseudonym "Saburō Yade." Within the limited demands of the

Merry Christmas in Summer

Japanese hero genre, and particularly the Metal Series in which the show appears, its innovations extend to Neross's treatment of his lieutenants. Rather than simply send a minion to destroy Metaldar, Neross allows his monsters to engage in gladiatorial combat for the right to do so, thereby ensuring that the baddies fight *each other* for part of each episode before the victor is permitted to go in search of our hero. Beginning in a primetime Monday slot, the show was moved to Sunday mornings halfway through its run.

Metaldar was later bought and adapted for the American market in a new form that combined it with its predecessor *Spielban* (see VR TROOPERS). The following year's show in the Metal Series chronology is JIRAIYA.

MIDDAY MOON *

1996. JPN: *Mahiru no Tsuki*. PRD: Yasuo Yagi. DIR: Nobuhiro Doi, Hirotake Katō. SCR: Kazuhiko Yūkawa. CAST: Yūji Oda, Takako Tokiwa, Yumi Shirakawa, Naoko Iijima, Takeshi Naitō. CHN: TBS. DUR: 45 mins. x 12 eps.; Thu 4 July 1996–19 September 1996.

Naoki (Oda) gamely struggles to make ends meet, running a cleaning company in order to support his sister. He meets Mae (Tokiwa) when they are both trying to help an abandoned puppy and the two fall in love. Mae wishes to be a TV announcer but seems to be having little success. She is making preparations to return to her hometown when she is finally accepted for the job. As she excitedly heads back to tell Naoki, she is set upon and raped by a group of strangers.

Naoki is unable to comprehend the enormity of Mae's trauma and tries to perk her up with a trip to Tokyo Disneyland. However, his superficial efforts are doomed to failure and Mae becomes increasingly distant. As she withdraws from him, Naoki is drawn to Mari (Shirakawa), the nurse who first treated Mae after the rape. Mae's behavior becomes erratic, as she alternately throws herself at Naoki in an attempt to wipe out her trauma, only to return once more to an apparently emotionless state. The rapists are eventually caught, though Naoki remains fearful that Mae's slow recovery will be halted if she is forced to identify them or give evidence in court.

A remarkably hard-hitting and controversial drama, *Midday Moon* jettisons much of the feel-good clichés of the genre in favor of a realistic and uncompromising portrayal of a victim's trauma. It also rejects the titillation common to later shows such as **CHEAP LOVE**, portraying some 1990s clichés such as dating clubs in a distinctly unflattering light. Compare to **FROM THE HEART** and **SLEEPING FOREST**, which approached Post Traumatic Stress Disorder from different angles, and **RED**, which also examined the aftermath of a rape.

Between 23 to 27 December in the same year, the series was rebroadcast in five feature-length TV specials, under the title *Midday Moon Complete Version: Wish You Were Here*. It was also released in a novelized form, credited to scenarist Yūkawa. Broadcast with English subtitles in the U.S. on KIKU TV. Theme: Swing Out Sister—"Anata ni Ite Hoshii" (Wish You Were Here). Peak rating: 23.2%.

MIDNIGHT RAIN *

2003. JPN: *Mayonaka no Ame*. PRD: N/C. DIR: N/C. SCR: N/C. CAST: Yūji Oda, Yasuko Matsuyuki, Hiroshi Abe, Misato Tanaka, Shunsuke Matsuoka, Maiko Yamada, Ikkei Watanabe, Ken Ishiguro, Kyōzō Nagatsuka. CHN: TBS. DUR: 45 mins. x ca. 11 eps.; Thu ?? January 2003–?? March 2003.
Takashi (Oda), a maverick new E.R. doctor at the prestigious Izumida hospital, disobeys his superiors on his first day at work by admitting a criminal who has been shot during a gunfight with police. He is miraculously able to save the man's life, a success which causes him to meet and begin a relationship with Yukiko (Matsuyuki), the broken-hearted officer who shot the criminal in the first place. Broadcast in the U.S. with English subtitles on KIKU TV.

MID-LIFE CRISIS *

1998. JPN: *Kamisan Nanka Kowakunai*. AKA: *We're Not Scared of Our Wives; Come Fly With Me*. PRD: Akira Isoyama. DIR: Makoto Kiyohiro. SCR: Seita Yamamoto. CAST: Masakazu Tamura, Isao Hashizume, Takuzō Kadono, Kyōko Koizumi, Hitomi Kuroki, Emi Wakui, Rie Miyazawa. CHN: TBS. DUR: 45 mins. x 11 eps.; Sun 12 April 1998–21 June 1998.
Gorō (Tamura) is left alone in Japan when his wife of 25 years flies to London to help their daughter get through her first pregnancy. He prepares to enjoy the bachelor life again for three trouble-free months, but immediately gains two unwelcome houseguests when his childhood friends arrive. Both Tamotsu (Hashizume) and Kenji (Kadono) have been thrown out by their wives for being unfaithful, but Gorō does not notice the obvious warning and sets about trying to charm every woman he sees (a succession of famous guest stars).

Mid-Life Crisis effectively forms a third season of the popular series **WIFE BASHING**—the names have been changed, but the relationships are the same. The three salacious old men relentlessly pursue the opposite sex with the energy of teenagers, trying to pick up women in a dentist's office, posing as famous people with similar names to charm gullible girls, and even trying to impress a pretty lady detective who is using an upstairs room as a stakeout location. Needless to say, they rarely get very far, and the much derided wives are sure to get their revenge in the end—most notably when one turns out not to be where she claimed but actually lying on a beach in Hawaii. Broadcast with English subtitles in the U.S. on KIKU TV. Theme: Frank Sinatra—"Come Fly With Me."

MIGHTY JACK *

1968. PRD: Yasuyoshi Itō, Yasuji Morita. DIR: Minoru Mitsuta, Mimachi Nonagase, Tsuneo Kobayashi. SCR: Tetsuo Kinjō, Shinichi Sekizawa, Bunzō Wakatsuki, Ichirō Ikeda, Saburō Shibahide, Tetsuo Kinjō, Naohiro Fuji, Hiroyasu Yamaura, Masahiro Yamada, Keisuke Fujikawa. CAST: Hideaki Nitani, Hiroshi Minami, Naoko Kubo, Akiyoshi Kasuga, Wakako Ikeda, Masaya Nihei, Hideyo Amamoto, Masayoshi Fukuoka, Yoshitaka Tanaka, Noriaki Inoue, Mitsuru Ōya, Gorō Mutsu, Anne Marie, Jirō Yanaga. CHN: Fuji. DUR: 25 mins. x 39 eps.; Sat 6 April 1968–29 June 1968 (#1); 6 July 1968–28 December 1968 (#2).
Prominent politician Gōnosue Yabuki (Yanaga) foresees the growing danger of Q, a high-tech terrorist organization, and decides to form his own elite group to combat it. The eleven members of Mighty Jack have different specialties, though some are more useful than others in fighting crime—leader Hachirō (Nitani) is a professional mountaineer and lieutenant Akira (Nihei) is a test pilot, but deputy Ippei (Minami) is a professional golfer.

Each time Q's cat-stroking mastermind attempts to seize control of the world, the heroic team meet at their secret hideout and board the flying battleship Mighty Jack, normally to be found in its underground base. They can then assemble what they need en route to the danger site, using Mighty Jack's onboard weapons factory.

The direct inspiration for *MJ* lay with **ULTRAMAN** creator Eiji Tsuburaya and his love of the British show *Thunderbirds* (NHK, 1966). Like *Thunderbirds* creator Gerry Anderson, Tsuburaya was keen to produce a spectacular sci-fi effects show but hoped to capture an audience beyond the usual children at whom such series were aimed. With a lead writer who was a native of Okinawa, an island at that time still occupied by the U.S. military, *MJ* grew out of the height of the Cold War and the first stirrings of U.S. involvement in Vietnam. In other media, James Bond was literally storming Japan in 1967's *You Only Live Twice,* while *The Man from U.N.C.L.E.* (NTV, 1965 as *0011 Napoleon Solo*) and *Wild Wild West* (Fuji, 1965) held primetime slots on Japanese television. However, a breakneck production schedule defeated some of *MJ*'s nobler aims—amid many explosions, there was little time to choreograph proper dogfights, and the audience drifted away.

Admitting defeat with the adult audience (a real shame, as *MJ* had true potential), the Tsuburaya studio retooled the series for younger viewers, renaming it *Tatakae! MJ* (*Fight! MJ*) for the final 26 episodes. With a completely different story, the protagonists were now a five-strong team who represented the Oriental Branch of the Association of People's Peace and Liberty on Earth (A.P.P.L.E.), led by general Fujii (Junya Usami). Early episodes simply replayed the previous season's mechanical battles and teamwork, but the latter part returned to the monster-of-the-week angle favored by *Ultraman*. Not only was this cheaper to produce than close-up modelwork, but it was easier for a young audience to understand. Music in the original series was by Isao Tomita.

MJ enjoyed one final flourish when the rights to the first season were purchased for English-language release by the Sandy Frank company. Instead of

Mighty Jack

© 1967 Tsuburaya Productions

releasing the entire series, the distributors chose to combine episodes 1 and 13 with pieces of bridging footage lifted from the other episodes to make the movie *Mighty Jack* (1986). As with the later Tsuburaya production **ARMY OF THE APES**, this feature-length edit is the only English-language incarnation of the series currently available.

MIGHTY MORPHIN' POWER RANGERS *

1992. JPN: *Kyōryū Sentai Jūranger.* AKA: *Dinosaur Battle Team Beast-Ranger; Zyuranger.* PRD: Kyōzō Utsunomiya, Jun Kaji, Takeyuki Suzuki, Shinichirō Shirokura. DIR: Shōhei Tōjō, Tarō Sakamoto, Takeshi Ogasawara, Keita Amemiya, Katsuya Watanabe. SCR: Noboru Sugimura, Kenichi Araki, Minehisa Arakawa, Susumu Takahisa, Toshiki Inoue, Kyōko Sagiyama. CAST: Yūta Mochizuki, Seiju Takayasu, Hideki Fujiwara, Takumi Hashimoto, Reiko

Chiba, Shirō Izumi, Machiko Soga. CHN: Asahi. DUR: 25 mins. x 50 eps.; Fri 21 February 1992–12 February 1993. One hundred seventy million years after she sold her soul to Satan, the evil queen Bandora (Soga) is freed from her prison on planet Nemesis by a passing astronaut. In her flying fortress of Dora Monstar (Wandering Mon-Star), she returns to Earth in order to restore it once more to its previous status of the Planet of Death. The aging wizard Barza, who has guarded a secret base all this time, recruits the valiant Zyuranger team to defend the planet, each of whom fights with a dinosaur as a totem creature. Their leader is Geki (Mochizuki), a prince of the Yamato tribe, who is also the red-clad Tyranno Ranger who fights with a Dragon Attack Sword. Kōji (Takayasu) is the black-clad Mammoth Ranger, a knight of the Shama clan who fights with the Mammoth Breaker. Dan (Fujiwara) is the blue-clad Triceranger who fights with the Tricerance (Triceratops Lance). Boy (Hashimoto) is the yellow-clad Tiger Ranger, knight of the Daimu clan who fights with the twin Saber Daggers. Kindhearted Mei (Chiba) is the Pteranger, a princess of the Rishia clan who fights with the Ptera Arrows. The team was later joined by a sixth member Burai (Izumi), the green-clad Dragon Ranger who wore special Dragon Armor. The team traveled around on their Roadsaura 1, 2, and 3 motorcycle-sidecar combinations, but also had robotic vehicles modeled after each of their totem animals. These dinosaur vehicles could combine to make the Daijūshin giant robot, which itself could be added to the Dragon Ranger's vehicle to create the Dragon Caesar super-robot and several other robot combinations.

Bandora and her minions try to seize control of the Earth with a series of monsters of the week, aided by her Golem cannon fodder troops, in what could have merely been yet another Super Sentai show, coming straight after JETMAN and with many similarities to the earlier KOSEIDON. However, this unremarkable entry in the long-running saga gained a new lease of life when it was picked up by Saban Entertainment and released in a substantially altered form in the U.S. and around the world.

The Saban version lifted special effects and combat from the original *Zyuranger* show and spliced it with new American footage. In the new version, the five-person team was a racially diverse mixture of all-American teenagers from the California suburb of Angel Grove—red Jason (Austin St. John), black Zach (Walter Jones), blue Billy (David Yost), yellow Trini (Thuy Trang), and pink Kimberley (Amy Jo Johnson), later joined by green Tommy (Jason Frank). They are recruited by Zordon (David Fielding), an interdimensional being who is attempting to save Earth from Rita Repulsa (the original Bandora), who has been freed from a distant prison

after a mere ten thousand years in captivity. When each episode develops into the inevitable fight, the new teenage American Power Rangers transform into the masked Japanese originals—in one case even changing sex, since Trini the Yellow Ranger was a girl in the U.S. version, while Boy in the original was demonstrably a boy. During the big fight, which often seemed to include Putty Patrollers (the Golems) and enemy monsters attacking Angel Grove's surprisingly large number of replica Tokyo landmarks, the Rangers would call on the power of their Dino Zord vehicles, which would eventually combine to make the Mega Zord supervehicle. Each episode would end with normality restored and the U.S. cast making a final appearance—essentially, Saban's version would comprise half a new episode and half an old one, but the ready-made material comprised all the expensive special effects footage, making it a relatively economical show to produce.

Caught in the middle of *Jurassic Park* dinosaur-hype and neatly occupying the kiddie craze vacuum between *Teenage Mutant Ninja Turtles* and the later *Pokémon* (*AE), the international success of *Mighty Morphin' Power Rangers* made it the most profitable Japanese TV drama ever in the U.S., albeit in a severely altered form. Still running to this day, its later seasons have incorporated successive Super Sentai shows, starting with the following year's DAIRANGER and continuing with KAKURANGER, OHRANGER, CARRANGER, MEGARANGER, GINGAMAN, GOGO FIVE, TIME RANGER, GAORANGER, and most recently HURRICANGER. It also encouraged many imitators to seek out more Japanese footage for re-versioning in the American market, leading to the U.S. release of other Japanese children's shows such as VR TROOPERS, SUPER SAMURAI SYBER SQUAD, BEETLEBORGS, and MASKED RIDER. The American cast also appeared in their own movie spin-off versions, *MMPR: The Movie* and *Turbo: A Power Rangers Movie*, using some of the Japanese

stunt players who made the original such a success. Music in the original series was by Akihiko Yoshida.

MIKAZUKI

2000. JPN: *Tekkōki Mikazuki*. AKA: *Iron Armor Machine Mikazuki*. PRD: N/C. DIR: Keita Amemiya. SCR: Toshiki Inoue. CAST: Yūta Kōchi, Jirō Hotaruyuki, Saori Nara, Yasuyo Shiratori, Fumina Hara, Saki Takasaki, Tetsuya Sugimoto. CHN: Fuji. DUR: 60 mins. x 6 eps. (1st ep 90 mins.); Mon 23 October 2000–24 March 2001.

One day, a huge watermelon marked with the letter K appears in the sky above Tokyo. If possible, school boy Kazeo Isurugi (Kōchi) is even more surprised than everyone else, as he knows it to be a replica of the watermelon he and his missing archeologist father ate a long time ago. Kazeo is lifted up toward the watermelon but saved by Akane, a high school girl who is also the chairperson of Akebono Heavy Industries. But, soon after, he is thrown out of the machine (it's not a watermelon after all) and falls until he is saved by the palm of a black Metal Giant. Kazeo accepts a new duty—facing monsters sent by the evil King Torpor, who wishes to rule the Earth.

A giant robot show from former JETMAN collaborators Toshiki Inoue and Keita Amemiya, *Mikazuki*'s large budget shows in copious special effects, truly investing it with great potential. However, in a bizarre broadcasting experiment, the producers chose to show it in *monthly* hour-long episodes. Consequently, although it ran no longer than the average series of 13 25-minute episodes, it had little opportunity to build up a following, and soon lost viewers who forgot the previous episode's plot, or missed one episode and had to wait a whole extra month to find out what happened next. A similar scheduling experiment was tried with the same year's *Figure 17: Tsubasa and Hikaru* (*AE). The music was produced by HATAKE of Sharan Q.

MIKE HAMA: PRIVATE DETECTIVE

2002. JPN: *Shiritsu Tantei Hama Mike.*
PRD: Yoshinori Horiguchi, Takenori
Sentō. DIR: Akira Ogata, Ryōsuke
Maeda, Hiroharu Hagiuta, Isamu
Ikusada, Hideaki Sunaga, Shinji
Aoyama, Tōru Iwamatsu, Sōgo Ishii,
Tetsuya Nakajima, Suguru Takeuchi,
Alex Cox, Tsuyoshi Toshishite. SCR:
Kenji Aoki. CAST: Masatoshi Nagase,
Miwako Ichikawa, Mika Nakajima,
Wakana Sakai, Haruka Igawa, Masashi
Yamamoto, Shunsuke Matsuoka,
Miyuki Matsuda, Sadao Abe, Kyōko
Koizumi. CHN: NTV. DUR: 45 mins. x 12
eps.; Mon 1 July 2002–16 September
2002.

Mike Hama (Nagase) is an impoverished Yokohama private detective,
whose stern exterior hides a sentimental softie who will do anything to help a
lady in trouble, particularly his sister
Akane (Nakajima). Preceded by three
Mike Hama movies, this series of TV
specials in the spirit of **DETECTIVE
STORY** featured a number of famous
directors, including Britain's Alex Cox,
whose eleventh episode features photography by Tom Richmond.
According to Japanese press releases of
the time, the series is slated to be
broadcast in the U.K., Germany, and
France. Theme: EGO-WRAPPIN'—
"Kuchibashi ni Cherry" (Cherry to the
Beak).

MINAMI'S SWEETHEART

1994. JPN: *Minami-kun no Koibito.* AKA:
Minami's Lover; A Girl in the Hand.
PRD: Kōtaro Takahashi. DIR: Shirō
Nakayama, Kazuhisa Imai. SCR:
Yoshikazu Okada. CAST: Yumiko
Takahashi, Shinji Takeda, Reiko Chiba,
Masao Kusakari, Rei Okamoto, Junji
Takada. CHN: Asahi. DUR: 45 mins. x 10
eps.; Mon 10 January 1994–21 March
1994; also 1 ep special, 10 April
1995.

As they look in through the window of
a high-class beach front restaurant, seven-year-old Hiroyuki Minami (Takeda)
makes a promise to his devoted friend
Chiyomi (Takahashi). On the day of
his eighteenth birthday, he will treat

Minami's Sweetheart

her to dinner in the self-same restaurant as a symbol of their eternal friendship. Ten years later, as graduation
nears, Hiroyuki plans a motorcycle ride
across America on Route 66, and
Chiyomi realizes that graduation could
separate them forever. She gently tries
to remind him of his promise but he is
more preoccupied with Risako
(Chiba), a sassy school troublemaker
who makes a show of kissing him while
the scandalized Chiyomi is busy on the
basketball court. Risako promises
Hiroyuki a *very* special birthday gift
and sends him photographs of herself

semi-nude. Meanwhile, Chiyomi discovers that her fearsomely handsome
widower father (Kusakari) is planning
to remarry and storms out of the house
to talk to Hiroyuki. Finding him
unsympathetic, she walks home in the
middle of a storm and is almost hit by
an out of control truck. Luckily (!), she
is struck by lightning and saved from
certain death by a miracle transformation that reduces her to mere inches in
height.

Worried about Chiyomi's failure to
appear at school the next day, Hiroyuki
rebuffs Risako's advances and heads

for the beach. Remembering his promise after all, he dutifully takes a seat at the restaurant, only to find the pint-sized Chiyomi clambering up to the window ledge. He takes her home in his jacket pocket, and she gets her secret wish—on Hiroyuki's first day as an adult, she wakes up beside him, albeit only inches tall.

Though initially prone to the clumsy acting that seems mandatory in so many teen dramas, *MS* soon reveals its true colors as a knowing pastiche of *Peter Pan*—compare to **NEVER LAND** or the similar second chances of **I'LL BE BACK**. Hiroyuki's love for Chiyomi is genuinely innocent, and as he approaches adulthood she is prepared to give anything to keep the two of them young forever. He crosses the threshold into adulthood, whereas she is transformed into a Tinkerbell figure—the only way she can cling to their childhood is by literally leaping into fairyland. The rest of the script obliges her by overstating all her troubles in the fairy tale terms familiar from **MASK OF GLASS**, particularly the evil stepsister figure of Risako, who zips around in her boyfriend's Porsche.

Knowing the Japanese appetite for crime and mystery, one wonders why nobody is suspicious that a girl disappears after she is last seen with her long-time male companion, leaving only her abandoned clothes by the roadside. Like **THE STAND-IN**, this could have been oh-so-sinister, but stays resolutely perky and innocent until the later episodes, when the story takes a decidedly unexpected turn.

Considering what must have been a low budget, the special effects are well executed, leading to numerous comedy incidents redolent of *Honey I Shrunk the Kids* (1989), such as Chiyomi cowering beneath the bed, terrified of the deafening howl of a vacuum cleaner pushed around the room by Hiroyuki's oblivious mother. In fact, the show picks up the moment Chiyomi shrinks, hiding its shortcomings beneath a series of set pieces such as her acquisition of suitable clothes (she gains a strangely shaped dress by pulling a fingerless glove over her head), or her panic-stricken escape from a menacing duck.

MS is based on the 1985 manga by Shungicu Uchida, the manga artist also responsible for *Water Story* and the notorious autobiography *Father Fucker*. As one of Uchida's earlier works, *MS* seems less controversial, though there are still odd throwaway moments, such as Hiroyuki's sister's preferred method of waking him up in the mornings—throwing back the bedclothes to get a look at his genitals! The story seems to have been a major influence on several unapproachable girlfriend anime of the years that followed, most notably the similarly pint-sized paramour of *Handmaid May* (*AE). It also has an irresistibly camp quality, particularly when Hiroyuki enlists the school sewing circle to make new clothes or buys doll's clothes originally made for the Japanese Barbie clone *Licca-chan* (*AE). Actor Takeda does his street cred no favors by wearing a silly scarf and a ridiculous pink denim jacket at inopportune moments. See also **AFTER SCHOOL**. Theme: Yumiko Takahashi—"Tomodachi de Ii kara" (Okay to be Friends).

MIRACLE MAN

1998. JPN: *Kiseki no Hito*. PRD: Kazutoshi Shimoda, Yoshinori Horiguchi. DIR: Kazuo Yamamoto, Masahiro Kunimoto. SCR: Rie Yokota. CAST: Masayoshi Yamazaki, Yuki Matsushita, Naho Toda, Kōsuke Toyohara, Hitoshi Ueki. CHN: Yomiuri. DUR: 45 mins. x 10 eps.; Mon 12 October 1998–14 December 1998. Yasuko (Matsushita) is the chief programmer at a software development company and troubled by glitches and bugs in a new game. She decides to seek the help of Katsumi (Yamazaki) the former programmer and eventually tracks him down to a remote Izu hospital. But Katsumi is recovering from a serious accident that has left him with the mind of an eight-year-old child—compare to **FROM THE HEART**, **ETERNAL CHILD,** and **TOWN WITHOUT ANGELS**. Theme: Masayoshi Yamazaki—"Boku wa Koko ni Iru" (Here I Am).

MIRACLE OF LOVE

1999. JPN: *Koi no Kiseki*. PRD: Toyohiko Wada, Motoshi Sasaki. DIR: Satoru Nakajima, Hiroshi Akabane. SCR: Miho Nakazono, Masahiro Yoshimoto. CAST: Riona Hazuki, Miho Kanno, Masato Hagiwara, Seiichi Tanabe, Jinpachi Nezu. CHN: Asahi. DUR: 45 mins. x 12 eps.; Thu 15 April 1999–1 July 1999. Taeko (Hazuki, in convincing prosthetics) is an obese girl who doesn't let her weight bother her, preferring to bask in the comfort of cake (see **ANTIQUE**) and the love of her parents. Her life is thrown into turmoil by the arrival of Yukino (Kanno), a beautiful thin girl who claims to be a relative and seems effortlessly perfect. Yukino stays with the family for four years, during which time she increasingly refers to Taeko as her "ugly sister." Eventually, Yukino seizes control of the family fortune and appears to have murdered Taeko's mother. Taeko flees into hiding, where she begins a year-long crash diet, before returning as a slim, attractive media personality (Hazuki, back to normal), ready to wreak her revenge. Theme: Fumiya Fuji—"Kaze no Jidai" (Age of Wind). Peak rating: 16.5%.

MIRACLE ROMANCE

1996. JPN: *Kiseki no Romance*. PRD: Katsu Kamikura. DIR: Nobuo Mizuta. SCR: Yasuhiro Koshimizu. CAST: Hidekazu Akai, Riona Hazuki, Yoshihiko Hakamada, Katsuhisa Namase, Ryūta Itō. CHN: NTV. DUR: 45 mins. x 10 eps.; Wed 10 January 1996–13 March 1996. Musashi (Akai) works in Osaka making paper lanterns but heads up to Tokyo for his sister's wedding. Losing his way in the big city, he meets bar hostess Makoto (Hazuki). After the wedding, he tracks her down using the book of matches she left him and the two begin a chalk-and-cheese romance contrasting the very different styles of the peoples of the Osaka and Tokyo regions.

Compare to SCENES FROM THE WATER TRADE and CAN'T HURRY LOVE. Theme: The Alfee—"Love Never Dies."

MIRRORMAN

1971. PRD: Toyoaki Awa, Minoru Mitsuta. DIR: Inoshirō Honda, Toshitsugu Suzuki, Yoshiyuki Kuroda, Shōhei Tōjō, Jun Ōki. SCR: Bunzō Wakatsuki, Keisuke Fujikawa, Hiroyasu Yamaura. CAST: Nobuyuki Ishida, Junya Usami, Takako Sawai, Toshiya Wazaki, Kentarō Kudō, Gen Sugiyama, Yōko Ichiji, Tadayoshi Kura, Sawako Kamizuki, Fujio Murakami, Mitsuru Saijō, Mamoru Kusumi, Shinichi Umeda, Michiharu Sakamoto. CHN: Fuji. DUR: 30 mins. x 51 eps.; Sun 5 December 1971–26 November 1972.

Kyōtarō Kagami (Ishida) is the offspring of a union between a father from a two dimensional universe and a mother from Earth. He is brought up by Dr. Mitarai (Usami), an expert in space physics, who has set up the Science Guard Members (SGM) in order to protect Earth from supernatural phenomena. The doctor also has made Kyōtarō the Mirror Man to confront the Invaders, the cause of the supernatural phenomena.

Based on an "original" idea Tetsuo Kinjō of Tsuburaya Productions, the *Mirrorman* project was later handed over to Narumitsu Taguchi. The concept was adapted into manga form to test it on the market, but no TV company was prepared to pick up a broadcast option. After an initial pilot starring SILVER MASK's Toshio Shiba, the series finally went into production with Nobuyuki Ishida in the lead. However, with SILVER MASK in the same time slot on rival network TBS, the two series were forced to compete against *each other* in the ratings. *Mirrorman* eventually fought back by taking the same kiddification route as the earlier MIGHTY JACK, transforming SGM from a group of scientists who order around the Air Defense Team into a combat-suited elite who do the fighting themselves. The Invaders' own forces were gradually transformed into a series of

monsters of the week in the manner of ULTRAMAN.

MIRUNA'S HOUSE

1972. JPN: *Miruna no Zashiki*. PRD: Kazuo Shibata. DIR: Minoru Hanabusa. SCR: Kuetsu Kawasaki. CAST: Yoshio Yamamoto, Emiko Ishizaki, Junkichi Hashimoto, Ichirō Sugai, Kazuya Kosaka, Noboru Mitani, Izumi Hara, Mayumi Miura. CHN: NHK. DUR: 30 mins. x 5 eps.; Sat 1 April 1972–29 April 1972.

Hidehiko (Yamamoto) and his sister Natsuko (Ishizaki) visit their uncle Tatsuzō (Hashimoto) during their spring vacation. In Tatsuzō's garden is a storehouse that *"belongs to Miruna,"* and is where he keeps all the possessions of his deceased daughter. The house is only opened twice a year on the anniversaries of her birth and death, and when the doors are unlocked this time, Tatsuzō reports that a statue of the Goddess of Mercy holding a golden baby has gone missing. The children speculate that the artifact may have been stolen by an escaped prisoner they have been warned about but the prisoner disproves their theory when he turns up dead. Folklorist Professor Tōyama (Mitani) tells Tatsuzō that the statue is not the Goddess of Mercy at all but the Virgin Mary holding an infant Jesus.

That night, Tatsuzō's servant Daizō (Kosaka) hands in his notice, claiming that he is going into business with a friend in Tokyo. Soon afterward, the Professor disappears, and the children find him tied up in Miruna's house. As the Professor suspected, it is Daizō who has been plundering Miruna's house and burying the treasures near the grave of his own parents. The priest of the local temple (Sugai) tells the children that they should keep quiet about the incident, and that he himself will ensure that Daizō learns the error of his ways.

MISFITS, THE *

1998. JPN: *Ao no Jidai*. AKA: *Blue Days, Le Periode Bleu*. PRD: Kazuhiro Itō. DIR:

Hiroshi Matsubara, Jun Nasuda, Osamu Katayama. SCR: Eriko Komatsu. CAST: Tsuyoshi Dōmoto, Megumi Okina, Takaya Kamikawa, Masanobu Andō, Kenji Kohashi, Ryōko Shinohara, Yū Yoshizawa, Jun Fubuki, Kei Yamamoto. CHN: TBS. DUR: 45 mins. x 11 eps.; Fri 3 July 1998–11 September 1998.

Disturbed youth Ryū (Dōmoto from the Kinki Kids) is always in trouble with the law. With his friends Toshi (Kohashi) and Masashi (Yoshizawa), he robs game center manager Honda (Yamamoto). Lawyer Haruna (Kamikawa) convinces Ryū to give himself up, though Ryū is held responsible not only for the bag snatching, but also for a later unrelated assault and the victim's false claim that the bag contained two million yen. After time in a youth correctional facility, Ryū is released into Honda's care, and tries to live a law-abiding life working at a *pachinko* parlor. However, his old cellmate Shuri soon arrives at his apartment. He stays with Ryū while he studies for his college entrance exams but is also seen flirting with Haruna's wife Kaoru. Haruna's behavior becomes increasingly erratic and when Kaoru and Shuri are injured in a car accident, Ryū suspects foul play.

Despite the outward appearances of lovable gangsters in the style of CHEAP LOVE or KISARAZU CATS EYE, *The Misfits* is also a cunningly concealed disability drama—the disability in question being multiple personality disorder, from which Haruna is suffering. Ryū's friend and confidante (at times) is also his deadly enemy (at times); we are never sure whether Haruna enters each scene as a helpful lawyer or a murderous thug, allowing for some entertaining switches in perspective. Compare to GIFT, SLEEPING FOREST, and *Fight Club* (1999). Broadcast with English subtitles in the U.S. on KIKU TV and KTSF TV. Theme: Kinki Kids—"Ao no Jidai" (Blue Period).

MISFORTUNE TASTES LIKE HONEY

1994. JPN: *Hito no Fukō wa Mitsu no*

© 1998 TBS

The Misfits

Aji. PRD: Keiko Take. DIR: Makoto Kiyohiro. SCR: Yumiko Kamiyama. CAST: Shinobu Ōtake, Pinko Izumi, Misa Shimizu, Haruko Sagara. CHN: TBS. DUR: 45 mins. x 11 eps.; Tue 11 January 1994–22 March 1994.
After finding accidental success at an early age, manga artist Mayuko (Ōtake) is a prima donna, bullying her assistants Megumi (Sagara) and Satoko (Shimizu) and demanding that she always gets her way. That changes with the arrival of her no-nonsense stepmother Sayuri (Izumi), who has no time for the tantrums of a spoiled brat. Compare to KING OF EDITORS. Theme: Akemi Ishii—"Anata no Mono" (It's Yours).

MISS DIAMOND

1995. PRD: Satoko Uchiyama. DIR: Ken Matsumoto. SCR: Yuki Kiyomoto. CAST: Asaka Seto, Masahiro Takashima, Hironobu Nomura, Satomi Kobayashi,

Jun Miho. CHN: Asahi. DUR: 45 mins. x 11 eps.; Thu 19 October 1995–14 December 1995.
After her father's sudden death, Nana (Seto) leaves university to help run the family tour company. While guiding a group around Bangkok, she is assaulted but rescued by the handsome Mr. Hayakawa (Takashima), a Japanese man. Theme: Asaka Seto—"Kono Jōnetsu wa Diamond" (This Passion is a Diamond).

MISS WITCH

1971. JPN: *Suki! Suki! Majō Sensei.* AKA: *We Love Witch Teacher.* PRD: Tōru Hirayama. DIR: Minoru Yamada, Itaru Orita, Katsuhiko Taguchi. SCR: Masaki Tsuji, Shinichi Ichikawa, Susumu Takahisa, Kiyohide Ōhara, Tadashi Endō. CAST: Yōko Kiku, Mantarō Ushio, Fuyukichi Maki, Leo Morimoto, Kuninobu Okumura, Ushio Akashi, Ayako Okumura, Yoshiyuki Fujie,

Tomonori Yazaki, Kazuko Sugiyama, Hideki Kawaguchi. CHN: Asahi. DUR: 25 mins. x 26 eps.; Sun 3 October 1971–26 March 1972.
A Japanese school gets a pretty teacher with magical powers, who not only brightens everyone's days with her winning smile but also helps defend the world from evil. Hikaru Tsuki (Kiku) is in fact the Queen of Star Alpha and a peaceful observer from the Andromeda Planet Union. Later in the series, she is promoted to A-class observer, also allowing her to transform into the heroine Andro Mask.

The story began life as *Teacher With a Thousand Eyes* (*Sen no Me no Sensei*), a manga by **MASKED RIDER** and **HARIMAO** creator Shōtarō Ishinomori, serialized in *Teen Look* magazine. As with its contemporary **COMET-SAN**, it took a woman with magical powers in the style of the American *Bewitched* and placed her in a situation where she could interact with children, with just a dash of *Bedknobs and Broomsticks* (1970). Ishinomori's story added references to Japanese myths and eventually had its title changed to *Teacher Princess Kaguya* (*Kaguya Hime Sensei*) in reference to the visitor from the moon who appears in the ancient *Taketori Monogatari*. Once the show began broadcasting, spin-off strips using the TV series title began appearing in the magazines *Shōjo Friend* and *Nakayoshi*. The main actress Yōko Kiku was recommended by Ishinomori personally and died in 1975, four years after the completion of the series, creating a personality cult that was to foreshadow those of Yūsaku Matsuda (see **DETECTIVE STORY**) and Masako Natsume (**MONKEY**). Theme: Mitsuko Horie—"Kaguya Hime Sensei no Uta" (Song of Teacher Princess Kaguya).

MITO KŌMON

1969. PRD: Minoru Itsumi. DIR: Tetsuya Yamauchi. SCR: Ichirō Miyakawa. CAST: Eijirō Tōno, Ryōtarō Sugi, Masashi Yokouchi, Ichirō Nakatani, Yumi Iwai, Isamu Yamagata, Shinya Ōwada, Yasushi Nagata. CHN: TBS. DUR: 45 mins. x

ca. 900 eps.; Mon 4 August 1969–
9 March 1970 (#1); 28 September
1970–10 May 1971 (#2); 29
November 1971–5 June 1972 (#3);
22 January 1973–17 September 1973
(#4); 1 April 1974–30 September
1974 (#5); 31 March 1975–
3 November 1975 (#6); 24 May
1976–10 January 1977 (#7); 18 July
1977–30 January 1978 (#8); 7 August
1978–5 February 1979 (#9); 13
August 1979–11 February 1980
(#10); 18 August 1980–9 February
1981 (#11); 31 August 1981–1 March
1982 (#12); 18 October 1982–11
April 1983 (#13); 31 October 1983–
9 July 1984 (#14); 28 January
1985–21 October 1985 (#15); 28
April 1986–19 January 1987 (#16);
24 August 1987–22 February 1988
(#17); 12 September 1988–1 May
1989 (#18); 25 September 1989–
16 April 1990 (#19); 22 October
1990–7 October 1991 (#20); 6 April
1992–9 November 1992 (#21); 17
May 1993–24 January 1994 (#22);
1 August 1994–15 May 1995 (#23);
11 September 1995–10 June 1996
(#24); 9 December 1996–27 October
1997 (#25); 9 February 1998–
17 August 1998 (#26); 22 March
1999–18 October 1999 (#27);
6 March 2000–20 November 2000
(#28); 2 April 2001–17 September
2001 (#29); 7 January 2002–1 July
2002 (#30); 14 October 2002–(#31).
Mitsukuni (Tōno) is an obscure member of the Tokugawa clan in the late
17th century, who also goes by the
name of Mito Kōmon—Mito being his
clan homeland in modern-day Ibaraki,
and Kōmon the "Yellow Gate" pen
name he adopted while compiling a
history of ancient Japan. Now that his
nephew is the Shogun Tsunayoshi
(reigned 1680–1709), Mitsukuni
decides to travel Japan incognito in
order to inspect the nation and ensure
that the country is prospering under
the Tokugawa. Disguised as a retired
merchant, the white-haired old man
travels in the company of his retainers
Kaku (Yokouchi) and Suke (Sugi), who
pretend to be his grandsons. They are

occasionally accompanied by Yahichi, a
former ninja, who fights to protect
Mitsukuni from assassins sent by
Yoshiyasu Yanagisawa (Yamagata), the
evil secretary of the shogun also seen
in CHŪSHINGURA.

Though Mitsukuni was a real historical figure, his fame grew during the
early 20th century thanks to a series of
novels by Sanjugo Aoki—compare to
similar fictional embellishments in THE
YAGYŪ CONSPIRACY. The *MK* series,
which has run intermittently for over
thirty years, was originally commissioned as a "home drama" like the family-oriented soaps already onscreen,
but with a period flavor. The show was
heavily influenced by Kōnosuke
Matsushita, whose electronics company
National was a sponsor for both *MK*
and NATIONAL KID, but also by TBS line
producer Minoru Itsumi. Itsumi
sketched out 13 basic plots for the wandering enforcers to encounter in innu-
merable variations, including evil
bailiffs, local agents of Yanagisawa, and
oppressed peasants, adding extra color
by keeping Mitsukuni constantly on
the move. Each week, the star would
have 45 minutes of screentime to
understand and solve the problem,
which he normally does by allowing
matters to come to a head and scowl-
ing meaningfully while his servants
reveal his true identity. Brandishing a
lacquered *inrō* case with the shogun's
crest as if it were a cop's badge, his
servants announce Mitsukuni's name
and rank, cowing all evildoers into
contrition.

For the first season, Mitsukuni travels to Takamatsu in Sanuki (now
Kagawa Prefecture), where his son
Yoritsune is governor. Mitsukuni
becomes involved in a quarrel over the
succession, as Yoritsune's six-year-old
son Karumaru is too young to rule
himself, while the other candidate
cousin Yorinō presents a dangerous
threat.

By the second season, Mitsukuni is
dispatched to northern Japan in an
attempt to prevent the rival clans of
Tsugaru and Nanbu from tearing each

other apart in a local conflict that has
been engineered by the wily Yanagisawa. Having dealt with the problem
(compare to similar issues in THE FIR
TREE LEFT BEHIND), Mitsukuni heads
for the southern island of Kyūshū to
solve a succession crisis in Kurume. En
route, he acquires a comedy sidekick,
Hachibei (Gentarō Takahashi) who
stays with the team thereafter.

A succession crisis at the top occupies Mitsukuni in the third season, as
the shogun is struck with illness, and
the three rival clan branches of Owari,
Kii, and Mito argue over his replacement. Yanagisawa allies with
Tsunamasa Owari and spreads rumors
in the southern land of Satsuma that
the Mito family are plotting to destroy
it. Some locals send messengers in
search of confirmation, while others
believe the propaganda and simply
send assassins, leading Mitsukuni to visit Satsuma and clear his family name.
Suke's role was handed over to Kōtarō
Satomi, who was to play the part for
another 16 years.

Though the cast rarely left the Tōei
stock samurai village near Kyoto, *MK*
began to acquire a reputation as a travelogue. Its star supposedly traveled the
length and breadth of Japan on many
occasions, and by the fourth season
TBS was exploiting it as a means of
advertising for domestic tourism, high-
lighting the handicrafts and delicacies
of Japan's many regions. Consequently,
season four sees Mitsukuni deciding to
follow the *Narrow Road to the Deep North*
popularized by the poet Bashō, traveling all the way to the topmost isle of
Hokkaidō.

Previous seasons always featured
Mitsukuni's outward and return journey, but for the fifth, he is called away
to help Princess Anri (Kaori
Kobayashi) of the Fukue clan on the
southern Gotō Islands near Nagasaki.
The journey takes the entire season,
while his leisurely return, sampling
many local dishes and tourist attrac-
tions, occupies much of the sixth.

Season seven sees Mitsukuni meet
with an accident while cutting the

branches of a pine tree. In need of some recuperation, he decides to visit a health spa in distant Tōhoku (the journey would have probably killed him in real life!), though his real reason is that he wishes to escort two sisters in their search of the region for their lost father. Similar ulterior motives govern the eighth season, in which Mitsukuni heads for Shimazu, ostensibly to congratulate the governor's wife (and shogun's daughter) Takehime on the birth of her son.

For the ninth season, Yashichi rescues a warrior from a group of assassins, who turns out to be a woman called Shino (Izumi Yamaguchi). She is the daughter of the lieutenant of the governor of the Kubota clan in Akita, whose family remain loyal to their lord despite a rival retainer's attempts to usurp power for his own son. Her father arrested and her stepbrother imprisoned, Shino seeks Mitsukuni's help. From this season onward, Kaku's role was played by Ōwada.

With Shino's family saved, the girl accepts an offer of marriage from the lovestruck Suke, but Mitsukuni is called away from their wedding in the tenth season in order to smooth another crisis. This time he must journey to Kyoto itself to report to the Emperor.

The eleventh season coincided with the tenth anniversary of the show, leading to the gimmick of a *Miss Mito Kōmon* contest on TBS. The winner, Kumiko Shimizu, got to play Miyo the hunter's daughter for the year, during which Mitsukuni travels to Dewa Shōnai to prevent the Sakai family from being torn apart in a local struggle. The same series saw the production of an animated spin-off, *Manga Mito Kōmon* (*AE), in which the traveling band encountered monsters, goblins, and ghosts.

Ninja similarly occupy Mitsukuni for the twelfth season, in which the team must struggle through ninja resistance to reach a clan whose overlord is suspected of plotting against the Shogun. The suspect is Mitsukuni's own son, who is being framed by the rival Sōzen

Honshō clan, who spread rumors that he intends to depose Tsunayoshi because his mother is of humble birth. The threat to the Shogun's life is revealed as genuine in the thirteenth season, in which Shogun Tsunayoshi is attacked by an assassin who leaves a sword behind bearing the crest of the Owari clan. However, Mitsukuni discovers that the "accident" is a double bluff and that it is in fact an attempt by the Hiraiwa clan to discredit their rivals. This season was the last in which Mitsukuni was played by Eijirō Tōno.

In the fourteenth series Mitsukuni (now played by Kō Nishimura) visits Nanbu to solve another succession conflict. Replacements were less troublesome behind the scenes, where the role of Kaku was handed over to Gorō Ibuki.

In an apparent retread of the ninth season, the fifteenth involved trouble at the Chikuzen clan in the southern town of Fukuoka. Mitsukuni meets a warrior woman who turns out to be the daughter of the governor. For the sixteenth season, he must go on the run from bounty hunters after a reward is put out for his life, but he returns for the seventeenth to save the Shima region from yet another plot by his nemesis Yanagisawa.

Prefiguring the story of the 1993 *taiga* drama WIND OF THE RYŪKYŪ ISLANDS, the eighteenth season focuses on the supposedly forbidden trade between the "closed country" of Japan and Imperial China. The Hirato clan plans to monopolize the illegal smuggling trade, until their efforts are halted by Mitsukuni and his followers, although the role of Suke was now played by Teruhiko Aoi. This was followed by a nineteenth season seemingly reprising the action of the eleventh. Despite the regular recycling of both episodic plots and the story arcs that occupied entire seasons, the 584 episodes of *MK* screened until this point still attained an average rating of 28.8%—however, there were rumblings at TBS that these ratings still demonstrated a decline from the 40%+ peak

enjoyed by the show in its early days. Viewer demographics demonstrated that the audience almost exclusively comprised viewers over 50—the story that had an old man at its center was appealing to an audience solely of old men, and without attention grabbing gimmicks, the show risked seeing its entire viewership eroded by old age.

To mark the twentieth season, another *Miss Mito Kōmon* contest was held and the three winners, Shima Yamashita, Yuki Waratani, and Yuka Yokota all secured roles as a result. The plot involved the non-appearance of Mitsukuni's son Yoritsune at court, and a quest back to Takamatsu in order to determine the cause.

The 21st series began with a two-hour special, and, amid Mistukuni's usual counterespionage work, this time in Okazaki, he also had to deal with an impersonator (Masao Komatsu) claiming to be him. This was the last season in which Mitsukuni was played by Nishimura.

For the 22nd, Mitsukuni (now played by Asao Sano) settles another succession crisis, this time by journeying to the central area of Kii (present day Wakayama Prefecture). Further assassin troubles, this time a band of criminals led by a killer nun, threaten the team in their 23rd season as they head off a dastardly plot in Kaga, an area governed by one of Mitsukuni's nephews.

The 24th season, including a two-hour special, sees Mitsukuni returning to Satsuma to fight pirates and more assassins. Behind the scenes, the period also saw the death of original producer Itsumi, and further dire portents from host channel TBS—advertisers no longer saw the show's viewership as a worthwhile audience, compared to the lucrative returns awaiting commercials run during trendy dramas.

However, even without Itsumi in charge, the show continued to soldier on. Rumors of its approaching demise proved to be untrue, and for the 25th season, Mitsukuni journeys to Chiba to see how soy sauce is made, before heading off to see his son in Takamatsu, helping local people along the route.

No doubt in an attempt to drag in younger audiences, the 26th season was crammed with ninja, as the team traveled to the assassins' spiritual homeland in Iga. Similar crowd pleasing tactics were attempted for the 27th season, in which the shogun arranges a marriage for Mitsukuni's granddaughter Princess Saya (Ai Sasamine). To assuage her fears, Mitsukuni agrees to travel to Morioka and see her husband-to-be for himself.

The year 2000 was the 300th anniversary of the death of the original Mitsukuni, celebrated in the 28th season by a journey along the 53 stages of the Tokaidō road, and a two-hour special in April. However, it also saw the end of the old style *MK,* to be replaced by a show with the same name, but with a different star and slightly different emphasis.

The 29th season saw a younger Mitsukuni (Kōji Ishizaka), accompanied by Suke (Yūji Kishimoto) and Kaku (Sumihiro Yamada) as usual, forced out of office by a new Yanagisawa (Jun Hashizume) and forced to wander the land upholding the law of the Shogun Tsunayoshi (Daijirō Tsutsui). This "new *MK*" played up its greater faithfulness to historical truth, and in its 30th season, Mitsukuni acknowledged this supposed factual edge by journeying to Nikkō Tōshōgū, the shrine dedicated to his grandfather Ieyasu Tokugawa (see TOKUGAWA IEYASU).

In 2002, Mitsukuni leads his team to Osaka in search of a solution to a financial crisis in the Edo government. However, on this occasion the lead was played by a new actor, Kōtarō Satomi, who had formerly played the part of the "young" Suke in the show for much of the 1970s and early 1980s. The series had run for so long that one of the former supporting cast members was old enough to play the old man himself. *MK* alternated in the same slot on TBS with another long-running

series ŌOKA ECHIZEN. Peak rating: 43.7% (in 1979).

The adventures of Mitsukuni were also parodied by the comedian Kenichi Enomoto in the NTV comedy *Enoken's Mito Kōmon Wanderings (Enoken no Mito Kōmon Manyūki,* 1954).

MOMOKO SAKURA LAND: TANIGUCHI INC.

1993. JPN: *Sakura Momoko Land: Taniguchi Mutsuzō Shōten.* PRD: N/C. DIR: Teruhiko Kuze. SCR: Momoko Sakura. CAST: Taishū Kase, Isako Washio, Shigeru Izumiya, Haruko Sagara. CHN: Asahi. DUR: 45 mins. x 12 eps.; Tue 13 April 1993–29 June 1993.

Taniguchi Inc., a rice cracker shop that has been in the same family for six generations, is still proudly run by 72-year-old grandfather Mutsuzō (Izumiya), who expects his descendants to carry on the tradition. Inconveniently, grandson Shinichi (Kase) announces that he has decided to marry Saby (Washio), a perfectly nice girl who does her best to charm the family. However, Saby is Indian and the family frets about the future of their traditional business if the next generation of heirs have a mixed heritage. A live-action drama created by Momoko Sakura, better known as the manga creator behind the immensely successful *Chibi Maruko-chan* (*AE). For other shows that approach the Japanese attitude toward foreigners, see LADY OF THE MANOR, GOOD MORNING TEACHER, and DOKU. Theme: YMO—"Pocket ga Niji de Ippai" (Pocket Full of Rainbows).

MONA LISA'S SMILE

2000. JPN: *Mona Lisa no Hohoemi.* PRD: Tōru Kawai. DIR: Kōzō Nagayama, Daisuke Tajima. SCR: Yasushi Fukuda, Yōko Iino, Jun Maekawa. CAST: Yōsuke Eguchi, Riona Hazuki, Kōshirō Matsumoto, Masato Ibu, Yoshizumi Ishihara, Satoko Ōshima, Hajime Okayama, Shirō Namiki. CHN: Fuji. DUR: 45 mins. x 11 eps.; Wed 12 January 2000–22 March 2000.

At the Weisz Tokyo auction house, a man and a woman get involved in a fierce bidding war over a Greek statuette. Eventually, it fetches four times the expected price and auctioneers approach the man to ask him to pay. He shocks them all by announcing that he never had any intention of doing so and that he was merely outbidding the female client so that she would never get the chance to notice that Weisz was trying to sell her a fake. The auctioneers are scandalized that anyone would accuse their world-famous company of selling counterfeit goods, but the man proves his point by smashing the statuette to reveal its modern construction. He is international art expert Masayuki (Eguchi), recently transferred to Tokyo from the Weisz London branch and already irritating his colleagues.

In a modern world where ethics are replaced by market forces, most Weisz Tokyo staffers think Masayuki is a madman—they would have happily sold the statuette and hoped that the buyer never noticed the deception. Only assistant manager Takurō (Junichi Okada), a former banker, sees Masayuki's point: that the Weisz corporation must retain its long-standing reputation for honor and good character. But Masayuki has not come to Tokyo to work as Weisz's conscience, he has come to witness the auction of the century—the Sad Mona Lisa.

There are many copies of Leonardo da Vinci's famous painting, but the Sad ML is notable for being the most perfect—since it only lacks the enigmatic smile, some even believe that it was painted by da Vinci himself and was intended to be one half of a pair. Formerly owned by Napoleon and Louis XIV, the Sad ML disappeared in France in 1911 and was supposedly returned two years later. However, Masayuki and several friends and rivals believe that the painting returned to France was itself a copy—his colleague Kaoru even has a photograph of Adolf Hitler admiring *two* Mona Lisas. The feverish detective work going on at the auction house is all observed with great interest by art restorer Chizuru (Hazuki), who dimly recalls a childhood memory of her artist father Orihara painting *"a picture of a sad woman"* and announces that the Sad ML to be sold at Weisz is actually *his* work. Masayuki realizes that for Orihara's fake to be so convincing, he must have been working from the original—the *real* Sad ML could still be in Japan. . . .

Mona Lisa's Smile is a mind-bending saga of forgery and counter-forgery, with Masayuki as the champion of art and honor, fighting off speculators, thieves, and counterfeiters in the quest to return Chizuru's birthright to her and also locate the priceless genuine article. Broadcast without English subtitles in the U.S. on KTSF TV. Theme: Dutch Training—"Stay."

MONJIRO

1972. JPN: *Kogarashi Monjirō*. AKA: *Monjirō of the Wintry North Wind*. PRD: Hideo Asano. DIR: Kon Ichikawa. SCR: Kon Ichikawa, Kei Hattori, Ikuko Ōyabu, Yasuko Ōno. CAST: Atsuo Nakamura, Mayumi Ogawa, Shun Ueda, Asao Koike. CHN: Fuji. DUR: 45 mins. x ca. 150 eps.; Sat 1 January 1972–26 February 1972 (#1); 1 April 1972–27 May 1972 (#2); 18 November 1972–31 March 1973 (#3); 5 October 1977–29 March 1978 (#4). In a time of lawlessness, a lone wanderer stalks the highways of Japan, clad in a ragged rush hat and unkempt cloak. Monjirō (Nakamura) is a peripatetic hero in the style of LONE WOLF AND CUB, but has no interest in justice. Instead, he only takes on the bad guy bailiffs, warlords, and bandits he encounters when they make him angry—contrast to MITO KŌMON, who similarly travels Japan but with the permanent objective of doing good.

Monjirō first appeared in a novel by Saho Sasazawa, but achieved new heights of fame in this starkly photographed adaptation. While NHK's annual *taiga* drama series continued to glorify the distant past in NEW TALE OF THE HEIKE, Japan was still reeling from the sight of student unrest and the predations of the Red Army terrorist group—times had clearly changed, and it was the Fuji network that met the challenge. The dawn of the nihilistic 1970s saw a new kind of anti-hero in Monjirō, whose oft-repeated catchphrase was *"It's nothing to do with me."* A samurai drama with the attitude and mood of a hard-boiled thriller, the solitary character caught the mood of the time and made a star out of Atsuo Nakamura, whose sexy sidelong glances won over an unexpected female audience. He also won over a number of bad girls on the road, as some of the female writers among the staff noted that the female audience loved it every time an encounter with Monjirō turned cruel bandit queens or vindictive samurai noblewomen into melancholy, lovestruck romantics.

His rumpled appearance was deliberately chosen by director Ichikawa as the most practical clothes to wear during a life spent eternally on the road. He was also famous for a toothpick permanently lodged in his mouth, although the traditional wood splinter of the novel was enlarged for TV to resemble something that looks more like a small chopstick. The "toothpick" occasionally doubled as a weapon and also functioned as a weather vane for observant fans of the series—while actor Nakamura remains eternally impassive, his toothpick gives away his inner mood. When fights did inevitably break out, they were filmed in a deliberately realistic fashion, more like savage street battles than the carefully choreographed play-fighting of other period dramas.

However, the show developed unexpected troubles offscreen, including the temporary absence of its leading man due to an injured Achilles tendon. The break in shooting was filled by the first broadcast of SURE DEATH, another show that presented a darker view of the noble samurai of old. More permanent damage was caused by the bankruptcy of the production company Daiei Kyoto, which led the staff to form their own organization and complete shooting without pay. The series briefly returned as *New Monjirō* in 1977, directed by Nobuhiko Ōbayashi, but its hero is such an icon that he has been pastiched in many media and is recognizable even to those who have never seen the original show. Headgear homages to Monjirō's distinctive straw hat have appeared in many martial arts movies, as well as in *Ninja Scroll* (*AE) and *Big Trouble in Little China* (1986).

After leading roles in both *Monjirō* and WATER MARGIN, actor Nakamura began to distance himself from period dramas. Following a cameo as the Emperor of Heaven in MONKEY and a lead in the modern romance *A Seashore Story* (1977), he presented the TBS documentary series *Atsuo Nakamura Discovers the World* (1984), which ran for four years. His credentials as both a hero and an educator thus established, he ran for political office as an independent candidate with unofficial backing from the Sakigake party and became a member of the Japanese Diet.

MONKEY *

1978. JPN: *Saiyūki*. AKA: *Journey to the West*. PRD: Tsuneo Hayakawa, Mineo Yamada. DIR: Jun Fukuda, Yūsuke Watanabe, Daisuke Yamazaki, Shōichi Ōta. SCR: James Miki, Hirokazu Fuse, Mamoru Sasaki, Isao Okishima. CAST: Masaaki Sakai, Masako Natsume, Toshiyuki Nishida, Shirō Kishibe, Tonpei Hidari, Shunji Fujimura. CHN: NTV. DUR: 45 mins. x 52 eps.; Sun 1 October 1978–1 April 1979 (#1); 11 November 1979–4 May 1980 (#2). Somehow managing to gate-crash the palace of the Emperor of Heaven, the mischievous Monkey King Sun Wukong (Sakai, formerly of the Spiders pop group) is given a sinecure position as master of the heavenly stables. Thrown out of heaven after eating the Peaches of Immortality and taking a leak on Buddha's hand, he is imprisoned beneath a mountain for 500 years, until he is offered a chance to redeem himself. He agrees to accompany the boy priest Tripitaka (Natsume, former spokesmodel for Kanebō Cosmetics) on a quest to retrieve sacred scrolls from the distant land of Gandhara. The pair are soon joined by reformed demons Sandy (Kishibe, formerly of the Tigers) and Pigsy (Nishida), both of whom were also once favored by heaven, but cast out after committing grave sins.

Commissioning a major series to mark its 25th anniversary, the NTV channel opted for a dramatization of Wu Cheng-en's 16th-century Chinese novel *Journey to the West*. A perennial favorite with Japanese children through several animated versions (*AE) and the 1977 puppet show **SUN WUKONG**, the story was designed to appeal to both parents and offspring, with a classical origin to guarantee a suitably worthy pedigree. Partnering *Son of Godzilla* director Jun Fukuda with longtime *taiga* scenarist James Miki, and featuring comedian Sakai (credited with inventing the Twist-inspired "Monkey" dance craze in his youth) in the title role, the show soon veered away from any pretense of historical accuracy, preferring humor, slapstick, and spectacular fight scenes amidst a flood of guest star cameos, such as **MONJIRŌ**'s Nakamura as the Emperor of Heaven in episode one. Despite running directly opposite the 1978 *taiga* drama **DAYS OF GOLD** on NHK, *Monkey* still picked up an average audience share around 20%—a remarkable feat considering *taiga*'s traditional stranglehold on Sunday ratings.

A second season followed in 1979, although Nishida had already accepted the lead role in **GENTA IKENAKA 80 KILOS** and was replaced by Tonpei Hidari as Pigsy. Tripitaka's "horse" (which was actually a shapeshifting dragon), occasionally assumed the cowardly human form of Yulong (Fujimura) as an extra cast member during the second season, but the story did seem to have lost its way and ended without its characters ever reaching their destination. The humor seems more desperate (Yulong is particularly

irritating) and the anachronisms assume unstable proportions, including a modern disco and a gambling den complete with roulette wheel. However, the series remained popular with the Japanese audience through reruns and a TV movie edit and received an extra burst of tragic publicity when actress Masako Natsume died of leukemia in 1985, aged just 31. When the channel's 40th anniversary rolled round in 1993, the series was unsuccessfully remade with a new cast, in a version filed in this book as **JOURNEY TO THE WEST**.

However, *Monkey*'s original success did not merely give it a high profile in the Japanese market. After the successful acquisition of NTV's earlier **WATER MARGIN**, the U.K.'s BBC also bought the English-language rights to *Monkey*—it remains possible that much of the extra budget seen onscreen, such as second season opening credits actually filmed *in China*, owes its opulence to the injection of BBC money. Adapted by *Water Margin*'s David Weir, the series was edited, simplified, and stripped of 13 later episodes before being broadcast in a primetime slot that enchanted an entire generation.

The BBC dub was broadcast around the English-speaking world, but not in the U.S., where *Monkey* was only seen in its original incarnation on local TV channels for Japanese immigrant communities. Instead, the best-known version of the story in America is the Chinese live-action version *Xiyouji*.

When the series eventually made it to British DVD in the early 21st century, distributors Fabulous Films included the previously unreleased episodes as bonus extras in subtitled form. In an era which took excessive care over its attitude toward media violence, some episodes of the series originally broadcast *for* children were rated by the British video censor as unsuitable for the under-12s. Theme: Godiego— "Monkey Magic." Both the opening theme and the closing "Gandhara" were released on record and entered the pop charts in both Japan and the

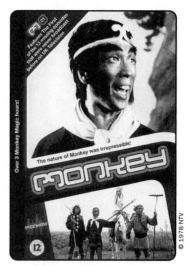

Monkey

U.K. The anime *Gandhara* (*AE) is said to have been inspired by the song.

MOON SPIRAL

1996. PRD: Masahiro Tsuburaya. DIR: Masahiro Tsuburaya, Ken Yumeno, Toshiyuki Takano, Takeshi Yagi. SCR: Kazuya Okada, Mihoko Sakai, Masakazu Migita. CAST: Hiroshi Miyasaka, Hideyo Amamoto, Mariya Yamada, Nobu Manno. CHN: NTV. DUR: 30 mins. x 3 eps.; Tue 7 May 1996–21 May 1996.

As the time of the prophecies of Nostradamus approach, the Moon Spiral secret organization of mutant psychics prepares to exterminate humanity. A similarly clandestine group is formed by the Japanese secret service, led by special agent Kessaku Yatsumata (Miyasaka), whose assistants include his psychic adopted daughter Chihiro (Yamada) and Nostradamus scholar Tōru (Amamoto). Meanwhile agents of Moon Spiral try to turn Chihiro to the Dark Side, as her powers could prove very useful to them in their plot to ensure that the meek never inherit the Earth.

Rushed into production in the wake of *The X-Files* (Asahi, 1995), this retread of **OPERATION MYSTERY** barely had the chance to begin before it was pulled from the airwaves. A last unbroadcasted episode was later included as a bonus on the show's video release. A different angle on the prophecies of Nostradamus formed part of the plot of **To Heart** three years later.

MOONLIGHT MASK

1958. JPN: *Gekkō Kamen*. PRD: Shunichi Nishimura. DIR: Sadao Funatoko. SCR: Yasunori Kawauchi. CAST: Kōichi Ōse, Kanichi Tani, Yukie Nunochi, Kazuya Oguri. CHN: KRT (TBS). DUR: 10 mins. x 72 eps.; 30 mins. x 69 eps.; Mon 24 February 1958–17 May 1958 (#1); 25 May 1958–12 October 1958 (#2); 19 October 1958–26 December 1958 (#3); 4 January 1959–29 March 1959 (#4); 5 April 1959–5 July 1959 (#5).

Wrapped from head to toe in a white suit, white turban, white cloak, white boots, and white gloves, Moonlight Mask (Ōse) is a lunar envoy sent to Earth to protect humanity from evil. His catchphrase is *"Don't hate, don't kill, but forgive,"* although while he never causes the deaths of his adversaries, he is not above a big fight at least once an episode. He rides a motorcycle to each crime fighting mission, which is often the most expensive prop on show—the advertising company that made *MM* was so impoverished that their chairman's office doubled as a set on many occasions and several bit parts were filled by passing employees in the style of the later **Vampire**.

Producer Shunichi Nishimura had always intended to make a period drama set in Japan's recent past, in the fashion of the many U.S. Westerns crowding Japanese TV schedules at the time. However, lack of funding caused him to shelve his planned adaptation of Jirō Osaragi's *Kurama Tengu* books about a man on a white horse righting wrongs in 19th-century Japan. Instead, he made *MM,* shooting in modern-day locations to save money. The first superhero show in Japan, *MM* was the inspiration for **Harimao** and **Eye of the Jaguar** and the ancestor of much

of modern-day Japanese children's TV, such as **Masked Rider**. With its tale of a strange visitor from another world who comes to Earth with powers and abilities far beyond those of mortal men, it owes an obvious debt to the George Reeves *Adventures of Superman* which, with a rating of 74.2%, was the highest rated show of *any* kind on Japanese TV by 1958. Broadcast on the same KRT channel that was the Japanese home of the Man of Steel, *MM* rode that wave of popularity, to secure its own rating of 60.8% the same year. The success of *MM* would allow Nishimura to make his long-awaited "Japanese Western," **The Samurai**.

The *MM* series can be subdivided into several separate story arcs, comprising the evil deeds of *Skull Mask* (*Dokuro Kamen*), followed by *The Secret of Paradai Kingdom* (*Paradai Ōkoku no Himitsu*), in which the evil Satan's Claw murders Prince Shapnash, the ruler of a country that needs MM's help. *Mammoth Kong* (*Kaijū Kong*) featured an international assassin's guild targeting the ten most important people in Japan and using a monster to attack police chiefs and government officials. *The Ghost Party Strikes Back* (*Yūreitō no Gyakushū*) features intrigues around a mine with a dark secret, which is jealously sought by the obligatory group of masked men in black. However, by the time the show had reached its fifth story, *Avoid Revenge* (*Sono Fukushū ni Te o Dasuna*), it was coming under fire from the media. In a foreshadowing of the violence debates that would plague its distant descendant the **Mighty Morphin' Power Rangers**, *MM* was removed from the air amid complaints from parents that their children were imitating its dangerous stunts and fight sequences. Consequently, the sixth story arc, *Dragon's Fang*, did not appear on TV, although it was continued in manga form in a strip drawn by Jirō Kuwata for *Shōnen Club*, as a novel serialized in *Shōnen Magazine* by original creator Yasunori Kawauchi, and eventually as part of the anime version screened on NTV in 1972 (*AE).

The live-action *MM* lived on at the movies, in six films made between 1958 and 1959. *MM*, directed by Tsuneo Kobayashi and featuring Fujitake Ōmura in the title role, ended on a cliffhanger and was completed by *Death Battle at Farthest Sea* (*Zekkai no Shitō*), followed by remakes of the Paradai, Kong, and Ghost Party arcs and the climactic *End of the Evil* (*Akuma no Saigo*), in which MM must track a serial killer known as The White-Haired Monster.

A new movie remake, updated for a new generation, followed in 1981, directed by Yukihiro Sawada and with the hero played by Daisuke Kuwabara. The hero was also reborn in 2000 as a kiddie cartoon (*AE). *MM* was also lampooned in Gō Nagai's erotic comedy *Kekkō Kamen* (*AE), in which the world is threatened by Satan's Toenail.

MŌRI MOTONARI *

1997. PRD: N/C. DIR: Takaharu Matsuoka. SCR: Makiko Uchidate. CAST: Hashinosuke Nakamura, Yasuko Tomita, Baijaku Nakamura, Tsurutarō Kataoka, Masao Kusakari, Tsuyoshi Morita, Toshiyuki Hosokawa, Takanori Jinnai, Masahiro Takashima, Keiko Matsuzaka, Ken Ogata. CHN: NHK. DUR: 45 mins. x ca. 50 eps.; Sun 5 January 1997–14 December 1997.

Motonari (1497–1571) hails from a powerful family in Aki (part of modern Hiroshima Prefecture) serving the Ōuchi clan. When a group of other Ōuchi vassals rebel against the family's autocratic rule, he stays out of the conflict, only to defeat the ringleader Harukata Sue in 1555 and become the lord, not only of his own region, but also of Suō and Nagato (modern-day Yamaguchi), Bingo (part of modern Hiroshima), and Bitchū (part of Okayama). As the ruler of much of the southwest of Japan's main island, an area known to posterity as Chōshū, he goes on to defeat Yoshihisa Amako, the ruler of the neighboring area of Chūgoku.

After the previous year's **Hideyoshi**, this 1997 *taiga* drama functions as a kind of prequel to the better-known events of Japan's civil war in the 16th century. The historical Motonari famously fought 200 battles in his lifetime, leading to an action-packed series of life-threatening crises that often seems more like *Die Hard* than a historical epic. Based on Michiko Nagai's novels *Yamagiri* (Mountain Mist) and *Motonari Soshite Onnatachi* (Motonari and His Women), *MM* cunningly appeals to both sexes by focusing on its lead as both an able general and a family man, depicting his life through the eyes of his powerful wife and children. Young Motonari was played by Tsuyoshi Morita (from V6).

The life of Motonari sets the historical stage for NOBUNAGA, whose prime opponent was Motonari's grandson Terumoto. Subsequently becoming a trusted general of Nobunaga's successor Hideyoshi, Terumoto would later be one of the five regents appointed to rule Japan in the name of Hideyoshi's infant son (see AOI). His luck would run out when he opposed a bid for power by Ieyasu Tokugawa (TOKUGAWA IEYASU), and his defeat would lead to a long-standing resentment between Tokugawa vassals and the people of Chōshū. Centuries later, this enmity would transform into the conflict dramatized in AS IF IN FLIGHT, in which the shogun would be overthrown and the Emperor restored to power. Broadcast in the U.S. with English subtitles on KIKU TV and KTSF TV.

MOTHER COMPLEX COP

1990. JPN: *Motherkon Keiji no Jikenbo*. PRD: N/C. DIR: Makihito Takai. SCR: Keiko Mukurochi. CAST: Hiroyuki Watanabe, Nobuko Otowa, Yuriko Ishida, Takeyuki Yue. CHN: TVT. DUR: 45 mins. x 6 eps.; Sun 25 February 1990–1 April 1990.
Rookie detective Yumie (Ishida) is investigating a high-profile case involving the murder of a wealthy girl. Her boss Detective Ōtani (Watanabe) leaves her in charge when he must rush off early in order to tend to his sick mother. Compare to the later Sylvester Stallone vehicle *Stop! Or my Mom Will*

Shoot (1992). Theme: Ayako Shimizu—"Sayonara o Mōichido" (Good-bye Again).

MPD PSYCHO

2000. JPN: *Tajū Jinkaku Tantei Saiko Amamiya Kazuhiko no Kikan*. AKA: *MPD Psycho: Return of Kazuhiko Amamiya*. PRD: Toshihiro Satō, Naoki Abe, Yoshihisa Nakagawa. DIR: Takashi Miike. SCR: Eiji Ōtsuka, Takashi Miike. CAST: Naoki Hosaka, Ren Ōsugi, Naoko Nakajima. CHN: WOWOW. DUR: 60 mins. x 6 eps.; Tue 2 May 2000–7 May 2000.
After witnessing his girlfriend's brutal murder, criminal profiler Yōsuke Kobayashi (Hosaka) begins to suffer from multiple personality disorder. Quitting his police job, he becomes his alternate persona "Kazuhiko Amemiya" and lives peacefully with his new wife Chizuko until his neighborhood suffers a spate of murder cases.

Reluctantly coming out of retirement like the hero of HYPNOSIS, Yōsuke investigates a series of bizarre deaths, including a corpse whose brain has been replaced with flowers, a pregnant murder victim whose fetus has been stolen, and a high school shooting at an institution that turns out to be a secret government experiment.

Based on Eiji Ōtsuka's manga in *Shōnen Ace* magazine, though greatly altered with the author's approval, *MPD Psycho* excels at thinking up macabre new ways of grossing out its audience. It is not enough merely to find a dismembered body, instead, the cast finds a dismembered body whose parts are numbered, seemingly for a grisly game of amputation bingo. Later episodes resolve questions about Yōsuke's own background in the style of FACE. Sequels were published in *Newtype* magazine in print form. See also THE MISFITS.

MRS. CINDERELLA

1997. PRD: Hiroyoshi Koiwai. DIR: Utahiko Honma. SCR: Taeko Asano. CAST: Hiroko Yakushimaru, Masaaki Uchino, Tetsuta Sugimoto, Kyōko

Enami, Mayuko Takada. CHN: Fuji. DUR: 45 mins. x 11 eps.; Thu 17 April 1997–26 June 1997.
Mizuho (Yakushimaru) lives with her husband Yasuyuki (Sugimoto) and her mother-in-law Ryōko (Enami), who bullies her constantly over her failure to produce a grandchild. When her pet Java sparrow escapes from the house, Mizuho welcomes the chance to follow it and tracks her errant pet down to a local park. There, she finds that the bird had flown to Mitsuru (Uchino), a handsome artist with whom Mizuho soon begins a torrid affair. Another drama from the producer/writer pairing of Asano and Koiwai that also gave us LOVE GENERATION and PLEASE GOD! JUST A LITTLE MORE TIME. Theme: Fumiya Fujii—"Do Not." Peak rating: 20.1%.

MS. KNOW-IT-ALL *

1998. JPN: *Nanisama!?*. AKA: *Who Do You Think You Are!?*. PRD: Hideki Isano. DIR: Akio Yoshida, Osamu Katayama. SCR: Toshio Terada. CAST: Gorō Kishitani, Yasuko Matsuyuki, Atsurō Watabe, Ryōko Shinohara, Yūko Takeuchi, Rina Uchiyama. CHN: TBS. DUR: 45 mins. x 11 eps.; Sun 11 October 1998–20 December 1998.
Salaryman Fūtarō (Kishitani) used to be a local hero at Chitose Foods—his talent at the relay race brought victory

in intercompany sports meets and his future looked bright. With his amateur sports career curtailed by an injury, Fūtarō finds himself shunted to a remote branch office and effectively removed from the promotional ladder, until he receives a summons to head-quarters. There, he is assigned to assist the ball-breaking food consultant Izumi (Matsuyuki), whose fierce nature is only tolerated at the company because of her expertise in Italian cuisine. She has personally asked for Fūtarō as an assistant because he has stamina, he seems to have no ambition, and she believes that it is impossible for her to fall in love with him.

Fūtarō soon discovers that Izumi's hard exterior hides a different person—she is a struggling single mother and has even changed her name to fit into the corporate world. Family members interfere in their lives—Izumi suspects that Fūtarō is conducting an affair with a woman who turns out to he his niece, while Izumi's countrified sister arrives to embarrass her in the big city. Though Fūtarō and Izumi constantly argue, their associates begin to realize that they are merely displacing their affections—compare to **Do We Love Each Other!** Fūtarō finally announces that he would like to become a father to Izumi's son but her ex-lover returns from Italy and offers to take both her and their son back with him.

For some reason, 1998 was the year of the sympathetic single mother in Japan, with **Tabloid** featuring a similarly proud parent, played by Rie Tomosaka. *Ms. Know-It-All* also has strong similarities to the same year's *His and Her Circumstances* (*AE), which also starred a couple engaged in constant one-upmanship, yet unable to confess their true feelings. Broadcast with English subtitles in the U.S. on KIKU TV and KSCI TV. Theme: Suga Shikao—"Bokutachi no Hibi" (Our Days). Peak rating: 15.6%.

MŪ
1977. PRD: Teruhiko Kuze. DIR: Teruhiko Kuze. SCR: Yōko Matsuda. CAST: Misako Watanabe, Hiromi Gō, Megumi Igarashi, Kentarō Shimizu, Kirin Kiki, Shirō Itō, Kayoko Kishimoto. CHN: TBS. DUR: 45 mins. x ca. 50 eps.; Wed 18 May 1977–9 November 1977 (#1); May 1978–February 1979 (#2).
During breakfast at the Usagiya store, maid Kaneda (Kiki) arrives and announces to her employers that she intends to quit. The family owners ask her to stay until the end of the day because it is the day their daughter Momoko (Igarashi) has an *omiai* marriage meeting with a prospective husband. Kaneda, however, has had enough and prepares to leave once and for all, only to beg to be reinstated when she sees how welcoming the family are to her replacement (Kishimoto, in her debut role), who has newly arrived from the country. However, when the family assemble in kimono for the marriage meeting, it is called off by a curt phone call from the would-be groom, who has just discovered that Momoko is deaf.

A slice-of-life drama in the style of **It's Time**, *Mū* is set in a shop that sells *tabi* (those quintessentially Japanese split-toe socks) in downtown Tokyo. Momoko's handicap is vigorously defended by her family, particular younger brother Takurō (Gō), although he still has time to ham it up by dancing with Kaneda. Better known as a feature of sci-fi stories such as *Super Atragon* (*AE), the original Mū is the sunken continent of Asian folklore, supposedly a utopia where everyone is blissfully happy, contrasted with the tribulations that surround the owners of the Usagiya. The series also featured opening titles designed by the artist Tadanori Yokoo. A second season, retitled *Mū no Ichizoku* (*Family of Mū*) followed in 1978. Theme: Kayoko Kishimoto—"Kitakaze yo" (The North Wind).

MUSASHI *
2003. PRD: Hisashi Ichii. DIR: Mitsunobu Nozaki. SCR: Toshio Kamata. CAST: Shinnosuke Ichikawa, Shinichi Tsutsumi, Ryōko Yonekura, Rina Uchiyama, Yukie Nakama, Masahiro Matsuoka, Makoto Fujita, Masanobu Takashima, Tsunehiko Watase, Beat Takeshi, Kankurō Nakamura. CHN: NHK. DUR: 45 mins. x 49 eps.; Sun 5 January 2003–?? December 2003.
At the Battle of Sekigahara in 1600, Musashi Miyamoto (Ichikawa) fights alongside his friend Matahachi Honiden (Tsutsumi), though Matahachi flees the battlefield. Although Matahachi is betrothed to Tsū (Yonekura), he is seduced by Kō, a camp follower who makes her living by stripping corpses on battlefields. Much to Matahachi's embarrassment, Kō hero-worships Musashi for famously defeating the bandit Tenma Tsumujikaze. Accompanied by Kō and her scavenging associate daughter Akemi (Uchiyama), Matahashi heads for Kyoto. Kō opens a teahouse while Matahachi enjoys the easy life, but Akemi is raped by one of her mother's customers and tries to commit suicide.

Jilted by Kō, Matahachi begins to wander the countryside once more, where he continues to hear stories about the legendary swordsman Musashi. Meanwhile, Akemi becomes a prostitute and gives birth to a child, while Musashi begins to fall for Tsū, who is an orphan like him.

Immortalized in the 20th century through Eiji Yoshikawa's *Musashi* series of novels, the samurai also known as "Sword Saint" flourished between the battle of Sekigahara (see **Aoi**) in 1600 and a famous duel 12 years later on Ganryū Island with Kojirō Sasaki. Based on Yoshikawa's books, this colorful adaptation was supposedly chosen to meet the public demand for a change from historical greats—unlike **Hideyoshi** and Ieyasu (**Tokugawa Ieyasu**), Musashi's life is chiefly a mystery. However, it remains likely that the real reason for the sudden change from history books to popular novels lies in the contemporary popularity of Takehiko Inoue's manga *Vagabond*. Other modern concerns dogged the series when the crew were forced to apologize to Kurosawa Productions for some overeager "borrowing" from *The Seven Samurai,* resulting in some recognizably similar scenes.

Musashi leaves Tsū behind when he leaves for advanced samurai training, but she secretly follows him around the country. After the Ganryū duel with Sasaki (played here by Matsuoka from TOKIO), the two live together, though their peaceful days do not last long. "Beat" Takeshi Kitano also appears in a cameo role as Musashi's father Munisai Shinmen. The story of this famous warrior continues in a different form in **FURTHER ADVENTURES OF MUSASHI**. The 2003 *Musashi* was shown in the U.S. on KIKU TV with English subtitles, and commenced its English-language run barely three months into the Japanese broadcast.

MY BLUE SKY

2000. JPN: *Watashi no Aozora.* PRD: Akio Suwabe. DIR: Takeshi Shibata, Kei Suzuki, Masaya Iseta, Tsuyoshi Inoue, Shō Yoshinaga. SCR: Makiko Uchidate. CAST: Tomoko Tabata, Takuma Shinoda, Michitaka Tsutsui, Shirō Itō, Mariko Kaga. CHN: NHK. DUR: 15 mins. x ca. 200 eps.; Mon 3 April 2000–30 September 2000 (#1); 1 April 2002–?? September 2002 (#2). Nazuna (Tabata) is a high school girl in northern Japan, jilted at the altar by her fiancé Kento (Tsutsui) who is dragged away by a female companion who tells him he must not give up his dream of becoming a championship boxer. Nazuna, however, pursues Kento to Tokyo, where she confronts him with the news that she is pregnant. Guiltily, Kento proposes to her a second time, but Nazuna realizes that his true ambition lies with his career. She rejects him and decides to bring up the child alone.

Six years later, Nazuna and her son Taiyō (Shinoda) are living in Tokyo, where Kento has just become the Japanese champion. Nazuna takes a part-time job cooking lunches at her son's elementary school and studies to become a nutritionist. Kento, however, loses his next bout. Taiyō still adores his father and Kento decides to quit for his son's sake, instead beginning a new career as a talent scout.

The template of the NHK *asa-dorama* is well established: 15 minutes of misery on a daily basis to entertain an audience of lonely housewives and reassure them that no matter how bad their lives might be, there is always someone who is suffering more than they. Where America has the *Jerry Springer Show,* the Japanese prefer their *schadenfreude* in fictionalized packages like **OSHIN**. Writer Uchidate, author of **ACCOMMODATING WOMAN**, commented at the time of the serial's release that her aim was to depict the new generation of women who believe that they want a baby, but not a husband; a sector of society also examined in **CROSS OF ROSES**. However, Uchidate's script questions whether it is possible for such women to accept that the father of their child is in love with someone else. She gained the chance to think further on the subject when NHK commissioned a second season to be broadcast in an *evening* slot—an unprecedented move for a "morning" drama, which normally exhaust their potential for suffering in the space of a single year, or half year in the case of more recent offerings. In the sequel, Nazuna is forced to give up her nutritionist studies to care for Taiyō. She discovers that Kento has indeed fallen in love with Koyuki (Rei Kikukawa), and resolves to win him "back" by numerous underhanded methods.

MY CHILD WOULD NEVER . . .

1984. JPN: *Uchi no Ko ni Kagitte.* PRD: Yasuo Yagi. DIR: Yukio Matsuda. SCR: Kazuhiko Ban. CAST: Masakazu Tamura, Aiko Morishita, Jōji Tokoro, Reiko Nakamura, Nobuko Miyamoto. CHN: TBS. DUR: 45 mins. x ca. 8 eps.; Fri 17 August 1984–28 September 1984. A satire of adult society told from the children's point of view, as a class full of elementary school children are able to manipulate the actions of their

gullible teacher Mr. Ishibashi (Tamura). *MCWN* was the first comic role for Tamura, who had previously been known as a playboy romantic lead. Compare to the later **SCHOOL TEACHER**. Theme: Checkers— "Hoshikuzu no Stage" (Stardust Stage).

MY DESTINY

1994. JPN: *Watashi no Unmei.* PRD: Seiichirō Kijima. DIR: Katsuo Fukuzawa. SCR: Shizuka Ōishi. CAST: Maki Sakai, Mikihisa Azuma, Yōko Nogiwa, Shirō Sano, Yasunori Danta. CHN: TBS. DUR: 45 mins. x 21 eps.; Tue 11 October 1994–21 March 1995. Chiaki (Sakai) meets fellow employee Jirō (Azuma) at the office ski club and the two are swiftly married. But only a few weeks after their wedding, Chiaki discovers that Jirō has lung cancer and is not expected to survive another six months. Compare to **PLEASE GOD! JUST A LITTLE MORE TIME**. Theme: Yūmi Matsutoya—"Suna no Wakusei" (Desert Planet) and "Inochi no Hana" (Flowers of Life).

MY FATHER THE OVER-ANXIOUS

1994. JPN: *Otōsan wa Shinpaishō.* PRD: Yoshio Gōda. DIR: Satoshi Tsuji. SCR: Akira Momoi, Kimiko Shimizu. CAST: Yasuo Daichi, Maki Mochida, Kie Arita, Taichi Kokubu, Jun Miho. CHN: Asahi. DUR: 45 mins. x 5 eps.; Tue 12 April 1994–17 May 1994. After the death of his wife, Kōtaro (Daichi) must single-handedly rear his daughters Noriko (Mochida) and Nana (Arita). He does his best to be a caring father but becomes increasingly paranoid when the teenage Noriko announces that she has a boyfriend, Kitano (Kokubu). Based on the 1983 *Ribbon* manga by Āmin Okada, who also wrote the later *Lunatic Handymen.* Theme: Atsushi Sarujima—"Mō Ichi Do" (One More Time).

MY LITTLE CHEF

2002. PRD: Motoyuki Suzuki, Takaaki Hirabe, Yūji Kajino. DIR: Takashi Minamoto, Kazuo Yamamoto. SCR: Takashi Minamoto, Noriko Gotō. CAST:

Akiko Yada, Hiroshi Abe, Aya Ueto, Heisuke Tōdō, Asahi Uchida, Masaru Nagai, Eri Kyokuyama, Yoshie Ichige, Sanako Hijikata, Morio Kazama. CHN: TBS. DUR: 45 mins. x 10 eps.; Wed 10 July 2002–11 September 2002.
Seri (Yada) is a cook at a rural retirement home but is really the daughter of a renowned chef. With her sister Nazuna (Ueto), she heads for the big city, where she meets unemployed restaurateur Kensaku (Abe). The group decide to open the Petit Étoile restaurant together, in a gourmet drama recalling ANTIQUE, SOMMELIER, and DELICIOUS LIAISONS.

MY LOVER

1995. JPN: Koibito yo. PRD: Reiko Kita. DIR: Michio Mitsuno, Kōzō Nagayama. SCR: Hisashi Nozawa. CAST: Honami Suzuki, Gorō Kishitani, Kōichi Satō, Kyōka Suzuki, Tomoya Nagase. CHN: Fuji. DUR: 45 mins. x 10 eps.; Thu 19 October 1995–21 December 1995.
Three hours before she is due to walk down the aisle with fiancé Ryōtarō (Satō), Manae (H. Suzuki) discovers that he has been having an affair. With meek resolve, she decides it is too late to cancel the wedding, but with just an hour to go, she meets Konpei (Kishitani). He is due to be married in the same place and confesses to her that his fiancée Shōko (K. Suzuki) is also seeing someone else. Since Shōko is already pregnant, Konpei suspects that the child may not be his. The spouses-to-be commiserate about their misfortune but still go through with the ceremony. Konpei and Manae stay in touch on rare occasions, but see increasingly more of each other a few months later when the couples accidentally become neighbors.
 With a flashback structure similar to writer Nozawa's later WEDNESDAY LOVE AFFAIR, ML depicts the horrifying gravity of modern customs, where Ryōtarō and Manae feel bound to keep vows they have not yet made, even when their prospective spouses have already broken them. The two shyly flirt with each other using private mailboxes—

an old-fashioned form of communication soon to be superceded by the e-mail of WITH LOVE and the mobile phones of WHERE IS LOVE? Needless to say, it all ends in tears—compare to PARFUM DE LA JALOUSIE. Theme: Celine Dion with Kryzler and Co.—"To Love You More."

MY OMIAI DIARY

1991. JPN: Boku no Omiai Nikki. PRD: N/C. DIR: Ken Yasaka. SCR: Yūki Shimizu. CAST: Takanori Jinnai, Shigeru Muroi, Mitsuko Baishō, Mitsue Suzuki. CHN: TBS. DUR: 45 mins. x 5 eps.; Sun 1 September 1991–29 September 1991.
Police officer Yūsaku (Jinnai) gets so annoyed with his nagging grandmother Tae (Suzuki) that he rashly promises he'll be married in Hawaii by the end of the following August. As the fateful day approaches with no sign of a bride, he approaches an introduction agency for help—compare to ARRANGED MARRIAGE and 101ST PROPOSAL.

MY TIME TRAVEL JOURNEY WITH MARI

1980. JPN: Boku to Mari no Jikan Ryokō. PRD: Kanae Mayuzumi. DIR: Minoru Hanabusa, Kazuya Satō. SCR: Hideyoshi Nagasaka. CAST: Masatsugu Ishibashi, Haruna Takase, Jō Shishido. CHN: NHK. DUR: 30 mins. x 4 eps.; Tue 12 August 1980–15 August 1980.
Tatsuo (Ishibashi) is an impoverished would-be private investigator, unable to find work anywhere but understandably troubled by the sudden appearance of a woolly mammoth in modern-day Tokyo. He is apparently the only person who can see it, and also the only person who can see what appears to be an exact double of himself, wearing clothes from the distant past. Could he be seeing a vision of one of his ancestors? Eventually, Tatsuo and his bewildered college girl companion Mari (Takase) are handed over to the Time Patrol, an enforcement organization whose 20th-century office operates out of an unassuming building in downtown Tokyo charged with

preventing criminals from the future from ruining the space-time continuum. Before long, Tatsuo and Mari are associate members of the Time Patrol, journeying (predictably, considering the holdings of Japanese TV prop departments) back to the Edo period. They must also delve into the origins of superhero Ultoreman (a thinly disguised ULTRAMAN homage), a comic book hero who seems to have been inspired by real-life fugitives from the 24th century. By the end, Tatsuo discovers the origins of the cosmic rays from the future that are bombarding the Earth and realizes that he has a pivotal role to play in the coming future. Based on the story Time Agent (Jikan Agent), by SF author Sakyō Komatsu—his answer to Yasutaka Tsutsui's TIME TRAVELER and Taku Mayumura's BAKUMATSU TIME TRAVELERS. The opening titles contained animation by Sadao Tsukioka, whose name appears on many 1960s anime, including Ken the Wolf Boy (*AE).

MY WIFE IS 18

1970. JPN: Okusama wa Jūhassai. PRD: Chiharu Kasuga. DIR: Ryūichi Okaya. SCR: Mamoru Sasaki. CAST: Yūki Okazaki, Tetsuo Ishidate, Manami Fuji, Akira Terao. CHN: TBS. DUR: 45 mins. x ca. 40 eps.; Tue 29 September 1970–8 June 1971.
In a lighthearted comedy, teen bride Hidori (Okazaki) is transferred to the school where her husband Tetsuya (Ishidate) is one of the teachers. Compare to the later HIGH SCHOOL TEACHER, which presented the same basic idea in a more salacious manner and without prior marriage to silence conservative complaints, or MAMA IS AN IDOL, which plays it all for laughs. PLEASE DARLING is a more blatant rip-off. A cheap way of remaking the many anime series like Mysterious Melmo (*AE) in which young girls were able to play at being an adult but devoid of actual transformation scenes. Theme: Yūki Okazaki—"Okusama wa Jūhassai" (My Wife Is Eighteen).

My Time Travel Journey with Mari

MYSELF IN CROQUETTE TOWN
1973. JPN: *Korokke Machi no Boku.*
PRD: Kazuo Shibata, Hiroshi Kubota.
DIR: Kanae Mayuzumi, Yoshiyuki Itō,
Minoru Hanabusa, Kazuya Satō. SCR:
Keisuke Tsutsui, Izuho Sudō. CAST:
Hisafumi Kurita, Akiji Nakayama,
Kaoru Natsukawa, Kōichi Nishimaki,
Sakiko Tamagawa, Tomoaki Hironaka,
Tetsuo Tsuno, Shinsuke Chikaishi,
Kyōko Jinbo. CHN: NHK. DUR: 30 mins. x
9 eps.; Sat 3 February 1973–31
March 1973.
Ichirō (Kurita), Kanako (Tamagawa),
and Dai (Hironaka) are nine-year-old
elementary school kids living in downtown Tokyo, united by their love for
croquette potatoes from the local deli
and their desire to live in a world without adults. Occupying an abandoned
apartment block owned by Kanako's
family, the children turn it into their
own private castle, and convince their
parents that they are going there for
private tutoring. They invite their
school teacher Kikuchi (Tsuno) to
come but have no lessons. Instead, he
eats the food packed by their grateful
parents and allows the children to play
in the complex. Wising up to the
deception after a while, Kanako's
father (Chikaishi) throws the children
out, but another teacher Ms. Iida
(Jinbo), formerly regarded by the kids
as snooty and unapproachable, talks
him round. Iida also moves into the
neighborhood and takes a room at
Kanako's grandmother's house, but
the new arrangement is disrupted by
council plans. It transpires that the
entire neighborhood is scheduled for
demolition to make way for a new
highway, causing the locals to band
together to fight for their beloved
"Croquette Town." The music was by
Nobuyoshi Koshibe.

MYSTERIOUS GIRL NILE
1991. JPN: *Fushigi Shōjo Nairu na
Thutmose.* PRD: Jun Higasa, Masayuki
Nishimura, Shigenori Takadera. DIR:
Shinji Murayama, Tarō Sakamoto,
Naoki Iwahara. SCR: Yoshio Urasawa.
CAST: Sanae Horikawa, Shigeru Saiki,
Fumiyo Haku, Manami Seki, Itsuka
Ishizaka, Hanako Nakamura, Tina
Gushiken, Tessen Yamane, Takashi
Tsumura, Masaru Okada. CHN: Fuji.
DUR: 30 mins. x 51 eps.; Sun 6
January 1991–29 December 1991.
Sanae (Horikawa) visits her ancestors'
graves to report that she has moved
house. However, her arrival damages
the family mausoleum, and releases 51
ancient spirits of the Nile that were for-
merly sealed inside. Sanae's ancestor,
Thutmose, orders her to recapture the
devils, using the secret identity of
Mysterious Girl Nile and her newfound
Egyptian magic powers. Based on
Shōtarō Ishinomori's manga—com-
pare to the later *CardCaptors* (*AE).
Theme: Hitomi Ishikawa—"Genki
Ageru ne" (Please Cheer Up).

MYSTERIOUS NEW STUDENT
1975. JPN: *Nazo no Tenkōsei.* PRD:
Tomoyoshi Hagiwara. DIR: Haruo

Yoshida, Kanae Kutsuzumi. SCR: Yūichirō Yamane. CAST: Hiroyuki Takano, Masaaki Maeda, Toshie Takada, Toshiharu Hoshino, Kaai Okada. CHN: NHK. DUR: 25 mins. x 9 eps.; Mon 17 November 1975–3 December 1975.

Junior high school student Kōichi Iwata (Takano) discovers that his new neighbor is also the new transfer student at his school. Norio Yamasawa (Hoshino) has a shiny blue star-shaped mark on his ear, and transfers into Kōichi's class, where he excels at both studying and sports. However, only Kōichi seems to notice that when he is confronted by the school bullies, Norio is able to repel them with an invisible force.

Four other new students, also bearing the mysterious star mark, mystify Kōichi's class teacher Ōtani with their excellent abilities and with their bizarre phobia of rain and the sound of jet engines overhead. Other schools all over Japan seem to have similar new arrivals, and Norio eventually confesses the truth to Kōichi. He and his friends are refugees from the distant world of D-3, destroyed by nuclear war but they are preparing to leave D-15 (or "Earth") soon because it too is threatened with nuclear destruction. Norio and his associates leave but Norio soon returns in a pale and wan state—their next destination proved to be a location where refugees were not welcome, and only a few of them were able to

evade the Refugee Hunters. Norio's father Ichirō (Kyūzō Kawabe) suggests that they should live on Earth, and Norio's family eventually move to Osaka (where, the authors would like to point out, *everybody* is an alien). The remaining refugees scatter over the rest of Japan, in this adaptation of the novel of the same name by Taku Mayumura (see **BAKUMATSU TIME TRAVELERS**).

MYSTERIOUS PEN-FRIEND

1974. JPN: *Maboroshi no Pen-friend*. PRD: Masaharu Morita. DIR: Kanae Kutsuzumi. SCR: Yoshiki Iwama. CAST: Yūji Yamaga, Masashi Hironaka, Kazuo Katō, Kazuko Aoki, Kimiko Ikegami, Sayoko Katō. CHN: NHK. DUR: 25 mins. x 9 eps.; Mon 15 April 1974–1 May 1974.

Junior high student Akihiko (Yamaga) believes he has lucked into the pen-friend of his dreams when he gets a letter from Reiko (S. Katō), an Osaka girl four years his senior who also sends along ten thousand yen. But a similar letter has been sent to his classmate Kumiko (Ikegami), and the suspicious Akihiko sends the money back, only to be informed that the return address does not exist. Another letter arrives from Reiko asking him for his clothes size, and Akihiko is surprised by some men in black, who photograph him before they are scared off by Kumiko. Meanwhile, down in Osaka, Akihiko's father is convinced that he has seen his

son's doppelganger walking into a local factory. Hearing that the mysterious Reiko is coming to visit, Akihiko and his brother Kazuhiko (Hironaka) go to the station to meet her. Akihiko evades capture by the men in black and returns home to find that a boy who looks exactly like him has arrived at the house. Captured and taken away in a flying truck, the real Akihiko finally meets Reiko, who turns out to be an android who resembles Megumi, a local shop girl whom Akihiko secretly loves. Reiko reveals that she and her fellow Inorganic Creatures have arrived from space and are plotting to rule the world by replacing children with androids.

Kumiko is also captured as part of an experiment to learn more about human emotion, but Reiko has begun to understand the human point of view and switches sides. Other androids decide to study a human family under laboratory conditions and send men in black to kidnap the rest of Akihiko's family. They arrive to find that the police, tipped off by Akihiko, are waiting for them and escape in panic. Reiko leads Akihiko and Kumiko to safety before the factory explodes—the escaping androids have set it to self-destruct to cover their tracks. Based on the novel of the same name by Taku Mayumura (see **BAKUMATSU TIME TRAVELERS**), and resembling a juvenile version of *The Stepford Wives*.

N

NAKED COP

1993. JPN: *Hadaka no Keiji*. PRD: Tōru Kinoshita. DIR: Hirokazu Fuse. SCR: Hirokazu Fuse, Kenichi Onishi, Toshimichi Ōkawa, Kazunari Kouchi, Toshio Okumura, Yū Kaneko. CAST: Hiroki Matsukata, Masanori Sera, Shigeru Muroi, Isao Hashizume, Kirin Kiki. CHN: NTV. DUR: 45 mins. x 30 eps.; Fri 8 January 1993–24 September 1993.
With "human interest" police shows such as **HAGURE KEIJI** seeming to win in the ratings war, NTV canceled its relatively successful **COP CLAN** to try this new drama, featuring Hiroki Matsukata and Hiroshi Fuse from the previous show. Recycling the "death on duty" formula introduced by **HOWL AT THE SUN**, the show even killed off the lady detective played by Shigeru Muroi, who was gunned down in the line of duty by criminal Kyūsaku Shimada. However, despite NTV's faith in the material, the ratings were lower than expected. Later episodes attempted to return to a more action-based format but the show was canceled. Although the NTV Friday slot had been dedicated to cop shows for 21 years since the first appearance of *Howl at the Sun*, the failure of *Naked Cop* brought it to an end. Theme: Eikichi Yazawa—"Tokyo."

NANAKO IN TRAINING

1997. JPN: *Kenshū I Nanako*. PRD: Hideki Ōno. DIR: Ikuhiro Saitō, Noboru Sugiyama, Hiroshi Ikezoe. SCR: Hiromi Kusumoto. CAST: Aiko Satō, Naoki Hosaka, Taichi Kokubu, Megumi Kobayashi, Shirō Itō. CHN: Asahi. DUR: 45 mins. x 9 eps.; Mon 13 October 1997–8 December 1997.
New surgical intern Nanako (Satō) is clumsy under pressure, which causes many problems for her with her stern medical resident observer (Hosaka). *NiT* is a comedy in the style of **IT STARTED WITH A KISS** with an added medical twist, based on the 1994 manga by Kozueko Morimoto. Theme: Every Little Thing—"Shapes of Love."

NANASE AGAIN

1979. JPN: *Nanase Futatabi*. PRD: Kanae Mayuzumi. DIR: Minoru Hanabusa, Haruo Yoshida, Kazuya Satō. SCR: Yoshio Ishidō. CAST: Yumi Takigawa, Yoshitaka Niigaki, Alexander Isley, Masami Horiuchi, Fumiaki Sakabe, Hajime Nakajima, Hiromi Murachi, Nagahide Takahashi. CHN: NHK. DUR: 30 mins. x 13 eps.; Mon 6 August 1979–18 August 1979.
Nanase (Takigawa) is a telepath, forced to stay constantly on the move for fear that people will discover her ability to read minds. One rainy night on a train, she meets two boys with similar powers. Tsuneo (Horiuchi) is a clairvoyant who predicts the train will meet with a terrible accident, while Norio (Niigaki) is an empath who confirms he is telling the truth. Trusting in their beliefs, the children escape from the train moments before it crashes. On the run from Norio's stepmother, who believes they are sorcerers, the trio hide out in Tokyo where they befriend bar worker Henry (Isley). Though hardly inconspicuous (three unaccompanied children and a towering black man!), the group travel to Hokkaidō, where they are able to prevent a would-be murderer from slaying his girlfriend. There, they meet Fujiko (Murachi), a girl who has no extrasensory powers but who reveals that she is a time traveler from the future.

Traveling into the past, Fujiko discovers that the trio are all descended from a family of telepaths who flourished in Hokkaidō 500 years earlier. Pursued in the present by journalist Yamamura (Takahashi), the group beg him to leave them alone and not to sensationalize their plight. Touched, he agrees to help them instead and takes Nanase to Macao, where she hopes to win the money to buy the land where the children want to live in Hokkaidō. However, Yamamura is kidnapped by the casino owner, who is assembling a posse of terrorists who specialize in slaying telepaths. Nanase rescues Yamamura and escapes to Japan with Princess Henide, a girl she meets at the casino, but the terrorists are intent on pursuing them and wiping the telepaths out.

Based on the series of books by **TIME TRAVELER** creator Yasutaka Tsutsui—compare to **INFRARED MUSIC**. Some of the earlier Nanase stories have been published in English as *Portraits of Eight*

Narita Divorce

Families, later retitled *What the Maid Saw*. The series was also remade as a **THURSDAY GHOST STORY**. Theme: Yoshikazu Fukano—"Hyacinth wa Doko ni" (Where is the Hyacinth?).

NAOMI

1999. PRD: Yū Moriya. DIR: Masato Hijikata, Hiroshi Nishitani, Makoto Hirano. SCR: Rumi Takahashi, Sumino Kawashima. CAST: Norika Fujiwara, Ryō, Aiko Satō, Masaya Katō, Leo Morimoto, Shunsuke Nakamura. CHN: Fuji. DUR: 45 mins. x 12 eps.; Wed 14 April 1999–30 June 1999.

Three very different female teachers, all called Naomi, try to get by at a Tokyo school. Naomi Tōdō (Fujiwara) is an enthusiastic type determined to win over the troublesome Class H. Naomi Kai (Ryō) is a stern, cold biology teacher uninterested in human emotions. Naomi Yashiro (Satō) is an innocent, gullible Japanese language teacher. They mainly face troubles caused by girls and Naomi Tōdō treats

them as grown-up women. In order to demonstrate how to deal with men, she even kisses a student in front of her class. Billed at the time as a female **GTO** or a deliberately sassy take on **KINPACHI SENSEI**, *Naomi* also bears some resemblance to the earlier **GODDESS OF VICTORY**. Peak rating: 17.7%. Theme: True Kiss Destination—"Girls Be Ambitious." A further musical piece, "Naomi's Theme," was provided by The Thrill, a band better known in the U.S. for *Blue Submarine Number Six* (*AE).

NARITA DIVORCE

1997. JPN: *Narita Rikon*. PRD: Atsuhiro Sugio. DIR: Masayuki Suzuki. SCR: Noriko Yoshida. CAST: Tsuyoshi Kusanagi, Asaka Seto, Rie Fukatsu, Hiroshi Abe, Leo Morimoto. CHN: Fuji. DUR: 45 mins. x 10 eps.; Wed 15 October 1997–17 December 1997. Ichirō (Kusanagi from SMAP) and Yūko (Seto) marry after a whirlwind courtship, realizing on their honey-

moon that they may have made a mistake. After a spectacular argument in Arrivals at Narita Airport, they decide to get a divorce and enlist Yūko's ex-boyfriend Takuya (Abe) and Ichirō's would-be girlfriend Reiko (Fukatsu) to help them. But as preparations progress, the capricious couple begin to question the wisdom of this decision, too. The divorce comes through but the sale of their apartment does not, forcing the now unmarried couple to live together. Yūko is invited to go to Greece with a writer she meets at her new publishing job, and Ichirō moves in with Takuya.

Giving up on Yūko, Ichirō prepares to accept an offer to study in Rome. However, on hearing from Takuya that she has been sacked from her publishing job and does not intend to go to Greece, he tries to arrange a reconciliation with her. Delayed by his boss, he is late for the meeting and subsequently quarrels with Yūko for what could be the last time. However, Yūko finds him at the airport before he flies off to Italy and returns the vinyl record that she lent him at their first meeting. Ichirō tells Yūko that she has always been the sunshine of his life, and the two walk off in separate directions . . . only to look back toward each other. They decide to get married again.

With a tagline of "Marriage is Not a Happy End," *Narita Divorce* set itself up as a radical change to the traditional conventions of TV romance, but, like the later **SHOTGUN MARRIAGE**, wasn't really all that different. Determined to approach the idea that it was easy to get married but that divorce was always hard, producer Sugio envisioned the show as a Hollywood romantic comedy, imagining his leading man as Dudley Moore and his leading woman as Goldie Hawn. Peak rating: 21.5%. Theme: Yumi Matsutōya—"Sunny Day Holiday."

NATIONAL KID

1960. PRD: N/C. DIR: Nagayoshi Akasaka, Jun Koike, Naruo Watanabe. SCR: Takashi Tanii, Nagayoshi Akasaka.

CAST: Ichirō Kojima, Shūtarō Tsubasa, Taeko Shimura, Kōji Komori. CHN: NET (Asahi). DUR: 30 mins. x 39 eps.; 4 August 1960–27 October 1960 (#1); 3 November 1960–29 December 1960 (#2); 5 January 1961–23 February 1961 (#3); 2 March 1961–27 April 1961 (#4).

Determined not to be outdone by the **MOONLIGHT MASK**, NET commissioned this relatively expensive series from Tōei. Though based on a story by Minoru Kisegawa, the premise was soon dragged in a new direction by the demands of sponsor National, the domestic brand name for the company better known abroad as Panasonic or Matsushita. So it was that the envoy from space who arrived to save the Earth from Venusian Aztec invaders and stayed on in later seasons to fight invading coelacanth monsters, underground invaders from the subterranean world of Hellstein, and finally aliens from planet Mazeran, had a "laser gun" which looked suspiciously like a National products flashlight. However, thanks to National's heavy investment, National Kid was the first flying superhero in Japanese TV history.

NATSUKO'S SAKE

1994. JPN: *Natsuko no Sake*. PRD: Yutaka Kiyono. DIR: Utahiko Honma. SCR: Fumie Mizubashi, Masaya Ozaki. CAST: Emi Wakui, Ken Ishiguro, Masato Hagiwara, Kiichi Nakai. CHN: Fuji. DUR: 45 mins. x 11 eps.; Wed 12 January 1994–23 March 1994.

Sake brewer's daughter Natsuko (Wakui) comes to Tokyo to be an advertising copywriter but quits after she sees an ad campaign that claims cheap booze is just as good as high quality sake. Her brother Yasuo (Nakai) confesses that it is his dream to make the best sake in Japan using special rice, but he dies unexpectedly before he can achieve his goal. Determined to do right by Yasuo's idea, Natsuko takes over the project to realize his dream, in a drama based on the 1988 manga in *Comic Morning* by

Akira Oze. Theme: Sachiko Kumagai—"Kaze to Kumo to Watashi" (Wind, Cloud, and Me).

NATURAL: FUTURE OF LOVE

1996. JPN: *Natural: Ai no Yukue*. PRD: Kazuo Yamamoto. DIR: Masahiro Kunimoto. SCR: Teruo Abe, Masaya Ozaki. CAST: Hikari Ishida, Toshirō Yanagiba, Yoshinori Okada, Tsuyoshi Ihara. CHN: Yomiuri. DUR: 45 mins. x 10 eps.; Mon 14 October 1996–16 December 1996.

Shiho (Ishida) is badly burnt in the same car accident that kills her friend Naoko outright. As Shiho recovers, she grows closer to Naoko's bereaved boyfriend Koba (Ihara), who was also in the car with the girls. A year after the accident, she agrees to marry Koba but also receives a proposal from Naoko's brother Katsuya (Yanagiba). Theme: My Little Lover—"Now and Then: Ushinawareta Toki o Motomete" (Now and Then: In Search of Lost Time).

NEVER LAND

2001. PRD: Mitsunori Morita. DIR: Mitsunori Morita, Shinjirō Kuranuki, Hideharu Takano, Yoshiharu Tazawa. SCR: Kazu Sunamoto. CAST: Tsubasa Imai, Ken Miyake, Maiko Yamada, Reiko Takashima, Sei Tanaka, Shingo Murakami, Tōma Ikuta, Yutaka Yamazaki, Takami Yoshimoto, Yōko Nogiwa, Misato Tachibana, Reiko Suō, Kōki Tanaka. CHN: TBS. DUR: 45 mins. x 11 eps.; Fri 6 July 2001–14 September 2001.

Claiming that his parents have gone abroad, 17-year-old Yoshikuni (Imai) elects to stay at the Seiran Academy dorm over the summer break. He joins fellow student Mitsuhiro (Miyake), who, as an orphan, always spends the summer at the deserted all-boys school, along with three other students and their disdainful dorm mistress Wakaba (Nogiwa), a strict harridan whom the boys joke must be a 100-year-old vampire. Mitsuhiro insists that they all observe each other's right to privacy, though it's immediately obvious that

every one of them has an impressive skeleton in the closet—not least of all Mitsuhiro whose mother committed suicide. Yoshikuni tries to break up with local girl Hiroko (Yamada) after a walk in the forest triggers suppressed memories of the day his own mother tried to strangle him. However, Hiroko takes it badly and overdoses on sleeping pills, supposedly by accident, though both her family and her best friend Aki (Suō) blame him for what they believe to be a suicide attempt.

Of course, Yoshikuni's parents aren't abroad at all, while the supercalm, quiet Mitsuhiro is busily having an affair with his young stepmother Keiko (Takashima), a sports car driving femme fatale who has recently purchased a beachside villa to be closer to her dear one.

Based on the book by Takashi Onda, this moody mix of palm trees, beach life, suppressed emotions, and dorm high jinks is also a vehicle for the Johnny's Jimusho pop factory—Miyake is a singer in boy band V6, who provides the theme tune. As suggested by the obvious reference to *Peter Pan*, these lost boys are less interested in suspense and mystery than they are in never growing up—pouting for the girlie audience who doubtless finds their shy misogyny incredibly endearing. Consequently, the acting has the wooden quality often seen in such enterprises; many of the boys behave as if they are rehearsing a school play, while the more experienced actors like Nogiwa run rings around them. In fact, the scenery often outacts the cast—unlike the frostbitten **BEACH WARS MIX**, this series genuinely appears to have been filmed in a bright, subtropical summer location, and the colors remain warm, even if most of the performances leave the audience cold.

NEW AIRPORT STORY

1994. JPN: *Shinkūkō Monogatari*. PRD: Masaru Takahashi. DIR: Kazuhiko Yamaguchi. SCR: Gorō Shima, Katsuaki Chaki. CAST: Hitoshi Ueki, Mikihisa Azuma, Anju Suzuki, Kazuko Katō. CHN:

Asahi. DUR: 45 mins. x 10 eps.; Thu 6 January 1994–17 March 1994. Shindō (Azuma) is the head of airport security who must share a working environment with the flight controllers. On his first day back at work, his investigations cause a plane to be delayed, throwing him into conflict with his workmates who just want to get the planes safely off the ground. Suspiciously similar to **AIRPORT 92** the "new" describes the airport, not the story.

NEW TALE OF THE HEIKE

1972. JPN: *Shin Heike Monogatari*. PRD: Ryūji Koga. DIR: Mitsuru Shimizu. SCR: Yumie Hiraiwa. CAST: Tatsuya Nakadai, Kanzaburō Nakamura, Yoshiko Sakuma, Isao Kimura. CHN: NHK. DUR: 45 mins. x ca. 50 eps.; Sun 2 January 1972–24 December 1972.

Japan has enjoyed a period of relative peace and prosperity, ever since the Taika reforms were drawn up about a generation after the death of prince **SHOTOKU TAISHI**. Now, nearly five hundred years later, two offshoots of the imperial family have started to exercise greater control in their home domains —the House of Taira (aka the Heike) and the House of Minamoto (aka the Genji). In 1155, a succession crisis causes separate factions within the clans to fight each other. The disturbance ends with the Hōgen Emperor in power and bestowing rewards on his chief supporters, Kiyomori Taira (Nakadai) and Yoshitomo Minamoto (Kimura). Yoshitomo is annoyed at this, since he believes he fought harder for Hōgen, only to see his sometime rival Kiyomori receiving all the best accolades.

Hōgen soon abdicates, preferring to exert influence from behind the scenes as Retired Emperor Go-Shirakawa, with Kiyomori the *de facto* ruler of Japan from 1167. The conflict between the Taira and Minamoto continues under the rule of the new Nijō Emperor until it turns into full-blown war, ending with the defeat of the Heike in the naval battle of Dannoura, at which Kiyomori's grandson, the child emperor Antoku, jumps to his death into the sea.

Adapted by **THANK YOU** writer Hiraiwa from a novel by **MUSASHI** author Eiji Yoshikawa that was itself seven years in the making, this tenth *taiga* drama centered on the life of Kiyomori (1118–1181) instead of the usual characters of interest, the warriors who did the bulk of his fighting for him. In ensuring that his wife's sister married the incumbent Nijō Emperor, Kiyomori's grab at power took on the appearance of a family melodrama, exactly the kind of angle likely to guarantee a male audience watching for the fights and a female audience watching for family intrigue and nice frocks— the period was particularly sumptuous in the *kimono* stakes.

The aftermath of the civil war did not see a return to peace, but instead the breakout of internal strife among the Minamoto, dramatized in **YOSHITSUNE** and **THE FIRE STILL BURNS**. The story was also turned into a movie by Kenji Mizoguchi as *New Tales of the Taira Clan* (1955) and a lavish 1993 puppet TV show by Kihachirō Kawamoto, with over 400 puppets. See also **TAIHEIKI**.

NEW YORK LOVE STORY

1988. JPN: *New York Koi Monogatari*. PRD: Kazuki Nakayama. DIR: Akiji Fujita. SCR: Toshio Kamata. CAST: Masakazu Tamura, Kayoko Kishimoto, Honami Suzuki, Mitsuko Oka, Hiroko Shino, Mari Torikoshi. CHN: Fuji. DUR: 45 mins. x 21 eps.; Tue 13 October 1988–22 December 1988 (#1); 18 October 1990–20 December 1990 (#2).

Akiko (Kishimoto) comes to New York, where she falls in love with handsome lawyer Eisuke (Tamura). For the second season, Tamura's hard-boiled attitude was toned down, turning him into more of a comical figure as he tries to juggle an affair with married woman Tomoko (Shino) and a simultaneous relationship with his young lover Ayumi (Torikoshi). New York remains an exotic destination for Japanese travelers and provides a glamorous location for **CHANCE!**, **HOTEL WOMAN**, and, abortively, **FRIENDS**. Actor Tamura would return there for the opening episode of **GOODBYE MR. OZU**. Theme: Yōsui Inoue—"Riverside Hotel."

NEWLY WED

1995. JPN: *Shinkon Nari!* AKA: *Just Married*. PRD: Naoyuki Yokoi. DIR: Takashi Hashimoto. SCR: Yū Yoshimura, Michiru Etō. CAST: Hiroshi Mikami, Riho Makise, Kōji Matoba, Manami Fuji, Chisato Yamazaki. CHN: TBS. DUR: 45 mins. x 12 eps.; Mon 17 July 1995–22 September 1995.

Masato (Mikami) is an only son of a Shintō priest who secretly dreams of becoming a film director. His childhood friend Yukari (Yamazaki), who is also the head of the temple council, appoints him as the new head priest. This outwardly kind gesture hides complex machinations, as Yukari suspiciously does so on the very day that Masato plans to marry his fiancée Nao (Makise), instantly annulling their wedding, and forcing the couple to wait the allotted three years until Masato has completed his advanced training. Compare to **FALSE LOVE**, in which a marriage is similarly upset by the plotting of another woman. Theme: Kome Kome Club—"Subete wa Honto de Uso Kamone" (Everything Might Be True and a Lie).

NEWS GUY

1992. JPN: *News na Aitsu*. PRD: N/C. DIR: Kazuhiro Onohara. SCR: Naruhito Kaneko. CAST: Masahiro Motoki, Tsurutarō Kataoka, Miyuki Imori, Tsuyoshi Ihara, Mie Yamaguchi. CHN: Yomiuri. DUR: 45 mins. x 12 eps.; Sat 4 July 1992–19 September 1992.

The ratings are sliding for International Television's prestigious early evening six o'clock news slot, causing upheavals in the studio. Veteran newscaster Reiko (Yamaguchi) fights to hang onto her job, constantly at odds with her deputy Kōhei (Motoki), who has transferred from a local subsidiary out in the sticks, and spunky rookie reporter Akane (Imori).

NEWS WOMAN

1998. JPN: *News no Onna*. AKA: *Channel 2, She's a News Maker; Anchorwoman*. PRD: Yūji Iwata, Takashi Ishihara. DIR: Hisao Ogura, Masataka Takamaru. SCR: Rumi Takahashi, Kumiko Tabuchi. CAST: Honami Suzuki, Hideaki Takizawa, Kyōzō Nagatsuka, Mitsuru Fukikoshi, Hironobu Nomura, Kyōko Fukada, Masahiko Nishimura, Norika Fujiwara, Hiroshi Abe. CHN: Fuji. DUR: 45 mins. x 11 eps.; Wed 7 January 1998–18 March 1998.

Tamaki Aso (Suzuki) has finally reached the top—married to the rich, handsome Dr. Kudō, she has also been made anchorwoman on the prestigious Channel Two News. She is a news reader of such steely professionalism that nothing will faze her, not even the realization that the victims of the fatal car accident she is reporting live are her husband and his ex-wife, returning from a high school reunion. Inside, Tamaki is distraught but resolves to carry on, only to discover that she has inherited more from her husband than she bargained for—compare to GOOD MOURNING. The legal executor, Kubota (Nagatsuka) informs her that the child of her husband's previous marriage has now lost both parents and his sole surviving relative is currently unreachable in Africa. Thus, Tamaki inherits Ryū (Takizawa from Johnny's Juniors), a sullen, resentful stepson who refuses to clean up after himself, breaks the dishes in the kitchen, and demonstrates his low opinion of Tamaki's cooking by ordering out for pizza while she is still slaving over a hot stove. Soon she discovers that they are *both* beneficiaries of the Doctor's will, and that unless she allows him to stay, *she* will be forced to find alternate accommodations.

News Woman cleverly interweaves its disparate plotlines to hold the viewer's attention. Those with little interest in the reluctant parenting drama between Tamaki and Ryū can still enjoy the understated romance that threatens to bloom between Tamaki and Kubota, while Tamaki's day job allows further diversions as her crew investigates

intriguing news stories. But the drama's greatest achievement lies in its study of TV news journalism itself—in the style of FEMALE ANNOUNCERS, it focuses on rivalries in the studio (between proponents of NHK-style Information and Fuji-style Variety) and the perilous, backstabbing aspects of life in the media. The series begins with the last bow of Tamaki's predecessor, whose departure is loaded with implications of behind-the-scenes skullduggery but before long, the scene is replayed with *Tamaki* as the outgoing anchorwoman, handing over her dream job to her more pliable replacement (Fukada, in a brief cameo). Just when the story might be flagging (the Ryū subplot is occasionally frustrating), Tamaki is thrown into troubled times like the heroine of TABLOID and forced to fight her way back up from square one at a new job—a run-down cable station whose ratings are negligible until she adds some pizzazz. Reputedly broadcast without English subtitles in the U.S. on KTSF TV. Theme: Judy and Mary—"Sanpo-Michi" (Strolling Along).

NEWSCASTER RYŌKO KASUMI

1999. JPN: *Newscaster Kasumi Ryōko*. PRD: Fumio Igarashi, Takamichi Yamada. DIR: Takamichi Yamada, Shingo Matsubara. SCR: Toshio Sekine. CAST: Chikako Kaku, Masahiro Takashima, Yōko Saitō, Ken Kaneko, Yumiko Takahashi. CHN: Asahi. DUR: 45 mins. x ca. 11 eps.; Thu 14 January 1999–?? March 1999.

A newscaster in her prime fights a network's attempts to replace her with a younger model. Doomed to failure in the ratings through comparison to the superior NEWS WOMAN and through being scheduled directly opposite the long-term favorite MAKING IT THROUGH. Compare to SCENES FROM THE WATER TRADE.

NIGHT HEAD

1992. PRD: Yūji Iwata. DIR: Jōji Iida, Masato Hijikata, Katsuyuki Motohiro, Masayuki Ochiai. SCR: Jōji Iida. CAST:

Etsushi Toyokawa, Shinji Takeda, Kanako Fukaura, Tarō Fujioka, Rie Yamaguchi. CHN: Fuji. DUR: 30 mins. x 21 eps.; Sat 8 October 1992–18 March 1993.

Naoto (Toyokawa) and Naoya (Takeda) are brothers who work as psychic investigators, each using his particular psychic power, utilizing the neglected dark side of the human brain—hence the "night head." With mysterious origins in a haunted forest (only truly explained in creator Jōji Iida's later novelization *Night Head Deep Forest*) the brothers are an intriguing mix—Naoto is telekinetic while Naoya is a telepath, and between them they make for a formidable team, as if the heroine of NANASE AGAIN had gained an extra ability.

Shown after midnight, *NH* is a deliberately moody, brooding thriller series after the fashion of the old British show *Sapphire and Steel*. The brothers are true anti-heroes—their first adventure begins when Naoto overhears comments in a crowded bar disparaging psychics and leads to a brawl when his powers start shattering glasses. Though he can hold off assailants by applying psychic pressure to their brains, Naoya is able to read the minds of his attackers, not only revealing who has slept with whom (everyone, it transpires!), but also that a woman seen leaving the bar is a murderess.

NH not only initiated the wave of

thrillers that prepared the Japanese for *The X-Files* and **RING**, it also proved to be a rich breeding ground for talent behind the scenes—the crew list includes early directorial credits for the parties who would go on to make **HYPNOSIS**, **ANOTHER HEAVEN**, and **BAYSIDE SHAKEDOWN**, among others. In addition to Iida's sequel, the series itself was novelized, reputedly with illustrations by the famous manga collective CLAMP. With a growing cult following, the series boasted a Christmas Eve TV special *NH: The Other Side* (1992) and a movie sequel *NH: The Trial* (1994). Composer Kuniaki Haishima would become better known later in the 1990s for his anime work, such as *Spriggan* (*AE).

NIGHT HOSPITAL

2002. JPN: *Night Hospital Byōki wa Nemuranai.* PRD: Yūya Fujii, Yoshinori Horiguchi, Kazuhiro Shimoda, Sadako Ikeda. DIR: Kihiro Karaki. SCR: Michiru Etō. CAST: Yukie Nakama, Reiko Takashima, Seiichi Tanabe, Kōji Imada, Mitsuru Fubuki, Naoto Takenaka, Yoon Yoon Son-ha. CHN: NTV. DUR: 45 mins. x 10 eps.; Mon 14 October 2002–16 December 2002.

Maki Morisawa (Nakama) is a pathologist posted as a physician to the graveyard shift at a hospital. Although she is an expert on many aspects of medicine, she has never had to practice on live patients before, and has little practical experience. She soon clashes with surgeon Hotaruko Ōkubo (Takashima), who would rather Maki was out of her way so she can get on with healing the sick. Theme: Tomoyasu Hotei—"Destiny Rose."

NIGHTS CANNOT BE SHARED

1996. JPN: *Yuzurenai Yoru.* PRD: Takayuki Sashida. DIR: Takemitsu Satō. SCR: Narihito Kaneko. CAST: Chikako Kaku, Shizuka Kudō, Masaki Kanda, Masahiro Matsuoka. CHN: Kansai. DUR: 45 mins. x 10 eps.; Tue 15 October 1996–17 December 1996.

Michiko (Kaku) has been married for 14 years to Shunpei (Kanda), the head chef at the prestigious Japanese restaurant Meigetsu. It is only with the death of Shunpei's mother Kiku that Michiko comes to realize that she has been held at arm's length by the old woman and never really permitted to participate in the running of the restaurant. The old woman kept something else from Michiko—the knowledge that Shunpei had been having an affair with young sake brewer Tae (Kudō) for the past three years. Shortly after introducing herself to Michiko, Tae serves her with divorce papers, with Shunpei's signature already obtained. Michiko only agrees to divorce if she gets to become the manageress of the Meigetsu, which she regards as her chance to stay close to Shunpei and win him back. However, as with so many new managers from **GOOD MOURNING** to **TAKE ME TO A RYOKAN**, it is only then that Michiko discovers how far in debt Meigetsu is. Determined to keep the restaurant afloat, Michiko borrows 60 million yen from Tae, offering *herself* as guarantee against the loan. The result is an outstandingly tense drama, as the two women are forced to cooperate on the business but continue to duel incessantly for the affections of Shunpei. Theme: Shizuka Kudō—"Gekijō" (Theater).

NIGHT'S EMBRACE

1994. JPN: *Yoru ni Dakarete.* PRD: Satoru Koyama. DIR: Hidemasa Hosono. SCR: Man Izawa. CAST: Shima Iwashita, Noriyuki Higashiyama, Masahiro Takashima, Tatsuya Yamaguchi, Eriko Watanabe. CHN: NTV. DUR: 45 mins. x 10 eps.; Wed 19 October 1994–21 December 1994.

Tokyo civil servant Sonoko (Iwashita) buys into Scarlet, a hostess bar fallen on hard times. As the new owner-manager, she intends to turn its fortunes around. Unknown to her, her former office subordinate Ryūsei (Higashiyama) is so deeply in debt to loan sharks that he is forced to moonlight at another job. He takes a job at a host club, but his first customer is Sonoko. Compare to **LAST LOVE**.

Theme: Toshinobu Kubota—"Yoru ni Dakarete."

NINZABURŌ FURUHATA

1994. JPN: *Keibuho: Furuhata Ninzaburō.* AKA: *Assistant Inspector Ninzaburō Furuhata.* PRD: Shizuo Sekiguchi. DIR: Mamoru Hoshi. SCR: Kōki Mitani. CAST: Masakazu Tamura, Masahiko Nishimura, Takeshi Kaga. CHN: Fuji. DUR: 45 mins. x ca. 33 eps.; Wed 13 April 1994–29 June 1994 (#1); 10 January 1996–13 March 1996 (#2); 13 April 1999–22 June 1999 (#3).

Assistant Inspector Ninzaburō Furuhata (Tamura) is the greatest detective in the homicide division. With his loyal sidekick Shintarō (Nishimura), he is assigned some of the most difficult cases, chiefly those in which the perpetrator is known to the police but evidence is sorely lacking.

As befits a TV series by a scriptwriter whose early work was for the theater, *NF* thrives not on car chases and gunfights but on one-on-one confrontations in the interview room. The criminal's identity is usually known to the audience already (see also **KIDNAP**), turning a matter of simple detection into a struggle to find enough evidence to justify charging and convicting the suspect. With flashes of insight and tirelessly jesuitical arguments, Ninzaburō eventually outwits his prey, forcing them into logical positions from which the only escape is confession or a slip of the tongue that provides a vital missing clue.

NF went into production after two important U.S. imports hit the Japanese market. Over a decade after the original *Columbo* ended its run, Peter Falk's shambolic but razor-sharp detective was resurrected for a longrunning series of TV movies. These new adventures reached the Japanese public at roughly the same time as *The Silence of the Lambs* (1990), which was by no means the first thriller to reveal the criminal's identity, but did so in a conspicuously successful manner that was guaranteed to encourage imitators.

Fearful that the protagonist's strange name would mislead viewers into thinking *NF* was a period drama in the style of **HEIJI ZENIGATA** or **HANSHICHI**, the series initially had the prefix "Assistant Inspector" to make it clear that it was set in the modern world. The prefix was dropped after the first season, when its cool, politely insolent, and comical protagonist had become a household name, along with star Tamura, who reportedly had little interest in mysteries until he fell in love with Mitani's script.

NF remains a regular fixture on Japanese TV, not merely in sequel seasons, but in four feature-length specials, shown on 12 April 1995, 27 March 1996, 4 April 1999, and 6 April 1999. In one of these, *NF vs. SMAP*, Ninzaburō took on four other 1990s icons. The second season was accompanied by a pastiche broadcast later in the evening after each episode. Entitled *Shintarō Imaizumi*, it featured Ninzaburō's long-suffering sidekick attempting to claim the credit for each case, using footage from the earlier broadcast with bridging material assembled by the production team. Note also the presence of surgeon Nakagawa (Kaga), a character lifted from Mitani's earlier drama series **TURN AROUND AND HE'LL BE THERE**. Peak rating: 28.3%.

NO CASH

1994. JPN: *Okane ga Nai!* PRD: Kōji Shiozawa. DIR: Setsuo Wakamatsu. SCR: Kazuyuki Morosawa, Masashi Todayama. CAST: Yūji Oda, Naomi Zaizen, Mikihisa Azuma, Akio Kaneda. CHN: Fuji. DUR: 45 mins. x 12 eps.; Thu 6 July 1994–21 September 1994.

With two young brothers to support, the impoverished Kentarō (Oda) takes a job with a cleaning firm and finds himself sweeping the floors at the multinational insurance company Universal, whose employees command salaries in the mid-six-figure region. He finds an important lost document and asks its grateful owner Ichirō (Azuma) if his discovery will earn him a job. However, Ichirō is not that grateful and Kentarō's request is rebuffed. Later, visiting bigwigs mistake him for an employee, and his unwitting impersonation of a Universal broker wins the company a huge contract. Winning the approval of Universal's chairman Himuro (Ryō Ishibashi), Kentarō is offered a job with the company for real and rises swiftly through the ranks. Meanwhile, Ichirō is fired after becoming a fraud victim and proposes to Michiko (Zaizen), Kentarō's childhood friend.

Becoming the chief of the sales division, Kentarō moves to an expensive apartment but is soon implicated in a bribery scandal. With his brothers taunted at school over a crime that Kentarō has not committed, he initiates his own investigation and discovers that he has been set up to take a fall on behalf of Himuro. Impressed with the new recruit's powers of deduction, Himuro offers him a partnership in the firm but Kentarō refuses in disgust and leaves the company. He arrives just in time to stop Ichirō's marriage to Michiko and proposes to her himself a year later, as he is now a successful independent businessman, back again in his old apartment.

A salaryman fairy tale in the style of *The Secret of My Success* (1987), *No Cash* was already late for the 1980s boom time but still worked as an amiable vehicle for its star Oda. Compare to its female flipside **EVIL WOMAN**. Theme: Yūji Oda—"Over the Trouble."

NO LONGER HUMAN

1994. JPN: *Ningen • Shikkaku: Tatoeba Boku ga Shindara.* AKA: *Failure as a Human: What If I Died; If I Die.* PRD: Kazuhiro Itō. DIR: Ken Yoshida. SCR: Shinji Nojima. CAST: Hidekazu Akai, Sachiko Sakurai, Taishū Kase, Megumi Yokoyama, Tsuyoshi Dōmoto, Yōsuke Saitō. CHN: TBS. DUR: 45 mins. x 12 eps.; Fri 8 July 1994–23 September 1994.

Former pro baseball player Mamoru (Akai) now runs a noodle restaurant and wants to send his son Makoto (Dōmoto) to a prestigious college. However, Makoto soon runs into trouble at his new school, when he attempts to intervene in a bullying incident and becomes a victim of bullying himself. He also witnesses his social science teacher Etsuo (Kase) shoplifting; the teacher confesses that he is a kleptomaniac and the softhearted Makoto agrees to keep his discovery secret. However, the wily Etsuo later appears at Mamoru's noodle bar and claims that Makoto has stolen his camera, not only framing the boy for theft, but also with taking a series of incriminating photographs of phys-ed teacher Miyazaki (Saitō) wearing women's clothes. The enraged Miyazaki blames Makoto for the appearance of the photographs around the school and subjects him to a cruel punishment regime.

Bullied by students and teachers alike, Makoto jumps to his death from the school roof. The distraught Mamoru finds a picture of his son being punished by Miyazaki and kills the teacher in a fit of rage. As Makoto's homeroom teacher Chihiro (Sakurai) tries to broker a deal between Mamoru and the police, Mamoru promises to turn himself in after consulting with his wife. However, when he fails to arrive, detectives suspect that he has traced the source of his son's misery to Etsuo and plans on killing him in revenge.

LIPSTICK creator Shinji Nojima is no stranger to dark tales, but this examination of bullying in Japanese schools

---

WEDDINGS FROM HELL

Sea of Love

As she heads off for her honeymoon on a helicopter in Tokyo Bay, a bride sees her drug addict ex-boyfriend in the crowd. When she is told she is forbidden to talk to him, she smiles at her new husband, opens the hatch, and jumps into the sea. ☞

suffered from uncharacteristically low ratings in the early part of its run. Nojima's usual popularity, peaking at 28.9%, soon returned when the bullying scenes abated to be replaced by a more traditional revenge tragedy—ironic, in that Chihiro tells her class that, through their apathy, ". . . *all of you are responsible for the death of Makoto*," while the TV audience was reluctant to face the same unpleasant scenes of bullying themselves.

Note that we have called this show *No Longer Human*, as that is the official English translation for the 1948 Osamu Dazai novel which shares the same Japanese title. The parallel was intentional on Nojima's part, as he intended to show that Mamoru forfeited his humanity the moment he sank to the same vengeful level as his son's tormenters. However, the homage was not appreciated by the Dazai estate, which threatened legal action and was fought off with the rather silly addition of a single dot in between the two words, thereby making the title sufficiently "dissimilar" to the novel it evokes. Theme: Simon and Garfunkel—"Hazy Shade of Winter."

NO VACANCIES

1972. JPN: *Manin Onrei*. PRD: Kazuo Shibata, Hiroshi Kubota. DIR: Kanae Mayuzumi. SCR: Izuho Sudō. CAST: Kokinji Katsura, Chieko Nakakita, Taeko Hattori, Mari Okamoto, Tomoharu Takeo, Toshi Shibazaki, Junichi Takeoka, Masanao Yamada, Tomomi Fujita, Yuka Noda, Kazuhiko Tsuchiya, Masao Imanishi, Matsuko Inaba, Masao Sugiura. CHN: NHK. DUR: 30 mins. x 7 eps.; Sat 12 February 1972–25 March 1972.

Portrait photographer Fukuichirō (Katsura) is blessed with nine children, while his brother Kanejirō (Imanishi) and his wife (Inaba) are childless. Kanejirō keeps asking his brother to allow him to adopt one of his, and eventually Fukuichirō asks the children for a volunteer. Though his second daughter Natsuko (Okamoto) agrees to move in with Kanejirō, she soon

becomes homesick and returns to her true family.

One day, a car crashes at the entrance of the family's photography studio. Nobody is hurt, and the driver Suguru (Sugiura) becomes a friend of the family. A former drive-in chef, he becomes close to the eldest daughter Shigeko (Hattori) when he offers to teach her how to cook. Second son Jōji (Shibazaki), who has been debating whether to go to college, decides instead to learn the culinary arts from Suguru as well.

This large family drama uses incidental events to build a tableau of a family's love for each other—compare to **MAKING IT THROUGH**. Later episodes concentrate on the love affair that becomes the drama's central theme, as a neighbor tries to introduce Shigeko to a young doctor. Fukuichirō and his wife Sumi (Nakakita) are surprised that their little daughter is already at an age for marriage, but Shigeko herself is more surprised by the feelings it brings out between her and Suguru. The chef and his student announce that they will marry and leave to tell Suguru's parents, a departure which finds Fukuichirō's wife Sumi musing on how all her children will soon leave the nest. Ever the optimist, Fukuichirō tells her that they are not losing nine children, but gaining nine in-laws.

NO WAITING

1992. JPN: *Mattanashi*. PRD: N/C. DIR: Hiroshi Yoshino. SCR: Chigusa Shiota. CAST: Yuki Saitō, Toshiyuki Nagashima, Sumiko Fuji, Sayuri Kokushō. CHN: NTV. DUR: 45 mins. x 11 eps.; Sat 4 July 1992–26 September 1992.

Former bank clerk Sakura (Saitō) marries former sumo wrestler Shūji (Nagashima), thereby becoming the unwilling mistress of the Naminokawa Stable. The grand mistress Yasuko (Fuji) teaches her the rules and the duties of her role in the traditional sumo world.

NO WAY! *

1998. JPN: *Akimahende!* PRD: Seiichirō

Kijima. DIR: Katsuo Fukuzawa, Makoto Kiyohiro, Natsuki Imai. SCR: Shizuka Ōishi. CAST: Yuki Uchida, Noriko Fujiwara, Tamao Nakamura, Masahiko Nishimura, Kazuya Ninomiya, Anne Suzuki. CHN: TBS. DUR: 45 mins. x 11 eps.; Fri 9 October 1998–18 December 1998.

Aristocratic old lady Katsura (Nakamura) meets Junichirō, her thrice-widowed old flame from the distant past. Junichirō proposes to her, and she agrees on the condition that she can get his four children to like her while he is away on a three-month business trip. Disguising herself as a housekeeper, she starts working at the house, only to discover that the children are not the little darlings that she has previously thought them to be. Son Daiki is surly and disrespectful and playing truant from school. Among the daughters, Ayame is planning on divorcing her husband, Sumire is conducting an affair with a married man, and Satsuki is troubled by ill health and prone to fainting episodes at school. The surrogate parent cliché is long established in Japanese drama but this particular one takes an obvious cue from the Hollywood movie *Mrs. Doubtfire* (1993). Americana also features heavily in the background, with Ayame desperately pursuing a career as an actress—she auditions for a foreign director who is supposed to be Steven Spielberg and temporarily disappears from the series to attend her Hollywood casting call. Broadcast in the U.S. with English subtitles on KIKU TV and KTSF TV. Theme: Pool Bit Boys—"Venus Accident."

NOBUNAGA

1992. AKA: *Nobunaga: King of Zipangu*. PRD: Keiji Shima. Takahiko Shigemitsu. SCR: Masataka Tamukai. CAST: Naoto Ogata, Ryūzō Hayashi, Keiko Takahashi, Hiromi Gō, Momoko Kikuchi, Miho Takagi, Mayumi Wakamura, Ken Utsumi, Mikijirō Hira, Frank Neal, Junji Inagawa, Michael Tomioka. CHN: NHK. DUR: 45 mins. x 51 eps.; Sun 5 January 1992–19 December 1992.

After the Portugese introduce firearms to Japan in 1543, the new technology is turned to military advantage by warlord Nobunaga Oda (Ogata). Defeating Yoshimoto Imagawa at the battle of Okehazama in 1560 and forming an alliance with Ieyasu Tokugawa (**TOKUGAWA IEYASU**), Nobunaga comes to the aid of Yoshiaki Ashikaga, the younger brother of the assassinated Shogun Yoshiteru. Entering Kyoto in 1568, Nobunaga makes Yoshiaki the new Shogun, becoming a powerful force in Japanese government. After a while, Yoshiaki and Nobunaga quarrel over political decisions, and Nobunaga banishes the nominal ruler in 1573 after a plot against him is discovered, effectively ending the Muromachi Period in Japanese history. This act causes unrest among many other warlords, who band together against Nobunaga. In the ensuing civil war, Nobunaga is initially defeated by **SHINGEN TAKEDA** but wins after Shingen is laid low by illness.

After consolidating his rule over central Japan, Nobunaga is thrown into opposition against his own lieutenant Mitsuhide Akechi (Tomioka). Confiscating Akechi's lands, Nobunaga promises him a domain in western Japan once he has seized it in an alliance with **HIDEYOSHI** (Tōru Nakamura). However, Akechi plots against his former ally, attacking Nobunaga while he is staying at the Honnōji Temple in Kyoto. Realizing that all is lost, Nobunaga sets fire to the temple and commits suicide to evade capture.

As demonstrated by the number of cross-references leading to entire TV series about incidental characters, the story of Nobunaga (1534–1582) is familiar to all Japanese. This 1992 *taiga* drama also shows the first stirrings of the sweeping changes introduced to the franchise by new producer Keiji Shima, who had been appointed in 1990. Whereas the original *taiga* producer Taiji Nagasawa concerned himself with the competition between the "new" medium of TV and the cinema world, Shima was an initiate of multi-

media, determined to exploit the TV drama across other platforms, particularly foreign sales. So it is that *Nobunaga* is presented from the point of view of Portuguese missionary Luis Frois (Neal) and the series highlights Nobunaga's protection of Christian emissaries. It even uses a variation of the Portuguese *Xipangu* to describe Japan—the term was in common use in Europe at the time and was, for example, the name of the land that Christopher Columbus hoped to find when he sailed toward the West. However, ratings were unremarkable for a *taiga*, possibly because mild-mannered lead actor Ogata was cast against his type as the sturdy warlord. The aftermath of Akechi's betrayal is examined in **KASUGA THE COURT LADY**, while Shima's policy of applied exoticism would come to fruition with the following year's **WIND OF THE RYŪKYŪ ISLANDS**. Peak rating: 33.0%.

NON-CHAN'S DREAM

1988. JPN: *Non-chan no Yume*. PRD: Tōru Shōji. DIR: N/C. SCR: Shigeko Satō. CAST: Tomoko Fujita. CHN: NHK. DUR: 15 mins. x ca. 150 eps.; Mon 4 April 1988–1 October 1988.
Irrepressibly enthusiastic Nobuko (Fujita), affectionately known as Non-chan, has come to the remote southern tip of the island of Shikoku in order to escape the American bombing raids on Tokyo in 1945. Her father, now dead, once encouraged his daughters with the phrase *"Girls, Be Ambitious,"* a paraphrase of the famous exhortation to *boys* made in Sapporo in 1877 by the American educator William Clark—see **NAOMI**, which steals the same gag for its theme song.

On the day the Emperor announces Japan's surrender, Nobuko acts as a midwife at the birth of her neighbor's child. The pretty Nobuko has two suitors—Hasumi is a dashing naval officer who instructs the local women in military drills, while Hiroshi is a simple local farmer. Nobuko makes a fool of herself at an *omiai* meeting with Hiroshi's parents, but soon reveals that

marriage is not top on her list of priorities. Instead, she wants to have a career—though her dream is initially greeted with ridicule from Hiroshi, he soon lends her moral support. This is partly because Hiroshi loves her and partly because he has a dream of his own: he wishes to link Shikoku to the mainland by building a bridge.

Nobuko begins to print a small newsletter in the town, and as its fame spreads, she sends a copy to a Tokyo publisher. After many hardships, she takes a job in Tokyo, eventually becoming the chief editor of the magazine *Dream*.

Though the series ended with the marriage of Nobuko and Hiroshi in 1951, it was deliberately timed so that real-life events would add a coda of their own. *Non-chan's Dream* straddles two periods of history, beginning with a shot of the statue of Ryōma Sakamoto (see **RYŌMA DEPARTS**) that overlooks Kōchi harbor, chronicling Japan's defeat and recovery and finishing with the prediction that Japan was about to enter a new age of prosperity. The year of broadcast saw the completion of the Seto Bridge, which famously linked Shikoku to the mainland and brought *"Hiroshi's dream"* to life. Peak rating: 50.6%.

NONOMURA HOSPITAL

1981. JPN: *Nonomura Byōin Monogatari*. PRD: Keiko Take. DIR: Hideo Sakurai. SCR: Norihiro Takahashi. CAST: Ken Utsui, Masako Natsume, Hiroshi Sekiguchi, Midori Kiuchi, Masahiko Tsugawa. CHN: TBS. DUR: 45 mins. x ca. 20 eps.; Tue 12 May 1981–13 November 1981.
After working in a large hospital for many years, Dr. Nonomura (Utsui) finally decides that he can better serve the public by opening his own clinic. The result is a mixture of a kitchen-sink family drama and a medical story, featuring **MONKEY**'s Masako Natsume as a loyal nurse. Theme: Shinji Tanimura—"Seinen no Ki" (A Tree of Youth). No relation to the anime of the same name (*AE).

Nurse Man

NOT ON SUNDAYS

1993. JPN: *Nichiyō wa Dame.* PRD: N/C.
DIR: Takeshi Inoue. SCR: Satoshi Oko-
reki. CAST: Misako Tanaka, Toshirō
Yanagiba, Toshiaki Karasawa, Hideo
Nakano, Masato Ibu. CHN: NTV. DUR: 45
mins. x 11 eps.; Sat 16 April 1993–26
June 1993.
Criminal psychology professor Fubuki
(Tanaka) has problems at home with
her teenage daughter and at work with
her ex-husband's younger brother
Masahito (Karasawa), who has newly
arrived in her department as a guest
lecturer. Theme: Corvettes—"Hitomi o
Boku ni Chikazukete" (Bring Your Eyes
Closer to Me).

NOTHING LASTS FOREVER

1999. JPN: *Jo-I.* AKA: *Female Doctors.*
PRD: Yoshinori Horiguchi. DIR: Masahiro
Kunimoto. SCR: Nao Morishita. CAST:
Miki Nakatani, Ryō, Ken Kaneko,
Shigeki Hosokawa, Yasufumi Terawaki.
CHN: Yomiuri. DUR: 45 mins. x ca. 11
eps.; Mon 5 July 1999–?? September
1999.
Life and loves in a Tokyo hospital, as
three lady doctors are implicated in a
murder trial. Based on the novel by
Sidney Sheldon, whose **OTHER SIDE OF
MIDNIGHT** has also been adapted into a
Japanese TV series.

NURSE MAN

2002. PRD: Hidehiro Kōno. DIR: Hitoshi
Iwamoto. SCR: Toshio Terada. CAST:
Masahiro Matsuoka, Satomi Kobayashi, Takako Uehara, Natsumi Abe,
Keiichi Yamamoto, Kyōko Kishida,
Masami Matsushima. CHN: NTV. DUR:
45 mins. x 10 eps.; Sat 19 January
2002–23 March 2002.
Yūjirō (Matsuoka from TOKIO) is a
newly graduated male nurse, who is
posted to the same hospital as his
friend Shinta (Yamamoto). However,
chief nurse Yoshie (Kobayashi) does
not believe that men should be permitted in her profession and announces
that only one of them will be allowed
to stay. Shinta is soon accepted by the
patients but Yūjirō's long list of mistakes appalls Yoshie and the attractive
Akane (Uehara), who is younger than
him in years but senior in nursing
experience. However, salvation arrives
in the form of his friendship with the
arrogant and demanding patient Miwa
(Abe), who is critically ill with heart
disease. Though she is shunned by the
other nurses, Yūjirō sympathizes with
her plight because she is suffering
from the same disease that killed his
sister. Though it does little more than
switch genders on **NURSE STATION** or
LEAVE IT TO THE NURSES, *Nurse Man* was
welcomed by the medical establishment for breaking with dramatic tradition and showing that not all medical
men are doctors and for not shying
away from the severity and hardship of
a nurse's life. In execution, however, it
is really nothing but **HALF DOC** without
a stethoscope.

NURSE STATION

1991. PRD: N/C. DIR: Osamu Tsuji. SCR:
Toshimichi Saeki, Kumiko Tabuchi.
CAST: Minoru Tanaka, Momoko Kikuchi,
Saya Takagi, Hiroko Moriguchi, Ritsuko
Tanaka. CHN: TBS. DUR: 45 mins. x 12
eps.; Tue 15 January 1991–19 March
1991.
After graduating from nursing college,
Mariko (Kikuchi) is assigned to
Kōhoku Hospital as a junior nurse,
sharing a room with fellow rookie
Yasuko (Moriguchi). As well as dealing
with patients, Mariko is excessively
occupied with handsome surgeon Dr.
Terasaki (M. Tanaka), who sends her
EEG into a flutter every time he walks
past. No relation to the 1991 Kyōko
Shimazu manga of the same name.
Compare to **LEAVE IT TO THE NURSES**
and **WHITE SHADOW**. Theme: Mi-Ke—
"Omoide no Kujūkurihama"
(Kujūkurihama in My Heart).

O

ODD APPLES

1983. JPN: *Fuzoroi no Ringotachi*. PRD: Katsumi Ōyama, Kenji Katashima. DIR: Shinichi Kamoshita, Yasuo Inoshita, Katsumi Ōyama, Shinichi Kamoshita. SCR: Taichi Yamada. CAST: Kiichi Nakai, Saburō Tokitō, Mariko Ishihara, Satomi Tezuka, Shingo Yanagisawa, Shōko Nakajima, Tomiyuki Kunihiro, Hitomi Takahashi, Kaoru Kobayashi. CHN: TBS. DUR: 45 mins. x 47 eps.; Fri 27 May 1983–29 July 1983 (#1); 15 March 1985–7 June 1985 (#2); 11 January 1991–22 March 1991 (#3); 11 April 1997–4 July 1997 (#4).

Nakategawa (Nakai), Iwata (Tokitō), and Nishidera (Yanagisawa) are students at a low-level university, who set up a hiking club in order to meet girls. Their first catches comprise Harue (Ishihara) and Yōko (Tezuka), who are studying to be nurses, and the plain Ayako (Nakajima) who attends an elite women's college. Nakategawa also gets to know a club hostess Natsue (Takahashi), who is living with the misanthropic Honda (Kunihiro), a Tokyo University graduate who runs a computer business from home.

As a coda to Japan's many educational dramas, *Odd Apples* features a new perspective on the importance attached to academic honors. Its characters chiefly lack any self-confidence and vision for the future but still make it through, regardless of their apparent failure to do well in the examination culture that so often defines "success."

Writer Taichi Yamada, who also created MEN'S JOURNEY, RIVER BANK ALBUM, and MAKING MEMORIES, kept his dialogue naturalistic and everyday, but uses it to contrast the caring, sharing central cast of supposed losers with the arrogant Kunihiro, thereby questioning the priorities of the 1980s bubble economy. Yamada's own comment on his work was that he was suspicious of a society that only accepted standardized, symmetrical apples, whereas natural apples came in all manner of sizes and shapes. Hitting an undercurrent of the materialistic 1980s, the show was a great success, returning three more times over 14 years and remaining in many viewer's all-time top tens.

Later seasons aged with the original cast and audience, depicting the characters struggling to find work in the job market, then dealing with marriage and divorce—compare to LEAVE IT TO THE NURSES. The final series found them taking stock in their thirties, as they faced a mid-life crisis about what they had achieved. Kiichi Nakai, Saburō Tokitō, and Mariko Ishihara were unknown actors who made their names with this series. Theme: Southern All Stars—"Itoshi no Elly" (My Dear Elly).

OFFICER ICHIRŌ

2003. JPN: *Keiji Ichirō*. AKA: *Detective Ichirō*. PRD: Mitsunori Morita. DIR: Mitsunori Morita, Katsunori Tomita. SCR: Mitsuo Kuroto. CAST: Haruhiko Katō, Rei Kikukawa, Yōko Nogiwa, Naoki Hosaka, Maho Toyota, Masahiko Tsugawa. CHN: TBS. DUR: 45 mins. x 9 eps.; Wed 15 January 2003–12 March 2003.

Ichirō is a new detective at the Tamagawa precinct, called to his first case—a family homicide. The idealistic young detective immediately begins pursuing the case but is soon shunted over to another crime, purportedly because he has disobeyed his superiors. The title takes its name from Ichirō, the baseball player currently with the Seattle Mariners, for whose name TBS happily paid a licensing fee.

OH, DAD! *

2000. JPN: *Oyaji*. PRD: Yasuo Yagi. DIR: Makoto Kiyohiro, Osamu Katayama. SCR: Kazuhiko Yūkawa. CAST: Masakazu Tamura, Ryōko Hirosue, Miki Mizuno, Junichi Okada, Yuriko Ishida. CHN: TBS. DUR: 45 mins. x 11 eps.; Sun 8 October 2000–31 December 2000.

Middle-aged father of three Kanichi (Tamura) is a doctor but also a complete disaster—when we first see him, he makes a fool of himself at his daughter Sayuri's *omiai* marriage meeting. Although he cannot comprehend why Sayuri remains single, his long-suffering wife Miyako knows exactly why—it's because Kanichi cannot help but interfere in the lives of his three children. Kanichi is also busily trying to ruin the marriage prospects of his younger daughter Suzu, this time

Odd Apples

deliberately because he disapproves of Tadashi, her choice as husband. Sayuri, who is trying to keep her pregnancy secret, has an assignation at a night club, where she is scandalized to see her father flirting with Machiko, the hostess—she realizes that there is a side to her father that she never suspected.

Every season of Japanese TV comes with at least one in-law appeasement drama, in which children try desperately to get on with their lives despite parental opposition. *Oh Dad!* inverts the standard motifs of the subgenre (see **SHOTGUN MARRIAGE** or **DAUGHTER-IN-LAW**), approaching the drama from the point of view of the interfering in-law himself.

Eventually, all of Kanichi's children move out of the family home—Kanichi collapses from the stress and discovers that the unidentified father of Sayuri's baby is a doctor at the hospital. Unable to resist snooping, he agrees to be kept under observation so he can locate the culprit. Meanwhile, however, Miyako has encountered someone from her past and threatens to leave him, pushing Kanichi even closer to Machiko. Screened in the U.S. with English subtitles on KTSF TV, KIKU TV, and Asahi

Homecast—and often confused with Tamura's later **LIFE WITH DAD**. Theme: Hana*Hana—"Sayonara Daisuki na Hito" (Goodbye to the One I Love).

OHRANGER *

1995. JPN: *Chōriki Sentai Ohranger*. AKA: *Super-Power Battle Team Ohranger; Power Rangers Zeo*. PRD: Jun Kaji, Susumu Yoshikawa, Takeyuki Suzuki, Naruki Takadera. DIR: Shōhei Tōjō, Masato Tsujino, Takeru Ogasawara, Hiroshi Furuta, Yoshiaki Kobayashi, Takao Nagaishi, Ryūta Tazaki. SCR: Noboru Sugimura, Toshiki Inoue, Shōzō Uehara, Hirohisa Soda, Susumu Takahisa. CAST: Masaru Shishido, Kunio Masaoka, Masashi Aida, Ayumi Asō, Tamao, Shōji Yamaguchi. CHN: Asahi. DUR: 25 mins. x 48 eps.; Fri 3 March 1995–23 February 1996.

In 1999, when the evil Machine Empire arrives to enslave the people of planet Earth, the United Armies (UA) of the world use the relics of an ancient, long-forgotten science to create the six-member Ohranger team of superpowered warriors. Their leader, Gorō (Shishido) is a captain in the UA and a master of Japanese martial arts who transforms into Oh Red. Shōhei (Masaoka) is a lieutenant in the UA and Oh Green on the Ohranger team. He likes boxing and ramen noodles. Soft-spoken Yūji (Aida), also a lieutenant, is Oh Blue on the team and a master of fencing. The team has two female members: Juri (Asō) is Oh Yellow, a strong-willed lieutenant in UA who is also an expert in martial arts; Momo (Tamao) is Oh Pink, a motherly girl next door who is also a lieutenant in UA and an expert in aikido and Chinese kung fu. They are later joined by young boy Riki (Yamaguchi) who transforms into the King Ranger, the legendary warrior who fought against the Machine Empire in the distant past. To aid them in their fight, the Ohranger team has a series of Egyptian-themed animal robots, each of which transforms into a humanoid version. These in turn can combine to make the Ohranger Robo, while five

other robots combine to make the Ohblocker robot. Other transforming weapons include Tackle Boy and Gun Machine, while the entire Ohranger vehicle is stored in the Pyramid Carrier Robot, which itself can transform into the King Pyramider robot.

Their enemies in the Machine Empire are led by Emperor Baxhund from Planet Paranoia, who sends his robot minions to seize control of the world, either by monsters of the week or with the aid of his cannon fodder Baro minions.

An important date for the Super Sentai series, marking as it did the 20th anniversary of the first Super Sentai show **GORANGER**, *Ohranger* seemed to derive much of its look and unifying theme from the previous year's Hollywood movie *Stargate*. It was soon picked up for American distribution as the next installment in the **MIGHTY MORPHIN' POWER RANGERS** series, under the title *Power Rangers Zeo*, where the drastic lineup changes forced some major reassignment of roles—the American Power Rangers version tried to maintain a year to year continuity, whereas most Super Sentai shows annually wiped the slate clean.

For the U.S. version, new bad guy Master Vile uses the Orb of Doom to turn back time and return the Power Rangers to their infant forms. Though Billy (David Yost, the last remaining member of the original cast) is able to restore himself to adult form, the rest of the Rangers are forced to go on a quest through time to find the pieces of the restorative Zeo Crystal. In the interim, Billy holds off enemy attack with the help of the Alien Rangers (see the previous year's **KAKURANGER**). Though the Rangers return with success, their base is destroyed during an attack by their archenemies Rito (Kerrigan Mahan) and Goldar (Bob Pappenbrook). They discover that their mentors Zordon and Alpha-5 have retreated to a super-secret underground base beneath the original secret underground base. Meanwhile, Vile, Rita Repulsa, and Lord Zedd (the entire menagerie of the Power Rangers' former archenemies) are attacked by the even more powerful, even more evil nemesis of the Machine Empire and flee to the distant galaxy of M-51. This leaves only the Power Rangers able to defend the Earth once more with the aid of the recovered Zeo Crystal, though most of them are forced to switch roles. Pink Ranger Catherine and Yellow Ranger Tanya retain their positions, while former Red Ranger Rocky (Steve Cardenas) is reassigned as the new Blue Ranger, former Black Ranger Adam (Johnny Yong Bosch) becomes the new Green Ranger, and Tommy (Jason Frank), who had already been the original Green Ranger and White Ranger, adds yet another color to his roster when he becomes the Zeo Red Ranger. Meanwhile, Billy chooses to relinquish his Power Ranger status and remains as their mentor, leaving for good later in the series. The Japanese version's King Ranger, when he eventually appears, is named the Gold Ranger in the U.S. version and is originally the intergalactic traveler Trey (Brad Hawkins). However, he disappears for a while to be replaced by Jason (Austin St. John), the original Red Ranger from the first U.S. series, who performed the Gold Ranger's tasks until Trey returned to take back his powers. Yes, it's *that* confusing.

Based, as usual, "on an idea by Saburō Yade," with music from prolific anime composer Seiji Yokoyama. *Ohranger* was followed in the Super Sentai chronology by **CARRANGER,** which was released in the U.S. as *Power Rangers Turbo.*

OK TO BE ALONE

1992. JPN: *Hitori de Iino.* PRD: N/C. DIR: Hiroshi Yoshino. SCR: Makiko Uchidate. CAST: Yasuko Sawaguchi, Hiroaki Murakami, Rina Katase, Tetsuya Bessho. CHN: NTV. DUR: 45 mins. x 11 eps.; Sat 11 January 1992–21 March 1992. The beautiful Madoka (Sawaguchi) is the center of the men's attention at her office. She eventually wins a mar-

Ohranger (U.S. cast)

riage proposal from the handsome elite salaryman Hoshino (Bessho) and the envy of her female colleagues. Her idyll is interrupted by the arrival of a new boss, Tsumura (Murakami), and the sparks start to fly.

OL POLICE

2000. AKA: *Office Lady Police.* PRD: Atsushi Satō, Kenji Ikeda, Toshio Akabane. DIR: Ryūichi Inomata. SCR: Keiko Nakamura, Yōko Nishimoto. CAST: Anna Umemiya, Rika, MIKI, Miwa Hosoki, Ritsuko Nagai, Shizuna Kasugai, Eriko Miura, Makoto Nonomura, Sayaka Fukuoka, Kinoko Morino. CHN: NTV. DUR: 22 mins. x 12 eps.; Sat 5 August 2000–26 August 2000 (#1); [2nd season broadcast dates unknown] (#2) ; 5 October 2001–26 October 2001 (#3). In a Japan with a rapidly decreasing crime rate, seven pretty policewomen resort to arresting passersby for jaywalking and minor littering offenses. As frustrated singletons, they also berate men who appear to have made the wrong choice in their girlfriends (i.e., anyone but them). One believes she has found the ideal man in the form of a TV advice lawyer and eagerly

allows herself to be seduced at a seedy love hotel, only to be surprised by his jealous wife. Taking the pair hostage at knife-point, the wife demands to be taken to the TV station for an on-air confession. However, as the girls ferry the couple through town in a convoy of police cars, they become affronted by the couple's lack of moral fiber and dump them by the roadside, refusing to press charges against either. Two other officers try another seduction method on a hapless pizza delivery boy, dueling for his affections with opposing little girl and older woman routines. The little girl technique wins, but the man later molests the "winner" at a karaoke bar. The girls discover that he uses his delivery job for "Pizza Hat" *(sic)* to survey the apartments of female customers, returning to sexually assault them once he has confirmed that they are alone. The girls organize a stakeout, much to the anger of their long-suffering lieutenant Yūichi (Nonomura), although he soon has problems of his own when he is framed by a girl who claims he has groped her on the night bus. . . .

An OL is an office lady—a pretty girl hired to do vague secretarial chores,

OL Police

though more likely to spend her time making coffee, doing the photocopying, and "brightening up the office." In a slumping economy less forgiving toward sinecures, the term has become a byword for bimbo. *OL Police*, as the name implies, is a feeble excuse for leggy, shapely Japanese girls to alternate between police uniforms, bikinis, and gym wear—in other words, hypnotically watchable. Screened as part of the late-night *ShinD* show, the script is a laughable mix of ham-fisted comedy business, fatuous moral messages, and airheaded girl talk (see YOU'RE UNDER ARREST), while the production values and continuity suggest the crew were keen to get out of this mess as swiftly as possible. One short conversation begins in the midday sun and ends in evening darkness—a sign of a cripplingly unforgiving shooting schedule. Meanwhile, a swarthy Indian man shuffles sneakily around in the background carrying a suspect package, hinting at a larger, more serious story-arc (and reinforcing the idea that only foreigners commit crimes in Japan). However, the girls are too wrapped up in their love lives to work out who he is. In fact, he disappears after episode two, and nobody mentions him again!

Like the girlie gangsters of TENNEN SHŌJO MANN, *OL Police* was never intended as anything more than tongue-in-cheek frippery, although its moral messages are half-hearted sops to the censor and often come after titillation of questionable tastefulness. There are some moments of genuine silliness, such as when the girls are forced to wait for the WALK sign before they can continue a chase, a couple of knowing pastiches (including the bed scene from *A Clockwork Orange*), and plenty of scenes of them sitting in the Jacuzzi talking about boys. This was clearly enough for some people, and the initial four-episode run was renewed for *OL Police 2* (aka *OL Police vs. Ko-gal Police*), and *OL Police 3* (aka *OL Police 2001*), in which the girls faced competition from cops played by the boy band Orange Prisoners. By the third series, several cast members had left, resulting in some new faces and a reduction of the core cast to six. Compare to SUKEBAN DEKA, BEAUTY SEVEN, and FIVE. Though technically broadcast early on a Saturday morning, most sources refer to it as a Friday night show. Theme: Do As Infinity—"Summer Days."

OL VISUAL BATTLE

2001. JPN: *OL Visual Kei*. PRD: Ikue Yokochi, Masaru Takahashi, Mayumi Akashi. DIR: Jun Akiyama, Naomi Tamura, Ikue Yokochi. SCR: Erika Seki, Natsuko Takahashi, Reiko Yoshida, Hisako Tajima. CAST: Sarina Suzuki, Sakura Uehara, Keiko Tōyama, Takeshi Masu, Ryūji Harada, Mai Hōshō, Jō Odagiri. CHN: Asahi. DUR: 45 mins. x 21 eps.; Fri 8 July 2000–16 September 2000 (#1); 13 April 2001–22 June 2001 (#2).

Manae (Suzuki) works for the Visual Textile fashion company and hides her plain features under a mask of expensive cosmetics. Tiring of making the best of what meager looks she has, she undergoes breast enhancement surgery, hoping that it will help her win her chosen man, work colleague Ryūtarō (Harada). However, her love

rival Sayuri discovers her secret and blackmails her, demanding that she give up Ryūtarō. The vengeful Manae tells her colleagues that *Sayuri* has had plastic surgery, a claim which ironically turns out to be true, as no inch of Sayuri's face and body has been spared the surgeon's knife—compare to PLASTIC BEAUTY.

Learning of the battle between the two girls, their plain colleague Mieko (Tōyama) decides that she too will enter the race for Ryūtarō's attentions, in the style of BEAUTY SEVEN. Though the object of their affections is transferred to the Osaka office, the girls continue to compete for the chance to impress him, reaching ludicrous heights when they enter the All Japan Miss Visual beauty contest. Though Sayuri wins the contest (and by default, the bet over who deserves Ryūtarō), it is Manae who wins his heart . . . temporarily.

In the second series, Ryūtarō returns to Japan after some time in New York to discover that Manae, under the mistaken impression that he likes fat girls, has put on a considerable amount of weight. Ryūtarō introduces the girls to his new significant other, the super-rich Reika (Hōshō), whose arrival on the scene inspires Manae to lose weight and win back "her" man—compare to MIRACLE OF LOVE. While she does so, she seems blind to the attentions of Katohiko (Odagiri), who likes her for who she is, not who she tries to be. Based on the manga by Kumi Kanatsu. Theme: Hiroko Anzai—"Necessary."

OL WAY OF SAVING

2003. JPN: *OL Zenidō*. PRD: Fumio Igarashi, Kazuyuki Morosawa, Yumiko Miwa, Naoki Satō, Yōichi Arishige, Yoshiaki Izumi. DIR: Renpei Tsukamoto, Seiichi Nagumo, Toshiyuki Tokuichi. SCR: Natsuko Takahashi, Hiroko Kanesugi. CAST: Rei Kikukawa, Kazuki Sawamura, Aiko Satō, Hiromi Kitagawa, Hitomi Arisaku, Seiko Takada, Yūko Fujimori. CHN: Asahi. DUR: 45 mins. x ca. 11 eps.; 11 April 2003–.

OL Ayame (Kikukawa) is an inveterate scrimper and saver, troubled by the sudden appearance of her profligate ex-boyfriend Shinichi (Sawamura), who has just found a job at her company. He has soon landed himself in trouble, when he believes a sob story from a salesperson with "a sick mother" and blows 600 thousand yen on an unnecessary English conversation course. Ayame cannot bear to see him waste money in that way and vows to help him avoid payment. Theme: Robbie Williams—"Something Beautiful."

ON A MOONLIT NIGHT

1997. JPN: *Tsuki no Kagayaku Yoru Dakara.* AKA: *Because It Was a Moonlit Night.* PRD: Yoshikazu Kobayashi. DIR: Isamu Nakae, Tōru Hayashi. SCR: Atsuko Hashibe. CAST: Makiko Esumi, Gorō Kishitani, Yoshino Kimura, Tatsuya Kamikawa, Hideo Murota. CHN: Fuji. DUR: 45 mins. x 12 eps.; Tue 1 July 1997–16 September 1997.
Office lady Tokiko (Esumi) accepts a marriage proposal from Tokyo University alumnus Takurō (Kamikawa). However, Takurō is in deep with the local criminal underworld, and, as a ramen-seller's daughter, Tokiko is unprepared for the coming trouble, or indeed for the experience of desiring the same man as her sister. Gorō Kishitani steals the show as a reformed gangster who tries to help out. Theme: Elephant Kashimashi—"Koyoi no Tsuki no Yōni" (Like the Moon Tonight).

ONE FOR ALL *

1999. JPN: *Sanbiki no Goinkyo.* AKA: *Three Retired Samurai.* PRD: Takashi Tōyama. DIR: N/C. SCR: Gorō Shima, Tatsuo Nogami, Kunio Fujii. CAST: Kōtarō Satomi, Tetsurō Tanba, Kei Tani. CHN: Asahi. DUR: 45 mins. x 9 eps.; Thu 21 October 1999–?? December 1999.
Kanbei (Satomi) is a rebel without a cause—an aging samurai determined to avenge the betrayal of his clan, but unable to find a foe he can blame. Sanshirō (Tanba) claims to have once

been the head of a samurai clan, but has been replaced as leader by his son and is no longer welcome there. Genmu (Tani) is another old man, who tells the others that he once enjoyed a flourishing career as the best ninja in Japan. The trio of has-beens decide to travel together to Edo, but soon become penniless and find ways to earn money. They encounter injustices. Whatever their pasts, they decide to live in the present and help common people in need, in a series that unites the old-school samurai stars of DAYS OF GOLD and THE FIRE STILL BURNS with former comedian Tani. A retread of MITO KŌMON with just a dash of *Grumpy Old Men* (1993), and a title deliberately designed to recall the earlier THREE SWORDSMEN, this series was broadcast with English subtitles in the U.S. on KIKU TV.

ONE HOT SUMMER

2001. JPN: *Sekai de Ichiban Atsui Natsu.* AKA: *Hottest Summer in the World.* PRD: Yasuhiro Yamada. DIR: Katsuo Fukuzawa, Susumu Ōoka, Akio Yoshida, Shunichi Hirano. SCR: Hiroshi Tsuzuki, Mutsuki Watanabe, Tomoko Matsuda. CAST: Gorō Kishitani, Emi Wakui, Shunsuke Kazama, Sachie Hara, Shingo Yanagisawa, Takehiko Ono, Moe Yamaguchi, Saori Nakane, Kunie Tanaka. CHN: TBS. DUR: 45 mins. x 10 eps.; Fri 6 July 2001–14 September 2001.
Daisuke (Kishitani) is secretary to powerful parliament member Yūji (Ono) and idolizes his boss as that rarest of creatures, the honest politician. Choosing a job because he wants to help the "little people" like himself, Daisuke hopes to pursue a political career one day but has trouble juggling his work with the time he wants to spend with wife Kimiko (Wakui) and daughter Chiemi (Nakane). However, Daisuke's life is turned upside down when colleague Ryōko (Hara) shows him a memo bearing his signature. Though Daisuke has no memory of it, he has supposedly signed a receipt for 50 million yen from a construction

company—compare to a similar deception in NO CASH. Yūji accuses him of trying to frame him, and Daisuke becomes the subject of intense pursuit by the police and the press.
One Hot Summer is an artful depiction of how swiftly the mighty can fall—compare to the similar jolt dealt to Japanese middle-class life in KIDNAP and OUT. On the run from the police with nowhere left to turn, Daisuke discards his ID badge, gives away his expensive watch, and prepares to throw himself from a bridge, only to be stopped at the last moment by Yabu (FROM THE NORTH's Tanaka). A straight-talking homeless man who regards rock bottom as an excellent place from which things can improve, Yabu helps get Daisuke back on his feet. Returning from hiding, he finds himself an unexpected guest at his own funeral, where his family believes that he has died in a fire. Secretly contacting Chiemi, he arranges a meeting at a nearby park, where he also finds Ryōko, who confesses that it was she who forged his signature. Officially a dead man walking, Daisuke sets out to clear his name, in a political drama loaded with suspense. The script is particularly good at showing the dark world that rests just beneath the surface of everyday life, such as a cop with a secret fetish for voyeurism or a high-level engineer who becomes homeless overnight. Nowhere is this more apparent than during Daisuke's initial flight from his office—thinking himself safe in a taxi, he begins to relax, only to realize that a radio dispatch about a "missing package" is actually a code taxi drivers use to inform the police of dangerous criminals in their cabs. Theme: Color—"Tsubasa Nakutemo" (Even Without Wings).

100 WAYS TO GET YOUR LOVER

1995. JPN: *Koibito o Tsukuru 100 no Hōhō.* PRD: Takayuki Urai. DIR: Ippei Suzuki. SCR: Akira Momoi, Junki Takegami. CAST: Yūko Natori, Taishū Kase, Megumi Kobayashi, Akiko Hinagata, Takashi Kashiwabara, Takeo

百年の物語

The Story of One Century

Nanako Matsushima Hitomi Kuroki
Yuichiro Yamaguchi Pinko Izumi Ryuji Harada
Mitsuko Kusabue Miho Kanno

Beat Takeshi Takao Osawa Hiromi Nagasaku
Shiro Ito Yuko Takeuchi Masami Hisamoto
Takuzo Kadono Takayuki Sorita

Atsuro Watabe Isao Hashizume Shiro Sano

VIDEO CD

© 2000 TBS

100 Years

Chii. CHN: Asahi. DUR: 45 mins. x 6 eps.; Tue 14 February 1995–21 March 1995.
Weather girl Misaki (Natori) is a single mother trying to bring up daughters Mia (Kobayashi) and Hiromi (Hinagata). Since splitting up with her husband Yoshinobu (Chii), she has had 99 disastrous blind dates and is ready to give up on men altogether. However, Mia tries to set her up one last time, with a Mr. Hibino (Kase) whom she has found herself. Premiering on Valentine's Day to catch viewers who couldn't find dates, *100 Ways* was an obvious retread of **101ST PROPOSAL** for a divorcée audience. Based on a manga by Fukami Kobayashi and Yukari Kawachi. Theme: Megumi Kobayashi—"Zap! Zap!"

100 YEARS *
2000. JPN: *Hyakunen no Monogatari.*
AKA: *Story of One Century; 100 Years: Taishō, Shōwa, Heisei.* PRD: Yasuo Yagi.
DIR: Yasuo Inoshita, Kenji Takenoshita, Nobuhiro Doi. SCR: Sugako Hashida, Seita Yamamoto, Kazuhiko Yūkawa.
CAST: Nanako Matsushima, Ryūji Harada, Miho Kanno, Takao Ōsawa,
Atsurō Watabe, Hitomi Kuroki, Yūichirō Yamaguchi, Takeshi Kitano, Hiromi Nagasaku, Isao Hashizume, Shirō Sano, Yūko Takenouchi, Pinko Izumi, Mitsuko Kusabue, Takuzō Kadono, Takayuki Sorita, Robert Hoffman. CHN: TBS. DUR: 90 mins. x 3 eps. (broadcast as 45 mins. x 6 eps. in U.S.); Mon 28 August 2000–30 August 2000.
[*Part One: Tempest of Love and Hate*] In 1920, landowner's daughter Aya (Matsushima) meets Kōta (Harada), a tenant farmer's son who wants to be an artist. He paints her portrait (actually, he daubs a ham-fisted caricature that looks more like Britain's Princess Anne!) but their burgeoning romance is cut short. Her father reveals that her prominent family is not as well-to-do as they once were and that he has been forced to agree to her wedding to Heikichi (Yamaguchi), an uncouth social climber from Kyūshū. The broken-hearted Kōta swears never to paint again, while Aya is thrown into a loveless marriage—Heikichi has a string of mistresses and never comes home, leaving Aya in the thrall of her domineering mother-in-law.
Three years later, Aya is separated from her in-laws by the Great Tokyo Earthquake. Rescued from the ruins by Kōta, now a landowner himself, she spends a blissful few days with him in the countryside before a glowering Heikichi retrieves her. Jealous of Kōta's love, Heikichi rapes Aya, and she eventually finds herself pregnant. Unwilling to bear Heikichi's child, Aya borrows money from Kōta to pay for an abortion. She is arrested by the police and imprisoned.
A year later, she emerges to discover that her own family has disowned her and that Heikichi's mother has died. The destitute Heikichi plans to start a new life in Manchuria, and Aya decides to give him a second chance. Kōta marries someone else and starts a family but is killed during the fighting in Shanghai. Full-scale war breaks out in Asia, leading to the deaths of Heikichi and Aya herself and leaving their two children to face the future as orphans.
[*Part Two: Love Surpasses Sorrow;* aka *When There is Love*] Aya's daughter Junko (Matsushima again) is a school teacher in 1949 Tokyo. Her brother Shinichi is a black marketeer and her class of school children are obsessed

with America as a land of opportunity, contrasted with the poverty of occupied Japan. Accidentally rounded up with prostitutes in the red-light district, Junko appeals for help to Japanese-American officer Kazuo (Ōsawa), who falls in love with her.

Shinichi nurses a deep-seated resentment against the GIs, blaming them for the death of his parents and the rape of his girlfriend Toshiko (Takenouchi). He pulls a knife on an American during a street brawl and is only saved by the timely arrival of Kazuo, though Shinichi continues to regard Kazuo as a foreign invader. Meanwhile, Junko's malaria-ridden uncle Kōsaku (Kitano) returns from an American internment camp, unsure of his place in his defeated homeland. Junko's friend Yoshie, who is seeing a GI called Steve (Hoffman), conspires to set her up with Kazuo but Shinichi remains opposed. In search of more cash, Shinichi takes to selling black market goods without paying a cut to his fellow gang members, and Kōsaku is killed trying to protect him. Kazuo dies fighting in the Korean War, and nine months later, Junko gives birth to his daughter Kazuko.

[*Part Three: Only Love*] In the year 2000, Junko's *grand*daughter Chiyo (Matsushima again) attends her funeral to thank her for raising her after she was abandoned by Kazuko. She also announces that she is pregnant, by a boyfriend with whom she does not want to associate. To secure a legal abortion, she press-gangs fugitive criminal Shinji (Watabe) into posing as the child's father. Little does she know that they have met at the site of the fateful first encounter between their respective great-grandparents, Aya and Kōta—a fact confirmed when Shinji unveils Kōta's much-traveled portrait of Aya.

Discovering that her mother is dying, Chiyo convinces Shinji to fly with her to America and pose as her husband again. Robbed by a truck driver outside Las Vegas, the pair bet the last of their money on a roulette game.

Winning enough to finish their journey, they head for Kazuko's home in Las Olivos, where Chiyo discovers that her mother is dead, but that she had always loved Chiyo (apparently). The pair prepare to return to Japan once more but Shinji is arrested at the airport. Six months later, he is released from prison and takes a job as a welder, only to be surprised at work by Junko, who is pregnant with his child . . . a child who will be born in 2001.

Unsurprisingly for a series that crams an entire century into just three movie-length episodes, *100 Years* falls short of its grandiose ambitions—compare to **OSHIN**, which has ten times the running time. It plays straight to the melodrama audience TBS hopes to win from NHK, delineating its men as sensitive love interests or moustache-twirling bad guys, while the women parade in a succession of nice frocks, occasionally even entering a room merely to exit and change clothes.

The Television magazine, organizers of Japan's "TV Academy Awards," gave a special prize to *100 Years* in the year of its release, perhaps more to honor the show's aims than its execution. *100 Years* could have been a monster miniseries with truly international appeal, but the result looks ironically like the U.K. broadcast of **INOCHI: LIFE**, which genuinely *was* a giant saga unceremoniously hacked into just a couple of hours. *100 Years* shares the whistle-stop pace of *Inochi*, hastily glossing entire decades with fleeting voice-overs. It's possible to discern discarded plot threads—Kazuo's tales of American internment camps "in the desert" seem to set up a visit by his granddaughter Chiyo that never comes, while Kazuko's life story, swept away in a couple of lines, could have been an entire extra chapter.

The central premise is a clever one, lifted from Yukio Mishima's novel *The Sea of Fertility,* which similarly chronicled an entire era through a recurring character. But although the theme of *100 Years,* regularly reiterated for the hard-of-thinking, is that women have

come a long way in the troubled 20th century, the lumpen script makes many characters seem to be irredeemably passive victims. Aya is raped by her husband, then sent to prison for vengefully aborting her child, and yet she returns dewy-eyed to Heikichi after he mutters a few half-hearted apologies—infuriatingly, he has even *agreed* to a divorce but she still accompanies him to Manchuria. This is supposedly a proud moment in women's rights because she has *decided* to go of her own free will, though she later mumbles something self-absorbed about "fate."

Though the superior 1940s sequence has time to discuss the U.S. internment camps and rapist GIs, World War II takes place conveniently off-stage—you'd be forgiven for thinking that "the war" comprised a surprise invasion of foul-mouthed, lecherous, drunken American thugs, who arrived in Japan and stole the population's food supply. The final episode presents America as a Babylon of gluttony, violence, and porn—though clearly not so awful as to scare off the actors and crew, who blew a fair proportion of the budget on filming the climactic road trip. Nevertheless, Shinji and Chiyo are a remarkably dim pair of tourists, who manage to get robbed in the middle of the Nevada desert—both contract diarrhea from suspect American prawns and are too busy squatting amid the cacti to notice that someone has driven out of nowhere and stolen their car.

The most surprising thing about the show's portrayal of the 20th century is how little seems to have changed—haircuts may vary and technology may improve, but a feminist audience would be no less aghast at Chiyo's 21st-century plight as they would be at Aya's a century earlier. Despite these flaws, or perhaps even because of them, *100 Years* is a fascinating document—its platitudes and blind spots speak volumes about what producers think a modern Japanese audience wants. For Western viewers, however, it is difficult to feel too much sympathy for five generations whose defining attributes seem to be a blinkered ignorance of the outside world and a complete inability to use contraception. Note also that, perhaps without the knowledge of the Japanese crew, the American costars use a stream of entertainingly bad language, making this the only Japanese drama we have seen that would require a parental warning in the U.S. Final insult is added to injury by the theme song, which is an ear-splittingly awful anthem by Nana Mouskouri. Shown subtitled in the U.S. on KIKU TV and other cable channels, where the local audience was not amused by the smell of burning martyr. Compare to **PEARL BEAUTY**.

101ST PROPOSAL

1991. JPN: *101-kaime no Propose*. PRD: Tōru Ōta. DIR: Michio Mitsuno, Eriko Ishizaka, Tōru Hayashi. SCR: Shinji Nojima. CAST: Atsuko Asano, Tetsuya Takeda, Yōsuke Eguchi, Ritsuko Tanaka, Yuriko Ishida, Hatsunori Hasegawa, Mika Iwata, Miyoko Asada. CHN: Fuji. DUR: 45 mins. x 12 eps.; Mon 1 July 1991–16 September 1991.

Kaoru (Asano) is a 30-year-old cellist, who still grieves over the death three years earlier of her fiancé Makabe. Her parents push her back into the social scene, arranging an *omiai* marriage meeting with Tatsurō (Takeda), a dull middle-aged man who has already been rejected by 99 other prospective brides. Turned down by Kaoru, Tatsurō refuses to give up and enlists the help of his brother Junpei (Eguchi) and Kaoru's sister Chie (Tanaka). Kaoru eventually accepts his proposal, only to find her decision called into doubt when she meets Tatsurō's new boss Fujii (Hasegawa), who is the spitting image of the dead Makabe. When Tatsurō sees Fujii proposing to Kaoru, he quits his job in shock, and an apologetic Kaoru returns his engagement ring.

Kaoru's best friend Momoko (Asada) encourages Tatsurō to try one more time. He studies to be a lawyer in the hope of winning her back and asks her to come to the church on the day the exam results are due. If he passes,

he promises to leave the engagement ring for her at the church; if he fails, he will never bother her again.

Kaoru is torn between the two men and also by the offer of a transfer to Germany. She asks Fujii what he will think of her in 50 years. Fujii replies simply that they are in love now and that the future is not important. However, Kaoru reveals that Makabe's answer to the same question was that he would still love her after 50 years—the incident reminds her that Fujii is only a lookalike of her beloved Makabe.

The day of the exam, she rushes to the church after a concert, only to find the empty ring box—Tatsurō has thrown the ring into the sea. Finding Tatsurō at the building site where he works, Kaoru asks *him* to marry her and the lovers seal their promise amid the bolts and rivets, with a ring fashioned from a spare nut.

Another early work by **LIPSTICK**'s Shinji Nojima, *101st Proposal* combined with the author's own **LOVE IS A WONDERFUL THING** and the same season's **TOKYO LOVE STORY** to create a heavy influence on 1990s romantic drama. With hindsight, the three dramas are regarded as the pinnacle of "pure love" trendy dramas. The show also made the unconventional casting choice of Tetsuya Takeda as a romantic lead, which proved to be an unexpected success. The actor reputedly improvised many of his scenes, suffusing his role with the homespun charm of his better-known **KINPACHI SENSEI**. The drama contains many "classic" scenes that are still often imitated, including a reconciliation in the rain where the couple share an umbrella—in Japan, a graffito of two names under an umbrella is the symbol of true love. It also features a faint premonition of writer Nojima's later dark side. Told of Kaoru's fear of losing another loved one, Tatsurō dashes in front of an oncoming truck, yelling "*I won't die. I won't die, because I love you.*" The older, sneakier Nojima would have probably let the truck hit him! *101st Proposal*'s

ratings peaked with the final episode's 36.7%, which was in excess even of the heights enjoyed by its chief rival **TOKYO LOVE STORY**. The theme song "Say Yes," by Chage and Aska, enjoyed a high chart success as a result of its appearance in the show, selling three million copies. The *Tree* album on which it later appeared kept both Michael Jackson and Madonna away from the number one spot on the Japanese charts.

ONE MORE KISS

2001. JPN: *Mō Ichido Kiss*. PRD: Kazuki Nakayama. DIR: Ryōko Hoshida, Shigeru Miki. SCR: Mika Umeda. CAST: Yōsuke Kubozuka, Yoon Son-Ha, Sachiko Kokubu, Erika Oda, Shūji Kashiwabara, Mitsunori Isaki, Nanae Akasaka, Tomomi Satō, Masaya Katō. CHN: NHK. DUR: 45 mins. x 10 eps.; Tue 9 January 2001–13 March 2001.

Ayumu (Kubozuka) is the privileged child of well-to-do parents, studying classical music at an elite academy and occasionally slumming it as the vocalist and guitar player in his buddies' rock band. When Ayumu's girlfriend Miwa (Kokubu) is harassed by a teacher, Ayumu forcefully defends her, leading to disciplinary action that places his school career in jeopardy. Trying to forget about the hazards ahead, he travels with his band to Seoul, where they play a set as part of an international youth festival. Backstage, he meets Sonya (Yoon), a Korean pop idol who likes the way he plays but is shocked to hear that he does not write his own songs.

Back in Tokyo, Ayumu loses his place at university and his girlfriend in swift succession, and is devastated by the death of one of his rock heroes—a member of the band "J" whose songs he has always admired. As he contemplates throwing himself from a footbridge, he sees Sonya getting out of a car and rushes over to return a bracelet she dropped in Seoul. Sonya, however, claims that her name is "Reika"—she is in Tokyo incognito at the behest of her agent. Ayumu hands her his phone number and soon receives a call from the pop idol, who is stuck in her hotel room with nothing to do. . . .

A critique of fame in the style of STAR STRUCK, *OMK* was originally trialed as *Seoul Love Story*, a working title that now seems more appropriate for FRIENDS (2), the suspiciously similar vehicle for Yoon's FIGHTING GIRL costar Kyōko Fukada, which followed a year later on TBS. Mika Umeda's script cleverly casts the demure Yoon as a fan bait Rapunzel figure, unable to enjoy life like a "normal" teenager—she travels the world, only to hide from the paparazzi in hotel rooms. The boundary between actress and character is blurred by Reika's Korean name—she is introduced as Yan Sonya, which seems perilously close to the name of the actress who plays her. All she needs, of course, is a good-hearted Joe Average to break the spell, though with his parents' money and his own musical talents, Ayumu is destined to be revealed as a Prince Charming soon enough.

Buried beneath the surface is an intriguing subplot about the nature of creativity. Sonya dismisses Ayumu for copying other people's songs, though as he comes to realize, if he were to follow his old dream of becoming a classical musician, he would be forced to play nothing *but* cover versions. Theme: Steve Barakat—"Love Affair."

ONE SUMMER'S LOVE LETTER

1995. JPN: *Hito Natsu no Love Letter*. PRD: Toshihiro Iijima. DIR: Takamichi Yamada. SCR: Masao Yajima. CAST: Yuki Matsushita, Masaki Kanda, Hitomi Kuroki, Katsunori Takahashi, Yōko Nogiwa. CHN: TBS. DUR: 45 mins. x 12 eps.; Thu 6 June 1995–21 September 1995.

After five years of marriage to biotechnician Kōichi (Kanda), Aki (Matsushita) has a four-year-old daughter and a happy life. That is, until one summer afternoon, when she rushes into an apparently deserted building to take shelter from a rainstorm. There, she meets Rei (Takahashi), with whom

she begins a torrid affair. As with the later PARFUM DE LA JALOUSIE, the change in their behavior with their respective spouses eventually leads their jilted partners to seek consolation in each other's arms as well. Theme: Miho Nakayama—"Heart to Heart."

1001 NIGHTMARES

1991. JPN: *Kaiki Senya Ichiya Monogatari*. PRD: Kenji Nagai, Hiroshi Abe, Kentarō Takahashi. DIR: Mitsunori Hattori, Tsugumi Kitaura, Teruyoshi Ishii, Shinichi Kamisawa, Shingo Kazami, Tomoyuki Imai. SCR: Keiki Nagasawa, Rumiko Asao, Akira Ishikawa, Tetsushi Moriyasu. CAST: Kimiko Amari, Toshihiro Takahashi, Sachiko Takato, Yūko Tsuburaya, Ryōsuke Suzuki. CHN: TBS. DUR: 15 mins. x 21 eps.; Sat 27 April 1991–14 September 1991.

Broadcast as part of the late-night Saturday show *Mascot!*, where it was forced to share the schedules with amateur shorts and members of the public performing party-pieces, *1001 Nightmares* was a series of mini-chillers in the style of THURSDAY GHOST STORY, featuring different guest stars each week. Reacting to the confidence and materialism of the bubble economy of the late 1980s, the show emphasized that the human capacity for terror and evil remained the same as it ever was, keeping the Japanese thriller genre alive ready for the next generation of creators, who would follow with NIGHT HEAD and RING. Stories included a boy possessed by a parasite from hell, a bride pursued by a vengeful doll, and a father stalked by the son he abandoned.

ONE-WAY TICKET TO LOVE

1997. JPN: *Koi no Katamichi Kippu*. PRD: Masaru Kamikura. DIR: Ryūichi Inomata, Futoshi Ōhira. SCR: Yuki Shimizu, Toshiya Itō. CAST: Makiko Esumi, Gorō Inagaki, Reiko Takashima, Takashi Naitō. CHN: NTV. DUR: 45 mins. x 10 eps.; Wed 15 October 1997–17 December 1997.

Narumi (Esumi) returns to Japan after

One More Kiss

ten years in Rio de Janeiro to discover a lot has changed. Her plane lands at a different airport, her guardian's baby sister is now all grown-up, and Narumi's own twin sister Harumi (Esumi again) has run away to Hokkaidō with her fiancé. She goes looking for the missing couple but instead finds Shinichi (Inagaki), a hapless boy who mistakes her for Harumi, on whom he has a crush. Her legal guardian Tatsuya (Naitō) offers her a place to stay in Tokyo, but she must fight off the enmity of Maiko, a girl who is convinced that Shinichi belongs to her and that Narumi/Harumi is determined to steal him away. Compare to similar double trouble in THE BRIDE IS SIXTEEN. Theme: Noriyuki Makihara—"Montage."

ONIHEI THE INVESTIGATOR

1969. JPN: *Onihei Hankachō*. PRD: N/C. DIR: Yoshiki Onoda, Masahiro Takase, Tokuzō Tanaka, Akira Inoue, Hitoshi Ōzu, Shōwa Ōta. SCR: Masato Ide. CAST: Kichiemon Nakamura, Yumi Takigawa, Toshinori Omi, Nekohachi Edoya, Meiko Kaji, Keizō Kanie (#4). CHN: Fuji. DUR: 45 mins. x 91 eps.; 7 October 1969–30 March 1972 (#1); 2 April 1975–25 September 1975 (#2); 1

Onihei the Investigator

April 1980–12 October 1982 (#3); 12 July 1989–2 February 1990 (#4); 3 October 1990–27 March 1991 (#5); 20 November 1991–13 May 1992 (#6); 2 December 1992–12 May 1993 (#7); 9 March 1994–13 July 1994 (#8); 19 July 1995–1 November 1995 (#9); 21 August 1996–4 September 1996 (#10); 16 April 1997–16 July 1997 (#11); 15 April 1998–10 June 1998 (#12); 17 April 2001–22 May 2001 (#13).

Heizō Hasegawa, aka Onihei (Devil Heizō), is the head of a special police force in the Edo period, charged with bringing violent robbers to justice. However, his job is made harder by a script that insists on portraying his quarries as three-dimensional characters with backstories, motivations, and troubles of their own, while he is often depicted as a sad individual, lacking the brightness and dynamism of a traditional hero. Instead of the simple evildoers deserving of a roadside death found in most period dramas, *Onihei*'s criminals often occupy a gray area—as the original novel by Shōtarō Ikegami says: "*People have both sides, good and evil.*" *Onihei*'s production values add to its charm, with an exacting recreation of Edo (Tokyo) as "the Venice of the East."

This hugely popular drama has been remade many times—Kōshirō Matsumoto played the main character from 1969–72, then Tetsurō Tanba in 1975, Kinnosuke Yorozuya from 1980–82, until Kichiemon Nakamura took over in 1990. The story was also adapted into a manga form by *Golgo 13*'s Takao Saitō in 1993. Though the twelfth season in 1998 was supposed to be the last one, "viewer requests" led to a final coda in the form of the 2001 season, based on five previously undramatized stories by original creator Shōtarō Ikenami, who also wrote LIVING BY THE SWORD.

ONLY YOU

1996. JPN: *Only You Aisarete*. AKA: *Only You Could Love Me*. PRD: Kazuo Yamamoto. DIR: Masahiro Kunimoto. SCR: Yumiko Kamiyama. CAST: Takao Ōsawa, Kyōka Suzuki, Izumi Inamori, Harumi Inoue, Gamon Kaai, Hinano Yoshikawa, Takeshi Ihara. CHN: Yomiuri. DUR: 45 mins. x 10 eps.; Mon 8 January 1996–11 March 1996. Beautiful model Chihiro (Suzuki) begins dating wealthy restaurateur Saitō (Ihara), but her appearances at his Saison bistro cause strife in the kitchen. Sumio (Ōsawa) is a mentally retarded man who has found a simple job as a dishwasher at the restaurant, but falls instantly in love with the unattainable Chihiro. *The Hunchback of Notre Dame* retold for a modern audience—compare to FLOWERS FOR ALGERNON. Theme: Primal—"Original Love."

ONLY YOU CAN'T SEE IT

1992. JPN: *Anata Dake Mienai*. PRD: Yasuyuki Kusuda. DIR: Yasuyuki Kusuda. SCR: Masahiro Yoshimoto. CAST: Hiroshi Mikami, Kyōko Koizumi, Masahiro Motoki, Haruko Sagara, Emi Shindō, Miho Takagi. CHN: Fuji. DUR: 45 mins. x 11 eps.; Mon 13 January 1992–23 March 1992.

Megumi (Koizumi) is given the diary of deceased millionaire Kōtarō Mamiya, which reveals that her "sister" Maiko (Takagi) is really his illegitimate daughter and entitled to a share of his inheritance. Posing as her sister, she visits Kōtarō's widow Hidemi (Shindō), who offers her 50 million yen to disappear and avoid causing the family embarrassment. However, soon after Megumi leaves, Hidemi orders her lawyer Kazuma (Mikami) to retrieve both the check and the incriminating diary.

Kazuma abducts the *real* Maiko, and while Megumi frets about her sister's whereabouts, she becomes the subject of a police investigation herself. By a remarkably unfortunate coincidence, Maiko has been accused of embezzling money from her company, and by recently banking a check for the missing amount (50 million yen), Megumi has just made herself the prime suspect.

Believing herself deserted by her boyfriend Mitsuhiko (Motoki), an intern at a psychiatric ward, Megumi returns to her apartment, where she is attacked by Kazuma. She regains consciousness to find herself tended to by the kindly Junpei (Mikami again). Falling for him, she dumps Mitsuhiko, who tells her that "Junpei" is a patient in the psychiatric ward and in need of treatment.

In fact, Mitsuhiko is lying and only wants Junpei to be admitted to the hospital so that he can hypnotize him into staying away from Megumi. He summons him for treatment, but discovers under hypnosis that Junpei genuinely *does* suffer from multiple personality disorder—he has a violent persona called Kazuma . . . .

Another drama with a twist from I'LL NEVER LOVE AGAIN creators Kusuda and Yoshimoto, *Only You Can't See It* was planned as the ultimate long-distance romance, with its lovers separated not by distance, but by mental illness. Compare to FACE: UNKNOWN LOVER and THE MISFITS. Peak rating: 16.3%. Theme: Date of Birth—"You're My Secret."

ŌOKA ECHIZEN

1970. PRD: Minoru Itsumi, Shunichi Nishimura, Michio Igarashi. DIR: N/C.

SCR: N/C. CAST: Gō Katō, Chiezō Kataoka, Muga Takewaki, Takashi Yamaguchi, Masayo Utsunomiya, Haruko Katō, Eiko Takehara, Kōtarō Satomi. CHN: TBS. DUR: 45 mins. x 398 eps.; 16 March 1970–21 September 1970 (#1); 17 May 1971–22 November 1971 (#2); 12 June 1972–15 January 1973 (#3); 7 October 1974–24 March 1975 (#4); 6 February 1978–31 July 1978 (#5); 8 March 1982–11 October 1982 (#6); 18 April 1983–24 October 1983 (#7); 16 July 1984–21 January 1985 (#8); 28 October 1985–21 April 1986 (#9); 29 February 1988–5 September 1988 (#10); 23 April 1990–15 October 1990 (#11); 14 October 1991–30 March 1992 (#12); 16 November 1992–10 May 1993 (#13); 17 June 1996–2 December 1996 (#14); 24 August 1998–15 March 1999 (#15).

Ōoka Echizen no Kami Tadasuke (Katō) is a town magistrate based in Edo, appointed by Shogun YOSHIMUNE in 1717 (the very first episode). Often preferring to wander among commoners in disguise, he actively keeps the peace in Edo and helps clear corruption out of local politics. From the second season, Tadasuke concentrates on defending the oppressed in unfair cases, and the third introduces troubles in his personal life, such as his relationship with his son. Like his fellow magistrate TOYAMA NO KIN-SAN, Tadasuke was a real historical figure (1677–1752), a judge in the Tokugawa period who was eventually awarded with a small hereditary domain by the grateful Shogun. His long-running TV adventures have alternated in the same slot with the similar MITO KŌMON for 30 years, with lead actor Gō Katō aging along with the character he plays—by this point in the original Tadasuke's life, the Shogun had died of old age! Though the episodes remain a formulaic blend of crime and punishment, they retain a peculiarly Japanese melancholy that has kept them popular with the local audience, though often regarded by foreign viewers as one step beyond a Martian soap opera in their alien quali-

Operation Mystery

ties. In one classic episode in the 13th season, a sick mother discovers that her husband is a suspected murderer. Meanwhile, her young son is selling splinters of wood as pills in a futile attempt to make some more money for his mother—in other words, he is a little match boy. Learning that Tadasuke is looking for her, the mother decides to commit suicide, and her loyal son announces that he will also kill himself. Instead of admonishing him for throwing away his life, the Japanese mother is exceedingly proud and suggests that they should die together. Although the viewers probably know how this ends before the opening credits have even finished rolling, such simple stories have retained audience attention for three decades. Peak rating: 33.2% (in 1970).

OPERATION MYSTERY
1968. JPN: *Kaiki Daisakusen*. PRD:

Yasushi Morita, Kōichi Noguchi. DIR: Toshihiro Iijima, Hajime Tsuburaya, Akio Sanesōji, Toshitsugu Suzuki, Shigeo Nakagi, Suguru Nagano. SCR: Shōzō Uehara, Tetsuo Kinjō, Mamoru Sasaki, Bunzō Wakatsuki, Jun Fukuda, Shinichi Ichikawa. CAST: Homare Katsuro, Shin Kishida, Shōji Matsuyama, Yasumi Hara, Reiko Kobashi, Akiji Kobayashi. CHN: TBS. DUR: 25 mins. x 26 eps.; Sun 15 September 1968–9 March 1969. In search of a new direction after the first ULTRAMAN series, Tsuburaya Productions commissioned a mystery drama focusing on "criminals who use science for nefarious purposes and the just people who protect science." The Science Research Institute (SRI) is a public-private partnership, whose members include the hotheaded athlete Kyōsuke Misawa (Katsuro) and cool intellectual Shirō Maki (Kishida). They are aided by their assistant

Hiroshi (Matsuyama) and token female secretary Saori (Kobashi).

The SRI missions amount to an intriguing collection of sci-fi ideas. In the first, *The Man Who Walks through Walls*, their quarry is a thief who has the ability to fade out of sight. In fact, he is found not to walk through walls at all, but instead owns a suit of retro-reflective material that allows him to apparently disappear—compare to the later "thermoptic camouflage" of *Ghost in the Shell* (*AE). Other innovative ideas include inspired murder mysteries in the style of *Sure Death*, such as *Killer Moth*, in which the titular insect's wings are daubed with the typhoid bacillus as part of a deadly conflict between the executives of two rival car corporations. In *Terror Telephone*, hypersonic waves are sent down a phone line to induce spontaneous human combustion in whoever picks up the receiver.

The SRI also face up to modern ills, such as the mistreatment of the elderly in *Blue Blooded Woman* and increased congestion on Japanese roads in *Endless Speeding*. With an eye on older audiences, *OM* concentrated not on the simple good versus evil of most children's dramas, but on the motivations of its wrongdoers. In *Lullaby of Death*, a boy inadvertently kills someone in the course of a series of experiments designed to save the life of his sister, who is dying from an incurable disease. In the penultimate episode, *Kyoto For Sale*, Maku falls in love with a girl called Miyako, who loves statues of Buddha. She is collecting signatures to "buy" Japan's old capital of Kyoto, in order to save its old-time streets from the advance of modernity. Though Maki sympathizes with Miyako (whose very name is a reference to *miyako*—the old term for capital city), he sees her fitting a teleportation device onto a statue and realizes that it is she who is responsible for a number of mysterious thefts.

At the close of the 1960s, when the early promise of science was eclipsed by paranoia about its price in pollution and rapid change, *OM*'s innovative and original scripts made it a masterpiece of early Japanese sci-fi. *OM*'s distant modern descendants include **NIGHT HEAD** and **UNSOLVED CASES**.

OR FOREVER HOLD HIS PEACE
1992. JPN: *Suteki ni Damashite*. PRD: N/C. DIR: Hiroshi Akabane, Toyohiko Wada. SCR: Yūki Shimizu. CAST: Masahiro Takashima, Hironobu Nomura, Kyōka Suzuki, Sayuri Kokushō. CHN: NTV. DUR: 45 mins. x 11 eps.; Wed 15 April 1992–24 June 1992.

Tetsuya (Takashima) and Kentarō (Nomura) are matrimonial swindlers, seducing gullible women and then absconding with their fortunes. After serving several years in jail, Tetsuya is released to discover that Kentarō has settled down with Akiko (Kokushō), the sassy owner of a pancake shop. While Tetsuya tries to determine whether Kentarō has really given up on his old career, Akiko begins to suspect the men's motives, leading to a series of misunderstandings and pre-emptive acts of revenge—compare to **PARFUM DE LA JALOUSIE**.

OSHIN
1983. PRD: Yukiko Okamoto. DIR: Hiroyuki Okada. SCR: Sugako Hashida. CAST: Ayako Kobayashi, Yūko Tanaka, Nobuko Otowa. CHN: NHK. DUR: 15 mins. x ca. 300 eps.; Mon 4 April 1983–31 March 1984.

Born in 1900, peasant girl Oshin (Kobayashi) is sent out at an early age to be a domestic servant. She soon demonstrates a sound business sense by applying what she has learned from the wealthy traders of the area, but is treated as a slave by a timber merchant and escapes to find employment at a rice shop. Accused of theft, she is rescued by a deserting soldier and (now played by Tanaka) eventually married off to a man from the notoriously chauvinist southern island of Kyūshū. Abused by her mother-in-law and weakened by the loss of a child, she also endures the slow decline and eventual suicide of her husband, who is tortured by memories of his collaboration in Japan's wartime military endeavors. Eventually, like the heroine of the later **INOCHI: LIFE**, Oshin eventually finds success and happiness toward the end of the reign of Hirohito, the third Emperor whose rule she has witnessed.

Oshin was the 31st of the NHK Serial TV Novels that stretched back to *My Daughter and I* (see Introduction), and commissioned as a celebration of the channel's 30th broadcast anniversary. Marshalling all the conventions of women's drama into one sprawling tale of almost a century of bad luck, abuse, in-law appeasement, loss, and misery, its peak rating of 62.9% made it the most popular drama in Japanese TV history.

Oshin also proved popular abroad, broadcast in 49 other countries, including Australia on SBS. The series exists in an animated remake (*AE) that concentrates on the early episodes featuring the child actress Kobayashi, who also provided the voice of the cartoon version. *Oshin* is much imitated in modern Japanese women's dramas, most recently in the TBS series **100 YEARS**. Some way into the filming of the series, a week's delay in filming was caused by the illness of lead actress Tanaka. NHK worked around the problem by taking the show off-air for a week, and replacing it with the short documentary series *Another Oshin*, introducing the area where the series was shot and tips such as recipes from the series for such delicacies as radish rice.

OTAMA AND KŌZŌ: A MARRIED COUPLE
1994. JPN: *Otama, Kōzō Fūfu Desu*. PRD: Shunji Ikehata. DIR: Teruhiko Kuze. SCR: Toshiharu Matsubara, Ryūji Mizutani. CAST: Kaoru Yachigusa, Kōichi Hamada, Masahiro Motoki. CHN: Yomiuri. DUR: 45 mins. x 12 eps.; Thu 7 July 1994–22 September 1994.

Kōzō (Hamada) is a former sumo wrestler, now the owner of a restaurant that serves the distinctive sumo wrestler meals known as *chanko*. The day before his daughter's wedding, he announces his intention to marry Otama (Yachigusa), a masseuse. The children are dead set against the idea, but Otama moves in anyway.

OTHER SIDE OF MIDNIGHT

1992. JPN: *Mayonaka wa Betsu no Kao.* PRD: N/C. DIR: Takemitsu Satō. SCR: Hiroshi Sotoyama. CAST: Hitomi Kuroki, Kōichi Iwaki, Isako Washio, Hiroshi Fuse. CHN: Asahi. DUR: 45 mins. x 10 eps.; Thu 9 January 1992–12 March 1992.

Noe (Kuroki) falls in love with Kanai (Iwaki) and agrees to marry him. However, soon after she has pledged herself to him, he disappears on a Malaysian business trip. The shocked Noe attempts suicide but eventually recovers. Eight years later, when she discovers that the callous Kanai is still alive, she plots an elaborate scheme of revenge, in this adaptation of Sidney Sheldon's best-selling novel.

The story was remade in 2002 by NHK, in a new version featuring a script by long-time *taiga* scenarist James Miki and music by Yōko Kanno. Miki was quoted as saying that the script was an ideal study of the "impact of passion," perhaps explaining why it has twice attracted the attentions of Japanese producers. Compare to PARFUM DE LA JALOUSIE, MIRACLE OF LOVE, and Sheldon's own NOTHING LASTS FOREVER.

O-TYPE ARIES

1994. JPN: *Ore wa O gata Ohitsuji za.* PRD: Yūko Hazeyama. DIR: Hiroshi Yoshino. SCR: Mieko Osanai. CAST: Tetsuya Takeda, Ippachi Kimura, Nene Ōtsuka, Tsurutarō Kataoka, Ayumi Ishida. CHN: NTV. DUR: 45 mins. x 9 eps.; Sat 22 October 1994–17 December 1994.

Takio (Takeda) is the production development chief of a large toy company, who always discusses his dreams with the toy company owner Shinozaki (Shirō Itō). One day, the director Satō (Kataoka) of Takio's company decides to cease the contract with Shinozaki

and have the toys made abroad. Theme: Kōji Tamaki—"Love Song."

OUR JOURNEY

1975. JPN: *Oretachi no Tabi.* PRD: Yoshio Nakamura, Shinkichi Okada, Daisuke Kadoya. DIR: Kōsei Saitō. SCR: Toshio Kamata. CAST: Masatoshi Nakamura, Masaaki Tsusaka (now Taisaku Akino), Ken Tanaka, Kaoru Yachigusa, Nana Okada. CHN: NTV. DUR: 45 mins. x 46 eps.; Sun 5 October 1975–10 October 1976.

Hotheaded Kasuke (Nakamura), wealthy but troubled Omeda (Tanaka), and laggard Guzuroku (Tsusaka) are in their final year at university. Refusing to be ordinary salarymen, they drop out to start their own handyman business, leading to a series which adequately portrayed the modern generation's lack of interest in following the traditional Japanese post-war work ethic. In opposition to youth dramas like ZEALOUS TIMES, which depict all goals as within reach so long as the protagonist gives it his all, *OJ* preferred to concentrate on harsh reality. Consequently, its characters soon decided that it was better to enjoy the present, instead of gambling for vague success in an unpredictable future by working hard. The series was originally planned for a six-month run, but its initial popularity led to a run that lasted almost a year. The cast returned in two feature-length specials in 1985: *Restart after Ten Years* (1985) and *Choice after Twenty Years* (1995). The series was remade as a ten-episode drama in July 1999, starring Tsuyoshi Morita, Ken Miyake, and Junichi Okada (all from V6).

OUR OLÉ!

1993. JPN: *Oretachi no Olé!* PRD: N/C. DIR: Tōru Kawashima. SCR: Yū Yoshimura, Takeo Kasai. CAST: Yasufumi Terawaki, Naomi Nishida, Kitarō. CHN: Mainichi. DUR: 45 mins. x 11 eps.; Thu 14 October 1993–23 December 1993.

Osamu (Gitan Ōtsuru) is a soccer player with the Brazilian national team. He

┌─────────────────────────────┐
│ **MT'S TOP TEN ACTRESSES** │
│ 1 ▪ Shima Iwashita   │
│ 2 ▪ Takako Tokiwa   │
│ 3 ▪ Shinobu Ōtake   │
│ 4 ▪ Yōko Nogiwa   │
│ 5 ▪ Miki Nakatani   │
│ 6 ▪ Tomoko Nakajima   │
│ 7 ▪ Sachiko Sakurai   │
│ 8 ▪ Shigeru Muroi   │
│ 9 ▪ Tomoko Yamaguchi   │
│ 10 ▪ Atsuko Asano   │
└─────────────────────────────┘

and tour guide Shimada (Terawaki) make extra money by moonlighting as ticket touts. One day, the head of a small Japanese village visits Brazil, leading Osamu and Shimada to suggest he form a village soccer team. This soccer drama capitalized on a renewed interest in soccer in Japan, which erupted with the formation of the "J-League" professional soccer organization in May 1993. From an obscure late-night curio (see FLY! YOUTHS), soccer became one of the highest-rated commodities on Japanese TV, with a Japan-Iraq qualifier on 28 October 1993 snagging a rating of 48%, in excess of all but the most historically significant drama serials. Although *Our Olé* rode this wave of interest, the popularity of soccer continued to grow in the years that led to the 2002 World Cup—see FRIENDS (2). Theme: Hideaki Tokunaga—"Boku no Soba ni" (By My Side).

OUT

1999. JPN: *Out: Tsumatachi no Hanzai.* AKA: *Out: Crimes of the Housewives.* PRD: Kazuo Kawakami, Reiko Ishizaka. DIR: Makoto Hirano, Yoshiko Hoshida. SCR: Yōichi Maekawa. CAST: Misako Tanaka, Naoko Iijima, Eriko Watanabe, Sachie Hara, Seiko Takada, Nasubi, Erika Oda, Shigeki Hosoda, Hideaki Itō, Yasunori Danta, Shō Aikawa, Akira Enomoto. CHN: Fuji. DUR: 45 mins. x 11 eps.; Tue 12 October 1999–21 December 1999.

Tokyo housewife Masako (Tanaka) has

lost her office job and now works the night shift at a food processing plant, where she has already gained the unwelcome attentions of lovelorn Brazilian immigrant boy Kazuo (Itō). Her son Nobuki is on probation after a drugs related offense, while her husband has become increasingly withdrawn—he has also lost his job but has yet to admit it. Masako's workmates at the factory are similarly luckless—Kumiko (Takada) is deeply in debt with *yakuza* loan shark Akira (Aikawa), while widow Yoshie (Watanabe) has a disabled mother-in-law, a freeloading sister, *and* an ungrateful daughter. Their friend Yayoi (Hara) has the worst problems of all—her husband Kenji (Danta) has returned to his gambling ways and has become increasingly abusive. One night, afraid for her own life, Yayoi strangles Kenji. Worrying for the future of her four-year-old son Takashi if she goes to jail, Yayoi begs Masako to help her dispose of the body.

Played completely straight, but with undeniable moments of black comedy, *Out* makes a succession of unlikely events and coincidences seem completely believable. At least part of this remarkable achievement lies in its surreal spin on *everyday* events. Before anything untoward has even happened, we see the women leaving for work in the middle of the night, going through a draconian decontamination process, and scrubbing in like surgeons, only to assemble mundane *bentō* boxes on a silent construction line dominated by a grim forewoman. The slow decline of Masako's life is artfully telegraphed with flashbacks to the last time she was truly happy—the day her family moved into their new house. Seven years on, and her husband forgets their wedding anniversary, her son is looking for a career in the Mob, and she has acquired a dead body that needs to be scattered around Tokyo.

Though concentrating on the housewives turned criminals in the style of Linda La Plante's *Widows*, *Out* makes full and economical use of its large cast, cleverly interweaving their tale with two more traditional TV genres. Masako has befriended her son's probation officer Noriko (Iijima), who calls round to boast that she has finally made the grade in the detective examinations. Finding herself in a police department riddled with sexism and corruption, Noriko's first case is to file a missing persons report for Yayoi's husband, a relatively simple job which soon runs out of control when parts of him keep turning up in trash cans all around the local park. The same story could easily have been shot as a straightforward cop drama from Noriko's point of view, or indeed as an offbeat gangster tale in the style of *The Sopranos*, since local ex-convict Mitsuyoshi (Enomoto) finds himself wrongly accused of the murder and is determined to find the true culprit. Later subplots include a dangerous liaison between Noriko's jilted boyfriend and the newly widowed Yayoi, as well as Mitsuyoshi's perverse relationship with Anna (Okinawan actress Oda faking a Chinese accent), a bar girl waif whose flirting with the drunken Kenji started the whole plot in motion.

But the wives steal the show—Masako and Yoshie are put-upon Japanese heroines, torn between their obligations and emotions, while Kumiko is a feckless troublemaker, ever ready to sell out her friends. It's her disregard for procedure that leads to the initial discovery of the murder, and her troubles with the *yakuza* that lead her to threaten to blow the whistle. Meanwhile, Yayoi has it easy—her friends must slice up Kenji in Masako's bathroom and deposit the grisly remains in random locations but she gets to stay at home rehearsing her "worried wife" performance. Later episodes play on this reversal of fortune, with Yayoi increasingly excited at the thought of her husband's insurance payout, while her friends are haunted by their guilt, dragged deeper into the underworld to cover their tracks, and reduced to nausea at the sight of raw meat or the rustling of plastic bags.

Based on a novel by Natsuo Kirino (who also wrote the original stories of the movies *A Tender Place* and *A Night Without Angels*), *Out* delivers revelations and cliff-hangers at exactly the right moments and exploits underused peripheral elements such as sound—Yayoi reports her husband's absence to the police while a wailing siren accusingly dominates the background noise. Piling on the suspense with oblique references to the works of Edgar Allan Poe (particularly a feline witness to the murder as in *The Black Cat* and ticking-bomb scraps of incriminating evidence in the style of *The Tell-Tale Heart*), it is an excellent example of what Japanese TV drama has to offer. Though the hackneyed finale finally crosses the ludicrous event horizon, this, too, is another literary nod, this time to Thomas Harris's *Silence of the Lambs* and *Hannibal*. It also provides some handy tips on dismembering corpses using standard household utensils and some wonderful dialogue, such as *"Which knife is best for sawing off a head? Steak or fish?"* A similarly entertaining thriller, **DANGEROUS LIAISONS**, also ran on Fuji during the same season. The story was remade for the cinema in 2002 by director Hideyuki Hirayama and writer Chung Ui-shin, with Mitsuko Baishō, Mieko Harada, Shigeru Muroi, and Naomi Nishida in the lead roles. The movie, however, cannot hold a candle to this excellent TV series. Theme: Masaharu Fukuyama—"Heaven."

OVER TIME

1999. PRD: Ichirō Takai, Chihiro Kameyama. DIR: Hideki Takeuchi, Kōzō Nagayama. SCR: Eriko Kitagawa. CAST: Takashi Sorimachi, Makiko Esumi, Yuriko Ishida, Naomi Nishida. CHN: Fuji. DUR: 45 mins. x 12 eps.; Mon 4 January 1999–22 March 1999. Natsuki (Esumi) finds herself falling for her friend's younger brother Sōichirō (Sorimachi), even though she has sworn to keep things purely platonic. They start sharing a house owned by Sōichirō's sister Haruko (Nishida) with

Natsuki's friend Fuyumi (Ishida). One day, Nazuna (Yoshino Kimura) visits Sōichirō and they start going out together. Meanwhile, Natsuki meets former private tutor Kuga (Kippei Shiina) and they become lovers. Nazuna becomes increasingly jealous of Natsuki and Nazuna and Sōichirō finally break up. Kuga leaves for the U.S. at around the same time, which, by the formula set up by **SEVEN PEOPLE IN SUMMER** and **ASUNARO CONFESSIONS**, gives Natsuki and Sōichirō one more chance to admit their feelings for each other. The result is an examination of the perennial question of whether men and women can be "just good friends," with a logo deliberately designed to recall writer Kitagawa's earlier **LONG VACATION**. However, with a peak rating of 21.9%, *OT* came nowhere near the popularity of its illustrious predecessor. Broadcast in the U.S. without English subtitles on the International Channel. Theme: The Brilliant Green—"Sono Speed de" (At That Speed).

OYOYO THE MONSTER

1972. JPN: *Kaijin Oyoyo*. PRD: Kazuo Shibata, Hiroshi Kubota. DIR: Yasuhiko Ishikawa. SCR: Tōru Ishiyama. CAST: Midori Hoshino, Yoshiaki Mine, Michiko Hirai, Tetsuya Kaji, Tadao Futami, Kuriko Etō, Nobuhiro Katō, Norio Nōya, Kazuko Makino, Aiko Nakayama, Toshiaki Suzuki. CHN: NHK. DUR: 30 mins. x 5 eps.; Sat 1 July 1972–29 July 1972.

"Oyoyo, the self-appointed boss of a violent criminal organization, is plotting to create a secret underground base in Japan. Detective Kimen is eager to catch Oyoyo." So begins *Oyoyo the Monster*, a TV show being written by scriptwriter Kazuhiko Ōsawa (Mine). As he tries to decide what happens next, he is approached by the mysterious Zhang Niantian (Futami), who offers him five million yen to hand over a letter he has just received from Switzerland. When Zhang meets with an untimely end, Kazuhiko is threatened by Oyoyo, who turns out to be a real person. Kazuhiko and his daughter Rumiko (Hoshino) are kidnapped, and shortly joined by two new hostages when Rumiko's boyfriend Jun (Katō) and the equally real Detective Kimen (Kaji) are captured in an ill-fated rescue bid.

Meanwhile, French detective Grunion (Nōya) goes in search of the missing people. Kazuhiko promises Oyoyo that he will hand over the letter if he is released, and the four are returned home. However, Oyoyo discovers that he has been handed a fake letter and he kidnaps Rumiko and Jun once more. Taken to Oyoyo's secret base and rescued by Grunion, they are looking through Oyoyo's stamp collection when they inadvertently initiate the base's self-destruct sequence. As they escape, Kazuhiko decides that the ending is too simple, and elects to add another twist to the story, even as he appears in it.

A highly experimental children's drama, *OtM* toyed with the idea of interactivity, among the world of drama, the world of the fictional writer, and the world of the viewers who are seen by the cast to be watching their actions on a TV screen. Based on the stories *Oyoyo Tō no Bōken* (Adventure on Oyoyo Island) and *Oyoyo Daitōryō* (President Oyoyo), by Nobuhiko Kobayashi. Music was by Jun Sakurai.

P

P.S. I'M FINE, SHUNPEI
1999. JPN: *P.S. Genki Desu, Shunpei.*
PRD: Yuka Nariai, Naoyuki Yokoi. DIR:
Ken Yoshida, Ryō Moriyama. SCR:
Tsukasa Kobayashi, Takako Suzuki.
CAST: Kōichi Dōmoto, Asaka Seto, Nenji
Kobayashi, Takaya Kamikawa. CHN:
TBS. DUR: 45 mins. x 12 eps.; Thu 24
June 1999–16 September 1999.
Shunpei (Dōmoto) will do anything to
get into prestigious Waseda University
and signs up for a cram school to help
him with the exams. However, he
meets a series of people for whom a
college education is an unattainable
dream or a living nightmare. His classmate at the cram school is Momoko
(Seto), a cynical dropout who must
cram to stay in the college. His neighbor Jirō (Kobayashi) is a Waseda graduate who makes no use of his education
at all, preferring to live off the ill-gotten gains of his bar hostess wife. Meanwhile, the only person who really seems
to deserve college is would-be author
Sentarō (Kamikawa), an uneducated
tough guy who works as a debt collector for a local loan shark agency. Based
on another manga by Fumi Saimon,
the prolific creator of **Tokyo Love
Story**. Peak rating: 13.7%. Theme:
Hysteric Blue—"Naze . . ." (Why).

PAIPAI
1989. JPN: *Mahō Shōjo Chūka na
Paipai.* AKA: *Magical Girl Chinese
Paipai.* PRD: Jun Higasa, Masayuki
Nishimura. DIR: Tarō Sakamoto, Tetsuji
Mitsumura, Fuji Saeki, Shinji Mura-
yama. SCR: Yoshio Urasawa, Kiyohide
Ōhara, Akiko Yamanaga. CAST: Natsuki
Ozawa, Shigeru Saiki, Takanobu
Yumoto, Kazuki Yamanaka, Daisuke
Ishigami, Rie Shibata, Toshi Ueda,
Hidekazu Nagae, Masakazu Arai. CHN:
Fuji. DUR: 25 mins. x 26 eps.; Mon 9
January 1989–9 July 1989.
Magical fairy Paipai (Ozawa) leaves her
Chinese-themed alternate dimension
in search of her fiancé in the human
world, where she stays with the mysti-
fied Takayama family. Based on an idea
by **Miss Witch** creator Shōtarō
Ishinomori—compare to **Comet-san**.
Theme: Hiroko Asakawa—"Ano
Musume ga Machi ni Yattekita" (That
Girl's Come to Town). Music by Yūsuke
Honma.

PAPA AND NATCHAN
1991. JPN: *Papa to Natchan.* PRD:
Yasuo Yagi. DIR: Jirō Shōno. SCR: Kiyota
Yamamoto. CAST: Masakazu Tamura,
Kyōko Koizumi, Junko Igarashi, Nenji
Kobayashi. CHN: TBS. DUR: 45 mins. x
10 eps.; Fri 19 April 1991–21 June
1991.
Gorō (Tamura) has brought his daughter Natsuki (Koizumi) up on his own
since his wife's death ten years ago.
The two of them have a friendly relationship and give little thought to the
difference in their ages. However, at
Natsuki's 20th birthday party, Gorō is
forced to confront the fact that his "little girl" is a fully fledged adult and has
to be left to make her own decisions,
make her own mistakes, and nurse her
own broken heart. Theme: Kyōko
Koizumi—"Anata ni Aete Yokatta" (I'm
Glad I Met You).

PAPA DON'T TRY TO BE COOL
1990. JPN: *Papa, Kakko Tsukanaize.*
PRD: N/C. DIR: Setsuo Wakamatsu. SCR:
Kenichi Iwasa. CAST: Kyōhei Shibata,
Kaho Minami, Satomi Tezuka, Shigeru
Muroi, Yūki Tsuchikura. CHN: Fuji. DUR:
45 mins. x 12 eps.; 5 July 1990–20
September 1990.
Tatsuo (Shibata) is an action star
known for his villain roles. Soon after
his idol singer wife walks out on him,
his house is surrounded by news
reporters. Tatsuo and his son Ryūji
(Tsuchikura) are forced to move out
and survive in the real world—compare to **Star Struck**. Theme: Kyōhei
Shibata—"Break Out."

PAPA IS A NEWSCASTER
1987. JPN: *Papa wa Newscaster.* PRD:
N/C. DIR: Kunimasa Kondō. SCR:
Kazuhiko Ban. CAST: Masakazu Tamura,
Jōji Tokoro, Atsuko Asano. CHN: TBS.
DUR: 45 mins. x 12 eps.; Fri 9 January
1987–27 March 1987.
A single newscaster, played by future
Ninzaburō Furuhata lead Masakazu
Tamura, receives an unexpected call
one day from three female strangers.
They reveal that they are his illegiti-
mate daughters and that his womaniz-
ing days have finally caught up with

him. Since the setup is hardly new, screenwriter Ban throws in a series of developments in the lead's media career, showing the life of a newscaster behind the scenes—compare to **Best Dad in the World** and **News Woman**.

PAPA SURVIVAL

1991. PRD: Kazunori Shiokawa. DIR: Shinichi Kamoshita. SCR: Toshio Sekine. CAST: Masaaki Sakai, Kōichi Iwaki, Hisako Manda, Pinko Izumi, Yasufumi Terawaki. CHN: TBS. DUR: 45 mins. x 12 eps.; Sun 2 July 1991–24 September 1991.

Drinking buddies Gorō (Sakai), Manabu (Iwaki), and Naoto (Terawaki) work in the same company and live in the same apartment block. Their friendship is put to the test when Gorō's wife Noriko (Izumi) unexpectedly serves him with divorce papers and runs for New York, leaving him to care for their daughter single-handed. The other men try to help out in the style of *Three Men and a Little Lady* (1990)—later imitators include **Don't Call Me Papa**, **After the Children Have Gone to Bed**, and **Basically Nice**. Theme: Fumiya Fujii—"Heartbreak."

PARADISE OF LOVE

1990. JPN: *Koi no Paradise*. PRD: Yoshiaki Yamada. DIR: Shunsaku Kawake. SCR: Kazuhiko Ban. CAST: Yūko Asano, Masahiro Motoki, Junichi Ishida, Takanori Jinnai, Honami Suzuki, Momoko Kikuchi. CHN: Fuji. DUR: 45 mins. x 12 eps.; Thu 12 April 1990–28 June 1990.

Divorcée dentist Tsunami (Asano) is unable to forget her former husband Yūsaku (Ishida) but moves in with her two sisters, office lady Moeko (Suzuki) and shy wallflower Shiori (Kikuchi). Tsunami rejects the advances of Masato (Jinnai) at an *omiai* marriage meeting, but Moeko finds him attractive and the two begin dating. The scandalized Tsunami takes pity on Moeko's jilted boyfriend Takashi (Motoki) and begins seeing him, unaware that Masato still has feelings for *her*. In what is to be a

complicated situation, even by the love polygon standards of Japanese romances, Tsunami finds herself receiving offers of marriage not only from Masato and Takashi, but also from Yūsaku, who has realized he made a mistake and wants to get back together.

After a while, Takashi is transferred to Canada and Yūsaku changes jobs. He invites Tsunami to cook for him in celebration (we haven't worked out how she is supposed to be impressed by this gesture), but he never arrives because he has been killed in a car accident.

Two months later, Masato asks the heartbroken Tsunami for her blessing, since he wants to marry Shiori. Takashi makes a last-minute appearance at their wedding in a whistle-stop visit from Canada, but instead of getting back together with him, Tsunami tells her two younger sisters that there is more to life than getting married—a somewhat ungracious speech to be making at your sister's wedding!

The horrified reaction of the girls was, it seems, mirrored by Japan's drama-watching audience of yuppie singletons, who looked up from their bridal magazines and matchmaking questionnaires for just long enough to vote *Paradise of Love* a resounding failure. Despite starring the ubiquitous Yūko Asano and repeating many of the tropes and traditions of trendy dramas (see **I Want to Hug You!**), *PoL* seemed to catch the Japanese audience in exactly the wrong mood. The yuppie boom economy was turning to bust, and conspicuous consumption was no longer fashionable—see the similar reaction to **You Are My Favorite in the World**. *PoL*'s heroine says nothing that wasn't also said in the more successful **In the Name of Love**, but Ban's script makes little use of the cast ensemble—if you're going to insist on having more than half a dozen leads, you need to keep them busy. In the wake of *PoL*'s spectacular flop, drama producers rethought their ideas of what constituted romance in the 1990s,

a brainstorming session that would result in the unparalleled success of **Tokyo Love Story**. Theme: Kyōsuke Himuro—"Jealousy o Nemurasete" (Put Jealousy to Sleep).

PARFUM DE LA JALOUSIE

2001. JPN: *Shitto no Kaori*. AKA: *Smell of Jealousy*. PRD: Michihiko Umezawa, Ikuhide Yokochi, Kōichi Tōda, Jinsei Tsuji. DIR: Shimako Satō, Renpei Tsukamoto, Akira Hibino. SCR: Reiko Yoshida, Noriko Gotō. CAST: Manami Honjō, Ayako Kawahara, Masato Sakai, Jō Odagiri, Yasufumi Terawaki, Nobuyoshi Kuwano, Maya Hamaoka, Maki Ikeda, Mireiyu, Hideaki Itō. CHN: Asahi. DUR: 45 mins. x 11 eps.; Fri 12 October 2001–?? December 2001.

Two couples chat at a high-class restaurant but the conversation contains a hidden edge. As they leave the table, the wife of one turns to the husband of the other and whispers: "*Can't you see, we have been betrayed?*" It all began seven days ago. . . .

Aroma therapist Minori (Honjō) has been living with her composer boyfriend Tetsushi (Sakai) for a year, but resists his offer of marriage. Although she loves Tetsushi, she still remembers being jilted at the altar by her ex-fiancé Naoki (Itō, as an intermittent guest star). Naoki claimed that she stifled him, and Minori fears that engagement to Tetsushi could bring out the clinging, dependent woman in her again. Meanwhile, Tetsushi has secured an excellent new contract, providing ambient music for a new garden project being designed by famous architect Eiji (Terawaki). However, Eiji's beautiful wife Saki (Kawahara) remembers Minori from their schooldays—how could she ever forget the "nice girl" for whom her onetime boyfriend Naoki dumped her? For the sake of their menfolk, neither woman mentions the Naoki incident, although Saki finds it hard to take Minori respectfully addressing her as *senpai* (senior).

Impressed by Minori, Eiji stuns a meeting of the garden project by

Parfum de la Jalousie

announcing that he will hire her to produce keynote fragrances for the garden—effectively dismissing the Paris perfumiers who were originally contracted for the job, with whom the French-speaking Saki has been negotiating. With nothing except circumstantial evidence, Saki begins to suspect that Eiji and Minori are having an affair.

Bearing high stylistic and thematic similarities to the April 2001 TBS drama **TO LOVE AGAIN** and Fuji network's **WEDNESDAY LOVE AFFAIR**, which ran during the same season, *PdlJ* is an entertaining and well-structured study of envy and mistrust. Playing like an inadvertent *Othello,* a series of chance asides, unsubstantiated gossip, meetings, and accidents lead Saki to reason that, although her husband has yet to cheat on her, the signs are all there that he will soon enough—this, for her, is case enough for "pre-emptive revenge," and so she seduces the hapless Tetsushi in the style of **ONE SUMMER'S LOVE LETTER**.

Saki isn't merely testing her relationship with her husband, but also avenging herself on Minori for their teenage years, when bad girl Saki lost out to good girl Minori for the affections of Naoki. Her plot is helped along by her loyal assistant Makoto (Odagiri), whose chaste devotion to her makes him excessively concerned for her well-being—partly because he cannot bear to see Saki hurt but subconsciously because he desires Saki for himself. He also first voices suspicions about Eiji's behavior with Minori, though his manipulations return to haunt him when Saki begins a series of noisy office assignations with Tetsushi instead of crying on Makoto's shoulder as planned. Meanwhile, Eiji's assistant Yūka (Ikeda) adores Eiji from afar, causing her to be bitterly resentful toward Minori and adding fuel to the flames.

Minori and Eiji inadvertently dine together when they are deserted by their colleagues; suspicious tongues wag when they are spotted entering a hotel room; Eiji comes home smelling of lavender after Minori accidentally splashes him with aroma oils; the couple emerge sweaty and disheveled from a stalled elevator—all these innocent events gain their own momentum, until *PdlJ* unfolds with all the unstoppable destruction of a slow-motion car wreck. Tetsushi fights desperately to extricate himself from Saki's web, while Minori innocently wonders why her boyfriend is behaving so strangely. In an attempt to mollify Tetsushi's fears, Minori agrees to marry him on Christmas Day *"if snow falls this year,"* but even this heartfelt promise is immediately twisted into something more sinister. Tetsushi's happy satisfaction is destroyed by Saki, who tells the innocent country boy that snow falls in Tokyo only once every ten years—Minori's reply was not a romantic yes but a devious no, she claims.

PdlJ is an excellent psychological drama that can be read on several levels. Beyond the entertainment of accidental, unavoidable tragedy lies a subtextual question—who is really to blame, and was this disaster waiting to happen all along but merely in search of a catalyst? With a heroine waiting a whole decade to avenge herself on a school rival, it has obvious appeal to younger viewers in Japan, while retaining an older cast likely to attract more mature audience members—Eiji is ancient in drama terms at 37. It also makes clever, albeit ludicrous, use of Minori's chosen profession. Each woman has a chosen perfume (lavender for Minori, jardin bagatelle for Saki), with which she marks her territory and her man. Meanwhile Tetsushi loves his girlfriend's natural smell (sometimes all the sniffing does get perversely distracting) and wishes she would not try to cover her true self with artificial scents—a homespun boy-next-door, slowly corrupted by the urban yuppie culture represented by Saki and Eiji. Compare to **COLD MOON** and **JEALOUSY**, though despite outstanding cruelty and histrionic vendettas, the ending of *PdlJ* still manages to be hopelessly romantic.

Based on the novel of the same name by Jinsei Tsuji, who also functioned as a producer on the show. Theme: Slow—"Echoes of Youth," also reprised in French during the show by Clementine and Jinsei Tsuji as "Tous Deux Tout Doux." Despite having one of TV drama's worst theme songs, *PdlJ* has one of the best scores—a wonderful Philip Glass pastiche, pulsing with minimalist menace.

PASSWORD IS BRAVERY, THE

2000. JPN: *Ai Kotoba wa Yūki*. PRD: Takashi Ishihara, Ken Hatano. DIR: Shunsaku Kawake. SCR: Kōki Mitani. CAST: Kōji Yakusho, Kyōka Suzuki, Shingo Katori, Masahiko Tsugawa, Kunie Tanaka, Toshiaki Karasawa. CHN: Fuji. DUR: 45 mins. x ca. 11 eps.; Thu 6 July 2000–30 September 2000. The sleepy, eccentric village of Tomashi is targeted by the ruthless Funamushi Corporation, which plans to dump toxic waste in the area and build a dangerous dioxin incinerator. The local residents have no idea what to do—they have elected the same mayor (Tanaka) for the past 40 years and now discover that they have been sold out to big business. Oyama (Katori from SMAP) is a local boy almost-

made-good, who failed in his attempt to become a pop star in Tokyo and has returned to Tomashi, where he tries unsuccessfully to attract the attention of the mayor's pretty daughter (Suzuki). The townsfolk prepare to fight an eco-terrorist resistance campaign, but Funamushi's slick lawyers have already secured approval from the prefectural government. Oyama and the mayor make a last-ditch trip to Tokyo in search of a lawyer of their own but nobody is prepared to fight such an airtight case. The mayor collapses from exhaustion and is hospitalized, and Oyama, unwilling to disappoint his simple hometown friends, hires an unemployed actor (Yakusho) who once played a TV lawyer.

In some ways, *PIB* picks up where **HERO** left off, far from the urban center of Japan with an attitude and a way of life under threat from soulless modernity. Like its contemporary **LADY OF THE MANOR**, the story's rural lifestyle is sometimes insanely overstated (we are supposed to believe that Suzuki has *never* left the town of her birth), but the occasionally odd behavior of the villagers is regarded by writer Mitani with an indulgent smile—as with **KING'S RESTAURANT**, he'd rather be simple and crazy than smart and boring. Compare to **COUNTRY LIVING**, another town and country conflict, or **DAISUKE HANAMURA** and **LOVE AND JUSTICE**, two other legal dramas that draw on the comedy touch of *Ally McBeal*. Industrial waste was also the subject of the following year's *Dioxin Summer* (*AE).

PASTURE OF STARS

1981. JPN: *Hoshi no Makiba*. PRD: Kanae Mayuzumi. DIR: Kazuya Satō. SCR: Minoru Betsuyaku. CAST: Katsuhiro Fukuda, Mariko Senju, Akira Senju, Yūsuke Kawazu, Toshie Takada, Akihiko Sugizaki. CHN: NHK. DUR: 40 mins. x 2 eps.; Mon 2 November 1981–3 November 1981. Ten years after the end of World War II, an amnesiac man (Fukuda) comes to the small village where Hanako (M.

Senju) lives. He finds abandoned blacksmith's tools and starts working at Hanako's family farm. Hanako calls him Momiichi and tries to help him restore his memory, but all he can remember is that he was once a blacksmith and had a horse called Tsukisumi. On a trip to the mountains, Momiichi meets a mysterious clarinet-playing gypsy (Sugizaki) who tells him of a gypsy community in the mountains. Over successive visits to the gypsies, Momiichi retrieves portions of his memory, recalling that he was on a sinking army transport ship and lost his beloved horse Tsukisumi in the water. In a state of deep depression, he finishes crafting the bell he has been working on but decides not to return to see the gypsies. However, that night, as he rings his bell alone, the gypsies come down to the pasture and start playing music together beneath a starry sky.

A short series based on a children's story by Eiji Shōno, *PoS* allegorized wartime grief in a fantasy setting—compare to Daisaku Ikeda's later *Rainbow Across the Pacific* (*AE). Although the war itself is more clearly depicted in the book, the original still focuses more on a Southeast Asian pastoral—the fantasy approach likely to have been a way of circumventing the reluctance of the media to discuss actual events and blame. Its stars Akira and Mariko Senju were famous musicians in Japan, and Akira would go on to compose the score for the decidedly less pacifist *Silent Service* (*AE). *PoS* was nominated for the 10th Munich International TV Youth Award.

PATHOLOGIST REIKO ISSHIKI

1991. JPN: *Jokyōju Isshiki Reiko: Hōigaku Kyōshitsu no Onna*. PRD: N/C. DIR: Tōya Satō. SCR: Yoshinori Watanabe, Nobuyuki Ishii. CAST: Hiroko Shino, Gitan Ōtsuru, Maki Mizuno, Shinji Yamashita, Masahiro Matsuoka. CHN: NTV. DUR: 45 mins. x 10 eps.; Sat 6 July 1991–7 September 1991. Reiko (Shino) is a forensic pathologist working with the police. When the chairman of a crooked business newspaper is killed under suspicious circumstances, Reiko's colleagues are prepared to accept the voluntary confession of high school student Keiichi (Matsuoka). Reiko, however, suspects foul play in a police procedural in the style of INVESTIGATOR MARIKO.

PEARL BEAUTY, THE

2002. JPN: *Shinju Fujin*. AKA: *Madame Pearl*. PRD: Keijirō Tsuru, Yasuhiro Tsukada. DIR: Yasuyuki Fujiki, Junichi Nishimoto, Kazuho Ōgaki. SCR: Takehiro Nakajima. CAST: Megumi Yokoyama, Shingo Katsurayama, Shinya Ōwada, Toshinobu Matsuo, Etsuko Nami, Ryōko Morishita. CHN: Fuji. DUR: 25 mins. x 65 eps.; 1 April 2002–28 June 2002.

Well-to-do Ruriko (Yokoyama) discovers that her family is not as rich as she previously thought. She is forced to break up with her true love Naoya (Katsurayama) and marry Tanehiko (Ōwada), a social climber whom the old Ruriko would have regarded as far beneath her notice. After she is widowed, she decides to avenge herself on the male gender by destroying the lives of the men she meets, but Naoya still carries a torch for her. Based on the newspaper story *Pearl Beauty* by Kan Kikuchi (one of Japan's most influential pre-war writers and editors), which ran in a newspaper during the Taishō period. The setting for this TV adaptation was moved to the first twenty years of the Shōwa period, covering the years up to and including 1945 and making the story look even more like the earlier OSHIN and 100 YEARS. Frocks and revenge for the daytime TV audience, with the added *frisson* of a "literary" source—although there is a certain irony to the change in setting; Kikuchi was a military collaborator during World War II and fell from favor after 1945.

PEDIATRIC DEPARTMENT: SEASONS OF FATE

1993. JPN: *Shōnibyōtō: Inochi no Kisetsu*. PRD: Fumio Igarashi. DIR: Ikuhiro Saitō. SCR: Man Izawa, Akiyo

Takizawa. CAST: Tomokazu Miura, Isao Hashimoto, Shigeru Muroi, Tatsuya Tamaguchi, Shō Aoyagi. CHN: Asahi. DUR: 45 mins. x 11 eps.; Sun 4 July 1993–12 September 1993.

Pediatrician Yoshihiro (Miura) is so devoted to his work that his wife has left him. He is forced to rethink his priorities when his son Keiichi (Aoyagi) is admitted to the hospital with a suspected tumor. Theme: Deen—"Sugao de Waratte Itai" (Want to Smile for Real).

PENNILESS CONSTABLE *

1998. JPN: *Binbō Dōshin Goyōchō*. PRD: Riichi Tanaka, Kengo Tanaka, Mika Kakuta. DIR: Toshihiro Iijima, Takuji Tominaga, Toshimasa Suzuki, Naoki Uesugi. SCR: Ichirō Miyakawa, Kunio Fujii, Gorō Shima, Norifumi Suzuki. CAST: Ikkō Furuya, Hitomi Takahashi. CHN: Asahi. DUR: 45 mins. x 9 eps.; Thu 9 July 1998–10 September 1998.

In Edo-era Japan, Kihachirō (Furuya) works as a constable for the Edo town magistrate. He also looks after nine orphans, which has attracted the attentions of two women—his boss's daughter and an attractive young geisha. He must look after his charges, keeping them out of trouble and protecting them from suspect individuals who claim to be their long-lost parents. Meanwhile, 18th-century Edo is beset with murders and crimes, which the permanently impoverished detective has to solve. The old-time setting of *PC* still finds Kihachirō faced with situations that could almost have been lifted from a contemporary drama—including illegal book makers, frame-ups, peddlers of banned books, blackmailers, and a once-popular singer fallen on hard times. Such story lines are not so much evidence of poor scripting, but an intriguing argument for the extremely modern concerns that troubled the ancestors of today's Japanese. While popular Western myth often holds that Japan was a medieval country, trapped in a time warp until its "liberation" by Perry's Black Ships in the late 18th century (see AS IF IN FLIGHT), *PC* suggests that Edo-era

Japan was an advanced quasi-modern society with all its attendant benefits and ills. Broadcast with English subtitles in the U.S. on KIKU TV. Theme: Shigeru Izumiya—"Ashita mo Kyō no Yume no Tsuzuki o" (Tomorrow Continues the Dream of Today).

PEOPLE OF THE LOTUS

1982. JPN: *Fuyō no Hito*. PRD: Kanae Mayuzumi. DIR: Kazuya Satō. SCR: Kaneto Shindō. CAST: Sakae Takita, Mariko Fuji, Mami Nakazato, Tsutomu Shimomoto, Kyōzō Nagatsuka. CHN: NHK. DUR: 40 mins. x 2 eps.; 1 April 1982–2 April 1982.

In 1895, Itaru Nonaka (Takita) climbs Mt. Fuji in October, convinced that significant meteorological results require a high observation point. His wife Chiyoko (Fuji) frets about his willingness to make solo trips up the mountain in severe winter weather in order to secure sets of data. Despite familial opposition and Itaru's own protestations, she follows him to a hut on the mountain and the couple becomes an inseparable team, taking observations once every two hours for two months. As winter sets in again, a combination of food shortage and exposure weakens the couple, until they are forcibly "rescued" from their hut by a group of engineers led by Wada (Nagatsuka). While recovering, they plan to recommence their observations but never manage to do so.

Chiyoko dies in 1923, but a National Meteorological Observatory is finally opened on Mt. Fuji in 1932, 37 years after Itaru's original observation. The aged Itaru is invited to the observatory and spends ten days there, in an adaptation of the book by Jirō Nitta, author of SHINGEN TAKEDA and THE SECRET OF WHISPERING REEF. Despite a greater resemblance to adult dramas like NON-CHAN'S DREAM, *People of the Lotus* was commissioned and made by NHK's children's division, presumably as a means of introducing young viewers to the science of weather.

PEOPLE OF THE NAMIKI FAMILY
1993. JPN: *Namiki ke no Hitobito*. PRD: N/C. DIR: Narimichi Sugita. SCR: Shunsaku Ikehata. CAST: Tetsuya Takeda, Takanori Jinnai, Narumi Yasuda. CHN: Fuji. DUR: 45 mins. x 10 eps.; Thu 14 January 1993–25 March 1993.
Hana (Yasuda) is the mistress of a married man, reluctant to attend the *omiai* marriage meeting set up by her eldest brother Kōhei (Takeda). She tries to enlist the help of her younger brother Kiyotsugu (Jinnai), but he is less concerned about his sister's social life than about his mounting debts. Theme: Kai Five—"Kaze no Naka no Hi no Yōni" (Just Like Fire in Wind).

PERFECT BRIDE *
2001. JPN: *Yome wa Mitsuboshi*. AKA: *Three Star Bride*. PRD: Akira Shimura, Mayumi Shimizu. DIR: Hiroshi Matsubara, Ikuhiro Saitō, Arata Katō. SCR: Yūki Shimizu. CAST: Yoshino Kimura, Gō Morita, Aya Ueto, Masahiko Nishimura, Isao Hashizume, Miyoko Asada, Ryūji Harada. CHN: TBS. DUR: 45 mins. x 11 eps.; Wed 11 April 2001–20 June 2001.
Miyuki (Kimura) is an engineer working for a construction firm. Mere moments after she has walked down the aisle with her new husband Makoto (Harada), he is called away to a troubled project in Africa, leaving her alone with her dreaded in-laws. She tries to make the best of a bad situation, but after her mother-in-law dies of a stroke and her father-in-law Masakichi (Hashizume) is hospitalized, she is left in charge of her new relatives and their struggling eel restaurant. Her work suffers because she is now juggling an impromptu career as a housewife, and when Masakichi comes home, his nurse daughter Kazuko (Asada) refuses to look after him. Meanwhile, two of her female in-laws plot to sell off Masakichi's beloved restaurant to land developers, and Miyuki's mother fakes an outbreak of food poisoning in order to hide from a stalker. The result is an intriguing mix of several drama clichés—the in-law

appeasement of **DAUGHTER-IN-LAW**, the gourmet intrigue of **THE CHEF**, and the reluctant parenthood of **TAKE ME TO A RYOKAN**. Broadcast in the U.S. with English subtitles on KIKU TV. Theme: Do As Infinity—"Week."

PERFECT LOVE *
1999. PRD: Hiroyoshi Koiwai. DIR: Masahide Takahashi, Isamu Nakae, Kōzō Nagayama. SCR: Taeko Asano. CAST: Masaharu Fukuyama, Yoshino Kimura, Yūsuke Santamaria, Tetsuya Takeda, Hiroko Hatano, Rina Takagi. CHN: Fuji. DUR: 45 mins. x 11 eps.; Mon 5 July 1999–20 September 1999.
Playboy dentist Taketo (Fukuyama) is still hung up on his ex-girlfriend, a would-be model who has found other priorities in her life. Regular office lady Chigusa (Kimura) falls in love with him but has trouble convincing him to let go of the past. Broadcast in the U.S. with English subtitles on KTSF TV and NGN TV. Theme: Glay—"Koko de wa Nai Dokoka e" (Anywhere But Here).

PHANTOM AGENTS *
1964. JPN: *Ninja Butai Gekkō*. AKA: *Ninja Platoon Moonlight*. PRD: Mikihiko Uemura, Minoru Tamura, Yoshiyuki Shindō. DIR: Keinosuke Tsuchiya, Yasuo Yoshino, Ken Yamada. SCR: Tatsuo Yoshida, Kazuo Nishida, Tatsuo Tamura, Tōru Sasaki. CAST: Jō Mizuki, Kenji Nagisa, Ryūji Ishikawa, Akira Yamaguchi, Makiko Mori, Yasunori Kojima, Isamu Yamamoto, Makiko Kagawa, Shōji Nakayama, Peter Williams, Akira Tomoda, Tōru Ōhira. CHN: Fuji. DUR: 25 mins. x 130 eps.; 3 January 1964–31 March 1966 (#1); 3 July 1966–2 October 1966 (#2).
"A gun is our last resort; we are Phantom Agents." With modern Japan infiltrated by crime organizations, the Japanese branch of Interpol forms a special espionage unit trained in the skills of the Iga and Koga ninja schools. They form the Ninja Platoon Moonlight, each with a codename derived from the Moon—Leader Gekkō (Mizuki), underlings Tsukikage (Nagisa),

Natsuki (Yamaguchi), Tsukinowa (Ishikawa), Hangetsu (Kojima), Mangetsu (Yamamoto), and token females Mikazuki (Mori) and Gingetsu (Kagawa). A forerunner of producer Yoshida's later *Battle of the Planets* (*AE) and the sentai shows such as **GORANGER**, *Phantom Agents* was based on an early 1960s manga that ran in *Shōnen King* magazine—in the original, the platoon were ninja co-opted into espionage missions in World War II. Drawing in equal parts on *Mission: Impossible* and *The Man from U.N.C.L.E.*, the ninja were kitted out in proto-sentai gear—crash helmets, leather jackets, tight trousers, and high boots. Each also had a sword strapped to his or her back. Unlike the true sentai shows, the budget affords little opportunity to impress the audience with a carefully designed monsters of the week. Instead, while the ninjas' adversaries remain typical besuited agent types, it is the ninja *techniques* that present much of the excitement. Walking everywhere in single file, the team could transform into their battle gear in seconds simply by ducking behind a tree. Similar trick photography is used to depict their incredible gymnastic powers—cameras shoot them jumping out of trees backward in order to give the appearance of incredibly high leaps.

Ninja themselves owe less to Japanese history than they do to 20th-century fiction, particularly the works

Platonic Sex

of Sanpei Shirato (*Manual of Ninja Martial Arts*, *AE) and Fūtarō Yamada (*Ninja Resurrection*, *AE). Thanks to the works of authors like them, Japanese popular culture had already established a set of "traditional" items for the ninja to use, including the *shuriken* throwing-stars, numerous cunning tricks such as roll-up walls to use as camouflage, special attacks, and incredible feats of contortion and escapology. These were augmented with a succession of high-tech gadgets in the spirit of the 007 movies, to make a truly entertaining hybrid of samurai epic and spy show. Their enemies were no exception and not averse to using their own bombs, gases, and razor-edged playing cards against the ninja, who were determined to stop their secret bacterial weapons factories and their numerous attempts to seize control of puppet regimes all around the world. Later episodes introduced a new brat member, young Tonfa, whose grandfather conveniently taught him ninjutsu before he died.

The story was picked up for the Australian market as *Phantom Agents*, with the evil Black Devil syndicate renamed the Black Flag and the central cast renamed Phanta, Cordo, Zemo, Antar, Mara, and Gina.

Broadcast in the wake of the success of **The Samurai**, the series created a brief boom in martial arts fanaticism among the young and was one of the most popular Japanese TV dramas shown abroad; compare its success with that of **Monkey** in the U.K. ten years later. The *Phantom Agents* version also made it to some U.S. stations and gained a fan following in the New York area. *PA* was the **Mighty Morphin' Power Rangers** of its time, albeit on a smaller scale, containing the seeds within it of much of the modern kids' sci-fi genre, from **Ultraman** to **Masked Rider**.

PLACE IN THE SUN, A

1994. JPN: *Hi no Ataru Basho.* PRD: Mamoru Koizumi. DIR: Kōzō Nagayama. SCR: Noriko Yoshida. CAST: Masatoshi Nakamura, Kōji Matoba, Minako Honda. CHN: Fuji. DUR: 45 mins. x 11 eps.; Thu 13 January 1994–24 March 1994.

Yūji (Nakamura) comes out of jail after serving several years for bribery. In an attempt to go straight, he finds a job at a yakitori restaurant, but soon clashes with both the employees and customers. Theme: Yōsuke Eguchi—"Ai wa Ai de" (Love For Love).

PLASTIC BEAUTY

2002. JPN: *Seikei Bijin.* AKA: *Artificial Beauty.* PRD: Hiroyoshi Koiwai, Kazuhiko Takahashi. DIR: Akiji Fujita, Junichi Tsuzuki. SCR: Tomoko Yoshida. CAST: Ryōko Yonekura, Kippei Shiina, Haruhiko Katō, Maiko Kikuchi, Noriko Aota, Yoshie Ichige. CHN: Fuji. DUR: 45 mins. x 11 eps.; Tue 9 April 2002–?? June 2002.

Honami (Yonekura) is a beautiful fashion model with a dark secret. She was born into a family of extremely ugly people, and although a series of operations in Europe have given her pristine looks, she is troubled that her secret will come out. Constantly fretting that her face-lifts are coming apart, deep down Honami is still the little girl who was bullied at school for her looks. She will do anything to stay ahead, but this arrogant attitude makes her personali-

ty as ugly to others as her face once was. There is one exception—Ryūsui (Shiina) is a master of flower arranging who gives no thought to her superficial beauty. Instead, he is attracted to her plucky personality, which he likens to hardy plants breaking through rocks. A cosmetic 21st-century spin on the disability dramas that flourished in the 1990s—compare to **Beautiful Life** and **Miracle of Love**. Shown unsubtitled in the U.S. on NGN TV.

PLATONIC SEX

2001. PRD: Kōzō Nagayama, Hidefumi Shōji. DIR: Kōzō Nagayama, Takeshi Tanaka, Isamu Nakae. SCR: Yukari Tatsui. CAST: Mari Hoshino, Toshiyuki Nagashima, Shirō Sano, Subaru Shibuya, Yoshiko Tanaka, Naoya Akama, Alison Raimondi, Karla Bruning, Tom Southern. CHN: Fuji. DUR: ca. 96 mins. x 2 eps.; 24 and 28 September 2001.

At midnight on the eve of her 16th birthday Kana (Hoshino) is out partying with her biker friends using stolen money, while her worried parents stare at the clock and a freshly baked cake. Arrested by the police and bailed out by her timid mother (Tanaka), Kana is manhandled by her angry father, who cuts off clumps of her hair and holds her head under a running faucet. This, apparently, is enough to make her leave home. She moves in with her boyfriend Taku but runs away when her father arrives and starts a fight. Hiding out with Taku's friends at a local bar, she is gang-raped after closing time and wanders the streets of Tokyo in a daze until she is recruited by nightclub scout Ishikawa (Sano).

Using the false name Ai Endō, Kana begins a new life as a nightclub hostess, which devolves into prostitution when she needs to raise the money to buy out her boyfriend Shun's gigolo contract at a gay bar. Jilted by Shun as soon as she buys his freedom, she drifts into the world of "adult" videos, where she becomes a star. Some years later, after a pointless interlude in New York, she finds a new love in the form of florist and sometime street busker Kazumi, only to lose him when she catches him in bed with her best friend Mai. Quitting the porn industry, she is reconciled with her family six years after leaving home.

It is difficult to tell whether *PS*'s sanitized and shallow approach should be blamed on the limitations of depicting controversial subjects on TV or on the failings of its original source material. It is supposedly based on a best-selling autobiography by Ai Iijima, a ubiquitous figure on late-night Japanese TV and radio, who also lent her name to the manga *Time Traveler Ai* and her reedy, expressionless voice to the anime *Adventure Kid* (*AE). However, despite these real-life origins, this story still bears a "fiction" disclaimer. Perhaps unjustly, its style of presentation manages to make Kana appear to be an impossibly spoiled brat, whose callow musings on the meaning of life do not deserve to grace a cornflakes box and whose genuinely traumatic real-life experiences are counterproductively toned down for the TV audience. Meanwhile, some of the show's most interesting moments focus on the people she leaves behind, presumably outside the scope of Iijima's original memoirs as she wasn't there to witness them.

We therefore assume that it is Yukari Tatsui, writer of **HEAVEN'S COINS** and **SEMI DOUBLE**, who is responsible for several key scenes which shift the focus away from the story's supposed lead. Once, Kana passes her father on the street, and the script is cleverly ambiguous as to whether he has not noticed her or simply ignored her. On another occasion, he is in a room when a fellow worker is watching a late-night TV program about "adult video star Ai Endō," whose name, of course, means nothing to him and whose face he cannot see from where he is standing. Tatsui's script also throws in some subtle subtextual sabotage to offset Kana's continual whining. Her parents argue about where they went wrong, resulting in a set of controversial accusations

in the style of **UNMARRIED FAMILY**, as Mom blames Dad for "always being at work," and he blames her for not being a "proper housewife." Similarly, Kana's former gang associate Chika later reappears as a respectable university graduate, undermining Ai's claim that her slump into sleaze was inevitable. In perhaps the most moving scene, her parents nervously sit down to watch one of her videos. As Ai spouts softcore pillow talk onscreen, Mom bursts into tears, simply because she now knows her long-lost daughter is still alive.

The story only really falters when it returns to Kana herself, who is happy to play the ingénue when she wants her latest squeeze to buy her a new wristwatch but retains this infantile attitude in her personal life. On two occasions, she rails self-righteously at cheating lovers, clinging to a muddled notion that only she is able to keep love and sex separate. This belief, that there is such a thing as "platonic sex," gives us the deliberately provocative title, but viewers hoping for nudity will be disappointed to hear that the only gratuitous thing in this drama is the sobbing, particularly in the outrageously weepy finale. Another notable point is the jaw-droppingly bad performances from the foreign actors, who join the long tradition of *gaijin* forced to declaim their lines as if speaking to a half-wit, slowly enough for the Japanese audience to pick out a word or two of English. Thanks to its mystifying popularity with sullen teenagers in search of an inappropriate role model, the story was also adapted into a movie the same year, starring Saki Kagami. Theme: Spitz—"Yume Oi Mushi" (Insect Chasing a Dream). Music by Tetsuya Komuro.

PLEASE DARLING

1993. JPN: *Onegai Darling*. PRD: N/C. DIR: Isamu Nakae. SCR: Junya Yamazaki. CAST: Yumiko Takahashi, Kenji Moriwaki, Hidetoshi Nishijima. CHN: Fuji. DUR: 45 mins. x 5 eps.; Thu 18 February 1993–18 March 1993. High school student Kaori (Takahashi)

marries college boy Keisuke (Moriwaki) at the age of sixteen. But when Keisuke graduates, he becomes a teacher and finds himself posted to Kaori's school. The couple agree to keep their marriage secret, which becomes increasingly difficult after Keisuke is put in charge of Kaori's class. Audiences were presumably expected not to notice that this was almost exactly the same as the earlier **MY WIFE IS 18**.

PLEASE DEMON

1993. JPN: *Onegai Demon*. PRD: Atsuhiro Sugio. DIR: Isamu Nakae. SCR: Junya Yamazaki. CAST: Naho Toda, Kenji Moriwaki, Emi Ōji, Shingo Katori. CHN: Fuji. DUR: 45 mins. x 5 eps.; Sat 27 November 1993–25 December 1993. Ichirō (Moriwaki) is the son and heir of King Demon, the lord of Hell. He comes up to the surface world in search of a wife, disguising himself as a teacher and falling in love with his work colleague Sanae (Toda). Not content with stealing from **MY WIFE IS 18**, the **PLEASE DARLING** team inverted the situations of *Bewitched* for this follow-up comedy. We leave it to later generations of sociologists to debate if a Japanese TV father finds the spawn of Hell to be a more attractive son-in-law proposition than, say, a foreigner. Theme: Modern Choki Chokis— "Jitensha ni Notte" (On a Bicycle).

PLEASE GOD! JUST A LITTLE MORE TIME

1998. JPN: *Kamisama! Mō Sukoshi Dake*. PRD: Hiroyoshi Koiwai. DIR: Hideki Takeuchi, Daisuke Tajima. SCR: Taeko Asano. CAST: Takeshi Kaneshiro, Kyōko Fukada, Haruhiko Katō, Yukie Nakama, Rie Miyazawa, Yukie Tanaka. CHN: Fuji. DUR: 45 mins. x 12 eps.; Tue 7 July 1998–22 September 1998. Masaki (Fukada) is an average middle-class teenager in a nuclear family, whose parents are staying together for the sake of the kids and whose mother is already having an affair. Neither happy nor unhappy, the only entertainment in her humdrum life is music produced by the pop producer Keigo (Kaneshiro). Losing a ticket to a concert given by one of Keigo's pop stars, Masaki decides to sell her body to recoup the money—see Last Love for details on the 1990s *enjo kōsai* (subsidized dating) scandal. Using the money to buy another ticket, she manages to get to the concert the next day and sees Keigo's car passing as she walks home in the rain. Throwing open her coat to reveal a T-shirt with the words "I LOVE KEIGO!" on it, she finds herself offered a lift home, which turns into drinks at Keigo's hotel and eventually a one-night stand.

Keigo, for his part, has no interest in relationships, as he is still nursing a broken heart over the death of his love Risa (Miyazawa) three years earlier. However, his self-absorption begins to crack and three months later he decides to give Masaki a call. He reaches her on the day she has just returned from the hospital, clutching a positive HIV test.

Initially, Masaki blames Keigo, though embarrassing questions asked of ex-lovers soon establish that it had nothing to do with him—Masaki has contracted the HIV virus from her single "client" in her short-lived flirtation with prostitution. Though Keigo discovers that he has a clean bill of health, he cannot shake off his feelings for the new girl. Standard drama conventions soon follow, including a misunderstanding when Masaki sees Keigo kissing one of his singers, Kaoru (Nakama), followed by a railroad track suicide attempt and a hospital reunion. Such clichés are relatively common in other dramas, though normally the star's problem is not infection but an unwanted pregnancy. Whereas a normal drama would, somewhat heartlessly, probably call for a miscarriage and subsequent return to "normality" at this point, HIV infection cannot be reversed as a script convenience.

Masaki returns to school, where rumors soon reach the press that she has contracted HIV through a one-night stand with a pop idol. Despite his

complete innocence, Keigo loses his recording contract and prepares to leave for America after an argument with Masaki. Calling in to see her on his way to the airport, he arrives in the nick of time to stop her throwing herself off a bridge. Proclaiming his love for her, he invites her to go to America with him but faces parental opposition from Masaki's stern father. After another misunderstanding involving her late arrival at the airport, the lovers part, each assuming that the other has jilted them.

Three years later, Keigo returns to Japan for a comeback tour, his career suitably revived by the adoration of the American public. Reconciled with the embittered Masaki, now an interior designer, he sleeps with her, only for her to collapse the following day with pneumonia, itself a symptom of the transformation of her HIV to full-blown AIDS. Entering the hospital, the recuperating Masaki discovers that she is now pregnant.

Now assuming a tragedy of Beautiful Life proportions, Masaki and Keigo decide to keep the baby, only for critical complications to develop during a premature labor, which comes on just as the couple complete their marriage vows. Now that he has become Masaki's next of kin after their wedding, Keigo must decide whether the doctors should save his wife or his baby.

An outstandingly weepy series with a triple-twist final episode (none of which we have given away, believe it or not!), *PGJaLMT* gained itself a rating of 28.3% and might well have been the most popular drama of the year but for the incredible success enjoyed by GTO, which followed it on Tuesday nights on Fuji. The series also exists in a novelization, credited to scenarist Asano. The series is now used in some Japanese classrooms to teach AIDS awareness, and presumably some innovative methods for schoolgirls to obtain extra spending money. Peak rating 28.3%. Theme: Luna Sea—"I for You."

POITRINE
1990. PRD: Jun Higasa, Masayuki Nishimura. DIR: Shinji Murayama, Tarō Sakamoto. SCR: Yoshio Urasawa. CAST: Yūko Kajima, Toshie Maeda, Shigeru Saiki, Makiko Otonashi, Ryūta Kobayashi, Yūji Shimoshima, Takehisa Yamazawa, Nobuhiro Tenma, Rie Shibata, Mayo Tanaka, Kiyonobu Suzuki, Jirō Hotaruyuki. CHN: Fuji. DUR: 25 mins. x 51 eps.; Sun 7 January 1990–30 December 1990.
Yūko Murakami (Kajima) meets a god at a shrine and is given the power to be the legendary Beauty Mask Poitrine in order to protect both the cosmos and her local community. Later in the series, Yūko's sister Momoko (Maeda) is given the power to transform into Poitrine Petite. Poitrine can transform herself into anyone she chooses to be, from a police woman to Tōyama no Kin-san (!). Based on Shōtarō Ishinomori's manga. Music by Yūsuke Honma.

POLE POSITION: FOR THE ONE I LOVE
1992. JPN: *Pole Position: Itoshi no Hito e*. PRD: Nobuo Mizuta. DIR: Tōya Satō. SCR: Izō Hashimoto. CAST: Taishū Kase, Yumi Morio, Ritsuko Tanaka, Saki Takaoka. CHN: NTV. DUR: 45 mins. x 11 eps.; Wed 8 January 1992–18 March 1992.
Racer Keiichi (Kase) joins the Formula Three racing team owned by Kashiwagi (Kazukiyo Nishikiori). However, his performance is rated as poor and he debates whether he should give it up. At a team meeting, he meets the attractive Makiko (Morio), who spurs him on to greater success. *PP* cashed in on the popularity of Formula One racing in Japan, itself inspired by Satoru Nakajima, the first Japanese F1 racer, who drove for the F1 Lotus team in 1987. Theme: Alfee—"Promised Love."

POWER OF LOVE
2002. JPN: *Koi no Chikara*. AKA: *Strength of Love*. PRD: Kōichi Funatsu, Takashi Ishihara, Yoshihiro Suzuki. DIR: Norio Wakamatsu, Masanori

Murakami. scr: Yūko Aizawa. cast: Eri Fukatsu, Shinichi Tsutsumi, Akiko Yada, Kenji Sakaguchi, Masahiko Nishimura. chn: Fuji. dur: 45 mins. x 11 eps.; Thu 10 January 2002–?? April 2002.

Thirtysomething career girl Tōko (Fukatsu) realizes that she is never going to get the dream man or dream career she has been waiting for and begins drinking heavily. She meets Kōtarō (Tsutsumi), whom she once adored but who now appears to have turned into an arrogant, self-centered man (suspiciously like Takumi in Fuji's FIRST TIME, which ran during the same season). In spite of herself, Tōko agrees to go into partnership with Kōtarō—her last chance for success in both love and business. Broadcast in the U.S. without English subtitles on the International Channel. Theme: Kazumasa Oda—"Kirakira" (Sparkling).

POWER OFFICE GIRLS

1998. jpn: *Shomuni*. aka: *General Affairs Section Two*. prd: Kōichi Funatsu. dir: Masayuki Suzuki, Masato Hijikata, Makoto Hirano. scr: Rumi Takahashi, Yūji Hashimoto. cast: Makiko Esumi, Kotomi Kyōno, Mai Hōshō, Keiko Toda, Kyōko Sakurai, Yumiko Takahashi, Leo Morimoto. chn: Fuji. dur: 45 mins. x ca. 36 eps.; Wed 15 April 1998–1 July 1998 (#1); 12 April 2000–?? July 2000 (#2); 3 July 2002–18 September 2002 (#3).

When her affair with a married man is discovered, office lady Sawako (Kyōno) is summarily demoted to General Affairs Section Two—compare to a similar fate in EVIL WOMAN. She arrives in the basement to discover that she is now a member of the Manpan Commerce corporation's most reviled section, a group of female misfits, led by a no-hoper man, charged with doing all the jobs in the company that nobody else will touch. Her fellow inmates include Rie (Takahashi), a flake who is convinced she has psychic powers, Kana (Sakurai), a self-confessed man-eater, and Azusa (Toda),

who is an ancient crone of 34. She immediately clashes with the head-strong Chinatsu (Esumi), who refuses to let her have the nearest free desk because *"it belongs to the cat,"* who sleeps in one of the drawers.

Based on the manga in *Comic Morning* by Hiroyuki Yasuda, *Shomuni* was given the unnecessarily ironic title of *Power Office Girls* by the foreign sales people at Fuji TV. A glorification of the "little people" of *Patlabor* (*AE) or even *Fight Club* (1999), it asks viewers if they can remember who it was who fixed the photocopier and changed the lightbulbs and then focuses on the life of a bizarre group of women who have supposedly been thrown on the corporate scrapheap, but in fact find themselves present at moments of pivotal importance.

General Affairs Two has achieved legendary status in the company—nobody is quite sure where it is or what it does, but they know that it is the corporate equivalent of Siberian exile and tell themselves that it is an asylum for the ugly and incompetent. It is all the more surprising, then, when the girls are joined by Ume (Hōshō), a superefficient secretary who has been relegated to their division after her cost-cutting plan led to a toilet paper shortage. Guiltily hoping she won't realize that *they* were responsible for the disappearing paper out of protest for the threatened removal of their beloved cat, the girls welcome her and hope that her exile will be temporary.

The series was followed by a special on 7 October 1998, in which the company takes a disastrous office trip to Atami. In the second 12-episode season, the girls are reunited from a disparate set of McJobs when their boss Mr. Inoue (Morimoto) reveals that the company is threatened by a draconian employee surveillance system. However, even after they have saved Manpan Commerce, they return to their old jobs and find that the company is as stuffy as usual. A *man* is sent to represent them at a women's conference, and the girls are forced to battle

Power Office Girls

a corporate directive forbidding company romances. Unsurprisingly, Manpan is soon bankrupted, causing the girls to be scattered, only to reunite once more and take revenge on the unscrupulous business partner who destroyed it. More of the same followed in the third season, *Shomuni Final*, in which the company recovers but enters lean times. Chinatsu marries a wealthy salaryman, but soon becomes bored and decides to run an office sweeps take on whether Sawako (Kyōno) can lose her virginity by June. The series was capped with a New Year's Day special in 2003, *Shomuni Forever*. Peak rating 28.5%.

Compare to LOCAL NEWS: DEPARTMENT THREE, PRETTY GIRLS, and the similar satire of BIG WING. Many cast members were reunited for the otherwise unrelated SCENES FROM THE WATER TRADE. Also released in a novelization, credited to "Fuji TV." Screened without subtitles in the U.S. on NGN TV. Theme: Izam with Astral Love—"Sunao no Mama de" (Just as Pliable as You Are).

PRECIOUS FRIEND

1997. jpn: *Ichiban Taisetsu na Hito*. aka: *Most Important Person*. prd: Hideki Isano, Yasuo Yagi. dir: Makoto

Kiyohiro, Hideki Isano. SCR: Yumiko Aoyagi. CAST: Shingo Katori, Arisa Mizuki, Ken Kaneko, Jinpachi Nezu. CHN: TBS. DUR: 45 mins. x 11 eps.; Fri 18 April 1997–27 June 1997.

Miwa (Mizuki) graduates from a two-year college, splits up with her college boyfriend, and finds a job at an insurance company. She moves back in with her family in Yokohama, a decision which brings her close to her childhood friend Kōhei (Katori from SMAP). The drama cuts in and out of their lives over a six-year period, showing the couple thrown together and pulled apart by a number of situations, until they finally confess that they have true feelings for each other. However, by this time, Kōhei has already found himself a fiancée, Hiroko. Eventually, he marries the woman chosen for him by his family, and the lovers tell each other that their feelings were nothing more than a crush. Later, Kōhei confesses that, whoever he may be married to, Miwa remains the most precious person in his life—a restatement of the Japanese traditional idea that romantic love and marriage should be kept very separate. Theme: John Lennon—"Just Like Starting Over."

PREGNANT

1994. JPN: Ninshin Desu yo. PRD: N/C. DIR: Masaaki Odagiri. SCR: Akemi Shimizu, Nobuyuki Fujimoto. CAST: Yoshikazu Miura, Gitan Ōtsuru, Saya Takagi, Eriko Tamura. CHN: Kansai. DUR: 45 mins. x 15 eps.; Mon 10 October 1994–21 November 1994; 16 October 1995–18 December 1995.

Obstetrician Daisuke (Miura) marries chief nurse Mariko (Takagi) and the couple enjoy six happy years of marriage, until Mariko suddenly announces that she is pregnant. Meanwhile, her brother Takayuki (Ōtsuru) is enjoying a bachelor life as a doctor. The short six-part first season was followed by a second in 1995, in which the parents juggled their medical careers while trying to find day care for their offspring—the medical establishment figures suddenly forced to look at life the way their patients have to every day. Theme: Masayuki Suzuki—"Yume Mata Yume" (Dream and Dream).

PRETTY GIRLS *

2002. JPN: Pretty Girl. PRD: Satoshi Suzuki. DIR: Akio Yoshida, Masahiko Hinako, Akira Okajima. SCR: Yumiko Aoyagi. CAST: Izumi Inamori, Seiichi Tanabe, Ryōko Yonekura, Nana Katase. CHN: TBS. DUR: 45 mins. x 9 eps.; Wed 9 January 2002–6 March 2002.

Dumped by her boyfriend and thrown out of her apartment, Tokyo girl Hana (Inamori) develops a crush on the broken-hearted Ryō (Tanabe), unaware that he is really the son of the wealthy owner of the Ginza's large Andrews department store. Hana takes a job with Andrews to be close to her prospective Mr. Right and soon becomes the confidante of the other girls who work there. After she befriends Ayumi, a shy wallflower who blows her chance at getting an in-house promotion to the design division, the two girls move in together. Hana also offers relationship advice to Rieko, a lowly receptionist who has unwisely boasted to her boyfriend that she works in the hallowed typing pool—as with EVIL WOMAN, would it have killed her to aim a little higher? Meanwhile Hana's colleague Tarō mistakes her clumsy attempts to impress Ryō for attempts to impress him and has to be gently discouraged from pursuing Hana any further. Hana's strange behavior leads Ryō to suspect that she is really a spy for his absent father, though such shenanigans cause the staff to be wholly unprepared for the true bombshell—office manager Mrs. Ino defects to a rival store, taking Andrews's client list with her. While the remaining staff try to pick up the pieces, the pretty new arrival Sayaka makes Ryō an offer he can't refuse. She promises to bail out the troubled store, but only if Ryō honors their parents' wishes that they should marry, leaving Hana in a difficult situation, faced with the loss of her job, or her love, or possibly both. Compare to DEPARTMENT STORE. Broadcast in the U.S. with English subtitles on KIKU TV. Theme: Hitomi Shimatani—"Chantilly."

PRIN PRIN

1979. JPN: Prin Prin Monogatari. PRD: N/C. DIR: N/C. SCR: Tōru Ishiyama. CAST: (voices) Hitomi Ishikawa, Akira Kamiya, Ayako Hori, Sanji Hase. CHN: NHK. DUR: 15 mins. x 656 eps.; Tue 2 April 1979–19 March 1982.

As a baby, Prin Prin (Ishikawa) was found floating in the sea in a box that also contained a monkey and a crown. Rescued by a fisherman from Arutoko City (i.e., "Somewhere City"), she spends her childhood there. After 15 years, she realizes that she is really a princess from a distant land and sets out in search of it. Her companions include Bonbon (Kamiya), Osage (Hase), Kaseijin (Hori), and a monkey called Monkey. So begins a puppet show that mixes the fairy tale odyssey of SUN WUKONG with the sci-fi antics of AERIAL CITY 008, infamous for its fearless inclusion of numerous satirical twists. In one notorious episode, the arms dealer Langer offers a free holiday to a high-level official if he agrees to buy a consignment of Gucci missiles—a parody of the Lockheed scandal in which politicians including former Prime Minister Kakuei Tanaka took kickbacks for promoting Lockheed aircraft. Another episode satirized the Middle East, in particular the ongoing Iran-Iraq war, by depicting three countries that were eternally at war with each other. One of the serial's best-loved characters was General Ruchi of Atata, a man with a giant head and an IQ of 1300. He dominated the show for six months, before revealing that he is an alien (as if you couldn't guess) and "escaping on a meteorite." Compare to HAKKENDEN and STAR FLEET. Note the presence of Akira Kamiya as one of the voices, better known in the anime world as City Hunter (*AE).

PRISON HOTEL

1999. PRD: Fumio Igarashi, Masaru Takahashi. DIR: Yukihiko Tsutsumi. SCR: Hajime Narita. CAST: Tetsuya Takeda, Akiko Matsumoto, Sōichirō Kitamura, Aya Ono. CHN: Asahi. DUR: 45 mins. x 10 eps.; 17 April 1999–19 June 1999.

Hotel Wakō ("Light of Peace"), aka Prison Hotel, is a hot spring resort where gangsters come to recover from their wounds. The owner Nakazō Kido (Takeda) is the gang boss. His niece Kōnosuke Kido (Matsumoto) is a novelist who was abandoned when she was very young, who is conducting an affair with her adoring secretary Seiji Tamura (Yoshihiko Inohara). The hotel manager, Hanazawa (Kitamura) has been head-hunted from the prestigious Crown Hotel and insists on running the operation as if it were a completely normal venture. However, matters are not helped by the presence of Yukie (Ono), the only surviving member of a family suicide pact, who is haunted by her disgruntled relatives, not to mention the eternally fractious clientele, who are not above settling disputes with guns and swords. A bittersweet comedy based on the manga of the same title by Jirō Asada. Later episodes concentrate on Kōnosuke's journey to find her lost mother.

PROFESSOR MIRAGE

1978. JPN: Shinkirō Hakase. PRD: Kyōzō Tsubaki. DIR: Takamasa Suzuki, Ryōzō Yoshida, Masami Kakuoka. SCR: Kuetsu Kawasaki. CAST: Akifumi Inoue, Jō Yoshikawa, Kenzō Tanaka, Tomonori Kenmochi, Akira Shima, Masayo Kawai, Kōhei Wakasugi. CHN: NHK. DUR: 20 mins. x 12 eps.; Mon 9 January 1978–26 January 1978.

Tadaaki Tōgehara (Kenmochi) claims to be able to murder from afar with the aid of psionic powers. Conjuror Shunsaku Kubodera (Inoue), aka Professor Mirage, who prides himself on unmasking psychic charlatans, receives a threat of murder from Tadaaki. He accepts the challenge, in a situation later reprised in the RING TV series.

PROMISE AT AGE 20

1992. JPN: Hatachi no Yakusoku. PRD: Tōru Ōta. DIR: Kōzō Nagayama. SCR: Yūji Sakamoto. CAST: Riho Makise, Gorō Inagaki, Michitaka Tsutsui, Eri Fukatsu. CHN: Fuji. DUR: 45 mins. x 11 eps.; Mon 12 October 1992–21 December 1992.

Boston-dweller Yuki (Makise) has become pen pals with Junpei (Inagaki), a member of her late brother's school baseball team, who has been sending her encouraging and tender letters in the three years since the funeral. She is also falling a little in love with him, even though they have never met, and he has yet to reveal that he is actually responsible for her brother's death. Matters are resolved when Junpei comes to Boston with his college baseball team. Peak rating: 16.5%. Theme: Motoharu Sano—"Yakusoku no Hashi" (The Agreed Bridge).

PROSECUTOR YOKO WAKAURA

1991. JPN: Kenji Wakaura Yōko. PRD: N/C. DIR: Tokizō Wakita. SCR: Akiji Imai. CAST: Chikako Kaku, Chōsuke Ikariya, Kazuko Yoshiyuki, Mariko Okada. CHN: NTV. DUR: 45 mins. x 12 eps.; Sat 13 April 1991–29 June 1991.

Prosecutor Yōko (Kaku) has just transferred to the Tokyo District Public Prosecutor's Office (see HERO) from Miyazaki. However, like all TV lawyers, she soon becomes enmeshed in the cases she is supposed to be processing, starting with an incident in which a young child appears to have been crushed by a large TV set. With her reluctant assistant Ōyama (Ikariya), she starts investigating.

PSYCHOMETER EIJI

1997. PRD: Yūko Hazeyama. DIR: Yukihiko Tsutsumi. SCR: Shinji Ohara, Akihiro Tago. CAST: Masahiro Matsuoka, Nene Ōtsuka, Toshiya Nagasawa, Yūki Ohara. CHN: NTV. DUR: 45 mins. x 20 eps.; Mon 11 January 1997–15 March 1997 (#1); 16 October 1999–18 December 1999 (#2).

High school student Eiji (Matsuoka) has psychometric ability—he is able to see inside people's minds. When he inadvertently touches the shoulder of pretty female detective Shima (Ōtsuka), he sees an image of the murder she is currently investigating and is unable to keep himself from interfering. Based on the 1996 manga of the same name serialized in the weekly Shōnen Magazine by Yūma Andō and Masashi Asaki, this mystery series in the tradition of NIGHT HEAD was soon recommissioned for a second season, with Shizuka Kudō taking over the role of Detective Shima. Theme: TOKIO—"Furarete Genki" (Fine After Being Rejected).

PUNCHING WOMAN

1998. JPN: Naguru Onna. AKA: Woman Striking a Blow. PRD: Yūji Iwata, Takashi Ishihara. DIR: Hisao Ogura, Masataka Takamaru. SCR: Kumiko Tabuchi. CAST: Emi Wakui, Mitsuru Fukikoshi. CHN: Fuji. DUR: 45 mins. x 10 eps.; Tue 13 October 1998–15 December 1998.

Kaori (Wakui) loses her job at an advertising agency and somehow ends up running a boxing gym, despite an avowed dislike of the sport. But soon she comes to value the camaraderie among her clients and visitors and agrees to get involved in an upcoming tournament. Often confused with the unrelated FIGHTING GIRL. Theme: Mr. Children—"Owari Naki Tabi" (Journey Without End).

PURE *

1996. PRD: Miwako Kurihara. DIR: Daisuke Tajima. SCR: Yukari Tatsui, Atsuko Hashibe. CAST: Emi Wakui, Katsunori Takahashi, Shinichi Tsutsumi, Ryōko Shinohara, Saki Takaoka, Jun Fubuki. CHN: Fuji. DUR: 45 mins. x 11 eps.; Mon 8 January 1996–18 March 1996.

Yuka (Wakui) has the outward appearance of a bright and cheerful girl, but she suffers from a pathologically low IQ and is borderline autistic. Her loving mother (Fubuki) has encouraged her in her singular talent, an artistic ability that she appears to have inherited from her late father, a painter. Her

Purple Eyes in the Dark

cousin Ryō (Takahashi) secretly enters one of Yuka's paintings in a competition sponsored by his company, and Yuka is unprepared for the attention of the outside world when she unexpectedly wins. However, she forms a lasting friendship with Tōru, a photojournalist for *Move* gossip magazine, who was once a hotshot reporter but has been moved to a low-rent title as punishment for earlier misdeeds—compare to **TABLOID**. Completely disinterested in Yuka's challenged mental condition, Tōru offers to go into business partnership with her and soon finds himself falling for the simple girl who only sees his good side. With a twist ending and a 23.5% rating, this disability drama in the style of **FROM THE HEART** was one of the most popular series of its season, though it was soon eclipsed by Fuji's **LONG VACATION** in April. However, its effect was felt for years to come, as its very name became a buzzword among producers and writers for the disability dramas that dominated the late 1990s. Broadcast in the U.S. with English subtitles on KTSF TV and WMBC TV. Theme: Mr. Children—"Na mo Naki Uta" (Song With No Name).

PURE SOUL
2001. JPN: *Pure Soul: Kimi ga Boku o Wasuretemo*. AKA: *Pure Soul: Lest You Forget Me*. PRD: Yoshinori Horiguchi, Motoko Kimura. DIR: Akihiro Karaki.

SCR: Michiru Egashira. CAST: Hiromi Nagasaku, Naoto Ogata, Yasufumi Terawaki, Jun Oguri, Masahiro Taguchi, Shigeru Muroi. CHN: Yomiuri. DUR: 45 mins. x 12 eps.; Mon 9 April 2001–25 June 2001.
Two couples are struck by tragedy that leads to memory loss and the eventual death of love—one through drug abuse and the other through the onset of Alzheimer's disease.

PURPLE EYES IN THE DARK
1996. JPN: *Yami no Purple Eye*. PRD: Osamu Tezuka (b). DIR: Takeshi Nakagawa. SCR: Michiru Tanabe, Junji Takegami. CAST: Akiko Hinagata, Haruhiko Katō, Kanako Enomoto, Sayaka Yamaguchi, Ayumi Hamasaki, Azusa Nakamura. CHN: Asahi. DUR: 45 mins. x 11 eps.; Mon 1 July 1996–9 September 1996.
Teenager Tomoko (Hinagata) is kissing her boyfriend Shinya (Katō), when she suddenly feels the leopard-shaped birthmark on her chest throbbing with heat. She is confused by the experience but thinks nothing more of it until she is attacked by school bullies and inadvertently transforms into a leopard. Her new biology teacher Miss Sonehara (Nakamura) takes an interest in her case and realizes that the girl carries feline DNA. She suspects that it may have something to do with Tomoko's late father, a zoologist

hounded out of the scientific establishment for his controversial research into animal transformation.
PEitD began as a 1984 manga in *Margaret* magazine by Chie Shinohara, an author who excels at dramatizing the life-changing transformations of puberty, in works such as *Sea's Darkness Moon's Shadow* (*AE) and *Anatolia Story*. Though sounding superficially like a rip-off of the U.S. series *Manimal* (1983) with bonus Japanese schoolgirls, it is actually much more cerebral than that, magnifying teenage obsessions to earth-shattering importance in the style of **MASK OF GLASS**. It also embraces Shinohara's own Freudian obsession with blood and bleeding, such as a scene in the opening episode when Tomoko savors a cut finger—this is also probably one of the kinkier drama series on Japanese TV. Like her U.S. relative *The Incredible Hulk* (1978), Tomoko requires anger or rage as a catalyst for her transformations, leading Miss Sonehara to kidnap Shinya, drug him, and seduce him in front of Tomoko in order to study her reaction. There is also an anime "image video" based on the story, in which scenes from the manga are recreated during seven musical interludes (*AE). Compare to **DAUGHTER OF IGUANA**. Theme: Iceman—"Dark Half."

PURSUIT OF TOMORROW

1976. JPN: *Asu e no Tsuiseki*. PRD: Tomoyoshi Hagiwara. DIR: Minoru Hanabusa, Masami Uehara. SCR: Yūichirō Yamane. CAST: Shōichi Sawamura, Yūsuke Takita, Miyako Osanai, Masako Kizaki, Satoshi Hasegawa, Takeo Nishizawa, Yūko Saitō, Akemi Morita. CHN: NHK. DUR: 20 mins. x 12 eps.; Mon 10 May 1976–27 May 1976.

When Motoi (Sawamura) and Fuyuko (Saitō) are visiting their classmate Reiko (Morita), they see a boy trying to break into her house. Motoi tries to catch him, but the boy escapes, using telepathy to broadcast his pleas that he is not a thief. The next day, the boy arrives as a new student in Motoi's class and is introduced as Kiyoharu (Hasegawa). Before long, Motoi's classmates begin losing their memories, and Motoi and Fuyuko begin investigating. They are warned off by Kiyoharu, but eventually piece together some evidence from abandoned diaries—it appears that Reiko has concealed the fact that she and Kiyoharu know each other from another school.

Journeying to the town near Kamakura where Kiyoharu and Reiko used to live, Motoi discovers that they only began behaving strangely after their visit to a forbidden cave. Fuyuko is kidnapped by Kiyoharu and Reiko, who demand Motoi's pendant as a ransom. The children reveal that they have been possessed by aliens who have fled the destruction of their own planet and who now plan on migrating to Earth. Motoi's pendant contains a secret report on the planet, written by Kiyoharu's father long ago. Motoi returns the pendant to Kiyoharu, and the alien boy leaves for his own planet, in a shameless rehash of MYSTERIOUS NEW STUDENT and INFRARED MUSIC.

Q

QUEEN OF LUNCH

2002. JPN: *Lunch no Jo-Ō*. PRD: Masatoshi Yamaguchi. DIR: Narihide Mizuta. SCR: Yūki Niki, Juri Takada, Mika Ōmori. CAST: Yūko Takeuchi, Satoshi Tsumabuki, Misaki Itō, Tomohisa Yamashita, Takayuki Yamada, Gō Wakabayashi, Shinichi Tsutsumi, Yōsuke Eguchi. CHN: Fuji. DUR: 45 mins. x 12 eps.; Mon 1 July 2002–16 September 2002.

Café worker Natsumi (Takeuchi) lives for lunch and savors every moment, from the stroll through the restaurant quarter in search of a suitable venue to the meal itself. One day she is enjoying a rice omelet when she is dragged from the restaurant by Kenichirō (Tsutsumi). He explains that his father is critically ill, and in order to make good with him after a two-year feud, Kenichirō must arrive at the family home with a fiancée on his arm. Natsumi reluctantly agrees to play along and goes ahead of Kenichirō to scout the venue—the family business is the restaurant Kitchen Macaroni. On arrival, Natsumi discovers that Kenichirō is the black sheep in a clan of brilliant cooks—his father and three brothers serve her the best rice omelet she has had in her life. However,

Kenichirō's past comes back to haunt him—Yūko, the girl he jilted at the altar, has stayed on in the family business as a waitress and is on the run from both the police and her gangster ex-boyfriend. Broadcast in the U.S. without English subtitles on Asahi Homecast. Compare to **ANTIQUE**.

QUIET DON, THE

1994. JPN: *Shizukanaru Don*. PRD: Yoshiki Tanaka. DIR: Yasuharu Hasebe. SCR: Takuya Nishioka, Yoshio Oka. CAST: Hideyuki Nakayama, Yuriko Ishida, Yōko Nogiwa, Takeshi Kaga. CHN: NTV. DUR: 45 mins. x 19 eps.; Fri 21 October 1994–17 March 1995.

Seiya (Nakayama) appears to be an ordinary salaryman working for a lingerie company. However, he is also the son and heir to the leadership of the "Shinsengumi," one of the largest *yakuza* groups in the Tokyo area, who is only slumming it in a day job because his mother Tae (Nogiwa) thinks that six months in the real world will get the urge out of his system. Based on a 1988 manga in *Shōnen Sunday* by Tatsuo Nitta. The story was originally released as a one-shot anime in 1990 (*AE). There were two specials shown after this live-action adaptation—*The*

Quiet Don Returns (1995) and *The Quiet Don Forever* (1996). Compare to *The Sopranos* and **GOKUSEN**. Theme: Keisuke Kuwata—"Matsuri no Ato" (After the Fiesta).

QUIZ

2000. PRD: N/C. DIR: Natsuki Imai. SCR: Mio Aiuchi. CAST: Naomi Zaizen, Takashi Naitō, Sarina Suzuki, Yūko Moriguchi, Tatsuhisa Namase, Yūichi Haba, Rina Uchiyama. CHN: TBS. DUR: 45 mins. x 11 eps. (last ep 65 mins.); Fri 14 April 2000–23 June 2000.

Kiriko (Zaizen) is a detective with mind-reading abilities, drawn into a battle of wits with a criminal. Mai, a local English conversation teacher, files an abduction report for her young son—the only evidence left at the scene of the kidnapping is a note that reads *"This is a quiz."* As the detectives try to solve the crime, they are taunted with a series of e-mail riddles sent by the kidnapper. Though seemingly in the tradition of **PSYCHOMETER EIJI** or **KIDNAP**, *Quiz* has a much older pedigree—the abduction is merely a distraction from an examination of other skeletons in the family's closet, making the series more similar to **RIVER BANK ALBUM**. Theme: Kirari—"Toy Soldiers."

R

R-17

2001. PRD: Tetsuya Kuroda, Satoko Uchiyama, Kazuo Yamamoto, Kōichi Tōda. DIR: Masahiro Kunimoto. SCR: Toshio Terada. CAST: Miki Nakatani, Kaori Momoi, Seiichi Tanabe, Hitomi Satō, Yū Kurosawa, Masahiko Nishimura. CHN: Asahi. DUR: 45 mins. x 12 eps.; Thu 12 April 2001–28 June 2001.

Despite low self-esteem, guidance counselor Sakurako (Nakatani) accepts a posting to a problem school. The teachers are either completely disinterested in their students or reduced to bleak depression after their efforts to help have failed. The students are the usual assembly of teenage pregnancies, drug addicts, subsidized daters, and bullies, although unlike KINPACHI SENSEI or even GTO, R-17 makes little attempt to make any of these more palatable for a TV audience. Instead, it presents a genuinely hard-hitting vision of a troubled school, more suitable for a late-night slot instead of the nine o'clock one this show had. Watch out in particular for the principal's daughter—a psycho who encourages others to commit suicide because she "*likes to watch.*" Theme: Miki Nakatani—"Air Pocket."

RABBIT'S EYE

1976. JPN: *Usagi no Me.* PRD: N/C. DIR: N/C. SCR: Yoshiki Iwama. CAST: Motoo Yamada, Midori Kanazawa, Daigo Kusano, Takato Igarashi, Takumi Nagase. CHN: NHK. DUR: 20 mins. x 16 eps.; Tue 26 October 1976–18 November 1976.

Tetsuzō (Yamada) is an autistic boy in a class taught by Fumi (Kanazawa), a teacher who realizes that some of his strange behaviors are in fact a cry for attention and for help—Tetsuzō's only "friend" is his pet fly. Fumi decides on a project to encourage Tetsuzō to become more sociable with his classmates, in a children's series that foreshadowed many of the disability dramas of the 1990s.

RAINBOWMAN *

1972. JPN: *Ai no Senshi Rainbowman.* AKA: *Warrior of Love Rainbowman.* PRD: Masayoshi Kataoka, Kōichi Noguchi. DIR: Takeshi Yamada, Suguru Nagano, Hiroyasu Sunahara. SCR: Tsunehisa Itō, Tatsuo Tamura, Takayuki Kase. CAST: Kunihisa Mizutani, Kakuko Motoyama, Eriko Ishikawa, Megumi Itō, Akifumi Inoue, Akihiko Hirata, Mayumi Yamabuki, Mieko Saegusa, Machiko Soga, Masao Murata, Hajime Kurata, Toki Shiozawa. CHN: NET (Asahi). DUR: 25 mins. x 52 eps.; Fri 6 October 1972–28 September 1973.

Thrown off his team for being too violent, champion wrestler Takeshi (Mizutani) goes in search of one-time master of the martial art Divadatta (Inoue, presumably his character is intended to refer to *Devadatta*, Buddha's cousin). Now living the life of a hermit in India, Divadatta becomes Takeshi's new mentor, and the sage teaches him discipline and the mastery of seven special transformations in the style of SEVEN COLORED MASK, each based on the Japanese names of the days of the week. Moonman (Monday) can shrink to a small size, Fireman (Tuesday) can spray fire from his fingers, Waterman (Wednesday) can breathe underwater and also spray water and/or ice at his enemies, Treeman (Thursday) has chameleon-like powers and can throw pine needles, Goldman (Friday) can throw thunderbolts and also fly short distances, and Earthman (Saturday) can cause earthquakes and also burrow underground. The prime incarnation, Sunman (Sunday) has numerous rainbow powers, including a heat ray. In later episodes, Takeshi develops the ability to combine separate attributes, allowing him to use three day powers at once. His enemy Mister K (Hirata) is an evil mastermind whose foreign allies are chiefly Chinese nationals determined to avenge themselves on Japan for humiliations suffered during World War II. Their activities include kidnapping Takeshi's friends and family and even finding his long-lost father in an African prison so that they can hold him for ransom. His later enemies include God Iguana (Shiozawa) and her mother (Soga), whose schemes are occasionally at odds with Mister K's, resulting in a three way battle at the end of each episode. Based an idea by

MOONLIGHT MASK creator Yasunori Kawauchi and reputedly broadcast with English subtitles on local television in Hawaii. The show was resurrected on its tenth anniversary as an anime series (*AE). Theme: Kenji Yasunaga—"Ike Rainbowman" (Go Rainbowman).

RED
2001. PRD: Takashi Kazeoka, Naomi Ōkubo. DIR: Akinori Yutani, Yasuyuki Fujiki, Tomoyuki Minagawa. SCR: Natsu Komori. CAST: Ryōko Yūi, Tomohiro Sekiguchi, Minori Terada, Katsuyuki Murai, Mayumi Asaka. CHN: Fuji. DUR: 15 mins. x 62 eps.; Tue 2 October 2001–28 December 2001.
Ever since childhood, Asami (Yūi) has been teased about her unnaturally red hair. Her parents appear to shun her, and the final straw comes when she is raped by a friend of her brother, who adds hurtful insult to criminal injury by sticking a paper bag over her head so he does not have to look at her "ugly" face. Running away to Tokyo, Asami befriends two men, Fuyuki and Naoya. The boys share the same father, but different mothers—Naoya was born in wedlock, whereas Fuyuki is the child of his father's mistress. Soon, Asami's interest in the boys becomes more than platonic, although her initial choice, Fuyuki, appears to let her down, causing her to turn to Naoya for solace. Based on the book by Erica Spindler. Compare to **MIDDAY MOON**.

RED BARON
1973. AKA: *Mach Baron, Ganbaron.* PRD: Harutoshi Kawaguchi, Hiroshi Uemura, Seizō Tamura (#1); Akira Yasuda, Harutoshi Kawaguchi, Toshio Ueda, Tetsuya Kobayashi (#2); Kazuhiko Watanabe, Akio Takahashi, Minoru Uchima, Kiyoshi Suzuki (#3). DIR: Kiyoshi Suzuki, Hirokazu Takano, Tōru Sotoyama (#1); Kiyoshi Suzuki, Kōichi Takano, Toshitsugu Suzuki, Masataka Yamamoto (#2); Shōhei Tōjō, Kengo Furusawa, Kiyosumi Fukasawa (#3). SCR: Shōzō Uehara, Keisuke Fujikawa (#1); Shōzō Uehara, Tomoji Inoue, Seiya Yamazaki (#2);

Hideyoshi Nagasaka, Shōzō Uehara, Narimitsu Taguchi (#3). CAST: Yōsuke Okada, Tetsuo Kinoshita, Toshi Katō, Pepe Hozumi, Rei Maki, Tetsuya Ushio, Isao Tamagawa, Hiroshi Ikaida, Nobuyuki Ishida, Sadako Amemiya, Yōichi Miyagawa, Akihiko Nagano, Tokio Yajima, Kunihide Kuruma (#1); Makoto Shimozuka, Yuri Kinoshita, Takashi Chikaraishi, Tamotsu Katō, Toshihiko Utsumi, Jirō Dan, Akiyoshi Fukae, Hiroshi Ikaida, Noboru Maro, Masaki Tokoro, Akihira Kimura, Yutaka Amano (#2); Kazuto Andō, Kiyotaka Ichikawa, Miwa Kawahata, Toshihiko Utsumi, Kumi Nishijima, Mami Kanetsuki, Katsuhiko Tanibe, Mayumi Harada, Susumu Ishikawa, Susumu Kurobe, Hideyo Amamoto, Gorō Hanamaki (#3). CHN: NTV. DUR: 25 mins. x 97 eps.; Wed 4 July 1973–27 March 1974 (#1); 7 October 1974–31 March 1975 (#2); 3 April 1977–24 December 1977 (#3).
The latest robots are gathered from all over the world for a Robot International Exhibition, which is then disrupted by the Iron Mask Party (IMP) led by the evil Deviller. The IMP intend to steal the robots and use them to enslave mankind. Kidnapped by the IMP, robot genius Dr. Kenichirō Kurenai leaves behind the superrobot Red Baron in the care of his brother Ken. IMP demands that he hand over Red Baron but he refuses and is killed. Ken and other members of Secret Science Institute (SSI), who are said to be modern ninja, fight IMP with the aid of Red Baron.
Often regarded as a live-action version of *Mazinger Z* (*AE), this robot show entered production at roughly the same time. Combining the action of **MASKED RIDER** and the stomping battles of **ULTRAMAN**, the first 26 episodes concerned the battle against the IMP, while the final 13 of the first season concentrated on the defeat of the real enemy—the Space Iron Mask Party who had been pulling strings from orbit.
The series was retooled the following year for Mach Baron, a follow-up in

which orphan Yō Arashida pilots the new Mach Baron robot in order to defeat the evil robot army of Dr. Rarahstein. Ratings, however, were not as impressive as for *Red Baron*, and the series was truncated after just 26 episodes.
However, the producers gave it another shot with *Chiisana Superman Ganbaron* (Little Superman Ganbaron), a 32-episode follow-up in which Mitsuru Tendō (Andō) is an ordinary 11-year-old boy who can turn into the superhero Ganbaron. While his parents are away in America, he lives, in the style of *Batman*, in a huge mansion with a butler called Musshu (Kurobe) and a supercomputer called Goemon, which is programmed to encourage him in his efforts and be a friend when he is depressed. His nemesis is Dr. Waruwaru (Amamoto), a childless friend of Mitsuru's grandfather to whom Mitsuru was rashly promised in a moment of weakness, and who has returned to wreak his revenge.
Starting off like a replay of **ASTRO BOY**, *Ganbaron* only shows its true nature as a sequel to *Mach Baron* and *Red Baron* with the arrival partway through the series of the giant robot Divaron. Idol groups such as the Four Leaves and The Lilies also made appearances, but the series will be best remembered for establishing many of the robot combat formula that would inform the later Super Sentai series—see **GORANGER**.
During the "retro boom" of the 1990s, in which old series were brought back in an attempt to sell to children *and* their nostalgic parents, the franchise made another appearance in the 49-episode anime series *Red Baron* (*AE).

RED MOON
1977. JPN: *Akai Tsuki.* PRD: Kanae Mayuzumi. DIR: Minoru Hanabusa, Haruo Yoshida, Masami Uehara, Tetsushi Nakamura. SCR: Yoshiki Iwama. CAST: Hiroyuki Takano, Hōsei Komatsu, Sumie Sasaki, Noboru

Ichiyama, Hiromi Murachi, Taeko Kobayashi, Sumako Nomura. CHN: NHK. DUR: 20 mins. x 20 eps.; Mon 4 April 1977–5 May 1977.

Teenager Ken (Takano) visits a local temple with his classmate Konishi (Ichiyama), who reports that he has seen a red moon and heard a dark voice in the marsh nearby. The following day, Konishi disappears. Ken visits the marsh and sees the red moon for himself. His would-be girlfriend Kanae (Murachi) suggests that Konishi may have been killed and hands him Konishi's notebook—full of poetry about the allure of death. Searching the mountain near the marsh the following day, the pair find traces of blood. When the police arrive, they immediately assume that Ken is the murderer, killing his schoolmate in an argument over Kanae. However, Ken realizes that a more apt suspect could be his own teacher Nakamura, who was seen walking out of the marsh on the day that Konishi disappeared. Nakamura claims he was merely collecting plant samples, but seems spooked by the enquiries. Ken visits the temple to get further evidence, but is ordered to stay away by the monk who lives there. The following day, *Nakamura* goes missing, but Ken remains determined to solve the mystery. This NHK children's series was based on a book by crime novelist Seichō Matsumoto and kept the hard-hitting edge of the adult books for which the author is better known.

RED PEACOCK

1978. JPN: *Benikujaku*. PRD: N/C. DIR: N/C. SCR: Yasuo Tanami. CAST: (voices) Toyokazu Minami, Aki Mizusawa, Akira Kamiya. CHN: NHK. DUR: 15 mins. x 223 eps.; 3 April 1978–16 March 1979.

When the kingdom of the Aztecs falls to the Spanish, the treasure of its last ruler Montezuma is somehow spirited away to Japan, where it becomes the prize in a fierce battle between the Swan and Skull clans. A puppet show based on a story by Toshio Kitamura,

which was itself a popular radio series back in 1954. Compare to *Nazca* (*AE).

RED SHADOW

1967. JPN: *Kamen no Ninja Akakage*. AKA: *Masked Ninja Red Shadow*. PRD: N/C. DIR: Junji Kurata. SCR: Masaru Igami. CAST: Yūzaburō Sakaguchi, Yoshinobu Kaneko, Fuyukichi Maki, Shirō Ōtsuji. CHN: Fuji. DUR: 25 mins. x ca. 50 eps.; Wed 5 April 1967–27 March 1968.

Red Shadow (Sakaguchi) is the son of the Shadow ninja clan. Working for Tōkichirō Kinoshita, later known as **HIDEYOSHI**, he fights alongside gadget man Blue Shadow (Kaneko) and master of disguise White Shadow (Maki). The *Red Shadow* series divides into four story arcs—the first comprises a battle to stop the Order of the Golden Eye, a conspiracy led by Yōgensai Kaga, who is plotting to take over Japan. Kaga's men include Oboro Ikkan, a giant who can make his body as thin as paper and float into the air; he is just one of many super-powered adversaries faced by the ninja in the style of **PHANTOM AGENTS**.

The villains of the second story arc are the Swastika Party, a Christian group attempting to obtain the Bells of Zeus, Satan, and Maria, sacred objects brought from Portugal as gifts for **NOBUNAGA**. As with **THE SAMURAI**, the new adversary is in fact an offshoot of the original—the Swastika Party has been formed by Yōgensai Kaga after the failure of his previous conspiracy. This time, Kaga's ultimate weapon is a flying saucer armed with missiles. For the third and fourth seasons, the enemies are rival clans of ninja—the Thirteen Activists of Nerai and the Silent Army of Fūma.

Though redolent of superhero shows like **ULTRAMAN**, *RS* was still classified as a period drama. This is supposedly because it has a historical basis! By a tortuous process of para-logic, the historical Nobunaga was reputedly interested in Dark Arts, which makes it *possible* that his subordinate Tōkichirō Kinoshita had contacts with ninja, who are (we are assured) genuine historical

characters, and not at all the concoctions of TV writers and pulp novelists. *RS* was actually based on a wholly fictional manga by Mitsuteru Yokoyama, creator of **JOHNNY SOKKO AND HIS GIANT ROBOT**.

One of the earliest products of the thaw in relations between the traditionally antagonistic TV companies and film companies (see Introduction), *RS* was made as a coproduction between Tōei and Kansai TV. It was the first all-color period drama on Japanese TV, luxuriating in its rainbow of hues so much that it often appears virtually psychedelic—compare to **INFRARED MUSIC**. The story was resurrected in 1987 as a 23-episode anime series (*AE) and again in 2001 as Hiroyuki Nakano's live-action movie, to mark the 50th anniversary of Tōei.

RED SUSPICION

1975. JPN: *Akai Giwaku*. PRD: Kazuko Nozoe. DIR: Masaharu Segawa, Toshiaki Kunihara. SCR: Akihiro Ishimatsu, Sugako Hashida. CAST: Momoe Yamaguchi, Ken Utsui. CHN: TBS. DUR: 45 mins. x ca. 29 eps.; 3 October 1975–16 April 1976.

Sachiko (Yamaguchi) is the 17-year-old daughter of radiotherapist Professor Ōshima (Utsui). After exposure to radiation in the hospital, she develops leukemia, and, as if that was not enough trouble for one lifetime, discovers that Ōshima is not her real father and that her boyfriend is really her half brother.

Just as Japan's cinemas once competed between Red and White chains, and the New Year's Eve song contest still divides the country into two color-coded blocks, TV in the 1970s found two competing star vehicles. The White series (see **WHITE RUNWAY**) mainly featured Jirō Tamiya in the lead roles, while his competitor in the Red series was Ken Utsui. Another regular in the Red series was singer Momoe Yamaguchi, who made her debut as an actress in *Red Labyrinth* (1975), and appeared in six successive serials. Her singing career famously interfered with

© 1972 Tsuburaya Productions

Redman

the shooting schedule, which may not have showed onscreen, but led to the resignation of fellow actress Kaoru Yachigusa in protest. Peak rating: 30%.

Other Red series are: *Red Destiny* (*Akai Unmei*, 1976), *Red Shock* (*Akai Shōgeki*, 1976), *Red Rapids* (*Akai Gekiryū*, 1977), *Red Bonds* (*Akai Kizuna*, 1977), *Red Crash* (*Akai Gekitotsu*, 1978), *Red Storm* (*Akai Arashi*, 1979), *Red Soul* (*Akai Tamashii*, 1980), and *Red Death Line* (*Akai Shisen*, 1980). One particular high point was *Red Crash*, in which Utsui dances for 13 hours while his mother undergoes critical surgery.

RED TURNIP

1992. JPN: *Akakabu Kenji no Gyakuten Hōtei*. AKA: *Prosecutor Red Turnip's Reversed Triumph at the Court*. PRD: N/C. DIR: Takeharu Hidaka. SCR: Tatsuhiko Kamoi. CAST: Frankie Sakai, Jun Miho, Tetsurō Tanba, Masumi Harukawa. CHN: Asahi. DUR: 45 mins. x

11 eps.; Mon 6 January 1992–16 March 1992.
Public prosecutor Shigeru (Sakai) gains the nickname "Red Turnip," on account of his love of the distinctive vegetable. He is posted to the Kaga branch of the Kanazawa District Public Prosecution Office, where he finds himself faced with a number of crimes to solve, with only his daughter Yōko (Miho), a Kyoto-based lawyer, volunteering to assist him.

Based on a crime novel by Shunzō Waku, the story first reached Japanese viewers in feature-length TV specials in the style of Columbo. The first, *Akakabu Kenji Funsenki* (*Prosecutor Red Turnip's Battle at the Court*), was shown on 17 April 1990 and was followed by two more in October and the following February, before this series in a more traditional 11-part mode. After the end of the TV series, *Red Turnip* returned in over a dozen further TV specials

throughout the 1990s and beyond. The most recent was shown on 19 October 2002.

REDMAN

1972. PRD: N/C. DIR: Kanji Ōtsuka, Tatsuki Adachi. SCR: N/C. CAST: N/C. CHN: NTV. DUR: 5 mins. x 138 eps.; Mon 24 April 1972–3 October 1972.
Broadcast as a part of the *Good Morning!* children's show, *Redman* features a superhero from planet Red, who fights with a monster each day to keep the Earth safe. Guest foes included costumes previously seen in **ULTRAMAN** and **MIRRORMAN**.

REFRAIN *

1998. JPN: *Meguriai*. AKA: *Twist of Fate*. PRD: Takashi Hashimoto, Yasuo Yagi. DIR: Tamaki Endō, Nobuhiro Doi. SCR: Noriko Yoshida. CAST: Takako Tokiwa, Masaharu Fukuyama, Kenichi Okamoto, Megumi Ōji. CHN: TBS. DUR: 45 mins. x 12 eps. (1st ep 70 mins.); Fri 10 April 1998–26 June 1998.
Graduate student Shūji (Fukuyama) falls in love with his neighbor, wannabe dancer Eri (Tokiwa). A year after they first meet, he asks her to marry him but she demurs, reminding him that she wants to study dance in New York and that marriage would ruin that plan. Shūji resents the implications in her answer, and after an argument, the couple split up. Two years later, Eri returns from New York and meets Shūji on the street. Shūji is with his fiancée Nahoko (Ōji) and assumes that Eri's doctor is also her boyfriend. Finding much in common, Nahoko and Eri meet in the Refrain coffee shop to gossip about Shūji, although Eri tries to cover a secret of her own— it turns out that Shūji was right about her dancing career and she should have listened to him. Meanwhile, Shūji's company suffers a financial crisis, causing Nahoko's snooty father to urge her to call the wedding off. Shūji and Eri commiserate about the downward turn in their luck, but their association only makes matters worse, as Nahoko now suspects they are having

an affair. However, matters are soon resolved, Shūji is married, and Eri throws herself into her work to forget him. As a result, she is hospitalized from overwork. Claiming he wants the best for her, Shūji confronts her about her friend Shimizu, who is about to leave for New York. Shūji urges her to admit her feelings for Shimizu, stop him at the airport in the style of many other Japanese dramas, and live happily ever after.

While that might be a suitable ending for most other series, that only takes us two thirds of the way through *Refrain,* which deliberately toys with the audience's expectations. Employing a similar time structure to the later **WEDNESDAY LOVE AFFAIR**, the story jumps ahead a further two years, to find Shūji struggling to deal with his father's death and heading toward imminent divorce from Nahoko. Getting into a taxi one day, he is shocked to discover that the driver is Eri, and that her "happily ever after" never happened, courtesy of an accident at the airport. The couple eventually move back in together, with Shūji trying to pursue a career as a photographer, while Eri supports him by working in a hostess bar. But the couple is split up once more by the reappearance of Shimizu, and Shūji leaves for Bosnia. He returns for the finale, only to discover that the Refrain is going to close down—an occurrence that will also lead to the demolition of the apartment he once shared with Eri. With this symbol of his happiness under threat, he prepares to make everything right—compare to **UNMARRIED FAMILY**, which similarly uses a demolished house as a metaphor for a lost way of life. Note that the Japanese title of *Sleepless in Seattle* (1993) is *Meguri Aetara,* or "If We Were Fated to Meet" while *Meguriai* was also the Japanese title of *An Affair to Remember* (1957). Theme: Masaharu Fukuyama—"Heart."

REIKO SHIRATORI I PRESUME

1993. JPN: *Shiratori Reiko de*

Gozaimasu. AKA: *I Am Reiko Shiratori.* PRD: Kōji Shiozawa. DIR: Masayuki Suzuki. SCR: Yoshikazu Okada, Yumiko Suzuki. CAST: Yasuko Matsuyuki, Masato Hagiwara, Chiharu Komatsu. CHN: Fuji. DUR: 45 mins. x 11 eps.; Thu 14 January 1993–11 February 1993 (#1); 16 October 1993–13 November 1993 (#2).

Reiko (Matsuyuki) is a wealthy brat, but she is innocent and clueless in matters of the heart. At kindergarten, she was bullied because she used to arrive in Daddy's stretch limo, but she was defended by schoolmate Tetsuya (Hagiwara), whom she has secretly adored ever since. She tries to win his love, but most of her efforts go horribly wrong.

*RSIP'*s 11-episode running time is that of a normal series, but was split into two halves across the year for reasons we have been unable to determine. The first five episodes ended on a definite high, with Reiko finally securing a marriage proposal from her beloved Tetsuya. However, in the second season, she cancels the wedding in order to encourage "the best love" between Tetsuya, making it possible for rival rich girl Ayame (Ritsuko Tanaka) to try and steal Tetsuya for herself.

A comedy in the style of the director's later **POWER OFFICE LADIES**, *RSIP* was based on the manga of the same title by Yumiko Suzuki, who also contributed to the TV series as a scriptwriter. *RSIP* the TV series was preceded by a one-shot anime video in 1990, in which Reiko was played by Maria Kawamura, the voice of Jung Freud from *Gunbuster* (*AE).

REMOTE

2002. PRD: Yūko Hazeyama, Masahiro Uchiyama. DIR: Tōya Satō. SCR: Shin Kirin, Yūji Sakamoto. CAST: Kyōko Fukada, Kōichi Dōmoto, Konishiki, Jun Nakura. CHN: NTV. DUR: 45 mins. x 10 eps.; 12 October 2002–14 December 2002.

Former traffic cop Kurumi (Fukada) is transferred to the Special Investigation Room for Unsolved Cases, where she

Remote

soon eventually tracks down her new boss Kōzaburō Himuro (Dōmoto from the Kinki Kids). Now with chronic agoraphobia after a traumatic incident, he refuses to leave his basement but continues to work remotely by phoning in his instructions to his partner. Based on a story by **YOUNG KINDAICHI FILES** writer Seimaru Amagi, *Remote* was also adapted into a manga version, drawn by Tetsuya Koshiba for *Young Magazine.* It mixes the investigative thrills of **UNSOLVED CASES** with the bickering partners of **BAYSIDE SHAKEDOWN**. Theme: Kinki Kids—"Solitude: Shinjitsu no Sayonara" (Solitude: True Goodbye).

RENDEZVOUS

1998. PRD: Takashi Hashimoto. DIR: Nobuhiro Doi, Susumu Ōoka, Fuminori Kaneko. SCR: Yoshikazu Okada. CAST: Misako Tanaka, Kaori Momoi, Katsunori Takahashi, Takashi Kashiwabara, Mitsuru Fukikoshi, Hiromasa Taguchi, Kyōko Kishida, Maiko Kikuchi, Sayaka Yamaguchi. CHN: TBS. DUR: 45 mins. x 11 eps.; Fri 3 July 1998–11 September 1998.

Two women flee to the Hotel Maria after disastrous marriages come to terrible ends. Asako (Tanaka) is an everyday housewife traumatized by the discovery that her husband cares more about his toy collection than he does about her. Mayumi (Momoi) is one half of a husband-and-wife authorial team, who has given up writing and withdrawn from public life after her husband's suicide. Compare to **HAPPY MANIA** and **SERIOUS AFFAIR**. Theme: Tomomi Kahara—"Here We Are."

RETURN OF THE GOLD WOLF

1999. JPN: *Yomigaeru Kinrō*. PRD: Ken Inoue, Yūichi Abe. DIR: Katsuyuki Motohiro, Tarō Ōya, Fuminori Kaneko, Hideki Isano. SCR: Shōichi Maruyama. CAST: Shingo Katori, Ryō Ishibashi, Takako Uehara, Manami Honjō, Chōsuke Ikariya, Shin Takuma, Takashi Itō. CHN: NTV. DUR: 45 mins. x 11 eps.; Sat 17 April 1999–26 June 1999.
Tetsuya (Katori from SMAP) applies for a job at the Shin Tōa company after a suicide attempt by its former chairman (his stepbrother) and the company's acquisition by the evil Mogi Corporation. By day, he puts on a perfect performance as a mild-mannered salaryman, but each night he becomes a hard-boiled detective, investigating the intrigues that led to the Mogi takeover and tracing the ownership of the various shares that caused his brother to lose control of the corporation. The result is a loving homage to the *noir* investigator of yesteryear, **DETECTIVE STORY**'s Yūsaku Matsuda, with just a touch of the Clark Kent/Superman secret identity. Peak rating: 21.4%. Theme: Miki Imai—"Sleep My Dear."

RETURN TO YESTERDAY

1993. JPN: *Ano Hi ni Kaeritai*. PRD: Hiroshi Akabane. DIR: Satoru Nakajima. SCR: Ryōichi Kimizuka. CAST: Shizuka Kudō, Momoko Kikuchi, Naoki Hosaka, Tetsuya Bessho, Karen Kirishima. CHN: Fuji. DUR: 45 mins. x 11 eps.; Mon 11 January 1993–22 March 1993.
Flighty younger sister Kayoko (Kudō) leaves Japan to study English in New York and asks her boxer boyfriend (Hosaka) to keep an eye on her elder sister Chiyoko (Kikuchi), a responsible

career woman who works in the film business. One day, Chiyoko is surprised to see Kayoko back in Japan, sitting among the journalists at the press call for a new movie. She is taken aback, not only because her sister has not warned her that she is returning to Japan, but also because during her absence, she and the boxer have fallen in love. Kayoko announces that she is back in Japan to stay and manages to get herself a job at the same film company. Theme: Shizuka Kudō— "Dōkoku" (Strong Emotion).

RICE CURRY

1986. PRD: N/C. DIR: Narimichi Sugita. SCR: Sō Kuramoto. CAST: Saburō Tokitō, Miwako Fujitani, Takanori Jinnai, Saburō Kitajima, Kiichi Nakai. CHN: Fuji. DUR: 45 mins. x 13 eps.; Thu 3 April 1986–26 June 1986.
Ken (Tokitō) and Akira (Jinnai) are invited by sushi chef Jirō (Kitajima) to follow him to Canada and open a Japanese restaurant. The pair drop everything and relocate to Vancouver, only to discover that Jirō has run away with his boss's wife. While they track down Jirō, they stay with BJ (Nakai), a student of log cabin architecture. Ken admires BJ's application and drive, only to see his hard-working friend crushed to death under a pile of logs. Akira and Ken soon have a falling out, though Ken eventually finds Jirō when he reads about him in the newspaper. Jirō has won the lottery and no longer has any desire to sell curry rice to the people of Canada. Instead, he wants to set up a very high-class Japanese restaurant, which is unlikely to require the services of inexperienced short-order cooks. Ken realizes that he has a dream of his own after all—he genuinely wants to set up a little curry rice restaurant, and it has taken this trip to Canada to prove it to himself. Made at the height of Japan's bubble economy, this tale from **FROM THE NORTH** writer Sō Kuramoto contains stern warnings about the perils of a get-rich-quick mentality.

RING

1999. JPN: *Ring Saishūshō*. AKA: *Ring— The Final Chapter*. PRD: Kazuhiko Takahashi. DIR: Yoshito Fukumoto, Hiroshi Nishitani. SCR: Kōji Makita. CAST: Toshirō Yanagiba, Tomoya Nagase, Kotomi Kyōno, Akiko Yada, Kei Yamamoto, Hitomi Kuroki, Yūta Fukagawa, Fumiyo Kohinata. CHN: Fuji. DUR: 45 mins. x 12 eps.; Thu 7 January 1999–25 March 1999.
Three years after the death of his wife Suzuka, former ace reporter Kazuyuki Asakawa (Yanagiba) has taken a voluntary transfer to the editorial department of the *Chūō Shinbun* newspaper—opportunities abound for a crossover story if he ever meets the cast of **TABLOID**. At the funeral of his niece Tomoko, Kazuyuki begins to suspect that several apparently unrelated deaths in his neighborhood were connected by an urban myth about a cursed videotape. He also discovers that his niece's recent trip to the countryside with friends was really a secret tryst with a local tough guy, who has also died under mysterious circumstances. Dumping his son Yōichi (Fukugawa) on his assistant Akiko Yoshino (Kyōno), Kazuyuki heads up to the remote Yatsugatake villa where the dead couples stayed. He finds and views the supposedly cursed video cassette, which seems to be nothing more than a pop promo for the idol singer Nao Matsuzaki. That night, he also finds the landlord dead—he, too, watched the tape precisely 13 days earlier.

Kazuyuki seeks the help of paranormal researcher Ryūji (Nagase), who discovers a series of subliminal messages embedded in the pop promo, including a baby's face, a picture of a woman at a mirror, and the text of a curse that sentences the viewer to death within 13 days. It also divulges that there is a way to break the spell, but cuts off before it can explain how. Further investigation reveals that while the original broadcast was quite innocent, viewers in one area received a garbled transmission that appeared to emanate from the brain of a troubled psychic.

Kazuyuki goes in search of Shizuko, a famous psychic from the post-war period, though her relatives on the remote island of Ōshima claim she died in the 1950s. In fact, Shizuko is still alive, but has been kept in seclusion ever since her predictions saved local villagers from the eruption of Mount Mihara in 1957. However, Shizuko is killed by supernatural forces before she can help Kazuyuki with the curse—the only clue she leaves is a fragment of her daughter's name, Sadako.

Based on the 1991 novel by Kōji Suzuki, *Ring*'s story is best known through the 1997 cinema version of the same name, directed by Hideo Nakata. It was the success of the film and its sequels that rushed this series into production, affording more opportunities to add extra scenes. Thus the *Ring* TV series takes two full episodes before it reveals the subliminal messages in the tape and also takes time out for much deeper investigations of the paranormal. Most notably, there are previously unseen subplots revolving around the dead Yatsugatake landlord, who scientist Rieko (Kuroki) finds to be infected with smallpox and Ryūji's traumatized stepsister Mai (Yada), who lurks in his house eating raw meat. Note also the presence of Shizuko herself as a character, whereas in the movie she was already dead. The audio message on the tape, translated in the movie version as "*Frolic in brine / Goblins be thine,*" (unnecessarily poetic in the movie translation: a more faithful version would be simply "*Play in the sea and a monster will get you*") becomes the more prosaic, but no less chilling "*Next year unto you / A baby will be born*" for television.

When Kazuyuki seeks Ryūji's assistance, the maverick researcher is already under a police investigation, suspected of causing the death of rival TV pundit Dr. Kaneda (Kohinata) through hypnotic suggestion in an early subplot. Kazuyuki and Akiko also get

to dissect some of Ryūji's powers, analyzing some of his parlor tricks and reiterating an early statement that most "magic" is either a con trick or has a perfectly reasonable scientific explanation. Scenarist Makita uses mundane modern evils to blind the characters to magical truths—when Tomoko is found dead in her bathroom, the police immediately suspect a drug overdose, and the true nature of the early human deaths goes almost unnoticed because of the false alibi concocted to hide the teenagers' secret sexual assignation. Furthermore, Ryūji is legally untouchable because putting a curse on someone is not a crime in modern Japan (see **THE CURSE**)— much of the police case against him is aimed at establishing more quantifiable methods for Kaneda's death.

However, while *Ring* worked well as a single feature, large parts of the TV serial's nine-hour duration seem like so much ballast. The movie switched the leads' genders to make *female* TV reporter Reiko Asakawa (Nanako Matsushima), who, with her lovelorn *male* assistant Yoshino (Yutaka Matsushige), joins forces with her *ex-husband and sometime psychic* Ryūji, played by Hiroyuki Sanada. If anything, the net result of the TV version of *Ring* is a renewed respect for the movie scenarist Hiroshi Takahashi, whose judicious editing of the story made for a much leaner and cleaner narrative.

Ring was screened at the very peak of Japan's post-*The X-Files* thriller boom (*The X-Files* was first screened on TV Asahi in November 1995), with **UNSOLVED CASES** running the following evening. It also played with the audience's expectations in a uniquely cheeky way, prefacing the first episode with an onscreen title that flashes past with almost subliminal swiftness—"*After 13 days, the people who videotaped this drama . . .*" This original form of copyright protection was inspired by a gimmick in Suzuki's novels, which were presented as case notes themselves infected with the Ring virus. Anyone

reaching the end of the novels would receive the chilling news that they, too, had just been cursed. The story was also adapted into manga forms, first by Kōjiro Nagai from Suzuki's novel and then by Misao Inagaki, using Hiroshi Takahashi's movie script as a source. Other parts of the *Ring* story were adapted into manga by the artist Meimu, who was also responsible for the manga version of *Gasaraki* (*AE). Peak rating: 21.1%. Theme: Original Life—"STARS."

The *Ring* series was not the first TV incarnation of the story. *The Complete Ring* (*Ring Kanzenban*, 1995) is a 95-minute TV movie shown on Fuji, directed by Chisui Takigawa, and written by **NIGHT HEAD**'s Jōji Iida with Taizō Soshiya. Featuring Katsunori Takahashi as Kazuyuki and Yoshio Harada as Ryūji, this version adheres closer to the plot of the novel, titillating the viewer with additional shots of Sadako (Ayane Miura) killing her victims in the nude.

The series **SPIRAL** is a sequel of sorts.

RINTARŌ *

1995. JPN: *Kagayake Rintarō*. AKA: *Blazing Rintarō, Lighten Up Rintarō*. PRD: Tamaki Endō. DIR: Tamaki Endō. SCR: Akio Endō. CAST: Toshiaki Karasawa, Kirin Kiki, Kyōzō Nagatsuka, Makiko Esumi, Miho Tsumiki. CHN: TBS. DUR: 45 mins. x 12 eps.; Sun 8 October 1995–24 December 1995.

Rin (Kiki) has brought up her son Rintarō (Karasawa) on her own, working sometimes as a nurse and sometimes as a cab driver. Rintarō becomes a sales person at an advertising company, where he meets and falls in love with a fellow co-worker (Tsumiki). However, his fiancée dies early on, leaving the distraught office worker to pick up the pieces of his life, unaware that the masked judo-girl who comes to his rescue in times of trouble is actually another woman (Esumi) who adores him from afar. Rintarō mixes the superheroics of **MOONLIGHT MASK** with the farce of a drama comedy, but caused some consternation on its original broadcast when it misleadingly gave SMAP's Masahiro Nakai a prominent role in its trailers. In fact, Nakai did not appear in the series until the sixth episode. Broadcast in the U.S. with English subtitles on KIKU TV. From the producer of **UNTIL THIS BECOMES A MEMORY**. Theme: Toshiaki Karasawa and Kirin Kiki—"Futari no Subete" (All About Us).

RISKY GAME

1996. PRD: Keisuke Miyakegawa. DIR: Yūichi Abe. SCR: Hiromitsu Nishida, Akiyo Takigawa. CAST: Yuki Matsushita, Yuriko Ishida, Maki Mizuno, Mikihisa Azuma. CHN: TBS. DUR: 45 mins. x 11 eps.; Thu 11 January 1996–14 March 1996.

Fashion designer Eiko (Matsushita), writer Shōko (Ishida), and teacher Tomomi (Mizuno) witness a high school girl throwing herself to her death. When they accidentally meet a few days later at a natural therapy salon, the three confess that the girl's death has affected their lives in different ways. A stranger's death provides the initial impetus, but otherwise compare to **ASUNARO CONFESSIONS** and its imitators.

RIVER BANK ALBUM

1977. JPN: *Kishibe no Album*. PRD: Tonkō Horikawa. DIR: Shinichi Kamoshita. SCR: Taichi Yamada. CAST: Naoki Sugiura, Kaoru Yachigusa, Yoshiko Nakada, Tomiyuki Kunihiro. CHN: TBS. DUR: 45 mins. x ca. 11 eps.; Fri 24 June 1977–30 September 1977.

An average-seeming Japanese family finally attains their dream of several years, building and moving into a house by the banks of the Tama River which runs through Tokyo. However, their happy story hides trouble beneath the surface. The father Kōsaku (Sugiura) is dabbling in criminal acts to save his company from going under. The children are grown-up, causing the mother Noriko (Yachigusa) to look for excitement in an affair, while the daughter (Nakada)

reveals that she is pregnant after being seduced by her American language-exchange partner. Meanwhile, son (Kunihiro) fails his university entrance exam and runs away from home. Eventually, as the family begins to realize how much they still rely on each other, the house is destroyed in a flood.

River Bank Album was based on the novel serialized in the *Tokyo Shinbun* newspaper by Taichi Yamada, creator of **HERE'S LOOKING AT YOU** and **MEN'S JOURNEY**. He refused to compromise for the sake of gaining good ratings and insisted on illustrating an ordinary family. It was a departure from conventional home dramas because it depicted the loneliness of a nuclear family in a big city and a housewife's search for a life beyond the kitchen—compare to its later imitator **FRIDAY'S WIVES**. The series was a landmark in 1970s drama, and won both the Television Grand Prize and the Broadcasting Society's Galaxy Award for this doom-laden family drama, which was repeated five times on Japanese TV during the 1980s. Theme: Janice Ian—"Will You Dance?"

RIVER WEEPS, THE

1990. JPN: *Kawa wa Naiteiru*. PRD: Takayuki Urai. DIR: Nozomu Amemiya. SCR: Sō Kuramoto. CAST: Ayumi Ishida, Kōichi Iwaki, Mikihisa Azuma, Megumi Yokoyama. CHN: Asahi. DUR: 45 mins. x 4 eps.; Thu 4 January 1990–25 January 1990.

Kōji (Azuma) is cramming classes in order to take the university entrance exam. His brother Kimisaku (Iwaki) finds him a job at a hospital cafeteria but expects a favor in return. He asks Kōji to keep his ear to the ground for news of any critical patients, as a nod to the right people at the right time could be turned to the advantage of Kimisaku's struggling funeral parlor business. Compare to **GOOD MOURNING**.

ROBOT DETECTIVE

1973. JPN: *Robot Keiji*. PRD: N/C. DIR:

Atsuo Okunaka, Itaru Orita, Kazunari Uchida. SCR: Masaru Igami, Shōichi Nakayama, Shōzō Uehara. CAST: Haruo Chiba, Kaku Takashina, Keiko Kurenai, Yumiko Kaga, Sakyō Mikami, Shinichi "Sonny" Chiba, Yūko Kimi, Ritsu Nakajima, Junji Yamaoka, Hideo Nakamura, Kiyoshi Kawakubo. CHN: Fuji. DUR: 30 mins. x 26 eps.; Thu 5 April 1973–27 September 1973.

Badoh is an organization that rents out killer robots to criminals. In an attempt to combat the onslaught of assassins, the special science investigation department of the Metropolitan Police hire the services of K (voiced by Nakamura), a robot detective. Though K is programmed to be a hardworking police officer, he immediately finds himself partnered with an antagonistic human cop. Old-timer Shiba (Takashina) has hated all machines every since the death of his beloved wife in an automobile accident—he likes to go with his experience and intuition, and loathes K's ceaselessly logical approach to every problem. K, meanwhile, tries to comprehend human emotion. Together with the action-hero younger cop Tsuyoshi Shinjō (Chiba), the mismatched detectives hunt down Badoh's various robot crimes, hoping to eventually trace them back to the criminal organization itself.

Created by Shōtarō Ishinomori, who also drew a manga that ran alongside the TV broadcasts, *Robot Detective* was way ahead of its time and often cited by Japanese sources as a forerunner of *Robocop*. Though it is unlikely that *Robocop*'s creators knew of this obscure foreign series, *RD*'s influence back in Japan was more palpable, particularly in the middle period Metal Series from **JIVAN** onward.

As *Robot Detective* went on, the curmudgeonly Shiba stopped calling him a "scrap pile" and began to accept him as just another police officer—a silly idea rendered utterly believable by Kaku Takashina's superbly straight performance. This matter-of-fact attitude was part of the serial's appeal; like the later *Patlabor* (*AE), *RD* excels at times when it simply tells a police story that happens to have a robot in it, though that's not to say that it does not have time for scenes of robot combat. For clues to the mood of K in any scenes you may see—his eyes are usually yellow, but turn red during combat and blue when he is sad. Music by Shunsuke Kikuchi.

ROCINANTE

2001. JPN: *Aiken Rocinante no Sainan: Mukai Arata no Dōbutsu Nikki.* AKA: *The Disaster of the Dog Rocinante: Arata Mukai's Animal Diary; Dog Diary.* PRD: Kenji Ikeda. DIR: Tarō Ōya, Hidenobu Hosono. SCR: Tomoko Yoshida, Takurō Fukuda, Chizuko Fukuda. CAST: Tsuyoshi Dōmoto, Maiko Yamada, Ken Ogata, Maki Mizuno, Natsumi Abe, Jun Akiyama, Sōichirō Kitamura, Toshiyuki Hosokawa. CHN: NTV. DUR: 45 mins. x ca. 11 eps.; Sat 21 January 2001–31 March 2001.

Arata (Dōmoto from the Kinki Kids) is a third-year veterinary student at Hachiōji University, a good-natured simpleton who never gets angry and whose kindness is often exploited by his classmates. During an exam, fellow student Emily (Yamada) tries to copy the crib sheet smuggled in by Michiru (Akiyama from Johnny's Juniors) and uses Arata as a go-between. The three are caught cheating and put in charge of 100 dogs who need cleaning, walking, and feeding. Rushed off their feet, the trainee vets are less than sympathetic to Haruna (Abe from Morning Musume), a pretty local girl who brings in her dying terrier and is harangued for expecting dogs to have the same life spans as humans.

When the dogs are eventually returned to their owners, Rocinante the golden retriever remains behind. The students try to return him but discover that his master (a train conductor) has been killed in an accident. Realizing that Rocinante must find a new owner or be sent to the pound, Arata claims that the dog is his, winning both the respect of Haruna and

his own eviction from his no pets accommodation. Reluctantly, man and dog move to a new abode, only to discover it is an all-girls dormitory run by Kanako (Mizuno).

A lighthearted, but also lightweight, comedy that places unwarranted faith in the star power of its pop idol leads and forces them to interact with a menagerie of animals, *Rocinante* merely adds four-legged troublemakers to the standard TV drama love polygon. Michiru pursues Haruna in vain, while Haruna tries to attract the unaware Arata, whose "calm" nature is so laid-back it verges on the autistic. He is anemic, and his regular fainting episodes lead him back to the nurse's office, where staff battle-ax Granny Haruko tries to convince him to give up veterinary science as a lost cause. Meanwhile, his two professors Tōno (Kitamura) and Murashima (Ogata) duel incessantly over everything and anything—from research grants to who can cycle the fastest. The plot remains formulaic, to the extent of confronting Dōmoto's character with a similar disaster to the one that beset him at the end of **SUMMER SNOW**, and the three writers' chief concern appears to be playing to the teenybop audience. Consequently there are cameo appearances both from fellow Kinki Kid Kōichi Dōmoto as a new student asking directions and also from Jun Matsumoto of Arashi, who was filming **YOUNG KINDAICHI FILES** at a neighboring studio and kindly popped by to make one of the ending credit sequences look more interesting.

As one might expect, it's the animals that make the show, particularly Rocinante himself, who narrates the whole series in a drawling, alien manner (with a voice provided by Hosokawa), commenting all the while on humans and their strange customs. This, however, is nothing new—Japanese fiction has been crawling with talking pets ever since Natsume Soseki's *I Am A Cat* (1905). Where *Rocinante* really scores is in its milking of sentimentality—a staple of all

Japanese drama, but all the more easy to achieve in the presence of fluffy animals. Though named after Don Quixote's horse, the titular dog is really modeled on Hachikō, the famously faithful hound whose statue is a Tokyo landmark, eternally waiting for a master who tragically will never return. The vets also get many speeches along the lines of *"a pet is not just for Christmas, it's for life,"* though such worthiness sits uneasily with a drama written as a vehicle for stars of the moment. Compare to **HAPPY** and **ANIMAL DOCTOR**.

ROCKET BOY

2001. AKA: *Rocket Boys.* PRD: Ichirō Takai. DIR: Shunsaku Kawake. SCR: Kankurō Kudō. CAST: Yūji Oda, Yūsuke Santamaria, Somegorō Ichikawa, Risa Sudō, Kotomi Kyōno, Ryō Iwamatsu, Nanae Akasaka, Ikkei Watanabe, Kei Yamamoto, Tomoko Nakajima, Machiko Washio, Toshihide Tonesaku. CHN: Fuji. DUR: 45 mins. x 8 eps.; Wed 10 October 2001–12 December 2001.

As a child, Shinpei (Oda) wanted to be an astronaut. But as 2001, the long-awaited year of space holidays and food pills, approaches, he is just another single salaryman, working at Galaxy Travel in Tokyo, where he has just been made supervisor. Ducking out of an unwelcome *omiai* marriage meeting, he watches a baseball game, where he and two other spectators are sprayed with beer from an exploding dispenser. The irate trio are paid off with a vast hoard of free beer coupons, which have to be redeemed at the newly opened Jaguar Club. Thrown together, like the cast of **WHERE IS LOVE?**, by their regular attendance, they become friends.

If *RB* seems to play like an average-length series shortened by a third, that's because it is. With lead actor Oda absent due to illness, production was suspended after the first two episodes. While Oda recuperated, the network showed old episodes of **BAYSIDE SHAKEDOWN** and the writer swiftly cut the remaining story line into a more manageable eight episodes.

Romance of the Three Kingdoms

Oda returned, his leg in plaster, to salvage what he could from the remains of the shooting schedule, guaranteeing a sympathy vote if not a drama with the popularity of his earlier TOKYO LOVE STORY.

RB owes its most obvious debt to the films of Wong Kar-Wai. Like one of Wong's Hong Kong singletons, Shinpei eats cratefuls of cheap noodles in order to amass competition coupons. He has been jilted by a girlfriend who insists on returning to see him (the script resolutely keeps them from getting back together) and has a speech comparing romance to pineapples in homage to *Chungking Express* (1994). But even before its production problems began, *RB* was a disappointment. Like the 21st century itself, *RB* promises spaceships and adventure, only to deliver a humdrum world of marketing, advertising, and tourism. Though there are occasional fantasy cutaways in the style of *Ally McBeal* as Shinpei fantasizes about life in space, *RB* is little different from any other drama. Mismatched friends meet by accident, help each other in matters of the heart, and one of them gets married. Its hero, meanwhile, is not the proactive *rocket* the title implies, but a kindhearted, conservative *boy*, who works in

the big city and stands to inherit the family inn business. Girls think he looks like Harrison Ford (no, really) but he has trouble finding that special someone. One is tempted to point out that it might have helped his dream career if he had studied rocket science instead of tourism.

Though *RB* offers hope for Shinpei in its final moments, he is also seen passing on the torch to the next generation—in other words, admitting that he's stuck in his rut. A character complains that instead of *playing* baseball, now all he does is watch it, but a similar accusation could be aimed at Shinpei, who tells parties of schoolchildren about space travel instead of actually doing it. Many dramas offer a conservative message, telling their viewers that it is important to be happy with their lot in life, but *RB* adds an extra twist of the knife, depicting a post-modern Japan where there is nothing but service industries. There are no adventurers any more, merely people who promote films about adventurers, play them in commercials, and dress up as them at product launches. Compare to **100 YEARS**, which similarly tried to celebrate the new century, only to inadvertently depict it as business as usual, and to **MANTEN**, which was caught up in the aftermath of a space tragedy.

ROMANCE

1999. PRD: Jun Kurosawa. DIR: Kazuhiro Mori, Masahiro Hinako. SCR: Yasuo Hasegawa, Kōhei Tsuka. CAST: Rie Miyazawa, Hiroyuki Ikeuchi, Tomonori Yoshida, Haruhiko Katō, Tokuma Nishioka, Morio Kazama, Pinko Izumi, Akiko Hinagata. CHN: Yomiuri. DUR: 45 mins. x ca. 11 eps.; Mon 2 June 1999–?? September 1999.
Would-be journalist Mizuki (Miyazawa) flirts with Shigeru (Ikeuchi), a swimmer in training for the Sydney Olympics, only to discover that she has a love rival in the form of Shigeru's male friend Junpei (Yoshida). Theme: trf—"Wired," Hitomi—"Made to Be in Love."

ROMANCE OF THE THREE KINGDOMS

1982. JPN: *Sankokuji Sangokushi*. PRD: N/C. DIR: Minoru Hanabusa, Susumu Yasue, Tōru Minegishi, Kazuya Satō. SCR: Hide Ogawa, Yasuo Tanami. CAST: (voices) Hayato Tani, Renji Ishibashi, Leo Morimoto, Mitsuo Senda, Noboru Mitani, Nobuto Okamoto. CHN: NHK. DUR: 15 mins. x ca. 600 eps.; Sat 2 October 1982–24 March 1984.
In the second century A.D., Han dynasty China collapses into the warring states of Wei, Shu, and Wu. Yuan De, aka Liu Bei (Tani), Guan Yu (Ishibashi), and Zhang Fei (Senda) exchange an oath to die together and lead a futile attack against the Yellow Turban rebels. Surrounded by the enemy and believing their lives at an end, they prepare to go down fighting, only to be rescued by government troops led by Caocao (Okamoto). Caocao suggests that the one who defeats Zhang Jue shall have the hand of the beautiful maiden Shu Ling. Both Yuan De and Caocao kill the brothers of Zhang Jue only to find that the man in question was already dead. Shu Ling, however, chooses Yuan De, and his involvement in the battle wins him a position as the magistrate of An Ding. An inspector from the capital tries to bribe the noble Yuan De, and when he refuses, tries to frame him. An angry Zhang Fei punches the man, forcing the trio of warriors to flee. Meanwhile, the Emperor dies, causing upheavals in the court. A princess is enthroned, but when the central court remains unstable, the warrior Dong Zhuo arrives at the head of an army. Dong Zhuo plans on enthroning his brother as Emperor, but Caocao refuses to allow this and plots to assassinate him. The assassination attempt fails and he escapes to the countryside, where he asks for the aid of his old rival Yuan De. However, Yuan De refuses, knowing that Caocao's indignation hides his desire to be Emperor himself.

Along with **WATER MARGIN** and **MONKEY**, *Rot3K* forms the bedrock of Chinese literature—here it is adapted as an epic puppet play narrated by comedy duo Shinsuke Shimada and Ryūsuke Matsumoto, with more than 400 puppets from the master puppeteer Kihachirō Kawamoto. Other aspects of the production were similarly lavish, with special effects, theme music from Haruomi Hosono, and a script from the writers of **HOWL AT THE SUN**. The narrators not only introduced the action in a modern studio, but also presented bridging explanations with maps and diagrams, and even entered the action themselves in puppet form as the bungling peasant characters Xin-Xin (Shimada) and Long-Long (Matsumoto). Kawamoto's later **TALE OF THE HEIKE** recycled some of the puppets.

ROOKIE!

2001. PRD: Takahiro Kasaoki, Yūji Tōjō, Tatsuya Date. DIR: Renpei Tsukamoto, Kazuhisa Imai. SCR: Masaya Ozaki. CAST: Kōichi Dōmoto, Rina Uchiyama, Toshio Kakei, Yoshizumi Ishihara, Shinji Yamashita, Hitomi Kuroki. CHN: Fuji. DUR: 45 mins. x ca. 11 eps.; Tue 10 April 2001–26 June 2001.

Makoto (Dōmoto from the Kinki Kids) is a new recruit at the "life safety" section of Tengenji Police Station. On his way to his first day of work, he is mistaken for a kidnapper and then on arrival he is treated like a student by his colleague Reiko (Kuroki). Makoto has only become a cop because he hopes for a stable career in the civil service and so has deliberately chosen the supposedly risk-free, bland posting of the life safety section. However, in the tradition of every single cop-buddy series since the dawn of time, he is paired with someone very different— Kitami (Kakei), an overenthusiastic go-getter, desperate to be a frontline detective, but somehow never quite making the grade. Meanwhile, the sharp-minded Reiko remains eternally passed over for promotion by her bosses. This is because she is a divorcée with a young son, even though she is easily the best officer on the team by far. And since it wouldn't be a cop dra-

ma without a snooping journalist, Makoto soon finds himself falling for rookie photographer Kaori (Uchiyama). Theme: Kinki Kids— "Jōnetsu" (Passion).

ROUGE

2001. PRD: Yoshikazu Tsubaki. DIR: Takehiko Shinjō, Seiichi Nagumo. SCR: Kumiko Tabuchi. CAST: Eriko Imai, Reiko Takashima, Naoki Hosaka, Hideki Tōgi, Hiroko Nakashima. CHN: NHK. DUR: 45 mins. x 6 eps.; 28 August 2001–10 September 2001.

Risa Tanigawa (Imai) is a 20-year-old graduate, determined to make a career in the competitive world of advertising. She applies for her dream job, working under the renowned creative director Reiko Motomiya (Takashima) at the Christina cosmetics corporation and, much to her surprise, is accepted as the newest recruit on the advertising team. Despite outrageous clumsiness and an apparent inability to succeed at any task she is given, the hapless girl soon wins the illogical approval of her workmates, even after she loses the Persian cat that a flighty foreign model has inexplicably brought along with her to a photo session.

Risa is promoted up the corporate ladder, and before long is working as a runner at an Okinawa photo shoot, where she continues to lose vital documents, wake up napping copywriters, and get distracted by dancing children. However, such an ingénue act, which only the Japanese could find endearing, attracts the attention of cameraman Shingo (Hosaka), in search of a new face to stick in front of the lens when the crew lose their star model. Consequently, Risa finds herself shunted out of her path to creative director and put through the rigorous training and primping required of a model, in an NHK riches-to-even-more-riches tale that bills itself as a "modern *Cinderella*." Compare to **BRAND**, and also to **MASK OF GLASS**, since *Rouge* takes the *Cinderella* subtexts of the famous acting drama and applies them to a group of people whose sole aim in life is con-

Rouge

vincing gullible women to spend more money on cosmetics. Based on a novel by Mie Yanagi, which hopefully made more sense in its original format. Theme: Yumiko Fukuhara—"Get Your Groove On."

RULES OF MARRYING FOR LOVE, THE

1999. JPN: *Ren'ai Kekkon no Hōsoku*. AKA: *The Rules*. PRD: Takuya Kanai, Hidefumi Shōji. DIR: Hidekazu Matsuda, Narihide Mitsuta. SCR: Seigo Kashida, Arisa Kaneko. CAST: Kyōko Koizumi, Toshirō Yanagiba, Takashi Kashiwabara, Satomi Kobayashi. CHN: Fuji. DUR: 45 mins. x 12 eps.; Wed 7 July 1999–22 September 1999.

Comedy in the style of **ARRANGED MARRIAGE**, as a group of romantics try to subvert the policies of a marriage referral service, hoping to find some kind of magical system for guaranteeing true love. With an alternate title in *katakana* that simply reads "Rules," it is highly likely that this series owes its original inspiration to the controversial American best-seller *The Rules: Time-Tested Secrets for Catching the Heart of Mr. Right* (1995), by Ellen Fein and Sherrie Schneider. See **HOW TO MARRY A BILLIONAIRE**. Peak rating: 14.5%. Theme: Kyōko Koizumi—"For My Life."

© 1968 NHK

Ryōma Departs

RUN

1993. PRD: N/C. DIR: Susumu Ōoka.
SCR: Yūki Shimizu. CAST: Tsuyoshi
Nagabuchi, Sayuri Kokushō, Saburō
Ishikura, Chōchō Miyako. CHN: TBS.
DUR: 45 mins. x 11 eps.; Fri 15
October 1993–24 December 1993.
Rinpō (Nagabuchi) is a fortune-teller
who operates out of an exclusive hotel
room in Shinjuku. However, he has a
parallel career, robbing from the unde-
servedly rich and redistributing their
ill-gotten money to the needy. The
original idea for the series came from
rock musician Tsuyoshi Nagabuchi (see
THE BODYGUARD and **TONBO**), who also
supplied the theme song: "Run."

RUNNING CIVIL SERVANT

1998. JPN: *Hashire Kōmuin*. PRD: Kōichi
Funatsu. DIR: Hiroshi Nishitani. SCR:
Arisa Kaneko, Yasuyuki Nojiri. CAST:
Tamao Satō, Megumi Okina, Ken
Kaneko. CHN: Fuji. DUR: 45 mins. x 8
eps.; Tue 13 October 1998–8
December 1998.
Unable to find a job anywhere else,
Nagisa (Satō) sits for the police
entrance exam as a last resort.
Unexpectedly passing the test, she

arrives at the police station to begin
her training, only to find herself posted to the White Lily Section. She is
shocked to discover that the White Lily
Section is a notorious dumping ground
for all the force's misfits and flakes—
compare to **EVIL WOMAN** and **POWER
OFFICE LADIES** for corporate variations
on the same theme.

RUNNING THROUGH THE NIGHT

1993. JPN: *Mayonaka o Kakenukeru*.
PRD: N/C. DIR: Ryōko Hoshida. SCR:
Akiko Yamanaga. CAST: Riona Hazuki,
Junko Sakurai, Megumi Okina, Miki
Mizuno, Katsuyuki Mori. CHN: Asahi.
DUR: 45 mins. x 6 eps.; Tue 16
November 1993–21 December 1993.
High school students Risa (Hazuki),
Chika (Mizuno), and Setsuna
(Sakurai) form their own band. After
hearing of the sudden death of pop
star Moriya, Risa visits the site of her
idol's death, where she meets his
younger brother Tokio (Mori). The
two begin a tentative relationship,
though Tokio has little time for the
girls' desperation to gain a foothold on
the self-same media train that killed his
brother. Based on the manga by Mito
Orihara, creator of *Emerald Princess*
(*AE), this drama was probably
inspired by the death the previous year
of the pop idol Yutaka Ozaki—see
EDGE OF THE WORLD. Theme: Akiko
Matsukura—"Dakedo" (But . . .).

RYŌMA DEPARTS

1968. JPN: *Ryōma ga Yuku*. PRD: N/C.
DIR: Ichirō Tsujimoto, Ben Wada. SCR:
Yōko Mizuki. CAST: Kinya Kitaōji, Ruriko
Asaoka, Hideki Takahashi. CHN: NHK.
DUR: 45 mins. x ca. 50 eps.; 7 January
1968–29 December 1968.
This 1968 *taiga* drama depicted the life
of Ryōma Sakamoto, who played a key
role at the end of the Edo period. He
was originally from a sake brewer's
family in Tosa (modern Kōchi
Prefecture). Influenced by Kaishū
Katsu, he came to support the move-

ment to open up the country. He set
up a trading company with the help of
Satsuma (modern Kagoshima
Prefecture) and, with Shintarō
Nakaoka, he managed to unite
Satsuma and Chōshū (modern
Yamaguchi Prefecture) in order to confront the central government in 1866.
In 1867 imperial rule was restored and
Emperor Meiji became the head of the
country. Ryōma contributed to the
construction of the modern system
with ideas such as having lower and
upper houses of parliament, establishment of the constitution, and forming
a standing army. However, he was assassinated in that very year at the age of
32. Based on a novel by Ryōtarō Shiba,
RD portrayed Ryōma as sharp minded,
foresighted, and a man of action.

The story was remade as the 1974
taiga drama *Kaishū Katsu*, from which
lead actor Tetsuya Watari had to bow
out halfway through, handing over his
role to Hiroki Matsukata. While
Matsukata complained to the press
about NHK's interference on the set,
scriptwriter Sō Kuramoto also publicly
argued with the producers. The scenarist, best known for **FROM THE NORTH,**
eventually quit the production, which
ran for its full year despite such misfortunes. Other *taiga* dramas based on the
same pivotal period of Japanese history
include **LIFE OF A FLOWER, KAJIN, TIME
OF THE LION, AS IF IN FLIGHT,** and
TOKUGAWA YOSHINOBU.

The story of Ryōma also formed the
basis for *Ryōma Forever* (1998), a TBS
broadcast starring Takaya Kamikawa.
Technically a very, very long TV movie,
shown over five hours in a single day,
Ryōma Forever was later broken up into
two movie-length sections and broadcast with English subtitles in Hawaii on
KIKU TV. The story of Ryōma
Sakamoto was also adapted into the
anachronistic and irreverent **LEAVE IT
TO RYŌMA.**

SAILOR SUIT REBEL ALLIANCE
1986. JPN: *Sailor Fuku Hangyaku Dōmei*. PRD: N/C. DIR: Mitsuo Ezaki. SCR: Hisashi Nishiki. CAST: Miho Nakayama, Nobuko Sendō, Risa Yamamoto, Kyōko Gotō, Kazuki Minamibuchi, Rikiya Yasuoka. CHN: NTV. DUR: 30 mins. x 23 eps.; Mon 13 October 1986–23 March 1987.
Kokuchō Academy used to be an elite school but it is now a nest of evil. Accordingly, spunky schoolgirls Miho (Nakayama), Yumi (Sendō), Ruri (Yamamoto), and Kei (Gotō) form the Sailor Suit Rebel Alliance to eliminate wrongdoers from the school premises, wearing heavy makeup in order to keep their secret identities hidden. Clearly an attempt by NTV to cash in on the success of the bad girls in Fuji TV's SUKEBAN DEKA, *SSRA* was originally commissioned for a mere 12 episodes, but had its broadcast run extended after unexpectedly high ratings. See also GIRL COMMANDO IZUMI. Theme: A-Jari—"Shadow of Love."

SAKURA
2002. PRD: Kōji Yoshikawa. DIR: Kazuhiko Shimizu, Yuzuru Satō, Kōichi Fujisawa, Shinzō Nitta, Akihiro Kimura, Kazuki Miki. SCR: Kumiko Tabuchi. CAST: Shiho Takano, Yukiyoshi Ozawa, Miyoko Asada, Gorō Noguchi, Takashi Sasano, Mami Kumagai, Hiromi Ōta, Kaori Takahashi, Ramos Ruy. CHN: NHK. DUR: 15 mins. x 156 eps.: 1 April 2002–28 September 2002.

Sakura (Takano) is a fourth generation Japanese-American who comes to Gifu as an English teacher. With an outwardly Japanese appearance, but the product of several generations of American society, Sakura suffers massive culture shock as she tries to adjust to the culture her ancestors left behind. A serial TV novel from NHK, *Sakura* was the first of this long-running series of housewives' dramas to feature an American citizen as its heroine—compare to BURNING MOUNTAINS AND RIVERS, which also focused on a Japanese-American.

SALARYMAN KINTARŌ *
1999. JPN: *Salaryman Kintarō*. AKA: *Kintarō*. PRD: Mitsunori Morita. DIR: Mitsunori Morita, Katsunori Tomita. SCR: Kenji Nakazono. CAST: Katsunori Takahashi, Masahiko Tsugawa, Michiko Hada, Miki Mizuno, Yōko Saitō, Naoki Hosaka, Noriko Aota, Ichirō Maeda, Masanobu Katsumura, Daisaku Akino, Yōko Nogiwa, Kanako Enomoto, Megumi Toshiaki, Chōichirō Moriyama, Hiroki Matsukata. CHN: TBS. DUR: 45 mins. x 34 eps. (eps. #13 and #14: 70 mins.); Sun 10 January 1999–21 March 1999 (#1); 9 April 2000–2 July 2000 (#2); 6 January 2001–17 March 2001 (#3).
Former motorcycle gang member Kintarō (Takahashi) saves the life of a company CEO and is rewarded with a managerial position. He moves to Tokyo with his son (his blind wife

Akemi having died sometime earlier) and is welcomed at the Yamato Company by an honor guard of his old biker associates. He is also shocked to meet Hitomi (Mizuno), a stranger who is the spitting image of his late wife—compare to BEAUTY. Kintarō's immediate boss Ryūnosuke (Tsugawa) is under threat from evil schemer Ōshima (Moriyama), and Kintarō is charged with finding the elusive computer password that will unlock Ōshima's activities and then swiftly packed off to a number of subsidiaries as a corporate troubleshooter. He turns around a troubled Sales Department and rescues a construction site that has fallen far behind schedule, before suggesting to the board that the company invest in a multilevel *pachinko* center. His activities soon attract the attention of the local gangsters, but Kintarō's ability with his fists and backup from his former associates on the other side of the law help him win through.

Based on the manga by Hiroshi Motomiya, who also created *Climbing on a Cloud* (*AE), *Goodfella* (*AE), *Don! Brutal Water Margin* (*AE), *Iron Man* (*AE), *My Sky* (*AE), and *Trusty Ginjiro* (*AE), *Salaryman Kintarō* capitalized on the vogue for gangsters-made-good in the wake of GTO and gained a respectable rating of 20.9%. Its hero soon returned for a second season, promoted now to Section Chief, and put in charge of the Yamato venture capital firm. Approached by Ling, a

Samurai, The

man he once saved from attackers, Kintarō tries to fund a chain of Chinese restaurants, only to face opposition from Chinese gangsters. Soon, however, he is involved in corporate intrigue again, as Yamato tries to sponsor a political candidate, and rival Heisei Construction tries to blacken Kintarō's name by sending his double into the streets to cause mayhem with a motorcycle gang. The gap between events in seasons one and two was bridged by a *Salaryman Kintarō* movie, directed by **MPD PSYCHO**'s Takashi Miike.

For the third season, Kintarō's firm has merged with another, and although he is promoted again, he is soon fired after he questions the new business partner's cost-cutting methods on a construction project. With a new child to support, Kintarō takes a job on the site as a humble construction worker. However, when the president of Yamato dies, he recommends Kintarō as his successor. Kintarō declines, but is soon dragged back into management, as Yamato tries to cut all of its ties with gangsters and corrupt politicians. Meanwhile, Kintarō's father, newly released from prison, engages in a battle of wits against Ōtake, an assassin hired to kill Kintarō.

As the third season drew to a close, *Kintarō* returned to Japanese television in cartoon form on the BS-1 cable channel, in a 20-episode anime series written chiefly by Sukehiro Tomita.

All three live-action seasons have been broadcast in the U.S. with English subtitles on KIKU TV. Peak rating: 20.9%. Themes: The Alfee—"Kibō no Kane ga Naru Asa ni" (Morning Rings the Bell of Hope), Tetsurō Oda—"Kizuna" (Bond), Katsunori Takahashi—"Atsuku Nare" (Get Hot).

SALE!

1995. PRD: Akira Shimura. DIR: Akiyoshi Imazeki. SCR: Yuki Kiyomoto, Takako Suzuki. CAST: Masaaki Sakai, Mami Yamase, Katsuyuki Mori, Chiharu Komatsu, Miho Kanno, Shiho Wakabayashi. CHN: Asahi. DUR: 45 mins. x 9 eps.; Tue 18 April 1995–27 June 1995.

The success of a discount store belonging to Ginjirō (Sakai) allows his four daughters to enjoy the highlife. However, he suddenly announces that his once prosperous company now faces bankruptcy, forcing his fun-loving daughters Beniko (Yamase), Midori (Komatsu), Aoi (Wakabayashi), and Momoe (Kanno) to tighten their belts, prepare for hard times, and even (the horror!) do a spot of work themselves. A jolt of reality played for laughs after the collapse of the bubble economy— compare to **WE HAVE TOMORROW**.

SAMURAI, THE *

1962. JPN: *Onmitsu Kenshi*. AKA: *Spy Swordsman*. PRD: Shunichi Nishimura. DIR: Sadao Funatoko, Tōru Tōyama, Akira Kikuchi. SCR: Masaru Igami, Yasushi Katō. CAST: Kōichi Ōse, Shunsuke Ōmori, Toshiyuki Katsuki, Bin Amatsu, Fuyukichi Maki, Yoshio Yoshida, Naoko Saga, Shinichirō Hayashi, Mizue Shiratori, Hideki Ninomiya. CHN: TBS. DUR: 25 mins. x 128 eps., *Onmitsu Kenshi* (featuring Kōichi Ōse), Sun 7 October 1962–28 March 1965 (#1-10); 25 mins. x 39 eps., *Shin Onmitsu Kenshi* (featuring Shinichirō Hayashi), 4 April 1965–26

December 1965 (#11); 25 mins. x 26 eps., *Onmitsu Kenshi* (featuring Shinichi Ogishima), 7 October 1973–31 March 1974 (#12).

Two years after eleventh Shogun Ienari comes to power (r. 1787–1837), his elder half brother Shintarō Akikusa (Ōse) renounces his inheritance and instead agrees to wander the country undercover, sniffing out any plots against the government in the style of his ancestor **MITO KŌMON**. For his first mission, he is sent to Japan's northern frontier, where Japanese settlers battle against the native Ainu people of Hokkaidō, and where he is soon made distinctly unwelcome by the local lord Jinjūrō (Katsuki).

Fresh from the success of **MOON-LIGHT MASK**, producer Nishimura was finally able to secure some funding for the children's period drama he had always wanted to make in imitation of American Westerns. Nishimura's original plan was only to use former *Moonlight Mask* star Ōse for a single season—his "Autumn Grasses" (*aki-kusa*) character was supposed to be replaced by someone called *Haruyama* (Spring Mountain) in early 1963 and later warriors also named after seasons. However, the original hero caught the public imagination, and Ōse remained in the lead role for the story-arcs that followed the initial 13-episode tale.

The second season, *Koga Ninja*, greatly outdid its predecessor with the introduction of Japan's famous assassins—supposedly ancient, but owing most of their popularity to the fictional work of authors like Fūtarō Yamada, creator of **THE YAGYŪ CONSPIRACY**. Shintarō and his newfound boy companion Shūsaku (Ōmori) compete against 13 ninja who are searching for the lost treasure of **SHINGEN TAKEDA**, in a story line so popular that ninja, not samurai, soon became a staple part of the series. For the third story-arc, *Iga Ninja*, Shintarō teams up with a group of the Shogun's own spies to fight the intrigues of a group of assassins from the Iga ninja clan. In the process, he gains the assistance of ninja Tonbei (former high school gymnast Maki). Though Shintarō and his allies are successful, they incur a vendetta proclaimed against them by the survivors of the Iga, for the fourth season *Black Ninja*. As James Bond 007 and other spy thrillers started to impact on Japanese media, Shintarō gains more fantastical adversaries for the fifth and sixth seasons, *Fūma Ninja* and *More Fūma Ninja*. Supposedly the ninja clan with advanced knowledge of gadgets and technology, the Fūma's leader Kōtarō (Amatsu) is looking for the lost treasure of the Hōjō family (see **HŌJŌ TOKIMUNE**). For season seven, a succession crisis in Wakayama leads to an all-out war between the Kishū and Negoro clans in *Ninja Terror,* followed by season ten, in which more Koga clansmen (in fact, Kōtarō of the Fūma, back from the dead) employ the titular *Phantom Ninja* in an attempt to depose local warlord Matsudaira. Season nine, *Puppet Ninja,* featured a group of smugglers disguised as itinerant puppeteers and lasted a mere ten episodes because of scheduling conflicts with the 1964 Tokyo Olympics. In the final season, *Contest of Death,* Kōtarō returns again to lead every ninja clan in Japan in a vendetta against Shintarō.

Two movies, *Onmitsu Kenshi* and *Zoku Onmitsu Kenshi,* appeared in 1964 as the series' popularity began to wane on TV. Faced with flagging ratings, the producers opted to introduce a new hero, Shinnosuke Kage (Hayashi), a samurai-ninja hybrid who teams up with the old Tonbei, new child companion Daisaku (Ninomiya), and token female Sanae (former child star Shiratori) to fight evil ninja in southwestern Japan. However, this new series (*Shin Onmitsu Kenshi*) was a flop, as audiences were already being attracted elsewhere by spy thrillers and Japan's first anime TV series *Astro Boy* (*AE).

After the death of director Funatoko, the franchise was briefly revived for 26 extra episodes in 1973 with Shinichi Ogishima in the lead role—Ōse had retired in 1969 to enjoy his investments. The new series,

Onmitsu Kenshi Tsuppashire! (*Run Spy Swordsman!*) tried to play up the fantastic elements of the original's *Fūma Ninja* peak, but such gimmicks were being done much better and cheaper in the era's new anime shows, particularly the sci-fi superninja of *Battle of the Planets* (*AE).

However, *The Samurai* enjoyed a new lease on life abroad, when 52 episodes from the second, third, and fourth seasons were broadcast in Australia on Sydney's TCN-9 channel. An unexpected, and to this day inexplicable, success with the local audience, this first-ever Japanese series to be broadcast in Australia led to a local tour by Ōse himself (bewildered at the foreign attention), the Australian acquisition of still more episodes, including the previously unseen first season, and the Australian broadcast of the unrelated **PHANTOM AGENTS**. The series was repackaged for Australian DVD in 2002.

SA-SHI-SU-SE-SO

1997. PRD: Jun Kurosawa. DIR: Kazunobu Yamauchi, Takashi Fujio, Jun Kurosawa. SCR: Noriko Nakayama, Atsuko Sagara. CAST: Hiroko Moriguchi, Raita Ryū, Chieko Matsubara, Akemi Ōmori, Kyōko Togawa. CHN: TBS. DUR: 30 mins. x 40 eps.; Mon 3 November 1997–26 December 1997.
Haruka (Moriguchi), an office lady in search of a change in her life, quits her job and becomes a chef, despite knowing virtually nothing about the culinary arts. Arriving at the exclusive Yoshino restaurant, she is trained hard by the head chef (Ryū) and the head waitress (Matsubara). Compare to **THE CHEF**. Theme: Hiroko Moriguchi—"Hitori ja Naiyo" (I'm Not Alone).

SAY HELLO TO BLACK JACK

2003. JPN: *Black Jack ni Yoroshiku.* PRD: Seiichirō Kijima, Hidenori Ikoshida. DIR: Shunichi Hirano, Shinichi Miki. SCR: Noriko Gotō. CAST: Satoshi Tsumabuki, Kyōka Suzuki. CHN: TBS. DUR: 45 mins. x ca. 11 eps.; Fri 11 April 2003–.

Eijirō (Tsumabuki) graduates from medical school and starts working as an intern at a university hospital, which is not quite the glamorous life he expected. Based on a comic of the same title by Shūhō Satō in *Weekly Morning* magazine, and sure to require comparison with **HALF DOC**. Theme: Ken Hirai—"Life is . . . ."

SAY YOU LOVE ME

1995. JPN: *Aishiteru to Ittekure.* PRD: Seiichirō Kijima. DIR: Jirō Shōno. SCR: Eriko Kitagawa. CAST: Etsushi Toyokawa, Takako Tokiwa, Akiko Yada, Kōki Okada, Ranran Suzuki, Yumi Asō. CHN: TBS. DUR: 45 mins. x 12 eps.; Fri 7 July 1995–22 September 1995.
Kōji (Toyokawa) is an artist with a hearing disability. Wannabe actress Hiroko (Tokiwa) falls for him and begins learning sign language in order to communicate with him. However, Kōji's sister Shiori (Yada) has become used to having her brother to herself and tries to break up the new relationship. Although Kōji and Hiroko start living together, Hiroko discovers a letter from Kōji's ex-girlfriend Hikaru (Asō). When she is unable to secure an absolute declaration of love from Kōji, she walks out and ends up in bed with her childhood friend Kenichi (Okada), now a lighting man at a nearby theater.

Kenichi decides to leave Tokyo for his native Sendai and asks Hiroko to come with him. Tipped off by Shiori, Kōji chases after her but misses her at her apartment. He sees her at the train station and attempts to call her name. Realizing it is he, Hiroko leaves the train and the two spend the night together. Kōji reveals that he desperately wishes he could hear her voice and asks her to say "I love you."

Though Hiroko returns to Kenichi, he realizes that her heart is not with him and leaves for Sendai on his own. Hiroko spends three years in Tokyo pursuing her acting career, until a fateful day when she is sent home early from a studio after her scene has been cut. Remembering that she first met Kōji under a nearby apple tree, she goes to revisit her past and meets Kōji himself, who has just ducked out of an award ceremony in his honor. Kōji plucks an apple from the tree for her and they both smile.

Where **HEAVEN'S COINS** kept the audience resolutely out of the sign language loop while its deaf characters communicated, *SYLM* subtitled its signing conversations—perhaps in imitation of similar sequences in *Four Weddings and a Funeral* (1993). It also recalls moments in the film adaptation of Mark Medoff's *Children of a Lesser God* (1986), particularly in the dramatic weight accorded to speech—Etsushi Toyokawa excels with expressive sign language in a world of silence. Peak rating: 28.1%. Theme: Dreams Come True—"Love Love Love."

SAZAE-SAN

1955. PRD: N/C. DIR: N/C. SCR: N/C. CAST: Chiemi Eri, Makoto Morikawa, Naritoshi Yoshihara, Yukari Uehara, Keizō Kawasaki. CHN: KRT, TBS. DUR: 25 mins. x ca. 120 eps.; Mon 3 October 1955–28 September 1957 (#1); 19 November 1965–29 September 1967 (#2).
Sazae Isono (Eri) is a hapless modern housewife in Tokyo, who shares a small house with her husband, two children, and her mother. An early success for the KRT network, the series successfully stole the thunder of NHK's foreign import *I Love Lucy*, which appeared to be an imitation of the Japanese "original" by the time it was broadcast in 1957. In fact, *Sazae-san*'s origins lie with a manga by Machiko Hasegawa serialized from 1946 in the *Asahi Shinbun*. The success of the story achieved new levels a decade later, when the channel was renamed TBS, and the serial was remade in color. Two years further on, it was revived in animated form on the rival Fuji TV network (*AE). The animated version of *Sazae-san* continues to this day, though it is only available in English in its manga incarnation.

SCARLET

1998. JPN: *Kurenai*. AKA: *Crimson*. PRD:

Shunji Okamoto, Yoshitaka Ōmori. DIR: Masaaki Odagiri, Daisuke Tanaka. SCR: Machiko Nasu. CAST: Naomi Kawashima, Takashi Naitō, Miki Sakai, Ikki Sawamura, Rumiko Koyanagi. CHN: Yomiuri. DUR: 45 mins. x 11 eps.; Mon 13 April 1998–22 June 1998.
Office worker Fumiko (Kawashima) has an affair with architect Masashi (Naitō), only to discover that she has become pregnant. When Masashi's wife Naoko (Koyanagi) finds out, she announces that she wants a divorce, leaving both Fumiko and Masashi stuck with each other—not a permanent situation they were planning on. Based on a novel by Junichi Watanabe, who also created the previous year's **LOST PARADISE**. Theme: Sarah—"Kurenai" (Scarlet).

SCARLET MEMORIAL

2003. JPN: *Hiiro no Kioku—Utsukushiki Ai no Himitsu*. AKA: *Scarlet Memorial—Beautiful Memory of Love*. PRD: Shunji Ikehata. DIR: Takayoshi Watanabe. SCR: Hisashi Nozawa. CAST: Kyōka Suzuki, Shigeru Muroi, Jun Kunimura, Hayato Ichihara, Ryōzō Tanaka, Isao Natsuyagi, Chō Ginpun. CHN: NHK. DUR: 43 mins. x 5 eps.; Mon 6 January 2003–27 January 2003.
Lawyer Naoyuki (Natsuyagi) agrees to defend his childhood friend Nana (Ginpun), a mentally distressed patient who has been arrested for murder. The task forces Naoyuki to dredge up unpleasant memories of his own. . . .
In 1963, art teacher Kaoru (Suzuki) is posted to a school in a rural town and lives in an isolated cottage by a lake. With her scarlet one piece dress and her European education, she causes a stir in the quiet community, particularly when she begins an affair with her married colleague and neighbor Fujieda (Kunimura). Suppressing his own feelings for Kaoru, Naoyuki volunteers to help Fujieda repair an old boat, thereby hoping to give the lovers an escape route from local gossip. However, the boat is smashed up by Fujieda's vengeful wife Shōko (Muroi).
Kaoru decides to quit her job and

refuses to see her lover. The relationship is probably over, but a careless comment from Naoyuki leads Shōko to believe that the lovers plan to elope. Blind with rage, Shōko decides to kill her husband, but instead drives her automobile into the lake, killing innocent bystander Maiko (Riho Akisada). Blaming himself for the incident, the widowed Fujieda commits suicide, and Kaoru leaves town, leaving a lone daughter driven to the edge of sanity.

This well-crafted NHK short series was based on the award-winning thriller *The Chatham School Affair* by Thomas H. Cook—compare to other adaptations of foreign books such as **FLOWERS FOR ALGERNON** and **THE OTHER SIDE OF MIDNIGHT**. Music by Tarō Iwadai.

SCENES FROM THE WATER TRADE

1999. JPN: *Omizu no Hanamichi*. AKA: *Bar Hostesses on the Central Path*. PRD: Masatoshi Katō. DIR: Makoto Hirano, Masato Hijikata. SCR: Mika Umeda. CAST: Naomi Zaizen, Takaya Kamikawa, Sae Isshiki, Sachie Hara, Hitomi Manaka, Kazushige Nagashima, Keiko Toda, Misaki Itō. CHN: Fuji. DUR: 45 mins. x ca. 22 eps.; Wed 6 January 1999–24 March 1999 (#1); Tue 10 April 2001–19 June 2001 (#2).
Akina (Zaizen) is a bar hostess in her thirties who is forced to consider retirement as she faces competition from younger models. She takes it as a message from the fates when the bar owner Matsushima dies and is replaced by the younger Ishizaki (Kamikawa). However, compliments from the silver-tongued Ishizaki keep her working in the bar, despite conflicts with the new number one girl Satsuki (Isshiki) and tempting offers from headhunters sent by an exclusive club. Later in the series, it is revealed that Ishizaki's life is in danger without life-saving surgery—perhaps a chance for these girls to prove that even if they don't have hearts of gold, they have other organs that might be just as useful?
The series returned two years later with *New Scenes from the Water Trade*

(*Shin Omizu no Hanamichi*). Compare to NIGHT'S EMBRACE. Based on a manga by Shizuka Kidoguchi, although the presence of several cast members from the earlier POWER OFFICE GIRLS makes it possible that this production was planned as a means of keeping the ensemble from the successful show without having to pay quite as much for the rights. A similar illegitimate relationship seems to link SISTER STORIES with LEAVE IT TO THE NURSES. Peak rating: 18.6%. Theme: Surface— "Nani Shitenno" (What Are You Doing?).

SCHOOL IN PERIL

1997. JPN: *Nerawareta Gakuen*. PRD: Yoshinori Chiba, Tomoyuki Imai, Kenichi Itaya. DIR: Katsuhito Ueno, Atsushi Shimizu, Iwao Takahashi. SCR: Sadayuki Murai, Minoru Kamio, Chiaki Konaka. CAST: Kazumi Murata, Shūji Kashiwabara, Erika Mabuchi, Hitomi Miwa, Saya Mochizuki, Akiko Andō, Futoshi Nakae, Ai Akai, Kaoru Namiki. CHN: TV Tokyo. DUR: 25 mins. x 9 eps.; Sun 3 August 1997–28 September 1997.

When their high school falls under the control of a sinister group known as the "Awakened," Kazumi (Murata) and Kōji (Kashiwabara) discover that the student rep Michiru Takamizawa (Mabuchi) is the leader. They unravel a conspiracy that began 17 years earlier, when a student called Kyōgoku received a message from the future that human beings would be eliminated in 2107. Deciding that the only way to save the human race is by forcing a new kind of evolution (see also INFRARED MUSIC), he commenced a series of experiments at the school but died before his work was complete. Michiru decides to complete Kyōgoku's work, in an adaptation of the story by Taku Mayumura, creator of MYSTERIOUS PENFRIEND, MYSTERIOUS NEW STUDENT, and BAKUMATSU TIME TRAVELER.

The story was previously filmed as CHALLENGE FROM THE FUTURE in 1977, an earlier *School in Peril* TV series star-

School in Peril

ring Tomoyo Harada in 1982, and a 1981 movie, directed by Nobuhiko Ōbayashi and starring Hiroko Yakushimaru. This 1990s version, partly written by a couple of famous anime scenarists, differs from the others chiefly in its depiction of its lead, who had previously been played as a powerful, fearsome psychic. Instead, this version's Michiru is quiet, understated, and smiling most of the time, which both adds extra creepiness and helps circumvent the more draconian broadcast restrictions placed upon onscreen violence at the end of the 20th century. Similarly, instead of going crazy in an orgy of violence, the students simply mutter strange incantations, laugh to themselves, or manage tricks such as balancing pencils effortlessly on their points—a more mundane form of weirdness which inadvertently made the series more, not less, believable. Bizarrely, however, the opening credits feature an unmistakable pair of naked breasts, so while the violence was out, nudity was obviously in. The series was topped off with a movie *School in Peril:*

Messiah from the Future (1997), directed by Atsushi Shimizu. Theme: Gisho— "Mizu no Waltz" (Water Waltz).

SCHOOL IS DANGEROUS

1992. JPN: *Gakkō ga Abunai*. PRD: Takamichi Yamada. DIR: Mitsunori Morita. SCR: Hideyoshi Nagasaka. CAST: Yumi Morio, Hitomi Takahashi, Ken Tanaka, Shin Takuma, Yumi Adachi. CHN: TBS. DUR: 45 mins. x 8 eps.; 4 August 1992–22 September 1992. Sakiko (Morio) sends her stepdaughter Mami (Adachi) off to her school, only to discover that her teacher Ichinose (Tanaka) has a *bad* reputation. Theme: ZARD—"In My Arms Tonight."

SCHOOL TEACHER

2001. JPN: *Gakkō no Sensei*. PRD: Kazuhiro Itō. DIR: Natsuki Imai, Shunichi Hirano, Noritaka Kajiwara. SCR: Eriko Komatsu. CAST: Tsuyoshi Dōmoto, Yūko Takeuchi, Naoki Tanaka, Mayumi Shintani, Atsuko Sakurai, Chōsuke Ikariya. CHN: TBS. DUR: 45 mins. x 11 eps.; Sun 7 October 2001–?? December 2001.

Fledgling school teacher Sentarō Sakuragi (Dōmoto from the Kinki Kids) travels from his native Osaka to take up his first teaching position in Tokyo. A warm-hearted lug with a thick Kansai accent, Sentarō has been warned that Tokyo people are cold and rude, but is still shocked by the behavior of a group of schoolgirls on the train who refuse to give up their seats for a heavily pregnant lady. He berates them in a scene of train rage similar to that which opens FIGHTING GIRL, much to the embarrassment of other passengers, including the pretty Motoko (Takeuchi). Motoko is even more shocked when she gets home to her father's noodle bar to discover that Sentarō is their new lodger and that he is coming to work at the same school where she teaches.

Sentarō arrives at Fujimigaoka School to discover an institution in disarray. Principal Atsushi (Tanaka) is a mollycoddled milksop who is unable to keep order in the classroom without his mother riding shotgun. In the mandatory love triangle, Atsushi lusts after Motoko, while Motoko carries a torch for Sentarō. Sentarō, in turn, falls for the picture of Motoko's elder sister on the mantelpiece, only to be told that the girl has been disowned over a family feud—her empty room is the reason that Motoko's father Chōichirō (Ikariya) has space for a lodger.

It is said of the drama business that one should never work with animals or children. Having pushed his luck with the veterinary comedy ROCINANTE, Dōmoto tempts fate again with this pallid rip-off of KINPACHI SENSEI. If the hype around the time of release is to be believed, Dōmoto took the part because he was keen to play a character from his native Kansai region, and while he pulls off the accent with predictable aplomb, the rest of the production is decidedly substandard.

The twist, such as there is, lies in the children, who are presented not as wide-eyed innocents but as fiercely unlikable tearaways with all the vices and none of the virtues of the adults—

see also MY CHILD WOULD NEVER . . . . Sentarō intervenes in what he believes to be a case of school bullying, only to discover that the suspected "bully" is really the injured party—the son of a prominent financier, he has been lending money to his classmates who have unsurprisingly allowed their debts to mount. Sentarō volunteers to take on the debts on behalf of the class, inadvertently causing new problems—the child discovers that now he is no longer owed money by his classmates, they no longer see any need to laugh at his jokes or pretend to be his friend.

But even this supposed twist to established school drama setups seems somehow lackluster—ST played during the same season as Fuji TV's marginally more entertaining GOODBYE MR. OZU, which featured another attempt to jump-start a clichéd formula. There is also something of an irony in that Ozu's teenage class still couldn't understand basic economics after an entire semester, while Sentarō's fifth-graders are able to calculate compound interest on variable rate loans before the end of episode one.

SCHOOL WARS
1984. JPN: *School Wars: Nakimushi Sensei no Shichinen Sensō*. AKA: *Mr. Blubberer's Seven-Year War*. PRD: Chiharu Kasuga. DIR: Kazuhiko Yamaguchi. SCR: Hiroshi Nagano. CAST: Shinji Yamashita, Jirō Sakagami, Tappei Shimokawa, Akiko Wada, Tatsuo Umemiya, Yūki Matsumura, Nana Okada, Yoshimi Iwasaki, Shingo Tsurumi, Hirokazu Takano. CHN: TBS. DUR: ?? mins. x 26 eps.; Sat 6 October 1984–6 April 1985.
Former All-Japan rugby player Kenji (Yamashita) becomes a gym teacher at Kawahara High School. Though the school is full of delinquent students, Kenji becomes manager of the rundown, unmotivated rugby club and hopes thereby to change the students' attitude through sports—compare to BLUE SCATTERS and GOODBYE MR. OZU. Kenji has particular trouble with Daisuke (Matsumura), a known trou-

blemaker since junior high and notorious for associating with local gangsters. Meanwhile, club member Hiroshi, aka Aesop (Takano), collapses one day and finds out that he has a brain tumor. The shocked boy decides to commit suicide, but is talked out of it by his classmates and encouraged to fight his condition. Though he eventually dies, his courage is an inspiration to the other club members, and by episode 14, they taste their first victory. By episode 22, they draw in the finals of the National Athletics Meet and finally make it to the hallowed Hanazono Ground, site of the All-Japan High School Championship, in the climactic episode.

Despite a heavy resemblance to the 1965 drama *What Is Youth?* (see Introduction), and initially appearing to be a rip-off of FLY! YOUTHS or ZEALOUS TIMES, *SW* was based on a true story. Former professional rugby player Yoshiharu Yamaguchi really did lead the notorious Fushimi Technical High to victory in the All-Japan Championships, through seven years of setbacks and hardship. The character of Daisuke was inspired by one Ōyagi, who became a player on Japan's own international rugby team. The story was novelized by Nobuhiro Baba under the title *Ochikobore Gundan no Kiseki* (*Miracle of the Dropout Group*).

SCHOOLMATES
1993. JPN: *Dōsōkai*. PRD: N/C. DIR: Hidenobu Hosono. SCR: Man Izawa. CAST: Yuki Saitō, Masahiro Takashima, Tetsuya Bessho, Minako Tanaka, Kazuhiko Nishimura. CHN: NTV. DUR: 45 mins. x 10 eps.; Wed 20 October 1993–22 December 1993.
Natsuki (Saitō) is engaged to Kōsuke (Takashima) but they break up at the last moment. Her childhood friend Fūma (Nishimura) comforts the heartbroken Natsuki, and the two end up marrying. However, Fūma demonstrates no interest in Natsuki at all because he secretly loves the *groom* she jilted at the altar. Fūma and Kōsuke unsuccessfully try to keep their gay

relationship secret from Natsuki—though once she finds out, she realizes that she still wants to give married life with Fūma another go. *Schoolmates* was the first time that Japanese TV covered both a gay relationship *and* a sexless marriage and encouraged further controversy with both male nude scenes and a screen kiss between two men.

SEARCHING FOR SOMEONE *

1996. JPN: *Kitto Dare ka ni Au Tame ni.* PRD: Hideo Amino. DIR: Takashi Komatsu. SCR: Akio Endō. CAST: Kyōzō Nagatsuka, Hiroshi Abe, Reiko Takashima, Seiichi Tanabe, Mai Kitajima. CHN: TVT. DUR: 45 mins. x 12 eps.; Sat 6 January 1996–23 March 1996.

A taxi driver (Nagatsuka) becomes involved in the lives and loves of his passengers, in a reversal of the traditional drama formula. Normally, in a cop show or journalist drama, for example, the stories come to the cast—here the cast goes in search of the stories.

SEARCHING FOR THE WAY I USED TO BE

1992. JPN: *Ano hi no Boku o Sagashite.* PRD: Yasuo Yagi. DIR: Makoto Kiyohiro. SCR: Akiko Yamanaga. CAST: Yūji Oda, Nobuko Sendō, Gitan Ōtsuru. CHN: TBS. DUR: 45 mins. x 11 eps.; Fri 17 April 1992–26 June 1992.

Three months before their wedding, Michi (Sendō) and Hiroki (Ōtsuru) decide to make a video to show at their reception, detailing how they met and fell in love. But while they are shooting, Michi spots her old classmate Morio (Oda) in the crowd and they start talking, raking up issues long thought forgotten. Theme: Gilbert O'Sullivan—"Tomorrow Today."

SEASON OF FLOWERS

1990. JPN: *Hana Aru Kisetsu.* PRD: Teruhiko Senno. DIR: Kōhei Kuno. SCR: Naruhito Kaneko. CAST: Kunihiko Mitamura, Yoshiko Miyazaki, Kōichi Miura, Yumiko Fujita. CHN: Asahi. DUR: 45 mins. x 5 eps.; Thu 23 August 1990–20 September 1990.

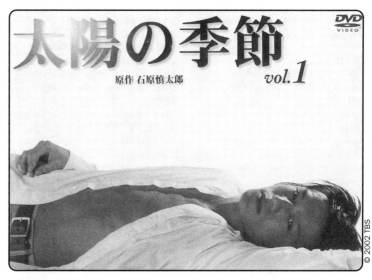

Season of the Sun

Freelance writer Shirō (Mitamura) has lived alone for five years, but is pressganged into moving in with his mother by his three persuasive sisters. The bachelor and his mother are now forced to adjust to each other's lifestyles against the backdrop of life in the town of Kamakura. Compare to **BEST DAD IN THE WORLD** and **MID-LIFE CRISIS**.

SEASON OF THE SUN

2002. JPN: *Taiyō no Kisetsu.* PRD: Sanae Suzuki, Noritaka Kajimura. DIR: Nobuhiro Doi, Ken Yoshida. SCR: Mutsuki Watanabe. CAST: Hideaki Takizawa, Chizuru Ikewaki, Yoshinori Okada, Rio Matsumoto, Sōsuke Takaoka, Shūgo Oshinari, Hirofumi Arai, Kei Ishibashi, Kōji Ōkura, Kenichi Endō, Hitomi Takahashi, Keiko Matsuzaka. CHN: TBS. DUR: 45 mins. x 11 eps.; Sun 7 July 2002–15 September 2002.

Tatsuya (Takizawa) is a charismatic student who hangs out with Shinji (Takaoka), the richest, most popular kid in school. In secret, Tatsuya is the impoverished son of a man who committed suicide over a decision made by Wakaba Bank, an organization owned by Shinji's father—compare to **I'LL**

NEVER LOVE AGAIN. He offers to help the disabled music student Eiko (Ikewaki) when she drops her sheet music while crossing the road. Meanwhile, Tatsuya attempts to seduce Yuki (Matsumoto), Shinji's fiancée, and plots to remove his childhood friend Kōhei (Okada) who knows his dark secret and has inconveniently joined the same athletics club.

Eventually, Eiko and Tatsuya move in together. Flushed with love for the disabled girl, Tatsuya decides to come clean and reveals his true origins and initial motivation for befriending Shinji. Yuki is particularly hurt by the news, not only because she realizes that she has been used, but also because she realizes that Tatsuya loves Eiko more than her.

The humiliated Shinji does his best to make life difficult for Tatsuya. Wakaba Bank ensures that Tatsuya's stipend is cut and that his mother loses her job. Fired up with a new desire for revenge, Tatsuya remembers that Eiko was never part of his long-term plans and dumps her. He plots with Orihara (Endō) to win Yuki's trust and thereby inveigle himself with her rich father, real estate agent Ryōzō (Akira Hamada). However, he does not realize that he is being played by the wily Orihara who intends to use Tatsuya as a fall guy in the coming scandal in the style of **ONE HOT SUMMER**.

Recognizing that he has been used, Tatsuya resolves to get Eiko back but ends up fighting with Shinji on Yuki's yacht—compare to *The Talented Mr. Ripley* (1999). Although Tatsuya throws himself into the sea, he is saved by Shinji, not out of altruism but because Shinji wants Tatsuya to pay for his crimes. Such plans, however, are not enough for Yuki, who begins vengefully stalking Tatsuya with a knife.

Despite the appearance of yet another disability drama, *SotS* originates in the 1956 novel by Shintarō Ishihara, the current Governor of Tokyo. The novel was adapted into a film in the same year, in which Ishihara's brother Yūjirō (see **HOWL AT THE SUN**) made his debut as an actor. Almost 50 years on, a story published in the earliest days of TV can still press the right buttons with the audience—particularly since it incorporates revenge, stalkers, sports competitions, hedonism in the style of the early trendy dramas, and a doomed subplot about a disabled girl. In other words, if only it had a couple of asides about cuisine, invading aliens, and a transforming robot, it would have every dramatic convention covered.

SECOND CHANCE

1995. PRD: Kazunori Itō. DIR: Ken Yoshida. SCR: Eriko Komatsu. CAST: Misako Tanaka, Hidekazu Akai, Tsuyoshi Dōmoto, Yuki Kuroda. CHN: TBS. DUR: 45 mins. x 12 eps.; Fri 14 April 1995–30 June 1995.
Widow Haruko (Tanaka) struggles to bring up her three boys by working in a supermarket, but her children are running out of control and she is at the breaking point. Then she meets Tsutomu (Akai), a lonely widower who has troubles of his own trying to bring up his daughter. Compare to **COLD MORNING**. Theme: Mayo Okamoto—"Tomorrow."

SECOND SON, SECOND DAUGHTER

1991. JPN: *Jinan Jijo Hitorikko Monogatari*. PRD: Keiko Take. DIR: Jirō Shōno. SCR: Toshio Kamata. CAST: Toshihiko Tahara, Toshirō Yanagiba, Momoko Kikuchi, Miyuki Kōsaka. CHN: TBS. DUR: 45 mins. x 11 eps.; Tue 17 October 1991–26 December 1991.
Shōhei (Tahara) and Keisuke (Yanagiba) are fighting for the affections of Junko (Kōsaka), though childhood friend Sayaka (Kikuchi) would much rather that at least *one* of them pay some attention to her, instead. Keisuke gives Junko up for Shōhei and starts going out with Sayaka, but the decisions comes back to haunt them. Theme: Yūko Imai—"Lovin' You."

SECOND TIME AROUND *

1996. JPN: *Sono Ki ni Naru Made*. AKA: *Till They Fall for Someone*. PRD: Keiko Take. DIR: Makoto Kiyohiro. SCR: Toshio Kamata. CAST: Sanma Akashiya, Hidekazu Akai, Shirō Sano, Satomi Tezuka, Yoko Akino, Kumiko Yamashita, Fumie Hosokawa. CHN: TBS. DUR: 45 mins. x 13 eps.; Sun 7 April 1996–30 June 1996.
Kenichi (Akashiya) has been forced to move back in with his mother after a messy divorce. He also has a miserable job as a personnel manager with a company that is laying off many staff members, and Kenichi has to break the news several times a day. He commiserates with two strangers on a train, Hideaki (Sano) and Makoto (Akai), and the trio of fellow divorcées agree to go on a blind date, attending a party thrown by four divorced women.

Next time the men meet on the train, Hideaki has already scored—he's heading home with Yuka (Hosokawa), who wants to *"help him clean his apartment."* Kenichi, however, has less luck. He encounters Kyōko shopping with her young son Takasuke, and when he tries to offer some fatherly advice, the irate Kyōko advises him to back off. Meanwhile Makoto pursues the elusive stewardess Midori, and finds himself house-sitting for her while she is

abroad—much to the annoyance of the other girls, who have become used to using the place as a crash pad after a night on the town. Hideaki's continuing success angers his ex-wife Chiharu, while Kyōko's friend Yayoi decides that she wants Kenichi for herself and that she will make a move unless Kyōko stakes her claim.

Another seven-way love polygon in the style of **WHERE IS LOVE?**, this time grappling not with the perils of first love, but with the hazards of beginning a relationship when both partners have a certain amount of baggage. Since it shares a writer and lead with **SEVEN PEOPLE IN SUMMER**, some drama fans treat it as a sequel of sorts, set a decade after the original's happy ending. Broadcast in the U.S. with English subtitles on KIKU TV. Theme: The Eagles—"Hotel California."

SECRET OF WHISPERING REEF, THE

1973. JPN: *Tsubuyaki Iwa no Himitsu*. PRD: Kazuo Shibata. DIR: Kazuya Satō. SCR: Toshio Kamata. CAST: Yōichi Sase, Shirō Iwakane, Kiyoko Nishiguchi, Yōko Kiku, Yōichirō Mikawa, Masugorō Kawabata. CHN: NHK. DUR: 30 mins. x 6 eps.; Mon 9 July 1973–19 July 1973.
Shirō (Sase) is a lonely boy who has lived with his grandparents on the remote Miura Peninsula ever since his parents died at sea. His daily route home from school takes him past Whispering Reef, an inlet where, according to local legend, careful listeners can hear the ghostly sound of a mother weeping for her child. Several days after Shirō witnesses a suspicious event at the reef, the body of a man is washed up on the shore. Investigating with his reluctant accomplice Keiko (Kiku), he discovers that Whispering Reef is the site of a secret World War II army base and that the treacherous cave network, which causes the eerie howling on a windy night, is also said to hold a vast treasure left over from a wartime bullion stockpile. Based on a story by Jirō Nitta, who also wrote **SHINGEN TAKEDA** and **PEOPLE OF THE**

LOTUS. Theme: Seri Ishikawa—"Tōi Umi no Kioku" (Memory of a Distant Sea).

SEESAW GAME, THE *

1996. JPN: *Futari no Seesaw Game*. AKA: *A Couple's Seesaw Game*. PRD: Hisao Yaguchi. DIR: Akimitsu Sasaki. SCR: Taketatsu Ishihara. CAST: Masatoshi Nakamura, Hiroko Shino, Kunio Murai, Satoko Ōshima. CHN: TBS. DUR: 45 mins. x 12 eps.; Sun 7 July 1996–29 September 1996.

It's nothing unusual for Kōhei (Nakamura) to be shunted around different subsidiaries of his company but he is completely unprepared for his "promotion" to resort manager. He and his two assistants are posted to a rural hot spring inn in Izu Peninsula, home of some of Japanese religion's most sacred shrines. There, they find the staff in revolt at the conglomerate's soulless business practices, and are reluctant to admit that the "traditional" way of running the inn has already driven it far into the red. In a series of hazing rituals, manageress Chiharu (Shino) forces them to work their way through all the jobs in the inn, including scrubbing out the baths—compare to TAKE ME TO A RYOKAN. In an attempt to put the inn back into profitability, Kōhei's assistant Kirino decides to compare the local fishmonger's prices with that of a nearby supermarket, causing further antipathy among the villagers. Kōhei is ordered to balance the books by firing the maid Kiku (Ōshima), but she trains her successor so diligently that Kōhei has second thoughts. As the city boys try to drum up a marketing campaign to bring in more clients, Kōhei's absent wife Ayako collapses in a psychosomatic seizure—she is stressed over her husband's prolonged stay in Izu and suspects him of having an affair with Chiharu. On Chiharu's suggestion, the convalescing Ayako is brought to the inn, where her relaxed attitude reminds the corporate bean counters that some things cannot be quantified or streamlined. Meanwhile, as Ayako begins to suspect

Kōhei and Chiharu once more, Kōhei is forced to embark on an elaborate deception to conceal the fact that Kirino has blown two million yen on a marketing pamphlet that has never materialized. As with so many other workplace related dramas, the series ends with the business under threat and the protagonist preparing to break the news to his staff, only to discover a last-minute ray of hope. Broadcast with English subtitles in the U.S. on KIKU TV. Theme: Smile—"Jigsaw Puzzle."

SEIBU POLICE

1979. JPN: *Seibu Keisatsu*. PRD: N/C. DIR: Takuya Watanabe, Yukihiro Sawada, Keiichi Ozawa, Tōru Murakawa, Yasuharu Hasebe. SCR: Hidekazu Nagahara, Hiroshi Kashiwabara, Tatsuya Asai, Takeo Ōno, Mitsuru Arai, Motozō Mineo. CAST: Tetsuya Watari, Yūjirō Ishihara, Akira Terao, Shunsuke Kariya. CHN: Asahi. DUR: 45 mins. x 234 eps.; Sun 14 October 1979–18 April 1982 (#1); 30 May 1982–20 March 1983 (#2); 3 April 1983–28 October 1984 (#3).

Daimon (Watari) is the section chief of the police investigation unit for Tokyo's Seibu Police. He and his men fight urban crimes with hard action and American style car chases, reputedly trashing 500 vehicles in the course of the show's 234 episodes. Though a hard-boiled cop show in the style of HOWL AT THE SUN, *SP*'s title was a subtle attempt to imply further American connections. Seibu genuinely is a Tokyo district, but the same characters were also used to mean "Wild West" in translations of many imported American TV shows—e.g., *Have Gun Will Travel* (*Seibu no Paladin*), *Hotel de Paree* (*Seibu no Yojinbō*), and *Stoney Burke* (*Seibu no Champion*).

SEMI DOUBLE

1999. PRD: Miwako Kurihara. DIR: Michio Mitsuno, Tatsuaki Kimura. SCR: Yukari Tatsui. CAST: Kiichi Nakai, Izumi Inamori, Tsunku, Vivian Hsu, Daijiro Kawaoka, Yū Yoshizawa, Shinobu Ōtake, Eri Kaneko, Eri Imai. CHN: Fuji.

DUR: 45 mins. x 12 eps.; Wed 14 April 1999–?? June 1999.

Shō (Nakai) is a tough psychology professor at Keisei University, who saves a beautiful woman from tripping at a train station. Taking a seat next to him on the train, she reveals that she is Misaki (Inamori), a model who depends on her looks for her career. Chattily, she confesses that the best-selling book she is reading is rather boring. Angrily, he reveals that he wrote it.

Some time later, Misaki contracts breast cancer. Recovering from a mastectomy that has ended her modeling career overnight, she turns once more to Shō's book and finds some comfort in its stern warnings that every living being faces unexpected adversity. She decides to enroll in his psychology course, but is bullied by the other girls (who still see her as a glamorous dilettante) and turned away by Shō, who does not know of her operation and assumes she is merely playing at changing careers.

The Japlish title, of course, is the romantic cliché that two lovers are halves of a predestined pair, as well as a blunt reference to Misaki's lost asset. Writer Tatsui is unafraid of tackling unpopular issues and treats the aftermath of breast cancer with the same sensitivity as her earlier infertility drama BORN OF LIES. She also presents an incisive portrayal of academic stagnation in the form of Shō, who turns to psychology to exorcise his abandon-

© 2001 Fuji

Serious Affair

ment by his father, only to find himself teaching a belief system that he does not even follow himself—his books are cynical hackery that he pumps out to pay the bills. Like the later **PLASTIC BEAUTY**, the heroine of *SD* lacks confidence in her attractiveness and waits expectantly for a man who will see her for who she truly is. Compare to **STAR STRUCK**, which presented a different view of a media darling's fall from grace. Broadcast unsubtitled in the U.S. on the International Channel and NGN. Peak rating: 16.2%. Theme: Ayumi Hamasaki and Tsunku from Sharan Q—"Love."

SERIOUS AFFAIR
2001. JPN: *Kabachitare.* AKA: *I Must Protest.* PRD: Masatoshi Yamaguchi. DIR: Hideki Takeuchi, Narihide Mizuta. SCR: Mika Ōmori. CAST: Takako Tokiwa, Eri Fukatsu, Takanori Jinnai, Ryōko Shinohara, Tomohisa Yamashita, Kōki Okada, Naoki Hosaka. CHN: Fuji. DUR: 45 mins. x 11 eps.; Thu 11 January 2001–22 March 2001.
Nozomi (Tokiwa) is a gullible, trusting girl who sees good in everyone and remains resolutely positive, no matter how badly her life may be going. Her friend Chiharu is a canny, sarcastic cynic who trusts nobody, and is convinced

that everyone is out to get her. After the sassy Chiharu helps the meek Nozomi get back at her boss for sexual harassment, the girls become inseparable. Each has something to teach the other, as they fight off con men and lame ducks, search for career happiness, and hunt for that elusive Mr. Right. Based on the manga in *Comic Morning*, written by Takashi Tajima and drawn by Takahiro Kochi. Theme: Mayu Kitaki—"Do You Remember Me?"

SEVEN-COLORED MASK
1959. JPN: *Nanairo Kamen.* AKA: *Multicolor Mask.* PRD: Masahiro Satō. DIR: Kōichi Shimazu, Atsuo Wada, Masukazu Iizuka, Satoru Ainoda, Toshirō Suzuki. SCR: Yasunori Kawauchi, Saburō Yūki, Yoshinari Matsubara. CAST: Susumu Namijima, Mitsuo Andō, Kenji Tsushio, Riki Iwaki, Mitsuko Kayama, Ken Hasebe, Shinichi "Sonny" Chiba. CHN: Asahi. DUR: 30 mins. x 57 eps.; Wed 3 June 1959–30 June 1960.
Private detective Kōtarō Ran (initially played by Susumu Namijima) has several secret identities—he is the Seven-Colored Mask, who is able to don different powers with different masks. Created by **MOONLIGHT MASK**'s Yasunori Kawauchi after the success of his earlier superhero, the Seven-Colored Mask also had seven superpowered opponents in the course of his year onscreen. The first was Cobra Mask, whose fortune was stolen by a group of kids during the war and who had used their ill-gotten cash to become wealthy. Cobra Mask, with his power over snakes, abducts the grown-up former thieves to exact his revenge. After the *Cobra Mask* arc, which was more of an adult detective mystery than the expected superhero combat, the Seven-Colored Mask had to track down King Rose, a master robber, forger, and jewelry thief. In the third, his adversaries were the international *Red Jaguar* crime syndicate, and in the fourth, he brought the masked thieves known as the *Three Aces* to justice. With

an emphasis on crime capers in the spirit of **HARIMAO** and **THE SAMURAI** (*AE), the fifth season pitted Seven-Colored Mask against *Golden Kin and Phantom Butankan*, thieves intent on finding a map that can lead them to buried treasure. The final two story arcs became somewhat more sinister, with the *Poisonous Spider* arc in which serial killer Don Noh attempted to amass a collection of grisly antiques, and the climactic *Dark Empire* chapter, in which Seven-Colored Mask fought against evil foreigner investors who were trying to seize control of Japan— compare to **SPACE GOVERNMENT MAN**. Part way through the series, the lead role was taken over by Shinichi "Sonny" Chiba, leading to a rise in ratings as the star introduced more action sequences. A manga spin-off was drawn by Daiji Kazumine.

SEVEN LADY LAWYERS
1991. JPN: *Shichinin no Onna Bengoshi.* PRD: N/C. DIR: Keiichirō Yoshida. SCR: Hideyoshi Nagasaka. CAST: Chikako Kaku, Izumi Igarashi, Tomomi Satō, Keiki Kobayashi. CHN: Asahi. DUR: 45 mins. x 31 eps.; Thu 10 January 1991–28 March 1991 (#1); 17 October 1991–19 December 1991 (#2); 7 January 1993–18 March 1993 (#3). Inheriting a law firm from her retiring father (Kobayashi), lady litigator Natsuko (Kaku) decides to hire only female staff. Though the effect might have been an all-girl lineup like **POWER OFFICE LADIES** or **OL POLICE**, the show's true inspiration can be discerned by its title. Beyond the implicit *Seven Samurai* gag, it also seems deliberately designed to imply some association with *L.A. Law* (1986), which was originally broadcast in Japan as *Shichinin no Bengoshi* (*Seven Lawyers*). Another Kurosawa reference, the cop show *Shichinin no Keiji* (*Seven Detectives*), ran on KRT from 1961 to 1968.

SEVEN PEOPLE IN SUMMER
1986. JPN: *Danjo Shichinin Natsu Monogatari.* PRD: Keiko Take. DIR: Jirō Shōno. SCR: Toshio Kamata. CAST:

Sanma Akashiya, Kimiko Ikegami, Tsurutarō Kataoka, Chikako Kaku, Midori Ogawa, Eiji Okuda, Shinobu Ōtake. CHN: TBS. DUR: 45 mins. x ca. 22 eps.; Fri 25 July 1986–26 September 1986 (Summer); 9 October 1987–18 December 1987 (Fall).
Ryōsuke (Akashiya) wakes up one morning in bed with Momoko (Ōtake), a complete stranger. After the initial embarrassment, the two continue to see each other, though they row continually in the style later popularized by **Do We Love Each Other!**. Ryōsuke introduces his friends Sadakurō (Kataoka) and Kimiaki (Okuda) to Momoko's friends Chiaki (Ikegami) and Kaori (Kaku) on a triple date that sets a series of interlocking love polygons in motion. Meanwhile, Momoko's friend Miwako (Ogawa) hopes to find love in an *omiai* marriage meeting, and Chiaki confesses her feelings for Ryōsuke, only to be rejected. She seeks comfort in the arms of Sadakurō, while Ryōsuke discovers that Momoko is shortly due to be posted to the U.S. for six months. Taking her to Narita airport to see her off, he tells her that he loves her and promises to wait for her.

To an audience reared on conservative values in the middle of an economic boom time, *Seven People in Summer* broke new ground by admitting that not everyone in Japan was married off by their mid-twenties. With its convincing depiction of women who were supposedly past their "sell-by" date, but successful in their careers, it gained a 31.7% peak rating, and is regarded as one of the best works by Toshio Kamata, scenarist of **Friday's Wives** and **Our Journey**. It also marked the first major serious acting roles for comedians Sanma Akashiya and Tsurutarō Kataoka. Akashiya gained extra plaudits for his witty rapid-fire exchanges with Shinobu Ōtake, in hilarious arguments about everything and nothing reminiscent of *Moonlighting* (NHK, 1986). The general attitude of *SPiS* was refined and sculpted to make **I Wanna Hug You!**, the

first of the trendy dramas that dominated the 1990s. Seven leads, or rather three couples and a busybody, have become a regular cast feature in many modern Japanese dramas, including later successes such as **Asunaro Confessions** and **In the Name of Love**. The overall effect keeps *SPiS* high on viewer polls nearly two decades after its first broadcast, with imitators to be found in most contemporary seasons, such as **Where Is Love?** and **The Way I Live**. Rare indeed is the Japanese romantic drama that does not steal at least something from *SPiS*, even if it is only a last-minute airport reunion—the drama even gets a name-check in **Wednesday Love Affair**, in a homage by the next generation of scriptwriters.

In a sequel the following year, titled *Seven People in Fall*, Momoko returns from the U.S., but shocks her friends by bringing a new boyfriend with her. Theme: Akemi Ishii—"Cha-Cha-Cha."

SHADOW OF YOUTH

1994. JPN: *Seishun no Kage*. PRD: Junichi Kimura. DIR: Keiji Tatara. SCR: Ryōichi Kimizuka. CAST: Yoshihiko Hakamada, Gamon Kaai, Chiharu Komatsu. CHN: Asahi. DUR: 45 mins. x 11 eps.; Mon 4 July 1994– 19 September 1994.
When a bunch of guys pick a fight with him in a public toilet, 18-year-old Takumi (Kaai) is rescued by Naoto (Hakamada). The boys start talking and Takumi mentions that he was punched by a lecturer at his cram school. The following day, Takumi discovers the lecturer in question has been attacked by a mob and begins to suspect his new friend's motives. Theme: Kenzō Fukuyama—"Ai o Kureyo" (Give Me Love).

SHADOW SPIES

1996. JPN: *Shōgun no Onmitsu! Kage Jūhachi*. PRD: Masaki Takahashi. DIR: Shinichirō Sawai, Tōru Murakawa, Shōji Hagiwara, Yūji Makiguchi. SCR: Kunio Fujii, Yoshinori Watanabe, Masahiro Shimura, Tetsu Kurumi,

Kimihiko Igawa, Tatsuo Nonami, Ayato Imamura. CAST: Kunihiko Mitamura, Yōko Minamino, Yūji Kishimoto, Bengal, Kyōko Tsujisawa, Kōtarō Satomi. CHN: Asahi. DUR: 25 mins. x 19 eps.; Sat 27 January 1996–29 May 1996.
Sōi Hitotsubashi (Satomi) disguises himself as masterless samurai Kurasuke Yasakanouchi and announces that he is a bridge between the "Eighteen Shadows" and their new shogun. Under his noble leadership, Amatarō (Mitamura) and his trusty samurai stand up against evil in Edo.

SHADOW WARRIORS

1980. JPN: *Hattori Hanzō: Kage no Gundan*. PRD: Yoshiyuki Kuroda. DIR: Eiichi Kudō. SCR: Takayuki Yamada, Mineyuki Nakazato. CAST: Shinichi "Sonny" Chiba, Teruhiko Saigō, Naomi Hase, Shōhei Hino, Junichi Kasuga, Akira Kume, Shōtarō Hayashi, Mikio Narita. CHN: Fuji. DUR: ?? mins. x 106 eps.; Tue 1 April 1980–30 September 1980 (#1); 6 October 1981–30 March 1982 (#2); 6 April 1982–30 September 1982 (#3); 2 April 1985–1 October 1985 (#4); 7 October 1985–30 December 1985 (#5, Bakumatsu, 13 eps.).
In 1651, the 11-year-old Ietsuna becomes the fourth Shogun, leading his influential chief retainers to plot against each other to take the reins of power. The Hattori family are the former vassals of Ieyasu (see **Tokugawa Ieyasu**) but have now fallen from grace, and their third-generation descendant Hanzō (Chiba) is now working as the master of a public bath. However, he also moonlights for the Shogun's right-hand man Masayuki Hoshina, leading his Iga ninja clan in a series of espionage missions—compare to **The Yagyū Conspiracy**.

Despite being as historically inaccurate as most other Japanese dramas, this long-running series in the style of **Sure Death** was characterized by impressive action sequences courtesy of its star, Chiba.

The second series dropped Hattori's

name from the title and moved the action one hundred years later, to 1752. Following the death of **YOSHIMUNE** the eighth Shogun, his personal attendant Tadamitsu Ōoka is put in charge of espionage and cuts off the scattered members of the Iga clan in the mountains near Edo. With only a few surviving members, their leader Shinpachi (Chiba), now working as a restaurant owner, swears revenge on the government.

The third series returned to the era of Shogun Ietsuna in 1657. Mitsusada, the ruler of Kishū, is plotting to make his son Tsunanori the next ruler but is locked in a battle of wits with Takako, the widow of the third Shogun Iemitsu. She is forced to flee from Edo Castle after an assassination attempt and becomes a nun, hiring Iga ninja Hanzō Tarao (Chiba again) to fight against Mitsusada. During the day, Tarao works as a fire guard at a public bath house.

After yo-yoing around the Edo period, the fourth and the fifth series were set at the end of the Edo period. This time, a namesake of the original Hanzō works as a handyman, but also leads a family of Iga ninja who are wanted by the shogunate for espionage. See also *Hattori the Ninja* (*AE).

SHALIBAN

1983. JPN: *Uchū Deka Shaliban*. PRD: Susumu Yoshikawa. DIR: Yoshiaki Kobayashi, Hideo Tanaka, Takeru Ogasawara, Satoru Tsuji. SCR: Shōzō Uehara, Susumu Takahisa, Keiji Kubota. CAST: Hiroshi Watari, Yumiko Takaya, Hitomi Yoshioka, Satoshi Kurihara, Saburo Andō, Masayuki Suzuki, Midori Nakagawa, Chieko Maruyama, Shōzō Iizuka. CHN: Asahi. DUR: 25 mins. x 51 eps.; Fri 4 March 1983–24 February 1984.

Earth is threatened by Psycho the Devil King (Iizuka) and his assistant Miss Akuma. Each week he sends at least one transforming "beast" to wreak havoc, and yet each week he is thwarted by Shaliban (Watari), the latest space cop to be charged with defending our planet. Shaliban's real identity is Igaden, a

man who was saved by **GAVAN** in the previous series. The second in the Metal Series that attempted to establish a rival brand to the same studio's Super Sentai shows such as **GORANGER**, *Shaliban* was followed by **SHIDER**.

SHARDS OF GLASS *

1996. JPN: *Garasu no Kakeratachi*. AKA: *A Kept Woman*. PRD: Tamaki Endō. DIR: Tamaki Endō. SCR: Akio Endō. CAST: Fumiya Fujii, Yasuko Matsuyuki, Kirin Kiki, Makiko Esumi, Tsurube Shōfukutei. CHN: TBS. DUR: 45 mins. x 11 eps.; Fri 12 July 1996–20 September 1996.

It's love at first sight for struggling video cameraman Atsuya (Fujii), and within a day he is kissing jewelry store owner Shōko (Matsuyuki). However, Shōko has a secret—she is a kept woman, and her sugar daddy is Atsuya's married boss Tokizō (Shofukutei). Tokizō refuses to release Shōko from her unwritten "contract" and soon avenges himself by firing Atsuya.

While the Atlanta Olympics dominated the Japanese ratings during the summer, the nation's few remaining drama-watchers were treated to a nasty tale of jealousy and revenge, updating the old kabuki cliché of doomed love between an indentured geisha and a commoner. Eventually, Tokizō is successful in his endeavors—Atsuya gets a new job at a TV station and moves in with aspiring actress Natsume, who had previously been offered a part in an adult video by Tokizō's henchman. However, as Tokizō prepares to attend his daughter's wedding, news comes out about his involvement in an earlier suspicious death, leading to one of TV drama's own traditions—the wedding scene showdown. Broadcast in the U.S. with English subtitles on KIKU TV. Theme: Fumiya Fujii—"Another Orion."

SHIDER

1984. JPN: *Uchū Deka Shider*. PRD: Susumu Yoshikawa, Itaru Orita, Jun Higasa. DIR: Michio Konishi. SCR: Shōzō

Uehara. CAST: Hiroshi Tsuburaya, Naomi Morinaga, Jun Yoshida, Kazuhiko Kubo, Masayuki Suzuki, Miho Hara, Toshiaki Nishizawa. CHN: Asahi. DUR: 30 mins. x 49 eps.; Fri 2 March 1984–8 March 1985.

After the early space detective stories of **GAVAN** and **SHALIBAN**, *Shider* was the last of the Metal Series to concentrate on sci-fi police. While the earlier shows in the series had older viewers, *Shider* specifically targeted younger children. In order to retain the older viewers, producers introduced Annie (Morinaga), the leader of a group of female fighters, whose influence would be felt later on in **KAKURANGER**.

SHINGEN TAKEDA

1988. JPN: *Takeda Shingen*. PRD: N/C. DIR: Atsuhiko Shigemitsu. SCR: Masataka Tamukai. CAST: Kiichi Nakai, Misako Konno, Mao Daichi, Yōko Minamino, Bunta Sugawara, Toshiyuki Nishida, Jō Shishido, Kankurō Nakamura, Kyōhei Shibata. CHN: NHK. DUR: 45 mins. x ca. 50 eps.; Sun 10 January 1988–18 December 1988.

Harunobu is a member of the Takeda family, a military clan rising to supremacy in the Kai region (modern Yamanashi Prefecture). Taking the name Shingen Takeda, he dedicates his efforts to the development of local mines and flood control and also falls in love with a girl he saves from danger during his first-ever battle. Their relationship endures through his turbulent life, as he goes into battle five times against his bitter rival Kenshin Uesugi—for Uesugi's view of the same historical events, see **HEAVEN AND EARTH**. After the death of Yoshimoto Imagawa in 1560, Shingen gains control of Suruga (part of modern Shizuoka Prefecture). He defeats Ieyasu Tokugawa (**TOKUGAWA IEYASU**) at the battle of Mikatagahara in early 1573 but dies of illness a few months later, leaving Japan open to the predations of **NOBUNAGA**. Based on the historical novel by Jirō Nitta, creator of **THE SECRET OF WHISPERING REEF** and **PEOPLE OF THE LOTUS**. The later *taiga* drama **MŌRI MOTONARI** is set at roughly the same time, but in the west of Japan. Peak rating: 49.2%.

SHINING BRIGHTLY

1998. JPN: *Kirakira Hikaru*. PRD: Masatoshi Yamaguchi. DIR: Shunsaku Kawake, Rieko Ishizaka. SCR: Yumiko Inoue. CAST: Eri Fukatsu, Yasuko Matsuyuki, Satomi Kobayashi, Kyōka Suzuki, Toshirō Yanagiba, Yasufumi Hayashi, Kenjirō Ishimaru, Yūjin Nomura, Ryōko Shinohara. CHN: Fuji. DUR: 45 mins. x ca. 20 eps.; Tue 13 January 1998–17 March 1998.

Forensic pathologist Yuriko (Suzuki) shows such care and respect for her "patients" that she inspires young doctor Hikaru (Fukatsu) to pursue the same career. Though her fellow pathologists ridicule her for her emotional reactions, Hikaru tries to imagine how the corpses she examines might have felt when they died, and her unique form of deduction often leads to the uncovering of previously unseen evidence. Mixing the Japanese love of detective mysteries and medical dramas with the dark mood of the late 1990s as seen in **UNSOLVED CASES** and **RING**, *Shining Brightly* was a great success in the style of the British *Silent Witness* or the American *Quincy, M.E.* (1976). The characters returned in two one-off specials in April 1999 and April 2000. Based on the 1995 *Mister Magazine* manga by Mamora Gōda, and since released as a novel, credited to scenarist Inoue. Theme: Mr. Children—"Nishi e Higashi e" (To East To West).

SHINJUKU PUNK RESCUE SQUAD

2000. JPN: *Shinjuku Bōso Kyūkyūtai*. PRD: Ryūichi Inomata. DIR: Takaya Kurata. SCR: Tetsuya Ōishi, Tomoko Yoshida, Noriko Gotō. CAST: London Boots, Takako Uehara, Takashi Naitō, Risa Gotō, Shin Yazawa, Nana Katase, Rika, Shinji Yamashita, Kensaku Kishida. CHN: NTV. DUR: 45 mins. x ca. 11 eps.; Sat 14 October 2000–?? December 2000.

A hospital "comedy" in which two sup-posedly wild and crazy tough guys become paramedics. Combining the lack of affect of **IKEBUKURO WEST GATE PARK** with the slapstick mishaps of **LEAVE IT TO THE NURSES**, the result is a soulless drama in which two guys who think they are funnier than they actually are chase girls who should know better and treat patients who must have done something really terrible in a past life to deserve their attention.

SHINKANSEN

1993. JPN: *Shinkansen Monogatari 93 Natsu; Shinkansen 97 Koi Monogatari*. AKA: *Bullet Train Story 93 Summer* (#1); *Bullet Train 97 Love Story* (#2). PRD: N/C. (#1). DIR: Masaharu Segawa. SCR: Yūichi Ikeda. CAST: Nenji Kobayashi, Masumi Miyazaki, Yūki Ayu, Shō Aikawa, Kimiko Ikegami (#1); Masanobu Takashima, Eriko Watanabe, Yōko Minamino, Mai Hōshō (#2). CHN: TBS. DUR: 45 mins. x 25 eps.; Fri 6 July 1993–21 September 1993 (#1); Thu 3 April 1997–26 June 1997 (#2).

Akiko (Miyazaki) is appointed Chief Purser on the prestigious Tōkaidō bullet train route, stretching from Tokyo, south past Mount Fuji, through the ancient capital of Kyoto, and down to the business metropolis of Osaka. However, she has only just completed her training and still has a lot to learn—like her predecessor in **TOP STEWARDESS** and her later counterpart in **BIG WING**, she seems at first to be a liability, but soon reveals that she has an empathy with the passengers in her care that makes her much loved and respected. Often with plots set up in one city, advanced on the train, and resolved on arrival, *Shinkansen* was able to unite Japan's famously antagonistic Kansai and Kantō regions by literally taking place in both of them.

A second season followed four years later, in which the format was dragged even further into the realm of emotional romances. New purser Daisuke (Takashima, in a blatant reprise of his role from **HOTEL**) finds himself right back where his predecessor started, but soon wins the respect of veteran trolley dollies Sayuri (Watanabe) and Kyōko (Minamino) and fellow rookie Misa (Hōshō). With passengers that needed reuniting, kidneys that needed transplanting, and families that needed healing on a weekly basis, it was described as "*Love Boat* on a Bullet Train," and not without cause, though the *Love Boat* never got up to speeds of 168 miles an hour. Theme: Akiko Wada—"Kaze no Yō ni, Sora no Yō ni" (Like the Wind, Like the Sky).

SHINSENGUMI *

1998. JPN: *Shinsengumi Keppūroku*. AKA: *New Chosen Group's Bloody Chronicle*. PRD: Kengo Tanaka, Katsuhiko Takei. DIR: Eiichi Kudō, Akinori Matsuo. SCR: Takeshi Yoshida, Katsumi Okamoto. CAST: Tetsuya Watari, Hiroaki Murakami, Shunsuke Nakamura, Yuki Amami, Miki Sakai. CHN: Asahi. DUR: 45 mins. x 10 eps. (1st ep 90 mins., shown in two parts in U.S.); Thu 8 October 1998–?? December 1998.

After 300 years of self-imposed isolation, Japan is jolted into the modern world by the arrival of Commodore Matthew Perry and his black ships. The shogunate, which has ruled Japan uncontested since the time of Ieyasu (**TOKUGAWA IEYASU**), is under great threat, and as the Japanese government splits into warring factions, only the loyal Shinsengumi group of Kyoto remains faithful to the old ways. Isamu Kondō (Watari) is responsible for one of the Shinsengumi's two factions and charged with keeping his men from petty vendettas against rival clans. Meanwhile, loyal Shinsengumi member Kotsuru begins a love affair with Lady Shinakai, possibly to the detriment of his knightly duties, while the rest of the men become steeped in jealousy and rivalry over the arrival of new recruit Sōzaburō Kano. Eventually, as Japan is plunged into a brief civil war, the Shinsengumi are abandoned by the very Shogun they are sworn to serve, and their leader is executed as a rebel.

Based on the book by Ryōtarō Shiba (see As If in Flight) and a remake of an earlier 1966 series—depending on where you stand, the Shinsengumi were either Japan's last bastion of samurai virtue or a group of bigoted vigilantes who terrorized Kyoto until torn apart by internal rivalries. Their dogged loyalty to a Shogun whose time had passed makes them a regular subject for Japanese writers, most recently in Nagisa Ōshima's movie *Taboo* (2000), which concentrates on the turmoil caused by the arrival of pretty boy Kanō—played in Ōshima's movie by Ryūhei Matsuda, the son of Detective Story's Yūsaku Matsuda. The Shinsengumi have also made a number of anime appearances, including *Shinsengumi Farce* (*AE) and *Zeguy* (*AE). Broadcast with English subtitles in the U.S. by KIKU TV. Theme: Chiharu Matsuyama—"Sayōnara."

The *Shinsengumi* was also the subject of the 2004 *taiga* drama from NHK, with a script written by Kōki Mitani and with Shingo Katori (from SMAP) in the lead role of Isamu Kondō.

SHIROBANBA

1973. PRD: Kazuo Shibata, Hiroshi Kubota. DIR: Kanae Mayuzumi. SCR: Sumie Tanaka. CAST: Hiroyuki Satō, Michiko Tsushima, Yōichi Miyagawa, Tayo Iwamoto, Sachiko Murase, Mitsue Suzuki, Miwako Kaji, Hideki Konno, Norimi Nishioka, Sumiko Hidaka. CHN: NHK. DUR: 25 mins. x 9 eps.; Mon 5 November 1973–21 November 1973. Around the beginning of World War I, Kōsaku (Satō) is a 10-year-old boy living with his grandmother Nui (Tsushima) in the mountains of Izu. The mistress of Kōsaku's grandfather, Nui has long been bullied by grandfather's true wife Shina (Murase), who lives upstairs with her daughter Mitsuko. This bizarre family arrangement is transformed by the arrival of Sakiko (Kaji), a distant relative who comes to the village to teach and moves in with Kōsaku's extended family.

After Kōsaku almost drowns in the river during the summer, his parents in Toyokawa demand that he come and live with them. However, the boy finds the idea unthinkable, as he cannot bear to leave the village or Sakiko, on whom he has a crush. The new term begins, and rumors abound that Sakiko has begun a relationship with her fellow teacher Nakagawa (Nishioka). Kōsaku is repelled at the thought and jealous, but within six weeks, Nakagawa is transferred to a village on the west coast and Sakiko quits her job to marry him. A year later, Sakiko develops pneumonia and dies. Three years later, after the death of Nui, Kōsaku has finally moved in with his parents. When his father is transferred to Taipei, he moves in with his Aunt Ume (Hidaka), but after several incidents of misbehavior he is assigned to the custody of a temple. Before he moves there, he asks for permission to visit Izu with his classmates, where he intends to compose poetry and visit Sakiko's grave.

An apparently directionless and picaresque series of incidents, justifiable because they are not fictional in origin but dramatizations of the early life of author Yasushi Inoue. Two years later, NHK would make another authorial biography, in A Life Scorned.

SHŌNAN GIRLS DORMITORY STORY

1993. JPN: *Shōnan Joshiryō Monogatari*. PRD: N/C. DIR: Kazuhiro Mori. SCR: Toshio Okumura, Yū Yoshimura. CAST: Yutaka Mizutani, Ritsuko Tanaka, Miyoko Asada. CHN: Asahi. DUR: 45 mins. x 10 eps.; Mon 5 July 1993–20 September 1993. Divorced professional surfer Shōichi (Mizutani) moves back to his parents' house in the resort area of Shōnan, only to find that the old public bath has now been converted into a dormitory for schoolgirls. He resolves to kick them out—compare to Beach Boys.

SHOPPING HERO *

2002. JPN: *Tsūhanman*. PRD: Noboru Sugiyama, Shintarō Suzuki, Tetsuya Kuroda. DIR: Masahito Yomo, Hidekazu Matsuda. SCR: Satoshi Suzuki. CAST: Shunsuke Nakamura, Ayako Kawahara, Masao Kusakari. CHN: Asahi. DUR: 45 mins. x 11 eps.; Fri 5 July 2002–20 September 2002. Mild-mannered Makoto (Nakamura) works for the fast-growing Paradise Corporation home shopping firm, where he soon develops a crush on Yūka (Kawahara), the beautiful girl who is the best-selling, highest-rated doyenne of the home shopping demonstrators. But when Yūka is unavoidably delayed for a broadcast, Makoto dons a Zorro costume and takes over her slot. His flamboyant deception deflects the scandalous gossip that might have otherwise accompanied Yūka's absence, but as the viewers react with great enthusiasm to the first appearance of the "Shopping Hero," other people at the Paradise Corporation begin to ask: "*Who was that masked man . . . ?*" He is ordered to return the following week for a repeat performance, in a humorous show that mixes marketing with the superhero genre. Broadcast with English subtitles in the U.S. on KIKU TV. Theme: Blossom—"Sweat."

SHOTGUN MARRIAGE

2001. JPN: *Dekichatta Kekkon*. PRD: Atsuhiro Sugio. DIR: Hideki Takeuchi. SCR: Noriko Yoshida. CAST: Ryōko Hirosue, Yutaka Takenouchi, Shinichi "Sonny" Chiba, Hiroshi Abe, Yuriko Ishida, Nana Katase, Satoshi Tsubuki. CHN: Fuji. DUR: 45 mins. x 11 eps.; Sun 1 July 2001–30 September 2001. Twenty-year-old Chiyo (Hirosue) discovers that she is pregnant after a one-night stand with 30-year-old commercial director Ryūnosuke (Takenouchi). The couple decide to get married, to the outrage of Chiyo's gruff police inspector father (Key Hunter's Chiba, who steals the show). Meanwhile, Ryūnosuke's widowed mother mistakenly believes that he has fallen in love with Reina (a Comedy Fat Girl), while his best friend Eitarō (Abe) anxiously avoids committing to Chiyo's sister Aki (Ishida), his girlfriend of ten years.

An amusing modern farce that manages to play at being risqué while delivering conservative entertainment—Chiyo and Ryūnosuke might have gotten naked with each other before the show begins, but they barely touch again for the rest of the series, just like the romantic leads in most other shows. No doubt for aesthetic reasons, the bulk of the drama focuses on the early weeks of the pregnancy: Chiyo's first trimester occupies ten whole episodes before she suddenly balloons and spawns in the space of the finale.

The drama is expanded in a developing relationship between 1970s fashion victim Aki and Chiyo's stoic obstetrician Dr. Komatsubara. Will he win her heart, or will she return to her long-standing, good-for-nothing boyfriend? Chiyo's mother earnestly tries to placate her scandalized samurai-era throwback of a husband (who has yet to forgive Ryūnosuke for impregnating his daughter *and* damaging one of his prized bonsai trees), while Ryūnosuke's flaky mother incessantly seeks advice from a photograph of her dead husband. Pushed even further into the background is a half-hearted romance between Ryūnosuke's assistant Takumi (Tsubuki) and Chiyo's friend Misato (Katase), who deserves an award for her unfeasibly tight jeans.

After a promising start, the tension begins to flag, as each successive misunderstanding leads to yet another *harrumph* from the Mifune-esque father (see also **LADY OF THE MANOR**), or yet another sulk from the ever-childish Chiyo. Her final test of Ryūnosuke's mettle (a revelation that is the cliff-hanger of the penultimate episode) is risibly contrived and only goes to show that *SM* might make a fun series, but would have been an even better two-hour special. Classic line when Ryūnosuke is late for a prenatal class: *"Everybody else came! Even the gaijin father-to-be! And he even took notes!"* Compare to **UNMARRIED FAMILY** (broadcast on the same channel and the same day) and **BRIDE-TO-BE**. Theme: Hitomi—"It's You."

SHŌTOKU TAISHI *

2001. AKA: *Prince Shotoku*. PRD: Kōki Kida. DIR: Mikio Satō. SCR: Shunsaku Ikehata. CAST: Masahiro Motoki, Miki Nakatani, Akira Takarada, Keiko Matsuzaka, Ken Ogata. CHN: NHK. DUR: 90 mins. x 2 eps.; 10 November 2001 (both).

Riding the coattails of the successful **YIN-YANG MASTER**, this NHK mini-series showcased the semilegendary life of Prince Shōtoku (574–622), son of the short-lived Emperor Yōmei. After Yōmei's illness, controversial conversion to Buddhism, and death, Shōtoku rose out of the ensuing unrest as an important government minister under his aunt, the Empress Suiko. Shōtoku is largely credited not only with bringing Buddhism to Japan, but with the re-establishment of diplomatic relations with China after two centuries of exclusion. His lifetime consequently spans a renaissance period in the seventh century, when the country embraced foreign crafts, customs, and philosophies. He also wrote the "Seventeen Article Constitution," a set of rather vague maxims that nevertheless transformed court life in Japan by introducing Confucian principles for the first time. After his death, he was canonized as a Buddhist saint. Broadcast with English subtitles in the U.S. on KTSF TV and KIKU TV—the KTSF version comprised four 45-minute episodes. Music by Isao Tomita.

SHOW NO MORE TEARS

1993. JPN: *Mō Namida wa Misenai*. PRD: Hiroshi Akabane. DIR: Takemitsu Satō. SCR: Masahiro Yoshimoto. CAST: Kumiko Gotō, Yūko Natori, Hisako Manda, Satomi Tezuka. CHN: Fuji. DUR: 45 mins. x 10 eps.; 20 October 1993–22 December 1993.

Midori (Gotō) was born in Quebec, abandoned by her mother as a baby, and raised in a convent. Now a famous idol singer, she discovers that her mother's initials were K.K. and begins searching for her, eventually narrowing the field down to one of Kaori

Shotgun Marriage

(Tezuka), Kiyomi (Natori), or Kayo (Manda). Theme: Ambience—"Saigo no Yakusoku: See You Again" (The Last Promise: See You Again).

SHOW-OFF, THE

1973. JPN: *Doterai Otoko*. PRD: Yasuo Nozoe. DIR: Yūji Utsumi. SCR: Kobako Hanato. CAST: Teruhiko Saigō, Ryō Tamura, Meiko Nakamura, Eiko Azusa, Emi Shindō. CHN: Kansai. DUR: 45 mins. x ?? eps.; Tue 2 October 1973–25 March 1977.

Mōzō Yamashita (Saigō), who only completed elementary school, becomes a successful merchant with his energy, combative spirit, and ideas as his weapons. This show was a masterpiece of the Osaka merchant's story. Kobako Hanato had written numerous dramas in which stoic heroes endure great hardships, but this time, the main character stands up and fights.

SIGN IS V, THE

1969. JPN: *Sign wa V*. PRD: Seiji Kuroda, Toshiyasu Doi. DIR: Susumu Takebayashi, Minoru Kanaya. SCR: Itsuo Kamijō, Toshio Kamata, Naohiko Kataoka. CAST: Jin Nakayama, Kaai Okada, Mari Nakayama, Bunjaku Han, Yuki Kishi, Mieko Nishio, Ikuko Koyama, Ryōko Wada, Yōko Aoki. CHN:

© 1969 TBS

The Sign Is V

TBS. DUR: 25 mins. x 45 eps.; Sun 5 October 1969–16 August 1970. Yumi Asaoka (Okada) is a brilliant high school volleyball player, but hates the sport with a vengeance. Her sister Miyo was a member of a corporate volleyball team, but died during a harsh training regime a year earlier. After winning her last college game, Yumi turns her back on volleyball forever, but is lured back to it by Keisuke Maki (Nakayama), the manager of the Tachiki Yamato Corporation team. Keisuke convinces her to join the company after graduation, which she eventually does along with captain Kaori and team members Chiiko (Koyama), Kimie (Wada), Sachiko (Aoki), and Mari (Nakayama).

The tribulations of a girls' volleyball team and their handsome male coach, *The Sign Is V* was based on the manga by Shirō Jinbo and Akira Mochizuki, which ran in *Shōjo Friend* from 1968 to 1970. It competed against *Attack Number One* (*AE) for the attentions of a female sports audience, as part of a sudden boom in Japanese volleyball fandom after the nation's "Witches of the East" female team unexpectedly won gold at the 1964 Olympics. As an indicator of the sport's popularity,

TSIV gained a rating of 39.3%, making it one of the most popular TV series of the last 30 years. The cast was also reunited for a 1970 movie, while the entire series was remade in 1974. Compare to **BEAUTIFUL CHALLENGER**. Theme: Keiko Mari—"Sign wa V."

SILICA

1960. JPN: *Uchūsen Silica*. AKA: *Spaceship Silica*. PRD: N/C. DIR: N/C. SCR: Bunpei Mori, Takehiko Maeda. CAST: (voices) N/C. CHN: NHK. DUR: 15 mins. x 227 eps.; Mon 5 September 1960–27 March 1963.
Boy scientist Pierrot and his big sister Nelly, a botanist, travel the galaxy with Captain Bob and his crew of robots, in the first of NHK's trilogy of science fiction puppet shows. Based on a story by science fiction writer Shinichi Hoshi, who also created **CAPRICIOUS INDEX**, the story was followed in the same slot by **SPACE PATROL** and **AERIAL CITY 008**. Prefiguring the later success of Gerry Anderson's *Stingray* (Fuji, 1964), Pierrot and Nelly's most popular destination was the water world of Sweta Penda, where they became embroiled in a war between the aquatic kingdoms of Ashveda and Iglec Alpha. Theme: Tokyo Broadcasting Children's

Choir—"Uchūsen Silica." Music was composed by Isao Tomita.

SILVER MASK

1971. JPN: *Silver Kamen, Silver Kamen Giant*. PRD: Yōji Hashimoto, Toshio Kobayashi. DIR: Akio Jissōji, Eizō Yamagiwa, Hiromi Higuchi, Jun Ōki. SCR: Mamoru Sasaki, Shōzō Uehara, Shinichi Ichikawa. CAST: Toshio Shiba, Seiichirō Kameishi, Saburō Shinoda, Junko Natsu, Isao Tamagawa, Shin Kishida, Yoshiko Kitamura, Shinya Saitō, Gena Matsuo, Hisashi Katō, Tetsuo Kubota. CHN: TBS. DUR: 25 mins. x 26 eps.; Sun 28 November 1971–21 May 1972.
Genius scientist Professor Kasuga successfully builds a photon rocket engine, but is murdered by an alien race that is convinced that humanity will invade *space* unless its military technology is kept primitive. Led by eldest son Kōji (Shiba), the Professor's five children realize that the secret to the photon technology has been hidden inside their bodies by their wily father, and they are recruited by their new mentor Professor Tsujiyama (Kishida). A team of humans in the **MIGHTY MORPHIN' POWER RANGERS** mode are thus turned into superheroes that fight aliens, although the underlying motive of the alien "invaders" is to protect the universe at large from the predations of mankind—compare to *Gunbuster* (*AE). An original twist on the superhero genre, defeated by the scheduling of the show directly opposite **MIRRORMAN**. Consequently, later episodes of *both* shows soon devolved into standard alien-of-the-week fare, in the style of **ULTRAMAN**.

SILVER WOLF

1996. JPN: *Ginrō Kaiki File*. AKA: *Silver Wolf Mystery Files*. PRD: Ken Inoue. DIR: Tōya Satō. SCR: Akihiko Tago, Tetsuya Ōishi. CAST: Kōichi Dōmoto, Mai Hōshō, Keizō Kanie, Ken Miyake. CHN: NTV. DUR: 45 mins. x 10 eps.; Sat 13 January 1996–16 March 1996.
Kōsuke (Dōmoto) is a shy 16-year-old high school student, who is a member

of the school newspaper club along with his 18-year-old stepsister Saeko (Hōshō). After an accident, Kōsuke suddenly develops a new personality (compare to **MPD PSYCHO**), calling itself "Ginrō" or "Silver Wolf." The sharper and more aggressive Ginrō begins solving mysteries and crimes around the school in the manner of **YOUNG KINDAICHI FILES**—a show which, ironically, would later steal actor Dōmoto for itself. In its concept of a cunning investigator in a child's body, it also owes a debt to *Conan the Boy Detective* (*AE), and shares the manga origins of the other series, being based on a comic in *Shōnen Magazine* by Masayoshi Ochibe. Paranormal detectives were big business in 1996, presumably following the success of *The X-Files* on TV Asahi the previous year. Themes: Kōichi Dōmoto—"Boku wa Omou" (I Think), Masahiko Kondō—"Midnight Shuffle."

SINCE I MET YOU

1996. JPN: *Kimi to Deatte Kara.* PRD: Kazunori Shiokawa. DIR: Katsuo Fukuzawa. SCR: Noriko Yoshida. CAST: Masahiro Motoki, Mayu Tsuruta, Yasufumi Terawaki, Harumi Inoue, Sawa Suzuki, Yōko Nogiwa. CHN: TBS. DUR: 45 mins. x 13 eps.; Fri 12 April 1996–28 June 1996.

Impoverished would-be art student Sachiko (Tsuruta) makes ends meet by working at a coffee shop, where she finds herself falling for one of her regulars, elite businessman Seiji (Motoki). Eventually, the couple agree to meet for a date, only for Seiji to realize that his company is directly responsible for the bankruptcy of a company owned by Sachiko's father. Torn with guilt, he is late for their meeting, electing instead to spend time with his ex-girlfriend (Suzuki). He eventually arrives two hours late, just in time to push the oblivious Sachiko out of the path of an oncoming truck. Seiji is left badly injured and with complete amnesia, while Sachiko resolves to nurse him back to health, not realizing that the restoration of his memory with also

cause him to remember what it was he was going to tell her. Compare to **HEAVEN'S COINS** and **SLEEPING FOREST**. Possibly inspired by the U.S. movie *While You Were Sleeping* (1995). Theme: Ryūichi Ōura—"Natsu no Gogo" (Summer Afternoon).

SINGLE LIFE *

1999. JPN: *Dokushin Seikatsu.* AKA: *Singles.* PRD: Yuka Nariai. DIR: Akio Yoshida, Makoto Kiyohiro. SCR: Masaya Ozaki. CAST: Makiko Esumi, Kōichi Satō, Noriko Katō, Shunsuke Nakamura, Haruko Mabuchi, Maki Sakai. CHN: TBS. DUR: 45 mins. x 10 eps.; Fri 6 July 1999–?? September 1999.

Fiercely competitive Tōwa Bank employee Kyōko (Esumi) rejects marriage as an option and struggles to make it to the top. She is accused of leaking information to a rival bank. Collapsing outside a Tokyo pub, she is rescued by the manager, who suggests that she could supplement her income with a second career. With her job in question, she begins to work as a call girl, though her first client Shinichi (Satō) makes his excuses and leaves. She soon finds out why, when journalist Shinichi turns up to interview her at the bank where she works. He later demands 380 million yen for his silence—Tōwa Bank is somehow responsible for the suicide of Shinichi's father and he is determined to extract revenge in some form.

Prostitution soon proves to be more dangerous than Kyōko imagined, particularly after a magazine article begins to circulate about a Tōwa Bank employee's double life. Soon, corruption is added to her list of crimes, as she is called to a hotel job and is photographed in a compromising position with one of her bosses. The scandal has been engineered by businessman Yoshikawa, who uses the incident to blackmail her into handing him a loan he will probably never repay. However, when Shinichi realizes that it is Yoshikawa who was responsible for his father's death, he decides to help Tōwa and Kyōko.

In 1997, **LAST LOVE** featured a woman forced into prostitution by financial desperation. After two years of Japanese media hysteria about *enjo kōsai* (subsidized dating), the heroine of *Single Life* decides to become a prostitute simply because she feels like it. However, unlike its ultimate inspiration *Pretty Woman* (1990), *Single Life* does not hypocritically romanticize a life on the streets. Some balance is offered in the shape of Ayumi, a bright and innocent girl who is lured into the world of adult videos by the sleazy recruiter Shimamura. For a while it looks as if her sweet nature will convince him to set aside his underworld life, but his spiteful girlfriend encourages him to ruin Ayumi, and her life spirals out of control as she is tempted by the deceptively easy returns of the porn industry.

Broadcast in the U.S. with English subtitles on KIKU TV under the title *Singles*—we have retained a more exact translation of the original name in order to distinguish it from the unrelated **SINGLES**. Theme: Toshinobu Kubota—"The Sound of Carnival."

SINGLES

1997. PRD: Kazuki Nakayama, Yūji Ōhira. DIR: Akiji Fujita, Hidekazu Matsuda. SCR: Yumie Nishiogi. CAST: Yūki Amami, Miki Mizuno, Yoriko Dōguchi, Takeshi Ihara, Ryūji Harada. CHN: Kansai. DUR: 45 mins. x 10 eps.; Tue 14 October 1997–16 December 1997.

Single camerawoman Asahi (Amami) discovers that she is pregnant after an encounter with her younger sister's exboyfriend Satoshi (Harada). Her old schoolfriend Yukiko (Mizuno) has given up on the idea of finding Mr. Right and instead has opted for artificial insemination. Their friend Chiho (Dōguchi) plans to find a more direct method, by tricking an unsuspecting one-night stand into getting her pregnant. See also **SINGLE LIFE**. Theme: Chicago—"Moonlight Serenade."

SISTER RETURNS EARLY IN THE MORNING

1994. JPN: *Oneesan No Asagaeri*. PRD: Kumio Ishizaka. DIR: Toshio Ōi. SCR: Yasuo Hasegawa. CAST: Maki Mizuno, Kenjirō Nashimoto, Akira Takarada, Mariko Kaga, Masanobu Takashima. CHN: Asahi. DUR: 45 mins. x 10 eps.; Tue 11 January 1994–8 February 1994; 24 March 1994–28 June 1994.

While still finishing her studies at a junior college, Nanako (Mizuno) meets journalist Sugita (Nashimoto), who offers her a part-time job on the magazine *Capital Sports*. It's a dream come true for Nanako, who always wanted to work in the media, and soon the plucky student is juggling classes with investigating a major scandal.

SREITM follows a typical pattern, and like NEWS WOMAN can be split into two distinct halves. However, *SREITM* was actually broadcast in two sections—after the first five episodes, viewers had to wait several weeks to see how Nanako's adventures panned out. She finds herself a full-time job with *Capital Sports*, only to be told that the company is in financial difficulties and that some staff members are going to have to be cut back. Themes: REV—"Dakishimetai" (Want to Hold You), Masataka Fujishige—"Aishiteru Nante Kotoba Yori" (Rather Than The Words 'I Love You').

SISTER STORIES

1999. JPN: *Tenshi no O-shigoto*. AKA: *Work of Angels*. PRD: Ayako Ōga, Kazuyuki Morosawa. DIR: Takao Kinoshita, Tōru Hayashi. SCR: Kazuyuki Sawamura, Mayumi Nakatani. CAST: Arisa Mizuki, Kyōzō Nagatsuka, Shigeru Jōshima, Sakura Uehara, Kazuko Yoshiyuki. CHN: Fuji. DUR: 45 mins. x 12 eps.; Wed 6 January 1999–24 March 1999.

Maria Abe (Mizuki) is the newest recruit at the run-down Santa Bianca Cruz convent, though the other nuns doubt she is really suitable for the religious life. She immediately annoys some of the old guard by asking for more salt in her morning gruel,

though the elderly Sister Sawaki (Yoshiyuki) warns the others not to judge her, lest they be judged themselves. Maria confesses to her fellow aspirant Sister Yoshino (Uehara) that she is the daughter of an ex-nun, who fell in love with a chapel renovator, and broke her vows to marry him.

Sister Yoshino offers Maria a midnight sip from her secret stash of booze, causing the tipsy aspirant to don her civilian clothes, clamber over the convent walls, and stagger to a nearby graveyard to commune with the spirit of her father. Local lawyer Mamoru (Nagatsuka) finds her sprawled over her parents' grave in a drunken heap and takes her back to his place to sleep it off. The couple are reunited when Mamoru and his assistant Hajime (Jōshima) arrive at the convent on legal business for evil property developer Mr. Maejima. The nuns are given three months to vacate the premises before demolition teams move in—though this breaks earlier promises made to them, Mamoru curtly reminds them that *"the law is stronger than faith."*

Mamoru's brusque exterior hides his grief at the murder of his Christian wife some five years earlier. His allegiances are torn between Maria and Maejima, who intends to use strong-arm tactics to scare the nuns away. Eventually, Mamoru refuses to do Maejima's dirty work and receives a severe beating at the hands of Maejima's heavies. Though he loses a client, the injured lawyer gains first a surrogate wife, as Maria moves into his apartment to cook and clean for him, and soon a surrogate family, as he is hidden in the convent by the local police. Mamoru resolves to help the nuns out of their predicament, but is forced to pose as a priest in order to keep his room at the convent.

Before the first episode is over we have already seen Hajime walking in on an irate, scantily-clad nun, and clubbing his boss repeatedly over the head with a heavy legal journal. The scene sets the farcical tone for *SS*, taking the

clichéd formula of a maverick with a heart of gold and weaving it into one of the strangest professions to be featured in a workplace related drama—*Sister Act* meets MASK OF GLASS, with a Japanese title that implies non-existent connections with the same stars' earlier LEAVE IT TO THE NURSES. Based on the manga in *Wani Magazine* by "U-K," *SS* merely takes the conventions of the school genre (clumsy transfer student, tough but fair principal, comedy fat girl) and dresses them up with a few religious trappings. But who can really resist singing nuns (yes, they sing), or the inevitable high jinks when Maria tries to cover up the fact she's broken a statue of the Virgin Mary? Note also that the lead's name is pronounced *Ave Maria*, when read in the Japanese fashion. Episodes are sprinkled with Biblical quotes, parables, and prayers, all cunningly woven into Maria's tribulations. Japanese drama loves to set duty against emotions, but Maria is in a true dilemma. Her duty to her father requires her to become a nun, and thereby somehow atone for his guilt in luring her mother away from the convent. But her emotional inheritance from her mother is one of a woman unsuited to a nun's life, who would much rather get married and settle down. For a different kind of Catholic do-gooder, see THE STAND-IN. Peak rating: 16.5%. Theme: Arisa Mizuki—"Asahi no Ataru Hashi" (Bridge in the Morning Sun).

SISTERS

1976. JPN: *Kyōdai*. PRD: Kanae Mayuzumi. DIR: Haruo Yoshida. SCR: Kei Hattori. CAST: Rika Miura, Mari Wada, Shōji Nakayama, Hiroko Kōda, Hōsei Komatsu. CHN: NHK. DUR: 20 mins. x 4 eps.; Mon 13 December 1976–16 December 1976.

In the late 1920s, 17-year-old Keiko (Miura) and 13-year-old Toshiko (Wada) are sent to the northern island of Hokkaidō, where they are expected to stay with their uncle and aunt, while attending school in Sapporo. When their grandmother dies, Keiko helps her mother with the preparations for the funeral, while Toshiko goes out to play with her friends. Her father admonishes her that it is a woman's duty to marry and have children, but Toshiko resolves that she will try to become a *better* woman by concentrating on her studies.

Two years later, the sisters debate marital morals after they witness a couple arguing—the husband is angry because the wife has taken a lover. Soon afterward, their aunt Sumiko leaves her husband because he has squandered his money on geisha and gambling. The next day, however, he apologizes and is taken back. The sisters find this adult behavior completely baffling.

In the spring, Keiko graduates from school. Lonely at home, she finds work as a seamstress, only to quit after a month. Soon afterward, she marries a man selected for her by her parents. Toshiko tells Keiko that she intends to go to Tokyo and find work after graduation. Based on the story by Fumi Azeyanagi.

SKY HIGH

2003. PRD: Tetsuya Kuroda, Yūji Ishida, Ikuhide Yokochi. DIR: Shun Nakahara, Manabu Asō, Norio Tsuruta, Tetsuo Shinohara, Ryūichi Takatsu, Ryūhei Kitamura. SCR: Mitsuru Tanabe, Naoya Takayama, Tomoko Ogawa. CAST: Yumiko Shaku, Hisashiro Ogura, Keita Miyatani. CHN: Asahi. DUR: 45 mins. x 10 eps.; Fri 17 January 2003–21 March 2003.

The pregnant Noriko (Kimika Yoshino) marries Masaru (Masato Sakai), incurring the vengeful wrath of her best friend Misato (Yuka Itaya), who wanted him for herself. Noriko is killed by Misato, and finds herself in the afterlife, where she is greeted by the mysterious woman Izuko (Shaku). Izuko reveals that she is the guardian of the Gate of Malice, a particular part of the afterlife where only suicides, murder victims, and those with undischarged grudges end up. It is her duty to grant such unfortunates a last wish. They may (a) accept their death and

journey on to Heaven in preparation for reincarnation, or (b) reject their death and wander the Earth as a ghost, or (c) reject the possibility of reincarnation, but avenge themselves on the living by placing a deadly curse on those who wronged them. There are no prizes for guessing which option Noriko chooses, though she is merely the first of several guest corpses in search of retribution. Not all go for the revenge option—some choose to wander among the living and observe what happens after their death, while others do not even realize they have been wronged until they find themselves at the Gate of Malice. One woman realizes that it is herself who is to blame, since everything that made her happy in life was stolen from her best friend; another, a student, has the opportunity to forgive and forget, or to exact divine retribution on the school bullies.

Based on the manga by Tsutomu Takahashi, *Sky High* takes the death-of-the-week premise of *Six Feet Under* (2001) and marries it to the divine intervention of *Touched by an Angel* (1994)—compare to LOVE SEPARATION SERVICE and HEAVEN CANNOT WAIT, and see also the similar revenge from beyond the grave found in the erotic anime *Rei Rei* (*AE). The manga had actually ended its run in the weekly *Young Jump* magazine, but was itself brought back to life for a new series to coincide with the broadcast of the TV adaptation. Japanese publicity hype at the time of the show's release claimed that the story had also been optioned for a Hollywood remake. Themes: Pornography—"Uzu" (Spiral), Wyolica—"Mercy Me—Itsuka Hikari o Dakeru Yō ni" (Mercy Me—Someday I May Embrace the Light).

SLEEPING FOREST

1998. JPN: *Nemureru Mori*. PRD: Reiko Kita, Chihiro Kameyama. DIR: Isamu Nakae, Kensaku Sawada. SCR: Hisashi Nozawa. CAST: Miho Nakayama, Takuya Kimura, Tōru Nakamura, Takanori Jinnai, Yūsuke Santamaria, Manami Honjō, Mieko Harada. CHN: Fuji. DUR:

> **WEDDINGS FROM HELL**
>
> **Here Come the Brides**
>
> This drama ends with the terrifying sight of the bride, in white, being walked up the aisle by her black-clad former best friend, who is also the jilted first wife of the groom. 🖙

45 mins. x 12 eps.; Thu 8 October 1998–24 December 1998.

For the last 15 years, Naoki (Kimura from SMAP) has been sending Minako (Nakayama) anonymous letters, urging her to meet him in the "sleeping forest." On the appointed day, Naoki sneaks out on his girlfriend Yuri (Honjō) to meet Minako, whom he has been watching ever since their childhood. Despite her impending marriage to salaryman Kiichirō (Nakamura), Minako cannot resist discovering the identity of her secret admirer but feels uneasy in his presence. She returns to her job in an orchid nursery, but after a series of harassment incidents, she confronts Naoki and warns him off. However, she begins to suspect that his appearance may have some connection to the strange visions she has been experiencing, and she begins to investigate her own past. She is shocked to discover that her family were not killed in a car accident as she had been told, but stabbed to death by her sister's crazed boyfriend Yoshiharu (Jinnai), who has recently been paroled after serving 15 years for multiple murder. Minako was the only witness, meaning that her entire past is a lie, concocted by a hypnotist in order to bury her childhood trauma. Her "visions" are the inevitable side-effects—after years of suppression, her original self is trying to break out.

Starting off as a retread of GIFT and HARMONIA, or a more thrilling take on the earlier Nakayama movie vehicle *Love Letter* (1995), *Sleeping Forest* fast becomes a masterpiece of TV drama, with a mind-bending story of Philip K.

Dick proportions, and plot twists to rival *Fight Club* (1999) and *The Sixth Sense* (1999). Quite literally nothing in the story can be taken for granted, since several of the characters are keeping secrets about their past (either consciously or otherwise), and each revelation changes the show's balance of power in a radical fashion. Fifteen years, it seems, is the time limit on repressed memories, a ticking bomb of trauma waiting to reassert itself—Naoki's sudden appearance in Minako's life is not the act of a malign stalker, but a last-minute rescue attempt before her entire personality falls apart. His hate-mail and smear campaign are designed to force her into hiding before the vengeful Yoshiharu arrives in town. In other words, the man we've assumed to be the bad guy is in fact a guardian angel, who has devoted his life to protecting the woman he loves. Other subplots include revelations of child abuse, incest, Oedipal longings, doomed love, and a second "ghost" in the form of Kiichirō's mother Makiko (Harada), declared dead after a seven-year absence, but still very much alive.

Nozawa's script revels in the deliciously Japanese idea that Minako's post-traumatic stress disorder is a form of living suicide and that her old self effectively died on the night she lost her old memories. Such a revelation turns *Sleeping Forest* into a very modern take on classical ghost stories, using modern science to retell a fairy tale—a phantom that haunts herself, if you will. But as with the writer's later **WEDNESDAY LOVE AFFAIR**, no single explanation suffices for long. Naoki's initially creepy claim that he and Minako are "one and the same" is revealed to be true, not in the expected TV drama sense of lovers made for each other, but quite spectacularly because she has been brainwashed with the use of his own childhood memories! Nozawa also offers intriguing thoughts on the presentation of self in everyday life—Minako's forthcoming wedding will gain her yet another new

surname and with it a new role and identity. Like the heroine of the earlier *Perfect Blue* (*AE), there are so many versions of her that she no longer knows which one is real. The true nature of the crime is revealed in a startling multiple-twist ending, with just minutes to spare before the legal statute of limitations allows the real criminal to get off scot-free.

A *Sleeping Forest TV Special* shown on 5 December 1998 comprised a feature-length edit of the first nine episodes, designed to lure in extra viewers for the final chapters. The story's powerful mix of psychological suspense and mystery resulted in the ultimate tribute—two years later, the suspiciously similar **ETERNAL CHILD** and **FROM THE HEART** fought for supremacy in the April season. Peak rating: 30.8%. Theme: Mariya Takeuchi—"Camouflage," also U2—"With or Without You."

SLEEPLESS CINDERELLA

2000. JPN: *Cinderella wa Nemurenai.* PRD: Kōichi Okamoto. DIR: Ryūta Inoue. SCR: Tomoko Yoshida. CAST: Sachie Hara, Yumi Adachi, Kumiko Akiyoshi, Akiho Sendō, Takaya Kamikawa. CHN: Yomiuri. DUR: 45 mins. x 9 eps.; Mon 10 January 2000–6 March 2000. Yōko (Hara) loses her mother when she is a child. She grows up and finds work as a welder, until the day she is informed that her long-lost father Sōsuke (Jinpachi Nezu) has died, but has also identified her as a beneficiary of his will. She becomes the chairwoman of Sōsuke's hotel group, but also inherits a half sister, Miyako (Adachi), who remains resentful of Yōko's overnight transformation. Sōsuke's wife Murasaki (Akiyoshi) is initially welcoming, but also secretly plots to bring down the unwelcome new arrival. Yōko's only ally is Sōsuke's secretary Yoshinori (Kamikawa), who is also Miyako's fiancé. However, Yoshinori has been having an affair with company employee Rikako (Sendō) who has helped him bury his criminal past and plots to take over the company with him.

Hospitality management drama ensues, in the style of **TAKE ME TO A RYOKAN** or **HOTEL**, but *SC*'s true inspiration lies in the put-upon heroines of dramas like **I'LL NEVER LOVE AGAIN**. Starting well with a good girl beset by evil plots on all sides, with only a single friend in the world who turns out to be the worst of the lot, *SC* collapses in its later episodes. Instead of engaging in the action, Yōko merely sits meekly by while her enemies are destroyed by their own schemes—a form of karmic retribution perhaps.

SLEEPLESS NIGHTS

2002. JPN: *Nemurenu Yoru o Daite.* PRD: Tetsuya Kuroda, Satoko Uchiyama, Takuya Nakagome, Shizuo Sekiguchi. DIR: Hiroshi Nishitani, Masanori Murakami, Manabu Kitagawa. SCR: Hisashi Nozawa. CAST: Naomi Zaizen, Tōru Nakamura, Toshio Kakei, Ryō, Naomi Akimoto, Arata Furuta, Seiichi Tanabe, Yūko Itō. CHN: Asahi. DUR: 45 mins. x 11 eps.; Thu 11 April 2002–27 June 2002. Ōta (Nakamura) is the chairman of the River Runs property development company, who moves to a new suburban home with his wife Yūko (Zaizen) and daughter Mina. They organize a party with their neighbors—Ōta's business protégé and former military man Tadamichi Yuzui (Furuta), J-League interpreter Kōhei Yamaji (Kakei), insurance 'total life planner' Yōji Shindō (Tanabe), and their families. But after a while, the Shindō family suddenly goes missing. In the second episode, the Yamaji family *also* goes missing. Remembering a mysterious comment she once heard from Kōhei, about a woman he is "unable to forget," former journalist Yūko decides to investigate.

As might be expected from the writer of **SLEEPING FOREST**, the past returns to haunt the present. For the current generation of Japanese thirtysomethings, the onset of marital, parental, and financial responsibilities came at the same time that the bubble economy of the 1980s gave way to recession. Yūko looks back on her salad days as a carefree time of champagne, fun, and money, contrasted with her present-day existence as a harassed and impecunious housewife. But there is more to *Sleepless Nights* than the yuppie hand-wringing of **WE HAVE TOMORROW**. What initially appears to be the early tensions of a mid-life crisis, as several thirtysomething couples question their achievements, is soon revealed to be something far more sinister. The menfolk of the various households all seem increasingly edgy with one another, while Ōta becomes overly fretful about the potential scandal—there are still 12 properties waiting to be sold in the development, and any bad publicity for the area is likely to place the sales in jeopardy. Yūko muses that although she has been married to Ōta for a decade, she really knows very little about him—he brought no guests to their wedding and told her that he has lived alone since the death of his mother when he was a child.

Yūko soon becomes convinced that the unexplained disappearances of Ōta's associates somehow relate to a disastrous bank robbery on Christmas Eve 1990, when a group of masked thieves held up a Japanese bank on Australia's Gold Coast. Though their guns were later found to be firing blanks, five live rounds also somehow made it into the magazines. According to press and police reports at the time, the robbers appear to have disagreed over something in the course of the robbery. One of the robbers and an innocent bystander were killed in the ensuing shoot-out. Yūko comes to suspect that the woman Kōhei is "unable to forget" is actually Ruiko Ōide (Itō), a bank teller who had only recently transferred to the Gold Coast branch from her native Japan, and whose killer has never been caught.

As Yūko's present-day life grows increasingly fraught in the style of **OUT** or **KIDNAP**, her story becomes interwoven with flashbacks detailing the events of the Australian bank robbery, gradually revealing the characters' actual relationship to events in a piecemeal form redolent of **GIFT**. Since the flashbacks have the consistency and apparent production values of a stand-alone movie, the series gives the impression that things really *were* better in the good old days—even the acting. *Reservoir Dogs* meets *The Firm*, and yet more proof if it were needed, that Hisashi Nozawa is one of the most thrilling writers working in Japanese TV today. Theme: The Brilliant Green—"Forever To Me—Owarinaki Kanashimi" (Forever To Me—Endless Grief). Note also the music by Hajime Mizoguchi, better known in the anime world as the composer for *Please Save My Earth* (*AE) and *Jin-Roh* (*AE).

SLOPE IN SPRING, THE

1971. JPN: *Haru no Sakamichi*. PRD: N/C. DIR: Toshio Kobayashi. SCR: Yoshinori Sugiyama. CAST: Kinnosuke Nakamura (later Kinnosuke Yorozuya), Chitose Kobayashi, Yoshio Harada, Ebizō Ichikawa X (Danjūrō Ichikawa XII), Hiroshi Arakawa, Sō Yamamura, Atsuo Nakamura, Chitose Kobayashi. CHN: NHK. DUR: 45 mins. x ca. 50 eps.; Sun 3 January 1971–26 December 1971.

This 1971 *taiga* drama depicts the life of Sōtan Yagyū (K. Nakamura), also known as Munenori, a retainer of the first three shoguns of the Edo period—Ieyasu, Hidetada (see **AOI**), and Iemitsu. At the age of 24, Sōtan fights at the battle of Sekigahara in 1600, alongside his father Sōgen or Sekishūsai (Arakawa), the founder of the Yagyū school of swordfighting. When the leader, Ieyasu (Yamamura) learns that his rival Mitsunari Ishida (A. Nakamura) has raised an army, he sends Sōtan to Sōgen with orders to harass the enemy's rear guard. After Sekigahara, the Yagyū family is granted land that has been confiscated from Ieyasu's enemy **HIDEYOSHI**. At age 31, Sōtan receives more land when he is appointed the martial arts tutor to Ieyasu's son Hidetada. He continues to work as an adviser to the Shogun, becoming chief superintendant in 1632 and a feudal lord in 1636. His wife Rin (Kobayashi), and later concubines, give birth to six male children between 1613 and 1636, who will grow up to become figures of legend—including Matajūro, the hero of kabuki, and Jūbei, the hero of 20th-century novels, movies, and the TV series **THE YAGYŪ CONSPIRACY**. Retiring to his estate in 1641, Sōtan becomes ill and dies in 1646 at the age of 76. This particular drama was based on the historical novel by Sōhachi Yamaoka, whose books were also adapted into the *taiga* dramas **TOKUGAWA IEYASU** and **MASAMUNE THE ONE-EYED DRAGON**.

SMILE HAS LEFT YOUR EYES, THE

2002. JPN: *Sora Kara Furu Ichi-Oku no Hoshi*. AKA: *One Hundred Million Stars Falling*. PRD: Ichirō Takai, Yoshihiro Suzuki, Takashi Ishihara. DIR: Takeshi Nakazawa, Makoto Hirano. SCR: Eriko Kitagawa. CAST: Sanma Akashiya, Takuya Kimura, Eri Fukatsu, Haruka Igawa, Kō Shibazaki, Kenya Ōsumi. CHN: Fuji. DUR: 45 mins. x 11 eps.; 15 April 2002–24 June 2002.

Scruffy cop Kanzō (Akashiya) takes on the case of a murdered college girl, but is forced to put it on hold when his sister Yūko invites him on a cruise. Her rich best friend Miwa (Igawa) is having a birthday party on the ship, but also begins an unexpected affair with the lowly apprentice cook Ryō (Kimura)—shades here of the cross-class romance in *Titanic* (1997). This is bound to cause problems with Miwa's wealthy fiancé Kashiwagi (Ōsumi), a partner selected for her by her domineering father. Yūko, however, doesn't see the attraction of Miwa's new beau. Unable to leave his detective sensibilities behind, Kanzō discovers that Ryō is two-timing Miwa with another girl called Yuki, a girl who seems to have had some kind of former association with the murder victim whose case Kanzō is investigating. Reuniting 21st-century star Kimura with Eriko Kitagawa, the writer of **LONG VACATION** and **BEAUTIFUL LIFE**, *SHLYE* was billed

© 2001 Asahi

The Sniper

from the outset as a drama with a series of twists lurking for the unsuspecting viewer—compare to **ETERNAL CHILD** or **SLEEPING FOREST**. Theme: Elvis Costello—"Smile."

SMILING THROUGH THE PAIN

1993. JPN: *Nikushimi ni Hohoende.* PRD: Mitsunori Morita. DIR: Takamichi Yamada. SCR: Toshio Terada. CAST: Tetsurō Yanagiba, Naoki Hosaka, Yoshiko Tanaka, Chiharu, Masahiko Tsugawa. CHN: TBS. DUR: 45 mins. x 11 eps.; Tue 12 October 1993–21 December 1993.

Fifteen years after he witnessed his mother throw herself to a watery death at sea, businessman Jun (Yanagiba) is recalled from New York by his businessman father Shinichirō (Tsugawa). His brother is presumed dead in a suicide pact with his lover, leaving Jun to take over the family business and welcome his new stepmother into the family. Since the brother is played by Naoki Hosaka, you know he's not going to remain "presumed dead" for long. Compare to **SLEEPING FOREST**. Theme: X-Japan—"Tears."

SNIPER, THE

2001. JPN: *Koibito wa Sniper.* AKA: *My Boyfriend is a Sniper.* PRD: Motoi

Sasaki. DIR: Eiichirō Hasumi. SCR: Ryōichi Kimizuka. CAST: Miki Mizuno, Teruyoshi Uchimura, Chōsuke Ikariya, Kaoru Yachigusa, Seiichi Tanabe, Naoto Takenaka, Shidō Nakamura. CHN: TV Asahi. DUR: ca. 100 mins. x 2 eps.; Thu 18 October 2001 and 24 December 2002.

Olympic-class marksman Wong Kaige (Uchimura) comes to Tokyo, ostensibly as an information technology student but really because he has been blackmailed into carrying out a series of assassinations on behalf of a Hong Kong crime syndicate. Completely by accident, he is assigned to a Japanese home stay family whose eldest daughter Kinako (Mizuno) is an undercover law enforcement officer. While Wong, under the pseudonym "Chan Hoi," receives his latest assignments from the local sleeper agent (Takenaka) who poses as his Japanese teacher, Kinako's squad tries desperately to track down the killer who is blowing away business leaders all over Tokyo. Meanwhile, Kinako and "Chan Hoi" overcome their initial reluctance and begin to fall for each other, each unaware of the other's secret identity. Wong has been promised a reunion with his missing mother (Yachigusa) if he carries out his mission, though his handlers have neglected to tell him that she has married a Japanese national who is to become one of his targets.

The Sniper is one of the most entertaining dramas we have seen. From its stunning opening sequence, in which Kinako single-handedly beats up an entire battalion of Chinese gangsters, to the chilling moment when actor Takenaka transforms from a camp language teacher into a gruff gang boss, it combines the terrorist romance of **LOVE 2000** with the lesser concerns of gourmet dramas, police thrillers, and classroom high jinks. It even has intercultural satire, with scenes played in Mandarin, and a comedy of manners in the style of **FALSE LOVE** after Kinako mischievously convinces Wong (and, by association, his classmates) that the Japanese for sorry is not "*Sumimasen*"

but "*Ki ni sunnatte*"—i.e., "*Just deal with it.*"

Reuniting many of the crew of **BAYSIDE SHAKEDOWN**, it leaves no cinematic trick unused, from an opening sequence inspired by *The Matrix* to scene changes that morph out of photographs onscreen and carefully lit flashbacks that allow Yachigusa to convincingly play herself 20 years younger. The story is leavened with liberal doses of kung fu action, modeled on the wire-work and stunts of the best Hong Kong action movies.

The producers claim that *The Sniper* was originally intended as a standard series, though how such a premise could have been stretched across 11 episodes remains questionable. Instead, the original pilot aired barely a month after the deaths of dozens of Japanese citizens in the 9/11 atrocities and sank without a trace—it only qualified for inclusion in this book at the last possible moment, when a TV movie sequel upgraded it to "series" status.

In the sequel, Kinako agrees to marry her work colleague Funaki (Tanabe), only for the lovers to be called away from their engagement ceremony on an emergency case. Leaving bewildered relatives behind, Kinako uses her kung fu skills to dispatch a number of Chinese gang members and pursues a fleeing suspect who is revealed to be Lau (Nakamura), a detective from the Hong Kong police. He claims to be hunting Wong Kaige, who appears to have resumed his career as a sniper, in contravention of the earlier promise he gave Kinako to retire.

SO I BOUGHT A HOUSE

1991. JPN: *Soredemo Ie o Kaimashita.* AKA: *Nevertheless I Bought a House.* PRD: Hiroshi Ōtani. DIR: Toshihiro Iijima. SCR: Kenichi Iwasa. CAST: Hiroshi Mikami, Misako Tanaka, Shin Takuma, Sayuri Kokushō, Hiroyuki Konishi. CHN: TBS. DUR: 45 mins. x 11 eps.; Fri 19 April 1991–28 June 1991.

Transferring from Kobe to their

company's Yokohama branch, newly-weds Yūsuke (Mikami) and Hiroko (Tanaka) are grateful for cheap accommodations at the corporate dormitory. However, they soon tire of the curfews, the thin walls, and the interfering concierge and decide that things could not possibly be worse if they simply bought a place of their own. Compare to ARE YOU ON THE MOVE? and EXCUSE ME AGAIN. Theme: Kumi Shōji—"Ano Koro no Yō ni" (Like That Time).

SO SWEET

1999. JPN: *Amai Seikatsu*. AKA: *Sweet Life, La Dolce Vita*. PRD: Nobuo Mizuta, Kenji Ikeda. DIR: Nobuo Mizuta, Rieko Ishizaka, Kensaku Sawada. SCR: Yasuhiro Koshimizu. CAST: Sanma Akashiya, Yuki Uchida, Reiko Takashima, Katsuhisa Namase, Toshiaki Megumi. CHN: NTV. DUR: 45 mins. x 12 eps.; Wed 7 July 1999–22 September 1999.
Rikimaru (Akashiya) is a middle-aged businessman conducting a clandestine affair with his secretary, until his wife and company find out. Rikimaru's wife is frosty but prepared to try again, whereas his less forgiving employers post him to a remote branch office and effectively end his rise up the promotional ladder. However, his biggest problem remains his jilted lover, who tracks him down and stabs him with a knife. Recuperating in the hospital, Rikimaru falls for his nurse. . . . Another mid-week adultery extravaganza—compare to WEDNESDAY LOVE AFFAIR. Broadcast without English subtitles in the U.S. on KTSF TV and NGN. Theme: Sophia—"Place."

SOAP BUBBLE

1991. JPN: *Shabon Dama*. PRD: Senji Nakasone. DIR: Setsurō Wakamatsu. SCR: Shōichirō Ōkubo. CAST: Tsuyoshi Nagabuchi, Satoshi Yamamura, Junichi Ishida, Misa Shimizu, Eiji Okada. CHN: Fuji. DUR: 45 mins. x 11 eps.; Thu 10 October 1991–19 December 1991.
Nanjō (Yamamura) is drawn into the shadowy underworld of West Shinjuku, as his normal life takes a series of dives in fortune. Threatened by bikers and

loan sharks, he falls in with Asakura (Ishida), a dealer prepared to trade anything if there's money in it for him and criminal doctor Teppei (pop star Nagabuchi). Reputedly based on an idea by Nagabuchi, which combined the long-running gangster genre with medical drama—or, if you prefer, looked a lot like Akira Kurosawa's *Drunken Angel* (1948). Theme: Tsuyoshi Nagabuchi—"Shabon Dama."

SOFT-BOILED EGG

1994. JPN: *Hanjuku Tamago*. PRD: Yasuyuki Kusuda. DIR: Yasuyuki Kusuda. SCR: Mika Umeda. CAST: Hiroko Shino, Yuki Uchida, Ritsuko Tanaka, Rie Tomosaka. CHN: Fuji. DUR: 45 mins. x 9 eps.; Fri 21 October 1994–16 December 1994.
In the six years since her husband's death, Machiko (Shino) has reared three daughters on her own. Yuka (Tanaka), Kana (Uchida), and Nao (Tomosaka) become concerned for their mother's future when their neighbor Yumiko (Akari Uchida) mentions that the widow has agreed to an *omiai* marriage meeting. Compare to ETCHAN. Theme: Yuki Uchida—"Tenka o Torō! Uchida no Yabō" (I'm Becoming a Ruler! Uchida's Ambition).

SOLBRAIN

1991. JPN: *Tokkyū Shirei Solbrain*. AKA: *Super Rescue Solbrain*. PRD: Kyōzō Utsunomiya, Jun Kaji, Nagafumi Hori. DIR: Masao Minowa, Michio Konishi, Takeru Ogasawara, Tetsuji Mitsumura. SCR: Shō Sugimura, Takahiko Masuda, Nobuo Ōgisawa, Kyōko Sagiyama. CAST: Kōichi Nakayama, Mitsue Mori, Hiroshi Miyauchi, Hidetoshi Iura, Mitsuru Onodera, Kaname Kawai, Mayuko Irie, Mitsutaka Tachikawa, Yū Yamashita. CHN: Asahi. DUR: 25 mins. x 53 eps.; Sun 20 January 1991–26 January 1992.
An unidentified flying object appears above Tokyo and starts attacking passing aircraft. The Solbrain team is sent to investigate, comprising leader Shunsuke Masaki (Miyauchi) and

members Daki Nishio (Nakayama), Reiko Higuchi (Mori), Jun Masuda (Iura), Takeshi Yazawa (Kawai), and the scientist Midori Aikawa (Irie). The UFO is found to be controlled by the biocomputer A320, developed by "dangerous scientist" Inagaki, who announces that nothing, not even he, can stand in the way of scientific evolution. A320 decides that it wants a physical body (compare to *Ghost in the Shell*, *AE) and demands that Inagaki sacrifice his own son, Kazuo. Inagaki agrees but the Solbrain team intervenes in the nick of time, leading the enraged A320 to drop the UFO onto Inagaki's lab. This in turn requires the arrival of the Solbrain team to rescue survivors from the rubble. The second Thunderbirds-inspired, rescue-oriented entry in the Metal Series, *Solbrain* also gained former WINSPECTOR member Night Fire Ryōma Kagawa (Yamashita) in its later episodes. The next entry in the Metal Series was the following year's EXIDRAFT.

SOMEBODY LOVES HER

1992. JPN: *Darekaga Kanojo o Aishiteru*. PRD: N/C. DIR: Michio Kōno. SCR: Kazuhiko Ban. CAST: Miho Nakayama, Kōji Matoba, Jinpachi Nezu, Junko Igarashi, Hiroko Nakajima. CHN: Fuji. DUR: 45 mins. x 11 eps.; Wed 14 October 1992–23 December 1992.
Manabu (Matoba) goes out to buy an engagement ring for his girlfriend Eriko (Nakajima), only to fall for the shop assistant Tsubasa (Nakayama). Later episodes introduce a surreal element, as Tsubasa seeks advice from her car—a sentient British Leyland Maxi that communicates to her by wiggling its windscreen wipers. Theme: Miho Nakayama & Wands—"Sekaijū no Dareyori Kitto" (More Than Anyone in the World).

SOMETIME SOMEWHERE

1998. JPN: *Konya Uchū no Katasumi de*. AKA: *Tonight Somewhere in the Cosmos*. PRD: Shizuo Sekiguchi. DIR: Keita Kawano. SCR: Kōki Mitani. CAST: Masahiko Nishimura, Naoko Iijima,

Takaaki Ishibashi, Yasukiyo Umeno, Masaji Yasui. CHN: Fuji. DUR: 45 mins. x 12 eps.; Thu 9 July 1998–24 September 1998.

Kōsuke (Nishimura) is a cameraman with a film company, who accidentally finds himself living on location in New York with an impromptu roommate, the flaky makeup artist Makoto (Iijima). The pair's antagonistic relationship takes on a new dimension when Kōsuke's freelance cameraman friend Higuchi (Ishibashi) also moves in. A comedy from the writer of NINZABURŌ FURUHATA with an exotic location—compare to NEW YORK LOVE STORY. Iijima's rival Kyōko Fukada also planned a romantic drama in New York, but was forced to relocate to Hong Kong for the opening of FRIENDS (2). Theme: Frank Sinatra—"But Not For Me."

SOMMELIER

1998. PRD: Hideki Inada, Yūji Ōhira. DIR: Mamoru Hoshi, Masanori Murakami. SCR: Mitsuru Tanabe, Rumi Takahashi, Masataka Kashida. CAST: Gorō Inagaki, Miho Kanno, Tetsuya Takeda, Anju Suzuki, Shigemitsu Ogi. CHN: Kansai (Fuji). DUR: 45 mins. x 11 eps.; Tue 13 October 1998–22 December 1998.

A troubled French restaurant in Tokyo hires Jō (Inagaki from SMAP), a maverick sommelier who doesn't play by the book. Jō believes that wine is the answer to most of the world's problems and enforces his superhero connoisseur outlook on patrons of the restaurant as well as innocent bystanders. Compare to ANTIQUE, which similarly places an incidental foodstuff at the center of the universe. Based on the manga by Shinobu Kaitani and Araki Jō. Peak rating: 15.4%.

SON OF THE GOOD EARTH *

1995. JPN: Daichi no Ko. PRD: Masakazu Kawamura. DIR: Takaharu Matsuoka. SCR: Sakae Okazaki, Toyoko Yamazaki. CAST: Takaya Kamikawa, Tatsuya Nakadai, Ken Utsui, Yoshiko Tanaka. CHN: NHK. DUR: 45 mins. x ca.

50 eps.; Sat 11 March 1995–20 March 1996.

In 1945, the Soviet army invades Manchuria and drives Japanese colonists off their land. With their father absent fighting elsewhere, the Matsumoto family is powerless to resist, and all the adults are killed. Daughter Atsuko is carried off to an unknown fate, while her amnesiac brother Katsuo is adopted by the Chinese Liu family, who name him Yisin. As a child of Japanese extraction, Yisin must face discrimination in his adopted homeland but as a man he finds a part to play in the construction and maintenance of the local iron company. A coproduction between NHK (celebrating its 70th anniversary as a broadcaster) and the People's Republic of China, SotGE is a sprawling saga of separated siblings and Yisin's conflicted feelings for his prodigal father set against the background of the Cultural Revolution. Compare to ANJU AND ZUSHIŌ, which approaches similar family trials but in a medieval Japanese setting. The story was based on a book by Toyoko Yamazaki, for which the author interviewed over 300 orphans who had endured similar circumstances—compare to the research that informed OSHIN. Shown with English subtitles in the U.S. by channels carrying Asahi Homecast programming.

SON-IN-LAW

2001. JPN: Muko Dono. PRD: Miwako Kurihara. DIR: Tatsuaki Kimura. SCR: Yoshihiro Izumi. CAST: Tomoya Nagase, Yūko Takeuchi, Anju Suzuki, Ryōko Shinohara, Yasunori Danta, Hironobu Nomura. CHN: Fuji. DUR: 45 mins. x ca. 22 eps.; Thu 12 April 2001–?? June 2001 (#1); 17 April 2003–?? June 2003 (#2).

Singer-songwriter Yūichi (Nagase) falls in love with Sakura, who appears at first to be a traditional Japanese girl keen to marry, settle down, and raise a family. However, Sakura's three sisters all have differing ideas about how to live a life—one is a single mother with a job, another is a traditionalist, and

the third is a radio announcer who is torn between family life and independence. The result is a tough case of in-law appeasement, since whatever Yūichi does to impress one sister is bound to annoy the others.

SONG OF CHIRIMENJAKO

1991. JPN: Chirimenjako no Uta. PRD: N/C. DIR: Shō Nagaoki. SCR: N/C. CAST: Masahiro Yanagimoto, Yū Matsuda, Hiromi Iwasaki, Kazue Itō, Rina Nishibe, Eigo Kawashima, Kentarō Nakaoka. CHN: NHK. DUR: 30 mins. x 4 eps.; Fri 11 January 1991–15 February 1991.

In 1947, Kenta (Yanagimoto) is an 11-year-old boy who has had to change schools three times in just five years, owing to his father's job as a police officer. The mournful boy transfers schools again and entertains his classmates by playing the harmonica. He joins the baseball team, but their manager "Akaoni" or the Red Devil (Matsuda) forces the boys to endure a harsh training regime, which none of the boys can quit without losing their food allowance. Realizing that his friend Akagire (Nakaoka) has failed to turn up for a few days, he visits him at home to find that Akagire's mother Michiyo is tending for Ōishi, an injured man. Other episodes include consumptive schoolgirl Sayuri (Iwasaki) and her classmate Sakurako (Nishibe), who is jealous of the attention that Kenta lavishes on his hospitalized friend. At the end, Kenta returns home to find that his goldfish has died. It is hoped that this is a symbol of the brevity of life and the need to hang onto friends, rather than a suggestion of what happens next—the chirimenjako of the title is a small dried fish delicacy.

SORROW IS THE COLOR OF THE SEA

1972. JPN: Kanashimi wa Umi no Iro. PRD: Kazuo Shibata. DIR: Kazuya Satō. SCR: Yasuo Tanami. CAST: Yōko Iijima, Satoshi Kadota, Isao Tamagawa, Toshikazu Kimura, Etsuko Kogawa,

Toshiaki Nishizawa. CHN: NHK. DUR: 30 mins. x 4 eps.; 3 June 1972–24 June 1972.

At the beginning of the fall semester, the dark, mysterious Kazuya (Kadota) transfers from distant Aomori to the Kōnan Middle School where Fumi (Iijima) is a pupil. Fumi recognizes his face, as he is the boy she saw during her vacation long ago with her friend Chikako, standing motionlessly by a body that had been pulled from the water off the Shimokita Peninsula. Fumi eventually discovers that Kazuya's mother deserted her husband and son, only to be killed in a car accident and that Kazuya's father followed his wife in death by committing suicide the following year—compare to SCARLET MEMORIAL. However, Fumi's parents seem to know a suspicious amount about Kazuya and his father. Kazuya and Fumi win a prize at an art competition and are invited to Europe. When they are applying for passports, Fumi finds out that she was *adopted* from an orphanage on Shimokita Peninsula. Realizing that she, too, has a connection to events in Shimokita, the distraught Fumi runs away from home, only to be found by Kazuya moments before she plans on throwing herself to her death. Based on the story by Takako Yamashita.

SORRY FOR CAUSING SUCH A COMMOTION

1985. JPN: *Maido Osawagase Shimasu*. PRD: Yūzō Abe. DIR: Yasuyuki Kusuda. SCR: Mineaki Hata. CAST: Eiji Bandō, Akira Onodera, Hiroko Shino, Emi Shindō, Kazuya Kimura, Miho Nakayama. CHN: TBS. DUR: 45 mins. x 27 eps.; Tue 8 January 1985–26 March 1985; 10 December 1985–25 March 1986.

Three families must deal with the hormonal whirl of their teenage children who are all intensely curious about sex. A deliberate attempt by OUR JOURNEY author Hata to try something different, this sex education comedy launched the acting careers of both Miho Nakayama and Kazuya Kimura. It also featured an appearance by female wrestler Dump Matsumoto.

SORRY TO INTERRUPT

1995. JPN: *Maido Ojama Shimasu*. PRD: Toyohiko Wada. DIR: Satoru Nakajima. SCR: Masahiro Yoshimoto. CAST: Yasuko Matsuyuki, Naoki Hosaka, Tōru Nakamura, Taishū Kase, Takashi Sorimachi. CHN: TBS. DUR: 45 mins. x 11 eps.; Tue 11 April 1995–27 June 1995.

Sakura (Matsuyuki) is studying design in Milan when she receives an urgent telegram from her family. Since it claims that her elder brother Kazuya (Hosaka) had a serious accident, she rushes home to Japan. On arrival, she discovers that it was an elaborate ruse and that Kazuya has merely run off with a bar girl, leaving three sullen children in need of a surrogate parent. Theme: Mink—"Zettai Kitto Suki" (Definitely Absolutely in Love).

SPACE GIANTS *

1966. JPN: *Magma Taishi*. AKA: *Ambassador Magma*. PRD: Kazuo Kamijima, Takaharu Bessho. DIR: Tatsuo Kuroda, Tōgo Wakabayashi, Keinosuke Tsuchiya, Mamoru Nakao, Shigeru Umeki. SCR: Susumu Takahisa, Hiroyasu Yamaura, Shigeru Umeki. CAST: Masumi Okada, Machiko Yashiro, Toshio Egi, Tetsuya Uosumi, Yoshio Kaneuchi, Tsuguaki Yoshida, Hideki Ninomiya, Shigeko Mitsuse, Hajime Shimizu, Tōru Ōhira, Gorō Mutsu, Edith Hanson. CHN: Fuji. DUR: 25 mins. x 52 eps.; 4 July 1966–25 September 1967.

The evil Goa (Ōhira) has conquered most of the planets in the universe and now sets his sights on Earth. But a good wizard whose name, confusingly, is also "Earth" (Shimizu), opposes him by bringing in a pair of warriors from the 2rf galaxy, the powerful robot fighters Magma (Uosumi) and Mol (Mitsuse), along with their robot son Gam (Ninomiya). Goa sends a series of monsters to attack the Earth but the family can be called from their secret mountain base to defend it. Their chief allies among the human race are journalist Atsushi Murakami (Okada), his wife Tomoko (Yoshiro), and their son Mamoru (Egi). In times of trouble, Mamoru can summon Gam to his aid with a single blow on his special whistle. Two blows will bring forth Mol and, in times of dire need, three blows will summon Magma himself. All members of the family can fight evil with the Gamma Rays they shoot from their antennae, and can also transform into torpedoes, while Magma can shoot missiles from his chest.

Based on a story by ASTRO BOY creator Osamu Tezuka, *Ambassador Magma* was a cheap early sci-fi show in the style of JOHNNY SOKKO AND HIS GIANT ROBOT. Monsters would often be defeated over several episodes, allowing for the same suit to be re-used across two, three, or occasionally four episodes. It was adapted into English as *Space Avenger* in 1972, but did not reach a wide audience until 1978 under its best-known title *Space Giants*. The dubbing was arranged by Peter Fernandez, who was responsible for many of the early American dubs of anime. In the U.S. adaptation, Goa was renamed Rodak, and Gam's parents were renamed Goldar and Silvar. Earth the wizard, not the planet, was renamed Methusan. Atsushi became Mr. Itamura, and his son became Mikko, although Tomoko and Gam inexplicably kept their original names. The story was remade in 1993 as the anime series *Ambassador Magma* (*AE).

SPACE GOVERNMENT MAN

1963. JPN: *Uchū G-Men*. AKA: *Space G-Men*. PRD: N/C. DIR: Morihei Magaya, Norio Mine, Jusaburō Deguchi. SCR: Akira Ōtani, Yūichi Kajiwara, Susumu Takahisa, Toshikazu Yamano. CAST: Masakazu Hirai, Shintarō Kuraoka, Hachirō Minamoto, Takako Azuma, Michel Higgins. CHN: NTV. DUR: 25 mins. x 8 eps.; Tue 20 August 1963–8 October 1963.

As the nations of Earth prepare to explore the vastness of space, Japan's Andromeda Institute is years ahead of the rest of the world, thanks to the

Space Government Man

genius of its supervisor Professor Kawanaka (Minamoto). However, the maiden flight of the Andromeda Institute's experimental vessel Radar One meets with disaster, and the elder brother of plucky all-Japanese boy Sakaze (Hirai) is lost in space, presumed dead. In fact, Radar One was just one of several Earth missions fated to accidentally cross the path of dastardly schemes from the Demon Empire, a secret society devoted to ruling the world. However, the Demon Empire's schemes are foiled at every turn by the people of the Andromeda Institute and by the occasional intervention of the "Space Government Man," a masked astronaut whose inspirational messages to young Sakaze sound suspiciously like speeches once delivered by his long-lost brother.

Ludicrous now, but a landmark in its time, *Space Government Man* sets the tone for much of children's TV that was to follow, including the entire **ULTRAMAN** series. Originally, 13 episodes were made, but only 8 episodes were broadcast. With a sepia color scheme that actually makes it look even older than it is and special effects to rival those of the Buster Crabbe *Flash Gordon*, it is a charmingly

camp approach to the sci-fi ideals of yesteryear. Its stories encapsulate the feelings of the Japanese in the early 1960s, as they recovered from World War II, tried to deal with the Korean War, and prepared for the Olympics. Consequently, Japan is great, the Japanese are great; there are people out there who want to hurt them, but there is a higher power that sees Japan's potential for peace.

Bonus entertainment value is supplied by the Demon Empire's agent in episode one, a beanpole *gaijin* who has to visibly struggle to allow himself to be bested in hand-to-hand combat by the show's diminutive hero. Meanwhile back at the base, the Professor muses about inventions, his pretty assistant swoons at the handsome hero, and an irritating child wanders around for no apparent reason—in other words, the very bedrock of Japanese science fiction.

The strange mix of plural and singular in the titles is explained by their origins—obviously we only see a single "Space Government Man," but the Japanese title implies a plural, presumably to draw non-existent links between this series and the American serials *Cowboy G-Men* (KRT, 1956) and *Dangerous Assignment* (released in Japan as plain *G-Men* on NTV in 1958).

SPACE PATROL

1963. JPN: *Ginga Shōnentai*. PRD: Susumu Yasue, Mushi Pro. DIR: Susumu Yasue. SCR: Osamu Tezuka, Ichirō Wakabayashi. CAST: (voices) Masako Ikeda. CHN: NHK. DUR: 15/25 mins. x 92 eps.: 7 April 1963–5 April 1964 (15 mins. x 43 eps.); 9 April 1964–1 April 1965 (25 mins. x 49 eps.).

The power of the sun begins to wane, endangering the future of all life on Earth. The Space Patrol, accompanied by Professor Hanajima and Rop the token child, go in search of material to revive the sun—compare to *Star Blazers* (*AE). Bridging the gap between **SILICA** and **AERIAL CITY 008**, this rare puppet show from Osamu Tezuka did

not achieve quite the same success as his more famous **ASTRO BOY**. No doubt with most of Tezuka's staff busy on the anime version of *Astro Boy, Space Patrol* only used minimal animation, for special effects and credits, using the puppets as a swifter method of shooting character-based sequences. Tezuka's puppet adventure was preceded on Japanese TV by Gerry Anderson shows such as *Supercar* (NTV, 1961) and *Four Feather Falls* (TBS, 1963)—the latter show perhaps explaining why Space Patrol has an incongruous cowboy, Tex, along with Pedro, a child with an unfeasibly large sombrero. Theme: Tokyo Broadcasting Children's Choir—"Ginga Shōnentai." Music was by Isao Tomita, who also provided scores for a number of Tezuka's animated works.

SPECIAL INVESTIGATIONS: FOREMOST

1977. JPN: *Tokusō Saizensen*. PRD: Yoriteru Saitō. DIR: Yasutada Nagano. SCR: Toshio Munakata, Ayato Imamura. CAST: Hideaki Nitani, Hiroshi Fujioka, Shūji Ōtaki, Toshiyuki Nishida, Shigeru Araki, Naoya Makoto, Kōjirō Hongō, Katsuhiko Yokomitsu. CHN: Asahi. DUR: 45 mins. x ca. 500 eps.; Wed 6 April 1977–26 March 1987.

Dandy detective superintendent Kamidai (Nitani) runs cases alongside veteran assistant inspector Ippei Funamura (Ōtaki) and young, eager assistant inspector Tetsuo Sakurai (Fujioka). Roughly contemporaneous with **HOWL AT THE SUN**, *SI* eschewed its rival's flashy action sequences and heartthrob actors in favor of solid, earthy human drama—a successful approach that lasted for ten years.

SPECTREMAN *

1971. JPN: *Uchū Enjin Golly*. AKA: *Golly the Space Monkey; Space Monkey Golly vs Spectreman; Spectreman*. PRD: Tomio Washizu, Takaharu Bessho. DIR: Keinosuke Tsuchiya, Takeo Sakai, Kōichi Ishiguro, Hiromi Higuchi, Yasuharu Hasebe. SCR: Masaki Tsuji, Keisuke Fujikawa, Kazuo Koike, Shōji

Nemoto, Susumu Takahisa, Tsunehisa Itō, Haruya Yamazaki. CAST: Takanobu Tōya, Kiyoshi Kobayashi, Ren Nishiyama, Tetsuo Narukawa, Tōru Ōhira, Takamitsu Watanabe, Kazuo Arai, Kōji Ozaki, Machiko Konishi, Sakurako Oya, Rumi Gotō, Taeko Sakurai, Kyōji Kobayashi, Seizō Katō, Hirotsugu Uenishi. CHN: Fuji. DUR: 25 mins. x 65 eps.; Sat 2 January 1971–25th March 1972.

Genius scientist monkey Golly (Tōya, voiced by Kobayashi and Nishiyama) escapes from Planet E after a failed coup. As he and his subordinate Rah (Uenishi) wander the cosmos, they discover the beautiful planet Earth and are incensed to see the environmental damage caused by its stupid inhabitants. Consequently, Golly punishes humanity by creating a number of ULTRAMAN-themed monsters out of pollution itself. However, Golly's plot is discovered by the inhabitants of Planet Nevilla 71, who have sworn to protect unsophisticated worlds from abuse at the hands of advanced civilizations. They send Spectreman to defend the planet . . . leading to a somewhat embarrassing change in emphasis in the series title. Though the series began with the title *Space Monkey Golly*, viewer response and plain common sense dictated that the title really ought to include the name of the giant cyborg who was fighting to save the Earth every week. From episode 21, it became known as *Space Monkey Golly vs Spectreman*, and from episode 40 onward, as just plain *Spectreman*. However, by this point, the serial's original pollution-inspired plotting was replaced by standard monsters of the week, and it never attained the heights of its early to middle period. Based on an idea by LIONMARU creator Sōji Ushio, and featuring a number of well-known anime scriptwriters on the staff, the series was also spun off into a manga by Daiji Ichimine and was released in *Bōken Ō* and *Shōnen Champion* magazines. The mind boggles at what might have happened if all superheroes began their adventures in such a strange way—would we all still be reading *Lex Luthor* comics?

The show made it to the U.S. in video form across 12 tapes, in a dubbed format that retained much of the original plotting. Some characters and situations first appeared in a failed pilot under the title *Elementman*, in which the lead was played by Kōji Uenishi.

SPIDER-MAN
1978. PRD: Susumu Yoshikawa, Hiroshi Ishikawa. DIR: Hirokazu Takemoto, Katsuhiko Taguchi, Kimio Hirayama, Yoshiaki Kobayashi. SCR: Shōzō Uehara, Susumu Takahisa, Kuniaki Oshikawa, Hirohisa Soda. CAST: Kōsuke Kayama, Rika Miura, Izumi Ōyama, Toshiaki Nishizawa, Mitsuo Andō, Yukie Kagawa, Fumiki Murakami, Tōru Ōhira. CHN: Tokyo Channel 12 (TV Tokyo). DUR: 25 mins. x 41 eps.; Wed 17 May 1978–14 March 1979.

Teenage motorcyclist Takuya (Kayama) is troubled by voices in his head. His scientist father Professor Yamashiro (Murakami) is killed while investigating a strange object approaching the Earth from space, and Takuya eventually goes looking for him. After fighting off hostile aliens at the crash site, Takuya finds Garia (Nishizawa), the last surviving crew member from Planet Spider. He warns Takuya of the approaching invaders from the Iron Cross Group and tells him that the crashed spaceship is a military vessel, The Marveller. Garia clips a special bracelet onto the unconscious Takuya, which injects him with Spider Extract. Garia then transforms into a spider, leaving Takuya to defend the Earth as the new superhero Spider-Man.

Unlike its Marvel comic origins, the Tōei *Spider-Man* series featured a formula typical to many other Japanese shows. The hero came equipped with supervehicles—the GP-7 car and the Marveller flying fortress, as well as a giant robot that allowed him to take on each monster of the week on equal terms. His true enemies were the evil Professor Monster (Andō) and his assistant Amazoness (Kagawa), a beau-tiful woman who dons glasses and a business suit so she can become a magazine editor and fight Spider-Man with the power of the poisoned pen. When such subtle means inevitably failed, the evil duo would fall back on their cannon fodder army of disposable minions. Spider-Man, in the meantime, can fight back with the aid of the Marveller, which can transform into the giant robot Leopardon. A feature-length movie version was also made.

Spider-Man was not the first Japanese adaptation of the Marvel character. In 1970, manga artist Ryōichi Ikegami had drawn a short-lived manga version of the story for *Shōnen Magazine*, but the story was defeated by "cultural differences" between Stan Lee's arachnid lone ranger and traditionally group-oriented Japanese children's superheroes. This later TV version learned from the previous mistakes, dumping much of the original's vigilante plot to create a story more like ULTRAMAN. The "original idea" for the series was credited to both Marvel Comics and "Saburō Yade"—a name which previously occurs on the anime *Combattler V* (*AE). Considering his incredibly prolific later career, the authors suspect that Yade ("Eight Hands"), like his Sunrise Studio counterpart Hajime Yadate, is a Tōei house pseudonym designed to keep series copyrights under corporate ownership. The same period also saw animated remakes of Marvel's *Frankenstein* and *Dracula* comics (*AE). Tōei planned a follow-up live-action adaptation of Marvel's *Captain America*, but the concept was eventually retooled to make BATTLEFEVER J. Music was by Michiaki Watanabe.

SPIRAL
1999. JPN: *Rasen*. PRD: Masatoshi Katō. DIR: Takao Kinoshita, Hiroshi Nishitani. SCR: Kazuhiko Tanaka, Kōji Makita. CAST: Gorō Kishitani, Takami Yoshimoto, Yūka Nomura, Akiko Yada, Tae Kimura, Risa Sudō, Seiichi Tanabe. CHN: Fuji. DUR: 45 mins. x 13 eps.; Thu 1 July 1999–23 September 1999.

Three months after the events of **RING**, surviving character Mai (Yada) is trying to readjust when she receives a warning. The vengeful Sadako (Kimura) could have somehow escaped from the abandoned well that has been her prison for many years. Mai forms an alliance with Mitsuo (Kishitani), a school teacher investigating an urban myth about a "cursed" videotape and Mitsuo's former student Natsumi (Yoshimoto). It transpires that there is a scientific explanation to the supposed "magical" curse of Sadako—the Ring Virus is a coded message stored in digital form that mutates human DNA to recreate Sadako anew. Terrifyingly for Mai and her associates, the Ring Virus has made its way onto a compact disc, the contents of which have already been broadcast to the surrounding area by an opportunistic TV station. Moreover, Mai has become impregnated with the new strain and is fated to shortly give birth to the new incarnation of Sadako (Yada, again). Growing fast to adult size, this new horror inexplicably attempts to strangle its victims, whereas the original was able to quite literally scare them to death.

However, after setting up this exciting continuation of Kōji Suzuki's *Ring* novels, *Spiral* degrades into a series of loosely connected paranormal investigations in apparent imitation of *The X-Files*. Made at the height of *Ring* fever after the release of the *Ring* movie and its 1998 *Spiral* follow-up, it deviates far from the author's intent, remodeling the original Mitsuo (a *pathologist* who performs the autopsy on Ryūji, protagonist of *Ring*) as a teacher who merely dabbles in sleuthing. The story also exists in a well-regarded 1999 manga version, drawn by Mizuki Sakura. Theme: Rough Laugh—"Taga Tame ni Kane wa Naru" (For Whom the Bell Tolls).

SPRING BRIDE JUMPS THE FIRE, THE

1998. JPN: *Tonde Hi ni Iru Haru no Yome*. PRD: Haruo Ōno. DIR: Kan Ishibashi. SCR: Hiroshi Takeyama. CAST: Nobuko Miyamoto, Yoshiko Tanaka, Keiju Kobayashi, Takuzō Kadono. CHN: TVT. DUR: 45 mins. x 11 eps.; Wed 15 April 1998–24 June 1998.

It's love at first sight for feisty nurse Yoshiko (Miyamoto) and sushi chef Akio (Kadono), but she is left widowed shortly after their wedding, when Akio drops dead from a surprise blood clot on the brain. The stunned Yoshiko is left to pick up the pieces of her life and to turn around the fortunes of Akio's struggling sushi restaurant, in the style of **GOOD MOURNING** and **TAKE ME TO A RYOKAN**. Theme: Kōsetsu Minami—"Watashi no Hana o Sakasetai" (I Want My Flower to Bloom).

SPRING FOR GRADE SIX, CLASS TWO

1975. JPN: *6-nen 2-kumi no Haru wa . . . .* PRD: Masaharu Morita. DIR: Yoshiyuki Itō. SCR: Masahiro Yamada. CAST: Keiko Kawahata, Ichirō Kanda, Mayumi Maehata, Shigekazu Nakajima, Akinori Umezu, Hirofumi Hoshino. CHN: NHK. DUR: 25 mins. x 6 eps.; Mon 3 March 1975–12 March 1975.

Grade six, class two is ruled by two rival groups: the boys led by the mischievous Toshio Murata (Kanda) and a girls' group led by principal's daughter Kyōko Kawahara (Maehata). On hearing that their new teacher, Kameno Hayata (Kawahara), has been hospitalized after an accident on the way to school on her first day, Toshio assumes that she is a mean old lady but is surprised to find that she is a beautiful woman when she finally arrives—compare to **24 EYES**. Toshio plans a number of pranks but the teacher fights back with her sharp wits. Matters reach a boiling point when Toshio's gang nail all the doors shut in the girls' lavatory, inadvertently trapping the school principal in one of the cubicles and leading to disciplinary action against Kameno. Kameno eventually discovers that Toshio's activities are designed to distract everyone from the fact that he rarely hands in homework on time—he is prevented from doing so by his no-nonsense father, who thinks that hard labor should come before homework on a child's list of priorities. Kameno tries to talk Toshio's father out of it but meets with stern resistance. Soon afterward, she collapses at school from complications arising from her accident, and her return to hospitalization threatens to break up the close-knit class and scatter them across other rooms. Based on the story by Hisashi Yamanaka, author of **ABARE HATCHAKU** and **TO BE AS I AM**.

SPRING IN BLOOM

2002. JPN: *Haru Ranman*. AKA: *Friendship*. PRD: Kazuhisa Andō, Yōko Matsui. DIR: Satoru Nakajima, Shinichi Iijima. SCR: Masayoshi Kashida. CAST: Manabu Oshio, Rie Tomosaka, Kazuki Kitamura, Emily Henmi, Hiroyuki Miyasako. CHN: Fuji. DUR: 45 mins. x 12 eps.; Tue 9 April 2002–25 June 2002.

Akane (Tomosaka) is a technical college graduate who nurtures ambitions of becoming an interior designer. At the moment, however, she is working in a design shop and slowly watching her dream career slip away. Falling in love with an expensive apartment in Daikanyama, a fashionable quarter of Tokyo that also features in **ALWAYS THE TWO OF US**, she advertises on the Internet for a roommate. She agrees to split the rent with Sōta (Oshio), a travel agent whose international commissions have all but disappeared in the wake of the 9/11 terrorist attacks in America. Akane secretly wonders if their platonic apartment-sharing will develop into something more serious, but her hopes are dashed on the first night, when Sōta brings home a female friend. Out for revenge, Akane invites her male friend Kansuke (Miyasako) back on the following evenings—though romance does not ensue between the respective couples, the chance series of meetings create a new network of friends in the style of **WHAT IS LOVE?** Meanwhile, Sōta has unwisely copied his housekey and rents his room out to acquaintances in his absence to use as an impromptu love hotel, much to Akane's disgust. Renamed *Friendship* in Fuji sales sheets, presumably in an attempt to associate it with the U.S. apartment-share comedy *Friends*. Theme: Revenus—"Acacia."

SPRING SWELL
1985. JPN: *Haru no Hatō*. AKA: *Wave of Spring*. PRD: N/C. DIR: Mitsuru Shimizu. SCR: Takehiro Nakajima. CAST: Keiko Matsuzaka, Masatoshi Nakamura, Morio Kazama. CHN: NHK. DUR: 45 mins. x ca. 50 eps.; Sun 6 January 1985–15 December 1985.
The middle part of a trilogy of 20th-century *taiga* dramas, beginning with the previous year's **BURNING MOUNTAINS AND RIVERS**, and continuing with **INOCHI: LIFE**, this 1985 series depicts the life of Sadayakko Kawakami (Matsuzaka). Born in 1871 and trained as a geisha from the age of seven, she becomes a popular party guest with the elderly statesmen of the Meiji Restoration, and is deflowered by Prime Minister Hirobumi Itō—see **AS IF IN FLIGHT**. At the age of 20 she falls in love with Otojirō Kawakami (Nakamura), an actor who is trying to cultivate a new form of theater. Quitting the geisha life to set up a drama troupe with her new husband, Sadayakko meets with a series of obstacles—not the least that she and her fellow Kawakami actresses are the first female theater performers in Japan since 1629. With no luck in Japan, she convinces her husband to try his luck abroad. Touring the U.S. with Kawakami's Imperial Japanese Theater company, she performs a number of famous kabuki scenes to foreign audiences and becomes a successful actress. After touring the U.K., France, and Russia, she appears onstage at the Paris Exhibition Theater in 1900, becoming the first Japanese international star, playing to crowds including André Gide, Claude Debussy, Auguste Rodin, and a young Pablo Picasso among their numbers.
Upon returning to Japan, the Kawakami theater troupe reverse their policies—instead of introducing

Japanese tradition to the West, they introduce Western drama to Japan, performing melodramatic adaptations of plays by William Shakespeare, Maurice Maeterlinck (see **BLUE BIRD**), and Victorien Sardou.
Following the death of her husband in 1911, Sadayakko has an affair with Momosuke Fukuzawa (Kazama), whom she knew from her geisha era. After helping Fukuzawa raise funds to build the Ōi dam, she later builds the Teishōji temple in Gifu, using donations from many of her contemporary actors from the kabuki theater.
In 1902, during a Milan performance, the historical Sadayakko was seen onstage by Giacomo Puccini and reputedly became a major influence for the composer's *Madama Butterfly* (1904). Though based on a story by Sonoko Sugimoto, itself inspired by true-life events, the broadcast of this *taiga* drama led to legal action by author Reiko Yamaguchi over alleged similarities between scenes it contained and pages from her own book, *Joyū Sadayakko* (*Sadayakko the Actress*). For different approaches to an actor's life, see **MASK OF GLASS** and **STAR STRUCK**.

SPY CATCHER J3
1965. PRD: N/C. DIR: Akira Kashima. SCR: Yūichi Ikeda, Yukiji Harima. CAST: Yūsuke Kawazu, Shinjirō Enohara, Tetsurō Tanba, Yuki Shirono. CHN: NET (Asahi). DUR: 25 mins. x ca. 26 eps.; Thu 7 October 1965–31 March 1966.
As the evil secret society known as Tiger tries to seize control of the world, the "Tulip" international crime fighting organization is set up to stop them. J3 (Kawazu) is the third-ranking agent responsible for keeping Japan safe, with the aid of his trusty air-car. Deliberately engineered as a Japanese answer to 007. Theme: Shunji Kanō—"Spy Catcher."

STAFF ROOM
1997. JPN: *Shokuin Shitsu*. PRD: Tonkō Horikawa, Yoshiharu Nakagawa. DIR: Tonkō Horikawa, Naoyuki Yokoi, Sanae Suzuki, Kazushi Ōki. SCR: Toshio

Kamata, Akira Hatamine. CAST: Atsuko Asano, Tōru Nakamura, Kōji Matoba, Miki Mizuno, Yōko Nogiwa. CHN: TBS. DUR: 45 mins. x 12 eps.; Fri 4 July 1997–19 September 1997.
Truck driver Yōko (Asano) is tempted back to her former career of teaching when she meets her ex-boyfriend Masashi (Nakamura). He now works at South Edogawa Middle School, a troubled institution whose principal Sugiura (Nogiwa) is determined to improve her students' grades at any cost. Theme: The Yellow Monkey—"Burn."

STAIRWAY TO HEAVEN
2002. JPN: *Tengoku e no Kaidan*. PRD: Yoshinori Horiguchi, Norihiko Imamura. DIR: Yasuo Tsuruhashi, Kōichi Okamoto. SCR: Shunsaku Ikehata, Masato Katō. CAST: Kōichi Satō, Morio Kazama, Yūko Kotegawa, Manami Honjō, Shunsuke Nakamura. CHN: NTV. DUR: 45 mins. x 12 eps. (ep 1: 90 mins.); 8 April 2002–24 June 2002.
Keiichi Kashiwagi (Satō) plots revenge against Tatsuya Enari (Kazama), who destroyed his father's life and stole his own girlfriend. Theme: hiro—"Eternal Place."

STALKER, THE *
1997. JPN: *Stalker Sasou Onna*. AKA: *A Woman Stalking*. PRD: Kazuko Nozoe. DIR: Mio Ezaki, Satoshi Isaka. SCR: Taketatsu Ishihara. CAST: Takanori Jinnai, Akiko Hinagata, Yumi Asō, Yoshiko Hakamada, Nenji Kobayashi, Takamasa Tanabe. CHN: TBS. DUR: 45 mins. x 11 eps.; Thu 9 January 1997–20 March 1997.
While his wife Kinuka (Asō) is away on a skiing trip, happily married father of two Shūji (Jinnai) foolishly agrees to meet with pretty coworker Michiru (Hinagata). After a drunken one-night stand, Michiru informs Shūji that she is pregnant, and though his first instinct is to encourage her to have an abortion, her contented attitude makes Shūji believe that Michiru can keep the child and also avoid embarrassing him with his wife.

After hearing of Shūji's recent odd behavior from her father, Kinuka starts to notice little things, like the fact that her husband returns home from work one day with one of his socks worn inside-out. Fearing for the repercussions, Shūji tries to talk his subordinate Kitagawa out of asking Michiru on a date, but that and her own claim that she is *already spoken for"* only encourages Kitagawa the more. Shūji comes to regard the simplest family outing as a minefield, as repeated "chance meetings" with Michiru reduce him to a nervous wreck. When his wife finds one of Michiru's earrings in his pocket, he is rescued by Kitagawa, who covers for him by claiming to be Michiru's boyfriend. This leads Kinuka to invite both him and Michiru to Shūji's house, only increasing her husband's panic.

As Michiru's behavior becomes progressively more outrageous, Shūji is forced to hide a telephone answering machine tape in which she attempts to reveal all to Kinuka. When Michiru repeatedly faxes divorce applications to Shūji, Kinuka finally moves out in disgust. She returns to talk things over with her husband, only to discover that Michiru has already invited herself round to cook dinner!

A hilarious entry in the bunny boiler subgenre, STALKER replays *Fatal Attraction* (1987) as a husband's infidelity returns to haunt him in increasingly histrionic episodes. A series of last-minute revelations increases the tension to fever pitch, as Michiru is hospitalized, plots to kidnap a member of Shūji's family, and eventually charges around his home wielding a kitchen knife. Compare to A STALKER'S INESCAPABLE LOVE, which premiered mere days before, the same writer's later STEALING LOVE *, DANGEROUS WOMAN, and WEDNESDAY LOVE AFFAIR. Broadcast with English subtitles in the U.S. on KIKU TV. Theme: Masahiko Kondō—"Ai wa Hitotsu" (One Love).

STALKER'S INESCAPABLE LOVE, A
1997. JPN: *Stalker Nigekirenu Ai.* PRD: Yoshinori Horiguchi, Mamoru Koizumi.

DIR: Nobuhiro Kamikawa, Akihiro Karaki. SCR: Miyuki Noe, Masaya Ozaki. CAST: Saki Takaoka, Atsurō Watabe, Harumi Inoue, Masaki Kanda. CHN: NTV. DUR: 45 mins. x 10 eps.; Mon 6 January 1997–10 March 1997. Umi (Takaoka) works at a golf practice range, where she is conducting a secret affair with the instructor Mr. Tadokoro (Kanda). While walking home on Christmas Eve, she unexpectedly bumps into local oddball Tatsuya (Watabe), who is scandalized to see that she is wearing a Christmas rose given to her by Tadokoro. Before long she has acquired an obsessed stalker, who eventually kidnaps her in a chilling drama portraying the flip side of the happy ending romances for which writer Noe is more famous. *A Stalker's Inescapable Love* was widely regarded as superior to the same season's better-known STALKER. It's difficult to guess which event prompted two rival channels to race into production on their own stalker dramas—our best guess is the close proximity of the Japanese video releases of *Unlawful Entry* (1992) and *Single White Female* (1992). The following year, the subgenre would be given a more juvenile slant in BOY CHASER. Theme: Ryūichi Sakamoto featuring Alluring Sister M—"The Other Side of Love."

STAND-IN, THE *
1998. JPN: *Private Actress; P.A.* PRD: Yoshiki Tanaka. DIR: Tōya Satō, Kazuki Kaneda, Tetsuhiro Ogino. SCR: Miyuki Noe. CAST: Kanako Enomoto, Kōichi Iwaki, Hisako Manda, Kumiko Mori, Ai Katō, Hiroyuki Ikeuchi. CHN: NTV. DUR: 45 mins. x 9 eps.; Sat 17 October 1998–12 December 1998. *"Who do you want me to be?"* Though 17-year-old Shiho (Enomoto) might look like just another pupil at Santa Maria Catholic Academy for Girls, she is really the secret love child of famously single actress Sayuri Nagasawa (Manda). Because her existence must be kept from the press, she has her own apartment, a conveniently incompetent maid/chaperone Machiko (Mori), and

only sees her mother on isolated occasions. One day, she is recruited by Yoshitaka (Iwaki), a fatherly figure whose Nikai Productions is not the talent agency it claims to be, but an undercover outfit that uses actors and actresses as agents in the real world. With her natural ability as a performer, Shiho becomes a Private Actress, charged with missions of espionage and surveillance. Her tasks include impersonating a dying businessman's long-lost daughter in order to deprive scheming relatives of their inheritance, posing as a womanizing doctor's fiancée to scare off his 13 mistresses, and pretending to be a young heiress when the real deal is too busy working as a bar girl. Not all her missions go according to plan, but the steely girl ensures that justice always wins out in the end.

The Stand-In is based on the 1991 *Flower Comics* manga by Michiyo Akaishi, whose many other girls' works include *Burning Alpine Rose* (*AE), *More Than the Sky and Stars,* and *Strawberry Moon.* The wish fulfillment of the original is aimed squarely at a teen audience, exploiting the idea of fame and glamour within arm's reach, secret identities, safely cosseted independence, and the conceit that a few minutes' cramming will afford easy access to the career of one's choice. The show also owes a distant debt to Gerry Anderson's *Joe 90,* though unlike the puppet hero of the 1960s, Shiho has no quasi-scientific explanation for her sudden mastery of a situation—instead the script fobs the viewer off with lightning flashes of artistic inspiration and explanations after the fact in the style of *Mission: Impossible.*

Despite the appearance of a "kidult" show like YOUNG KINDAICHI FILES, *The Stand-In* was screened at nine on a Saturday evening at the height of the *enjo kōsai* (subsidized dating) scare which rocked the Japanese media with apocryphal tales of teenage prostitution—compare to LAST LOVE. While *The Stand-In*'s original motive may have been innocent enough, there was

Stand-In, The

doubtless a part of the audience that derived its own personal entertainment from the sight of a uniformed school-girl asking the viewer who he wanted her to be.

Shot on video with a thumping Tetsuya Komuro muzak track to conceal moments of bad location sound, *The Stand-In* often presents a surreal and hallucinatory view of the world—you decide whether this is poor writing or an artful evocation of Shiho's modern *ennui*. Like the "private dancers" whose place she sublimates for a conservative audience, Shiho must harden herself to deal with some of society's real lowlifes: in the first episode alone she is nearly killed by a client seeking to add a touch of realism to her performance in trials redolent of **MASK OF GLASS**. Shiho has a strangely amoral attitude toward her job—she rarely questions the ethics of her mission, leaving such issues to her avuncular boss. Instead, her performances are generally depicted as white lies undertaken to defeat much greater evils, against an array of pantomime foes

who sneer and spit to demonstrate which side they're on. That's not to say she doesn't question the motives of some of her clients, warning one arrogant customer that *"Someday a woman is going to stab you to death,"* but only after she's taken his money. Shown subtitled in the U.S. on KIKU TV. Peak rating: 18.7%. Theme: Globe—"Perfume of Love."

STAR BOY

2000. JPN: *Star Bōzu*. PRD: N/C. DIR: N/C. SCR: N/C. CAST: Masashi Ogata, Atsushi Ishino. CHN: BS-i (TBS). DUR: 45 mins. x 13 eps.; Fri 8 December 2000–3 January 2001.
A long time ago in a galaxy far away, the Magadras Empire almost succeeds in brainwashing its subjects. However, a small band of revolutionaries, the Pijorina Federal Army, fights back. They are defeated in a great battle, but one ship escapes to fight another day, in a late-night sci-fi comedy that featured computer-generated spaceships and robot suits designed by Kunio Ōkawara of *Gundam* (*AE) fame. Some

schedules list it as a Thursday night show, although it was technically broadcast at one o'clock on a Friday morning.

STAR FLEET *

1980. JPN: *X Bomber*. PRD: Kimio Ikeda. DIR: Michio Mikami, Akira Takahashi. SCR: Keisuke Fujikawa. CAST: (voices) Toshio Furukawa, Shigeru Chiba, Naoki Ryūta, Mami Koyama, Yūji Mitsuya, Mikio Terashima, Hidekatsu Shibata, Tōru Furuya, Rihoko Yoshida, Reizō Nomoto, Toshiaki Iwamoto, Shū Tanaka. CHN: Fuji. DUR: 25 mins. x 25 eps.; Sat 11 October 1980–27 December 1980.
In the year 2999, the evil space emperor Gelma (Tanaka) invades the Solar System and conquers Pluto Alpha Base, forcing its commander Captain Custer (Iwamoto) to change sides. With no other options, the Terran Star Fleet orders aging scientist Ben Robinson (Terashima) to hold off the enemy assault with the prototype X Bomber warship. Ben assembles Shirō Ginga (Furukawa), the son of the X Bomber's

missing inventor, gunner Bigman Lee (Ryūta), and jive-talking pilot Bongo Herakles (Chiba) as his crew, and also takes along Lamia (Koyama), the pretty alien orphan for whom he is a guardian. The mismatched crew hold off the first assault by Gelma's psychotic general Bloody Mary (Yoshida), who claims to be looking for an ultimate weapon known only as the F-01. Lamia correctly assumes that *she* is the F-01 and has to be deterred from handing herself over to the enemy. Meanwhile, Lamia is in telepathic contact with Halley (Furuya), the captain of the alien vessel The Skull, who eventually reveals that Lamia is indeed the F-01 and that she will inherit great powers on the eve of the coming millennium.

The puppet show *X Bomber* was conceived as a deliberate attempt to outdo NHK's AERIAL CITY 008 and its ultimate inspiration *Thunderbirds*, utilizing the design talents of Gō Nagai, creator of *Devilman* (*AE) and *Getter Robo* (*AE). With only a fraction of the *Thunderbirds* budget available, *X Bomber* was deemed a failure on its original Japanese broadcast and was taken off-air after just 12 episodes. However, it gained a new lease on life in the U.K., when it was dubbed into English and broadcast as *Star Fleet*. Under this title, it introduced the clichés and traditions of Japanese children's sci-fi to an entire generation—from the attack craft that combine to form the Dai X giant robot to the shocking deaths of major characters adding genuine pathos. Though common knowledge today in the wake of MIGHTY MORPHIN' POWER RANGERS, the attitude and style of Japanese sci-fi made *Star Fleet* an impressive and much-loved example of the genre. There was also some renaming—Ben Robinson became Doctor Benn, Shirō Ginga became Shiro Hagen, Bongo Herakles became Barry Hercules, and Bigman (presumably a reference to a similar character in Isaac Asimov's *Space Ranger*) became John Lee. Among the supporting cast Bloody Mary was transformed into Commander Makara, her lieutenant Kozslo

became Orion, and Captain Custer became Captain Carter.

The new voices included long-time Gerry Anderson collaborator Denise Bryer and actors such as Garrick Hagon, Liza Ross, and Peter Marinker, who would also star in WATER MARGIN and a succession of Manga Entertainment anime dubs. The 24-episode British series (which lost one from the grand total by combining episodes 18 and 19) was later brought to the U.S., where it died a second ignominious death, hacked into an eight-part series of straight-to-video features. In 2002, *X Bomber* was re-released in Japan on DVD, with one of the English language movie edits included as an extra. The Japanese characters also appeared in a 1980 manga spin-off, drawn by Eiichi Saitō, while the U.K. incarnation was adapted into a separate six-month comic strip in the British children's weekly *Look-In*, by Angus Allan and Alan Noble. Theme: Vow Wow—"Soldier in the Space." Note: It is a common misconception that the music for the series was by Queen guitarist Brian May. Although May did release his own version of the English theme song, the original U.K. version was by Paul Bliss, a former keyboardist with the Moody Blues.

STARGAZING

2002. JPN: *Tentai Kansoku.* AKA: *Searchin' for My Polestar.* PRD: Yū Moriya, Takahiro Kasaoki, Masako Watanabe. DIR: Hiroshi Nishitani, Junichi Tsuzuki, Naoki Tazawa. SCR: Keiko Hata, Chiho Watanabe. CAST: Hideaki Itō, Kenji Sakaguchi, Jō Odagiri, Koyuki, Tomoko Tabata, Manami Konishi, Shigenori Yamazaki. CHN: Fuji. DUR: 45 mins. x 12 eps.; Tue 2 July 2002–17 September 2002. It's been three years since the seven members of the Seiwa University Sagittarius Astronomy Club enjoyed an idyllic summer watching the stars. It was the first and last time they did any real stargazing, but they continue to meet regularly to have fun and catch up on old times—all except Tomoya

(Sakaguchi), who went traveling after graduation and whose whereabouts are unknown. The only genuine astronomer in the group, Kenta (Yamazaki) now has to get up early to work in the family fish shop and has no time to look at the stars. Satomi (Tabata) invites her friends to her wedding but harassed salaryman Kyōichi (Itō) is delayed by a presentation at work. Kyōichi still has feelings for trainee teacher Mifuyu (Koyuki), his college girlfriend, though the two have long since split up. Meanwhile, fellow Sagittarian Yuri (Konishi) is despised at her workplace by colleagues who believe she is having an affair with her boss. Yuri's real boyfriend since college days, Takeshi (Odagiri) tries to set Kyōichi up with a date through an Internet dating service, though Kyōichi is disgusted when he discovers Takeshi is running it as a business venture.

Unable to take time off for a honeymoon, Satomi returns to her job at a nursing home, where she receives a surprise visit from Tomoya, back from Mexico. Satomi organizes a grand reunion at their old hang-out, the Jupiter restaurant, where she hopes that Mifuyu and Tomoya will get together. Or that Kyōichi and Mifuyu will get back together. Or that Takeshi will explain his recent bad behavior. . . .

Seven, the magical number for love polygon dramas since SEVEN PEOPLE IN SUMMER, is here applied to the seven stars of the Big Dipper, and their earthbound counterparts. *Stargazing* throws in an unrequited love, a prodigal return, an anonymous Internet relationship, a just-married couple, and a relationship on the rocks, and waits to see how the group dynamic shifts. Compare to ASUNARO CONFESSIONS, WHERE IS LOVE?, and GREATEST FEELING.

STAR STRUCK

2001. JPN: *Star no Koi.* AKA: *Love with a Super Star.* PRD: Yūji Iwata. DIR: Masayuki Suzuki, Masanori Murakami. SCR: Miho Nakazono. CAST: Tsuyoshi Kusanagi, Norika Fujiwara, Masanobu

Katsumura, Hiroko Anzai, Keiko Toda, Toshio Kakei, Hiromi Kitagawa, Leo Morimoto, Takashi Ukaji. CHN: Fuji. DUR: 45 mins. x 11 eps.; Thu 11 October 2001–20 December 2001.

Sōsuke (Kusanagi from SMAP) is a low-level employee at San Marco Ham, a high-class butcher. Deserted by his fellow workers when a film crew is in town, he is alone in the office when famous movie star Hikaruko (Fujiwara) drops in and falls asleep at a desk. She inadvertently leaves with his jacket, and he tries to retrieve it from her but is blacklisted by her manager Saegusa (Ukaji) as just another stalker. When Hikaruko realizes the mistake, she sends him an invitation to her star-studded birthday party. Out of his depth amid the celebrities, Sōsuke strikes up a conversation about meat products with Torao (Morimoto), a bored-looking man who turns out to be an incredibly famous director. Impressed with Sōsuke's innocence, Hikaruko meets him outside and returns his jacket. It contains a silver brooch, which he had been intending to give to his would-be fiancée Mina, but since she has just dumped him over the phone, he gives it to Hikaruko. As she has just discovered that *her* boyfriend Tsujikata (Kakei) has been having an affair with her rival Reiko (Anzai), she accepts it with a kiss. Later that evening at a press conference, Hikaruko proclaims that she has fallen in love with Sōsuke. For her, it is just another prank but everyone else takes it seriously. Soon, Sōsuke is hounded by the media, and the two would-be lovers are forced to confront the very different worlds they live in, in a distinctly Japanese take on *Notting Hill* (1999).

As with the film that inspired it, *SS* flirts with the notion of fame, casting one star as a celebrity and another as an everyday joe—see also **ONE MORE KISS**. It also plays up the godlike status of its Princess Charming—everywhere Sōsuke goes he is confronted with her figure on giant billboards and TV screens, most noticeably in a touching

scene where his lonely figure appears to be cradled in her hand. However, his world of salaryman camaraderie and homespun wisdom is cleverly juxtaposed with her glitzy media sham— Hikaruko's latest movie having been a box-office disaster, the money is running out. Her canny agent (Toda) encourages her to fake an affair with Sōsuke in order to generate media hype for her next project and retain her appeal with "the common people." Sōsuke agrees to help, and the couple timidly spend the night at a hotel, whiling away the hours by building a house of cards.

Trapped in the media machine since her teens, Hikaruko treats Sōsuke's mundane life with the wide-eyed glee of a Martian tourist, obsessively seeking the company of "normal people," excitably observing Laundromat rituals, and eagerly learning the correct way to address fast food vendors. Meanwhile, fortunes are on the slide at San Marco, and Hikaruko must return Sōsuke's kindness when his boss rashly promises her face as the poster image for the Tokyo Ham Festival. Though her normal appearance fee is ¥2 *billion*, she agrees to do it for a single sandwich. This initially touching gesture soon becomes more sinister, as her psychiatrist reveals that she has always suffered from stress-induced flakiness, and the pressure is mounting as she passes idol retirement age. In one clever moment, a graffiti artist paints "Agony" across the chest of the giant Hikaruko billboard that watches over Sōsuke's trip to the office. Later that day, the actress develops a heart condition.

Hikaruko tries to change her image by taking a part in a period drama, with Sōsuke as her archery teacher— his interest in *kyūdō* was forgotten after the opening scene, only to be clumsily dredged up again halfway through the series. Other undeveloped last-minute subplots include Jean-Pierre, the French racing driver whose death left Hikaruko all but widowed seven years earlier. Unmentioned for nine

Star Struck

episodes, he is brought up mere moments before he appears in a dream sequence, only to disappear again from the script.

The final episode cunningly subverts at least some of the viewer's expectations by introducing a new framing device. Perhaps inspired by the same year's *Millennium Actress* (*AE), *Star Struck* is revealed to be the work of a young journalist in the year 2041, who has been sent to interview the aged Hikaruko about her acting glory days. As the journalist writes the lines that opened the first episode, the finale dares the viewer to watch the series again with the knowledge that it genuinely *is* the work of a writer from "a different world," and that many of Hikaruko's bizarre observations may not be true to character at all, but the editorial annotations of a historian from the future.

STAR WOLF *

1978. JPN: *Star Wolf, Uchū no Yūsha Star Wolf.* AKA: *Cosmic Hero Star Wolf.* PRD: Hiromi Katō, Masunosuke Ōhashi, Noboru Tsuburaya, Akira Tsuburaya. DIR: Kiyosumi Fukuzawa, Minoru Kanaya. SCR: Keiichi Abe, Hiroyasu Yamaura, Yoshihisa Araki, Bunzō

Star Wolf

Finally accepted into the crew after demonstrating that he has the strength of ten men, Ken accompanies them on their new mission to Kararu, a world with a Middle Eastern theme, where the pugnacious Ken soon lands himself in prison after killing a brawler in a local bar. Meanwhile, Ken is pursued by Reeja/Rita (Shimazaki), his former lover, now on a vendetta because she is also the sister of the partner he killed in the first episode! She is shot by prison guards but not before revealing to Ken that his "treachery" was only to be expected, as he is not a true Valnastarian at all but the child of missionaries from Earth.

Escaping back to the Bakkus III, Ken foils an attempted mutiny by crewman Yorōlin (Muramatsu) and steers the ship through a black hole to escape. After almost getting caught in a supernova, the crew reach Yorōlin's homeworld of Sassar (Sissar in the English version), where they are ordered to destroy a doomsday device. Crash landing in the "Devil's Desert," Ken helps them infiltrate the enemy base by bodily throwing his fellows over the fence. They destroy the doomsday device with a bomb, although the turncoat Yorōlin dies trying to deactivate it.

For the second half of the series, renamed *Cosmic Hero Star Wolf* from episode 14 onward, Ken and his colleagues must defend the universe from a succession of monsters of the week, including Nipopo the Space Dinosaur, an "android" that looks suspiciously like a man in a fireman's outfit painted gold, and a "space bounty hunter."

The success of *Star Wars* (1977) created a new wave of interest in science fiction, met in Japan by such productions as the *Star Blazers* movie (*AE) and the animated adaptations of E. E. "Doc" Smith's *Lensman* (*AE) and Edmond Hamilton's *Captain Future* (*AE). Not to be outdone, the Tsuburaya studio tried this live-action adaptation of Hamilton's *Star Wolf* books—*Weapon from Beyond* (1967), *The Closed Worlds* (1968), and *World of the Star Wolves* (1969). As with *Star Wolf*'s

Wakatsuki, Hideyoshi Nagasaka, Toyohiro Andō. CAST: Tatsuya Azuma, Miyuki Tanigawa, Tsutomu Yukawa, Hiroo Tachikawa, Nagahide Takahashi, Jō Shishido, Katsumi Muramatsu, Shōhei Yamamoto, Nana Shimazaki, Akihiko Hirata. CHN: NTV. DUR: 25 mins. x 24 eps.; Sun 2 April 1978–24 September 1978.

In the 21st century, Earth is attacked by raiders from Valnastar. One of their number, Ken (Azuma), realizes that one of the Earth people he is about to shoot is a boy with the same name as his and refuses to kill the boy or his mother. When his partner attempts to execute them himself, Ken kills him in the ensuing scuffle. Ken is forced to steal a ship to evade capture but is set upon by fighters that leave his vessel crippled. After drifting for a while in space, he is picked up by the crew of the Terran ship Bakkus III: captain Joe (Shishido), pilot Ryū/Rocky (Takahashi), computer expert Hime/Tami (Tanigawa), navigator Dan (Yukawa), and cadet Billy (Tachikawa). Ken helps them escape another Valnastar attack. The crew take him to seek medical attention but he runs away, afraid that their kindness will evaporate when they discover that he was once one of the invaders who are attacking their home world.

fellow Tsuburaya serials TIME OF THE APES and MIGHTY JACK, the first 14 episodes of *Star Wolf* were re-edited into two features, dubbed into English, and broadcast in the United States, under the titles *Fugitive Alien* (1978) and *Star Force: Fugitive Alien II* (1978). In this format, both movies appeared on *Mystery Science Theater 3000*. For another adaptation of famous American science fiction, see FLOWERS FOR ALGERNON.

STATION

1995. PRD: Atsushi Satō. DIR: Nozomu Amemiya. SCR: Akihiro Tago, Yutaka Kaneko. CAST: Eisaku Yoshida, Kunihiro Matsumura, Seiichi Tanabe, Naomi Zaizen, Miki Nakatani. CHN: NTV. DUR: 45 mins. x 9 eps.; Sat 14 January 1995–11 March 1995.

Tōru (Yoshida) is a hardworking manager at Shinjuku train station, who finds himself helping an old lady search for her son Yōji (Matsumura), only to discover that Yōji is his new subordinate. The cast remains in one spot while their workplace brings new stories to them, in the style of BIG WING, based on the *Big Comics* manga by Kenichi Ōishi and Mitsuo Hashimoto. See also WINDY DETECTIVE. Theme: J-Walk—"Ienakatta Kotoba o Kimi ni" (The Words I Never Said to You).

STEALING LOVE * DANGEROUS WOMAN

1998. JPN: *Ryakudatsu Ai * Abunai Onna*. PRD: Kazuko Nozoe, Akiko Ōnishi. DIR: Mio Ezaki, Satoshi Isaka. SCR: Taketatsu Ishihara. CAST: Hidekazu Akai, Izumi Inamori, Yoshihiko Hakamada, Sarina Suzuki, Nenji Kobayashi. CHN: TBS. DUR: 45 mins. x 11 eps.; Fri 9 January 1998–27 March 1998.

Takeshi (Akai) is a happily married neuropathologist who lives with his wife Shigeko (Inamori) and daughter Hana. However, their life is thrown into upheaval by the arrival of Shigeko's mentally unstable sister Suzu (Suzuki), who is determined to have Takeshi for herself. In the style of the writer's earlier STALKER, she is pre-

Steel Angel Kurumi—Pure

pared to try any method to achieve this goal, including murder. Theme: Glay—"However."

STEEL ANGEL KURUMI—PURE

2002. JPN: *Kōtetsu Tenshi Kurumi—Pure*. PRD: Kenji Kume, Hideki Ōyanagi. DIR: Hiroaki Hobo. SCR: Tsunehisa Arakawa. CAST: Aya Matsui, Hiromi Teramon, Ayano Tachibana, Nobuyuki Mihara, Emi Yamamoto, Rie Arai, Hirotaka Suzuoki, Makoto Kamijō. CHN: Fuji. DUR: 15 mins. x 24 eps.; [broadcast dates unknown].

The day after tomorrow, teenager Nakahito (Kamijō) receives a giant package from the Ayanokōji Company. It's Kurumi (Matsui), a robot maid programmed to answer to his every need and, it would seem, to address him at all times in an irritatingly shrill voice, break into "song" on a whim, and dance like a puppet with cut strings. She also breezily enjoys stripping off and jumping into the bath with him, though the shy couple both seem to keep their underwear on. Before long, Nakahito's misery is compounded by the arrival of Kurumi's robot "sisters" Saki (Tachibana) and Karinka (Teramon) who join forces to

run amok in his apartment like the three little maids from Hell.

SAK is ostensibly based on the manga in *Shōnen Ace* by the pseudonymous Kaishaku, which also exists in an earlier anime variant (*AE), though its origins stretch back further into the past. With a magical interloper interfering with the life of a hapless boy, it owes a heavy debt to *I Dream of Jeannie*, which was broadcast in Japan on MBS in 1966 and is partly responsible for the slightly suspect "magical girlfriend" genre that exists to this day in titles such as *Oh! My Goddess* (*AE) and *Handmaid May* (*AE). However, Kurumi's name acknowledges an even older inspiration—*The Nutcracker* (1892), which similarly allegorizes a child crossing the threshold into adulthood through interaction with a "toy." In Japanese, a *kurumi* is a walnut.

However, such lofty origins are little help when faced with the fiendishly low production values of *SAK*. Chiefly shot on a single set, and with an understandably inexperienced cast failing to achieve the slapstick and timing that comes easily to animation, this is very poor late-night fare that makes OL POLICE look like *The West Wing*.

Straight News

Though it is a common war cry among anime fans that the genre is not just for kids, the medium has not been well-served in many of its recent adaptations for live-action TV—compare to **YOU'RE UNDER ARREST**. Insult is added to injury by the Japanese DVD release, which puts just three 15-minute episodes on each disc. For a better approach to the same kind of material, see **MINAMI'S SWEETHEART**. Theme: The Pure Angels (i.e. the cast)—"Egao Kudasai" (Wish I Could See You Smile).

STEWARDESS SWEETHEART

1994. JPN: *Stewardess no Koibito*. PRD: Kazuko Nozoe. DIR: Noriaki Asai. SCR: Buryū Ishihara. CAST: Shin Takuma, Naho Toda, Takeshi Naitō, Masumi Miyazaki, Yumi Morio, Harumi Inoue, Mitsuko Imai, Ken Ogata. CHN: TBS. DUR: 45 mins. x 12 eps.; Tue 12 April 1994–17 May 1994.

Natsu (Toda) is determined to become an air stewardess, and finds herself falling for would-be 747 co-pilot Kazuki (Takuma). That is, until Kazuki's wife, who has been presumed dead for some time, turns up to claim him back. Theme: Yōsui Inoue—"Ai wa Kimi" (Love Is You).

STORY OF LOVE

1993. JPN: *Aijō Monogatari*. PRD: Chihiro Kameyama. DIR: Tatsuaki Kimura. SCR: Toshiharu Matsubara. CAST: Masatoshi Nakamura, Kyōko Mano, Keiko Saitō, Fuyuki Moto, Makoto Ayukawa. CHN: Fuji. DUR: 45 mins. x 11 eps.; Thu 15 April 1993–24 June 1993.

When he loses the last member of his amateur pop band, marketing consultant Shūhei (Nakamura) decides to form a new group with his work colleagues Akira (Ayukawa) and Yōjiro (Moto). Not to be confused with **LOVE STORY**. Theme: Mi-Ke—"Please Please Me, Love."

STRAIGHT NEWS

2000. PRD: Kyō Itō. DIR: Tōya Satō. SCR: Kazuhiko Ban. CAST: Hiroshi Mikami, Tomoyo Harada, Ryōko Yonekura. CHN: NTV. DUR: 45 mins. x ca. 11 eps.; Wed 11 October 2000–31 December 2000.

After a long sojourn as a war reporter in Eastern Europe, veteran broadcaster Yajima (Mikami) returns to Tokyo. He seems to be a tough, unlikable man with few friends and a daughter he never sees, but the straight-talking newsman is determined to shake up Japan's traditionally conservative, timid reporting. On his first day in the new job, he airs hidden camera footage of himself talking to a prominent politician about a bribery scandal, securing critical praise but enemies in high places.

Almost unrecognizable underneath a severe crew cut, actor Mikami turns Yajima into one of TV drama's greatest anti-heroes—imagine if the cantankerous Rocket Romano were suddenly placed in charge of America's *ER*. When we first see him, he is chasing a one-night stand from his hotel room, callously offering her money when he sees her putting on a school uniform. His colleagues tell tall stories about him, including the time in a war zone when he supposedly used another journalist's body to shield himself from a gunman's bullets. But like the series itself, Yajima's character peels away successive layers that continually hold the audience's interest. He breaks real news by screening the interview, but to do so he betrays his politician friend. However, it soon transpires that the politician was in on the deal from the beginning—leading staffers to question if Yajima has broken any "news" at all, or if he has merely found a more flamboyant way of toadying to the establishment like his rivals. Compare writer Ban's later **LET'S GO NAGATACHO**.

Straight News is both the name of the series and of the show within the show, thus avoiding the pitfalls of Channel 2 in **NEWS WOMAN** or News Planet in **FEMALE ANNOUNCERS**. Of all the broadcast/journalism dramas of the 1990s, *Straight News* remains the most serious and realistic, lacking any of the cartoonish antics of its predecessors. Some of Yajima's activities may be distinctly comedic, but the show remains resolutely straight-faced and is all the better for it. Broadcast unsubtitled in the U.S. on KDOC TV.

STRANGEST STORY I'VE EVER HEARD, THE

1990. JPN: *Yo ni mo Kimyō na Monogatari*. PRD: Kōji Shiozawa. DIR: Masayuki Suzuki, Shunji Iwai, Mamoru Hoshi, Yukihiko Tsutsumi. SCR: Tokio Tsuchiya, Eriko Kitagawa, Kōki Mitani, Jōji Iida, Fumie Mizuhashi. CAST: Tamori. CHN: Fuji. DUR: 15 mins. x ca. 26 eps.; Thu 19 April 1990– ?? September 1992.

An umbrella show in the style of **100 GHOST STORIES**, in which narrator Tamori (presenter Kazuyoshi Morita) introduces a series of spooky modern tales, in which horror appears in deceptively everyday settings. The result is a variable mixture of shows, as new talents experiment with their ideas on a late-night show, with truly original hits but also some spectacular misses. The show is said to have created the interest in modern horror that paved the way for **NIGHT HEAD** and *The X-Files* in Japan, which in turn created the late 1990s environment that gave us **RING** and **UNSOLVED CASES**.

STRAWBERRY ON THE SHORTCAKE

2001. AKA: *SOS*. PRD: Kazuhiro Itō. DIR: Nobuhiro Doi, Hiroshi Matsubara. SCR: Shinji Nojima. CAST: Hideaki Takizawa, Kyōko Fukada, Yōsuke Kubozuka, Rina Uchiyama, Yuriko Ishida. CHN: TBS. DUR: 45 mins. x 10 eps.; Fri 12 January 2001–16 March 2001.

Pathologically shy schoolboy Manato (Takizawa from Johnny's Juniors) has developed a crush on Yui (Fukada), a free and somewhat infantile spirit who has just become his stepsister by marriage. Yui, however, has eyes only for Tetsuya (Kubozuka), who has become the toughest kid in the school by default, since a mysterious illness has kept him in the same class for two years. Love triangles in Japan, of course, are never that simple—Tetsuya has *really* failed his exams twice in a row because he is conducting a secret affair with his schoolteacher Mariko (Ishida), a confused twentysomething who nurses a broken heart over the death of her fiancé. Meanwhile, as if you couldn't guess, Manato's balcony backs onto that of his neighbor Haruka (Uchiyama), a literal girl next door who adores him.

The characters' various natures are simplified, in women's magazine shorthand to a simple question: when you eat a shortcake, do you start with the cake or with the strawberry on top? Thus Manato and Haruna are passive, gratification-deferring cake eaters who save the best until last, while Yui and Tetsuya are active, go-getting strawberry eaters who want everything now and give little thought to the consequences.

The opening episode of *SoS* is truly fascinating, as it slowly dawns on the viewer that nobody seems to pay any heed to Yui and Tetsuya, that Yui seems unafraid of death, that Mariko frets over a lost lover, and that Tetsuya's "illness" seems to have kept him forever young. . . . Could it be, in the style of *The Sixth Sense*, that they are dead and that only Manato can see them? Sadly, no. Nobody notices them because the acting and direction is so limited—the

central cast have eyes only for each other, and the rest of the world might as well be a cardboard cutout for all the impact it exerts. The agonizing over who loves whom does become very wearing, though as a drama from the writer of LIPSTICK, things are soon pepped up with some innovative virginity-losing (most notably to a predatory artist who seems to subsist on paint and boys) and, in a major first for the writer, an ending that actually appears to be happy. With theme music from Abba, the show is also notorious for whipping up a brief revival for the '70s group in Japan, particularly in the last episode, which contained a glorified pop video run-down of top moments from the series, set to the tune of, naturally, "SOS."

SUBMARINER 8823 HAYABUSA

1960. JPN: *Kaiteijin 8823*. PRD: N/C. DIR: N/C. SCR: N/C. CAST: N/C. CHN: Fuji. DUR: 25 mins. x 26 eps.; Mon 3 January 1960–28 June 1960.

Once the most advanced civilization in the Pacific, the legendary Elde culture sank beneath the waves over 500,000 years ago. Though most of the inhabitants were killed in the disaster, a handful survived to set up their own secret undersea kingdom, run on strict scientific and logical principles. One of the Elde, #8823 (pronounced *ha-ya-bu-sa*, coincidentally modern Japanese for "peregrine falcon"), comes ashore and is rescued by Japanese schoolboy Isamu and Dr. Oikawa. Thus 8823 came to protect Isamu and his mentor Dr. Oikawa, who has discovered the important mathematical formula X132.

With the explorations of Jacques Cousteau popularizing oceanography all over the world and the televisual exploits of Lloyd Bridges in *Sea Hunt* (1957), underwater adventure was in fashion. The idea of an undersea kingdom reasserting its power in modern times would be recycled a few years later in *Brave Raideen* (*AE). Music by Masayuki Yokota.

Strawberry on the Shortcake

SUKEBAN DEKA

1985. AKA: *Bad-Girl Cop*. PRD: N/C. DIR: Tarō Sakamoto, Hideo Tanaka, Michio Konishi. SCR: Noboru Sugimura, Tokio Tsuchiya, Akira Unno, Ichirō Yamanaka, Izō Hashimoto. CAST: Yuki Saitō, Kōji Naka, Yasuyoshi Masuda, Chiaki Watanabe, Mika Kaneko, Natsumi Arai, Mayumi Shimizu, Miho Hayashi, Hitomi Takahashi, Hiroyuki Nagato. CHN: Fuji. DUR: 25 mins. x 109 eps.; 11 April 1985–31 October 1985 (#1); 7 November 1985–23 October 1986 (#2); 30 October 1986–29 October 1987 (#3).

Saki Asamiya (Saitō) is an undercover police officer sent to investigate high school crime. Dolled up in a traditional sailor suit uniform, she fights with a yo-yo that bears the crest of the Metropolitan Police—sometimes flashing it at her victims in the style of Mito Kōmon.

Based on the 1976 manga by Shinji Wada in *Hana to Yume* magazine, *SD* returned for a second season, in which Saki was replaced with Yōko Godai (Yōko Minamino) and gained two schoolgirl subordinates Kyō (Haruko Sagara) and Yukino (Akie Yoshizawa). The third season introduced elements lifted from ninja movies, along with a new lead in the form of actress Yui

Summer Snow

Asaka. However, Minamino returned to her role in the *SD* theatrical movies in 1987 and 1988. The story's most recent incarnation came in the form of a 1991 anime series (*AE), in which the voice of Saki was provided by Kazue Ikura. Compare to TENNEN SHŌJO MANN and GIRL COMMANDO IZUMI.

SUMMER PROPOSAL *

1996. JPN: *Hito Natsu no Propose.* AKA: *One Summer's Proposal.* PRD: Mitsunori Morita. DIR: Mitsunori Morita. SCR: Takako Suzuki. CAST: Maki Sakai, Yōko Nogiwa, Naoki Hosaka, Tōru Nakamura, Yasufumi Terawaki, Saki Takaoka, Izumi Inamori. CHN: TBS. DUR: 45 mins. x 12 eps.; Fri 5 July 1996–20 September 1996.
Shortly before she is due to walk down the aisle, Megumi (Sakai) discovers that her fiancé is seeing someone else. She dumps him and, because they worked together, also quits her job. Meanwhile her mother Mitsuko (Nogiwa), a radio DJ who often uses Megumi and her friends as inspiration for material, tries to cheer her up. Megumi falls for Mitsuko's colleague Takashi (Hosaka), but he not only fails to recall their first meeting, he also

appears to be taking an active interest in her friend Akiko.
With "seven people in summer" united by a common point of contact (in this case, Mitsuko) and entering into a series of halting courtships, *Summer Proposal* is a typical love polygon drama in the mold of SEVEN PEOPLE IN SUMMER or WHERE IS LOVE?. Drawing equally on *Ally McBeal* and the technology-conscious 1990s, it also introduces the concept of the reality gap between people's vision of the world and how it really is. Megumi and Takashi are clearly made for each other but unable to express their true feelings, instead trying to bury their desires in dating others. Meanwhile, the two would-be lovers have inadvertently struck up an anonymous Internet flirtation (compare to WITH LOVE) and both share an interest in the care of "e-mail fish" virtual pets. The reality gap is emphasized even further in the show's final episodes, in which everything appears to be resolved an episode early, only to be rearranged in an epilogue set one year later, in which many of the previous happy ending assumptions turn out to be false. Broadcast in the U.S. with

English subtitles on KIKU TV. Theme: Glay—"Beloved."

SUMMER SNOW *

2000. AKA: *The Nobles.* PRD: Kazuhiro Itō. DIR: Hiroshi Matsubara, Tamaki Endō, Shunichi Hirano. SCR: Eriko Komatsu. CAST: Tsuyoshi Dōmoto, Ryōko Hirosue, Tsubasa Imai, Chizuru Ikewaki, Shun Oguri, Ryōko Kuninaka, Shunsuke Nakamura, Takuzō Kadono, Hideko Hara. CHN: TBS. DUR: 45 mins. x 11 eps.; Fri 7 July 2000–15 September 2000.
Natsuo (Dōmoto) is teaching a young boy how to ride a bike, but the child collides with Yūki (Hirosue), a sickly bank employee who has spent her whole life avoiding anything that might be "bad for her." Yūki and Natsuo find they have a lot in common, particularly since Natsuo's brother has a hearing defect. Natsuo's other obsession is diving—a sport that would prove fatal to Yūki, though she feels she is unable to tell him about her medical condition for fear that she would lose him. Meanwhile, their associates Chika (Ikewaki) and Hiroto (Imai) discover that they are to become parents. The child stands a high chance of having a birth defect itself, but they eventually decide that *all* children must struggle to survive and that an abortion would be the wrong course of action. Yūki rebels against her stern father, who clashes with Natsuo, claiming that his draconian rules are designed to save his daughter's life, not destroy her opportunities for fun. Meanwhile, Yūki discovers that, like the heroine of BEAUTIFUL LIFE, her days are numbered without a heart transplant and her chances of getting one are greatly reduced if she stays in Japan to be with Natsuo, instead of doing the sensible thing and heading for America— where, presumably, fresh human hearts are handed out to Japanese tourists on a daily basis. A transplant opportunity eventually presents itself, but it is not quite the happy ending for which viewers might have been hoping. Broadcast in the U.S. with English subtitles on

KIKU TV. Theme: Kinki Kids—"Natsu no Ōsama" (King of Summer).

SUMMER STORM

1992. JPN: *Natsu no Arashi*. PRD: N/C. DIR: Hidekazu Nakayama. SCR: Takashi Ezure. CAST: Yūzō Kayama, Masahiko Kondō, Akira Nagoya, Jun Fubuki, Michiko Haneda. CHN: TBS. DUR: 45 mins. x 7 eps.; Thu 13 August 1992–24 September 1992.

Kentarō (Kayama) is a former public prosecutor, now the owner of a small café who has become estranged from his son Kensuke (Kondō). One day, he is approached by Shiho (Fubuki), the wife of a man implicated in a banking scandal seven years earlier, who wants the help of Kentarō, the man who prosecuted him. Not to be confused with the 1989 *Summer Storm*, a sequel to the unrelated EYE OF THE STORM.

SUMMER WITH YOU

1994. JPN: *Kimi to Ita Natsu*. PRD: Chihiro Kameyama. DIR: Utahiko Honma. SCR: Eriko Kitagawa. CAST: Michitaka Tsutsui, Issei Ishida, Asaka Seto, Maju Ozawa, Takao Ōsawa. CHN: Fuji. DUR: 45 mins. x 12 eps.; Mon 4 July 1994–19 September 1994.

With his wife away abroad looking after her sick father, Irie (Tsutsui) finds himself spending the summer vacation alone with his rebellious daughter Asami (Seto). Their strained relationship is put under further tension by the arrival of Irie's old school buddy, the handsome Sugiya (Ishida). Peak rating: 19.4%. Theme: Yumi Matsutoya—"Hello My Friend."

SUN DOES NOT SET, THE

2000. JPN: *Taiyō wa Shizumanai*. AKA: *Sun Shines Forever*. PRD: Masatoshi Yamaguchi. DIR: Isamu Nakae, Narihide Mizuta, Shinichi Sakuraba. SCR: Fumie Mizuhashi. CAST: Hideaki Takizawa, Yasuko Matsuyuki, Yūka, Keiko Takeshita, Ran Itō, Ren Ōsugi, Rena Komine, Hitomi Satō, Isao Bitō, Masaki Kyōmoto. CHN: Fuji. DUR: 45 mins. x 11 eps.; Thu 13 April 2000–22 June 2000.

Nao (Takizawa from Johnny's Juniors) is a tough brawler who adores his mother Teruko (Takeshita) and often gets into fights on her behalf. When she suddenly collapses and dies, Nao begins to suspect that her death may have been caused by malpractice at the hospital—his suspicions are given further plausibility when he goes to pick up her ashes from the crematorium and finds what he believes to be a scalpel blade among her remains. In the company of his lawyer Setsu (Matsuyuki), he begins to investigate, while gradually falling in love with Ami (Yūka) the daughter of chief surgeon Keizō (Ōsugi), who could be a prime suspect.

As with KIDNAP, this drama questions the formerly unassailable honor of Japan's authority figures, as private individuals take on an establishment that jealously guards its inner knowledge. Cunning and brutal, Setsu is reluctant to take the case unless Nao is simply in it for the money, since a single charred blade found near the ashes is hardly evidence, particularly when family members were encouraged to say goodbye to their mother by placing small tokens in the coffin. She reasons that they can probably embarrass the hospital into a monetary settlement, but that finding out what actually killed Nao's mother is a near impossibility. The only evidence of malpractice, or indeed, information about the cause of death, will come from the medical establishment itself, which Nao is just about to take on.

The script plays with the viewers' expectations—many times in shows such as WHITE SHADOW and 24-HOUR ER, we have seen medical protagonists unjustly accused of malpractice, and the case is soon put to Etsushi (Kyōmoto), a kindly surgeon who admits he may have dropped his scalpel, but only *after* Teruko was pronounced dead when he insisted on performing a last-ditch attempt at open heart massage. However, Nao refuses to believe the explanation is that simple, doggedly going over his mother's last hours minute by minute, until he discovers that it was the *absence*, not the presence, of something crucial that caused his mother's death. Among several good performances, the show is stolen by Matsuyuki as Setsu, who proves to be an unstoppable, amoral legal machine, ready to hunt down guilt even when Nao realizes it is in his best interests to give up. In the final courtroom showdown, it is Nao who tries to stop her from opening a whole new can of legal worms and he who is dragged from the court as she pounces on the true culprit, whether Nao wants her to or not. Theme: Elton John—"Goodbye Yellow Brick Road."

SUN VULCAN

1981. JPN: *Taiyō Sentai Sun Vulcan*. AKA: *Sun Battle Team Sun Vulcan*. PRD: Susumu Yoshikawa, Takeyuki Suzuki. DIR: Hirokazu Takemoto, Kimio Hirayama, Yoshiaki Kobayashi, Kazushi Hattori, Minoru Yamada, Shōhei Tōjō, Atsuo Okunaka, Akira Kashima. SCR: Shōzō Uehara, Hirohisa Soda, Susumu Takahisa, Akiyoshi Sakai, Mikio Matsushita, Tomomi Tsutsui. CAST: Ryūsuke Kawasaki, Takayuki Godai, Yoshiya Sugi, Asao Kobayashi, Hideaki Kusaka, Machiko Soga. CHN: Asahi. DUR: 25 mins. x 50 eps.; Sat 7 February 1981–30 January 1982.

The Black Magma Machine Empire wants to defeat the human race and replace life on Earth with mechanized minions. To defend the Earth, a secret task force is assembled—one warrior each from Sky, Sea, and Land, each with special powers. Takano (Godai) is the red-clad Vul-Eagle, Yoshiya (Sugi) is the blue-clad Vul-Shark, and Akio (Kobayashi) is the yellow-clad Vul-Panther, while their vehicles (Jaguar, Cosmo, and Sand Vulcan) can combine to form their ultimate weapon, the Sun Vulcan Robo. In times of great need, the trio can also attack with their secret weapons, color-coded American footballs that can be kicked at the enemy for devastating effect.

Their archenemy is Hell Satan

(Kusaka), the president of the Black Magma Machine Empire, whose anonymous Machine Men provide the cannon fodder. As well as the obligatory monster of the week, *Sun Vulcan* also features Queen Hedorian (Soga), paramount baddie from the earlier **DENZIMAN** series. Following her defeat at the hands of the Denziman Team, Hedorian has been restored to life with an artificial heart, and serves Hell Satan as his faithful cyborg lieutenant. Based once more "on an idea by Saburō Yade." The next in the Super Sentai series would be the following year's **GOGGLE-V**. Music by Michiaki Watanabe. Soga would return once more as another invader in **MIGHTY MORPHIN' POWER RANGERS**.

SUN WUKONG

1977. JPN: *Tobe! Son Gokū*. AKA: *Fly! Sun Wukong*. PRD: N/C. DIR: N/C. SCR: N/C. CAST: (voices) Chōsuke Ikariya, Ken Shimura, Boo Takagi, Kōji Nakamoto, Cha Katō. CHN: TBS. DUR: 25 mins. x ca. 100 eps.; Tue 11 October 1977–27 March 1979.
Cast out of Heaven for making mischief, monkey king Sun Wukong (Shimura) is offered a last chance for redemption—he must guard the priest Tripitaka (Ikariya) on his long journey to the fabled land of Gandhara, where he hopes to acquire some priceless Buddhist scriptures. Preceding the more famous **MONKEY** by several months, this puppet show ran concurrently on Japanese TV with yet another retelling of Wu Cheng'en's *Journey to the West*—Fuji TV's sci-fi cartoon adaptation *Spaceketeers* (*AE). Intended as a parody of the original story, the voices were played by members of the comedy group The Drifters, and the puppets were made to look as much like them as possible—hence the presence of **BAYSIDE SHAKEDOWN**'s Ikariya in the role of Tripitaka.

SUNFLOWERS ON THE HILL

1993. JPN: *Oka no Ue no Himawari*. PRD: Tonkō Horikawa. DIR: Makoto Kiyohiro. SCR: Taichi Yamada. CAST:

Kaoru Kobayashi, Yōko Shimada, Keiko Takeshita, Michitaka Tsutsui, Yasuo Daichi. CHN: TBS. DUR: 45 mins. x 12 eps.; Sun 11 April 1993–27 June 1993.
Film company engineer Kōhei (Kobayashi) is on his way home one night when he sees a woman taken ill at a train station. He ensures that she gets home safely, at which point the woman, Fumi (Shimada), tells him that, unbeknownst to him, she has conceived, birthed, and reared his child. Adapted from his own novel by writer Yamada, who also created **HERE'S LOOKING AT YOU**. Theme: Garth Brooks—"Omoide ni Yurete" (What She's Doing Now).

SUNSET WAR

1974. JPN: *Yūbae Sakusen*. PRD: Kazuo Shibata. DIR: Minoru Hanabusa. SCR: Yoshihiro Ishimatsu. CAST: Takao Yamada, Isamu Nagato, Tayo Shimada, Tadayoshi Kura, Midori Utsumi, Yoshiki Imamura. CHN: NHK. DUR: 25 mins. x 6 eps.; Mon 14 January 1974–23 January 1974.
Shigeru (Yamada) likes tinkering with machinery. His friend Akio (Imamura) loves science and sci-fi, while another friend Gorō loves ninja comics and judo. Unwisely pressing a button on a machine he finds in a junkyard, Shigeru is transportd to the Edo period, where he is thrown into jail by suspicious law enforcers. Luckily for him, the jail is attacked by ninja, and he manages to use his machine to return himself to the present amid all the confusion.
   Akio insists, somewhat redundantly, that Shigeru has found a time machine, and the three boys concoct a series of modern devices designed to impress the ninja. Returning back in time, they impress the chief magistrate with their futuristic wizardry, and Shigeru is appointed as the new town official in charge of dealing with the local "ninja problem." However, Shigeru's first ninja captive turns out to be a pretty girl called Yōko, who pleads for clemency—her family have

only turned to a life of crime because the evil government has stolen their land.
   The boys leapfrog back and forth in time in an attempt to stop the ongoing battle between ninja and the Edo authorities. On one trip, they accidentally bring Yōko with them to the present, and the peasant girl is incredibly impressed to find that the world does eventually become a peaceful place. However, the boys' interference only makes things worse, and eventually Yōko is killed, along with many other combatants in the past. The disenchanted boys return to their own time and throw away the time machine, which mystifyingly takes to the air and paints the sky pink. Based on a story by Ryū Mitsuse, author of **WIPE OUT THE TOWN** and **DAWN IN SILVER**. Music by Katsuhisa Hattori.

SUPERHERO

1997. JPN: *Seigi no Mikata*. AKA: *Ally of Justice*. PRD: Toshikazu Tanaka. DIR: Masahiro Kunimoto. SCR: Kazuyuki Morosawa. CAST: Taichi Kokubu, Maki Mizuno, Reiko Takashima, Takeshi Naitō. CHN: Yomiuri. DUR: 45 mins. x 11 eps.; Mon 14 April 1997–23 June 1997.
Junpei (Kokubu) has a dream of becoming a superhero. He grows up and becomes a police officer to fight against evil in the best way he knows in the real world. One day, he becomes smitten by Kyōko (Mizuno), a girl he meets while on patrol. He is unable to stop thinking about her, but does not realize that the woman of his dreams is really a call girl. Theme: TOKIO—"Julia."

SUPERHUMAN SAMURAI SYBER SQUAD *

1993. JPN: *Denkō Chōjin Gridman*. AKA: *Electrolight Superman Gridman*. PRD: Kazuo Tsuburaya, Nobuyuki Koyama, Hiroshi Inoue. DIR: Kimihiko Soga, Shinichi Kamisawa, Hirotaka Muraishi, Kyōta Kawasaki, Kazuya Konaka, Yoshiki Kitamura, Teruyoshi Ishii, Toshiyuki Takano. SCR: Yasushi Hirano,

Hiroyuki Kawasaki, Isao Shizutani, Kazuhiko Kōbe, Toshimichi Ōkawa. CAST: Masaya Obi, Jun Hattori, Takeshi Sudō, Takeshi Sugawara, Ed Yamaguchi, Miru Ichiyanagi, Gorō Kataoka. CHN: TBS. DUR: 25 mins. x 39 eps.; Sat 3 March 1993–8 January 1994.

Khandejifer, the incarnation of pure evil, manifests itself on the hard drive of one Takeshi Tōdo (Sugawara), a lonely rich kid who toys with computer programs for kicks. Takeshi's malevolent virus creations are able to travel through the ether and inhabit other computers and any other electronic device possessing a circuit board, prompting the hyperspatial law enforcer Gridman to take action. Recruiting three Earth children to help him, he uses their computer expertise to fight evil in the digital realm and can even combine with Earth boy Naoto (Obi) to give himself a body in the real world suitable for combating any monsters that make it out of the digital world to threaten our own planet.

Modernizing their own **ULTRAMAN** franchise for the digitally conscious 1990s, Tsuburaya threw in computer graphics and an Internet-inspired subplot for what was otherwise a standard tale of monster of the week, transformation, little fight, and climactic bigger fight. Popular for its flashy computer graphics and impressive Pythagorean-solid cyberspace, *Gridman* was soon picked up for the American market in the wake of the **MIGHTY MORPHIN' POWER RANGERS**. Given a suitably alliterative new title and a wholly unnecessary spelling error, it became *Superhuman Samurai Syber Squad* in its new English-language incarnation. In this version, all-American teenager Sam Collins (Matthew Lawrence) is sucked into one of his computer games by an energy surge, developing the powers and persona of his online "Servo" personality. Meanwhile, rogue artificial intelligence Kilokahn escapes from a military test site and finds its way to the hard drive of troubled child Malcolm (Glen

Beaudin), causing Sam and his buddies to begin a quiet battle behind the scenes to prevent Kilokahn and its minions from seizing control of the world.

SUPERMARKET WAR, THE *
1998. JPN: *Ryūtsū Sensō*. PRD: N/C. DIR: N/C. SCR: Toshimichi Saeki. CAST: Eisaku Yoshida, Hideko Yoshida, Makoto Ōtake, Ken Utsui. CHN: NHK. DUR: 45 mins. x 3 eps.; Sat 10 January 1998–24 January 1998.

Sanae (H. Yoshida) is the manager of a small NEOS supermarket franchise and the owner of the land on which the store is built. She and her assistant Daisuke (E. Yoshida) try to get on with local businesses, but are thrown into adversity by some cold-hearted decisions made by Shimazaki at head office. Shimazaki moves Daisuke to headquarters and instructs him to oversee the construction of a giant superstore close to Sanae's. The construction of the new outlet is liable to destroy Sanae's operation, devalue her land, and put local shops out of business. Daisuke and Sanae resolve to fight back. Broadcast with English subtitles in the U.S. on KIKU TV.

SURE DEATH SERIES
1972. JPN: *Hissatsu*. PRD: Hisashi Yamauchi. DIR: Hiroki Matsuno. SCR: Tatsuo Nogami. CAST: Sō Yamamura, Ken Ogata, Yoichi Hayashi, Makoto Fujita, Tsutomu Yamazaki, Masaya Oki, Takahiro Tamura, Ichirō Nakatani, Yōsuke Kondō, Kōji Ishizaka, Ryūzō Hayashi, Mitsuko Kusabue, Katsutoshi Shin. CHN: TBS (1972–1975); Asahi (1975–1992). DUR: 45 mins. x 768 eps.; 2 September 1972–14 April 1973 (#1); 21 April 1973–13 October 1973 (#2); 20 October 1973–22 June 1974 (#3); 29 June 1974–28 December 1974 (#4); 4 January 1975–27 June 1975 (#5); 4 July 1975–9 January 1976 (#6); 26 January 1976–23 July 1976 (#7); 30 July 1976–22 October 1976 (#8); 29 October 1976–14 January 1977 (#9); 8 May 1977–4 November 1977 (#10); 18 November 1977–10 February 1978

Superhuman Samurai Syber Squad

© 1993 Tsuburaya Productions

(#11); 17 February 1978–18 August 1978 (#12); 25 August 1978–24 November 1978 (#13); 8 December 1978–11 May 1979 (#14); 18 May 1979–30 January 1981 (#15); 6 February 1981–1 May 1981 (#16); 8 May 1981–25 June 1982 (#17); 2 July 1982–24 September 1982 (#18); 8 October 1982–1 July 1983 (#19); 8 July 1983–14 October 1983 (#20); 21 October 1983–24 August 1984 (#21); 31 August 1984–28 December 1984 (#22); 11 January 1985–26 July 1985 (#23); 2 August 1985–8 November 1985 (#24); 15 November 1985–25 July 1986 (#25); 8 August 1986–31 October 1986 (#26); 7 November 1986–6 March 1987 (#27); 13 March 1987–31 July 1987 (#28); 7 August 1987–25 September 1987 (#29); 8 October 1991–24 March 1992 (#30). In the Edo period, a secret society is formed to avenge the impoverished on the rich and powerful who think they are above the law. Hanemon Otowaya (Yamamura) is the boss of assassins, whose guiding principle is that he only kills those who are evil. He is assisted by Sanai Nishimura (Hayashi), a swordsman who teaches at a dōjō but who also works as a hitman for Hanemon when required. Another of

Sure Death Series

© 1972 TBS

their number is Baian Fujieda (Ogata), an acupuncturist who specializes in lethal injections. He is also a womanizer, who is caught in bed with his latest lover by her husband. Trying to extricate herself from the situation, Baian's lover claims that she has been raped, causing the angry Baian to extract his own revenge and murder her. The bereaved husband hires other assassins to kill Baian, leading to a vendetta on the streets of Edo.

Dominating 20 years of broadcast history in Japan, the *Sure Death* series owes a certain debt to the James Bond movie series, with amoral killers working undercover for their own definition of the greater good. It also specialized in innovative ways of killing, using everything from hairpins and bamboo skewers to gadgetry in the style of 007. It was based on the book *Shikakenin Baian* by Shōtarō Ikenami—*shikakenin* being the author's newly

coined word for an avenging assassin. Part of the show's appeal to the Japanese audience lay in the double lives of its protagonists. By day, they were humble citizens with few cares except the constant search for money, women, and good sake. By night, they transform into avenging equalizers, whose ethics were considerably more flexible and less admirable than the old style champions of justice like **MITO KŌMON**.

The first sequel, *SD Punisher* (*Hissatsu Shiokinin*) introduced a new element—instead of merely killing evil-doers, the assassins would ensure that they died in as unpleasant a way as possible, often torturing them to death. Despite frequently making the assassins look more evil than their targets, this new spin proved very popular with audiences, and also made a star of the season's new recruit—Mondo Nakamura (Fujita) starred as a civil ser-

vant, who dons assassin's garb at night to clear up the corrupt system. He was joined by Tetsu (Yamazaki), a womanizing Buddhist priest whose specialist area was dislocating joints. The smart Mondo and the monstrous Tetsu were joined by hotheaded brawler Jō (Oki) to make the season's trio of avengers.

However, the second season of *SD* backfired when events on screen were linked in the Japanese media to a real-life murder case. This scandal led TBS to reform the series for the third season, laying the emphasis on helping, not killing, renaming it *Sure Death— Helpers on the Run* (*Tasukebito Hashiru*). Corpses, however, still piled up on screen, as lordless samurai Bunjūrō Nakayama (Tamura) wandered Japan in the style of **LONE WOLF AND CUB**, bringing justice to those in need and also carousing with all the local pretty girls. Losing his sword partway through the season, Bunjūrō fought henceforth with an iron bar, accompanied by another lordless retainer, Hiranouchi Tsuji (Nakatani), whose preferred method of killing was a needle concealed in a tobacco pipe. In another change mid-season, the assassins were apprehended and brought to justice, their sentence comprising an order to return to their former duties, but this time with government supervision!

Mondo stayed on as a series regular, returning for the third season with two new assistants, stone mason Daikichi (Kondō) and widowed scholar of Dutch Mitsugu (Ishizaka). Determined to take out his grief on the world, Mitsugu becomes increasingly cruel as the series progresses and eventually dies at the end, leaving Mondo to ponder the meaning of life.

The fourth season was arguably the high point of the *SD* series, featuring noodle seller Hanbee (Ogata again) teaming up with itinerant gambler Masakichi (Hayashi). Their boss was a woman, Masakichi's mother Osei (Kusabue).

Mondo returned once more for the fifth season, working with Ichimatsu (Oki, again!), a professional killer with a soft spot for children. The third member of the trio was Ingen (Shin), a womanizing Buddhist priest who enjoys killing people. The series ended with Mondo springing Ichimatsu from jail, in contravention of his own role as a civil servant.

The series continued in this vein for many more years, with minor variants on the killing for a cause theme. The series was presumed to come to an end in 1993, with the release of the film *Hissatsu! Mondo Shisu* (*SD Mondo Dies*). However, rumors of the "sure death" of the series were greatly exaggerated—it began without Mondo, and demonstrably was able to continue without him. Another *SD* movie followed in 1994, and in 1996 the assassins' guild gained another unlikely member with the arrival of the movie *SD: Samisen Shop-Owner Yūji* (*Hissatsu Shamisenya Yūji*). There have also been 19 TV specials. Compare to **THE HANGMAN**. Peak rating: 33.9% (in 1984).

SURGEON SAEKO ARIMORI

1990. JPN: *Gekai Arimori Saeko*. PRD: Yasuhiko Kawahara. DIR: Hidenobu Hosono. SCR: Man Izawa. CAST: Yoshiko Mita, Masahiro Takashima, Pinko Izumi, Kōichi Iwaki. CHN: NTV. DUR: 45 mins. x 23 eps.; Sat 14 April 1990–30 June 1990 (#1); 10 October 1992–19 December 1992 (#2).

Surgeon Saeko (Mita) is a 43-year-old divorcée in the process of starting her own hospital. Arriving for the first time at the hospital in a helicopter with an emergency patient, she organizes a successful operation, but the people at the hospital find her attitude difficult to take. This is doubtless because she is an uncompromising maverick, like **SURGEON SANSHIRŌ NATSUME**. Themes: Masatoshi Nakamura—"Negai" (Wish), Junko Ōhashi—"Ai wa Toki o Koete" (Love Beyond Time).

SURGEON SANSHIRŌ NATSUME

1998. JPN: *Gekai Natsume Sanshirō*. PRD: Tetsuya Kuroda. DIR: Hiroyuki Mutō. SCR: Mitsuo Kuroto. CAST: Takeshi Naitō, Kuniko Yamada, Harumi

Inoue, Mirai Yamamoto, Aki Takejō. CHN: Asahi. DUR: 45 mins. x 10 eps.; Thu 15 October 1998–10 December 1998.

Sanshirō (Naitō) is a top-class surgeon, who immediately causes trouble at his new hospital when he arrives *with* the victim of an accident he has witnessed. The patient is ordered to go to another hospital but the maverick surgeon refuses to compromise, like a whole pile of other uncompromising maverick surgeons in **HALF DOC** and **24-HOUR ER**, and come to think of it, **SURGEON SAEKO ARIMORI**. Theme: Tsuyoshi Nagabuchi—"Yubikiri Genman" (Promise).

SUZURAN *

1999. PRD: N/C. DIR: Rintarō Mayuzumi. SCR: Yūki Shimizu. CAST: Nagiko Tōno, Yumi Hiiragi, Chieko Baishō, Isao Hashizume, Rina Uchiyama, Tsuyoshi Ujiki, Isao Bitō. CHN: NHK. DUR: 15 mins. x ca. 150 eps.; Mon 5 April 1999–2 October 1999.

At the end of the Taishō era (mid-1920s), Jirō Tokiwa (Hashizume), the stationmaster of Ashimoi in Hokkaidō, finds an abandoned baby in the waiting room. Adopting the girl and naming her Moe, he raises her as his own, though the girl still has trouble dealing with the stigma of her abandonment. When she grows up, she decides to leave Hokkaidō and search for her mother in Tokyo, but instead finds herself thrown into the terror of World War II. Moe was played by Hiiragi as a girl, Tōno as a young woman, and Baishō in her later life. Perhaps capitalizing on its early similarities to *Poppoya the Railroad Man* (1999), it was also adapted into a movie the following year—only the third time such a fate has awaited an NHK morning drama after 27 years of broadcasts. The *suzuran*, or lily of the valley, is a flower that endures severe winter and waits for the happiness of spring—supposedly a symbol of Moe's life, though it would also appear to apply to every other NHK morning drama heroine. Shown

on KDOC Los Angeles with English subtitles.

SWEET DEVIL

1998. PRD: Tetsuya Kuroda, Kōsuke Matsuo. DIR: Nobuhiro Kamikawa, Hiroshi Tomizuka. SCR: Yasushi Fukuda, Masaki Fukasawa. CAST: Lina (Noriko Matsuda), Mina (Minako Amahisa), Reina (Reina Miyauchi), Nana (Nanako Sawashi), Ai Katō, Takeshi Naitō. CHN: Asahi. DUR: 45 mins. x 9 eps.; Mon 13 July 1998–7 September 1998.

Anthropology students Izumi (Nana), Riku (Reina), and Nagi (Lina) are all keen members of the course run by Professor Danhara (Naitō). One day, they acquire an ancient book of magic from Greece and believe that some of its spells actually appear to work. Enlisting a fourth student Tōko (Mina), who claims to have powers of extrasensory perception, they try to investigate a local serial murder case, only to find the criminal's magical powers have put a curse on them. Despite apparent similarities, this vehicle for the Okinawan pop group MAX preceded the American *Charmed* (1998) by a full season—its influences are more likely to rest with the movie *The Craft* (1996) and the TV series *Buffy the Vampire Slayer* (1997).

SWEET HOME

1994. PRD: Seiichirō Kijima. DIR: Jirō Shōno. SCR: Yumie Nishiogi. CAST: Hiroshi Fuse, Tomoko Yamaguchi, Maho Toyota, Saya Takagi, Keita Masuda, Yōko Nogiwa. CHN: TBS. DUR: 45 mins. x 12 eps.; Sun 9 January 1994–27 March 1994.

Transferred by his company, Minoru (Fuse) and his family move from Hokkaidō to Tokyo. His wife Wakaba (Yamaguchi) soon finds out that mothers in Tokyo are more uptight about their children's education, since when she takes her son Akira (Masuda) to kindergarten, her fellow attendees are *already* sending their children to cram schools, hoping to secure the best elementary place for them. Since elementary school admissions test not just the children, but also their parents, Wakaba persuades the reluctant Minoru to join the race. They attend a parents' cram school run by the super-strict Yoriko (Nogiwa). Meanwhile, Minoru faces potential redundancy at work and Wakaba has to take on a part-time job to help pay the school fees. Both the parents and child become nostalgic for their carefree days of a simple "sweet home," in a drama from **GOOD MOURNING** writer Yumie Nishiogi. Cleverly applying the traditions of in-law appeasement to a school setting, with Yamaguchi as a put-upon young "bride," and Nogiwa as the fearsome "mother-in-law," Nishiogi's satire on Japan's hothouse education system attracted official complaints from a real-life cram school, which only added to its ratings. Compare to **CRAM SCHOOL BOOGIE**. Peak rating: 26.9%. Theme: Kyōko Koizumi—"My Sweet Home."

SWEET MARRIAGE

1998. JPN: *Amai Kekkon*. PRD: Hideki Inada, Kō Wada. DIR: Masanori Murakami, Ikuo Kamon. SCR: Mayumi Nakatani, Hiromi Kusumoto. CAST: Noritake Kinashi, Naomi Zaizen, Seiichi Tanabe, Sayaka Yamaguchi. CHN: Fuji. DUR: 45 mins. x 11 eps.; Thu 8 January 1998–19 March 1998. Kitarō (Kinashi) mistakenly believes that his life with his wife Asako (Zaizen) and son is happy and content, until hidden tensions come to the forefront when his wife writes a novel that wins a major literary prize. Theme: Every Little Thing—"Time Goes By."

SWEET SEASON

1998. PRD: Seiichirō Kijima. DIR: Katsuo Fukuzawa. SCR: Yumiko Aoyagi. CAST: Nanako Matsushima, Kippei Shiina, Maho Toyota, Keizō Kanie, Yoshihiko Hakamada, Yoshihiko Inohara, Yoshie Ichige. CHN: TBS. DUR: 45 mins. x 11 eps.; Thu 15 January 1998–26 March 1998. Single girl Matsushima has separated from her colleague Yutaka (Hakamada), and is now secretly dating her married boss Akira (Shiina). The situation dredges up a large amount of family guilt, since she herself still blames her father Shinya (Kanie) for having an affair in the past which led to the death of Matsushima's brother. Matters are made palpably worse by the revelation that Matsushima is pregnant with Akira's baby, but is unable to tell him for fear of what the news might do to his invalid wife Chikako (Toyota). When he finally finds out, Akira asks her to keep the baby, but she has a miscarriage. Realizing that his true feelings lie with Matsushima, Akira leaves his wife. The distraught Chikako tells the whole sorry story to Matsushima's parents, leading to an argument which causes Matsushima to move out of the family home and in with her lover.

Meanwhile, Shinya keeps receiving calls from a man called Shinji (Inohara), who claims to be his son by his former mistress. Shinya decides to travel to Sendai to visit Shinji and his mother, which in turn leads to a row between Shinya and Kayako (Ichige), his wife of 30 years.

For her exploration of illicit love affairs, **IDEAL MARRIAGE** scriptwriter Yumiko Aoyagi chose to concentrate on two generations of the same family in order to add volume to the story. Needless to say, later episodes develop along traditionally histrionic drama lines, as Akira meets with an accident that causes him to lose his memory. Though he eventually regains it, he does not reveal to Matsushima that he recognizes her and leaves for Hong Kong. Three years later, Chikako visits Matsushima to tell her that she is divorcing Akira and that she has arranged for the couple to meet at a bar called Sweet Season. Theme: Southern All Stars—"Love Affair: Himitsu no Date" (Love Affair: Secret Date).

T

TABLOID

1998. PRD: Masatoshi Yamaguchi. DIR: Shunsaku Kawake, Rieko Ishizaka, Narihide Mizuta. SCR: Yumiko Inoue. CAST: Takako Tokiwa, Kōichi Satō, Rie Tomosaka, Takashi Kashiwabara, Hiroyuki Sanada. CHN: Fuji. DUR: 45 mins. x 10 eps.; Wed 14 October 1998–16 December 1998.

Saki (Tokiwa) is a snooty journalist with the high-class *Chūo Shinbun*, who embarrasses her conservative bosses by asking impertinent questions at a government press conference. Although she is counting on the support of her superiors, she is drummed out of the press club and, much to her disgust, re-assigned to the down-market *Evening Top* tabloid—compare to a similar downward career path in **NEWS WOMAN**. Her hard-won journalistic values are immediately questioned by her new editor Taku (Satō), a no-nonsense hack who reminds her that tabloids do not have the captive, habitual audience of broadsheets, but must instead fight for their audience on a daily basis. Taku stresses that average commuters have only 120 yen in change, which will be squandered on canned coffee unless *Top* can catch their eye with lurid headlines and scandalous photographs.

Taku assigns Saki to Kurumi (Tomosaka), a tough reporter unafraid of bending the truth to get a good story. Although the girls are initially at odds (Saki once publicly rebuffed Kurumi in her *Chūo Shinbun* days), they soon become friends in the quest to make news, particularly when Saki's newshound sixth sense sniffs out a good story. Her chief project is Toshihiko Manabe (Sanada), a creepy murder suspect in a high-profile trial, though Saki becomes convinced that he is innocent.

Inspired in equal parts by *The Paper* (1994) and *I Love Trouble* (1994), two U.S. movies that hit Japanese video stores at roughly the same time in 1995, *Tabloid* artfully contrasts quality journalism with the gutter press. Saki soon learns to play by a different set of rules, winning the respect of her workmates through her willingness to adapt and through the contacts and skills she acquired in her former life at *Chūo Shinbun*. It is an excellent introduction to the world of newspaper people, assembling media archetypes like the office burnout, the flighty designer, and the ultra-cool photographer and putting them to good use. **DANGEROUS LIAISONS** writer Inoue's script also fore-grounds issues in journalistic ethics, such as the invasion of privacy and confidentiality in the pursuit of a good story. She also imparts equal weight to the contradictory powers of the press—sometimes the journalists burn the midnight oil to file a scoop that nobody reads, whereas on other occasions a trivial story attracts undue attention in the style of **FEMALE ANNOUNCERS**. Meanwhile, Saki dogged-ly pursues justice in the Manabe case, whose subject alternates between hounded innocent and sinister criminal—actor Sanada keeps the viewer guessing to the very end. The story examines every tier of the newspaper trade, from the humble newspaper seller outside the building (who also babysits Kurumi's daughter) to *Evening Top*'s stern owner in the penthouse, who threatens to close the paper down unless sales improve within three months. Naturally, Saki throws herself into delivering a scoop that can save the day—stunning her colleagues from her old job. Compare to **LOCAL NEWS: DEPARTMENT THREE** and the suspiciously similar premise of **MESSAGE**. The *Chūo Shinbun* newspaper was also the supposed location of much of the action in **RING**. Peak rating: 16.1%. Theme: Glay—"Be With You."

TAEKO SASHOW'S LAST CASE

1995. JPN: *Sashō Taeko no Saigo no Jiken.* PRD: Akira Wada. DIR: Shunsaku Kawake. SCR: Jōji Iida. CAST: Atsuko Asano, Toshirō Yanagiba, Shirō Sano, Naoko Iijima, Takeshi Masu, Keizō Kanie. CHN: Fuji. DUR: 45 mins. x 11 eps.; Wed 12 July 1995–20 September 1995.

Taeko Sashow (Asano) is a detective at the Metropolitan Police, who formerly belonged to the Crime Psychology Profiling Team (CPPT). She believes that her ex-boyfriend Keigo (Masu), the former leader of the CPPT, has developed a condition that causes him to enjoy killing and that his recent disappearance is related to the murder of Taeko's best friend. Taeko and her assistant Yukio (Yanagiba) pursue the perpetrators of a series of murders, only to see them die mysteriously. Former CPPT colleague Ikenami (Sano) insists that Keigo is already dead, but Taeko does not believe him, claiming that she has been seeing visions of him. Ikenami prescribes a drug for her to combat the "hallucinations," though Taeko comes to suspect that it is Dr. Ikenami who has been orchestrating the murderers and their murders from behind the scenes. However, before she can act on the suspicion, Ikenami disappears, and Yukio's girlfriend Rie (Iijima) turns up dead. Yukio swears vengeance, but he in turn is trapped by Ikenami and almost killed. Taeko arrives just in time and arrests Ikenami, but the doctor escapes from custody when he is taken to the hospital for profiling, killing a nurse and a detective in the course of his escape.

Ikenami arranges to meet Taeko at a secret rendezvous, where he tells her that he killed Keigo himself over a swindle, and that her visions were drug-induced—he has been supplying her with hallucinogens mixed with Keigo's own powdered bones, in a set-up redolent of COLD MOON. Taeko tackles Ikenami and is almost killed, but saved in the nick of time by her colleagues.

The case seems closed, but Taeko refuses to believe that Keigo is dead. She eventually tracks him down to a hospital, where the injured Keigo is attached to a life-support machine. He confesses that it is in fact *he* who has been behind all the murders, intending to "send his love to her" from the hospital bed. An irate Taeko unplugs his life-support machine and walks away.

Heavily inspired by *The Silence of the Lambs* (1990), this sophisticated suspense from NIGHT HEAD creator Jōji Iida features Atsuko Asano, queen of

the early trendy dramas, in a serious role. The TV movie *Sashō Taeko: Kikan no Aisatsu* (Taeko Sashow's Return Greeting) followed on 25 March 1997. Set three years later when Taeko is still recuperating from her ordeal in a sanatorium, it features the detective dragged back into service by her former colleague Kōsaka (Kanie) after a series of copycat murders—presumably a copy of *Copycat* (1995). Music by Tarō Iwadai. Theme: Rod Stewart—"Lady Luck."

TAIHEIKI

1991. PRD: Yasuo Takahashi. DIR: Mikio Satō. SCR: Shunsaku Ikehata. CAST: Hiroyuki Sanada, Yasuko Sawaguchi, Ken Ogata. CHN: NHK. DUR: 45 mins. x 49 eps.; Sun 6 January 1991–6 December 1991.

Born in 1305 to the Ashikaga clan, Takauji Ashikaga grows up in a time when emperors and aristocrats plot to retrieve their lost power from the regent Takatoki Hōjō—last of the inheritors of the events described in THE GRASS AFLAME. In fact, the Hōjō family, long the manipulators of power through puppet emperors and puppet shoguns, have now become puppets themselves; Takatoki comes to power aged only eight, thanks to the manipulations of the Nagasaki family. Takauji, however, tries not to involve himself in such intrigues, as he prefers to enjoy life. Eventually, Takatoki Hōjō is attacked in Kamakura by the forces of Yoshisada Nitta—Takatoki commits suicide, bringing about the long-delayed end of Japan's Kamakura Period.

With the fall of the regency, the Emperor Go-Daigo becomes the de facto ruler of Japan, though he immediately favors the aristocracy over the warrior class and the common people. Unwilling to submit to the authority of another family, he appoints his son Prince Morinaga as the new Shogun, turning down Takauji's own "request" for the position. Taxes rise, resulting in a rebellion by the peasantry, and although Takauji is awarded the former lands of the Hōjō, he takes the

opportunity to set up his own military government in the area.

After a succession of battles, Takauji seizes the imperial capital of Kyoto and puts his own puppet, Emperor Kōmyō, on the throne. Effectively, this makes Takauji and his brother Naoyoshi the rulers of Japan, much to the annoyance of the supporters of Emperor Go-Daigo, who continues to "reign" from the Yoshino mountains south of the nearby city of Nara, itself a former imperial capital. Consequently, allegiances in Japan are divided between the "Northern Dynasty" supported by Takauji and the "Southern Dynasty" supported by the backers who put Go-Daigo on the throne. With Go-Daigo's death in 1339, the rival factions refuse to back down, and a second "Southern" Emperor is put on the throne, widening the rift. Takauji falls out with his brother, plunging the nation into another civil war. Takauji dies in 1358 from illness, but the enmity between the rival factions is not healed until 1392, when his grandson Yoshimitsu unifies the country once more, becoming prime minister under Emperor Gokomatsu, who has already been the Northern Emperor for several years, and whose authority is finally recognized by the Southern supporters.

Since it takes years to plan a *taiga* drama, producers must have decided to put *Taiheiki* into production during the long illness of Hirohito, the Shōwa Emperor. This makes NHK producer Reo Endō's decision to adapt Eiji Yoshikawa's novel all the more surprising, as the period of the Northern and Southern Courts had long been avoided by TV companies, unwilling to invite controversy by dramatizing a period in which the Imperial family itself was demonstrably corrupt. Over footage of the collapse of the Berlin Wall, the opening narration noted that the world itself was entering a time of change, and audiences seemed to support it, with favorable ratings and little sign of the feared backlash from the Japanese Right. Novelist Yoshikawa's NEW TALE OF THE HEIKE and MUSASHI were also dramatized as *taiga* dramas. Peak rating: 34.6%.

TAIL OF HAPPINESS *

2002. JPN: *Shiawase no Shippo.* PRD: Hisao Yaguchi, Andrew Tamon Tanba, Junko Abe. DIR: Akimitsu Sasaki. SCR: Fumie Mizuhashi. CAST: Miki Mizuno, Kyōzō Nagatsuka, Kenji Sakaguchi, Sachie Hara, Shirō Sano, Sachiko Kokubu, Kyōtarō Koizumi, Chiharu Niiyama. CHN: TBS. DUR: 45 mins. x 12 eps.; Thu 11 April 2002–27 June 2002.

In the two years since her mother's death, Mio (Mizuno) has tried to get on with her life while suppressing her love for her childhood friend Riku (Sakaguchi), who persists in asking *her* for advice about his girlfriend Shōko (Hara). But Mio's existence is thrown into turmoil by the arrival of her father (Nagatsuka), whom she has not seen since her parents' divorce when she was a child. Dad claims that he has mended his ways and wants to bond with his child—when Mio reluctantly assents, Riku mistakenly believes that the male underwear he sees on the washing line belongs to Mio's new boyfriend. As Mio and Riku struggle to admit their feelings for each other, she continues to spar with her very different father in the style of **BEST DAD IN THE WORLD**. Broadcast with English subtitles in the U.S. on KIKU TV. Theme: Every Little Thing—"Kioku" (Memory).

TAINTED LOVE SONG

2001. JPN: *Kizudarake no Love Song.* AKA: *For Your Sanctuary.* PRD: Yoshishige Miyake, Yūji Tōjō, Tatsuya Itō. DIR: Hiroyuki Ninomiya, Kazuhisa Imai. SCR: Masaya Ozaki. CAST: Katsunori Takahashi, Ai Katō, Mika Nakajima, Hiroko Hatano, Yoshizumi Ishihara, Tokuma Nishioka, Naomi Kawashima, Ken Kaneko. CHN: Fuji. DUR: 45 mins. x 11 eps.; Tue 9 October 2001–18 December 2001.

Kōsuke (Takahashi) is a former pop music producer, now fallen on hard times after accusations of plagiarism. Kicked out of the music world, he now

Tale of an Announcer's Woes

© 2003 Steve Kyte

runs a small noodle bar. Meanwhile, Mirai (Nakajima) is a troubled teenager already known to the police, who has been raised single-handedly by her mother, bar owner Aya. Kōsuke hears Mirai singing on the street and senses in her a true musician—he resolves to turn her into a professional singer. However, Kōsuke's sister Yuka (Katō), tries to stop him out of jealousy for his interest in Mirai, while his producer rival Ezaki (Kaneko), now top dog in his absence, will do anything to keep Kōsuke out of the music business. The result is a behind-the-scenes drama about a media profession in the style of **PAPA IS A NEWSCASTER**, recycling the familiar archetypes yet again. Theme: Mika Nakajima—"Stars."

TAKE ME TO A RYOKAN

2001. JPN: *Watashi o Ryokan ni Tsuretette.* AKA: *You Said You'd Take Me to a Ryokan.* PRD: Takashi Ishihara, Hideki Inada. DIR: Hisao Ogura, Masanori Murakami. SCR: Tomoko Aizawa. CAST: Arisa Mizuki, Akiko Yada, Ken Kaneko, Yūko Asano, Morio Kazama. CHN: Fuji. DUR: 45 mins. x 12 eps.; Wed 11 April 2001–27 June 2001.

Gold digging publicist Rinko (Mizuki) thinks she has landed the perfect man—a guy who owns seven hotels. However, shortly after their marriage, her husband dies while supervising the construction of a new franchise in Australia. Rinko discovers that the construction company has embezzled such vast amounts of money from the project that her husband died penniless. Although she inherits his estate, she is forced to sell off six of the hotels. She arrives at the seventh, a run-down *ryokan* (Japanese-style inn) and is ready to sell it too, until she discovers that it is her late husband's ancestral home. She decides to stay and turn around the fortunes of the inn, but is hindered by the other item left to her in her husband's will—a teenage daughter from an earlier marriage. Compare to **GOOD MOURNING** and **NEWS WOMAN**.

TALE OF AN ANNOUNCER'S WOES

1987. JPN: *Announcer Puttsun Monogatari.* PRD: N/C. DIR: Tomoji Fujita. SCR: Mineaki Hata. CAST: Kayoko Kishimoto, Masaki Kanda, Maiko Takai. CHN: Fuji. DUR: 45 mins. x 5 eps.; Mon 6 April 1987–11 May 1987.

Following the success of **PAPA IS A NEWSCASTER** in the previous season, this behind-the-scenes drama at a news station broke new ground by featuring actual media figures. Whereas other shows such as **FEMALE ANNOUNCERS** or **NEWS WOMAN** would conceal true identities and change names, *Tale of an Announcer's Woes* was almost exclusively shot in and around the Fuji building, with a supporting cast of real journalists and newscasters in cameo roles.

TAMING OF THE SHREW, THE

1993. JPN: *Jaja Uma Narashi.* AKA: *Taming the Wild Horse.* PRD: Yūji Iwata. DIR: Mamoru Hoshi. SCR: Masashi Todayama, Yoshikazu Okada. CAST: Kiichi Nakai, Arisa Mizuki, Yuki Uchida, Mayu Tsuruta, Issei Ishida. CHN: Fuji. DUR: 45 mins. x 12 eps.; Mon 5 July 1993–20 September 1993.
Ryūichirō (Nakai) is an ordinary businessman. He marries the director of the company he is working for, but she dies soon after the wedding. Ryūichirō finds himself living with his wife's daughter Natsumi (Mizuki) in a huge estate. NB: Though the Japanese title refers to a wild horse, our translation reflects its common usage in Japan, as the local title for the play by William Shakespeare. Peak rating: 21.8%. Theme: T-Square and the Royal Philharmonic Orchestra—"Tomorrow's Affair."

TANAKA CLAN DETECTIVES

2002. JPN: *Tantei Kazoku.* AKA: *Detective Family.* PRD: Kenji Ikeda, Takeshi Takase, Satoshi Suzuki. DIR: Makoto Naganuma. SCR: Taketatsu Ishihara. CAST: Motoki Fukami, Izumi Inamori, Takanori Jinnai, Ryūnosuke Kamiki, Ryōko Kuninaka, Hiroyuki Miyasako, Shigeru Muroi, Airi Taira. CHN: NTV. DUR: 45 mins. x 9 eps.; Sun 13 July 2002–14 September 2002.
After the death of her private investigator father, Sayuri (Inamori) and her mother decide that it is probably best to shut down the family business. After all, none of the surviving family members knows anything about being a detective. However, prodigal son Ichirō (Jinnai) returns at the last moment and offers to keep the business running. Initial enthusiasm on the part of other family members soon turns sour when Ichirō reveals that he is now a truck driver and knows little about the detective business except what he picked up while playing cops and robbers as a kid. Compare to **DON'T WORRY**.

TARŌ

1975. PRD: Masaharu Morita. DIR: Minoru Hanabusa. SCR: Yōko Matsuda. CAST: Yutaka Usami, Noboru Nakatani, Miyako Osanai, Shōichi Kuwayama, Masanao Yamada, Kumi Somayama. CHN: NHK. DUR: 25 mins. x 6 eps.; Mon 20 January 1975–29 January 1975.
Tarō (Usami) is a 17-year-old high school student from an urban middle-class family. His father Seijirō (Nakatani) is a professor and his mother Nobuko (Osanai) is a translator. He adores Motoko (Somayama), who is a year older but has a boyfriend. She also comes from a relatively poor family, who are unable to pay for her higher education. While Tarō decides to follow his father into anthropology, albeit at a minor university that does not meet with his parents' approval, Motoko leaves school and gets a job as a waitress. Tarō is impressed that she has already found a place in the adult world, but upset when he realizes that she is intimate with her boyfriend— Tarō and Motoko are separated by time and class, and by the fact that as they leave their teens, they are each heading toward very different worlds. Based on a story by Ayako Sono, *Tarō* illustrates the impatience of those in their late teens in their desire to become adults, unaware of the relationships or attitudes they may be forced to leave behind.

TEACHER BINBIN STORY

1988. JPN: *Kyōshi Binbin Monogatari.* PRD: Chihiro Kameyama. DIR: Hiroshi Akabane. SCR: Masao Yajima. CAST: Toshihiko Tahara, Misako Konno, Hironobu Nomura, Izumi Igarashi, Junko Igarashi. CHN: Fuji. DUR: 45 mins. x 26 eps.; Mon 4 April 1988–27 June 1988 (#1); 3 April 1989–26 June 1989 (#2).
Ryūnosuke Tokugawa (Tahara) and his junior Enomoto (Nomura) are idealistic teachers at a troubled elementary school in Ginza, the heart of Tokyo. Ryūnosuke falls in love with a cram school lecturer Mayumi (Konno), even as his own institution is threatened with closure. The second series relocated the characters to a different school. Compare to **KINPACHI SENSEI** and **GTO**. Peak rating: 26.0% (series #2). Theme: Toshihiko Tahara—"Dakishimete Tonight" (Hold Me Tonight).

TEACHER! TEACHER! *

1998. JPN: *Sensei Shiranai no!?* AKA: *Don't You Know, Teacher!?* PRD: Tamon Tanba. DIR: Sanae Suzuki, Kanji Takenoshita. SCR: Yūki Shimizu. CAST: Tsuyoshi Kusanagi, Yuriko Ishida, Tomoe Shinohara, Katsuhisa Namase, Ryō Fukawa, Momoko Kurosawa. CHN: TBS. DUR: 45 mins. x 12 eps.; Fri 10 April 1998–26 June 1998.
Former delinquent Yūsaku (Kusanagi from SMAP) becomes a fifth grade teacher at East Asakusa School. His charges are initially extremely unresponsive to his efforts to teach them, and his attempt to gain their approval with a yo-yo contest lapses into farce when two boys fight over the attentions of a female classmate. He deals with the standard problems of any classroom (bullying, a lonely transfer student, a schoolgirl-teacher crush, etc.), but with a unifying theme of individualism—Yūsaku is scandalized that the children are already afraid to buck group trends at eleven years old and exhorts them to be proud of being themselves. Other problems include an abandoned child unable to write the "letter to mother" homework assigned by Yūsaku, a girl who flirts with bulimia as she struggles to make it as a model, a rich kid who falls from grace when his father is arrested, and an unpopular girl who becomes even

more despised when she is labeled the "teacher's pet." In other words, yet another remake of **KINPACHI SENSEI**, although this turncoat delinquent story was broadcast a whole season ahead of the better-known **GTO**. Broadcast in the U.S. with English subtitles on KIKU TV. Theme: Tatsurō Yamashita—"Itsuka Hareta Hi ni" (On Some Clear Day).

TEACHER'S PET

1991. JPN: *Sensei no Okini-iri*. PRD: N/C. DIR: Akio Yoshida. SCR: Rin Takagi. CAST: Takanori Jinnai, Miwako Fujitani, Kirin Kiki, Kyōzō Nagatsuka, Sae Isshiki. CHN: TBS. DUR: 45 mins. x 12 eps.; Fri 28 June 1991–13 September 1991.

Hitoshi (Jinnai) is a former music prodigy, fallen on hard times and forced to make ends meet by playing the piano in a bar. He receives a letter from Shinobu (Kiki), his late brother's ex, informing him that the school of the performing arts where she works is looking for a new teacher. He takes the job, though he soon proves to be wholly unsuited to teaching, while the memory of his dead brother both pushes him toward Shinobu, while somehow also keeping them apart. Theme: Junko Ōtsuka—"Tears."

TEACHER'S SUMMER HOLIDAY

1992. JPN: *Kyōshi Natsuyasumi Monogatari*. PRD: N/C. DIR: Setsuo Wakamatsu. SCR: Shōichirō Ōkubo. CAST: Ryō Ishibashi, Isao Bitō, Atsushi Kondō, Masahiko Tsugawa. CHN: NTV. DUR: 45 mins. x 12 eps.; Wed 1 July 1992–23 September 1992.

After the death of his brother, night-club host Shūji (Ishibashi) decides to become a high school teacher. His attitude does not impress conservative members of staff, but gradually they come to notice Shūji's charm and natural way with his students. However, Ayatarō (Kondō) confronts him at every opportunity. Compare to **GTO** and **KINPACHI SENSEI**, as usual.

TEAM

1999. JPN: *Team: Saiaku de Saikō na Futari*. AKA: *Best Men, Worst Place*. PRD: Shizuo Sekiguchi, Takashi Ishihara. DIR: Keita Kōno, Hiroshi Nishitani. SCR: Ryōichi Kimizuka. CAST: Tsuyoshi Kusanagi, Masahiko Nishimura, Miki Mizuno, Hitomi Kuroki, Naho Tōda, Ken Koba, Kazuo Mizuhashi, Ren Ōsugi, Naoki Shimada. CHN: Fuji. DUR: 45 mins. x 11 eps.; Wed 13 October 1999–22 December 1999.

Yūsuke (Kusanagi from SMAP) is a career civil servant on the political fast track at the Ministry of Education, with a highly idealized view of children and teenagers. He finds himself shunted onto a four-month internship program to a local police station, where he is expected to observe juvenile offenders in their natural habitat. The reluctant transfer is assigned an equally reluctant babysitter Hajime (Nishimura also from SMAP), a tough cop given the job as punishment after he mishandled a hostage situation and caused a fellow officer to be wounded in a gunfight. The government employee's interest in counseling and touchy-feely initiatives immediately annoys the cop, who has to deal with violent teenage criminals on a daily basis. A harder-hitting series than the usual reluctant buddy drama, *Team* replays writer Kimizuka's mismatched partners of **BAYSIDE SHAKEDOWN**. The cast returned in feature-length TV specials on 3 November 2000, 5 October 2001, and 20 September 2002. Theme: Canna—"Kaze no Muku Mama" (As the Wind Changes).

TEEN STORY

1975. JPN: *Suekko Monogatari*. PRD: Masaharu Morita. DIR: Kanae Mayuzumi. SCR: Noboru Yokomitsu. CAST: Mariko Endō, Kazuya Oguri, Keiko Tsushima, Taeko Hattori, Masahiko Kametani. CHN: NHK. DUR: 25 mins. x 6 eps.; Mon 6 January 1975–15 January 1975.

Fourteen-year-old Keiko (Endō) is the youngest in her family and a tomboy who shuns her schoolwork. Her father Taichi (Oguri) is an eccentric writer

who likes climbing up on the roof of the house. During summer vacation, Keiko's elder siblings Kazue (Hattori) and Akio (Kametani) return home from college. Their neighbor sets up an *omiai* marriage meeting for Kazue, who soon starts dating a boy called Toshio. Meanwhile, Akio has passed his driving test but is sternly informed by Taichi that he does not need a car.

A year later, another summer holiday begins with Kazue at home, preparing to be a wife. Keiko will have to face a high school entrance exam in the winter but still does not like studying. Consequently, Akio and Toshio decide to teach her during the summer, causing Keiko to lament that her holiday might as well be more weeks spent enduring school. Sent to collect Kazue's wedding kimono, Keiko accidentally leaves it on the train and waits hours at the station until it can be returned. After the wedding ceremony, Keiko joins her father on the roof and tells him that Kazue's wedding has changed her mind—henceforth she will study hard.

TELL ME YOU LOVE ME SOMEDAY

1993. JPN: *Itsuka Suki da to Itte*. PRD: Masayuki Morikawa. DIR: Shirō Nakayama. SCR: Taketatsu Ishihara. CAST: Masahiro Motoki, Kyōka Suzuki, Miho Tsumiki, Naoto Takenaka, Shingo Tsurumi. CHN: TBS. DUR: 45 mins. x 12 eps.; Tue 5 January 1993–24 March 1993.

Slacker Ryūsei (Motoki) does his best

to do as little as possible in life. He tells his brother-in-law Kōsaku (Takenaka) that his dream is to work as a toy maker, only to have his bluff called when Kōsaku offers him work in his toy factory. Theme: Misato Watanabe—"Itsuka Kitto" (Maybe One Day).

TEMPTATION

1990. JPN: *Yūwaku*. PRD: Kunimasa Kondō. DIR: Kunimasa Kondō. SCR: Haruhiko Arai, Satoko Okudera. CAST: Hiroko Shino, Ryūzō Hayashi, Misako Konno, Eisaku Yoshida, Mari Nishio. CHN: TBS. DUR: 45 mins. x 12 eps.; Fri 13 April 1990–29 June 1990.

Two strangers on a train are thrown into melodrama when Taeko (Konno) confesses to fellow passenger Yoshiyuki (Hayashi) that she has just gotten married, only to be jilted by her husband in the space of just five hours. The couple ends up sleeping together, but when Yoshiyuki returns to Tokyo he discovers that there is more to the story than that—in fact, Taeko's husband committed suicide under suspicious circumstances. Taeko comes back into his life and also begins conducting an affair with his son (Yoshida). Theme: Tatsurō Yamashita—"Endless Game."

TEN BILLION MAN

1995. JPN: *100-oku no Otoko*. PRD: Yoshikazu Hattori. DIR: Hidekazu Matsuda. SCR: Akiko Yamanaga. CAST: Naoto Ogata, Isao Bitō, Keiko Saitō, Eisuke Kadota, Tomorō Taguchi, Mikijirō Hira. CHN: Kansai. DUR: 45 mins. x 13 eps.; Mon 3 July 1995–25 September 1995.

When his mother's business fails, leaving her 10 billion yen in debt, average salaryman Takuya (Ogata) is forced to guarantee the repayment of the loan. With no hope of ever paying it off, he is made an offer he can't refuse. Underworld boss Amayoshi (Hira) offers to buy Takuya's body for 10 billion yen—with little choice, Takuya signs away his freedom. Based on the 1993 manga in *Big Comics* by Yasuyuki Kunitomo, who also created *Junk Boy* (*AE). Compare to **FIVE** and **HEAVEN**

CANNOT WAIT. Theme: Tube—"Ano Natsu o Sagashite" (Searching for that Summer).

TEN BRAVE WARRIORS OF SANADA

1975. JPN: *Sanada Jūyūshi*. PRD: N/C. DIR: N/C. SCR: Akishige Narusawa. CAST: (voices) Shōji Matsuyama, Akira Nagoya, Shin Kishida, Noboru Mitani, Momoko. CHN: NHK. DUR: 15 mins. x 445 eps.; Mon 7 April 1975–25 March 1977.

Yukimura Sanada was an intelligent warlord who fought side by side with **HIDEYOSHI**. He enlists a group of ninja to help him in the war against Ieyasu Tokugawa, including Sasuke Sarutobi (*AE), the son of a warrior who was ruined by Nobunaga. Others were the white-skinned foreigner Saizō Kirigakure, and the blonde-haired beauty Kiyomi Miyoshi, in a puppet show based on a story by **GOKENIN ZANKURŌ** creator Renzaburō Shibata. The puppets were created by Juzaburō Tsujimura, who had previously enjoyed great success with **HAKKENDEN**.

TEN URARA

1989. PRD: N/C. DIR: N/C. SCR: N/C. CAST: Risa Sudō, May Kiuchi, Hideko Hara, Takeshi Katō, Kaoru Kobayashi, Junko Ikeuchi. CHN: NHK. DUR: 15 mins. x ca. 150 eps.; Mon 6 April 1998–3 October 1998.

After her father's death in 1970, seven-year-old Urara Kawashima (Kiuchi) leaves Nikkō with her illustrator mother Tomoko (Hara), moving in with Tomoko's father Kōjirō (Katō). She meets Ryōji (Kobayashi), a carpenter, and she becomes interested in his work. Tomoko quarrels with her mother Hatsuko (Ikeuchi), leading her and Urara to move out of the parental home into their own accommodation, where Urara befriends anime fan Kazumi.

Some years later, in 1981, Urara (Sudō) is 18 years old and unsure about her future. She discovers that downtown Tokyo is losing its craftsmen and decides to be a carpenter, asking the aged Ryōji to teach her.

TENAMONYA STRAW HAT

1962. JPN: *Tenamonya Sandogasa*. PRD: N/C. DIR: Ryūji Sawada. SCR: Toshio Kagawa. CAST: Makoto Fujita, Minoru Shiraki, Ichirō Zaitsu. CHN: TBS. DUR: ca. 30 mins. x 309 eps.; Sun 6 May 1962–31 March 1968.

The chivalrous Tokijirō (Fujita) is a respected member of the Osaka Tennōji clan, but has made so many mistakes in his life that he decides to travel far away to re-assess his life and train to be a better warrior. Setting off in the company of his sidekick Chinnen (Shiraki), he heads along the famous Tōkaidō road, and high jinks ensue, in the first major TV role for Fujita, who would go on to star in **SURE DEATH**. Heavily laden with Osaka-style humor and the area's distinctive dialect, *TSH* was particularly popular in the Kansai region, where its viewing rate peaked at over 60%. Renewed for a second season after the initial journey was complete, Tokijirō and Chinnen were obliged to return to Osaka, and with audiences still tuning in, continued through the south of Japan, down to the Ryūkyū Islands, and then back home via Shikoku. Soon becoming a Japanese travelogue in the style of **MITO KŌMON**, the series followed its leads north again toward Hokkaidō. Comedian Ichirō Zaitsu joined them en route for added humor, while an espionage element was added in later episodes as the travelers became embroiled in an attempt by smugglers to deliver a Russian cannon to would-be revolutionaries. The series returned in two later spin-offs *Tenamonya Ipponyari* (1969) and *Tenamonya Nitōryū* (1971). The Kansai dialect of the *Tenamonya* is best translated as *Konnamonda* "Here's Your . . . ," while *Ipponyari* is a single spear, i.e., a single guiding principle, and *Nitōryū* is fighting with two swords. See also the sci-fi anime homage *Tenamonya Voyagers* (*AE).

10–4 10–10

1972. JPN: *Kinkyū Shirei 10–4 10–10*. AKA: *Emergency Order 10–4 10–10*. PRD: Takuzō Ōmura. DIR: Nobuhiko

Hamano, Hidetaka Ueno, Inoshirō Honda, Yukimitsu Murase, Kiyosumi Fukasawa. SCR: Junji Tashiro, Toshiyuki Shibata, Susumu Takahisa, Keisuke Fujikawa, Narimitsu Taguchi. CAST: Toshio Kurosawa, Noboru Mizuki, Shunsuke Ikeda, Rei Maki, Shirō Ōno, Kazuaki Yuhara, Junichi Matsuoka, Tomoyuki Nemoto, Yūko Fukasawa. CHN: NET (Asahi). DUR: 25 mins. x 26 eps.; Mon 3 July 1972–25 December 1972.

Professor Haruhiko Mōri (Kurosawa) sets up a special private investigation team that utilizes Citizen's Band (CB) radios, hoping to use their network to solve crimes that leave the police baffled. When trouble strikes, the Professor sends out a 10–34 ("SOS") message to associates under the command of Iron Mask (Mizuki). He then organizes team members with handles like Snow White and the Tokyo Silvervine Rider, who employ gadgets and special weapons developed in the Professor's lab.

Made in the middle of a mini-boom of mystery shows as the Tsuburaya studio capitalized on the success of **ULTRA Q**, *10–4 10–10* took its name from the CB code numbers for "Roger" and "Out." The team's cases varied from mundane searches for missing persons to battles against evil, such as a giant mutant rat, a mud monster, a mutant vampire from the Amazon, and killer mold. As with **UNBALANCE** and **OPERATION MYSTERY**, the show attempted to move away from the monster battles for which the Tsuburaya studio had become known—only one city-stomping giant appears in its entire six-month run.

Though CB radio had been licensed in the U.S. since the 1940s, Japanese TV seems to have been ahead of the times in exploiting it as a dramatic gimmick. It would be several years before the West was treated to Sam Peckinpah's CB demolition derby in *Convoy* (1978) and the dubious short-wave delights of the early Nicole Kidman movie *BMX Bandits* (1984). The whole thing seems almost impossi-

10–4 10–10

© 1972 Tsuburaya Productions

bly quaint in these days of the Internet and instantaneous global communication, but see **HEIJI ZENIGATA** for details of his mobile phone wielding granddaughter. Music by Takeo Watanabe.

TENNEN SHŌJO MANN
1999. AKA: *Permanent Make-Up Girl Mann*. PRD: Nobuaki Murooka. DIR: Takashi Miike. SCR: Itaru Era. CAST: Jun Matsuda, Yoshihiko Hakamada, Natsumi Yokoyama, Luna Nagai, Megumi Asakura, Reina Suzuki, Yūki Matsuoka, Shion Nakamaru, Mai Andō, Masako Ikeda, Shunsuke Matsuoka. CHN: WOWOW. DUR: 70 mins. x 3 eps.; Mon 22 February 1999–24 February 1999.

Ever since she was bullied as a child, Mann (Matsuda) has nurtured her own natural abilities in the martial arts. A few years of living abroad in Hong Kong and Thailand have allowed her to hone her skills in kickboxing, which

comes in handy on the tough streets of Shinjuku. Mann finds herself in the middle of a turf war between four different groups of sailor-suited schoolgirls over who gets to hang around on which street corner and who gets to the lonely businessmen first—*TSM* was made at the tail end of the "subsidized dating" scandal that also influenced **THE STAND-IN**. Mann herself, however, remains aloof like a latter-day **YOJIMBŌ**, punching out any perverts she meets and refusing to attach herself to any one gang.

Based on the 1993 *Young Magazine* manga by Tetsuya Koshiba, *TSM* was adapted for the TV screen by film director Takashi Miike, who turns it into a cross between the movie *Bounce Ko-gals* and an episode of *Kung Fu*. It's a testament to Miike's skill with the pulp medium that *TSM* isn't completely unbearable, since under his firm guidance, the film avoids the cheap

Tennen Shōjo Mann

camera tricks, unnecessary zooms, and overt "fan service" one could expect from a lesser director. Instead of trying to confine himself to episodic TV, Miike wisely plays to his strengths and experience in the cinema, shooting the original series as three TV movies entitled *TSM: Violence at Spain Hill, TSM: Revenge at Kōendori,* and *TSM: War in Shibuya.* The result is a comedy schoolgirl version of the *Godfather* trilogy, with, as the Japanese title hints, "made-up girls" instead of "made men" as the criminal footsoldiers.

Though *TSM* does not take itself as seriously as other underworld dramas like **CHEAP LOVE**, it still portrays a sanitized image of life on the edge of the criminal world—Mann's friends might act like desperate street kids, but they all seem to have nice middle-class homes to return to at the end of the day. To be fair however, this is at least part of the gag, as demonstrated when two groups of girls greet each other with cheery waves, only to remember they're supposed to be hanging tough.

With sixteen (count 'em!) female leads, all making up in looks what they lack in any discernable acting ability, and noisy wham-bang sound effects laid over Mann's fights, there's plenty here to keep WOWOW's late-night audience happy, and enough to lead to two more feature-length episodes in November, subtitled *TSM Next,* in which Mann and her friends fought against vampires. Sadly, however, this is not as good as it sounds. Compare to **SUKEBAN DEKA**. Theme: Momoe Shimano and Maestro T—"45°C."

TEPPEN

1999. AKA: *Hong Kong Bag-Snatcher Story.* PRD: Yoshikazu Sugimura, Yoshiyuki Tanaka. DIR: Takehiko Shinjō, Ten Shimoyama. SCR: Masaki Fukasawa, Sumino Kawashima, Michiru Egashira. CAST: Maki Sakai, Naoki Hosaka, Kumiko Endō. CHN: Asahi. DUR: 45 mins. x ca. 11 eps.; Thu 8 July 1999–16 September 1999. Teppen (Sakai) is a tough Hong Kong street kid, who makes her money by

snatching bags from tourists. Her criminal life is interrupted when a scheming company boss (Hosaka) attempts to evict her grandmother from the condemned tenement where Teppen grew up. The old lady chooses this moment to confess to Teppen that she is a foundling, and that the only facts known about her real mother are that she was Japanese and that she wrote her name on the amulet Teppen wears around her neck.

Seemingly planned as an international drama in the style of **FALSE LOVE** or **LADY OF THE MANOR**, *Teppen* was presumably intended as a star vehicle for a bilingual actress such as Vivian Hsu or Faye Wong. Sakai is suitably hard-bitten in the role, but her fluent Japanese requires some suspension of disbelief. Perhaps she was a last-minute replacement for an actress who would have been able to perform more effectively in Chinese, until the standard *Cinderella* formula takes hold and the story moves to Japan. Theme: Nanase Aikawa—"Sekai wa Kono Te no Naka ni" (World in My Hand).

THANK YOU

1970. JPN: *Arigatō.* PRD: Fukuko Ishii. DIR: Kimiaki Kawamata. SCR: Yumie Hiraiwa. CAST: Kiyoko Suizenji, Hisano Yamaoka, Kōji Ishizaka, Hiroshi Ishii, Nobuko Otowa, Aiko Nagayama, Masako Izumi, Masami Sawada, Nobuto Okamoto, Miyako Osanai. CHN: TBS. DUR: ca. 45 mins. x 187 eps.; Thu 2 April 1970–22 October 1970 (#1); 27 January 1972–18 January 1973 (#2); 26 April 1973–25 April 1974 (#3); 2 May 1974–24 April 1975 (#4).

Hikaru (folk singer Suizenji) only realizes what she had when it is gone—her policeman father was killed in the line of duty, and now she misses him terribly. Living with her mother Katsu (Yamaoka) at a kindergarten run by a friend's husband, Hikaru has been secretly attending the police academy for six months, but feels she cannot tell her broken-hearted mother. However, she is forced to admit to her career choice when a friend inadvertently turns up at her house with a textbook.

Capitalizing on the success of such 1960s dramas as her own *Mother Intrepid* (see Introduction), *TY* writer Yumie Hiraiwa highlights the tendency of modern families to take each other for granted until it is too late. The initial 30-episode show was so successful that it was brought back two years later (Hiraiwa having dropped out of sight for the first year while writing **New Tale of the Heike**) for a 52-episode sequel, which maintained the same cast dynamics, but gave them completely different roles. Hence, season #2 concentrates on Arata (Suizenji again), a nurse who is occasionally forced to liaise with her supervisor mother Yū (Yamaoka again) who is occasionally assigned to the hospital where she works. Arata's father is dead (again), this time killed in World War II. This second series gained a peak rating of 56.3%, making it the most popular drama show of the entire 1970s, beating out the year's NHK *taiga* **The Fir Tree Left Behind**, and even the news.

The third season, also a year long, moved the action to a fishmongers where yet another orphan daughter (Suizenji yet again), lives with a mother widowed at the tender age of 24. Meanwhile, romance beckons in the form of Genki (Ishizaka), the local grocer's son.

Suizenji never gave up her singing career while she performed in the *TY* serials, and eventually quit, pleading pressures of work. The production team pressed on with a fourth year-long series, replacing the leads with Naomi Sagara and the original *Mother Intrepid* herself, Masako Kyōzuka. However, the new line-up and setting (a curry restaurant) failed to retain viewers of the old series, and *TY* bowed out in the middle of the 1970s. Powerful family dramas would continue to be the forte of Fukuko Ishii, who would go on to produce **Making It Through**. Hiraiwa would resurface in the 1990s, storylining **Artistic Society**.

THEIR TIME
1999. JPN: *Kanojotachi no Jidai*. PRD: Ichirō Takai. DIR: Hideki Takeuchi, Rieko Ishizaka, Kensaku Sawada. SCR: Yoshikazu Okada. CAST: Eri Fukatsu, Miki Mizuno, Shinobu Nakayama, Kippei Shiina, Sei Hiraizumi, Kaoru Okunuki. CHN: Fuji. DUR: 25 mins. x 12 eps.; Wed 7 July 1999–22 September 1999.
Fukami (Fukatsu) is a telephone operator bored with the constant grind of inquiries and complaints, who visits a night school in search of a change. There, she meets Chizu (Mizuno), who is signing up for Bible study, and Tsuguko (Nakayama), who wants to qualify as an accountant and work in America. Meanwhile, Fukami's brother-in-law Keisuke (Shiina) is transferred to a dead-end posting, and is tempted to leave his job, staying only because of the need to support his wife (Okunuki).

Three women in their mid-twenties from wildly differing backgrounds discover that they have more in common than they first thought. They help each other out in careers and relationships, in much the same way as the men of the writer's earlier **All about Young People**, or its original inspiration, **Our Journey**. See also the similar **Making Memories**. Theme: Nina—"Happy Tomorrow."

THEIR WEDDING
1997. JPN: *Kanojotachi no Kekkon*. PRD: Yū Moriya, Takashi Ishihara. DIR: Takao Kinoshita, Toshinori Nishimae. SCR: Kumiko Tabuchi. CAST: Kyōka Suzuki, Akiko Matsumoto, Takashi Naitō, Izumi Inamori, Ikki Sawamura, Shigeki Hosokawa. CHN: Fuji. DUR: 45 mins. x 11 eps.; Thu 9 January 1997–20 March 1997.
Fast-food franchise manager Kiriko (Suzuki) arrives at a friend's wedding, only to be beckoned aside by an anonymous man, who asks her to deliver a letter to the bride. Kiriko dutifully does so and discovers that the letter is from the groom saying he is leaving her. Kiriko now feels obliged to set matters right—although her own life is far

from perfect, she cannot bear the thought of ruining others', even inadvertently. Theme: Globe—"Face."

THEN SHE STOLE MY HEART
1992. JPN: *Sonotoki Heart wa Nusumareta*. PRD: N/C. DIR: Utahiko Honma. SCR: Eriko Kitagawa. CAST: Sae Isshiki, Yuki Uchida, Takuya Kimura, Chieko Matsubara, Tomoko Ikuta. CHN: Fuji. DUR: 45 mins. x 5 eps.; Thu 19 November 1992–17 December 1992.
Teenager Hiroko (Isshiki) adores high school basketball player Masayuki (Kimura) and decides that he will be the lucky recipient of her first kiss. However, before she has the chance to plant one on him, her kiss is "stolen" when new arrival Saki (Uchida) gets there first. A school drama with a sapphic twist. Theme: Yumi Matsutōya—"Fuyu no Owari" (End of Winter).

THERE'S ALWAYS TOMORROW
1991. JPN: *Ashita ga Arukara*. PRD: Tamaki Endō. DIR: Susumu Ōoka. SCR: Makiko Uchidate. CAST: Miki Imai, Nobuko Sendō, Ryō Ishibashi, Tomoko Nakajima, Kunio Murai, Michiyo Ōkusu. CHN: TBS. DUR: 45 mins. x 10 eps.; Fri 18 October 1991–20 December 1991.
Reiko (Imai) is promoted to division chief of her company's special planning division, ostensibly because of her bright ideas. She later discovers the real reason—her mother (Ōkusu) is having an affair with the company director (Murai). Theme: Miki Imai—"Piece of My Wish."

THERE'S YOUR ANSWER!
1997. JPN: *Sore ga Kotae da!*. PRD: Kazuhiko Takahashi, Takashi Ishihara. DIR: Setsurō Wakamatsu, Hiroshi Nishitani. SCR: Masashi Todoyama. CAST: Hiroshi Mikami, Miki Sakai, Masato Hagiwara, Kyōko Fukada, Tatsuya Fujiwara, Sayaka Yoshino, Kenji Anan. CHN: Fuji. DUR: 45 mins. x 12 eps.; Wed 2 July 1997–17 September 1997.
Once a brilliant conductor, now an embittered recluse, Narumi (Mikami)

© 2003 Steve Kyte

They Were Eleven

is lured out of retirement by music teacher Ikeda (Hagiwara), who convinces him to take over the school orchestra in the remote mountain village where he has made his home. The rest of the story takes on the form of a sports drama, as Narumi knocks the amateur musicians into shape and finds a form of romantic redemption for himself. Compare to **TIME OF YOUR LIFE** and **LxIxVxE**, which seem to have been similarly inspired by the British movie *Brassed Off* (1997). Theme: Ulfuls—"Wonderful World."

THEY WERE ELEVEN
1977. JPN: *Jūichinin Iru!* PRD: Kanae Mayuzumi. DIR: Tōru Minegishi. SCR: Mamoru Sasaki. CAST: Haruka Yamashiro, Taizō Sayama, Tsuguaki Yoshida, Satoshi Shibazaki, Pepe Hozumi, Toshio Nakamura, Yūji Mitsuya, Tadayoshi Kura, Isao Kataoka, Masato Yamada, Keizaburō Ishigaki, Kei Satō. CHN: NHK. DUR: 40 mins. x 1 ep; Wed 2 January 1977.
Launched into space on a team-building exercise, the cadet crew of the Hakugō (Blank Number) are allowed to return to Earth at any time, but they will all fail the course if they do so before the end of the full 53-day mission time. As their ship heads out into the void, they realize that there is an extra, uninvited crew member. Someone on the ship is an imposter, but the cadets are unable to radio Earth for advice because that will mean instant disqualification. Though some argue that discovering the interloper's identity may even be part of their mission, cadet Floru (Yamashiro) is struck by a deadly virus. Crewman Tada (Sayama) runs for the panic button but is prevented from pressing it by Fourth (Shibazaki), who argues that the mission must go on. Eventually, one crew member reveals that he is an alien carrying the virus, and crewman Ōsama (Yoshida) presses the panic button. The crew return to their university expecting the worst, but are told that despite their alien infestation, they have lasted twenty days longer than every other cadet ship. Based on the 1975 manga by **DAUGHTER OF IGUANA** creator Moto Hagio, *They Were Eleven* is a science fiction story written for girls, but with an all-male cast to hold the interest of the genre's traditional male viewers—the androgyne Floru (though quite obviously played by an actress in this adaptation) is supposed to be the point-of-view character for Hagio's original female readership. It is also a departure from traditional NHK science fiction, which usually concentrates on contemporary dramas about telepathic powers (e.g., **INFRARED MUSIC**) or time travel stories that recycle sets from period dramas (e.g., **BAKUMATSU TIME TRAVELERS**). The story was retold in 1986 as a one-shot anime (*AE), and both anime and manga versions have been released in English. This TV curio, however, remains unknown in the West.

THIRD TEMPTATION, THE
1994. JPN: *Sankenme no Yūwaku.* PRD: Masa Tomita. DIR: Masa Tomita. SCR: Masakuni Takahashi. CAST: Yukiyo Toake, Akira Nishimura, Ittoku Kishibe, Kazuhiko Nishimura, Megumi Ōji,

Mayuko Fujita. CHN: Yomiuri. DUR: 45 mins. x 12 eps.; 14 April 1994–30 June 1994.

Housewife Kyōko (Toake) is dragged into volunteering to help out at an old people's club by her old school friend Noriko (Fujita), but starts receiving unwelcome letters from the aged Mr. Yoshimoto (Nishimura). The result is presumably a geriatric version of **THE STALKER**, based on a story by Ryō Ueno. Theme: Keiko Tōge—"Kowareyasui Monogatari" (A Fragile Story).

13TH SUMMER

1977. JPN: *Jusansai no Natsu*. PRD: Kyōzō Tsubaki. DIR: Ryōzō Yoshida. SCR: Hiroko Kishi. CAST: Sachiyo Kuki, Jun Funaki, Shigeko Takabe, Masa Yamada, Yōko Ōta, Aritsune Amano, Chigusa Iwano. CHN: NHK. DUR: 20 mins. x 16 eps.; Mon 3 March 1977–29 March 1977.

As she begins her first year of middle school, Toshie (Kuki) is hit by a succession of calamities. After her mother's death, she must live with her father and grandmother, though her father passes away, as does her last living relative. Her English teacher Sachiko (Takabe) agrees to be her guardian, but that only causes further resentment among the other children, until Toshie makes a new friend, Minako (Iwano). Based on the story by Toshiko Otsubone.

THIS IS HONIKEGAMI POLICE STATION

2002. JPN: *Kochira Honikegami Sho*. PRD: Kazukiyo Morishita, Takashi Hashimoto. DIR: Tokizō Wakita, Jun Kurosawa, Tatsuya Ikezawa, Munenobu Yamauchi. SCR: Yoshi Yokota. CAST: Masanobu Takashima, Maki Mizuno, Ken Kaneko, Maho Nonami, B-saku Satō, Rina Chinen, Bengal, Hiromasa Taguchi, Mansaku Ikeuchi, Ai Kago, Masako Motai, Tsuyoshi Ihara, Yuriko Hoshi, Isao Hashizume. CHN: TBS. DUR: 45 mins. x 11 eps.; Mon 8 July 2002–16 September 2002.

Keisuke (Takashima) is a quiet, unas-suming police chief who has been assigned to the working-class precinct of Honikegami. His wife is abroad translating children's books (for some reason), so he lives with his mother-in-law Toshie Hoshi (Hoshi) and his daughter Yumi (Kago). On his first day at the precinct, he arrives in the middle of a training exercise and volunteers to take the place of the officer playing the role of the criminal. Consequently, for most of his staff, the first time they see their new chief he is being bailed out of jail by some other officers, much to the chagrin of Keisuke's straight-laced deputy Jūzō (Hashizume). The other officers are an off-the-peg lineup assembled from **BAYSIDE SHAKEDOWN** leftovers—former neighborhood flat-foot Kenji (Kaneko), new transfer Azusa (Nonami), and widowed chief detective Mai (Mizuno), who is still searching for the criminal who shot her husband. Based on the manga by Gen Takamochi in *Comic Morning*—compare to the similarly titled *Kameari Park Precinct* (*AE).

THIS THING CALLED LOVE

1993. JPN: *Ai Suru to Iu Koto*. PRD: Yasuo Yagi. DIR: Jirō Shōno. SCR: Seita Yamamoto. CAST: Naoto Ogata, Kyōko Koizumi, Kazue Itō, Takuzō Kadono, Isao Hashizume. CHN: TBS. DUR: 45 mins. x 11 eps.; Fri 8 January 1993–19 March 1993.

Salaryman Ryōsuke (Ogata) finds himself falling for Tomomi (Koizumi), a girl who he meets at a kiosk in the business district that sells *bentō* packed lunches. When he asks her out, he discovers that she has just lost her job, but soon helps her find one in the building where he works. Theme: Kyōko Koizumi—"Yasashii Ame" (Gentle Rain).

THOSE WERE THE DAYS

1996. JPN: *Hakusen Nagashi*. PRD: Utahiko Honma. DIR: Tatsuaki Kimura. SCR: Keiko Nobumoto, Hiroki Harada. CAST: Tomoya Nagase, Miki Sakai, Kotomi Kyōno, Takashi Kashiwabara, Tatsu Nakamura, Masami Shimojō, Erika Mabuchi, Ryōko Yūi. CHN: Fuji.

DUR: 45 mins. x 11 eps.; Thu 11 January 1996–21 March 1996.

High school junior Sonoko (Sakai) falls for Shō (Nagase), a night school student who dreams of becoming an astronomer, but is unlikely to be able to afford to go to the required college. Shō, however, does not reciprocate her feelings, as he is already going out with Kayano (Yūi). Meanwhile, their "friend" Yūsuke (Kashiwabara) wants Sonoko for himself and does everything he can to keep her away from Shō. Or if you prefer, just watch **ASUNARO CONFESSIONS** again.

Madoka (Kyōno) gives up her university place in order to tend to her boyfriend Shinji (Nakamura), who has lost his memory after a mountaineering accident. Recovering from his amnesia, Shinji is inspired to help others by Gen (Shimojō), the sushi chef in the next bed, who tells him about an old high school tradition called *hakusen nagashi*. . . .

Shinji decides to join the Nagano Police Mountain Rescue team, while Madoka decides her vocation is to be a nurse. Yūsuke plans to go to university in Kyoto, while Sonoko's friend Fuyumi (Mabuchi) gets ready to travel to Tokyo to become an actress. Shō is invited to work at an observatory in Hokkaidō, and it appears that almost all seven characters are attaining their dreams, except Sonoko, who has no idea what she should be doing—compare to the fate that awaits Takako in **IN THE NAME OF LOVE**. Their high school graduation complete, Sonoko suggests that they also "graduate" from their shortcomings by performing the *hakusen nagashi* ceremony. The girls take off the scarves from their sailor-style uniforms and the boys remove the white ribbon from their hats, each writing on them what they want to leave behind. Sonoko wishes to leave cowardice, Fuyumi her hypochondria, Madoka her sweet tooth, Kayano her bad attitude, Shinji his indecisiveness, and Yūsuke his armchair theorizing. With Shō adding his black tie (to symbolize his melancholy, perhaps), the pieces of cloth are tied together and thrown into a stream in a self-indulgent ritual that, thankfully, did not catch on and clog Japanese sewers every year.

It is only after Sonoko has seen her friends off to their various destinations that she makes a decision of her own. Returning to her old school, she tells her former mentor that her dream is to help other people find theirs—she wants to be a teacher.

A mawkish drama that sits between the high school nostalgia of KIMPACHI SENSEI and the lost twentysomethings of SEVEN PEOPLE IN SUMMER, TWtD was a rare foray into the trendy drama world by Keiko Nobumoto, better known abroad as a lead writer on *Macross Plus* and *Cowboy Bebop* (*AE). Nobumoto also wrote a novelization of the series, as well as *TWtD: Summer of 19* (1997) and *TWtD: Wind of 20* (1999), two later TV specials that looked in on the characters' later lives, presumably in an attempt to kickstart an irregular franchise in the style of FROM THE NORTH. Peak rating: 12.6%. Theme: Spitz—"Sora mo Toberu Hazu" (We Might Even Fly).

THREE CORNERED HEART

1995. JPN: Sankaku Heart. PRD: Keiji Tatara. DIR: Keiji Tatara. SCR: Akio Endō. CAST: Kōji Yamamoto, Hiromi Nagasaku, Shigeru Muroi, Reiko Katō, Chiharu Kawai. CHN: Asahi. DUR: 45 mins. x 11 eps.; Mon 9 January 1995–20 March 1995.

Tomoo (Yamamoto) is a shy young man, pathologically nervous in the company of young women, who can trace this condition back to the child-hood bullying he received at the hands of his cousin Ikuko (Nagasaku). But when his parents go abroad for a long trip, the fearful Tomoo is forced to move in with his relatives, only to discover that the horrible Ikuko has grown into a beautiful young woman. Another not-quite-incest drama, to be filed alongside STRAWBERRY ON THE SHORTCAKE. Theme: East End x Yuri—"MAICCA" (Oh Well).

THREE FIGHTING MISTRESSES

1995. JPN: Okami Sandai Onna no Tatakai. AKA: Battles of Three Generations of Inn Mistresses. PRD: Hisao Yaguchi. DIR: Akimitsu Sasaki. SCR: Taketatsu Ishihara. CAST: Yumiko Takahashi, Keiko Takahashi, Hisano Yamaoka. CHN: TBS. DUR: 45 mins. x 11 eps.; Thu 12 January 1995–23 March 1995.

Pursued by creditors after her father's debts become impossible to pay off, 18-year-old Satsuki (Y. Takahashi) is apprehended by Shizue (Yamaoka), the grand mistress of a traditional inn, where the new arrival is introduced as the new manager. Theme: Yumiko Takahashi—"Namida no Machikado" (Street Corner of Tears).

THREE GROWN MEN *

1997. JPN: Otona no Otoko. AKA: Middle-Aged Bachelors. PRD: Takashi Hashimoto. DIR: Akio Yoshida, Susumu Ōoka. SCR: Shizuka Ōishi. CAST: Kōji Yakusho, Yasunori Danta, Masahiko Nishimura, Akiko Matsumoto, Kimiko Yo, Maiko Kikuchi, Mitsuru Fukikoshi. CHN: TBS. DUR: 45 mins. x 13 eps.; Sun 6 July 1997–28 September 1997.

Advertising executive Daijirō (Yakusho) discovers that his old flame Miyuki (Matsumoto) is now a divorcée working at his company. Meanwhile, the boss forces Daijirō's colleague Hitoshi (Danta) to have an *omiai* marriage meeting with Hinako (Kikuchi), the daughter of a valued client. Hinako, however, prefers Daijirō, who is ordered to take her out on a date. Daijirō's friend Yūsaku (Nishimura) sees Hinako waiting for Daijirō and delivers the news that Daijirō has been delayed—much to his chagrin, he has been asked to sit in on Miyuki's new project, all about finding the ideal partner. Yūsaku has dinner with Hinako, but is seen by his would-be fiancée Yōko, who immediately assumes that the two are having an affair and that she is just about to be jilted. Hitoshi, for his part, is not bothered about losing out to Daijirō in the affections of Hinako because he finds

himself falling in love with Miyuki, although her availability is called into question by the reappearance of her ex-husband. In other words, seven people in a complex love polygon, some of whom will form new attachments before the end and some of whom will restore a love once thought lost—compare to SEVEN PEOPLE IN SUMMER and its many imitators. Broadcast in the U.S. with English subtitles on KIKU TV. Theme: Tōko Furuuchi—"Daijōbu" (All Right).

THREE SISTER DETECTIVES

1998. JPN: San Shimai Tanteidan. AKA: Spark Girls Be Cute! Be Cool! PRD: Tomoaki Koga, Atsushi Satō. DIR: Hitoshi Ōhira, Makoto Naganuma, Hiroshi Yoshino, Tomoaki Koga. SCR: Izō Hashimoto. CAST: Ranran Suzuki, Hinano Yoshikawa, Yūka Nomura, Junji Takada. CHN: NTV. DUR: 45 mins. x 10 eps.; Sat 10 January 1998–21 March 1998.

Sisters Ayako (Suzuki), Taeko (Yoshikawa), and Shumi (Nomura) suspect that their father Junpei (Takada) was killed under suspicious circumstances. As they investigate, they become accomplished detectives and solve cases for other people they encounter. Commissioned as an all-girl answer to YOUNG KINDAICHI FILES, with just a hint of the earlier anime series *Cat's Eye* (*AE), *Three Sister Detectives* is based on a story by HANDS OFF THE THIEF creator Jirō Akagawa, who also created *Holmes the Tortoiseshell Cat* (*AE).

THREE SISTERS

1967. JPN: Sanshimai. PRD: N/C. DIR: Mitsuru Shimizu. SCR: Naoyuki Suzuki. CAST: Mariko Okada, Shiho Fujimura, Komaki Kurihara, Tsutomu Yamazaki, Osamu Takizawa, Shinsuke Ashida. CHN: NHK. DUR: 45 mins. x ca. 50 eps.; Sun 1 January 1967–24 December 1967.

Masterless samurai Kingorō (Yamazaki) comes to know three beautiful sisters, whose brother is a servant of the Shogun Yoshinobu (see TOKUGAWA YOSHINOBU). Based on the novels by Jirō Osaragi, this was the first *taiga* drama to concentrate on anonymous commoners as the main characters—observing historical events from a new point of view. Some costumes and sets were probably recycled the following year, when the same series of events was repeated in RYŌMA DEPARTS.

THREE SWORDSMEN *

1987. JPN: *Sanbiki ga Kiru*. PRD: Tamotsu Sugisawa, Michinao Fukasawa, Norimichi Matsudaira, Masato Kameoka. DIR: Kazuyoshi Yoshikawa, Akinori Matsuo, Tokuzō Tanaka, Kiyoshi Miyakoshi. SCR: Tatsuo Nogami, Gorō Shima, Akira Ogawa, Kunio Fujii, Masahiro Shimura. CAST: Hideki Takahashi, Kōji Yakusho, Koasa Shunpūtei, Kaoru Sugita. CHN: Asahi. DUR: 45 mins. x 144 eps.; Thu 22 October 1987–31 March 1988 (#1); 1 December 1988–11 May 1989 (#2); 4 April 1990–28 June 1990 (#3); 11 April 1991–24 October 1991 (#4); 9 July 1992–25 February 1993 (#5); 23 December 1993–2 June 1994 (#6); 6 April 1995–31 August 1995 (#7); 15 April 2002–24 June 2002 (#8).

Three anti-authoritarian samurai leave Edo for Kyoto, encountering many troubles on the way as they try to earn their living day by day in the style of LONE WOLF AND CUB. Heishirō Yasaka aka Tonosama (Takahashi), Shinnosuke Kuji aka Sengoku (Yakusho), and Jinnai Tsubame aka Tako (comedian Shunpūtei) stand up to wrongdoers and often quarrel among themselves, as they display an anachronistically modern set of attitudes—compare to the stoic values of MITO KŌMON and ŌOKA ECHIZEN, particularly in later episodes when Jinnai is revealed to be an undercover magistrate.

In the second season *Zoku Sanbiki ga Kiru* (*More Three Swordsmen*), Jinnai asks the other two for help. He has been spying on corrupt officials who have been pocketing public money, and now stands accused of murder. He quits his job as a magistrate, and the three old friends head for Edo to clear his name. For season three *Zokuzoku Sanbiki ga Kiru* (*Even More of the Three Swordmen*), the trio are obliged to travel from Chikuzen to Sengoku's hometown in Satsuma (modern Kagoshima Prefecture), where the warrior reveals that he is really a ninja. This time, they are accompanied by Chō (Yōko Nagayama), a pretty girl who has fallen in love with Tonosama. The fourth season, *Matamata Sanbiki ga Kiru* (*Yet Again The Three Swordsmen*), adds a number of plotlines based on supernatural phenomena, as the trio and Chō head for Edo once more, and the true identity of Tonosama is finally revealed.

With the original story now complete, the characters supposedly go their separate ways, but meet up again in Nikkō for *Shin Sanbiki ga Kiru* (*New Three Swordsmen*), in which they must travel to Echigo. The series ends with Jinnai's marriage to Princess Sayuri, and with the breakup of the original team, chiefly due to Kōji Yakusho's wish to pursue other roles. Consequently, the sixth season *New* [in English] *Sanbiki ga Kiru*, former idol singer Masahiko Kondō joined as new cast member Ukon Kira aka Senryō, while Yūsuke Tanaka became a fourth member of Jinnai's son Jinnosuke. Kōji Yakusho was not absent for long—his character Sengoku soon reappeared in the seventh season *Tsūkai Sanbiki ga Kiru* (*The Thrilling Three Swordsmen*), claiming that he has already tired of the monastic life and setting off on a new journey with Jinnai and Ukon, who now uses the new pseudonym Wakatono.

Three Swordsmen was itself a remake of a series that was first seen in the 1960s between October 1963 and March 1969 on Fuji TV, made with three newcomers in the roles—Tetsurō Tanba, Mikijirō Hira, and Isamu Nagato. The use of the term *sanbiki* emphasized the characters' wild outlaw natures as –*biki* is a suffix only used when counting animals, not humans. The characters also appeared in a movie spin-off in 1964.

The series was remade a second time in 2002, with Sakyō Samonji aka Gokuraku (Takeshi Naitō) and Hanbee Yūki aka Sensei (Nenji Kobayashi), and Masanobu Takashima as Takuma Aoyagi aka Wakadaishō—literally "Young Blade" but also a reference to the movie character: see CHAIRMAN WAKA DAISHŌ. This newest incarnation of the story was broadcast in the U.S. with English subtitles on KIKU TV.

THUNDER MASK

1972. PRD: Yoshikazu Morita, Hiromi Saitō, Kazuo Horie. DIR: Inoshirō Honda, Susumu Tanaka, Akira Okazaki. SCR: Shōzō Uehara, Keisuke Fujikawa, Maru Tamura. CAST: Kazutaka Sugawara, Kazumi Inoguchi, Hidehiko Kuroda, Kentarō Kachi, Toshio Fujii, Norio Yamashita, Kōtarō Tomita, Masao Imanishi, Eiko Takaoka. CHN: NTV. DUR: 25 mins. x 26 eps.; Tue 3 October 1972–27 March 1973.

Earth is threatened by a series of beasts, including devils, fire-breathing Parajudon, vampire shark Samera, and zombie lord Gyadabiran. In the tradition of ULTRAMAN, only the mild-mannered Japanese youth Kōichi (Sugawara) can save us, when he transforms into the giant superhero Thunder Mask.

ASTRO BOY creator Osamu Tezuka's Tezuka Pro studio had long planned to move into live-action, but went bust shortly after completing the pilot for *Devil Garon*. Several staff members from Tezuka Pro's abortive live-action division formed the new Hiromi Pro, clearly with Tezuka's blessing—*Thunder Mask* was reputedly "based on the manga by Osamu Tezuka," though the creator did not begin publishing it in *Shōnen Sunday* until the week after the TV show started. The most likely explanation is that the all-new story was deliberately initiated after the collapse of Tezuka Pro for copyright reasons. The presence of some incredibly strange samurai-style pseudonyms among the crew implies that there was more trickery behind the cameras—conceiveably Hiromi Pro was calling in favors with fellow ex-Tezuka Pro staffers, who were now under contract elsewhere.

The manga serialization ended in January, shortly before the series itself. Japanese sources list a 29-episode production schedule of which only 26 were made, a curious number since it would have been a strange TV company indeed that wanted Hiromi Pro to run three episodes over a traditional second season.

THURSDAY DINNER TABLE

1992. JPN: *Mokuyō no Shokutaku*. PRD: Takeshi Matsumoto. DIR: Takeshi Matsumoto. SCR: Kenichi Iwasa. CAST: Ikkō Furuya, Hiroko Shino, Shigeru Izumiya, Tetsuya Bessho, Yui Natsukawa. CHN: TBS. DUR: 45 mins. x 11 eps.; Thu 15 October 1992–24 December 1992.

The day-to-day existence of the Miyazawa family is disrupted when eldest daughter Chinami (Natsukawa) announces that she plans to marry. With mixed feelings about the first of their three children to flee the nest, mother Tōko (Shino) makes plans for redecorating the departing girl's room. But that is before Tōko finds a pregnancy testing kit among Chinami's things. Theme: Mariya Takeuchi—"Ie ni Kaerō" (Let's Go Home).

THURSDAY GHOST STORY

1995. JPN: *Mokuyō no Kaidan*. PRD: Akira Wada, Shunji Matsumura, Hideki Inada, Masatoshi Katō, Kōichi Funazu. DIR: Kenji Nakanishi (#7); Toshinori

Nishizen (#8); Daisuke Shimada (#3); Takao Kinoshita (#1, #9, #11, #17); Katsuyuki Motohiro (#12, #18); Yūichi Satō (#14); Masahito Hijikata (#15); Masato Tsujino (#2, #9); Takashi Shimoyama (#4); Hiroki Yamada (#5); Daisuke Tajima (#6, #10, #13); Toshikazu Nagae (#16). SCR: Junki Takegami (#2, #7, #10, #12, #13); Naoya Takayama (#1, #9, #11); Kazuhiko Tanaka (#18); Masaki Fukuzawa (#14, #15); Yasushi Fukada (#16); Masaya Ozaki (#17); Shigenori Nakamura (#3); Rika Nakase (#4); Hitoshi Munei (#5); Masahito Kagawa (#6); Junya Yamazaki (#8). CAST: Hideaki Takizawa, Yuka Nomura, Naoki Kawano (#1, #9, #11); Maki Mizuno, Yūshi Sōda, Yoshihiko Hakamada (#2); Gorō Inagaki (#3); Kōichi Dōmoto, Yukihei Murakami, Daisuke Uchiyama (#4); Yukinobu Satō, Miho Kanno (#5); Tsuyoshi Kusanagi, Rieko Miura (#6); Yumi Adachi, Shingo Tsurumi, Mayu Emoto, Arima Yamada, Maya Soda (#7); Ryōko Hirosue, Hiromasa Taguchi, Haruhiko Katō, Kazumi Murata (#8); Hidemasa Nakayama, Shigeki Hosokawa, Tomohiro Sekiguchi, Maya Hamaoka (#10, #13); Kōichi Dōmoto, Takeshi Masu, Naoki Takahashi, Mayumi Asaka, Hiroko Sakurai (#12); Hideaki Takizawa, Emily Nakayama, Mayuko Takada, Mikihisa Azuma (#14); Ryōko Hirosue, Jun Toba, Akio Kaneda, Mari Hoshino, Yukie Nakama (#15); Yuka Nomura, Ai Maeda, Maya Hamaoka, Seito Hagiwara (#16); Ranran Suzuki, MIE, Tarō Yamamoto (#17); Rie Tomosaka, Ken Izawa, Tokuma Nishioka (#18). CHN: Fuji. DUR: 45 mins. x 116 eps.; Thu 19 October 1995–14 March 1996 (#1); 19 October 1995–11 January 1996 (#2); 19 October 1995 (#3); 2 November 1995 (#4); 7 December 1995 (#5); 14 December 1995 (#6); 11 January 1996–14 March 1996 (#7 and #8); Thu 18 April 1996–12 September 1996 (#9 and #10); 17 October 1996–28 November 1996 (#11); 17 October 1996–21 November 1996 (#12); 5 December 1996–12 December 1996 (#13); 9 January 1997–27 February 1997 (#14); 1 May

1997–22 May 1997 (#15); 29 May 1997–26 June 1997 (#16); 3 July 1997–14 August 1997 (#17); 4 September 1997–11 September 1997 (#18).

Noboru (Takizawa from Johnny's Juniors, barely out of diapers!) and his friends solve crimes and investigate strange phenomena around his school in *Mystery Club*. This 15-episode tale was only the first in a long-running series of weekly seven-thirty thrillers and mysteries, aimed squarely at a young audience. With the same management office behind much of the casting, the guest stars include members of SMAP, TOKIO, Johnny's Juniors, and the Kinki Kids, guaranteeing ratings from fans of teenybop music. This audience also led to a drift in the nature of the stories, away from the earlier thrillers and chillers to more spectacular sci-fi in the spirit of TIME TRAVELER or SCHOOL IN PERIL.

Thursday Ghost Story usually squeezes two tales in 45 minutes. *Mystery Club* ran concurrently with a remake of NANASE AGAIN (#2) and four one-off stories. These included *Midnight Blood* (#3), in which Akira (Inagaki from SMAP) tries to resurrect his dead wife with magic, and *Mario* (#4), a story about a bullied teenager (Dōmoto from the Kinki Kids) who realizes that if he dreams that his tormentors meet with a terrible end, they appear to do so. Other stars appearing in the one-offs included Miho Kanno in *Cindellera's Shoes* (#5), and the first drama appearance by SMAP's Tsuyoshi Kusanagi in *Secret Companion* (#6), where he plays a boy sucked into the underworld of gamblers and gangsters.

The serial length *Ghost Hunter Saki* (#7) featured Yumi Adachi as a modern woman who dabbles in the occult and finds herself successfully summoning a ghost. The ghost reveals that it is searching for a lover, killed 50 years earlier in a wartime raid—a neat combination of the 50-year limbo of Stanley Kwan's movie *Rouge* (1988), with an acknowledgement of the 50th anniversary of the end of World War II.

Ghost Hunter Saki ran concurrently with the nine-episode *Magical Feeling* (#8), in which the handsome Masashi (Katō) confesses to his adoring girlfriend Nozomi (a very young Hirosue) that he is *"not like other guys."*

At this point, the *Thursday Ghost Story* slot was moved half an hour later, closer to the "real" adult dramas. *Mystery Club* (#9) was resurrected, this time as a 16-episode drama set in a junior high, shown concurrently with the 16-episode *MMR Unidentified Flying Object* (#10), which is also available on video, suggesting it was more highly regarded than its predecessors. In it, disbelieving writer Tōru (Nakayama), who has no time for the occult or UFOs, is moved from his regular job on a fashion journal to *Magazine Mystery Research,* a publication that concentrates on the unexplained. His first job is to interview a girl who claims she has spoken to "angels," in an adaptation of the *MMR UFO* story by Yūki Ishigaki. Possibly, part of the series' success may have been born from a general trend toward horror—by the time *MMR UFO* ended on TV, the long-running YOUNG KINDAICHI FILES had arrived on NTV, while TV Asahi began broadcasting *The X-Files* only a few weeks later in December.

For the 11th to 13th serials, the umbrella series was renamed *New Thursday Ghost Story*. In the 7-episode return of *Mystery Club* (#11), subtitled *Seven Wonders in the School*, Noboru (Takizawa again) refuses to believe that a strange purple mirror is a cursed relic. However, his colleague Erika (Nomura) knows that the mirror has been stolen from a sacred shrine, and suspects that a demon dwells somewhere inside it. *Mystery Club* ran concurrently with *Cyborg* (#12) directed by NIGHT HEAD's Motohiro, in which foreign exchange student Akira (Dōmoto from the Kinki Kids) is supposedly killed in America, but returns to Japan as a cyborg operative for a secret criminal organization. This series was followed by two further episodes of *MMR UFO*, which we file as story #13.

Graduating from his school sleuthing, Hideaki Takizawa returned in the supposedly "Final" season, the 10-episode *Time Keepers* (#14), in which average teenager Kentarō is enlisted by time cop Kei (Nakayama) to help her track down a murderer from the future, who has sought refuge in 1990s Japan.

The "Final" season was nothing of the sort, and several further stories duly arrived the following year, now with the suffix "97." In *Haunted School* (#15) teenager Haruka (Hirosue again) is approached by a guardian spirit, who tells her to stop chasing boys and take up her duty to preserve the family honor by guarding a sacred treasure—compare to *Devil Hunter Yohko* (*AE).

In the four-episode *Ghostly News* (#16), based on the story by Tomokazu Satō, two "normal" teenagers are forced to enlist the help of the school "ghost *otaku*," when they discover green spirits in the stump of a tree that has just been struck by lightning.

The five-episode *Magical Fū* (#17) is set in the troubled Toy Division of a large corporation. The toys magically come to life to help employee Asuka (Suzuki) save the company. The last of the *Thursday Ghost Stories* was three-episode *Explosion! Girl with Another Persona* (#18). Yumi (Tomosaka) drinks a chemical that creates another Yumi, a Jekyll-and-Hyde opposite who creates problems for her at school. By this time, both the teen stars and their audience were getting older, and as the audience stayed up later, the evening shows they viewed in the late 1990s would often feature the stars they had grown up watching.

TIME OF THE LION, THE
1980. JPN: *Shishi no Jidai*. PRD: Susumu Kondō. DIR: Mitsuru Shimizu. SCR: Taichi Yamada. CAST: Bunta Sugawara, Gō Katō, Reiko Ōhara, Shinobu Ōtake. CHN: NHK. DUR: 45 mins. x ca. 50 eps.; Sun 6 January 1980–21 December 1980.
Senji Hiranuma (Sugawara) and Yoshitaka Kariya (Katō) meet at the

Paris Exhibition when they come to the aid of geisha Mon (Ōhara). The two young men become friends, but are soon caught up in history in the making. Senji is a samurai from Aizu, a domain that supports the central government in Edo, while Yoshitaka is a reformist samurai from Satsuma—compare to similar tensions in AS IF IN FLIGHT. The two friends find themselves on opposite sides in the conflicts that close the Edo period, see the overthrow of Yoshinobu Tokugawa (see TOKUGAWA YOSHINOBU), and witness the Meiji Restoration, in the first *taiga* drama to knowingly fictionalize some events and also not to be based on a pre-existing book. The story was an original idea from Taichi Yamada, creator of MEN'S JOURNEY, RIVER BANK ALBUM, and ODD APPLES. Music by Ryūdō Uzaki.

TIME OF YOUR LIFE *
1997. JPN: *Kimi ga Jinsei no Toki*. PRD: Toshihiro Iijima. DIR: Takamichi Yamada, Ikuhiro Saitō, Toshimasa Suzuki. SCR: Toshio Sekine. CAST: Masanobu Takashima, Nanako Matsushima, Misa Shimizu, Megumi Okina, Ikkei Watanabe, Keiko Tsushima. CHN: TBS. DUR: 45 mins. x 10 eps.; Fri 17 January 1997–21 March 1997.
Municipal worker Shinichi (Takashima) is present when his old elementary school is demolished and decides to rescue his classmates' "time capsule" from the foundations. He resolves to return the contents to their original owners, inadvertently reuniting his old high school band in the process. Former child prodigy pianist Tomomi (Matsushima) is an embittered burnout, Kana (Shimizu) is now married and working at a TV company, while their old mentor Ritsu (Tsushima) is now a widow, who rediscovers her husband's last musical composition amid the time capsule contents. Reminded of their former, younger, selves, Shinichi's friends go into a form of social meltdown as they attempt to reform their current lives.

Time Ranger

Kana has a miscarriage and reveals to her husband that the baby was not his. Tomomi asks Shinichi to "make her a woman," while former band member Gorō tries a similar tactic on Shinichi's impressionable sister Mayu. As a band performance looms and the old friendships spin apart, Shinichi realizes that he will need to drag his former associates back for one last performance. With an innovative way of assembling the traditional former schoolmates love polygon, *ToYL* also draws on the "last concert" theme of the U.K. movie *Brassed Off* (1996), which was also purloined for the later **LxIxVxE**. Broadcast in the U.S. with English subtitles on KIKU TV. Theme: Toshinobu Kubota—"Cymbals."

TIME RANGER *
2000. JPN: *Mirai Sentai Time Ranger.* AKA: *Future Battle Team Time Ranger.* PRD: Ken Fukuyoshi. DIR: Satoshi Morota, Noboru Matsui, Hajime Konaka, Tarō Sakamoto, Hiroshi Futsuda, Shōjirō Nakazawa. SCR: Yasuko Kobayashi, Toshiki Inoue, Ryōta Yamaguchi, Noboru Takemoto. CAST: Masaru Nagai, Yūji Kido, Masahiro Kuranuki, Tomohide Koizumi, Mika Katsumura, Shinji Kasahara, Ryūzaburō Ōtomo. CHN: Asahi. DUR: 25

mins. x 51 eps.; Sun 13 February 2000–11 February 2001.
Don Dorneo (Ōtomo) is the boss of the Launders crime family, who escapes from the 30th century and hides at the dawn of the 21st. Four Time Protection Team (TPT) officers pursue him from the future, but decide they need reinforcements upon arrival and recruit unwilling passerby Ryūya (Nagai) to be the Red Time Ranger—conveniently he is good at karate. His four TPT associates include Ayase (Kido), an agile man diagnosed with a fatal disease that will kill him in just a couple of years who fights as Time Blue; Sion (Kuranuki) who transforms into Time Green and is responsible for intelligence and communications; Domon (Koizumi), a master of the 30th-century martial art of Grapp, who transforms into Time Yellow; and Yūri (Katsumura), a girl from the Intercity Anti-Organized Crime Squad, who has an encyclopedic knowledge of weapons, and transforms into Time Pink.

Their chief enemy, Don Dorneo, has conveniently hijacked an entire prison on his flight from the future and periodically thaws out monstrous inmates in order to commit crimes in the year 2000, in an innovative excuse for the

monster-of-the-week fighting that has come to characterize so many of these "original ideas by Saburō Yade" that form the Super Sentai series. Like **GOGO FIVE** before it and its successor **GAORANGER**, *Time Ranger* was swiftly adapted for American audiences, forming the ninth season of the **MIGHTY MORPHIN' POWER RANGERS**, under the title *MMPR: Time Force.*

The American version changes the Dorneo character to Ransik (Vernon Wells), the leader of a mutant uprising in A.D. 3000, who escapes to the year 2001 after seriously wounding Alex (Jason Faunt), the original Red Time Ranger. The other members, Pink Jen (Erin Cahill), Green Trip (Kevin Kleinberg), Yellow Katie (Deborah Estelle Philips), and Blue Lucas (Michael Copon) pursue Ransik through time, recruiting Alex's presumed ancestor Wesley (Faunt again) as their newest member once they arrive. With the recuperating Alex monitoring their actions from the future, the Time Force fight off both the predations of Ransik's minions, as well as the unexpected interference of the Silver Guardians, whose Quantum Ranger Eric (Dan Myers) is initially an embittered rival of Wesley's. As with earlier incarnations of the series, the Quantum Ranger is eventually found to have a good heart, as does Ransik's formerly evil daughter Nadira (Kate Sheldon), who realizes there's more to life and switches sides after she helps a woman give birth. The script is even able to be a little more hard-hitting than normal in places, thanks to the time travel options available to the writers—Wesley actually *dies* at one point, only to have the events that led up to his sacrifice altered by the concerned Time Force. Music in the original was by Kōichirō Kameyama.

TIME TRAVELER
1972. PRD: Kazuo Shibata. DIR: Kazuya Satō. SCR: Tōru Ishiyama. CAST: Junko Shimada, Kiyoshi Kinoshita, Akira Hamada, Fumiko Kashiwabara, Etsuko Ogawa, Reiko Takao, Teresa Noda,

Setsuko Horikoshi. CHN: NHK. DUR: 30 mins. x 6 eps.; Sat 1 January 1972–5 February 1972.

Losing consciousness in a laboratory, Kazuko (Shimada) wakes up with a memory of the scent of lavender and finds herself lying outside in the snow on what appears to be the following day. She witnesses a badly aimed snowball break a window and injure one of her classmates and then finds herself just as suddenly returned to the present. When the events she witnessed come true the next day, her classmate Kazuo Fukamachi (Kinoshita) reveals that she has inhaled a chemical he has made—his real name is Ken Sogol and he is a time traveler from the future, stranded in the distant past of his world until he can somehow find a chemical that can move its user *forward* rather than back in time.

One day Kazuko receives a telepathic distress call from Ken, in which he claims to be trapped in August, and in Hokkaidō. Kazuko obtains some of the lavender chemical to help him, but realizes that she does not know how to initiate the time-leap required. On the advice of her teacher Mr. Fukushima (Hamada), she visits a psychiatrist, who determines that she only leaps in time when she has an unexpected shock. Fukushima dutifully threatens her with a stick, causing the desired effect and allowing her to rescue Ken.

Ken finally completes the chemical he requires, only to discover that the cleaning lady has sniffed it herself. They track her 27 years back in time, to a World War II hospital, where she is intent on using the Forward chemical to bring her dying daughter back to the future. However, her body disappears, and Ken explains that she has been erased because she broke one of the cardinal rules of time travel. Soon after, Ken reveals that he intends to return to his own time and that he is going to wipe out the memories of his friends. Though Kazuko forgets all about him, the scent of lavender always makes her feel nostalgic, for reasons she can't quite recall.

Time Traveler is the very first of the NHK juvenile drama series, a hundred TV serials made for the children of the first generation to grow up with a TV in the home. Based on the 1965 story *Toki o Kakeru Shōjo* (*Girl Across Time*) by Yasutaka Tsutsui, this perennial favorite has also been adapted into a 1983 movie starring Tomoyo Harada, a feature-length TV special on Fuji in 1985 (starring Yōko Minamino), the later TV series GIRL ACROSS TIME, and yet another film in 1997, starring Nana Nakamoto. Its most recent appearance was in January 2002 as one of three short TV specials under the umbrella title of *Morning Musume Love Stories*. Featuring starlets from the titular girl group, the story shared the screen with adaptations of *Smart-san* (*AE) and Yasunari Kawabata's novel *The Izu Dancer*.

TO BE AS I AM

1973. JPN: *Boku ga Boku de Aru Koto*. PRD: Kazuo Shibata. DIR: Yoshiyuki Itō. SCR: Yoshiki Iwama. CAST: Yoshito Arima, Hitoshi Takagi, Akemi Negishi, Ryūta Mine, Hiromi Tsuru, Mayumi Komatsu, Akitake Kōno, Eri Naraoka, Fumio Kirihara, Izumi Hara, Sakae Koike. CHN: NHK. DUR: 24 mins. 30 sec x 6 eps.; Mon 17 September 1973–26 September 1973.

Hidekazu (Arima) is a mischievous 12-year-old boy who overhears a man and a woman plotting a money-making scheme when he is in the park discarding an embarrassingly poor exam record. His sister Mayumi (Komatsu), however, retrieves the incriminating exam, and Hidekazu is grilled by his concerned family. He promises that his end of term report card will be more impressive, only to discover that it is actually even worse. Afraid of returning home, he hides in a truck and wakes up to discover that it has been driven away by one of the plotters he saw in the park.

After witnessing the driver run over a pedestrian and fail to report the incident, he realizes something is afoot and escapes from the truck at the next stop. In a nearby house, he meets old man Mr. Tanimura (Kōno) and a girl called Natsuyo (Naraoka), who inform him that the driver fits the description of the village headman's wayward son. Subsequently, Hidekazu learns that local legend describes the lost treasure of SHINGEN TAKEDA buried somewhere in the hills nearby, and he realizes that he has stumbled on an attempt by criminals to steal the objects for themselves. Based on a children's book by Hisashi Yamanaka, who also created IF A CHILD COULD FLY and AFTER SCHOOL.

TO HEART *

1999. JPN: *To Heart: Koishite Shinitai*. PRD: Kazuhiro Itō. DIR: Hiroshi Matsubara, Jun Nasuda, Tamaki Endō. SCR: Eriko Komatsu. CAST: Tsuyoshi Dōmoto, Kyōko Fukada, Sachie Hara, Hidekazu Akai, Reiko Azechi, Hisashi Yoshizawa, Matsuo Matsutoshi, Kōki Okada. CHN: TBS. DUR: 45 mins. x 12 eps.; Fri 2 July 1999–17 September 1999.

Determined to fall in love before the prophecies of Nostradamus come true, lonely crepe-seller Tōko (Fukada) overcomes her initial dislike of rookie boxer Yūji (Dōmoto from the Kinki Kids). He is initially disinterested because he has a long-standing crush on the owner of the florist's shop where he works part time. However, as Yūji begins training in earnest with a former Olympic pugilist Yoshi (real-life ex-boxer Akai), Tōko appoints herself as the head of his fan club. No relation to the anime series *To Heart* (*AE), which was released the following year. For similar millennial angst, see LAST SONG and I'LL BE BACK. Broadcast in the U.S. with English subtitles on KIKU TV and KTSF TV. Peak rating: 17.7%. Theme: Kinki Kids—"To Heart."

TO LOVE AGAIN *

2001. JPN: *Mukashi no Otoko*. AKA: *Man From the Past, Ex-Boyfriend, Endless Sorrow*. PRD: Hisao Yaguchi, Takashi Hashimoto. DIR: Akimitsu Sasaki, Takashi Fujio. SCR: Makiko Uchidate. CAST: Norika Fujiwara, Takao Ōsawa, Yasuko Tomita, Hiroshi Abe,

NORIKA FUJIWARA TAKAO OSAWA YASUKO TOMITA HIROSHI ABE
KAZUMA SUZUKI TOMOKA KUROTANI TAKAKO KATO

© 2001 TBS

To Love Again

Kazuma Suzuki, Tomoka Kurotani, Takako Katō. CHN: TBS. DUR: 45 mins. x 12 eps.; Fri 6 April 2001–22 June 2001.

Twenty-nine-year-old jeweler Akari (Fujiwara) feels stuck in a rut with Hayato (Abe), a boyfriend who refuses to commit and has a demeaning part-time job as a jewelry model, for which she knows she was hired solely for her looks. Invited to a school reunion, she accepts on the condition that her old flame Arashi (Ōsawa) won't be there, but her reluctance hides a secret— though she pretends to have no desire to see him, she still has his number stored in her mobile phone. Arashi, of course, soon turns up back in her life, and the two begin meeting secretly. After one of their encounters, Arashi goes home to his wife Mari (Tomita) with Akari's telltale perfume on his clothes (compare to **PARFUM DE LA JALOUSIE**). He denies everything but is soon planning a trip to the famous Hōryūji temple with Akari, believing that his wife and father will be going to the nearby Tōdaiji temple instead—of course, their plans change!

Confronted by Mari, Akari confides her troubles to her friend Satako (Kurotani), who reacts eagerly to the realization that Hayato, whom she has long desired, might soon be back on the singles market and ready for her. Mari and Hayato join forces to investigate the behavior of their respective partners and witness them locked in an embrace. In a last-ditch attempt to win her back, Hayato finally proposes but Akari refuses as she has already made plans to leave on a weekend trip with Arashi. Arashi, however, reacts with unexpected annoyance to the news— he would *prefer* her to return to Hayato, causing Akari to doubt his motives. By now, Mari is on the verge of mental breakdown and seems determined to win Arashi back at all costs. A melodramatic tale of dual infidelity in the style of **ONE SUMMER'S LOVE LETTER**, *To Love Again* unites the regular clichés of investigating spouses and absurdly hysterical revenge. Amid all the melodrama, it seems churlish to pick at a single narrative hole, but advanced though Japanese phones may be, were they really programmable with phone num-

bers all that long ago? Presumably, Arashi's number was never simply "left" on Akari's phone, but entered into its memory some time after the lovers first parted. Broadcast in the U.S. with English subtitles on KIKU TV and reputedly on Channel 18 in Los Angeles. Writer Uchidate approached the folly of fairy-tale endings in other dramas, including **LOVE AND LIES** and **ACCOMODATING WOMAN**. Theme: Ayumi Hamasaki—"Endless Sorrow."

TOKUGAWA IEYASU
1983. PRD: N/C. DIR: Makoto Ōhara. SCR: Mieko Osanai. CAST: Sakae Takita, Tetsuya Takeda, Shinobu Ōtake. CHN: NHK. DUR: 45 mins. x ca. 50 eps.; Sun 9 January 1983–18 December 1983. Born to a lowly samurai family in 1543, the young Takechiyo's family is torn apart by conflicting clan allegiances, causing him to lose contact with his mother at the age of two. Sent as a hostage to the Imagawa family at the age of four, the boy who would grow up to become Ieyasu (Takita) learns about warfare and politics from an early age. Leaving his small home domain

of Matsudaira behind, he becomes a trusted lieutenant of Yoshimoto Imagawa and Nobunaga Oda (see NOBUNAGA), having his first taste of defeat when his lords are defeated in the events also depicted in LAND THIEF. Eventually helping Nobunaga defeat Imagawa at the battle of Okehazama, Ieyasu is placed in charge of Imagawa's conquered lands. Defeated in battle by SHINGEN TAKEDA at the battle of Mikatagahara in 1573, Ieyasu returns with a vengeance after Takeda falls ill—events also depicted in HEAVEN AND EARTH. Gaining control of the realms of Kai and Shinano, he marries Princess Asahi, and forms an alliance with her brother Hideyoshi. He makes further advances toward the end of the 16th century, as the power of the Hōjō family begins to wane—see GRASS AFLAME and HŌJŌ TOKIMUNE. Ieyasu risks censure by refusing to embark on Hideyoshi's ill-fated invasion of Korea.

After the death of Hideyoshi in 1598 leaves an heir too young to rule, Ieyasu becomes one of the council of regents, eventually defeating his rival Mitsunari Ishida at the battle of Sekigahara, and thereby becoming Shogun. Two years later, in events also described in AOI, he resigns in favor of his son Hidetada, but marches into battle again in order to remove Hideyoshi's true heir Hideyori. In 1616, a year after Hideyori's defeat, Ieyasu dies, leaving Japan under the rule of his descendants for the next 250 years, until events depicted in TOKUGAWA YOSHINOBU.

Tokugawa Ieyasu was an adaptation of a sprawling historical novel by Sōhachi Yamaoka, which had been serialized in a newspaper between 1950 and 1968. Yamaoka later confessed that he saw his story as an allegory of the Cold War, with Nobunaga as the Soviet Union and Imagawa as the U.S. Between them, of course, is the seemingly insignificant Matsudaira clan (the author's representation of Japan), which patiently waits until the time is right to take power in the region. "Patience" was the buzzword of the day

in 1983, which saw not only Ieyasu enduring the unendurable on NHK, but also the stoic OSHIN. Peak rating: 37.4%.

TOKUGAWA YOSHINOBU

1998. PRD: N/C. DIR: N/C. SCR: Masakatsu Tamukai. CAST: Masahiro Motoki, Hikari Ishida, Masaaki Sakai, Reiko Ōhara. CHN: NHK. DUR: 45 mins. x ca. 50 eps.; Sun 4 January 1998–13 December 1998.

Born in 1837, Yoshinobu (Motoki) is the seventh son of Nariaki, a prominent Tokugawa nobleman in Mito. He is adopted by the Hitotsubashi family, a branch of the Tokugawa without a male heir, hence greatly increasing his chances of being nominated as the next Shogun. When Iesada, the thirteenth Shogun, dies without issue in 1858, Nariaki attempts to push Yoshinobu as a successor but is overruled. Instead, power brokers select Iemochi, an easily manipulated boy whose accession forces Yoshinobu and other Tokugawa notables to go into seclusion. However, Iemochi dies after only five years in office, and Yoshinobu becomes the fifteenth Tokugawa Shogun at the young, but not particularly pliable age of 21. An ardent reformist and politician, Yoshinobu uses his new authority to reform the government, modernizing along European lines and restructuring the armed forces.

In 1867, he arranges a number of meetings with foreign ambassadors in order to establish himself as Japan's true ruler in the eyes of the world, but faces opposition from Satsuma and Chōshū, two southern domains whose activities also feature in LIFE OF A FLOWER and AS IF IN FLIGHT. Shōjirō Gotō tries to reconcile the opposing factions and suggests that everyone agrees to Ryōma Sakamoto's proposition for a united democratic government under the Emperor. The Meiji Emperor is "restored" to true temporal authority on 9 December 1867, with Yoshinobu fully expecting to retain some form of power as the Emperor's

new chief minister. However, the new government is dominated by vassals of the rebellious domains of Satsuma, Chōshū, and Tosa, who demand that this "last Shogun" not only give up his powers, but also hand over government land to the Emperor. The furious Yoshinobu realizes too late that his reforms have created a new order without any need for a Shogun (an antiquated office dating back centuries), and leads a last-ditch assault on Chōshū. Meeting with a disastrous defeat in Kyoto at the battle of Toba Fushimi, Yoshinobu flees to Edo, where a new government dominated even more by Satsuma and Chōshū forces him to surrender to Saigō Takamori on the advice of Kaishū Katsu (see RYŌMA DEPARTS). The defeat of Yoshinobu represents the end of the era begun by the ascension of Ieyasu Tokugawa (see TOKUGAWA IEYASU), and represents the entry of Japan into the modern world. Based on a story by Ryōtarō Shiba.

TOKYO ASSEMBLY

1976. JPN: *Daitokai*. PRD: Kensuke Ishino. DIR: Yasuo Furuhata. SCR: Sō Kuramoto. CAST: Tetsuya Watari, Yūjirō Ishihara, Yūsaku Matsuda. CHN: NTV. DUR: 45 mins. x ?? eps.; Tue 6 January 1976–3 August 1976 (#1); 4 April 1977–28 March 1978 (#2); 3 October 1978–11 September 1979 (#3).

Targeted by gangsters because of his successes at Nara police station, detective Kuroiwa (Watari) discovers that his sister Keiko (Akiko Nishina) has been raped in retribution. He joins forces with his friend Takigawa (Ishihara), the editor of the *Tōyō Shinbun* newspaper, in an attempt to bring justice back to the streets, in a drama that was uncompromising in its depiction of life on the streets. The first season was given the subtitle *Tatakai no Hibi* (*Battling Days*), and depicts cops as ordinary human beings rather than the guardians of the law, with a script from Sō Kuramoto, the creator of FROM THE NORTH.

TOKYO BAY BLUES

1990. JPN: *Tokyo Wan Blues*. PRD: N/C. DIR: Mitsuo Kuroto. SCR: Mitsuo Kuroto. CAST: Naoto Ogata, Yasuo Daichi, Rina Katase, Chizuru Azuma. CHN: Asahi. DUR: 45 mins. x 5 eps.; Thu 18 October 1990–15 November 1990.

Yōhei (Ogata) gives up his dream of becoming a pilot to help his half brother Jinpei (Daichi) run a boat rental business. Jinpei is initially ungrateful as he has other things to worry about—chiefly his wife Kumi (Katase) and her decision to walk out on him.

TOKYO CINDERELLA LOVE STORY

1994. JPN: *Imōto yo*. AKA: *Sister Mine*. PRD: Tōru Ōta. DIR: Kōzō Nagayama. SCR: Fumie Mizuhashi. CAST: Emi Wakui, Toshiaki Karasawa, Gorō Kishitani, Mayu Tsuruta, Katsumi Watanabe, Kōsuke Toyohara, Izumi Igarashi, Naomi Nishida. CHN: Fuji. DUR: 45 mins. x 10 eps.; Mon 17 October 1994–19 December 1994.

When her brother Kikuo (Kishitani) comes to visit Tokyo, single girl Yukiko (Wakui) agrees to meet him at the station. While he waits for her, he is mistaken for a chauffeur by Masashi (Karasawa), a company director newly arrived in town. Though the error is soon corrected, Yukiko lends Masashi her umbrella out of a sense of duty—Masashi idly mentions that he has a "sister like her."

He throws away the umbrella, not expecting to meet her again, but the two bump into each other at a hot dog stand (whence Yukiko has fled from the high prices of a French restaurant). He invites her and Kikuo to a forthcoming company dinner, where he hopes they will insulate him from his colleagues' attempts to set him up with the boss's daughter Hatsue (Igarashi).

This "invitation to the ball" is only one of many references to *Cinderella*—compare to the similar GLASS SLIPPERS. Masashi, of course, is the handsome prince, but this retelling of the story flirts more with the attitudinal difference between rich and poor—possibly because its inspiration may have come indirectly, through the materialistic fable of *Pretty Woman* (1990). Masashi is blissfully unaware that his world is too sumptuous for the impoverished Yukiko, and while his attempts to impress her may have a fairy-tale sheen (the two of them get to play all alone in one of his corporate theme parks after dark), they also have a dark and arrogant underside. In particular, he almost gives up on her before the relationship has begun when she speculates she's not good enough for him, and he even sends a company minion to offer her parents work in Tokyo, almost as if he feels he can buy her affection. His ex-girlfriend Misaki is much more accustomed to the jet-set lifestyle of yachting and luxury and is determined to win him back. Meanwhile, Masashi's chauffeur Shinji (Toyohara) has split up with his bar-girl lover Hitomi. She begins a relationship with Kikuo, and it soon becomes apparent that Hitomi is Masashi's long-lost sister. With two brother-sister couples and three orbiting ex-lovers, the stage is set for the traditional seven-way romantic drama established in SEVEN PEOPLE IN SUMMER. Reputedly broadcast without subtitles in the U.S. on WNYC TV. Peak rating: 24.6%. Theme: Chage and Aska—"Meguriai" (Refrain).

TOKYO ELEVATOR GIRL

1992. PRD: Kazuhiro Itō. DIR: Akio Yoshida. SCR: Eriko Komatsu. CAST: Rie Miyazawa, Mikihisa Azuma, Hidekazu Akai, Tomoko Nakajima, Kae Okuyama, Daisuke Shima. CHN: TBS. DUR: 45 mins. x 11 eps.; Fri 10 January 1992–20 March 1992.

After graduating from college on the remote Japanese island where she grew up, the kindly, perky Tsukasa (Miyazawa) heads for Tokyo, where she lands herself a job as an elevator girl at a department store. With her colleague Naoko (Okuyama), she must ensure that all the company employees get to their floors on time, or risk the wrath of the handsome but strict communications manager Mr. Takagi (Shima). She comes to realize that although her post may be lowly, she is privy to every elevator conversation and is one of the few employees known to every sector of the company, from management to cleaning staff. Words fail us, but see BIG WING.

Released in the midst of media hype about 19-year-old Miyazawa's best-selling nude photo album *Santa Fe*, *TEG* was the height of her first TV career. She then moved into films and entered a slump from which she only recovered with a return to TV in CONCERTO. Writer Komatsu would continue to come up with original twists on the mundane—see TO HEART and HOUSEWIFE AND DETECTIVE. Theme: Rie Miyazawa—"Kokoro Kara Suki" (Love from the Heart).

TOKYO LOVE STORY

1991. PRD: Tōru Ōta. DIR: Kōzō Nagayama. SCR: Yūji Sakamoto. CAST: Honami Suzuki, Yūji Oda, Narimi Arimori, Akiho Sendō, Yōsuke Eguchi. CHN: Fuji. DUR: 45 mins. x 11 eps.; Mon 7 January 1991–18 March 1991.

Rika (Suzuki) is sent by her company to welcome a new staff member transferring from Ehime. She resolves to behave in a big sisterly manner toward Kanchi (Oda, in the role that made him a star), but is secretly forced to admit that she has feelings for him. Kanchi, however, does not seem interested, primarily because he still carries a torch for his old flame Satomi (Arimori).

Discovering that Satomi's heart truly belongs to his best friend Kenichi (Eguchi), Kanchi does the gentlemanly thing and bows out. However, he is still shocked by the realization that Kenichi and Satomi have become lovers and ends up sharing a bed with Rika in a moment of weakness. Their relationship enters an awkward phase, as Kanchi now feels obliged to feign a genuine romantic attraction to Rika, which only makes her realize all the more that she has made a mistake. Meanwhile (as if that wasn't enough melodrama!), Satomi discovers that Kenichi is having an affair with his former classmate Naoko (Sendō) although she is engaged to someone else. The heartbroken Satomi seeks consolation in the arms of Kanchi, which only serves to rub salt into Rika's wounds. When Kanchi finally tells Rika that he and Satomi are now hoping to be an item, Rika refuses to give him up.

Unlike many other love stories of the period, this adaptation of Fumi Saimon's manga avoids a truly happy ending. Like many later characters who finish a serial in a form of self-imposed exile, Rika gets on a plane for Los Angeles, leaving her true love to marry someone else. A last meeting three years later follows as a coda, but even then Rika's decision remains absolute—a gesture of passive independence much imitated in later dramas such as IN THE NAME OF LOVE. However, as she stares out at a Tokyo sunset from a rooftop vantage point, she admonishes the viewer not to dwell on her solitude, but on the good times that she and Kanchi spent together. Regarded as a dramatic risk at the time, this "unexpected" twist has since become so overused that it is now a cliché in its own right. In spite, or perhaps because of this, *TLS* remains one of the best-loved dramas of the 1990s with a peak rating of 32.3% and remains on many all-time Top Tens to this day. It was the most successful and highly regarded inheritor of the trendy dramas that began with producer Ōta's earlier I WANT TO HUG YOU! and led to numerous other adaptations of manga by Fumi Saimon, including AGE 35, ASUNARO CONFESSIONS, CLASSMATES, KOWLOON RENDEZVOUS, P.S. I'M FINE, SHUNPEI and UNMARRIED FAMILY. Saimon, incidentally, is the wife of Kenshi Hirokane, creator of the best-selling *Kachō Shima Kōsaku* manga that formed another defining work in 1990s popular culture. Although their works have rarely been animated or translated into English, and hence escaped the notice of most foreign fans, they

remain one of the most influential couples in the modern manga business.

A feature-length TV special broadcast on 12 February 1993, re-cut footage to present the entire story solely from the viewpoint of Rika. Theme: Kazumasa Oda—"Love Story wa Totsuzen ni" (Sudden Love Story). The theme itself has achieved classic status, and is often voted the all-time favorite among drama fans.

TOKYO MONEY PIT

2002. JPN: *Tokyo Niwatsuki Ikkodate.* AKA: *Tokyo Detached House with Garden.* PRD: Hidehiro Kawano, Takaomi Saegusa, Yuki Inoue. DIR: Takaomi Saegusa, Noriyoshi Sakuma, Yūichi Abe. SCR: Yoshiko Morishita, Yūko Matsuda. CAST: Saki Kagami, Rei Kikukawa, Yoshio Harada, Akiko Matsumoto, Aiko Morishita, Papaya Suzuki, Takashi Tsukamoto, Eriko Yamakawa. CHN: NTV. DUR: 45 mins. x 9 eps.; Wed 10 July 2002–4 September 2002.

After he retires, professor Kazuo Tameyama foolishly believes that it would be a nice idea to unite all his five daughters under one roof and live as a happy family. He searches for a house with a suitably central location for his grandchildren to attend school, and soon moves into what appears to be the ideal home for all nine Tameyama family members. However, the house is not all that it seems, and the Tameyamas are soon struggling to keep their sanity as a succession of problems come to light—compare to ARE YOU ON THE MOVE?, EXCUSE ME AGAIN, and the U.S. movie *The Money Pit* (1985).

TOKYO UNIVERSITY STORY

1994. JPN: *Tokyo Daigaku Monogatari.* PRD: Masaru Takahashi. DIR: Kazuhisa Imai. SCR: Junya Yamazaki. CAST: Gorō Inagaki, Asaka Seto, Yoshihiko Hakamada, Kaoru Ide, Midori Hagio. CHN: Asahi. DUR: 45 mins. x 10 eps.; Mon 10 October 1994–19 December 1994.

Handsome teenager Naoki (Inagaki

GREAT OPENINGS

Cupid's Arrow

Shot with a harpoon gun by a woman maddened with jealousy over the loss of her ex-lover to a former arsonist whose last three fiancés have all met with sticky ends, an insurance investigator falls bleeding into icy waters, and watches as his life flashes before him. ☞

from SMAP) is very popular with the local girls and is sure to ace his exams and make it to a prestigious university in the capital. But that's before he encounters Haruka (Seto) and falls in love with her at first sight. His attention is diverted and he loses his focus on his exams, placing his entire future in jeopardy. Based on the 1993 manga by Tatsuya Egawa, who also created *Magical Talruto* (*AE), *Be Free* (*AE), and *Golden Boy* (*AE). It is safe to assume that both manga and drama titles were to some degree intended to evoke the earlier success of TOKYO LOVE STORY. Theme: Kumiko Yamashita—"Drive Me Crazy."

TOMMY AND MATSU: DETECTIVES

1979. JPN: *Uwasa no Keiji Tommy and Matsu.* AKA: *Renowned Detectives Tommy and Matsu.* PRD: Chiharu Kasuga, Hiroshi Senhara, Yūzō Higuchi, Kiyoshi Nomura. DIR: Yoshio Inoue, Jitsuo Ezaki, Shigeru Doi. SCR: Hiroshi Nagano, Shōji Imai, Takashi Ezure. CAST: Tomiyuki Kunihiro, Shigeru Matsuzaki, Etsuko Shihomi, Hisashi Igawa, Tetsuo Ishidate, Megumi Ishii. CHN: TBS. DUR: 45 mins. x 106 eps.; Wed 17 October 1979–25 March 1981 (#1); 13 January 1982–22 December 1982 (#2).

Detective Tomio (Kunihiro) is a single nerd who lives with his sister Satchi (Shihomi) and suffers from vertigo. The only thing that drags him out of his shell is being teased with the girl's name Tomiko, which causes him to fly into a berserk rage. Predictably, the laws of cop-buddies dictate that his partner should be the hotheaded womanizer Susumu (Matsuzaki), with whom Tomio solves cases on the streets of Tokyo.

Heavily inspired by *Starsky and Hutch* (TBS, 1977), this comedy cop show ran alongside it on the same channel, breathing new life into the detective genre dominated by stern stoics like HANSHICHI and HAGURE KEIJI.

After their original run drew to a close along with its inspiration, Tommy and Matsu were overhauled for *Tommy and Matsu: Cop Bikers*, which shamelessly ripped off the American series *CHiPs* (NTV, 1979). Their last appearance was in the movie *The Great Switch* (*Daigyakuten*), which lifted the central premise of the movie *Trading Places*, and was something of a flop. Theme: Shigeru Matsuzaki—"Wonderful Moment."

TOMOKO AND TOMOKO

1997. JPN: *Tomoko to Tomoko*. PRD: Yasuo Yagi. DIR: Katsuo Fukuzawa, Ken Yoshida, Hiroshi Matsubara. SCR: Kazuhiko Yūkawa. CAST: Misako Tanaka, Naoko Iijima, Takashi Kashiwabara. CHN: TBS. DUR: 45 mins. x 12 eps.; Thu 3 July 1997–18 September 1997.

Tomoko #1 (Tanaka) and the younger Tomoko #2 (Iijima) first meet as children, when they become stepsisters through marriage. The relationship, however, is short-lived, as Tomoko #2's mother dies, and she moves away to live with blood relatives. The two girls meet again 23 years later at the funeral of Tomoko #1's father, who was briefly Tomoko #2's stepfather. They decide to move in together in order to preserve what little family ties remain, but they have very different personalities—the elder is a genteel lady, obsessed with tidiness, while the younger is a tough, rebellious wild child who talks like a gangster. Theme: Wham—"Club Tropicana."

TOMORROW FOR JUN

1975. JPN: *Jun no Ashita*. PRD: Masaharu Morita. DIR: Kanae Mayuzumi, Yoshiyuki Itō. SCR: Yoshiki Iwama. CAST: Mariko Endō, Sumio Takatsu, Hitomi Nakahara, Mari Wada, Miki Sanbongi, Junkichi Orimoto, Sumie Sasaki, Midori Tamura, Kimiaki Kawasaki, Toshiko Fujita. CHN: NHK. DUR: 25 mins. x 12 eps.; Mon 16 June 1975–9 July 1975.

Junko (Endō) is a 13-year-old junior high school student, who must face new hardships when her father (Takatsu) goes missing, and her mother (Nakahara) and two younger sisters (Wada and Sanbongi) have to struggle to make ends meet. Based on Akiko Inoue's story *Namidayo Sayōnara* (*Farewell to Tears*). Music by Seiichi Suzuki.

TOMORROW WILL BE OKAY

1996. JPN: *Asu wa Daijōbu*. PRD: Ken Michisoto. DIR: Kazuhisa Imai. SCR: Makoto Hayashi, Keiki Nagasawa. CAST: Michitaka Tsutsui, Naomi Zaizen, Kyōzō Nagatsuka. CHN: Kansai. DUR: 45 mins. x 8 eps.; Mon 8 January 1996–26 February 1996.

Widower Motoki (Tsutsui) is literally left holding the baby when he is forced to rear his eight-month-old son alone. The child is too young to be left at a daycare center, forcing Motoki to take him along with him to work, until the day he is interviewed by Koharu (Zaizen), a writer for a baby magazine. Theme: Tokyo Q Channel—"Sunao na Mamade Koi o Shiyōyo" (Let's Fall In Love As We Are).

TONBO

1988. AKA: *Dragonfly*. PRD: Mitsuru Yanai. DIR: Susumu Ōoka. SCR: Mitsuo Kuroto. CAST: Tsuyoshi Nagabuchi, Kumiko Akiyoshi, Shō Aikawa, Nobuko Sendō. CHN: TBS. DUR: 45 mins. x ca. 11 eps.: ?? October 1988–?? December 1988.

Eiji (Nagabuchi) is released on parole after two years behind bars, only to discover that his girlfriend has left him and that his former gangster associates

no longer trust him. Once prepared to go to jail to protect his chosen lifestyle, he finds himself questioning it, in another vehicle for pop star Nagabuchi, who also created and starred in THE BODYGUARD and RUN. He also sang the theme song, "Tonbo," which was a hit in its own right.

TOP STEWARDESS

1990. JPN: *Top Stewardess Monogatari*. PRD: Kazuko Nozoe. DIR: Toshiaki Kunihara. SCR: Shizuka Ōishi, Takayuki Kase. CAST: Kuniko Yamada, Miyuki Imori, Narimi Arimori, Junko Akisawa. CHN: TBS. DUR: 45 mins. x 11 eps.; Tue 17 April 1990–26 June 1990.

The adventures of Ann (Yamada), an assistant purser with JAL, who is given a new responsibility on an important airline route and must whip her three bumbling assistants into shape. Compare to the later SHINKANSEN and BIG WING.

TOSHIIE AND MATSU *

2002. JPN: *Toshiie to Matsu*. PRD: Kazuko Asano. DIR: Mineyo Satō. SCR: Hiroshi Takeyama. CAST: Toshiaki Karasawa, Nanako Matsushima, Takashi Sorimachi, Yutaka Takenouchi, Noriko Sakai, Yūki Amami, Mika Yamaguchi, Tomokazu Miura, Ken Matsudaira, Teruyuki Kagawa, Yūichirō Yamaguchi. CHN: NHK. DUR: 45 mins. x 49 eps. (first episode 60 mins.); Sun 6 January 2002–29 December 2002.

In 1550 Inuchiyo (later Toshiie, played by Karasawa) is a son of the Maeda clan in 16th-century Owari, an active and aggressive boy with a heart of gold. His younger cousin Matsu (M. Yamaguchi) is adopted into his family, and the good-natured Toshiie looks after her. Discovering that he is unlikely to stand a chance against the local warlord NOBUNAGA (Sorimachi), Toshiie volunteers to become his retainer. Returning to his hometown several years later, he meets an older Matsu (now played by Matsushima), who still cherishes a gift he gave her as a child.

Toshiie angers Nobunaga, who

orders him to commit suicide and omits him from any benefits accruing from his successful military campaigns. Toshiie remains out of favor until 1561, when he slays a bitter enemy and is forgiven. He befriends fellow retainers HIDEYOSHI (Kagawa) and Narimasa (Yamaguchi), whose wife Haru (Amami) in turn befriends Hideyoshi's wife One (Sakai) and Matsu herself, now married to Toshiie.

Eventually, after a number of intrigues and battles, Nobunaga appoints Toshiie as the leader of the Maeda clan in 1569. Suddenly become the lord and lady of their own fief, Toshiie and Matsu are forced to balance an escalating military budget. Toshiie becomes the lord of Echizen (modern Fukui Prefecture) after helping in the defeat of SHINGEN TAKEDA's cavalry, but Nobunaga asks for Matsu to stay with him so she can care for his sick concubine Yoshino.

Toshiie and Matsu's daughter Kō falls in love with Nagatane, a member of her own Maeda clan, but is ordered by Nobunaga to marry a relative of his new favorite Ieyasu (TOKUGAWA IEYASU). Although realizing his new appointment to an even bigger fief is conditional on the marriage, Toshiie refuses—wishing instead for his daughter to find happiness with Nagatane.

As the years pass, Matsu becomes a close confidante of the dying Hideyoshi, and Toshiie is made one of the five regents charged with ruling until Hideyoshi's son achieves maturity—events dealt with in the earlier AOI.

Revisiting the fertile dramatic turf of Japan's civil wars, *TaM* focuses not only on Toshiie (1538–1599), but accords equal weight to his wife in true *taiga* tradition. The final episode features a coda in 1614, the year of Matsu's death, but also that of the couple's eldest son Toshinaga, who famously plotted with Ieyasu and eventually achieved a domain that was second in size only to that of the Tokugawa Shogunate itself. There was, of course, the usual massaging of plots and facts—most noticeably a reduction in

the age difference between the leads. Though Matsu is presented in the drama as only five years younger than Toshiie, the genuine historical figures were separated by a much larger gap— when they married, he was 22 and she was only 12. Broadcast in the U.S. with English subtitles on KIKU TV.

TOWN WITHOUT ANGELS
2000. JPN: *Tenshi ga Kieta Machi*. AKA: *Angels Left Town, The*. PRD: Hidehiro Kōno. DIR: Nozomu Amemiya, Tomoaki Koga, Tetsuhiro Ogimo. SCR: Yūki Shimizu. CAST: Kōichi Dōmoto, Fumiya Fujii, Noriko Sakai, Yuka Itaya. CHN: NTV. DUR: 45 mins. x ca. 11 eps.; Wed 12 April 2000–28 June 2000.
Teru (Fujii) is an autistic boy who works in a factory, pushed out into an unforgiving world when the factory is closed down. With nowhere else to go, he moves in with his brother Tetsurō (Dōmoto), a lowlife heavily in debt to loan sharks, reduced to boxing in the street for 1000 yen a minute, and wholly unprepared for the arrival of a family member in need of care and attention. As yet another disability drama, tracing its origins back through the 1990s to *Rain Man* (1988), *Town without Angels* was swamped in the schedules by the success of BEAUTIFUL LIFE the previous season. Theme: Kinki Kids—"Mō Kimi Igai Aisenai" (Don't Love Anyone But You).

TŌYAMA NO KIN-SAN
1970. PRD: Tamotsu Sugizaki, Norimichi Matsudaira, Masato Kameoka (#8–#14). DIR: Nobunori Hayashi (#1), Masatake Matsuo (#3), Takeshi Arai (#4), Toshio Masuda (#8). SCR: Ayato Imamura (#1, #3), Arata Morita (#3), Akira Ogawa (#4, #8), Masahiro Shimura (#8). CAST: Umenosuke Nakamura, Maki Mizuhara, Michiyo Kogure, Kōtarō Satomi (#1); Danjūrō Ichikawa, Ginnosuke Ichikawa, Kentarō Kudō, Miyako Tazaka (#2); Yukio Hashi, Tarō Yamada (#3); Ryōtarō Sugi, Shirō Kishibe (#4, #5); Hideki Takahashi, Susumu Miyao (#6, #7); Hiroki Matsukata, Gō Wakabayashi

(#8–#14). CHN: Asahi. DUR: 45 mins. x ca. 364 eps.; Sun 12 July 1970–30 September 1973 (#1); 7 October 1973–22 September 1974 (#2); 29 September 1974–30 March 1975 (#3); 2 October 1975–29 September 1977 (#4); 15 February 1979–18 October 1979 (#5); 8 April 1982–19 September 1985 (#6); 15 October 1985–16 September 1986 (#7); 21 April 1988–24 October 1988 (#8); 25 May 1989–30 November 1989 (#9); 5 July 1990–27 December 1990 (#10); 7 November 1991–2 July 1992 (#11, 28 eps.); 4 March 1993–16 December 1993 (#12); 9 June 1994–19 January 1995 (#13); 7 September 1995–21 March 1996 (#14).
Kinshirō Tōyama is a samurai-era playboy who loves sake. However, like MITO KŌMON and ŌOKA ECHIZEN before him, this is merely a false identity. He is really a magistrate, whose girlfriend works as a spy to find evil deeds and corruption in Edo. Not above ambushing criminals in person, Kinshirō's modus operandi normally involves baring his distinctive cherry blossom tattoo, in order to convince wrongdoers that justice has finally found them out. When brought in front of a judge (who invariably turns out to be Kinshirō himself, out of disguise), the criminals are apt to claim that there is no evidence, thereby allowing him to bare his tattoos once more, with the words "*Do you not see this blizzard of cherry blossoms?*" Realizing that the magistrate himself is a witness to their crimes, the criminals resign themselves to their fate, while Kinshirō, or "Kin-san" as he soon became known, gets to say "*Ikken rakuchaku*" (Another case solved)—Japanese TV's answer to "*Book 'em, Danno*."

The original Tōyama no Kin-san (1753–1855) was a genuine magistrate in the 1830s, whose exploits were first dramatized in an 1893 kabuki play. The character has gone on to appear in movies, plays, and particularly the novels of Tatsurō Jinde, from whose work this TV version was drawn. The series has had a number of titles,

Transparent

beginning as *Gozonji Tōyama no Kin-san* (*Behold TnK*) with Umenosuke Nakamura in the lead role, before becoming *Tōyama no Kin-san Torimonochō* (*Investigations of TnK*) once the role passed in the second series to kabuki actor Danjūrō Ichikawa XII. Combining the two elements with *Gozonji Kin-san Torimonochō* for season three, Yukio Hashi took over the title role, only to hand it over once more to Ryūtarō Sugi in the simply named *TnK*. Sugi stayed with the role until the seventh series, when he was replaced by Hideki Takahashi.

With the death of novelist Jinde in 1986, the series was rebranded *TnK II,* and the same period saw the release of a sci-fi anime spin-off, known in English as *Samurai Gold* (*AE). The 9th to the 14th series featured Hiroki Matsukata, and were renamed *Meibugyō Tōyama no Kin-san* (*Famous Judge TnK*).

Matsukata returned in 1997 for *TnK versus the Lady Rat* (*Tōyama no Kin-san vs. Onna Nezumi*), in which he himself is falsely accused of a crime, and robber's daughter Kon (Yūko Kotegawa) dons a disguise in order to locate the true culprit. A second season featured Kon and Kin-san teaming up to fight

crime, in a franchise that remains as long-lasting as **HANSHICHI** and **HAGURE KEIJI**.

TRANQUIL SCENE, A

1990. JPN: *Nagi no Kōkei.* PRD: Takako Kitazaki. DIR: Kōhei Hisano. SCR: Eizaburō Shiba. CAST: Yoshiki Kobayashi, Machiko Kyō, Shigeru Yazaki, Midori Kiuchi, Saori Tsuchiya, Jun Negami. CHN: Asahi. DUR: 45 mins. x 6 eps.; Thu 8 February 1990–15 March 1990.

Nobuko (Kyō) has looked after her school teacher husband Jōtarō (Kobayashi) for more than forty years of their marriage. One day, encouraged by Narumi (Negami), a lecturer at a culture center, Nobuko decides to become independent from her husband. Based on a story by Aiko Satō.

TRANSPARENT

2002. JPN: *Satorare.* PRD: Arihide Yokose, Kōichi Tōta, Tetsuya Kuroda. DIR: Masataka Takamaru, Renpei Tsukamoto, Naomi Tamura. SCR: Masaya Ozaki, Reiko Yoshida. CAST: Mayu Tsuruta, Jō Odagiri, Uno Kanda, Hiroko Hatano, Jun Fubuki, Tetta Sugimoto. CHN: Asahi. DUR: 45 mins. x

10 eps.; Thu 4 July 2002–12 September 2002.

In near-future Japan, the entire country becomes involved in a coverup. The government reveals that certain individuals with genius-level intelligence are vitally important national treasures, and should be afforded all possible help in getting on with their work— which can include scientific breakthroughs, works of artistic genius, and inventions that bring massive foreign investment into Japan. There's just one snag: the geniuses have a crippling side effect to their high IQs, which causes them to inadvertently broadcast their innermost thoughts to everyone around them. Were they to find out, the embarrassment could destroy them—consequently, the "transparents" are kept separate in remote small towns, each of which receives tax breaks if the inhabitants conspire to pretend that nothing unusual is going on.

Kenichi (Odagiri) is one such transparent, a brilliant biotechnician who has annoyed his minders by pigheadedly insisting on a career as a surgeon. His handlers try desperately to conceive of a way for him to change his mind—each day that he practices as a normal doctor is another day he won't be inventing new vaccines, while the hospital staff will never permit him to fully qualify because his telepathic affliction makes it impossible for him to keep bad news from his patients. Eventually running out of options, the government sends in Yōko (Tsuruta), an undercover military psychiatrist whose job it is to change his mind at any cost.

Although dramatic parallels are most obvious in **FROM THE HEART**, *Transparent*'s origins lie in a story by Makoto Satō, which achieved greater recognition when it was turned into the 2001 movie of the same name by **BAYSIDE SHAKEDOWN** director Katsuyuki Motohiro. However, the underlying theme of *Transparent*, that Big Brother is busily watching the hero's every move, actually owes more to *The Truman Show* (1998).

TREMBLING FEELING, A

1995. JPN: *Yureru Omoi*. PRD: Tetsuo Ichikawa. DIR: Akira Sakazaki. SCR: Michiko Nasu. CAST: Yōko Minamino, Tetsuya Bessho, Keiko Oginome, Hiroshi Takano, Maju Ozawa. CHN: TBS. DUR: 45 mins. x 11 eps.; Fri 13 January 1995–24 March 1995.
Lady lawyer Kanako (Minamino) marries her boss and inherits a four-year-old stepson. Though her marriage initially seems like bliss, she soon realizes that she has also inherited a cantankerous father-in-law and an interfering sister-in-law. Theme: ZARD—"Just Believe in Love."

TRICK

2000. PRD: Kiyoshi Kurata, Kōji Makita, Akihiro Yamauchi. DIR: Yukihiko Tsutsumi, Hiroaki Hobo. SCR: Kōji Makita, Makoto Hayashi. CAST: Yukie Nakama, Hiroshi Abe, Katsuhisa Namase, Yōko Nogiwa. CHN: Asahi. DUR: 45 mins. x 21 eps.; Fri 7 July 2000–15 September 2000 (#1); 11 January 2002–22 March 2002 (#2).
Circus conjuror Naoko Yamada (Nakama) finds herself jobless and in debt, until she sees a small ad from physicist Jirō Ueda (Abe), who offers to pay a reward to any persons who can scientifically convince him that they have psychic powers. Naoko successfully fools him and collects the reward, only to discover that the competition was itself a ruse, designed to find Jirō a genuine psychic to help him on a mission. His colleague's daughter has been indoctrinated into a sinister religious cult, and Jirō needs someone with ESP to help him investigate the cult leader Sumiko Kirishima. Realizing that she will not be able to admit she cannot help him without forfeiting the reward, Naoko prepares to storm out, only for Jirō to beg her to stay, claiming that he only has four days to live. Sumiko has cursed him, and since she did so while floating in midair, he has reason to believe that her powers certainly are genuine.

Back at her apartment, Naoko discovers that Jirō has paid off her out-standing rent, obligating her to help him. She reluctantly agrees to accompany him to the cult headquarters, where the couple incur the wrath of Sumiko and are forced to go on the run from a murderous and vengeful religious organization.

Crossing DEVIL'S KISS with UNSOLVED CASES (or if you prefer, *Jonathan Creek* with *The X-Files*), *Trick* soon returned for a second season in which Naoko continues to solve mysteries using her knowledge of magic and sleight-of-hand. A movie followed in November 2002, in which the pair are invited to portray gods in a local festival, only to find themselves in a village where all the inhabitants genuinely believe themselves to be divine. Theme: Chihiro Onizuka—"Gekkō" (Moonlight).

TRIPLE FIGHTER

1972. PRD: Akira Tsuburaya, Takeshi Shimizu. DIR: Tatsumi Andō, Toshitsugu Suzuki, Kanji Ōtsuka. SCR: Bunzō Wakatsuki, Keisuke Fujikawa, Tadashi Kondō, Setsuko Nakagawa. CAST: Hiroshi Takizawa, Kōsaburō Onokawa, Mayumi Fue, Hideto Ishii, Shōichi Yoshinaka. CHN: TBS. DUR: 10 mins. x 26 eps.; Mon 3 July 1972–25 December 1972.
Desiring to rule the entire universe, invaders from Planet Devil use an army of "Demon Monsters" to carry out their bidding. Down on Earth, the Space Attack Team (SAT) is formed to protect the world from the Demons—the Japan bureau of the SAT comprises the three siblings Tetsuo (Takizawa), Yūji (Onokawa), and Yuri (Fue), who are actually alien agents from the friendly Planet M. Transforming into the Green, Red, and Orange Fighters, the three agents save the planet from regular monsters of the week, in the style of the same studio's ULTRAMAN.

TROUBLESOME

1977. JPN: *Komattana*. PRD: N/C. DIR: Takamasa Suzuki. SCR: Yukio Doi. CAST: Rieko Hiramatsu, Tomono Itō, Michiko Tsushima, Eiko Yamagishi, Kazuki

Saitō. CHN: NHK. DUR: 20 mins. x 12 eps.; Mon 7 March 1977–24 March 1977.
Thirteen-year-old Momoko (Hiramatsu) lives with her mother (Itō), who runs a fashion school, selfish grandmother (Tsushima), and Miss Yamamoto (Yamagishi). Momoko is attracted to her classmate Saburō Noda (Saitō) because his name is similar to idol singer Gorō Noguchi (himself). Based on the novel of the same title by Aiko Satō, with music by Kenichi Kumagai.

TROUBLESOME TEACHER

1994. JPN: *Sensei wa Wagamama*. PRD: Takayuki Urai. DIR: Osamu Tsuji. SCR: Akira Momoi. CAST: Yūko Natori, Masaki Kyōmoto, Tomoya Nagase, Kaori Takahashi, Masahiro Matsuoka. CHN: Asahi. DUR: 45 mins. x 12 eps.; Mon 4 July 1994–30 August 1994.
A new principal introduces sweeping changes at an old-fashioned girls' school, transforming it overnight into a coed establishment. Haruki (Nagase from TOKIO) and his two friends are the first three boys to begin their studies at what has previously been an all-female establishment. Theme: Hiromasa Ijichi—"Ano Natsu no Futari" (That Summer's Couple).

TROUBLESOME WOMEN

1992. JPN: *Wagamama na Onnatachi*. PRD: N/C. DIR: Masaaki Odagiri. SCR: Miyoko Nagase. CAST: Yūko Kotegawa, Gitan Ōtsuru, Satomi Tezuka, Masaki Kanda, Kumiko Yamashita. CHN: Fuji. DUR: 45 mins. x 11 eps.; Thu 15 October 1992–24 December 1992.
Junko (Kotegawa) tires of marriage to Seiichirō (Kanda), and decides to divorce him after five years together. She meets Chitose (Tezuka) and Midori (Yamashita), two women the same age as her, and the three unlikely friends decide that they will cooperate in creating their own rules and in searching for a lifestyle that pleases *them*, not society at large. Theme: EPO—"Ano Asa, Kaze ni Fukarete" (That Blustery Morning).

TURBORANGER

1989. JPN: *Kōsoku Sentai Turboranger*. AKA: *High-Speed Battle Team Turboranger*. PRD: Kyōzō Utsunomiya, Takeyuki Suzuki. DIR: Takao Nagaishi, Shōhei Tōjō, Kiyoshi Arai, Masao Minowa. SCR: Hirohisa Soda, Kunio Fujii, Toshiki Inoue, Asami Watanabe. CAST: Kenta Satō, Fumiaki Ganaha, Keiji Asakura, Junichirō Katagiri, Shigeko Kinohara, Takeru Watabe, Yoshinori Tanaka, Masako Morishita. CHN: Asahi. DUR: 25 mins. x 51 eps.; Sat 25 February 1989–23 February 1990. Two thousand years ago, the evil Demon tribes were defeated by an alliance of humans and fairies. In order to prevent the human race from destroying itself, the power of the fairies was sealed away. The fairy Sealon, however, has recruited five noble teenagers from Class 3A at Musashino High and bestowed special powers and vehicles upon them, so that they can form the Turboranger team to protect the Earth from the resurgent power of the Demons. Enriki (Satō) is Red Turbo, captain of the school baseball team and wielder of the GT Sword. Daichi (Ganaha) is Black Turbo who fights with the T Hammer. Yōhei (Asakura) is Blue Turbo, heartthrob captain of the school swimming team and a deadly shot with the J Gun. Shunsuke (Katagiri) is Yellow Turbo, star of the school gymnastics team and wielder of the B Bow-Gun. Haruna (Kinohara) is Pink Turbo, president of the school student council, leader of the majorettes, and wielder of the deadly W Stick. The team's five Turbo Machine automobiles launch from their base and combine make the Turbo Robo, but the base itself is also a transforming robot and can re-form to create the truly massive Turbo Builder. Perhaps there is some connection to the previous year's Hollywood movie *Big*, in which Tom Hanks's character ridiculed the notion of a transforming building ... *nothing* is too ridiculous for a Super Sentai show! They also had a larger mobile jet vehicle, the Rugger Fighter, which could transform into the Big Rugger Gun, yet another giant robot.

Their enemies comprise the various different Demon tribes, reunited under a new leader, the evil Emperor Rargon (voiced by Watabe). Each provides a monster of the week to fight the Turboranger team, aided by the many cannon fodder Oolah minions. Based "on an idea by Saburō Yade," and featuring music by Akihiko Yoshida. *Turboranger* was preceded in the Super Sentai continuity by **LIVEMAN** and followed by **FIVEMAN**.

TURN AROUND AND HE'LL BE THERE

1993. JPN: *Furikaereba Yatsu ga Iru*. PRD: Shizuo Sekiguchi. DIR: Keita Kōno. SCR: Kōki Mitani. CAST: Yūji Oda, Masahiko Nishimura, Ken Ishiguro, Takeshi Kaga, Akiho Sendō, Yuki Matsushita. CHN: Fuji. DUR: 45 mins. x 11 eps.; Wed 13 January 1993–24 March 1993. Genius surgeon Kōtarō Shima (Oda) is a pragmatist who regards medicine as a mere tool to earn money—compare to the mercenary doctor *Black Jack* (*AE). His colleague Gen Ishikawa (Ishiguro) is an idealist who believes that doctors have a sacred duty, leading to numerous conflicts between the two. Gen is often scandalized by Kōtarō's words and deeds, and frequently reports him to chief surgeon Nakagawa (Kaga, who would reprise the role in **NINZABURŌ FURUHATA**), who merely waves off his complaints.

Gen eventually discovers evidence that there is a sinister reason for Nakagawa's disinterest. A botched operation by Nakagawa once led to Kōtarō misdiagnosing a patient as brain dead and turning off the life-support machine—an incident leading both surgeons to cover for each other in a pact of mutually assured destruction. Meanwhile, Gen himself causes a patient's death through malpractice, pushing him onto a stressful run of meetings, accusations, and an eventual out of court settlement as the hospital management avoids legal action.

Believing the stress has given him a stomach ulcer, he consults with colleagues, who agree with him—all except Kōtarō who bluntly tells him that he has cancer.

Theater dramatist Kōki Mitani's second drama series hides a revenge tragedy premise beneath hospital trappings, as two fierce rivals duel for ward supremacy. Gen plans to have Kōtarō fired for taking kickbacks from a medical supply company, but Kōtarō skillfully manages to pin the blame on fellow doctor Hiraga (Nishimura). As Hiraga is fired, the desperate Gen leaks to the press the true story that Kōtarō euthanized an incurably ill patient, leading Kōtarō to face inevitable resignation.

However, Kōtarō is called back to the hospital when Gen begins vomiting blood—he is the only surgeon who can save him, in a homage to **WHITE TOWER**. Gen refuses to sign a consent form, causing Kōtarō to shrug and walk out with his customary coldness, only for colleagues to talk Gen into agreeing. The operation is successful, leading the two antagonists to call an embarrassed truce on the hospital ward, but as Kōtarō prepares to head home, he is repeatedly stabbed in the back by the vengeful Hiraga.

Predating *E.R.* (NHK, 1995) with its day per episode per week time structure and the writer's own **KING'S RESTAURANT** with its almost theatrically low number of sets, Kōki Mitani's drama serial gained a respectable 22.7% peak rating. Since one of the leads was presumed dead, fans were surprised by the appearance of a feature-length TV special on 29 December 1993 that picked up the story shortly after Kōtarō's stabbing, as the dying surgeon crawls through the snow toward a phone box and remembers many years earlier, on a day he agreed to remove a bullet from a wounded gangster when he should have been preparing for a complex heart operation. Theme: Chage and Aska—"Yah Yah Yah."

24 EYES

1974. JPN: *Nijūyon no Hitomi*. PRD: Masaharu Morita. DIR: Kazuya Satō. SCR: Sumie Tanaka. CAST: Keiko Sugita, Tomoko Ayano, Isao Tamagawa, Masaaki Okabe, Kō Hamada. CHN: NHK. DUR: 25 mins. x 12 eps.; 11 November 1974–20 November 1974 (#1); 5 January 1976–14 January 1976 (#2).

In 1928, the sleepy island of Shōdoshima is shaken up by the arrival of Miss Ōishi (Sugita), a new school teacher with scandalous modern views and ideas. She is an immediate hit with the twelve schoolchildren in her care, who are determined to visit her when she injures her leg. It is only then that they realize just how far she has to cycle to teach them each day—they find out the hard way when they have to walk it.

As with any other drama that spans the war years, (compare to **PEARL BEAUTY**), the innocent beginnings of *24 Eyes* soon take a new direction. This was the original author's intention all along; the story began as a novel by pacifist Sakae Tsuboi, motivated by the sight of Japan re-arming during the 1950s, with apparent amnesia about the horrors of World War II. The second half of the story aired just over 12 months later, with an older Miss Ōishi leaving teaching to become a housewife and struggling to make ends meet with her mother-in-law, as her husband is conscripted. She remains in touch with the class of children that she originally taught and frets maternally about what is to become of the boys in the class as they grow to manhood. After World War II has brought many tragedies, she comes out of retirement to teach once more and finds herself teaching a class that contains several relatives of her original students.

Adapted into movies in 1954 and 1987 (as *Children on the Island*), and as an anime in 1980 (*AE), *24 Eyes* remains a perennial favorite with Japanese audiences. Part of its appeal lies in its accidental resemblance to the traditional tales of hardship and depri-vation such as **OSHIN** or **INOCHI: LIFE**, and it certainly ticks all the boxes of women's melodrama—start with pre-war proto-feminism, show stoic bravery in the face of food shortages and wartime utility, followed by the loss of loved ones through the horrors of battle, and a weepy denouement in which a life is found not to have been wasted. This final high point, of course, is also a common feature in classroom dramas from **KINPACHI SENSEI** to **GTO**, ensuring that *24 Eyes* has a place in most genre by genre accounts of 20th-century television. However, its most impressive accomplishment lies in its use of the teacher-oriented framing device, which essentially allows Ōishi and the viewer to travel in time through important moments in her students' lives.

24 HOUR EMERGENCY ROOM

1999. JPN: *Kyūmei Byōtō 24 Ji*. PRD: Akira Wada, Kumiko Nakajima. DIR: Daisuke Tajima. SCR: Kiyoshi Fukuda. CAST: Yōsuke Eguchi, Yasuko Matsuyuki, Hiroshi Abe, Hideaki Itō, Nana Katase, Tomoko Tabata, Hiroyuki Miyabe, Risa Sudō, Tae Kimura, Fumiyo Kohinata, Nanako Matsushima. CHN: Fuji. DUR: 45 mins. x 24 eps.; Tue 5 January 1999–23 March 1999 (#1); 3 July 2001–18 September 2001 (#2).

Hospital trainee Kaede (Matsushima) witnesses a horrific accident on the way to her first day at Kōhoku Hospital Emergency Ward. She is unable to accomplish her duties in the ambulance, but hands the patient over to supercop doctor Issei Shindō (Eguchi), who saves the patient's life and informs her of Kōhoku's perma-nent state of crisis—"*Open 24 hours a day, 365 days a year, and that includes New Year and Golden Week.*" Meanwhile, rumors among the new staff members that Doctor Shindō is dating a patient turn out to be a misunderstanding of personal tragedy: Shindō's wife Saki (Misa Takada) is in an irreversible veg-etative state on one of the hospital life-support machines, making the

24 Hour Emergency Room

handsome Shindō a *de facto* widower.

Made five years after the American *E.R.* premiered on NHK, this superb and unashamed clone even adopts a similar set of archetypes—genius sur-geon Shindō, harassed chief resident Odagiri, overworked deputy Kanbayashi (Kohinata), comedy maver-ick Baba (Miyabe), rich hospital man-ager's daughter Sakurai (Sudō), kind-hearted intern Yabe (Itō), super-capable chief nurse Saeko (Kimura), and stern-but-goodhearted hospital chief Jingū. Director Tajima saturates the elevated entranceway in light, shooting the white-clad staff as if they were angels on a mission, and it is somehow moving to see the staff bow every time they must call a time of death—an intriguing mix of blatant copying and innovative remodeling for a different culture. It even pastiches other Japanese shows—Dr. Baba sets off to do good deeds in Africa like **DOCTOR HIIRAGI**, only to return with a recurring bowel infection.

In the second season, snooty cardio-thoracic specialist Dr. Tamiki Kosaka (Matsuyuki) is, in her opinion, "demot-ed" to the E.R., and tries to convince Dr. Shindō to return from his leave of absence. She claims that he has a duty to stay in medicine, though her true motive is to increase her own chances of rotating back to heart surgery. Shindō's comatose wife has since died, and he agrees to return, though Kosaka is forced to remain on the E.R. staff as the love interest of the season.

As in other hospital shows, transient patients bring weekly subplots of their own, including a doctor who pricks herself with an infected needle, a resentful fire chief who blames the hospital for the loss of one of his men, and an assault victim who accidentally receives a cubicle next to her wounded attacker. Japanese characterization also brings some original moments— notably a salaryman determined to commit suicide, and a dying cancer patient obsessively folding lucky *origami* paper cranes because *"nobody else will do it for her."* Anyone who has struggled to learn Japanese will also appreciate the timeless moment when Yabe tries to soothe a widow who suspects that her husband died in bed with a mistress. Secretly reading the records over her shoulder, he lies that her husband died asking for his beloved wife Fumiko, only to discover later the name should have been pronounced *Ayako*.

The show has some wonderful throwaway moments, such as a ghoulish insurance saleswoman who stalks the staff, and an entire student fancy-dress party that comes down with food poisoning, thereby swamping the already chaotic ward with girls dressed as sexy nurses. There is also a distinct obsession with off-the-wall solutions— Shindō likes nothing better than performing a midair tracheotomy with a coat hanger and penknife, or firing up an oxyacetylene torch to disinfect a workman's drill, with which he operates on a cranial blood clot.

For the penultimate three episodes, Kōhoku Hospital seems to become "the place where everybody knows your name," with admissions of many ex-girlfriends, old flames, and former schoolmates to crank up the emotional tension. The death of a prominent staff member is dealt with innovatively— instead of a clichéd TV funeral, donor

reps arrive to collect him like agents of the Grim Reaper, and the procession to the organ-harvesting operation takes on a moving, ritualistic quality. Unlike earlier episodes, the action also interlocks in a series of interdependent and sequential story-arcs—these excellent later episodes leading some latecomers to believe that the entire *series* took place over a single "24-hour" period. The E.R. is threatened with closure for being the only department at Kōhoku that doesn't make a profit, and the staff is encouraged to prescribe expensive medications and unnecessary treatments. As they become increasingly disillusioned, Yabe is drawn to pediatrics, while Kosaka is made an offer from an unnamed hospital in Chicago—the home of both *E.R.* and *Chicago Hope*, of course. Meanwhile, pro-E.R. candidate Jingū is running for election as hospital chief against academic Anzai, who is determined to shut it down, and Kanbayashi is found to be writing a tell-all newspaper column under the pseudonym Dr. Bean. The central crisis involves the admission of a comatose accident victim, found to have already been unconscious for over a year. His arrival leads to conflict between Yabe and Kosaka over medical ethics (is a suspected suicide attempt an implicit Do-Not-Resuscitate order?) and intense pressure to keep him comfortable—his daughter is Yabe's ex-girlfriend, now a powerful prosecutor hungry for a malpractice suit. The man is revealed to be the central witness in an infamous financial scandal—the hospital will make powerful enemies whether they cure him or kill him!

The final crisis, set a week after the three-episode multi-arc, has a phosgene gas outbreak threatening the entire district during the hospital manager elections, with staff from other departments drafted into the E.R. to assist. They are forced to confront the value of the E.R. to the hospital, both in medical and public relations terms, and there is a neat narrative closure, as Kosaka berates her former surgical colleagues with exactly the same

"Toughest Job in Medicine" pep talk she received from Shindō on arrival.

The cast returned for a feature-length New Year's Day special in 2002, in which Shindō and Baba puzzle why so many detectives should be in attendance at the admission of an eight-year-old boy who has fallen down some stairs. In fact, their patient Ryōta (Ryūnosuke Kamiki) was pushed down the stairs by Shigeru (Manabu Oshio), a criminal who attacked an office worker in the same building. Shigeru, meanwhile, has hijacked a cruise party armed with a rifle. Shindō is dropped onboard to attend to a wounded crew member, only to discover that Kosaka is already there—she is on vacation from her new Chicago posting and doing her best to help with limited materials. Shindō must dive into the water to save Kosaka's life when a SWAT team arrives with inadvisable timing and Shigeru begins firing into the crowd. Compare to NURSE STATION, WHITE SHADOW, and LEAVE IT TO THE NURSES. Peak rating: 24.0%. Theme: Dreams Come True— "Itsu no Ma ni" (When?).

29TH CHRISTMAS

1994. JPN: *29-sai no Christmas*. PRD: Kazuki Nakayama. DIR: Masayuki Suzuki. SCR: Toshio Kamata. CAST: Tomoko Yamaguchi, Toshirō Yanagiba, Yuki Matsushita. CHN: Fuji. DUR: 45 mins. x 10 eps.; Thu 20 October 1994–22 December 1994.

Noriko (Yamaguchi)'s 29th birthday turns into a nightmare when she arrives late for work, is demoted, and loses her boyfriend. She is consoled by her friends Ken (Yanagiba) and Aya (Matsushita) and moves in with them, in a drama that might at first glance appear to be a Christmas-themed romance. In fact, however, it is a gentle assertion of female independence in the spirit of IN THE NAME OF LOVE. Instead of finding a man for Christmas Eve, which has become a night for romance in modern Japanese custom, Noriko *chooses* to spend the evening with her female friends, not as lonely singletons but as friends with the power to make that decision. The drama also saw the first flourishing of the star power of Tomoko Yamaguchi, who would later appear in LONG VACATION. Peak rating: 26.9%. Theme: Mariah Carey—"All I Want For Christmas Is You."

TWINS TEACHER

1993. JPN: *Twins Kyōshi*. PRD: N/C. DIR: Ikuhiro Saitō. SCR: Taketatsu Ishihara, Yoshikazu Okada. CAST: Masahiro Takashima, Ken Ishiguro, Kyōka Suzuki, Miho Kanno, Mitsuko Oka. CHN: Asahi. DUR: 45 mins. x 11 eps.; Sun 12 April 1993–28 June 1993.
School principal Mitsuko (Oka) hires teachers Takai (Ishiguro) and Kurosaki (Takashima) to turn around the fortunes of Class Two—a group of hopeless kids at the bottom of the academic leagues and notorious for bad behavior. At the time, she is unaware that the two teachers are actually twins separated as children—a somewhat pointless refinement of the KINPACHI SENSEI formula. Theme: Masahiro Takashima— "Kowarerugurai Dakishimetai" (I Want To Hug You Till It Hurts).

TWO PEOPLE

1997. JPN: *Futari*. PRD: Teruyoshi Shimura, Ryōichi Satō. DIR: Takehiko Shinjō, Ryōichi Itsukida. SCR: Noriko Yoshida. CAST: Megumi Okina, Sae Isshiki, Rena Komine, Sayaka Yamaguchi, Kenji Kohashi, Ryūichi Kawamura. CHN: Asahi. DUR: 45 mins. x 11 eps.; Mon 14 April 1997–23 June 1997.
Mika (Okina) is a shy, retiring wallflower with low self-esteem, eternally outshone by her overachieving, superpopular big sister Chizuko (Isshiki). After Chizuko is mortally injured saving Mika from an out-of-control truck, Mika is left with a bad case of survivor's guilt and the seething resentment of Chizuko's old friends. That, and the newfound ability to communicate with the dead, as the supercompetent Chizuko returns in ghost form to offer help and encouragement in Mika's new life. Her dead sister's voice saves her from a potentially dangerous encounter with a would-be rapist, but also seems to be pushing her toward a relationship with Chizuko's ex-boyfriend—is this really for Mika's good, or is Chizuko still dominating her sister's life, even from beyond the grave? The result is a sentimental but moving rip-off of *Truly Madly Deeply* (1990) and *Always* (1990). Reputedly shown unsubtitled in the U.S. on KTSF TV. Theme: Spitz—"Yume ja Nai" (Not a Dream).

U

UGLY DUCKLING *

1996. JPN: *Minikui Ahiru no Ko*. PRD: Yoshikazu Kobayashi. DIR: Tōru Hayashi. SCR: Fumie Mizuhashi. CAST: Gorō Kishitani, Takako Tokiwa, Gamon Kaai, Yōko Moriguchi, Hiromasa Taguchi. CHN: Fuji. DUR: 45 mins. x 11 eps.; Tue 16 April 1996–25 June 1996.

When girlfriend Masako (Tokiwa) moves away from Hokkaidō to pursue her dream of being a hair stylist in the big city, her country boyfriend Gansuke (Kishitani) decides to follow her there. As an elementary school teacher, he reasons that urban children could not possibly be that different from the well-behaved country kids he is used to teaching. The result is a classroom drama in the spirit of KINPACHI SENSEI, just with younger kids. Broadcast in the U.S. with English subtitles on KTSF TV. Theme: Chiharu Matsuyama—"Kimi o Wasurenai" (I Won't Forget You).

ULTIMATE LAWYER

2003. JPN: *Saigo no Bengonin*. AKA: *The Last Lawyer*. PRD: Ken Inoue, Kyō Itō, Yasuyuki Ōtsuka. DIR: Hitoshi Iwamoto, Norika Sakuma. SCR: Keiko Hata. CAST: Hiroshi Abe, Risa Sudō, Tsubasa Imai, Yūko Asano, Hideharu Ōtaki, Akio Kaneda. CHN: NTV. DUR: 45 mins. x 10 eps.; Wed 15 January 2003–19 March 2003.

Ryōko (Sudō) always wanted to be a lawyer, but instead finds herself working at a bank. Moved to the Investigation Section, she is given the job of collecting money from debtors, in the course of which she is sent to a struggling law firm. Instead of finding a huge building, she finds Kazuaki Yūdō (Abe), a good-hearted man operating out of a one-room apartment, without the money to hire a secretary or pay off his loans. Fired from her banking job, Ryōko volunteers to be Kazuaki's assistant when the glamorous Michiko (Asano) from the Japan Lawyers' Association hires him to defend a murder suspect. Toshiya (Imai) protests his innocence, but he has a previous criminal record and was a coworker of the victim at a local blacksmith's. Once Toshiya's innocence is proved by Kazuaki, he too comes to work at the law firm, in a mixture of the inadvertent work colleagues of MEN'S JOURNEY and the legal farce of HERO. Theme: hiro—"Baby Don't Cry."

ULTRA Q

1966. PRD: Eiji Tsuburaya, Hitoshi Shibusawa, Takai Soni. DIR: Hajime Tsuburaya, Kōji Kajita, Harunosuke Nakagawa, Toshihiro Iijima. SCR: Kitao Sensatsu, Tetsuo Kinjō, Masahiro Yamada, Hiroyasu Yamaura, Kyōko Kitazawa, Shōzō Uehara, Mieko Osanai. CAST: Kenji Sahara, Hiroko Sakurai, Yasuhiko Saijō, Ureo Egawa, Yoshifumi Tajima, Tadashi Okabe, Kōji Ishizaka. CHN: TBS. DUR: 25 mins. x 28 eps.; Sun 2 January 1966–14 December 1966.

"For the next 30 minutes, your eyes will apart (sic) from your body, and going into the mystery zone." Hoshikawa Airlines pilot Jun Majōme (Sahara) moonlights as a science fiction writer, occasionally finding inspiration by investigating strange phenomena in the company of his copilot Ippei (Saijō) and lady newspaper photographer Yuriko (Sakurai). The trio can also call on the advice of Professor Ichinotani (Egawa), a venerable scientist.

As audiences grew for Japanese domestic television after the 1964 Tokyo Olympics, the TBS network dabbled in reproducing the successes of other channels. After KRT's successful duplication of *The Adventures of Superman* with its MOONLIGHT MASK, TBS looked to the new show of the moment, the NTV broadcasts of *The Twilight Zone*, for a new direction. Snatching the second season of *The Twilight Zone* for itself in 1964, TBS then imitated its U.S. import with this homegrown production. Produced by Eiji Tsuburaya, whose greatest previous success had been as the special effects technician on *Godzilla*, the first planned episode of the new series was the enjoyably camp *Mammoth Flower*, which featured a giant plant like an oversized triffid, extending its roots around central Tokyo, and only defeated by Jun flying overhead in his Cessna and dropping an acid bomb. However, producers soon discarded *The Twilight Zone*'s emphasis on stories with twists in the tale or nature run wild—though *Mammoth Flower* was eventually incorporated into the series as broadcast episode #4. The original plan to imitate Rod Serling's show was shelved for a while, and eventually dusted off as UNBALANCE. Meanwhile, the untitled project in development was named in honor of "Ultra C," the name of a difficult gymnastics move that had entered Japanese slang in the wake of the Tokyo Olympics. The *Ultra Q*[uestion] series proper preferred to introduce at least one costumed monster each week that would then cause havoc while the investigators looked on. Plots included creatures awakened from prehistoric sleep, alien invaders, and everyday animals exposed to scientific widgets or potions that turned them into gigantic monsters. Forces of nature such as Gorgos the rock monster rubbed shoulders with creatures such as Mongura, formed when a garden-variety mole ingests royal jelly extracted from mutant bees. Even the more traditional thriller plots have a monster connection—it is not enough for the newly inaugurated "Inazuma" train to run out of control in episode #10, the incident has to be caused by M-1, an escaped artificially engineered lifeform that soon grows into a monster. Similarly, a story that clearly started out as a "ghost ship" chiller along the lines of the *Flying Dutchman*, is soon pepped up with the arrival onboard of a giant bird.

With a long 15-month production schedule that swiftly used up Tsuburaya's supply of monster suits as fast as the effects department could make them, later episodes soon brought back monster "favorites" for repeat performances, or cameos with slightly altered appearances. The search for monster-free plots led to one of the series' most memorable stories, in which Yuriko investigates the "1/8 Project," and discovers that it is a science experiment designed to miniaturize the population of Japan in order to free up more living space and allow the better distribution of food. Needless to say, Yuriko is soon miniaturized, allowing the producers to shoot an entire episode in which her fellow investigators get to stomp around a model city looking for her. The ending of that episode features Yuriko waking up to discover it "was all a dream," only to look out the window at the teeming population of the city below. . . .

The later *Ultra Q* episodes also used several more monster-free episodes that were originally filmed for the abortive *Unbalance,* including a tale of demonic possession in which the only "monster" is a psychic schoolgirl. However, TBS wanted more monsters, forcing Tsuburaya to come up with a means of defeating a terrifying menace every week. The straightforward answer was to find a superhero who could deal with them on equal terms. Accordingly, the 28th episode, a complicated tale about an innocuous looking train that could travel through time and relative dimensions in space, was dropped from the initial broadcast run in favor of a pilot episode for a new show. Utilizing a new version of the *Ultra Q* credit sequence and part of the series name in order to break the audience in gently, the new series was called **ULTRAMAN**. *Ultra Q* was brought back as a color movie in 1990.

ULTRAMAN *
1966. PRD: Eiji Tsuburaya, Hajime Tsuburaya, Kazuo Tsuburaya. DIR: Hajime Tsuburaya, Toshihiro Iijima, Toshitsugu Suzuki, Akio Jissōji, Yūzō Higuchi, Shingo Matsubara, Teruyoshi Ishii. SCR: Tetsuo Kinjō, Shinichi Sekizawa, Masahiro Yamada, Ryū Minamigawa, Keisuke Fujikawa, Bunzō Wakatsuki, Tarō Kaidō, Shōzō Uehara, Hiroshi Yamaguchi, Kazunori Itō, Budd Robertson, John Douglas, Chiaki Konaka, Hidenori Miyazawa, Hideyuki Kawakami, Minoru Kawasaki, Hiromi Muraishi, Kazunori Saitō, Akio Satsugawa, Keiichi Hasegawa. CAST: Susumu Kurobe, Akihiko Hirata, Shōji Kobayashi, Masaya Nihei, Hiroko Sakurai, Ichiki Ishii; Susumu Fujita; Kōji Moritsugu, Yuriko Hishimi; Jirō Dan; Keiji Takamine, Mitsuko Hoshi; Ryū Manatsu; Hatsunori Hasegawa, Hitoshi Nakayama, Sayoko Hagiwara, Mayumi Asano, Ikuko Wada, Eri Ishida; Dore Krause; Kane Kosugi, Sandra Gilbert, Rob Roy Fitzgerald; Hiroshi Nagano, Mio Takagi, Akitoshi Ōtaki, Takami Yoshimoto, Shigeki Kagemaru, Yukio Masuda; Takeshi Tsuruno; Takeshi Yoshioka; Takayasu Sugiura. CHN: TBS, BS-2, NTV, MBS. DUR: 25 mins. x 495+ eps.; Sun 10 July 1966–9 April 1967 (#1); 1 October 1967–8 September 1968 (#2/Seven); 2 April 1971–31 March 1972 (#3/Returns); 7 April 1972–30 March 1973 (#4/A); 6 April 1973–5 April 1974 (#5/Tarō); 12 April 1974–28 March 1975 (#6/Leo); 2 April 1980–25 March 1981 (#7/"80"); 23 December 1991–4 January 1992 (#8/Great—on BS-2); 8 April 1995–1 July 1995 (#9/Powered); 7 September 1996–30 August 1997 (#10/Tiga); 6 September 1997–29 August 1998 (#11/Dyna); 5 September 1998–28 August 1999 (#12/Gaia); 7 July 2001–8 June 2002 (#13/Cosmos—see below).

Ultraman is a kindly alien from the Land of Light, who travels three million light-years from his home nebula of M-78 to help the people of Earth defend themselves against monsters. His mission begins badly when he collides with an aircraft piloted by good-hearted Earthman Hayata (Kurobe). To save the life of his innocent victim, Ultraman merges with the dying human—the new symbiotic lifeform created retains Hayata's consciousness, but also permits Ultraman to lie dormant inside him, unaffected by the atmosphere of Earth, which would otherwise prove fatal to him. Hayata joins the Science Special Investigation Team, an organization devoted to protecting the Earth from scientific disasters, alongside Captain Muramatsu (Kobayashi), marksman Arashi (Ishii), comic relief gadget man Ide (Nihei) and token female communications officer Akiko (Sakurai). When Hayata's colleagues find themselves in a life-

© 1966 Tsuburaya Productions

Ultraman

combat between men in rubber suits standing in the ruins of model cities. *Ultraman*'s best "loved" foe was probably the alien Baltan, which resembled a cross between a beetle and a lobster, though the show's most famous guest-star was Godzilla, who appeared in episode 10 as "Jirass" (U.S.: Kira), disguised with the addition of a collar frill, which Ultraman soon pulled off anyway. The hero's most dangerous foe was arguably Zetton, the space dinosaur who broke his Color Timer in the final episode, leading to the arrival of Ultraman Zoffy, leader of the Space Garrison, who took Ultraman home.

Ultraman's associate *Ultraman Seven* soon arrived on Earth as a replacement—for Tsuburaya is keen to stress that later *Ultraman* serials are not "sequels," but self-contained stories that happen to share continuity. It may sound like an arbitrary distinction, but every *Ultraman* is someone's first, and viewers like to think they are not simply watching a remake. Ultra Seven takes on the identity of Dan Moroboshi (Moritsugu), who secretly defends the Earth from yet more invaders, while trying not to fall in love with the pretty Anne (Hishimi). Never calling on help from his alien brothers and taking a considerable amount of punishment in his battles, *Seven* is regarded with hindsight by many fans as one of the peaks of the franchise. However, ratings at the time showed a notable dip, and TBS determined that *Seven* would be the end of *Ultraman*.

The Tsuburaya studio attempted to jump-start other franchises such as **MIGHTY JACK** and **OPERATION MYSTERY** in the years that followed, only to resurrect Ultraman with a third season *Ultraman Returns* (1971), competing with the new **MASKED RIDER** series for children's affection and pocket money. Although, as the title implies, the studio initially planned to bring back the original, it was decided that it would be more profitable for merchandising purposes to create an all-new character—eventually named Jack after years of being known simply as "the one

threatening situation, he is able to secretly use his Beta Capsule to transform into Ultraman, growing into a 40-meter tall alien giant in a red and silver suit, who is able to take on the giant city-stomping monster menaces on their own terms, defeating them with his Specium Ray and Ultra Slash. However, the moment Hayata transforms, the Earth's savage environment begins to affect Ultraman, leading the alien to develop a blue three-minute Color Timer that sits on his chest at all times. When the blue timer turns red and begins to flash, Ultraman has only seconds left of his three-minute safe period, and must swiftly dispatch his enemy or risk injury and death.

Film effects specialist Eiji Tsuburaya was originally approached by Fuji TV in the early 1960s and asked to come up with an idea for a weekly mystery series. His initial pitch was for a series called *Woo* (or possibly "*U*"), about a

creature from Andromeda who comes to Earth to save the planet from monsters. He intended to follow it up in later seasons with two other tales of alien superheroes, with working titles of *Rappa* and *Space Horse*. *Woo* fell through at Fuji, by which time Tsuburaya had already invested in an expensive optical printer to set up special effects. He was able to sell the device to Fuji's rival channel TBS, who, having acquired the technology to make a monster show, shelved the **UNBALANCE** show then in development and instead authorized the production of **ULTRA Q**. Six months into *Ultra Q*, the ghost of *Woo* reasserted itself with the first broadcast of *Ultraman*. Many monsters were set up as sympathetic creatures, desperate to escape from the Earth or otherwise avoid human contact. However, whatever their inner motivations, many were also threats to human civilization that needed to be stopped, normally by

from the third season." Consequently, although the monster-of-the-week plotting remained essentially unchanged, Ultraman Jack bonded with mechanic and would-be racing driver Hideki Gō (Dan), who "dies" in an automobile accident in episode one. The monsters were not aliens like the majority of Seven's enemies, but homegrown dangers, and the first in the franchise to appear in "families," with parents or children of earlier creatures avenging their wronged relatives.

For the fifth season, *Ultraman Ace* (aka *Ultraman A*), humble baker Seiji (Takamine) witnesses his bakery being destroyed by an attacking monster, and is then killed along with kindhearted Minami (Hoshi) when the pair try to save a wheelchair-bound hospital patient from dying beneath the wheels of a runaway truck. The pair both bond with Ultraman Ace, requiring them to touch their Ultra Rings together to transform into a creature with a man's courage and a woman's love for peace. Ace's enemies included a number of Super-Beasts created by the Yapool invaders, although Minami later revealed that she was really an agent from the Moon, and left for her home after Ace defeated the Lunatyx monster halfway through the season. Thereafter, Seiji was left to transform into Ace alone, but all through the season he called upon the help of his brothers, leading to cameos from many of the earlier Ultras.

Though many sources refer to the Ultra Family or the Ultra Brothers, few of the Ultramen are actually related. However, the hero of the fifth season, Ultraman Tarō, was genuinely the son of the Ultra rulers Ultra Father and Ultra Mother, and reputedly the cousin of Ultra Seven. The youngest of the Ultramen, and prone to repeated death scenes and revivals, Tarō's year as an agent ended when he turned in his badge to the Ultra Mother and left to *"walk the Earth."*

As the 1970s wore on, Japan began to suffer a recession, chiefly initiated by the Oil Shocks. The situation

inspired the dire portents of **JAPAN SINKS**, but also led to a round of belt-tightening in the media business. To producers with falling budgets, men kicking over model buildings started to look less appealing than the savings afforded by animated productions, and rubber monster shows began to decline even as the giant-robot anime gained in popularity. The sixth show saw the arrival of the Ultras' distant relative *Ultraman Leo* from the nebula L-77 in the constellation of Leo. Adopting Earth as his home after the destruction of his native world, Leo is tutored by Dan Moroboshi, the former Ultra Seven, now hobbling around on crutches after an accident has deprived him of his ability to transform. Made at the height of Bruce Lee's posthumous fame after *Enter the Dragon* (1973), *Ultraman Leo* concentrated on martial arts skills, and often featured its hero defeating monsters with karate alone. Taking over Seven's mission of defending the Earth, gymnastics instructor Gen (Manatsu) trains under Dan and occasionally leans on his mentor's "Ultra Willpower" as a form of telepathic backup.

Ultraman left Japanese screens after Leo, returning in an animated incarnation in 1979 (*AE), known as *The Ultraman* or sometimes *Ultraman Joneus* or Joe. Technically, this should be listed as the next season, as a recreation of its hero's costume does eventually turn up in the later live-action movie *Ultraman Monster Grand Battle.* However, his presence in the continuity is arguable, as the prologue to *Ultraman 80* claims that the Earth has been safe from monsters *"for five years."* At any rate, the *Ultraman* anime ran from 4 April 1979–26 March 1980, setting the scene for the next live-action *Ultraman* series, *Ultraman 80.*

In an unexpected homage to **KINPACHI SENSEI**, the *actual* seventh season sees a new Ultraman adopting the form of Earth schoolteacher Takeru Yamato (Hasegawa), in charge of Year One, Class E. Loved by his students,

but eternally at odds with the prissy deputy principal Kumi (Wada), Takeshi chastely pursues the pretty gym teacher Kyōko (Asano), in whose presence he becomes bashful and tongue-tied. Of course, Takeshi is not merely a schoolteacher, but moonlights as a member of the secret OGM organization, in which capacity he helps in the secret battle against space monsters and transforms into his giant form. A loner who rarely calls on the other Ultras, Ultraman 80 is later joined by Yullian, the Queen of the Land of Light, who takes the Earth name of Ryōko (Hagiwara) and gives the Ultramen one of their rare female fighting companions. Their secret identities eventually revealed, the couple return to their place of origin at the end of the series.

The eighth and ninth seasons represented attempts by the Tsuburaya studio to sell the series to foreign franchisees. The 13-episode *Ultraman Great* (aka *Ultraman: Toward the Future*) was made in Australia, and not initially broadcast on TBS in Japan, but shown on the NHK satellite channel BS-2, where little of its potential fanbase had a chance to see it. When it finally aired on TBS, it did so *after* the ninth season, further confusing continuity. Written by Noboru Aikawa and Terry Lansen and directed by Andrew Browse, *Ultraman Great* featured new hero Jack Shindō (Dore Krause?) fighting to defend a land of cacti and kangaroos from invading monsters, and unable to maintain his heroic form for longer than three minutes, this time on account of the Earth's pollution.

Ultran Seven then bizarrely went over to NTV for two 1994 TV specials, *Solar Energy Wars* and *Alien Earth*, before returning to TBS the following year for another foreign-made incarnation. *Ultraman Powered*, featured Kenichi Kai (Kosugi) defending Earth from a number of earlier monsters, dusted off for another attempt to break into the franchise in the lucrative North American market after the success of the **MIGHTY MORPHIN' POWER RANGERS**. In fact, however, some earlier *Ultraman* serials had already reached the U.S., including the original, which was dubbed for U.S. TV by long-time anime adaptor Peter Fernandez, and *Ultra Seven*, which was shown in Hawaii and then redubbed for Turner Network Television.

The franchise entered a period of self-parody with *Ultraman Zearth*, a 30th anniversary movie released as part of a Tsuburaya triple bill in 1996 and followed by *Zearth 2* in 1997. In it, gas station janitor Katsuto is obsessed with cleanliness, an interest which conceals his secret identity as Zearth, an Ultra who has come to Earth to help clean up the planet's pollution, and the terrible monsters it sometimes engenders.

The franchise moved to MBS for the tenth season, *Ultraman Tiga*, which discarded much of the previous continuity and started with a clean slate. In the year 2007 (2049 in the U.S. dub), Tiga is an ancient giant of light brought back to life in the form of human agent Daigo (Nagano from V6), in order to defend the Earth from an ancient evil. This Ultra is able to assume different modes, discarding power for speed in Purple Mode or switching speed for power in his heavy duty Red Mode, in addition to his normal Omni Mode position, which includes both colors. The only one of three stone Ultra statues rescued from the Tiga pyramid in Japan before monsters destroy it, Tiga becomes the weapon of choice used by GUTS, the Global Unlimited Task Squad. With many scripts from anime scenarists such as Chiaki Konaka of *Armitage III* (*AE), and Akio Satsugawa of the contemporary hit series *Evangelion* (*AE), *Tiga* drew its influences from the popular anime of the day—somewhat ironically in that, for example, the bio-robots in *Evangelion* had time limits on their operational power in homage to the original *Ultraman*. GUTS Captain Megumi Iruma (Takagi) is constantly at odds with her superiors in the Terrestrial Peaceable Consortium, leaving tactical decisions to her deputy

Munekata (Ōtaki), who is in charge of a group of misfits that includes Osaka-born comic-relief technology geek Horii (Masuda), impossibly handsome ladies man Shinjō (Kagemaru), and Rena (Yoshimoto), the female pilot who is the best soldier of the bunch.

Continued in movies and on video, *Tiga* was followed by the 11th season *Ultraman Dyna*, clearly intended as a direct sequel and featuring several returning characters and situations. Now set in the year 2017, as humanity terraforms Mars and heads out into space on the "Neo Frontier," *Dyna* features Earth boy Shin Asuka (Tsuruno), who teams up with some surviving members of the GUTS team, now known as SuperGUTS, as well as the children of the previous season's Horii. Shin's interest in fighting monsters from space is not merely altruistic, his baseball-loving father was lost in space many years ago in an early encounter with aliens, and Shin maintains that he might still be alive out there. During reruns, *Dyna* was complemented with a series of one-minute infomercials under the title *Ultraman Nice*, in which an all-new comic-relief Ultra fought a number of new monsters.

For the 12th season, *Ultraman Gaia*, the producers ignored both the back-story of the original series and the newly-established continuity of the *Tiga/Dyna* days, now setting their story in the not particularly futuristic year of 2000. *Gaia* features both the titular Ultra and his occasional ally Ultraman Agul, a completely blue Ultra whose loyalties lie not with the human race, but with planet Earth itself. This makes for occasional internal conflicts, as Agul is not above letting the entire human race die if it will improve chances for the Terran biosphere as a whole. Capitalizing on the same end-of-the-century angst that informs **MOON SPIRAL**, the story has a think-tank realize that the Earth faces imminent destruction at the hands of an approaching evil. Forming the cumbersomely titled Globalcentric Universal Alliance against Radical Destruction

(or GUARD), the authorities dispatch eXpanded Interceptive Guards (or XIGs) to defend the planet, one of whom is genius scientist Gamu (Yoshioka), who works alongside a number of specialized three-man teams, including Lightning, Falcon, Crow, Marlin, and Seagull, taking the cast roster up into crowded double figures. Notable for a number of foreign actors as permanent Japanese-speaking team members, the series concludes with an incredible Armageddon, as the skies are darkened by an approaching supermonster, and the human race unites with Ultras and all the fearsome monsters of the Earth, who have come out to fight to save their own planet from alien invasion.

Bad luck struck in the 13th season, *Ultraman Cosmos*, which was released at roughly the same time as the *Ultraman Cosmos: First Contact* movie, and was deliberately first broadcast on 7 July 2001, the centenary of the birth of studio founder Eiji Tsuburaya. In an attempt to avoid increasingly strict censures on "onscreen violence," the *Cosmos* series introduced Musashi (Sugiura), whose Ultra transformation often took the pacifist "Luna" Mode, in which form he was unable to harm any opponents. The later Corona and Eclipse Modes permitted more traditional fighting, but it was the Luna Mode that caused the greatest controversy, first because an Ultraman that tried not to fight was not popular with many old-school fans, but mainly because of later events that would cripple the series in 2002. The show was pulled off-air in June 2002 after lead actor Sugiura was arrested by Osaka Prefecture Police. An acquaintance of Sugiura's younger brother accused him of assault two years earlier, when the 19-year-old Sugiura had supposedly attacked the boy in retaliation for the theft of some money. While inquiries continued, *Cosmos* was concluded in two hastily assembled final episodes, dropping all of Sugiura's appearances. Similarly, the film distributor Shōchiku, sitting on the completed

second *Cosmos* movie *The Blue Planet*,
rereleased the film to Japanese cinemas with Sugiura's scenes hacked out.
In the new version, the child actor who
played the young Musashi is shown
scenes from his future—cunningly
ensuring that his adult face is never
seen. MBS filled the on-air gap left by
the show's departure by screening
Ultraman Neos, a seven-year-old failed
Ultra pitch, mothballed by Tsuburaya
as a direct-to-video title, and only dusted off to plug the hole left by *Cosmos*.

However, the tables had turned by
the end of June, when it was revealed
that the plaintiff had withdrawn much
of his previous accusations against
Sugiura. Those who had so readily
exiled the actor from the public eye
now discovered that his accuser was
indeed a thief, and that while big
brother Sugiura did not deny giving
him a bloody nose in an earlier incident, the plaintiff's actual injuries had
been sustained in a wholly unrelated
brawl with ten other people, which
took place at a time when Sugiura had
demonstrably spent the entire day on a
film set on the other side of town. As a
result, the red-faced MBS reversed its
previous decision, ignored the continuity problems caused by the previous
"ending," pulled *Neos* from the air, and
ran the rest of *Cosmos* as originally
intended. The Sugiura footage was also
restored to the movie, and the series
limped to its close later in the year
than initially planned. A third movie,
Ultraman Cosmos vs. Ultraman Justice
(2003), features Suigiura again, who
now prefers that his given name is pronounced Taiyō, not Takayasu.

There have been many other spin-
offs, cartoons, movies, TV specials, and
reunions in the course of *Ultraman*'s
36-year history, but space does not
allow for us to cover them here. In
spite of the ignominious scandal over
its most recent incarnation, *Ultraman*
remains a central pillar of Japanese TV
and arguably the most quintessentially
Japanese of the nation's many superheroes.

Unbalance

UNBALANCE

1973. JPN: *Kyōfu Gekijō Unbalance*.
AKA: *Frightening Theater Unbalance*.
PRD: Ken Kumagai, Yoshiyuki Shindō.
DIR: Kiyonori Suzuki, Toshiya Fujita,
Yasuharu Hasebe, Eizō Yamagiwa,
Tatsumi Kamidai, Tokihisa Morikawa.
SCR: Yōzō Tanaka, Mieko Osauchi,
Bunzō Wakatsuki, Shinichi Ishikawa,
Mari Takizawa, Hiroyasu Yamaura,
Shōzō Uehara. CAST: Misako
Watanabe, Yūsuke Kawatsu, Yūko
Ninagawa, Ichirō Zaitsu, Eiji Okada,
Masumi Harukawa, et al. CHN: Fuji. DUR:
55 mins. x 13 eps.; Mon 8 January
1973–2 April 1973.
Unbalance was an anthology series of
chills of the week, including *A Mummy's
Love, The Girl Who Planned for Death,
Assassin's Game, The Masked Grave, The
Cat Saw It, Scream of the Vampire*, and *The
Butterfly Girl*. Though many were
dreamed up for the series, about half
acknowledged a literary inspiration,

including *The Woman Selling Title Deeds*
by Seichō Matsumoto and *Should Dawn
Break* by Fūtarō Yamada.

Unbalance was the original setup for
the series that became ULTRA Q, mothballed for several years and brought
back after ULTRAMAN entered a hiatus,
alongside other *The Twilight Zone* imitators such as OPERATION MYSTERY.
Originally titled *Frightening Theater
Unbalance Zone* in admission of its original inspiration, initial plans called for a
team of amateur paranormal
researchers meeting up in the
Unbalance coffee shop in Tokyo's
swish Ginza area. However, that idea
was later dropped in favor of a linking
device after the fashion of *The Twilight
Zone*'s Rod Serling, in which narrator
Tatsuo Aojima introduced each
episode with a creepy voice-over. Cast
and crew otherwise changed with each
episode, including a rich variety of
writers whose other credits included

productions as diverse as KEN-CHAN, COMET-SAN, and MIGHTY JACK. Music by Isao Tomita.

UNDER ONE ROOF

1993. JPN: *Hitotsu Yane no Shita*. AKA: *Our House*. PRD: Tōru Ōta. DIR: Kōzō Nagayama. SCR: Shinji Nojima. CAST: Yōsuke Eguchi, Noriko Sakai, Masaharu Fukuyama, Issei Ishida. CHN: Fuji. DUR: 45 mins. x 24 eps.; Mon 12 April 1993–28 June 1993 (#1); 14 April 1997–30 June 1997 (#2). Tatsuya (Eguchi) is the oldest son in a family that was dispersed after the death of his parents. A retired marathon runner, he comes to Tokyo to marry his boss's daughter and looks up his other estranged siblings. Brother Masaya (Fukuyama) was adopted by a doctor's family and is now studying at a medical school. Sister Koyuki (Sakai) is an office lady conducting an ill-advised affair with a married coworker. Kazuya (Ishida) has just been released from juvenile detention and risks a criminal career unless he can stay out of trouble. Koume (Megumi Ōji) is preparing for her high school entrance exam. The youngest of the family, Fumiya (Kōji Yamamoto), is wheelchair-bound and presumed autistic.

When Tatsuya's engagement is canceled, Tatsuya invites all his brothers and sisters to live under one roof with him. Though times are occasionally tough the reunited family get alone well, until they discover that Koyuki was actually adopted. Now that she has been magically deprived of sisterly status, Masaya confesses his romantic feelings for her. Koyuki leaves in search of her real mother, but is talked into returning by Tatsuya, in one of several incidents in the style of MAKING IT THROUGH, as the family's impromptu guardian tries to keep everything on an even keel.

A deliberate and successful attempt by screenwriter Shinji Nojima to update the 1960s series *The Young Ones* (see Introduction), *UOR* not only returned for a second season, but suc-

cessfully proved that he was not limited to "difficult" dramas like HIGH SCHOOL TEACHER and IN THE NAME OF LOVE. Later episodes feature the family trying to come to terms with the rape of Koyuki and Tatsuya's steely determination to bring the perpetrator to justice—compare to MOON AT MIDDAY. The reunited family is broken up once more as Kazuya runs away and Koyuki elopes with Masaya, but are brought back together when they hear that Tatsuya has decided to run a marathon in their honor. Peak rating: 37.8% (series #1). Theme song: Kazuo Zaitsu—"Saboten no Hana" (Cactus Flowers).

UNDERAGE

1995. JPN: *Miseinen*. PRD: Kazuhiro Itō. DIR: Ken Yoshida. SCR: Shinji Nojima. CAST: Issei Ishida, Takashi Sorimachi, Shingo Katori, Gamon Kaai, Masaki Kitahara, Sachiko Sakurai, Nagiko Tōno, Ayumi Hamasaki. CHN: TBS. DUR: 45 mins. x 11 eps.; Fri 13 October 1995–22 December 1995. Third-year high school student Hiroto (Ishida) falls for college girl Moeka (Sakurai) while working part time as a bouncer at a pop concert. She, however, announces that she has just become engaged to his brother, who is the star of the college rugby team and his father's pride and joy. Unable to expect much support from his buddies Tanabe (Kitahara) and Kamiya (Kaai), Hiroto tries to keep his feelings to himself when Moeka volunteers to give him extra tutoring in his weakest subject—home economics. Meanwhile, Hiroto befriends Deku (Katori from SMAP), a retarded boy with a heart of gold, who hangs out at the local amusement arcade. He also renews his acquaintance with Goro (Sorimachi), a former classmate at junior high, who was thrown out for delinquency and now has connections in gangland. In other words, a replay of ALL ABOUT YOUNG PEOPLE, but with some high-powered staffers, particularly in writer Nojima and supporting cast member Sorimachi—if playing lovable tough

guys were a football shirt, he would have to retire his number after the later GTO. Peak rating: 23.2%. Theme: The Carpenters—"Top of the World."

UNENDING SUMMER

1995. JPN: *Owaranai Natsu*. PRD: Katsumi Kamikura. DIR: Nobuo Mizuta. SCR: Mika Umeda. CAST: Asaka Seto, Kumiko Akiyoshi, Ryūichi Ōura, Megumi Kobayashi, Tetta Yamashita. CHN: NTV. DUR: 45 mins. x 10 eps.; Wed 19 July 1995–20 September 1995. Since her parents divorced when she was three, Himawari (Seto) has been raised solo by her artist mother Kaoru (Akiyoshi). The situation changes when Kaoru announces that she will remarry again, but her new husband comes with a son of his own—compare to STRAWBERRY ON THE SHORTCAKE. Theme: My Little Lover—"Hello Again: Mukashi kara Aru Basho" (Hello Again: Back Where We Were).

UNMARRIED FAMILY

2001. JPN: *Hikon Kazoku*. PRD: Hiroyoshi Koiwai, Tomoyuki Hayashi. DIR: Michio Kōno. SCR: Rumi Takahashi. CAST: Hiroyuki Sanada, Kyōka Suzuki, Ryōko Yonekura, Makoto, Yuki Izumisawa, Ryūdō Uzaki. CHN: Fuji. DUR: 45 mins. x 12 eps.; Sun 1 July 2001–20 September 2001. Forty-year-old Yōsuke (Sanada) is a selfish marketing man at a food and confectionery company, charged with pushing a substandard product at the fashion magazine *Maybell*. Much to his surprise, *Maybell*'s chief editor is his 35-year-old ex-wife Chikako (Suzuki). Though he fantasizes that she wants him back, she is far too smart for both him and his pitch—she curtly informs him that his "tasty diet drink" is anything but, and shows him the door. Demoted to the sales division at his company, he returns home to find that his pretty 28-year-old second wife Hikaru (Yonekura) wants a divorce. A capricious dancer who married him straight out of college, she has tired of raising their son Shiota (Izumisawa) single-handedly, and forces Yōsuke to learn about household drudgery first-hand when he leaves him in charge.

The opening credits of *UF* say it all—a beautifully executed tracking shot that takes Yōsuke from newlywed home, to foreign business trips, through whistle-stop visits to his wife and son across several seasons, only to end with him in a lonely hotel room. Here is a man who has sacrificed every-thing for what was once known as the Japanese work ethic, incisively summa-rized by Chikako as a "dinosaur" atti-tude destined for extinction. She, on the other hand, has positively flour-ished without him, pragmatically describing a woman's choice as one between *"either money and a career, or free time and a man."* Though she occasion-ally frets that she is doomed to remain a born-again spinster (a dilemma also approached in the same creator's **AGE 35**), she forces Yōsuke to admit that having a spouse and child has left him no less lonely. In one of the most touching scenes, the couple revisit the site of their first home, now an empty lot, and draw the floor plan of their house in the dirt—here was the living room, this was the kitchen, and *here*, they glance meaningfully at each other . . . a place for a baby's crib.

UF is yuppie drama in the tradition of *Sex and the City*, and even uses a piece from the American show's soundtrack as background music. The influence of *Ally McBeal* (see also **HERO**) shows through, not only in the concept of former lovers forced togeth-er by chance, but also occasional sequences in which Yōsuke imagines how things *ought* to be, before harsh reality catches up with him. Based on a manga in *Big Comics Superior* by Fumi Saimon, creator of **TOKYO LOVE STORY**, *UF* cleverly inverts the world view of *It's a Wonderful Life*—all the *bad* things that happen to Yōsuke are ultimately his own karma. Even the heartless Hikaru is painted as a sympathetic character, with a subtext that she has only devel-oped her seven year itch because Yōsuke rushed her into marriage and motherhood in the first place.

After further demotion, Yōsuke quits his job, loses his company-spon-sored housing, and happily takes up Chikako's offer of a place to stay, there-by replaying the cozy career woman with surrogate family story line of **NEWS WOMAN**. Chikako must deal with an unexpected stepson, while Yōsuke becomes driver and confidante for Shinya (Uzaki), the married photogra-pher with whom Chikako has recently ended an affair.

First portrayed as a jerk and a bitch, Yōsuke and Chikako are soon com-pletely reformed, leading them (and the audience) to wonder why they ever divorced in the first place. Consequently, the latter half of the series is almost solely occupied with tying up peripheral loose ends, such as winning over Shiota and placating Shinya. Halfway through, Yōsuke gains another rival for Chikako's affections in the form of ambitious young jour-nalist Jun (Makoto from the boy band Lucifer), parachuted into the plot to extend the conflict for the requisite number of episodes.

UF's only real failing is that there is little tension in the Hikaru-Yōsuke-Chikako triangle. This is partly because Sanada and Suzuki are such likable, charismatic actors that it is impossible not to want their characters to get back together, but chiefly because Hikaru switches motivations at the drop of a hat. Initially claiming that she wants to leave Yōsuke *"to have sex with a variety of different men,"* she then demands cus-tody of her son, but embarks on a career doing tango demonstrations in a late-night bar. Like Chikako, she has a schizophrenic attitude toward mod-ern mores: she warns Shiota that dili-gently doing his homework *every* day will only turn him into a salaryman fail-ure like his father, but is this a heartfelt bohemian pep talk, or simply a ruse to extend her own quality time with him? Compare to **NARITA DIVORCE**. Shown unsubtitled in the U.S. on the International Channel. Theme: Amber—"Taste the Tears."

Unmarried Family

UNRINGING BEEPER, THE

1993. JPN: *Pokebell ga Naranakute.* PRD: Nobuo Komatsu. DIR: Nozomu Amemiya. SCR: Akio Endō. CAST: Ken Ogata, Nae Yūki, Maki Sakai, Yōko Agi, Satoru Ikeda, Katsunori Takahashi. CHN: NTV. DUR: 45 mins. x 12 eps.; 3 July 1993–25 September 1993.
Stressed at work and shut out of family life, middle-aged businessman Seiji (Ogata) begins an affair with the much younger Ikumi (Yūki), much to the annoyance of her former boyfriend Kyōhei (Takahashi). Melodrama of great proportions soon ensues, since Ikumi is the best friend of Seiji's daughter Shōko (Sakai). An object les-son in how technology can make a series age too fast—the personal pager is now a museum piece, though its suc-cessor, the mobile phone, plays a criti-cal part in many modern dramas, such as **WHERE IS LOVE?** and **TO LOVE AGAIN**. Theme: Mari Kokubu—"Pokebell ga Naranakute."

UNSOLVED CASES

1999. JPN: *Keizoku.* PRD: Hiroki Ueda. DIR: Yukihiko Tsutsumi, Hideki Isano. SCR: Yumie Nishiogi. CAST: Miki Nakatani, Atsurō Watabe, Gorō Noguchi, Sarina Suzuki, Raita Ryū, Yū Tokui, Hidekazu Nagae, Kenichi Yajima,

Masashi Arifuku, Shigeru Izumiya, Mari Nishio, Shōta Takagi, Katsuyuki Murai. CHN: TBS. DUR: 45 mins. x 11 eps.; Fri 8 January 1999–19 March 1999.

Jun Shibata (Nakatani) is a haunted, nervous Tokyo University graduate, hired by the Tokyo Metropolitan Police and partnered with the embittered, cynical Tōru Mayama (Watabe)—a detective who once had prospects, but who has now transferred to the dead-end Department of Unsolved Cases. Little more than a PR exercise so that chiefs can assure the public that the police are "still working on" certain crimes, the department has little hope of making headway. However, Jun's enthusiasm and a few lucky breaks prove infectious, and soon the UC office is solving a crime a week. Their cases include a supposedly cursed painting, a distraught widow determined to avenge herself on her husband's mistress, a case of pre-emptive revenge (see PARFUM DE LA JALOUSIE), and some clever "locked room" mysteries, such as a dying security guard, determined to clear his name after an incident 13 years earlier when he discovered the body of his client packed in the freezer he was supposed to be guarding.

UC happily admits its inspirations, and even toys with the viewer's expectations—when we first see Tōru, he is being watched in the street by a crow straight from the works of Edgar Allan Poe, which then drops dead from the cold. The series also teases with fairytale references in the midst of story lines that are uncompromisingly unmagical. When retiring officer Kunio (Izumiya) asks the team to investigate an unsolved parcel bombing from his youth, his nickname Enma allows writer Nishiogi to frame the case as a quest on behalf of Japan's mythical King of Hell. The "snow woman" story, a folktale from the samurai era also revisited in 100 GHOST STORIES and WARASHI, is replayed here as an unsolved case from 1947, when a soldier returning from the Pacific War meets with a strange end. The UC offi-

cers (literally) blow the dust off it one last time, before the files are discarded for being past the statute of limitations—compare to a similar situation in SLEEPING FOREST. However, despite its paranormal trappings, there is very little in UC that is not grounded in reality—it is less The X-Files than Sherlock Holmes, since a perfectly rational explanation is inevitably forthcoming. Unlike Fox Mulder, the UC team don't want to believe in the unexplained—when a TV psychic predicts a murder live on air, they immediately assume he is the prime suspect, using media dazzle to cover his tracks—compare to similar shenanigans in RING.

Although there are earlier precedents, such as NIGHT HEAD, the most obvious influence on this mismatched couple are Mulder and Scully from The X-Files. Jun is cold and analytical, able to solve complex math problems in her head, but still hitting the books when it comes to love—we see her immersed in trashy romances, self-help manuals, and horoscopes. She also has a family connection, as her father's death is itself an unsolved case. Tōru is the disenchanted one, doggedly working his way through the shelves of crimes that have been abandoned by less diligent officers and trying to elicit new evidence from witnesses who have all but forgotten the events. Later, we also discover that he is haunted by the death of his sister Saori. The supporting cast are a menagerie of comedy washouts like their counterparts in BAYSIDE SHAKEDOWN, including the cowardly Seiichi (Yajima), work-to-rule stickler Akio (Tokui) who has an alarm to tell him when it's time to clock off, and Aya (Suzuki), an attractive assistant with residual street smarts from her previous career as a nightclub hostess.

Humor dilutes some of the chills, such as Jun's unerring ability to help students with their homework on the bus, Tōru's attempt to explain to Aya that he is unable to lend her any money because he is speaking to her from a mobile phone while being held prisoner in a giant refrigerator, or Jun's

bemused reaction to a malfunctioning sign outside a pachinko parlor (missing its "pa," it spells out a slang term for "penis"). However, UC is also an accomplished thriller, and much of its appeal stems from its gleefully dark nature, typified by a scene in which a group of police officers joke and laugh in a scene of office banter while a giant screen behind them shows a bloody corpse whose murderer they have been unable to trace. Jun, in particular, becomes increasingly traumatized by her harrowing experiences—one of which involves her waking up in bed, believing herself to have been raped by the corpse found lying next to her. The series becomes increasingly sinister as it continues, reaching a dramatic and controversial conclusion that helped propel it to a rating of 15.7%, but also angered as many fans as it pleased. In retrospect, however, UC has been recognized as one of the better dramas of the 1990s and continues to rate high on viewer polls. Theme: Miki Nakatani—"Chronic Love."

The franchise was revived for the Christmas Eve TV movie Phantom Special (1999), in which an amnesiac Jun is appointed as the chief of Hachiōji Police Station, and finds a former informant dead under a supposedly magical tree. A later movie Keizoku (2000) has UC officers sent to investigate a series of murders on a remote island, with a chief suspect who claims to be able to control the minds of others.

UNTIL THE DAY WE LEAVE THE NEST

1976. JPN: Sudatsu Hi Made. PRD: Tomoyoshi Hagiwara. DIR: Yoshiyuki Itō, Tōru Minegishi. SCR: Shirō Ishimori. CAST: Kimiaki Kawasaki, Kaoru Sakamoto, Sanae Nakahara, Kikunojō Segawa, Keiko Tsushima, Kazuto Andō, Sumiko Kakizaki, Yumiko Tanaka, Makoto Miyata, Sakiko Tamagawa, Miyuki Murata. CHN: NHK. DUR: 20 mins. x 16 eps.; Mon 6 September 1976–10 October 1976. Yasushi (Kawasaki), Masahiko

(Sakamoto), and Yoshio (Miyata) are the "Three Idiots," class clowns at their junior high, who find three girls to fall in love with—Taeko (Tamagawa), Kyōko (Tanaka), and Sachiko (Murata). But just when everything seems to be going well, they are struck by a series of revelations and tragedies. Sachiko collapses and is revealed to be suffering from a terminal disease, while Yasushi's grandfather is bankrupted by the collapse of a friend's company, in which he was the primary creditor.

The children are still dazed by the sudden death of Sachiko, when Masahiko learns that his father is being transferred to distant Kagoshima and moving his family with him. Yasushi seeks comfort from Taeko, only for her to reveal that her family is North Korean, and that her father has decided to take his family back to their homeland. Meanwhile, Kyōko reveals that she is shortly to leave for the U.S., where she will rejoin her parents. Realizing all too late that the days of their carefree childhood have passed them by, the Three Idiots hold a farewell ceremony to mark Masahiko's departure. Based on a story by Hiroshi Sugao. Theme: Yumiko Tanaka— "Sudatsu Hi Made."

UNTIL THIS BECOMES A MEMORY

1990. JPN: *Omoide ni Kawaru Made*. PRD: Tamaki Endō. DIR: Tōru Moriyama. SCR: Makiko Uchidate. CAST: Miki Imai, Junichi Ishida, Kazuo Zaitsu, Yuki Matsushita. CHN: TBS. DUR: 45 mins. x 12 eps.; Fri 12 January 1990–30 March 1990.
Ruriko (Imai) is engaged to Naoya (Ishida), but starts to have second thoughts when a new man enters her life. While she prevaricates, her sister (Matsushita) moves in and steals her fiancé, leading to a series of shocks and twists in the style of screenwriter Uchidate's later I'LL NEVER LOVE AGAIN. Peak rating 21.4%. Theme: Diana Ross—"If We Hold on Together."

UNTRUE SMILE

1976. JPN: *Itsuwari no Bishō*. PRD: Tomoyoshi Hagiwara. DIR: Kazuya Satō, Haruo Yoshida. SCR: Toshio Ide. CAST: Kimiko Ikegami, Kazuko Aoki, Ryōko Hara, Noriyuki Murata. CHN: NHK. DUR: 25 mins. x 20 eps.; Mon 5 April 1976–6 May 1976.
After the death of her mother Haruko, teenage country girl Misao (Ikegami) discovers that she was adopted. She goes to live with movie star "relative" Natsuko in Tokyo, who asks to be called Auntie, even though she is *really* Misao's mother. Natsuko is so preoccupied with her career and success that she couldn't care less about her children—compare to a similar media mother in THE STAND-IN. Natsuko plans, in the style of MASK OF GLASS, to turn Misao into the perfect actress, although this revelation is greeted with outright hostility by her personal assistant Yasuko (Yumiko Kawamura), who was rather hoping that *she* would become the actress's protégé. The newly formed family unit soon shakes apart as Natsuko quarrels with her husband Yūsaku (Yoshiharu Hisatomi), Yasuko quits and then demands to be reinstated, and Natsuko dies in a car crash with her lover—compare to SCARLET MEMORIAL.

After Natsuko's death, Misao stays with Yūsaku, and her half brother Yōichi (Murata). However, she becomes envious of their housekeeper Toshiko (Masako Yagi), who becomes too close for comfort with the widowed head of the household, and is soon agreeing to be addressed as "Mother" by the impressionable young Yōichi. Before long, Yūsaku and Toshiko have announced their intention to marry, and Misao has stormed off to a holiday resort with a friend, who talks her into welcoming her "Third Mother." But when Misao returns home, she discovers that Toshiko plans on marrying someone else, and that it is now up to her to talk her out of it and back into living with her stepfather.

An interesting reversal of the wicked stepmother subgenre as typified by the same year's CHILDHOOD, *Untrue Smile* features a parent in denial about her daughter, before switching to the standard formula of a daughter in denial about her parent. Based on the story by Noriko Tsujimura—compare to THE STAND-IN and MASK OF GLASS.

URADEKA

1992. AKA: *Inner Cop*. PRD: N/C. DIR: Yasuharu Hasebe. SCR: Yū Tagami, Kuniaki Kasahara. CAST: Tatsuya Fuji, Naomi Zaizen, Masaomi Kondō, Kyōko Togawa, Kazuhiko Nishimura. CHN: Asahi. DUR: 45 mins. x 12 eps.; Tue 14 April 1992–30 June 1992.
Upstanding undercover police officer Sasaki (Fuji) is mortally wounded when he is caught by the cocaine-smuggling biker gang he has infiltrated. Left for dead, he is saved by agents of the Super Law organization, a group in the style of the SURE DEATH stories, devoted to taking down the criminals that the regular police cannot touch. He is offered the chance to become an *uradeka*—a cross between undercover cop and vigilante. Theme: Takao Kisugi— "Tameiki no Ato de" (After the Sigh).

URBAN FOREST

1990. JPN: *Tokai no Mori*. PRD: Mitsunori Morita. DIR: Takamichi Yamada. SCR: Hideyoshi Nagasaka. CAST: Masanobu Takashima, Misako Tanaka, Hitomi Kuroki, Yōsuke Eguchi, Masatō Ibu. CHN: TBS. DUR: 45 mins. x 11 eps.; Fri 6 July 1990–14 September 1990.
Rookie lawyer Shinsuke (Takashima) meets Miwako (Kuroki), a girl from a couple of years ahead of him at college, who has now found herself a job at a law firm. She helps him get hired there too, and Shinsuke is placed under the wing of ace lady lawyer Aki (Tanaka). However, Aki and Miwako compete at everything, particularly where men are involved. Theme: Hideaki Tokunaga—"Kowarekake no Radio" (Breaking Down Radio).

V

VAMPIRE

1968. PRD: Osamu Tezuka. DIR: Tsutomu Yamada. SCR: Yasuhiro Yamaura, Masaki Tsuji, Toshirō Fujinami, Tomohiro Andō, Shunichi Yukimuro, Yoshiyuki Fukuda. CAST: Yutaka Mizutani, Hiroshi Satō, Fumio Watanabe, Kiyomi Kiteuchi, Yoshiaki Yamamoto, Osamu Tezuka. CHN: Fuji. DUR: 25 mins. x 26 eps.; Thu 3 October 1968–5 April 1969 (moved to Saturdays after ep 14).

Toppei Tachibana (Mizutani) is an everday worker at the Mushi Pro animation company, who is secretly one of the Clan of Night's Weeping, a secret organization of were-creatures including his associates Chippei (Yamamoto) and Locke (Satō), involved in an age-old battle with other supernatural beings. His secret is discovered by Morimura (Watanabe), a reporter with the *Daily Times* who witnesses Toppei's full-moon transformation into a wolf.

Vampire is notable for several reasons in Japanese TV, not the least because it features **ASTRO BOY** creator Osamu Tezuka playing himself—he was Toppei's fictional boss, but also the owner of the real-life Mushi studios that provided all the animated special effects that augment the live-action footage. Though *Vampire* was an intriguing idea, the integration of live-action and animated effects did not quite go according to plan, chiefly because the script required animal cast members, a difficult group at the best of times (see **ROCINANTE**), to react to effects they plainly cannot see. A short-lived attempt by Tezuka to move into the live-action world of **ULTRAMAN** and its imitators—compare to the later **BORN FREE**. Theme: Yoshiaki Matsukawa—"Vampire."

VINGT-CINQ ANS MARRIAGE

1991. PRD: Kazuki Nakayama. DIR: Akiji Fujita. SCR: Shizuka Ōishi. CAST: Narumi Yasuda, Momoko Kikuchi, Ken Ishiguro, Azusa Nakamura, Nenji Kobayashi, Kazuhiko Nishimura. CHN: Fuji. DUR: 45 mins. x 12 eps.; Thu 4 July 1991–19 September 1991.

Asako (Yasuda) is a press officer for a fashion label, who has been scared to begin a new relationship in the year since she broke up with her married ex-boss, Ryūji (Kobayashi). She meets doctor Kunpei (Ishiguro) when the pair both miss their stop on the train, but Asako's fragile new relationship is soon under threat from her man-eating college buddy Migiko (Kikuchi). Meanwhile, Ryūji's friend Kiyoshi (Nishimura) has secret feelings for Migiko, but is unable to express them.

Ryūji tries fervently to win Asako back, and although she accepts a marriage proposal from Kunpei, she is unable to resist paying a visit to Ryūji when he is hospitalized with hepatocirrhosis. This leads to Kunpei's discovery of Asako's past association with Ryūji, and the couple eventually break up. In a twist that was remarkable in its day, the former wild child Migiko decides to settle down and marry Kiyoshi, while Asako, regarded by everyone as the "marrying type," decides to stay single for now. This first serious TV drama from Shizuka Ōishi examines the phenomenon of the "Christmas Cake," in which women were regarded as unmarriageable if they had not found a man by 25—so the saying went, such women, like Christmas Cakes, were useless after the 25th. With **TOKYO LOVE STORY** and **IN THE NAME OF LOVE**, it forms a trio of early 1990s drama serials in which women daringly pushed themselves past the Christmas Cake barrier until 1996, when a single woman's sell-by date was officially upgraded to **AGE 35**. Also available in a novelization credited to Ōishi, the show attained a respectable peak rating of 20.2%. For another drama that aims for sophistication through the use of a French title, see **PARFUM DE LA JALOUSIE**. Theme: Chika Ueda—"I Will."

VIRGIN ROAD *

1997. PRD: Miwako Kurihara. DIR: Michio Mitsuno, Tatsuaki Kimura. SCR: Yukari Tatsui. CAST: Emi Wakui, Takashi Sorimachi, Tetsuya Takeda, Yasufumi Terawaki, Mai Hōshō, Masaki Kitahara. CHN: Fuji. DUR: 45 mins. x 11 eps.; Mon 6 January 1997–17 March 1997.

Stubborn wild child Kazumi (Wakui) disobeys her widowed father Hikaru (Takeda) and leaves to study jewelry design in New York. As New Year approaches, she takes a plane home, not only to reconcile with the angry Hikaru, but to gently break the news that she is pregnant by her ex-boyfriend and wants to keep the baby. Stricken with morning sickness, she vomits on fellow passenger Kaoru (Sorimachi), and, having broken the ice with this innovative opening move (compare to YAMATO NADESHIKO), asks him if he will help her by posing as her fiancé (compare to MARRY ME!). Kaoru agrees, but the couple immediately run into difficulty when their deception is almost exposed by Kiri (Hōshō), Kaoru's plucky ex-girlfriend from Osaka, who happens to bump into them at the airport.

As with the later 100 YEARS, *Virgin Road* both opposes and affirms traditional values—Kazumi may be an unmarried mother-to-be with a maverick writer (a freelance, she is shocked to discover!) posing as her fiancé, but the elaborate deception is designed to save face and avoid angering her conservative father. Hikaru, for his part, is such a stick in the mud that he actually protests at her wearing contact lenses. These handy items have fallen out in the past, allowing for the dreamlike flashback blur which frames her first sighting of Kaoru—unbeknownst to her, they have met before.

As the family reassembles for New Year, Japanese tradition is presented as something that comforts even as it stifles (compare to LADY OF THE MANOR), while America is openly described by Kaoru as the *"land of broken dreams."* He calls Kazumi's attention to their fellow passengers—all downhearted, downtrodden Japanese, returning to their homeland, as that is the only place where they will be truly accepted. As with the international dramas that would follow in the years after (such as FRIENDS), a foreign country is presented as a nice place to visit, but not an

environment in which a *real* Japanese person would want to live. Peak rating: 21.4%. Broadcast with English subtitles in the U.S. on KTSF TV, where the local audience was presumably more likely to notice the blatant steals from Alfonso Arau's movie *A Walk in the Clouds* (1995). "Virgin road," incidentally, is the Japlish term for a wedding aisle. Theme: Namie Amuro—"Can You Celebrate?"

VIRTUAL GIRL
2000. PRD: Yoshiki Tanaka. DIR: Tōya Satō, Ryūichi Inomata. SCR: Tetsuya Ōishi. CAST: Kanako Enomoto, Takanori Jinnai, Tomoe Shinohara, Yumi Adachi. CHN: NTV. DUR: 45 mins. x 9 eps.; Sat 15 January 2000–11 March 2000.
Enomoto plays an amnesiac teenager, recruited by a psychiatric researcher to test the Virtual Reality 2000 machine that permits her to try on the minds, personalities, and desires of others. Compare to THE STAND-IN and VR TROOPERS.

VR TROOPERS *
1986. JPN: *Jikū Senshi Spielban*. AKA: *Dimension Warrior Spielban*. PRD: Susumu Yoshikawa, Itaru Orita, Yūyake Usui. DIR: Osamu Tsuji, Takeru Ogasawara, Michio Konishi, Yoshiaki Kobayashi, Yoshiharu Tomita. SCR: Shōzō Uehara, Yoshiaki Kobayashi, Noboru Aikawa, Kazunori Takizawa, Yasushi Ichikawa, Noboru Sugimura. CAST: Hiroshi Watari, Naomi Morinaga, Makoto Sumikawa, Mickey Curtis, Michiko Nishiwaki, Toshimichi Takahashi, Machiko Soga. CHN: Asahi. DUR: 25 mins. x 44 eps.; Mon 7 April 1986–9 March 1987.
In desperate need of water, the Warler Empire decides to invade Earth, kidnapping Helen (Morinaga), the sister of the heroic Yōsuke (Watari). Yōsuke resists, in the company of his group of combat-trousered female associates (the supporting cast having moth-

balled the miniskirts of previous Hero Series outings). Space queen Pandora (Soga, compare to her later role as *Bandora* in MIGHTY MORPHIN' POWER RANGERS) sends a variety of bizarre monsters to defeat Earth's defenders, including the Megafreezer, the Doorbeller, the Blender, and the Car Mirror (*miira* being Japanese for *mummy*). With sci-fi siblings in vogue after *Return of the Jedi* (1983), Yōsuke must rescue his sister from Warler's clutches, then join forces with her to save the world.

Coming after JUSPION in the Metal Series chronology, *Spielban* reunited several cast members and stunt players from earlier shows, including Watari from SHALIBAN, Morinaga from SHIDER, and Soga from DENZIMAN. It also unexpectedly made it to the West during the 1990s boom in Japanese action shows—as with fellow series such as BEETLEBORGS and SUPER SAMURAI SYBER SQUAD, *Spielban* was drastically rewritten. Theme: Ichirō Mizugi—"Jikū Senshi Spielban," with music by the series composer Michiaki Watanabe.

Brought to the U.S. by Saban Entertainment under the title *VR Troopers*, the show was combined with the next Metal Series show in the chronology, the following year's METALDAR. A new story now highlighted industrialist Carl Ziktor (Gardner Baldwin), who uses Grimlord, a virtual reality version of himself, to assemble an army of warrior robots. Ryan (Brad Hawkins) is an all-American kid whose father disappeared two years earlier while investigating the Ziktor case—now Ryan and his friends Kaitlin (Sarah Brown) and JB (Michael Bacon) must tool up as the VR Troopers to stop Ziktor's scheme before Grimlord seizes control of the world. The second of *VR Troopers*'s two seasons also incorporated some fight footage from the earlier SHIDER.

W

WALKING ON UP

1994. JPN: *Ue o Muite Arukō*. PRD: Miwako Kurihara. DIR: Rieko Ishizaka. SCR: Kazuhiko Ban. CAST: Hikaru Nishida, Hiroshi Tachi, Yuriko Ishida, Katsunori Takahashi, Rie Tomosaka. CHN: Fuji. DUR: 45 mins. x 12 eps.; Mon 11 April 1994–27 June 1994.

Aki (Nishida) gets a job at a TV station, hoping to work her way through the ranks so that she can produce drama series. On arrival, she finds herself assigned to *Monday 21*, exactly the kind of trivial contemporary talk show she cannot bear, and forced to work with former baseball pitcher Samejima (Tachi). Compare to TABLOID, in which another media worker is forced into a job she doesn't want. Peak rating: 15.5%. Theme: Kōmi Hirose— "Dramatic ni Koi shite" (Love Me Dramatically).

WAR OF FLOWERS

1994. JPN: *Hana no Ran*. PRD: N/C. DIR: Yūji Murakami. SCR: Shinichi Ichikawa. CAST: Yoshiko Mita, Danjūrō Ichikawa XII, Kinnosuke Yorozuya, Machiko Kyō, Mansai Nomura, Takako Matsu. CHN: NHK. DUR: 45 mins. x ca. 30 eps.; Sun 3 April 1994–25 December 1994.

The Ashikaga Shogunate has ruled Japan since the events of TAIHEIKI, but the eighth Ashikaga Shogun Yoshimasa (Ichikawa) has little interest in politics. Having become Shogun aged just 13, he prefers to lead a decadent life, while he leaves the running of the country to his ministers, the eternally feuding Katsumoto Hosokawa (Nomura) and Sōzen Yamana (Yorozuya). However, the Shogun's profligate lifestyle is threatening to bankrupt the country, and matters are not helped by the interference of Yoshimasa's wife Tomiko Hino. She lends money at a high interest rate and then tries to recoup her bad debts by imposing road tolls on all routes into Kyoto.

Aged 29, Yoshimasa decides to officially retire, and nominates his brother Yoshimi as his successor. However, Tomiko soon gives birth to a son, Yoshihisa, and demands that Yoshimasa recognize him as the official heir. Yamana supports her decision, leading Hosokawa to ally himself with the insulted Yoshimi. By 1467, the rival factions have become armies, in the decade-long Ōnin War that devastates areas of Kyoto and spreads out into the surrounding countryside. Despite massive loss of life, the war ends in stalemate, by which time Yoshimasa has officially abdicated in favor of Yoshihisa. However, Yoshihisa soon dies, leading Yoshimasa to attempt to undo the rivalry by nominating his Yoshimi's son as his successor. But the damage has already been done, and with the capital itself a scene of strife, the country is plagued by a series of civil conflicts for the ensuing century, until it is finally reunified by NOBUNAGA.

Scriptwriter Shinichi Ichikawa concentrated on the life of Tomiko Hino, one of the most infamous women in Japanese history. However, despite NHK's educational remit and the failure of such similar works as James Clavell's *Shogun* (see Introduction), Ichikawa also strayed far from historical facts. The poor ratings for *War of Flowers* led NHK to cancel the experiment in running shorter *taiga* dramas that began with WIND OF THE RYŪKYŪ ISLANDS, and the following year's YOSHIMUNE lasted the full 50 weeks. The drama included a number of kabuki and kyōgen actors, including Mansai Nomura who would go on to star in the movie version of YIN-YANG MASTER, as well as the debut of Takako Matsu, the daughter of a kabuki family who would go on to find fame in many contemporary dramas.

WARASHI

1991. PRD: Kenji Nagai, Hiroharu Abe, Masamine Ryūhō. DIR: Hiromi Muraishi, Teruyoshi Ishii, Shinichi Kamisawa, Seika Abe. SCR: Bunzō Wakatsuki, Kazuhiko Kōbe, Chiaki Konaka, Junki Takegami, Noboru Aikawa, Masanobu Uzuki. CAST: Takumi Nishio, Arika, Narumi Tokita. CHN: TBS. DUR: 25 mins. x 24 eps.; Thu 3 October 1991–25 March 1992.

Paranormal researchers Kyōko (Arika) and Yuri (Tokita) scout out pretty boy Hiroshi Midō (Nishio) to help them with their studies—by a curious coincidence, *midō* translates as "pretty boy."

He's ideal for their purposes, as he takes *everything* seriously, including their ditzy psychobabble, and seems to have no interest whatsoever in chasing girls. The trio then become involved in a series of mysteries of the week, including the usual demonic possessions, a demonic computer virus (see **DEVIL SUMMONER**), a poltergeist, the ubiquitous "snow woman," dolls that come to life, and even an infestation of Japan's native *tengu* crow spirits. A succession of guest stars add to the fun—compare to **100 GHOST STORIES** and **1001 NIGHTMARES**. Based on the manga in *Shōnen Magazine* by Daisuke Terasawa, who also created *Mister Ajikko* (*AE) and **KING OF SUSHI**. Although billed in some sources as a Wednesday night show, it was actually broadcast at one o'clock on Thursday mornings.

WATCH OUT, KINDERGARTEN CHIEF

1993. JPN: *Chotto Abunai Enchō-san.* PRD: N/C. DIR: Yoshiharu Ueki. SCR: Tomoko Ayabe. CAST: Nenji Kobayashi, Shinobu Nakayama, Miho Takagi, Miyoko Asada, Junji Takeda. CHN: NTV. DUR: 45 mins. x 11 eps.; Sat 9 January 1993–20 March 1993.
Kōtarō (Kobayashi) refuses to play by the book at the kindergarten founded by his father. The maverick child minder is constantly scolded by his father and brother, who wish he would turn up on time and put more effort into the business, which has fallen on extremely hard times. Theme: Mariko—"Kono Sora wa Ashita desu" (This Sky is Tomorrow).

WATER MARGIN, THE *

1973. JPN: *Suikoden.* AKA: *Heroes of the Marsh.* PRD: Kensuke Ishino, Toshio Katō, Kazuo Morikawa. DIR: Toshio Masuda. SCR: Kaneo Ikegami, Toshio Masuda. CAST: Atsuo Nakamura, Kei Satō, Sanae Tsuchida, Yoshiyo Matsuo, Hajime Hana, Takeshi Ōbayashi, Isamu Nagato, Teruhiko Aoi, Ryōhei Uchida, Toshio Kurosawa, Kō Satō, Yoshirō Kitahara, Tsutomu Yamagata, Hitoshi Ōmae, Tetsurō Tanba. CHN:

NTV. DUR: 45 mins. x 26 eps.; Tue 2 October 1973–26 March 1974.
"Do not despise the snake for having no horns, for who is to say it will not become a dragon. So may one just man become an army." When his wife commits suicide rather than submit to the wanton lusts of the covetous politician Kao Chiu (Satō), vengeful Chinese weapons master Lin Chung (Nakamura) is framed and imprisoned. Lamenting that the government has fallen into the hands of evil men and that true allegiance to the Emperor can only be expressed through rebellion, he escapes with a handful of like-minded individuals. They hide in the Marshes of Liang Shan Po, where they join the outlaw band of Sung Chiang (Ōbayashi). Though Lin Chung is often offered the leadership of the group, he turns it down, claiming that he is not worthy. Instead, he and his associates fight a prolonged war of attrition against the evil Kao Chiu, with recruitment made easier by Kao Chiu's unerring habit of persecuting and looting all over China, thereby ensuring that every week sees a new influx of embittered, vengeful exiles. The outlaws swell in number until they are a veritable army—including 108 larger-than-life characters such as concubine turned warrior Hu Sanniang (Tsuchida), who fights with twin blades and worships the chaste Lin Chung from afar, giant Buddhist monk Lu Ta (Nagato), who combines the religious background of a Friar Tuck with the brute strength of a Little John, Wu Sung the Tiger Man (Hana), and Shih Chin the Tattooed Dragon (Aoi), recognized by schoolage viewers as the only person who could conceiveably be cooler than Lin Chung. Note that in the romanizations of these character names, we have favored those used by the program's English adapters, not by Sinologists or *WM* scholars.
Like its fellow historical novel **ROMANCE OF THE THREE KINGDOMS**, *WM* has its origins in the legends that grew up around a genuine historical event, in this case roughly contemporary with the stories of **YOSHITSUNE** and Robin

The Water Margin

Hood. Twelfth-century Chinese chronicles mention 36 rebels led by one Sung Chiang, who harried the Northern Song Dynasty for several years, before being co-opted into the government itself. Folklore about these "outlaws of the marsh" grew over the next few generations, along with estimates of their number, becoming a recurring theme of Yuan Dynasty theater, and eventually committed to paper by Luo Guanzhong and Shi Nai'an sometime in the 14th century. The magical figure of 108 (the number of earthly temptations) recurs in fiction all over Buddhist Asia, from the anime series *UFO Robot Dai Apollon* (*AE) to the Korean movie *Volcano High* (2001). Often adapted in China and Japan, *WM* made it into manga form courtesy of Mitsuteru Yokoyama, creator of **COMET-SAN**, **GIGANTOR**, and **JOHNNY SOKKO AND HIS GIANT ROBOT**. Published in the magazine *Kibō Life* in 1969, it is this Yokoyama version that led to the TV series—the onscreen titles cite both Shi and Yokoyama as the co-creators of the story, which typically focuses less on the ensemble of supporting characters and more on Lin Chung as an archetypal rōnin figure.
Picked up by the BBC in 1977,

adapted by David Weir, and dubbed by Michael Bakewell (who would go on to direct many English anime adaptations for Manga Entertainment in the 1990s), *WM* became many children's first encounter with the Far East—compare to the effect of THE SAMURAI in Australia and MIGHTY MORPHIN' POWER RANGERS in the U.S. It remains available on U.K. video to this day, despite being virtually forgotten in its native Japan until the release of a DVD edition in 2003. Weir also wrote a novelization of the series.

Among the many other versions of the story are Chang Cheh's Cantonese movie *Seven Blows of the Dragon* (1972), the Billy Chan movie *All Men Are Brothers: Blood of the Leopard* (1992), a second 1988 manga by Sentarō Kubota and Kiyoshi Numata, the sci-fi anime *Demon Century Suikoden* (*AE), and the gangster remake *Don! Brutal WM* (*AE). Theme: Godiego—"The Water Margin." NB: Since it is sung in Japanese, the song presumably had a different original name, probably "Tomorrow is Another Day." However, it was under the former title that it reached number 35 on the U.K. pop charts in October 1977.

WAY I LIVE, THE

2003. JPN: *Boku no Ikiru Michi*. PRD: Keiichi Shigematsu, Yūji Iwata. DIR: Mamoru Hoshi, Yūji Satō. SCR: Ayako Hashibe. CAST: Tsuyoshi Kusanagi, Akiko Yada, Shōsuke Tanihara, Kazuyuki Asano, Jun Toba, Kinya Kikuchi, Aiko Morishita, Fumiyo Kohinata, Ren Ōsugi. CHN: Kansai. DUR: 45 mins. x 11 eps.; Tue 7 January 2003–18 March 2003.

Twenty-eight-year-old biology teacher Hideo (Kusanagi from SMAP) discovers that he has inoperable stomach cancer and hence probably less than a year to live. He decides to try and make a difference in the world around him, which comprises an entire staff room of single teachers—the chairman's daughter Midori (Yada), her handsome, adoring math teacher cohort Masaru (Tanihara), staff room baby

Chikara (Toba), bluff, brash games teacher Sadao (Kikuchi), and wild child English teacher Reiko (Morishita). Throw in Hideo's doctor Benzō (Kohinata) to make up the numbers, and you get what the producers must have been after—SEVEN PEOPLE IN SUMMER crashed into Akira Kurosawa's *Ikiru* (1952). Compare to the previous year's KISARAZU CATS EYE, which featured a similar lead without long to live.

WAY YOU WERE WHEN WE FIRST MET, THE

1994. JPN: *Deatta Koro no Kimi de Ite*. PRD: Satoshi Koyama. DIR: Hiroshi Yoshino. SCR: Makiko Uchidate. CAST: Takanori Jinnai, Noriko Sakai, Tōru Kazama, Mariko Kaga, Anna Nakagawa. CHN: NTV. DUR: 45 mins. x 12 eps.; Wed 13 April 1994–29 June 1994.

Discovering that her father isn't dead at all, but living in Morocco, trading company office lady Nana (Sakai) manages to get herself posted to Casablanca. There, she tries to search for him with help from company branch manager Keisuke (Jinnai). In the process, the couple fall in love, although Keisuke reveals that he has a wife and child back in Japan. The story began life as a 1990 manga, drawn by Yōko Okino from a script by Machiko Uchidate, who also wrote LUCKILY I WASN'T SO IN LOVE and TO LOVE AGAIN, and several other stories in which women chase unsuitable men, and lament that they are never so attractive to them as they were the moment they first met. Theme: Mariya Takeuchi—"Jun'ai Rhapsody" (Pure Love Rhapsody).

WE ARE ANGELS

1979. JPN: *Oretachi wa Tenshi Da*. PRD: Yoshiji Kaga. DIR: Tōru Kinoshita. SCR: Hiroshi Nagano. CAST: Masaya Oki, Yumi Takigawa, Atsushi Watanabe, Kyōhei Shibata, Masaki Kanda. CHN: NTV. DUR: ?? mins. x ?? eps.; [broadcast dates unknown].

Penniless detective Asō (Oki) and his

minions solve mysteries, in a comedy antidote to the same year's tough SEIBU POLICE and cool DETECTIVE STORY. Leading man Oki had often played romantic leads before, but deliberately took this role to widen his range.

WE HAVE TOMORROW *

2001. JPN: *Ashita ga Aru sa*. PRD: Hidehiro Kawano. DIR: Takaomi Saegusa. SCR: Mitsukiyo Takasu. CAST: Masatoshi Hamada, Kanpei Hazama, Takashi Fujii, Hitoshi Matsumoto, Kōji Higashino, Toshirō Yanagiba. CHN: NTV. DUR: 45 mins. x 11 eps.; Sat 21 April 2001–20 June 2001.

Section manager Hamada (Hamada from Downtown) has bright prospects—a graduate of a French university, he now works in the massive Tōaru Corporation and has just accepted a transfer to the company's Osaka branch. While it's not the nerve center, it's clearly a test of his management mettle and may help him rise faster up the promotional ladder when he returns to the capital. His first mission involves a last-minute dash to get the right paté for a forthcoming French Market event, for which his company has promised to supply food—compare to similar culinary goings-on in STAR STRUCK. It soon transforms into a desperate attempt to get an expensive crate of Lafite Rothschild into the building, and when it is inevitably smashed to bits, it is the canny Hamada who remembers the wise words of a taxi driver, that most people can't tell good wine from bad—see DANGEROUS LIAISONS.

WHT is TV for the recession, setting up the pseudo-sophistication of the early trendy dramas, only to demolish it with successive waves of belt-tightening and double-dealing. In fact, its origins lay not in a novel or a manga, but in a hugely popular series of commercials for tinned coffee.

As in IDEAL BOSS, ROCKET BOY, and FRIENDSHIP, the staff must deal with a succession of difficult decisions, which they solve in outlandish ways—such as when ordered to save money by firing one of his underlings, Hamada organizes a bowling contest to make his decision for him. Hamada's staff thrash desperately around in search of new ideas to keep their jobs, but nothing goes according to plan. At a publicity demonstration, a combination wristwatch and tape recorder plays back one employee's confession of love for another. The staff fight to secure the rights to reproduce their favorite noodle bar's specialty in an instant form, but a go-getting American-educated rookie smashes a "priceless" vase and neglects to apologize. Plans for a theme park are almost thwarted by a knife-wielding environmental activist determined to protect the local water fowl, while attempts to secure a children's merchandising contract are ruined when the client's young son almost eats a battery while in the care of Hamada's staff.

In the final episode, the company is taken over by a French multinational, whom Hamada tries to impress with a new champagne brand, the titular "Tomorrow." Deeply symbolic of the carefree times of Japan's economic boom now turned to bust, "tomorrow" is something that the staff cling to in more ways than one. Not to be confused with THERE'S ALWAYS TOMORROW, which was a product of the very economic bubble whose loss this 21st-century show continually mourns. A movie version followed in 2002, in which Hamada and his team are stuck with selling crockery to bars while the elite division led by Mochizuki (BAYSIDE SHAKEDOWN's Yanagiba) is handed a much more interesting project and asked to develop a rocket. Theme: Re/japan—"Ashita ga Aru sa."

WEDDING PLANNER

2002. PRD: Atsuhiro Sugio. DIR: Hideki Takeuchi, Eiichirō Hazumi, Tsuyoshi Nanataka. SCR: Yasushi Fukuda. CAST: Yūsuke Santamaria, Naoko Iijima, Yoshino Kimura, Satoshi Tsumabuki, Ayumi Itō, Hiroshi Abe. CHN: Fuji. DUR: 45 mins. x 11 eps.; Wed 10 April 2002–?? June 2002.

Tōru (Santamaria) is a company man at a large conglomerate, shuffled, like his fellows in WE HAVE TOMORROW, LOVE GENERATION, and EVIL WOMAN, to a new posting. Unable to contest this latest move, he winds up managing the troubled Sweet Bridal affiliate, a company that promises to organize every last detail of the perfect wedding. His vice president is Kanako (Iijima), a divorced mother who nevertheless retains a hopelessly romantic streak and cannot bear to hear Tōru's talk of bottom lines and the bridal "industry." She was also the organist at Tōru's own disastrous wedding a year earlier, at which he was left at the altar in a pastiche that reverses the viewpoint of the final scene of *The Graduate* (1967). Tōru's other underlings are no more sympathetic: Misaki (Kimura) is an obsessive perfectionist, whose attention to detail hides problems in her personal life, although her act has fooled the young Kurumi (Itō), a perky girl in love with the idea of marriage, who has now developed a complex about never measuring up to "Miss Perfect." Outnumbered by the women, Tōru tries to even things out by hiring his old high school buddy Shūhei (Tsumabuki) as a photographer, but Shūhei has zero interest in weddings.

As with the similar CEREMONIAL OFFICIATOR, these misfits are the least likely people to organize the happiest day of other people's lives, but they gamely attempt to do their jobs in the face of impossible odds. Wedding dresses need to be altered at the last minute, bizarre flower arrangements need to be made by special request, gospel singers need to be vetted for tunefulness and dancing ability, and the lovelorn staff members have to keep themselves from falling in love with their clients. Weddings are such a staple of Japanese drama that it was inevitable someone would think of a show about the people who organize them, combining the traditional workplace oriented plot with a multiplicity of the sentimental romantic event that

so often adorns a serial's final episode. Ironically, however, the impetus to get this particular show off the ground seems to have come from a foreign movie, *The Wedding Planner* (2001).

WEDNESDAY LOVE AFFAIR, A *

2001. JPN: *Suiyōbi no Jōji*. PRD: Kōzō Nagayama, Reiko Kita, Kimiyasu Hiraga. DIR: Masaki Nishiura, Kōzō Nagayama. SCR: Hisashi Nozawa. CAST: Masahiro Motoki, Yuki Amami, Taizō Harada, Hikari Ishida, Misaki Itō, Shōsuke Tanihara, Sayaka Kaneko, Kazuki Kitamura. CHN: Fuji. DUR: 45 mins. x 11 eps.; Wed 10 October 2001–19 December 2001.

One man confides in another at a bar. His mistress wants him to kill his wife, and has even supplied him with a murder weapon. He wishes he could set the clock back to a month ago. . . .

Eiichirō (Motoki) is a young editor at Bunyō Publishing, with, it has to be said, the world's most ridiculous haircut. His latest project is Kōsaku (Harada), a young crime novelist who specializes in hard-boiled thrillers. Eiichirō lures him away from his former publisher, and convinces him to broaden his horizons by writing a romance. Meanwhile, Eiichirō's marriage is taking on the appearance of a novel in real life. His wife Ai (Amami), an interior designer, hears that her former schoolfriend Misao (Ishida) has just lost her husband of two years. Though the women have not spoken for 15 years, Ai decides to attend the funeral, and Eiichiro dutifully accompanies her. During the service, he sees Misao mouthing the words of a song at him: that old Chiyo Okumura favorite "Make Me Your Love Slave." The couple try to set Misao up with Kōsaku, since Eiichirō believes he will be inspired to write a great romance if he can only find a girlfriend. However, Kōsuke has already fallen for bar girl Yukako (Itō). Later at a clandestine meeting, Misao confesses to Eiichirō that she wants him for herself, even if he is her best friend's husband.

In the wake of LOST PARADISE, there was a glut of publishing oriented dramas—*WLA*'s contemporaries LOVE STORY and WHERE IS LOVE? also featured editors trying to wrest manuscripts from recalcitrant authors. Unlike them, *WLA* wears its literary influences on its sleeve—the first episode alone drops references to authors Ryōtarō Shiba (see AS IF IN FLIGHT), Junichirō Tanizaki, Tōson Shimazaki, and Shintarō Ishihara. It also demonstrates an insider's knowledge of the publishing world, most evident in Yukako's guerilla marketing operation in a Tokyo bookshop. She spreads Kōsaku's books out on the bestseller table, knowing that the starstruck manager will ask for autographs, and that signed books, even if signed by the author, are "spoiled goods" and cannot be returned. *WLA* also throws in pop culture signifiers, not only with nods to Hollywood movies such as *Terminator* and *Swordfish*, but even to other dramas—the women fell out in 1986, "*when SEVEN PEOPLE IN SUMMER was big on TV,*" while Kōsaku sports a threadbare parka coat in homage to Yūji Oda's in BAYSIDE SHAKEDOWN.

Despite these superficial trappings, *WLA* remains a masterful study of adultery and deceit. Thursday and Friday are for entertaining clients, Saturday and Sunday are for the family, and Monday and Tuesday are taken with catching up on work. That just leaves Wednesday for illicit affairs—since the show was broadcast *on* a Wednesday, it probably led to a few viewer speculations about why their spouses were home late that evening.

Writers are often encouraged to write about what they know, and all too often stories about writing itself tend to become swamped in self-referentiality. *WLA* avoids this trap by concentrating on the temptation of Eiichirō, with Kōsaku as an incredulous witness, accomplice, and confessor. After a confusing start in which the viewer is inundated with information and flashbacks, it settles into a compelling series of revelations. Eiichirō is not only desired by Ai and Misao, but by bar owner Shimako and Ai's business partner Shōgo (Kitamura, in what has to be one of Japanese TV's rare occurrences of a sympathetic gay character). Ai warns Eiichirō to be wary of her "best friend," claiming that the girls haven't spoken since the pregnant Misao was deserted by Ai's brother Akihiro (Tanihara). However, later episodes challenge the viewer's allegiances with a series of narrative switches. Misao reveals that she and Ai *"always fall in love with the same man,"* and that Ai forced Akihiro to seduce her in order to snare another man for herself. The claims and counter-claims come thick and fast—Ai's "first kiss" was not with a man but with Misao, in something both women dismiss as harmless experimentation, but could it be something more sinister? Ai claims that Misao's abortion left her barren, so why does Misao talk hopefully of having a child? Is Misao just a vulnerable widow, or does she have a score to settle? If so, is Ai really the guileless innocent that Eiichirō once thought her to be? These questions only add to his torment and to the viewer's unease—we learn to look for heroes in drama, but *WLA* regularly forces us to question whose side we should be on. In the space of a few episodes, Eiichirō changes from a fiercely loyal husband to a scheming adulterer, Misao from a depressed loner to a passionate black widow (whose husband's death may not have been through overwork but through sexual exhaustion!), and Ai from the perfect wife into an anguished woman scorned. In one of many classic scenes, Misao reveals that she has Eiichirō's missing wedding ring in her mouth, and forces him to fish it out with his tongue in the scant seconds before Ai re-enters a room. The ultimate test comes on 9 November, which is both Misao's birthday and Eiichirō's wedding anniversary—with whom should he spend the night . . . ?

The story's biggest switch comes at its midpoint, shortly after the flashbacks catch up with the opening moments. After setting up a disaster of *Fatal Attraction* proportions, *WLA* discards much of the previous tension in the style of the writer's earlier BLUE BIRD, spooling a year into the future for a story with a very different tone. As Eiichirō and Ai prepare to separate (compare to NARITA DIVORCE), yet more flashbacks retell the previously unseen story of their courtship. Eiichirō realizes how stupid he has been, but though he wants to rekindle his love for Ai, he meets opposition from Kōsaku, who has realized that he has feelings for her himself! Despite a feel-good finale set a further three years later, the last seconds of the final episode hint Eiichirō's love troubles are anything but over. See also the similar PARFUM DE LA JALOUSIE, which was screened on TV Asahi during the same season. Shown subtitled on NGN TV in the U.S.

WEEKEND MARRIAGE
1999. JPN: *Shūmatsu Kon.* PRD: Hisao Yaguchi. DIR: Akimitsu Sasaki, Takashi Fujio. SCR: Makiko Uchidate. CAST: Hiromi Nagasaku, Yuki Matsushita, Hiroshi Abe, Kazuki Sawamura, Tōru Nakamura, Ayako Kawahara, Hitomi Nakahara, Kyōko Togawa, Kurume Arisaka, Shūji Kashiwabara, Mika Satō, Emi Makino. CHN: TBS. DUR: 45 mins. x ca. 13 eps.; Fri 9 April 1999–2 July 1999.

Resentment boils under the surface in a "normal" Japanese family, as eldest daughter Yōko (Nagasaku) basks in the praise and attention of her parents, while little sister Tsukiko (Matsushita) seems to live permanently in her shadow. But the situation changes when Tsukiko enjoys a string of successes at work, and also announces that she has just found herself the perfect fiancé. Not to be outdone, Yōko decides to ruin Tsukiko's life, to ensure that she's the one who gets all the attention. Another drama from the crew who made **YOUNGER MAN** and **TO LOVE AGAIN**. Theme: Solitude—"Favorite Blue."

WE'LL MEET AGAIN

1995. JPN: *Itsuka Mata Aeru.* PRD: Tōru Ōta. DIR: Kōzō Nagayama. SCR: Fumie Mizuhashi. CAST: Masaharu Fukuyama, Sachiko Sakurai, Kōji Imada, Nene Ōtsuka, Kippei Shiina. CHN: Fuji. DUR: 45 mins. x 12 eps.; Mon 3 July 1995–18 September 1995.
A group of old high school buddies from Shimane find themselves all moving to Tokyo at roughly the same time and rekindle their friendship. Though this rarely extends beyond occasional drinking sessions in a local bar, they eventually gain an unexpected additional member. Now in Tokyo too, Tsuyumi (Sakurai) was in the year below them at school and still carries a torch for Kazutoshi (Shiina)—a fact unknown to Shinichi (Fukuyama) when he brings her along to one of their nights out. Theme: Southern All Stars—"Anata Dake o: Summer Heartbreak" (Only You: Summer Heartbreak).

WE'RE ROOKIE COPS

1992. JPN: *Oretachi Rookie Cop.* PRD: N/C. DIR: Yasuharu Hasebe. SCR: Shōichi Maruyama. CAST: Tōru Nakamura, Isako Washio, Seito Hagiwara, Tōru Watanabe, Toshihiko Sakakibara. CHN: TBS. DUR: 45 mins. x 14 eps.; Tue 14 April 1992–14 July 1992.
After graduating from police academy in the northern city of Sendai, Takeshi (Hagiwara) is posted to the central precinct in urban Yokohama. He begins his new career as rookie cop, unable to mention to his detective boss

Ryō (Nakamura) that this posting has placed him in close proximity to family members he would rather forget about—including local gangster Yukio (Sakakibara).

WHAT ABOUT LOVE?

1992. JPN: *Ai wa Dō da?* PRD: Tamaki Endō. DIR: Tamaki Endō. SCR: Akio Endō. CAST: Ken Ogata, Misa Shimizu, Miho Tsumiki, Kotono Shibuya, Eriko Watanabe. CHN: TBS. DUR: 45 mins. x 10 eps.; Fri 17 April 1992–26 June 1992.
In the eight years since the death of his wife, salaryman Shinichi (Ogata) has dated a number of women. His three daughters Ayame (Shimizu), Kanae (Tsumiki), and Sanae (Shibuya) are not happy with their father's flings. Theme: Minori Yukijima—"Anata wa Shiranai" (You Don't Know).

WHAT DID THE SALES LADY SEE?

1993. JPN: *Sales Lady wa Nani o Mita?* PRD: N/C. DIR: Toshio Ōi. SCR: Chigusa Shiota. CAST: Kayoko Kishimoto, Takeshi Naitō, Yōko Minamida. CHN: Asahi. DUR: 45 mins. x 11 eps.; Thu 15 April 1993–24 June 1993.
A year after the death of her husband, Takeko (Kishimoto) struggles to make a living as a life insurance saleswoman. Her new boss Muraki (Naitō) thoughtlessly promises to hit a ten million yen sales target before the end of the year, leaving her to get the contracts signed by whatever means it takes. Theme: Tetsurō Oda—"Asa ga Kuru Made" (Until the Morning Comes).

WHAT THE HOUSEKEEPER SAW

1983. JPN: *Kaseifu wa Mita!* PRD: Hiromi Yanagida. DIR: Kazuo Ikehiro. SCR: Eizaburō Shiba, Yū Tagami. CAST: Etsuko Ichihara, Akiko Nomura, Yoshiko Miyazaki, Naomi Matsui. CHN: Asahi. DUR: 45 mins. x 12 eps.; 2 July 1983 (#1); 13 October 1984 (#2); 29 June 1985 (#3); 12 April 1986 (#4); 11 April 1987 (#5); 9 January 1988 (#6); 8 April 1989 (#7); 6 January 1990 (#8); 5 January 1991 (#9); 4 January 1992 (#10); 3 October 1992

(#11); 2 January 1993 (#12); 9 April 1994 (#13); 8 April 1995 (#14); 13 April 1996 (#15); 5 July 1997 (#16); Thu 9 October 1997–25 December 1997 (#17); 6 February 1999 (#18); 8 March 2000 (#19); 17 February 2001 (#20); 9 March 2002 (#21).
Housekeeper Akiko (Ichihara) is naturally curious and often finds herself working for wealthy families that appear to be happy, but whose outward appearance hides anguish and scandal. Based on *Atsui Kūki (Hot Air)* by detective novelist Seichō Matsumoto, this alluring combination of the peripatetic sleuthing of *Murder She Wrote,* the movie-length episodes of *Columbo,* and the snooping maid of **NANASE AGAIN** led to a successful franchise for the last two decades, that only became a fullfledged TV series in 1997. With its emphasis on poking into other people's business and occasional cleaning tips, it has remained a popular audience choice among housewives. See also **NO WAY!** and **THE HOUSEKEEPER**.
For the TV series, Akiko gains an extra level of stress when she is forced to share an apartment with Kinuyo (Nomura), the woman who assigned her many disastrous jobs in the past. Kinuyo sets her up with a new introduction that cannot *possibly* go wrong—the family of a judge. Theme: Etsuko Ichihara—"Kitto Shiawase" (Maybe Happy).

WHAT WOMEN SAY

1994. JPN: *Onna no Iibun.* PRD: Fukuko Ishii. DIR: Yasuo Ishita. SCR: Kimiko Ishii. CAST: Kaoru Yachigusa, Kōji Ishizaka, Hisano Yamaoka, Kōji Utsumi, Akina Nagayama. CHN: TBS. DUR: 45 mins. x 11 eps.; Thu 13 October 1994–22 December 1994.
After 25 years of happy marriage in Tokyo, Tarō (Ishizaka) and Ai (Yachigusa) finally own a house of their own. However, the couple soon find out that Tarō is to be transferred to Hokkaidō. Based on an idea by **OSHIN** writer Sugako Hashida. Theme: Paul Mauriat—"Bara-iro no Minuet" (Rose-Colored Minuet).

WHEN I MISS YOU YOU'RE NOT AROUND

1991. JPN: *Aitai Toki ni Anata wa Inai.* . . . PRD: Chihiro Kameyama. DIR: Utahiko Honma. SCR: Kazuhiko Ban. CAST: Miho Nakayama, Gitan Ōtsuru, Kenji Moriwaki, Azusa Watanabe, Risako Shitara. CHN: Fuji. DUR: 45 mins. x 11 eps.; Mon 7 October 1991–16 December 1991.

Nurse Miyoko (Nakayama) and salaryman Yūsuke (Ōtsuru) have dated for a year, but are forced to begin a long-distance relationship when Yūsuke is transferred to Sapporo. As soon as they are alone in their respective cities, potential new partners make a move—Miyoko attracting attention from both travel agent Nakanishi (Tōru Kazama) as well as Takase (Fumiya Fujii), the father of a patient. Meanwhile, Yūichi has to fight off the attentions of local girl Kozue (Shitara). Misunderstandings begin to pile up until the couple break off their relationship. A vengeful Miyoko decides to perk herself up with a hotel assignation with Nakanishi, but discovers that she cannot go through with it because she is still in love with Yūsuke. She desperately tries to get to Hokkaidō to see him, but events seem to conspire against her. Eventually, she is able to fly to Sapporo for a reunion on 23 December, but has to fly back to Tokyo to carry on with her job on Christmas Eve. Peak rating 26.3%. Theme: Miho Nakayama—"Tōi Machi no Dokoka de" (Somewhere in a Faraway Town).

WHEN THE SAINTS GO MARCHING IN

1998. JPN: *Seija no Kōshin.* AKA: *Walk of Idiot.* PRD: Kazunori Itō. DIR: Ken Yoshida, Hiroshi Matsubara, Jun Nasuda. SCR: Shinji Nojima. CAST: Issei Ishida, Ryōko Hirosue, Noriko Sakai, Masanobu Andō, Akiko Hinagata, Megumi Matsumoto, Masahiro Kobayashi, Yōsuke Saitō, Yasunori Danta, Chōsuke Ikariya. CHN: TBS. DUR: 45 mins. x 11 eps.; Fri 9 January 1998–27 March 1998.

Towa (Ishida) and his mentally handi-capped associates find menial jobs at a toy factory, though behind the closed company doors they are physically and sexually abused by their employers. The result is a dark and depressing drama from LIPSTICK's Shinji Nojima, in which a building devoted to creating joy for children is also home to continual bouts of rape and assault on innocents unable to comprehend why they are being treated in this way or how they can put a stop to it. Nojima was reputedly inspired by real events—in 1997, a factory owner in Mito was indicted for abusing his mentally handicapped staff, while the same year saw a scandal about nurses at an asylum keeping their charges heavily sedated at all times. Theme: Miyuki Nakajima—"Inochi no Betsumei" (Another Name for Life).

WHERE IS LOVE? *

2001. JPN: *Koi ga Shitai! Koi ga Shitai! Koi ga Shitai!* AKA: *I Want to Be in Love! I Want to Be in Love! I Want to Be in Love!; Broken Heart Story About Ryōsuke; Love Love Love.* PRD: Yasuo Yagi. DIR: Osamu Katayama, Ken Yoshida. SCR: Kazuhiko Yūkawa. CAST: Atsurō Watabe, Miho Kanno, Maki Mizuno, Mitsuhiro Oikawa, Takayuki Yamada, Kumiko Okae, Jōji Tokoro. CHN: TBS. DUR: 45 mins. x 11 eps. (1st ep 70 mins.); 8 July 2001–?? September 2001.

Hotel chambermaid Mikan (Kanno) misses the chance to buy the red shoes she has been promising herself as a gift and instead spends a lonely birthday in a Tokyo snack bar. Her reverie is interrupted by two other patrons, celebrity author Ichirō (Oikawa) and girlfriend Ai (Mizuno), who spice up their failing relationship by staging fights in public places. Not realizing it is a setup, high school teacher Ryōsuke (Watabe) intercedes, impressing the female clientele with his chastisement of Ichirō. As he leaves, Mikan tries to return a bag he has left behind, but he gives it to her—she opens it to discover the very same shoes she had coveted for herself. Ryōsuke bought them as a gift for his fiancée Reiko, but she has jilted him and fled to Paris to be a model, leaving him just seven days to cancel the ceremony, which was to be held at the hotel where Mikan works.

Mikan is not the only customer to be affected by the incident. Middle-aged housewife Orie (Okae), a devoted follower of Ichirō's crowd-pleasing advice program, rightly suspects that her salaryman husband is having an affair (in fact, he is meeting his lover at Mikan's hotel), and half-seriously rings a telephone dating service, claiming to be a 24-year-old air stewardess. When she records a message proclaiming her love for Edouard Manet's 1882 painting *A Bar at the Folies Bergère*, she excites the interest of art-loving teenager Wataru (Yamada) and begins a flirting phone relationship, with him claiming to be a graphic designer in his thirties. In fact, he is yet another of the customers on the day of the fateful lovers' quarrel, though he regularly eats at the snack bar because its manager, Bunpei (Tokoro), is his long-lost father.

WIL is a charming retread of SEVEN PEOPLE IN SUMMER, with the fates of seven individuals interlaced through a series of chance meetings. The title song is "Rainbow Connection" by the Carpenters, a theme also buried in the characters' names: Ryōsuke *Akai* (red), Orie *Kōda* (yellow), Wataru *Aoshima* (blue), Bunpei *Midorikawa* (green), Ichirō *Shimura* (violet), and *Ai* Haneda (indigo). A *mikan* is a small orange—she even apologizes for her strange name, presumably on behalf of a frustrated writer unable to include the color or by other means.

Though it could easily have centered on Mikan's workplace à la HOTEL, *WIL*'s focal point is actually Bunpei's "Suki Ie" establishment—a name best translated as Happy Eater, or for the subtextually minded, The Love Hut. It draws on two popular 1990s romantic traditions—for the girls, Mikan's innocently Japanese take on the heroine of *Bridget Jones's Diary*, while Ryōsuke resembles the protagonists of Haruki Murakami's novels, benignly stalked by adoring women. Ai's problems soon create extra tension: dumped by the fickle Ichirō, she creates additional links between the characters through her dual careers as beauty parlor masseuse and nightclub hostess—a tiring life she has chosen in order to avoid her rich father's attempts to set her up with an arranged marriage.

Miho Kanno is enchanting as Mikan, a Japanese everygirl who believes in love at first sight, but is forced to confront the vomit strewn, blocked toilet aftermath of many a hotel guest's illicit union. Before long, she is sneaking into Ryōsuke's house to wash his car, while he still pines for the coldhearted Reiko. Comedian Jōji Tokoro is similarly delightful as Bunpei, the chef who worships Mikan from afar. Seeing her ordering bowl after bowl of *gyūdon* (beef rice bowl) while pretending *not* to wait for Ryōsuke, he presses some indigestion medicine into her hands. However, he is too late, which ultimately leads to a questionable first for TV drama— Mikan perched on the toilet, discussing romance with her mother, while the repercussions of a rice binge escape noisily from her troubled bowels. Shown subtitled on KIKU TV and KSCI TV in the U.S.

WHERE THE MEN ARE
1994. JPN: *Otoko no Ibashō*. PRD: Tetsuo Ichikawa. DIR: Kagenobu Kuwahata. SCR: Tatsuo Kobayashi. CAST: Tomokazu Miura, Yōko Akino, Kayako Sono, Shizuo Nakajō, Saburō Ishikura. CHN: TBS. DUR: 45 mins. x 13 eps.; Sun 3 July 1994–25 September 1994.
Naoki (Miura) is the Head of Sales for Kogane Beer, suddenly shuffled into the Secretarial Division. His wife Yuriko (Akino), a former secretary for the company, does not think he is suited for the job, but his mother-in-law Sakurako (Sono) is pleased at this "promotion." Compare to another interfering relative in **LADY OF THE MANOR**. Theme: Kaoru Okui—"Kiseki no Toki" (Time of Miracles).

WHICH IS WHICH? (1)
1972. JPN: *Dotchi ga Dotchi*. PRD: Kazuo Shibata. DIR: Michiyasu Kaji. SCR: Kiiko Wakagi, Masahiro Yamada. CAST: Takako Matsushita, Masako Matsushita, Eiken Shōji, Midori Katō, Sakae Inoue. CHN: NHK. DUR: 30 mins. x 5 eps.; Sat 30 September 1972–28 March 1972.
Natsuko (T. Matsushita) and Fumiko (M. Matsushita) are twins. Natsuko is older by a few minutes and insists on taking charge, but Fumiko is the one who likes helping people. Her friend Gai (Inoue) has lost his father in a car accident and needs to find 100,000 yen to keep his family from the poverty line, leading the twins to volunteer to help him win the money. There are advantages to having an exact double, particularly when there's always one person left in the neighborhood who doesn't know about the twins. Hence, later episodes see the girls using their unique talents to turn around the fortunes of a tennis match and to gently fend off the advances of Mr. White, the Japan manager of a foreign company, who would like to marry a Japanese girl, but thinks that *"they all look the same."* Thinner premises have been stretched for longer on Japanese TV, but this comedy of errors bowed out after just five episodes. Based on the book of the same name by Kei Ōki.

WHICH IS WHICH? (2)
2002. JPN: *Dotchi ga Dotchi*. PRD: Masayoshi Sentani. DIR: Takashi Komatsu. SCR: Yūko Miyamura. CAST: Miko Iida, Kento Shibuya, Kenjirō Nashimoto, Jun Miho, Maggie Shirō, Takahiro Furukawa. CHN: NHK. DUR: 30 mins. x ca. 11 eps.; Sat 5 October 2002–28 December 2002.
Ririka (Iida), a 12-year-old school girl who loves ballet, evades some local bullies by climbing into a magic box owned by magician Jun (Shirō), which unexpectedly switches their brains. Now Jun's body is controlled by Ririka's mind, and the pragmatic girl simply ignores the taunts and challenges of Jun's class rival Kajira

(Furukawa). Meanwhile, Ririka's body is controlled by Jun's mind, and the vengeful boy uses his new girl disguise to throw Kajira around the judo hall. Eventually, the boy in the girl's body ends up enjoying ballet, and the girl in the boy's body finds that she quite enjoys throwing enemies hard onto judo mats, in a remake of **AFTER SCHOOL**, based on a story by Hisashi Nakayama. Unlike its original inspiration, it is not played solely for laughs, but includes a developing relationship as the pair, unable to talk to anyone else about their condition, discuss their problems and ambitions.

WHITE RIDGE
1977. JPN: *Shiroi Tōge*. PRD: Kanae Mayuzuki. DIR: Minoru Hanabusa, Masami Uehara. SCR: Mamoru Sasaki. CAST: Yūji Hasegawa, Kei Tani, Taizō Sayama, Hiroyuki Satō, Manabu Tezuka, Kaori Kobayashi, Kazutaka Nishikawa, Kaoru Sugita. CHN: NHK. DUR: 30 mins. x 20 eps.; Mon 31 October 1977–1 December 1977.
Gentarō (Hasegawa) is a son of Shinzaemon Ikeda, one of the retainers of Akō made famous in **CHŪSHINGURA**. He vows to avenge his dead father, but nobody takes him seriously on account of his age. He decides to go back to Akō and live with his friends, but when his friend is slain by a local official during the journey, he kills the man and is pursued by government agents. Unable to remain in Akō, they flee to a southern island, but Gentarō's brother Shinnosuke (Sayama) is killed covering their escape. A junior version of the story of the 47 rōnin, in every sense of the word.

WHITE RUNWAY
1974. JPN: *Shiroi Kassōro*. PRD: Hajime Sasaki, Saburō Ōuchi. DIR: Yoshiaki Banshō. SCR: James Miki. CAST: Jirō Tamiya, Yōko Yamamoto, Keiko Matsuzaka, Hideo Takamatsu. CHN: TBS. DUR: 30 mins. x ca. 26 eps.; Fri 5 April 1974–27 September 1974.
Sugiyama (Tamiya) returns to Japan

© 2001 TBS

White Shadow

after passing the grueling U.S. airline pilot training regime and examinations, only to discover that his wife Ayako is missing. He begins a new job as a pilot and continues to search for her, with the aid of his former colleague's widow Satoko (Yamamoto) and the assistance of smitten stewardess Kaoru (Matsuzaka). *WR* was the second of six "White" TV serials used as star vehicles for Jirō Tamiya and sought to capitalize on the success of the earlier airline drama ATTENTION PLEASE. Other "White" dramas in the series include the original WHITE SHADOW (1973), *White Horizon* (*Shiroi Chieisen*, 1975), *White Secret* (*Shiroi Himitsu*, 1976), *White Wilderness* (*Shiroi Kōya*, 1977), and WHITE TOWER. See also the serial's "Red" rival, filed here under RED SUSPICION. Music by Kōsuke Kida.

WHITE SHADOW

2001. JPN: *Shiroi Kage*. AKA: *Life (and Love) in the White*. PRD: Shinichi Miki. DIR: Katsuo Fukuzawa. SCR: Yukari Tatsui. CAST: Masahiro Nakai, Yūko Takeuchi, Risa Junna, Akemi Ōmori, Kumiko Aimoto. CHN: TBS. DUR: 45 mins. x 10 eps.; Sun 14 January 2001–?? March 2001.
Nurse Tomoko (Takeuchi) begins work

at Gyōda Hospital, where she meets the handsome surgeon Naoe (Nakai from SMAP). He soon orders her to assist in an operation on terminal cancer patient Ishikura, despite the opposition of his colleague Kobashi, who sees no point in prolonging the patient's suffering. Tomoko sees that the optimistic Naoe is merely giving the patient what everyone deserves—a chance, however small.

Naoe is suspended from work for punching a suicidal patient, and returns to discover that Ishikura has run out of money and can no longer afford chemotherapy. Naoe struggles to save him, but Ishikura dies, leaving a note that thanks to Naoe for all his efforts. For his part, Naoe reveals that he has contracted multiple myeloma, a cancer of the bone marrow that will soon lead to his own death. Kobashi offers to treat him, but Naoe refuses, pointing out that the moment his treatment begins, he would have to give up working as a doctor. The ailing Naoe convinces Tomoko to come to Hokkaidō with him, where he insists on showing her a lake he regards as his favorite place in the world. He sends her back the next day, claiming he has business to attend to and then commits suicide at the same beautiful spot.

Based on a novel by LOST PARADISE creator Junichi Watanabe, *WS* was first adapted for television by Sō Kuramoto in 1973, as another installment of the "White" series of star vehicles for Jirō Tamiya (see WHITE RUNWAY). This 2001 version was generally regarded as a pale imitation of the original—a criticism not helped by the later 2003 TV movie, which seemingly resurrected Naoe at a new hospital.

WHITE TOWER

1978. JPN: *Shiroi Kyotō*. PRD: Shunichi Kobayashi. DIR: Shunichi Kobayashi, Masao Aoki. SCR: Naoyuki Suzuki. CAST: Jirō Tamiya, Etsuko Ikuta, Gaku Yamamoto, Yōko Shimada, Meichō Soganoya, Nobuo Nakamura. CHN: Fuji. DUR: 45 mins. x 31 eps.; Sat 3 June 1978–6 January 1979.

After the death of his father, would-be medical student Gorō (Tamiya) has no chance of affording the fees to complete his medial training. His local doctor helps him financially, and after graduation, he is offered the chance to be (literally) adopted into the Zaizen family, owners of the prestigious Zaizen Obstetrics and Gynecology Hospital. As an only child, he refuses, but his pragmatic mother signs him over anyway for the sake of his future career.

Gorō soon makes a name for himself as an expert surgeon, and rises to the position of assistant professor at a university teaching hospital. However, chief professor Azuma (Nakamura) resents Gorō, and decides to appoint an outsider as his successor. Gorō fights for the position that he believes is rightfully his, using his adopted father's power and influence to get his way, but tragically neglects a patient to attend an international surgical conference in Germany. He must then face a legal inquiry into the patient's death while simultaneously undergoing his final interviews for the professorial post—he wins the post, but loses the malpractice suit. He is also suffering from cancer and forced to throw himself on the mercy of the only surgeon who can possibly save him, the same Professor Azuma who has opposed him for so long. His former colleagues try to hide the severity of his condition from him, and he eventually dies calling for his mother.

The granddaddy of all Japanese medical dramas, *WT* began as a series of novels by Toyoko Yamazaki, and was made into a movie in 1966 by director Satsuo Yamamoto, and a TV series in 1967. This 1978 remake was regarded as the best of all, not only for the cast and direction, but possibly also for the tragic circumstances that surrounded its completion. Shortly after filming ended on this sixth of the "White" dramas that were to make him a star, leading man Tamiya shot himself.

WHO DID THIS TO ME?

1996. JPN: *Konna Watashi ni Dare ga*

Shita. PRD: Atsuhiro Sugio. DIR: Masayuki Suzuki. SCR: Masashi Todayama. CAST: Michitaka Tsutsui, Shinji Takeda, Makiko Esumi, Takako Matsu, Ryōko Hirosue. CHN: Fuji. DUR: 45 mins. x 10 eps.; Tue 15 October 1996–17 December 1996.

Daichi (Tsutsui) and Kenji (Takeda) dream of becoming comedians, but for now have to settle for working as dishwashers at the Punchline comedy club. One day, they encounter Yōko (Esumi), the manager of a popular *manzai* comedy duo and beg her to become their manager. She agrees, neglecting to mention that she needs a new star even more than they need a lucky break—compare to **STAR STRUCK**, **GOLDEN KIDS**, and the U.S. movie *Punchline* (1988), though *WDTtM* is similarly low on laughs, despite a cast sparkling with stars. Theme: Yūko Sōma—"Hoshi ni Negai o" (Wish Upon a Star).

WHY I WON'T BE A DOCTOR

1990. JPN: *Boku ga Isha o Yameta Riyū.* PRD: Atsushi Satō. DIR: Hideyuki Hirayama. SCR: Kazuki Ōmori, Etsuko Kitagawa. CAST: Hiroshi Abe, Nagare Hagiwara, Hiroyuki Nagato, Miyoko Asada, Akiko Nomura. CHN: TV Tokyo. DUR: 45 mins. x 6 eps.; Mon 27 May 1990–8 July 1990.

Keisuke (Abe) is a trainee doctor at a large Yokohama hospital who starts to doubt his vocation, in an adaptation of a story by Akira Nagai. Compare to **HALF DOC**. Theme: Takako Okamura—"Kiss."

WIDESHOW, THE

1994. JPN: *Za Wideshow.* PRD: Nobuo Mizuta. DIR: Toshio Tsuchiya. SCR: Yasuhiro Koshimizu. CAST: Kiyoshi Nanbara, Teruyoshi Uchimura, Kyōka Suzuki, Takako Tokiwa, Ai Sasamine. CHN: NTV. DUR: 45 mins. x 9 eps.; Fri 14 January 1994–18 March 1994.

The TV news program *Last Wide* gets the scoop of the century when staff discover that pop star Yui Murakami (Sasamine) has been raped. However, they broadcast the news without thinking through the consequences, leading to Yui's brother/manager Ichio (Uchimura) accusing them of violating his sister's human rights. In a stroke of innovative casting, actor Uchimura's longtime comedy collaborator Nanbara plays his bitter enemy in the press corps. Compare to **DIVORCE PARTY**, **MIDDAY MOON**, and **STRAIGHT NEWS**. Theme: Kōji Yoshikawa—"Rambling Rose."

WIFE BASHING

1993. JPN: *Kamisan no Waruguchi.* AKA: *Speaking Badly of the Wife.* PRD: Yasuo Yagi. DIR: Shinichi Kamoshita. SCR: Seita Yamamoto. CAST: Masakazu Tamura, Hiroko Shino, Akiko Matsumoto, Isao Hashizume, Takuzō Kadono, Marina Watanabe. CHN: TBS. DUR: 45 mins. x 23 eps.; Sun 17 October 1993–26 December 1993 (#1); 8 January 1995–26 March 1995 (#2).

Kei (Tamura) and Yukiko (Shino) have been married for 18 years and have no children but enjoy each other's company. Their life is thrown into turmoil by the arrival of Shūichirō (Hashizume), an old friend from Kei's school days. The series had a second sequel of sorts in the form of **MID-LIFE CRISIS**, which recycled the same actors and situations. Broadcast without English subtitles in the U.S. on KTSF TV. Themes: China Boom—"Shun-ka-shū-tō Asahiru-yoru" (Spring Summer Autumn Winter Morning Noon and Night), Maki Kanzaki—"Jishin Kaminari Kaji Watashi" (Earthquakes, Thunder, Fire, Me).

WILD 7

1972. PRD: N/C. DIR: Yasuharu Hasebe, Sadao Nozaki, Mio Ezaki, Hideo Rokka. SCR: Kan Saji, Michio Sobu, Fumio Kannami, Hisashi Takahata, Hidekazu Nagahara, Shōzō Uehara. CAST: Shinya Ono, Yūsuke Kawazu. CHN: NTV. DUR: 25 mins. x 25 eps.; Mon 9 October 1972–26 March 1973.

A group of condemned killers are offered a different way off death row, if they agree to become a special unit of the police, licensed to terminate criminals with extreme prejudice. Based on Mikiya Mochizuki's 1969 manga, itself inspired by *The Dirty Dozen* (1967), this tale of motorcycling heroes was distinguished by the lack of transformation (they *always* wore biker gear!) and by their criminal origins. Compare in later years to **SURE DEATH** and **THE HANGMAN**, which similarly glorify vigilantes in apparent opposition to Japan's conventional respect for authority. However, precedents extend much further into Japan's past—since the **SHINSENGUMI**, rebels have always spin-doctored their actions as those of loyalty toward a higher power. Such arguments were not good enough for TV violence watchdogs and PTAs, who ensured that the violence was toned down considerably from the original manga, much to the dissatisfaction of the viewing audience. A long-running manga that spanned several decades and 33 compilation volumes, *Wild 7* was reborn as a two-part anime video series in 1994 and 1995 (*AE) and dusted off again in 2002 for the anime TV series *Wild 7 Another.*

WIN THE FISH AND WIN THE BRIDE

1998. JPN: *Gyoshin Areba Yomeshin.* PRD: Hiroaki Kondō. DIR: Yukio Fukamachi. SCR: Naruhito Kaneko. CAST: Kaoru Yachigusa, Yukiyo Toake, Ikkei Watanabe, Rina Katase. CHN: TVT. DUR: 45 mins. x 11 eps.; Wed 7 January 1998–18 March 1998.

Proud mother Tomoe (Yachigusa) is taken aback by an announcement from her son Shōichirō (Watanabe). Now aged 37, he has decided to get married to Yayoi (Toake) who is 12 years older than him. The happy couple move in with Tomoe, ready for a new in-law appeasement drama in the style of **COME TO MAMA'S BED** or **LADY OF THE MANOR**. Theme: Masashi Sada—"Yasuragi Hashi" (Relaxing Bridge).

WIND, CLOUD, AND RAINBOW

1976. JPN: *Kaze to Kumo to Niji to.* PRD: N/C. DIR: Toshihiko Kishida. SCR: Yoshiyuki Fukuda. CAST: Gō Katō, Ken

Ogata, Sayuri Yoshinaga. CHN: NHK. DUR: 45 mins. x ca. 50 eps.; Sun 4 January 1976–26 December 1976. Tenth-century Kyoto is a place of great culture and power, particularly for the Fujiwara family that has carefully married into the imperial house, and rules Japan from behind the throne. Meanwhile, the common people are burdened with heavy taxation by a disinterested central government. In A.D. 935, Masakado Taira, a descendant of Emperor Kammu (r. 781–806), raises an army in the Kantō region (the site of modern-day Tokyo), and leads a revolt against the Fujiwara. He proclaims himself the new Emperor, and leads a resistance movement primarily supported by farmers and disenchanted warriors.

At the same time, the government makes Sumitomo Fujiwara (Ogata) the governor of the maritime region of Iyo, and instructs him to deal with the increasing incidents of pirate attacks on Japan's Inland Sea. Though his tour of duty supposedly elapses in 934, he refuses to return to Kyoto. Instead, he joins the very pirates he was supposed to defeat and begins attacking royal possessions. Sumitomo is eventually killed in 941, the year after Masakado met his own death. Based on Chōgorō Kaionji's novels *Masakado Taira* and *Wind, Cloud, and Rainbow*, this drama represented the earliest historical period to be examined by the *taiga* series to date. Masakado Taira is a popular figure in Japanese fiction, chiefly as a vengeful ghost, and can also be found in **YIN-YANG MASTER** and the anime *Doomed Megalopolis* (*AE) and *Tokyo Revelation* (*AE). Another of Kaionji's novels was turned into the *taiga* drama **HEAVEN AND EARTH**.

WIND OF THE RYŪKYŪ ISLANDS

1993. JPN: *Ryūkyū no Kaze*. PRD: N/C. DIR: Yoshiyuki Yoshimura. SCR: Nobuo Yamada. CAST: Noriyuki Higashiyama, Atsurō Watabe, Tomoyo Harada, Yuki Kudō, Show Kosugi, Isao Hashizume, Akira Kobayashi, Hideo Murota, Tōru Emori, Toshio Kakei. CHN: NHK. DUR: 45

mins. x ca. 26 eps.; Sun 10 January 1993–13 June 1993. The Ryūkyū Islands, stretching southwest toward Taiwan from the tip of Japan, are still an independent kingdom in the early 1600s. There is, however, a threat from the Shimazu clan ruling the southern Japanese domain of Satsuma—particularly from Yoshihisa Satsuma, a warlord who wants to conquer the region. The islands are still officially a client kingdom of the declining Chinese Ming Dynasty, and local brothers Qi Tai (Higashiyama) and Qi Shan (Watabe) are determined to resist the Japanese grab for power. However, there are other forces at work—Japan is slowly closing itself to foreign trade and ambassadors as it enters a period of self-imposed isolation. For as long as the Ryūkyū Islands are under both Japanese and Chinese influence, they provide a secret corridor of trade for merchants such as merchant Shirōjirō Chaya (Kakei). Meanwhile, Ieyasu Tokugawa (see **TOKUGAWA IEYASU**) attempts to profit from both sides of the conflict, in a *taiga* drama that was beautiful to look at but was regarded as "shallow" in comparison to other NHK historical series. Such criticism may be unfair, as *WotRI* was part of an experiment in running shorter *taiga* dramas—it was followed the same year by the similarly truncated **THE FIRE STILL BURNS** and by **WAR OF FLOWERS** in 1994. The story was based on a book by Shunshin Chin, a native of Kōbe whose family and academic background allowed him to specialize in a broader East Asian historical perspective than many other NHK sources. His other books include *The Opium War, Heaven of the Taipings*, and *Coxinga*, none of which, sadly, have attracted the interest of NHK.

WINDY DETECTIVE

1995. JPN: *Kaze no Keiji Tokyo Hatsu!* PRD: Eiichi Fujiwara. DIR: Naosuke Kurosawa. SCR: Kenji Kashiwabara. CAST: Kyōhei Shibata, Kenichi Okamoto, Tomoko Ōga, Hideo Nakano,

Jun Karaki. CHN: Asahi. DUR: 45 mins. x 19 eps.; Wed 18 October 1995–20 March 1996. A killer is stalking passengers at Tokyo Station, placing the duty officer at the local police precinct in an impossible position. Detective Kazama (Shibata) has literally millions of potential suspects coming through the station every day, and escape routes by bullet train to almost every part of Japan. *WD* seems inspired by the terminus cop of **STATION**, broadcast earlier in the year on NTV, and ran in the slot that led into the long-running detective series **HAGURE KEIJI** later each Wednesday. Theme: Kyōsuke Himuro—"Tamashii o Daitekure" (Embrace the Spirit).

WINSPECTOR

1990. JPN: *Tokkei Winspecter*. AKA: *Special Rescue Police Winspector*. PRD: Kyōzō Utsunomiya, Nagafumi Hori. DIR: Shōhei Tōjō, Takeru Ogasawara, Tetsuji Mitsumura, Michio Konishi. SCR: Susumu Takahisa, Noboru Sugimura, Junichi Miyashita, Ryūji Yamada. CAST: Suguru Yamashita, Hiroshi Miyauchi, Mami Nakanishi, Masaru Ōbayashi, Sachiko Oguri, Ryō Yamamoto, Yō Hoshikawa, Shinichi Satō. CHN: Asahi. DUR: 25 mins. x 49 eps.; Sun 4 February 1990–13 January 1991. Superintendent Shunsuke Masaki (Miyauchi) forms an elite unit of the police force, designed to cope with crimes that other divisions simply cannot handle. He selects the scientific genius and linguist Ryōma to help him, and gives him an experimental suit of police armor, resistant to bullets and "low-level" lasers, but so taxing on its wearer that prolonged use can put his life in danger—compare to **MASKED RIDER**. Ryōma's "Fire" suit also protects him from extremes of heat, and will kill anyone else who tries to put it on.

Ryōma is aided by Madock, the Winspector team's vast mainframe A.I., and his obligatory female sidekick, sharp-shooter Junko (Nakanishi). The Winspector team also comprises two robots, transforming ground assault vehicle Biker and aerial-capable Walter.

Wipe out the Town

Later, Biker gains Demitas, a small talking tin can to keep him company.

Based, as usual, "on an idea by Saburō Yade," *Winspector* forms the seventh of the Metal Series that began with **GAVAN**, and was preceded by **JIVAN**. Eventually, the Winspector team would leave to join Interpol and fight foreign crime, leaving their former boss Shunsuke to come up with another team of enforcers: the following year's **SOLBRAIN**. Though the show was not adapted for the American market, it was dubbed into German in a European attempt to cash in on the success of **MIGHTY MORPHIN' POWER RANGERS**. Theme: Takayuki Miyauchi—

"Kyō no Ore kara Ashita no Kimi e" (From Today's Me to Tomorrow's You).

WINTER VISITOR
1994. JPN: *Fuyu no Hōmonsha*. PRD: Nobuo Koga. DIR: Yoshiyuki Fuji. SCR: Tsuyoshi Yoshida. CAST: Gō Katō, Nagare Hagiwara, Yoshiko Tanaka, Taisaku Akino, Misato Hayase. CHN: Kansai. DUR: 45 mins. x 4 eps.; Mon 21 October 1994–19 December 1994. On the run from a troubled past, Muroi (Katō) signs up as a merchant seaman, only to put ashore at Yokohama. There he meets Mika (Hayase), a blind girl whose father is

struggling to build a nursery school for foreign children. Based on a story by Mitsuteru Kazama. Theme: Toshinori Yonekura—"Fragile."

WIPE OUT THE TOWN
1978. JPN: *Sono Machi o Kese*. PRD: Kanae Mayuzumi. DIR: Haruo Yoshida, Tōru Minegishi. SCR: Yūichirō Yamane. CAST: Azusa Koyama, Sakiko Tamagawa, Toshiya Kumagai, Hiroko Saitō, Kumon Awata. CHN: NHK. DUR: 25 mins. x 16 eps.; Mon 20 January 1978–23 February 1978. Teenager Tetsu (Koyama) and his school friends believe that they are tracking down ghosts in their

neighborhood, but they are actually pursuing the echoes and shadows of a parallel universe. Tetsu finds himself crossing over to a parallel Japan in the grip of fascism, where citizens fear the secret police and freedoms have been crushed. The children are sent to a concentration camp for inferior citizens, while the ruling class of the alternate world prepare to leave forever, planning to make their home in our own universe. Tetsu and his friends escape from the camp, along with local love-interest Chizuko (Saitō). Tetsu plans on taking her back to his own universe with him, but she is revealed to be a spy. The boys find Dr. Shirato (Tamagawa), the inventor of the dimensional transport machine, and use it to return to their place of origin. Based on two stories by Ryū Mitsuse (see **DAWN IN SILVER**)—*Out the Town* and *Don't Look at That Flower* (*Sono Hana o Miru na!*)

WIPE YOUR TEARS

2000. JPN: *Namida o Fuite*. PRD: Atsuhiro Sugio. DIR: Kōzō Nagayama, Isamu Nakae, Hideki Hirai. SCR: Noriko Yoshida. CAST: Yōsuke Eguchi, Kazuya Ninomiya, Yuki Uchida, Tortoise Matsumoto, Chōsuke Ikariya, Ayumi Ishida. CHN: Fuji. DUR: 45 mins. x ca. 11 eps.; Wed 11 October 2000–31 December 2000.
Carpenter Katsuo (Eguchi) agrees to become the temporary guardian of four children when he learns that their father (his old American football buddy) has died in a fire, and their mother is still in a coma. The reluctant parent discovers that his logical way of looking at things doesn't always work, though his enthusiasm eventually begins to rub off on the listless children. Compare to the earlier Eguchi vehicle **UNDER ONE ROOF**. Theme: Yuzu—"Tobenai Tori" (Flightless Bird).

WITCHES AT KUNI'S HOUSE

1994. JPN: *Kunisanchi no Majotachi*. PRD: Toshiaki Iwaki. DIR: Mitsunori Morita. SCR: Toshio Terada, Naoko Harada. CAST: Ken Ishiguro, Akira Onodera, Hitomi Kuroki, Shōko Tamura, Fumie Hosokawa, Akane Oda. CHN: Asahi. DUR: 45 mins. x 12 eps.; Tue 11 April 1994–27 June 1994.
TV weatherman Kunitaka (Ishiguro) comes home one day to discover that his father Haruo (Onodera) has inherited four daughters after paying off the debts of a recently deceased friend. Amid the usual chaos expected to descend on a household that has suddenly gained four feisty female members out of the blue, the series also spun off into the animated adventures of the family dog, in *Junkers Come Here* (*AE). Theme: Yui Nishiwaki— "Kanojo ni Naritakatta Hi" (The Day I Wanted To Be Your Girlfriend).

WITH LOVE

1998. PRD: *Reiko Kita*. DIR: Utahiko Honma, Daisuke Tajima. SCR: Kazuhiko Ban, Masaya Ozaki. CAST: Yutaka Takenouchi, Misato Tanaka, Mitsuhiro Oikawa, Sachie Hara, Daijirō Kawaoka, Norika Fujiwara, Kaori Kawamura. CHN: Fuji. DUR: 45 mins. x 12 eps.; Tue 14 April 1998–30 June 1998.
Takashi (Takenouchi) is a former musician with rock band Ash, who lost his nerve after breaking up with lead singer Rina (Kawamura) and now works as a corporate jingle writer for the AVA studio. He meets banker Amane (Tanaka), a prim young lady who works on another floor, although she initially assumes that AVA stands for Adult Video Actors and that Takashi's company is making pornographic films in her building. She also sees what Takashi cannot—that pretty DJ Kaori (Fujiwara) already adores him, and Amane assumes that the two are already an item. Takashi and Amane continue to meet at various social occasions and coincidences, though they rarely get on well—it does not help that Takashi tries to open an account at Amane's bank, only to be mistaken for another man with the same name and accused of credit-card fraud. Amane is having a difficult time at the bank, chiefly because an office Romeo has recently tried to involve her in an embezzlement scheme, and she is being framed for a number of missing transactions. According to Takashi's boss, the quality of *his* work is sliding because too many years have passed without any experience of being in love.
There is a twist, of course. Takashi has inadvertently e-mailed one of his compositions to the wrong address, and it has arrived in Amane's mailbox. Charmed by the anonymous composer of the tune, Amane begins flirting online with "hata@," as she knows him, claiming to be a Paris-based career woman, using the pseudonym "Teru Teru Bōzu." Takashi lies, too, and pretends to teach music to elementary school children. The two begin an online relationship, unaware that they have already met in real life.
With Love is clearly inspired by Nora Ephron's *You've Got Mail* (1998), though the title recalls the more epistolary communication of the ultimate source for both—Ernst Lubitsch's *Shop Around the Corner* (1940). However, screenwriter Ban is able to do so much with the material in 12 episodes, including some notable twists. Paramount among them is a second inadvertent relationship, in that Takashi befriends Haruhiko (Oikawa), a slimy banker who wants Amane for himself. Not realizing that Amane is Teru Teru Bōzu, Takashi finds himself advising Haruhiko on the way to win Amane's heart—throwing elements of *Cyrano de Bergerac* into the mix. The online lovers finally agree to meet up in episode six, which builds up to a tense climax on the top of Tokyo Tower, only to end on the cliff-hanger that *Haruhiko* has come along—he is prepared to pose as "hata@" in order to seduce Amane.
The tension becomes quite unbearable for the final episodes, which see Haruhiko preparing to whisk Amane away to Paris, and even booking her new favorite musician ("that guy from Ash," naturally) to entertain them at their party. Ban's script boldly avoids the full closure demanded by happily-

ever-after romantics, preferring to end with weepy joy, but also with the acknowledgement that the two lovers still have a lot to learn about each other before they can truly call themselves a couple. The perils of e-mail relationships also appear in FRIENDS and SUMMER PROPOSAL, while similar false identities form part of the plot of WHERE IS LOVE?. Peak rating: 23.5%. Theme: My Little Lover—"Destiny."

WIZARD OF DARKNESS

1997. JPN: *Eko Eko Azaraku*. PRD: Yoshinori Chiba, Tomoyuki Imai, Kenichi Itaya, Hiroki Ōta. DIR: Atsushi Shimizu, Mitsunori Hattori, Hiroyuki Muramatsu, Katsuhito Ueno, Mikio Hirota, Higuchinsky. SCR: Chiaki Konaka, Yūki Okano, Jun Koshō, Tamio Hayashi, Yūsuke Akamatsu, Sadayuki Murai. CAST: Hinako Saeki, Rie Imamura, Tokio Dan, Rumi Sakakibara. CHN: TV Tokyo. DUR: 25 mins. x 18 eps.; Sat 1 February 1997–31 May 1997. Misa Kuroi (Saeki) is a schoolgirl with magical powers, who has achieved semi-mythical status among local children. With a name that is a homonym for "Black Mass," this faintly creepy teen witch fights evil in modern Japan, in several linked mini-arcs, as well as one-off stories. After three episodes set in and around school, Misa leaves to wander the city for the rest of the series.

The initial 13 episodes proved to be an unexpected ratings hit, leading to the commissioning of 13 more that concentrated on Misa's own past—she is, for example, found to be carrying two dolls with her that turn out to be her cursed parents. However, only a few episodes in to the extended run, a juvenile murder case in Japan prompted the channel to pull the last eight episodes from the air—compare to similar self-censorship in MASKED RIDER. The entire 26 episode run is now available on video.

WoD began as a manga by Shinichi Koga, serialized in *Shōnen Champion* magazine from 1975 to 1979. The series was also spun off into a 1970s radio show, and three 1990s movies, released in the U.S. as *Wizard of Darkness I* and *II*, and *Misa the Dark Angel*. "Eko Eko Azarak," the origin of the series' Japanese title, is an incantation from the pagan manual *The Witches' Rune*.

WIZARD OF OZ

1974. JPN: *Oz no Mahō Tsukai*. PRD: Shūji Terayama. DIR: Hisaya Kondō, Nobuhiro Shige. SCR: Hiroshi Migiwa, Akira Adachi, Jirō Mio. CAST: (voices) Shelly, Hiroshi Satō, Ei Takami, Fujio Tsuneta. CHN: NTV. DUR: 30 mins. x 26 eps.; Sat 5 October 1974–29 March 1975.

Dorothy (Shelly) is transported to the distant land of Oz, where she soon acquires traveling companions—the Scarecrow, the Cowardly Lion, and the Tin Woodman. Acquiring a magical pair of Oz Spectacles in episode five, she encounters mysterious fruits, ghosts, a shooting star, and a prison of mists, before attending a witch's 2001st birthday party. After a disappointing meeting with the "King of Oz," who is not all he appears to be, the group sets out in search of a means of getting home—the ideal method would seem to be a secret Oz rocket project. Traveling onward, Dorothy's companions prove themselves in a series of missions, as the Tin Woodman successfully fights off a dragon, the Cowardly Lion proves his bravery, and the Scarecrow falls in love. Finally, Dorothy is able to launch the Oz rocket *Sayōnara*, and returns home over the rainbow to her native Kansas.

Based, somewhat loosely it seems, on *The Wonderful Wizard of Oz* (1900) by L. Frank Baum, this musical puppet show was not afraid of trying something new. Its most notable gimmick was the pair of Oz Spectacles, with telltale green and red lenses that gave away their true nature as 3D glasses. From episode five onward, sequences of the show were broadcast in 3D, and children were encouraged to obtain their own Oz Spectacles in order to get the full effect. Adaptations of the story

also exist in several anime versions, including *The Wizard of Oz* (*AE) and *Galaxy Adventures of Space Oz* (*AE). Some Japanese video catalogues also list a feature-length tape of the later Pikkari Theater puppet musical production of *The Wizard of Oz* (1991), in which Fumi Hirano, the voice of Lum from *Urusei Yatsura* (*AE), plays Dorothy.

WOMAN DREAM

1992. PRD: Yoshiki Miruta. DIR: Junji Kadō. SCR: Takuya Nishioka. CAST: Nae Yūki, Takeshi Naitō, Yoshimi Satō, Miyoko Yoshimoto, Shizuo Nakajō. CHN: Kansai. DUR: 45 mins. x 11 eps.; 5 October 1992–14 December 1992. Rina (Yūki) works at a nursery school in Shinshū. She has been raised from childhood by her grandmother and has no memory of her parents. She is therefore shocked to discover a letter from the mother she has always believed to be dead, announcing that she plans on coming to find her in Tokyo. Based on a story by Nobuhiko

Kobayashi. Theme: T-BOLAN—"Bye For Now."

WOMEN OF THE ONSEN *
1999. JPN: *Onsen e Ikō.* AKA: *Let's Go to a Hot Spring.* PRD: Hisao Yaguchi. DIR: Munenobu Yamauchi. SCR: Yuki Kiyomoto. CAST: Takako Katō, Kumiko Fujiyoshi, Michiko Ameku, Minoru Tanaka, Shiho Fujimura. CHN: TBS. DUR: 25 mins. x 179 eps.; Mon 13 September 1999–10 December 1999 (#1), 27 November 2000–23 February 2001 (#2), 28 January 2002–?? December 2002 (#3).

After resigning from her job at a bank, Kaoru (Katō) travels to the remote hot spring resort where her mother Shizue runs an inn. Offered jobs as maids, Kaoru and two friends are initially ostracized by the other staff, particularly when Shizue tells them that Kaoru is in training to take over the business. Yuriko, the wife of Kaoru's disgraced half brother Atsushi, had formerly believed that the job would be hers and makes life as difficult as possible for Kaoru's circle, first in an attempt to dissuade her, and then in revenge for Kaoru's success. Kaoru eventually cannot take any more hazing, but is prevented from resigning when she discovers that Shizue is dying from cancer. Just as the situation in the inn seems to settle down, the staff are beset by a number of visitors that cause them to question the stories they have told each other. One maid is revealed to be a former nurse hiding under a false identity and resumé, while Kaoru must deal with the reappearance of her prodigal half brother, who has been missing for seven years following a business scandal. Atsushi's arrival alters the fragile peace at the inn, leading Yuriko to recommence her intrigues.

Unlike most of the other serials in this book, *Women of the Onsen* is a daytime show, broadcasts in the *Ai no Gekijō* (Love's Theater) slot designed like the NHK *asa-dorama* to entertain an audience of housewives who enjoy watching people whose lives are more miserable than theirs. Combining the

Cinderella torments of **HOUSE OF THE DEVILS** with the hotelier drama of **TAKE ME TO A RYOKAN**, it was also broadcast with English subtitles in the U.S. on KIKU TV.

WOMEN'S COMPANY
1998. JPN: *Oshigoto Desu!* AKA: *It's a Job.* PRD: Ayako Ōga, Kazuyuki Morosawa. DIR: Hitoshi Iwamoto, Takao Kinoshita, Tōru Hayashi. SCR: Kazuyuki Sawamura, Mayumi Nakatani. CAST: Mayu Tsuruta, Yuki Matsushita, Akiko Hinagata, Taichi Kokubu, Yoshihiko Inohara, Takao Ōsawa. CHN: Fuji. DUR: 45 mins. x 12 eps.; Thu 16 April 1998–2 July 1998.

Dissatisfied with back stabbing and office politics after four years at a large company, Natsuko (Tsuruta) is looking for a way out. With fellow office lady Kotori (Matsushita) and receptionist Miki (Hinagata.), she opens her own shop. Based on the manga by **TOKYO LOVE STORY** creator Fumi Saimon, which ran in *Big Comics Superior.* Peak rating: 19.5%. Theme: Ulfuls— "Makasenasai" (Leave it to Me).

WONDERFUL FAMILY VACATION *
1998. JPN: *Subarashii Kazoku Ryokō.* PRD: Akira Sasaki. DIR: Kōhei Kuno. SCR: Toshio Kamata, Mineaki Hata. CAST: Pinko Izumi, Yōko Nogiwa, Raita Ryū, Hironobu Nomura. CHN: TVT. DUR: 45 mins. x 12 eps.; Wed 1 July 1998–16 September 1998.

Ten years after Sachiko (Izumi) married Tadahiro (Nomura), a man ten years her junior, the couple move in with Tadahiro's frail grandmother. Though their motives are wholly honorable, Tadahiro's other relatives are convinced that Sachiko is merely a gold digger with her eyes on the family fortune. An in-law appeasement drama in the style of **DAUGHTER-IN-LAW** soon ensues, and was later shown in the U.S. with English subtitles on KTSF TV. Theme: Shanghai Typhoon—"Tsubasa ga Hoshii" (I Want Wings).

WONDERFUL FRIEND
1975. JPN: *Subarashiki Yūjin.* PRD: Seiji

Akiyama. DIR: Noriaki Sasahara, Tōru Kusakabe. SCR: Isamu Seki. CAST: Toshimasa Kamei, Akifumi Inoue, Masaki Yasuda, Takahiro Yoshimoto, Yōko Hirai, Tomomi Saitō. CHN: NHK. DUR: 25 mins. x 12 eps.; Mon 20 October 1975–12 November 1975.

After his younger brother Akira (Yoshimoto) is in a bicycle accident with Kasumi (Saitō), Hiroshi (Kamei) avoids difficult questions by simply claiming the accident was all his responsibility. At the hospital, he discovers that Kasumi's elder sister is Beniko (Hirai), a girl who has been admiring him from afar for some time. Determined to make amends, Hiroshi promises to take the girls to school every day on his bicycle cart, prompting the admiration of his brother, but also providing an excuse to meet them again.

WONDERFUL LIFE
1993. JPN: *Subarashiki Kana Jinsei.* PRD: Tōru Ōta. DIR: Michio Mitsuno. SCR: Hisashi Nozawa. CAST: Atsuko Asano, Yūji Oda, Kōichi Satō, Ken Tanaka, Yasuko Tomita, Rie Tomosaka. CHN: Fuji. DUR: 45 mins. x 12 eps.; Thu 1 July 1993–16 September 1993.

Yume (Asano) finds herself single and pregnant after her boyfriend Kunio (Tanaka) disappears. She marries her childhood friend Shinpei (Satō) but divorces him when she discovers his numerous affairs, and now struggles to rear her child single-handedly, while teaching at a culinary school. Meanwhile, Kunio's younger brother Mitsugu (Oda) becomes a teacher in a high school, and finds himself teaching Yume's teenage daughter Haruka (Tomosaka). Although he is already living with Hatsune (Tomita), he realizes that the only person he has ever loved is Yume. Mitsugu proposes to Yume, but so does Shinpei, who has dumped his new wife.

As if two marriage proposals at once were not enough drama in her life, Yume discovers that she has breast cancer—compare to **SEMI DOUBLE**. Though the absent Kunio soon returns and also tries to win her back, Yume agrees to marry Mitsugu, unaware that Hatsune is pregnant with his child. When Hatsune commits suicide, Mitsugu goes missing, and Yume tracks him down and prevents him from following suit. Mitsugu decides to go to Hokkaidō for three years to "find himself," and Yume leaves for London to be a chef. Three years later, the family are reunited at Haruka's wedding, and Yume resolves to enjoy life as much as she can, since she is unlikely to live more than another two years. As with his earlier **DEAR BELOVED** and **LIVE FOR THIS LOVE**, scriptwriter Nozawa takes to the institution of marriage with a wrecking ball, questioning what's really important in life, and decides that culinary art is a big chunk of it. Peak rating 25.0%. Theme: Yōsui Inoue—"Make-up Shadow."

WORLD OF ICE

1999. JPN: *Kōri no Sekai*. AKA: *Inanimate World*. PRD: Reiko Kita. DIR: Michio Mitsuno, Katsunori Tomita. SCR: Hisashi Nozawa. CAST: Yutaka Takenouchi, Nanako Matsushima, Tōru Nakamura, Yuki Uchida, Ken Kaneko, Reiko Matsuo, Tomoko Nakajima, Tae Kimura, Ryōsei Tayama. CHN: Fuji. DUR: 45 mins. x 11 eps.; Mon 11 October 1999–20 December 1999.
Eiki (Takenouchi) is an investigator for Rose Life Insurance faced with a succession of suspicious and shocking cases, including a mother who has thrown burning oil over her daughter in order to collect on a recent policy. He is sent to snoop around the events surrounding the death of an English teacher at Eiwa Girls' School and immediately clashes with police detective Takeshi (Nakamura), who objects to amateurs involving themselves in the serious business of solving crimes. Since even the police believe it to be murder, the school principal also secretly hires the coldhearted geology teacher Tōko (Matsushima) to conduct her own investigation. Her behavior makes Eiki suspicious and he begins to doubt her vacation alibi, particularly when he dis-

covers that her former fiancé recently met with an untimely end, mangled in the propellers of a cruise ship.
Circumstantial evidence seems to mount up against Tōko, particularly when it is revealed that she had an earlier fiancé who died of a suspected drug overdose. He was a psychiatrist, who met her when she was undergoing treatment for the trauma of losing yet *another* fiancé, who was killed while working as a photojournalist in Northern Ireland. But although Eiki is under pressure from his company to prove a case of foul play, his own growing feelings for Tōko lead him to believe she has been framed.
The sense of impending menace is accentuated by the presentation of the series as Eiki's last moments. Episode one opens with the bleeding, drowning Eiki watching his life flash before him—the succession of fast images slowing to a real-time crawl as it reaches the events of the series itself. With the entire series being told in flashback already, writer Nozawa is unafraid of adding further re-enactments of past events, notably the spectacular ends of Tōko's family members and lovers.
As the police and insurance investigations dig deeper, they discover that Tōko is an orphan—her debt-ridden parents died when she was 15 in a fire presumed to be a form of double suicide. The payout on the life insurance policy not only cleared their debts, but allowed sufficient money for the impoverished Tōko to go to college. Eiki thinks he sees a habit-forming, life-changing event in the manner of their death, and its effect on Tōko, and he is *almost* right.
Tōko's childhood friend Shōgo (Kaneko) is presented to the viewer as a prime suspect—he has worshipped her from afar, but that still offers no reason for the death of the English teacher. A far better motive rests with three schoolgirls who were falsely accused of *enjo kōsai* (subsidized dating) (see **LAST LOVE**) by the victim, but they are unlikely to have had the wherewithal to kill her. As with the

same writer's earlier **SLEEPING FOREST**, the truth is actually a complex web of overlapping intrigues, only actually settled in a shocking ending. In one of many surprise moments, Eiki even fills out a life insurance policy, makes Tōko the beneficiary, and begs her to marry him, as proof that he believes she is innocent.
As with the same year's **FORBIDDEN LOVE**, which also starred Matsushima, the Japanese title contains multiple meanings. Superficially, it alludes to the Ice Storm bar where some of the action takes place, though it is also a reference to an event from Eiki's youth, when he nearly died walking on an iceberg—ground that appears to be solid can open up at any moment and plunge the unwary into icy seas. Also, of course, it refers to Tōko's apparently emotionless state, a traumatized condition symbolized by blue-themed lighting and backgrounds, gradually overwhelmed by the warm oranges of Eiki's feelings. Gaining a peak rating of 24.4%, *WoI* continues to score high in viewer polls. Theme: Kyōsuke Himuro—"Diamond Dust."

WOULD YOU SAY I WAS UGLY?

1993. JPN: *Watashitte Busu Datta no?* PRD: N/C. DIR: Takamichi Yamada. SCR: Shizuka Ōishi. CAST: Seiko Matsuda, Renji Ishibashi, Saburō Tokitō, Junko Sakurai, Shūhei Aikawa. CHN: TBS. DUR: 45 mins. x 12 eps.; Fri 16 April 1993–2 July 1993.
Advertising copywriter Yūko (Matsuda) has a love-hate relationship with director Seo (Tokitō). Compare to **SHOTGUN MARRIAGE**. Theme: Seiko Matsuda—"Taisetsu na Anata" (You Are Important).

WOUNDED ANGEL

1974. JPN: *Kizudarake no Tenshi*. PRD: Kinya Shimizu. DIR: Eiichi Kudō, Kinji Fukasaku, Tatsumi Kamidai. SCR: Shinichi Ichikawa. CAST: Kenichi Hagiwara, Yutaka Mizutani, Kyōko Kishida, Shin Kishida. CHN: NTV. DUR: ca. 30 mins. x ca. 26 eps.; Sat 5 October 1974–29 March 1975.

Osamu (Hagiwara) is an uneducated pauper who lost his parents as a child and harbors a fierce sense of justice. He teams up with Tōru (Mizutani), a private detective who takes generosity and gullibility to insane lengths, and the mismatched pair undertake a series of dirty, dangerous missions for the evil Takako (Kishida).

Directed by several top Japanese movie directors and featuring acclaimed acting from Kenichi Hagiwara, *WA* was a colorful and comedic depiction of life at the bottom of the 1970s social ladder. Hagiwara's clothes and attitude were much imitated at the time, and the series still makes it onto top ten lists 30 years after its original broadcast.

WOUNDED WOMAN, A
1999. JPN: *Kizudarake no Onna*. PRD: Yūji Tōjō, Kōichi Tōda, Kazuhisa Andō. DIR: Renpei Tsukamoto, Takashi Komatsu. SCR: Kazuyuki Morosawa, Izō Hashimoto. CAST: Reiko Takashima, Tatsuya Yamaguchi, Masato Furuoya. CHN: Fuji. DUR: 45 mins. x 11 eps.; Tue 13 April 1999–?? June 1999. When her husband and daughter are murdered by gangsters, Kyōko (Takashima) goes into the bodyguard business, hoping to save other families from the same fate and ultimately track down the parties responsible for the deaths of her loved ones. Yamaguchi (from TOKIO) plays her loyal male assistant—compare to THE BODYGUARD. Peak rating: 16.0%. Theme: Takurō Yoshida—"Kokoro no Kakera" (Fragments of Heart).

Y

YAGAMI'S FAMILY TROUBLES

1994. JPN: *Yagami-kun no Katei no Jijō*. PRD: Kumio Ishizaka. DIR: Osamu Tsuji. SCR: Akira Momoi, Shōji Imai. CAST: Taichi Kokubu, Maki Mochida, Mari Natsuki, Takuzō Kadono, Junichi Yamamoto. CHN: Asahi. DUR: 45 mins. x 11 eps.; Tue 11 October 1994–2 February 1995.

Yūji Yagami (Kokubu) is the offspring of a marriage between the worlds—his pretty, eternally young mother Nomi (Natsuki) is a witch from another dimension, while his father Yōji (Kadono) is an everyday salaryman. Yūji has inherited his mother's magical talents, but has supposedly agreed never to use them. But teenage times are troublesome, and he realizes that a little magical help couldn't possibly hurt in his attempts to attract female attention. So begins just one of the romantic entanglements in this retread of *Bewitched* (1964), almost presented as a sequel to the American show by focusing on the child of the original couple. Dad is pursued at work by a feisty secretary, who loses interest in him when she sees how pretty his wife is. Accordingly, she switches her attentions to Yūji himself. Meanwhile, Yūji's mother's good looks have charmed the boys in his class, who fight over who loves her the most, and how best to rid themselves of her inconvenient husband.

Yagami's Family Troubles began as a 1986 manga by Kei Kusunoki, who also created *Ogre Slayer* (*AE). The story was previously adapted as an anime (*AE) in 1990. Theme: Tomohisa Kawazoe—"Oh Yes! Kiss o Shiyō yo" (Oh Yes! Let's Kiss).

YAGYŪ CONSPIRACY, THE

1978. JPN: *Yagyū Ichizoku no Inbō*. AKA: *Plot of the Yagyū, Rampage of the Yagyū*. PRD: Tadashi Iwasaki, Norimichi Matsudaira, Naoyuki Sugimoto, Yūji Makiguchi, Kanō Namura. DIR: Kinji Fukasaku, Akinori Matsuo, Kazuo Ikehiro, Yoshiyuki Kuroda, Yūji Makiguchi. SCR: Tatsuo Nogami, Masahiro Shimura, Tsutomu Nakamura, Hideaki Yamamoto, Takayuki Yamada. CAST: Sō Yamamura, Ryō Tamura, Shinichi "Sonny" Chiba, Etsuko Shihomi, Mikio Narita, Ken Nishida, Michiyo Kogure, Etsushi Takahashi, Fumio Watanabe, Asao Koike, Yumi Takigawa, Hiromi Okamoto, Mariko Okada, Daijirō Harada, Yōko Kino, Fumiyoshi Maki, Kazuko Yoshiyuki, Yūki Meguro. CHN: Kansai. DUR: 45 mins. x 39 eps.; Tue 3 October 1978–26 June 1979.

In the time of Shogun Hidetada (see **SLOPE IN SPRING**), swordmaster Munenori Yagyū (Yamamura) teaches the heir Iemitsu (Tamura) how to fight. Munenori's son Jūbei (Chiba) becomes firm friends with the young Shogun-to-be, and hopes that his father, a close ally of the Bakufu government, will not be called upon to oppose the Shogun's authority. There are already many others prepared to do that, as the Shogunate has abolished over 60 samurai clans, which has resulted in literally thousands of masterless swordsmen roaming the country and adding to civil unrest.

As Hidetada's death approaches, he rightly suspects that his wife Oeyo (Kogure) and her faction at court will try to usurp Iemitsu and place his younger brother Tadanaga (Nishida) in power instead. To the surprise of all present at a banquet, Hidetada announces that he wishes Tadanaga to replace him, before collapsing into a coma. After his death, a group of ninja break into the mausoleum and cut out the corpse's stomach. Intercepted by the Yagyū family, they are apprehended, and the stolen stomach is found to contain proof that the late Shogun was poisoned.

The lines are now drawn for a battle of intrigue—Hanzō Hattori, leader of the Iga (see **SHADOW WARRIORS**), has secretly given his backing to the Tadanaga faction. Ranged against them are the Ura Yagyū, an organization of spies devoted to defending Iemitsu through intrigue and counterespionage led by Jūbei's father, with members including Jūbei's younger brother Samon (Meguro), sister Akane (Shihomi), and members of the mysterious Negoro ninja clan. Opposed to both sides is a third faction, who do not want anyone as Shogun, and would instead rather restore the figurehead Emperor to true authority over Japan.

As the feudal lords of Japan form, break, and re-form alliances behind the scenes, the Yagyū are charged with the job of defeating assassins before they can close in, dissolving potential threats, and fighting off disgruntled rōnin. Jūbei himself leads an ill-fated band of Negoro on a mission to kill Sakai (Watanabe), a chief elder on the Shogun's staff, who has been charged with assassinating Iemitsu. Ambushed by forces of the Imperial supporter Karasumaru (Narita), the warring ninja clans must fight their way out. Jūbei saves Iemitsu's life by shielding him from the attack, but one of Karasumaru's arrows strikes Jūbei in the eye, ruining his field of vision and calling his future as a swordsman into doubt.

Though claiming an ancient pedigree back to legends told about the strange disappearance of a genuine historical figure, The Yagyū Conspiracy has a much more modern origin. A 1950s pulp samurai novel by Fūtarō Yamada, this TV version was made for the 20th anniversary of Kansai TV (compare to MONKEY) and featured a first episode directed by Kinji Fukasaku known better abroad in its movie edit Shogun's Samurai (1978). Chiba would return to the movie screen as Jūbei in Darkside Reborn (1981), itself remade as Samurai Armageddon (1995). Characters called Jūbei also appear in Ninja Scroll (*AE) and Ninja Resurrection (*AE), which similarly confuse the historical figure with the Yamada version, adding a ninja emphasis also found in the Hiroshi Inagaki movie Secret Scrolls (Yagyū Bugeichō, 1957).

The Yagyū family returned in 1982 for a second series, Yagyū's Secret Quest (Yagyū Jūbei Abaretabi). In it, Jūbei Yagyū reputedly goes mad in 1639 and attempts to assassinate Shogun Iemitsu. His father Munenori is dishonored and faced with a difficult situation. With Jūbei on the run and his other son unable to leave the Yagyū headquarters, Munenori cannot afford to leave the Shogun's side, but someone has to inspect the Nakasendō

route that links Edo to the Imperial capital of Kyoto. With little choice, Munenori decides to send his daughter Akane on the perilous mission, which is likely to involve regular confrontations with the many bandits who must be cleared from the route to keep travelers safe.

Taking the false name of Nuinosuke and disguising herself as a man, Akane begins her journey, accompanied by three fellow Ura-Yagyū: old family friend Tarobei, and brother/sister team Arisuke and Akemi. Meanwhile, Jūbei is not mad at all, but on a secret mission of his own that follows the same route, in the company of several other Yagyū spies who have joined a troupe of acrobats to cover their tracks. On occasion, he also comes to the rescue disguised as a creature called the Maboroshi Tengu (Phantom Goblin). Compare to the anime Jūbei-chan the Ninja Girl (*AE). The cunning Iga leader Hanzō Hattori would, according to another TV series, build the temple where THE SAMURAI was trained.

YAMATO NADESHIKO *

2000. AKA: *Perfect Woman*. PRD: Takashi Ishihara, Yūji Iwata. DIR: Setsurō Wakamatsu, Makoto Hirano. SCR: Miho Nakazono. CAST: Nanako Matsushima, Shinichi Tsutsumi, Akiko Yada, Masahiko Nishimura, Risa Sudō, Toshio Kakei, Mikihisa Azuma. CHN: Fuji. DUR: 45 mins. x 11 eps.; Mon 9 October 2000–31 December 2000.

Air stewardess Sakurako (Matsushima) is a social climber determined to escape from her impoverished upbringing by marrying a wealthy man. She walked out on her old life the moment she graduated ten years ago and came to Tokyo with a new hairstyle and a new attitude. She meets Ōsuke (Tsutsumi) and immediately shows a flirtatious interest in him, since she believes him to be a doctor and the owner of thoroughbred horses, and hence rich enough to make her happy. However, Ōsuke is really an assistant in his mother's fish shop, having returned to Japan to help her run the

place after his father's death, leaving behind a promising career as a mathematician at MIT in the Boston area. Ōsuke's interest in Sakurako is equally suspect, since he is initially less interested in her than in her resemblance to his ex-girlfriend in America. Meanwhile, Sakurako's no-nonsense fellow flight attendant friend Wakaba (Yada) loves Ōsuke for what he is and does not care if he is rich or not.

YN mixes the relationship comedy of ARRANGED MARRIAGE (Sakurako and friends are forever going on group dates, or gōkon) with the multiplicity of misunderstandings of SHOTGUN MARRIAGE. Boy-crazy flight attendants pursue gullible rich men and starstruck poor men, lovers break up at the altar and reconcile with teary-eyed melodrama, and a Tokyo minx delivers lectures on the ideal way to meet men—which would appear to be pouring scalding hot drinks on their hands and then offering to take them home for medical attention. In terms of the fairy tale formula which often informs Japanese TV, this is Cinderella from the point of view of the ugly sister, who must mend her ways before she will ever get her Prince Charming.

The nadeshiko (fringed pink) flower is the epitome of Japanese womanhood, as also referenced in the anime series Nadesico (*AE). Lead actress Matsushima would return as an idealized Japanese woman in 100 YEARS. Also compare to the dating movie Go-Con! (2000). Broadcast with English subtitles in the U.S. on NGN TV and KTSF TV. Theme: Misia—"Everything."

YASHA

2000. AKA: *Demon*. PRD: Kōtarō Takahashi, Takayuki Urai. DIR: Shimako Satō. SCR: Shimako Satō. CAST: Hideaki Itō, Nene Ōtsuka, Kōichi Iwaki, Hiroshi Abe, Mitsuru Fukikoshi, Shūji Kashiwabara, Kasumi Nakane, Sayaka Taniguchi, Satoshi Jinbo. CHN: Asahi. DUR: 45 mins. x 11 eps.; Fri 21 April 2000–30 June 2000.

Shizuka (Itō) is a genetically engineered genius working as a head researcher at the U.S. headquarters of Neo Genesis, the world's largest pharmaceutical company. After eight years in the States, he is sent to Tokyo to investigate a strange viral outbreak on the island of Kirishima. Setting up a lab at Rakuhoku University, he meets his childhood friend Shigeichi (Kashiwabara), who is blind but has developed a keen sense of hearing. With nowhere to stay, Shizuka moves in with Shigeichi and his sister Tōko, but soon gets a major shock when he encounters Rin Amemiya (Itō again), the long-lost twin he never knew he had.

Shizuka creates viral analysis software to determine the cause of the deaths at Kirishima, but realizes that Tōko has developed similar symptoms since she was bitten by her pet parakeet. In the nick of time, he identifies the virus as "A80," and successfully concocts a serum that saves Tōko's life. However, he secretly knows that A80 is a virus created by his own company, and that the only person in the world who could have brought it into Japan is Kyōichirō Amemiya (Iwaki), Rin's father. Shizuka tries to persuade his twin to leave Amemiya's home, but when he fails, moves in himself in search of evidence.

However, Rin confesses that the Kirishima incident was *his* doing, and invites Shizuka to join his secret project to decimate the world's population by releasing a plague genetically engineered to kill only the elderly—compare to **KEYS TO THE CITY**. Shizuka refuses to cooperate, but Rin eventually "persuades" him by shooting an infected person in front of Shigeichi, contaminating him in the process. Shizuka uses his own blood to create an antiserum, but cannot save his friend's life. He vows revenge on Rin, even as the virus begins to spread through the population and panic ensues. Uniting the late 20th-century thriller traditions of **NIGHT HEAD** and **RING**, this late-night show was based on the ongoing manga by *Banana Fish* creator Akimi Yoshida, originally pub-

lished in a supplement to *Shōjo Comic*. The more recent DVD release is adorned with a "GCATGCT" DNA sequence, inviting unfair dismissal as a rip-off of the Hollywood movie *Gattaca* (1997), whereas the original manga was published in Japan over a year before the film's release. Note the director and adaptor Shimako Satō, better known as the director of the movie version of **WIZARD OF DARKNESS**, and also *Tale of a Vampire* (1992). Theme: Sting—"Desert Rose."

YELLOW CARD

1993. PRD: N/C. DIR: Makoto Kiyohiro. SCR: Mitsuo Kokudo. CAST: Takanori Jinnai, Momoko Kikuchi, Daisuke Toshikura, Ryūji Harada, Keiju Kobayashi. CHN: TBS. DUR: 45 mins. x 13 eps.; Fri 2 July 1993–24 September 1993.

Three years after he walked out on his wife and children, Masao (Jinnai) returns in search of forgiveness and reconciliation, only to discover that he is a widower. His wife was running a noodle bar with her sister Noriko (Kikuchi) and cook Shunpei (Harada). His son Kazushige (Toshikura) cannot forgive him and holds him personally responsible for the death of his mother.

YES, HATSU-SAN

1973. JPN: *Hatsu-san, Haai (sic)*. PRD: Kazuo Shibata. DIR: Minoru Hanabusa. SCR: Genyō Takahashi. CAST: Masami Yomo, Shigeyuki Sunouchi, Kazuo Katō, Hizuru Takachiho, Masao Itō, Midori Yoshihara, Rumi Gotō. CHN: NHK. DUR: 30 mins. x 4 eps.; Sat 6 January 1973–27 January 1973. The rich, Tokyo-based Kajiki family mention to their retired nanny that they are looking for a maid. Before long, country girl Hatsu (Yomo) is at their doorstep applying for the job, even though the lady of the house would prefer someone more sophisticated. Despite her snooty reception from the family, particularly lady of the house Umeko (Takachiho), Hatsu gets the job. She befriends the lonely younger son Katsumi (Sunouchi), and

he confides in her that he is secretly keeping a pet dog in an outbuilding.

Umeko's fur coat goes missing, and she immediately accuses Hatsu of stealing it. Meanwhile, Katsumi's older brother discovers his dog and reports it, leading Umeko to order him to get rid of the animal. Katsumi locks himself in the outbuilding until he is allowed to keep his pet, but when Hatsu retrieves him, she sees that the dog's bed has been made from Umeko's missing fur coat. Without thinking, she hides it in her own trunk, and heads off for a New Year break with her family.

Katsumi runs away from home when Umeko makes him get rid of the dog anyway, but Hatsu brings him back for a family reconciliation, for which even the dog manages to find its way home. However, just as everything seems resolved, Umeko finds the missing fur coat in Hatsu's trunk, and fires her loyal employee. Based on the novel *Jochūkko* (*Little Maid*) by Shigeko Yuki. Compare to **GOOD PERSON**.

YESTERDAY'S ENEMY IS TODAY'S

1995. JPN: *Kinō no Teki wa Kyō mo Teki*. PRD: Tonkō Horikawa. DIR: Kazufumi Ōki. SCR: Toshiharu Matsubara. CAST: Junichi Ishida, Hitomi Kuroki, Shirō Itō, Shiho Fujimura. CHN: TBS. DUR: 45 mins. x 12 eps.; Sun 9 April 1995–25 June 1995. Privileged rich kid Kōhei (Ishida) fully expects to become the president of the company established by his late father, only to discover that his mother (Fujimura) and the company vice president have other plans. Theme: Sachiko Kumagai—"Ohayō Funny Girl" (Good Morning, Funny Girl).

YIN-YANG MASTER, THE

2001. JPN: *Onmyōji*. PRD: Susumu Kondō, Yoshinori Komiyama (#1); Kenichiro Yasuhara (#2). DIR: Masaaki Odagiri (#1); Satoshi Hayashi (#2). SCR: Eriko Komatsu, Chikako Nagakawa, Erika Tanaka (#1); Atsuhiro Tomioka (#2). CAST: Gorō Inagaki, Tetta Sugimoto, Manami Honjō, Sayaka Yamaguchi (#1); Hiroshi Mikami, Naoki Hosaka, Michiko Hada, Takayuki Yamada, Yasutaka Tsutsui, Yasunori Danta, Takanori Jinnai (#2). CHN: NHK (#1); Fuji (#2). DUR: 45 mins. x 10 eps. (#1); 45 mins. x 5 eps. (#2); Tue 3 April 2001–5 June 2001 (#1); 2 July 2002–30 July 2002 (#2).

In Japan's 10th-century capital Heian Kyō (modern Kyoto), royal sorcerer Abe no Seimei (Inagaki from SMAP) undertakes projects to dispel evil spirits from the lives of the local nobility. Phantoms and demons are brought into being by people's frustrations and desires, leading much of Seimei's work to resemble that of a modern detective, pathologist, or doctor—just with bonus scenes of hauntings and hallucinations.

The semi-mythical figure Abe no Seimei (921–1005) has cameo roles in several works of Japanese literature, including the *Tale of the Heike, Tales of Past and Present, Tales from the Uji Collection*, and the Noh play *Kanawa*. In modern times, *Yin-Yang Master* began as a series of novels by Baku Yumemakura, but first achieved mass popularity in 1999 when the books were adapted into manga form by artist Reiko Okano. A Brian Eno "image album" followed, and the manga eventually won the Tezuka Manga Award, issued in the name of Okano's father-in-law, ASTRO BOY creator Osamu Tezuka.

Perhaps it was the same end-of-the-century angst that gave us I'LL BE BACK and the LAST SONG, but for some reason, Abe no Seimei was a popular character in Japanese media during the time. A movie *Yin-Yang Master* (2001), starring kabuki actor Mansai Nomura as Seimei alongside drama regulars Hideaki Itō and Hiroyuki Sanada, conspicuously credited its origin to "the novel by Baku Yumemakura," with no mention of Okano in the same manner as the first TV series. Only a year later, a second *Yin-Yang Master* TV series arrived, this time on the Fuji network, loudly proclaiming that it was based on the manga version. This latest adaptation, *YYM: Evil Spirits of the Imperial City*, features Hiroshi Mikami as Seimei. With Princess Aya (Hada) under a powerful curse that no sorcery seems to be able to defeat, Seimei sets out with his friend Masayuki (Hosaka) to find the only thing that can save her, Raikirimaru, the Thunder-Cutting Sword.

YOJIMBO

1967. JPN: *Ore wa Yōjinbō*. AKA: *I am Yōjimbō*. PRD: N/C. DIR: Shunichi Kōno. SCR: Shinji Kessoku. CAST: Akira Kurizuka, Miki Nakasone, Jūshirō Konoe, Masako Kishi. CHN: NET (Asahi). DUR: 30 mins. x ca. 100 eps.; Mon 3 April 1967–25 September 1967 (#1); 29 January 1968–22 July 1968 (#2); 29 July 1968–31 March 1969 (#3); 7 April 1969–29 December 1969 (#4).

Yōjimbō, or "The Bodyguard," is a wandering warrior in the style of LONE WOLF AND CUB, who is prepared to undertake any mission as long as the money's right. As opposed to the obvious good and evil of other samurai dramas, Yōjimbō was often a character operating in gray areas (compare to MONJIRŌ), and his sense of justice was often frustrated by the actions of supposedly "good" government officials. Original leading man Kurizuka was replaced by Yūnosuke Itō for the second season, *Yojimbo in Waiting*, but his stage schedule forced him to leave the program after the 18th episode. Kurizuka was back for the third season,

Yojimbo Returns, and the fourth, *I am Yojimbo*.

YOSHIMUNE

1995. JPN: *Hachidai Shōgun Yoshimune*. AKA: *Tokugawa Yoshimune; Yoshimune the Eighth Shōgun*. PRD: N/C. DIR: Makoto Ōhara. SCR: James Miki. CAST: Toshiyuki Nishida, Nenji Kobayashi, Tōru Emori, Masahiko Tsugawa, Sakae Takita, Shiho Fujimura, Mitsuko Kusabue. CHN: NHK. DUR: 45 mins. x 48 eps.; Sun 8 January 1995–10 December 1995.

Yoshimune is born in 1684 as the third son of Mitsusada Tokugawa, a minor noble in the Tokugawa family who rules the fief of Kii (modern Wakayama and Mie prefectures) on behalf of the Shogun. He stands little chance of inheriting any wealth or power, until the untimely death of his father and two elder brothers makes him the next male heir to run the region. Kii is beset by a number of difficulties, particularly financial, but Yoshimune successfully keeps his domain running well, even after a disastrous tidal wave ruins the coastal area in 1707. When the seventh Shogun Ietsugu dies in childhood, the main branch of the Tokugawa lose their last male heir, forcing a search among more distant relatives for a successor. Yoshimune becomes the eighth Shogun in 1716, inheriting a Japan that is virtually bankrupt.

Yoshimune introduces a series of sweeping changes, the Kyōhō Reforms, limiting the size of the nobility, organizing the cultivation of new arable areas, and even issuing edicts on women's fashion. Among his sumptuary edicts, or economy orders, are instructions to reduce conspicuous consumption at weddings, limits on the amount of gold thread to be used in women's clothes, a ban on expensive lacquerware goods, and traffic restrictions on palanquins. His strict reforms were to save Japan from economic crisis, restore the power and authority of the Shogunate for another century, and ensure his place in the history books as the greatest ruler since Ieyasu (**TOKUGAWA IEYASU**). He retires in favor of his son in 1745, and dies in 1751.

With Japan's 1980s bubble economy in tatters, several TV writers wrote in praise of frugal living and belt-tightening, resulting in shows such as **HIS AND HER TEA CUPS** and **SALE!**. Ratings for the traditional Sunday *taiga* dramas had been falling since **WIND OF THE RYŪKYŪ ISLANDS** in 1993, leading NHK to call in veteran screenwriter James Miki. Eschewing the traditional samurai battles in favor of humor, Miki deftly compares the 1990s experience to Japan at the turn of the 18th century, when the cultural flowering of the Genroku period (1688–1704) gave way to a time that required harsh measures of austerity. His chosen setting also allows for cameo appearances from the many famous people of the day, including haiku poet Bashō, and author Saikaku Ihara. The story itself is narrated by an actor playing Monzaemon Chikamatsu, "Japan's Shakespeare." *Yoshimune* shared schedules with the sixth season of **ABARENBŌ SHŌGUN**, a fictionalized account of Yoshimune's life. Hence, throughout 1995, it was possible to see someone playing the eighth Shogun every Saturday *and* Sunday night. *Yoshimune* reversed the decline of the *taiga* series, clawing its way up to a respectable peak rating of 26.4%.

YOSHITSUNE

1966. JPN: *Minamoto no Yoshitsune.* PRD: N/C. DIR: Naoya Yoshida. SCR: Motozō Murakami. CAST: Kikunosuke Onoe, Junko Fuji, Ken Ogata. CHN: NHK. DUR: 45 mins. x 52 eps.; Sun 2 January 1966–25 December 1966.

In 1180 amid the same Taira/Minamoto internecine struggles covered in **THE GRASS AFLAME**, the nobleman Minamoto no Yoshitsune meets his half brother Yoritomo. Instead of welcoming him, the power hungry Yoritomo treats his newfound sibling as just another retainer, eventually sending him to Kyoto in 1183 to defeat his cousin Yoshinaka. Enjoying the patronage of the Retired Emperor Go-Shirakawa, Yoshitsune lives in Kyoto for a while, where he becomes reacquainted with his mother Tokiwa and fights a duel with **BENKEI**, who swears undying allegiance to him. He then leaves for the northern city of Hiraizumi (see **THE FIRE STILL BURNS**), returning in 1184 to help his half brother lead an army against his family's enemies at the Battle of Ichinotani. The grateful Go-Shirakawa offers the victorious Yoshitsune an honorary title, in a ruse that successfully causes friction between the two siblings. Ordered by Yoritomo to reject the title, Yoshitsune instead accepts it, snubbing his half brother further by declining an offer of marriage to the daughter of one of his lieutenants. An irate Yoritomo excludes Yoshitsune from his army, but is forced to seek his help at the Battle of Yashima. Yoshitsune turns the war in his half brother's favor once more and inflicts a crushing defeat on the Taira at the naval battle of Dannoura. It is only in the aftermath that he realizes that many of his adversaries have thrown themselves into the sea to resist capture—losses include the child Emperor Antoku, along with some of his Imperial sacred artifacts.

Ostracized by a half brother jealous of his success, Yoshitsune is approached by agents of the Gyō clan while in Kyoto, and invited to raise an army and join their rebellion. He refuses on Benkei's advice, but leaves town ahead of Yoritomo's men, losing much of his army in a disastrous storm. Welcomed to Hiraizumi by his old friend Hidehira Fujiwara, Yoshitsune believes he is safe, but soon finds himself caught up in a Fujiwara family quarrel. After the death of the aging Hidehira, his son Yasuhira assassinates his pro-Yoshitsune brother Tadahira. Yasuhira attacks Yoshitsune in 1189, and Benkei dies defending him. Realizing that his time has come, Yoshitsune commits suicide.

The tale of this young tragic hero is so popular that it has appeared on Japanese TV on numerous occasions. In kabuki form, an incident from the story of Yoshitsune also formed the first official drama broadcast on Japanese TV in 1953 (see Introduction). A 1959 series was specially commissioned to mark the establishment of the NET channel (now known as TV Asahi), in which a 13-year-old Kinya Kitaōji played the young Yoshitsune. The story was remade for a 1991 NTV drama special. See also **NEW TALE OF THE HEIKE**. Peak rating: 32.5%.

YOU ARE MY FAVORITE IN THE WORLD

1990. JPN: *Sekai de Ichiban Kimi ga Suki!* PRD: Yoshiaki Yamada. DIR: Michio Mitsuno. SCR: Toshiharu Matsubara. CAST: Atsuko Asano, Hiroshi Mikami, Shizuka Kudō, Hiroshi Fuse, Tōru Masuoka. CHN: Fuji. DUR: 45 mins. x 12 eps.; Mon 8 January 1990–19 March 1990.

Hana (Asano) and Kōji (Mikami) have both argued with their lovers in Kyoto and get on the same bullet train back to Tokyo. Kōji's friend Mankichi (Fuse) boards the train with him and falls in love with Hana at first sight. The trio agree to meet up in town, where a series of situations maneuver four more of their friends into a complicated love polygon. Four years after **SEVEN PEOPLE IN SUMMER**, its formula was still being repeated on a regular basis, but *YAMFitW* was badly received by an audience tiring of the unrealistically glamorous lifestyles on TV. Along with **PARADISE OF LOVE**, it came to symbolize the end of the original trendy dramas that began with **I WANT TO HUG YOU!**.

YOU ARE MY PET

2003. JPN: *Kimi wa Pet.* PRD: Sanae Suzuki, Akiko Hamada. DIR: Fuminori Kaneko, Arata Katō. SCR: Mika Ōmori. CAST: Koyuki, Jun Matsumoto, Seiichi Tanabe, Wakana Sakai, Eita, Misa Uehara. CHN: TBS. DUR: 45 mins. x ca. 11 eps.; Wed ?? April 2003–?? June 2003.

Career woman Sumire (Koyuki) loses her boyfriend, and then punches her boss after he sexually harasses her. She finds Takeshi (Matsumoto), a ballet dancer fallen on hard times, who has run away from home and is now cowering in a cardboard box after being attacked by some bullies. Sumire tells Takeshi that she wants a pet like the dog she had as a child, and when the boy agrees, she renames him Momo and takes him home with her. The two begin a strange relationship, but while Sumire soon finds a new love in the form of Hasumi (Tanabe), she is unable to give up on her "Momo." Based on the manga by Yayoi Ogawa—compare to ROCINANTE.

YOU LIKE IT HOT? *

1998. JPN: *O-atsui no ga O-suki?* PRD: Masaru Kamikura, Toshio Akabane. DIR: Ryūichi Inomata. SCR: Yasuhiro Koshimizu. CAST: Kippei Shiina, Misato Tanaka, Katsuhisa Namase, Toshiaki Megumi, Shunji Fujimura, Toshiyuki Hosokawa. CHN: NTV. DUR: 45 mins. x 11 eps.; Wed 1 July 1998–9 September 1998.

Bunzaemon (Fujimura) is the aging owner of a venerable public bath house, the Yumeyu, a registered cultural attraction where traditional methods are rigidly observed. But with his son Shunpei (Hosokawa) missing, he is unsure of who can take over the family business until his grandson Keiichirō (Shiina) volunteers. High jinks, predictably, ensue in this retread of IT'S TIME. Broadcast in the U.S. with English subtitles on KIKU TV and KTSF TV. Theme: Blanky Jet City—"Dandelion."

YOUNG GENERATION

1996. JPN: *Wakaba no Koro.* AKA: *About the Young Generation.* PRD: Kazuhiro Itō. DIR: Hiroshi Matsubara. SCR: Eriko Komatsubara. CAST: Tsuyoshi Dōmoto, Kōichi Dōmoto, Jinpachi Nezu, Megumi Okina, Tomoe Kitaura. CHN: TBS. DUR: 45 mins. x 12 eps.; Fri 12 April 1996–28 June 1996.

Although they start off on the wrong foot, two Tokyo teenagers eventually become friends and lend their support to each other until their attachment is tested by a tragic betrayal. Takeshi (Tsuyoshi Dōmoto from the Kinki Kids) has to hold down two jobs to support his brother and sister because his drunken father has been in no state to work since the death of his mother. His newfound friend Kai (Kōichi Dōmoto, the other Kinki Kid) is the estranged son of the town doctor—compare to a similar friendship on opposite sides of the tracks in Akira Kurosawa's *Drunken Angel* (1948). Friendships are placed under further strain by Izumi (Okina), Takeshi's lifelong friend, for whom he now has stronger feelings, but who herself has eyes only for Kai. Sometimes confused with ALL ABOUT YOUNG PEOPLE, the title of which sounds similar in Japanese. Theme: Bee Gees—"First of May."

YOUNG KINDAICHI FILES

1995. JPN: *Kindaichi Shōnen no Jiken File.* PRD: Yūko Hazeyama. DIR: Yukihiko Tsutsumi. SCR: Masaki Fukasawa, Tetsuya Ōishi. CAST: Tsuyoshi Dōmoto, Rie Tomosaka, Masato Furuoya. CHN: NTV. DUR: 45 mins. x 26 eps.; 15 July 1995–16 September 1995 (#1); 13 July 1996–14 September 1996 (#2, 9 eps.); 14 July 2001–15 September 2001 (#3, 9 eps.).

Hajime Kindaichi (Dōmoto from the Kinki Kids) is the teenage descendant of a famous detective who swears he will solve every crime he comes across. With his sidekick and childhood friend Miyuki (Tomosaka), a girl who remains chaste but fiercely jealous of every other woman he meets, he solves crimes for the adult detective Isamu Kenmochi (Furuoya).

Hajime Kindaichi's first TV appearance was a feature-length special on 8 April 1995, although even the series tends to break into story-arcs across more than one episode. Thus, in both anime and live-action versions, chapters of *YKF* readily lend themselves to re-editing as stand-alone TV features. Before that, *YKF* began life as a 1992 manga by Yozaburō Kanari and Fumiya Satō in *Shōnen Magazine*, originally inspired by Kanari's viewing of *Lupin*

III (*AE)—the adventures of another modern hero with a famous grandfather. However, as with *Lupin III*, copyright issues came into play—the manga survived unopposed, but the broadcast of this TV drama version led to public success and legal action from the estate of author Seishi Yokomizo. Lawyers argued that *Kōsuke* Kindaichi had first appeared in *Hōseki* magazine in 1946, and that by featuring his grandson, the manga was passing itself off as a sequel. The wrangle was averted with an out-of-court legal settlement, freeing the franchise to continue as an anime series (*AE) and as a remake with the all-new cast of Jun Matsumoto, Anne Suzuki, and Takashi Naitō. In celebration, the third season began with Kindaichi on a cruise ship, allowing for several cheesy gags at the expense of *Titanic* (1997), before the crew start dying and he is able to put his brain to work.

The third season of *YKF* was broadcast in the U.S. on KTSF TV, presumably without English subtitles. Several *Young Kindaichi* novels and manga stories are also available in English. *YKF* became a calling card for the director Yukihiko Tsutsumi who later created PSYCHOMETER EIJI and IKEBUKURO WEST GATE PARK. For another grandchild taking after her detective ancestor, see *Ai Zenigata* in the HEIJI ZENIGATA entry.

YOUNG ORPHEUS

1972. JPN: *Shōnen Orfée.* PRD: Kazuo Shibata. DIR: Kanae Mayuzumi. SCR: Hiroyuki Yokota. CAST: Shinji Osada, Mari Wada, Shōji Ōki, Kōichi Hayashi, Kyōko Satomi. CHN: NHK. DUR: 30 mins. x 4 eps.; Sat 2 September 1972–23 September 1972.

The Land of the Dead is not a mythical place, but a small planet far off in the cosmos. Its solitary ruler falls in love with the sight of a girl's smile and the sound of her laugh, and decides to bring her to his world to be his companion. Back on Earth, Susumu (Osada) is traumatized by the sudden death of his sister Fūko (Wada), but manages to hitch a ride on the spaceship that transports departed souls to the Land of the Dead. Though he is almost killed with a poison drink, Susumu manages to stow away on another ship, piloted by the Boss's former servant Pierrot (Ōki). The pair search for Fūko and for a means of returning to Earth. They are told by an old man (Hayashi) that the secret lies in a particular drop of water, but they are swamped by a heavy rainstorm, in which every drop comprises a single human soul. Eventually retrieving Fūko, they discover that she has amnesia, and that consequently they must seek a cure in the Cactus Kingdom on the Flower Planet. Captured by the Queen (Satomi), Susumu is ordered to beat her champion knight in single combat or forfeit his sister's life. He wins the duel and finds out that her champion was the abductor of his sister. Susumu wakes up in the hospital back on Earth, where Fūko has made a miraculous recovery, in a strange mixture of *The Little Prince* (*AE) and *Night Train to the Stars* (*AE), based on a book by Yukio Misawa. Its most obvious debt, of course, is to the classical legend of Orpheus and Eurydice, in which a musician must descend into the underworld to rescue his beloved.

YOUNG PAPA
2002. JPN: *Yan Papa*. PRD: Hideki Inada. DIR: Ryōko Hoshida, Nobuyuki Takahashi. SCR: Yumie Nishiogi. CAST: Tomoya Nagase, Miwako Fujitani, Ai Katō, Maki Gotō, Miku Ishida. CHN: TBS. DUR: 45 mins. x 10 eps.; Wed 9 October 2002–11 December 2002.
Twenty-five-year old Yūsaku (Nagase) falls in love with Yui (Fujitani), a manga artist many years older than him. Despite opposition from Yui's bratty children from a previous marriage, the couple make preparations for a wedding ceremony. However, Yui is killed on the way to the wedding. Because Yui has already signed legal documents making Yūsaku her next of kin, he inherits her possessions. Among her papers, Yūsaku discovers the outline for a new manga series, in which Yui

had planned to make amends to her children, whom she has neglected in favor of her work for so long. Despite the temptation to walk away from the hellish children, Yūsaku moves into the house they share with their aunt, intending on bringing Yui's dream to life, whatever the cost. Reluctant parenting in the style of NEWS WOMAN, with a manga twist in the style of KING OF EDITORS.

YOUNG SHŪSAKU *
2000. JPN: *Nekketsu Shūsaku ga Yuku*. PRD: Katsuhiko Takei. DIR: Kiyoharu Izumi. SCR: Chigusa Shiota. CAST: Shunsuke Nakamura, Hiroshi Fujioka, Shirō Itō. CHN: Asahi. DUR: 45 mins. x 9 eps.; Thu 19 October 2000–14 December 2000.
Morioka swordsman Shūsaku (Nakamura) comes to the big city of Edo, where his countryside swagger is soon bested by the superior swordsmanship of TOYAMA NO KIN-SAN (Fujioka). He begins studying the way of the sword at the Nakanishi School, where the stern master refuses to give him much praise. However, in the style of HANSHICHI, young Shūsaku and his new friend Kin-san become involved in several local crime cases, including the murder of a kabuki actress and the arrest of one of their lady friends on a false murder charge. Shūsaku falls for local girl Yae, for whose friend Oyō he and Kin-san temporarily work as bodyguards, but is unable to makes his feelings known. A combination of *Hanshichi*'s detection with a little proto-sports drama in the training sessions and *dōjō* rivalries of the swordsmen soon ensues. Broadcast in the U.S. with English subtitles on KIKU TV.

YOUNGER BROTHER
1981. JPN: *Otōto*. PRD: Kanae Mayuzumi. DIR: Noriaki Sasahara. SCR: Isamu Seki. CAST: Kumiko Akiyoshi, Hiroyuki Takano, Mizuho Suzuki, Kyōko Kishida. CHN: NHK. DUR: 30 mins. x 2 eps.; Thu 27 August 1981–28 August 1981.
In the early years of the 1920s, teenage Gen (Akiyoshi) lives with her writer

WEDDINGS FROM HELL

Here Come the Brides

This drama ends with the terrifying sight of the bride, in white, being walked up the aisle by her black-clad former best friend, who is also the jilted first wife of the groom. ☞

father (Suzuki) and stepmother (Kishida). She is also responsible for looking after her little brother Tamao (Takano), who pines for his dead mother. His attitude worsens until he is arrested by the police, and his parents wash their hands of him. The family are finally reunited at his bedside when he is diagnosed with terminal pneumonia, and Tamao dies mere days after he receives the maternal love he craves. Another cheery Japanese children's drama, based on the book by Aya Kōda.

YOUNGER MAN
2003. JPN: *Toshishita no Otoko*. PRD: Hisao Yaguchi, Takashi Hashimoto. DIR: Akimitsu Sasaki, Takashi Fujio. SCR: Makiko Uchidate. CAST: Izumi Inamori, Katsunori Takahashi, Jun Fubuki, Toshiki Kashū, Yumi Asō, Mitsuru Hirata. CHN: TBS. DUR: 45 mins. x ca. 11 eps.; Thu 9 January 2003–?? March 2003.
Office lady Chikako (Inamori) falls for a man she meets at her gym, but finds her advances politely yet firmly rejected. Her mother Hanae (Fubuki) enjoys far more success with her own boyfriend, a mystery man that Chikako has never met, but who appears to have spurred the middle-aged lady into a second youth. Imagine, then, Chikako's surprise and revulsion, when she discovers that her mother's new boyfriend is Shun (Takahashi), the same man she has been pursuing herself. Chikako resolves to win Shun for herself, no matter what the cost, in another drama from the people who brought you TO LOVE AGAIN and

WEEKEND MARRIAGE. Hype at the time claimed it was another innovative approach to romance from writer Uchidate, forgetting any similarities with the earlier **COME TO MAMA'S BED.** Theme: Sinba—"Hana" (Beauty).

YOUR TOWN

1973. JPN: *Anata no Machi*. PRD: N/C. DIR: Ryūnosuke Sano, Hiroshi Watanabe. SCR: Tadaaki Yamazaki. CAST: Tōru Ōe, Teruaki Satō, Tadao Futami, Mitsuko Tsutsumi, Tetsuharu Taniguchi, Kiriko Kamihara. CHN: NHK. DUR: 30 mins. x 6 eps.; Mon 11 June 1973–20 June 1973.

Wanderers Ken (Ōe) and Hiroshi (Satō) stumble into a new town to discover that everything is cheap, everyone is friendly, and there's plenty of work available. They settle down for a while and enjoy the good life, but eventually tire of their new life and decide to hit the road again. It's only then that they discover the town's secret law—that nobody may ever leave. Four years after the Japanese broadcast of the British series *The Prisoner* (NHK, 1969), this Japanese children's TV clone finds two partners in crime trying a number of escape schemes. Music by Kenichi Kumagai.

YOUR YUKICHI IS CRYING

2001. JPN: *Omae no Yukichi ga Naiteiru*. PRD: Keiko Morishita. DIR: Kazuhisa Imai. SCR: Kazuhiko Yūkawa. CAST: Noriyuki Higashiyama, Taichi Kokubu, Yuki Matsushita. CHN: Asahi. DUR: 45 mins. x ca. 11 eps.; Thu 11 January 2001–?? March 2001.

Yukichi (Kokubu) is a privileged, shy mother's boy, who inherits a school from his departed grandmother. With no aptitude or acumen, Yukichi becomes the principal of a school with serious financial difficulties. Consequently, he tries to buy help in the form of master educator Seiji (Higashiyama). A teaching drama that introduces the "renegade master" convention more often seen in gourmet shows such as **SOMMELIER, THE CHEF,** and **ANTIQUE.**

YOU'RE UNDER ARREST

2002. JPN: *Taiho Shichauzo*. PRD: Jun Akiyama. DIR: Hiroshi Akabane. SCR: Tetsuya Ōishi. CAST: Sachie Hara, Misaki Itō, Kazushige Nagashima. CHN: Asahi. DUR: 45 mins. x 9 eps.; Thu 17 October 2002–12 December 2002.

The Tokyo Bokutō Station traffic department gains two new officers in the form of shy, reserved ace driver Miyuki (Hara) and impulsive, bad-tempered martial artist Natsumi (Itō). Supposedly charged with no duty heavier than ticketing bad drivers, the over-enthusiastic girls immediately start taking the law into their own hands, eagerly rushing in to stop a robbery without asking for backup, only to scare the living daylights out of a group of store employees being run through a simulation by motorcycle cop Ken (Nagashima). Despite numerous dressings down from their boss, the girls insist on doing what they think is right, even when it risks their jobs. After preventing local girl Yūka from committing suicide, they hunt down the man who drove her to despair.

Needless to say, they also luck into big-league crimes, such as when they find a badly parked car whose driver is just about to hijack a bus. The girls stop the incident, only to discover that their criminal had an accomplice onboard who takes them prisoner. Ken, who harbors secret feelings for Miyuki, saves the day on his motorcycle, but Miyuki is forced to commandeer the bus herself in order to drive a patient to the hospital in time for a vital operation.

As with *YuA*'s spiritual cousin **OL POLICE,** this is not so much a police series as an excuse for mawkish flirting. Matters reach an early peak when Ken wakes up in bed with Natsumi, incurring the wrath of Miyuki, although the girls soon patch up their relationship over a bomb scare at Yūka's school. Natsumi surprises them by announcing that she is intending to marry, but Miyuki soon discovers that her friend's fiancée is a serial wife-killer. And so on.

First published in manga form in 1986, Kōsuke Fujishima's *You're under Arrest* (*AE) was animated straight-to-video in 1994, remade as TV cartoon serials in 1996 and 1999, released as an animated movie in the same year, and then brought back as another animated TV series in 2001. This live-action version seems intended to capitalize on the fact that the manga's original fans are now likely to be thirtysomething TV viewers, and ready for a drama adaptation of one of their childhood favorites. However, *YuA* suffered in the ratings war through comparison with the same season's **REMOTE,** and drew to a close after nine episodes, with Natsumi facing recruitment to the Metropolitan Police's criminology unit. Theme: Mariah Carey—"Through the Rain."

YOUTH FAMILY

1989. JPN: *Seishun Kazoku*. PRD: N/C. DIR: Toshiki Miyazawa. SCR: Man Izawa. CAST: Ayumi Ishida, Misa Shimizu, Isao Hashizume, Takanori Jinnai, Gorō Inagaki. CHN: NHK. DUR: 15 mins. x ca. 30 eps.; Mon 3 April 1989–30 September 1989.

Departing from the usual conventions of morning drama, *YF* dumps in-law appeasement and uxorial misery in favor of the life of a nuclear family, both of whose parents are working. Mako (Ishida) holds down a day job at a department store and supports her daughter Saki (Shimizu), who is a wannabe manga artist. As with its later imitator **YOUNG PAPA,** friction between the couple arises over the disparity in their incomes—Mako earns more than her husband, who decides that he needs a complete career change.

YOUTH OFFSIDE: FEMALE TEACHER AND THE HOT-BLOODED ELEVEN

1993. JPN: *Seishun Offside: Onna Kyōshi to Nekketsu Eleven*. PRD: N/C. DIR: Tatsuzō Inohara. SCR: Masahiro Kobayashi. CAST: Rina Katase, Kenichirō Kikuchi, Hiroshi Fuse, Tetsurō Tanba. CHN: Asahi. DUR: 45 mins. x 4 eps.; Tue 19 October 1993–9 November 1993.

Yōko (Katase) is an uncompromising school teacher in her home town of Machida, pressed into service as the coach for the troubled high school soccer team, the Machida Jurassics. This is partly because she has inherited the team from her father, and partly because she feels she owes it to the boys, one of whom, the 15-year-old Kenichi (Kikuchi), has developed a crush on her. Not to be confused with *Red-Blooded Eleven* (1970), which was the first animated soccer series to be screened on Japanese television.

YŪHI'S THE KING OF THE HILL
1978. JPN: Yūhigaoka no Sōridaijin. PRD: Yoshio Nakamura. DIR: Terumasa Saitō. SCR: Mineaki Hata. CAST: Masatoshi Nakamura, Masaki Kanda, Kaoru Yumi, Masao Komatsu, Miwako Fujitani. CHN: NTV. DUR: 30 mins. x ca. 50 eps.; Wed 11 October 1978–10 October 1979.

Yūjiro (Nakamura) is an idealistic yet unconventional English teacher who returns to Japan after picking up a number of unorthodox teaching methods in the zany United States. The result is an antidote to the same era's earnest teaching drama ZEALOUS TIMES, which could be said to be the spiritual ancestor of **GTO**. Based on the manga by Akira Mochizuki, creator of **THE SIGN IS V**.

YUTA AND HIS WONDROUS FRIENDS
1974. JPN: Yuta to Fushigi na Nakamatachi. PRD: Masaharu Morita. DIR: Kazuya Satō. SCR: Akira Hayasaka. CAST: Toshiya Kumagai, Sachiko Itō, Taiji Tonoyama, Gajirō Satō, Kokan Katsura, Masato Tsujimura, Fumiaki Sakabe, Setsuo Wakui, Kunio Ōtsuka. CHN: NHK. DUR: 24 mins. 30 sec x 3 eps.; Mon 6 May 1974–8 May 1974.

After the death of his father in a factory accident, city boy Yuta (Kumagai) returns to his mother's home village amid the northern mountains of Tōhoku. The family runs a hotspring resort, but Yuta has no playmates and is left to keep himself amused. Old man Torakichi (Tonoyama) tells him of the local legend of the *zashiki warashi*—bare-kneed, shy boys in indigo kimono who hardly ever speak to strangers. Later, as Yuta sleeps on the night of the full moon, he is awoken by five mischievous boys, all played by adult actors—Pedoro (Satō), Hinodero (Sakabe), Senro (Wakui), Monze (Katsura), and Jinjo (Tsujimura). Yuta accompanies the *zashiki warashi* in a trip up the mountain and eventually even takes them with him to school, although only he can see them. Later, we discover that the "boys" are in fact the spirits of dead children—the poverty-struck Tōhoku region has often been forced to make harsh decisions to keep the local population down, and the *zashiki warashi* are the result. Abandoned by their parents before they were given proper names, the *zashiki warashi* all have "birthdays" that are really their memories of the day they died. Pendoro takes his name from where he was found, in the mud (*doro*) among the shepherd's purse flowers (*penpengusa*) in 1695. Senro died on a railway track (*senro*) in 1929. Monze was left at the front gate of a temple (*monzen*) in 1783. Jinjo was abandoned in front of a guardian statue (*jizō*) in 1833, and Hinodero takes his name from that of the geisha house to which his mother was sold in 1902.

Eventually, the *zashiki warashi* reveal that they cannot come to see Yuta any more, because a new road being built into the hills will banish them—"*We're not meant for anything modern.*" Compare to *My Neighbor Totoro* (*AE) and *Pompoko* (*AE).

Z

ZATŌICHI

1974. JPN: *Zatōichi Monogatari*. PRD: Suguru Kadoya. DIR: Kazuo Mori, Yoshiyuki Kuroda, Shintarō Katsu, Kenji Misumi, Mikiyoshi Yasuda, Tokuzō Tanaka, Junji Kurata, Akira Inoue. SCR: Hajime Takaishi, Kinya Naoi, Fumi Takahashi, Shōzaburō Asai, Ichirō Ikeda, Seiji Hoshikawa, Masao Hoshida, Takayuki Yamada. CAST: Shintarō Katsu, Sanae Tsuchida, Masahiko Tsugawa, Tamao Nakamura, Kinya Kitaōji, Kiwako Taichi, Toshio Kurosawa, Yukiji Asaoka, Yūjirō Ishihara, Makoto Fujita. CHN: Fuji. DUR: 45 mins. x 100 eps.; Thu 3 October 1974–17 April 1975 (#1); 4 October 1976–25 April 1977 (#2); 9 January 1978–26 September 1978 (#3); 16 April 1979–19 November 1979 (#4).

Zatōichi (Katsu) is a blind swordsman who works as a masseur—all the better to be close to his hobbies, women and gambling. He is bullied and discriminated against, but he endures it all with good humor, chiefly because he is a master swordsman and unafraid of taking up arms to defend the weak.

Zatōichi began in the movie theaters with Kenji Misumi's movie *The Blind Swordsman* (1962). A sequel followed the same year, and the movie series continued throughout the 1960s, with a notable high point at Kihachi Okamoto's *Zatōichi Meets Yōjimbō* (1970). The 17th movie, *Zatōichi Challenged* (1967) was supposedly the original inspiration for the Rutger Hauer vehicle *Blind Fury* (1989).

The movie series came to a temporary close with its 25th episode, *Zatōichi's Conspiracy* (1972), but leading man Shintarō Katsu simply moved his role onto the small screen. It was a good time for samurai shows, particularly with the challenge provided by **SURE DEATH** and **MONJIRŌ**, and Zatōichi lasted throughout the 1970s, before a final 26th movie, called simply *Zatōichi* (1989), closed the story once and for all. A versatile martial artist who also trained the leading man in **ABARENBŌ SHŌGUN**, Shintarō Katsu also appeared in **MASAMUNE THE ONE-EYED DRAGON**, and died in 1997. He was long regarded as inseparable from the *Zatōichi* role, until the release of Takeshi Kitano's own remake in 2003. The three later seasons of the TV show contained the suffix Shin ("New"), and were shown in the U.S. on NGN without English subtitles. Shintarō Katsu also sang the theme song "Otentosan" (The Sun).

ZEALOUS TIMES

1978. JPN: *Netchū Jidai*. PRD: N/C. DIR: Tomomi Tanaka. SCR: Hirokazu Fuse. CAST: Yutaka Mizutani, Etsuko Shihomi, Mikiko Otonashi, Kimiko Ikegami, Ichirō Ogura, Yōsuke Ōkawa, Mitsuko Kusabue, Eiji Funakoshi. CHN: NTV. DUR: ?? mins. x ca. 50 eps.; Fri 6 October 1978–30 March 1979 (#1); 5 July 1980–28 March 1981 (#2).

Kōdai Kitano (Mizutani) is a rookie teacher from Hokkaidō who genuinely likes children and finally gets a posting to a Tokyo elementary school. Principal Amagi offers to let him stay at his house, and Kōdai agrees, only to discover that several other teachers are already doing so.

ZT set the tone for an entire subgenre of comical but passionate teachers in school dramas that continues to this day with **KINPACHI SENSEI** and **GTO**. Previously typecast as a gangster in serials such as **WOUNDED ANGEL**, Mizutani jumped at the chance to expand his range, announcing that he had hoped the series would be a success in the same vein as *Bad News Bears* (1976), the American movie that similarly inspired the creation of **KING'S RESTAURANT**. The production team was initially reluctant to use so many untrained children, but the mix of actors and amateurs paid off, the final episode hit a peak of 40%, and the series remains in top ten lists two decades on. In the gap between the first and second season, Mizutani appeared in a brief cop show spin-off *Zealous Times Detective Story* (7 April 1979–6 October 1979).

ZONE FIGHTER

1973. JPN: *Ryūsei Ningen Zone*. AKA: *Meteor Man Zone*. PRD: Kimihiko Etō, Nobuyuki Takahashi, Yoshio Nishikawa. DIR: Jun Fukuda, Inoshirō Honda, Kengo Furusawa, Akiyasu

Kikuchi. SCR: Shōzō Uehara, Masaru Takeue, Satoshi Kurumi, Motoo Nagai, Susumu Takeuchi, Shinichi Kamisawa, Kazuhisa Hattori. CAST: Kazuya Aoyama, Kazumi Kitahara, Kenji Satō, Shōji Nakayama, Sawako Kamizuki, Shirō Amakusa, Hideaki Ohara, Tōru Kawai, Yuzuru Kusumi. CHN: NTV. DUR: 25 mins. x 26 eps.; Mon 2 April 1973–24 September 1973.

The Gorga Empire, a race of gargoyle aliens with antennae they can pull off their heads and use as whips, destroy the home planet of the Zone. The last survivors of the Zone clan take refuge on planet Earth, where they adopt human names and disguises. However, their new homeworld proves to be the next target in the Gorgan plan to con-quer the universe. Zone refugees Hikaru (Aoyama), Hotaru (Kitahara), and Akira (Satō) use their alien powers to transform into Zone Fighter, Zone Angel, and Zone Junior to protect their adopted home from regular monsters of the week called Terro-Beasts, dropped to Earth in Gorgan capsules. Inevitably, the monster proves to be too much for the Zone people to handle, and Hikaru is forced to transform into a giant version of himself to take the monster on under equal terms.

As the popularity of the *Godzilla* movies began to wane, the Tōhō Studios utilized some of the talent and props from the movies to concoct their own answer to Tsuburaya's **ULTRAMAN** franchise. Despite relative obscurity in TV terms, *Zone Fighter* has retained a cult following among fans of monster movies, who watch for the appearance of the movie monster King Ghidorah in episodes five and six, and the arrival of Godzilla himself in episode 11. In one of five appearances in the series, the famous lizard took on Gigan, the same creature he would fight in the same year's movie *Godzilla vs. Megalon*, which was also directed by ZF's Jun Fukuda. The adverse economic climate of the early 1970s, exploited to some extent by the later **JAPAN SINKS**, was to cause the serial's premature end and the *Godzilla* movies themselves experienced a long hiatus after 1975.

Appendices

Foreign TV Shows

Chinese Titles

Next Season's Shows

Bibliography

Index

FOREIGN TV SHOWS

In the course of preparing this book, we have found information on over 1,100 foreign TV shows broadcast on Japanese TV since 1954. They are listed below along with the original title, Japanese title where different, a translation where required, and date and channel where available. Dates marked with an asterisk (*) are of U.S. broadcast when the Japanese date was unknown to us. Where a show was not broadcast on a major channel, but instead syndicated on a minor network, we have filed the channel as "Synd." Later shows broadcast on cable channels, such as The Mystery Channel (Myst) or The Super Channel (Supe) have been so filed. Our list is by no means exhaustive, but presents a helpful guide to some of the shows that share the Japanese airwaves with local productions. Data we have been unable to confirm has been marked "??."

26 Men = Arizona Rangers • NET • 1959

42nd on Film = Hidōsuji no Michi • NHK • 1961

77 Sunset Strip = Sunset 77 • TBS • 1960

79 Park Avenue = Ai no Arashi ni [In a Storm of Love] • TBS • 1981

87th Precinct = 87 Bunsho • Fuji • 1962

A Rumor of War = Shirarezaru Senjō • Fuji • 1984

ABC Afterschool Specials = Jidōgeki Eiga [Children's Theater] • NHK • 1979

Abbott and Costello = Cartoon • NTV • 1970

Abbott and Costello Show, The = Dekoboko Gekijō [Uneven Theater] • NTV • 1958

Absolutely Fabulous • NHK • *1992

Adam 12 = Tokusōtai Adam 12 [Special Investigation Team Adam 12] • Fuji • 1970

Addams Family, The =Addams no Obake Ikka [Addams Family of Ghosts] • TVT • 1968

Adventurer, The = Himitsu Sōsain Note • TVT • 1973

Adventures in Paradise = Nankai no Bōken [South Sea Adventure] • NET • 1965

Adventures in Rainbow Country = Mori to Mizuumi no Kuni no Bōken [Adventures in the Land of Forests and Lakes] •

Synd • 1979

Adventures of a Jungle Boy = Jungle Boy • NTV • 1963

Adventures of ARK = Animal Rescue Kids • NHK • *1997

Adventures of Black Beauty = Kurouma no Monogatari [Story of the Black Horse] • NHK • 1974

Adventures of Champion = Meiba Champion no Bōken [Adventures of Champion the Famous Horse] • KRT • 1957

Adventures of Hiram Holliday = Hiram-kun Kampai [Cheers to Hiram] • NTV • 1960

Adventures of Kit Carson = Seibu no Yūsha Kit Carson • NTV • 1957

Adventures of Ozzie and Harriet = Yōki na Nelson [The Cheerful Nelsons] • NHK • 1960

Adventures of Rin Tin Tin = Meiken Rin Tin Tin [Famous Dog Rin Tin Tin] • NTV • 1956

Adventures of Robin Hood = Robin Hood no Bōken • NTV • 1956

Adventures of Sherlock Holmes = Sherlock Holmes no Bōken • NHK • 1985

Adventures of Sindbad Junior = Shōnen Sindbad • YTV • 1965

Adventures of Superman = Superman •

KRT • 1956

Adventures of the Gummi Bears = Gummi Bears no Bōken • ABC • 1987

Adventures of the Sea = Seaspray-gō no Bōken [Adventures of the Seaspray] • CBC • 1968

Adventures of Tin Tin = Tin Tin no Bōken • Fuji • 1964

Adventures of Tom Sawyer = Tom Sawyer no Bōken • NHK • 1962

Adventures of Young Gulliver = Gulliver to Kobitotachi [Gulliver and the Little People] • NHK • 1969

Agatha Christie Hour, The • Synd • 1987

Airwolf = Chō'onsoku Kōgeki Heli Airwolf [Supersonic Attack Helicopter Airwolf] • NTV • 1986

Alcatraz: The Whole Shocking Story = Datsugoku Alcatraz [Escape From Alcatraz] • NTV • 1987

Alcoa Goodyear Theater = Sunday Star Gekijō • TBS • 1965

Alcoa Premiere Theater = Star no Meisaku Gekijō • TBS • 1966

Alfred Hitchcock Hour = Hitchcock Suspense • KTV • 1963

Alfred Hitchcock Hour = Shin Hitchcock Series [New Hitchcock Series] • Fuji • 1965

Alfred Hitchcock Presents = Hitchcock

Gekijō [Hitchcock Theater] • NTV • 1957

Alfred Hitchcock Presents = Hitchcock Gekijō 96 [Hitchcock Theater 96] • TVT • 1986

Alias Smith and Jones = Seibu no Futari-gumi [Western Twosome] • NHK • 1972

Alice in Wonderland = Fushigina Kuni no Alice • NHK • 1988

All-Star Theater = Star Gekijō • NHK • 1958

Ally McBeal = Ally My Love • NHK • 1998

Alvin and the Chipmunks = Alvin to Chipmunk • CN • *1983

Alvin Show, The = Wanpaku Sanningumi [Mischievous Trio] • TBS • 1964

American Girls, The • TVT • 1979

Americans • Fuji • 1961

Amos Burke Secret Agent • NTV • 1966

Andy Griffith Show, The = Mayberry 110-ban [110 Mayberry] • NTV • 1964

Anna and the King = Ōsama to Watashi [The King and I] • Synd • 1975

Annie Oakley = Annie yo Teppō o Tore [Annie Get Your Gun] • KRT • 1957

Aquaman • Synd • *1967

Aquanauts, The • NET • 1963

Archie Show, The = Archie de Nakucha [It's Gotta Be Archie] • NET • 1970

Archie's TV Funnies = Manga TV Funny • Synd • *1971

Arnie • NET • 1972

Around the World = Sekai o Kakeru Dai Bōken [Great Round-the-World Adventure] • Synd • *1967

Arthur Rank Children's Theater = Shōnen Eiga Gekijō • TBS • 1966

Asphalt Jungle, The • KTV • 1966

Assignment Underwater = Bill Sencho [Captain Bill] • NET • 1961

Assignment Vienna = Wien Chōhōmō • Fuji • 1975

A-Team, The = Tokko Yarō [Special Attack Guys] • Asahi • 1985

Atom Ant Show, The = Kairiki Ant • NET • 1966

Avengers, The = Oshare Mitsu Tantei

[Dandy Secret Detectives] • NET • 1967

Aventures de Tom Sawyer = Tom Sawyer no Bōken • NHK • 1970

Avventure di Pinocchio = Pinocchio • NHK • 1973

Awakening Land, The = Kaitakusha • Fuji • 1979

Award Theater = Golden Theater • TBS • 1965

B.B.C. Family Classics I = Sekai Kodomo Meisaku Gekijō • Asahi • 1978

B.B.C. Family Classics II = Kodomo Sekai Meisaku Gekijō • Asahi • 1979

B.B.C. Shakespeare Plays = Shakespeare Gekijō • NHK • 1980

B.B.C. World Famous Novels = Sekai Meisaku Dorama Series • TVT • 1974

B.J. and the Bear = Truck Yarō BJ [Truck Guy BJ] • NTV • 1980

B.J. and the Ladies = BJ & Truck Gal • NTV • 1983

Bachelor Father = Ojisama wa Hitorimono • NTV • 1961

Backstairs at the Whitehouse = Whitehouse Monogatari [Whitehouse Story] • TVK • 1981

Bad News Bears = Ganbare Bears [Go For It Bears] • NTV • 1979

Baggy Pants and the Nitwits = Manga Wakiwaki Land [Cartoon Crazy Land] • TBS • 1980

Banacek = Banacek Hatsujo [Enter Banacek] • Fuji • 1977

Banana Splits Adventure Hour = Manga Daibōken • TVT • 1970

Band of Brothers • WOW • 2002

Banyon = Shiritsu Tantei Banyon [Private Investigator Banyon] • NET • 1973

Barba Papa • TVT • 1977

Barefoot in the Park = Hadashi de Kōen o • Fuji • 1973

Baretta = Keiji Baretta [Detective Baretta] • NET • 1976

Barnaby Jones = Meitantei Jones [Famous Detective Jones] • NTV • 1975

Baron, The • Fuji • 1966

Barrier Reef = Endeavor-gō no Tanken [Investigations of the Endeavor] • NHK • 1971

Bat Masterson • NET • 1959

Batfink Show, The = Mōretsu Bat-kun [Burning Bat] • NTV • 1969

Batman • Fuji • 1966

Battlestar Galactica = Uchū Kūbo Galactica [Space Carrier Galactica] • NTV • 1981

Baywatch • Supe • *1989

Beany and Cecil = Beany no Bōken Ryokō [Beany's Adventure Journey] • NET • 1963

Bearcats =Tsūkai! Jidōsha Yarō [Thrill! Car Guys] • KTV • 1973

Beauty and the Beast = Bijo to Yajū • Lala • *1987

Beavis and Butthead • MTV • *1993

Beetle Bailey, Barney Google = Shinpei Bailey [Bailey the New Recruit] • Synd • 1966

Belphegor ou Phantome du Louvre = Belphegor wa Dare da [Who is Belphegor] • MBS • 1965

Ben Casey • TBS • 1962

Benson = Mr. Benson • TVT • 1980

Best of the Post, The • NTV • 1960

Betty Boop = Betty-chan • NTV • 1959

Beulah Land • TVK • 1983

Beverly Hillbillies, The = Jajauma Okumanchōja [Wild Millionaires] • NTV • 1962

Beverly Hills 90210 = Beverly Hills Kōkō Hakusho [Beverly Hills High School Confessions] • NHK • 1992

Bewitched = Okusama wa Majo [My Wife is a Witch] • TBS • 1966

Big Mac Show, The = Tonchinkan Sōdōki [Chronicle of Absurd Disturbances] • NET • 1963

Big Valley, The = Big Valley Bokujō [Big Valley Ranch] • NET • 1965

Big World of Little Adam = Apollo-kun to Dai-Uchū [Little Apollo and Big Space] • NET • 1969

Bill Cosby Show, The • TBS • 1987

Bill Dana Show, The = Bakushō Hotel [Hysterical Hotel] • NET • 1965

Billy Bang Show, The • Fuji • 1964

Bionic Woman, The = Bionic Jamie • NTV • 1977

Birdman = Chōjin Birdman [Superman Birdman] • Synd • 1981

Birdman and the Galaxy Trio = Denshi Chōjin U Bird [Electric Aviator U Bird] • NET • 1971

Blondie • KTV • 1962

Blue Angels = Jet Pilot • Fuji • 1961

Blue Knight = Los Keisatsu 25ji [L.A. 25 Hour Cop] • Fuji • 1981

Blue Light = Blue Light Sakusen [Blue Light Battle] • Fuji • 1966

Blue Thunder • TVT • 1984

Bob & Carol & Ted & Alice = Yōki na Couple [Vivacious Couples] • NTV • 1976

Bobby Sherman Show, The • TVK • 1974

Bold Venture = Calypso Yarō [Calypso Guy] • TBS • 1966

Bonanza • NTV • 1960

Bonanza = Bonanza/Cartwright Kyōdai [Cartwright Brothers] • NTV • 1960

Bonheur Conjugale, Le = Aijō Senka [Love Speciality] • Fuji • 1965

Boots and Saddles = Daigo Kiheitai [Fifth Cavalry] • NTV • 1960

Born Free = Yasei no Elza [Elza of the Wild] • Fuji • 1975

Bourbon Street Beat • TVT • 1967

Boy Meets World • NHK • *1993

Bozo the Clown = Yukai na Bozo • Fuji • 1960

Bracken's World, The = Kareinaru Sekai [The World Become Glorious] • TBS • 1973

Brady Bunch = Yukai na Brady-zoku [Pleasant Brady Family] • Fuji • 1970

Brady Kids, The = Wanpaku Brady [Mischievous Bradys] • TVT • 1976

Branded = Kōya no Nagaremono [Wilderness Wanderer] • KRT • 1959

Brave Eagle • KRT • 1958

Breaking Point • NET • 1963

Brenner • NET • 1959

Broadside = Dansei Pinch Sakusen [Battle Trouble with Men] • NTV • 1965

Broken Arrow • Fuji • 1961

Bronco • TBS • 1961

Bronk = Keiji Bronk [Detective Bronk] • TBS • 1977

Brooklyn South = Brooklyn 74 Bunsho [Brooklyn 74th Precinct] • WOW • *1997

Brotherhood of the Blue Seagull = Kamome-gō Nakamatachi [Companions of the Gull] • NHK • 1972

Brothers Brannagan = Brannagan • MBS • 1962

Buccaneers/Dan Tempest = Kazokubune Sultana-gō [Pirate Ship Sultana] • KRT • 1957

Buck Rogers in the 25th Century = Captain Rogers • NTV • 1984

Buckskin = Seibu Shōnen Jody [Western Boy Jody] • NET • 1965

Bucky and Pepito • Fuji • 1964

Buffalo Bill Jr. = Buffalo Bill no Bōken [Adventures of Buffalo Bill] • KRT • 1957

Buffy the Vampire Slayer = Buffy Koi Suru Jūjika [Buffy Loving Crucifix] • FOX • *1997

Bugs Bunny Show, The • MBS • 1961

Burke's Law = Burke ni Makasero [Leave It to Burke] • NTV • 1964

Buster Keaton Comedy = Keaton Gekijō [Keaton Theater] • NHK • 1976

Butch Cassidy = Yatta ze Mukimuki Daisakusen [We Did It! Silly Battle] • NET • 1969

Byline Big Town = Tokudane o Nigasuna [Don't Let the Scoop Get Away] • TBS • 1965

C.B. Bears = Itazura Dōbutsu Tengoku [Mischievous Animal Heaven] • Synd • *1977

Cade's Country = Hoankan Sam Cade [Sheriff Sam Cade] • NTV • 1974

Cadfael = Shūdōshi Cadfael [Friar Cadfael] • Myst • *1994

Cagney and Lacey = Onna Keiji Cagney and Lacey [Female Detectives C&L] • YTV • 1983

Cain's 100 = Tokusōkan Nick Cain [Special Investigator Nick Cain] • TVT • 1967

Californians, The • Fuji • 1966

Call of the West = Seibu no Yobigoe • Synd • 1978

Calvin and the Colonel = OK Calvin •

TVT • 1967

Camp Runamuck = Wanpaku Camp Gakkō • Synd • 1979

Cannon = Tantei Cannon [Investigator Cannon] • NHK • 1975

Cannonball • KRT • 1959

Captain Caveman = Mukamuka Oyaji to Go-Go Gals [Angry Old Man and the Go-Go Girls] • Synd • *1971

Captain Fathom • NTV • 1967

Captain Gallant = Gaijin Butai [Foreigner Platoon] • CBC • 1965

Captain Nice • Fuji • 1968

Captain Power • Asahi • 1988

Captain Scarlet • TBS • 1968

Car 54, Where Are You? = Dassen Pato-car 54 [Patrol Car 54 Off-Course] • NTV • 1962

Cara Williams Show, The = Okusama Sha-in [My Wife is a Company Employee] • Fuji • 1966

Caroline in the City = Caroline in NY • Lala • *1995

Casablanca Series • NHK • 1959

Case of Dangerous Robin = Kiken o Kau Otoko Scott [Scott, the Man Who Buys Danger] • NET • 1960

Casey Jones • KRT • 1968

Casper, Funday Funnies = Dete Koi Casper [Come On Out, Casper] • Fuji • 1962

Catweazle = Mahōtsukai Catweazle [Catweazle the Sorcerer] • NHK • 1970

Celebrity Deathmatch • MTV • *1998

Centennial = Harukanaru Seibu [The Far West/Centennial] • NHK • 1982

Champions, The = Dengeki Spy Sakusen [Explosion Spy Battle] • Fuji • 1968

Channing = Channing Gakuen [Channing Academy] • TVT • 1964

Chaplin's Comedy = Kigeki no Ōsama Chaplin [King of Comedy Chaplin] • NET • 1965

Charles Boyer Show, The = Charles Boyer Dorama • TBS • 1964

Charlie Brown Specials • NHK • 1975

Charlie Brown Specials = Peanuts • NHK • 1971

Charlie Chaplin Short Subjects = Chaplin

Shōgekijō • NHK • 1976

Charlie Chaplin's Comedy = Ōatari Chaplin [That's Right Chaplin] • NTV • 1963

Charlie's Angels = Chijō Saikyō no Bijotachi Charlie's Angel [Strongest Beautiful Women in the World *CA*] • NTV • 1977

Charmed = Majo no Sanshimai [Three Sister Witches] • NHK • *1998

Chase = Tokusō Tsuisekiban Chase [Special Pursuit Unit Chase] • NTV • 1977

Checkmate • Fuji • 1961

Chevalier de la Maison Rouge = Kurenai no Yakata • TBS • 1963

Cheyenne • KRT • 1960

Chicago Hope • FOX • *1994

Chiefs = Keisatsu Shochō [Police Chiefs] • NHK • 1985

Chiffy Kids, The = Wanpaku Goningumi [Naughty Five] • NHK • 1980

Children's Theater Features = Jidōgeki Eiga Series • NHK • 1971

ChiPs I = Shirobai Patrol John and Ponch [White Bike Patrol John and Ponch] • NTV • 1979

ChiPs II = Shirobai Patrol Ponch and Bobby [White Bike Patrol Ponch and Bobby] • NTV • 1985

Chopper One = Chopper One Sky Patrol • NHK • 1977

Chopper Squad = Umi no Kyūjotai Rescue 5 [Marine Rescue Team Rescue 5] • NTV • 1980

Christie Comedies = Chocomaka Sakusen • TBS • 1964

Chrysler Theater = Kaigai Shūsaku Drama Hour • TBS • 1973

Chuckleheads = Hassuru Chuck • TBS • 1965

Cimarron Strip = Kettō Cimarron Machidō • TBS • 1972

Circus Boy • NTV • 1957

Cisco Kid, The • KRT • 1956

Citizen Soldier = Senjō [Battlefield] • MBS • 1963

City Detective = Sōsa Memo [Investigation Memo] • NTV • 1958

Cliffhangers = Bōken Gekijō [Adventure

Theater] • NET • 1963

Clue Clue = Otoboke Tanteidan no Daibōken [Silly Detective Team's Great Adventures] • Synd • ??

Clutch Cargo = Bōken-ō Clutch [Adventure King Clutch] • Fuji • 1961

Code 3 = Hijōsen [Crime Line] • ABC • 1957

Colditz = Colditz Daidassō [Great Escape from Colditz] • NTV • 1974

Colonel Bleep = Super Cat • NTV • 1964

Columbia Adventure Serials = Jungle Theater • NET • 1964

Columbo = Keiji Columbo [Detective Columbo] • NHK • 1973

Combat! • TBS • 1962

Comedy Capers = Atafuta Ojisan • TBS • 1966

Commander Cody Sky Marshall = Uchū Senshi Cody [Space Warrior Cody] • NET • 1963

Commonwealth Cartoons = Manga Gekijō [Manga Theater] • TBS • 1961

Condominium • Fuji • 1982

Conflict Series • NHK • 1959

Connaissez-Vous Bigot = Bigot Shitteimasu ka [Do You Know Bigot?] • NHK • 1982

Convoy = Zenkan Hasshin [All Vessels Advance] • Fuji • 1967

Cool McCool = Manga Cool McCool • Synd • *1966

Coronet Blue = Coronet Blue no Nazo [The Enigma of Coronet Blue] • NHK • 1968

Count of Monte Cristo = Kenshi Monte Cristo [Knight of Monte Cristo] • KTV • 1967

Courageous Cat • NHK • 1961

Courtship of Eddie's Father = Eddie no Suteki na Papa [Eddie's Wonderful Papa] • NET • 1971

Cowboy G-Men • KRT • 1956

Cowboy in Africa = Africa Daibokujō [Great African Pasture] • NHK • 1968

Cowboys, The = Shōnen Cowboy [Young Cowboys] • NHK • 1974

Crisis/Suspense Theater • NET • 1964

Crunch and Des/Charter Boat = Senchō

Crunch [Captain Crunch] • MBS • 1959

Crusader Rabbit = Susume Rabbit [Onward Rabbit] • Fuji • 1959

CSI Crime Scene Investigation = Kagaku Sōsaban [Science Investigation Team] • WOW • *2000

Curtain Time • KTV • 1967

D.A.'s Man, The = Dazman S • NET • 1962

Dakotas, The = Dakota no Otoko [Men of Dakota] • NTV • 1963

Daktari = Mitsurin Ōkoku Daktari [Jungle Kingdom Daktari] • NET • 1966

Dalgliesh: A Certain Justice = Shijin Keishi Dalgliesh [Poetic Superintendant Dalgliesh] • Myst • *1997

Dallas = Karei Naru Warui Ichizoku [The Bad Family That Became Glorious] • Asahi • 1981

Dan August = Keibu Dan August [Inspector Dan August] • NET • 1971

Danger Man = Himitsu Meirei [Secret Command] • ABC • 1960

Dangerous Assignment = G-Men • NTV • 1958

Daniel Boone = Seibu no Ōja Daniel [Daniel King of the West] • NET • 1968

Danny Thomas Hour, The = Kaigai Shūsaku Series [Overseas Super Show] • NHK • 1967

Dark Angel • Asahi • *2000

Dark Secret of Harvest Home = Akuma no Sumu Mura [Village Where the Devil Dwells] • TBS • 1981

Dark Skies • AXN • *1996

Dastardly and Muttley = Sky Kid to Ma-ō [Sky Kid and Devil-King] • NET • 1970

David Niven Show, The • TBS • 1964

Dawson's Creek • WOW • *1998

Deadline • KTV • 1967

Debbie Reynolds Show, The = Debbie no Okusama Sakusen [Battles of Wife Debbie] • Fuji • 1971

Decoy/Policewoman = Sōsamō [Dragnet] • ABC • 1960

Defenders, The = Bengoshi Preston

[Lawyer Preston] • NHK • 1962

Delvecchio = Keiji Delvecchio [Detective Delvecchio] • TBS • 1980

Dennis O'Keefe Show = Nani Shitenno Papa [Papa What Are You Doing?] • KRT • 1960

Department S = Himitsu Shirei S [Secret Order S] • NTV • 1969

Deputy Dawg Show, The = Wanwan Hoankan [Woof-Woof Sheriff] • Fuji • 1961

Deputy, The = Mune ni Kagayaku Hoshi [A Star Shining on His Breast] • Fuji • 1961

Derrik = Keiji Derrik [Detective Derrik] • TVK • 1979

Desilu Playhouse = Desilu Gekijō • Fuji • 1963

Detectives, The = Mystery 61 • NTV • 1961

Dexter's Laboratory • Synd • 1998

Dharma and Greg = Futari wa Saikō D&G [Best Couple Dharma and Greg] • NHK • *1997

Dick Francis Mystery • NHK • 1982

Dick Powell Drama Series, The • TBS • 1964

Dick Powell Showcase, The = Dick Powell • NTV • 1963

Dick Tracy • NET • 1962

Die Maus = Anime Maus • NHK • 1981

Diff'rent Strokes = Arnold Bōya wa Ninkimono [Boy Arnold Is Popular] • Synd • 1983

Dirty Sally • Synd • 1978

Divorce Court = Rikon Saiban • NTV • 1963

Doctor Snuggles = Snuggles Hakushi no Bōken [Adventures of Professor Snuggles] • NHK • 1977

Dodo the Kid from Outer Space = Yūsei Bōya Dodo-kun • NTV • 1966

Dog and Cat = Onna Keiji JJ Kane [Female Detective JJ Kane] • TVT • 1980

Donna Reed Show, The = Uchi no Mama wa Sekai-ichi [Best Mama in the World] • Fuji • 1959

Doris Day Show, The = Mama wa Taiyō • NHK • 1970

Dr. Christian • NHK • 1957

Dr. Kildare • NET • 1962

Dr. Simon Locke = Keisatsu-I Simon Locke [Police Doctor Simon Locke] • Synd • 1976

Dragnet • NTV • 1957

Dream Merchant = Yume o Uru Otoko • Synd • 1987

Duck Tales = Wanpaku Duck Yume Bōken [Mischievous Duck Dream Adventures] • TVT • 1988

Dukes of Hazzard = Bakuhatsu! Duke [Explode! Duke] • Fuji • 1980

Dusty's Trail = Dusty Trail • Synd • 1981

Dynamutt = Chinken Tantei Dynamutt [Curious Dog Investigator Dynamutt] • Synd • ??

Dynasty • NHK • 1987

E.B.I. = Uchū Teishintai [Space Volunteer Corps] • TVT • 1969

E.R. = ER Kyūkyū Byōshitsu [ER Emergency Room] • NHK • 1995

East of Eden = Eden no Higashi • Asahi • 1981

East Side West Side • TBS • 1966

Ed = Ed Boring Bengoshi [Ed Boring Lawyer] • Fox • *1999

Eddie Cantor Comedy Theater = Eddie Cantor Show • Fuji • 1959

Eischied = Tokusō Keibu Eischied [Special Inspector Eischied] • TVT • 1981

Eleanor and Franklin = Waga Shōgai no Daitōryō [The President of My Life] • NET • 1977

Elephant Boy = Mamore! Jungle [Protect! Jungle] • NTV • 1972

Eleventh Hour, The • NET • 1963

Ellery Queen • Fuji • 1978

Emergency +4 = Kinkyū Shirei Rescue [Priority Order Rescue] • Asahi • 1977

Emil = Itazurakko Emil [Mischievous Emil] • NHK • 1976

Empire • NTV • 1965

Espionage • TBS • 1964

Evening in Byzantium = Hijack 78 • TVT • 1979

Everglades, The = Jungle Patrol • NTV • 1962

Evil Touch = Akuma no Tezawari [Devil's

Touch] • NTV • 1982

F Troop • TBS • 1968

Fall Guy = Bokutachi Shōkinkasegi [We're Bounty Hunters] • NTV • 1984

Fame = Fame/Seishun no Tabidachi [Young Travelers] • TBS • 1984

Family • TVT • 1979

Family Affair, The = New York Papa • Fuji • 1967

Family Ties • TVT • 1986

Famous Playhouse = Meiga Hour • NTV • 1958

Fantastic Four • Synd • 1970

Fantastic Four = Uchū Ninja Gormus [Space Ninja Gormus] • NET • 1969

Fantastic Voyage = Micro Kesshitai [Micro Suicide Squad] • NHK • 1973

Fantasy Island • Synd • 1982

Farmer Alfalfa = Alfalfa Ojiisan • Synd • 1970

Farmer's Daughter = Suteki na Katy [Wonderful Katy] • NET • 1963

Farscape • ?? • *1999

Fat Albert and the Cosby Kids = Soreyuke Donpan [Go For It Fatso] • Synd • *1972

Fatal Vision = Giwaku [Misgivings] • NHK • 1985

Father Knows Best = Papa wa Nandemo Shitteru [Papa Knows Everything] • NTV • 1958

Father of the Bride = Hanayome no Chichi • NHK • 1962

Favorite Story = Sekai Meisaku Monogatari • NHK • 1958

Fawlty Towers = Mr. Chonbo [Mr. Cock-Up] • TVT • 1979

FBI • TBS • 1965

Felicity = Felicity no Seishun [Felicity's Youth] • WOW • *1998

Felix the Cat = Felix-kun no Bōken • NHK • 1960

Felony Squad, The = Tokusō Keiji Sam [Special Investigation Detective Sam] • MBS • 1967

Fireball XL-5 = Uchū Bōken XL-5 [Space Adventure Fireball XL-5] • Fuji • 1963

Fitz (i.e. U.S. Cracker) = Shinri Sōsa Tantei Fitz [Psychological Investigation

Detective Fitz] • Myst • *1997

Five Fingers = Spy/Gohon no Yubi • Fuji • 1965

Flamingo Road • TBS • 1981

Flesh and Blood = Champion no Michi [Way of the Champion] • MBS • 1984

Fliet d'Acier, Le = Hijōsen [Crime Line] • TBS • 1964

Flight • NTV • 1959

Flintstones, The = Kyōsai Tengoku/Genshi Kazoku [Strong Wife Heaven/Prehistoric Family] • Fuji • 1961

Flipper = Wanpaku Flipper [Naughty Flipper] • Fuji • 1966

Flying Doctor, The = Soratobu Doctor • Fuji • 1964

Flying High = American Girls • TVT • 1979

Flying Nun = Itazura Tenshi [Mischievous Angel] • TBS • 1968

Follow the Sun • NTV • 1962

For the People = Kenji Koster [Prosecutor Koster] • KTV • 1967

Forest Rangers = Shinrin Keibitai [Guardians of the Forest] • NHK • 1967

Four Feather Falls = Mahō no Kenjū [The Magic Pistol] • TBS • 1963

Four Just Men, The • KRT • 1959

Frasier = Soryanai ze!? Frasier [Frasier, You're Kidding!?] • Supe • *1993

Freaks and Geeks = Ushimitsu Show • WOW • 2002

French Atlantic Affair = Taiseiyō o Nottore • Asahi • 1981

Friends • WOW • *1994

From a Bird's Eye View = Hana no Stewardess [Lively Stewardess] • NTV • 1971

From Here to Eternity = Chijō yori Endō ni • TBS • 1981

Frontier • NTV • 1958

Frontier Circus = Circus wa Seibu e Iku [Circus Heads West] • NTV • 1961

Fugitive, The = Tōbōsha • TBS • 1964

Full House • Lala • *1987

Funky Phantom = Dobochon Ikka no Yūrei Ryokō • NET • 1972

Funny Company, The • TVT • 1964

Funny Face/Sandy Duncan Show = Suteki na Sandy [Wonderful Sandy] • NTV • 1973

Funny Manns, The = Teketeke Ojisan [Nutty Old Men] • Fuji • 1962

Further Adventures of Doctor Dolittle • NHK • 1972

Fury/Brave Stallion = Meiba Fury [Famous Horse Fury] • KRT • 1958

G.I. Joe • Synd • 1982

Gale Storm Show, The = Oh! Susanna • KRT • 1959

Gallant Men, The • NET • 1963

Gambler, The = Kōya no Gambler [Wilderness Gambler] • NHK • 1975

Garrison's Gorillas = Tokkō Garrison Gorilla [Special Attack Force Garrison Gorilla] • NET • 1968

Gemini Man • Fuji • 1978

Gentle Ben = Kuma to Mark Shōnen [The Bear and Mark the Boy] • TBS • 1969

George = Aiken George [Beloved Dog George] • Synd • 1979

Gerald McBoing-Boing = Boing Boing Bōya [Boing Boing Boy] • Synd • 1960

Get Christie Love! = Onna Keiji Christie [Female Detective Christie] • NTV • 1976

Get Smart = Soreyuke Smart • NET • 1966

Ghost and Mrs. Muir, The = Mrs. To Yūrei [Mrs. and Ghost] • NTV • 1968

Ghost Squad, The = Kage Naki Tsuisekisha [Pursuers Without Shadows] • TBS • 1966

Ghost Story = Mayonaka no Kyōfu [Fear at Midnight] • Fuji • 1975

Gideon C.I.D./Gideon's Way = Gideon Keibu/Hijō no Michi [Road of Sin] • KTV • 1967

Gidget = Gidget wa 15-sai [Gidget is 15] • TBS • 1970

Gilligan's Island (Gilligan-kun SOS) • NTV • 1966

Girl From U.N.C.L.E., The = 0022 U.N.C.L.E. no Onna • NTV • 1967

Glowing Summer = Onboro Kuruma no Donna Obasan [Aunt Donna and Her Broken Down Car] • NHK • 1974

Glynis = Okusama Jiken desu [My Wife's on the Case] • Fuji • 1964

Godfather Saga, The • Fuji • 1987

Going My Way = Wagamichi o Yuku • NHK • 1963

Goliath Awaits • TVT • 1983

Gomer Pyle USMC = My Pace Nitōhei [My Pace 2nd Rank Private] • TBS • 1965

Good Life, The = Sokonuke Otoboke Untenshu [Bottomless Clumsy Driver] • NET • 1975

Great Adventure, The = Daibōken • TVT • 1964

Great Grape Ape, The = Jumbo Gorilla no Daibōken [Great Adventures of the Jumbo Gorilla] • TVT • 1977

Greatest American Hero = American Hero • NTV • 1982

Greatest Heroes of the Bible = Shin Tenchi Sōzō [The New Creation of Heaven and Earth] • NET • 1963

Greatest Show on Earth = Sekai Saidai no Circus • NET • 1963

Green Acres = Nōen Tengoku [Farm Heaven] • NHK • 1967

Green Hornet, The • NTV • 1967

Grindl • NET • 1964

Guestward Ho = Papa to Watashi to de Ichinin mae [Papa and I Are One] • TBS • 1964

Gumby = Gumby-kun no Daibōken [Gumby's Great Adventure] • MBS • 1964

Guns of Will Sonnette, The = Gunman Mujō [Unfeeling Gunman] • NET • 1968

Gunslinger • TBS • 1963

Gunsmoke • Fuji • 1959

Hamish Macbeth = Macbeth Junsa [Patrolman Macbeth] • Myst • 2002

Hammer House of Horror = Akuma no Ikei [Devil's Fantasy] • Fuji • 1984

Hank = Gakuen wa Ōsawagi [Uproar in Academia] • Fuji • 1966

Hanna Barbera New Cartoons = Terebi Obachama • NTV • 1962

Happy = Boku wa Happy • Fuji • 1961

Happy Days • TVT • 1978

Harbor Command • NTV • 1957

Hardcastle and McCormick = Tantei Hard and Mac [Investigator Hard and Mac] • NTV • 1985

Hardy Boys and Nancy Drew = Shōnen Mystery Series [Young Mystery Series] • NHK • 1979

Harlem Globetrotters = Harlem Trotters • Synd • 1973

Harold Lloyd's Comedy = Lloyd Shōgekijō [Lloyd's Laughter Theater] • NHK • 1977

Harper Valley PTA = Waga Machi Harper Valley wa Ōsawagi [Our Noisy Town HV] • TBS • 1984

Harry O = Tsuisekisha [The Pursuer] • NET • 1976

Harry's Girls = Utatte Odotte Ai Shite [Sing, Dance, and Love] • Fuji • 1964

Harsh Realm • ?? • *1999

Hart to Hart = Tantei Hart & Hart [Detectives Hart and Hart] • TBS • 1981

Hathaways, The = Gokigen Tin Pan-kun [Good Humored Tin Pan] • NET • 1962

Have Gun Will Travel = Seibu no Paladin [Paladin of the West] • NHK • 1960

Hawaii Five-O • Fuji • 1970

Hawaiian Eye • MBS • 1963

Hawk, The = Yakan Sōsakan Hawk [Night Investigator Hawk] • NET • 1967

Hawkins = Tantei Hawkins [Investigator Hawkins] • TVT • 1975

Hazel = Hazel Obasan [Aunt Hazel] • NET • 1962

He and She = Oatsui Futari [Hot Couple] • Fuji • 1970

Heckel and Jeckel Show, The • KRT • 1957

Hector Heathcote Show, The = Let's Go Hector • NTV • 1964

Heidi = Alps no Shōjo Heidi (1975) • NHK • 1976

Heidi = Alps no Shōjo Heidi (1980) • TVT • 1983

Hello Oswald • WOW • 2003

Help! It's the Hair Bear Bunch = Kumakun Trio Daidassō [Great Escape of the Bear Trio] • NHK • 1972

Hennesey = Gun-I-san wa Honnichi Tabō [Pressure of Daily Work for the Military Doctor] • MBS • 1962

Herculoids, The • Synd • 1970

Here Comes Double Deckers = OK Seven Sakusen [OK Seven Great Battle] • TVT • 1972

Here Comes the Bride • TVT • 1972

Here Comes the Grump = Ijiwaru Jiisan Daitsuiseki [Great Pursuit of the Bullying Old Man] • NTV • 1973

Here's Boomer = Gasahiare Boomer [Keep It Up, Boomer] • NTV • 1981

Here's Lucy = Yōki na Lucy [Lively Lucy] • TBS • 1971

Hero, The = Papa wa Hero [Papa Is a Hero] • NTV • 1968

Hey It's the Key = Henshin Jumbo to Bōken Trio [Transforming Jumbo and the Adventure Trio] • Synd • ??

Hey, Landlord = Yanushi wa Nice Guy • NTV • 1967

High Chaparral • TVT • 1968

Highway Patrol • NHK • 1956

Hill Street Blues • KTV • 1984

Hogan's Heroes = 0012 Horyo Shūyōjo [Prison Camp 0012 (sic)] • TVT • 1966

Hollywood Star Playhouse = Hollywood Gekijō • NTV • 1958

Holocaust = Holocaust/Sensō to Kazoku [War and Family] • Asahi • 1978

Homicide: Life on the Street = Homicide Satsujin Sōsaka [Homicide Division] • Supe • *1993

Hondo = Kōya no Apache [Wilderness Apache] • TVT • 1968

Honey West = Honey ni Omakase [Leave it to Honey] • NET • 1966

Hong Kong Phooey = Moeyo 0011! [Burn 0011, i.e. "Enter the" 0011] • Synd • *1974

Hopalong Cassidy = Warera no Cassidy [Our Cassidy] • NTV • 1958

Hotel de Paree = Seibu no Yōjinbō [Western Guardsman, i.e. Western Yojinbo] • NET • 1967

Hound for Hire = Manga de Ikō [Let's Go With Manga] • Fuji • 1963

Houndcats, The • TVT • 1977

How to Marry a Millionaire = Okumanchōja to Kekkon Suru Hōhō • Fuji • 1959

HR Pufunstuff = Kaijūtō [Monster Island] • TVT • 1971

Huckleberry Hound = Chinken Huckle [Curious Dog Huckle] • NET • 1959

Hunter = Keiji Hunter [Detective Hunter] • ABC • 1988

I Dream of Jeannie = Kawaii Majo Jeannie [Cute Witch Jeannie] • MBS • 1966

I Love Lucy • NHK • 1957

I, Spy • NET • 1966

Ida Lupino Theater = Ida Lupino Show • TBS • 1964

If Tomorrow Comes = Mayonaka no Angel [Midnight Angel] • TVT • 1987

If You Had a Million = Hyakuman-doru Morattara • Fuji • 1959

Ike: The War Years = Shōgun Ike • NHK • 1980

I'm Dickens He's Fenster = Mina-san Donkachi Combi Desu [Everyone, We Are the Slapstick Team] • NET • 1964

I'm the Law/G.Raft Casebook = Sōsamō [Investigation] • MBS • 1962

Immortal = Fujimi no Otoko • Fuji • 1971

Impossibles and Frankenstein Jr. = Super Three • NET • 1967

Inch-High Private Eye = Chibi Tantei no Dai Bōken [Little Detective's Big Adventure] • Synd • *1973

Incredible Hulk, The = Chōjin Hulk • NTV • 1979

Inner Sanctum, The = Kyōfu no Tobira [Door of Fear] • Fuji • 1959

Inspector Wexford = Wexford Keibu • Myst • ??

Inspector, The • Fuji • 1972

Interns, The • TBS • 1971

Interpol Calling = Kokusai Hijōsen [International Crime Line] • KTV • 1960

Invaders, The • NET • 1967

Invasion = Shinryaku: Praha no Higeki [Invasion: Tragedy in Prague] • Fuji • 1981

Invasion America • ?? • 1999

Investigators = Crime 13 • Fuji • 1962

Invisible Man = Tōmei Ningen • NTV • 1960

Invisible Man = Tōmei Ningen • Fuji • 1978

Iron Horse = Mōretsu Apache Tetsudō [Wild Apache Railroad] • MBS • 1969

Ironside = Oni Keibu Ironside [Devil Inspector Ironside] • TBS • 1969

Islanders, The • NET • 1963

It Takes a Thief = Pro Spy, Spy no License • TBS • 1969

It's a Living = Restaurant Ōsawagi [Restaurant Chaos] • TVT • 1984

It's a Man's World = Wakamono no Kawa [A Young Person's River] • Fuji • 1965

It's About Time = Mac to Hec no Prehistoric Ryōko [Mac and Hec's Prehistoric Journey] • TBS • 1968

Ivanhoe • KRT • 1958

Jabber Jaws = Wanpaku Jaws [Mischievous Jaws] • Synd • ??

Jack and Jill • Supe • *1999

Jack Benny Show, The • NHK • 1961

Jack Webb's G-E "True" = Ano Toki Kono Toki Mitsuroku [That Time This Time Secret Record] • NTV • 1963

Jason King/Department S = Sakka Tantei Jason King [Author Detective *JK*] • NTV • 1976

Jennifer Slept Here = Yōki na Yūrei Jenny [Jenny the Merry Ghost] • TVT • 1984

Jericho • NET • 1967

Jesse Owens Story = Kuroi Inazuma Owens Monogatari [Black Lightning Owens Story] • NTV • 1986

Jet Jackson/Captain Midnight • KRT • 1957

Jetsons, The = Uchū Kazoku [Space Family] • NHK • 1963

Jim and Judy in Teleland = Terebi Bōya no Bōken [Adventures of TV Boy] • NTV • 1955

Jim Backus Show, The = One-man Henshūchō [Autocratic Editor-in-Chief] • Fuji • 1961

Jimmy Stewart Show, The = Yōki na Howard-zoku [Cheerful Howard Family] • NET • 1972

Joe 90 = Super Shōnen Joe 90 [Super Boy Joe 90] • NET • 1968

Joe Forrester = Keikan Forrester [Policeman Forrester] • ANB • 1982

Joe McDoakes Show, The = Yumemiru Otoko Show [Dreaming Man Show] • TBS • 1968

John and Yoko: A Love Story • TBS • 1988

John Wayne Westerns = John Wayne Seibugeki • NTV • 1957

Johnnie Ringo = Hayauchi Ringo [Quick-Draw Ringo] • TBS • 1963

Johnny Cypher in Dimension Zero = Johnny Cypher • Fuji • 1968

Johnny Midnight = Mayonaka no Johnnie • NET • 1965

Johnny Quest: File 037 = JQ • TBS • 1965

Johnny Staccato • NET • 1962

Josie and the Pussycats = Doradora Koneko to Chaka-musume • NET • 1971

Journey to the Center of the Earth = Chitei Daitanken [Great Underground Investigation] • Synd • 1971

Judd for the Defense = Bengoshi Judd [Lawyer Judd] • NHK • 1968

Julia • TVT • 1969

Julie Lescaut = Onna Keibu Julie Lescaut • ?? • *1992

June Allyson Theater, The = Hollywood Meisaku Hour • NET • 1960

Jungle Bomba = Bomba the Jungle Boy • NTV • 1963

Jungle Jim • Fuji • 1964

Kane and Abel • Asahi • 1986

Karen • Fuji • 1965

Kate Loves a Mystery = Miss Kate no Bōken [Adventures of Miss Kate] • NHK • 1981

Kaz = Nekketsu Bengoshi Kaz [Hot-Blooded Lawyer Kaz] • TVT • 1980

Kentucky Jones = Hello Ōsama [Hello King] • NTV • 1966

Key to Rebecca = Rebecca no Kagi • NHK • 1986

Kids From 47A = Anne-dori 47-banme • NHK • 1977

King Kong • NET • 1967

King Leonardo and His Subjects = Manga no Ōsama Leonardo [Cartoon King Leonardo] • Fuji • 1963

King of Diamonds = Dia no Johnny • NTV • 1962

King of the Hill • Sky • *1997

King's Row Series • NHK • 1959

Kingston Confidential= Tokuhō Kisha Kingston [Special Journalist Kingston] • TVT • 1981

Klondike = Fū-Un Klondike [Windy-Cloudy Klondike] • NTV • 1960

Knight Rider • ANB • 1987

Kojak = Keiji Kojak [Detective Kojak] • TBS • 1975

Kolchak the Night Stalker = Jiken Kisha Kolchak [Investigative Journalist Kolchak] • NTV • 1976

Krazy Kat Cartoon • NHK • 1957

KTK Cartoons = Manga no Kuni I [Cartoon Land I] • TVT • 1967

Kung Fu = Moeyo! Kung Fu [Burn Kung Fu, i.e. "Enter the" Kung Fu] • NET • 1976

Kung Fu Shaolin = Hong Kong Kung Fu Shōrin-ji • TVT • 1983

L.A. Law = Shichinin no Bengoshi [Seven Lawyers] • ?? • *1986

La Femme Nikita = Nikita • AXN • *1997

Ladies' Man • Synd • 1982

Lady Blue 2 = Onna Keiji Lady Blue 2 • Asahi • 1988

Lancer = Taiketsu Lancer Bokujō [Confrontation at Lancer Ranch] • TVT • 1969

Land of the Giants = Kyōjin no Wakusei [Planet of the Giants] • TVT • 1969

Laramie = Laramie Bokujō [Laramie Ranch] • NET • 1960

Laredo • Fuji • 1966

Lassie = Meiken Lassie [Famous Dog Lassie] • KRT • 1957

Lassie in the Forest = Mori no Ken Lassie 66 • TBS • 1966

Lassie in the Forest = Mori no Ken Lassie • KTV • 1975

Lassie's Rescue Rangers = SOS! Hashire Lassie [SOS Run Lassie!] • Synd • *1973

Laurel and Hardy • NTV • 1964

Laverne and Shirley • TVT • 1980

Law and Mister Jones, The = Bengoshi Jones [Lawyer Jones] • NHK • 1965

Law of the Plainsman = Apache Hoankan [Apache Sheriff] • KTV • 1966

Lawbreaker, The = Sōsa File X [Enquiry File X] • TBS • 1964

Lawless Years, The • NET • 1962

Lawman = Renpō Hoankan [Federal Marshall] • Fuji • 1959

Leave it to Beaver = Beaver-chan • NTV • 1959

Legend of Custer = Sōretsu! Dainana Kiheitai [Heroic! Seventh Cavalry] • Fuji • 1970

Legend of Jessie James = Jessie James • TVT • 1968

Life and Legend of Wyatt Earp = Hoankan Wyatt Earp [Sheriff Wyatt Earp] • NTV • 1961

Life at Stake = Documentary Drama • NHK • 1979

Life of Riley, The = Yōki na Riley [Jovial Riley] • NET • 1959

Line-up, The = Sōsasen • TBS • 1961

Linus the Lionhearted = Zukkoke Lion [Bumbling Lion] • NET • 1969

Little House on the Prairie, The = Daisōgen no Chiisana Ie • NHK • 1975

Little People, The = Yōki na Oishasan [Cheerful Doctor] • NET • 1973

Little Rascals = Chibikko Gang [Cute Kids Gang] • NET • 1961

Little Women = Wakakusa Monogatari [Tale of Young Grasses] • NHK • 1980

Littlest Hobo, The = Meiken Rocky [Famous Dog Rocky] • TVT • 1980

Lock Up • NET • 1959

Logan's Run • NTV • 1978

Lone Ranger • KRT • 1958

Lone Ranger the Cartoon = Manga Lone Ranger • Synd • 1965

Loner, The = Yūsha Colton [Heroic Colton] • Fuji • 1967

Long Chase, The = Futari no Tsuigeki [A Couple's Chase] • NHK • 1975

Long Hot Summer = Nagaku Atsui Natsu • TVT • 1987

Longstreet • TVT • 1974

Loretta Young Show, The • NHK • 1960

Lost in Space = Uchū Kazoku Robinson [Space Family Robinson] • TBS • 1966

Lost Islands, The = Kotō no Himitsu [Secret of the Lone Island] • NHK • 1977

Lou Grant = Jiken Kisha Lou Grant [Investigative Journalist Lou Grant] • TBS • 1984

Love American Style = America-shiki Ai no Technique • TVT • 1977

Love and Marriage = Mama wa Fuku Shachō [Mama is the Company Vice-President] • KRT • 1960

Love Boat • NTV • 1980

Love on a Rooftop = Kawaii Tsuma Julie [Cute Wife Julie] • MBS • 1968

Love, American Style = Ren'ai Senka [Course on Love] • Fuji • 1972

Lucille Ball/Desi Arnaz Comedy Hour = Lucy Show II • TBS • 1965

Lucy Show, The • TBS • 1963

M Squad = Chicago Tokusōtai M [Chigaco Special Investigation Team M] • Fuji • 1961

M*A*S*H = Mattaku Kono Yo wa Subarashii [It's Quite a Wonderful World] • Synd • 1977

Mack and Myer For Hire = Mack to Myer • Fuji • 1964

Madigan = Oni Keiji Madigan [Devil Detective Madigan] • TVT • 1979

Mafalda = Omasena Mafalda • NHK • 1978

Magician, The • TVT • 1974

Magilla Gorilla Show, The = Gorilla no Gin-chan • TBS • 1966

Magnificent 6 1/2 = OK Seven Sakusen [War of the OK Seven] • NHK • 1975

Magnum P.I. = Shiritsu Tantei Magnum [Private Investigator Magnum] • TBS • 1984

Man and the Challenge, The = Chōsen [The Challenge] • NET • 1959

Man Called Intrepid, A = Intrepid to Yobareta Otoko • NHK • 1983

Man Called Shenandoah, A = Shenandoah • MBS • 1966

Man from Atlantis, The = Atlantiskara Kita Otoko • NHK • 1980

Man from Blackhawk, The = Shiritsu Tantei Logan [Private Investigator Logan] • TBS • 1964

Man from U.N.C.L.E. = 0011 Napoleon Solo • NTV • 1965

Man in a Suitcase = Ginpatsu no Ōkami [Silver-haired Wolf] • TVT • 1969

Man of the World = Sekai o Kakeru Otoko • NET • 1963

Man Undercover = Senkō Keiji Dan [Undercover Cop Dan] • TVT • 1979

Man Who Never Was, The = Kako no Nai Otoko [Man Without a Past] • NTV • 1966

Man With a Camera = Cameraman Kovac • NET • 1960

Man Without a Gun, The = Teppōji Adam [Gunman Adam] • NET • 1963

Manhunt • Fuji • 1960

Mannix • NTV • 1968

Many Happy Returns = Tenteko Depāto [Bustling Department Store] • Fuji • 1968

Many Loves of Dobie McGillis = Dobie no Seishun [Dobie's Youth] • KRT • 1960

Marco Polo • TBS • 1982

Marcus Welby MD = Doctor Welby • NHK • 1971

Margie = Konnichiwa Margie [Hello Margie] • NET • 1964

Marilyn: The Untold Story = Marilyn Monroe: Sono Ai to Shi [MM: Her Life and Death] • TBS • 1984

Martian Chronicles, The = Kasei Nendaiki • TBS • 1983

Martin Beck = Keiji Martin Beck [Detective Martin Beck] • WOW • *1997

Martin Kane, Private Eye • KRT • 1957

Masada = Honoo no Toride Masada [Burning Stronghold Masada] • NTV • 1984

Master of the Game = Game no Tatsujin • Fuji • 1988

Master, The = Ninja no John to Max [John and Max the Ninja] • TVT • 1985

Matinee Theater • NHK • 1960

Maverick • NET • 1961

Maya = Kyōzō Maya [Maya the Great

Elephant] • NTV • 1968

McCallum = Kenshikan McCallum [Medical Examiner McCallum] • Myst • *1995

McCloud = Keibu McCloud [Inspector McCloud] • NET • 1974

McCoy = McCoy no Yarōdomo [McCoy and the Guys] • NHK • 1978

McKeever and the Colonel = Totsugeki McKeever [Charge, McKeever] • Fuji • 1963

McKenzie's Raiders = Susume Kiheitai [Onward Cavalry] • TVT • 1967

McMillan and Wife = Shochō McMillan • NHK • 1976

Me and the Chimp = Yukai na Chimpan [Amusing Chimp] • TVT • 1974

Medic • NET • 1959

Medical Center = Geaikai Cannon [Surgeon Cannon] • TVT • 1974

Meet Corliss Archer = Yōki na Corliss [Jovial Corliss] • NTV • 1957

Mel-O-Toons = Otogi no Kuni Manga [Manga Fairytale Land] • NHK • 1961

Memory of Eva Ryker = E. Ryker no Kioku • NTV • 1984

Men Into Space = Uchū Tanken [Space Investigation] • NHK • 1959

Merry Melodies Show, The = Nigero Speedy [Run Speedy] • TVK • 1974

MGM Cartoon = Manga Uchūsen [Manga Spaceship] • Synd • 1975

MGM Cartoons = Manga Mangadon • NTV • 1963

Miami Undercover = Miami Senritsu [Shocking Miami] • MBS • 1961

Miami Vice = Tokusō Keiji Miami Vice [Special Detectives Miami Vice] • TVT • 1986

Michael Shayne, Private Detective = Tantei Michael [Investigator Michael] • Fuji • 1961

Mickey Rooney Show, The • KRT • 1957

Mickey Spillane's Mike Hammer = Mike Hammer • Fuji • 1961

Mighty Hercules, The • Fuji • 1963

Mighty Mightor, The = Astro Chōjin Jumbo [Astro Superman Jumbo] • TVT • 1970

Mighty Mouse Playhouse, The = Mighty

Mouse • KRT • 1957

Mike Hammer = Tantei Mike Hammer [Investigator Mike Hammer] • Fuji • 1988

Millionaire, The • NET • 1960

Mischief Makers = Chibikko Taishō [Leader of the Cute Kids] • TBS • 1963

Mission: Impossible = Spy Daisakusen [Spy Great Battle] • Fuji • 1967

Moby Dick = Ganbare Moby [Go For It Moby] • NHK • 1969

Mod Squad, The = Mods Tokusōtai [Investigation Team Mods] • TVT • 1969

Mole Series, The = Yukai na Mogura • NHK • 1979

Mona McClusky = Okusama wa Dai-Star [My Wife Is a Big Star] • NTV • 1966

Moneychangers, The • NHK • 1977

Monkees, The • TBS • 1967

Monroes, The = Wyoming no Kyōdai [Brothers of Wyoming] • NHK • 1967

Monty Nash = Tokumei Sōsakan [Special Duty Investigator Monty Nash] • TVT • 1977

Monty Python's Flying Circus = Soratobu Monty Python [Flying Monty Python] • TVT • 1976

Moonlighting = Kochira Blue Moon Tanteisha [This Is the Blue Moon Detective Agency] • NHK • 1986

Moses the Lawgiver = Moses • Synd • 1985

Most Deadly Game = Zig Zag • NET • 1971

Most Wanted = Tokusō Buchō Evers [Special Investigation Team Leader Evers] • TVT • 1981

Motor Mouse and Auto Cat = Nigeroya Nigero Dai Race [Run Run Great Race] • NHK • 1971

Mouse Factory • NET • 1973

Movin' on = Hassō Truck 16 Ton • TVT • 1976

Mozart • NTV • 1982

Mr. Magoo = Ganbare Magoo [Go For It Magoo] • NET • 1963

Mr. District Attorney = Chihō Kenshi • KRT • 1956

Mr. Ed = O-Uma no Ed-san [Ed the Horse] • KTV • 1962

Mr. Lucky = Tsuiteiru Otoko • NTV • 1964

Mr. Novak • NTV • 1963

Mr. Roberts • TBS • 1967

Mr. Smith Goes to Washington = Smith Miyako e Iku • Synd • 1980

Mr. Terrific = Flyman • NTV • 1967

Mrs. G. Goes to College = Mama wa Daigaku Ichinensei • Fuji • 1964

Mrs. Columbo • NHK • 1980

Mumbly = Super Keiji Borongo [Super Detective Mumbler] • NHK • 1977

Munsters, The • Fuji • 1965

Murder in Texas = Texas Satsujin Jiken • TBS • 1984

Murder She Wrote = Jessica Obasan Jikenbo [Aunt Jessica's Case Files] • NHK • 1988

Murphy Brown = TV Caster Murphy Brown • Supe • *1988

Mutant X • AXN • *2001

My Favorite Martian = Bravo Kaseijin [Bravo Martian] • NTV • 1964

My Friend Flicka = Meiba Flicka [Famous Horse Flicka] • Fuji • 1960

My Little Margie = Kawaii Maggie [Cute Maggie *(sic)*] • TBS • 1964

My Living Doll = Hokuro ni Goyōjin [Mind the Moles] • TVT • 1968

My Mother the Car = Obasan wa 28-Nensei [Mother is a '28 Model] • Fuji • 1966

My Three Sons = Papa Daisuki [We Love Papa] • Fuji • 1961

My World . . . É and Welcome to it = Papa wa Meromero [Henpecked Papa] • NTV • 1970

Mystery Series = Mystery Eiga Gekijō [Mystery Movie Theater] • KTV • 1961

N.Y.P.D. = New York Keisatsu Honbu • KTV • 1970

Naked City I, The = Hadaka no Machi • NET • 1959

Naked City II, The = Hadaka no Machi • TBS • 1962

Nana = Shōfu Nana [Nana the Prostitute] • TVT • 1983

Nancy = Nancy wa Toshigoro [Nancy is of Marriageable Age] • TVT • 1972

Nanny and the Professor = Bokura no Nanny [Our Nanny] • NHK • 1971

Nash Bridges = Keiji Nash Bridges [Detective Nash Bridges] • AXN • *1996

National Velvet = Hashire, Chess [Run, Chess] • NHK • 1960

New Adventures of Batman (Cartoon) • NTV • 1985

New Adventures of Black Beauty = Shin Kurouma no Monogatari [Story of the Black Horse] • NHK • 1975

New Adventures of Gilligan = Bōken Gilligan [Adventure Gilligan] • Synd • *1974

New Adventures of Huckleberry Finn = Yattaze Huck no Bōken • NHK • 1970

New Adventures of Superman = Superman: Shin • NTV • 1971

New Archie/Sabrina = Archie to Sabrina • Synd • 1981

New Breed, The • NET • 1962

New Funday Funnies: Casper = Casper to Asobō [Let's Play with Casper] • Fuji • 1975

New Loretta Young Show, The = Mama to Shichinin no Kodomotachi [Mama and Seven Children] • NHK • 1963

New Scooby Doo Movies = Shin Yowamushi Kuruppa [New Coward Kuruppa] • Synd • *1972

New Three Stooges Show = Trio The San Baka [Trio the Three Idiots] • NET • 1966

New York Confidential = New York Monogatari [New York Story] • NHK • 1959

Next Step Beyond = Shin Yo ni mo Fushigi na Monogatari [New Mysterious Tales of Another World] • NTV • 1982

Nichols = Hoankan Nichols [Sheriff Nichols] • NET • 1972

Night Gallery = Yojigen e no Shōtai [Passage to the Fourth Dimension] • NET • 1973

Night the Bridge Fell Down, The = Yoru no Bridge Down • NTV • 1983

No Time For Sergeants = Ultra 2 Tō Hei

[Ultra 2nd Grade Soldiers] • MBS • 1965

Noah's Ark = Dōbutsu Sensei Noah [Animal Doctor Noah] • NTV • 1961

Northern Exposure = Tadori Tsukeba Alaska [Ended up in Alaska] • Supe • *1990

Northwest Passage = Sōretsu! Seibu Yūgekitai [Heroic! Western Raiders] • Fuji • 1963

Nurses, The = Kangofu Monogatari • NHK • 1963

Nutty Squirrel's Tales, The = Nutty Dreamland • NET • 1963

NYPD Blue • TVK • *1993

O.K. Crackerby = Oyaji wa Okumanchōja [Dad's a Millionaire] • Fuji • 1967

Occasional Wife = New York Kekkon Sakusen [New York Marriage Scheme] • YTV • 1968

Odd Ball Couple, The = Soreyuke Wan-Nyan [Go For It Woof-Miaow] • TVT • 1977

Oh, Those Bells = Sokonuke Brothers [Clumsy Brothers] • TBS • 1963

O'Hara U.S. Treasury = Himitsu Sōsakan O'hara [Secret Investigator O'hara] • TBS • 1972

One Step Beyond = Yo ni mo Fushigi na Monogatari • NTV • 1959

Orson Welles' Great Mysteries = Orson Welles Theater • NET • 1977

Our Gang Comedy = Chibikko Gang [Cute Kids Gang] • NET • 1962

Our House • NHK • 1987

Out of the Inkwell = Noppo no Koko • TBS • 1966

Outcasts, The = Nihiki no Nagaremono [Two Wanderers] • TVT • 1968

Outer Limits, The • NTV • 1964

Outlaws, The • NET • 1961

Outsider, The • NTV • 1973

Oz • Supe • *1997

Panic! • NET • 1959

Paper Moon • TVT • 1977

Partners in Crime = Futari de Tanken o [Investigate Together] • NHK • 1985

Partners, The = Soreyuke Partners • ANB • 1977

Party of Five = San Francisco no Sora no Shita [Beneath the San Francisco Sky] • CSN1 • *1994

Passport to Danger = Kiken e no Passport • ABC • 1956

Partridge Family, The = Ninki Kazoku Partridge [Popular Partridge Family] • TVT • 1971

Patty Duke Show, The • TBS • 1964

Pearl = Shinju Wan: Unmei o Kaeta Yokkakan [Pearl Harbor: Four Days that Changed Fate] • Asahi • 1979

People's Choice = Seishun Buranko [Youth Swing] • Fuji • 1959

Perils of Penelope Pitstop = Penelope Zettai Zetsumei [Penelope's Certain Death] • NHK • 1970

Perry Mason • Fuji • 1959

Persuaders, The = Dandy Kareinaru Bōken [Glorious Dandy Adventures] • NET • 1975

Pete and Gladys = Yōki na Fūfu [Cheerful Husband and Wife] • NHK • 1963

Pete Smith Specialities • Fuji • 1964

Peter and Gustaf • NHK • 1969

Peter Gunn • ABC • 1961

Peter Potamus Show, The = Kaba no Kabacho [Kabacho the Hippo] • TBS • 1966

Peter the Great = Pyotr Taitei • NHK • 1987

Petit Theatre, Le = Grand Prix Theater • Fuji • 1960

Petrocelli = Bengoshi Petrocelli • Fuji • 1976

Petticoat Junction = Petticoat Sakusen [Petticoat Battle] • TBS • 1964

Peyton Place = Peyton Place Monogatari • MBS • 1965

Philip Marlowe = Senpūko Marlowe [Whirlwind Child Marlowe] • MBS • 1959

Pick a Letter = Alphabet Asobi [Alphabet Play] • TVT • 1964

Picket Fences = Picket Fences Block Sousa Memo [PF Block Investigation Memo] • Myst • *1992

Pink Panther Show, The • Fuji • 1972

Pippi Longstocking = Nagakutsushita no

Pippi • NHK • 1975

Pirate, The = Moeru Sekai no Otoko [Man of the Burning World] • TBS • 1981

Pistols and Petticoats = Teppō to Petticoats • TBS • 1968

Planet of the Apes = Saru no Wakusei • Fuji • 1975

Planet of the Apes the Cartoon = Manga Saru no Wakusei • TBS • 1977

Playhouse 90 • TVT • 1964

Playhouse, The • KRT • 1957

Please Don't Eat the Daisies = Bokura Ippiki Rokunin [We Six Are One Creature] • Fuji • 1967

Poirot = Meitantei Poirot [Famous Detective Poirot] • NHK • 1991

Police Story • Fuji • 1976

Police Surgeon = Keisatsu-I Monogatari • TVT • 1974

Police Woman = Onna Keiji Pepper [Woman Detective Pepper] • Fuji • 1975

Polizei Funkruft = Patrol-tai Shutsudō [Patrol Move Out] • TBS • 1968

Polly = Bokura no Polly [Our Polly] • NHK • 1962

Polly a Venice = Pippo to Kotori [Pippo and the Little Bird] • NHK • 1971

Polly in Spain = Circus no Polly • NHK • 1972

Pony Express = Western Tokkyū [Western Express] • NET • 1961

Popeye I • KRT • 1959

Popeye II • NHK • 1962

Popeye the New Cartoon Show = New Popeye Show • NHK • 1980

Porky Pig = Porky-kun • NHK • 1956

Possible Possum Show, The = Nandemo Chūdo • Fuji • 1966

Pow Wow = Pow Wow Bōya [Pow Wow Boy] • NTV • 1961

Powers of Matthew Star = Chōnōryoku Prince Matthew Star [Super Powered Prince Matthew Star] • Synd • 1985

Practice, The = The Practice: Boston Bengoshi File [Boston Lawyer File] • FOX • *1997

President's Plane is Missing, The = Daitōryō Senyōki Sōnansu • NET • 1975

Pretenders, The = Arano no Ōji [King of the Wilderness] • NHK • 1974

Prime Suspect = Daiichi Yōgisha • NHK • *1982

Primus = Aoi Tanken Primus [Blue Investigator Primus] • TVT • 1978

Prisoner, The = Prisoner No. 6 • NHK • 1969

Private Secretary = Jomissho • KRT • 1958

Professionals, The = Professional CI5 Tokusōhan [Professional CI5 Special Investigation Team] • NTV • 1982

Profiler = Hanzai Shinri Bunseikan [Criminal Psychology Analyst] • Supe • *1996

Project UFO • TVK • 1983

Protector, The • NTV • 1972

Psychiatrist, The = Doctor Whiteman • NET • 1974

Puccini • NHK • 1973

Pursuers, The = Keisatsuken Ivan [Ivan the Police Dog] • NTV • 1965

Q & Q = Mori no Himitsu [Secrets of the Forest] • NHK • 1976

Q.T. Hush = Tantei Skat [Investigator Scat] • Fuji • 1962

Queen's Bench Court VII = QB Seven • Fuji • 1977

Quick-Draw McGraw = Hayauchi McGraw • NET • 1960

Quincy, M.E. = Dr. Keiji Quincy [Dr. Detective Quincy] • ANB • 1979

Rafferty = Doctor Rafferty • Fuji • 1979

Rage of Angels, The = Tenshi no Okori • Asahi • 1987

Ramar of the Jungle • KRT • 1958

Randall and Hopkirk = Yūrei Tantei Hopkirk [Ghost Investigator Hopkirk] • Fuji • 1970

Range Rider, The • NET • 1960

Rat Patrol, The • NTV • 1966

Rawhide • NET • 1959

Real McCoys, The = McCoy Jiisan • NHK • 1962

Rebel, The = Seibu no Hangyakuji [Western Rebel] • Fuji • 1960

Rebels/The Seekers = Jiyū to Ai no Daichi [Land of Freedom and Love] • TBS • 1982

Red Dwarf = Uchūsen Red Dwarf-gō • NHK • 1998

Red Skelton Show, The = Skelton Daishō Gekijō [Skelton Big Laugh Theater] • NET • 1961

Remington Steele = Tantei Remington Steele [Investigator Remington Steele] • NTV • 1987

Rendezvous • NTV • 1959

Reporter, The • TBS • 1969

Republic Super Serials = Tsūkai Series [Thrill Series] • NET • 1963

Rescue 8 = Daihachi Kyūjotai • Fuji • 1958

Restless Gun, The • TBS • 1961

Retour d'Arsene Lupin= Kaiketsu Lupin Kaette Kita Arsene Lupin [Return of Arsene Lupin] • Myst • *1989

Return of Sherlock Holmes = Sherlock Holmes no Bōken 2 • NHK • 1988

Rex the Runt • WOW • *1998

Rheinemann Exchange, The = Rheinemann Spy Sakusen [Rheinemann Spy Battle] • NHK • 1980

Rich Man, Poor Man • NHK • 1979

Richard Boone Show, The • Fuji • 1966

Richard Diamond/Call Mr. D = Meitantei Diamond [Famous Detective Diamond] • Fuji • 1960

Rifleman, The • KRT • 1960

Ripcord • NTV • 1962

Riptide = Riptide/Tantei 24 Hour [24 Hour Investigation] • Synd • 1986

Riptide = Umi no Bōkensha [Marine Adventurer] • TVT • 1976

Road Runner Show, The • Synd • 1970

Roaring 20's, The • ABC • 1961

Rocket Robin Hood • KTV • 1971

Rockford Files, The = Rockford-shi no Jiken Memo • NET • 1975

Rocky and His Friends = Rocky to Yukaina Tomodachi • NHK • 1961

Rocky Jones Space Ranger = Susume! Uchū Patrol [Advance! Space Patrol] • NET • 1967

Rod Rocket • TVT • 1964

Rodeo/Wide Country • TBS • 1963

Roger Ramjet = Jet no Roger • TBS • 1967

Rookies, The • Fuji • 1975

Room 222 = Kokujin Kyōshi Dix [Black Teacher Dix(on)] • TVT • 1970

Room for One More = Wagaya wa Ippai [Our House is Full] • Fuji • 1963

Roots • Asahi • 1977

Roots: The Next Generation • Asahi • 1979

Roswell = Roswell Hoshi no Koibitotachi [Star Lovers] • NHK • *1999

Rounders, The = Cowboy Yarō • NET • 1969

Route 66 • NHK • 1962

Rovers, The = Nankai no Mike [Mike of the South Seas] • NTV • 1970

Roy Rogers Show, The = Roy Rogers • NET • 1963

Ruff and Ready Show, The = Tsuyoi zo Ruffty [You're Strong, Ruffty] • Fuji • 1961

Rules of Marriage = Kekkon no Hōsoku • NHK • 1983

Run Buddy Run = Nigeroya Nigero! • TBS • 1967

Run For Your Life = Paul Bryan • YTV • 1967

Run Joe Run = Ganbare Meiken Joe [Keep It Up, Famous Dog Joe] • TBS • 1977

Ryan = Shitsuritsu Tantei Ryan [Private Investigator Ryan] • TVT • 1977

S.A. 7 = Tokusō SA 7 [Special Investigation SA 7] • TBS • 1966

S.W.A.T. = Tokubetsu Sogekitai SWAT [Special Assault Team SWAT] • TVT • 1976

Sabrina and the Groovy Ghoulies = Yūreijo no Dobochon Ikka [Scary Family in the Haunted Castle] • NET • 1970

Saint, The = Saint Tengoku Yarō [Heaven Guy] • NTV • 1965

Sam and the River = Boku no Thames-gawa [My River Thames] • NHK • 1975

Samson and Goliath • Synd • 1970

San Francisco Beat • TBS • 1964

San Francisco International = San Francisco Daikūkō [Great San Francisco Airport] • NET • 1974

Scarlet and Black • KTV • 1984

Scener ur ett Aktenskap = Aru Kekkon no Fūkei [Scenes at a Wedding] • Asahi •

1980

Science Fiction Theater = Kūsō Kagaku Gekijō • NHK • 1956

Scooby Doo Where Are You = Yowamushi Gruppa [Cowardly Gruppa] • NHK • 1970

Scotland Yard = London Keishichō [London Metropolitan Police Headquarters] • KTV • 1959

Scrappy • NHK • 1958

Screen Directors' Playhouse = Kore ga Dorama da! [This is Drama!] • NET • 1960

Sea Hunt = Sensuiō Nelson [Undersea King Nelson] • KRT • 1958

Seagull Island = Chichūkai Kamomejima Satsujin Jiken [Murder Files of Seagull Island] • MBS • 1987

Search and Rescue = Dōbutsu Kyūjotai [Animal Rescue Squad] • Fuji • 1984

Search, The/Probe = Probe Tanken Shirei [Order Probe Investigation] • NET • 1973

Seaway, The = Hatoba no G-Men [Waterfront G-Men] • TVT • 1969

Sebastian et la Mary Morgane = Umi no Sebastian [Sebastian of the Sea] • NHK • 1973

Second Hundred Years, The = Papa no Oyaji wa 30-sai [Papa's Father Is 30] • NET • 1968

Secret Agent = Himitsu Chōhōin Drake [Secret Intelligence Agent Drake] • Fuji • 1965

Secret Agent Man • WOW • *2000

Secret Life of Waldo Kitty = Niji o Tsukamu Neko [The Cat Who Caught the Rainbow] • NHK • 1976

Secret Service, The = London Shirei X [London Order X] • NHK • 1970

Secret Squirrel Show, The = Himitsu Tantei Kurukuru • NET • 1966

Seinfeld = Tonari no Seinfeld [My Neighbor Seinfeld] • Lala • *1990

Sergeant Preston of the Yukon = Keisatsuken King [Police Dog King] • KRT • 1961

Serpico = Keiji Serpico [Detective Serpico] • TVT • 1984

Seven Little Australians = Riverhouse no

Niji [Rainbow over the Riverhouse] • NHK • 1975

Sex and the City • WOW • *1998

Shaft = Kuroi Jaguar [Black Jaguar] • NTV • 1975

Shane • TVT • 1970

Shannon • NTV • 1961

Shazzam! = Dai Maō Shazzam [Great Magic King Shazzam] • NET • 1968

Sheena Queen of the Jungle = Jungle no Jo-ō [Queen of the Jungle] • KRT • 1957

Sheriff of Cochise = Morgan Keibu I [Inspector Morgan I] • NTV • 1958

Shirley Temple Show, The = Otogi no Kuni • NHK • 1961

Shirley Temple Story Book = Otogi no Kuni • NHK • 1961

Shock! Pictures, The = Shock! • NET • 1964

Shōgun • Asahi • 1981

Shotgun Slade • NTV • 1962

Silent Force = Chinmoku Butai • Synd • 1986

Silent Service = Raigeki Sen Yōi [Thunder Assault Prepare for Battle] • Fuji • 1963

Simpsons, The • WOW • *1989

Sir Francis Drake = Captain Drake • Fuji • 1963

Six Million Dollar Man, The = Cyborg Kikai Ippatsu [Narrow Escape, Cyborg] • NET • 1974

Ski Boy = Alps no Ski Boy • NHK • 1973

Skippy the Bush Kangaroo = Kangaroo Skippy • NTV • 1968

Sky King • NTV • 1963

Skyhawks, The • NHK • 1971

Slattery's People = Slattery Monogatari [Slattery Story] • NHK • 1966

Sledge Hammer = Ore wa Hammer da! [I'm Hammer!] • TVT • 1987

Smith Family, The = Keiji Kazoku [Detective Family] • TVT • 1976

Smokey the Bear = Susumeya Susumeya Smokey [Move It Move It Smokey] • NHK • 1970

Smurfs = Mori no Smurfs [Smurfs of the Forest] • TVT • 1985

Snoop Sisters, The = Tantei Snoop Shimai

[Investigators Snoop Sisters] • NHK • 1977

Snuffy = Otoboke Snuffy [Silly Snuffy] • Synd • 1979

So Little Time = Futari wa Otoshigoro [Marriageable Couple] • NHK • *2001

Soap • TVT • 1978

Soldiers of Fortune = Inochi Shirazu no Kelly [Reckless Kelly] • TBS • 1962

Soleil de Minuit, Le = Mayonaka no Taiyō • NHK • 1964

Sopranos, The = The Sopranos Aishū no Mafia [Sorrowful Mafia] • WOW • *1999

South Park • WOW • *1997

Space 1999 • TBS • 1977

Space Angel = Captain Zero • TBS • 1963

Space Ghost, The = Uchū Kaijin Ghost [Space Monster Ghost] • NET • 1967

Space Kiddett = Uchū Wanpaku Tai [Space Mischief Team] • NHK • 1969

Space Patrol • TVT • 1964

Speed Buggy = Hassō Buggy Dai Race • NET • 1976

Spider-Man • TVT • 1974

Spin City • Supe • *1996

Spunky and Tadpole = Ganbare Spunky [Go For it Spunky] • Fuji • 1961

Spy! = Hijō no Shirei Spy [Merciless Spy Under Orders] • TBS • 1982

Stagecoach West = Ekibasha Nishi • NTV • 1961

Star Maker = Ginmaku o Irodoru Ai no Henreki [Travels in Love of the Silver Screen] • Synd • 1987

Star Performance = Star no Meisaku Series • TBS • 1964

Star Trek = Uchū Daisakusen [Great Space Battle ST] • NTV • 1969

Star Trek the Cartoon = Manga Uchū Daisakusen • TVT • 1977

Stargate SG-1 • AXN • *1997

Starlost, The = Uchūkan Ark [Space Ark] • NHK • 1975

Starsky and Hutch = Keiji Starsky and Hutch [Detectives Starsky and Hutch] • TBS • 1977

Steve Canyon = Jet Fighter • NTV • 1963

Stingray = Kaitei Daisensō Stingray

[Undersea Great War Stingray] • Fuji • 1964

Stoney Burke = Seibu no Champion [Champion of the West] • TBS • 1965

Straightaway/The Racer • NET • 1962

Strange Report, The = Tantei Strange [Investigator Strange] • NHK • 1970

Streets of San Francisco, The = San Francisco Sōsasen [San Francisco Investigation] • NET • 1975

Strike Force = Los Keisatsu Tokusōtai [L.A. Police Special Investigation Team] • TBS • 1985

Strong Medicine = Dana and Lou: Little House Josei Clinic [D&L Little House Women's Clinic] • Lala • *2000

Studs Lonigan = Ai to Kanashimi no Ki [Trees of Love and Sorrow] • TBS • 1983

Suddenly Susan = Hello! Susan • Supe • *2000

Sugarfoot = Arizona Tom • NHK • 1960

Sun Also Rises, The = Taiyō wa Mata Noboru • NTV • 1988

Super 6 = Super President I • Fuji • 1970

Super President = Super Series • Fuji • 1971

Super Train = Genshiryoku Chōtokkyū Super Train [Atomic Powered Super Express Super Train] • Asahi • 1981

Supercar • NTV • 1961

Superman the Cartoon Series = Manga Superman • KRT • 1955

Surfside 6 • TBS • 1961

Sweeney, The = London Tokusōbu Sweeney [London Special Investigation Team Sweeney] • ANB • 1977

Switch = Karei na Tantei Pete and Mac [Splendid Detectives Pete and Mac] • NET • 1976

Sword of Freedom = Jiyū no Ken • KRT • 1959

Sylvester and Tweety • Synd • 1980

T.H.E. Cat = Cat • MBS • 1967

T.J. Hooker = Pato-car Adam 30 • NTV • 1985

Tab Hunter Show, The = Koi no Tehodoki Oshiemashō [Let's Learn About Love] • Fuji • 1960

Taggart = Keiji Taggart [Detective

Taggart] • Myst • *1983

Tales of St. Petersburg • Asahi • 1980

Tales of the Texas Rangers = Texas Kesshitai [Texas Suicide Corps] • KRT • 1960

Tales of the Unexpected = Kyōfu to Kaiki no Sekai [World of Fear and Strangeness] • TVT • 1977

Tales of the Unexpected = Yokisenu Dekigoto • TVT • 1980

Tales of the Vikings = Viking Daikaizoku [Viking Great Pirates] • NTV • 1960

Tales of Wells Fargo = Kenjū Machidō [Way of the Pistol] • Fuji • 1962

Tall Man, The = Seibu no Taiketsu [Western Confrontation] • Fuji • 1961

Tallahassee 7000 = Dial 7000 • TBS • 1964

Tammy = Suteki na Tammy [Wonderful Tammy] • YTV • 1968

Target = Unmei no Hyōteki [Fateful Target] • ABC • 1960

Target: The Corruptors = Corruptors • Fuji • 1962

Tarzan (1966) • NET • 1967

Tarzan (b&w serial) • NET • 1966

Tarzan: Lord of the Jungle = Jungle no Ōja Tarzan • Synd • 1980

Temps de Copains = Sannin no Wakamono [Three Young People] • NHK • 1964

Tennessee Tuxedo and His Tales = Tuxedo Penguin • TVT • 1968

Terrahawks = Chikyū Bōeigun Terrahawk • NHK • 1985

Terrific Adventures of the Terrible Ten = Bōken Shōnentai Terrible Ten [Boy Adventurers TT] • NTV • 1963

Terry in the South Seas = Nankai no Terry • NHK • 1963

Terrytoons Cartoons = Merry Go Round • KRT • 1957

Testimony of Two Men, The = Ishi Jonathan [Doctor Jonathan] • TBS • 1978

Texan, The • MBS • 1963

That Girl = Suteki na Ann [Wonderful Ann] • NET • 1967

Then Came Bronson = Sasurai no Rider Bronson [Wandering Rider Bronson] • TVT • 1974

Thin Man, The = Kage Naki Otoko [The Man Without a Shadow] • NTV • 1964

Third Man, The = Daisan no Otoko • NET • 1961

Third Watch • WOW • *1999

This is Alice = Kawaii Alice [Cute Alice] • NET • 1959

This Man Dawson • NTV • 1960

Three Stooges, The = Sanbaka Taishō • NTV • 1963

Thriller • NET • 1961

Thunderbirds • NHK • 1966

Tightrope = Himitsu Shirei Tightrope [Secret Order Tightrope] • NET • 1960

Time Tunnel, The • NHK • 1967

To Rome With Love = Sannin Musume [Three Daughters] • TBS • 1970

Today's FBI = FBI Formation 5 • TBS • 1965

Tom and Jerry • TBS • 1964

Tom Ewell Show, The = Furefure Papa [Hardbitten Papa] • NTV • 1961

Tom Terrific = Tom no Bōken [Tom's Adventures] • NET • 1959

Toma = Keiji Toma [Detective Toma] • NTV • 1975

Tombstone Territory = Hayauchi Hoankan [Quick-Draw Sheriff] • Fuji • 1965

Tomorrow People, The = Chikyū Boeitai [Earth Defense Force] • NHK • 1976

Toonsylvania • WOW • *1998

Top Cat = Doraneko Taishō [Leader of the Stray Cats] • NET • 1963

Topper = Yōki na Yūrei [Jovial Ghost] • TVT • 1964

Touch of Frost, A = Frost Keibu [Inspector Frost] • Myst • *1992

Tour de France par Deux Enfants = Lecrel Kyōdai no Tabi [Journey of the Lecrel Brothers] • NHK • 1959

Trackdown • NET • 1962

Trapper John MD = Doctor Trapper • NTV • 1982

Travels of Jaimie McPheeters = Jaimie no Bōken Ryokō [Jamie's Adventure Journey] • Fuji • 1964

Treasure Island = Takarajima • NHK • 1969

Trial of Lee Harvey Oswald = Daitōryō o Neratta Otoko [The Man Who Targeted the President] • Asahi • 1978

Trouble With Father • TBS • 1963

Troubleshooters, The • Fuji • 1968

Trouble with 2B, The = B Class Itazura Sakusen [Mischief Tactics of Class B] • NHK • 1975

Turnabout • TVT • 1979

TV Reader's Digest = Shin Aijō Monogatari [New Love Stories] • ABC • 1964

Twelve O'clock High = Tōjō Tekki Hatsugeki Shirei [Enemy Above Order to Open Fire] • NET • 1965

Twentieth Century Fox Hour = Nijū Seiki Fox Hour • NET • 1961

Twilight Zone I = Michi no Sekai [The Unknown World] • NTV • 1963

Twilight Zone II • TBS • 1964

Twin Peaks • Fuji • 1992

Two Faces West = Kenjū Kyōdai [Pistol Brothers] • KTV • 1966

Two of a Kind = Futari wa Futago [The Two Are Twins] • NHK • *1998

Tycoon, The = One-man Sadōki [Autocratic Uproar] • TVT • 1965

Tyrant King = London Daitsuigeki [Great London Chase] • NHK • 1973

U.F.O. = Nazo no Enban UFO [Mysterious Saucer UFO] • NTV • 1970

U.S. Border Patrol = Border Patrol • MBS • 1959

U.S. Marshall = Morgan Keibu II [Inspector Morgan II] • NTV • 1960

Unbroken Arrow, The = Shōnen Robin Hood [Young Robin Hood] • NHK • 1981

Underdog Show, The = Ultra Wan-chan [Ultra Doggie] • Fuji • 1968

Unexpected, The = Yokisenu Dekigoto • TBS • 1964

Union Pacific = Taiheigen [Great Plains] • Fuji • 1959

Unsuitable Job For a Woman • ?? • *1997

Untouchables, The • NET • 1961

UPA Cartoons = Manga no Kuni II [Cartoon Land II] • TVT • 1967

V.I.P. • AXN • *1998

Valley of the Dinosaurs = Genshi Kyōryū Jidai [Age of the Dinosaurs] • Synd • 1977

Valley of the Dolls = Ai to Kanashimi no Hollywood [Hollywood of Love and Sadness] • TBS • 1985

Vanished = Daitōryō no Scandal [The President's Scandal] • NHK • 1974

Vega$ • NTV • 1979

Virginian, The • NET • 1964

Visitor, The = Aru Hōmonsha • TBS • 1963

Vita di Leonardo da Vinci = Leonardo da Vinci no Shōgai • NHK • 1972

Voyage to the Bottom of the Sea = Genshiryoku Sensuikan Sea View-gō [Atomic Powered Submarine Sea View] • NET • 1964

Wacky Races = Chikichiki Machine Mō Race [Furious Crazy Machine Race] • NET • 1970

Wagner = Wagner no Shōgai [Life of Wagner] • TBS • 1983

Wagon Train = Horo Basha Tai • NTV • 1960

Wait Till Your Father Gets Home = Oyaji Tengoku [Father Heaven] • Synd • *1972

Walker Texas Ranger • Supe • *1993

Wally Gator = Wani no Gator • Synd • 1966

Walter Winchell File, The = Tanken Kisha Winchell [Investigative Journalist Winchell] • NET • 1960

Waltons, The = Wagaya wa 11-nin [Our House Has Eleven People] • TBS • 1973

Wanted Dead or Alive = Kenjū Mushuku [Wanderer with Gun] • Fuji • 1959

Washington: Behind Closed Doors = Kenryoku to Inbō: Daitōryō no Misshitsu [Power and Intrigue: The President's Secret Room] • NHK • 1978

West Wing, The = The White House • NHK • *1999

Westerner, The = Harukanaru Seibu [The Far West] • Fuji • 1961

Westwinds to Hawaii = Hawaii no Bōken • NHK • 1979

What's New Mr. Magoo = Shin Kingan

Magoo [New Near-Sighted Magoo] • Synd • ??

Wheelie and Chopper Bunch = Hassō Kuruma-kun [Racing Kuruma] • Synd • *1974

Wheels = Jidōsha • NHK • 1979

Whiplash = Muchi to Kenjū [Whips and Guns] • TBS • 1962

Whirlybirds = Soratobu Bōken Helicopter [Aerial Adventure Helicopter] • KRT • 1957

Whispering Smith = Smith to Iu Otoko [A Man Called Smith] • Fuji • 1961

Whistler, The = Kuchibue o Fuku Otoko • NHK • 1956

White Stone, The = Himitsu no Shiroi Ishii [Secret of the White Stone] • NHK • 1974

Whiz Kids = Maikon Daisakusen • NHK • 1984

Wild Wild West = Wild West • Fuji • 1965

Will and Grace = Futari wa Tomodachi? W&G [A Couple Who Are Friends? W&G] • NHK • *1998

William Tell, The Adventures of • NTV • 1959

Winds of War = Senjō no Arashi • Asahi • 1983

Wire Service = Tokumei Kisha • Fuji • 1965

WKRP in Cincinatti = Kattobi Hōsō WKRP [Chaotic Broadcaster WKRP] • MBS • 1983

Wonder Woman • Fuji • 1977

Wonder Years, The • FOX • *1988

Wonderful Stories of Professor Kitzel = Kuruguri Hakushi no Machine • NHK • 1973

Woobinda Animal Doctor = Dōbutsu Sensei Nikki [Diary of an Animal Doctor] • NHK • 1969

Woody Woodpecker Show, The • NTV • 1961

World Famous Drama Series = Sekai Meisaku Gekijō • NHK • 1964

World of the Giants = Shukushō Ningen Hunter [Shrunken Human Hunter] • NET • 1960

World War Three = Daisanji Sekai Taisen • TVT • 1982

X-Files, The • Asahi • 1995

Yippie, Yappy and Yahooey • Synd • 1968

Yogi Bear = Kumagorō • NET • 1964

Yogi's Gang = Kumagorō no Chin Patrol [Kumagorō's Strange Patrol] • Synd • 1980

You Are There = Anata wa Mokugekisha [You Are the Witness] • NTV • 1963

Young Lawyers = Wakaki Bengoshitachi • NHK • 1972

Zero One • NTV • 1962

Zorro = Kaiketsu Zorro [Magnificent Zorro] • NTV • 1961

CHINESE TITLES

Listed below are official and unofficial Mandarin titles of over 140 Japanese dramas, to aid identification in Chinese-speaking countries.

101-ci Qiuhun = 101st Proposal

2001-nian de Nanren Yun = Fate in 2001

20-sui de Jiehun = Promise at Age 20

24 Xiaoshi Jizhenshi = 24-Hour E.R.

29-sui de Shengdanjie = 29th Christmas

Ai de Huatou = Harmonia

Ai Shang Da Ming Xing = Star Struck

Aiqing Baipishu = Asunaro Confessions

Aiqing Geming = Love Revolution

Aiqing Menghuan = Imagine

A-Nan de Xiao Qingren = Minami's Sweetheart

Ba Quan Zhuan 2001= Dive Deep

Bai Nian Wuyu = 100 Years

Bai Xian Liu = Those Were The Days

Bai Ying = White Shadow

Bainian Wuyu = 100 Years

Benjia zhi Jia = Lady of the Manor

Bian Shen = Daughter of Iguana

Bianju Wang = King of Editors

Bing zhi Shijie = World of Ice

Cainiao Xingjing = Rookie

Chabao Si Jiedi = No Way!

Channel 2 = News Woman

Chengtian Lihun = Narita Divorce

Chenshui de Senlin = Sleeping Forest

Chidai Xikou Gongyuan = Ikebukuro West Gate Park

Chu Jia Shi Tianmi = Perfect Bride

Chuanshuo de Jiaoshi = Legendary Teacher

Cuimian = Hypnosis

Dahe Fuzi = Yamato Nadeshiko

Dai Wo Qu Lüguan = Take Me to a Ryokan

Dongjing Aiqing Gushi = Tokyo Love Story

Dongjing Guoji Konggang Wuyu = Big Wing

Dongjing Xianzhiqiyuan = Tokyo Cinderella

E Zuo Ju zhi Wen = It Started with A Kiss

Erqian Nian de Ren = Love 2000

Fang Ke Hou = After School

Fanghao Manfang = Full House

Feihun Jiazu = Unmarried Family

Feizhou de Ye = Africa Nights

Feizhou zhi Ye = Africa Nights

Fen Shou Zhuoying Hui = Love Separation Service

Fengzi Chenghun = Shotgun Marriage

Fuqin = Oh, Dad!

Ganying Shaonian = Psychometer Eiji

Gei Wo Ai Ba! = Love Me

Gen Wo Shuo Ai Wo = Say You Love Me

Guai Zhan Yi Ke Guai Shengfu de Nüren = Match Point

Gui no Qijia = House of the Devil

Haitan Nanhai = Beach Boys

Hao Xiaoxi = Good News

Haomen Nuhai = Fighting Girl

Huacun Dajie = Daisuke Hanamura

Huojian Nanhai = Rocket Boys

Huoshi Wuyu = Leave It to the Nurses

Jiaru Haomen de Fangfa = How to Marry

a Billionaire

Jingdu Yuangong Jingnei = Kyoto Unsolved Cases

Jintailang = Kitarō

Jintian yi Shaonian Shijianbo = Young Kindaichi Files

Jishi Xinwen= Straight News

Jixu = Unsolved Cases

Junei Da Zhangfu = Come Fly with Me

Kesouyan zhi Nü = Investigator Mariko

Kouhong = Lipstick

Letai de Shousi = King of Sushi

Li Tianguo Zuijin de Nanren = Heaven Cannot Wait

Lian'ai Qiji = Miracle of Love

Lian'ai Shiji = Love Generation

Liang ge Ren = Sisters

Lianhou = Refrain

Lianjia de Ai = Cheap Love

Lianlian Qingliang = Long for Love

Ling Yige Tian = Another Heaven

Liwu = Gift

Lixiang zhi Jiehun = Ideal Marriage

Mei Nü Da Zuo Zhan = OL Visual Battle

Meili de Ren = Beauty

Menglong Tejing Dui = G-Men 75

Mingpai = Brand

Mofa Mei Shaonü = Sweet Devil

Monü de Tiaojian = Forbidden Love

Naiyou Dangao Shang de Caomei = Strawberry on the Shortcake

Nanqing Shidai = Down and Out

Ni de Chaopiao Zai Kuqi = Your Money Is Crying

Ni Suo Jiao Wo de Shi = From the Heart

Nongjia Cheng Zhen = False Love

Nü Xu Da Ren = Son-in-Law

PS Wo Hen Hao, Junping = P.S. I'm Fine, Shunpei

Putaojiu Zhuanjia = Sommelier

Qianmian Nülang = Mask of Glass

Qin Bu Ru Jin = Family Values

Qing Cadiao Yanlei = Wipe Your Tears

Qing zhi Shidai = The Misfits

Qingchun Wu Hui = All about Young People

Ren Jian Shige = No Longer Human

Renzhu Gaochu Pa = Friends in Need

Sanshi la Jingbao = Overtime

Shen de Ezuoju = Capriccio

Shen Zhi shi Zai Duo Yidian = Please God! Just a Little More Time

Shengzhe zhi Xingjin = When the Saints Go Marching In

Shi Shui Touzou Wo de Xin = Then She Stole My Heart

Shiji Mo no Shi = The Last Song

Shijie Qimiao Wuyu = Miracle World

Shijie Shang Zui Re de Xiatia = One Hot Summer

Shiliu Sui Xinniang = The Bride Is Sixteen

Shoulie Nanhai = Boy Hunt

Shuang Shen = Daughter of Iguana

Shuo Laopo de Huaihua = Wife Bashing

Shuwu Er Ke = Shomuni

Suiyue = Days

Taiyuan Bu Hui Xiachen = The Sun Does Not Set

Tianguo zhi Wen = Heaven's Kiss

Tianmi de Jijie = Sweet Season

Tianshi de Gushi = Sister Stories

Tongyi Wuyan Xia = Under One Roof

Wanglu Qingren = With Love

Weiman Dushi = Miman City

Weixian Guanxi = Dangerous Liaisons

Weixian zhi Fei = E.S.

Wo Liang de Weilai = I'll Be Back

Woliang de Weilai = Back to Our Future

Wuji Shentan = Geisha Detective

Xia Ri Xue = Summer Snow

Xiang Lian'ai Xiang Lian'ai Xiang

Lian'ai = Where Is Love?

Xiangbing Huangtai zhi Dongwu Riji = Rocinante

Xiao Bao = Tabloid

Xiaoshile Tianshi de Jiedao = Street of Disappearing Angels

Xie Xin = Trick

Xiezouqu = Concerto

Xingji Jinbi = Heaven's Coins

Xinsugong Zoujiu Jidui = Shinjuku Punk Rescue

Xiri Nanyou = To Love Again

Yi Zhang Ban Shuangren Chuang = Semi Double

Yinyangshi = Yin-Yang Master

Youchang Jiaqi = Long Vacation

Zai Wen Yi Ci = One More Kiss

Zaoxingshi = Style

Zaoyi Nü = Beach Wars Mix

Zhengyi Bisheng = Justice for All

Zhongxia de Shengdan Kuai le = Merry Christmas in Summer

Zhuijin er Renzu = Serious Affair

NEXT SEASON'S SHOWS

The drama world moves fast; there are approximately 30 new series each season, of which perhaps a dozen will go out in primetime, and only a handful will comprise remakes or sequels to earlier shows. In order to help you guess what the story-lines might be for as-yet unmade series like *Hairdresser Detective, My Boyfriend Is an Alien, Get Away from My Husband You Bitch,* and who knows, perhaps *Undertaker Cop,* we offer this handy plot generator. Delete as applicable, or add your own variables:

Janet is a (reporter / photographer / traffic cop / nurse / princess / florist / teacher / stewardess / designer) **who finds herself falling for John, who is a** (detective / bail jumper / salary-man / architect / doctor / samurai / pilot / musician / student/ undercover alien / terrorist). **After first meeting during a** (wedding / crime investigation / blind date / robbery / sword-fight), **they initially fail to get on with each other, but are miraculously thrown back together by their** (interfering parents / shared interest in an unlikely hobby / unexpected relocation to shared lodgings). **However, their burgeoning relationship is threatened by** (old flames / intrigues at their workplace / the fact they've switched bodies / their removal to a different time period), **and by the fact that Janet is** (already married / a celebrity / impersonating someone else / on the run from the police / diagnosed with only three months to live / on an undercover mission / pick one from the next list) **and that John is** (leaving the country / in love with someone else / supposed to defend the world from attacking aliens / pick one from the previous list). **Nor is anyone expecting the sudden mid-season appearance of** (an old flame / a long-lost relative / an ultimatum that could ruin their careers). **They must also deal with a dark secret, because one of them is** (also married / still getting over the death of a loved one / a parent / suppressing the memories of a terrible trauma / actually a ghost / hell-bent on revenge against the other's father). **Luckily, they grow closer thanks to an incident involving** (zany friends / a talking dog / someone's parent / a wacky DJ) **and the fact that they are forced to cooperate on** (rearing a child or children / chasing a story / an arrest / saving the planet). **Though the story appears to resolve itself, a surprise twist involving** (another murder / a revelation about the boss / a sudden hospitalization) **leads to a last-minute reunion at** (Narita airport / a wedding / a sports meet / the hospital). **And everybody lives happily ever after, including two supporting cast members who have unexpectedly fallen in love, unless there is a second season, in which case at least one of the leads will** (turn up with an unexpected spouse / change jobs / lose his or her memory).

Aoyagi, M., ed. *Kettei!! Terebi Dorama*

BIBLIOGRAPHY

Best 100 [It's Settled!! Best 100 TV Dramas]. Tokyo: Enterbrain, 2001.

———, ed. *TV Dorama o 100-bai Tanoshimō: Dorama DVD Super Guidebook [Twice the Excitement from 100 TV Dorama DVDs]*. Tokyo: Enterbrain, 2002.

Barnouw, E. *Tube of Plenty: The Evolution of American Television*. New York: Oxford University Press, 1990.

Brooks, T. and E. Marsh. *The Complete Directory to Prime Time Network and Cable TV Shows 1946-Present*. New York, Ballantine Books, 1999.

Buckley, S. *Encyclopedia of Contemporary Japanese Culture*. London: Routledge, 2002.

Clements, Jonathan and Helen McCarthy. *The Anime Encyclopedia: A Guide to Japanese Animation Since 1917*. Berkeley: Stone Bridge Press, 2001.

[Doramap Project] *TV Dorama Koko ga Rokechi da!! [TV Dorama: This is the Location!!]*. Tokyo: Sun Books, 2000.

Fujita, K., ed. *TV Star Meikan 2002/5700 TV Persons 2002 Star's Directory (sic)*. Tokyo: Tokyo News, 2001.

[Fukuka Shoten Editorial Staff]. *2001 Comic Catalog*. Tokyo: Fukuka Shoten, 2001.

Galbraith, S. *Japanese Science Fiction, Fantasy and Horror Films*. Jefferson, NC: McFarland, 1994.

Gill, T. "Transformational Magic: Some Japanese Super-Heroes and Monsters." In *The Worlds of Japanese Popular Culture: Gender, Shifting Boundaries and Global Cultures*, edited by D. Martinez. Cambridge: University Press, 1998.

Gitlin, Todd. *Inside Prime Time*. Berkeley: University of California Press, 1994.

Harvey, P. "Interpreting *Oshin*—War, History and Women in Modern Japan." In *Women, Media and Consumption in Japan*, edited by L. Skov and B. Moeran. London: Curzon Press, 1995.

———. "*Nonchan's Dream:* NHK Morning Serialized Television Novels." In *The Worlds of Japanese Popular Culture: Gender, Shifting Boundaries and Global Cultures*, edited by D. Martinez. Cambridge: University Press, 1998.

Hiramatsu, K., ed. *Terebi 50-nen in TV Guide: The TV History of 50 Years*. Tokyo: Tokyo News Tsūshinsha, 2000.

Inui, N. *That's TV Graffiti: Gaikoku Terebi Eiga Sanjūnen no Subete [All About 35 Years of Foreign TV and Films]*. Tokyo: Film Art-sha, 1988.

Ishida, Y., ed. *Minna no Terebi Jidaigeki: Dai Hit-saku kara Chō-Cult Sakuhin made [Everybody's TV Period Dramas: From Great Hits to Super-Cult Works]*. Tokyo: Aspect, 1998.

———, ed. *TV Dorama All File: 90's Minpō-ban*. Tokyo: Aspect, 1999.

Iyoda, Y., et al., eds. *Terebi Shi Handbook [TV History Handbook]*. Tokyo: Jiyūkokuminsha, 1998.

Kobayashi, Y. *Dorama o Aishita Onna no Dorama [The Drama of a Woman Who Loved Drama]*. Tokyo: Kusaosha, 1995.

Komatsu, K. *That's Terebi Dorama 90's*. Tokyo: Diamond Graphic-sha, 1999.

Krauss, E. *Broadcasting Politics in Japan: NHK and Television News*. Ithaca, NY: Cornell University Press, 2000.

Masuyama, H. *NHK Shōnen Dorama Series no Subete [All About NHK Juvenile Drama Serials]*. Tokyo: Ascii, 2001.

Matsuo, Y. *Terebi Dorama o "Yomu": Eizo no Naka no Nihonjinron ["Reading" Television Drama: Japanese Uniqueness Onscreen]*. Tokyo: Metropolitan Publishing, 2002.

Nakajima, S., et al. eds. *Tsuburaya the Complete*. Tokyo: Kadokawa, 2001.

Nakano, Y. "Who Initiates Global Flow? Japanese Popular Culture in Asia." In *Visual Communication*, Vol. 1, No. 2. London: Sage Publications, 2002.

Nomura, Y. *Terebi Jidaigeki Shi— Chambara Chronicle 1953–1998 [History of Television Period Drama]*. Tokyo: Tokyo Shinbun, 1999.

Odagiri, M. *Terebi Shokai no Butai Ura [Behind the Scenes on Television]*. Tokyo: Mitsui, 1994.

Okada, Y. *Dorama o Kaku [To Write*

Drama]. Tokyo: Diamond, 1999.

Painter, A. *The Creation of Japanese Television and Culture*. Ph.D. dissertation. University of Michigan, Department of Anthropology, 1992.

Phillips, A. *Trendy or Timeless? The Classical Heritage of Contemporary Japanese Television Love Stories*. M.A. dissertation. University of Alberta, Department of East Asian Studies, 1999.

Sata, M. and H. Hirahara, eds. *A History of Japanese Television Drama: Modern Japan and the Japanese*. Tokyo: Japan Association of Broadcasting Art, 1991.

Schilling, M. *The Encyclopedia of Japanese Pop Culture*. New York: Weatherhill, 1997.

Stronach, B. "Japanese Television." In *Handbook of Japanese Popular Culture*, R. Powers and H. Kato, eds. New York: Greenwood Press, 1989.

"Suspense Junkies." *Ni Jikan Dorama Daijiten [Dictionary of Two-Hour Drama]*. Tokyo: Mitsui, 1999.

Takahashi, M. *The Development of Japanese Television Broadcasting and Imported Television Programs*. M.A. dissertation. Michigan State University,

Department of Telecommunications, 1992.

Thompson, R. *Television's Second Golden Age: From* Hill Street Blues *to* ER. New York: Syracuse University Press, 1997.

Toriyama, H. *Nihon Terebi Dorama Shi [History of Japanese Television Drama]*. Tokyo: Eijinsha, 1986.

Uesugi, J. and F. Takakura. *Terebi Dorama no Shigotonin-tachi [People Who Work in TV Drama]*. Tokyo: KK Best Sellers, 2001.

Yokose, M., ed. *Sentai Hero Super Visual: Super Sentai Series 25th Anniversary 1975–2001*. Tokyo: Tokuma Shoten, 2001.

ONLINE SOURCES (JAPANESE)
http://www.tvdrama-db.com

http://www.jmdb.ne.jp

http://www3.justnet.ne.jp/ ~a_matsu/Ashi.HTM

http://tvgroove.com

http://www.fujitv.co.jp

http://www.tv-asahi.co.jp

http://www.ntv.co.jp

http://www.tbs.co.jp

http://www.ktv.co.jp

http://www.ytv.co.jp

http://www.nhk.or.jp

ONLINE SOURCES (ENGLISH)
http://nt2099.com/DORAMA

http://jdorama.com

http://www.kikutv.com

http://www.jstv.co.uk

http://www.geocities.com/ doramatalk/index.html

http://www.dalekempire.com/ KaijuFanOnLine.html

http://www.henshinonline.com

http://www.japanhero.com

http://www.rangercentral.com

http://www.waynebrain.com/ ultra/index.html

http://www.akadot.com

COMMERCIAL SITES
http://www.amazon.co.jp

http://www.cdjapan.co.jp

http://www.yesasia.com

INDEX

Doramas whose titles begin with numerals are listed *twice* in this index, at the very beginning in numerical order and within the alphabetical entries according to spelling based on pronunciation; e.g., the dorama *100 Years* appears at the beginning of the listings as well as under the reasonably assumed pronunciation/spelling *One Hundred Years*. Alphabetization is by the "word first" method, so that *All Men Are Brothers* is listed before *Allah no Shisha*. **Boldface type** indicates a main entry for a dorama.

JONATHAN CLEMENTS is a Contributing Editor of *Newtype USA* magazine. His publications include *The Anime Encyclopedia, The Moon in the Pines, The Kid's Movie Guide,* and *Chinese Life*. He is also a scriptwriter and director for the Big Finish company on audio adventures for *Judge Dredd, Strontium Dog,* and *Doctor Who*. In 2000, he received a Japan Festival Award for outstanding contributions to the understanding of Japanese culture.

MOTOKO TAMAMURO was a regular contributor to *Manga Max* magazine, for which she wrote groundbreaking articles on modern Japanese icons, including *GTO* and *The Young Kindaichi Files*. She was a research assistant on *The Anime Encyclopedia* and has translated interviews with many famous Japanese figures, including Takeshi Kitano and Yoshitaka Amano.

STEVE KYTE has worked as a freelance illustrator since 1980, drawing video and book covers, comic strips, and film and TV pre-production designs. His interest in Japan dates back to his childhood, but he was seriously bitten by the anime and manga bug in the early eighties and his work in that vein includes art for the magazines *Anime UK* and *Manga Max*, the Broken Sky series of novels, and the character designs for the 2003 UK/Japan anime co-production *Firestorm*.

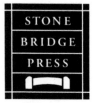

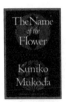